Movies and Methods

VOLUME II

Movies and Methods
VOLUME II

An Anthology

EDITED BY Bill Nichols

UNIVERSITY OF CALIFORNIA PRESS
BERKELEY   LOS ANGELES   LONDON

University of California Press
Berkeley and Los Angeles

University of California Press, Ltd.
London, England
Introductory materials copyright © 1985 by Bill Nichols
Other new material copyright © 1985 by The Regents of
the University of California

Printed in the United States of America
5 6 7 8 9

Library of Congress Cataloging in Publication Data
(Revised for volume 2)
Main entry under title:
Movies and methods.
Includes bibliographical references and indexes.
1. Moving-pictures.   I. Nichols, Bill.
PN1994.M7   791.43   74-22969
ISBN 0-520-03151-2 (alk. paper: v. 1)
ISBN 0-520-05409-1 (alk. paper: v. 2)

The paper used in this publication meets the minimum
requirements of American National Standard for
Information Sciences—Permanence of Paper for
Printed Library Materials, ANSI Z39.48–1984. ∞

CONTENTS

Part 3   FEMINIST CRITICISM

Part 4   STRUCTURALIST SEMIOTICS

Part 5   PSYCHOANALYTIC SEMIOTICS

Part 6   COUNTERCURRENTS

ACKNOWLEDGMENTS

A number of individuals offered helpful suggestions regarding the selection of articles for this anthology. I want to extend my gratitude to Blaine Allan, Dudley Andrew, Peter Baxter, Thomas W. Benson, Patricia Erens, Tag Gallagher, Douglas Gomery, E. Ann Kaplan, Bruce Kawin, Noel King, Chuck Kleinhans, Julia Lesage, John Locke, Judith Mayne, Joe Medjuk, Dana Polan, William Rothman, Jerry Salvaggio, Alexander Sesonske, Vivian Sobchack, Peter Steven, Thomas Waugh, Marion Weiss, Paddy Whannel, and Robin Wood.

Julianne Burton provided me with considerable assistance both in the selection of articles and in the preparation of the introductory material. Her trace, as it were, is securely embedded in the organization and texture of the work, and for that I am profoundly thankful.

Joanne Marion gave me considerable help with the appreciable amount of correspondence required and with the negotiation of permission to reprint articles. Frances Timleck and Caroline Kingsman helped in the final stages of assembling the completed manuscript.

I extend my appreciation to Ernest Callenbach, my editor, for his enthusiastic support and generous advice. He has helped to reduce the difficulties of publishing more often than I can recall. The Queen's University Advisory Research Committee provided a modest grant that helped to complete the process of assembling the articles and securing permission to reprint them; the Committee's help is gratefully acknowledged. I also want to thank my colleagues at Queen's University, whose own work and spirit of engagement and exchange have been a constant source of stimulation: Blaine Allan, Peter Baxter, Peter Morris, and Peter Pearson. Above all, I must thank the person who makes working at Queen's a source of joy and pleasure, Jill Spettigue.

Special thanks to the following sources for permission to reprint articles:

Introduction to Bazin's "The Stalin Myth in Soviet Cinema," from *Film Criticism* 3, no. 1 (Fall 1978), reprinted by permission of Dudley Andrew and *Film Criticism*. "The Stalin Myth in Soviet Cinema," from *Film Criticism* 3, no. 1 (Fall 1978), translated by Georgia Gurrieri, first published in *L'Esprit* (July–August 1950), reprinted by permission of *Film Criticism*. "Technique and Ideology: Camera, Perspective, Depth of Field," from *Film Reader*, no. 2 (1977), reprinted by permission of Jean-Louis Comolli and *Film Reader*. "Technological and Aesthetic Influences on the Development of Deep-Focus Cinematography in the United States," from *Screen* 13, no. 1 (Spring 1972), reprinted by permission of Patrick Ogle and *Screen*. "Sound and Color," from *Jump Cut,* no. 17 (1977), reprinted by permission of Edward Buscombe and *Jump Cut*. "Notes on Columbia Pictures Corporation 1926–1941," from *Screen* 16, no. 3 (Autumn 1975), reprinted by permission of Edward Buscombe and *Screen*. "Writing the History of the American Film Industry: Warner Brothers and Sound," from *Screen* 17, no. 1 (Spring 1976), reprinted by permission of Douglas Gomery and *Screen*. "Color and Cinema: Problems in the Writing of History," from *Film Reader,* no. 4 (1979), reprinted by permission of Edward Branigan and *Film Reader*. "Mass-Produced Photoplays: Economic and Signifying Practices in the First Years of Hollywood," from *Wide Angle* 4, no. 3 (1980), reprinted by permission of Janet Staiger, *Wide Angle,* and Johns Hopkins University Press.

"Tales of Sound and Fury: Observations on the Family Melodrama" from *Monogram,* no. 4 (1972), reprinted by permission of Thomas Elsaesser and the British Film Institute. "Minnelli and Melodrama," from *Screen* 18, no. 2 (Summer 1977), reprinted by permission of Geoffrey Nowell-Smith and *Screen*. "An Introduction to the American Horror Film," from *The American Nightmare: Essays on the Horror Film* (Toronto: Festival of Festivals, 1979), reprinted by permission of Robin Wood and Richard Lippe. "Entertainment and Utopia," from *Movie,* no. 24 (Spring 1977), reprinted by permission of Richard Dyer and *Movie*. "Beyond *Vérité:* Emile de Antonio and the New Documentary of the Seventies," from *Jump Cut,* nos. 10–11 (1976), reprinted by permission of Thomas Waugh and *Jump Cut*. "The Voice of Documentary," © 1983 by The Regents of the University of California, reprinted from *Film Quarterly* 36, no. 3 (Spring 1983), by permission of Bill Nichols and The Regents. "Beyond Observational Cinema," from *Principles of Visual Anthropology,* edited by Paul Hockings (The Hague: Mouton Publishers, 1975), reprinted by permission of David MacDougall and Mouton Publishers. "The Avant-Garde: History and Theories," from *Screen* 19, no. 3 (Autumn 1978), reprinted by permission of Janet Bergstrom, Constance Penley, and *Screen*.

"Visual Pleasure and Narrative Cinema," from *Screen* 16, no. 3 (Autumn 1975), reprinted by permission of *Screen*. "Towards a Feminist Film Practice: Some Theses," from *Edinburgh Film Festival Magazine,* no. 1 (1976), reprinted by permission of Claire Johnston. "*Jeanne Dielman:* Death in Installments," from *Jump Cut,* no. 16 (1977), reprinted by permission of Jayne Loader and *Jump Cut*. "In the Name of Feminist Film Criticism," from *Jump Cut,* no. 19 (1978), revised and reprinted in *Heresies,* no. 9, reprinted by permission of B. Ruby Rich and *Jump Cut*. "The Right of Re-Vision: Michelle Citron's *Daughter Rite,*" © 1981 by The Regents of the University of California, reprinted from *Film Quarterly* 35, no. 1 (Fall 1981), by permission of Linda Williams, B. Ruby Rich, and The Regents. "Gentlemen Consume Blondes," from *Wide Angle* 1, no. 1 (1979), reprinted by permission of Maureen Turim, *Wide Angle,* and Johns Hopkins University Press. "The Place of Woman in the Cinema of Raoul Walsh," from *Raoul Walsh,* edited by Philip Hardy for Edinburgh Film Festival (Colchester: Vineyard Press, 1974), reprinted by permission of Claire Johnston and Pam Cook.

"Signification in the Cinema," from *Diacritics* 4, no. 3 (Fall 1974), reprinted by permission of Paul Sandro and *Diacritics*. "The Anatomy of a Proletarian Film: Warner's *Marked Woman*," © 1973 by The Regents of the University of California, reprinted from *Film Quarterly* 27, no. 2 (Winter 1973–1974), by permission of The Regents. "*The Searchers*: An American Dilemma," © 1980 by The Regents of the University of California, reprinted from *Film Quarterly* 34, no. 2 (Winter 1980–1981), by permission of Brian Henderson and The Regents. "*Mildred Pierce* Reconsidered," from *Film Reader,* no. 2 (1977), reprinted by permission of Joyce Nelson and *Film Reader.* "The Spectator-in-the-Text: The Rhetoric of *Stagecoach*," © 1975 by The Regents of the University of California, reprinted from *Film Quarterly* 34, no. 2 (Winter 1975–1976) by permission of Nick Browne and The Regents. "*S/Z* and *The Rules of the Game*," from *Jump Cut,* nos. 12–13 (1976), reprinted by permission of Julia Lesage and *Jump Cut.* "Godard and Counter Cinema: *Vent d'Est*," from Afterimage, no. 4 (Fall 1972), reprinted by permission of Peter Wollen and New Left Books, London. "*Jaws,* Ideology, and Film Theory," from *Times Higher Education Supplement,* no. 231 (March 26, 1976), reprinted by permission of Stephen Heath and *Times Higher Education Supplement.*

"Psychoanalysis and Cinema: The Imaginary Discourse," from *Quarterly Review of Film Studies* 2, no. 3 (August 1977), reprinted by permission of Charles F. Altman and *Quarterly Review of Film Studies.* "Ideological Effects of the Basic Cinematographic Apparatus," from *Cinéthique,* nos. 7–8 (1970), reprinted by permission of Jean-Louis Baudry and *Cinéthique;* translation © Alan Williams, first printed in *Film Quarterly* 28, no. 2 (Winter 1974–1975) and revised for publication here. "Story/Discourse: Notes on Two Kinds of Voyeurism," from *Psychoanalysis and Cinema: The Imaginary Signifier* (Bloomington: Indiana University Press and London: Macmillan Press, 1982), reprinted by permission of Christian Metz, Macmillan Press, and Indiana University Press. "A Note on Story/Discourse," from *Edinburgh Film Festival Magazine* (1976), reprinted by permission of Geoffrey Nowell-Smith. "On the Naked Thighs of Miss Dietrich," from *Wide Angle* 2, no. 2 (1978), reprinted by permission of Peter Baxter, *Wide Angle,* and Johns Hopkins University Press. "The Voice in the Cinema: The Articulation of Body and Space," from *Yale French Studies,* no. 60 (1980), reprinted by permission of Mary Ann Doane and *Yale French Studies.* "The Avant-Garde and Its Imaginary," from *Camera Obscura,* no. 2 (Fall 1977), reprinted by permission of Constance Penley and *Camera Obscura.* "Masochism and the Perverse Pleasures of the Cinema," © 1984 by Gaylyn Studlar, reprinted by permission of the author.

"The Neglected Tradition of Phenomenology in Film Theory," from *Wide Angle* 2, no. 2 (1978), reprinted by permission of Dudley Andrew, *Wide Angle,* and Johns Hopkins University Press. "Colonialism, Racism, and Representation: An Introduction," from *Screen* 24, no. 2 (1983), reprinted by permission of Robert Stam, Louise Spence, and *Screen.* "Responsibilities of a Gay Film Critic," from *Film Comment* 14, no. 1 (January–February 1978), © *Film Comment*, reprinted by permission of Robin Wood and *Film Comment*. "A Brechtian Cinema? Towards a Politics of Self-Reflexive Film," from *Jump Cut,* no. 17 (1978), reprinted by permission of Dana Polan and *Jump Cut;* revised by Dana Polan for publication here. "The Point-of-View Shot," from *Point of View in the Cinema: A Theory of Narration and Subjectivity in Classical Film* (New York and Berlin: Mouton Publishers, 1984), originally published in different form in *Screen* 16, no. 3 (Autumn 1975), reprinted by permission of Edward Branigan, *Screen,* and Mouton Publishers. "Statistical Style Analysis of Motion Pictures," © 1974 by The Regents of the University of California, reprinted from *Film Quarterly* 28, no. 1 (Fall 1974) by permission of Barry Salt and The Regents. "The Space between Shots," from *Screen* 15, no. 1 (Spring 1974), reprinted by permission of Dai Vaughn and *Screen*. "Class and Allegory in Contemporary Mass Culture: *Dog Day Afternoon* as a Political Film," from *College English,* 38, no. 8 (April 1977), reprinted by permission of Fredric Jameson and The National Council of Teachers of English.

Original spellings and punctuation have been preserved in articles that first appeared in British, Canadian, or Australian sources.

INTRODUCTION

CHANGING TIMES

To borrow from the title of a recent publication, there is definitely "ferment in the field" of film. This phrase comes from a special issue of *The Journal of Communication,* in which communications scholars addressed the issues raised, in large measure, by the same varieties of cultural studies that have characterized recent film scholarship. Empirical, sender-receiver studies involving the measurement of "effects" have come under increased criticism, leading some communication specialists to give closer consideration to cultural theories of ideology, subjectivity, enunciation, narrative, genre, and viewer positioning—theories whose application is well established in film. But the application and establishment of such theories continue to stimulate new ideas within film study as well. The discipline is clearly alive and well, extending itself into new domains—notably television and video—and consolidating some sense of distinct historical development.

In fact, film study may now be reaching the end of one phase in its development. Between the late 1960s and the late 1970s, it separated into a continuing tradition of amateur or semiacademic writing and a widespread and by now reasonably well-entrenched academic scholarship. One indicator of the second development is that the number of Ph.D.'s in film in the United States rose from approximately two hundred in 1964 to more than two thousand today.[1] Other indicators range from the creation and growth of film departments to the increasing professionalization of the main academic film societies—the Society for Cinema Studies and the University Film and Video Association, groups that fifteen years ago were little more than pretexts for the social gathering of kindred spirits, such as filmmakers, journalists and critics, students of popular culture, humanists, and, mingling indistinguishably with them, a few academic film scholars.

This volume is itself a mark of the establishment of an institutional base for film study inasmuch as it complements the first volume of *Movies and Methods* (Berkeley: University of California Press, 1976). The first selection of essays in the early 1970s marked the emergence of a new area of scholarship while developing its own distinctive mix of methodologies; this second selection of essays, made mostly in the early 1980s, confirms the existence of an established field of study. The methods and concepts that ten years ago were considered controversial and potentially damaging to the humanistic tradition of film appreciation (a tradition that preserved the kinship between early university scholarship and popular, non-academic criticism) have now become the working assumptions and principles passed on in graduate programs by the "new film scholars," who have now become part of the academic establishment. Semiotics, poststructuralism, linguistics, psychoanalysis, phenomenology, Marxism, feminism, formal analysis, cognitive and perceptual psychology, anthropology, literary and rhetorical criticism, and cultural history are now the coin of the realm.

Even so, there is a paradox here. A lively, productive ferment exists in the field for several reasons. One reason is that the new methodologies just cited have not gained universal acceptance. They stand largely in opposition to a staunchly defended humanistic tradition. Moreover, many scholars, including myself, have adopted these methods without accepting them wholeheartedly and dispute the political tendencies or strategies that they often involve, some of which are discussed later in the introduction. Another reason is that these methods are not intrinsic to film. Their adoption by film scholars (partly to distinguish academic from nonacademic writing, partly because of their productiveness for research) erodes the sense of film study as a distinct discipline. Most of the articles collected here, for example, depend on a conceptual framework extrinsic to film study per se to sharpen our understanding of film. The question arises: Is film study a coherent area of study, or is it necessarily a part of that larger field—perhaps identifiable as cultural studies—from which so many of its principles come? My own view is that film study makes little sense as a distinct area (in contrast to English, say, in the period of the New Criticism) but that its essentially interdisciplinary nature has not been emphasized because of the practical need to gain an autonomous base within the academy, which is normally measured in terms of departmental status.

Other paradoxes surround the ferment in the field. The sense of a discipline with a body of knowledge, a set of diverse methodological principles, a tradition (albeit a short one), and an institutional base arises precisely at the time when the phenomenon of "the movies" is becoming anachronistic, marginal to a visual culture increasingly centered on television, video, and new forms of electronic communication and exchange. Some lag between culture and its scholarly study may be inevitable. Hence, television studies, which now have some of the excitement of film studies in the 1960s, are gaining prominence at the very moment when traditional broadcast television is beginning to be threatened by cable and pay television, videocassettes, videodiscs, computer games, and two-way information networks, such as Telidon in Canada and Prestel in England.

This lag between the prevalence of cultural forms and the study of those forms has some advantages in the university. The study of film has gained an added dimension of respectability precisely because it is increasingly aligned with one of the great missions of Western humanism: the preservation and conservation of our cultural heritage. But this gain also means that film study is losing some of the strength it once derived from its contemporaneousness, its immediate relevance to the cultural experience of students and their need to understand this experience. Instead, film study increasingly derives its importance from an historical dimension that has, ironically, itself come under fire from the same poststructuralist theories that have been crucial to the development of film studies as a discipline in the 1970s.

In sum, film study has developed into a discipline at the very moment when traditional humanistic concepts regarding our cultural heritage have been placed into crisis, even though some of these concepts have helped film study to gain respectability inside the academy. Notions of a single, unified heritage and of an historical method that stands apart from the poetic strategies of narrative that it employs can no longer be taken for granted. For example, Hayden White, in *Metahistory: The Historical Imagination in Nineteenth-Century Europe* (Baltimore: Johns Hopkins University Press), proposes a purely formal taxonomy of nineteenth-century histories based on the way in which the historical field is cast into one of four linguistic tropes. White argues (p. xi) that "in any field of study not yet reduced (or elevated) to the status of genuine science, thought remains the captive of the linguistic mode in which it seeks to grasp the outline of objects inhabiting its field of perception."

Film study cannot therefore rest comfortably with its role of conservator when the theories and practices underlying the process of conservation are themselves under challenge. Poststructuralism, an approach comprising elements of structural, semiotic, Marxist, feminist, and psychoanalytic thought, carries White's formal challenge still further. It casts doubt on basic assumptions about human nature, subjectivity, the individual as a given whose aesthetic responses need only to be fine-tuned, and art as somehow fundamentally beyond ideology. Terry Eagleton, in *Literary Theory: An Introduction* (Minneapolis: University of Minnesota Press, 1983), argues that the boundaries of literary theory are undefendable because literary (and, by clear extension, film) theory merges indistinguishably with philosophy, semiotics, sociology, cultural history, and other zones of thought. But more important, such boundaries are illusory, because nothing can conclusively distinguish literature or art from discourse in general. For Eagleton and other poststructuralists, the aesthetic is subsumed by the ideological. (We will return to this point later in this Introduction.) In this view, film study can become nonillusory only by refusing to claim autonomy for its object of study.

But to deny autonomy to the object of study is also to deny autonomy to the field of study. Film study thus becomes a part of cultural studies, investigating the form and meaning of social relationships as manifested in texts (films, novels, television programs) or in everyday life (sports, dress, speech). Whatever specificity can be assigned to the study of film possesses significance only when it is drawn back into the general arena of culture and ideology. It is here that film-viewing pleasure can be related to class, race, sex, and nationality, to questions of social structure and the position of the individual (including the question of how a sense of individuality or spectatorship itself arises or is created).

Thus, we face three paradoxes: First, film study depends on non-film-specific methodologies for its research paradigms. Second, it has the academic status of a "new" discipline, although its object of study is becoming part of an "old" culture. Third, its autonomy as a discipline is partly illusory, because some of the methods that have distinguished it also challenge the traditional justifications for disciplinary autonomy.

The result, however, has been ferment, not paralysis; debate, not resignation; and diversity, not homogenization. These outcomes have occurred not within a neutral arena conducive to a pluralism of methods but within an institutional, bureaucratic structure governed by material practices, internal hierarchy, and struggles for power. (Poststructural methods have been quite central to these struggles for the past ten years, and I shall return to this point in the last section of this Introduction.)

One reason for the centrality of these methods, and one explanation for their appearance, has been the increasing importance of culture to contemporary social structure. We have witnessed not only the rise of the mass media in an industrial age but also the transformation of our economy into a postindustrial, information or service economy. Production, distribution, dissemination, and consumption increasingly function within the terms of the communication and exchange that poststructuralism has studied. Cultural study is thus not on the periphery, as it is in the conventional Marxist model, for which the economic base determines the cultural superstructure. Instead, contemporary capitalism places cultural processes at the center of any understanding of society. We live under the sign of the spectacle, as Guy Debord has argued in *Society of the Spectacle* (Detroit, Mich.: Black and Red, 1973), or within a prison-house of discourse, to modify Fredric Jameson's apt title *The Prison-House of Language* (Princeton, N.J.: Princeton University Press, 1972). Language and culture do not allow us to express our relation to the world so much as they constitute that relation.

Thus, the need to improve our understanding of the social functions of culture and ideology assumes high priority. The cultural comes to be seen less as a privatized realm of personal enrichment and more as a socializing realm of ideological significance. It is within this framework that most of the articles in this volume develop their particular position. They show that a situation rife with paradox can stimulate rigorous inquiry and meaningful debate. They overcome paradox to exhibit both disciplinary strength *and* methodological borrowing, historical awareness *and* contemporary pertinence, formal analysis *and* contextual placement. As such, these articles are cause for celebration as well as paradigms for further study. My role here is to contextualize them, to point up the debates that persist among them, to show how they are fueled by the struggle to make methods and past achievements address continuing, sharply felt needs, and how that struggle can stimulate our own experience of film and our writing about it.

ON METHOD

Critical method in film study means something different from an analytic formula or from scientific method. Method generally involves a coherent cluster of shared assumptions about the nature of the world, what populates it, and what our relationship to it is. Scientific method subjects theory to rigid checks: If its predictions cannot be verified, it disappears (or lies dormant at best, pending verification). Cultural theory depends on a looser form of consensus. Its success depends on generating what we might call a "comprehension effect": It replaces curiosity with a sense of knowledge; it establishes assumptions, provides guidance or protocols for analytic procedures, and facilitates mutual understanding. The results of cultural theory are shared perspectives, not provable predictions, which, of course, means that questions of ideology, purpose, and institutional context are even more crucial in cultural theory than they are in science. Cultural study is a form of purposeful social activity possessing (sometimes hidden) agendas involving class, race, or sex; self-interest; and the dynamics of group formation and maintenance. Not even in science is there anything like pure theory, and certainly there is no such thing in cultural study.

Questions of consciousness and the unconscious, of subjectivity, of intentionality, of purpose and feedback or constraint are integral to culture. Such questions are not aberrations, errors, or fallacies to be bracketed, nor are they phenomena to be reduced to simplistic formulas. The only invariable is the continually shifting relationship between meaning and context. There are no absolutes or givens, nothing finally "objective." No formula can fully describe or fix the historically variable relationship between ourselves and the traces left by others that form our culture. Each object of study must be sighted and fixed repeatedly. Times and categories change. Perspectives differ.

Certainly, methodologies themselves come and go. An imaginative, bold new perception appears with broad explanatory power and compelling arguments, such as Michel Foucault's conception of history, Lévi-Strauss's of myth, Jacques Lacan's of psychoanalysis, Saussure's of language, or Bateson's of systems theory. Other individuals adapt, extend, champion, and implement some of the original principles in relation to new problems, demonstrating the viability of these principles over a range of issues and beginning the process of establishing an institutional discourse and practice. Still others amplify, illustrate, popularize, and defend the growing body of knowledge as a received way of doing things in which questions of professional or bureaucratic status and power become increasingly central. A paradigm or method evolves and with it an institutional apparatus that supports it. Such is the trajectory of social revolutions, industries, and scientific paradigms as well as of critical methods. The success of every new method depends on two things: first, its ability to fill a perceived lack or need as well as or better than alternative proposals or paradigms (this motivates people to adopt its assumptions and procedures); and second, its success in securing a position of power that it can maintain against competitors.

SOME COMMON THEMES

The five areas of methodological application represented by the articles collected in this volume—historical, genre, and feminist criticism along with structuralist semiotics and psychoanalytic semiotics—have all addressed perceived lacks or needs compellingly, and they have all gained positions of prominence within film study. (The articles in Part 6 exemplify methods that offer compelling indications both of problems in need of address and of ways of solving them, but these methods have yet to gain a position of institutional authority.)

All the methods represented in this volume strive for consistency and rigor but often in different and sometimes contrary or contradictory ways. Phenomenology stresses the open-endedness of interpretation and the primacy of experience, while structuralist semiotics stresses operating procedures that come close to generating replicable results (on the level of structure if not of meaning, since the "rules" for the construction of meaning are less variable than meaning itself). At the same time, these alternative methods have some things in common. In fact, the articles share a number of general preoccupations, which the reader is apt to encounter in other examples of contemporary film scholarship. These preoccupations concern the status of the text as a category, the level of generalization appropriate to cultural analysis, and the contentious issue of the individual or subject: Is the subject a workable category?

The Status of the Text

The very term *text* signals a desire for precision and specificity at the same time as it renders a more diffuse connotation: Film criticism uses methods developed for the criticism of texts to inspect its object in the hopes of understanding its working principles better. *Text* conveys a greater sense of methodological exactitude than the terms *movie* or *film,* partly because it implies that films are manifestations of certain characteristics found across a range of works that many non-film-specific methods are adept at analyzing.

In addition, from an historical perspective, the relations between text and reality (so central to realist theorists, such as Bazin and Kracauer) and between text and author (the main concern of auteur criticism) have yielded to a new set of relations: between text and context on the one hand, particularly in the articles in Parts 1 and 2 (for example, those by Ogle, Buscombe, Gomery, Wood, Dyer, and Waugh) and between text and viewer on the other, particularly in many of the articles in Parts 3 and 5 (for example, those by Mulvey, Baudry, Metz, and Studlar). In addition, the text is a particularly important site for the examination of discourse or language. As such, it can be scrutinized as a manifestation of rhetoric (as in Nick Browne's "The Spectator-in-the-Text: The Rhetoric of *Stagecoach*"), of narrative (as in Charles Eckert's "The Anatomy of a Proletarian Film: Warner's *Marked Woman*"), or of ideological contestation (as in Claire Johnston's "Towards a Feminist Film Practice: Some Theses"). The text can also serve as a proving ground for general theories about cinematic codes, as in Christian Metz's analysis of *Adieu Phillipine* in *Film Language* (New York: Oxford University Press, 1974) or in the assorted essays in *Film Reader,* no. 1 (1975), which all consider *Citizen Kane* in relation to Metz's *grande syntagmatique.* Thus, textual criticism could be considered a methodological category in itself (approximately twenty of the articles in this volume pay extended attention to particular films), but the assumptions of those who use the method are so heterogeneous that it seems preferable to indicate how important the method has become to all forms of analysis.

The Question of Generalization

How general can generalizations be? In some ways, the question is the other face of the textual analysis coin: If we try to group texts together in order to discover some general features, how far can we go? Of course, genre study builds on the assumption that texts can be grouped in telling ways. Often, historical study does, too; in discussing the coming of sound or of color in terms of economics and technology, what early examples of sound or color film have in common carries more weight than what they do not. In his early writings, Christian Metz attempted to characterize the cinema as a semiotic system. And many writers seek to identify the characteristics of modes of film production (such as artisanal, collective, or studio), or of movements, schools, genres, and oeuvres. In these cases, general categories take priority over the properties of specific films.

Debate about ideological effects sharpens the issue. Do narrative films or the cinematic apparatus—the entirety of the system of production, exchange, and consumption—have particular ideological effects? And if we grant that they do, to what extent do they dominate local or textually specific effects? Nick Browne's use of rhetorical concepts to examine how we read *Stagecoach* "against the grain" of general rules of spectator positioning developed in the articles by Christian Metz and Jean-Louis Baudry disputes the determining nature of any general form of positioning. Thomas Elsaesser's excellent essay, "Primary Identification and the Historical Subject: Fassbinder and Germany," in *Cine-tracts* 3, no. 3 (1980), which I was unable to include, carries the dispute from textual onto historical terrain, lending valuable specificity to the generalized use of the psychoanalytic concept of identification.

These challenges to easy generalization raise important questions about ideological determinations and aesthetic value. They cast doubt on the notion that any film, however innovative or radical, must produce certain "effects" at another, more controlling level. They also help to remind us that art gets lost in the rush to theory. Generalizations about ideological effects, semiotic features, and psycho dynamics apply to every text; aesthetic merit or quality may no longer be a central consideration at all. Traditionally, critics regard the effect of a text as dependent on its distinctive qualities. When this effect is cast in terms of "textual system," as Metz calls it, tension may well remain between textual analysis and general theory or between ideology as a function of an overarching system or apparatus and as a function of a specific textual instance. Even if we choose not to formulate a canon of good taste or to enforce prescriptions for good form, we must still account for the pleasure and fascination that some texts give, pleasure and fascination that seem to be functions of aesthetic principles as well as of ideological, psychoanalytic, or semiotic ones. These problems cannot be made to vanish merely by subsuming aesthetics under ideology, as Eagleton claims they can or as Laura Mulvey does in "Visual Pleasure and Narrative Cinema," where she argues that all Hollywood narrative conforms to the general requirement of providing viewing pleasure for men. Nor can we retreat to the higher ground of Art—of cinema as opposed to movies. Fredric Jameson contends that our choice is not between a crude mass culture and the refined high culture of previous generations but between mass culture and modernism as two sides of a contemporary effort to represent the conflicts of everyday life; see Jameson's "Reification and Utopia in Mass Culture," *Social Text,* no. 1 (1979): 130–48. But even within this slightly restricted field, questions of specificity and the link between aesthetics and ideological effect—questions ranging from issues of quality to issues of narrative structure raised by story/plot, voice, or *mise-en-scène*—remain the focus of a continuing debate. This debate also hinges on the question, For whom?—that is, who is the recipient of textual address?

The Death of the Subject

Today, the desire to resurrect a bygone aesthetic tied to great works of art that we can learn to appreciate is also a desire to resurrect the subject of humanism, namely, individual man [sic]. This man exists as the homotropic center of a natural universe available to consciousness and of a social universe governable by conscience. Is this "man" dead or alive? If he is not extinct, he is at least endangered. Feminism alone has seen to that, exposing as it has the extent to which the sublime nobility of humanist study rests on the celebration of the achievements of men by men. But the severest blows come from poststructuralism, which places the determinations of system and structure over those of individual volition.

Paul Ricoeur speaks of two great critical schools: the School of Revelation and the School of Suspicion. The first belongs to a humanism that seeks in art revelations of the human spirit in material form. The second belongs to a posthumanism that sees in texts the symptomatic display of the social order that produced them. The author becomes a fictitious unity masking the patterns of regulation and control that characterize the systems or codes of which the subject is only an expression. The humanist engagement with meaning and value as part of a search for ethical models and aesthetic standards is contextualized by the poststructuralist engagement with the production of meaning and values, models and standards as aspects of the belief systems that a given social order uses to win the consent of those whose consciousness, identity, and desire it regulates. Poststructuralist thought turns away from art, aesthetics, value, and man to question texts, codes, effects, and subject positions. It argues that the subject, "I," who believes that it exerts conscious control is actually subject to the systems—verbal language, semiotic codes—through which it speaks or that speak it. "I" is also subject to that locus of being which speaks but is never recognized, the unconscious. The subject as a rational individual exercising free will and self-determination becomes a fiction that facilitates acquiescence to the determinations of language and the unconscious, and, through them, of the social order—capitalist, patriarchal society in our case. When poststructural thought is regarded as political, it is usually because of its radical critique of the fundamental conception of the individual or subject. However, the political efficacy of such a critique, like the determining nature of generalizations, has yet to be fully demonstrated.

I will have a bit more to say about poststructuralist thought later in the Introduction, but its massive consequences for criticism should already be apparent. A gulf opens between our experience of a text and our understanding of that text, between effect and the production of effects, between the phenomenology of revelation and the psychodynamics of identification, between language as a vehicle for self-expression and language as an instrument of subject construction, between the self and other as poles of an ultimate unity and the unity of self and other as the ultimate fiction. The poststructuralist enterprise, whose influence is evident throughout this volume, situates pleasure in relation to sexuality and desire, and it situates sexuality and desire in relation to the hegemony of sexual difference, the dominance of male sexuality, the phallus, and patriarchy.

Hence, it becomes possible to say of a film that it "is constituted by a set of discourses," as Colin MacCabe does without naming the active agent ("Theory and Film: Principles of Realism and Pleasure," *Screen* 17, no. 3 [1976], p. 11). The use of the passive voice, like the discussion of effects, points to a problem: Can we assign an active agent to such effects? In the poststructuralist paradigm, the agency cannot be a subject, since the subject is itself an "effect." The agency can only reside in systems, structures, apparatuses, codes. To use the active voice is to anthropomorphize the analyst's abstract constructs. Perhaps a set of discourses constitutes a film, but how, by what agency? This "set,"—something akin to what anthropologists call culture—must still be placed in relation to human agency. Otherwise, poststructuralism paints itself into a deterministic corner. Humanist concepts of free will and determinism, with their limited grasp of system and structure, are no longer acceptable solutions. Film scholarship, under the influence of poststructuralism, has not found a way out of this corner. Effects just happen to us. Ideology is controlling. Hopes get pinned to counter cinema—modernist texts that produce "knowledge effects" about ideology and the cinematic apparatus. To a remarkable degree, the majority of poststructuralist writers has neglected to seek solutions from other methods, such as the systems theory concepts of goal seeking and constraints, which replace free will and determinism. The heterogeneity of research methods at work in film study may not yet be quite as eclectic as it should be.

The status of these three terms—*text, generalization,* and *subject*—has assumed a broad importance. Regardless of methodology, almost all writers today have definite assumptions about these terms in mind when they analyze the cinema. What kind of object is under scrutiny, how general can our discussion be, and what relationship does the object have to those who encounter it? Historical, genre, feminist, semiotic, rhetorical, phenomenological, and Marxist answers will vary, but, to an appreciable degree, writers using these different approaches ask very similar questions. Concern with a few central, highly problematic issues often characterizes critical inquiry and artistic practice within a given period of intellectual and artistic crisis. As a result, this volume, like the first volume of *Movies and Methods,* can be thought of not as a series of monologues by writers indifferent to each other's speech but as an extended dialogue that, through cross-references and common preoccupations, sustains a debate on most of the basic questions posed about culture today.

Poststructuralism stands at the storm center of this debate. That may well be another sign that film study has achieved institutional status: Debates about methodology begin to predominate over debates about substance. It becomes more important to determine the writer's methodological and political orientation than it is to determine the substantive nature of an issue. Concomitantly, the sense that film represented a potent means for engaging with pressing topical issues, which motivated much of the interest in film in the 1960s, has been sustained most actively by individuals who maintain some distance from the poststructural paradigm. For example, compare these two statements about the practice of filmmaking:

Any relation of history in cinema risks simple reactionary effects if not passed through reflection on the current reality of such a practice, which reality includes the fact—the present history and institution—of cinema. (Stephen Heath, *Questions of Cinema* [Bloomington: Indiana University Press, 1981],p. 238)

Can filmmakers afford to undertake an abstract analysis or make an educational statement *about* representation if it is politically imperative that they represent a "brutal actuality" in order to counteract its ideological version? (Jane Gaines, "Women and Representation," *Jump Cut,* no. 29 [1984]: 26)

Attempts to address an issue without formally engaging the mediating agency of discursive means can be seen as naive, amateur, untheorized, or nonacademic. And the method that has been most influential in its insistence on the theoretical primacy of language and the production of meaning is poststructuralism. Although other methods might have made the same claim, poststructural semiotics, especially psychoanalytic semiotics, has presented itself as serious theoretical scholarship of a progressive nature because of the attention that it pays to the question of how meaning and spectator positions get produced. For this reason, poststructuralism occupies a position in film study not unlike that of the existential Other. In its Lacanian, ideologically engaged form, poststructuralism has come to represent an authoritative theoretical discourse with which its alternatives must come to terms. Alternative views acknowledge their own departure from or indebtedness to this model far more often than they do for any other methodology. It is clear that such acknowledgment is due in part to the primacy that poststructuralism has claimed for itself, sometimes inappropriately.

Poststructuralism poses the question of methodological primacy on two levels. Both levels involve questions of hierarchy or logical typing, not an either-or choice. On one level is the concept that the higher logical type—a class of objects, such as a methodology or a language—constrains the lower logical type—members of the class of objects or statements made using a given method or language. This is not to say that membership in a class determines all the qualities or characteristics of the members of that class. Although this claim is often made, it is quite simply wrong. If it were correct, no process of dialectical transformation (*Aufhebung*) would be possible in either natural or social systems. Thus, method or language exerts a constraining influence on any statements made within its frame, and that influence has some important consequences. But the messages also matter, and they are not fully determined by the method or language system that organizes them. In this regard, poststructuralist critics, especially psychoanalytic critics, have overemphasized methodological orthodoxy as an evaluative criterion.

On the other level is the question of logical typing within poststructuralism. A psychoanalytic theory of the construction of the subject has a different order of generality than a social theory of the actions of constructed subjects does. Any theory of how individuality is constituted constrains any theory of how individuals engage with their world, but these are two different levels of theory, and one cannot simply determine the other. In giving priority to theories of the construction of the subject and subjectivity, especially in relation to language, poststructuralism has sometimes overstated its claims and assumed that such theories are determining. That assumption is wrong, although the limits or constraints proposed by poststructuralism for the subject may be of major consequence, as the articles in Part 5 show.

In the introductions to individual articles, I have undertaken to sharpen the sense in which poststructuralism has served as a significant Other in both positive and negative terms: as a radical challenge to received notions of individual subjects and their socialization and as a dangerous distraction from the immediate political issues that confront us as preconstituted individuals.

THE METHODS THEMSELVES

Each of the methods represented in this volume has considerable explanatory power, and each has engendered appreciable research activity. And, although each method has addressed questions of text, generalization, and the subject, it has done so in a distinctive way. For example, the authors of the articles in Part 1 rely on concrete details to substantiate general propositions. These details are not always textual. Such scholars as Douglas Gomery and Janet Staiger use new kinds of source material to reconstruct such events as the coming of sound or the standardization of film production, and Jean-Louis Comolli turns from primary source material to the claims that others have made about the early cinema. For the most part, historical writing has benefited immensely from the development of an academic base for film scholarship, both in the study of textual matters of style or structure and in the study of contextual matters of economics or technology. Archival deposits of films and documents have facilitated extensive revision of the received wisdom of earlier film histories. In its recent, revisionist phase, film history has insisted as much on specifics as on generalizations and on the subject as an historical agent as much as on the subject as an ideological effect.

Like genres themselves, genre criticism remains remarkably durable. Interests shift—from westerns to melodrama, from genre in relation to auteurs to genre in relation to structure or history and ideology. But the need both to group films into meaningful categories that indicate significant elements in common and to follow the transformation of those elements over time remains strong. At the same time, despite the explanatory power of genre criticism and despite its ability to sustain research, its steps to resolve this need have run contrary to some of the central tendencies of poststructuralist work, which Paul Willemen described in his "Presentation" for *Genre* (ed. Stephen Neale [London: British Film Institute, 1980], p. 3) as "the need to account for cinema as a specific signifying practice involving questions regarding the relation between texts and viewers (problem of the look, questions of address and subject construction, problem of identification/distanciation, etc.)."

Of course, genre study does account for cinema as a specific signifying practice, but the terms that it uses are more structural and intertextual than they are viewer oriented. Often, the stress on genre structure or textual strategy obtains its full significance from the implications that it is seen to have for viewers—as the articles by Wood, Nichols, MacDougall, and Penley and Bergstrom suggest—but the nature or construction of the viewer usually is not a central problematic. Genre criticism and structuralist semiotics provide an extremely valuable methodology for the derivation of general principles from specific instances, whether in relation to fiction, or documentary, or the avant-garde.

The articles collected in Part 3 show that feminist film criticism and theory have an urgently political tone that is only sometimes characteristic of other methods. Several articles in the other parts of this volume—notably those by Joyce Nelson, Robin Wood, Gaylyn Studlar, and Peter Baxter—adopt a feminist perspective, concerned as they are with sexual difference in the cinema. The need that feminist criticism addresses—to examine the representation of sexual difference and the sexual positioning of the spectator—is immediately personal and ideological. Certainly, feminist criticism has substantially improved our understanding of how meaning gets constructed within a highly charged social context that makes the notion of pure entertainment an impossible fiction.

One strand of feminist writing, represented most forcefully by Laura Mulvey's article, "Visual Pleasure and Narrative Cinema," assumes that the sort of semiotic psychoanalytic theory associated with Jacques Lacan is a necessary prerequisite for a specifically feminist film theory. In film study generally, Lacan's work has helped to shift consideration to a high level of theoretical abstraction, where the key questions involve the cinematic apparatus, the production of meaning, representation, narrative, and the constitution of spectator positions. These operations, it is argued, explain how the commercial cinema functions to address predominantly male pleasure. Understanding these operations in turn valorizes a feminist film practice that focuses critically on these same operations—a practice associated with the work of Chantal Akerman, Yvonne Rainer, and Marguerite Duras.

Other feminists—represented here by the articles by Loader, Rich, Williams and Rich, and Turim—regard this tendency to valorize the most theoretical feminist filmmakers and to stress the determining power of the broadest generalizations as useful but constricting. These writers differentiate among specific uses of narrative, realism, spectator positioning, or the cinematic apparatus without insisting in every instance on addressing the general issues that these practices raise. Nor do they attribute determining power to abstract generalizations, although they readily acknowledge their importance. (*Jump Cut,* no. 29 [1984] offers an extremely valuable state-of-the-art summary of both tendencies.) The second tendency in feminist criticism stresses the importance of working to develop a more historically and socially specific understanding of sexual difference, a less phallocentric conception of the female than that of lack or castrating threat, and a more diverse canon of exemplary feminist filmmaking.

Structuralist semiotics originates in Metz's early efforts to describe the cinema as an object, efforts well summarized in Paul Sandro's article, "Signification in the Cinema." Metz's initial concern was with codes, not texts; with general regulating principles, not specific applications. However, this taxonomic effort flagged rather quickly and soon became attached to the analysis of specific texts—as in Charles Eckert's exemplary essay, "The Anatomy of a Proletarian Film: Warner's *Marked Woman*"—or to a psychoanalytic current that sought to account for desire, the unconscious, and the spectator, work exemplified by the articles in Part 5. Eckert has subsequently questioned whether a synthesis of structuralism, Freudianism, and Marxism is either desirable or possible. The authors of the remaining articles in Part 4 have demonstrated that an affirmative answer is possible. Stephen Heath's essay, "*Jaws*, Ideology, and Film Theory," sketches a rationale for the transition to psychoanalytic theory: An analysis of the *operation* cinema (its capacity to mark out positions and possibilities for the viewer) is a necessary complement to an anatomy of the *object* cinema.

Psychoanalytic semiotics has tended to occupy the high ground of theoretical generalization and to focus its attention on the question of the subject. For example, the very generality of Lacan's notion of woman as lack or castrating threat makes it a controlling perspective. It has a potentially large "comprehension effect," since it covers virtually all narrative film. Such a notion of the female subject also addresses a noticeable problem, since previous generalizations about cinema tended to be based on moral presumption and to lack much methodological buttress. The corrupting or merely entertaining cinema of popular writing yields to the phallocentric cinema of academic scholarship.

The two articles that make the most vivid and compelling argument for the determining power of fundamental operations underlying the great majority of films are Laura Mulvey's "Visual Pleasure and the Narrative Cinema" and Jean-Louis Baudry's "Ideological Effects of the Basic Cinematographic Apparatus."[2] These essays offer a powerful explanatory framework, and they have stimulated considerable research activity. Of all the articles in this volume, they best establish the terms and conditions of the poststructural Other; the movement of other writers toward and away from their assumptions and arguments—the articles by Studlar and Browne are good examples of departures—give a sound measure of the force field organized by poststructural, psychoanalytic methodology.

Part 6, Countercurrents, conveys some of the diversity now at work in film studies. The articles in Part 6 point to needs or problems not yet addressed or not satisfactorily addressed by the prevalent methodologies. Some, like Branigan's "The Point-of-View Shot," give priority to specific questions involving the text. Others, like Wood's "Responsibilities of a Gay Film Critic" and Andrew's "The Neglected Tradition of Phenomenology in Film Theory," give priority to general questions of methodology and the kind of results they produce. Some, like Polan's "A Brechtian Cinema? Towards a Politics of Self-Reflexive Film," dispute the notion of broad, determining ideological effects; others, like Salt's "Statistical Style Analysis of Motion Pictures," help to correct false generalizations about directorial style at the level of the shot. Each article indicates the explanatory power of an alternative way of looking at films and suggests, at least implicitly, some of the research issues that its methodology might address fruitfully.

These essays also give some hint of things to come, of methods that may well gain ascendancy in the years ahead. Prominent among these, I would suggest, are empirical research, viewer-response criticism, neoformalism, and continuing efforts to find a compelling synthesis of Freud and Marx. Film study, developing as it has within a humanities context, has vigorously eschewed empirical research. The tendency for film study to align with the general field of cultural studies and the resulting overlap of interests with the objects of study and the methods of the social sciences (most notably in regard to television) make it quite likely that film studies will take up, and give special inflection to, the use of empirical methodologies. Efforts to move away from broad effects that constitute subjects and positions toward concepts of negotiation and active reading make viewer-response-oriented work an area of considerable promise, while neoformalism has introduced a vital specificity that often challenges historical, aesthetic, and ideological conclusions reached by other methods. And the need to achieve some theoretically satisfying combination of the personal and the political, the social field of interaction and the unconscious domain of desire, will certainly continue to motivate extensive effort. Together with other methods, such as phenomenology, these nascent tendencies seem to indicate that the next period will be quite different from the one that extended from the mid seventies to the early eighties, where one method, poststructuralism, proved strikingly dominant. Rather than concluding the volume with the sense of an ending, with the sense of methodological debate resolved, Part 6 serves to convey a sense of open-endedness. It acknowledges that the process of matching method to need, meaning to purpose, is a continuing one and that diversity is itself a source of the new.

POSTSTRUCTURALISM AS OTHER:
SOME FURTHER THOUGHTS

Although poststructuralism has dominated film study for the past decade or so, it has its share of internal contradictions and inconsistencies, which produce gaps or fissures where paradox shows through. They point to issues that may not be able to be resolved within the methodological frame within which they are posed. As I show in *Ideology and the Image* (Bloomington: Indiana University Press, 1981), poststructuralism has introduced powerful concepts of ideology, representation, and the subject. But it also has its limits. A brief survey of six points of tension can clarify both the power of the method and its limits.

(1) *Identification.* The authors of several articles in this volume liken the film experience to what Jacques Lacan has called the *mirror-phase,* although they differ about the particulars. The gist of the argument is that we enter into a primary identification with the succession of images on a screen regardless of content. "All that remains is the brute fact of seeing: the seeing of an outlaw," as Metz argues (see his article, "Story/Discourse," in this volume). In contrast to theories of viewing as a dreamlike state expressed in early Freudian accounts of the cin-

ema, this argument establishes a relationship that pivots on voyeurism, fetishism, and narcissism to establish a controlling, ahistorical relation between viewer and screen. To that identification, viewers then add a secondary identification with particular images, namely characters, especially with their faces.

Poststructuralism asks what are the consequences of these conditions of relation to the screen and the representations that appear on it. Through the notion of suture (discussed in Dayan's "The Tutor-Code of Classical Cinema" in the first volume of *Movies and Methods*), identification becomes understood as a process, a continual displacement of positions that undermines the traditional notion of identification as a simple attachment between subject and object, viewer and image. And yet the consequences of such identification remain deeply engrained in the Lacanian model that produced them. Individuals become positioned as viewers or spectators. Their collective relation to the screen as an audience, with the accompanying particularities of class, race, sex, and place—in short, history—is suppressed by the particularities of individual subject formation. Poststructuralist work claims political value for its insights into this formation process, but, because it remains historically dimensionless, that political value is in acute need of supplementation.

(2) *Analogy.* Poststructuralist work draws a number of analogies regarding the cinema and also raises the issue of analogy as an analytic procedure in its own right. The sheer number of analogies is striking. In recent years, cinema has been likened to Plato's cave, the Lacanian mirror-phase, Freudian dreamwork, and Lévi-Straussian myth, to name only a few. All have served a valuable, stimulating role, broadening the range of comparisons by which we can come to know cinema. However, analogies are imprecise, because they propose likenesses, not identities. Charles Altman's article, "Psychoanalysis and Cinema: The Imaginary Discourse," pursues this point quite vividly. Altman argues that we risk creating an imaginary unity and coherence to cinema by likening it all to a single thing. In an exceptionally polemical and prolix critique of Stephen Heath's work not included in this volume, Noël Carroll disputes the rigor of all analogies, which he describes as primarily rhetorical devices designed to persuade the reader that a certain perspective is useful.[3] To liken the cinema to something else is one thing, but, in the absence of an adequate elaboration of differences, it leaves us with allegorical or formulaic readings: The cinema repeats the experience of the mirror-phase, primary narcissism, or the dream without transforming these experiences into a pattern peculiar to its own historical conditions of existence. The articles in this volume by Browne, Andrew, and Jameson all seek to provide some redress by calling for greater textual and historical precision.

(3) *Effects.* As already noted, poststructuralism tends to speak more frequently of effects than of causes. Cinema is said to produce ideological effects. There are effects of the basic cinematic apparatus and of narrative, suture, point of view, and an *énonciation* that masks its own production. There is the effect of producing a subject position for the viewer—through linear perspective, or scopophilia, or illusionism. Poststructuralism seeks to describe more general, nonmeasurable effects that usually involve the construction by films of the very con-

ception of the subject or individual. As a methodological perspective, it brackets empirical research, which it sees as complicit with the very assumptions about the constitution of the subject and human agency that it calls into question. Verification is irrelevant for a method based on speculative metaphors, analogies, and psychoanalytic hypotheses about the structure of the unconscious.

The absence of verification procedures causes some to balk. Because it lacks such procedures, poststructuralism conforms to Popper's description in *Conjectures and Refutations* (London: Routledge and Kegan Paul, 1963) of a nonscience, although the extremely radical nature of its critique of the subject, subjectivity, and language makes the desire for proof all the greater. The explanatory power of the critique and its capacity to stimulate new work that stands outside the humanist tradition, that offers a political perspective from which to criticize the implicit deficiencies and biases of that tradition, however limited that perspective may be, is proof enough that poststructuralism has use value, but, by emphasizing effects, it has failed to provide an adequate model for process, change, or history. It remains primarily a deterministic and synchronic model, not a dialectic and diachronic one.

(4) *Language and Ideology.* Poststructuralist work does not regard language or, by extension, film as the neutral means by which we understand ourselves, others, and our world. Rather, it draws on versions of the Whorf-Sapir hypothesis, which describes a world constructed in, by, and through language. In this view, language or film offers entry into a realm of symbolic exchange, but, via an elaborate linkage to Freudian theory, it does so only on condition that we accept a resolution of the Oedipus complex. This requires us to accept the phallus as the signifier of difference par excellence and gender difference as male dominated. Language or interdiction breaks down the special bond between child and mother in the mirror-phase. The father's prohibition against incest, which breaks the bond, is also a positive injunction to represent oneself in language, to demand with words what one cannot have or sustain by more direct means. That is, the special, potentially incestuous bond with the mother—henceforth the union of full relationality— can be achieved only through representation and then only in part. The child enters a symbolic realm of spoken exchange in which the vocable "I" can represent his or her physical body. And, gradually, that "I" becomes a central feature of the individual.[4]

The cinema, in speaking to us, also proposes an "I" who speaks, although it is usually masked, so that stories appear to tell themselves. As a cultural institution, however, the "I" of the dominant cinema speaks a social discourse that is patriarchal and capitalist, among other things. Much poststructural writing has examined how this is so, primarily in relation to patriarchy. Many of the feminist and semiotic articles included in this volume consider the ideological function of language or discourse to be tied to the question of gender in powerful ways. Gay criticism has pursued the same premise, examining how heterosexuality becomes posited as a norm and how the union of the heterosexual couple becomes a standard definition of narrative closure. (Robin Wood's article "An Introduction to the American Horror Film" shows how the monster represents the variety of forces, which include homosexuality, that threaten the bourgeois nuclear family.)

The linkage of language to ideology invites new strategies of reading. The text can be considered troubled, and its troubles—the displacements and evasions, the structuring absences—can be considered symptomatic of irresolvable social contradiction. Nowell-Smith's article, "Minnelli and Melodrama," does precisely that. But troubled texts are only half the story. There are also troubling texts. Colin MacCabe, in "Realism and Cinema: Notes on Some Brechtian Theses," *Screen* 15, no. 2 (Summer 1974): 7–17, refers to the same difference when he speaks of strategies of subversion. Troubling texts subvert expectations. They use formal structuring principles against the grain of normal usage. They jar, disorient, and block the construction of conventional subject positions. MacCabe, like many, cites Brecht and Godard as prime examples. Others turn to Japanese and Third World examples; see, for example, Kristin Thompson and David Bordwell, "Space and Narrative in the Films of Ozu," *Screen* 17, no. 2 (Summer 1976): 41–73, and Julianne Burton's "The Politics of Aesthetic Distance: The Presentation of Representation in *São Bernardo*," *Screen* 24, no. 2 (March–April 1983): 30–53.

Reading for symptoms and effects further differentiates poststructuralist analysis from the traditional approaches. Direct links between texts and social action are mediated by the need to interrogate the language of cinema itself and by the view that effects do not prompt actions but establish positions from which actions can follow. Hence, cathartic and imitative theories of identification fall into disrepute. To take one example, male-oriented heterosexual pornography could be regarded as a source of catharsis, because it releases male sexual energies vicariously. However, it could also be seen as a stimulus to imitation—harmlessly through masturbation or dangerously through sexual aggression or rape. Finally, it could be read as symptomatic of the construction of gender identity in our culture and of the forms of action that these identities render probable.

This last position, which is the position of poststructuralism, clearly has value, not least because it avoids simplified notions of causality that might otherwise plague any theoretical critique or political opposition to a "specific signifying practice," such as pornography. The insistence on reading texts as semiotic utterances, not as the direct equivalent of physical actions (usually violent or sexual actions, or both), maintains the correct form of logical types (what lies inside the frame, pornography, cannot cause what occurs outside the frame, society; if anything, it will be the contrary)—and it gives priority to the ideological implications of discursive practices. The danger lies in not recognizing that there are also illogical types: For a few viewers, a genuine short circuit occurs in which the viewing of pornography leads to criminal actions; poststructuralism has no theory for such occurrences. There is another danger as well: Poststructuralism cannot step beyond discourse as an object of theoretical inquiry. The analysis of the ideological implications of language, especially in relation to gender, is one thing; the step beyond to an agenda that translates the political perspective into political intervention is another. (For a method rooted in the traditions of academic discourse, that may be a step beyond the academy and its internal criteria for use value.) This danger creates a gap or fissure between poststructural methodologies and Marxism, even when those methodologies are conceived of politically.

(5) *The Mirror of Production.* Jean Baudrillard's book *The Mirror of Production* (St. Louis: Telos Press, 1975) poses a question that reveals yet another problematic analogy: Must we conceptualize the text within a framework of production and consumption? Like phallocentrism, ethnocentrism, and logocentrism, econocentrism takes one quality to be the measure of humankind, that is, labor power. Poststructuralism adapts the metaphor of productive labor to the text. The text produces effects through specific signifying practices; it embodies a production of meaning. The critic's task is to deconstruct that production and to point to or suggest new constructions.

Many poststructuralists take up this form of diagnostic, deconstructive argumentation, which resembles Marx's, in order to free us from the hegemony of the dominant mode of signification, the discourse of phallocentric capitalism. The question remains, Are the basic assumptions that they contest repeated in the critique itself? Is Lacanian psychoanalysis itself phallocentric, and is the critique of textual production itself econocentric? As Mark Poster writes in his introduction to Baudrillard's book, "Far from transcending political economy, Marxism, to Baudrillard, strengthens and extends its most basic propositions. Man is conceptualized as a producing animal just as in political economy, except that Marx wants to liberate his productive potential. This still leaves us with a metaphor or 'mirror' of production through which alone every aspect of social activity is intelligible. And so contemporary French theorists remain trapped in this conceptual cage: Althusser sees theory as 'production,' Deleuze and Guattari give us an unconscious that is a 'producer' of desire, the *Tel Quel* group refers to textual 'production'" (p. 3).

As a consequence of such entrapment by the metaphor of production, poststructuralism has difficulty granting that texts or culture can overcome the sphere of production and the constraints of ideology. Production and ideology become so all-inclusive that they have no outside. The position of a Marxist like Herbert Marcuse who grants to art the possibility of "the great refusal," especially in his *Eros and Civilization*, becomes just another vain hope. At best, the text or culture can lay bare the means of its own production and construct a critique of discursive practices and their effects; this, however, remains a matter of production—a matter of good over bad production, an ethics of productive practice. It seems to be a position at one with the divided self, the split subject, the schizophrenia of an identity based on an Other it can never match. Texts become cadavers that can be diagnosed both for subversive strategies and for malignancies that infect the body politic. But struggle inside a cycle of production and consumption requires some vision of existence beyond, some merger of the hermeneutics of suspicion with the hermeneutics of revelation cast not in the spiritual, idealist terms of Paul Ricoeur but in secular, material terms. It is one thing to be asked to labor to produce meaning from difficult, troubling texts that refuse the ideologically loaded pleasures of easy, merely troubled texts; it is another thing to know that these labors are for some transforming end. That consideration leads directly to the sixth area of potential crisis.

(6) *The Work Ethic*. Some texts demand that we work vigorously to comprehend them. As Peter Wollen's article, "Godard and Counter Cinema: *Vent d'Est*," indicates, much modernist and postmodernist art presents a dense surface that is hard to penetrate. The pleasure of watching Chantal Akerman's *Jeanne Dielman*, a film to which several feminist articles refer, is very different in kind from the pleasure of watching *Singin' in the Rain* and the other musicals that Richard Dyer examines in his article, "Entertainment and Utopia." Many contemporary artists want us to confront our usual mode of engaging with cultural products that have been fabricated for uncritical consumption. Clearly, this is an issue of some importance. It implies that pleasure cannot be taken as innocent, since many cultural products ultimately demean or diminish us by reproducing and representing the relations of production that exploit and oppress us. However, the sharpest opposition is not between a corrupt popular culture and a progressive avant-garde that refuses ideology by refusing conventional means of expression— a point vividly pursued by Constance Penley in "The Avant-Garde and Its Imaginary"—but between different ways of seeing or reading culture in any form.

It is too easy to say merely that viewers of popular film are passively positioned or fixed by ideological effects and that viewers of modernist work actively confront these effects. Most viewers bring resistance strategies, selective responses, and active skepticism to bear on their experience. That fact is sometimes overlooked. An understanding of viewers' active, resistant, "deviant" readings of texts cannot be subordinated to the hard work of critics who "produce" a deconstructive reading in hope of offsetting the work's production of ideological effects. (Tania Modleski's *Loving with a Vengeance: Mass-Produced Fantasies for Women* [Hamden, Conn.: Archon Books, 1982] pays careful attention to the active processes required in reading formulaic fiction, such as soap operas. Modleski's book provides a vivid example of a method that responds to the actual practice of reading.) Many poststructuralist articles that draw inspiration from Bertolt Brecht, such as Peter Wollen's article here on *Vent d'Est* or Martin Walsh in his *Brechtian Aspects of Radical Cinema* (London: British Film Institute, 1982), appear to endorse a disconcerting blend of Calvinism and Marxism. The need to move beyond a politics of discipline, refusal, and work derived from an ethical and religious heritage is a challenge that poststructuralism has yet to address adequately.

The work ethic returns in another way as well. That is, the critic is not a guide or an apologist but a clinician. When ideology was thought of as a set of ideas or as false consciousness, art was considered subversive. But thinking of ideology as an unconscious pattern of lived relations causes criticism to become the subversive art. The old aesthetics of pleasure is now seen as a pathology of pleasure. Feminist and psychoanalytic writers argue that narrative structures address their pleasure to men. Women exist to be looked at; they appear as images of veneration or lust. To accept the pleasures that these images provide is to share the neurotic pathologies imposed by a patriarchal regulation of gender and thus to accept complicity with sexism.

For that reason, criticism must make the Great Refusal. That is, we must learn how to refuse the pleasures that excuse and perpetuate contradictions of sex, race, class, and nation. What was once the subject matter of aesthetics—representation, illusionism, fascination, pleasure, the idealized image of women—is now seen as symptoms of neurosis. Voyeurism and fetishism become diagnostic categories; the threat of castration and the power of the gaze become key elements in a calculus of sexual domination. A counter aesthetics of psychopathology has emerged that takes it upon itself to tear the veil of innocence from the face of culture.

One might well question whether the social is not slighted in such reliance on a particular psychoanalytic model, but revision of our understanding of desire, pleasure, ideology, and narrative is not itself the problem. There is a risk in valorizing an analytic diagnostics of culture that, in refusing ideologically complicit pleasures, backs into a position of denying pleasure entirely or of withholding pleasure until social conditions can be changed. Denial does not have to follow from caution, but vestiges of a peculiarly leftist Calvinism again complicate the picture. The mirror of production applies to criticism as well as to art. In our culture, work, labor, analytic logic, the will to knowledge can all too readily take precedence over play, leisure, poetic or dialectical logic, and the pursuit of pleasure. The reality principle looms large for critics, too. Within the poststructuralist school of suspicion, critical interrogation can pride itself on its ability to resist the lure of the text in order to deconstruct it. The danger lies in allowing that resistance to become an end in itself. If it does, we return to a distrust of art and nonanalytic reason that is at least as old as Plato.

The fact that the field of film study has become increasingly institutionalized, more and more the province of professional scholars, is another inducement to valorize the sober-minded work ethic. However, for most people, including critics, culture is interesting precisely because it embodies the reasons of the heart that analytic reason does not understand. Whatever our methodological bent or political commitments, we do well to remain suspicious of a methodology founded on poetic metaphors and analogies that seeks to limit us to a Cartesian logic that can analyze desire but not fulfill it.

LANGUAGE AND AUTHORITY

The final and most contextual question regarding poststructural criticism involves its use of language, which is more than a question of so-called good English. It is also a matter of the pragmatics of communication, the effect of messages on others, and of its particular inflection within an institutionalized context.

The basic objection to poststructuralism at this level is that too much of the writing is "difficult" and that it uses this difficulty to tyrannize the reader. Frequently, such writing strains, or even violates, grammatical conventions. Often its meaning remains elusive, even after much rereading. And more than one scholar has thrown up his or her hands in exasperation at what Dana Polan calls "terrorist semiotics."[5]

The issue of poststructuralism's use of language invites polemic, because it touches on so many deeply felt beliefs about the nature and purpose of language and because it intersects with so many complicating factors involving institutions, discourse, and power. However, it is essential for us to address the issue, because it gives us a final opportunity to estimate the place of poststructuralism in film study.

Difficult language has no monopoly on tyranny. Most religious cults indoctrinate their participants into a set of beliefs that could be (and sometimes are) articulated by anyone with a grade-school education. A "tyranny of lucidity," as Catherine Belsey calls it in *Critical Practice* (London and New York: Methuen, 1980), informs all advertising, most religious cults, and a great deal of everyday conversation. In a (suspiciously) lucid passage, Belsey thus summarizes the most widespread defense for difficult language:

The transparency of language is an illusion. Partly as a consequence of [post-Saussurean] theory, the language used by practitioners [of such theory] is usually far from transparent. The effect of this is to alert the reader to the opacity of language, and to avoid the "tyranny of lucidity," the impression that what is being said must be true because it is so obvious, clear and familiar. The discourses of post-Saussurean writers like Louis Althusser, Roland Barthes, Jacques Derrida and Jacques Lacan, though different from each other in very important ways, share this property of difficulty, and not simply from a perverse desire to be obscure. To challenge familiar assumptions and familiar values in a discourse which, in order to be easily readable, is compelled to reproduce these assumptions and values, is an impossibility. New concepts, new theories, necessitate new, unfamiliar and therefore initially difficult discourses. (pp. 4–5)

Difficulty may then be regarded as a necessary condition for challenging familiar views, especially views about language. A semiopaque form of discourse is part of the radical critique of the classical humanist conception of self, world, and language. Instead of the means by which the self expresses its understanding of the world, language becomes this self and mediates, if not determines, its conception of the world. Difficult language reminds us of the material, mediating presence of language through the effort that it demands.

However, whether semiopacity is helpful, let alone necessary and sufficient, for the articulation of an alternative social and linguistic theory is not proved conclusively by making an analogy between conceptual difficulty and discursive difficulty. Difficult, innovative concepts that have profound implications, such as biological evolution or the Copernican theory of a heliocentric universe, can be communicated in simple, clear prose. But more is involved. Difficult language has an institutional as well as a theoretical context, and the institutional context has considerable bearing when we move from theory in the abstract to the institutional production, distribution, and consumption of knowledge, which take place mainly in the academic realm.

In an historical context, difficult language can be classified by type and by purpose. Some writing is conceptually difficult. Its notions may violate common sense or reject habitual ways of seeing. No matter how clearly written such writing is, it may still be difficult. Other writing is stylistically or syntactically difficult. It may use complex figures of speech or rhetorical devices; it may be highly

metaphorical or allegorical; or it may use numerous subordinate clauses, preposi-
tional phrases, or parenthetical expressions. Such writing may convey relatively
commonplace ideas in a way that makes them difficult to grasp.

What purpose does difficult writing serve? Belsey suggests that it produces a
"comprehension effect" regarding our understanding of the force of language in
the constitution of our own subjectivity, at least in poststructuralist theory. That is
not one of the usual reasons for using difficult language. The use of difficult language is more commonly associated with the rise of institutions relying on bureaucratic, rational-legal authority to wield considerable social power and marginally with the self-preservation of persecuted minority groups, which often use
guileful, opaque language as a necessary defense. In contrast to charismatic authority, institutional authority requires clearly defined protocols, channels of
communication, and a fixed, determinate hierarchy. An elite—legal, medical,
theological, political, or intellectual—controls special means of linguistic articulation as a necessary consequence of its institutional basis. Part of the elite's
training as experts lies in learning how to use the language of the profession with
precision. Using the language with precision requires the ability to present what
George Orwell called a "defense of the indefensible"; at the least, it means possessing the rhetorical skill needed to legitimize institutional practices.

Thus, language in the service of institutional, hierarchical authority sustains
the positions of elites; the presence of social divisions, such as those based on
class, race, or sex; and the perpetuation of institutional power. In the context of
normalized conceptual categories, stylistically or syntactically difficult language
normally operates to achieve either precision or obfuscation. As Robert Bo-
guslaw notes in his book, *The New Utopians* (Englewood Cliffs, N.J.: Prentice-
Hall, 1965), "gobbledygook is *not* simply semantic folderol. It is a mechanism for
dealing with deeply rooted ambiguity." From this perspective, the function of
difficult language is to set up meticulous specifications and conditions so as to
forestall argument (for example, legal contract phraseology) and for obscuring
indefensible acts with euphemism and evasion.

Poststructuralist writing contests institutional authority in the university by
contesting the intellectual legitimacy of the humanist, homocentric paradigm.
That is one level of conceptual difficulty, but that is not the level that seems to
cause the greatest debate. It is the level of stylistic or syntactic difficulty that
provokes charges of obscurantism, hostility or diffidence toward the reader, and
contempt for the popularizing impulse. The authors of a collectively written critique of *Screen*'s seeming endorsement of semiotic psychoanalysis ("Psychoanalysis and Film," *Screen* 16, no. 4 [1975–1976]: 119–30), pointed to two types of
obscurity in previous articles. One type was the result of "the attempt to com-
press complicated ideas." Though understandable, they found its frequency disturbing, since it suggested to them that *Screen* was impatient with readers who
needed summaries. The second type of obscurity was "a matter of a particular
strategy of writing." They cite this example of such writing from *Screen*:

The problem is to understand the terms of construction of the subject and the modalities of
the replacement of this construction but also, more difficultly, the supplacement—the over-

placing: supplementation or, in certain circumstances, supplantation (critical interruption) of that construction in its place of repetition. (*Screen* 16, no. 2 [Summer 1975], p. 87)

The authors of the critique analyze the difficulty (pp. 122–23):

This is an example of a strategy of writing derived from Roland Barthes in which the use of "precise" terms from other intellectual disciplines is combined with an interest in the play of language (a play in this instance of the similar sounds in the words "supplacement," "overplacing," "supplementation," "supplantation"). The strategy seems to us a confusing one with the play of language undermining the attempt to be precise.

This critique remains compelling. It has not been rebutted, and much poststructuralist writing remains highly vulnerable to it. Intolerant attacks on poststructuralism as elitist and obscurantist or imprecise made by those already entrenched within the academy may, of course, simply be part of struggles for institutional power, struggles in which poststructuralism remains the underdog. It deserves limited political support for precisely that reason: Even if the university has become an institution like any other, vestigial concepts, such as academic freedom and tenure, support a model of genuine pluralism that confounds notions of bureaucratic authority and instrumental knowledge; the struggle to retain even vestiges of this utopian and frequently idealistically conceived model is important. The defense of difficult language as poststructuralism has used it is a defense of the indefensible. The pattern that characterizes the formation of elites (master/ disciple, expert/client), of rational-legal authority (the models of a "mirror of production," analytic logic, and the work ethic in particular), the use of difficult language in the context of hierarchies of power, and the obfuscational character of much of its linguistic difficulty all suggest that poststructuralism is repeating the patterns of institutional authority that it challenges theoretically. The poststructuralist use and defense of difficult language on theoretical grounds in almost complete disregard of the institutional context and consequences is a powerful indictment of its politics as simply more of the same. As a political agenda, that is inadequate.

For a prime example of the retrograde politics of poststructuralism as institutional and institutionalized discourse, we can look to the psychoanalytic semiotic critique of patriarchy that posits woman as lack or deficiency and the symbolic realm of language as the province of men. This critique holds that the representation of women is controlled by the principles of male scopophilia (narcissism, voyeurism, sadism, fetishism), and it makes these principles its central target. As a critique, it is sorely lacking: lacking in any sense of feminist determination apart from what men can offer; lacking in any analysis of the social (as opposed to the psychical or unconscious) production of gender identity or of the ways in which the social intersects the psychical; and lacking in any recognition that images of women could function as objects of desire for someone other than the male voyeur. Lesbian psychodynamics, lesbian politics, and lesbian aesthetics remain the great unspoken, perhaps because they are considered to be evidence of minor psychopathology or uninstructive social deviance.

Equally problematic is the inability of this form of academic critique to establish a foothold elsewhere in society. An institutional base can be politically valuable if it provides a means for reaching outside a specific institution. But the psychoanalytic poststructuralist critique of sexuality has not left the academy. Feminists working in other institutions, in other social settings, or on issues other than phallocentrism and discourse theory—that is, on such issues as equal rights, gay and lesbian rights, day care, and sexual harassment—find little in the post-structuralist critique to guide them. Neither the concepts nor the articulation of the concepts presents a very useful political model.

In sum, poststructuralism has played a dominant role in film theory for the last ten or fifteen years. The scope, complexity, and difficulty of its critique earned it a central position in the debate about film study between the late seventies and the early eighties, a centrality threatened by sharpened critiques and compelling alternatives in the mid eighties.

NOTES ON THE ORGANIZATION OF THIS BOOK

The articles here, like those in the first volume of *Movies and Methods,* have been chosen for their instructive, often imaginative use of methodological principles. The arrangement aims at helping them to refer to and build on one another. Many of the articles were chosen to convey some of the density and cross-referentiality of recent film literature. This organization also has the advantage of allowing the reader to approach a given issue—for example, a particular film, such as *Jeanne Dielman, 23 Quai du Commerce–1080 Bruxelles–*from several perspectives.

All the articles are printed in their entirety so as to prevent the authors from finding that the editor's judgment of the key portions of an article did not correspond to their own. This decision meant that a number of important articles could not be included because of their length; these articles include Stephen Heath's essay on *Touch of Evil,* "Film and System, Terms of Analysis" (*Screen* 16, no. 1 [1975]:7–77, and no. 2 [1975]:91–113) and Christian Metz's "The Imaginary Signifier" (*Screen* 16, no. 2 [1975]:14–76). All the articles were published in journals, not in books; journal articles can be hard to find, and worthy journal articles need to be preserved in book form.

The introductions to individual articles seek to distill their main points and place them in context. They point out interrelationships between individual articles, and they sometimes take issue with an article's content—not because I doubt its importance but because I want to exemplify and encourage an active, skeptical reading that sees each article as making a contribution to a continuing collaborative process of formulating knowledge.

Notes

1. Raymond Fielding, "A Bibliography of Theses and Dissertations on the Subject of Film," *University Film Association Monograph,* no. 3 (1979).

2. Some other important examples are Christian Metz's "The Imaginary Signifier," in his *The Imaginary Signifier* (Bloomington: Indiana University Press, 1982); Stephen Heath's collection of essays, *Questions of Cinema* (Bloomington: Indiana University

Press, 1981); *Communications,* no. 23 (1975), a special issue on psychoanalysis and cinema; numerous essays in the journal *Camera Obscura*; selections in three American Film Institute monographs (*Re-Vision: Essays in Feminist Film Criticism, Cinema History/Cinema Practices,* and *Cinema and Language*) whose contents are drawn from predominantly poststructuralist conferences; and the proceedings of the 1978 Center for Twentieth Century Studies conference, *The Cinematic Apparatus.*

3. See Noël Carroll, "Address to the Heathen," *October,* no. 23 (Winter 1982): 89–163, especially 153–157. The debate continues with Stephen Heath's reply, "Le Père Nöel," *October,* no. 26 (1983): 63–115, and Carroll's "A Reply to Heath," *October,* no. 27 (1983): 81–102.

4. Some of the articles collected in this volume—notably those by Laura Mulvey, Charles Altman, and Mary Ann Doane—summarize Jacques Lacan's notion of the mirror-phase. Other summaries occur in Daniel Dayan, "The Tutor-Code of Classical Cinema," *Movies and Methods* (Berkeley: University of California Press, 1976, 438–51); Colin MacCabe, "Presentation," *Screen* 16, no. 2 (Summer 1975): 7–13; Christian Metz, "The Imaginary Signifier," *Screen* 16, no. 2 (Summer 1975): 14–76, especially 48–52; and Anthony Wilden, *System and Structure,* 2 ed. (London: Tavistock, 1980). Lacan's essay, "The Mirror-Phase as Formative of the Function of the I," appeared in English translation in *New Left Review,* no. 51 (1968): 71–77.

5. A terse but pointed exchange that illustrates all these basic contentions appears in *Enclitic* 7 no. 1 (Spring 1983) between Larry Crawford, who in "Textual Analysis" offers a poststructural critique of David Bordwell's article, "Textual Analysis, Etc.," published in *Enclitic,* nos. 10–11 (1982), and David Bordwell, who in "Textual Analysis Revisited," offers a trenchant response.

Part 1
Historical
Criticism

THE STALIN MYTH IN SOVIET CINEMA

ANDRÉ BAZIN

Dudley Andrew's introduction sets the historical context for Bazin's article, reminding us of the lively debate and struggle to create a socialist France in the immediate postwar period and of André Bazin's intimate involvement in that struggle. By turning to the then extremely timely question of Joseph Stalin's depiction in three Soviet films, this article brings to the fore Bazin's concern with the uses of film in history. Polarized by a recalcitrant American anti-Communism and a monolithic Stalinism, the French left sought to define an appropriately French socialism. Many supported Stalin as at least an expediency, just as many American Communist Party members supported the hard line called for in the Duclos letter of 1945. Bazin breaks with such expediency and risks alienating those who insisted that French socialism had to develop in relation to Soviet Union policy directives.

Bazin's essay is clearly not a contribution to the history of film as an industry or art form, but it provides a compelling argument for the no less important question of how films represent historical reality, particularly how they represent contemporary figures and events, where there is a very real possibility of shaping not only the popular perception of historical figures and historical events but also the self-perceptions of the historical figures themselves. Bazin refers to this possibility in his appendix of 1958, where he quotes Khrushchev's claim that Stalin learned more about the Soviet countryside from Soviet films than from first-hand experience. Certainly, we have seen other major political figures help to shape fictional representations of themselves that they then appear to internalize. Ronald Reagan is only the most obvious recent example. Richard Nixon's Checkers speech suggests that the creation of a mythic self that then becomes part of the historical figure's public persona is a common process in contemporary political life.

Bazin's concern with the specific ways in which Stalin the historical figure becomes "Stalin" the cinematic signifier opens up a rich line of investigation into the relationship between history and myth, ideology and narrative —areas of great interest to contemporary research. Bazin's frame of reference is different. For example, ideology *is not a word that he uses, but he does demonstrate how careful textual study and broad reflection can give the cinema and its representations the contextual placement they need in order to be understood. In that regard, too, his references to relatively obscure Soviet films that we have probably never seen need not be taken as evidence of a marginal issue. Older, lesser-known films often provide the impetus for new theories and revised histories. For example, the retrospective of French cinema organized by the Museum of Modern Art in 1981 that was expanded to 113 films by the Los Angeles County Museum of Art and the UCLA film archives made it possible to reassess decades of French cinema (and François Truffaut's evaluation of it in his "A Certain Tendency of the French Cinema," which is included in the first volume of* Movies and Methods*). Historians and critics frequently discover new meanings in old films, such as* Young Mr. Lincoln *or* Marked Woman. *Such a process of discovery fosters the need to reassess our representation of cinematic history and test it against the changing present.*

•

INTRODUCTION, by Dudley Andrew

What follows is not some minor or long-lost article, recently unearthed. No, this is without question the most talked about and controversial essay André Bazin ever wrote. He even lodged it in the very center of his first volume of collected works. It has escaped translation no doubt because it deals with three forgettable Russian films and because it comes out of an era, militant Stalinism, most people would like to forget.

From 1944–48 Bazin associated himself with countless left-wing journals and cultural organizations in the exhilarating struggle for a socialist France freed from the class and monied interests of the Third Republic. In 1948, as the idealism of these groups began to wear off and as the old order surfaced unchanged, outside pressure completely factionalized these groups. First of all, the Marshall Plan arrived from the USA promising incredible financial aid to those countries which would form an alliance against the Soviet Union. In part as a response to this, international Stalinism spread into France, a dogmatic form of communist ideology based on the supreme and unquestioned prominence of one man, Joseph Stalin.

In my biography of Bazin I describe the effect of these tensions on him and the organizations to which he belonged. The internecine warfare took an incredible toll upon him emotionally and physically. He was forced out of one group for refusing to knuckle under to the Stalinist line and he stopped writing for *L'Ecran Français.* His general despondency concerning the cultural situation in France was multiplied by his complete physical breakdown in March of 1950. He wrote this essay for *Esprit* from a sanitorium for consumptives. When he returned to Paris the article had just come out and, I've been told, he had to duck in and out of the *Esprit* office for fear of running into a verbal or physical battle. *Esprit,* the premier Christian socialist organ of France and Europe, was the perfect forum for his views. Its overall posture could not be questioned: socialist, even communist, but based on a liberal humanism and dead set against all demagoguery. While *Esprit* preached the values of collectivism and nodded to Russia as often as possible, few of its writers could in good faith pursue the Stalinism which was required of Party members in that age.

Of course Bazin has been proved correct, as he gloats in an appendix written in 1958, the year he collected his essays and the year also of his death. Even Khrushchev can chuckle at Stalin's limitless presumption. And nearly all of those who were alienated from Bazin because of this essay (George Sadoul above all) were reconciled to him within a few years. Bazin's integrity, together with his winning personality, amply evident in the sly humor and moral passion of this essay, would not be withstood for long.

We shouldn't let the rootedness of this essay confine it to a position of mere "historical interest." As always Bazin was after bigger game, bigger even than the Stalinists. He wanted to come to terms with the issues of history, myth, and propaganda after having been barraged with a decade's worth of films about the war, its leaders, its causes. He felt that cinema flirted with dual and contradictory powers: to freeze a moment of history and to raise that moment to the status of eternal truth on a big screen. Because of this he knew that producers (be they governments or studios) must be scrupulously watched lest they misuse or confound these powers. His analysis, as you will see, is ingenious and is full of implications for today's cinema and today's politics. I urge you to brave the references to a bygone age and to some of its forgotten films. As you will see, this essay quickly turns into the kind of argument you wish you could have dreamt up and written down yourself.

[D.A.]

Part of the Soviet cinema's originality is its audacity in portraying living historical figures. This phenomenon was a logical extension of the new communist art— an art by living craftsmen which exalts very recent history. Perhaps it is logical from an historical materialist perspective to treat men as facts, assigning them a place in the representation of an event, which is usually forbidden in the West before "historical distance" removes the psychological taboo. Even 2,000 years were not enough for Cecil B. De Mille to dare to show more than just the feet of Christ in *Ben Hur*. This artistic "prudishness" could never withstand a Marxist criticism, nor hold up in a country where the comrades who "committed treason" were erased from paintings (except for Lenin, who is embalmed there). Nonetheless, it seems to me that the mise en scène of living historical figures has taken on central importance only with Stalin. Films about Lenin were not made until after his death, except by accident, whereas since the war Stalin has appeared on screen not just in newsreels but in historical films as well. Gelovani, the actor who (dare I say) "incarnates" him in *The Vow* is a specialist whom the Russians had, since 1938, already seen play Stalin many times. Although Gelovani doesn't appear as Stalin's counterpart in *The Battle of Stalingrad* nor in *The Third Blow*, he was particularly well known for *The Siberians, Valeri Schklov,* and *The Defense of Czaritsin*. Naturally, Stalin did not have the privilege of playing himself. The first version of *The Vow*, severely edited for the French market, evidently had Georges Bonnet doing the lambeth walk and the scenes in which Hitler appeared were much longer (Hitler's role was played by a Czechoslovakian railwayman whose resemblance to the Führer was uncanny). In *The Battle of Stalingrad*, not only did Hitler appear, but also Churchill and Roosevelt. But significantly enough, these last "portrayals" were much less convincing than that of Stalin, especially with regard to Roosevelt, where the likeness, although favorable, was almost nil, and Churchill, who was frankly (and intentionally) caricatured.

Of course, this procedure is not entirely original; one could go back to Méliès's *The Dreyfus Affair*, or to another of his films which comically anticipates plans for a tunnel under the English Channel (in which President Fallières and King George V inaugurate the project). At that time, the "news" had not yet imposed its demands—naval battles reconstructed in cisterns could appear as if they were "recorded on site." This cinematic reconstruction of news events is to current news reporting what the polychromatic covers of *Petit Journal* are to our modern photographic reporting. Twenty years before Eisenstein, Georges Méliès reconstructed the revolt on the Potemkin. But since then we have learned to distinguish documentation from reconstruction, to the point of preferring an authentic view, however incomplete or awkward, to the most perfect of imitations—or at least treating them as two entirely different cinematic genres. The Soviet cinema (with Dziga Vertov's famous theory of the "camera-eye") was primarily responsible for making this distinction. That is why a modern spectator feels somewhat ill at ease when an actor portrays a famous historical character, whether living or dead— such as Napoleon, St. Vincent de Paul, Queen Victoria, or Clemenceau. This uneasiness can be compensated for by the semi-prodigious aspect of the spectacle in itself, as well as by an actor's exceptional performance. But this uneasiness is even greater when the historical person portrayed is still alive. Imagine the R.P.F. making a propaganda film about General de Gaulle in which all the historical events are reconstructed and the General's role played by, let's say, Louis Jouvet with a fake nose. Enough!

Obviously, many scriptwriters have been inspired to do biographies of famous contemporary figures. But significantly enough, they only treat people (especially contemporary political figures) who are "living legends"—such as famous singers or musicians whose biographies have been popular with Hollywood producers in recent years. An even better example might be the two films about Cerdan, played by Cerdan himself. But you might answer that it's Cerdan himself, in the flesh. That is true, but there isn't really very much difference. Actually, this case clearly illustrates the ultimate limits of the phenomenon's process: it is visibly about the identification of the man Cerdan with his own myth (from this point of view *The Man with the Clay Hands* has a naive, limpid script). Here the cinema constructs and consecrates the legend: it definitively transports the hero to Olympus. The operation works only with people who are already deified in the public mind; that is, primarily with "stars," whether in sports, theater, or cinema. Scientists and saints (lay or religious) can be included. But again, the process of identification doesn't get started until the people in question are dead—for example, Pasteur, Edison, or Dunant. If you want, a distinction can be made between the myth of the "star" and the glorious edifying legend which surrounds the scientist. Until now, however, the biographies of great men were not considered to be edifying until after these men had died. In the West, the cinematic representation of living figures has involved only one area which can be called para- or posthistorical—the hero must belong to the mythology of an art, sport, or science, and the historical sequence in which he participates must be considered closed.

Theoretically, the audacity of the Soviet cinema could be considered as an admirable application of historical materialism. Doesn't the taboo which we have acknowledged in Western cinema come from an idealism, or at least a "personalism," which is not applicable to historical materialism? And furthermore, doesn't this taboo also come from a chronic uncertainty concerning History? In other words, we attach too much value to the individual, yet we are not capable of assigning the individual a place in History until History comes to a close. For a French person today it's easy to be proud of Napoleon. But for a communist, a great man is, *hic et nunc*, one who helps make History for himself—a History whose meaning is defined, without possible error, by the dialectic process and the Party. The greatness of the Hero is objectified, that is, relative to the unfolding of the History in which he is at that moment both the means and its consciousness. A materialist dialectical perspective maintains the human dimension of the hero, emphasizing only psychological and historical traits to the exclusion of the sort of transcendence which characterizes capitalist mystification best exemplified by the mythology of the "star."

From this point of view, the masterpiece of Soviet film with the historical hero is by far *Chapayev* (1934; Vasiliev). If you get the chance to see the film again, notice how sensitively Chapayev's weaknesses are insinuated—even his most obviously heroic actions are undercut without diminishing the psychological level at all. It is the political adjunct commissioner who represents historico-political objectivity. The film does glorify Chapayev, but at the same time it is against him, showing the primacy of a long-term political view over the action of a temporarily useful leader of an heroic group. Even though it relates to a more distant past, *Peter the Great* is an equally instructive and human film, rich in the same dialectic of man and History. Peter's greatness comes primarily from the correctness of his historical vision. In other respects, Peter has his flaws—drunkenness and lechery. His most loyal companion is basically an errant rogue, but he shares Peter's illustriousness because, remaining faithful, he has the truth of History on his side. In *Chapayev* the opposite occurs. Although the white guards and their colonel are just as courageous as the little troop with the red leader, they are, nonetheless, in "error."

Pursuing this point, the headquarters in *The Great Decision* gives me a strong feeling for the responsibilities of men facing History. The generals' dialogue is not aimed at showing off their personal brilliance. The point is to show, through the character, friendships and weaknesses of the men who serve History, their groping toward an infallible historical consciousness.

Compare these examples to the image proposed in three recent Soviet films: *The Third Blow, The Battle of Stalingrad*, and *The Vow*. Considerations of mise en scene, which greatly favor the first two films, will not be taken into account. In the first two war films there is an obvious unity of construction—opposition between the battlefield and the Kremlin, the apocalyptic disorder of the military battle and the studious silence of Stalin's office. In *The Battle of Stalingrad* this pensive serenity is also juxtaposed with the hysteria of Hitler's headquarters. In *The Great*

Decision the radical division of labor between the leader and the soldier has already been pointed out. (This is a long way from the potato-pelting strategy of a Chapayev, who had barely progressed from medieval chivalry or brigadeering.) These generals are expected to think correctly, not to risk their lives. Without romanticizing or being demagogic, one would admit that this is really the role of the headquarters in modern war, although we have seen many generals who have neither risked their lives nor judged correctly. If, despite everything, this radical division of labor and danger is a universal fact, it would be hard to imagine how Western civil and military leaders could glorify themselves. Clemenceau felt the need to tour the trenches regularly to maintain his popularity. For Westerners, the immunity, or I should say impunity, of headquarters does not merit glory—we usually prefer seeing a commander-in-chief in motorized reconnaissance on the front rather than at his desk. The glorification of the pensiveness and invulnerability of headquarters needs at its basis the utmost confidence of soldiers in their leader—a confidence, a priori, without irony, acknowledging equal validity in the risks taken by the general in his underground shelter and those of the soldier before a flame-thrower. After all, this confidence is logical in a truly socialist war. In *The Great Decision*, the battle itself is hardly noticeable. The only interest in individual heroism brought out by the scriptwriter is related to the repair, under German machine-gun-firing, of a telephone line which is indispensable to headquarters—a neurological operation.

In *The Battle of Stalingrad* and in *The Third Blow*, however, this dichotomy between the head and members is so absolute that it goes beyond the historical and material realism we accorded to it above. Even endowing field marshal Stalin with hyper-Napoleonic military genius and with the principle merit of conceiving victory, it is still extremely dangerous to assume that things took place inside the Kremlin the way they are shown in the film: Stalin, completely alone, meditating in front of a map decides, after long and intense reflection and a few puffs on his pipe, what measures should be taken. When I say completely alone, I mean that, although Vassiliewsky is always there, he doesn't talk, playing the part of a confidant obviously to avoid the ridiculousness of Stalin talking to himself. This centralizing or cerebral concept of war is confirmed even by the way in which the battle is presented. In contrast to *The Great Decision*, the battle comprises the major portion of the film. But although the reconstruction attains an ampleness and exactitude unequalled since Griffith's *Birth of a Nation*, the vision is in effect equivalent to Fabrice's at Waterloo—not materially, since the spectacle of war has not been spared, but essentially, because the camera's placement of us as spectators makes it impossible to create order out of the chaos. This image of war, equivalent to "on the spot" news reporting, is in some ways amorphous, without cardinal points or visible evolution—as an anthill that's just been kicked. The camera and the montage carefully avoid choosing amid the chaos (which we secretly know is organized) any significant fact, detail, beginning, middle, or end of the military events, Ariadnean thread of significant action, or act of individual heroism. The few exceptions to this vision only confirm the rule. In *The Battle of Stalingrad* (first part) the military tableau is framed by two precise actions: the withdrawal of the militia in the beginning, and the defense of the post at the end. But between these two significant events—one of collective enthusiasm, the other of individual courage—stretches the enormous magma of the battle. Imagine witnessing the operation from an invulnerable helicopter which gives you as general a view of the battle as possible, yet without in any way distancing you from the fate, development, or positions of the armies. All the meaning of the war is therefore transferred to the interpolated commentary, to the animated maps, and especially to Stalin's vocalized meditations.

This way of presenting facts and events has, as a result, the apocalyptic incoherence of the battle at its base and the singular omniscient mind which orders and resolves this apparent chaos at its summit. Between the two—nothing. No intermediary section in the cone of the plot, no significant image of the psychological and intellectual processes which affect men's destinies or the outcome of the battle. The relationship between the pencil mark of the commander-in-chief and the soldier's sacrifice seems direct, or at least the intermediary mechanism is insignificant—it is purely a transmitting organ whose analysis, consequently, can be left out.

This presentation of events does have a certain truth if you retain not the facts, but a sort of simplified, essential schema. The intellectual procedure is neither truly Marxist nor compatible with the strictly documentary character of the two terms of the represented process. But, as we are told, these films pretend to be more than historical: scientific. No expense was spared in order to reconstruct the battle as perfectly as possible, so why would we doubt the strict objectivity of the other end of the chain of events? Why would they fool us concerning the events inside the Kremlin?

Here Stalin's properly ontological, rather than psychological, attributes are made apparent—his omniscience and infallibility. Just a glance at a map, or a look at a tractor engine, are enough for him to win the greatest battle of History or to see that "the spark plugs are fouled up."

In *Nouvelle Critique*, Francis Cohen wrote that Stalin, objectively speaking, was the greatest sage of all time because he incarnated the knowledge of the communist world. I wouldn't necessarily deny Stalin the personal and historical merits these films attribute to him but what I would object to, with slight reservation, is that the image of Stalin presented as "real" conforms exactly to what a myth of Stalin would have him be—to what would be useful for him to be.

For propaganda purposes, no better model could have been constructed. Either Stalin really is a superman, or else we are in the presence of a myth. It is beyond my purpose here to discuss whether or not the idea of a superman is Marxist. But I would dare say that "Occidental" or "Oriental" myths function esthetically the same way. From this point of view, the only difference between Stalin and Tarzan is that the films about the latter don't pretend to be documentaries.

Formerly, all the great Soviet films were characterized by a realist humanism, in opposition to Western cinema's mystifications. Recent Soviet cinema claims to be even more realistic than ever, but this realism serves as an alibi for the intrusion of a personal myth which is foreign to all the great pre-war films and whose appearance necessarily upsets the economic esthetics of the work. If Stalin, even while living, could be the main character of a film, it is because he is no longer "human," engaging in the transcendence which characterizes living gods and dead heroes. His esthetic physiology is not fundamentally different from that of the Western "star." Both elude psychological definition. Presented this way, Stalin is not, nor could he ever be, a particularly intelligent man or "genius" leader, but rather a familiar god or incarnated transcendence. That is why, despite his real existence, his cinematic portrayal is possible today—not because of an exceptional effort at Marxist objectivity, nor as an attempt at artistic application of historical materialism, but on the contrary, because, properly speaking, the portrayal is no longer of a particular man, but of a social hypostasis, a transition toward transcendency—a myth.

If the reader rejects this metaphysical vocabulary, another can be used in its place. The phenomenon can be explained as arriving at the end of History. To make Stalin (even if he acts in conjunction with the populace) the principal hero and determiner of a real historic event while he is still alive, implies that from now on he is invulnerable to any weakness, that the meaning of his life has already and definitively been attained, and that he could never subsequently make a mistake or commit treason. It wouldn't be the same if these were actual news photos—we already have the Yalta interview and Stalin's appearance at the Red Square. Obviously, these documents can be used to glorify a living political figure, but precisely because of their reality they remain fundamentally ambiguous. It is the use made of them that gives them their apologetic meaning. They are only valuable within and in relation to a certain discourse. To a democratic spectator, Leni Riefenstahl's montage on the Nuremberg Congress, *Triumph of the Will*, seems to be an argument against Hitler. The images used outside the specified discourse can become an anti-Nazi montage. But obviously in Stalin's case something else occurs. It is already surprising that Stalin appears episodically in historical films the way other great Soviet or Western political figures do in the films we talked about. But the fact that he is the dramatic motivation in these films implies even more—that his biography is literally identical with History and shares the absoluteness of History. Until now, only death could identify the hero or martyr with his works. It used to be possible to tarnish a memory or to discover a treason retrospectively. But death remained a necessary if not sufficient condition. For Malraux, it is death which transforms our life into destiny; for the communist it is death which can reabsorb all the subjectivity of an event. At 80 years old the "conqueror of Verdun" can become the "traitor of Montoire," or at 85, the "martyr of Yeu Island" precisely because, whatever a man's genius or qualities, he is only significant in the light of History "when eternity finally transforms him just as it does History."

The astonishingly subjective character of the political processes in popular democracies can be accounted for within this point of view. From a purely Marxist perspective it is enough to say that Bukharin, Radek, or Kostov incarnated certain tendencies that the Party had decided to combat as historically erroneous. Their physical liquidation was just as unnecessary as it would have been to liquidate our retired ministers. But as soon as a man is said to have participated in History, to have been involved in this or that event, a part of his biography is irremediably "historicized." An intolerable contradiction is set up between this definitively objectified part, petrified in the past, and the present physical existence of a Bukharin, a Zinoviev, or a Radek. You cannot reduce a man to nothing but History without in turn compromising that History by the subjective presence of the individual. A living communist leader is an officially confirmed god in History because of his past actions. The idea of objective treason, which seems to stem so clearly from Marxism, has not stood up in political practice. According to the Soviet "Stalinist" communist perspective, no one can "become" a traitor. That would imply that he wasn't always a traitor, that there was a biographical beginning to this treason, and that, conversely, a person who became a menace to the Party would have been considered useful to the Party before becoming evil. The Party could not simply bust Radek to the lowest rank, or condemn him to death. It was necessary to proceed with a retroactive purge of History, proving that the accused was, since birth, a willful traitor whose every act was satanically camouflaged sabotage. Of course, this operation is highly improbable and far too serious to be used in every case. That is why the public *mea culpa* can be substituted concerning minor figures whose historical action is indirect—such as artists, philosophers, or scientists. These solemn hyperbolic *mea culpa*s can seem psychologically improbable or intellectually superfluous to us if we fail to recognize their value as exorcism. As confession is indispensable to divine absolution, so solemn retraction is indispensable to the reconquering of historical virginity. There again lies the scandal of subjectivity—it is implicitly recognized as the vehicle of History, and yet proclaimed elsewhere as pure objectivity.

Our "hypercritical," "idealist," "bourgeois" consciousness can maintain simultaneously that Pétain is both the "conqueror of Verdun" and the "traitor of Montoire," whereas in Russia, old comrades that have been liquidated must disappear completely from the Soviet's painting of history. History, at least in its public manifestations, postulates a severe idealism, assuring a radical equivalent between subjectivity and its social value—an absolute Manichaeism in which anti-historical forces come directly from the Devil and from diabolic possession.

Within these perspectives, the cinematic representation of Stalin cannot be underestimated. It implies that the identification between Stalin and History is henceforth definitively established—that with regard to Stalin the contradictions of subjectivity don't apply. This phenomenon can be explained by the fact that Stalin furnished sufficient proof of his devotion to the Party, as well as of his genius, and that a hypothetical treason was so improbable that there was no risk involved in treating him, while alive, as a dead hero. In "Beotie's Little Statues," Prévert tells us of the misfortunes of an admiral who goes crazy the same day his statue is inaugurated—that is to say, in matters of biography one can never be certain of anything. The feeling of complete certainty which comes out of Soviet films implies, not the virtual death of Stalin, already a living statue, but the reciprocal truth—the end of History or at least the end of the dialectical process at the heart of the socialist world.

Lenin's mummification in his mausoleum and Stalin's obituary—"Lenin Lives"—marked the beginning of the end. Stalin's cinematic mummification is no less symbolic than Lenin's embalmment. The former signifies that Stalin's relationship to Soviet politics and to what we normally refer to as "humanness" is no longer contingent or relative. The asymptote of "Man" and "History" is surpassed. Stalin is History incarnate.

As such, he could not be endowed in character, psychology, or personality with the qualities of the common herd (something which Vasiliev's Chapayev and Petrov's Czar Peter still have): these existential qualities are not relevant since everything is derived from theology. Stalin is presented as himself throughout these films as pure allegory.

As History, he is omniscient, infallible, irresistible—his destiny is irreversible. As a human, his psychological make-up is reduced to the qualities which best conform to allegory—pensiveness (opposed to Hitler's hysteria), reflectiveness or rather consciousness, a decisive mind, and goodness (this last characteristic, which is emphasized in *The Vow,* is indispensable in connecting the people to History, a History which, from a Marxist viewpoint, is the expression of the people's will). Any other human trait would only disrupt this almost hieratic image, reducing it to our contingency. In the beginning of *The Vow* there is a highly significant scene which can be called the "Rite of History." Lenin has just died, and Stalin goes off in the snow on a pilgrimage to meditate at their last places of conversation. There, near the river bank, where Lenin's shadow seems to be inscribed in the snow, the voice of the dead man speaks to him. Just in case the metaphor of a mythic anointment and the hearing of the Ten Commandments were not enough, Stalin looks *to the sky.* Through the evergreen branches a ray of sunlight strikes the forehead of the new Moses. We see it all there, even down to the horns of fire. With the light coming from above, it is very significant that Stalin, and only Stalin, is the one who benefits from this Marxist Pentecost, even though there were twelve apostles. Next we see him, slightly bent from the weight of this grace, returning to his friends. From this point on, he will be distinguished from them, set apart—not only because of his wisdom and genius, but because of the presence in him of History.

In a more familiar mode, there is another scene in *The Vow* worth recounting—the scene with the tractor. The first agricultural tractor made in Russia arrives at the almost deserted Red Square. With tears in his eyes, a communist critic says: "The child isn't strapping yet, but he's a country boy." Spitting and coughing, the engine suddenly breaks down. The mechanic desperately looks everywhere, hitting this and that. A few sympathetic passersby advise him and try to help (it is precisely this dozen or so good people that we find everywhere whenever we need them and whose biography symbolizes that of the Soviet people— Russia is large, but the world is small!). But just at this moment Stalin comes walking by with several colleagues from the Supreme Soviet. He asks what the problem is, in avuncular friendliness. They tell him that the tractor is broken. Bukharin remarks, with a diabolical chuckle, that they'd be better off buying them from America, to which the *vox populi,* in the form of the mechanic, answers that to say that is merely defeatism and that Russia will be better off making her own tractors, even if it takes a few breakdowns. Then you see Stalin approach the engine, tapping it with the tip of his fingers and diagnosing the problem under the admiring stare of the mechanic: "It's the spark plugs." (I'm trusting the subtitles.) He jumps into the driver's seat and makes three small circles in Red Square. Close-up of Stalin at the wheel—he thinks; he sees the future; superimposition of thousands of tractors in the factory, more tractors, tractors plowing the fields, dragging behind them the long claws of multi-bottomed plows. . . . Enough.

Unfortunately for our zealous communist critic, we have already seen tractors before. There were tractors in Eisenstein's *The General Line* (1929), including the famous scene of the breakdown. The awkward and enraged driver, having just been outfitted with new leathers, gradually strips himself of his gloves, his helmet, and then his glasses, to become a peasant again. There is also a peasant woman who laughingly rips up her dress to make rags for him. (At that time, Stalin did not yet play radio-electric mechanics.) At the end of the film there were parades of tractors, a colossal epic of foreign steel insects scratching the ground, inscribing their mark as they had inscribed the sky with their smoke.

As long as the Stalinist apologetics remained on the verbal or even on the iconographic level, one could say that it was a relative phenomenon, reducible to rhetoric or to propaganda, and therefore reversible. In this way the supremacy of Stalin's genius is neither opportunist nor metaphorical—it is properly ontological. The cinema is in its essence as incontestable as Nature and History—not only because cinema's meaning and persuasiveness is incomparably greater than any other means of propaganda, but especially because the cinematic image is other, seeming completely superimposable with reality. A portrait of Petain or de Gaulle or Stalin, even if it's blown up to 100 meters square, decomposes as it composes—in the end, it engages nothing. However, a cinematic reconstitution of Stalin, especially when it is centered on him, is enough to define forever his place and meaning in the world—enough to fix his essence irrevocably.

APPENDIX (1958)

Except for a few stylistic corrections and some lightening of tone, I haven't wanted to change this article which first appeared in the July–August 1950 edition of *L'Esprit*. It was not surprising that *L'Humanité* and *Les Lettres Françaises* reacted the strongest. Since then, certain events have occurred which, to say the least, have confirmed the theses advanced here. You will judge whether or not they have since become peripheral.

Without going so far as to imply that Mr. Khrushchev carefully kept this copy of *L'Esprit,* I can't help but remember with satisfaction some passages from his famous report.[1] Regarding Stalin's omniscience which allowed him not only to decide the outcome of a battle but also to locate a bad spark plug in a broken tractor, Khrushchev states: "Stalin would say almost anything and believe that it was so. After all, he was a genius, and a genius only has to glance and he can immediately say what it is." Stalin himself, in his own abridged "Biography," wrote: "Stalin's military mastery worked as well in defense as in offense. Comrade Stalin's genius gave him the ability to guess the enemies' plans and to foil them."

But what is really amazing is that Stalin started to inform himself on Soviet reality through the cinema's myth of him. Once again Khrushchev confirms this. Not having stepped foot in a village since 1928, "it was through movies that he [Stalin] knew the countryside and its agriculture, and these films greatly embellished reality. Numerous films painted the kolkhosian way of life by showing us tables tottering under the weight of turkeys and geese. Obviously, Stalin believed it was really like that."

The circle was closed. Cinematic mystification even closed in around its subject. It would hardly be exaggerating to say that Stalin got to the point where he was convinced of his own genius by watching films about Stalin. Even Jarry could not have thought of a more pompous way to inflate the morality of his Father Ubu.

Note

1. Khrushchev's February, 1956, "secret" speech to the Party Central Committee, which the CIA published abroad. This report marked the beginning of de-Stalinization in the Soviet Union.

Translated by Georgia Gurrieri.

TECHNIQUE AND IDEOLOGY: CAMERA, PERSPECTIVE, DEPTH OF FIELD

JEAN-LOUIS COMOLLI

In the preceding article, André Bazin relies primarily on his own critical reflections to place a set of films within a historical framework; in the next article, Patrick Ogle relies on technical journals and trade reports to trace the development of deep-focus photography. Here, Jean-Louis Comolli exemplifies a third kind of historical investigation: Comolli's article is a contribution to and intervention in the contemporary debate on the origins of cinema and the relation of technology to science and ideology. His references are largely to other French historians of the cinema, who see technology as neutral, free of ideological bias. For them, technology provides the tangible means of realizing humanity's lofty vision and ideals. Comolli does not introduce new facts as such or derive new

*evidence from the rereading of early films but instead places an ongoing debate
into a different frame of reference. Thus, what is most strongly at issue for
Comolli is the terms of debate: Can we begin by asking whether allowing the
motion picture camera to stand for cinematic technology and its effect, as J.-P.
Lebel does, creates a distortion? Does this distortion not continue to repress
what the cinema normally represses —the invisible processes that generate a
recognizable, moving picture of the world: photochemistry, frame lines, sound
track, the projector positioned behind us, and so forth? Comolli argues that this
repression of the invisible corresponds directly to an "ideology of the visible (and
what it implies: the masking and effacement of work)" that posits the centrality of
sight (seeing is believing). Even so, a crisis had to be overcome: the potential of
cinema to supplant the eye's supremacy through scientific research that would
throw the ideology of the visible itself into question. Comolli goes on to discuss
how illusion —the ability to project "life as it is" —rather than science —the
study of the underlying principles of movement and vision —took precedence
once fantasy became channeled through commercially viable enterprise. In this
discussion, he contrasts the historical arguments of Lebel, which are part of a
larger debate involving Marcelin Pleynet, Jean-Louis Baudry, and Comolli on one
side and Lebel on the other, with those of his predecessors Jacques Deslandes and,
of course, André Bazin. Comolli undertakes to provide a perspective that allows
us to understand not only how economics and ideology contribute significantly to
the "birth" of the cinema but also how certain interpretive strategies can will
these factors out of existence.*

*Above all, Comolli's article shows us how important our basic assumptions are
for any critical investigation that we undertake and how important it is to subject
those assumptions to close scrutiny if we are to determine whether they in fact
capture the conditions that are necessary and sufficient to a study of the subject
at hand.*

Only Part I of Comolli's article appears here.

•

CAMERA, PERSPECTIVE, DEPTH OF FIELD

Most film criticism has now (under pressure) come round to admitting
that all film is a product of ideology, made in and expressing an ideology, and
therefore in some way related to politics—whatever claims to 'art' it may make
for itself in the first instance. Signs of this acceptance of film's ideological status
can be seen in two areas:

(1) in the increasing number of special issues (of journals up to now predominantly cinephile) on 'political cinema' or 'politics and cinema'; and
(2) in the increased market value of films with explicitly political themes.

But at a certain point the strongest resistance is shown to any critical analysis of
the ideological character of cinema. Curiously, this is not expressed as a claim for
the autonomy of the aesthetic processes. Everything involved in the field of film

technology—equipment, methods, standards, conventions—is vigorously *defended* from any ideological implications by a number of critics, filmmakers and, naturally, by the majority of technicians themselves. They'll agree (more or less) that film has a relationship to ideology on the level of themes, production (system of economic relations), distribution (interpretations) and even on the level of its realization (by the *metteur en scène*/subject), but never any in the area of the technical practices which *manufacture* film from beginning to end. They demand a place apart for film technology, beyond ideologies, outside history, social movements, and the construction of meanings. Film technique we are told is precisely that—a technique, and *neutral*. It is capable of expressing everything without expressing anything of itself, expressing only what one (the filmmaker and the technician) wants it to express. It has a vehicle, a means, something which transmits and has as its end the obliteration of any trace of itself from this transmission. And indeed, common sense has no lack of examples to demonstrate that the camera gives disinterested services to both the fascist and the communist film, that the use of close-up is characteristic of both Eisenstein and Hollywood, etc.

Let's take note of this *demand* for 'a place apart' for cinematographic technique, and question it. Why is the diffuse and insistent discourse of technicians (often backed up by filmmakers and critics now that the question is becoming important) so anxious to defend the field of technical and mechanical practices from any influence from or bearing on ideology; and to place it so firmly in the wings rather than on the stage where meanings are in play? For setting technique to one side and keeping it in reserve is also giving it a place—making it fill a slot in the ideological discourse of technicians and in the technological and/or technicist ideology. For this discourse to happen, a particular concept—an *image*—of film technique had first to be constituted. The discourse then had as its function to confirm and perpetuate it.

Because it has the virtue of formulating the implications of the technological discourse, the long article by Jean-Patrick Lebel, "Cinema and Ideology,"[1] will serve as my main reference here (purely for the problems under discussion: other points raised by Lebel call for separate discussion).

Lebel writes:

... film is clearly a scientific invention, not a product of ideology, since it is founded on a real body of knowledge and on the properties of the matter which it activates: the proof is that it functions, and that by activating specific matter (various instruments + the properties of light + persistence of vision) in order to film a material object, it produces a material image of that object.[2]

or:

... it is not the filmmaker, but the camera, a passive recording instrument, which reproduces the object or objects filmed in the form of an image-reflection constructed according to the laws of the rectilinear propagation of light waves (which in fact define the effect known as perspective). The phenomenon is perfectly capable of scientific explanation and has nothing to do with ideology.[3]

Implicit in these extracts, backing up Lebel's argument and providing a focus for the discourse of technicians under discussion here (discourse which can be heard or read in the film schools, the universities where technique is taught and in the textbooks which propagate it, etc.) is

(1) the fact that film technique inherits something from science (the legitimacy and importance of this inheritance will be examined in Part III; for the moment the principle is taken as given);

(2) from which it is deduced that film technology also inherits the scientific character of Science—in this case the double virtue of accuracy and neutrality. Before examining the various ideological embodiments of depth of field—a specific technological process selected here for its exemplary qualities—I will have to go through a number of questions about the process known by the *mythical name* of THE INVENTION OF THE CINEMA: in other words, about the ideology, the mythology even, which has grown up around the relationship of film technique and its 'founding *sciences.*' (I will do no more than indicate a number of directions for research, to be taken up and developed more systematically since the complexity of the problem—as yet unexplored—demands extended consideration from more than one direction.)

PART I. A DUAL ORIGIN

The Ideological Place of 'the Basic Apparatus'

When he wrote "Cinema and Ideology," J.-P. Lebel was intervening in a debate initiated by Marcelin Pleynet in *Cinéthique* and developed by that journal and by *Cahiers.*[4]

Pleynet had said:

Have you noticed how all the many possible discourses on the cinema assume the *a priori* existence of a non-signifying apparatus/producer of images which gives impartial service in any situation, to the left and to the right? Before thinking about their 'militant role' wouldn't filmmakers be well advised to think about the ideology produced by the basic apparatus (the camera) which defines the cinema? The film camera is an ideological instrument in its own right, it expresses bourgeois ideology before expressing anything else . . . It produces a directly inherited code of perspective, built on the model of the scientific perspective of the Quattrocento. What needs to be shown is the meticulous way in which the construction of the camera is geared to 'rectify' any anomalies in perspective in order to reproduce in all its authority the visual code laid down by Renaissance humanism . . . The point at which photography was invented is not without interest: Hegel was closing off the History of Painting; painting itself was showing signs of awareness that the science of perspective governing its figurative relationships arose out of a specific cultural system . . . It was at this point that Niepce invented photography (Niepce [1765–1833] was a contemporary of Hegel [1770–1831]), called in to reinforce the Hegelian closure and to produce the standards and prohibitions of the reigning code of perspective by mechanical means.

In my view, only when we have thought through this phenomenon, and the way in which the camera determines the structure of the cinematic reality it represents, will cinema be able to consider its relations to ideology in an objective way.[5]

Let's take as our basis the questions raised by this text:

(1) the relation between the photographic—then cinematic—image and the pictorial representation of space set out by the Quattrocento code of perspective,

which dominated Western painting for five centuries, though not exclusively: on this point see the works of Francastel which refer to the coexistence of several figurative systems.[6] How this relationship acts on the level of ideologies and cultural performances.

(2) the relation between the invention of photography and the invention of the cinema, between photography and cinema: correspondences and differences. The question of the technical birth of the cinema.

(3) the determining role of the 'camera' apparatus in thought about the ideology of film technique. This last question will be my starting point.

When first Pleynet, then the editors of *Cinéthique,* and then Jean-Louis Baudry[7] pose the question of the inscription of emergent cinema into a given socio-historical moment (the second half of the 19th century) and into the dominant ideology of the time, they pass over film technique as a whole to center directly on the apparatus which "determines the structure of the cinematic reality it represents."

The notion of 'the basic apparatus' (Baudry) is thus put forward: the camera is what produces the 'visible' in accordance with the system of 'monocular' perspective governing the representation of space: it is therefore in the area of the camera that we should seek, for the materials of cinema as a whole, the perpetuation of this code of representation and the ideology it sustains or reasserts. Once filmmaking's key factor (the camera) falls to ideology, it is in fact difficult to see how film could claim to escape.

It is striking that when J.-P. Lebel criticizes the positions taken by Pleynet and ourselves—in his attempt to disprove the 'accusation' of 'an ideological nature' of the cinema—he too chooses the camera as the object and dominant figure in his demonstration. True, since he wants to meet the adversary on his own ground and ideology has been placed 'in' the camera, he has to banish it from the camera, replacing it with the guarantee of an affiliation with Science. But it's still the camera which comes into question, *alone* once again; and again it has the difficult position of both *representing* film technique as a whole and *transposing* on to that whole its 'perfectly scientific' nature (in contradistinction to the theories which would have it 'purely ideological').

One of Lebel's initial observations it's true seems to reflect a certain uneasiness, which is a kind of symptom of the distortion involved in making the camera the centerpiece of the debate:

Note that the word camera here (and in everything that follows[8]) doesn't just designate that usually black object which goes under the name of 'camera': it takes in the whole of the technical operation, from filming to projection, which brings about the mechanical reproduction of reality in the form of images. This is also sometimes referred to as 'the camera effect' by the ideological school in question here. In other words, the term camera should not be understood in the limited sense of the object itself; as used here it comprehends the whole operation and its system of technical processes (all based on the same scientific principles deriving from the laws of propagation of light), which are precisely what characterize the cinema as a means of production.[9]

Lebel gives a clear explanation—but no criticism—of the way in which the 'ideological tendency' operates a hypostasis of the camera; but there is nothing in the remainder of his work to indicate that he is not doing the same. The contrary, in fact, since the cornerstone of his discourse is the scientificity of the camera:

The camera is not an ideological instrument in itself, it does not produce a specific ideology, any more than its structure inevitably condemns it to reflecting the dominant ideology. It is an instrument, and ideologically neutral precisely because it is an instrument/apparatus/machine. Its basis is scientific and it is constructed on this scientific basis, not *according to* an ideology of representation (in the speculative sense of the term).[10]

The Camera Then

For it is here in this *camera-situation* that a confrontation occurs between the two discourses—one locating film technique in ideology, the other locating it in science. Note that, whether we are told [that] the essentials of the technical system which produces film have their founding origins in the body of scientific knowledge, or that this system is governed by the ideological representations and demands dominant at the time it was perfected, in both cases (discourse of technicians on the one hand, attempts to elaborate a materialist theory of cinema on the other) the example given is *always* the instrument which produces the cinematic *image,* and it alone, seen solely from the point of view of optics. (With Pleynet in fact the focus of attention is somewhat arbitrary and in the *early* stages bore on just *one* of the components of the camera—the *lens.* For Lebel, though he mentions persistence of vision, the Scientific frame of reference—which is constantly invoked—is *Geometrical Optics*—the 'laws of propagation of light.')

We are therefore dealing with a specific *image* of the camera: it is used metonymically to *represent* the whole of film technique—*the part which stands for the whole.* It's *brought forward* as the *visible* part standing for *the whole of technique.* This symptomatic *displacement* has now to be questioned in the very way we formulate the relationship between Technique and Ideology.

Deputizing the camera to represent the whole of film technique is not only taking 'the part for the whole'—it's also a reductive operation (from the whole to the part). It needs to be questioned because *on the level of theory* it reproduces *the separation which still marks* the technical practice of cinema—*between the visible part* of film technique and its *'invisible' part.* (This is evident in the practice of filmmakers and technicians; in the spontaneous ideology of that practice; but also in the 'idea' or ideological image which the film-going public constructs for itself of film work—concentrating on shooting and the studio to the exclusion of laboratory processes and editing.) The visible part of film technique (camera, shooting, crew, lights, screen) *suppresses* the invisible part (frame lines, chemistry, fixing and developing, baths, and laboratory processing, negative, the cuts and joins of montage technique, sound track, projector, etc.) and the latter is generally relegated to the unreasoned, 'unconscious' part of cinema. It is significant that Lebel, who is so anxious to claim the regulation of the cinema by scientific principles, deduces this claim solely from geometrical optics, only once mentioning persistence of vision, which is after all what specifically distinguishes the cinema from photography—the synthesis of movement (and the scientific work which made it possible, cf. below). He overlooks altogether that other patron science of cinema and photography—photochemistry—without which the camera would still be only a *camera obscura*. As for Pleynet's observations, they apply equally to the Quattrocento *camera obscura*, the 17th-century magic lantern, the various projection devices which were the forerunners of the cinematograph and the still camera; their chief concern is clearly to note connections between these various mechanisms and the camera, but they risk missing precisely what the camera conceals (which doesn't include the lens). In the final analysis, film, the film feed systems, emulsion, frame lines, and not just the lens, are all essentials of cinema, without which there would be no cinema.

It is not clear therefore that what is happening at the moment on the level of practice should be reproduced on the level of theory: the reduction of the hidden part of technique to its visible part carries the risk of reasserting the domination of the visible, i.e., *the ideology of the visible* (and what it implies: the masking and effacement of work). Defining the ideology of the visible Serge Daney said:

[The cinema] postulates that from the 'real' to the visual and from the visual to its reproduction on film, the same truth is reflected infinitely without any distortion or loss.

And in a world where 'I see' is automatically said for 'I understand' such a fantasy has probably not come about by chance. The dominant ideology, which equates the real to the visible, has every interest in encouraging it . . . But we could retrace the process back further still and bring into question what both serves and precedes the camera: a blissful confidence in the visible, the hegemony gradually acquired by the eye over the other senses, taste, the need a society has to turn itself into a spectacle, etc. . . . The cinema therefore is in partnership with the Western metaphysical tradition and its vested interest in seeing and sight which the cinema as an optical system is called on to concretize. What is the science of light, and what can the language of light be? Teleological surely, if teleology consists in "neutralizing duration and action in favor of an *illusion* of simultaneity and form" (Derrida).[11]

Undoubtedly it was this that Pleynet had in mind when he stressed the impregnation of the basic apparatus by the Quattrocento code of perspective: the hegemony of the eye, 'visual-ization,' and the ideology of the visible linked to the Western tradition of systems centered on a single point. The image produced by the camera could not fail to confirm and reinforce 'the visual code defined by renaissant humanism' which placed the human eye at the center of the system of representation, thereby excluding other systems and assuring the domination of the eye over all the other organs of senses: the eye (Subject) enthroned in the place of the divine (humanism's critique of Christianity).

A situation of *theoretical paradox* is thus reached, constituted as follows: on the one hand, a desire to expose the camera as subject to the dominant ideology of the visible in its conception and construction; on the other hand, an attempt to bring about this exposure by stressing the dominance of the camera (the visible) over film technique as a whole, which it is assumed to represent, inform and program (in the role of *model*).

The argument places the camera in a privileged position in order to make it the source of an ideological chain into which the cinema has been integrated. The theoretical ground for singling out the camera in this way clearly includes the principal and determining role of the camera in film production. If, however, this ground also includes everything that is implicated in this apparatus, then the act which singles out the camera must be taken further—otherwise it risks remaining imprisoned in the same chain.

The perspective has therefore to be changed. That is, it has to take into account what the act of designating the camera in this way thrusts aside, to ensure that this emphasis on the camera—necessary and productive though it is—is not itself pushed back into the very ideology it is aimed at.

A materialist theory of cinema (it seems to me) must bring out the ideological 'heritage' of the camera (and its 'scientific heritage,' the two being not at all mutually exclusive as Lebel seems to think); at the same time it must bring out the ideological investments which have been made in the camera. For neither in the production of film nor in the history of the invention of the cinema is the camera alone at issue. If the way that it involves technique, science and/or ideology is in fact determining, it is only so in relation to other determining factors. These may well be secondary in relation to the camera, but then this *secondary status* has to be examined—the status and function of all that the camera conceals.

To emphasize once again the danger implicit in making the cinema as a whole function on the *reduced model* of the camera (the risk is one of mystification since the camera then acts as an ideological screen in the very discourses which assign it this ideological place) it is enough to note the almost complete lack of any theoretical work on either the sound track, for instance, or on laboratory technique. (As if the vision of light—Geometrical Optics—had cancelled out its work: the chemistry of light.) The lack can only be explained by the domination of the visible in the practice of cinema as in reflection on the cinema.

For example, it is surely time *to expose* the ideological role of two techniques (where instruments + processes + knowledge + practice which back each other up are combined to realize an *aim*—an objective which then constitutes, founds and sanctions the technique). The techniques in question, *grading* and *sound mixing,* are located in the hidden and unreasoned area of cinema (except with very rare filmmakers, Godard, Rivette, Straub . . .). We will attempt to deal with this in Part III.

'BIRTH' = DELAY

The Invention of the Cinema

The long period of gestation of the cinema (which was not without its 'inexplicable' blanks and gaps during practically the whole of the 19th century) has been widely studied but poorly understood;[12] it also appears to be a list of often unrelated events which seem more or less accidental, fortuitous, even contradictory—so much so that it is scarcely possible to see any reassuring 'progress' there. Probably for these reasons this 'birth' period is the haven and source of strength for the majority of the fantasies and myths current on the cinema. Theoreticians and historians in search of its origins seem to have been motivated by the same desires as André Bazin: "If the origins of an art allow one to see something of its essence . . . "[13] So it should come as no surprise if this fleeting 'essence' is never more fleeting than in that space—already the realm of mythology—in which it is sought.

Nor if the decisive intervention of science in that space is far less certain than Lebel would have us believe. Bazin himself for instance—on these questions it's useful to refer to him frequently because the idealism and humanism of the interpretations he advances themselves serve as pointers to the ideological basis of the invention of the cinema: they re-mark it and therefore constitute a valuable and revealing instrument of work. Anticipating the arguments of the historian Jacques Deslandes, Bazin puts the emphasis on the 'craft' character of the discoveries which led to the cinema in order, of course, to marvel at it the more. In order, too, to reintegrate this invention of a machine into the sphere of man's myths and dreams—literally to *humanize* it by showing how insignificant and backward a part was played by technology, machines, and the sciences themselves, in comparison to the power of the ancient and clearly mythical dream of 'fixing' the image of life, of *representing* the living:[14]

What a reading of Georges Sadoul's admirable book on the origins of the cinema (*L'Invention du Cinéma,* Denoël) paradoxically reveals is, despite the author's Marxist viewpoint, a sense of the inversion of the relations between economic and technical evolution and the imagination of the investigators. Everything seems to have happened as if historical causality which moves from economic infrastructure to ideological superstructure had to be reversed here; and as if basic technical discoveries had to be considered as fortunate accidents, essentially secondary in relation to the preliminary idea of the inventors. The cinema is an idealist phenomenon. The idea of it existed already armed in men's minds, like in some platonic heaven, and what strikes us most of all is the obstinate resistance of matter to the idea rather than any help offered by techniques to the imagination of the pioneers. Its fathers are not scientists (with the exception of Marey, but it is significant that Marey was only interested in the analysis of movement, not in the inverse process which allowed for its reconstruction).[15] Even Edison was basically no more than a genius of do-it-yourself, a giant in the Inventors' Contest. Niépce, Muybridge, Leroy, Demeney, Louis Lumière himself, were faddists, reckless dabblers, or at best, ingenious industrialists . . . A real understanding of the discovery of the cinema will not be reached through the technical discoveries which made it possible . . .[16]

Note how Bazin brings every argument to bear, offers all the ways out: the 'dream's' primacy over science carefully set in the idealist framework emphasized by Bazin himself—for *Cinéthique,* this was inevitably supporting 'evidence' of cinema's 'natural ideological bent':

Bazin always stressed the idealism which had presided over the invention of the camera, and the non-scientific artificial character of its construction. The camera fulfilled man's ancient dream—of reproducing reality and reproducing himself.[17]

It is to this text (and via it to the words of Bazin quoted above) that Lebel opposes his discourse on the scientificity of the camera. But in this case the opposition is not restricted to Bazin and *Cinéthique*: pressure against the recognition of any determining role in the affair to science is characteristic of the great majority of historians, including Sadoul and Deslandes (whose works correct certain errors but finally persist in the same direction). Lebel therefore shows some uncertainty in both the counter-arguments he produces.

(1) He rightly observes that prior to the industrial stage of social development, all technical-scientific inventions could only be made in craft conditions:

[This is] confusing type of production (artisanal/industrial) with scientific research proper, as if all the great inventors and investigators of history up to the 20th century had not *all* been artisans.[18]

We are in complete agreement: it's not a question of knowing whether the 'inventors' of the cinema were artisans or not (they were, more or less inevitably), but to what extent in spite of, or because of, their craft status, their preoccupations and work can also claim a scientific status. This is in the end the only important question, and precisely the one which Lebel evades.

(2) The inconsistency of his other argument is more striking still.

When the reference to the artisanal character of the invention of photography and the cinema bases itself on the fact that the cinema concretized one of man's ancient 'dreams' whose ideological aspect is obvious (and/but historically determined) in an effort to invalidate their claim to scientific status, it is simply straying into irrelevance. It's like bringing a complaint against the aeroplane—also invented in artisanal conditions—for concretizing an ancient dream of man's whose ideological content is no less clear (and also historically determined). And as if therefore in order to struggle against the ideological effect of the myth of Icarus the constructors of socialist (or materialist) aircraft were called upon to denounce the ideology produced by the aeroplane by 'deconstructing' it—if not quite systematically, at least enough to assure its passengers sufficient discomfort to break down the fascination of the sky and constantly remind each traveler that it is not he who is flying, but that he does so only thanks to and through an *apparatus* and that consequently his relations to the real world remain unchanged.[19]

Lebel does it's true take the trouble to add: "of course I'm caricaturing the argument," but this scarcely attenuates the excesses of his comparison: misled by his concern to make the cinema (or the camera) a *scientific object* and a pure, technical system, he doesn't see that to compare it to another technical system like the aeroplane is simply to exclude the cinema from the field in which it acts (and in which the aeroplane doesn't act, even if it is a means of 'communication'), i.e., that of the process of signification—of ideology itself. It is because the cinema (scientific object or not) is a signifying practice that the fact that it fulfills 'an ancient dream of man's' has weight, that this debate concerns us, and that Lebel found it necessary to intervene.

By way of a preliminary observation, it is significant that all film historians (including Deslandes, whose work is referred to below) are uneasy when it comes to fixing an anterior limit to their field of work. The factors which make them choose one event, date, or invention rather than another as inaugural to their work are of the most arbitrary kind. This is because the prehistory of the cinema is *lost* in the obscurity of mythical times: the cinema doesn't just fulfill an 'ancestral human dream,' it also perpetuates a series of 'old empirical realities,' and 'old' techniques of representation.

Deslandes for example chooses 1826 and the invention of photography (in fact, just of the light-sensitive photographic plate) by Niépce and Daguerre, but this is giving a privileged status to just one of the constitutive techniques of the cinema—the one for which it's possible to fix an exact historical date. For the remainder (camera, breakdown and synthesis of movement) he is inevitably obliged by their weighty and ancient history to go further back.

As an optical system, the camera as we know it is simply a—barely perfected—adaptation of the Quattrocento *camera obscura*. But this dark chamber was known to the Egypt of the Pharaohs 347 years before Christ, and to Arab science of the 9th century, while Bessy and Chardin's *Dictionnaire du Cinéma* details its various manifestations and improvements since Bacon (1620).

Given its long existence, the *camera obscura* as an instrument was not just known, but handled, used and studied by scientists and artists from century to century throughout our history, well before there was any concern to question and understand the why and how of the small, inverted image which could be seen faintly in its depths.

Things become rather more disturbing when one observes that the same situation applies for the phenomenon which constitutes the other major pivot of the technical specificity of the cinema: the phenomenon which has been called 'persistence of vision' since the 19th century but which was known and studied at least since the Arab astronomer Al Hazen (965–1038).

Al Hazen was the author of *The Elements of Optics* (which also mentions the *camera obscura*); he not only criticized the then dominant theory of vision—which postulated the emission of 'luminous rays' by the eye—noting the persistence of luminous impressions after the eyelids were closed; but he also described perfectly the continuous circle which the eye perceives when a flaming torch is rotated in front of it at great speed.

Thus the major lines of the invention of the cinema—the production of an *image* of the world and the illusion of *continuity* brought about by the movement of objects—were established long before the light-sensitized plate which brought the photograph into being was produced. This must already modify considerably the role played by science as such since

(1) the two phenomena in question arose out of empirical observation ('optical illusions,' on the importance of which we will return later) and

(2) they were observed, described and 'explained' in each period in terms of dominant philosophies, i.e., ideologically, even if the systems of explanation were graced by the name of science: the 'epistemological break' for the *camera obscura* only came with the slow and erratic establishment of Geometrical Optics (17th century), and for visual perception with psycho-physiology in the 20th century.

The situation is much the same if one approaches the official date of the invention of the cinema.

First of all, there is, as Bazin observed, the relatively modest role played by both science and the scientist as such in the production of this instrument. As we have already seen, the *camera obscura,* while it demonstrated the linear propagation of light—without as yet being its experimental proof—was conceived and improved outside virtually any established scientific knowledge on the nature of light and vision. The only scientific practice with which it has any real connection is in fact the system of laws which structured *perspectiva artificialis*.[20] It is not therefore in this area that the decisive development came. The perfecting of the photographic plate was to stand out more: it represented a leap, prepared for it's true by the researches of Niépce on lithographic processes and ways of copying engravings by a chemical process. It remains true nevertheless that this leap was effected without the help of any scientific hypothesis on either the physics of light or its chemistry. One has only to read Niépce to be convinced:

to discover among the emanations of luminous liquid an agent which would be capable of imprinting in an accurate and durable way images transmitted by optical processes: I don't mean of course in all their vivid variety of colour, but in all the gradations of tone between black and white.[21]

As for Daguerre, it's well known that what led him to research the possibilities of "a new method of fixing the views found in nature without recourse to an artist" were the *trompe l'oeil* shows of the Diorama (which operated with great success from 1822 and in which light, noise and everything else competed to give the viewer a perfect illusion of reality).[22] It should be added that it was only more than a century later (1940–45) that the action of light on a sensitized plate could be explained theoretically.[23]

It was undoubtedly for persistence of vision that scientific research was of greatest importance: in 1824 the English mathematician Roget published a series of experiments on what he called "a curious optical illusion," the stroboscopic effect. A few years later, and almost simultaneously, Faraday in England and especially Plateau in Belgium published the results of their experiments with cogged wheels rotated in the same or in opposite directions. From these experiments Plateau derived the *Phenakistiscope* or *Fantascope* (1833), a scientific curiosity which became a fashionable toy. At the same time (once again) Stampfer, Professor of Applied Geometry at the University of Vienna, produced his stroboscopic discs, which became the *Zoetrope*—in fact identical to Plateau's invention.

Deslandes attributes this sudden density of research and instruments to a revival of interest in scientific circles in problems raised by the mechanism of sight. Bazin also expresses astonishment:

It is worth noting that, without any scientifically necessary connection, the work of Plateau and Niépce was almost contemporaneous; it was as if investigators had held back their interest in the synthesis of movement for centuries, waiting for chemistry for its part— quite independently of optics—to interest itself in the automatic fixation of the image.

What we have to account for therefore are the causes of this 'delay'—or of the contemporaneity of work on photography and movement. It seems clear that these are not located in the respective state of the sciences concerned. We must look rather at the crack which photography forced in the systems of figurative representation of the world, at the new questioning which it provoked of the central role of the human eye, its solar place and its intimate relations with the world (intimacy of Subject to Life, henceforth mediated and disturbed by a machine). It was this central role of the human eye which photography tended to duplicate or replace—substituting itself as a perfected version of the eye and its privileged representative. In other words we must look in the area of ideology.

At a certain point, therefore, the human eye was abruptly seen as neither alto-gether unique, nor quite irreplaceable, nor very perfect. Our position (advanced as a hypothesis and a reworking of Bazin's proposition) is that this point was arrived at when the invention of photography (of the sensitized plate) perfected the *camera obscura* and thereby achieved what generations of painters had for centuries demanded from the technique of artificial perspective—the possibility of copying nature faithfully: "the most excellent painting manner is the one that imitates best and makes the painting resemble the natural object it represents most closely," wrote Leonardo da Vinci. The first photograph, as we know, shows a *perspective* of roofs—where the triumph of monocular perspective as a system of representation in which the eye of the spectator (painter, Subject) occupies the center, directs the vanishing lines, governs the points of departure and conver-gence of the light rays, seems therefore to be assured. This is the moment when the supremacy of the eye is challenged (the simple lens of the *camera obscura*, which, as da Vinci had observed, corresponded to the crystalline lens of the hu-man eye, becomes the 'objective' of the camera). What we have in other words is a development which backs up the eye by perpetuating its principles of representa-tion of the world and the codes constructed on the standards of its 'normality,' but which at the same time undermines the hegemony of the eye and transcends it.

The probable effects of such a double development are: a strengthening of confidence in a perspective and analogous representation of the world (the photo-graphic image can't be argued with, it shows the real in its truth), and a crisis of confidence in the organ of vision, which till then had reigned over all representa-tion as its official standard scientifically—through 'the laws of scientific perspec-tive.' One is reminded of Leonardo da Vinci's advice:

. . . for the first tree, take a firmly fixed sheet of glass and carefully fix the position of your eye as well. Draw the outline of the first tree onto the glass upright until the outline of the tree you have drawn touches the outline of the real tree; then color your drawing so that it corresponds to the original in color as well as shape, and if you shut one eye they both seem to be painted on the glass an equal distance away.[24]

Science's sudden interest in optical illusions can be seen as a symptom of this crisis of confidence: devalorized and deposed from its central place by the eye of the camera, the human eye could once again become the object of scientific re-search and experiment. Aberrations reappeared, acting both within and against the ideology which set the eye up as a standard sanctioned by the laws of perspec-tive. As we have said, it was not that these 'illusions' had not been known for a long time, even to the point where for scientists and some philosophers they had undermined any possibility of total confidence in the human eye. But the doubt on the scientific level in some sense provoked a compensating and cushioning reac-tion on the level of ideology, so that the inscription of the doubt and deficiency was systematically compensated for by the inscription of the normality and cen-trality of the eye.[25] It is in this sense that we can agree with Marcelin Pleynet that the code of the *perspectiva artificialis* has acted as a repressive system.[26] Finally, if further proof is needed that the invention of the cinema only came about as a response to an ideological demand, it can be found in the total contradiction evi-

dent between the projects, inventions and declarations of the majority of the successive inventors of the cinema and the position of one of their number—the
physiologist Marey, who undoubtedly came closest to producing the definitive
apparatus, but saw no advantage in it from a scientific point of view. What dominates what Deslandes calls "the search for the absolute" and Bazin, "the myth of
total cinema" is a general striving for the perfect and complete reproduction of
life: photographic image + depth + movement + color + sound (as a *Temps*
journalist rather naively put it—science was advancing in giant strides and would
little by little succeed in overcoming death, its only obstacle and enemy). Marey
on the other hand perfected the *chronophotograph*, which was distinguished from
the camera chiefly by the fact that it used photographic paper rather than film;
but, as Deslandes points out:

A gulf separated the chronophotograph from the film camera and this was not just a technical specificity . . . It was the object of the apparatus. The film camera has as its essential
object the production of a long ribbon of images, which when run through a projector will
create an illusion of movement. The chronophotograph's sole function was to record
movement, to 'fix' it.[27]

The physiologist was thus concerned with the destructuring and analysis of
movement, and if he studied the possibilities of projecting his images and perfected a number of models of the *chronophotographic projector,* it was so that he
could observe the movement recorded several times over. This is why he had no
thought of working with film but was satisfied with rolls of paper film:

In order to grasp the nature of movement in a clear way it is useful to be able to reproduce it
several times over. This happens naturally with the apparatus which functions on a rotating
disc. But, as we have to use a roll of paper film in order to produce images, the ends have to
be joined so that it will run continuously and pass the series of images through the lens over
and over again.[28]

The same concerns led him to condemn the cinema in specific terms:

Animated photographs have permanently fixed essentially fleeting movements but what
they show, the eye could have seen directly; they add nothing to the power of our eyes,
remove none of the illusions. The real value of a scientific method is the way that it compensates for the inadequacy of our senses and corrects their errors.[29]

As Deslandes says, "He saw no interest in projecting onto the screen life as it
is."[30] Moreover in his own field of research—the physiology of movement—
Marey soon experienced the realism of the photographic image as an obstacle,
which led him to de-naturalize his scene: black background, black clothing, one
leg often swathed in black to avoid blurring the trace of the other, and finally
reflector bands on the arms and legs, these being the only thing recorded by the
camera to result in a kind of graphics:

The animated images have been 'fixed' into geometric figures. The illusion of the senses
has faded, but it has made way for the satisfaction of the intellect.[31]

A fairly careful reading of the history of the invention of the cinema thus
reveals the distortion involved in exaggerating, in the interests of objectivism, the

theoretical and practical role played by science in its invention. But while this history (and I have done little more than reformulate some of its specific problems here) may lack pointers towards Science it does point to Economics as a major determining factor in the establishment of film technique; and, through a double, social demand/response process, Economics are linked to ideology. It is in fact as both plural and fragmented that the 'birth' of the cinema emerges from all its 'Histories': scattered and sporadic, starting over again with each new 'apparatus,' each additional technical detail and each new patent; at the same time it is held back, postponed again for a time by the lack in each successive apparatus of some technical detail, of the new solution to a new problem. So much so that what changes from one apparatus to the next is infinitesimal, and so is what they lack. With the Lumière brothers' 'new' invention (prefigured a thousand times) this dual action of advance and delay in the progress of one technique over another comes to an abrupt end. A qualitative leap—but at what price? As Bazin and Sadoul point out, there had been nothing to prevent the production of a *Phenakistiscope* or a *Zoetrope* since ancient times:[32] it could be said too that nothing stood in the way of photography from the moment (1680 apparently) that a lens was added to the *camera obscura,* just as nothing separated Emile Reynaud's *Praxinoscope* and its public screenings of animated pictures from the Lumière *Cinématographe,* except that the pictures were drawn, not filmed (even though the photograph had existed for some time). What we are faced with therefore is chains of research (on the production of the image, on its fixation and reproduction, on the synthesis of movement) running in a disorganized way more or less parallel, but independent of each other; and chains of often simultaneous and identical inventions (disputes over patents play a large part in histories of the cinema), developing on the common basis of old empirical observations to converge and complete each other much later—a half century after Faraday, Plateau and Stampfer's experiments on stroboscopic effect and visual persistence, and a half century after the invention of the sensitized photographic plate. On the other hand, in the last years of the 19th century, the race for patents was frantic, as numerous virtually identical recording/projecting instruments came on to the market simultaneously: the competitors reached the finishing line together.

Bazin interprets this series of delays and lags as proof of a "resistance on the part of matter," a backwardness, even, of technique and science in relation to the idea and the myth, since the majority of the inventors had a very clear idea of the aim and bearing of their work—to produce a faithful and complete representation of life, and "realize man's ancient dream." But the real reason for this delay is not just a part of the (inevitable, according to Bazin) dislocation between the 'dream' and its 'realization.' Rather, while it's true that the 'scientific' conditions for the production of the definitive camera apparatus had come together more than half a century before its completion, the scientists themselves, as we saw, were scarcely preoccupied with straightening out the technical-practical difficulties of its manufacture because they had little interest in that manufacture. On the other hand, from the moment the production of the camera was integrated into a social demand and an economic reality, things were precipitated and efforts unleashed.

Deslandes, whose viewpoint is in no sense marxist, notes:

The importance of the Edison Kinetoscope (1892–3) is commercial and economic, not technical. It would in fact be a waste of time to try to show that some particular apparatus from 1895 or 1896 intended for the projection of moving pictures derives more or less directly from the principle and the mechanism for which Edison took out a patent . . . It's useless reviving the disputes over priority concerning the technical details of the first instruments of film projection and recording. This is not where the connection lies . . . The essential fact and starting point of the process which finally led to the practical realization of animated projections was the 'nickel' which the American viewer dropped into the slot of the Edison Kinetoscope, and the 25 centimes which the Parisian stroller paid in September 1894 to glue his eye to the viewer of the Kinetoscope . . . This is what explains the birth of the cinema show in France, England, Germany and the United States in 1895. Moving pictures were no longer just a laboratory experiment, a scientific curiosity; from now on they could be considered a commercially viable public spectacle. The origins of the Lumière Cinématographe, Robert William Paul's Theatrograph, or Skladinowsky's Bioscope should be sought not in the technical descriptions of earlier patents, but in the columns of figures in the account books kept by Ralph and Gammon's Kinetoscope Co., which was entrusted with the exploitation of Edison's instruments (more than $48,000 in under a year). The men who in 1895 completed the apparatus which made possible the screening of moving photographs for commercial ends were not disinterested researchers pursuing some Promethean dream, they were practical men.[33]

Which had already been said by the English historian Brian Coe:

The introduction of the Kinematograph was the turning point in the story of kinematography; not only were motion pictures shown to be practical—this had been in little doubt for many years—but they were shown to be profitable too.[34]

It is to the mutual reinforcement of an ideological demand ("to see life as it is") and the economic demand to make it a source of profit that cinema owes its being. It is no different from the majority of techniques—all bent towards the realization of an objective assigned to them by these two demands, which constitute the technique in question in terms of this objective. This is what seems to be important to establish and not lose sight of in the case of the cinema; for if we are in agreement with Lebel in refusing to stamp the cinema with some "natural ideological blemish," it is not in order to conjure away under an inconsistent "scientific basis" the fact that it was under the impact of an economic demand and as an ideological instrument that the cinema was conceived, made and bought from start to finish.

Notes

1. In *La Nouvelle Critique*, nos. 34, 35, 37 and 41; reference should of course be made to the whole of this study, which has since (1971) been published by Editions Sociales; but my discussion is limited to particular arguments from the first part (no. 34).

2. "Cinéma et idéologie," *NC*, no. 34, p. 70.

3. Ibid., p. 71.

4. Cf. *Cinéthique*, no. 3, "Economique, idéologie, formel," discussion with Marcelin Pleynet and Jean Thibaudeau; various issues of *Cinéthique*, particularly no. 5, "Direction" (Gérard Leblanc), "La parenthèse et le détour" (Jean-Paul Fargier); "Notes sur l'appareil de base" (Jean-Louis Baudry, no. 7/8), as well as the long collective article in no. 9, pp. 51–59;

nos. 216 and 217 of *Cahiers* ("Cinéma/idéologie/critique," 1 & 2); "Travail, lecture, jouissance" (Serge Daney and Jean-Pierre Oudart, no. 222), "Film/politique" (Pascal Bonitzer, no. 222), "La vicariance du pouvoir" (Jean Narboni, no. 224), and "La suture" (Jean-Pierre Oudart, nos. 211 and 212), "Le concept de montage" (Jacques Aumont, no. 211), "Montage" (Jean Narboni, Sylvie Pierre, Jacques Rivette, no. 210); "Le détour par le direct" (J.-L. Comolli, nos. 209 and 211), "L'effet de réel" (Jean-Pierre Oudart, no. 228).

  5. *Cinéthique*, no. 3, p. 10.

  6. Cf. especially *Peinture et société*, Idées-Arts, Gallimard.

  7. Op. cit., *Cinéthique*, no. 7/8.

  8. Where Lebel criticizes the positions of Pleynet, those of *Cinéthique*, and our own.

  9. Op. cit., *NC*, no. 34, p. 68.

  10. Op. cit., *NC*, no. 34, p. 72.

  11. "Sur Salador," in "Travail, lecture, jouissance," *Cahiers*, no. 222.

  12. In fact Volume I of *L'Histoire comparée du cinéma*, by Jacques Deslandes, Casterman, which covers the period 1826–1896, completes (and in some cases corrects) the works of Georges Sadoul: it has the particular merit of quoting the statements of inventors, the texts of depositions of patents, etc., thereby unfolding an interesting ideological panorama.

  13. "Le mythe du cinéma total," in *Qu'est-ce que le cinéma?*, I, p. 25, Editions du Cerf.

  14. Note, on the other hand, that in his "Ontologie de l'image cinématographique" (*Qu'est-ce que le cinéma?*, I), Bazin links *representation* to death and particularly to the Egyptian practice of embalming. Current research by Jean-Louis Schefer also poses this connection, though it's true on quite different theoretical assumptions.

  15. Cf. below.

  16. "Le mythe du cinéma total," op. cit., pp. 21–22.

  17. Gérard Leblanc, in "Welles, Bazin et RKO," *Cinéthique*, no. 6, p. 30. Part II of my study criticizes certain positions taken in this article.

  18. Op. cit., p. 18.

  19. Ibid., p. 71.

  20. It is relevant that the word *prospectiva*, or *perspectiva*, in medieval Latin designates the science of optics itself (see the treatise on optics by John Peckham [d. 1292] entitled "Perspectiva"). After the words of Alberti, which provide a mathematical and geometrical foundation for perspective, painters and theoreticians of the Quattrocento and Cinquecento distinguished between *perspectiva* (or *prospectiva*) *communis* or *naturalis*, which seems to have designated both the science of sight and the act of seeing itself ("things fixed by a particular angle of vision," Schefer) and *artificialis* (which, inversely, establishes Alberti's geometrical perspective allowing "accurate constructions to be made," Schefer).

  21. Quoted by André Vigneau in "Une brève histoire de l'art de Niépce à nos jours," Laffont, p. 63.

  22. Quoted by Jacques Deslandes, op. cit., pp. 63–65.

  23. On the 'backwardness' of photochemistry and the theory of the physics of light in relation to the practice of photography, cf. *La science de la photographie*, Gérard de Vaucouleurs, Elzevir:

> We have had to wait until very recently for the appearance of a coherent theoretical explanation of the subtle and mysterious mechanism of the action of light on a light-sensitive layer, an explanation which had been vainly sought for a century. This is because the mechanism activates extremely complex phenomena involving the intervention of elementary particles: ions, electrons, photons, which can only be interpreted by the most modern theories of matter and light.

  24. In *Leonardo da Vinci, le peinture*, texts collected and translated by André Chastel, Hermann, p. 172. For da Vinci, even more than for Alberti, the eye of the observer is the

criterion of the truth of what is represented: we know that da Vinci came to criticize Alberti's linear perspective because, confronted with a painting composed in accordance with the laws of perspective, the eye of the spectator could only see this flat surface free of distortions of any kind from a certain prescribed distance—a distortion of the lateral parts of the canvas occurring as the eye drew nearer the center of the painting.

25. The program of a conference in London in 1881, quoted by Deslandes (op. cit., p. 247): the propagation of light; light waves; concave and convex mirrors; Darker's Kaleidoscope; refraction; the light spectrum; mirages; diffraction; interference; Newton's rings; the iridescence of pearls, feathers and soap bubbles; chromatic and monochromatic light; luminous persistence on the retina; the Thaumotrope; the Kalotrope; the photodrome; Bayle's Choreutoscope.

26. See below.

27. Op. cit., p. 141.

28. Quoted by Deslandes, op. cit., p. 143.

29. Ibid., p. 144.

30. Op. cit., p. 130.

31. Quoted by Deslandes, op. cit., p. 144. Note further that another scientist, Albert Londe, appointed by Charcot to direct the medical photographic laboratory at La Salpetrière, perfected chronophotographic instruments but, like Marey, declared the *cinématographe* without interest from a scientific point of view: "The cinematographic representation places the observer in the same situation as in front of the model itself." However, Londe emphasizes that the situation is changed if the cinematograph is used at a *reduced* or *accelerated* speed: "by slowing down the operation of the instrument synthesizing movement, you reveal movements which normally escape the eye . . . Inversely certain movements escape the eye because of their extreme slowness, for example the growth of animals and plants. By taking a series of photographs at suitably spaced intervals and screening them at high speed, one can reproduce the complete phenomenon in a moment." This is a foresight of one of the important directions taken by *scientific film,* and it is worth noting that it was from the first integrated into the area of 'trick photography,' i.e., into the transgression of the impression of realism. It is not enough, as Lebel says, to "attach a camera to a microscope and film some operation on a slide" to produce scientific film "where the result has nothing to do with ideology . . ." The filming of microscopic images still requires a break with the 'normality' of 'realist' frequency.

32. Cf. André Bazin in "Le mythe du cinéma total," op. cit., p. 22.

33. Op. cit., pp. 213–214.

34. Quoted by Deslandes, op. cit., p. 213.

Translated by Diana Matias.

[Note: References to "persistence of vision" here and in other articles usually represent an inaccurate grasp of our current understanding of the perception of apparent movement in film. For a detailed discussion of apparent movement in film, see Teresa de Lauretis and Stephen Heath, eds., *The Cinematic Apparatus* (London: Macmillan, 1980).—BN]

TECHNOLOGICAL AND AESTHETIC INFLUENCES ON THE DEVELOPMENT OF DEEP-FOCUS CINEMATOGRAPHY IN THE UNITED STATES

PATRICK OGLE

Patrick Ogle's study represents one of the first efforts in a recent wave of historical revisionism that has carefully scrutinized the received wisdom of film history in the light of a return to primary source material. To a remarkable degree, many of the film histories and introductory film appreciation texts that appeared in the late 1960s based their facts and chronology on existing film histories, not on such reexamination. Ogle does not repeat the received wisdom about a prodigy from New York (Orson Welles) who arrived in Hollywood and showed the old-timers bold new ways to make movies. Instead, he situates Welles and Citizen Kane *within a web of interrelated technological and aesthetic developments that had left a trace on the previous twenty-five or so years of theatrical film production. Ogle does not try to explain why styles of soft and deep focus came and went in any detail, although he does note that magazine styles of photography may have been a significant factor. That begs the question, since we have only "explained" one succession of styles with another. To go farther would require placing aesthetic and technological developments within the kind of broad cultural or ideological context that Jean-Louis Comolli, for one, adopts. Such placement also occurs in another early piece of historical revisionism, Peter Baxter's "On the History and Ideology of Film Lighting,"* Screen *16, no. 3 (Autumn 1975), which provides an elaborate explanatory framework for the predominance of certain aesthetic choices in lighting practice. Nonetheless, Ogle's article is a superb example of careful scholarship and clear exposition. It serves as an excellent introduction to the revision of traditional film history now under way.*

•

A matter of continuing concern and some puzzlement to the author is the matter of the range and weight of relative emphases in film scholarship. Film is, as seems readily apparent, an art form and communications medium that has arisen from, and continues to be dependent upon, a relatively high level of technology. It is therefore surprising that most critical and scholarly work on film seems almost consciously to eschew any concern for film technology and the relationship it bears to many aesthetic and historic trends in the cinema. Just as aesthetic-communicative desires on the part of filmmakers have tended to affect the direction and aims of research and problem solving in film technology, so has the ever-changing state of the art in film technology tended to define the 'band-width' within which the visual and aural styles of film art and communication could operate. Deep-focus cinematography, the subject of this paper, furnishes a particularly good example of the degree to which a style of film-making can be dependent upon both aesthetics and technology.

Deep- or pan-focus cinematography as a recognized visual style in film-making first came to critical and public attention with the release of Orson Welles's film *Citizen Kane* in early to middle 1941.[1] Unusual for the time, much note was taken of the contributions of Gregg Toland, ASC, who directed the photography of the film. Toland's name has become synonymous with deep-focus cinematography even though some other cameramen were working along similar lines at the time, and one of them, James Wong Howe, ASC, seems to have produced a proto-deep-focus film in his photography of *Transatlantic* ten years earlier.[2] As practised by Toland and others, deep-focus cinematography constituted perhaps the first coherent alternative seen in American films to the editing-centred film theories of Eisenstein, Pudovkin, and Kuleshov. Whereas to the Russians the content of a given shot was subordinate to the feelings generated by its juxtaposition with those preceding and succeeding it, in deep-focus cinematography the individual shot and the action recorded within it came to be of primary importance. In this sense the American deep-focus school may be thought more cameraman-oriented than editor-oriented, and shared in common certain qualities with the German silent film tradition (not surprising, considering the number of old UFA cinematographers, such as Karl Freund, who were enjoying influential careers in the American industry) of concern with camera angle, camera motion, set lighting, and actor positions and movements within a take. Deep-focus cinematography tended toward long duration sequences, the avoidance of cutaways and reaction shots, the employment of a meticulously placed camera that only moved when necessary, and the use of unobtrusive, virtually invisible editing.

The most noticeable quality of deep-focus cinematography, however, was, as its name implies, the cultivation of crisp focus throughout an unprecedented depth of field in the scene photographed. In reviewing *Citizen Kane,* the *American Cinematographer* (house organ of the American Society of Cinematographers) commented:

The result on the screen is in itself little short of revolutionary: the conventional narrow plane of acceptable focus is eliminated, and in its place is a picture closely approximating what the eye sees—virtually unlimited depth of field, ranging often from a big head close-up at one side of the frame, perhaps only inches from the lens, to background action twenty, thirty, fifty, or even a hundred feet away, all critically sharp. The result is realism in a new dimension: we forget we are looking at a picture, and feel the living, breathing presence of the characters.[3]

While succumbing to the lingering misconception that the human eye as a lenticular system possesses extreme depth of field (for this is not the case, the eyes and brain having instead a remarkable ability to follow focus on various points of interest almost instantaneously without normal conscious awareness on the part of the viewer), the *American Cinematographer* reviewer did properly emphasize the startling crispness of focus and sense of presence conveyed by the technique. It is in this conveyed sense of presence (to be usefully distinguished from the general concept of realism— for in the light of thirty years *Citizen Kane* is seen to be anything but realistic in style) that the chief distinguishing characteristic of deep-focus cinematography may reside, for in providing the viewer with visually acute high information imagery that he may scan according to his own desires without the interruptions of intercutting, deep focus in André Bazin's words 'brings the spectator into a relation with the image closer to that which he enjoys with reality'.[4] In one way, then, the deep-focus aesthetic was an attempt to achieve a simulation of certain effects of theatre performance both by the elimination of certain film characteristics that pointed up the fact of there being an intermediary between viewer and performance, and by the employment of other inherently filmic characteristics that enhanced the theatrical sense of presence while simultaneously preventing any occurrence of the wretched 'canned theatre' effects of some early sound films. Chief among these latter characteristics was that of composition in depth, for the common deep-focus 'all-in-one' shot of the type described in the *American Cinematographer* review involved spatial relationships impossible to experience in the theatre. Deep-focus cinematography foreshadowed, in a sense, the development of the wide-screen formats of a dozen years later, techniques that, while using different technology and composing in breadth instead of depth, shared with deep focus the goals of sense of presence and many other qualities of the long duration take aesthetic.

While not all examples of deep-focus cinematography were necessarily realist in nature or style, the primary influences upon the development of deep focus were strongly involved with the concept of realism as a proper means of expression and communication. There had always been a tradition of sharply focused and realistic American film camera work, especially in outdoor footage, as much of Billy Bitzer's work for David Wark Griffith will attest. While largely eclipsed by the heavily diffused photographic style of the later 1920's and 1930's, the realistic style was still to be seen in certain genre films (such as westerns and gangster films) whose subject matter had a certain adamantine quality inconsistent with the softness of the prevailing camera style. (It is not surprising that the director for whom Gregg Toland filmed the partially deep-focus *The Grapes of Wrath* and *The Long Voyage Home* in 1940 and for whom Arthur Miller, ASC, filmed the deep-focus *How Green Was My Valley* in 1941 should be John Ford, whose experience with raw and realistic film-making had gone back to *The Iron Horse* of 1924 and before. Ford's *Stagecoach* of 1939, as photographed by Bert Glennon, ASC, looked forward very much to *Citizen Kane* in its use of ceilinged sets, wide-angle lenses, and distinctly 'un-Hollywood' lighting.[5]) Thus in the controversy surrounding the visual style of *Citizen Kane* it was possible for intelligent and presumably fair-minded cinematographers of such eminence as Leon Shamroy, ASC, and Gaetano Gaudio, ASC, to take the extreme position that there was really nothing new about deep focus, and that it consisted essentially of a return to practices of a quarter century earlier.[6, 7]

Probably more important to the development of the deep-focus style were influences toward realism that came from outside Hollywood and, to a large extent, from outside motion picture making. The 1930's saw the rise of the documentary film as an international movement. Some of the better American examples, such as Pare Lorentz's *The Plow that Broke the Plains* of 1936 (cinematography directed by Paul Strand, widely known as a still photographer) and *The River* of 1937, were to prove enduring examples of crisp *plein air* photography. The work of Jean Renoir in France during that decade was also of a very realistic sort, even looking forward—in his *Toni* of 1934—to post-war Italian Neorealism. Renoir's filming style tended toward the preservation of a greater depth of field than usual for the time, and toward the use of compositions that exploited this somewhat expanded depth by the inclusion of realistic background activities often dispensed with by more theatrically influenced directors. Renoir's actors usually moved about in evenly lit naturalistic settings, and takes tended to be of rather long duration. Significant actions were highlighted by judicious use of the moving camera, but one which moved only for good reason, not in the wilful and near-gratuitous fashion of the German silent era 'camera as actor'.

The attitudes toward realism and practices in filming of Jean Renoir provide an important link with some non-cinematic factors that were tending to move American cinematographic styles in a more realistic direction. One of Renoir's assistants during the middle 1930's was Henri Cartier-Bresson, who has become world-renowned in his own right as a still photographer of the unposed and candid 'decisive moment'. Cartier-Bresson's photographs (always taken, interestingly enough, with a Leica camera, which uses motion picture film and was originally developed by Oscar Barnack during the early 1920's as an economic method of making film exposure and lighting tests in the German UFA film studios) were seen by millions of people, along with the similarly realistic work of other photojournalists, in magazines such as *Life* and *Look*. James Wong Howe, whose lifelong interest has been in the cultivation of realism in cinematography, made a perceptive remark in mid-1941:

> There is one thing about modern cinematography which I feel no one has emphasized sufficiently. This is the profound influence the photographic and picture magazines, which have become so popular during the last ten years, have had on styles in studio camera work.[8]

Howe felt that the tendency toward crisper definition, greater depth, and occasional use of higher contrast was primarily due to a change in public taste 'directly traceable to the growth in popularity of miniature camera photography, and to the big picture magazines'[9] in which the public saw the stark realism of miniature camera photojournalism every week. This change in public taste, Howe considered, had evoked a change in cinematographic style 'so slowly and subtly that we ourselves have scarcely been conscious of it. . . .'[10]

The popularity of miniature camera photojournalism may have had more effect on changes in cinematographic style than just changes toward 'slice-of-life' realism. For reasons that have never been clear, the so-called 'normal' lenses for motion picture cameras (those which supposedly give the most natural perspective effects and which are consequently used in the majority of picture-taking situations) have always been of approximately twice the focal length of normal focal length lenses for still camera lenses of similar negative size. A 35mm (film gauge) motion picture camera has a normal lens of 50mm focal length, the same focal length as that of a 35mm still camera, such as the Leica, whose negative size area is twice that of the motion picture camera frame. The fact that the Leica normal lens focal strength is (relatively speaking) half that of the motion picture camera means that most pictures made with the still camera take in an angle of view twice as wide as that taken in by a motion picture camera filming the same event from the same distance. For cinematographers to duplicate on film the perspective and foreground-background image size relationships normally seen in the picture magazines, they would have to use what were considered in motion picture terms distinctly wide-angle lenses. As this was precisely what the deep-focus cinematographers did, much of the 'realism' attributed to deep focus may be due to the unconscious awareness on the part of the viewer that the object sizes and spatial relationships correspond more closely to those of still photography (and, in truth, to the way one's eyes tend to see) in deep focus than in conventional cinematography.

While the tendencies toward realism mentioned in the preceding paragraphs had a noticeable effect both on the general American cinematographic style and upon the development of the deep-focus style, it should not be thought that the appearance of deep focus was either entirely inevitable or predictable on the basis of those tendencies alone. A number of changes in motion picture technology were necessary to provide the range of capabilities from which Toland and others chose those suitable for synthesis into the mature deep-focus style. The significance of these changes can perhaps best be appreciated by a brief historical survey of the evolution in film stocks and developers, lenses, and lighting from the early 'hard edge' style of circa 1915, through the heavily diffused 'fuzzygraph' era[11] of the later 1920's and early 1930's, to the coming of the deep-focus style in 1941.

The era of silent film-making that extended from the time of David Wark Griffith's *The Birth of a Nation* (1915) until the coming of sound in the later 1920's has often been painted as one of great art prevailing over woefully deficient technology. Such a viewpoint may be based excessively on hindsight. Many a contemporary student of film history will dutifully shake his head in thinking of the agonies doubtless suffered by cinematographers confined to the use of orthochromatic film. What he will likely not be aware of is that orthochromatic film (a type sensitive to green, blue-violet, and ultra-violet light) constituted a very real improvement over the 'ordinary' or non-colour-sensitised emulsions (sensitive only to blue-violet and ultra-violet)[12] that had been the basic material of even earlier film-making. (Blue-sensitive film, semi-ironically, was to reappear in modified form in 1939 as Fine Grain Release Positive film, an important ingredient in the deep-focus technique.) As panchromatic film emulsions (a type reasonably sensitive to the entire visible spectrum rather than just the shorter wavelengths) had been first introduced in 1913[13] but had not proved popular, it would appear that cinematographers of the era may have preferred to use orthochromatic film. Most of this preference may have been due to the innate conservatism of many cinematographers (upon whose heads much wrath would inevitably descend in the event of photographic mishap), but some of it may have been due to the conduciveness of orthochromatic film to the crisp contrasty style of cinematography (which had its parallels in the 'f-64' school of still photography) that prevailed until sometime into the 1920's. While orthochromatic film was an intrinsically slow (i.e., not particularly light-sensitive) emulsion type, this factor may not have been very obvious at the time as the extremely strong and contrasty developers then in use compensated in large measure for the deficiencies in film speed, albeit at a great cost in excessive graininess. Cinematographers often found themselves having to stop their lenses down to f-45 for filming exteriors,[14] indicating that the violent developing chemicals of the time gave the film an effective speed of over 160 ASA, similar to that of medium to fast black-and-white panchromatic emulsions of today. An f-45 lens aperture set on a normal 50mm motion picture camera lens provided an extreme depth of field, such that objects would be rendered sharp at distances from just under two feet to infinity. The full deep-focus potentials of this great depth of field seem rarely if ever to have been explored at the time, however.

The sharp, contrasty qualities of orthochromatic film were well matched by the characteristics of the lenses in use at the time, critically sharp-cutting anastigmats, such as Dagors and Tessars,[15] whose maximum apertures of f-3.5 gave measurably greater depth of field than those of later, faster lenses.

Lighting during the era of orthochromatic film was chosen for compatibility with the green-blue-violet sensitivity of the stock. As this was the era of the silent film, much filming was done outside, where sunlight and skylight provided rich and free sources of light concentrated toward the shorter wavelengths of the visible spectrum. At one time indoor filming had been accomplished largely by the use of studios with glass skylights, but as time went on production companies began to eschew the vagaries of weather by turning exclusively to the use of artificial illumination. Banks of mercury vapour lamps (identical in concept and similar in spectral distribution to modern street and highway lamps) were used for broad, general lighting, and provided the suitable bluish light needed with high electrical efficiency. The other primary light source at the time was the carbon arc lamp (which in later improved form was perhaps to be the crucial element in deep-focus cinematography). The carbon arc lamp produced a very blue light (similar to that emitted by a contemporary electric arc welder) of high intensity per watt of electricity consumed. Unlike the mercury vapour lamp, the carbon arc lamp emitted light from a very small area. This point-source lighting tended to bring out textures and cast very sharp shadows, adding strongly to the sense of crispness and contrast already evoked by the film and lens types.

Some time into the 1920's the extremely hard and sharp look in cinematography began to give way to a softer, more diffused style, paralleling a similar trend in still photography. This was first achieved by the optical means of fitting layers of gauze over the camera lens and placing optical diffusers called 'silks' over the lights. Some visual softening appeared with the introduction of a number of newer and more complex motion picture lenses, the designs of which traded off a degree of lens correction in order to achieve greater light-gathering power. These lenses, with maximum apertures of about f-2.3, also possessed intrinsically less depth of field at maximum aperture (which came to be used as the normal filming aperture) than had the older, simpler lenses. This increased softness was optical rather than tonal, for orthochromatic film remained contrasty by nature. As part of the trend toward softening of shadows and lowering of contrast, Lee Garmes, ASC, began experimenting with the use of 'Mazda' incandescent lamps for lighting films during the mid-1920's.[16] The Mazda lamp was initially at a disadvantage when used with orthochromatic film as much of its light was in the yellow-orange region to which orthochromatic film was blind, and its electrical efficiency was significantly lower than that of either arcs or mercury vapour lamps. The initial value of the Mazda lamp was in the non-point-source quality of the light, for it cast significantly softer shadows and tended to suppress textures. This single advantage of the Mazda lamp would probably not have been enough to ensure its success had not other events intervened, however, for 'as late as 1927 the majority of motion picture productions were made using orthochromatic negative with mercury vapour and arc lamps . . .'[17]

Nineteen twenty-eight was a pivotal year for the American film industry, witnessing as it did the first significant amount of sound film production, the introduction of the soft-looking finer grain Type 1 panchromatic film by Eastman Kodak, and the beginning of the metamorphosis from arc to Mazda for studio lighting.[18] Panchromatic film stock and Mazda lighting proved well matched to each other, the film being sensitive to the longer wavelengths of visible radiation, in which Mazda illumination was particularly rich. Intensive testing by the American Society of Cinematographers

definitely proved the Incandescent to be superior for use with Panchromatic film; but I doubt if the innovation would have been accepted so readily had not sound arrived to force the issue. The 'Inkie' was the only really silent lamp available, and it naturally sprang overnight into general use.[19]

With the at least temporary discontinuance of the use of arc lamps owing to noise problems on the newly built sound stages, American film-making entered a period of heavily diffused images, soft tonality, and shallow depth of field that was to characterise Hollywood films until into the later 1930's. Whil softness and diffusion was the prevailing aesthetic style of cinematography, it must be admitted that for much of the period it may not have been possible to achieve the earlier crispness even if cinematographers had wanted to, so encumbering were the demands of early sound film-making. The soft tonality panchromatic emulsions, while intrinsically more light-sensitive than orthochromatic, came to be processed in milder, more fine-grain borax-type developers (such as D-76) that greatly improved picture resolution quality but reduced effective film speed and contrast. Soft shadow Mazda lighting, crucial to sound film-making due to its silence, was less efficient electrically than arc and available only in lighting units of comparatively low power. The newer and faster lenses had almost by necessity to be used at maximum aperture, further softening the image and reducing depth of field.

While the coming of the sound film had had a strong influence on moving cinematography away from the crisp, contrasty, depthy style of much of the silent era, another new film type and technology had a similarly strong influence in making possible a return to more realistic cinematography styles in the later 1930's and in furnishing much of the technology crucial to the deep-focus style. This was Technicolor (which also, in a McLuhan sort of way, may have given monochrome cinematography the possibility of becoming an art by supplanting it as the basic medium of mass popular visual entertainment). If the silencing of cameras and lights in order to record speech and music satisfactorily had been one of the major efforts of sound film technology, one of the primary problems in developing the three-colour subtractive Technicolor process was to maintain the silence of lighting equipment while enormously increasing its power and significantly shifting its colour balance. As the film stocks used in the Technicolor process had a very low effective speed and were balanced for the predominantly green-blue of daylight, Mazda incandescent lighting could no longer be relied upon as a primary lighting source. Consequently a new generation of arc lamps appeared, incorporating a number of improvements that rendered them quiet and flicker-free. Changes in the chemical formulas for the carbons used shifted the spectral distribution of the light produced such that arc could match daylight with only mild filtration by means of a straw-coloured Y-1 filter. The modern arc lamp of the middle to later 1930's retained the crisp shadow-casting and texture-revealing point-source light of its forebears, and models of remarkable intensity and carrying power began to appear.[20] While much of the Mazda incandescent lighting equipment commonly used in black-and-white production after 1935 dated back (in design and often in construction) to the beginning of the sound era almost a decade earlier, virtually all arc lighting developed for Technicolor work was of 1934 or later vintage and possessed substantial advantages in uniformity, controllability, and power.[21, 22] Confined initially to use in colour production work (due both to scarcity and—one thinks—to power beyond that needed by most workers in monochrome), the new arc lights later began to be used in black-and-white production with fair frequency, the arrival of faster Technicolor film stocks in 1939[23] having allowed a sizeable reduction in colour lighting power requirements (and having even sparked something of a resurgence in the use of filtered Mazda lighting on Technicolor sets).

Developments in filmstock technology proceeded apace. The soft and fine-grain (in comparison to orthochromatic) Eastman Type 1 panchromatic emulsion of 1928 was followed later the same year by the slightly faster and even softer Type 2 emulsion. February 1931 saw the introduction of the first super-sensitive panchromatic emulsion, Eastman Super Sensitive Panchromatic Negative, a stock at once materially faster, finer-grained, and softer than its predecessors. Rather than stopping down lens apertures (and thus risk losing the then-fashionable softness of image), cinematographers initiated a trend toward ever lower-key light levels on the sets (a trend that, in some quarters, continues to the present day). The introduction of Eastman Super X Panchromatic Negative in March 1935 continued the trend toward somewhat higher speed with much lower grain and improved picture quality. Super X film remained an inherently soft, low-contrast emulsion, as indicated by the recommendation of the manufacturer that the film be developed to the comparatively high gamma of .70 for normal results. This characteristic of tonal softness in film stocks was abruptly reversed in late October 1938, however, when Eastman introduced Plus-X Panchromatic Negative as a new general-use film, an emulsion with twice the speed of Super X, finer grain, similar developing characteristics, but with such noticeably higher contrast that many cinematographers, having grown accustomed to working with soft tonality films, were to experience real difficulty in lighting sets properly for the new film.

Two weeks after the introduction of Plus-X came the announcement of Eastman Super XX, a film possessing grain characteristics comparable to those of the standard Super X previously used, but with a film speed four times as great. Developed initially for newsreel work and other specialised and realistic filming done under difficult lighting conditions (and also developed, one suspects, to regain first place in the film speed derby from Agfa-Ansco, whose Agfa Supreme Negative and Agfa Ultra-Speed Negative emulsions had been introduced eleven months previously and had won a Class I Academy Award for the manufacturer[24]). Super XX film quickly came to be used in ways far different from those intended or envisaged by Eastman Kodak. A few cinematographers, such as Victor Milner, ASC, became immediately aware that the high-speed film widened the potential expressiveness of the medium in that:

It makes it possible for us to run the scale between extremely soft, naturalesque low-level lightings (50 foot candles or less), shot with full lens apertures, to the opposite extreme of higher-level illumination (perhaps as high as 200 foot candles or more) exposed at greatly reduced apertures for a new and greater depth and crispness.[25]

Only a very small number of cinematographers opted for the possibilities of increased crispness and depth of field, however. A greater number followed the path of James Wong Howe in maintaining full aperture filming while further lowering set lighting levels almost to those of conventional roof lighting,[26] thus providing more naturalistic settings within which the actors could perform. By far the greatest number of cinematographers (Milner included), however, utilised Super XX film in a strange (but fully explainable) way. Conservative by nature and distressed by the increased contrastiness of the new general-use Plus-X emulsion, these cinematographers began to employ Super XX as a production film with deliberate underdevelopment, a procedure that gave them lowered contrast similar to the old Super X film they had been used to, and fine grain similar to the new Plus-X emulsion.[27] The great loss of film speed entailed in underdevelopment was desirable to them, as it permitted the use of lighting levels and lens apertures little different from those of previous practice. The armchair paleontologist would find this a classic example of the evolutionary principle that, within a modified environment, new or changed behaviours or forms in an organism arise in the organism's attempt to return to the homeostasis of the previous environment. Ironic indeed is the realisation that, while Super XX film was to prove an important ingredient in the development of the crisp, deep-focus style, the main impetus toward its use as a production filmstock was the desire to preserve the soft tonality and low depth of field of the older type of cinematography!

A final important development in film technology occurred in 1939 with the introduction of a new emulsion type in the relatively unglamorous category of release print stocks. This film, Fine Grain Release Positive, was an extremely slow stock sensitive only to blue-violet and ultra-violet light, and required printing by means of modified high-pressure mercury arc light sources. To offset these inconveniences, Fine Grain Positive had the major advantage of being virtually grainless, and thus free from the problem of successive image degradation common to printing stocks before it. Picture quality improved noticeably, and the new freedom from grain multiplication through the various print generations from camera to release print allowed cinematographers to use high-speed films, such as Super XX, without the fear of excessive graininess. Sound quality improved even more than did picture quality on Fine Grain Positive Film: high frequencies were reproduced far better, and emulsion ground noise was reduced $6-8$ decibels,[28] factors that would be highly important to films in which the sound track was to play a strong role.

In contrast to the relative flux that had been occurring in the areas of lighting and film stocks, the field of camera lens design had changed little since the introduction of the fast and relatively soft lenses of the late silent era. Small incremental improvements had been made in lens correction and sharpness, but a ceiling seemed to have been reached, dictated largely by the design compromises that had to be struck in dealing with the conflicting requirements of lens speed and optical quality. Revolutionary, therefore, were the implications of the announcement by two independent researchers in 1939 of the principle of lens coating, by which a microscopically thin layer of magnesium fluoride was deposited on the lens surfaces with resulting improvements in light transmissions of more than 75 percent under some conditions. As might be expected concerning a process that promised much more efficient use of light, the lens coating principle proved of great interest to Technicolor Corporation, and the first commercial application of lens coating techniques was by Bausch & Lomb in delivering coated projection lenses to twenty-five Loew theatres in the larger cities for the first showings of *Gone with the Wind,* where improvements in screen illumination, image contrast, and sharpness of focus were noted.[29] Similar benefits were noted when coatings were applied to camera lenses. A typical uncoated high-speed motion picture anastigmat lens, such as the Astro Pan-Tachar, suffered light losses in excess of 41 percent due to reflections from the eight air-to-glass surfaces comprising its lens formula. Such light losses were reduced to negligible proportions with the application of optical coatings. In addition internal reflection and fog-producing scattered light within the lens were largely eliminated, allowing the lens to capture a great deal of shadow detail normally lost.[30] William Stull, ASC, noted that lens coatings produced

. . . a practical increase in speed of virtually one full stop. . . . Thus a normal f-2.3 lens, when treated, is the equivalent in speed of an f-1.6 objective, but still retains the depth of field, definition, and optical quality of the f-2.3 design!

The elimination of the internal reflections gives a marked increase in the apparent definition of scenes photographed with treated lenses. . . . The picture as a whole is visibly more crisp, and details not previously evident are suddenly revealed. In the same way depth of field is apparently considerably increased by the treated lens. It is quite possible that the circle of confusion is affected, since the resolving power is known to be increased.[31]

A point not made by Stull is that another great increase in depth of field became possible with coated lenses simply because the greatly increased efficiency of light transmission demanded a physically smaller lens diaphragm aperture to transmit the same amount of light as a larger aperture had previously. This smaller aperture increased both depth of field and lens sharpness.

Looking back at the technological state of the movie-making art in 1940, a determinist could well argue that the conjunction of powerful point-source arc lights, fast film emulsions, and crisp coated lenses rendered inevitable the emergence of deep-focus cinematography. The argument has some merit, for, indeed, a number of cinematographers seem at the time to have looked over their newly improved tools and commenced semi-independent investigations into increased-depth photography. Aware as he is of the crucial importance of much of this technology to the deep-focus style, the author nevertheless feels that for deep focus to appear and develop as it did, a number of essentially aesthetic choices and creative syntheses had to occur. These choices and syntheses seem largely to have been made by one man, Gregg Toland, for, while other cinematographers may have been working rather haphazardly toward a cinematographic style of increased depth, crispness, and contrast, Toland was the first person to draw together and elaborate the series of attitudes and technical tool usages that became the coherent body of filming practices constituting the deep-focus style. The matter of timing and opportunity also seems very important, for, without the fertile creative environments provided by William Wyler, John Ford, and especially by Orson Welles, the deep-focus style might never have come into being.

Gregg Toland was an atypical cinematographer in a number of respects. In an industry given to constant shifts of personnel and employment, such that a cameraman was often literally 'only as good as his last picture', Toland remained under steady contract with Samuel Goldwyn from 1926 until his death in 1948,[32] and managed to retain the same personnel on his camera crew for most of that time. Although Toland and his crew were often loaned out to other studios, the relative security of employment under the Goldwyn contract and stability of competent operative personnel on his film crew probably did much to provide Toland the kind of breathing space needed for coherent creative endeavour.

Although he had been a director of photography since the beginning of the decade, Toland did not reach prominence among Hollywood cinematographers until early 1938, when his expertise in filming Goldwyn's *Dead End* for William Wyler (completed the previous summer) was noted in the April issue of the *Amer-*

ican Cinematographer. Most of the film was made on a single indoor set of a New York City street, and Toland made an unusual (for the time) effort to achieve the realistic look of sunshine illumination by bunching eight powerful arc lamps together to simulate the crisp, single-source parallel-ray illumination of sunlight.[33] Toland's name soon became familiar to readers of the ASC magazine. A few months later, in discussing his work on *Kidnapped* (the version with which Otto Preminger was very briefly involved), the magazine was to allude to Toland's innovative and adaptive nature in mentioning that:

The lighting of the picture followed his general custom of using a low key unless some reason out of the ordinary indicated to the contrary. In spite of his preference for a low key, there is no hesitation on his part in using lamps when in his judgment there is photographic occasion.[34]

Toland had also just finished his first film in colour, *The Goldwyn Follies.* As this film was photographed on the slow, pre-*GWTW* emulsions that required set key lighting not much below the 800–1,000 foot candle level common in 1936,[35] Toland was thus by the middle of 1938 quite proficient at simulating realistic lighting on indoor sets and knowledgeable in the use of arcs at very high lighting levels; both practices were to be elemental to deep-focus cinematography.

Although the use of Eastman Super XX film as a production filmstock seems to have originated with Joseph Valentine, ASC,[36] a number of other cinematographers (including Toland, William Daniels, ASC, and Rudolph Maté, ASC) began to use the stock regularly soon after. The film in whose production Toland first used Super XX is not known to the author, but it would not seem unlikely for the stock to have been used at least sporadically in William Wyler's *Wuthering Heights* of 1939, a film in which Toland experimentally employed deep focus in a few scattered scenes,[37] and a film for whose black-and-white photography he was to receive the Academy Award in 1940. Similarly, Toland's first production use of coated lenses is difficult to pinpoint, although he was later noted as one of the first cinematographers, if not the first, to experiment with coated lenses and use them in important productions.[38] John Ford's *The Grapes of Wrath* of 1940, though involving a masterful use of hard, low-fill source lighting for a realistic documentary look, seems to have been filmed too early (later 1939)[39] to claim the honour. Toland very probably did use coated lenses in filming Ford's *The Long Voyage Home,* however, which was in production toward the middle of 1940,[40] and in which, as in *The Grapes of Wrath,* some still rather tentative deep-focus effects were used.

In Orson Welles's *Citizen Kane* of 1941, any qualities having to do with the tentative or provisional in photographic style (or anything else, for that matter) had disappeared, and the mature deep-focus style emerged. As well as constituting the first full-fledged example of the deep-focus style, *Citizen Kane* may also be the best example, displaying as it does an uncompromised self-assuredness of visual style that many later deep focus films could not match. The coherence of *Citizen Kane's* visual aspect (a coherence shared by the dialogue, sound, and music of the film) is due in large measure to the conditions under which the film

was produced, for the making of *Citizen Kane* constituted a major coming together of technological practice with aesthetic choice in an environment highly
conducive to creativity.

Judging that therein lay an unusual opportunity for photographic innovation,
Toland actively sought the assignment to shoot the film, and brought his veteran
operative crew with him to the RKO studios to do so. Unusual in a Hollywood
production of the time, Toland was on the job for a full half year, including preparation and actual shooting.[41] The importance of Orson Welles, both in terms of his
own creative contributions and his encouragement of innovative behaviour in others, cannot be overemphasised. Toland was later gratefully to acknowledge Welles's
willingness to let him experiment with photographic effects that often took weeks to
achieve, remarking that 'such differences as exist between the cinematography in
Citizen Kane and the camera work on the average Hollywood product are based on
the rare opportunity provided me by Orson Welles, who was in complete sympathy
with my theory that the photography should fit the story'.[42]

Coming to his first turn at film direction from a notoriety-filled period of work
in radio and live theatre, Welles was determined to give *Citizen Kane* the kind of
unique imprint that he had made upon his efforts in the other media. Whether due
to his theatrical experience (in which action occurs within specific spatial bounds
primarily within real-time duration) or that in radio (in which events take place in a
fluidly homogeneous 'field' very different from the discrete segmentation of visually perceived space), Welles became strongly desirous of creating a film in
which actions were to flow smoothly into each other by means of imperceptible
transitions, with intercutting and inserts to be eliminated as completely as possible. In achieving this, according to Toland:

We arranged our action so as to avoid direct cuts, to permit panning or dollying from one
angle to another whenever that type of camera action fitted the continuity. By way of
example, scenes which conventionally would require a shift from close-up to full shot were
planned so that the action would take place simultaneously in extreme foreground and
extreme background.[43]

Although the fluidity of effect in storytelling desired by Welles seemed almost
ideally suited in concept to the deep-focus style with which Toland had been
experimenting, the cinematographer no doubt found his technological and innovative expertise fully tested, for nothing quite like this had ever been attempted
before. That *Citizen Kane* remains a visually exciting film over thirty years after
its release is a testament to the rightness of Toland and Welles's aesthetic choices
and furnishes an example of creative exploitation of the then-current limits of
technology to which the much-abused term 'classic' does not seem inappropriate.

Citizen Kane was one of the first important productions filmed with the Mitchell BNC motion picture camera, a device whose quiet operation was achieved by
means of internal sound dampening measures.[44] The elimination of the bulky
external blimp previously required had important consequences for filming in the
deep-focus style. Simply dispensing with the need for shooting through the optical glass plate of the blimp sharpened up the photographed image and increased

light transmission over ten percent.[45] Lens focus, depth of field, and photographic composition could easily be checked without having to open up a blimp. The relative compactness and light weight of the self-blimped Mitchell BNC must have proved of distinct value under the conditions of use imposed by the generally small, deep sets within which *Citizen Kane* was filmed, allowing the camera to be raised, lowered, panned, and dollied (no doubt often by means of an hydraulic tripod and dolly-track system previously developed by Toland)[46] with comparative ease. An additional psychological advantage may have accrued in the use of this camera, as its comparatively small size surely rendered its presence less intimidating to the actors, who often found themselves having to perform only two or three feet away from it.

While the 25mm focal length wide-angle lens was a standardised item in most cinematographers' inventories of equipment, it was normally used only in situations where the camera could not be moved back far enough to capture all the relevant action within the field of view of the normal 50mm lens. The distinguishing feature of Toland's wide-angle lens was in the way he used it. Like Howe and Glennon before him, Toland was both aware of the inherently greater depth of field of the wide-angle lens (following the rule of thumb that depth of field varied inversely as the square of the magnification of the lens)[47] and of the fact that the different perspective given by the lens could be used for dramatic effect. Where Toland went beyond Howe and Glennon's occasional semi-standardised use of the wide-angle lens was in using his stopped down to f-8, f-11, or even f-16, extending depth of field in some cases from less than two feet to infinity! With Toland's small-aperture wide-angle lens, a cinema aesthetic of non-intercut compositions in depth became fully realisable.

The use of a coated lens (the 'Vard' opticoating system, developed at Cal Tech)[48] was highly important to the deep-focus cinematography of *Citizen Kane,* for the minutely thin chemical deposit (amounting in thickness to a fraction of the wavelength of light) on the air-to-glass surfaces of the lens doubled light transmission, sharpened the imagery and contrast, and made possible filming practices previously considered quite unattainable. As a coated lens at f-8 transmitted the same amount of light as an uncoated optic at f-5.6, scenes could be filmed with the increased depth of field of the former aperture, but with the halved lighting requirements of the latter. The most noticeable new filming technique afforded by the use of coated objectives was that of shooting into lights, examples of which are seen in the several sequences dealing with Susan Alexander's opera debut in *Citizen Kane.* Without lens coatings such shots would have been unusably washed out and diffuse.

Employment of Eastman Super XX film as a production stock joined with coated lenses in helping permit the use of the small lens apertures necessary to Toland's compositions in depth. Unlike most cinematographers, Toland used the stock at full rated speed, developing time, and contrast. While the film speed of Super XX (128 ASA for daylight or arcs, 80 ASA for tungsten Mazda) may not seem remarkable by contemporary standards, the two points should be borne in mind that Super XX did constitute an enormous advance over the Super X stock

(32 ASA for daylight, 20 ASA for Mazda) that for all practical purposes had preceded it, and that the American Standards Association criteria for determining film speeds have been modified since that time, such that by the current measurement system Super XX would have a daylight ASA film speed of slightly over 250—reasonably fast even by today's standards. The relatively new (and by no means universally used) Eastman Fine Grain Release Positive filmstock was utilised for the final release prints to motion picture theatres, ensuring protection of the Eastman Super XX footage from grain multiplication or other image degradation and significantly improving the reproduction fidelity of *Citizen Kane's* sound track, itself as revolutionary as the film's photographic style.

Granting that camera, lenses, and filmstocks played important roles in the deep-focus cinematography of *Citizen Kane,* nevertheless the true *sine qua non* of the style seems to have involved the lighting equipment and its method of employment. Faced with the desire to film at diminished apertures within narrow, deep, roofed-over sets, Toland had to rely entirely on floor-level lighting of very considerable intensity and carrying power. 'The answer, of course, was to use arcs very extensively. It is safe to say that *Citizen Kane* could not have been made without modern arc lighting'.[49] As the spectral distribution of arcs resembled that of daylight in that the preponderance of energy was to be found among the shorter wavelengths of visible radiation, all the inherent light sensitivity of the Super XX emulsion could be utilised, for the stock was half again as fast under daylight arc conditions than when exposed to Mazda incandescent illumination. While also electrically more efficient in terms of lumens per watt, the primary advantage of arc lighting as used on *Citizen Kane* was in terms of sheer power. Toland's general practice was to use arc broads (specifically, the Mole-Richardson 'Duarc' developed for colour work)[50] set back about twice as far (20–30 feet) from the players as incandescent broadsides would have been, thus increasing the depth of field of uniform illumination. Toland commented that:

. . . the use of arcs permitted us to light this way [floor lighting from front of set] and yet to avoid the unevenness of exposure which might normally be expected under such circumstances. . . . With the [Mazda-type] lamp nearer the action, its depth of illuminative field might be a matter of two or three feet. With an arc placed further back, your subject can move freely over an area of ten feet or more in depth without undesirable changes in exposure value. Arc illumination, in a word, gives you depth of field in lighting to match the optical depth modern technique affords.[51]

To permit filming at reduced lens apertures, lighting levels on the *Citizen Kane* sets were very high, quite atypical for the time.[52] While cinematographers such as James Wong Howe would prefer a key light level of 35 foot candles when using Super XX film,[53] Toland was using at least 320 foot candle key lighting for his set-ups at f-8, rising to more than 1,300 foot candles in the occasional shots made at f-16. The fact that arc illumination was somewhat easier to look into than that from reflectors or Mazda lighting must have been only of small comfort to the actors!

Another (and final) way—besides allowing deep-focus compositions—in which Toland's lighting for *Citizen Kane* furthered Welles's desire to avoid direct cutting or traditional transitions occurred in the lap dissolves that provided most transitions in the film. A pair of dimmers were used so that an overlapped sequence—(1) background of first shot dims; (2) players in first shot dim; (3) background of second shot fades in; (4) players in second shot fade in—could occur in which both imagery and lighting worked together in smoothing the transition almost to imperceptibility. This sense of various elements working smoothly together seems to characterise all of the film, and in intelligently blending compositional and tonal desires with technological capabilities, Gregg Toland created mature deep-focus cinematography.

Considering Orson Welles's own flair for publicity and the pseudo-exposé qualities of the film's screenplay, *Citizen Kane* could hardly help attracting much notoriety and controversy upon its release. Part of this notoriety and controversy surrounded the cinematography and the cinematographer, a most unusual occurrence in the American film industry. Gregg Toland's name came closer to becoming a household word than any other cameraman's before or since. Mass circulation magazines published photo stories demonstrating the principle of deep focus and featuring its creator.[54] Controversy raged among cameramen: some hailed it as a breakthrough, other considered it a slightly silly retrogression to the early days of film-making. Other films began to appear soon after in essentially the deep-focus style. Arthur Miller, ASC, filmed *How Green Was My Valley* for John Ford in 1941 in a somewhat toned-down deep focus that won him the Academy Award for black-and-white photography (defeating Toland's *Citizen Kane*) in 1942. Toland himself filmed *The Little Foxes* in 1941 for William Wyler (and was thoroughly unhappy in having done so, as delays on the set made it impossible for him to film *How Green Was My Valley,* for which he seems to have originally been slated),[55] and *Ball of Fire* for Howard Hawks the same year. A comedy, *Ball of Fire* is of interest as perhaps the only high-key deep-focus film, Toland himself feeling that in many ways the Hawks work posed greater technical problems than had Welles's.[56] Arthur Edeson, ASC, filmed John Huston's first film, *The Maltese Falcon* of 1941, in a strong deep focus, outdoing Toland in using an even wider-angle (21mm focal length) lens. Stanley Cortez, ASC, retained much deep focus in Welles's second film, *The Magnificent Ambersons* of 1942.

The coming of the Second World War submerged the deep-focus cinematographic style (as it did so much else) in the flood of mundane but important matters having to do with fighting and winning a global conflict. Many cinematographers spent the duration in military service, filming real events with 16mm equipment that gave inherently greater depth of field than had the 35mm studio cameras. Thus, though deep-focus cinematography did not reappear as a specific style after World War II, many of its qualities found their way, in modified form, into standard Hollywood usage by way of these returning cinematographers. In the postwar years, as today, crisp deep-focus cinematography came to be seen for what it finally is—one possible visual means of conveying experience, just as is diffused shallow-focus cinematography. The primary contribution of Gregg Toland and others in developing deep focus may have been in demonstrating that such a range of choice exists.

ADDITIONAL NOTES

In the course of research for the preceding paper, the author had occasion to come upon a number of items that, though not all related directly to the techniques employed in achieving extreme depth of field in the deep-focus style, are interesting enough to merit inclusion and brief comment.

Gregg Toland himself continued experimentation toward the end of achieving yet greater depth of field during the postwar period. No results of these experiments seem to appear in any of his postwar films, however. At the time of his death in late 1948, Toland was about to begin filming *Roseanna McCoy,* in which he planned to employ a so-called 'ultimate focus' lens with an aperture of f-64. Although such a phenomenally small lens opening would have required the full measure of postwar advances in film speed and lighting power to achieve proper exposure of the film, the lens offered a tantalising capability: depth of field extending from less than six inches to infinity![57]

In September 1936, the well-known cinematographer Hal Mohr, ASC (whose credits run the range from *The Jazz Singer* of 1927 to *The Wild One* of 1954 and beyond) described a system he had developed to selectively extend focal depth in certain scenes contained in the films *The Green Pastures* and *Bullets or Ballots.*[58] Utilising the optical principle of the 'swinging back' that allows users of certain still cameras to adjust the plane of focus to run through objects at different distances from the camera, Mohr had developed a ball-and-socket lens mount that permitted a specially chosen Leica Summar 50mm f-2 still camera lens to pivot about its nodal point. Using his swing-mount lens, Mohr was able to angle the plane of focus such that a figure in close-up on one side of the frame would share equal sharpness with a distant figure on the other side. Alternately, an entire group of faces could be in focus, from children at the bottom of the frame in front to adults near the top of the frame much further back. An obvious drawback of the swinging lens, as Mohr himself allowed, was that action and composition had to be planned so that important parts of the scene were disposed along the diagonal line of focus, for sharpness fell off quickly in front or behind the plane of focus just as in conventional lenses. The inventor felt the swing lens to be of value despite its drawbacks, however, noting that it had allowed him to avoid focus shifts or the breaking up of scenes into individual closer shots. Although his device did not gain widespread popular acceptance among his peers, Hal Mohr was prophetic in taking concrete personal action toward achieving a cinematographic style of increased depth and reduced intercutting. The possible influence of Mohr's two increased focal depth films upon the sensibilities of other cinematographers might be an interesting topic for further research.

During the 1941–2 heyday of deep-focus cinematography, several systems were proposed that endeavoured to achieve deep-focus effects without the need for small lens apertures and strong lighting of the Toland systems or the special compositional requirements of Mohr's method. One such approach was the 'IR System', developed by a design team headed by a past president of the Society of Motion Picture Engineers, who described it in a very lengthy article in the January 1942 issue of the *American Cinematographer*.[59] Briefly, the IR system involved splitting up the depth of the scene to be photographed into as many as four separate spatial regions. These separate zones were lit either by electronic flash-tube or mechanically shuttered conventional lighting that made it possible to illuminate each zone separately for a precisely delimited time. The zoned and timed lighting system connected electromechanically with a specially modified motion picture camera that, in addition to the conventionally rotating shutter disc, possessed another rotating disc within which reposed a number of specially ground lenticular elements called 'diffo plates'. Each diffo plate instantaneously changed the focus of the camera lens when rotated into place behind it, adjusting the focus of the lens to that region of the scene being briefly illuminated by the synchronised zone lighting. In operation, therefore, each frame of film recorded four separate exposures at four different points of focus. The IR system did seem to work, although as can be imagined simplicity was not its keynote. Strong efforts had to be made to prevent lighting spillover between illumination zones lest mysterious hot spots occur in the frame. Whether due to the exigencies of the war effort or to its own deficiencies, the IR system was not heard of again. Considering their ability to design and develop an incredibly complex method of achieving an effect rather simply arrived at by Gregg Toland, the author has little doubt but that the people who developed the IR system quickly and easily found rewarding and congenial work in areas such as military hardware development.

Another approach to increasing depth in cinematography was described in the very next issue of the *American Cinematographer*.[60] This device, called the Electroplane camera, shared with the IR system the attempt to provide a sense of depth similar to that of the eye by means of an electromechanical analogue to the focus-changing scanning through which the eye constantly cycles. Much simpler than the IR system, the principle feature of the Electroplane camera was its lens. The so-called 'Detrar' lens was an otherwise rather conventional optic, but with a rapidly oscillating internal element that shifted focus back and forth from four feet to infinity many times a second. The oscillation was provided by an electromagnetic assembly very similar to the voice coil of a loudspeaker, the system relying upon the optical principle that light energy levels (the ability to form a latent image on the film) reach their highest when an image is in sharpest focus. As the lens rapidly scanned focus back and forth during the exposure of a single frame, images affected the film most strongly at sharpest focus, tending to overwhelm blurs. While one might imagine a problem arising with regard to a 'halo' of unfocused image surrounding the sharp image, this did not seem to present any major obstacle to the design. Alas, like the IR system, the Electroplane camera was not heard from again, but a recent patent by Pathé of France indicates that the principle of increased depth through oscillating focus may yet return to use in Super Eight-millimeter motion picture cameras, where the convenience of focus-free filming may well outweigh the slight image degradation probable with such a system.[61]

As a final aside, the three-dimensional picture would seem to be the next logical step beyond deep-focus cinematography. Unfortunately, where deep focus had Orson Welles, 3-D had Arch Oboler, and gimmick supplanted art. Three-dimensional films proved a short-lived fad that died with the coming of Cinemascope in 1953. While the form may yet return (and the author rather hopes it will), the lesson, it is hoped, has been learned: technology can only advance an art form when intelligently applied to significant subject matter.

Notes

As many of the notes are from issues of the *American Cinematographer*, such references will be abbreviated to *AC*.

1. Bosley Crowther, "The Screen Review: Orson Welles' Controversial *Citizen Kane* Proves a Sensational Film at Palace," *New York Times*, May 2, 1941, p. 25.

2. Charles Higham, *Hollywood Cameramen: Sources of Light* (Bloomington and London: Indiana University Press, 1970), pp. 83–85.

3. "Photography of the Month" *American Cinematographer*, May 1941, p. 222.

4. André Bazin, *What Is Cinema?*, trans. Hugh Gray (Berkeley and Los Angeles: University of California Press, 1967), p. 35.

5. John Castle, "Bert Glennon Introducing New Method of Interior Photography," *AC*, February 1939, pp. 82–83.

6. Walter Blanchard, "Aces of the Camera V: Leon Shamroy, ASC," *AC*, May 1941, pp. 215, 254.

7. Walter Blanchard, "Aces of the Camera XV: Tony Gaudio," *AC*, March 1942, pp. 112, 137.

8. Walter Blanchard, "Aces of the Camera VII: James Wong Howe, ASC," *AC*, July 1941, p. 346.

9. *Ibid.*

10. *Ibid.*

11. Charles G. Clarke, ASC, "Are We Afraid of Coated Lenses?" *AC*, April 1941, p. 199.

12. Emery Huse, ASC, "The Characteristics of Eastman Motion Picture Negative Film," *AC*, May 1936, p. 190.

13. Emery Huse and Gordon A. Chambers, "Three New Negative Emulsions: Background X, Plus-X, and Super XX," *AC*, December 1938, p. 487.

14. Elmer G. Dyer, ASC, "Films I Have Used," *AC*, March 1936, p. 122.

15. Walter Blanchard, "Aces of the Camera V: Leon Shamroy," *AC*, May 1941, p. 215.

16. Walter Strohm, "Progress in Lighting Means Economy," *AC*, January 1936, p. 16.

17. Emery Huse, *op. cit.*, p. 190.

18. Huse and Chambers, *op. cit.*, p. 487.

19. Walter Strohm, *op. cit.*, p. 16.

20. C. W. Handley, "Advanced Technique of Lighting in Technicolor," *AC*, June 1937, pp. 230–31.

21. William Stull, ASC, "Technicolor Bringing New Charm to the Screen," *AC*, June 1937, p. 235.

22. Elmer C. Richardson, ASC, "Recent Developments in Motion Picture Lighting," *AC*, August 1937, p. 319.

23. "Faster Colour Film Cuts Light a Half," *AC*, August 1939, pp. 355–56.

24. *AC*, March 1938, p. 120.

25. Teddy Tetzlaff *et al.*, "Lighting the New Fast Films," *AC*, February 1939, p. 70.

26. Walter Blanchard, "Aces of the Camera VII: James Wong Howe," *AC*, July 1941, p. 346.

27. Victor Milner, ASC, "Super XX for 'Production' Camerawork," *AC*, June 1941, p. 269.

28. George Blaisdell, "Fine Grain Films Make Strong Advance," *AC*, November 1939, pp. 486–88.

29. "Bausch & Lomb Increase Lens Light Transmission," *AC*, March 1940, p. 104.

30. William Stull, ASC, "Non-Glare Coating Makes Lenses One Stop Faster" *AC*, March 1940, p 109.

31. *Ibid.*

32. "Gregg Toland, 44, Cameraman, Dies," *New York Times*, September 29, 1948, p. 30.

33. "Toland's 'Dead End' Selected in Caucus One of Three Best,' *AC*, April 1938, pp. 141–42.

34. "Toland with 20th's 'Kidnapped' Awarded Camera Honors for May," *AC*, July 1938, p. 274.

35. C. W. Handley, *op. cit.*, pp. 230–31.

36. Victor Milner, *op. cit.*, p. 269.

37. Walter Blanchard, "Aces of the Camera XIII: Gregg Toland, ASC," *AC*, January 1942, pp. 15, 36.

38. *Ibid.*

39. Frank S. Nugent, "The Screen in Review: Twentieth Century Fox Shows a Flawless Film Edition of John Steinbeck's 'The Grapes of Wrath,' with Henry Fonda and Jane Darwell, at the Rivoli," *New York Times*, January 25, 1940, p. 17.

40. Lewis Jacobs, "Watching Ford Go By: The Toughest Director Is Seen at Work on 'The Long Voyage Home'," *New York Times*, May 26, 1940, Section IX, p. 4.

41. Gregg Toland, ASC, "I Broke the Rules in 'Citizen Kane'," *Popular Photography*, June 1941, p. 55.

42. *Ibid.* p. 91.

43. *Ibid.* p. 90.

44. H. Mario Raimondo Souto, *The Technique of the Motion Picture Camera* (New York: Hastings House, 1969), p. 61.

45. William Stull, *op. cit.*, p. 109.

46. Gregg Toland, ASC, "Practical Gadgets Expedite Camera Work," *AC*, May 1939, pp. 215 18.

47. J. F. Westerbury, ASC, "Size of Image as a Guide to Depth of Focus in Cinematography," *AC*, June 1932, p. 15.

48. Gregg Toland, "I Broke the Rules in 'Citizen Kane'," *Popular Photography*, June 1941, pp. 55, 90.

49. Gregg Toland, ASC, "Using Arcs for Monochrome," *AC*, December 1941, p. 558.

50. "M-R Introduces Duarc, New Automatic Broadside," *AC*, October 1938, p. 407.

51. Gregg Toland, "Using Arcs for Monochrome," *AC*, December 1941, pp. 558–59.

52. William Stull, ASC, "Surveying Major Studio Light Levels," *AC*, July 1940, pp. 294–96, 334.

53. Walter Blanchard, "Aces of the Camera VII: James Wong Howe," *AC*, July 1941, p. 346.

54. "Orson Welles, Once a Child Prodigy, He Has Never Quite Grown Up," *Life*, May 26, 1941, pp. 108–116.

55. Thomas Brady, "Peace Comes to 'The Little Foxes'," *New York Times,* June 22, 1941, Section IX, p. 4.

56. Gregg Toland, "Using Arcs for Monochrome," *AC,* December 1941, pp. 558–59, 588.

57. "Gregg Toland, 44, Cameraman, Dies," *New York Times,* September 29, 1948, p. 30.

58. Hal Mohr, ASC, "A Lens Mount for Universal Focus Effects," *AC,* September 1936, pp. 370–71.

59. Alfred N. Goldsmith, "Increasing Focal Depth with the IR System," *AC,* January 1942, pp. 8, 9, 38–44.

60. Edwin P. Holden, Jr., "The Electroplane Camera, A New System for Obtaining Natural Depth," *AC,* February 1942, pp. 56–57.

61. Norman Goldberg, "Shop Talk: Is Lens Focusing Pathé?" *Popular Photography,* November 1970, pp. 60, 62, 128.

Bibliography

(with comments where appropriate)

BOOKS:

Bazin, André, *What Is Cinema?,* trans. Hugh Gray. Berkeley and Los Angeles: University of California Press, 1967.

Higham, Charles. *Hollywood Cameramen: Sources of Light.* Bloomington and London: Indiana University Press, 1970.

Mascelli, Joseph V. (ASC) (ed.). *American Cinematographer Manual,* Second Edition. Hollywood: American Society of Cinematographers, 1966.

Souto, H. Mario Raimondo. *The Technique of the Motion Picture Camera.* New York: Hastings House, 1969.

PERIODICALS:

American Cinematographer:

"Bausch & Lomb Increase Lens Light Transmission," March 1940, p. 104. Indicates first commercial use of lens coatings was with regard to *projection* lenses for a Technicolor film (*GWTW*).

"Faster Color Film Cuts Light a Half," August 1939, pp. 355–56. More use of incandescent Mazda possible, less fill light needed. Technicolor lighting levels brought down to Super X (ASA 32–20) levels. Used in filming *GWTW.*

"How Lighting Units Are Developed Today," May 1937, pp. 189, 193. Changes in film speeds and lighting styles. Information on fresnel-type spotlights, parabolic types, and condensor spots.

"M-R Introduces Duarc, New Automatic Broadside," October 1938, pp. 407, 416. Developed for Technicolor use; successor to the SideArc, also developed for Technicolor. Relied on heavily by Toland for deep-focus filming.

"Photography of the Month: *The Battle of Midway,*" October 1942, p. 456. Citation of value of 16mm for combat footage. Use of colour (Kodachrome), great intrinsic depth of field. John Ford as director and cameraman.

"Photography of the Month: *Citizen Kane,*" May 1941, p. 222. ASC as impressed as everyone else. Some reservations noted, mostly with regard to several of Toland's moving camera usages.

"Photography of the Month: *How Green Was My Valley,*" February 1942, pp. 66–67, 94. Comparison with *Citizen Kane* in terms of use of deep focus.

"Photography of the Month: *Ladies in Retirement,*" October 1941, p. 475. Filmed by George Barnes, ACC (AA that year for *Rebecca*) and considered an example of extremely good use of pan-focus compositions.

"Photography of the Month: *The Little Foxes,*" September 1941, p. 425. Toland's first release after *Kane* was faulted for apparent bad choice of deep- vs. shallow-focus in several parts of the film.

"Photography of the Month: *The Maltese Falcon,*" November 1941, p. 548. Arthur Edeson, ASC, used his personal 21mm lens for much of the shooting. Considered a good example of how deep-focus techniques could be applied to what was considered a 'programme' film.

"Technical Progress in 1940," January 1941, pp. 6–7, 36. Summary including information on high-speed camera emulsions and lens coating techniques.

"Technical Progress in 1941," January 1942, pp. 6–7, 45. Summary including information on Toland's use of Super XX film contrasted with that of other cameramen.

"Toland's 'Dead End' Selected in Caucus One of Three Best," August 1938, pp. 141–42. Toland's use of indoor sets, 8,000 amps of lighting, sunlight simulation by grouping arcs. Mention of Toland working on his colour film, *The Goldwyn Follies.*

"Toland With 20th's 'Kidnapped' Awarded Camera Honors for May," July 1938, p. 274. Shot almost entirely indoors. Use of low key except when strong light needed. Toland's adaptability noted.

"What's Wrong With Cinematography," November 1938, pp. 449, 457. Report of meeting at which cameraman complained that the labs were underdeveloping film and otherwise losing picture quality in relation to what the cameramen themselves were able to achieve by the use of Leicas and fine-grain developers.

"Lab Chief's Disagree with Cameramen," December 1938, pp. 491–92. Rebuttal by lab chiefs to above article.

Blaisdell, George. "How Joe Valentine Built Alpine Crispness into Sea-Level Shots—Just a Matter of Balancing Incandescent and Arcs, Having Regard to Color of Respective Lights and Color Sensitivity of Film Employed—Uses Arc Designed for Technicolor," February 1938, pp. 52, 82. Early example of use of Technicolor lighting in monochrome production on indoor set for expressive effect. Valentine was later to originate use of Super XX film as a production stock.

Blaisdell, George. "Fine-Grain Films Make Strong Advance," November 1939, pp. 486–88. Mention of improved image and sound.

Blanchard, Walter. "Aces of the Camera V: Leon Shamroy, ASC," May 1941, pp. 215, 254. Discourse on changing camera styles and the coming of deep focus in the inimitable Shamroy manner. Shamroy considered the coming of colour to be potentially more important for realism than deep-focus monochrome.

Blanchard, Walter. "Aces of the Camera VII: James Wong Howe, ASC," July 1941, pp. 322, 346, 348. Howe's approach to Super XX usage. Minicam and picture magazine influence on cinematography. Realism of the Edward Weston variety and relation to film styles.

Blanchard, Walter. "Aces of the Camera XIII: Gregg Toland, ASC," January 1942, pp. 15, 36. First uses of deep focus, coated lenses, etc.

Blanchard, Walter. "Aces of the Camera XV: Tony Gaudio," March 1942, pp. 112, 137. Gaudio, who had been a cameraman since about 1942, considered deep focus an old idea and set of basic principles brought up to date with new materials and technology. Noted shifts of photographic style through his career.

Castle, John. "Bert Glennon Introducing New Method of Interior Photography," February 1939, pp. 82–83. Use of roofed sets, 25mm lens, low light levels. Avoided conventional Hollywood backlight. Used in *Stagecoach*.

Clarke, Charles G. (ASC). "Are We Afraid of Coated Lenses?" April 1941, pp. 161, 199. Cites aesthetic use of anti-flare qualities in dealing with coated lenses, related to differing styles of cinematography.

Clarke, Charles G. (ASC). "How Desirable Is Extreme Focal Depth?" January 1942, pp. 14, 36. Short history of filming styles from sharp to diffused and back again. Plea for avoidance of dogmatism and use of styles appropriate to subject matter.

Dyer, Elmer G. (ASC). "Films I Have Used," March 1936, pp. 122, 128–29. Recollections of orthochromatic film and its qualities. Dyer was the dean of aerial cinematographers, and filmed the aerial sequences for most of the classic flying films.

Edouart, Farciot (ASC). "25 Years of Progress," November 1945, pp. 368–69, 378, 405. Information on the quieting of arcs and the historical trends in matching lighting spectral distribution to film colour sensitivities.

Goldsmith, Alfred. "Increasing Focal Depth with the IR System," January 1942, pp. 8–9, 38–44. Long but not overly informative article on the lens focus scanning and timed lighting IR system.

Greene, W. Howard (ASC). "Low-Key Lighting May Be as Easy in Color as It Is in Monochrome," April 1938, pp. 146, 151. Improvements in selective lighting, etc. moving Technicolor away from the even floodlit style of earlier days.

Handley, C. W. "Advanced Technique of Lighting in Technicolor," June 1937, pp. 230–31. Lists 1,936 foot candle levels for black-and-white and Technicolor key lighting.

Holden, Edwin P., Jr. "The Electroplane Camera: A New System for Obtaining Natural Depth," February 1942, pp. 56–57. Description of the oscillating lens deep-focus system.

Howe, James Wong (ASC). "Reflections on Making His First Color Production," October 1937, pp. 408–12. Use of realistic, non-brilliant colours for costumes, etc. Use of arcs for fill in outdoor shooting; less squinting.

Howe, James Wong (ASC). "The Documentary Technique in Hollywood," June 1944, pp. 10, 32. *Grapes of Wrath* mentioned. Influences of combat footage on Hollywood technique noted. Prediction of movement toward realism and increased depth of field during postwar years.

Huse, Emery (ASC). "The Characteristics of Eastman Motion Picture Negative Film," May 1936, pp. 190–92, 202. Short history of films, differentiation between "ordinary emulsions" and orthochromatic. Changes in developers.

Huse, Emery, and Gordon A. Chambers. "Three New Negative Emulsions: Background X, Plus-X, and Super XX," December 1938, pp. 487–90, 525. Short history of Eastman films. Characteristics of new films discussed.

Lang, Charles B., Jr. (ASC). "Filtering Arcs for Matching Quality in Monochrome," June 1939, pp. 269–70. Mazda-panchromatic compatibility. Changes in arc light designs.

Lightman, Herb. "Psychology and the Screen," May 1946, pp. 160–61, 178–79. Some examples cited referring to *Citizen Kane*.

Lightman, Herb. "Mood in the Motion Picture," February 1947, pp. 48–49, 69. Mentions Garmes, Howe, Toland. Examples of use of low key and deep focus.

Marley, Peverell (ASC). "Bottleneck of the Movies," December 1941, pp. 564, 589. Orthochromatic film anecdotes: exposure, lighting, make-up, etc.

Mescall, John (ASC). "Pan-Focus for Your Home Movies," December 1941, pp. 576, 593. Description of Toland's methods. Comment that deep focus is even easier in 16mm and 8mm filming.

Miller, Arthur (ASC). "Putting Naturalness into Modern Interior Lighting," March 1941, pp. 104–105, 136. Considered natural-looking lighting had only become possible shortly before with development of faster films and selective lighting.

Milner, Victor (ASC). "Super XX for 'Production' Camerawork," June 1941, pp. 269, 290. Description of the use of the stock in the usual "overexpose-underdevelop" mode in which most cameramen used it.

Mohr, Hal (ASC). "A Lens Mount for Universal Focus Effects," September 1936, pp. 370–71. Ball-and-socket swing mount lens for shifting plane of focus.

Mole, Peter. "The M-R 'Brute', A New Super High Intensity Carbon Arc Lamp," December 1946, pp. 438–39. A 225 amp lamp, also developed primarily for colour work.

Polito, Sol (ASC). "Polito Matches Daylight with Arcs in Technicolor Film at Warners," February 1938, pp. 54, 84. Use of daylight arcs and filtered Mazda in outdoor settings.

Rayton, Dr. Wilbur B. "Recent Developments in Photographic Optics," February 1947, pp. 44–45, 54, 56, 66. Mentions exposure problems due to light fall-off with wide-angle lenses.

Richardson, Elmer C. "Development of a Wide-Range Studio Spot Lamp," July 1935, pp. 282–83, 296. Basic description of the Solarspot fresnel lamp from which the modern arc lamp light controls were developed.

Richardson, Elmer C. (ASC). "Recent Developments in Motion Picture Lighting," August 1937, p. 319. Note taken of advances in colour lighting over that of black-and-white.

Strohm, Walter. "Progress in Lighting Means Economy," January 1936, pp. 12, 16. Mazda-sound-panchromatic film interrelationship.

Stull, William (ASC). "Technicolor Bringing New Charm to the Screen," June 1937, pp. 234–37, 242. Superiority of Technicolor lighting to that of monochrome.

Stull, William (ASC). "Maté Blends Arcs and Inkies to Light 'Marco Polo' Stages," June 1938, pp. 234, 238–39. Choice of different lighting for different moods. Reminiscences of old arcs in relation to new Technicolor-type arcs. Maté also worked for Goldwyn.

Stull, William (ASC). "Amateur Progress in 1939 Exceeded Professional," January 1940, pp. 16–17. Fine-grain release stocks as major development of the year. Faster Technicolor emulsions. Great changes in Technicolor lighting. Principle of lens coating discovered.

Stull, William (ASC). "Non Glare Coating Makes Lenses One Stop Faster," March 1940, pp. 108–109, 142. General description of advantages of lens coatings.

Stull, William (ASC). "Surveying Major Studio Light Levels," July 1940, pp. 294–96, 334. Survey of key light foot candle levels and f-stops in use by cameraman and studio. Extremes were 25 FC and 36 FC, with most between 38 and 280 FC, tending toward the lower end. Lenses normally used at full aperture (f-2.3 or so), though Twentieth Century Fox had standardised at f-3.5 and 150 FC for all crews.

Stull, William (ASC). "Through the Editor's Finder," May 1941, p.221. Concern expressed that *Citizen Kane's* photographic style might be thoughtlessly duplicated under pressure of producers' demands in films not given to deep focus.

Tetzlaff, Teddy, William Mellor, Arthur Edeson, L. William O'Connell, Gaetano Gaudio, Theodor Sparkuhl, Victor Milner, and Charles Rosher. "Lighting the New Fast Films," February 1939, pp. 69–70. Milner the only one of the contributors at the time considering the use of small f-stops and high light levels for crisper, deeper focus. Milner may not have ever made a deep-focus film, though Edeson did so with *The Maltese Falcon*.

Toland, Gregg (ASC). "Practical Gadgets Expedite Camera Work," May 1939, pp. 215–18. Description of basher lights, hydraulic tripod, remote follow focus, dolly and track system developed by Toland.

Toland, Gregg (ASC). "Realism for 'Citizen Kane'," February 1941. Missing from Northwestern University collection. Not consulted.

Toland, Gregg (ASC). "Using Lights for Lighting Monochrome," December 1941, pp. 558–59, 588. Information on filming *Citizen Kane* and *Ball of Fire*.

Westerberg, J. F. (ASC). "Size of Image as a Guide to Depth of Focus in Cinematography," June 1932, p. 15. Some basic rules of thumb as to depth of field in relation to image size, lens focal length, and subject distance from camera.

Popular Photography:

Goldberg, Norman. "Shop Talk: Is Lens Focusing Pathé?" November 1970, pp. 60, 62, 128. Information on recent oscillating film gate camera patent, similar in principle to Electroplane camera.

Toland, Gregg (ASC). "I Broke the Rules in 'Citizen Kane'," June 1941, pp. 55, 90–91. A popularised article on the techniques Toland used in filming *Citizen Kane,* it is nevertheless quite informative, especially with regard to Welles's desires.

NEWSPAPERS:

The New York Times:

"Gregg Toland, 44, Cameraman, Dies; Pictorial Supervisor of Many Leading US Films, He Began on Coast at 15," September 29, 1948, p. 30. Vital statistics of life, development of deep focus, plans for "ultimate focus" lens at time of death, work on *Citizen Kane,* etc. Much confused terminology related to deep focus.

Brady, Thomas. "Peace Comes to 'The Little Foxes'," June 22, 1941, Section 9, p. 4. Notation of Toland's extreme disappointment in not being able to film *How Green Was My Valley,* due to delays caused by Bette Davis–William Wyler row.

Crowther, Bosley. "John Ford's Odyssey in 'The Long Voyage Home'; He Presents a Brooding Drama of Wanderlust," October 9, 1940, p. 30. Note taken of Toland's "splendid photography."

Crowther, Bosley. "The Screen in Review: Orson Welles' Controversial 'Citizen Kane' Proves a Sensational Film at Palace," May 2, 1941, p. 25. Unusual inclusion of Toland's name in the credits at the beginning of the article. Crowther emphasised that Toland's contributions should not be overlooked.

Crowther, Bosley. "The Ambiguous 'Citizen Kane'; Orson Welles, in His First Motion Picture, Creates a Titanic Character Which Does Everything but Explain Itself," May 4, 1941. Section 5, p. 1. Elaboration of preceding article. Notes important contribution of Toland, notes use of camera as commentator as well as recorder. Crowther's objections to the method of story telling seem little different from his objections to films of twenty years later.

Crowther, Bosley. "The Screen in Review: 'The Little Foxes,' Full of Evil, Reaches the Screen of the Music Hall," August 22, 1941, p. 19. Noted aid of Toland in telling story by means of sharp focus and hard, realistically textured images.

Jacobs, Lewis. "Watching Ford Go By; the Toughest Director Is Seen at Work on 'The Long Voyage Home'," Sunday, May 26, 1940, Section 9, p. 4. Information on Ford-Toland filming practices.

Nugent, Frank S. "The Screen in Review: Twentieth Century Fox Shows a Flawless Film Edition of John Steinbeck's 'The Grapes of Wrath,' with Henry Fonda and Jane Darwell, at the Rivoli," January 25, 1940, p. 17. Noted Ford's use of camera as "reportage and editorial and dramatisation by turns or all in one." Comparison with work of Russian realists.

Nugent, Frank S. "About 'The Grapes of Wrath'; Twentieth Century Fox's Magnificent Film of the Steinbeck Novel Becomes a Testament to the Power of the Screen," Sunday, January 28, 1940, Section 9, p. 5. Elaboration of preceding review. Toland mentioned as having "photographed it so beautifully."

SOUND AND COLOR

EDWARD BUSCOMBE

Edward Buscombe's examination of the history of two major technological inno-vations, sound and color, attempts to situate change in relation to economics, technology, ideology, and aesthetics. That scope makes this an admirable essay, which is all the more remarkable for its brevity and clarity. In the first section, Buscombe argues that economics always contributes the necessary *criterion for innovation (the extraction of surplus value or, in different terms, the long-term survival of a given film), but economics alone cannot provide a sufficient crite-rion. After showing how the economic criterion relates to the coming of sound, Buscombe reveals what the usual story of the introduction of sound obscures: the need for an innovation that satisfies aesthetic and ideological criteria as well. Sound did so, almost "naturally," by enhancing the realist effect of cinema. Color did not. In the second section, Buscombe shows how the tardy introduction of color was determined not only by economic or technological factors but also by an aesthetic and ideological factor: the need to make color compatible with a style of realism that at first it disrupted. Like Ogle's account of cinematographers, who used the advantages of faster film stock to reduce lighting levels rather than lens apertures, so that the same shallow-focus style could be maintained despite the opportunity to alter it, Buscombe's discussion suggests that filmmakers attempted to restrict color to uses, such as fantasy sequences, that perpetuated the domi-nance of the prevailing black-and-white aesthetic.*

Buscombe's discussion of the actual effects of sound and color, pegged as it is to reports of audience response and film industry claims, opens up a speculative dimension that close examination of actual film practices might be required to substantiate. Whether audiences resisted color or 3-D and to what degree, or whether a more complex set of resistances was at work, which a few statements on effect or use by Hollywood practitioners only begin to explore, invites the kind of careful scrutiny that might compel Buscombe's thesis to be revised. For example, he notes that color became prevalent only after film sales to color television be-came a major source of income for the Hollywood studios, since black-and-white prints had a lower value in that market. But he has already shown that color was resisted as inappropriate to the realist aesthetic. Why, then, did it become the pre-ferred practice in television? This question raises issues involving the same set of terms that Buscombe has already introduced—economics, technology, aesthetics, and ideology—but they now are applied to television and another instance of technological innovation that requires an explanation in its own right.

•

The last issue of *Film Reader*[1] devoted half of its total space to examining the relations between industry, technology and ideology in the cinema. *Film Reader's* initiative is a welcome sign that film theory is paying more attention to economic and technological determinants and that film history is increasingly moving out of the era of mere facts and figures towards consideration of more substantive matters.

However, an article by J. Douglas Gomery in this issue,[2] though providing valuable detailed information on the introduction of sound into Hollywood, raises some problems concerning the extent to which economics can assist our understanding of the cinema. Gomery claims that "economic theory can explain the coming of sound."[3] Gomery has in mind the theory of technological innovation.[4] This theory seeks to explain the factors governing the invention, innovation and diffusion of new technology in any given industry: in what circumstances new techniques or products are first invented and then introduced as practical and commercial propositions subsequently adopted by the industry as a whole. A considerable literature exists on this subject, but we may take as representative the work of one author cited by Gomery. Edwin Mansfield, in his book *Technological Change*,[5] lists several factors governing a decision to innovate once an invention has been produced:

To begin with, the firm should estimate, of course, the expected rate of return from intro-ducing the new product or process. In the case of a new product the result will obviously depend on the capital investment that is required to introduce the innovation, the fore-casted sales, the estimated costs of production, and the effects of the innovation on the costs and sales of the firm's existing product line. . . . In addition the firm should estimate, as best it can, the risks involved in innovating.[6]

Mansfield also enumerates those factors affecting the rate at which an innovation will become diffused:

(1) the extent of the economic advantage of the innovation over older methods or products, (2) the extent of the uncertainty associated with using the innovation when it first appears, (3) the extent of the commitment required to try out the innovation, and (4) the rate of reduction of the initial uncertainty regarding the innovation's performance. (Mansfield, p. 88)

Mansfield also suggests that a number of factors might be expected to affect the speed of any single firm's response to a new technique: (1) the size of the firm (one would expect larger firms with more resources to be quicker at innovating); (2) the degree of expectation of profit from the new technique; (3) the rate of growth of the firm (expanding firms might innovate more easily); (4) the firm's profit level (prosperous firms would have the necessary capital or credit); (5) the age of the firm's management personnel (younger management might be more receptive to new ideas); (6) the liquidity of the firm (the more liquid the firm the better it might be able to find finance); (7) the firm's profit trend (firms with declining profits might look harder for new profits or techniques) (Mansfield, pp. 93–95).

There is nothing very profoundly "theoretical" about Mansfield's formulations, yet they do have some explanatory power in relation to the coming of sound. Gomery has shown that Warner Brothers did pay careful attention to the question of costs and to the problem of finding the necessary capital.[7] Furthermore Mansfield's four factors affecting the rate of diffusion help to explain why the changeover to sound was so rapid. The economic performance of the new product and the speedy reduction in the uncertainty regarding that performance more than outweighed the original uncertainty itself and the high costs of installing new equipment.

The seven factors characterizing those firms most likely to innovate should provide an explanation for the fact that it was Warners, one of the smaller companies, which led the way in sound. Unfortunately, the theory of technological innovation breaks down at this point, since Mansfield can find no statistically significant correlations across a range of industries for factors 3, 4, 5, 6 and 7. The only factors known to affect a firm's willingness to innovate are its size (bigger firms do innovate faster) and the expected rate of profit. The latter point seems fairly obvious; while the former shows Warners to be an exception to the rule. Gomery is forced to look elsewhere for an explanation of Warners' actions, which were, he claims, the result of the farsightedness of Waddill Catchings, the entrepreneur who master-minded the firm's strategy. Gomery's theoretical position therefore ends up not so far as he thinks from that of the film historians he takes to task. He sets out to prove that sound was introduced as the result of an economic law which "theory" can explain. But instead sound turns out to be the result of one man's initiative. The only substantial difference between Gomery's explanation and that of previous historians is a dispute over which individuals should get the credit, Catchings or the Warner brothers themselves.

Thus the theory of technological innovation seems of limited use, and Gomery reverts from a search for economic explanations back to a kind of "great man" theory of history. But could a different kind of economic theory explain the coming of sound? This would depend on what kind of explanation we are looking for. The theory Gomery wants to use could only explain why it is that innovation takes the course it does. It doesn't explain why there should be innovations in the first place, a more fundamental and surely more interesting question. To answer it we cannot adopt a simple notion of supply and demand, since the public could hardly be said to have demanded sound pictures until it had seen and heard them. True, once sound had been successfully demonstrated demand affected the rate of diffusion. But the initial investment in research and development had to be made when future demand could only be guessed at.

One must start with the fundamental law that in a free market economy a firm is motivated by, to use the terms of capitalist economics, a desire to maximize profits; or, in the terms of Marxist economics,·a desire to maximize the rate at which it extracts surplus value. In any given economic situation this can be done in a number of ways. For example, a firm can attempt to develop fresh markets and so achieve economies of scale. In the late 20s the film industry had no easy way of finding fresh markets—domestic and foreign penetration of the market being near saturation point. (In 1926 U.S. attendances ran at 100 million a week. In Britain, for example, American films had 74¼ percent of the market at this time.)[8]

Another possibility is for a firm to lower its costs of production. Given that constant capital costs, both fixed and circulation (that is, the costs both of buildings and machinery, and of raw materials) were relatively inelastic, this could be done only be reducing the cost of variable capital, i.e., labor. (I am assuming, though I cannot prove it, that in the film industry in the late 20s the costs of constant capital were in fact inelastic.) But in a labor-intensive industry such as filmmaking, and one in which automation had at that time gone as far as it could go (another assumption I cannot actually prove) it seems as though there was little opportunity for cutting costs. However, it is worth noting in this respect that Warners' original motive in developing sound was to use it as a means of recording vaudeville acts and musical sound tracks for silent pictures. In other words, sound was at first intended to increase the productivity of vaudeville performers and theatre musicians. Only subsequently was it seen as a means of creating an entirely new product.

Another way for a firm to increase the rate of surplus value is to increase its share of the existing market at the expense of its competitors. This can sometimes be achieved by price cutting. But the American film industry had evolved by the end of the 1920s into a mature oligopoly in which the sale of the product (i.e., exhibition) was tightly regulated by the major firms dominating the market, in co-operation with each other. Each production company needed the sales outlets (theatres) of the others in order to market its products. Thus none of the large companies could involve itself in a price war against the wishes of the others. The smaller companies, who might have had most to gain from price competition, were in the weakest position to do anything of the kind, because few of them had theatres of their own and because the majors controlled the most important theatres.

Only one way remains in such a situation for a company to secure an advantage over its competitors. It can create a new product. In a sense, of course, this happened all the time in Hollywood since every picture was unique and its uniqueness was protected by copyright. But precisely because all products were unique no company possessed a decisive advantage. This required an innovation of a different order. Such an innovation was sound, a wholly new kind of product which would make all other kinds obsolete. And the possession of this invention did indeed, for a time, give Warners a chance to increase its share of the market. (It seems likely also that it did for a while increase the absolute size of the market, bringing new customers into the theatres. And it may have helped postpone the decline in attendances brought on by the Depression.) The profits which a monopoly on a new product make possible are known in Marxist economic theory as "technological rent"[9] and the search for this monopoly explains why innovation should be a necessary feature of the economic system even when business seems good.

From this perspective, we should not view innovation in the film industry as a rational and sought-for outcome of attempts on the part of altruistic inventors to "improve" film technology, nor as proof of capitalism's success in combining profit with the satisfaction of human needs. Human needs are many, but capitalism will produce only those innovations from which rent can be extracted, since the whole basis of the system is production for exchange value rather than use value. Sound would not have succeeded, admittedly, had not the public found a use for it, but the public was given "what it wanted" only because sound offered the opportunity for a monopoly. And the same principle applies, *mutatis mutandis,* to any other technological innovation. The history of the invention of the camera itself is written largely in the patents taken out for each new modification.

Gomery argues convincingly against those film historians who claim that Warners decided to produce sound films in a desperate gamble to ward off bankruptcy; Gomery shows that the decision formed part of a carefully thought-out strategy to upgrade the company's status to that of a major.[10] But the case of sound (introduced by Warners and Fox, at that time two of the smaller studios) does not show that technological innovation in the cinema results only from a special set of circumstances. An oligopoly reduces competition in certain areas; it does not eliminate it altogether. Firms continue to compete with each other, but the main form of competition takes the shape of a search for new products. Innovation and technological rent are functions of the system as a whole, not just the result of attempts by small firms to break into the big time. The first three-component Technicolor film, for example, was released by RKO and the first CinemaScope picture by Twentieth-Century-Fox, both majors.

Economic theories can only partially explain technological innovations, since economics cannot say why innovations take the form they do, only why they are an essential part of the system. Economics can explain the necessary but not the sufficient conditions for innovation. No new technology can be introduced unless the economic system requires it. But a new technology cannot be successful unless it fulfills some kind of need. The specific form of this need will be ideologically determined; in the case of cinema the ideological determinant most frequently identified has been realism. Whether the search for greater realism has been welcomed, as in the case of Bazin's discussion of deep focus or Charles Barr's of CinemaScope,[11] or whether realism is subjected to a fundamental critique, as in the case of writings by Comolli and Baudry,[12] theorists appear to agree that realism indeed dictates the formation of the needs which technology satisfies.

But to define "realism" is no simple matter; and while we may agree that realism is dominant, it may not always be the only ideological need fulfilled by technological innovations. The history of the use of color in the cinema provides an interesting test case for the precise role of realism. The scientific principles of color, like those of sound, were known long before sound or color films became technically and commercially feasible. With color, as with sound, the delay in its introduction resulted in part from technical problems in producing a system that would work under commercial operating conditions (early color films were very prone to scratching, for example). But again as with sound there was also resistance on aesthetic grounds. Douglas Fairbanks, whose picture *The Black Pirate* (1927) was produced in two-component Technicolor, complained that color had

always met with overwhelming objections. Not only has the process of color motion picture photography never been perfected, but there has been a grave doubt whether, even if properly developed, it could be applied without detracting more than it added to motion picture technic. The argument has been that it would tire and distract the eye, take attention from acting and facial expression, blur and confuse the action. In short it has been felt that it would militate against the simplicity and directness which motion pictures derive from the unobtrusive black and white.[13]

Such objections appear rather strange if one supposes that the demand for realism in the cinema has always been merely a question of the literal rendering of appearances. We perceive the world as colored, after all, and therefore an accurate representation of it should also be colored. (Leaving aside the fact that complete accuracy is impossible since color in film only approximates the colors perceived in the real world.) But in fact it has never been a question of what *is* real but of what is *accepted* as real. And when it first became technically feasible, color, it seems, did not connote reality but the opposite.

This may in part be for historical reasons, since the very first uses of color involved the tinting of certain sequences in films shot in black and white. Such a usage was extremely conventional, a long way from a literal representation of the world. And as I suggest below, there may be more important reasons why color was not accepted as connoting reality. At any rate, the objections to which Fairbanks refers are clearly consistent with a realist aesthetic. Color would serve only to distract the audience from those elements in the film which carried forward the narrative: acting, facial expression, "the action." The unity of the diegesis and the primacy of the narrative are fundamental to realist cinema. If color was seen to threaten either one it could not be accommodated.

It thus becomes possible to understand why color took so much longer to take hold than sound. The technical problems were probably no greater, nor was it simply force of habit—audiences accustomed to silent pictures adapted to sound practically overnight. Color, on the other hand, has become universal only since the advent of color television, which lowered the relative resale (to television) value of theatrical features made in black and white. Color technology has taken so long to diffuse, we can conclude, partly because unlike sound it could not be instantly accommodated to the realist aesthetic.

Further evidence of color's "unreality" for early spectators can be found in the use actually made of it. For example, in the first few years after the introduction of three-component Technicolor (originally used in the Disney cartoon *Flowers and Trees* in 1932) the great majority of films employing the process were produced within genres not notably realistic in the sense of their being accurate representations of what "life" is "like." It can be argued, of course, that not many Hollywood pictures represent what life is like; but it nevertheless remains true that a kind of hierarchy ranks genres according to the extent to which the world they portray, fictional or not, is close to what the audience believes the world to be like. Thus at one end of the scale we find newsreels, documentaries, war films, crime films, etc. and at the other cartoons, musicals, westerns, costume romances, fantasies, comedies. Virtually all the early three-component Technicolor pictures are in these latter genres.[14] Thus by the 1930s the original objection to color, that it would detract from the narrative, had given way to the extent that color was permissible in *some* films, and so therefore no longer totally incompatible with audience concentration on a story. (Of course such an objection as Fairbanks describes must always have been an extreme position since certain uses of color, such as tinting, became quite common very early on.) Yet it was still considered sufficiently unrealistic to be taboo for films with "realistic" subject matter.[15]

We must now return to the question of why color was not perceived as realistic. Why was its use during the 1930s restricted to unrealistic genres, whereas the use of sound was not? Color must surely have connoted something else. What that something else was could, I think, be demonstrated by an analysis of the color films produced. But I propose instead to take a short cut and consult an industry manual published in 1957—*Elements of Color in Professional Motion Pictures*.[16] Written by a committee of film industry personnel, it distills the collective theory and practice of color photography in Hollywood up to the late 50s. By this time the use of color was no longer restricted to certain genres; by the date of publication, the authors suggest, two-thirds of all features were produced in color. Nevertheless, certain of their remarks on the relation of color to realism shed some light on why for a long time color was restricted to special uses.

For the authors of this book, one should note first of all, realism is never to be equated with naturalism, strict fidelity to the world as it appears:

> This psychological factor can be of great importance in creating an atmosphere of reality or verisimilitude on the screen. With the filming of a historical or "period" picture, for example, research is done not only on architecture and decoration, but also on the colors in use during the particular period and in the specific country. Yet the use of the actual colors of the period or the country are very rarely employed (sic). Because of psychological factors governing the response of a modern viewing audience, far better results are achieved by the use of a *desaturated tonality of the times,* that is, a less saturated range or "palette" of color and pattern, but adequately punctuated with authentic identifying colors so that the end result stands to be identified as historically accurate yet believable. (*Elements,* pp. 41–42)

The colors we accept as real are therefore a compromise between what we are accustomed to and what used to be. The need to make the audience believe in what is depicted on the screen permits, indeed demands, a distortion of what actually is, or was. Such a practice can of course be observed in other aspects of Hollywood filmmaking, though the practitioners are rarely so honest about what they are doing.

The authenticity of what the producers know to be false is guaranteed by the other "realities" of the film, principally the narrative. The authors of this textbook are in no doubt that it is to the narrative that color must ultimately be subordinate, "the objective being to have color 'act' with the story, never being a sepa-

rate entity to compete with or detract from the dramatic content of the picture"
(*Elements,* p. 41). Such a position is exactly what we should expect. But the book
allows, interestingly, for some exceptions to this rule; other values, it seems, may
conflict with the necessity of realism. First, there is the value of the star:

> The feminine star, for example, whose appearance is of paramount concern, must be given
> undisputed priority as to the color of make-up, hair and costume which will best comple-
> ment her complexion and her figure. If her complexion limits the colors she can wear
> successfully, this in turn restricts the background colors which will complement her
> complexion and her costumes to best advantage. (*Elements,* pp. 40–41)

Thus it is not simply the appearance of the real world (modified to make it "be-
lievable") or the requirements of the narrative which dictate the use of color. The
values of stardom must have their place, even if they are in conflict with the
dictates of realism (which presumably might demand background colors which
did not suit the star). That the reference is to "feminine" stars alone makes it
fairly clear what kind of values are in question here.

But the authors challenge realism most strikingly in their remarks on musical and fantasy pictures. In these genres, it seems, color may escape the demands of realism; it need no longer be subordinate to plot and the appearance of
the real world:

> Musicals and fantasy pictures are open to unlimited opportunities in the creative use of
> color. Here we are not held down by reality, past or present, and our imaginations can soar.
> Musicals and fantasies are usually designed to provide the eye with visual pleasure in the
> way that music pleases the ear. (*Elements,* p. 42)

Thus these genres are privileged; here the bonds of realism may be slipped and
the audience may give itself up to "pleasure." The musical, interestingly, offers
another means whereby the dictates of narrative can be avoided, for although
musical numbers are often motivated by the plot they do sometimes succeed in
cutting free of narrative altogether and functioning outside it.

Color, then, need not serve realism. It may simply provide pleasure. Yet pleasure in the cinema is never a simple matter. The pleasures cinema offers—the
pleasures of realism itself or other kinds—are always within ideology. What ideological forms do the purely visual pleasures of color take? On this point the
manual is silent and we must return to the films themselves.

The ideological appeal of color suggests two possibilities. First, color must
signify luxury or spectacle. Whether employed in the western to enhance the
beauties of nature, in the costume drama to portray the sumptuousness of the
Orient or the Old South, or in musicals to render the dazzle and glamor of show-
biz, color serves to embody a world other than our own into which, for the price of
a ticket, we may enter. We should not suppose, of course, that color must always
signify luxury or spectacle, since such a signification depends in part upon its
scarcity value and even on the mere fact of its costliness. Once color has become
normal in the cinema it begins to lose these connotations. One should add,
though, that in certain kinds of documentaries and even occasionally in features
black and white is still used as a guarantor of truth, which would not be possible
unless their opposite, color, signified something other than truth.

Second, color in early Technicolor pictures operates as a celebration of technology: "look how marvellous the cinema is!" Color, far from providing a recognizable portrait of the real world, lifts us out of that world, above its mundane problems and unreconcilable contradictions into a new world where the limitations of the old are swept away and its difficulties transcended. (Consider, for example, the relation between the black-and-white and color sequences in *The Wizard of Oz*.) Early Technicolor functions as a form of self-reflexiveness, which instead of deconstructing the film and destroying the illusion effects a kind of reification of technology. Other forms of film technology function in the same way: Cinerama, 3-D, even spectacular crane or helicopter shots all having the effect satirised in the Cole Porter song in *Silk Stockings*: "glorious Technicolor and breathtaking CinemaScope and stereophonic sound." So we might see color working to confirm Ernest Mandel's statement that "Belief in the omnipotence of technology is the specific form of bourgeois ideology in late capitalism."[17]

That color can function to signify luxury or celebrate technology does not mean that these two uses of it are necessarily subversive of the dominant cinematic ideology. Not everything which is not realism is counter-cinema. Nevertheless, color clearly did function to an extent as a contradiction of realism. Realism, though dominant, could not provide all the things which were in demand. Realist ideology held out against color first by denying its compatibility with narrative and then by confining it to certain genres. Color, however, was able to satisfy needs which realism could not. Were this not so it is hard to see how, given its unrealistic connotations, it could ever have been introduced at all. Since the 1930s, however, color has become progressively absorbed back into realism, with the result that the audience's need for spectacle and for technological wonders has had to be satisfied by a succession of further technological developments: wide screen, 3-D, Sensurround and so on. Even wide screen has now (though in a form less wide than the original CinemaScope) been absorbed into conventional technique. It seems at least possible that a similar fate might have befallen 3-D and other marvels had not they been too expensive for a contracting industry.

Notes

1. *Film Reader* 2 (1977).

2. Douglas Gomery, "Failure and Success: Vocafilm and RCA Innovate Sound," *Film Reader* 2 (1977): 213–21.

3. *Ibid.*, p. 219.

4. This is outlined in some detail in Gomery's doctoral thesis: *The Coming of Sound to the American Cinema: A History of the Transformation of an Industry*, University of Wisconsin–Madison, 1975.

5. Edwin Mansfield, *Technological Change* (New York: 1971) is a shortened version of his work *The Economics of Technological Change* (New York: 1968), which Gomery cites.

6. Mansfield, *Technological Change*, pp. 77–78.

7. Douglas Gomery, "Writing the History of the American Film Industry: Warner Brothers and Sound," *Screen* 17, no. 1 (Spring 1976).

8. Benjamin B. Hampton, *History of the American Film Industry* (New York: 1970) pp. 362, 357.

9. Ernest Mandel in *Late Capitalism* (London: 1975) states: "The continuous and systematic hunt for technological innovations and the corresponding surplus-profits becomes the standard hallmark of late capitalist enterprises and especially of the late capitalist large corporations" (pp. 223–24).

10. Gomery, *op. cit.*

11. André Bazin, "The Evolution of the Language of Cinema" and Charles Barr, "CinemaScope: Before and After," both reprinted in *Film Theory and Criticism,* ed. Gerald Mast and Marshall Cohen (New York: 1974).

12. Jean-Louis Comolli, in a series of articles "Technique et Idéologie" beginning in *Cahiers du Cinéma* no. 231, reprinted here in part; Jean-Louis Baudry, "Ideological Effects of the Basic Cinematographic Apparatus," *Film Quarterly* 28, no. 2 (Winter 1974–75): 39–47, reprinted here.

13. Quoted in *A Technological History of Motion Pictures and Television,* ed. Raymond Fielding (Berkeley and Los Angeles: 1967), p. 54.

14. Among the early three-component Technicolor films were: *Becky Sharp* (1935), *The Garden of Allah* (1936), *Trail of the Lonesome Pine* (1936), *Snow White and the Seven Dwarfs* (1937), *Nothing Sacred* (1937), *Drums* (1938), *The Adventures of Robin Hood* (1938), *Goldwyn Follies* (1938), *Sweethearts* (1938), *Dodge City* (1939), *Gone with the Wind* (1939), *Northwest Passage* (1939), *The Wizard of Oz* (1939), *Jessie James* (1939), *The Thief of Bagdad* (1939).

15. I would not wish to assert that the slow diffusion of color technology was *solely* due to ideological factors. Undoubtedly there were technical problems, possibly greater than those encountered with sound films. And because color was more expensive there was an economic rationale for reserving its use for pictures which were expensive in other ways and which could be given special treatment by exhibitors (restricted runs in large urban theatres, etc.). *Gone with the Wind* would be an example. My main point, however, is that economic factors never exist in isolation, and that in the case of color economics and ideology are mutually reinforcing. See the remarks about luxury and scarcity below.

16. *Elements of Color in Professional Motion Pictures* (New York: 1957).

17. *Op. cit.*, p. 501.

NOTES ON COLUMBIA PICTURES CORPORATION 1926–1941

EDWARD BUSCOMBE

Buscombe begins this article by addressing a basic problem of film literature: How can we bring precision to an understanding of the relationships among film as art, film as industry, and film as ideological form? He argues convincingly that "reflection theory" assumptions —films reflect the sensibilities of their makers; films reflect the relations of production; films reflect the dominant ideology —

simply will not do. In industrial terms, a company's need to ensure the long-term survival of the system that allows it to exist may conflict with its desire for profits. And in film, as Janet Staiger reminds us in her article, the attempts to differentiate individual films as well as to standardize successful formulas can encourage attempts to express attitudes, values, and sentiments that challenge aspects of the existing social system. The profit incentive does not neatly correspond to conservative political attitudes. And certainly the production of complex texts does not remain under conscious, calculated control, even in a culture industry. Crosscurrents, contradictions, tensions seep in; some may very well point to flaws in the premises of the dominant ideology. No studio executive, no matter how astute and no matter how reactionary, could eliminate them totally.

However, Buscombe does not pursue the path of textual production as a complex signifying practice, as the Cahiers du Cinéma *editors do in their article on* Young Mr. Lincoln, *reprinted in the first volume of* Movies and Methods. *Instead, he concentrates on what the* Cahiers *editors gloss over: the degree to which a particular film can be correlated with specific political attitudes and goals. At one point, Buscombe warns about the hazards of overpoliticization that makes a film the purveyor of a single, historically specific message, but later he tests the viability of such an approach addressed to individual studios.*

Buscombe uses Columbia Pictures as his example and American Madness *as his particular instance. Some of the criticisms of studio and industry history that he makes along the way are important reminders of work yet to be done — the lack of basic research resources, the second- and third-hand nature of most so-called studio history. Some studio archives are now available — R.K.O., Universal, Warner Brothers, and United Artists records are all on deposit — but there are still major gaps: For example, few revelatory memos survive, and none of the R.K.O. documents relating directly to Howard Hughes or to the studio's complicity with the industry blacklist are in the material deposited at UCLA. And, although Douglas Gomery in the rejoinder that begins his article illustrates what can be done with existing information (some from sources Buscombe neglects to consider, such as court records), there still remain the basic problems with which Buscombe begins: The recent upsurge in film history scholarship still has not produced an effective synthesis of aesthetic achievement, industry practice, and ideological functions within cinema. In this regard, Buscombe's article is a very healthy reminder of the global outlook still needed as a guide for detailed studies. If Buscombe himself perpetuates some auteurist assumptions by focusing on the personnel at Columbia in his attempt to correlate an individual's party politics, degree of influence, and overall studio policy, he also reminds us that we need to seek comprehensive models that are capable of addressing the problems of art and ideology in relation to the motion picture industry.*

•

I

'The film industry': 'the cinema'. How are these terms related in film criticism? 'The film industry' describes an economic system, a way (or ways) of organising the structure of production, distribution and consumption. Historically such organisation has, in Britain and America, conformed to the usual pattern of capitalist activity; film can be seen as an industry like any other. It has passed from the primitive stage of small-scale entrepreneurial activity to the formation of large-scale monopolies, securing their position by vertical integration, spreading from production into distribution and exhibition. Since the War the industry has, like other forms of business, developed towards diversification and the formation of multinational corporations. In other respects too film has developed like other industries. Production in particular has been based on a division of labour, of a fairly extreme kind. From early days the industry has employed the techniques of mass advertising, and it has required the injection of huge sums of capital, resulting in turn in the passing of control of the industry from its original owners and from the primary producers.

In film criticism, then, the term 'film industry' implies a way of looking at film which minimises its differences from other forms of economic activity; a way which is of course predominantly that of those who actually own the industry. Its characteristic descriptions are sufficiently indicative of a perspective: 'the trade', 'marketing', 'exploitation', a 'package', 'product'.

'The cinema' suggests something else. While the term might, notionally, encompass the industry, the pull is surely in a different direction. 'The cinema' implies film as art. As Raymond Williams has shown with convincing detail in *Culture and Society*, the opposition between art and industry has a long history in our culture. The division between the two is experienced everywhere as deep, but nowhere deeper than in film. On the one hand we are given to understand is the industry, churning out product for financial gain. On the other are artists, creating enduring works of personal expression or comment on life and society. Such an opposition has taken different forms at different times. Sometimes it has been geographical. In America there was Hollywood, the industrial system par excellence. In Europe (usually excluding Britain, apart from its documentaries) there were artists: Renoir, Dreyer, Bergman, Antonioni, etc. Later the auteur theory, as applied to American cinema, changed the emphasis. Though Hollywood was still an industry, through diligent critical work some artists could be winnowed from the chaff, artists who against the odds managed by luck, cunning or sheer genius to overcome the system, the industry. The auteur theory, whatever its 'theory' may have been, did not in practice abolish the distinction between art and industry; it merely shifted the line of demarcation.

One might suppose that a little common sense would tell us that such a distinction is nonsense, that all film is both industry *and* art, in some sense. Even the lowest, most despised products (choose your own examples) are made with some kind of art. Do they not share the same language as the acknowledged masterpieces: do they not tell a story, try to affect the spectators' emotions? They may do it more or less effectively, but isn't this a difference of degree, not of kind? Conversely, in the making of the most spiritual and sublime films grubby bank notes change hands. The film stock on which the masterpiece is recorded may come from the same batch used to shoot the potboiler on the adjoining stage.

Yet proof that the mutual exclusion of art and industry operates at a level too deep to be affected by mere common sense can be found not only in the dominant critical attitudes but in the organisation of social institutions. To give an example close to home: the British Film Institute was set up, as its Memorandum of Association states, 'to encourage the development of the art of the film'. At the same time it is stated that the BFI is not permitted 'to control nor attempt to interfere with purely trade matters'. Art not only can but must be divorced from industry. And the split is preserved even in the structure of government. Whereas the BFI is administered by the Department of Education and Science, the film industry comes under the Department of Trade and Industry. Thus the opposition art/industry has to be seen not merely as a 'mistake' in film criticism which can be easily rectified by a more careful look at the facts, but as the result of a whole practice of thinking, talking, writing and disseminating inscribed in institutions like the BFI, those parts of the education system that handle film, plus also exhibition/viewing practice—the art-house circuit and its audience(s)—the 'immaterial' thought both reflecting and being part of this apparatus; in short, as part of an ideology.

The main concern here, however, is not with the origins of such an opposition but with its consequence for film criticism. This may be baldly stated: there has been scarcely any serious attempt to think the relationship between art and industry with regard to films produced in what have historically been for us the two most important film-making countries, namely our own and the United States. Criticism has been devoted not to relating them but to separating them out, and in practice this has meant that critics have concentrated on the beauties and mysteries of art and left the industry, presumably a tougher plant, to take care of itself. Study of the industry might require knowledge of, say, economics or of how films are actually made, knowledge which critics have not been expected to acquire. The main effort of criticism, therefore, has gone into the study of film texts viewed as autonomous, self-sufficient entities; or, occasionally, as reflections of society, but certainly not as reflections of the industry which produced them, unless they are being dismissed as rubbish. Even recent work deriving from structuralism and concerned to open up the text, to 'deconstruct' it, has tended to take the film as 'given' and has ignored questions of how the organisation of a film text might relate to the organisation of an industry or to specific working practices.

It is in respect of Hollywood, the largest field of activity in both film-making and criticism, that the lack of a history of the industry is most glaring. Of course there is a certain amount of information around. Statistics have occasionally been assembled (a number of government and trade reports on Hollywood in the 1930's are listed in the notes of Leo C. Rosten's *Hollywood: The Movie Colony, The Movie Makers,* a book which has some useful material on this period). There are one or two books, again on the 1930's, which assemble some facts about the economics of the industry (for example, F. D. Klingender and Stuart Legg, *The Money Behind the Screen* and Mae D. Huettig, *Economic Control of the Motion Picture Industry).* But of course they don't attempt to make any connections between the economics and the actual films produced. There is also the ragbag of publicity releases, inaccurate box-office returns and general gossip which makes up the trade press (*Film Daily, Motion Picture Herald, Variety, Hollywood Reporter,* etc). To this may be added a host of 'biographies' (or ghosted autobiographies) of prominent industry figures, of which *Hollywood Rajah* by Bosley Crowther (on Louis B. Mayer) and *King Cohn* by Bob Thomas (on Harry Cohn) are representative examples. Little that is useful can be gleaned from such works, which mostly string together collections of anecdotes about the 'great men'. On such questions as the financial structures within which they were obliged to operate or the actual working methods of their studios they are for the most part silent. Of studio histories, properly speaking, there are none, with the possible exception of Richard Schickel's book *The Disney Version,* which is hampered by his failure to get any cooperation from the Disney studio itself; a fact, of course, that is not without its significance, since it indicates the difficulties of this kind of work.

Indeed, the neglect of industry history is not only a consequence of critical attitudes and priorities which have abandoned the field to those whose interest does not go beyond 'personalities'. It is also the result of very real practical problems. The fact is that the history of the American film industry is extremely difficult to write, because many of the basic materials that would be needed are simply not available. The statistics are incomplete and unreliable. The trade press presents only the acceptable face of the business, even when one can get access to it (the BFI Library, virtually the only collection of such periodicals in Britain, has no run of *Variety,* though there are plans to acquire one). The biographies, and studio histories, where they exist at all (for example Bosley Crowther's *The Lion's Share,* on MGM), are largely based on reminiscences. Concrete documented evidence in the form, say, of studio memoranda, accounts and other records, is almost totally lacking. If such records still exist they are mostly locked away in studio vaults. And the history of technological development in Hollywood has still to be written. Lastly, the films themselves; such prints as have been preserved are often impossible to see. The situation is little different from that which exists in relation to the history of the Elizabethan stage, with this exception, that infinitely less method and application has gone into researching it.

The result is that when Hollywood has been written about its industrial dimension has been ignored. Much of the writing has been based on an idea of history as one damned thing after another. Even such a prestigious work as Lewis Jacobs's *The Rise of the American Film* scarcely rises above this, most sections being simply annotated film lists. The only principle to compete has been auteurism, which leaves film history at the stage which history proper reached in the nineteenth century when Carlyle defined it as the lives of great men. Deliberate attempts to get away from auteurism, such as Colin McArthur's *Underworld USA* (on the crime film) and Jim Kitses's *Horizons West* (on the Western) are ultimately broken-backed books. Genres may be related to aspects of American history, but in the end it is the auteurs who dominate the account.

Some recent, more promising directions have been pursued. Patrick Ogle's work on deep focus [*Screen* 13 no. 1; reprinted here] or that of John Ellis and Charles Barr on Ealing Studios (*Screen* 15 nos. 1–2, 16 no. 1) have from different perspectives tried to make connections between films and the nature of the industry which produced them. *The Velvet Light Trap* has brought to light valuable material on the studio system, though the use that has been made of it has often been disappointing. But the gaps in our knowledge are still enormous.

II

One consequence of the existence of such gaps has been that attempts to relate Hollywood films to the society which produced them have simply by-passed the industry altogether. The result has been a series of short circuits. Hollywood films are seen as merely 'reflecting' society. On the one hand is society, seen as a collection of facts, attitudes, psychological patterns or whatever. On the other are the films, where one sees such facts, attitudes, etc. mirrored. Though it may be conceded that the mirror sometimes distorts, in so far as there is a theory behind such a view it is a naively realist one, and indeed how could it be otherwise? If there is no conception of Hollywood as an industry with its own history, specific practices, economic relationships, technological and other material constraints, if film is seen as something that somehow mysteriously appears and having appeared is simply there, fixed and given, then how is one to understand the nature of any mediation? To confine ourselves again to the period of the 1930's, a book such as Andrew Bergman's *We're in the Money* devotes a mere four pages to 'A Note on the Movie Industry and the Depression,' which ends thus: 'The preliminaries completed, we proceed to the black-and-white footage itself.' And in the black-and-white footage the social comment can simply be read off as if the films were so many sociologists' reports. Here is an admittedly rather extreme example: 'Tod Browning's 1932 MGM film, *Freaks,* had a cast made up of pinheads, human torsos, midgets, and dwarfs, like nothing ever seen in the movies. And what more stunted a year than 1932 for such a film?' (p. 168).

One might expect that more specifically Marxist attempts to relate Hollywood to American society would display a little more rigour and subtlety. Bourgeois cultural theories, with their assumptions about the values of artistic freedom and personal expression, are obviously ill-equipped to deal with a medium so conditioned by money, technology and organisational structures. Books such as Bergman's, which dispense with most of that theory (though never completely; some auteurs, such as Capra and Vidor, make an appearance) seem to have no theory at all to replace it. Marxism, on the other hand, proposes a sophisticated understanding of the relations between society, a system of production and the actual product. Yet such Marxist models as have been put forward for understanding Hollywood have suffered from a crudity which has had the effect of deadening further thought. The crudest model of all is that encapsulated in Godard's phrase 'Nixon-Paramount'. The model implied in such a phrase has had obvious attractions for the political avant-garde and indeed contains some truth. But the truth contained in such vulgar Marxism is so vague and general as to have scarcely any use at all. Ideological products such as films are seen as directly caused by the nature of the economic base of society. A capitalist system produces capitalist films, and that is all there is to it. Alternatively, but the slight sophistication is scarcely a modification, the products of Hollywood are bourgeois and capitalist because the particular industry which produces them is capitalist. And the more specific the model becomes the more its crudity is exposed. Thus in the first section of the *Cahiers du Cinéma* text on *Young Mr. Lincoln* (translated in *Screen* 13 no. 3) we are told that since Hollywood is involved with big business its ideology is not just a generally capitalist one. It supports the more reactionary wing of the political spectrum represented by the Republican Party.

The *Cahiers* text is only one example of a desire to show not only that Hollywood is a part of bourgeois ideology in general but that some Hollywood films are intended to carry a specific and reactionary message which has a direct reference to a particular political situation. Another example of such over-politicisation comes in a recent issue of *Jump Cut* no. 4 (November–December 1974), which contains an interpretation of *King Kong* as an anti-Roosevelt tract. The article conveniently states its premises in a footnote:

This article is built round two suppositions. First, that all huge business corporations (such as RKO) are conservative Republican unless demonstrated otherwise, and that their products (like *King Kong*) will reinforce their interests instead of betraying them. Second, that the auteur theory in its standard application is not a germane approach when dealing with a political film, especially under the tight studio control of the 1930's. A political film would only be allowed release if its philosophy was in line with that of the studio which made it. Therefore, RKO studio will be regarded as the true 'auteur' of *King Kong,* despite the innumerable personal touches of its artistic crew.

Although the phrase 'unless demonstrated otherwise' indicates that the author, Gerald Peary, is aware of the dangers of over-simple generalisations, his assumptions still seem open to two major objections. Firstly, is it not possible that even in Hollywood (not noted perhaps for its political sophistication) there were in the 1930's people who could see that the survival of capitalism (and hence of their 'huge corporations') was not necessarily synonymous with the victory of the Republican Party, especially a Republican Party so discredited as the one which had been led to electoral disaster and intellectual bankruptcy by Herbert Hoover? Secondly, what exactly *are* the interests of such corporations? In the long term, obviously, the survival of a system which allowed them to make profits. But in the short term surely it was those profits themselves. Is it to be assumed that studio executives saw the possibility of profits in attacking a leader who had so recently demonstrated his popularity at the polls (especially among the cinema-going section of the public)? Or should we assume that the political commitment of the studio executives overcame their dedication to profits?

It seems unlikely, but our ignorance about Hollywood generally and about the particular organisation of RKO is such that we cannot answer these questions. Precisely for this reason we ought to beware of assuming any answers. Even if we do assume, with the authors in *Cahiers* and *Jump Cut,* that a studio is owned by big business and that one of its products promotes the political and hence economic interests of the company (I say apparently because the actual interpretation of the films seems open to question), it does not necessarily follow that the political meaning is the result of who owns the studio. *Post hoc* is not *propter hoc.*

The lack of any detailed knowledge of industry history, then, suggests caution on the question of the political orientation of Hollywood in the 1930's. Firstly, is it true that the film industry was controlled by big business? And is this the same as the Republican Party (there was business influence among the Democrats too)? Secondly, if it is true can one assume a direct effect on the ideology of Hollywood films? Even the term 'ideology' seems to pose a problem here. It is one thing to argue that, using the term in its classical Marxist sense (or as refined by Althusser) to mean a general world view or structure of thought situated primarily below the conscious level, Hollywood films are ideological expressions of bourgeois society. It is quite another to argue that they support a specific set of political attitudes. Bourgeois society is more than simply the Republican Party. And in any case Marxist theory only claims that ideological products are determined *in the last instance* by the economic relations existing at the base of society. The arguments about *Young Mr. Lincoln* and *King Kong* appear to assume that facts about who controls the film industry can provide a sufficient explanation of a film's ideology, ignoring the dimension of the institutional structures which may intervene between the economic base and the final product. Without a knowledge of these structures one cannot say that these films are *not* propaganda; but if they were intended as such, as the *Cahiers* and *Jump Cut* articles imply, it is a strange sort of propaganda which requires an ingenious interpretation thirty or forty years later to make its point. Surely it would have to be demonstrated that such a reading was available to an audience at the time.

III

These problems were thrown into relief by a viewing some time ago of *American Madness,* directed for Columbia in 1932 by Frank Capra. The story of the film concerns Dickson, the manager of a small-town bank (played by Walter Huston). The directors of the bank are financiers of the old school (pre-Keynesians), dedicated to tight money policies, which they pursue ruthlessly and selfishly. Dickson, however, has a different view of what the function of a bank should be. He believes that money should be put to work to create jobs and opportunities. His policy is to lend to small businessmen, trusting in his own assessment of their good intentions rather than in the security they can offer. His beliefs are put to the test when a run on the bank occurs; the run is stopped and his faith in his clients vindicated when the little people he has helped rally round to deposit money and so restore confidence in the bank.

The programme note which accompanied the screening of the film at the National Film Theatre suggested that the character of Dickson might have been based on A. H. Giannini, a California banker who was influential in Columbia's affairs in the 1930's. Such a suggestion raises one immediate difficulty, in that it seems to assume that the apparent, or manifest, meaning of the film is the only one, and ignores the possibility that the latent meaning may be quite different. The film might be about other things besides banking. It excludes, that is, the possibility of analysing the film along the lines of the *Young Mr. Lincoln* text, which finds that, despite the film's apparent project of supporting the Republican cause in the 1940 presidential election, the 'real' meaning of the film undermines this. (The problem of such readings, despite their obvious attractions, is that it is never explained how in practice the subversive meaning of the film becomes available to the people to whom it might be of some use, i. e., the working class.) Nevertheless, the suggestion seemed worth following up because of the possibility that it might throw some light on the question of Hollywood's relation to politics in the 1930's, and on the nature of the production system generally. And this might in turn tell us something about Capra's films.

Robert Mundy, in a review of Capra's autobiography in the American *Cinema* (7 no. 1 [Fall 1971]: 56), speculates on how it was that Capra was able to make films which so closely embodied his personal ideas. He suggests two reasons: firstly, that Capra was working for a small studio where freedom was greater, and secondly, that Capra's vision 'was unusually consonant with the vision of America which Hollywood purveyed with such commercial success in the 1930's. Ideologically his films were rarely at odds with the image of life which the studios believed the public wanted to see.' Mundy avoids the facile assumption that Capra was 'in touch' with America, and that his films arise out of some special relationship to the people and the mood of the time. Instead, he suggests that his work is an expression of the point of view of his *studio.* He concludes, however, that we need to know more: 'A persuasive history of Columbia in the 1930's [is] needed before an informed critical account of Capra's work can be written.' Quite. The problem is to know where to start, given the problems of such research outlined above. Mr. Giannini seemed to offer a way in.

He is referred to in a number of books about Hollywood, but as far as I know never more than in passing, as a prominent Californian banker who was involved in movie financing. In several of the references there is a curious uncertainty about his initials. Sometimes he is called A. P. Giannini, sometimes A. H. Thus Philip French in his 'informal' history of the Hollywood tycoons *The Movie Moguls* mentions him on p. 25: 'In fact the first banker to take the cinema seriously was the Californian A. P. Giannini, the son of an Italian immigrant, whose Bank of Italy (later renamed the Bank of America) has played an important part in movie finance since before the First World War.' On p. 79 we read: 'A. H. Giannini, the influential movie financier whose Bank of Italy had a special claim on Hollywood consciences of whatever religious denomination'.

The mystery of A. H. or A. P. was only cleared up when I looked up Giannini in the *National Cyclopaedia of American Biography.* It appears that there were two of them. (Obviously I am not the first person since Mr. Giannini père to be aware of this fact, but it seems as though Philip French was not when he wrote his book. Of such confusions is film history made.) It's worth giving some details of their careers, since they are relevant to Capra's film. A. H. and A. P. (or to give them their full names, Attilio Henry and Amadeo Peter) were brothers. Both their parents were natives of Italy; their father had been a hotel keeper but had come to California to try farming. Amadeo was born in 1870 and his brother four years later. The older brother had gone to work at the age of twelve in his stepfather's firm of wholesale commission agents in San Francisco, and while still in his twenties he formed the Columbus Savings and Loan Society. In 1904 he founded the Bank of Italy. Giannini's bank was at the time of a novel kind. Branches were set up in small towns across the country to attract the savings of the man in the street and Giannini even started savings schemes in schools. His bank specialised in making loans to small businesses with minimal collateral and introduced the practice of lending money for house purchase repayable in monthly instalments. He appears to have been a man of some determination and imagination; during the great San Francisco earthquake and fire of 1906, Giannini was the first to reopen his bank, setting up his desk on the waterfront while the fire still raged. By 1930 he had built up his banking interests to the point where the holding company, the Transamerica Corporation, was the largest of its kind in the world with assets of $1,000 million. Giannini's unorthodox methods did not endear him to more conservative financiers on Wall Street; particularly deplorable was his policy of encouraging wide public ownership of his corporation and of assisting his employees to become stockholders through profit-sharing schemes.

His brother Attilio (sometimes called Dr. Giannini, though he abandoned medicine when made vice-president of his brother's Bank of Italy) was involved in various movie companies between the world wars. In 1920 he lent Chaplin half a million dollars to make *The Kid*. In 1936 he became president and chairman of the board of United Artists and though he resigned from this position in 1938 he retained an influential position in the film industry by virtue of his place on the voting trust which controlled Universal Pictures. He was also involved with several so-called independent production companies, such as Selznick International Pictures and Lesser-Lubitsch. It's worth pointing out that none of these organisations possessed large chains of movie theatres. It was the tangible assets of real estate which tempted the Wall Street banks into movie finance in the 1920's. Giannini does at least seem to have been more interested in making pictures.

Giannini's main importance for present purposes is his role in Columbia. The company was originally formed in 1920 as CBC, the letters standing for the names of the three men who set it up: Harry Cohn, Joe Brandt and Harry's brother Jack. All of them had previously worked for Carl Laemmle at Universal. Attilio Giannini lent them $100,000 to get started. In 1924 the company changed its name to Columbia Pictures Corporation (possibly an echo of the Columbus Savings and Loan Society?). Giannini continued to be closely involved. Although in 1929 the studio decided to establish their stock on the New York exchange, 96 percent of the voting stock was concentrated in the hands of a voting trust. In 1932 Joe Brandt was bought out by Harry Cohn (after Jack Cohn had attempted to enlist Giannini's support in a coup against his brother) and thereafter the voting trust which controlled the company consisted of the two Cohns and Giannini. Unlike most studios at this time Columbia had no debts to the New York investment banks and instead was run as a family business.

Giannini's position was therefore a powerful one. Unfortunately one has no actual knowledge of how he used it. All that can be done is to suggest what his influence might have been, given the kind of background from which he and his brother came. The Gianninis were quite separate from the New York banking establishment. Not only was theirs a different kind of business (deposit as opposed to investment banking), involving them with different kinds of clients; they were Catholics (unlike the Rockefellers and Morgans), they were second-generation immigrants, they came from the other side of the country, and their social attitudes were, as far as one can tell, less patrician. A. P.'s entry in the *National Cyclopaedia* says that he 'has ever been known as a friend of the poor and struggling' and if ever a banker could be so described it seems likely that he was. Not surprisingly, therefore, he supported the Banking Act introduced by Roosevelt in 1935 because, he said, he preferred a measure of government control to domination of the banks by the Wall Street establishment. In 1936 he actively supported Roosevelt's campaign for a second term, at a time when Wall Street considered FDR as no better than a Communist. It seems reasonable to assume that his brother shared his liberal views.

The Gianninis might, then, be seen as a kind of contradiction in terms: populist bankers. The populists of the nineteenth century had regarded bankers as the physical embodiment of all that was evil, and believed that the agricultural problems of the Midwest were largely caused by a conspiracy of monopolists on Wall Street keeping interest rates up and farm prices down. (Amadeo Giannini was, we are told, greatly interested in agricultural progress.) The little man, the populists contended, stood no chance against those who commanded such resources and used them for selfish purposes. But the Gianninis believed in deliberately aiding such small businessmen and farmers who got no help from Wall Street. In this respect they are in line with the policies of the New Deal, which attempted to get big business under some kind of government control while at the same time trying to raise farm prices and help small firms and individuals by encouraging banks to make loans, by refinancing mortgages and so on.

This too is Dickson's policy in *American Madness* and it seems plausible that the character is indeed based on Dr. Giannini. The question then is, what do we make of it? A simple and tempting theory might be constructed: Capra's film doesn't so much capture what 'people' were thinking at the time as represent the thinking of a New Dealer on the voting trust controlling Columbia. Such a theory certainly has its attractions. Firstly, it provides a corrective to the crude assumption that Hollywood = big business = the Republican Party. Secondly, other Capra films, such as *Mr. Deeds Goes To Town, Mr. Smith Goes To Washington, You Can't Take It with You,* also embody the populism that was a powerful element in the New Deal. Thirdly, the situation of Columbia itself, quite apart from the beliefs of those in control, might well be seen as impelling it towards the New Deal coalition of anti-establishment forces. Despite the Academy Awards Capra collected for the studio in the 1930's it never entirely freed itself from its Poverty Row origins. Although the company bought its own studio in 1926 and in 1929 set up a national distribution organisation, at the beginning of the 1930's Columbia was still producing less than thirty features a year (to MGM's forty-three) and most of these were destined for the lower half of a double bill. Output increased steadily during the decade, but the studio was never in the same league as the majors. In 1935, for example, the total volume of business of Loew's, the parent company of MGM, was $85 million; Columbia's was $16 million. Thus Loew's had nearly 22 percent of the total volume of business of the industry, Columbia only 4 percent. And despite the characteristically violent swings in the film industry each year from profit to loss and back again, these relative percentages did not change for the rest of the decade. The reason why Columbia was unable to increase its share of business is that, unlike the major studios, it had no chain of theatres of its own which could serve as a secure outlet for its product. All the money it made came from the sale of its own pictures to theatres owned by other studios. MGM and the other majors could, and frequently did, recoup losses on their own films by profits on the exhibition of other companies' output.

But a potential advantage of this relative weakness was that Columbia preserved its financial independence. It had not had to borrow heavily from the banks to finance the acquisition of theatre chains, and as a result the studio was still in the control of the men who founded it, the two Cohns and Giannini. Its independence of Wall Street meant that it might well become the focus of anti-establishment forces, and that if it did it had the freedom to make films which reflected that, always providing of course that it could sell them to the theatres.

But caution is necessary even before trying to test out such a thesis. Capra in his autobiography devotes several pages to recording how charmed he was by Roosevelt's personality; yet, he says, this only made him 'almost a Democrat'. One might suppose that Capra, a first-generation immigrant, an Italian Catholic born in Sicily, was a natural Democrat. But the political content of his films, while embodying support for the underdog, does not attach itself to any party. His belief in the people goes hand in hand with a classically populist distrust of *all* their leaders. And other tendencies in his films, such as a pervasive anti-intellectualism and a hostility to central government, are certainly not characteristic of the New Deal.

Nevertheless there is a kind of radicalism in his films which would certainly not have commended itself to the fiercely Republican Louis B. Mayer, for example, and it therefore seems worth pursuing the thesis that Columbia might have been a focus for Roosevelt sympathisers. Harry Cohn, who controlled the production side of the company throughout the period, appears to have had no interest in politics at all. It is true that he visited Mussolini in 1933 after Columbia had released a complimentary documentary entitled *Mussolini Speaks*. But Cohn seems to have been more impressed with the intimidating lay-out of the dictator's office than with his politics. When he returned to Hollywood he rearranged his own office in imitation. Capra remarked in an interview at the National Film Theatre that Cohn didn't care what the politics of his studio's films were. His concern was with their money-making potential, which he estimated with a 'fool-proof device. . . . If my fanny squirms it's bad. If my fanny doesn't squirm it's good. It's as simple as that' (quoted in *King Cohn,* p. 142). If Giannini had wanted the studio to take a pro-New Deal stance, then it seems as though Cohn would have had no particular objections.

The only way of testing whether there was such a policy, in default of any access to whatever records of the company may still exist, is to look at the films that Columbia made during the period and to find out what one can about the people who made them. It's at this point that the sheer physical difficulties of this kind of work intrude. Taking the period 1926–41, from just before the introduction of sound to a year or so after Capra left Columbia (an arbitrary choice, but less arbitrary than some, and one which corresponds very roughly to the period of the Depression and the consequent New Deal, as far as World War II), Columbia, despite being one of the smaller studios, made on my calculations 627 feature films. (The figure may not be exact because the *Film Daily Year Book,* from which the calculation is made, lists the films of each year twice, once under each studio and once in alphabetical order for the whole industry. Titles appearing in one list don't always appear in the other.) To make those films the company employed 67 different producers, 171 directors, and 269 writers. (The figure for writers is from 1928; they are not credited in the *Year Book* before that date.) By writers is meant those credited with a screenplay. Authors of the original stories from which the films were made might amount to another two or three hundred people. There are also fifteen people whose names appear at one time or another as directors of the company, Columbia Pictures Corporation.

These are the people within the organisation whose position would have allowed them to influence the political content of the films. One might wish to argue that everyone, actors, cameramen, designers, right down to the studio policemen, had some kind of influence, however small. Melvyn Douglas, for example, who acted in many films for Columbia in the 1930's, was active in liberal causes. I have excluded these workers from consideration mainly because, given the nature of the production process, as far as one understands it, and the rigid division of labour, their control over the political content (if any) of a film would have been less. Actors didn't make up their own lines. In any case one has to stop somewhere, and it's not too easy to find out who the studio policemen were.

One is thus faced with a preliminary list of 522 people; to be precise, it is slightly less because the division of labour was not absolute and some writers directed or vice versa. But there is not much overlapping, and the total must be around 500 (this for one small studio during a mere fifteen years of its fifty-year existence). The BFI Library has a card index system which allows one to check whether the Library has entries on individuals in books, periodicals or on microfiche. I accordingly looked up everyone who worked on more than the occasional film. Very few of these names appear in the index and when they do it is often merely a reference to a tiny cutting in *Variety* recording the person's death and giving a short list of the films they worked on. (This is not a criticism of the state of the Library but of the state of film history.)

A few things do emerge. Columbia seems to have been, in the higher echelons, a tight-knit community (one precondition perhaps of a consistent policy). One of the producers was Ralph Cohn, the son of Jack. Everett Riskin, another producer, was the older brother of Robert, who wrote several of Capra's screenplays. Sam Briskin, general manager of the studio in the early 1930's and executive in charge of production from 1938 to 1942, was the brother-in-law of Abe Schneider, treasurer of the company for most of this period. Briskin's brother, Irving, was another producer at Columbia. Yet this doesn't tell us much about an industry where the pull of family relationships was always strong and where 'the son-in-law also rises' was a standard joke.

On the political affiliations of the vast majority, I found no information at all, nor even any information on their lives which would permit a guess. Some very few wrote books or had books written about them, but with the exception of Cohn and Capra their careers were peripheral to Columbia. A few more have been the subject of articles in film magazines, and from these one can glean scraps of information. Richard Maibaum, who wrote a few scripts for the studio, was the author of some anti-lynching and anti-Nazi plays before coming to Hollywood. Dore Schary, whose Democrat sympathies were well known, was also a writer at Columbia in the 1930's. So, very occasionally, were Donald Ogden Stewart, associated with left-wing causes at the time, and Edward Chodorov, involved with committees for refugees from Spain and Germany and later more or less blacklisted. But this scarcely amounts to much. Stewart, after all, wrote a lot of scripts for MGM.

More significant, at first sight, than the presence of 'liberals' is the fact that exactly half of the Hollywood Ten were actually employed at Columbia during the 1930's; namely Edward Dmytryk, Dalton Trumbo, Herbert Biberman, John Howard Lawson and Lester Cole. But a concerted Communist effort at the studio is hardly likely. Only Dmytryk worked there more than occasionally, and he during his time as a contract director was making routine B-feature films (musicals, horror pictures, thrillers) which, one must assume, offered little scope for the kind of social comment Dmytryk later put into *Crossfire*. There were one or two other Communists working at Columbia who testified before the House Un-American Activities Committee four years after the 1947 hearings which sent the Ten to jail. Paul Jarrico, who wrote for Columbia the screenplays of *No Time to Marry* (1938) and *The Face Behind the Mask* (1941), was called before the Committee in 1951 but refused to testify and pleaded the 5th Amendment. Another called before the Committee in 1951 was Sidney Buchman. One of Harry Cohn's favourite writers, Buchman specialized in comedy. Among his credits for Columbia are: *Whom the Gods Destroy* (1934); *I'll Love You Always, Love Me Forever, She Married Her Boss* (1935); *The King Steps Out, Theodora Goes Wild, Adventure in Manhattan, The Music Goes Round* (1936); *Holiday* (1938); *Mr. Smith Goes to Washington* (1939); *The Howards of Virginia* (1940); *Here Comes Mr. Jordan* (1941). Buchman admitted that he had been in the Communist Party from 1938 to 1945, but refused to supply the Committee with the list of names of other members they required and was cited for contempt. He was found guilty and given a one-year suspended sentence and a $150 fine.

Buchman clearly occupied an influential position at Columbia. He was a producer as well as a writer and was associated with some of Columbia's greatest successes in the late 1930's and early 1940's. But if *Mr. Smith* is satirical about Washington life, it retains an unswerving, even touching, faith in American political institutions, and it is difficult to see that Buchman's membership in the Communist Party had any great effect on what he wrote. Indeed many of his associates appear to have been surprised to learn that he was a Communist.

It may be that a more detailed search through such records as are available would turn up some decisive evidence. But on what has been presented so far it seems unlikely that, Dr. Giannini notwithstanding, there was any deliberate policy of favouritism to the New Deal or left causes. The same conclusion seems likely to follow from the films. Here again one is attempting generalisations based on woefully inadequate knowledge, because, apart from those directed by Capra, I have seen very few of the films Columbia made during the period. Nevertheless some impressions can be gained from looking at the records. In the late 1920's and early 1930's the staples of the studio's output were adventure and action films, comedies, often mildly risqué, and the occasional exposé (one of Jack Cohn's first successes at Universal was to convince Carl Laemmle of the box office potential of *Traffic in Souls,* a sensationalist feature on the white slave trade). Westerns and thrillers made up the rest of the production schedule. Of course titles can be misleading, but a list of the films produced in 1928 probably gives a fair indication of at least the type of films being made:

That Certain Thing, The Wife's Relations, Lady Raffles, So This Is Love? Woman's Way, Sporting Age, Matinee Idol, Desert Bride, Broadway Daddies, After the Storm, Golf Widows, Modern Mothers, Name the Woman, Ransom, Way of the Strong, Beware of Blondes, Say It with Sables, Virgin Lips, Scarlet Lady, Court Martial, Runaway Girls, Streets of Illusion, Sinners' Parade, Driftwood, Stool Pigeon, The Power of the Press, Nothing to Wear, Submarine, The Apache, The Lone Wolf's Daughter, Restless Youth, The Sideshow.

Besides Capra, directors working regularly for Columbia at this time included the veteran director of serials George B. Seitz *(The Perils of Pauline),* and Erle Kenton, another veteran who had been in pictures since 1914. The policy, one guesses, was one of efficient professionalism dedicated to getting the most out of Columbia's meagre resources. Not only did Columbia make fewer films; they also spent less on each production than the major studios. (Few of their films at this time ran more than seventy minutes.) This would seem to leave little room for the carefully considered personal statements of the kind Capra aspired to later in the 1930's. This is not to say that there was no possibility of social or political comment, however, as the history of Warners at the same time shows.

After Capra's astonishing success with *It Happened One Night* in 1934, which won Columbia its first Oscars and enormously increased the studio's prestige, pictures of the earlier type were supplemented by the occasional more expensive production. Though Columbia had contract players of its own (for example Jack Holt, Ralph Bellamy or, in Westerns, Buck Jones and Charles Starrett), they could not compare in box-office appeal with the stars of bigger studios. Columbia could not afford the budgets which having bigger stars would have entailed. On the other hand it could never break into the big time without them. Harry Cohn's solution to this vicious circle was to invite successful directors from other studios to make occasional pictures for Columbia, pictures which would be given larger than usual budgets and which would have stars borrowed from other studios. Careful planning permitted short production schedules and kept costs down to what Columbia could afford. Capra too was given increasingly larger budgets and outside stars. Thus a number of big-name directors came to work at Columbia during the later 1930's, often tempted by the offer of being allowed to produce their own films. Among the titles produced at Columbia during the period after *It Happened One Night* were:

1934: *20th Century* (dir. Howard Hawks, with John Barrymore and Carole Lombard), *The Captain Hates The Sea* (dir. Lewis Milestone, with Victor McLaglen and John Gilbert); 1935: *The Whole Town's Talking* (dir. John Ford, with Edward G. Robinson), *She Married Her Boss* (dir. Gregory La Cava, with Claudette Colbert), *She Couldn't Take It* (dir. Tay Garnett, with George Raft and Joan Bennett), *Crime and Punishment* (dir. Josef von Sternberg, with Peter Lorre); 1936: *Theodora Goes Wild* (dir. Richard Boleslavski, with Irene Dunne); 1937: *The Awful Truth* (dir. Leo McCarey, with Cary Grant and Irene Dunne); 1938: *Holiday* (dir. George Cukor, with Cary Grant and Katherine Hepburn); 1939: *Let Us Live* (dir. John Brahm, with Maureen O'Sullivan and Henry Fonda), *Only Angels Have Wings* (dir. Howard Hawks, with Cary Grant, Thomas Mitchell and Richard Barthelmess), *Golden Boy* (dir. Rouben Mamoulian, with Barbara Stanwyck and Adolphe Menjou); 1940: *His Girl Friday* (dir. Howard Hawks, with Cary Grant and Rosalind Russell), *The Howards of Virginia* (dir. Frank Lloyd, with Cary Grant), *Angels Over Broadway* (dir. Ben Hecht and Lee Garmes, with Douglas Fairbanks Jr.), *Arizona* (dir. Wesley Ruggles, with William Holden); 1941: *Penny Serenade* (dir. George Stevens, with Cary Grant and Irene Dunne), *Texas* (dir. George Marshall, with William Holden, Glenn Ford and Claire Trevor), *You Belong To Me* (dir. Wesley Ruggles, with Barbara Stanwyck and Henry Fonda), *The Men in Her Life* (dir. Gregory Ratoff, with Loretta Young).

But despite this sprinkling of prestige productions the basic recipe remained much the same as before. There were lots of low-budget Westerns (a dozen or so in 1940) directed by Lambert Hillyer, a veteran of the Columbia lot, or Joseph H. Lewis, and starring Bill Elliott or Charles Starrett. The studio made several series: a number of films based on Blondie, the cartoon character, the Lone Wolf series of thrillers, an Ellery Queen mystery series and so on. There were light comedies from Alexander Hall, more light comedies and musicals from Walter Lang, and plenty of crime films (a few titles at random from 1938: *Women in Prison, When G-Men Step In, Penitentiary, Highway Patrol, Reformatory, Convicted, I Am the Law, Juvenile Court, Smashing the Spy Ring*).

What is one to conclude from what emerges of Columbia's production policy in this period? Aware that a viewing of all the films might prove one wrong, it could be said that there is no evidence of Columbia's deliberately following a line favourable to the New Deal. Of course it could be objected that a similar scanning of the titles of Warner Brothers films of the same time would fail to reveal what an actual viewing of the films shows, a detectable if not pronounced leaning towards Rooseveltian attitudes. But this much seems likely: the policy of bringing in outside stars and directors (and writers too) for big-budget productions would have worked against the continuity required for a deliberate political policy. Whereas at Warner Brothers a nucleus of stars, writers, producers and directors was built up capable of producing pictures that fused the thrills of crime with social comment, at Columbia the occasional film (such as *A Man's Castle*, directed by Frank Borzage in 1933) which took the Depression as its subject was a one-off, with the exception of Capra. And it does seem as though Capra *was* an exception. As far as one can tell the directors who did not have his freedom at the studio did not follow him in the direction of social comment, and neither did directors brought in from outside with a similar amount of freedom. And Capra's films, after all, despite his standing within the studio, are only a tiny proportion of all the films Columbia made in the 1930's.

If one can say that the presence of Giannini on the trust controlling Columbia did not lead to films predominantly favourable to the New Deal, then can one not also throw doubt on the assumption that control of a studio by interests favourable to the Republican Party led to films (such as *Young Mr. Lincoln* and *King Kong*) designed to make propaganda for that party? No one would argue that there was a total lack of correlation between ownership and the content of films. No studio in the 1930's would have tolerated outright Communist movies, or anything very close to that. (Nor for that matter would a Fascist film have stood any chance of being made.) But within these parameters considerable diversity was possible, a diversity, moreover, which it is dangerous to reduce by the simple expedient of labelling all the films as bourgeois. The difference in political attitudes between, say, *The Good Earth* (MGM, 1937) and *The Grapes of Wrath* (20th Century-Fox, 1940)—two films with not totally dissimilar subjects—are not negligible and relate to real political and social events of the time. But they cannot be explained simply in terms of who owned the studios or in terms only of social attitudes at the time. Any explanation would require that a number of factors be taken into account, and not least of these would be the exact nature of the institutions which produced them.

The history of the American film industry, then, forms a kind of missing link in attempts, Marxist and otherwise, to make connections between films and society. As we have seen, many of the materials needed to forge that link are missing, which is why the title of this essay, 'Notes on Columbia Pictures Corporation 1926–1941', is intended to imply more than the customary academic modesty. The problems of producing such a history are both practical and the result of a massive ideological prejudice, and I am aware that the information I have produced on Columbia in the 1930's amounts to very little in the way of real knowledge. But this information has been the result of a few hours in the library, not of a large-scale research programme. If one considers how much has been learned, for example, about British labour history in the nineteenth century the possibilities for further research do not seem hopeless. As a subject it would appear equally as unpromising as the history of the film industry. Apart from newspapers there are few written sources and the people involved are all dead. The history therefore has to a great extent to be reconstructed from the material objects which survive: buildings, institutional structures, the customs and practices of a people. But full-time academics and research students have been working in the field for years. The study of the history of the American film industry has scarcely begun.

WRITING THE HISTORY OF THE AMERICAN FILM INDUSTRY: WARNER BROTHERS AND SOUND

DOUGLAS GOMERY

Taking up the challenge issued by Edward Buscombe in the preceding article, Douglas Gomery begins by reminding us of the sources of data that scores of film scholars have ignored over the decades: court records, hearings of federal regulatory agencies, studio archives now on deposit, and, for some topics, local and municipal records. Gomery then shows how these sources of evidence give us a radically different picture of the coming of sound. Instead of being forced by impending bankruptcy to try sound, Warner Brothers appears to have embarked on a farsighted policy of expansion. The exploitation of talking pictures was not an act of desperation but part and parcel of a strategy designed to strengthen Warners' position in the film industry. As Gomery says, the bankruptcy that scholars have cited since the 1930s may well have been simply a case of well-financed, well-planned short-run indebtedness.

The way in which Gomery makes his point is as important as the point itself. Gomery shows clearly how previously unused sources can be brought into play. For that reason, his footnotes are as instructive as his main argument. Gomery also asks how this revision would affect theories about the relation between technology and ideology that such writers as Jean-Louis Comolli propose. He does not answer this question, but it seems reasonable to suppose that the effect will be slight. Gomery's historical revisionism dwells exclusively on the film industry as a facet of American business. Edward Buscombe's article points to the hazards in tying the history of a whole industry to the ideology or ideological effect of a particular film, even a particular group of films. There appears to be considerable latitude between what those in the industry do to secure a profitable market position and the ideological operations and effects of the industry's products. Clearly, the two are related; few film critics or historians would deny that. However, that the financial strategies and maneuvers of a single company give us an insight into the ideology of sound still needs to be demonstrated. The absence of any direct correspondence, however, does not detract from Gomery's exemplary investigation into the history of the American film industry.

•

I

Edward Buscombe raises important questions concerning film analysis, ideology and economics in his article, 'Notes on Columbia Pictures Corporation 1926–41' (*Screen* 16 no. 3 [Autumn 1975]: 65–82). It is indeed regrettable that critics must base ideological criticism of American films on problematic histories of the American film industry, such as Lewis Jacobs's *The Rise of the American Film,* or 'pop' biographies like Bosley Crowther's *Hollywood Rajah.* Yet Buscombe gives the wrong reason for this lack of industrial history. The problem is *not* the non-existence of data, it is one of theory and methodology. Buscombe reveals his own bibliographical limitations in citing a lack of primary documents. For example, from 1940 to 1960 American economists interested in anti-trust issues directed their energies toward the mounds of data unearthed in the court proceedings leading to the United States Supreme Court decision, *United States* v. *Paramount Pictures et al.,* 334 US 131 (1948). Conant's admirable book, *Antitrust in the Motion Picture Industry,* lists over 175 separate court decisions, and more than a dozen governmental investigations of the industry on this one topic alone. All are part of the public record. Only Conant and his fellow economists have ever probed this mountain of data. Historians of the American film industry have chosen thus far to ignore it. Moreover court records, and other data generated by numerous private and governmental agencies, exist for all periods and topics in the history of the American film industry. We must not simply trust the old bibliographies or faulty recollections, but go out and seek the evidence wherever it may be.

The more difficult undertaking is the creation of a theory and method for writing the history of any film industry. Certain film scholars, notably Thierry Kuntzel, have suggested that this task be left to economists (*Screen* 14 no. 3 [Autumn 1973]: 44). True, economists have developed a powerful set of tools for analysis. But film historians should and must ask different questions. Economists, typically, pose the problem in the most general terms. They test their hypotheses, and slowly add parts to their total theoretical framework. For example, their interest in *United States* v. *Paramount Pictures et al.* is *not* in motion picture history, but rather how the industry responded to a most unusual remedy set forth by the United States Supreme Court (see A.D. Neale: *The Anti-Trust Laws of the United States of America,* Cambridge 1970, pp. 84–85, 166–70 and 404–7). Film historians would ask a different set of questions, looking toward the formation of a closed set of generalisations concerning cultural artifacts created in the past. The history of any film industry ranges over a limited set of economic phenomena, but an almost infinite set of socio-cultural phenomena. Here the court *records,* not the effects of its decisions, are of greater concern. They provide data about the structure and conduct of the industry in question, the primary documents so vital to the writing of any history. Simply put, the writing of the history of any film industry is too important, too wide-ranging and too synthetic to be left to economists.

In the past, historians of the American film industry have not even followed the most basic practices of the field. Few explain the basic methodologies they employ. More surprisingly, almost as few cite their sources. Footnotes by film historians are rare items. No other brand of history is so casual in violating this basic attribute of scholarship. Edward Buscombe himself falls into this trap. Except for two internal citations, one with no page given, his 12-page history of Columbia Pictures is note free. One must only wonder how he created his historical passages concerning the rise of this firm in the 1920's. A cursory examination of Bob Thomas's 'pop' biography, *King Cohn,* seems to reveal his source. Is Buscombe just recycling the very myths he asks us to question? Without footnotes, or even a bibliography, the reader can never know.

II

In relation to these problems I should like to confront a conclusion in the history of the American film industry now accepted almost as gospel: Warner Brothers' impending bankruptcy caused its innovation of sound. Numerous writers of the history of the American film industry have set forth this claim. Lewis Jacobs in his *The Rise of the American Film* (New York 1939, p. 297) writes:

On August 26, 1926 [sic], Warner Brothers, in a desperate effort to ward off bankruptcy, premiered a novelty, the first motion picture with sound accompaniment, *Don Juan.*[1]

Textbook author Gerald Mast repeats the same assertion using slightly different language (*A Short History of the Movies,* Indianapolis 1971, p. 227):

Western Electric offered Vitaphone in 1926 to Warner Brothers, a family of struggling film producers whose company was near bankruptcy. The Warners had nothing to lose.

Elsewhere Kenneth MacGowan, David Robinson, Laurence Kardish, Peter Cowie, Kevin Brownlow, Jean Mitry and Georges Sadoul echo this conclusion.[2]

Other writers, coming after Jacobs's standard work, were not so bold. Some, like Arthur Knight, A. R. Fulton and Henri Mercillon, ignore the issue of motivation.[3] Presto! Warner Brothers adopted the new technology. Other accounts are a little more expansive, containing a sentence or two. Benjamin Hampton and Charles Higham (twice) credit Warner Brothers' desire for more theatres, D. J. Wenden the overall industry structure, and Robert Sklar the industry's costly movie palaces.[4] Harry M. Geduld provides the longest account of the coming of sound in *The Birth of the Talkies* (New York 1975). Yet he avoids, and thereby complicates this issue. For Geduld Warner Brothers first learned about sound because of an investment in radio. It then, for no apparent reason, adopted sound. Bankruptcy almost resulted when Warner Brothers overcommitted itself in this one area (pp. 107–8, 113). Nowhere does Geduld explain why Warner Brothers chose to gamble all its assets on an idea and system all its richer competitors had rejected, or how it financed all this new investment.

Warner Brothers' published financial statements seem to support the Jacobs-inspired, traditional version. Using the data in Table I, a narrative could be constructed in the following fashion: the company was losing large amounts of money, when about March 1926, it presumably decided to risk all on sound. Despite the mild success of *Don Juan,* the losses continued, albeit at a somewhat slower pace. But it was *The Jazz Singer* and its subsequent revenues in the beginning of 1928 which saved the company. Bankruptcy was averted; the turnabout was complete.

The 'bankruptcy hypothesis' is so well accepted that at least two scholars have employed it as a basis for their analysis of film and ideology. In 'The Movie Jew as

Table 1 WARNER BROS. PICTURES, INC.: NET PROFIT AND LOSS

FISCAL YEAR ENDING	PROFIT (LOSS)
	$
March 31, 1924	103,000
March 31, 1925	1,102,000
March 27, 1926	(1,338,000)
August 28, 1926 (5 months)	(279,000)*
August 27, 1927	30,000
August 31, 1928	2,045,000
August 31, 1929	14,514,000

*A $669,000 loss at an annual rate.

Source: Warner Bros. Pictures, Inc. A *Financial Review and Brief History: 1923–1945* (New York: privately printed, 1946), p. 28.

an Image of Assimilationism, 1903–1927,' *Journal of Popular Film* 4 no. 3 (1975): 190–207, Thomas Cripps writes:

Warner Brothers, a studio of modest proportions and in straitened circumstances, saw 'talking film' as a gimmick that would attract revenue, while Al Jolson, a Broadway song-and-dance man, gambled on sound as a way to score a point on his rival, George Jessel. For the vehicle that would either carry Hollywood into the sound era or destroy both Jolson's career and the studio, they chose Samson Raphaelson's *The Jazz Singer* (1927).

Even as sophisticated an analyst of film and ideology as Jean-Louis Comolli accepts the traditional explanation. In 'Technique et idéologie (5): Caméra, perspective, profondeur de champ, *Cahiers du Cinéma,* nos. 234–235 (December–February 1971–1972), pp. 99–100, he writes:

It was necessary that Warner Brothers, a small company almost on the edge of bankruptcy, and which had nothing to lose, try its luck; the risk was, in August, 1926, the release and success of *Don Juan,* 'the first sound and singing film'.

Comolli goes on to conclude from this and other evidence that for the coming of sound technological change was not the moving force, but rather the effect of the specific ideological functions served by the entrepreneurs of the American film industry. How much is Comolli's conclusion tied to this historical construct? Would it still hold if Warner Brothers was *not* bankrupt?

III

Several factors can be isolated that are important for analysing any technological change. The innovating firm must, directed by its entrepreneurs, raise the necessary capital and devise a strategy to crack the market held by its competitors. Hence the innovator's situation vis-à-vis its competitors and the state of the business cycle must not be ignored. For Warner Brothers' innovation of sound, every account of these factors has remained mere speculation, or has been sketched out only in the most superficial detail. Yet rich primary data does exist with which one can begin to answer these questions. During the 1930's Warner

Brothers and its principal licensor of sound equipment, Electrical Research Products, Inc. (ERPI), a wholly-owned subsidiary of the American Telephone and Telegraph Company (AT&T), tangled in three major patent and contractual suits.[5] Secondly, in 1937 the United States Congress investigated AT&T's operations in non-telephone areas, including sound motion pictures. This probe produced several file drawers full of testimony, confidential memoranda, and almost all of ERPI's financial records.[6] Finally motion picture trade publications, such as *Variety* and *Moving Picture World,* and general business publications like *Barrons* also charted the film industry's activities in the late 1920's. With these as yet unused sources, one can begin to revise the standard histories of the introduction of sound outlined above.

For Warner Brothers one man secured the financial backing and provided much of the necessary business acumen. He was Waddill Catchings, the chief investment banker of Wall Street's Goldman, Sachs Company. A Mississippi-born graduate of the Harvard Law School, Catchings joined Goldman, Sachs in 1918. Not only an investment banker, he also authored treatises on economic problems. With William T. Foster he organised the Pollack Foundation for Economic Research in 1921, and co-authored two books during the 1920's on economic problems: *Business Without a Buyer* in 1926 and *The Road to Plenty* in 1928. Central to Catchings's economic theory was the necessity for the businessman-entrepreneur to take bold action. Only this behavior, coupled with an adequate money supply, could ensure prosperity and eliminate severe depressions such as had occurred in 1920–1. Catchings demonstrated his faith in this principle in his investment work at Goldman, Sachs; during the boom of the 1920's he was the most optimistic of all the 'New Era' financiers.[7]

Warner Brothers first came to Catchings's attention in December 1924. Henry A. Rudkin, senior partner of McClure, Jones and Reed, another New York investment house, advised Catchings that Warner Brothers sought to expand and needed Wall Street help. McClure, Jones and Reed was too small to provide large-scale assistance. Was Goldman, Sachs interested? This seemed an extremely risky proposition even to Catchings. Up to this point, Wall Street had done little large-scale financing of motion picture firms, with the exception of Famous Players. On at least two prior occasions even the risk-loving Catchings had refused to issue securities for motion picture corporations; he deemed none stable enough for Goldman, Sachs support. Moreover, Catchings had never even heard of Warner Brothers. Nevertheless on Rudkin's recommendation he undertook the usual routine investigation as to the credit standing and expected economic future of Warner Brothers.[8]

Several aspects of the Warner Brothers' operation impressed Catchings. One was its strict control of production budgets. Goldman, Sachs had never previously been sufficiently confident to finance motion picture concerns because it had received no guarantee that their production departments could set limits for the cost of films. Warner Brothers' rigid cost-accounting procedures, especially the day-to-day audits by production manager Jack Warner, set Warner Brothers apart from the other firms he had considered. He also learned Warner Brothers used extremely economical methods in building their studio lot and acquiring props. Catchings agreed to finance Warner Brothers, but *only* if it would allow him to dictate a master plan for long-term growth. Catchings had helped build up other companies. Both Woolworths and Sears-Roebuck had associated themselves with Goldman, Sachs as small, regional businesses and with its backing had grown into large, national corporations. Only with this long-term control could Catchings interest important banks in generating the necessary capital.[9]

Both Catchings and Warner Brothers' president, Harry Warner, knew that financing was the first and most important part of the company's operations that Goldman, Sachs, or any investment house must change.[10] During its short existence Warner Brothers had used two methods to obtain capital for film production. For a limited number of films Harry Warner would approach a rich individual and trade an interest in the profits of a film for a contribution to its backing. Warner Brothers had to pay extremely high interest rates, sometimes as high as 100 percent, for these loans. The more frequent method was the 'franchise system', under which Warner Brothers divided the United States and Canada into twenty-eight zones and secured one franchise holder per zone, usually a major exhibitor. It would then obtain from each backer an advance toward a set number of films to be repaid with a percentage of the expected profits. The franchise holder in turn would then distribute the film within his exclusive territory. Warner Brothers would pay extraordinary fees for these required advances. For the typical film, each of the twenty-eight backers would contribute several thousand dollars. For this, in most cases, Warner Brothers returned double (and sometimes more) the original amount. Thus the effective interest rate was greater than 100 percent. Catchings was sure he could procure cheaper rates. Moreover Warner Brothers also lacked a distribution network to reap the significant advantages of economies of scale, a theatre circuit, and the publicity machinery to differentiate its films from those of other independent producers.[11]

Negotiations between Catchings and Harry Warner commenced in January 1925. One month later, upon hearing that Warner Brothers was trying to make a deal with Goldman, Sachs, the franchise holders rebelled. Normally unorganized, they appointed a committee to meet with Harry Warner. They were afraid that Warner Brothers would try to terminate what had been an extraordinarily profitable relationship. At this point Harry Warner pursued an alternative. He knew that Vitagraph, a pioneer motion picture producer with an international distribution network of fifty exchanges, was in severe financial difficulty. Its operations had generated extremely large losses for each of the past five years. Harry went directly to Vitagraph's president, Albert E. Smith, and offered to buy the corporation. Smith's most immediate problem was paying off $980,000 of current liabilities. Harry Warner offered to take over these debts, and purchase the shares of Smith, J. Stuart Blackton and the estate of William T. Rock for $800,000. Warner Brothers would then possess majority control (*Variety*, February 4, 1925, p. 23).

Harry Warner closed the deal in March 1925, and announced it to the surprised franchise holders in April 1925. Warner Brothers now had twenty-six exchanges in the United States, four in Canada, ten in England and ten in Continental Europe. It also acquired one studio in Brooklyn, New York, another in Hollywood, a large laboratory, a film library, real estate and story rights. This takeover was the first move in Warner Brothers' gamble to break the bind of the franchise holders and move up in importance in the industry. It was also the last financial maneuver done without the direct approval of Waddill Catchings. Its daring captured Catchings's imagination and he agreed to finance Warner Brothers' future operations. In March 1925, Goldman, Sachs and McClure, Jones and Reed underwrote 170,000 new shares of Warner Brothers stock to finance the Vitagraph deal. In May, Catchings joined the Warner Brothers board of directors and was named chairman of the board's finance committee.[12]

Immediately Catchings set out to obtain the necessary permanent financing for production. After much effort he established a revolving credit line of $3,000,000 at 5 percent interest. To secure such a sizeable loan Catchings went right to the top of the American banking fraternity. The leading commercial bank in the United States at the time was the National Bank of Commerce in New York; it had never granted a loan to *any* motion picture company. Catchings managed to persuade board chairman, James S. Alexander, at least to study the matter. The National Bank of Commerce completed an extremely thorough study and decided to make an exception with Warner Brothers. Alexander added an extra 1 percent call-charge to the normal 5 percent demanded of its best customers. This charge would accrue even if the account were never used. Having persuaded the National Bank of Commerce, Catchings then approached the Colony Trust Company of Boston. Again he achieved success. With agreement from these two conservative giants, four other large banks easily fell into line. Pooling the loans, the revolving credit was established. Catchings had solved the short-term crisis for funding production.[13]

He next turned his attention to acquiring funds for capital expansion. He and Harry decided Warner Brothers needed more exchanges, first-run theatres, better promotion and the remodelling of existing production facilities. In the fall of 1925 Catchings orchestrated a $4,000,000 three-year, 6½ percent debenture. Warner Brothers expanded in the required directions. It acquired ten medium-sized first-run theatres in cities including Seattle, Baltimore, Cleveland, and Pittsburgh. These theatres became the nucleus of its new chain with Sam Warner in charge. Warner Brothers also leased first-run theatres in key locations, beginning with an eleven-year commitment to the Orpheum in Chicago's Loop.[14] The only available Broadway theatre was the Piccadilly; this Warner Brothers purchased for $800,000, and immediately re-named the Warners'. Unfortunately it was the smallest major theatre in the Broadway area, seating only 1,500. Warner Brothers began planning its biggest theatre: the 3,600-seat, $2,000,000 Warners' in Hollywood. Moreover it signed an agreement with Alexander Pantages to use his vaudeville artists as presentation acts in its new theatres. In the second area, Warners opened eight new distribution exchanges in the United States and Canada to provide a complement equal to Famous Players. It added twenty-one new exchanges in South America and the Far East. The return was immediate. Sales throughout the world helped offset some of its new investments. Warner Brothers also added $250,000 in improvements to Vitagraph's Hollywood studio (see *Variety*, August 12, 1925, p. 23; December 2, 1925, p. 36; December 16, 1925, p. 7).

Catchings and Harry Warner set their sights on the top. In July 1925, Warner Brothers opened a $500,000 national advertising campaign in the major general-interest magazines and selected newspapers, including a special coordinated blitz through the Hearst newspapers.[15] Catchings and Harry Warner wanted the Warner Brothers name to become as well known as Famous Players or First National. In July 1925, Catchings even bid $8,500,000 to take over Universal. Carl Laemmle wanted $10,000,000. Catchings considered this a reasonable price. However, Laemmle and Robert Cochrane would not let Catchings's accountants examine Universal's books. Without this information to convince bankers, Catchings called off the deal. This was Catchings's first attempt at a merger, but not his last. Ultimate success would come with the takeover of First National itself in October 1928 (*Variety,* July 15, 1925, p. 26; October 28, 1925, p. 27).

As a final expansionist move towards acquiring more publicity, Warner Brothers sought to buy a radio station. Sam Warner was fascinated with the new technological improvements in radio that seemed to appear almost daily. He and Warner Brothers chief electrician, Frank N. Murphy, coordinated the purchase of the necessary equipment to set up a station. KFWB opened in the spring of 1925. Warner Brothers was the second motion picture producer with a station, and the only one in Hollywood. KFWB openly copied the publicity methods of the then nationally popular radio master-of-ceremonies and theatre entrepreneur, Samuel Rothafel (Roxy). Harry Warner even advised the Motion Pictures Producers and Distributors Association to establish a station for the whole industry (*Moving Picture World,* February 21, 1925, p. 769; March 21, 1925, p. 286; April 11, 1925, p. 592).

It was as an outgrowth of these radio dealings that Sam Warner, through Western Electric salesman Nathan Levinson, became interested in Western Electric's newly developed sound (on-disc) system. Together they convinced Harry to see a demonstration in the early part of May 1925. However they did not tell him the nature of the films because, as Harry later recalled (*General Talking Pictures,* 18 F. Supp. 650, Record, p. 1108):

if [they] had said talking picture, I never would have gone, because [talking pictures] had been made up to that time several times, and each was a failure. I am positive if [they] said talking picture, I would not [have] gone.

Nevertheless Harry went. In a small screening room he first saw a man speaking. Next a five-piece jazz orchestra appeared on the screen. Harry became interested. His companion, Sidney J. Weinberg, Catchings's assistant, was ecstatic. Spurred on by the banker's enthusiasm, Harry conceived of an idea of how to use this new invention. He later remarked to Catchings: 'If it can talk, it can sing.' Warner Brothers could record the greatest vaudeville and musical acts and present them in small- to medium-sized theatres. This would provide for these theatres presentations equal to, or better than, those currently available, at a much lower cost. It was an entrepreneurial vision that would require the large amounts of financing only Catchings could provide.[16]

In June 1925, Warner Brothers signed a contract with Western Electric, and its representative, Walter J. Rich, to produce vaudeville shorts experimentally. Slowly the two parties cooperated on the problems of production, and jockeyed for the best market position vis-à-vis Famous Players, Loews and First National. The *Don Juan* show was the product of the year-long production effort. Contractual complications arose on the financial side. Warner Brothers signed two sets of agreements with Western Electric—one in April 1926 and a second in May 1927. Constant negotiations stalled any major thrust into the market. Slowly Harry carried out and perfected his strategy of 'vaudeville shorts'. Success would come in the first part of 1928 when these shorts, *The Jazz Singer* and the new part-talkies would begin to generate revenues commensurate with the $3,000,000 investment Warner Brothers had accumulated in three years, most of it during the first year.[17]

Although the investment in sound in 1925 and 1926 was sizeable, it represented only one-fifth of Warner Brothers' increase in assets. The other phases of its growth continued. Warner Brothers even began to experience some return on these investments. Ernest Lubitsch's *Lady Windemere's Fan* established box-office records on its debut in January 1926 at the Warners' theatre in New York City; crowds had to be turned away. Lubitsch, guaranteed at least $150,000 per year, was Warner Brothers' top director (*Moving Picture World,* January 9, 1926, p. 161; *Variety,* April 14, 1926, p. 23). In February 1926, *The Sea Beast* with John Barrymore also proved to be exceptionally popular. In an attempt to duplicate the successful 'road-show' strategy of the 'Big Three', Warner Brothers even worked out a deal with legitimate theatres to showcase the film at two dollars top admission. In April 1926, at its first sales convention (of three) Harry Warner announced twenty-six features for the 1926–27 season, sixteen less than the previous season. However these twenty-six 'Warner Winners' would cost more than the previous year's forty-two features. In addition he announced nine new 'road-show' specials, including John Barrymore in *Don Juan* and *Manon Lescaut* and Syd Chaplin in *The Better 'Ole*.[18] Moreover Harry had just signed George Jessel to duplicate his popular role of *The Jazz Singer*. Waddill Catchings, in the closing address to this April convention, praised Warner Brothers for its solid advance during the past year, and predicted a bright future with greater potential than any other firm in the industry.[19]

Warner Brothers had extended itself in still other areas in the first half of 1926. It opened its second radio station, WBPI, in New York City. Headquartered at the Warners' theatre, and under the direction of Sam Warner, it generally employed vaudeville talent currently at the theatre (*Moving Picture World,* January 16, 1926, p. 220). On May 4, Sam Warner launched a transcontinental tour of a 'radio station'. Controlled by KFWB, Frank Murphy and his crew could set up the portable station in twenty minutes at any theatre using a Warner Brothers' film. It would then broadcast the stage show, sponsor contests and generally create publicity for Warner Brothers pictures and exchanges. The 'station' toured throughout the summer months. Sam also oversaw yet another new aspect of Warner Brothers operations. In April 1926, Warner Brothers re-equipped Vitagraph's Brooklyn laboratory with modern apparatus; it had a capacity to process four million feet per week. Warners also expanded into foreign production by closing a deal to co-produce ten films with the Bruckman Film Company of Germany.[20]

With all this capital outlay, it was not unexpected that the yearly financial state-ment, issued in March 1926, stood in the red. The loss was large, $1,338,000, but the company had more than doubled its asset base. It now possessed an interna-tional distribution network, owned a growing chain of theatres, and was producing higher-priced films. Moreover it had the support of the nation's best banks in its climb toward the top of the industry (*Moving Picture World,* May 1, 1926, p. 2; July 10, 1926, p. 88; *Variety,* June 30, 1926, p. 49). By August 1927, revenues had grown sufficiently to cut its rate of loss in half. Foreign operations had become quite lucra-tive. Rentals in Great Britain improved substantially even in 1926, and would grow by more than $2,000,000 for the fiscal year ending August 31, 1927. Yet Catchings and Harry Warner continued to invest, especially in higher-priced pictures. By August 1927, despite having tripled its asset base in two years, Warner Brothers had turned the corner and even registered a small profit. The gigantic success of sound motion pictures, built on the solid base of earlier investments, would turn potential long-run gain into immediate rewards in 1928.[21]

Throughout this period Catchings continued to secure the necessary finance. As soon as the Vitaphone operations began to demand larger amounts of credit, Catchings was commensurate to the task. The initial Vitaphone contract called for a $500,000 investment; by February 1927, Warner Brothers had accumulated over $3,000,000 in assets. To obtain this capital, Catchings kept refinancing the revolving credit of $3,000,000. Catchings continued his persuasive cajoling; the bankers remained cooperative. In fact in August 1926, the Central Union Trust Company of New York agreed not even to notify Warner Brothers' creditors of their pledged accounts receivable when it extended Warner Brothers a new loan for $1,000,000. In September 1926, he secured yet another $1,000,000 from S. W. Strauss and Co.; Harry Warner used this to improve the former Vitagraph studio in Hollywood. Catchings would continue this adroit financing until 1930. By then Warner Brothers' asset base had grown from slightly more than $5,000,000 in 1925 to $230,000,000, a 4,600 percent increase in five years.[22]

IV

Several specific and general conclusions emerge from this short history. In terms of the question posed concerning the cause of Warner Brothers' innova-tion of sound, the firm was never 'near bankruptcy'. In its early years it was a profitable operation, but one that could only become more profitable with a size-able expansion in several important areas. To effect this growth, Waddill Catch-ings and Harry Warner secured funds for production, distribution, exhibition and promotion. These investments created short-term losses. In fact it was simply a case of well-financed, well-planned short-run indebtedness. Moreover Catchings had the support of America's most important banks throughout this period of expansion. And sound was only one part, albeit a very risky one, of the invest-ment surge. It succeeded only because the early expansion had created the neces-sary structural base.

Warner Brothers' expansionary activities in the boom of the mid-1920's were part of a plan to move it up in the industry. At the time the industry's Big Three, Famous Players, Loews and First National, dominated the industry. Fox, Film Booking Office (FBO), Universal, Pathé-Producers Distributing Corporation, and Warner Brothers composed a second tier. Fox and Warner Brothers would, and did, successfully challenge the Big Three. In fact, Warner Brothers was so successful it acquired First National in 1928. FBO and Pathé-PDC would become the basis of Radio-Keith-Orpheum. Universal was too conservative and fell in importance to join United Artists, a special case, and the only independent of the 1920's to emerge as an important firm, Columbia. The other independent producers of the 1920's either went out of business or became an almost insignificant part of the market.

On a larger scale this account of Warner Brothers' expansion is only one example of a possible revisionist history of the American film industry. For the bankruptcy question, *a priori* one would begin to challenge the usual conclusion, as well as the terms in which that explanation is written. Other areas should be subjected to similar probes. But we must be careful. We must create our first principles, and methods. We must examine the accepted notions of bias and cause, and begin to search out new sources of primary data. Only then can the type of history of the American film industry emerge that Buscombe demands, and Cripps, Comolli and other film-and-ideology analysts so vitally need.

Notes

1. The premiere took place on August 6, 1926; see *Variety,* August 11, 1926, pp. 4, 5 and 10.

2. Kenneth MacGowan, *Behind the Screen,* New York, 1965, p. 283; David Robinson, *The History of World Cinema,* New York, 1973, p. 162; Peter Cowie, ed., *A Concise History of the Movies,* New York, 1972, p. 197; Laurence Kardish, *Reel Plastic Magic,* New York, 1972, p. 103; Kevin Brownlow, *The Parade's Gone By,* New York, 1968, p. 657; Jean Mitry, *Histoire du cinéma,* Paris, 1964, vol. 2, pp. 353–54; Georges Sadoul, *Histoire du cinéma mondial,* Paris, 1949, p. 228.

3. A. R. Fulton, *Motion Pictures,* Norman, Okla., 1960, p. 155; Arthur Knight, *The Liveliest Art,* New York, 1957, p. 146; Henri Mercillon, *Cinéma et monopoles*, Paris, 1953, p. 18.

4. Robert Sklar, *Movie-Made America,* New York, 1975, p. 152; D. J. Wendon, *The Birth of the Movies,* New York, 1975, p. 173; Charles Higham, *The Art of the American Cinema,* New York, 1974, p. 85; Charles Higham, *Warner Brothers,* New York, 1975, p. 41; Benjamin B. Hampton, *History of the American Film Industry,* New York, 1931, pp. 379 and 381.

5. *General Talking Pictures Corporation et al.* v. *American Telephone and Telegraph Company et al.,* 18 F. Supp. 650 (1937); *Electrical Research Products, Inc.* v. *Vitaphone Corporation,* 171 A. 738 (1934); *Koplar (Scharaf et al., Interveners)* v. *Warner Bros Pictures, Inc. et al.,* 19 F. Supp. 173 (1937).

6. U.S. Federal Communications Commission, *Staff Report on Electrical Research Products, Inc.*, Vols. I, II and III (Pursuant to Public Resolution No. 8, 74th Congress, 1937).

7. Arthur M. Schlesinger, Jr., *The Crisis of the Old Order,* Boston, 1956, pp. 134–36; William T. Foster and Waddill Catchings, *The Road to Plenty,* New York, 1928, pp. 84–93;

"Warner Brothers Pictures," *Fortune,* December 1937, p. 98; *Koplar,* 19 F. Supp. 173, Record, pp. 279–83 (Waddill Catchings's direct testimony; the case concerns a stockholder's suit against the Warner brothers for manipulation of stock prices at the expense of other stockholders, and the testimony cited here was background to the crucial facts disputed in the case).

8. *Koplar,* 19 F. Supp. 173, Record, pp. 283–85 (Catchings's direct testimony), pp. 1100–1101 (Harry Warner's direct testimony).

9. *Koplar,* 19 F. Supp. 173, Record, pp. 320–24 (Catchings's direct testimony), pp. 1106–7 (Harry Warner's direct testimony); *Electrical Research Products, Inc.* v. *Vitaphone Corporation,* 171 A. 738 (1934), Affidavit of Waddill Catchings, pp. 1–2.

10. The four Warner brothers had a clean division of labour regarding their motion picture firm at this time. Harry, the eldest, was chief operating and financial officer, Abe ran the distribution branch, Sam the technical and exhibition activities and Jack the production.

11. *Koplar,* 19 F. Supp. 173, Record, pp. 320–24 (Catchings's direct testimony); *Motion Picture News,* April 4, 1925, p. 1409; February 7, 1925, p. 557.

12. *Moving Picture World,* May 2, 1925, p. 25; *Motion Picture News,* May 2, 1925, p. 1925; May 2, 1929, p. 2020; *Koplar,* 19 F. Supp. 173, Record, pp. 330, 1101–11.

13. *Koplar,* 19 F. Supp. 173, Record, pp. 353–63 (Catchings's direct testimony); John Sherman Porter, ed., *Moody's Manual of Industrials 1925,* New York, 1926, pp. 1899–1900.

14. *Moving Picture World,* September 5, 1925, p. 74; *Variety,* August 26, 1925, p. 21; September 23, 1925, p. 36; July 5, 1925, p. 21; *Koplar,* 19 F. Supp. 173, Record, pp. 390–400 (Catchings's direct testimony).

15. *Variety,* June 10, 1925, p. 30; *Moving Picture World,* August 1, 1925, p. 550; *Variety,* September 23, 1925, p. 36; *Moving Picture World,* June 13, 1925, p. 769; *Variety,* April 1, 1925, p. 27; April 8, 1925, p. 29.

16. *Koplar,* 19 F. Supp. 173, Record, pp. 366–68 (Catchings's direct testimony), p. 1101 (Harry Warner's direct testimony). For a similar, less detailed account, see Joseph P. Kennedy, ed., *The Story of the Films as Told by the Leaders of the Industry,* New York, 1927, pp. 320–22.

17. The innovation of Vitaphone by Warner Brothers and the reaction of Fox and the rest of the film industry are described in the author's Ph.D. dissertation, *The Coming of Sound to the American Cinema: A History of the Transformation of an Industry,* University of Wisconsin–Madison, 1975, pp. 110–253.

18. *Variety,* February 24, 1926, p. 24; *Moving Picture World,* May 8, 1926; May 15, 1926, pp. 212–13; *Variety,* January 30, 1926, p. 446; *Moving Picture World,* May 8, 1926, p. 116.

19. *Moving Picture World,* May 1, 1926, p. 44; April 24, 1926, p. 582; Warner Brothers Pictures, Inc., *A Financial Review and Brief History,* New York, 1946 (privately printed), p. 30.

20. *Moving Picture World,* May 1, 1926, p. 2; May 15, 1926, p. 226; September 18, 1926, p. 173; April 17, 1926, p. 2; March 20, 1926, p. 4.

21. *Moving Picture World,* March 5, 1927, p. 18; *Electrical Research Products,* 171 A. 738, Plea, Exhibit D, p. 335.

22. *Koplar,* 19 F. Supp. 173, Record, pp. 455–59, 479, and 560–65 (Catchings's direct testimony); John Sherman Porter, ed., *Moody's Manual of Industrials 1927,* New York, 1928, pp. 385–86; *Variety,* September 1, 1926, p. 5; November 24, 1926, p. 10.

COLOR AND CINEMA: PROBLEMS IN THE WRITING OF HISTORY

EDWARD BRANIGAN

Branigan's 1979 article is an excellent model of practical historiography. Rather than discussing the general principles that can be used to organize history, Branigan examines four particular examples of film history writing in order to compare and contrast their assumptions and procedures. (Comolli's, Ogle's, and Gomery's articles are included here; the fourth is Terry Ramsaye's A Million and One Nights. *) But what makes Branigan's essay even more valuable is that he extrapolates governing principles from the texts he examines and applies them to a new, common topic: the history of color cinematography. In this way, not only do the differences in methodology of the original texts become apparent, but the way in which they might govern each author's approach to another set of "facts" is also illuminated.*

Although Branigan does not emphasize it, his analysis also points out how each of the four authors chooses somewhat different sources for his information. Ramsaye's facts derive largely from biography or autobiography and tend toward the anecdotal. Patrick Ogle relies on technical trade journals and, to a lesser degree, on the comments of cinematographers. Douglas Gomery goes to corporate records, economic journals and newspapers, and court records involving film industry firms. Comolli depends heavily on Marxist theories of culture, art, and ideology to reread and challenge the claims of previous film histories. He places less emphasis on independent research than the other authors, and he, like Branigan, pays careful attention to the use of these sources in a construction of history. Thus, Comolli's primary sources are less historical than they are theoretical.

Each of these four perspectives generates a different history and a different view of what constitutes history. Branigan's comparative method could be used to examine other writers, like Edward Buscombe, Barry Salt, and Janet Staiger, who are represented here. If Branigan sometimes makes assertions that other authors would dispute (for example, that color enhances the reality effect —a view quite different from Buscombe's), he nonetheless demonstrates how much can be learned about other writers' approaches by comparing them one with another. If it is correct to say that a firm conception of previous film history is necessary for the construction of new historiographic models, then the work that Branigan carries out here is not only a helpful summary and dissection of other texts but also a prolegomenon to film histories yet to come.

•

I wish to examine the subject of color, and more specifically, the early history of color in cinema. Underlying this subject, however, is a more important issue and my major concern: the different ways in which that early history of color *has* been told or *might* be told. It should be emphasized at the outset that my purpose is not to work toward an eclecticism or pluralism where the history of color becomes the sum of all the histories of color, or all the methods of writing that history. Such a history is really only *one* more history, and a peculiarly indigestible one at that. Of much greater interest to me are the different *ways of seeing* the history of color. What forces and events are singled out by a given historian as "significant" and how are they arranged into a narrative of time? In this manner I hope to expose the assumptions (framework, theory) which a historian uses to generate a history—all of which is normally obscured beneath apparently neutral and unassuming titles, such as "The Development of Colour Cinematography"[1] or "Refinements in Technique."[2] I take this "history of histories" approach because I'm convinced that one cannot write about the history of color without a particular conception of that history.

In a practical sense, a conception of history depends upon a set of categories which are used to analyze (break up, articulate) the world. Michel Foucault, in a preface to his history of sixteenth- and seventeenth-century European science, discusses the following passage from a Borges story which, in turn, quotes a "certain Chinese encyclopaedia." In this encyclopaedia it is written that

animals are divided into: (a) belonging to the Emperor, (b) embalmed, (c) tame, (d) sucking pigs, (e) sirens, (f) fabulous, (g) stray dogs, (h) included in the present classification, (i) frenzied, (j) innumerable, (k) drawn with a very fine camelhair brush, (l) *et cetera,* (m) having just broken the water pitcher, (n) that from a long way off look like flies.[3]

What is important for us in this passage is the recognition that categories arranged in a scheme are not just a way of looking at the world but in some sense determine[4] *what we see.* The world is not out there holding a secret which at best has already been recorded in an encyclopedia and at worst remains to be discovered by the persistent and perceptive analyst. Instead the world is constructed by the analyst in the act of analyzing. Analysis proceeds via a set of categories which are selected—consciously or unconsciously—to suit a particular purpose.

I will now examine four types of histories of color which might be constructed from the perspectives of (what I will term) adventure, technology, industrial management, and ideology. In each case I will focus on the analytical method characteristic of the approach and ask how such an approach might conceive the history of color in the cinema. In particular, what data from the early history of color might these approaches select, what arguments would be made, and how would the data be organized into a historical narrative? In this way I hope to illustrate how one might proceed in the writing of at least four different histories of color technology. These four histories, of course, do not exhaust the ways one might write the history of color.[5]

I will employ the three criteria of cause, change, and subject in order to distinguish the analytical methods of the four histories.[6] By *cause* I mean a historian's reasoning about the determinants or conditions of a state. By *change* I mean a reasoning about the difference between temporal states. That logic may appear in innumerable guises; for instance, change may be characterized in terms of a transition, evolution, progression (progress), regression, transformation, mutation, permutation, repetition, substitution (exchange), mediation, and in many other ways. By *subject* I mean that role or function ascribed to the individual with respect to a historical process. That role may run a spectrum from the individual as a psychological agent to the individual as one constructed (placed, positioned) by large-scale forces.

I. THE ADVENTURE OF COLOR

Terry Ramsaye devotes one chapter in his history of the motion picture to color. Entitled "Adventures of Kinemacolor," the chapter traces the fortunes of two film companies exploiting the Kinemacolor process: Natural Color Kinematograph Co. Ltd. (England) and the Kinemacolor Company of America. The title of Ramsaye's book, with its reference to *The Arabian Nights or The Thousand and One Nights,* is suggestive of his method. The second sentence of the chapter states that "the course of color history in the films has been as romantically adventurous as the story of the screen."[7] The history of color for Ramsaye is a romantic adventure story, a tapestry of tales. This assertion is more than a metaphor or a rhetorical flourish. It reveals a way of conceiving history which is characteristic of nineteenth-century historians. Such histories are structured as dramas of disclosure, with a stress on conflict and climax. They are written in a dramatic, staccato rhythm and in a vivid, even inspirational way.[8] For example, Ramsaye describes the work of the inventor Edward R. Turner, an early contributor to Kinemacolor, as follows:

Turner set to work to seek a new approach to the problem.
One day in 1902, as Urban sat at his desk nearby, there came a crash from the workshop where Turner was striving with his perplexities.
Urban ran into the room and found Turner dead on the floor.
Turner's notes, models and formulae were scattered about in confusion. No one else knew the meaning of half of them. The most of what Turner had attained died with him.[9]

Note that the first three paragraphs in the description contain only a single sentence each, and the last paragraph only three. This helps create a dramatic rhythm in which the telling of the death is more important than the date of the death. The anecdote is arranged to create suspense and surprise ("a crash from the workshop"), and its ending to perpetuate a mystery about the man and his work. It is not that the anecdote leaves something unexpressed but that it suggests the inexpressible, a mystery lingering beyond death in the ambiguity of the real.[10] (What did Turner discover? What was he thinking? If only his notes and models could speak . . .)

Another history of Kinemacolor—in many ways more comprehensive than Ramsaye's account—devotes one sentence to the death of Turner: "Unfortunately Turner died of a heart attack while working in his laboratory soon afterwards."[11] A third history says only, "A short time later, Turner died."[12] Ramsaye's selection of this event and his expansion of it reveals a preoccupation of nineteenth-century history writing: the concentration on an event-centered time span of short duration. History is reduced to a point—often to the decision-making individual. The reduction is rendered, whenever possible, in an anecdote about an individual which serves to concentrate history further to a particular time, place, and circumstance. For example, Technicolor's abrupt (?) change from a two-color additive to a two-color subtractive process is explained in terms of a "decisive" event, "one terrible night in Buffalo."[13] The event was a particular showing of the film *The Gulf Between* (1917) attended by Dr. Herbert Thomas Kalmus, one of the directors of Technicolor, Inc. It is not important in this type of history writing whether the anecdote is true or false or unverifiable because even if false[14] it may yet (metaphorically) serve its purpose, which is to explicate the past as a *linear* chain of events; that is, historical cause is linear. It is not accidental that such histories choose a literary style which obeys the neo-Aristotelian unities (time, place, action); nor is the style chosen merely to capture the interest of a lay reader; rather, the drama is itself evidence of a way of seeing and articulating the world.

What then is linear narrative? Such a narrative depends on a logic of reducing the set of future possibilities by events already realized in the past and thus a "climax"—that archetypal figure of the linear narrative—quite rightly assumes the shape of a pyramid where every element in the signifying space redoubles and builds consistently in one direction until there remains but one (inevitable) possibility. Thus, what is inevitable in a linear narrative is only the certainty of a climax or decisive event.[15] We see that the linear narrative depends on reducing signification to points—an individual, a decision, an event, the new invention, a pithy anecdote—and then linking the points one by one, through conflict and struggle, to a climax or decisive point which reveals/resolves what has gone *before,* that is, history. In this way the linear narrative is always looking back, repeating itself, summing up grandly, reducing; and most importantly, preparing the climax. Hence the charge that the linear history is "presentist"; that is, depends on a backward projection of current events (or rather, current beliefs about events) in order to seek the elements of a climax in their pure state. These elements are then arranged into a narrative which climaxes in the present. The present is also taken as an absolute reference point in order to measure *change.* Linearity, with its devices of foreshadowing, suspense, and surprise, often produces teleological overtones to the causal chain. Jacobs asserts that "After almost half a century of progress, the American film has achieved a degree of maturity. It now moves forward toward a more profound destiny."[16] Note the implicit view of historical change in the words "forward," "progress," "maturity," and "destiny."

If the relation of events to one another is stipulated in linear causal terms, what about long-term change? In the adventure story type of history, change is specified as an evolution, a gradualism, usually based on an organic growth metaphor.[17] Hence the common break-down of time into the periods of birth, youth, maturity (peak), decline (sterility), death, and then perhaps rebirth. This schema may be overlaid on anything—technology, film style, genre, studio, the film industry—in order to account for change. (Witness the table of contents of many film history books.) Jacobs, for example, asserts that D. W. Griffith's career falls into three periods—apprenticeship, maturity, and decline.[18]

In summary, the adventure history is written on the assumption that historical cause is one-to-one; in it, a chain of pithy anecdotes and events marks a linear progression of time. Change in such histories often takes the form of an organic evolution. The source of this evolution is, again, located in a point: a decisive event, the genius of an individual, a revolutionary invention.

I now wish to consider a history which seizes on new inventions and uses their developments to model historical cause and change.

II. THE TECHNOLOGY OF COLOR

A second way one might approach the early history of color in cinema is to trace the technology which made it possible. In a technological reading of history, the artistic text is seen as a product of (1) the resources available and (2) the resources preferred by the artist. From an ever-expanding pool of materials, the artist makes certain selections. This schema translates into the categories of (1) technology and (2) aesthetics. If the project is a writing of *history,* the result combines a history of technology and a history of aesthetics. Thus is founded the autonomy of aesthetics and the search for the criteria which isolate the various arts, for example, the Russian Formalist and early structuralist search for cinematic "specificity" or "pure" cinema. The aim is to discover a unique, and permanent (i.e., timeless) place for film beyond history. Hence the technological approach perpetuates a split between history and aesthetics.

Often included in the category of technology is what might be called technique. The difference between the two is that between a process, or apparatus—such as a camera dolly—and a procedure involving that apparatus in a text—such as a dolly-in or a close-up shot. The justification for blurring the distinction between technology and technique is the implicit belief that many new techniques depend on new technologies; for example, the zoom shot depends on a new type of lens. It matters little that such a connection cannot always be made so readily (what technology gave rise to the "jump cut"?); in each case an aesthetic *form* is discovered which may receive any content. For example, Lewis Jacobs measures the developing potential of the film medium in part by what techniques have been "invented" or "discovered" and laid up for future filmmakers like nuts in a squirrel burrow. Jacobs, in a chapter entitled "D. W. Griffith: New Discoveries," says that with the film *After Many Years* (1908), Griffith "saw the chance to use his new device, the close-up." The film is important not only for adding the "dramatic" close-up to the long shot and full shot but for "another surprise, even more radical": breaking up a scene by cutting to a distant space, a second scene.[19] For Jacobs this means, in the broadest sense, the discovery of editing as a tool and resource. In a now famous analysis Jean-Louis Comolli demonstrates that the isolation of technique (especially from narrative) leads to a search for "first times," and rapidly piles up meaningless distinctions, such as the first "enlargement" close-up, the first "dramatic" close-up, etc.[20]

In many ways the common etymology of the words "technology" and "technique" provides a fortunate confusion for the writers of a technological history, because the terms reinforce each other's autonomy and obscure questions about the social and economic forces which propel technology in certain directions and the ideological investment which creates and maintains techniques. Advances in technology make possible new techniques while at the same time the desire for new forms of expression in the film medium engenders advances in technology. Each justifies the other in a hermetic circularity.

An example of a technological approach is Patrick Ogle's 1972 study of the technique of deep focus. The title of his history, appropriately, points to the split between technology and aesthetics mentioned above: "Technological and Aesthetic Influences upon the Development of Deep-Focus Cinematography in the United States."[21] Ogle traces how improvements and changes in design of film stocks, lenses, and lighting affected deep focus in cinema. The question now arises, if one were to write a history of color processes in technological terms, what sort of "facts" would be selected?

First, one might attempt to list various technological and technical devices and their impact on color. Thus when Ogle notes that a new lens coating for cameras and projectors greatly increased light transmission, the color historian could interject that this development would have a much greater impact on color films than on black-and-white films, since improved screen brightness and image contrast affect not only lightness but also the saturation of color (the colors black, white, and grey are without saturation).[22] The first commercial application of coated projection lenses was for the opening of *Gone With The Wind* (1939) in twenty-five Loew's theatres, and the color effects were stronger than any previously seen.

Along with new technology, one would also be interested in the "discovery" by filmmakers of techniques which affect color; for instance, compositions utilizing large blocks of homogeneous color, or juxtaposed primary colors, or a certain edited sequence of colors—all of which increase the perceived saturation of color and open the way for various aesthetic effects based on saturation (e.g., increased tension, unnaturalness, heightened emotion).[23] Perhaps the single most cited example of editing for color effect is the succession of colors in the ballroom scene in *Becky Sharp* (Mamoulian, 1935). As the sound of cannon fire is heard and panic begins, the colors in the scene change, principally through the costume and lighting, from cool—greys, blues, greens—to a "climax" in the reds—yellow, orange, scarlet.[24]

Secondly, a technological history of color would examine not only new discoveries but the interaction between color and other technologies and techniques. For example, with the arrival of Technicolor came a new sort of film stock which was very slow and balanced for the blue-green of daylight. This meant that the light sources used in filming needed to be enormously increased in power, their color balance (color temperature) significantly shifted, the rate of burning made uniform, the area of illumination controlled, and, since this was also the time of the sound film, the lights had to be quiet. Technology rose to the challenge. A whole new generation of arc lamps was developed to replace Mazda incandescent lamps, and these new arc lamps were, in turn, necessary to the deep-focus style of the late thirties.[25] Thus color technology was tied to deep focus.

Color technology also bore a relation with sound technology. In the early twenties, 80–90 percent of American films were tinted in some manner.[26] The chemical baths used in tinting, however, interfered with the sound track and so color disappeared as filmmakers elected sound. The resulting flurry of activity led in 1929 to the introduction of Sonochrome by the Eastman Kodak Co., in which color was reintroduced by tints in the film stock itself. Sonochrome was a black-and-white positive film on one of sixteen tinted bases or a neutral base.[27]

When change is measured by "perfection" it follows a rhythm similar to that of an evolution: inspiration, invention, modification, advance, improvement, new advance. The series can be extended in both directions: inventions are foretold by persons "ahead of their times" (mad visionaries) and fall into disuse when replaced by bold, new inventions. The problem with the technological approach is that science does not march triumphantly along—independent and autonomous—toward perfection. This approach commonly "explains" failure with the statement that a device "wasn't practical"—but again, not practical with respect to what purpose? The demand for good quality, synchronous sound, for instance, is rooted in social forces larger than technology; and to say that Sonochrome is a response to the problem of tinting avoids such questions as what social and economic interests were served by color which forced its return in the form of Sonochrome (realism? profit?).

If failure is what is "impractical," success is often explained by the mere fact of newness or novelty. Arthur Knight says that

At the very moment that sound arrived, a practicable color process was also ready.
And with the overwhelming success of their sound experiments, the producers were now willing to try almost any novelty.

However, only two paragraphs before, Knight explains the *failure* of early color by saying it was "merely a novelty."[28] What is missing is an analysis of the social forces which make a device a "novelty" or "merely a novelty." It is not perfection which makes an invention successful but social and economic purpose. It is not enough to speak of the "spirit of the age," the movies' "loss of innocence," or a "conservatism." The last explanation is a particular favorite where a gap exists between available technology and actual practice (e.g., the very slow acceptance of panchromatic film despite its many "technical" advantages over orthochromatic film). Ogle speaks of the film industry as "conservative by nature," and of the "innate conservatism of many cinematographers."[29]

It is true that many innovations in film—color, sound, widescreen—were imposed on the industry from outside. But to speak of the conservatism of an industry apart from an institutional and economic context explains nothing; and to speak of the conservatism of an individual leads to the construction of psychic or hereditary profiles and the view that history is generated by great men, great innovators with ideas whose time had come. In either case, the technological history is told at the expense of greater forces. Technology is not neutral or spon-

taneous but is a product of social and economic circumstances and only secondar-
ily of great men.[30]

III. THE INDUSTRIAL EXPLOITATION OF COLOR

I now consider a third model for writing a history of color—one suggested by Douglas Gomery with respect to sound in "The Coming of the Talkies:
Invention, Innovation, and Diffusion."[31] Like the technological model, Gomery
separates out questions of aesthetics,[32] but in place of technology he employs a
principle capable of a more supple analysis:

[The] advent [of sound] can be appreciated by viewing it in terms of the economic theory
of technological innovation, which posits that a product or process is introduced to increase profits in three systematic phases: invention, innovation, and diffusion. . . . In each
of the three phases, the producers and suppliers of sound equipment carried out their business decisions with a single view toward maximizing long-run profits.[33]

Gomery, therefore, concentrates on (1) those management decisions which (2)
maximize the long-run profits of a business. The approach is that of industrial
organization economics—a branch of neo-classical economic theory.

According to Gomery's analysis the first stage of technical development is
invention, which spans everything concerning the technical device from an "archaeology" to a time just short of commercial exploitation. Gomery discusses the
beginnings of sound and the failure of some eighty-one small companies attempting to market their own versions of a sound system.[34] He begins with commercial
attempts to link sound and image for a viewer through the playing of a phonograph during the projection of the images (either synchronized to the images in
some way or nonsynchronized) or through a sound-on-film method. He does not
consider the development of the phonograph itself as a commercial device, nor
does he examine the dominant method of linking sound and image in the early
cinema (i.e., live musical and/or vocal accompaniment).

When we turn from sound to the relation of color and image, things become
more complex. Do we begin with the black-and-white photograph? An accurate
color record depends on a film emulsion which is uniformly sensitive to all the
colors of the spectrum. If, for instance, the film were not sensitive to red and
yellow then those colors would be rendered as black (absent) and there would be
no hope of distinguishing red from yellow. The silver halides in a film emulsion
are chiefly sensitive to blue, violet, and ultraviolet radiation. (Since the human
eye does not see ultraviolet, its reproduction on film will somewhat "distort" the
other colors.) The addition of certain chemical dyes by 1884 increased the sensitivity of "ordinary" film to include green and brought about "orthochromatic"
film. Further advances in dyes expanded sensitivity to the reds and led to "panchromatic" film stocks in 1903 and 1905. Color photographs from nature were
made in the late 1870s and the first commercially successful color photographic
process was the Lumière Autochrome in 1907. Continual progress in sensitizing
dyes made possible the great advances in color photography after 1930.

There are still earlier important dates in natural color photography: 1798 (the development of lithography by Senefelder), 1813 (the principle of the dye and bleach color film), and 1861 (Maxwell's demonstration of a three-color process). In fact by the time of Technicolor film (1932) there already existed a bewildering array of color processes and companies vying for success. There have been over 100 major color processes, about half of which originated or were used in the United States.[35] Many were rarely or never used to make a film. It is enough to note, without exploring the details,[36] that natural color processes are usually divided into two types—additive color systems (e.g., Kinemacolor, early Technicolor, and modern television) and subtractive color systems (e.g., Technicolor, Eastman Color, Kodachrome)—and that each type may be further classified according to whether it is based on a set of two or three primary colors.

So far we have considered the invention of color with respect to the photograph (natural color), but a second line of development lies closer to painting. Hand-painted daguerreotypes appeared around 1839[37] and hand-painted films appeared with the very first films in 1894.[38] Hand coloring became a large and important industry. Factories of women applied as many as six colors to each frame of the film. A variation on the technique—stenciling—existed into the 1930s. Other techniques, related to painting, involved the use of chemical baths either to dye the gelatin ("tinting," which colors the light areas) or to replace the silver image of positive film ("toning," which colors the dark areas) or a combination of tinting and toning. One might even add a third line of color development, closer to the theatre than to either photography or painting: the use of separate, colored spotlights during the projection of a film. Griffith used the technique, which one reviewer called "revolutionary," in the projection of *Broken Blossoms* (1919).[39]

We see, then, that color experimentation appeared with the earliest photographs and the earliest films. The major techniques—additive color, subtractive color, painting, stenciling, and chemical baths—were all well under way in the early 1900s. In fact there is such a remarkable diversity that it is not immediately clear with which industries to begin a study of color, or how far back to go. One company, however, which was clearly involved in the invention phase of color was the Natural Color Kinematograph Co. (Kinemacolor).

Kinemacolor enjoyed considerable success in the years 1909–1915. Thereafter it declined and failed. If we were to follow Gomery's model, we would not search for the failure of Kinemacolor in a failure of technology, such as the requirement of outdoor sunlight for film exposure (thus no studio shooting); excessive wear on the film due to projection at twice the speed of black-and-white films; the need for special, complicated projectors; and other problems like fringing and reduced screen illumination related to the additive process.[40] Rather, Gomery suggests that in the failure of the eighty-one or so early sound companies "technological inferiority played only a small role"[41] or no role at all.[42] More important were such factors as a solid financial underpinning for the business, a strong research and development laboratory, and superior marketing and managerial skill.[43] It has, in fact, been claimed that poor management was a factor in the decline of Kinemacolor.[44]

Let us consider a set of data—an event in the history of Kinemacolor—and see how it might be used by different historians. In February 1912, Kinemacolor premiered its film of the Delhi Durbar of 1911 which recorded the pageantry and celebration in Bombay, Delhi, and Calcutta in honor of the coronation of King George V and his visit to India. *The Durbar at Delhi* ran 2½ hours (16,000 feet) whereas the longest films produced before 1912 were 45–60 minutes. Black-and-white films of the same event, which preceded the Kinemacolor film, closed after three weeks. The immensely profitable Kinemacolor film, however, ran for 15 months and grossed three-quarters of a million dollars.[45] What can one say beyond the fact that *The Durbar at Delhi* was Kinemacolor's "greatest success"?[46]

For Terry Ramsaye the film provides material for several stirring anecdotes, including the image of Charles Urban burying the negatives of each day's shooting and sleeping on top of them to guard against sabotage by rivals. The reels are referred to by Ramsaye as "precious" which further prepares for the climax three sentences later: "He slept with his treasure."[47] Ramsaye almost certainly based his account on the typewritten notes of Urban.[48] An alternate explanation for burying the Durbar films—which would not suit Ramsaye's purpose at all—is that the films were buried to protect them from the intense heat of the Indian sun.[49]

Ramsaye also asserts that Urban lost a knighthood at the hand of the King because he fell ill and could not attend a royal showing of the Durbar film. Urban was "on the verge of death," says Ramsaye, and he continues: "It was a tragedy reminiscent of the unfortunate death of Turner, the first of the color inventors, in Urban's office years before."[50] Earlier we noted how Ramsaye portrayed Turner's death as a dramatic event, but why is it now mentioned again (and with certain details repeated) seven pages later? What is the connection between Urban's illness—from which he recovered—and Turner's death? Precisely this: to reinforce a *narrative* of history, to remind the reader of the story Ramsaye is telling— that the story connects up its events and is an organic whole. For Ramsaye, Urban is (here) a particular kind of *character*—a player in a "tragedy"[51] and the victim of an "unkind fate."[52] Thus, in an important way Ramsaye's history depends on a conception of character derived from classic literary narrative. He wishes to remind us that Turner, as a character, is important to the story.

Ramsaye says that at the time of the Durbar film Kinemacolor "was on the high tide of success."[53] Note the use of the word "tide." The metaphor points to a theory of historical *change* (discussed earlier) based on an evolutionary model; more precisely, change according to an organic and natural growth process. Ramsaye does not deal with the decline of Kinemacolor (though he speaks obliquely of an "interruption" due to World War I[54]), but instead chooses in the final page and a half of an eleven-page chapter to mention Prizma color, Kelley-color, and Technicolor which are represented as carrying on the work of Kinemacolor ("The Kinemacolor method became in consequence the basis of practically all subsequent color processes"[55]). For Ramsaye, Kinemacolor *is* color and color is continuing to grow and evolve. The financial demise of a particular business is incidental.

How would Patrick Ogle deal with the Durbar film? He would undoubtedly cite it as proof that a certain level of technical perfection had been achieved in the camera, film stock, and projection of Kinemacolor movies. More difficult would be the question of why the company failed. Ogle might cite continuing technical problems which were never resolved, such as the frequent allegation that projection of the films near the threshold frequency needed for persistence of vision resulted in eyestrain and headaches for viewers.[56] Ogle would more likely avoid the question and concentrate on the relations of Kinemacolor technology to subsequent color processes and the eventual "perfection" of color. Perfection in these terms would be measured against the state of color technology today or "foreseeable" by today's standards.

Gomery would probably view the Durbar film as evidence of the long-term profit potential of the Kinemacolor enterprise, but would not attach special importance to the event because it does not provide answers to the sorts of questions he asks about financial stability, research facilities, and bold management decisions, though it does bear somewhat on the marketing of color. (Compare the Durbar film with Gomery's treatment of early sound programs and films, like *The Jazz Singer*.[57]) For Gomery the success of the Durbar film is for the most part irrelevant to the success or failure of Kinemacolor.

Although I have limited my inquiry to the early history of color, it may be useful to sketch the two phases of technological development which follow "invention"—innovation and diffusion. In the innovative phase of sound, Gomery discusses how sound was adapted for profitable use by Warner Brothers, Fox Film Corporation, the Big Five (after the expiration of the Big Five Agreement), and RKO. It is in this phase that Gomery's criterion of "creative management" is especially prominent. The principal hero for Warner Brothers is Waddill Catchings. The management of both Warners and Fox is characterized as "bold,"[58] the actions of the Big Five as "decisive,"[59] and the management of RKO as "superior."[60] For Gomery it is in the context of "management" that the individual—if he is also "creative"—has the chance to enter history.

A history of color in the innovation phase would certainly include the Technicolor Company. Its president, Herbert Kalmus, would be portrayed as "unquestionably the man who put Technicolor over."[61] Taken to an extreme, this reliance on the individual corporate leader leads to the following description of Kalmus in a *Fortune* magazine article: "The Doctor shaves with a Gillette razor, likes his fried eggs done on one side only, reads a great deal of biography and physics but very little fiction."[62]

In the diffusion phase economists study how other firms in an industry react to what has become profitable for a competitor. In the diffusion of sound, Gomery includes the general adoption and conversion to sound by the large motion picture companies chiefly through mutual cooperation (the Hays Office and the Academy of Motion Picture Arts and Sciences played major roles). Smaller companies with little capital were forced out of business or merged with the majors.[63] A history of color in the diffusion phase would include the antitrust and patent problems of the Technicolor Company in the late 1940s.[64] The diffusion phase completes an economic cycle of change which is driven by a desire for long-run profit. The individual's place in such a history is one of business management.

IV. THE IDEOLOGY OF COLOR

I will now consider a final approach to the writing of a history of early color. Jean-Louis Comolli, writing from an avowedly Marxist perspective, asserts in "Technique et idéologie" that a history of technology and technical forms is not enough. He does not reject technical explanations[65] but calls for the analysis of a larger context which locates and determines technology. This larger context is composed of two social demands—the ideological and the economic. Comolli states that "It is to the mutual reinforcement of an ideological demand ('to see life as it is') and the economic demand to make it a source of profit that cinema owes its being."[66] Before I consider in more detail the problem of ideology, it may be useful to indicate briefly in what ways Comolli's theory of historical *cause* is nonlinear and his theory of historical *change* is nonevolutionary; that is, how Comolli differs from the sort of history written by Ramsaye.

What is the alternative to linear cause? For Comolli it is "a history characterized by discontinuous temporality, which is recursive, dialectical, and not reducible to a single meaning but rather, is made up of types of signifying practices whose plural series has neither origin nor end."[67] The reference to "neither origin nor end" is crucial to Comolli because, for the traditional historian, the beginning and the end points pose special problems in the linear narrative (a special embarrassment). In Aristotle's words: "A whole is that which has a beginning, a middle, and an end. A beginning is that which does not itself follow anything by causal necessity."[68] To seek after beginnings and origins, then, in order to unify a historical narrative is in some sense an ahistorical inquiry: that which has no cause (a beginning) lies outside of time and history. The problem for the materialist historian is that in utilizing language to *name,* one has already cut out a point, a potential origin. The alternatives are either to no longer use language or to name a *plurality* of beginnings—a series of points which may even be contradictory— and thereby defeat the notion of an event—a coalescence of points into the master point or origin. This is what Comolli attempts by deconstructing the origin of cinema into a scattered series of events—visible and invisible, continuous and discontinuous, from yesterday to twenty-five centuries ago.[69] By naming a great many events, Comolli hopes to block the very notion of a single event, a first cause, which leads (through the neo-Aristotelian unities) to a climax.

What is the alternative to evolutionary change? For Comolli change is measured in the Marxist terms of an unremitting class struggle. He thus attacks metaphors based on evolution and natural growth, such as the "birth" of cinema.[70] Although modern theories of biological evolution have lost much of their "perfection" element—an organism's inherent tendency toward perfection—there remains a weak "directional" component shaped by natural processes.[71] In this respect the Marxist notion of change is not unlike evolutionary change. Evolution, however, is still characterized by gradualism, continuity, and adaptation to the environment, factors foreign to Marxism. Thus Comolli especially seizes on those "gaps" or discontinuities in the growth of technologies and techniques which are potentially damaging to a theory of smooth evolution. One such gap, he says, is the disappearance of deep-focus cinematography—widespread in early cinema—and its reappearance in the late thirties. Another gap is the delay in moving from ordinary and orthochromatic film stocks to panchromatic films.

What is the role of the individual—the subject—in the process of history? In a system of linear cause, the individual is easily singled out: he or she is largely autonomous and often the decision-maker, the event-maker. In a system of evolutionary change, the individual again is easy to identify: change is based on the metaphor of the body—birth, growth, death. By a curious alchemy, even gaps in the evolution may be referred to the body. Thus Robert Sklar in *Movie-Made America* says that D. W. Griffith's *After Many Years* is a "*rediscovery* of cinema's fundamental resources," which "would not be *lost* again."[72] The references to rediscovery and loss are the very figures of a linear and evolutionary history, which can pose a gap or even retrogression only in such terms as a failure of "memory," something which was "forgotten" but is now assured. In this way the subject is continually present and reinscribed in the traditional history.

For Comolli, on the other hand, the subject exists only in relation to *ideology*. For present purposes I shall define an ideology as a possible relation between individual consciousness and its social ground. It is a largely coherent and logical system of images, ideas, values, feelings, and actions by which, and through which, persons experience their societies at various times; for instance, a "philosophy" or theology, although an ideology need not be formalized in this way.[73] (Strictly speaking, an ideology is not an image or an idea but a representational system through which the individual encounters the material conditions of existence.) Comolli therefore asks an epistemological question: What are the conditions that make it possible to know man? How does man represent himself to himself?

Comolli attempts to steer a middle course between those who claim that technology is neutral, independent of use (Ogle, Lebel)[74] and those who claim that technology is *inherently* ideological. In the latter group is Jean-Louis Baudry, who claims that certain features of the cinematic apparatus (lens, camera, projector) mark it with an original sin so that cinema will never truly escape bourgeois illusionism.[75] For Comolli, technology is already and always a part of an ideology and it functions along with "institutions" to hold the members of a society in a certain set of relationships or bond. Technology is produced by and functions in an ideology; thus it is not "neutral." But neither is it determined forever by its past or present functions, for it may be adapted to serve in another set of social relations.

Let us consider ideology at work in the cinema through three concepts: science, art, and realism. We will then ask how color functions in each of these areas.

Comolli argues that cinema arose out of an attempt to compensate for the imperfections of the human eye by substituting the objective, scientifically accurate eye of the camera lens.[76] Cinema was vision perfected; science guaranteed the truth of cinema's reproduction of reality. According to Comolli this belief (or "myth," if one is outside of that ideology) was part of a complex of beliefs which shaped the development of cinema and its technology. Although Comolli does not work the argument out in detail, one can suggest evidence which would be marshalled in support of such a position. Thomas Edison or, indeed, Dr. Herbert Kalmus, for example, would be approached not as biographical figures but in the way in which these men *were sold to the public*.[77] Thus Edison, the man of science and invention, was almost universally referred to in his day as the Wizard of Menlo Park, or simply the Wizard—for how else to explain the miracles of science? Ramsaye's history furthers the Edison myth with such chapters as "In the House of the Wizard." The Edison product was sold as a triumph of science. The 1902 Sears, Roebuck and Co. catalogue advertises the improved model of the Edison 1901 Kinetoscope as follows:

This season we shall handle the Edison Kinetoscope for projecting moving pictures exclusively. The moving picture apparatus is known as one of the greatest of the Edison inventions, and on it the Wizard of Originality has spent much time in the perfection of the present type of machine, embodying every improvement and every convenience which science, mechanical skill and research have been able to add to the first invention.[78]

The marketing of Kinemacolor, too, emphasized its scientific character and how "the colours obtained are due to the agency of LIGHT only. No painting, hand-work, stencil-work or similar devices are used."[79] The program for the first showing of Kinemacolor in the United States (December 1909) repeatedly stresses science, not just to differentiate its product from hand-painting and tinting but to claim a superior legitimacy derived from Science:

It has been pointed out in an American print by a critic, who, by the way, had never seen the results, that "THE MAIN PRINCIPLES OF THE URBAN-SMITH PROCESS WERE KNOWN TO THE SCIENTIFIC WORLD BEFORE EITHER MR. URBAN OR MR. SMITH TOOK UP THE MATTER!" Exactly! Messrs. Urban and Smith admit the fact and take special pride in it. Their invention *is* based upon the solid foundation of established scientific truths. If it were based upon some fantastic notion not in accordance with the principles of pure science there would be little hope for its future. It is just *because* Kinemacolor is based upon the solid rock of scientific fact that distinguished scientists all over Europe have been enthusiastic in its praise and have predicted a brilliant future for the young art, which has been born to the world for the entertainment and instruction of the people.

Messrs. Urban and Smith's only claim is that with the expenditure of much time and money they are the *first* to take up these sound scientific principles and materialize them into practical, everyday results, and it is for that reason that the Patent offices of every civilized country in the world have granted Letters Patent for the process.[80]

The fact that cinema was taken to be a perfected form of the human eye is revealed in Ramsaye's history when he concludes his account of Kinemacolor by speaking of the "extraordinary possibilities yet to be explored . . . with light entirely below the visual range of the human eye."[81] Ramsaye speaks of the development of a new film stock sensitive to infrared. The ideology which links science, camera, vision, and truth is as current as today's magazines. One advertisement for a camera invites the reader to "explore the world of 1/500 second." The Canon camera "can literally make you master of your visual domain. . . . If you want a look at a world you've never seen before, look at the AE−1."[82]

A second center of ideology is the notion of Art (and its Aesthetics). Art is conceived to be, not a discourse, a kind of text, but a special, even sacred access to knowledge, the Human Condition, Truth (the complex, ambiguous, and ineffable), etc. Art, especially Great Art, is approached with reverence for it has universal and timeless value. Thus to the extent that cinema can become Art—and more than a "movie"—it is able to escape history. For example, Griffith's *Broken Blossoms* (1919) was marketed in a series of elaborate ways as an Art object.[83] Its color effects were distinguished from the ordinary so as to become the very *sign* of Art. Thus cinema promised the reconciliation of science and art in a technologically precise reproduction of reality where science became the guarantor of the truths of Art.

A third area for the investigation of ideology is the insistence on realism. Since the cinema was linked to science, it became the perfect tool to record reality with precision. The 1902 Sears catalogue described the Kinetoscope as follows:

THE UNRIVALLED EDISON KINETOSCOPE, moving picture machine, giving a pictorial presentation, not lifelike merely, but apparently life itself, with every movement, every action and every detail brought so vividly before the audience that it becomes difficult for them to believe that what they see before them can be other than nature's very self.[84]

Color, of course, perfectly enhances a reality effect. An ad for a 1910 hand-painted film asserted that "the flesh tints [are] so natural that it is hard to believe that the people are only pictures on a screen."[85] Natural color processes offered even greater possibilities for realism.[86] Earlier I discussed the possible significance of Kinemacolor's *The Durbar at Delhi* for three historians. For Comolli the film would probably be important insofar as it demonstrates the new powers of realism provided by color. He would find significant the comments of the Russian Dowager Empress writing to her son, Nikolai, from London (April 29, 1912) after seeing the Durbar film:

We are lunching today with Georgie and May at Buckingham Palace. They both send you greetings. Last night we saw their journey to India. Kinemacolor is wonderfully interesting and very beautiful and gives one the impression of having seen it all in reality . . .[87]

The only danger in all this was that "color experimenters are apt to go arty and prevent even *natural colors from producing natural illusions*."[88] Many critics of early natural color processes spoke of the dangers of "gaudy," unrealistic color ("garish" was another favorite word). And Technicolor soon recognized the important investment they had in realistic uses of color. They insisted that anyone renting their color equipment also hire a color consultant from the company in order to "properly" orchestrate color combinations.[89]

It may be useful to consider a specific set of technological changes, related to the problem of realism, and to contrast the ways that these changes would be seen by different historical methods. In 1936−37, new and more efficient lighting equipment, and improvements in the laboratory processing of Technicolor film, along with new techniques of photographing color, made possible lighting levels extremely close to average black-and-white standards.[90] One director of photography, Ray Rennahan, testified, "I now light almost exactly as I would for monochrome."[91] In 1939 Technicolor introduced a film stock three to four times faster yet, which meant a 50 percent reduction in normal lighting levels (the reduction was not greater because of the continued necessity for color filters and beam-splitting devices in the camera). This meant that color correcting filters became practical, allowing the use of smaller, more flexible incandescent light sources (which are also softer). In addition the film offered a wider exposure latitude and so allowed better rendition of shadows. Lighting levels approached those of black-and-white on Eastman Kodak Super X (ASA 40). Many other techniques of black-and-white photography also became feasible (e.g., the use of diffusion and of small spotlights for precise lighting of faces in close-ups) with the result that color became less garish, more natural. Director of photography Ernest Haller concluded:

Now that we have this fast film, which enables a cinematographer to use all the little tricks of precision lighting he has used in monochrome to glamorize his stars, I am sure that color is going to be more flattering than ever to the women![92]

At least the representation of women, it seems, was secure.

How might these changes be interpreted by the four historians we have discussed? For Ramsaye the data has a decidedly technical, unexciting cast about it. If he were to use it, he would want the data to coalesce about a personality or culminate in a dramatic event. One source of dramatic events in film history, of course, is the Great Film and it would be even better if some of these technical changes were *first* used in that great film. Thus Ramsaye would probably structure his presentation around the making of *Gone with the Wind* (1939), the first production to use the faster Technicolor film and on which both Rennahan and Haller worked.

For Ogle these technological changes would be evidence of a logical, natural perfection of technique. He would assert that the changes were largely scientific and so independent of cultural demands. The resulting techniques would be neutral in that they could be used in any way: in realistic and unrealistic films. The fact that cinematographers tended to reestablish monochrome techniques—that is, to conceive color in terms of black and white—would be due to the "conservatism" of the profession.

For Gomery the changes would be of interest to the extent that, for example, new lighting equipment might be more cost-effective and techniques resulting in less "garish" color might influence the demand for, as well as the marketing of, color. Were black-and-white techniques employed on color films because they were cost-effective? How should color be introduced? Through shorts and newsreels (as in the marketing of sound) or through some combination of roadshows, cartoons, special attractions, big budget features, etc.? These marketing decisions, in turn, have aesthetic implications. Nevertheless, the general return to black-and-white techniques would have less interest for Gomery and would probably fall into the province of "aesthetics."

Comolli, however, would find these changes of major significance. For him it would be an illustration of technology acting to reinvest the old in new ways. Technology, here, is responding to a deeper structure—a realistic order of discourse. This argument does not contend that all black-and-white films were realist films, but only that the realist codes were by the late 1930s well worked out and well established in black-and-white. Directors and cinematographers continued to think in terms of the black-and-white codes and with the increased importance of color, the demand was there to "improve" color film and equipment in line with the existing state of black-and-white technology. "Improve" in this context means to make a technological change so as to be able to deploy the familiar codes.

Comolli could cite as support the detailed advice of cinematographer James Wong Howe on the best use of background, costume, rim lighting, illumination levels, light placement, colored beams, composition, and other variables in order to achieve with color the same "illusion of naturalness"[93] as in black-and-white. Technology reveals itself here through color and lighting codes in the text. Hence, for Comolli, technological refinements are important in the writing of film history, but only insofar as they are related to the social and economic matrix in which they find their function. Culture, for him, is a series of codes and textual systems accessible to semiotic analysis.

In summary, Comolli points to an ideology in which man defines himself by redefining his sight in terms of the cinema. He discusses the ideology of science and how the human eye is represented as being replaced by the camera eye— by the lens of science, which cannot lie. Color serves to increase the camera's claim to scientific accuracy, and when used realistically is able to repeat the dominant forms of the culture. In this sense color does not begin with Technicolor, nor even with the hand-painting of film in 1894 but much further back in Western culture: at least to the colors and linear perspective of the paintings of the Renaissance. Comolli would suggest that in order to understand color in film one must first study the uses of color in the other arts, and the forms of intelligibility they sustain.

V. CONCLUSION

The accompanying Table presents in schematic form a comparison of the four types of history writing which I have explored. The problem I deal with is how one might uncover the various assumptions a historian makes about time, or rather the social view implicated in a conception of time. Using these assumptions one can construct at least four different histories of color technology in early film. The purpose, however, is not to settle historians into categories or reveal distinctive schools of historiography. It is not uncommon for a historian to make different assumptions in different portions of the same history. (I have indicated, for example, that Lewis Jacobs has written both an adventure and a technological history in *The Rise of the American Film*.) I am not strictly analyzing what might be termed the "style" of a particular type of writing.[94] My purpose in utilizing the criteria of cause, change, and subject is to provide a way of comparing the different types of questions that a historian may ask and thereby to reveal what kind of

A COMPARISON OF THE ASSUMPTIONS OF
FOUR TYPES OF HISTORICAL INQUIRY

Aspects of Historical Time	RAMSAYE *Adventure History*	OGLE *Technical History*	GOMERY *Industrial History*	COMOLLI *Ideological History*
CAUSE	Linear (events, anecdotes; neo-Aristotelian unities)	Relations among technologies (science)	Economic context (long-run profits; industrial organization theory)	Social and economic context (Marxist economic theory)
CHANGE	Evolution (birth, growth, death)	Perfection of technique	Economic cycle (invention, innovation, diffusion)	Marxist class struggle (dialectical change)
SUBJECT (ROLE OF INDIVIDUAL)	Organic metaphor and anecdotes about individuals (psychology)	Inventors and cinematographers	Creative management	Member of economic class and subject in ideology

history arises from those questions. Thus I am primarily interested in historical logic rather than syntax.

I am not searching for the one, true, and genuine type of history writing because much can be learned from asking different sorts of questions, applying various time schemes, and using a variety of perspectives. If I tend to privilege the sort of history written by Comolli, it is because he is explicit about his method, conscious of the theoretical implications, and asks interesting questions which have produced new interpretations of certain data. Comolli attempts to use his theory at every level of his writing and in the process recasts technology, techniques, and their role in the cinematic machine.

Notes

Reprinted with minor corrections and additions from *Film Reader* 4 (Evanston, Ill.: Northwestern University Press, 1979), pp. 16–34. This essay has emerged in part from two courses at the University of Wisconsin–Madison, Spring 1977: Tino Balio's "History of the Motion Picture Industry" and Russell Merritt's "Historiography of Film." It is a revision of a paper presented at the International Film Conference IV, The University of Wisconsin–Milwaukee, February 22–24, 1978. I wish to thank Douglas Gomery for his comments and Roberta Kimmel for her editorial assistance.

1. Roger Manvell, ed., *The International Encyclopedia of Film* (New York: Crown Publishers, 1972), pp. 29–48.

2. Lewis Jacobs, *The Rise of the American Film* (New York: Teachers College Press, 1968), chap. XXII.

3. Michel Foucault, *The Order of Things* (New York: Vintage Books, 1970), p. xv. Cf. Christian Metz's comments on the disorder and inconsistent methodology in film histories, "The Imaginary Signifier," *Screen* 16 (Summer 1975), pp. 23–24.

4. It is important to qualify the word "determine," for if the historian is not independent of an analytical schema or language neither can we go to the other extreme and assert that the historian is fully defined by the choice of a language. It is enough to emphasize the crucial role played by the schema in the production of a history. See generally, Dan Slobin, *Psycholinguistics* (Glenview, Ill.: Scott, Foresman and Co., pp. 120–133; Umberto Eco, *A Theory of Semiotics* (Bloomington: Indiana University Press, 1976), pp. 76–81; E. H. Gombrich, *Art and Illusion* (Princeton: Princeton University Press, 1969), pp. 181–287; Nelson Goodman, *Languages of Art* (Indianapolis: Hackett Publishing Co., 2nd ed., 1976), pp. 7–8.

5. Cf. Charles F. Altman, "Towards a Historiography of American Film," *Cinema Journal* 16 (Spring 1977) and the essays in *Film: Historical-Theoretical Speculations,* Ben Lawton and Janet Staiger, ed. (Pleasantville, N.Y.: Redgrave, 1977).

6. These criteria were suggested by the remarks of Michel Foucault in his "Foreword to the English Edition" of *The Order of Things,* pp. xii–xiv. They are useful because of their generality and because they address the logic of a historical argument.

7. Terry Ramsaye, *A Million and One Nights* (New York: Simon and Schuster, 1926), p. 562.

8. Fernand Braudel, "Histoire et sciences sociales: la longue durée," *Annales* 4 (October–December 1958), pp. 725–53 (trans. by Sian France, "History and the Social Sciences: The Long Term," in Fritz Stern, ed., *The Varieties of History* [New York: Vintage Books, 1973], pp. 404–429). See generally Hayden White, *Metahistory* (Baltimore: Johns Hopkins University Press, 1973); Geoffrey Nowell-Smith, "Facts About Films and Facts of Films," *Quarterly Review of Film Studies* 1, no. 3 (August 1976): 272–75.

9. Ramsaye, p. 563.

10. Cf. Roland Barthes, *S/Z* (New York: Hill and Wang, 1974), pp. 216–17.

11. D. B. Thomas, *The First Colour Motion Pictures* (London: Her Majesty's Stationery Office, 1969), p. 10.

12. James Limbacher, *Four Aspects of the Film* (New York: Brussel & Brussel, 1969), p. 14.

13. Herbert Kalmus, "Technicolor Adventures in Cinemaland," *Journal of the Society of Motion Picture Engineers* 31 (December 1938), pp. 565–66. This article may be found in Raymond Fielding, ed., *A Technological History of Motion Pictures and Television* (Los Angeles: University of California Press, 1967), p. 52. Other accounts draw on Kalmus's recollections, which, significantly, he views as an adventure story. See Roderick Ryan, *A Study of the Technology of Color Motion Picture Processes Developed in the United States* (Ph.D. Diss., University of Southern California, 1967), pp. 133–34; Limbacher, pp. 25–26.

14. Robert Sklar repeats a "story which may or may not be true" (in fact, almost certainly not true) because it nevertheless illustrates his theory of the importance of D. W. Griffith's years at Biograph. Robert Sklar, *Movie-Made America* (New York: Vintage Books, 1975), pp. 50–51.

15. The definition of linear narrative is derived from Edward Branigan, "Subjectivity Under Siege—From Fellini's *8½* to Oshima's *The Story of a Man Who Left His Will on Film,*" *Screen* 19 (Spring 1978), p. 39.

16. Jacobs, p. 539.

17. Oswald Spengler develops an explicit "organic logic" whereby cultures simply *are*

organisms with the same cycles as animals, trees, and flowers; *The Decline of the West,* trans. Charles Atkinson (New York: Knopf, 1926).

18. Jacobs, p. 98 and Chaps. VII, XI, and XIX.

19. *Ibid.,* pp. 102–103. Griffith is still generally held to be the "father of film technique"; Arthur Knight, *The Liveliest Art* (New York: New American Library, 1957), p. 31. Barry Salt chronicles the "discovery" of devices such as the "cinematographic angle" within an explicit model of evolutionary change; "The Early Development of Film Form," *Film Form* 1 (Spring 1976), pp. 92, 95, 96, 100 and "Film Form: 1900–06," *Sight and Sound* 47 (Summer 1978), p. 149.

20. Comolli, part 3, pp. 47–49 and note 12 (pp. 3.5–3.8; 3.10–3.11), see note 65 *infra.*

21. Patrick Ogle, "Technological and Aesthetic Influences upon the Development of Deep-Focus Cinematography in the United States," *Screen* 13 (Spring 1972), pp. 45–72.

22. Hans Kreitler and Shulamith Kreitler, *Psychology of the Arts* (Durham, N.C.: Duke University Press, 1972), p. 39.

23. *Ibid.;* Edward Branigan, "The Articulation of Color in a Filmic System," *Wide Angle* 1, no. 3 (1976): 20–31.

24. Rouben Mamoulian, "Colour and Emotion," *Cinema Quarterly* 3 (Summer 1935), p. 225 and "Colour and Light in Films," *Film Culture* 21 (Summer 1960), pp. 74–75; John Gallagher and Marino Amoruco, "An Interview with Rouben Mamoulian," *The Velvet Light Trap* no. 19 (1982), pp. 21–22; Forsyth Hardy, "The Colour Question," *Cinema Quarterly* 3 (Summer 1935), pp. 232; Allen Chumley, "The Screen: Movies in Motley," *New Masses* 16 (July 2, 1935), p. 44; Jacobs, p. 472; William Johnson, "Coming to Terms with Color" in Lewis Jacobs, ed., *The Movies as Medium* (New York: Farrar, Straus & Giroux, 1970), p. 215 n. 8.

25. Ogle, p. 52.

26. L. A. Jones, "Tinted Films for Sound Positives," *Transactions of the Society of Motion Picture Engineers* (May 1929), p. 199.

27. Ryan, pp. 21–23.

28. Knight, p. 149.

29. Ogle, pp. 54, 50.

30. See in general, note 65 *infra;* Christopher Williams, "The Deep-Focus Question: Some Comments on Patrick Ogle's Article," *Screen* 13 (Spring 1972): 73–76; James Spellerberg, "Technology and Ideology in the Cinema," *Quarterly Review of Film Studies* 2 (August 1977): 288–301.

31. J. Douglas Gomery, "The Coming of the Talkies: Invention, Innovation, and Diffusion," in Tino Balio, ed., *The American Film Industry* (Madison: University of Wisconsin Press, 1976), pp. 192–211. Gomery draws on his more extensive study, "The Coming of Sound to the American Cinema: A History of the Transformation of an Industry," (Ph.D. Diss., University of Wisconsin–Madison, 1975).

For a useful comparison between the technological and industrial management approaches to the history of sound in film, see Patrick Ogle, "Development of Sound Systems: The Commercial Era," pp. 198–212 and Douglas Gomery, "Failure and Success: Vocafilm and RCA," pp. 213–221 in *Film Reader* 2 (Evanston, Ill.: Northwestern University, 1977).

Other work by Gomery on the problem of sound includes the following: "The Coming of Sound to the German Cinema," *Purdue Film Studies Annual* 1 (August 1976): 136–143; "Tri-Ergon, Tobis-Klangfilm, and the Coming of Sound," *Cinema Journal* 16 (Fall 1976): 51–61; "Problems in Film History: How Fox Innovated Sound," *Quarterly Review of Film Studies* 1 (August 1976): 315–330; "The Warner-Vitaphone Peril: The American Film

Industry Reacts to the Innovation of Sound," *Journal of the University Film Association* 28 (Winter 1976): 11–19; "Toward an Economic History of the Cinema: The Coming of Sound to Hollywood," paper delivered at the International Film Conference IV, University of Wisconsin–Milwaukee, February 22–24, 1978.

For criticism of Gomery's approach see Edward Buscombe, "Sound and Color," *Jump Cut* 17 (April 1978), p. 23.

32. Aesthetics is mentioned only once, Gomery, "Talkies," p. 210.

33. *Ibid.,* pp. 193–94; Gomery, "Transformation of an Industry," chap. 1.

34. *Ibid.,* pp. 194–98; Gomery, "Failure," p. 213.

35. Ryan, pp. 1–2.

36. There are four major surveys of all the color processes: E. J. Wall, *History of Three-Color Photography* (Boston: American Photographic Publishing Co., 1925); Joseph Friedman, *History of Color Photography* (Boston: American Photographic Publishing Co., 1944); Ryan, *op. cit.;* Adrian Cornwell-Clyne, *Colour Cinematography* (London: Chapman and Hall, Ltd., 1951). The first three are now available from Focal Press, New York. Three other surveys of a more summary nature are Limbacher and Manvell, *op. cit.,* and see note 64 *infra.*

37. Thomas, p. 1.

38. Ramsaye mentions *Annabelle-the-Dancer* made in the summer of 1894 at West Orange, N.J. for the Edison Kinetoscope, pp. 194–95.

39. Julian Johnson, "The Shadow Stage," *Photoplay Magazine* 16 (August 1919): 55–56 in George Pratt, ed., *Spellbound in Darkness* (Greenwich, Conn.: New York Graphic Society, rev. ed., 1973), p. 251.

40. Thomas, pp. 31–33; Ryan, pp. 19, 132–33, 384–85.

41. Gomery, "Failure," pp. 213–14, 218.

42. Gomery, "Talkies," p. 197.

43. Gomery, "Failure," p. 218.

44. Thomas, p. 35.

45. Ramsaye, p. 570. Charles Urban, head of Kinemacolor and present during the filming, gives the figure of £150,000+ in typewritten notes dated 1921 quoted by Thomas, p. 27.

46. Thomas, p. 26.

47. Ramsaye, p. 570.

48. There is a striking similarity in wording between Ramsaye and the typewritten notes of Urban. Portions of the latter are presented in Thomas, pp. 26–27, 13.

49. Limbacher, p. 15.

50. Ramsaye, p. 570.

51. *Ibid.*

52. *Ibid.,* pp. 570–71.

53. *Ibid.,* p. 570.

54. *Ibid.,* p. 571.

55. *Ibid.*

56. Thomas, p. 32.

57. Gomery, "Talkies," pp. 201–7.

58. *Ibid.,* pp. 194, 199, 206. See also J. Douglas Gomery, "Writing the History of the American Film Industry: Warner Brothers and Sound," *Screen* 17 (Spring 1976): 40–53.

59. Gomery, "Talkies," p. 210.

60. Gomery, "Failure," p. 218.

61. "What? Color in the Movies Again?", *Fortune* 10 (October 1934), p. 93.

62. *Ibid.,* p. 166.

63. J. Douglas Gomery, "Hollywood Converts to Sound: Chaos or Order?" in Evan William Cameron, ed., *The Coming of Sound to the American Cinema 1925–1940* (Pleasantville, N.Y.: Redgrave, 1979).

64. George Frost and S. Chesterfield Oppenheim, "Technical History of Professional Color Motion Pictures" (Washington, D.C.: The Patent, Trademark, and Copyright Foundation, George Washington University), mimeograph.

65. Jean-Louis Comolli, "Technique et idéologie," six parts in *Cahiers du cinéma* no. 229 (May–June 1971), pp. 4–21; no. 230 (July 1971), pp. 51–57; no.231 (August–September 1971), pp. 42–49; no. 233 (November 1971), pp. 39–45; nos. 234–235 (December–January 1971–72), pp. 94–100; no. 241 (September–October 1972), pp. 20–24.

The first four parts are translated by Christopher Williams, "Ideas About Film Technology and the History of the Cinema, with Reference to Comolli's Texts on Technology (*Cahiers du Cinéma*)," British Film Institute, mimeograph, part 1 (pp. 1.1–2a.9), part 2 (pp. 2b.1–2b.10), part 3 (pp. 3.1–3.11), and part 4 (pp. 4.1–4.10). Half of the first part is translated by Diana Matias, "Technique and Ideology: Camera, Perspective, Depth of Field," *Film Reader* 2 (Evanston, Ill.: Northwestern University Press, 1977), pp. 128–140, reprinted here.

The reference in the text is to Comolli, part 4: pp. 40–41, 43 (pp. 4.1, 4.2, 4.5).

66. *Ibid.,* part 1: p. 15 (p. 1.16). Edward Buscombe argues that economics can explain the necessary but not sufficient conditions for the innovation of color. He goes on to examine the needs and ideology served by color; Buscombe, pp. 24–25.

67. *Ibid.,* part 3: p. 44 (p.3.2); see especially part 2: pp. 56–57 n. 13 (pp. 2b.9–2b.10).

68. *Aristotle's Poetics* trans. S. H. Butcher (New York: Hill and Wang, 1961), chap. VII.3.

69. Comolli, part 1: pp. 7–8, 11 (pp. 1.5, 1.6, 1.10).

70. *Ibid.,* part 1: p. 9f. (p. 1.7f).

71. See Ernst Mayr, "Evolution," *Scientific American* 239 (September 1978), pp. 47–55.

72. Sklar, p. 51 (my emphasis).

73. See Louis Althusser, "Ideology and Ideological State Apparatuses" in *Lenin and Philosophy and Other Essays,* trans. Ben Brewster (New York: Monthly Review Press, 1971), pp. 127–186; Paul Narboni and Jean-Louis Comolli, "Cinema/Ideology/Criticism," three parts in *Screen* 12 (Spring, Summer 1971) and *Screen* 13 (Spring 1972); Terry Eagleton, *Marxism and Literary Criticism* (Los Angeles: University of California Press, 1976), pp. viii, 16–19; Philip Rosen, "*Screen* and the Marxist Project in Film Criticism," *Quarterly Review of Film Studies* 2 (August 1977): 273–87; Branigan, "Subjectivity Under Siege," p. 10 and "Foreground and Background: A Reply to Paul Willemen," *Screen* 19 (Summer 1978), p. 139.

74. Jean-Patrick Lebel, *Cinéma et idéologie* (Paris: Editions sociales, 1971).

75. Jean-Louis Baudry, "Cinéma: effects idéologiques produits par l'appareil de base," *Cinéthique* 7–8 (1970), pp. 1–8; trans. "Ideological Effects of the Basic Cinematographic Apparatus," *Film Quarterly* 27 (Winter 1974–75), pp. 39–47.

76. Comolli, part 1: p. 13 (p. 1.13).

77. Frank Taylor, "Mr. Technicolor," *The Saturday Evening Post* (October 22, 1949).

78. *The 1902 Edition of the Sears Roebuck Catalogue* (New York: Crown Publishers, Inc., 1969), p. 170.

79. Kinemacolor Programme, New York, Madison Square Garden (Dec. 11, 1909), reprod. in Ryan, pp. 438–43.

80. *Ibid.*

81. Ramsaye, p. 572.

82. *Time* (May 9, 1977), p. 20. See also *Time* (February 13, 1978), p. 62: "A camera can explore the world in ways your eyes can't." The ideology of Art is also commonly invoked; see *ibid.*, p. 5: "For me, photography has become a magic window to two minds: my subject's and my own."

83. Vance Kepley, Jr., "Griffith's *Broken Blossoms* and the Problem of Historical Specificity," *Quarterly Review of Film Studies* 3 (Winter 1978): 37–47.

84. 1902 Sears catalogue, p. 156.

85. Quoted by Limbacher, p. 4.

86. See, e.g., the comments by a prominent Hollywood cinematographer on the added realism of Technicolor; Walter Blanchard, "Aces of the Camera V: Leon Shamroy, A.S.C.," *American Cinematographer* (May 1941), p. 254.

87. Quoted by Jay Leyda, *Kino* (New York: Collier Books, 1960), p. 47n.

88. *Fortune, op. cit.,* p. 168 (my emphasis).

89. Lansing Holden, a color designer for Selznick International, and Gilbert Betancourt, a color coordinator, offer some comments in "Color! The New Language of the Screen," *Cinema Arts* 1 (July 1937), p. 64 and "Present Color Trend Is Toward Subdued Hues," *American Cinematographer* (August 1937), p. 317. The color consultant was one of several tie-in services (including processing and printing) which were to cause antitrust difficulties for Technicolor. See note 64.

90. C. W. Handley, "Advanced Technique of Lighting on Technicolor," *American Cinematographer* (June 1937), pp. 230–31; William Stull, "Technicolor Bringing New Charm to Screen," *American Cinematographer* (June 1937), p. 236; Elmer Richardson, "Recent Developments in Motion Picture Lighting," *American Cinematographer* (August 1937), p. 319; W. Howard Greene, "Low Key Lighting May Be as Easy in Color as It Is in Monochrome," *American Cinematographer* (April 1938), p. 151.

91. Stull, p. 236.

92. "Faster Color Film Cuts Light a Half," *American Cinematographer* (August 1939), p. 356. The faster film also allowed the use of large background projection screens which reduced the necessity for location shooting; William Stull, "Amateur Progress in 1939 Exceeded Professional," *American Cinematographer* (January 1940), p. 16; Barry Salt, "Film Style and Technology in the Thirties," *Film Quarterly* 30 (Fall 1976): 31–32.

93. James Wong Howe, "Reaction on Making His First Color Production," *American Cinematographer* (October 1937), p. 411. See also, J. A. Ball, "The Technicolor Process of Three-Color Cinematography," *Journal of the Society of Motion Picture Engineers* 25 (August 1935), p. 136; Winton Hoch, "Technicolor Cinematography," *Journal of the Society of Motion Picture Engineers* 32 (August 1942), p. 102; and several articles in the July 1941 issue of *American Cinematographer*. The reduction of illumination levels allowed new techniques to be used to create natural effects; Arthur Miller, "Putting Naturalness into Modern Interior Lightings," *American Cinematographer* (March 1941), p. 104.

94. There is, though, much to be learned from a stylistic analysis of historical writing; see Peter Gay, *Style in History* (New York: Basic Books, 1974) and Erich Auerbach, *Mimesis: The Representation of Reality in Western Literature* trans. Willard Trask (Princeton, N. J.: Princeton University Press, 1953).

MASS-PRODUCED PHOTOPLAYS: ECONOMIC AND SIGNIFYING PRACTICES IN THE FIRST YEARS OF HOLLYWOOD

JANET STAIGER

The greatest value of Staiger's contribution to this volume no doubt lies in its attempt to specify some of the relations between economics and aesthetics. Unlike Buscombe and Comolli, who argue that economic constraints may limit the range of the aesthetically possible and that they position what remains within an ideological arena, Staiger tries to portray an intimate relationship between the two that affirms a continuing series of tensions. Instead of sound's becoming part of cinema's technological repertoire when it was ideologically and economically advantageous, Staiger sees signifying practices continuing to exist in tension with economic demands. How a technological or stylistic innovation becomes economically coopted is less her thematic starting point than the assumption that economic considerations operate to hold a potentially much broader range of aesthetic practices perpetually in check and that this tension becomes a central feature of the cinema as institution and apparatus. Our own desire for the cinema takes form around the contradictory tendencies that pulse between the economic and the aesthetic—between the uniqueness that ads for a particular film proclaim and the standardization that recurrent industry patterns or practices enforce.

In this way, Staiger proposes a highly dynamic model of industrial and signifying practice that seems both more subtle and more powerful than the models that Branigan examines. Like Gomery, Staiger introduces us to a rich range of source material and to a highly suggestive, interdisciplinary methodology. An excellent example of that methodology lies in her adaptation of the art history tactic of examining contracts between patrons and artists to determine what values or qualities in a painting received the highest value: She examines moving picture ads to see what qualities were promoted the most heavily, and she contrasts them with the qualities promoted by intraindustry guidelines and statements.

The difficulties in positing determining linkages between levels of activity that possess their own internal dynamic and that yet are clearly related, such as economic and aesthetic practices, are only partially resolved by metaphors and vocabulary that reduce one to the other. In some historical accounts, the resort to rhetorical persuasiveness, the use of such terms as productive practices *and* production of meaning *to refer to the realm of discourse as well as to economic activity, seems poorly based, because it relies on a loose impression of both film*

*style and studio method. Staiger eschews this easy out and makes a number of
intriguing points about early filmmaking. A study of how the tensions she
identifies have played themselves out over an extended period of time would be
the next logical step.*

•

In a 1917 handbook for freelance writers of movies, Marguerite Bertsch writes,
"By the subjective we mean all that takes place within the mind or soul of a
character, either in thought or feeling, influencing his future behavior." She then
describes two techniques: the double exposure, in which both the character and
the subjective thoughts are represented simultaneously in the image, and editing
with dissolves, in which the subjective material is presented sequentially in shots
bracketed by the cues of dissolves. She continues: "All subjective matter, such as
a retrospection into the past, a looking forward into the future, or the hallucinations of a troubled mind, is possible to either, and so these two devices may be
used one in place of the other." Of course, Bertsch is disseminating and formalizing conventions we recognize, as did she, as part of the standard techniques of the
Hollywood film of 1917.[1]

As an analyst of films, one area of research is how we explain historically
particular representational systems. An apparent explanation of films at least is
that the narrative moving pictures the United States film industry produced took
theirs initially from representational systems already available in fiction, theater,
pantomime, vaudeville, opera, from systems in painting, engraving, still photography, lantern and stereopticon shows, illustrated comic strips and so on. In other
words, the industry took representational systems available from other extant
products in the culture and adapted them where necessary to suit the moving
pictures. The production of these objects constitutes a culture's signifying practices, which include its ideologies of representation, its conventions, its aesthetics. We are familiar with the characterization of the representational system
which Hollywood produced: a linear, "closed" sequence of events with emphasis
on individual character psychology as motivation for narrative action; the dominance of causal action over spatial and temporal continuity justifying the breaking
down, the analyzing of space and time—but a continuity reconstituted through
certain rules of linkage, such as matches-on-action, frame cuts, establishing and
re-establishing shots, systems of screen direction (the 180-degree rule, shot–
reverse shot, eyeline and point-of-view constructions). We are familiar with its
photographic aesthetics: valuing a "three-dimensional," "stereoscopic" depth;
clear, steady images in which the narrative event "stands out" within the site of
its occurrence; human bodies made up and lit for cultural representations of
beauty, realism and typage as well as for narrative legibility. At any point of
choice for this representational system other possibilities exist, and within the
mode there are historical changes as well.[2]

Economic practices, the other part of this process, are also products of and
producers of cultures and social institutions. These practices are the economic
modes of production—the forces and relations of production. Clearly, signifying

and economic practices are not separate. On the one hand, the creation of a product that signifies involves some mode of economic production, even if it is a single individual positioned in relation to a single object. On the other hand, any product of an industry (including the tools and technology produced to create the product) potentially has some signification which may be as basic as an expression of the function of the object. This object is for drinking. That one is for measuring the amount of reflected light. The difference between the two practices, really, is what part of the progress one is emphasizing at the moment.

In order to make this more concrete, I want to consider how economic practices in the first years of Hollywood might be related to the development of its representational systems such as, for instance, Bertsch's statement of the equivalence of two methods to signify subjectivity. I shall concentrate on what became the dominant practices, not the options which might have been. To study this, I am going to construct, first of all, a general description of the economic practices in the society contemporaneous with the initiation of the U.S. film industry. In this description I am going to identify a tension in the economic practices between standardization and differentiation. Second, I am going to describe some of the economic practices of the film industry between 1907 and 1917 which repeat this general tension. Third, I will suggest how and where these economic practices had an effect on the representational systems.

THE CONTEMPORARY ECONOMIC PRACTICES

Economic practices in the United States shifted significantly during the nineteenth century. The introduction of a machine tool industry in the 1810s and 20s permitted an industrial revolution which emphasized mass production through standardization and interchangeable parts.[3] These machines centralized the location and formalized the labor process into a factory mode of production. Companies formed to capitalize on inventions, such as the telegraph and telephone, and massive capital investment in transportation systems rapidly promoted national and international markets. Aided by state institutions in the form of laws and court decisions, a corporate business structure developed. An unanticipated effect of the Fourteenth Amendment was the court's decision to define business corporations as "persons," giving them due process of law.[4]

When the Standard Oil trust was broken up in 1892, it re-incorporated as a holding company in New Jersey, a state which had in 1889 foreseen the advantages of creating a liberal incorporation law. The New Jersey law permitted corporations, like persons, to buy and hold stock in other companies, allowing combinations to develop and to capitalize "without regard to the actual cost of existing plant[s]."[5] From 1896 to 1904, consolidation of firms occurred at an incredible rate, the high point of which was the incorporation of U.S. Steel for over $1,000,000,000, while Moody's listed 318 other industrial combinations with more than 5,300 plants and a combined capital of over $7,000,000,000. A thousand railroad lines were consolidated into six systems controlling over $10,000,000,000 in capital.[6] Supreme Court decisions made the Sherman Anti-

Trust Act of 1890 almost irrelevant, except when applied to striking unions.[7] Big business produced increasing capital and goods with the United States rivaling Europe as an industrial giant.

With this came the business concept of efficiency as the means to economic success. Efficiency justified the division of labor into smaller and smaller units and the motions of the worker into more and more predetermined sequences of actions. General interest in labor conditions developed after 1900 in the United States due to attacks by labor organizations and muckrakers and by comparisons to the Europeans who adopted Taylorism before U.S. businesses did. "Scientific management" caught on in the early 1910s.[8]

Efficiency through economies of scale justified the creation of trusts and then holding companies and other legal business structures.[9] John D. Rockefeller sought an end to "'idiotic, senseless destruction,' 'the wasteful conditions' of competition."[10] Discussing in 1902 the reorganization and recapitalization of the railroads, M. G. Cunniff said that Huntington's and Morgan's idea of a "community of interest" had brought the lines to "the best condition they have ever known, with the cheapest freight rates, the best equipment, the fastest service, and the largest dividends in the world."[11]

Efficiency justified the standardization of products. Trade associations which dated from the Civil War provided a means of sharing information, developing standard cost accounting systems, and pooling patents.[12] "Efficiency" spilled over into political and legal decisions. In 1901 Theodore Roosevelt considered "handling the tariff problem through 'scientific management,'"[13] and court decisions on wage rates and working conditions for women were made on the basis of business efficiency.

If efficiency justified standardization, another process was simultaneously at work—differentiation of products by advertising. Although advertising is ancient as an economic practice, in the early 1800s in the United States most goods were sold generically. By the mid-1800s companies began advertising goods by name brands, and by the 1870s retailers spent money on local and national printed materials to the consumer and began outdoor display advertising. In 1870, 121 trademarks were registered with the U.S. Patent Office, in 1906 more than 10,000 and by 1926 over 70,000. An early advertising agent set up business in 1841 in Philadelphia, soon expanding to Boston and New York. In 1899 Ayer's became a full-service ad agency, did national campaigns, conducted market surveys and created trade names. Advertising expenditures in 1904 were over $800 million and at 3.4 percent of the gross national product, the same percentage level current today. In the 1890s as the corporations consolidated, they moved into vertically integrated structures, directly controlling their own retailing and associated advertising to consumers. By the late 1920s only one third of U.S. goods went through independent wholesalers; the other two thirds were marketed directly or through corporation-owned outlets.

Thus, the film industry begins in a general industrial structure of a well-developed corporate capitalism which is positioned between the economic practice of standardization for efficient mass production and the economic practice of product differentiation.

THE ECONOMIC PRACTICES OF
THE FILM INDUSTRY

The people who entered the film industry had these contemporary examples as their standards for successful economic competition. The formation of a moving pictures patent pool at the end of 1908 followed the general pattern of consolidation of communities-of-interest to end "vexatious and expensive litigations."[14] In a brief prepared by the Patents Company for the 1912 investigation by the Department of Justice into their trust, the lawyers argued that without a combination of patents no business could be conducted. A series of lawsuits had determined three patents essential to the industry, which were split between three different concerns and their licensees.

The only solution for the industry to continue was cross-licensing. Lawyers cited patent pool precedents in the farm machinery industry as justification for the formation of the company.[15] At the point of organization, all significant manufacturing and importing firms were included in the company.[16] The organizing of the Patents Company seemed to indicate a stable business climate, and the individual firms, assured of regular unrestricted national and international sale of their products through the Patents Company, began to run off up to one hundred copies of each negative rather than the ten to twelve previously struck. The increased income provided capital for expanding their operations.

Unfortunately for the Company, however, while patents seek a monopoly of control over an invention, publication of patent information upon application also provides knowledge for other inventors.[17] Even if the Patents Company had legal rights, the cameras and projectors were easily manufactured by others. Furthermore, the growth of the exhibition sector of the industry seemed to suggest high profits—warranting a calculated risk of being caught for patent infringement. With low barriers to entry and high profits to tempt new competitors, it is not surprising that in the next twelve months Powers Picture Plays, the Independent Motion Picture Company, the New York Motion Picture Company, Thanhouser, Rex and other firms incorporated.[18]

Meanwhile, the manufacturing firms of the Patents Company followed general economic practices of vertically integrating into distributing and retailing by establishing the General Film Company in April 1910. The independents followed suit and consolidated at the distribution level.[19] In 1912 Livingston and Co., members of the New York Stock Exchange, organized the public financing of the distributing firm of Mutual Film, and $1,700,000 common stock and $800,000 cumulative preferred at 7 percent were authorized for sale. Price, Waterhouse in 1916 issued a fifty-four-page manual on how standard accounting for the film industry should be done.[20]

The mode of production was similarly sophisticated by 1916. Once the industry seemed potentially capable of a regular supply of films with a widespread demand in the exhibition sector, mass production began. Multiple shooting units for each company were created to increase the number of releases per company, thus increasing profit potentials. The "logic" of this economic practice was described in 1911:

When an industry has reached such a magnitude that many people are employed in its work . . . some employees will develop greater ability in some lines than in others, and the lines of activity become so divergent that they are best cared for separately. As in any manufacturing industry, the manufacture of motion picture films for exhibition in a modern factory has its division of labor, and a film picture is the joint product of the various departments and specialists who in turn take it and perfect it with their skills.[21]

This divided labor split into a "line-and-staff" structure with administrators in New York or Chicago handling general operations and distributing and advertising the films, producers and studio managers administering the nationally distributed studio and on-location production units, departments handling set construction, costuming, properties, special effects, casting, developing negatives and editing, and units headed by directors doing the shooting. In late 1916, an "efficiency system" in one studio had a four-page manual given to new employees which listed rules, regulations and the duties of every job position. Given a number within the system, the employee entered into a production schedule already organized.[22]

The pattern for the product was the scenario produced by the director and writers.[23] By 1913, detailed continuity scripts were regularly produced by scenario departments. These departments were split into two major functional operations: the writing of original screenplays for the firm and the transference of original plots from freelancers and increasingly from plays, novels and short stories. Trade papers announced as early as 1909 that manufacturers were accepting freelance contributions of stories. In a 1909 article entitled "Motion Picture Play Writing as an Art" (three months after the new copyright law went into effect and following the court ruling that Kalem's film *Ben Hur* infringed on copyright protection), the Edison company announced the filming of Mark Twain's "The Prince and the Pauper" and the hiring of famous writers to produce scenarios. By 1911 trade papers were regularly publishing articles such as "Outline of How to Write a Photoplay," and books contained sample scenarios.[24]

Producing standard scripts had at least two functions: (1) saving costs and (2) controlling quality. It is easy to see how preplanning the scenes saves costs. Since labor was paid by time, not unit of production, all employees needed to be used efficiently. Furthermore, detailed scripts permitted initial estimates of the cost of the film and allowed prior trimming if the film was likely to go over budget.

The second function, quality control, relates to two events simultaneous with the development of this mode of production. Between 1910 and 1915, multiple-reel films increased in number. At the same time, Frank Woods of the *New York Dramatic Mirror* and other writers began reviewing films and responding to patrons' questions and reactions in the general and trade papers. This formalized network of interaction began a dissemination of rules and categories of conspicuous skill and quality in the photoplay.

A study of some of these conceptions of quality and skill should suggest how certain representational systems held in esteem influenced economic practices. (Again, this is a two-sided process.) As examples, two reviews of Woods in March 1911 should indicate an ideological reason for the development of the continuity script:

His Daughter (Biograph, February 23)— . . . the old father's fall was not convincing, and the girl's intention to leave the town was told only by the subtitle, as she ran out bareheaded and with no traveling equipment. There was also a technical error in the management of the scenes: exits from the interiors are to the right, but the immediate entrances to the exteriors are also from the right.[25]

Attention has been called frequently in *Mirror* film reviews to apparent errors of direction or management as to exits and entrances in motion picture productions. . . . A player will be seen leaving a room or locality in a certain direction, and in the very next connecting scene, a sixteenth of a second later, he will enter in exactly the opposite direction. Now it may be argued quite logically that this need not necessarily be inartistic because the spectator himself may be assumed to [have] changed his point of view, but . . . the spectator will not look at it that way. Any one who has watched pictures knows how often his sense of reality has been shocked by this very thing.[26]

What the continuity script provides is a precheck of the quality of spatial, temporal and causal continuity and *vraisemblance.* This became more problematic as the length of the films developed and as the aesthetics refined to include frame cuts, matches-on-action, inserts, cut-backs, flashes, mixing of interior and exterior sets and narrative "punch."

That the industry paid attention to reviews and critics was evident in Woods's column of March 22, 1911, in which he rather gleefully recounts an incident of a film company arguing for half an hour, citing Woods as an authority, whether or not the son in a photoplay should turn toward the camera as he said farewell to his mother.[27] The solution was that the turn was deemed realistic because of spatial positions, but that the son should avoid playing to the camera, an acting practice Woods and others considered unnatural.

The dispersal of these standards of quality and of format was supplemented by the appearance of trade associations in the film industry. In July 1908 a craft union of projectionists formed, in 1911 New York motion picture exhibitors incorporated, in 1913 cinematographers in New York formed the Cinema Camera Club, in 1914 the Photoplay Authors' League was established and in 1916 the Society of Motion Picture Engineers formed with the "avowed purpose of 'the advancement in the theory and practice of motion picture engineering and the allied arts and sciences, the standardization of the mechanism and practices employed therein and the dissemination of scientific knowledge by publication.'"[28]

Furthermore, and this is something I want to stress, the quality control function was placed legally by the courts in the hands of the company. Two law suits in 1917 are typical of this. Charlie Chaplin sued Essanay for stretching a two reeler of his into a four reeler after he left. His suit was denied because, among other considerations, the photoplay was declared Essanay's property. In a second case, the director Herbert Brenon unsuccessfully contested Fox's reediting of *A Daughter of the Gods.*[29]

If these practices provided efficient, standardized mass production of photoplays, simultaneous with them came the need to differentiate the product—to appeal to the exhibitors to order one firm's films rather than another's. It should be pointed out that direct, nationwide, organized advertising to the consumer by the producing and distributing companies did not begin until 1915.[30] At first, exhibitors chose their own films from the distributors who advertised to them, and the exhibitors created their own advertising to attract customers: newspapers, billboards and lobby displays. With the formation of the Patents Company, some aids were offered to the exhibitors. In November 1909 the A.B.C. Company of Cleveland was delegated as official supplier of posters: "These posters are not 'fakes,' made up from dead stock previously printed for some melodramatic production, but *real pictorial posters made from actual photographs of scenes in the pictures they advertise."* [31] At the same time in Edison's catalogue, "stars" (its term) and stock players were being introduced to the exhibitors.[32] (These stars were established theatrical stars; the film companies began to develop their own about a year later.[33]) From this period on, the companies supplied cuts for newspapers and information about the actors and actresses to exhibitors so that they, in turn, could "boom" the films.

The rise of multiple-reel films coincides with this shift in attack to more controlled advertising of individual films. What was special about each film was specified to the consumer. The concept of a *feature* film goes back at least to this 1904 advice to exhibitors by Kleine Optical Company:

The exhibitor who purchases a small quantity of films, say from 300 to 500 feet, is necessarily compelled to confine himself to short subjects. But if the purchase is 1,000 feet, we advise one feature film of 400 to 500 feet, the balance from 50 to 100 feet each; if 2,000 feet, there should be at least one long feature film, such as *The Great Train Robbery,* 740 feet, or *Christopher Columbus,* 850 feet. These long films admit of special advertising, that is to say, special emphasis on one subject, which is more effective than equal emphasis on a number of shorter films. The public has been educated to appreciate these long films, which tell an interesting story and need few words of explanation.[34]

In October 1909 Pathé released *The Drink* in two parts over two days. Quickly exhibitors shifted from sequential days to running the multiple reels on one day and advertising something "extra and of more importance than the ordinary single reels."[35] Since business was thriving, more money could be expended on these "De Luxe" films, which went together with better advertising and timing release dates to take advantage of the advertising, which permitted higher admission prices and which could pay the costs of theatrical stars and production values. As a result, the film had a longer exhibition life, providing more income to cover the geometrical increases in cost.[36] In April 1914, a year before the release of *The Birth of a Nation,* one fifth of New York City's theaters were running multiple-reel features, and people were paying $1.00 on Broadway to see a film that cost $50,000 to produce.[37] In 1915 Paramount, seeking higher rental rates for a feature film, decided to assist directly the exhibitors in their promotion, reasoning that to get the higher rentals they would need to increase receipts. Advised by an advertising agency to direct ads to the patrons, Paramount's new Department of Exploitation began their initial national advertising with primary demand ads— ones that emphasized the institution of movie-theater-going.[38]

In *Painting and Experience in Fifteenth-Century Italy,* Michael Baxandall talks about the difficulties of determining what a patron of the arts might see in an individual work. To locate the "period eye," as he calls it, he examines written contracts between painters and patrons and notes that during the first part of the 1400s the quality of the materials to be used was carefully specified. By the second half of the century, what parts of the work the master artist was to paint became important. This leads Baxandall to the conclusion that cultivated people expected to be able to perceive the *conspicuous skill* of the artist.[39] These perceptible skills, of course, were formally taught by rules and categories of discussion within the culture.

What Baxandall is suggesting, I think, is generalizable to the U.S. film industry. An historian can construct where *value* in the product lies as a means, in part, of determining the relationships between economic and signifying practices. In this mode of production, advertising is an economic practice directing consumers to the apparent areas of exchange-value in the product. In the culture in this time, novelty, originality and uniqueness are areas of heavy advertising stress.[40] Additional ones are conspicuous display of certain "unique" personalities, specific popular genres, "realism" and expensive means of production (for instance, spectacles in which massive sets and hundreds of people are involved).

These are parts of the catalogue and review descriptions of three early films:

Life of an American Fireman (Edison, 1903, Edwin S. Porter): It will be difficult for the exhibitor to conceive the amount of work involved and the number of rehearsals necessary to turn out a film of this kind. We were compelled to enlist the services of the fire departments of four different cities . . . and about 300 firemen appear in the various scenes of this film.[41]

The Great Train Robbery (Edison, 1903, Edwin S. Porter): It has been posed and acted in faithful duplication of the genuine 'Hold Ups' made famous by various outlaw bands in the far West, and only recently the East has been shocked by several crimes of the frontier order, which fact will increase the popular interest in this great Headline Attraction.[42]

Il Trovatore (Pathé, 1911): Pathé has an "innovation": The novelty lies in the special music that goes with the picture. The score of the opera has been carefully arranged by a competent musician so that it times exactly with the dramatic action of the film.[43]

We have, then, in the first years of Hollywood, economic practices with a tension: simplify, standardize and consolidate for efficiency and mass production but differentiate, direct the consumers' attention to the originality and production values of the feature product.

ECONOMIC PRACTICES AND FILMIC REPRESENTATIONAL SYSTEMS

In the U.S. film industry, co-extensive with its history of economic practices is a complex history of signifying practices—ideologies, aesthetics, conventions. What might be economically cheap might simultaneously "violate" an aesthetic of beauty or composition or a convention of *vraisemblance* or continuity or counter ideologies of value and representation. I have suggested a tension between the economic practices of standardization and differentiation. Likewise, I theorize, in general, two other tensions within the processes. First, that of economic practices versus signifying practices: the tension of low cost—an economic goal for profit maximization—versus high cost—ideologies of value in originality, spectacles, displays of labor and conspicuous skills, such as technological tours de force. The other major tension is within the signifying practices themselves: a tension between codes of *vraisemblance,* what seems "ordinary life," and codes of novelty, variation, "art," beauty, the non-ordinary. One can begin to postulate the possibilities had the economic or signifying practices been different, had, for instance, on the broader scale, *repetition* rather than originality been valued.

This prevents a simplistic assertion that such and such economic practice determined such and such signifying practice and makes the historical representation more complex, mediated and non-linear. Locating single causes also becomes impossible. This means that, in an individual instance, specific historical inquiry will be necessary to understand the impact of the particular practices operating at that time and place on the formation of specific films or groups of films. But this model likewise permits that precision without lapsing into a reflectionism.

In this concluding section, I am merely going to suggest areas in which economic practices of the period pressured the construction of certain signifying practices. I have already indicated how the mode of production, the trade media and trade associations worked toward standardizing the representational systems and how advertising and reviews promoted perception of specifiable values in the product. Now I will suggest some further sites of influence.

Cost factors promoted the reuse of sets and costumes, thus stimulating serials, genres and series. Serials, like the multiple-reel films, were usually shot at one time so that locations and sets were used only once even though the episodes might extend for weeks in release.[44] Price, Waterhouse, in their 1916 memorandum, advises accountants to charge all scenery and costume costs to the original film since reuse was unpredictable but would thereafter be free any time such reuse could be managed.[45] Companies often called for scenarios that would use established sets. Sometimes an extensive initial investment channeled subsequent films. William Selig's zoo, purchased in 1908 for an African safari film, was used for a series of animal films. Bison's hiring of the Miller Brothers 101 Ranch Wild West Show resulted in several years of Westerns and the Civil War films using large casts.[46] Connected to this, a 1913 manual advises freelance writers:

Unity of place is also of economic importance for the production and will permit the use of the same settings for many scenes. In this way the producer feels justified in spending more money upon the settings themselves. He is more or less limited by the owner of the motion picture company as to the outlay for each picture—and the result is more elaborate and artistic stage effects.[47]

The writer also advises creating few characters for the plot:

At the same time more attention could be given by the director to the production; more time taken, because less wasted on supernumeraries; and more money to spend on settings and costumes and additional film, because of the reduced cost of salaries.[48]

Cost factors promoted a limited number of retakes. Price, Waterhouse suggests that there were several ways to distribute overhead costs, but the preferred method was to divide them by the number of exposed feet of negative film on the assumption that "managers who take many feet of discarded negative are careless, wasteful, and expensive. . . . "[49] Rehearsals of actors were considered cheap compared to the costs of all laborers, electricity and film stock involved in actual shooting time. Such an economic practice might also weigh against long takes, which are more susceptible to error as the length of the take or its complexity increases.[50]

A more tenuous connection, but one that occasionally surfaces, is that cost factors related to techniques of style. A handbook author writes that dissolves are usually used instead of double exposures to indicate a character's thoughts because they are cheaper, less complicated and less time consuming. The practice of having the characters "discovered" in the scene rather than using entrances is cited as saving thirty to forty feet of film. The technique of cutbacks (the period term for cross-cutting) can be used to abbreviate the length of the action and save film footage by cutting away to parallel action and then cutting back with the former action completed.[51] Obviously, there are other reasons for the cut-back: it is a means to avoid censorable material, an explicit aesthetics of variation of shots is functioning in the period and it provides a simpler, cheaper technique than a split screen or an unusual set for representing parallel action—not to mention the narrative effects of suspense and complexity which constitute a process for the subject.

Expenditures of funds on spectacles and trick work are often balanced against the effect they produce. Writers of advice to freelancers continually caution against writing photoplays that require wrecking trains, burning mansions and building extravagant sets. John Emerson and Anita Loos go so far as to advise that, although night scenes can be done with "sunlight arcs, mercury lights and spotlights," the cost of each is $2,500, and they are hard to transport. "It is well," they write, "to keep your characters indoors by night."[52]

On the other hand, the expenditures might be justified. In describing the production technology, one writer in 1913 points out that the camera is heavy and mounted on a "massive tripod." Despite this, it is shifted to difficult set ups:

The body of the camera, without the tripod, may be placed upon the overhead beams in a studio in order to get some novel scenic effect below; or a special platform may be built for the camera and operator, when the producer is determined to get a scene on the side of a cliff.[53]

The reason? ". . . [A]n unusually strong story that justifies the special effort. . . . " Innovation of such effects seems motivated by this ideology of value in originality supported by the economic and signifying practices. It explains the occurrence *within the system itself of optional signifying practices* without resorting to a model of these options deconstructing the system.[54] For example, Fred Balshofer describes the decision to use a complicated camera movement rather than analytical editing in a 1915 film:

Besides being an outstanding picture, *The Second in Command* contained a technical innovation. . . . While going over the script for our first picture, it seemed to us that we would have to come up with something new in production to match the class of our new star, [Francis X.] Bushman. We decided to plan the action of some scenes to make it possible to follow the actors, especially Bushman, and to move to a close-up without making a cut. We certainly weren't thinking of anything as elaborate as we wound up with. We drew a rough sketch of a platform large enough to set the tripod on with the camera and cameraman that could be moved on four wheels. When it was constructed, we found we would have to enlarge it to accommodate a second person. As the platform was pushed forward, it became difficult for Adler to crank the camera, watch the actors to judge distance as the platform moved, and to follow the focus all at the same time. And so it went. We were continually taking the rolling platform in to our small carpenter shop and having it altered to meet our needs as they became more and more complex. . . . Making a film this way took more time but after looking at the rushes, we thought it worthwhile. Besides, it added that something extra to the production of the picture.[55]

Of course this sort of "first-itis" was useful to the individual companies in promoting a studio style and identity for brand-name advertising. The reviewers and trade papers contributed to a perpetuation of searching for novelties and innovations. One reviewer in 1912 writes:

Biograph's influence on picture production has been important. It was the first company— at least in America— to introduce heroic figures in its pictures. It was the first in America to present acting of the restrained artistic type, and the first to produce quiet drama and pure comedy. It was the first to attempt fading light effects. It was the first to employ alternating flashes of simultaneous action in working up suspense.[56]

Triangle initiated the use of art titles as an "experiment" in 1916 which "served to distinguish still further the highly individual character of the Ince plays,"[57] and in an article entitled "Very Latest Thing in Photoplay Subtitles," Triangle explains that their Photographic and Art Department head had "set to work to develop the subtitle to a maximum of efficiency."[58]

Something successful was widely and rapidly imitated by the industry. Classical Hollywood films are not only typified by genres and series but by cycles. This was made possible by short-term production plans, often made less than a year in advance even in the 1930s and 40s for program features. This was partially due to the standardization which made rapid production possible. In 1913, critics were complaining that the "time is ripe for another shift," that everything is a "repetition" of what had come before.[59] The search for originality leads to some amusing results. Emerson and Loos say that "the very latest thing" in 1920 is the "pictorial pun. For example, in *A Virtuous Vamp,* a leading character says to the flirtatious heroine: 'Woman, you make me see red.' The scene is instantly tinted red."[60] Emerson and Loos think this "novelty" will last a couple months. Or the case cited in 1913:

Death is seldom dramatic. It is even capable of being turned to farce if overdone. One of the funniest stories that was ever screened ended with the suicide of the sole remaining member of the cast. All the others had been murdered. It was meant by producer and author alike to be tremendously sensational, but there is but a short step from the ultrasensational to the travesty of sensation.[61]

Economic practices affected the signifying practices in another way. To some writers they even became part of the aesthetic rationales for the signifying practices. Victor Freeburg in the 1923 book *Pictorial Beauty on the Screen* incorporates efficiency into his theory of aesthetics: "The pictorial beauty discussed in this book is really a kind of pictorial efficiency, and therefore must have practical economic value." "A practical proof is dramatic utility. The motions of a photoplay are in the service of the story. They should perform that work well without waste of time and energy." "One might say that the artistic efficiency of a motion picture may be partly tested in the same way as the practical value of a machine. In either case motions are no good unless they help to perform some work."[62]

In my initial example, Bertsch's equation of the two procedures for representing subjectivity may have been a bit naive. Technically and economically, a double exposure provided more production complexity than editing with dissolves. By 1917 the perceptible value of the *novelty* of either device may have made them equivalent in signifying subjectivity with the double exposure used for production value and editing with dissolves used when the subjective sequence was extensive or not worth the additional cost. (There are also different implications about the representation of space and subject.) In either case, however, they are incorporated into a general representational mode, the classical Hollywood film. To determine the value and function of any individual practice requires an extensive construction of the history of *both* economic and signifying practices within the culture in order to provide satisfactory production of knowledge about signification by subjects.[63]

Notes

1. Marguerite Bertsch, *How to Write for Moving Pictures: A Manual of Instruction and Information* (New York: George H. Doran Company, 1917), pp. 97 and 99.

2. In using the term signifying practices, I want to emphasize that the representational systems produced have meaning in the act of the subject's constitution of the signifying object. Assumed, then, are issues of subjectivity. See Rosalind Coward and John Ellis, *Language and Materialism: Developments in Semiology and the Theory of the Subject* (London: Routledge & Kegan Paul, 1977), pp. 80–81 and 122–52 *passim,* and Stephen Heath, "The Turn of the Subject," *Ciné-Tracts* 7/8, 2, No. 3 and 4 (Summer, Fall 1979), 42–45. Several instances of the characterization of the classical Hollywood mode of representation are: Jean-Louis Comolli, "Technique et Idéologie (4): Caméra, perspective, profondeur de champ," *Cahiers du Cinéma,* no. 233 (November 1971), pp. 39–45; Kristin Thompson and David Bordwell, "Space and Narrative in the Films of Ozu," *Screen* 17, no. 2 (Summer 1976): 42–43; and Noël Burch, "Porter, or Ambivalence," *Screen* 19, no. 4 (Winter 1978–1979): 91–105.

3. This section relies heavily on three general economic histories: Harry N. Scheiber, Harold G. Vatter and Harold Underwood Faulkner, *American Economic History,* 9th ed. (New York: Harper & Row, 1976); Alex Groner, *The American Heritage History of American Business and Industry* (New York: American Heritage Publishing Co., 1972); John Chamberlain, *The Enterprising Americans: A Business History of the United States,* rev. ed (New York: Harper & Row, 1974).

4. On the shift from the formation of corporations for public interests to those for private profit, see Groner, *The American Heritage History,* pp. 60 and 91. Chamberlain, *The Enterprising Americans,* pp. 132 and 154 details the court decisions and laws in the

second half of the century as does Scheiber et al., *American Economic History,* pp. 299–300, and Groner, *The American Heritage History,* p. 197.

5. Chamberlain, *The Enterprising Americans,* p. 174, and see U.S. Industrial Commission, *Preliminary Report on Trusts and Industrial Combinations,* 56th Cong., 1st Sess., House Document No. 476, Part 1 (Washington, D.C.: Government Printing Office, 1900), pp. 9–13, 16–20, 32–34 rpt. in *American Economic Development Since 1860,* ed. William Greenleaf (New York: Harper & Row, 1968), pp. 216–33.

6. The government's investigation in 1900 produced a detailed description and explanation of these mergers; see U.S. Industrial Commission, *Preliminary Report,* pp. 216–33. For a contemporary unsympathetic version which was widely read see William J. Ghent, *Our Benevolent Feudalism* (New York: The Macmillan Company, 1902). On the findings of the Pujo Committee of Congress, which investigated community-of-interest holdings in 1913, see *Great Issues in American History,* ed. Richard Hofstadter (New York: Alfred A. Knopf and Random House, 1958), pp. 298–301.

7. Groner, *American Heritage History,* pp. 198–99; Hofstadter, *Great Issues in American History,* pp. 121–22, 125.

8. On the history of scientific management in the U.S. see Don D. Lescohier, "Working Conditions," in *History of Labor in the United States,* ed. John R. Commons, vol. III (1935; rpt. ed., New York: Augustus M. Kelley, 1966), pp. 304–15; Thomas C. Cochran and William Miller, *The Age of Enterprise,* rev. ed. (New York: Harper & Brothers, 1961), pp. 184 and 243–48; Groner, *American Heritage History,* p. 217; Hofstadter, *Great Issues in American History,* pp. 242–43.

9. Magnus W. Alexander, *The Economic Evolution of the United States: Its Background and Significance* (New York: National Industrial Conference Board, 1929), p. 35.

10. John D. Rockefeller, cited in Chamberlain, *The Enterprising Americans,* p. 150.

11. "Increasing Railroad Consolidation," *World's Work* 3 (February 1902): 1775–1780, rpt. in *American Economic Development Since 1860,* pp. 106–15. Not everyone agreed with this assessment of holding companies; see Richard Hofstadter, *The Age of Reform* (New York: Vintage Books, 1955), p. 232, and Ghent, above.

12. Alexander, *The Economic Evolution of the United States,* pp. 34–38; Monte Calvert, *The Mechanical Engineer in America, 1830–1910* (Baltimore: Johns Hopkins University Press, 1967), p. 172; Cochran and Miller, *The Age of Enterprise,* p. 243; Ray M. Hudson, "Organized Effort in Simplification," *The Annals of the American Academy of Political and Social Science* 87 (May 1928): 1–8; and Frank L. Eidmann, *Economic Control of Engineering and Manufacturing* (New York: McGraw-Hill Book Company, 1931), pp. 261–68.

13. William Appleton Williams, *The Contours of American History* (1961; rpt. ed., New York: Franklin Watts, Inc., 1973), pp. 405–6.

14. M. B. Phillipp and Francis T. Homer for the Motion Picture Patents Co., "Memorandum for the Motion Picture Patents Company and the General Film Company concerning the investigation of their business by the Department of Justice," TS, 18 May 1912 (Museum of Modern Art), p. 17.

15. Phillipp and Homer, "Memorandum," pp. 1–17. The precedents were *Bement* v. *National Harrow Company,* 186 U.S. 70 and *Indiana Manufacturing Company* v. *J. I. Case Threshing Machine Company,* 154 F. R. 365.

16. Ralph Cassady Jr., "Monopoly in Motion Picture Production and Distribution: 1908–1915," *Southern California Law Review* 32, no. 4 (Summer 1959): 328–29, 335, 346. On page 363, Cassady lists five manufacturers not included in the company in early 1909 and another list is available in "The Independent Movement," *The Nickelodeon,* no. 1

(February 1909), pp. 39–40. The latter article gives a contemporary account of the exhibitors' reaction to the company's formation and the organization of a counter alliance, the Independent Film Protective Association.

17. Jeanne Thomas Allen, [untitled paper], The Cinematic Apparatus: Technology as Historical and Ideological Form, Conference at the Center for Twentieth-Century Studies, University of Wisconsin–Milwaukee, 22–24 February 1978. In the main argument of the essay Allen points out how the general business practice of standardization of technology relates to the history of the invention of the motion picture machines.

18. Robert C. Allen, "Motion Picture Exhibition in Manhattan 1906–1912: Beyond the Nickelodeon," *Cinema Journal* 18, no. 2 (Spring 1979): 11. On contemporary accounts of the expanding exhibition industry, see "Motion Picture Films," *Complete Illustrated Catalog of Moving Picture Machines, Stereopticons, Slides, Films* (Chicago: Kleine Optical Company, November 1905), pp. 206–07, rpt. in George C. Pratt, *Spellbound in Darkness: A History of the Silent Film*, rev. ed. (Greenwich, Conn.: New York Graphic Society, 1973), pp. 39–42; "Growth of the Film Business," *Billboard* 18, no. 37 (15 September 1906): 16, rpt. in Pratt, *Spellbound in Darkness*, pp. 42–43; Joseph Medill Patterson, "The Nickelodeons: The Poor Man's Elementary Course in the Drama," *The Saturday Evening Post* 180, no. 21 (23 November 1907): 10–11, 38, rpt. in Pratt, *Spellbound in Darkness*, pp. 46, 48–52. The details of the formation of the independents are: Powers Picture Plays—1909 (Anthony Slide, *Early American Cinema* [New York: A. S. Barnes & Co., 1970], p. 98); IMP—1909 (Slide, *Early American Cinema*, p. 96); the New York Motion Picture Company—early in 1909 incorporated in New York with $10,000 capital (Fred F. Balshofer and Arthur C. Miller, *One Reel a Week* [Berkeley, California: University of California Press, 1967], p. 22); Thanhouser—fall 1909 (Anthony Slide, *Aspects of American Film History Before 1920* [Metuchen, New Jersey: The Scarecrow Press, 1978], pp. 68–73); and Rex—1909 by Edwin Porter, Joe Engel and William Swanson (Balshofer and Miller, *One Reel a Week*, p. 48, and Slide, *Early American Cinema*, p. 14).

19. Phillipp and Homer, "Memorandum," pp. 42–46; "H. E. Aitken," *Reel Life* 3, no. 26 (14 April 1914): 17–18; "C. J. Hite's Career," *Reel Life* 3, no. 16 (3 January 1914): 3; "Spectator," "'Spectator's' Comments," *New York Dramatic Mirror* [hereafter *NYDM*] 65, no. 1691 (17 May 1911): 28; for a list of 1,911 manufacturers, brand names and distribution groups, see David Sherrill Hulfish, *Cyclopedia of Motion Picture Work*, vol. 1 (Chicago: American School of Correspondence, 1911), pp. 277–282.

20. "Financing the Motion Picture Wall Street's Latest Move," *Reel Life* 3, no. 22 (14 February 1914): 34. Other firms were organized as stock companies but without public sale; for details of early stock issues see Paul H. Davis, "Investing in the Movies [part 7]," *Photoplay* 9, no. 3 (February 1916): 71–73. His series of eleven articles runs from August 1915 through August 1916. Price, Waterhouse & Company, *Memorandum on Moving Picture Accounts* (New York: Price, Waterhouse & Company, 1916).

21. Hulfish, *Cyclopedia*, vol. 2, p. 76.

22. "The Higher Efficiency," *Cinema News* 1, no. 1 (15 December 1916): 6.

23. For a description of the development in one company of the mode of production using the producer as quality controller and the continuity script as the pattern, see Janet Staiger, "Dividing Labor for Production Control: Thomas Ince and the Rise of the Studio System," *Cinema Journal* 18, no. 2 (Spring 1979): 16–25. The standard script format is detailed there.

24. "Motion Picture Play Writing as an Art," *The Edison Kinetogram* 1, no. 3 (1 September 1909): 12; Archer McMackin, "How Moving Picture Plays Are Written," *The Nickelodeon* 2, no. 6 (December 1909): 171–73; Everett McNeil, "Outline of How to

Write a Photoplay," *Moving Picture World* 9, no. 1 (15 July 1911): 27; Hulfish, *Cyclopedia,* Vol. 2, pp. 78–90.

25. "Reviews of Licensed Films," *NYDM* 65, no. 1680 (1 March 1911): 31.

26. "Spectator," "'Spectator's' Comments," *NYDM* 65, no. 1681 (8 March 1911): 29.

27. "Spectator," "'Spectator's' Comments," *NYDM* 65, no. 1683 (22 March 1911): 28. Also see "Significant Praise for 'Mirror,'" *NYDM* 65, no. 1674 (18 January 1911): 34. Woods is undoubtedly "biased," but Epes Winthrop Sargent of *Moving Picture World,* William Lord Wright of *Motion Picture News* and other contemporaries continually acknowledge his (as well as their own) influence on the "art" of the photoplay.

28. Phil Whitman, "Western Correspondent," *Motion Picture News* 5, no. 3 (20 January 1912): 35; "Exhibitors Incorporate," *NYDM* 66, no. 1718 (22 November 1911): 25; Lewis W. Physioc, "The History of the Cinema Camera Club," *Cinema News* 1, no. 5 (15 February 1917): 5–6; "Woods Heads Authors' League," *NYDM* 70, no. 1840 (25 March 1914): 31; Society of Motion Picture Engineers, *The Society of Motion Picture Engineers* (New York: Society of Motion Picture Engineers, 1930), p. iii. The Cinema Camera Club was a forerunner of the American Society of Cinematographers, which formally incorporated in 1919; George Blaisdell, "Arnold Again Head of A.S.C.," *American Cinematographer* 20, no. 5 (May 1939): 198.

29. Louis D. Frohlich and Charles Schwartz, *The Law of Motion Pictures Including the Law of the Theatre* (New York: Baker, Voorhis, & Co., 1918), pp. 169–71; Slide, *Early American Cinema,* pp. 92–95.

30. For a general history see John Francis Barry and Epes W. Sargent, *Building Theatre Patronage: Management and Merchandising* (New York: Chalmers Publishing Company, 1927), pp. 15–27; Howard Thompson Lewis, *Cases on the Motion Picture Industry* (New York: McGraw-Hill Book Company, 1930), pp. 435–43. A taste of 1915 exhibitor advertising practices may be had from Epes Winthrop Sargent, *Picture Theatre Advertising* (New York: Chambers Publishing Company, 1915).

31. "Advertising the Pictures," *The Edison Kinetogram* 1, no. 7 (1 November 1909): 14 (their italics).

32. "The Edison Stock Company," *The Edison Kinetogram* 1, no. 4 (15 September 1909): 13; "Our Stock Company," *The Edison Kinetogram* 1, no. 5 (1 October 1909): 13; "Our Lobby Display Frames," *The Edison Kinetogram* 1, no. 9 (1 June 1910): 2.

33. Anthony Slide, "The Evolution of the Film Star," *Films in Review* 25 (December 1974): 591–94.

34. "About Moving Picture Films," *Complete Illustrated Catalog* (October 1904), pp. 30–31, rpt. in Pratt, *Spellbound in Darkness,* pp. 36–37.

35. "Spectator," "'Spectator's' Comments," *NYDM* 65, no. 1676 (1 February 1911): 29.

36. This list does not mean to suggest any causality or priority of factors. It notes only a conjunction that worked together to promote multiple-reel films. L. F. Cook, "Advertising the Picture Theater," *The Nickelodeon* 3, no. 9 (1 May 1910): 331–32; "Laemmle Plans New Series of Imp Films De Luxe," *Motion Picture News* 4, no. 15 (15 April 1911); "Spectator," "'Spectator's' Comments," *NYDM* 66, no. 1709 (20 September 1911): 26; "Spectator," "'Spectator's' Comments," *NYDM* 66, no. 1721 (13 December 1911): 28; "Spectator," "'Spectator's' Comments," *NYDM* 67, no. 1728 (31 January 1912): 51.

37. Most of these films were two and three reelers, but a shift in exhibition practices was occurring, "The Listener Chatters," *Reel Life* 4, no. 3 (4 April 1924): 6.

38. Barry and Sargent, *Building Theatre Patronage,* pp. 19–21; Lewis, *Cases on the Motion Picture Industry,* pp. 435–43.

39. Michael Baxandall, *Painting and Experience in Fifteenth-Century Italy: A Primer in the Social History of Pictorial Style* (Oxford, England: Clarendon Press, 1972), pp. 14–39.

40. Leonard B. Meyer in *Music, The Arts, and Ideas: Patterns and Predictions in Twentieth-Century Culture* (Chicago: University of Chicago Press, 1967) also suggests that novelty as a value is a cultural ideological system for the West from about 1500 to now (pp. 89–133). He does not, however, tie this into the economic supports which perpetuate an appearance of novelty, assuming instead that a shift in our conception of authorship will dilute the force of "novelty" as a value.

41. *Edison Films,* Supplement no. 168 (Orange, New Jersey: Edison Manufacturing Company, February 1903), pp. 2–3, rpt. in Pratt, *Spellbound in Darkness,* pp. 29–30.

42. *Edison Films,* Supplement no. 200 (January 1904), pp. 5–7, rpt. in Pratt, *Spellbound in Darkness,* pp. 34–36.

43. "Spectator," "'Spectator's' Comments," *NYDM* 65, no. 1672 (4 January 1911): 28.

44. Epes Winthrop Sargent, *The Technique of the Photoplay,* 2nd ed. (New York: The Moving Picture World, 1913), p. 123.

45. Price, Waterhouse, *Memorandum,* pp. 11–12.

46. Slide, *Early American Cinema,* p. 23; "Bison Gets 101 Ranch," *NYDM* 66, no. 1720 (6 December 1911): 29; "Bison Company Gets 101 Ranch," *Moving Picture World* 10, no. 10 (9 December 1911): 810; William Lord Wright, *Photoplay Writing* (New York: Falk Publishing Co., 1922), pp. 105–108.

47. Eustace Hale Ball, *The Art of the Photoplay* (New York: Veritas Publishing Company, 1913), p. 50.

48. Ball, *The Art of the Photoplay,* p. 43; also see for example James Irving, *The Irving System* (Auburn, New York: The Authors' Press, 1919), p. 159.

49. Price, Waterhouse, *Memorandum,* p. 12–15.

50. See for instance Balshofer's description below of the choice of a long take rather than analytical editing in *The Second in Command.* Another reason may be the inability of the studio to have as many final cut options available with a long take style.

51. The problem of footage length was more serious when exhibition practices limited the narrative to one, two, or three reels. Catherine Carr, *The Art of Photoplay Writing* (New York: The Hannis Jordan Company, 1914), pp. 41–43; Ball, *The Art of the Photoplay,* pp. 52–53; Epes Winthrop Sargent, "The Photoplaywright," *Moving Picture World* 23, no. 12 (20 March 1915): 1757; Irving, *The Irving System,* p. 179.

52. Sargent, *The Technique of the Photoplay,* p. 117; J. Berg Esenwein and Arthur Leeds, *Writing the Photoplay* (Springfield, Mass.: The Home Correspondence School, 1913), pp. 222–24; Louella O. Parsons, *How to Write for the 'Movies,'* rev. ed. (Chicago: A. C. McClurg & Co., 1917), p. 46; John Emerson and Anita Loos, *How to Write Photoplays* (1920 rpt., Philadelphia: George W. Jacobs & Company, 1923), p. 55.

53. Esenwein and Leeds, *Writing the Photoplay,* p. 206.

54. After all, for example, a long take rather than editing does not in itself challenge the general Hollywood classical mode. See its classical function in Balshofer's description. Nor does analytical editing always subordinate itself to a causal chain. Without continuity links, it may function in other ways; see the obvious examples of Eisenstein and Godard.

55. Balshofer and Miller, *One Reel a Week,* pp. 117–18. Unfortunately, this description was written many years after the event, but it is still useful I think. Kevin Brownlow writes that the film had "several beautifully executed and surprisingly intricate traveling shots. The movement was absolutely smooth, even when the camera, mounted on two dollies, slid

backward and then sideways." *The Parade's Gone By* (Berkeley, California: University of California Press, 1968), pp. 23–26.

56. "A Blot in the 'Scutcheon-Biograph,'" *NYDM* 67, no. 1728 (31 January 1912): 56.

57. "The Wonderful Year in Three Corners of Triangle Film," *The Triangle* 3, no. 3 (4 November 1916): 5.

58. "Very Latest Thing in Photoplay Subtitles," *The Triangle* 3, no. 7 (9 December 1916): 1.

59. "William Lord Wright's Page," *Motion Picture News* 7, no. 16 (19 April 1913): 13–14.

60. Emerson and Loos, *How to Write a Photoplay,* p. 88.

61. Sargent, *The Technique of the Photoplay,* p. 104.

62. Victor Oscar Freeburg, *Pictorial Beauty on the Screen* (1923, rpt., New York: Arno Press & The New York Times, 1970), pp. 10, 96 and 97.

63. I would like to thank the participants of the 1980 Ohio University Film Conference, Edward Branigan and David Bordwell for their very useful comments on a draft of this paper.

Part 2
Genre Criticism

TALES OF SOUND AND FURY: OBSERVATIONS ON THE FAMILY MELODRAMA

THOMAS ELSAESSER

First published in Monogram *magazine in 1972, this article belonged to a larger collective project justifying an intense, rigorous interest in the American cinema. Although* Monogram *was sympathetic to auteurism as an analytic principle, the magazine also sought to identify stylistic and formal qualities of Hollywood cinema that related to generic and historical dimensions as well as to directorial ones. Elsaesser's discussion of Hollywood melodrama remains the most exemplary single article in that effort. He traces the evolution of melodramatic form in several European countries and links that evolution to the playing out of class struggle (notably to the ascendancy of the middle class over the aristocracy).*

The characteristics that he assigns to melodrama help to explain its durability and its attraction. Inherently neither progressive nor conservative, it is an ambivalent form capable of various political inflections. Melodrama is also internally polyvalent, capable of a tension-producing counterpoint between form and content, a point that Nowell-Smith pursues in the next article. In the use of vocal inflection, mise-en-scène, and everyday actions, such as eating a meal or having a drink, melodrama can construct a powerful set of tensions between a character's physical embodiment and the expectations that we and the other characters have of him or her. Through the melos *side of melodrama, rhythms, tonalities, and textures emerge that set the narrative on edge. The very constriction implied by the focus on the individual and domestic space; on small actions and events; and on codings of dress, demeanor, and action that let resonance accrue in terms of the film and contemporary reality, not of a broader, iconographic or symbolic tradition, becomes the source of aesthetic achievement and ideological input in the hands of auteurs. (This contrasts with metteurs-en-scène, such as Curtiz, Lumet, or Mankiewicz, who aspire to present ideas and value conflicts more directly, as European films do.) The films exhibit a "contents under pressure" that usually erupts in the moments of emotional excess on which the popular definition of melodrama depends. That excess reverberates with the basic historical tensions of class, race, and sex that are expressed more than they are resolved as characters live out the impossible contradictions that have turned the American dream into a nightmare.*

Elsaesser's essay marks out a terrain that many others have since examined, including its extensions into television soap opera and prime-time melodrama, such as Dallas, Paper Dolls, Falcon Crest, *and* Dynasty. *His pioneering venture is all the more valuable for his use of Freudian concepts of how representations become manipulated in the unconscious through dreamwork as an analogy for the workings of melodrama and for his refusal to append these concepts to Lacan's interpretation of them. In this approach, he shares ground with Charles Eckert, whose article on* Marked Woman *appears in Part 4.*

•

HOW TO MAKE STONES WEEP

Asked about the colour in *Written on the Wind,* Douglas Sirk replied: 'Almost throughout the picture I used deep-focus lenses, which have the effect of giving a harshness to the objects and a kind of enamelled, hard surface to the colours. I wanted this to bring out the inner violence, the energy of the characters, which is all inside them and can't break through.' It would be difficult to think of a better way of describing what this particular movie and indeed most of the best melodramas of the fifties and early sixties are about. Or for that matter, how closely, in this film, style and technique is related to theme.

In this article I want to pursue an elusive subject in two directions: to indicate the development of what one might call the melodramatic imagination across different artistic forms and in different epochs; secondly, Sirk's remark tempts one to look for some structural and stylistic constants in one medium during one particular period (the Hollywood family melodrama between roughly 1940 and 1963) and to speculate on the cultural and psychological context which this form of melodrama so manifestly reflected and helped to articulate. Nonetheless this isn't a historical study in any strict sense, nor a *catalogue raisonné* of names and titles, for reasons that have something to do with my general method as well as with the obvious limitations imposed on film research by unavailability. As a consequence I lean rather heavily on half a dozen films, and notably *Written on the Wind,* to develop my points. This said, it is difficult to see how references to twenty more movies would make the argument any truer. For better or worse, what I want to say should at this stage be taken to be provocative rather than proven.

Bearing in mind that (whatever one's scruples about an exact definition) everybody has some idea of what is meant by 'melodramatic', any discussion of the melodrama as a specific cinematic mode of expression has to start from its antecedents—the novel and certain types of 'entertainment' drama—from which script-writers and directors have borrowed their models.

The first thing one notices is that the media and literary forms which have habitually embodied melodramatic situations have changed considerably in the course of history, and, further, they differ from country to country: in England, it has mainly been the novel and the literary gothic where melodramatic motifs persistently crop up (though the Victorian stage, especially in the 1880s and 1890s, knew an unprecedented vogue for the melodramas of R. Buchanan and G. R. Sims, plays in which 'a footbridge over a torrent breaks under the steps of the villain; a piece of wall comes down to shatter him; a boiler bursts, and blows him to smithereens');[1] in France, it is the costume drama and historical novel; in Germany 'high' drama and the ballad, as well as more popular forms like *Moritat* (street songs); finally, in Italy the opera rather than the novel reached the highest degree of sophistication in the handling of melodramatic situations.

Two currents make up the genealogy. One leads from the late medieval morality play, the popular *gestes* and other forms of oral narrative and drama, like fairytales and folk-songs to their romantic revival and the cult of the picturesque in Scott, Byron, Heine and Victor Hugo, which has its low-brow echo in barrel-organ songs, music-hall drama, and what in Germany is known as *Bänkellied,* the latter coming to late literary honours through Brecht in his songs and musical plays, *The Threepenny Opera* or *Mahagonny.* The characteristic features for our present purposes in this tradition are not so much the emotional shock-tactics and the blatant playing on the audience's known sympathies and antipathies, but rather the non-psychological conception of the *dramatis personae,* who figure less as autonomous individuals than to transmit the action and link the various locales within a total constellation. In this respect, melodramas have a myth-making function, insofar as their significance lies in the structure and articulation of the action, not in any psychologically motivated correspondence with individualised experience.

Yet, what particularly marks the ballad or the *Bänkellied,* i.e., narratives accompanied by music, is that the moral/moralistic pattern which furnishes the primary content (crimes of passion bloodily revenged, murderers driven mad by guilt and drowning themselves, villains snatching children from their careless mothers, servants killing their unjust masters) is overlaid not only with a proliferation of 'realistic' homely detail, but also 'parodied' or relativised by the heavily repetitive verse-form or the mechanical up-and-down rhythms of the barrel organ, to which the voice of the singer adapts itself (consciously or not), thereby producing a vocal parallelism that has a distancing or ironic effect, to the extent of often criss-crossing the moral of the story by a 'false', i.e., unexpected, emphasis. Sirk's most successful German melodrama, *Zu Neuen Ufern,* makes excellent use of the street ballad to bring out the tragic irony in the court-room scene, and the tune which Walter Brennan keeps playing on the harmonica in King Vidor's *Ruby Gentry* works in a very similar way. A variation on this is the use of fairgrounds and carousels in films like *Some Came Running* and *Tarnished Angels,* or more self-consciously in Hitchcock (*Strangers on a Train, Stage Fright*) and Welles (*Lady from Shanghai* and *The Stranger*) to underscore the main action and at the same time 'ease' the melodramatic impact by providing an ironic parallelism. Sirk uses the motif repeatedly, in, for instance, *Scandal in Paris* and *Take Me to Town.* What such devices point to is that in the melodrama the *rhythm* of experience often establishes itself against its value (moral, intellectual).

Perhaps the current that leads more directly to the sophisticated family melodrama of the 40's and 50's, though, is derived from the romantic drama, which had its heyday after the French Revolution and subsequently furnished many of the plots for operas, but which is itself unthinkable without the 18th-century sentimental novel and the emphasis put on private feelings and interiorised (puritan, pietist) codes of morality and conscience. Historically, one of the interesting facts about this tradition is that its height of popularity seems to coincide (and this remains true throughout the 19th century) with periods of intense social and ideological crisis. The pre-revolutionary sentimental novel--Richardson's *Clarissa* or Rousseau's *Nouvelle Héloise,* for example—go out of their way to make a case for extreme forms of behaviour and feeling by depicting very explicitly certain external constraints and pressures bearing upon the characters, and by showing up the quasi-totalitarian violence perpetrated by (agents of) the 'system' (Lovelace who tries everything, from bribing her family to hiring pimps, prostitutes and kidnappers in order to get Clarissa to become his wife, only to have to rape her after all). The same pattern is to be found in the bourgeois tragedies of Lessing (*Emilia Galotti,* 1768) and the early Schiller (*Kabale und Liebe,* 1776), both deriving their dramatic force from the conflict between an extreme and highly individualised form of moral idealism in the heroes (again, non-psychological on the level of motivation) and a thoroughly corrupt yet seemingly omnipotent social class (made up of feudal princes and petty state functionaries). The melodramatic elements are clearly visible in the plots, which revolve around family relationships, star-crossed lovers and forced marriages. The villains (often of noble birth) demonstrate their superior political and economic power invariably by sexual aggression and attempted rape, leaving the heroine no other way than to commit suicide or take poison in the company of her lover. The ideological 'message' of these tragedies, as in the case of *Clarissa,* is transparent: they record the struggle of a morally and emotionally emancipated bourgeois consciousness against the remnants of feudalism. They pose the problem in political terms and concentrate on the complex interplay of ethical principles, religious-metaphysical polarities and the idealist aspirations typical of the bourgeoisie in its militant phase, as the protagonists come to grief in a maze of economic necessities, *realpolitik,* family loyalties, and through the abuse of aristocratic privilege from a still divinely ordained, and therefore doubly depraved, absolutist authority.

Although these plays and novels, because they use the melodramatic-emotional plot only as their most rudimentary structure of meaning, belong to the more intellectually demanding forms of melodrama, the element of interiorisation and personalisation of primarily ideological conflicts, together with the metaphorical interpretation of class conflict as sexual exploitation and rape, is important in all subsequent forms of melodrama, including that of the cinema. (The latter in America, of course, is a stock theme of novels and movies with a 'Southern' setting.)

Paradoxically, the French Revolution failed to produce a new form of social drama or tragedy. The Restoration stage (when theatres in Paris were specially licensed to play 'melodramas') trivialised the form by using melodramatic plots in exotic settings, and providing escapist entertainment with little social relevance. The plays warmed up the standard motif of 18th-century French fiction and drama, that of innocence persecuted and virtue rewarded, and the conventions of melodrama functioned in their most barren form as the mechanics of pure suspense.

What before the Revolution had served to focus on suffering and victimisation—the claims of the individual in an absolutist society—was reduced to ground-glass-in-the-porridge, poisoned handkerchiefs and last-minute rescues from the dungeon. The sudden reversals of fortune, the intrusion of chance and coincidence had originally pointed to the arbitrary way feudal institutions could ruin the individual unprotected by civil rights and liberties. The system stood accused of greed, wilfulness and irrationality through the Christ-like suffering of the pure virgin and the selfless heroism of the right-minded in the midst of court intrigues and callous indifference. Now, with the bourgeoisie triumphant, this form of drama lost its subversive charge and functioned more as a means of consolidating an as yet weak and incoherent ideological position. Whereas the pre-revolutionary melodramas had often ended tragically, those of the Restoration had happy endings, they reconciled the suffering individual to his social position, by affirming an 'open' society, where everything was possible. Over and over again, the victory of the 'good' citizen over 'evil' aristocrats, lecherous clergymen and the even more conventional villains drawn from the lumpenproletariat, was re-enacted in sentimental spectacles full of tears and high moral tones. Complex social processes were simplified either by blaming the evil disposition of individuals or by manipulating the plots and engineering coincidences and other *dei ex machina,* such as the instant conversion of the villain, moved by the plight of his victim, or suddenly struck by Divine Grace on the steps of Nôtre-Dame.

Since the overtly 'conformist' strategy of such drama is quite evident, what is interesting is certainly not the plot structure, but whether the conventions allowed the author to dramatize in his episodes actual contradictions in society and genuine clashes of interests in the characters. Already during the Revolution plays such as Monvel's *Les Victimes cloîtrées* or Laya's *L'Ami des lois,* though working with very stereotyped plots, conveyed quite definite political sympathies (the second, for instance, backed the Girondist moderates in the trial of Louis XVI against the Jacobites) and were understood as such by their public.[2]

Even if the form might act to reinforce attitudes of submission, the actual working out of the scenes could nonetheless present fundamental social evils. Many of the pieces also flattered popular sympathies by giving the villains the funniest lines, just as Victorian drama playing east of Drury Lane was often enlivened by low-comedy burlesque put on as curtain raisers and by the servants' farces during the intermission.

All this is to say that there seems a radical ambiguity attached to the melodrama, which holds even more for the film melodrama. Depending on whether the emphasis fell on the odyssey of suffering or the happy ending, on the place and context of rupture (moral conversion of the villain, unexpected appearance of a benevolent Capuchin monk throwing off his pimp's disguise), that is to say, depending on what dramatic mileage was got out of the heroine's perils before the ending (and one only has to think of Sade's *Justine* to see what could be done with the theme of innocence unprotected), melodrama would appear to function either subversively or as escapism—categories which are always relative to the given historical and social context.[3]

In the cinema, Griffith is a good example. Using identical dramatic devices and cinematic techniques, he could, with *Intolerance, Way Down East* or *Broken Blossoms,* create, if not exactly subversive, at any rate socially committed melodramas, whereas *Birth of a Nation* or *Orphans of the Storm* are classic examples of how melodramatic effects can successfully shift explicit political themes onto a personalised plane. In both cases, Griffith tailored ideological conflicts into emotionally loaded family situations.

The persistence of the melodrama might indicate the ways in which popular culture has not only taken note of social crises and the fact that the losers are not always those who deserve it most, but has also resolutely refused to understand social change in other than private contexts and emotional terms. In this, there is obviously a healthy distrust of intellectualisation and abstract social theory— insisting that other structures of experience (those of suffering, for instance) are more in keeping with reality. But it has also meant ignorance of the properly social and political dimensions of these changes and their causality, and consequently it has encouraged increasingly escapist forms of mass entertainment.

However, this ambivalence about the 'structures' of experience, endemic in the melodramatic mode, has served artists throughout the 19th century for the depiction of a variety of themes and social phenomena, while remaining within the popular idiom. Industrialisation, urbanisation and nascent entrepreneurial capitalism have found their most telling literary embodiment in a type of novel clearly indebted to the melodrama, and the national liberals in Italy during the *Risorgimento*, for example, saw their political aspirations reflected in Verdi's operas (*cf.* the opening of Visconti's *Senso*). In England, Dickens, Collins and Reade relied heavily on melodramatic plots to sharpen social conflicts and portray an urban environment where chance encounters, coincidences, and the side-by-side existence of extreme social and moral contrasts were the natural products of the very conditions of existence—crowded tenement houses, narrow streets backing on to the better residential property, and other facts of urban demography of the time. Dickens in particular uses the element of chance, the dream/waking, horror/bliss switches in *Oliver Twist* or *Tale of Two Cities* partly to feel his way towards a portrayal of existential insecurity and moral anguish which fiction had previously not encompassed, but also to explore depth-psychological phenomena, for which the melodrama—as Freud was later to confirm—has supplied the dynamic motifs and the emotional-pictorial decor. What seems to me important in this form of melodrama (and one comes across a similar conception in the sophisticated Hollywood melodramas) is the emphasis Dickens places on discontinuity, on the evidence of fissures and ruptures in the fabric of experience, and the appeal to a reality of the psyche—to which the notions of sudden change, reversal and excess lend a symbolic plausibility.

In France it is the works of Sue, Hugo and Balzac that reflect most closely the relation of melodrama to social upheaval. Sue, for example, uses the time-worn trap-door devices of cloak and dagger stage melodrama for an explicitly sensationalist, yet committed journalism. In a popular form and rendered politically palatable by the fictionalised treatment, his *Mystères de Paris* were intended to crusade on such issues as public health, prostitution, overcrowding and slum housing, sanitation, black-market racketeering, corruption in government circles, opium smoking and gambling. Sue exploited a 'reactionary' form for reformist ends, and his success, both literary and practical, proved him right. Twenty years later Victor Hugo, who had learnt as much from Sue as Sue had picked up from *Nôtre-Dame de Paris,* produced with *Les Misérables* a super-melodrama spectacular which must stand as the crowning achievement of the genre in the novel. The career of Jean Valjean, from convict and galley slave to factory owner and capitalist, his fall and literal emergence from the sewers of Paris to become a somewhat unwilling activist in the 1848 Revolution, is staged with the help of mistaken identities, orphans suddenly discovering their noble birth, inconvenient reappearance of people long thought dead, hair-breadth escapes and rescues, multiple disguises, long-suffering females dying of consumption or wandering for days through the streets in search of their child—and yet, through all this, Hugo expresses a hallucinating vision of the anxiety, the moral confusion, the emotional demands, in short, the metaphysics of social change and urban life between the time of Waterloo and 1848. Hugo evidently wanted to bring together in a popular form subjective experiences of crises, while keeping track of the grand lines of France's history, and he succeeds singularly well in reproducing the ways individuals with different social backgrounds, levels of awareness and imaginations, respond to objective changes in the social fabric of their lives. For this, the melodrama, with its shifts in mood, its different tempi and the mixing of stylistic levels, is ideally suited: *Les Misérables,* even more so than the novels of Dickens, lets through a symbolic dimension of psychic truth, with the hero in turn representing very nearly the id, the superego and finally the sacrificed ego of a repressed and paranoid society.

Balzac, on the other hand, uses melodramatic plots to a rather different end. Many of his novels deal with the dynamics of early capitalist economics. The good/evil dichotomy has almost disappeared, and the Manichean conflicts have shifted away from questions of morality to the paradoxes of psychology and economics. What we see is a Schopenhauerian struggle of the will: the ruthlessness of industrial entrepreneurs and bankers, the spectacle of an uprooted, 'decadent' aristocracy still holding tremendous political power, the sudden twists of fortune with no-good parasites becoming millionaires overnight (or vice versa) through speculation and the stock exchange, the antics of hangers-on, parvenus and cynical artist-intellectuals, the demonic, spell-binding potency of money and capital, the contrasts between abysmal poverty and unheard-of affluence and waste which characterized the 'anarchic' phase of industrialisation and high finance, were experienced by Balzac as both vital and melodramatic. His work reflects this more in plot and style than through direct comment.

To sum up: these writers understood the melodrama as a form which carried its own values and already embodied its own significant content: it served as the literary equivalent of a particular, historically and socially conditioned *mode of experience.* Even if the situations and sentiments defied all categories of verisimilitude and were totally unlike anything in real life, the structure had a truth and a life of its own, which an artist could make part of his material. This meant that those who consciously adopted melodramatic techniques of presentation did not necessarily do so out of incompetence nor always from a cynical distance, but, by turning a body of techniques into a stylistic principle that carried the distinct overtones of spiritual crisis, they could put the finger on the texture of their social and human material while still being free to shape this material. For there is little doubt that the whole conception of life in 19th-century Europe and England, and especially the spiritual problems of the age, were often viewed in categories we would today call melodramatic—one can see this in painting, architecture, the ornamentation of gadgets and furniture, the domestic and public mise-en-scène of events and occasions, the oratory in parliament, the tractarian rhetoric from the pulpit as well as the more private manifestations of religious sentiment. Similarly, the timeless themes that Dostoyevsky brings up again and again in his novels—guilt, redemption, justice, innocence, freedom—are made specific and historically real not least because he was a great writer of melodramatic scenes and confrontations, and they more than anything else define that powerful irrational logic in the motivation and moral outlook of, say, Raskolnikov, Ivan Karamasov or Kirilov. Finally, how different Kafka's novels would be, if they did not contain those melodramatic family situations, pushed to the point where they reveal a dimension at once comic and tragically absurd—perhaps the existential undertow of all genuine melodrama.

PUTTING MELOS INTO DRAMA

In its dictionary sense, melodrama is a dramatic narrative in which musical accompaniment marks the emotional effects. This is still perhaps the most useful definition, because it allows melodramatic elements to be seen as constituents of a system of punctuation, giving expressive colour and chromatic contrast to the storyline, by orchestrating the emotional ups and downs of the intrigue. The advantage of this approach is that it formulates the problems of melodrama as problems of style and articulation.

Music in melodrama, for example, as a device among others to dramatize a given narrative, is subjective, programmatic. But because it is also a form of punctuation in the above sense, it is both functional (i.e., of structural significance) and thematic (i.e., belonging to the expressive content) because used to formulate certain moods—sorrow, violence, dread, suspense, happiness. The syntactic function of music has, as is well known, survived into the sound film, and the experiments conducted by Hanns Eisler and T. W. Adorno are highly instructive in this respect.[4] A practical demonstration of the problem can be found in the account which Lilian Ross gives of how Gottfried Reinhard and Dore Shary re-edited John Huston's *Red Badge of Courage* to give it a smooth dramatic shape, with build-ups and climaxes in the proper order, which is exactly what Huston had wanted to avoid when he shot it.[5]

Because it had to rely on piano accompaniment for punctuation, all silent film drama—from *True Heart Susie* to *Foolish Wives* or *The Lodger*—is 'melodramatic'. It meant that directors had to develop an extremely subtle and yet precise formal language (of lighting, staging, decor, acting, close-up, montage and camera movement), because they were deliberately looking for ways to compensate for the expressiveness, range of inflection and tonality, rhythmic emphasis and tension normally present in the spoken word. Having had to replace that part of language which is sound, directors like Murnau, Renoir, Hitchcock, Mizoguchi, Hawks, Lang, Sternberg achieved in their films a high degree (well recognised at the time) of plasticity in the modulation of optical planes and spatial masses which Panofsky rightly identified as a 'dynamisation of space'.

Among less gifted directors this sensitivity in the deployment of expressive means was partly lost with the advent of direct sound, since it seemed no longer necessary in a strictly technical sense — pictures 'worked' on audiences through their dialogue, and the semantic force of language overshadowed the more sophisticated pictorial effects and architectural values. This perhaps helps to explain why some major technical innovations, such as colour, wide screen and deep-focus lenses, crane and dolly, have in fact encouraged a new form of sophisticated melodrama. Directors (quite a sizeable proportion of whom came during the 30s from Germany, and others were clearly indebted to German expressionism and Max Reinhardt's methods of theatrical mise-en-scène) began showing a similar degree of visual culture as the masters of silent film drama: Ophuls, Lubitsch, Sirk, Preminger, Welles, Losey, Ray, Minnelli, Cukor.

Considered as an expressive code, melodrama might therefore be described as a particular form of dramatic mise-en-scène, characterised by a dynamic use of spatial and musical categories, as opposed to intellectual or literary ones. Dramatic situations are given an orchestration which will allow for complex aesthetic patterns: indeed, orchestration is fundamental to the American cinema as a whole (being essentially a dramatic cinema, spectacular, and based on a broad appeal) because it has drawn the aesthetic consequences of having the spoken word more as an additional 'melodic' dimension than as an autonomous semantic discourse. Sound, whether musical or verbal, acts first of all to give the illusion of depth to the moving image, and by helping to create the third dimension of the spectacle, dialogue becomes a scenic element, along with more directly visual means of the mise-en-scène. Anyone who has ever had the bad luck of watching a Hollywood movie dubbed into French or German will know how important diction is to the emotional resonance and dramatic continuity. Dubbing makes the best picture seem visually flat and dramatically out of sync: it destroys the flow on which the coherence of the illusionist spectacle is built.

That the plasticity of the human voice is quite consciously employed by directors for what are often thematic ends is known: Hawks trained Lauren Bacall's voice so that she could be given 'male' lines in *To Have and Have Not*, an effect which Sternberg anticipated when he took great care to cultivate Marlene Dietrich's diction, and it is hard to miss the psychoanalytic significance of Robert Stack's voice in *Written on the Wind,* sounding as if every word had to be painfully pumped up from the bottom of one of his oil-wells.

If it is true that *speech* in the American cinema loses some of its semantic importance in favour of its material aspects as sound, then conversely lighting, composition, decor increase their semantic and syntactic contribution to the aesthetic effect. They become functional and integral elements in the construction of meaning. This is the justification for giving critical importance to the mise-en-scène over intellectual content or story-value. It is also the reason why the domestic melodrama in colour and wide screen, as it appeared in the 40's and 50's, is perhaps the most highly elaborated, complex mode of cinematic signification that the American cinema has ever produced, because of the restricted scope for external action determined by the subject, and because everything, as Sirk said, happens 'inside'. To the 'sublimation' of the action picture and the Busby Berkeley/Lloyd Bacon musical into domestic and family melodrama corresponded a sublimation of dramatic conflict into decor, colour, gesture and composition of frame, which in the best melodramas is perfectly thematised in terms of the characters' emotional and psychological predicaments.

For example, when in ordinary language we call something melodramatic, what we often mean is an exaggerated rise-and-fall pattern in human actions and emotional responses, a from-the-sublime-to-the-ridiculous movement, a foreshortening of lived time in favour of intensity—all of which produces a graph of much greater fluctuation, a quicker swing from one extreme to the other than is considered natural, realistic or in conformity with literary standards of verisimilitude: in the novel we like to sip our pleasures, rather than gulp them. But if we look at, say, Minnelli, who has adapted some of his best melodramas (*The Cobweb, Some Came Running, Home from the Hill, Two Weeks in Another Town, The Four Horsemen of the Apocalypse*) from generally extremely long, circumstantially detailed popular novels (by James Jones, Irving Shaw *et al.*), it is easy to see how in the process of having to reduce 7 to 9 hours' reading matter to 90-odd minutes, such a more violent 'melodramatic' graph almost inevitably produces itself, short of the narrative becoming incoherent. Whereas in novels, especially when they are staple pulp fare, size connotes solid emotional involvement for the reader, the specific values of the cinema lie in its concentrated visual metaphors and dramatic acceleration rather than in the fictional techniques of dilation. The commercial necessity of compression (being also a formal one) is taken by Minnelli into the films themselves and developed as a theme—that of a pervasive psychological pressure on the characters. An acute sense of claustrophobia in decor and locale translates itself into a restless and yet suppressed energy surfacing sporadically in the actions and the behaviour of the protagonists—which is part of the subject of a film like *Two Weeks in Another Town,* with hysteria bubbling all the time just below the surface. The feeling that there is always more to tell than can be said leads to very consciously elliptical narratives, proceeding often by visually condensing the characters' motivation into sequences of images which do not seem to advance the plot. The shot of the Trevi fountain at the end of a complex scene where Kirk Douglas is making up his mind in *Two Weeks* is such a metaphoric condensation, and so is the silent sequence, consisting entirely of what might appear to be merely impressionistic dissolves, in the *Four Horsemen,* when Glenn Ford and Ingrid Thulin go for a ride to Versailles, but which in fact tells and foretells the whole trajectory of their relationship.

Sirk, too, often constructs his films in this way: the restlessness of *Written on the Wind* is not unconnected with the fact that he almost always cuts on movement. His visual metaphors really ought to have a chapter to themselves: a yellow sports-car drawing up the gravelled driveway to stop in front of a pair of shining white Doric columns outside the Hadley mansion is not only a powerful piece of American iconography, especially when taken in a plunging high-angle shot, but the contrary associations of imperial splendour and vulgar materials (polished chrome-plate and stucco plaster) create a tension of correspondences and dissimilarities in the same image, which perfectly crystallizes the decadent affluence and melancholy energy that give the film its uncanny fascination. Sirk has a peculiarly vivid eye for the contrasting emotional qualities of textures and materials, and he combines them or makes them clash to very striking effect, especially when they occur in a non-dramatic sequence: again in *Written on the Wind,* after the funeral of Hadley Sr., a black servant is seen taking an oleander wreath off the front gate. A black silk ribbon gets unstuck and is blown by the wind along the concrete path. The camera follows the movement, dissolves and dollies in on a window, where Lauren Bacall, in an oleander-green dress, is just about to disappear behind the curtains. The scene has no plot significance whatsoever. But the colour parallels black/black, green/green, white concrete/white lace curtains provide an extremely strong emotional resonance in which the contrast of soft silk blown along the hard concrete is registered the more forcefully as a disquieting visual association. The desolation of the scene transfers itself onto the Bacall character, and the traditional fatalistic association of the wind reminds us of the futility implied in the movie's title.

These effects, of course, require a highly self-conscious stylist, but they are by no means rare in Hollywood. The fact that commercial necessities, political censorship and the various morality codes restricted directors in what they could tackle as a subject has entailed a different awareness of what constituted a worthwhile subject, a change in orientation from which sophisticated melodrama benefited perhaps most. Not only did they provide a defined thematic parameter, but they encouraged a conscious use of style-as-meaning, which is a mark of what I would consider to be the very condition of a modernist sensibility working in popular culture. To take another example from Minnelli: his existential theme of a character trying to construct the world in the image of an inner self, only to discover that this world has become uninhabitable because it is both frighteningly suffocating and intolerably lonely (*The Long, Long Trailer, The Cobweb*) is transformed and given social significance in the stock melodrama theme of the woman who, having failed to make it in the big city, comes back to the small-town home in the hope of finding her true place at last, but who is made miserable by mean-mindedness and bigotry and then suffocated by the sheer weight of her none-too-glorious, still ruefully remembered past (*Hilda Crane, Beyond the Forest, All I Desire*).[6] But in Minnelli, it becomes an opportunity to explore in concrete circumstances the more philosophical questions of freedom and determinism, especially as they touch the aesthetic problem of how to depict a character who is not constantly externalising himself into action, without thereby trapping him in an environment of ready-made symbolism.

Similarly, when Robert Stack shows Lauren Bacall her hotel suite in *Written on the Wind,* where everything from flowers and pictures on the wall to underwear, nailpolish and handbag is provided, Sirk not only characterizes a rich man wanting to take over the woman he fancies body and soul, or the oppressive nature of an unwanted gift. He is also making a direct comment on the Hollywood stylistic technique that 'creates' a character out of the elements of the decor, and that prefers actors who can provide as blank a facial surface and as little of a personality as possible.

Everyone who has at all thought about the Hollywood aesthetic wants to formulate one of its peculiar qualities: that of direct emotional involvement, whether one calls it 'giving resonance to dramatic situations' or 'fleshing out the cliché' or whether, more abstractly, one talks in terms of identification patterns, empathy and catharsis. Since the American cinema, determined as it is by an ideology of the spectacle and the spectacular, is essentially dramatic (as opposed to lyrical, i.e., concerned with mood or the inner self) and not conceptual (dealing with ideas and the structures of cognition and perception), the creation or reenactment of situations which the spectator can identify with and recognise (whether this recognition is on the conscious or unconscious level is another matter) depends to a large extent on the aptness of the iconography (the 'visualisation') and on the quality (complexity, subtlety, ambiguity) of the orchestration for what are trans-individual, popular mythological (and therefore generally considered culturally 'lowbrow') experiences and plot structures. In other words, this type of cinema depends on the ways 'melos' is given to 'drama' by means of lighting, montage, visual rhythm, decor, style of acting, music—that is, on the ways the mise-en-scène translates character into action (not unlike the pre-Jamesian novel) and action into gesture and dynamic space (comparable to 19th-century opera and ballet).

This granted, there seems to be a further problem which has some bearing on the question of melodrama: although the techniques of audience orientation and the possibility of psychic projection on the part of the spectator are as much in evidence in a melodrama like *Home from the Hill* or *Splendor in the Grass* as they are in a Western or adventure picture, the difference of setting and milieu affects the dynamic of the action. In the Western especially, the assumption of 'open' spaces is virtually axiomatic; it is indeed one of the constants which makes the form perennially attractive to a largely urban audience. This openness becomes problematic in films that deal with potential 'melodrama' themes and family situations. The complex father-son relationships in *The Left-Handed Gun,* the Cain-Abel themes of Mann's Westerns *(Winchester 73, Bend of the River),* the conflict of virility and mother-fixation in some of Tourneur's Westerns (*Great Day in the Morning, Wichita*) or the search for the mother (-country) in Fuller's *Run of the Arrow* seem to find resolution because the hero can act positively on the changing situations where and when they present themselves. In Raoul Walsh's adventure pictures, as Peter Lloyd has shown,[7] identity comes in an often paradoxical process of self-confirmation and overreaching—but always through direct action, while the momentum generated by the conflicts pushes the protagonists forward in an unrelentingly linear course.

The family melodrama, by contrast, though dealing largely with the same Oedipal themes of emotional and moral identity, more often records the failure of the protagonist to act in a way that could shape the events and influence the emotional environment, let alone change the stifling social milieu. The world is closed, and the characters are acted upon. Melodrama confers on them a negative identity through suffering, and the progressive self-immolation and disillusionment generally ends in resignation: they emerge as lesser human beings for having become wise and acquiescent to the ways of the world.

The difference can be put in another way. In one case, the drama moves towards its resolution by having the central conflicts successively externalised and projected into direct action. A jail-break, a bank robbery, a Western chase or cavalry charge, and even a criminal investigation lend themselves to psychologised, thematised representations of the heroes' inner dilemmas and frequently appear that way (Walsh's *White Heat* or *They Died with Their Boots On,* Losey's *The Criminal,* Preminger's *Where the Sidewalk Ends*). The same is true of the melodrama in the *série noire* tradition, where the hero is egged on or blackmailed by the *femme fatale*—the smell of honeysuckle and death in *Double Indemnity, Out of the Past* or *Detour*—into a course of action which pushes him further and further in one direction, opening a narrowing wedge of equally ineluctible consequences, that usually lead the hero to wishing his own death as the ultimate act of liberation, but where the mechanism of fate at least allows him to express his existential revolt in strong and strongly anti-social behaviour.

Not so in the domestic melodrama: the social pressures are such, the frame of respectability so sharply defined that the range of 'strong' actions is limited. The tellingly impotent gesture, the social gaffe, the hysterical outburst replaces any more directly liberating or self-annihilating action, and the cathartic violence of a shoot out or a chase becomes an inner violence, often one which the characters turn against themselves. The dramatic configuration, the pattern of the plot makes them, regardless of attempts to break free, constantly look inwards, at each other and themselves. The characters are, so to speak, each others' sole referent, there is no world outside to be acted on, no reality that could be defined or assumed unambiguously. In Sirk, of course, they are locked into a universe of real and metaphoric mirrors, but quite generally, what is typical of this form of melodrama is that the characters' behaviour is often pathetically at variance with the real objectives they want to achieve. A sequence of substitute actions creates a kind of vicious circle in which the close nexus of cause and effect is somehow broken and—in an often overtly Freudian sense—displaced. James Dean in *East of Eden* thinks up a method of cold storage for lettuce, grows beans to sell to the Army, falls in love with Julie Harris, not to make a pile of money and live happily with a beautiful wife, but in order to win the love of his father and oust his brother—neither of which he achieves. Although very much on the surface of Kazan's film, this is a conjunction of puritan capitalist ethic and psychoanalysis which is sufficiently pertinent to the American melodrama to remain exemplary.

The melodramas of Ray, Sirk or Minnelli do not deal with this displacement-by-substitution directly, but by what one might call an intensified symbolisation of everyday actions, the heightening of the ordinary gesture and a use of setting and decor so as to reflect the characters' fetishist fixations. Violent feelings are given vent on 'overdetermined' objects (James Dean kicking his father's portrait as he storms out of the house in *Rebel Without a Cause*), and aggressiveness is worked out by proxy. In such films, the plots have a quite noticeable propensity to form a circular pattern, which in Ray involves an almost geometrical variation of triangle into circle and vice versa,[8] whereas Sirk (*nomen est omen*) often suggests in his circles the possibility of a tangent detaching itself—the full-circle construction of *Written on the Wind* with its linear coda of the Hudson-Bacall relationship at the end, or even more visually apparent, the circular race around the pylons in *Tarnished Angels* broken when Dorothy Malone's plane in the last image soars past the fatal pylon into an unlimited sky.

It is perhaps not too fanciful to suggest that the structural changes from linear externalisation of action to a sublimation of dramatic values into more complex forms of symbolisation, and which I take to be a central characteristic of the melodramatic tradition in the American cinema, can be followed through on a more general level where it reflects a change in the history of dramatic forms and the articulation of energy in the American cinema as a whole.

As I have tried to show in an earlier article (*Monogram,* no. 1), one of the typical features of the classical Hollywood movie has been that the hero was defined dynamically, as the centre of a continuous movement, often both from sequence to sequence as well as within the individual shot. It is a fact of perception that in order to get its bearing, the eye adjusts almost automatically to whatever moves, and movement, together with sound, completes the realistic illusion. It was on the basis of sheer physical movement, for example, that the musicals of the 30's (Lloyd Bacon's *42nd Street* being perhaps the most spectacular example), the gangster movie and the B-thriller of the 40's and early 50's could subsist with the flimsiest of plots, an almost total absence of individual characterisation and rarely any big stars. These deficiencies were made up by focusing to the point of exaggeration on the drive, the obsession, the *idée fixe,* that is to say, by a concentration on the purely kinetic-mechanical elements of human motivation. The pattern is most evident in the gangster genre, where the single-minded pursuit of money and power is followed by the equally single-minded and peremptory pursuit of physical survival, ending in the hero's apotheosis through violent death. This curve of rise and fall—a wholly stylised and external pattern which takes on a moral significance—can be seen in movies like *Underworld, Little Caesar, The Roaring Twenties, Legs Diamond* and depends essentially on narrative pace, though it permits interesting variations and complexities, as in Fuller's *Underworld USA*. A sophisticated director, such as Hawks, has used speed of delivery and the pulsating urgency of action to comic effect (*Scarface, 20th Century*) and has even applied it to films whose dramatic structure did not naturally demand such a treatment (notably *His Girl Friday*). In fact Hawks's reputed stoicism is itself a dramaturgical device, whereby sentimentality and cynicism are played so close together and played so fast that the result is an emotional hot-cold shower which is apt to numb the spectator's sensibility into feeling a sustained moral charge, where there is more often simply a very skilled switchboard manipulation of the same basic voltage. (I am thinking especially of films like *Only Angels Have Wings.*)

This unrelenting internal combustion engine of physical and psychic energy, generically exemplified by the hard-boiled, crackling aggressiveness of the screwball comedy, but which Walsh diagnosed in his Cagney heroes as psychotic (*White Heat*) and a vehicle for extreme redneck republicanism (*A Lion in the Streets*), shows signs of a definite slowing-down in the 50's and early 60's, where raucous vitality and instinctual 'lust for life' is deepened psychologically to intimate neuroses and adolescent or not so adolescent maladjustments of a wider social significance. Individual initiative is perceived as problematic in explicitly political terms (*All the King's Men*), after having previously been merely stoically and heroically anti-social, as in the *film noir*. The external world is more and more riddled with obstacles which oppose themselves to personal ambition and are not simply overcome by the hero's assertion of a brawny or brainy libido. In Mann's Westerns the madness at the heart of the James Stewart character only occasionally breaks through an otherwise calm and controlled surface, like a strong subterranean current suddenly appearing above ground as an inhuman and yet somehow poetically apt thirst for vengeance and primitive Biblical justice, where the will to survive is linked to certain old-fashioned cultural and moral values—of dignity, honour and respect. In the films of Sirk, an uncompromising, fundamentally innocent energy is gradually turned away from simple, direct fulfilment by the emergence of a conscience, a sense of guilt and responsibility, or the awareness of moral complexity, as in *Magnificent Obsession, Sign of the Pagan, All That Heaven Allows* and even *Interlude*—a theme which in Sirk is always interpreted in terms of cultural decadence.

WHERE FREUD LEFT HIS MARX IN THE AMERICAN HOME

There can be little doubt that the postwar popularity of the family melodrama in Hollywood is partly connected with the fact that in those years America discovered Freud. This is not the place to analyse the reasons why the United States should have become the country in which his theories found their most enthusiastic reception anywhere, or why they became such a decisive influence on American culture, but the connections of Freud with melodrama are as complex as they are undeniable. An interesting fact, for example, is that Hollywood tackled Freudian themes in a particularly 'romantic' or gothic guise, through a cycle of movies inaugurated possibly by Hitchcock's first big American success, *Rebecca*. Relating his Victorianism to the Crawford–Stanwyck–Davis type 'women's picture', which for obvious reasons became a major studio concern during the war years and found its apotheosis in such movies as John Cromwell's *Since You Went Away* (to the front, that is), Hitchcock infused his film, and several others, with an oblique intimation of female frigidity producing strange fantasies of persecution, rape and death—masochistic reveries and nightmares, which cast the husband into the role of the sadistic murderer. This projection of sexual anxiety and its mechanisms of displacement and transfer is translated into a whole string of movies often involving hypnosis and playing on the ambiguity and suspense of whether the wife is merely imagining it or whether her husband really does have murderous designs on her: Hitchcock's *Notorious* and *Suspicion,* Minnelli's *Undercurrent,* Cukor's *Gaslight,* Sirk's *Sleep My Love,* Tourneur's *Experiment Perilous,* Lang's *Secret Beyond the Door* all belong in this category, as does Preminger's *Whirlpool,* and in a wider sense Renoir's *Woman on the Beach.* What strikes one about this list is not only the high number of European émigrés entrusted with such projects, but that virtually all of the major directors of family melodramas (except Ray)[9] in the fifties had a (usually not entirely successful) crack at the Freudian feminist melodrama in the forties.

More challenging, and difficult to prove, is the speculation that certain stylistic and structural features of the sophisticated melodrama may involve principles of symbolisation and coding which Freud conceptualised in his analysis of dreams and later also applied in his *Psychopathology of Everyday Life.* I am thinking less of the prevalence of what Freud called *Symptomhandlungen* or *Fehlhandlungen,* that is, slips of the tongue or other projections of inner states into interpretable overt behaviour. This is a way of symbolising and signalling attitudes common to the American cinema in virtually every genre. However, there is a certain refinement in the melodrama—it becomes part of the composition of the frame, more subliminally and unobtrusively transmitted to the spectator. When Minnelli's characters find themselves in an emotionally precarious or contradictory situation, it often affects the 'balance' of the visual composition—wine glasses, a piece of china or a trayful of drinks emphasise the fragility of their situation—e.g., Judy Garland over breakfast in *The Clock,* Richard Widmark in *The Cobweb* explaining himself to Gloria Grahame, or Gregory Peck trying to make his girlfriend see why he married someone else in *Designing Woman.* When Robert Stack in *Written on the Wind,* standing by the window he has just opened to get some fresh air into an extremely heavy family atmosphere, hears of Lauren Bacall expecting a baby, his misery becomes eloquent by the way he squeezes himself into the frame of the half-open window, every word his wife says to him bringing torment to his lacerated soul and racked body.

Along similar lines, I have in mind the kind of 'condensation' of motivation into metaphoric images or sequences of images mentioned earlier, the relation that exists in Freudian dream-work between manifest dream material and latent dream content. Just as in dreams certain gestures and incidents mean something by their structure and sequence, rather than by what they literally represent, the melodrama often works, as I have tried to show, by a displaced emphasis, by substitute acts, by parallel situations and metaphoric connections. In dreams one tends to 'use' as dream material incidents and circumstances from one's waking experience during the previous day, in order to 'code' them, while nevertheless keeping a kind of emotional logic going, and even condensing their images into what, during the dream at least, seems an inevitable sequence. Melodramas often use middle-class American society, its iconography and the family experience in just this way as their manifest 'material', but 'displace' it into quite different patterns, juxtaposing stereotyped situations in strange configurations, provoking clashes and ruptures which not only open up new associations but also redistribute the emotional energies which suspense and tensions have accumulated, in disturbingly different directions. American movies, for example, often manipulate very shrewdly situations of extreme embarrassment (a blocking of emotional energy) and acts or gestures of violence (direct or indirect release) in order to create patterns of aesthetic significance which only a musical vocabulary might be able to describe accurately, and for which a psychologist or anthropologist might offer some explanation.

One of the principles involved is that of continuity and discontinuity (what Sirk has called the 'rhythm of the plot'). A typical situation in American melodramas has the plot build up to an evidently catastrophic collision of counter-running sentiments, but a string of delays gets the greatest possible effect from the clash when it does come. In Minnelli's *The Bad and the Beautiful* Lana Turner plays an alcoholic actress who has been 'rescued' by producer Kirk Douglas giving her a new start in the movies. After the premiere, flushed with success, self-confident for the first time in years, and in happy anticipation of celebrating with Douglas, with whom she has fallen in love, she drives to his home armed with a bottle of champagne. However, we already know that Douglas isn't emotionally interested in her ('I need an actress, not a wife', he later tells her) and is spending the evening with a 'broad' in his bedroom. Lana Turner, suspecting nothing, is met by Douglas at the foot of the stairs, and she, at first too engrossed in herself to notice how cool he is, collapses when the other woman suddenly appears at the top of the stairs in Douglas's dressing gown. Her nervous breakdown in the car is conveyed by headlights flashing against her windscreen like a barrage of footlights and arc-lamps.

This letting the emotions rise and then bringing them suddenly down with a thump is an extreme example of dramatic discontinuity, and a similar, vertiginous drop in the emotional temperature punctuates a good many melodramas—almost invariably played out against the vertical axis of a staircase.[10] In one of the most paroxysmic montage sequences that the American cinema has known, Sirk has Dorothy Malone in *Written on the Wind* dance on her own, like some doomed goddess from a Dionysian mystery, while her father is collapsing on the stairs and dying from a heart-attack. Again, in *Imitation of Life,* John Gavin gets the brush-off from Lana Turner as they are going down the stairs, and in *All I Desire* Barbara Stanwyck has to disappoint her daughter about not taking her to New York to become an actress, after the girl has been rushing downstairs to tell her father the good news. Ray's use of the staircase for similar emotional effects is well known and most spectacular in *Bigger than Life,* but to give an example from another director, Henry King, I'd like to quote a scene from *Margie,* a film following rather closely Minnelli's *Meet Me in St. Louis,* where the heroine, Jeanne Crain, about to be taken to the graduation ball by a blind date (whom we know to be her father) since her poetry-loving bespectacled steady has caught a cold, comes tearing down from her bedroom when she hears that the French master, on whom she has a crush, has dropped in. She virtually rips the bouquet of flowers out of his hands and is overwhelmed by joy. With some embarrassment, he has to explain that he is taking somebody else to the ball, that he only came to return her papers, and Margie, mortified, humiliated and cringing with shame, has just enough time to get back upstairs before she dissolves in tears.

While this may not sound terribly profound on paper, the visual orchestration of such a scene can produce some rather strong emotional effects and the strategy of building up to a climax so as to throttle it the more abruptly is a form of dramatic reversal by which Hollywood directors have consistently criticised the streak of incurably naive moral and emotional idealism in the American psyche, first by showing it to be often indistinguishable from the grossest kind of illusion and self-delusion, and then by forcing a confrontation when it is most wounding and contradictory. The emotional extremes are played off in such a way that they reveal an inherent dialectic, and the undeniable psychic energy contained in this seemingly so vulnerable sentimentality is utilised to furnish its own antidote, to bring home the discontinuities in the structures of emotional experience which give a kind of realism and toughness rare if not unthinkable in the European cinema.

What makes these discontinuities in the melodrama so effective is that they occur, as it were, under pressure. Although the kinetics of the American cinema are generally directed towards creating pressure and manipulating it (as suspense, for example), the melodrama presents in some ways a special case. In the Western or the thriller, suspense is generated by the linear organisation of the plot and the action, together with the kind of 'pressure' which the spectator brings to the film by way of anticipation and *a priori* expectations of what he hopes to see; melodrama, however, has to accommodate the latter type of pressure, as already indicated, in what amounts to a relatively 'closed' world.

This is emphasised by the function of the decor and the symbolisation of objects: the setting of the family melodrama almost by definition is the middle-class home, filled with objects, which in a film like Philip Dunne's *Hilda Crane,* typical of the genre in this respect, surround the heroine in a hierarchy of apparent order that becomes increasingly suffocating. From father's armchair in the living room and mother's knitting to the upstairs bedroom, where after five years' absence dolls and teddies are still neatly arranged on the bedspread, home not only overwhelms Hilda with images of parental oppression and a repressed past (which indirectly provoke her explosive outbursts that sustain the action), it also brings out the characteristic attempt of the bourgeois household to make time stand still, immobilise life and fix forever domestic property relations as the model of social life and a bulwark against the more disturbing sides in human nature. The theme has a particular poignancy in the many films about the victimisation and enforced passivity of women—women waiting at home, standing by the window, caught in a world of objects into which they are expected to invest their feelings. *Since You Went Away* has a telling sequence when Claudette Colbert, having just taken her husband to the troop train at the station, returns home to clear up after the morning's rush. Everything she looks at or touches, dressing gown, pipe, wedding picture, breakfast cup, slippers, shaving brush, the dog, reminds her of her husband, until she cannot bear the strain and falls on her bed sobbing. The banality of the objects combined with the repressed anxieties and emotions force a contrast that makes the scene almost epitomise the relation of decor to characters in melodrama: the more the setting fills with objects to which the plot gives symbolic significance, the more the characters are enclosed in seemingly ineluctable situations. Pressure is generated by things crowding in on them, life becomes increasingly complicated because cluttered with obstacles and objects that invade their personalities, take them over, stand for them, become more real than the human relations or emotions they were intended to symbolise.

It is again an instance of Hollywood stylistic devices supporting the themes, or commenting on each other. Melodrama is iconographically fixed by the claustrophobic atmosphere of the bourgeois home and/or the small-town setting, its emotional pattern is that of panic and latent hysteria, reinforced stylistically by a complex handling of space in interiors (Sirk, Ray and Losey particularly excel in this) to the point where the world seems totally predetermined and pervaded by 'meaning' and interpretable signs.

This marks another recurrent feature, already touched on, that of desire focussing on the unobtainable object. The mechanisms of displacement and transfer, in an enclosed field of pressure, open a highly dynamic yet discontinuous cycle of non-fulfilment, where discontinuity creates a universe of powerfully emotional but obliquely related fixations. In melodrama, violence, the strong action, the dynamic movement, the full articulation and the fleshed-out emotions—so characteristic of the American cinema—become the very signs of the characters' alienation, and thus serve to formulate a devastating critique of the ideology that supports it.

Minnelli and Sirk are exceptional directors in this respect not least because they handle stories with four, five or sometimes six characters all tied up in a single configuration, and yet give each of them an even thematic emphasis and an independent point of view. Such skill involves a particularly 'musical' gift and a very sensitive awareness of the harmonising potential contained in contrasting material and the structural implications of different characters' motives. Films like *Home from the Hill, The Cobweb, Tarnished Angels* or *Written on the Wind* strike one as 'objective' films, since they do not have a central hero (even though there may be a gravitational pull towards one of the protagonists) and nonetheless they cohere, mainly because each of the characters' predicaments is made plausible in terms that relate to the problems of the others. The films are built architecturally, by a combination of structural tensions and articulated parts, and the overall design appears only retrospectively, as it were, when with the final coda of appeasement the edifice is complete and the spectator can stand back and look at the pattern. But there is, especially in the Minnelli movies, also a wholly 'subjective' dimension. The films (because the parts are so closely organised around a central theme or dilemma) can be interpreted as emanating from a single consciousness, which is testing or experiencing in dramatic form the various options and possibilities flowing from an initially outlined moral or existential contradiction. In *The Cobweb* John Kerr wants both total self-expression and a defined human framework in which such freedom is meaningful, and George Hamilton in *Home from the Hill* wants to assume adult responsibilities while at the same time he rejects the standards of adulthood implied in his father's aggressive masculinity. In the latter the drama ends with a 'Freudian' resolution of the father being eliminated at the very point when he has resigned himself to his loss of supremacy, but this is underpinned by a 'Biblical' one which fuses the mythology of Cain and Abel with that of Abraham blessing his first-born. The interweaving of motifs is achieved by a series of parallels and contrasts. Set in the South, the story concerns the relations of a mother's boy with his tough father, played by Robert Mitchum, whose wife so resents his having a bastard son (George Peppard) that she won't sleep with him again. The plot progresses through all the possible permutations of the basic situation: lawful son/natural son, sensitive George Hamilton/hypochondriac mother, tough George Peppard/tough Robert Mitchum, both boys fancy the same girl, Hamilton gets her pregnant, Peppard marries her, girl's father turns nasty against the lawful son because of the notorious sex-life of his father, etc. However, because the plot is structured as a series of mirror-reflections on the theme of fathers and sons, blood ties and natural affinities, Minnelli's film is a psychoanalytical portrait of the sensitive adolescent—but placed in a definite ideological and social context. The boy's consciousness, we realise, is made up of what are external forces and circumstances, his dilemma the result of his social position as heir to his father's estate, unwanted because felt to be undeserved, and an upbringing deliberately exploited by his mother in order to get even with his father, whose own position as a Texan land-owner and local big-shot forces him to compensate for his wife's frigidity by proving his virility with other women. Melodrama here becomes the vehicle for diagnosing a single individual in ideological terms and objective categories, while the blow-by-blow emotional drama creates the second level, where the subjective aspect (the immediate and necessarily unreflected experience of the characters) is left intact. The hero's identity, on the other hand, emerges as a kind of picture-puzzle from the various pieces of dramatic action.

Home from the Hill is also a perfect example of the principle of substitute acts, mentioned earlier, which is Hollywood's way of portraying the dynamics of alienation. The story is sustained by pressure that is applied indirectly, and by desires that always chase unattainable goals: Mitchum forces George Hamilton to 'become a man' though he is temperamentally his mother's son, while Mitchum's 'real' son in terms of attitudes and character is George Peppard, whom he cannot acknowledge for social reasons. Likewise, Eleanor Parker puts pressure on her son in order to get at Mitchum, and Everett Sloane (the girl's father) takes out on George Hamilton the sexual hatred he feels against Mitchum. Finally, after his daughter has become pregnant he goes to see Mitchum to put pressure on him to get his son to marry the girl, only to break down when Mitchum turns the tables and accuses him of blackmail. It is a pattern which in an even purer form appears in *Written on the Wind:* Dorothy Malone wants Rock Hudson who wants Lauren

Bacall who wants Robert Stack who just wants to die. *La ronde à l'américaine.* The point is that the melodramatic dynamism of these situations is used by both Sirk and Minnelli to make the emotional impact 'carry over' into the very subdued, apparently neutral, sequences of images that so often round off a scene and which thereby have a strong lyrical quality.

One of the characteristic features of melodramas in general is that they concentrate on the point of view of the victim: what makes the films mentioned above exceptional is the way they manage to present *all* the characters convincingly as victims. The critique—the questions of 'evil', of responsibility—is firmly placed on a social and existential level, away from the arbitrary and finally obtuse logic of private motives and individualised psychology. This is why the melodrama, at its most accomplished, seems capable of reproducing more directly than other genres the patterns of domination and exploitation existing in a given society, especially the relation between psychology, morality and class-consciousness, by emphasising so clearly an emotional dynamic whose social correlative is a network of external forces directed oppressingly inward, and with which the characters themselves unwittingly collude to become their agents. In Minnelli, Sirk, Ray, Cukor and others, alienation is recognised as a basic condition, fate is secularised into the prison of social conformity and psychological neurosis, and the linear trajectory of self-fulfilment so potent in American ideology is twisted into the downward spiral of a self-destructive urge seemingly possessing a whole social class.

This typical masochism of the melodrama, with its incessant acts of inner violation, its mechanisms of frustration and over-compensation, is perhaps brought most into the open through characters who have a drink problem (cf. *Written on the Wind, Hilda Crane, Days of Wine and Roses*). Although alcoholism is too common an emblem in films and too typical of middle-class America to deserve a close thematic analysis, drink does become interesting in movies where its dynamic significance is developed and its qualities as a visual metaphor recognised: wherever characters are seen swallowing and gulping their drinks as if they were swallowing their humiliations along with their pride, vitality and the life force have become palpably destructive, and a phoney libido has turned into real anxiety. *Written on the Wind* is perhaps the movie that most consistently builds on the metaphoric possibilities of alcohol (liquidity, potency, the phallic shape of bottles). Not only is its theme an emotional drought that no amount of alcohol, oil pumped by the derricks, or petrol in fast cars and planes can mitigate, it also has Robert Stack compensate for his sexual impotence and childhood guilt feelings by hugging a bottle of raw corn every time he feels suicidal, which he proceeds to smash in disgust against the paternal mansion. In one scene, Stack is making unmistakeable gestures with an empty Martini bottle in the direction of his wife, and an unconsummated relationship is visually underscored when two brimful glasses remain untouched on the table, as Dorothy Malone does her best to seduce an unresponsive Rock Hudson at the family party, having previously poured her whiskey into the flower vase of her rival, Lauren Bacall.

Melodrama is often used to describe tragedy that doesn't quite come off: either because the characters think of themselves too self-consciously as tragic or because the predicament is too evidently fabricated on the level of plot and dramaturgy to carry the kind of conviction normally termed 'inner necessity'. Now, in some American family melodramas the inadequacy of the characters' responses to their predicament becomes itself part of the subject. In Cukor's *The Chapman Report* and Minnelli's *The Cobweb*—two movies explicitly concerned with the impact of Freudian notions on American society—the protagonists' self-understanding as well as the doctors' attempts at analysis and therapy are shown to be either tragically or comically inadequate to the situations that the characters are supposed to cope with in everyday life. Pocket-size tragic heroes and heroines, they are blindly grappling with a fate real enough to cause intense human anguish, which as the spectator can see, however, is compounded by social prejudice, ignorance, insensitivity on top of the bogus claim to scientific objectivity by the doctors. Claire Bloom's nymphomania and Jane Fonda's frigidity in the Cukor movie are seen to be two different but equally hysterical reactions to the heavy ideological pressures which American society exerts on the relations between the sexes. *The Chapman Report,* despite having apparently been cut by Darryl F. Zanuck Jr., remains an extremely important film partly because it treats its theme both in the tragic and the comic mode without breaking apart, underlining thereby the ambiguous springs of the discrepancy between displaying intense feelings and the circumstances to which they are inadequate—usually a comic motif but tragic in its emotional implications.

Both Cukor and Minnelli, however, focus on how ideological contradictions are reflected in the characters' seemingly spontaneous behaviour—the way self-pity and self-hatred alternate with a violent urge towards some form of liberating action, which inevitably fails to resolve the conflict. The characters experience as a shamefully personal stigma what the spectator (because of the parallelisms between the different episodes in *The Chapman Report,* and the analogies in the fates of the seven principal figures of *The Cobweb*) is forced to recognise as belonging to a wider social dilemma. The poverty of the intellectual resources in some of the characters is starkly contrasted with a corresponding abundance of emotional resources, and as one sees them helplessly struggling inside their emotional prisons with no hope of realising to what degree they are the victims of their society, one gets a clear picture of how a certain individualism reinforces social and emotional alienation, and of how the economics of the psyche are as vulnerable to manipulation and exploitation as is a person's labour.

The point is that this inadequacy has itself a name, relevant to the melodrama as a form: irony or pathos, which both in tragedy and melodrama is the response to the recognition of different levels of awareness. Irony privileges the spectator vis-à-vis the protagonists, for he registers the difference from a superior position. Pathos results from non-communication or silence made eloquent—people talking at cross-purposes (Robert Stack and Lauren Bacall when she tells him she's pregnant in *Written on the Wind*), a mother watching her daughter's wedding from afar (Barbara Stanwyck in *Stella Dallas*) or a woman returning unnoticed to her family, watching them through the window (again Barbara Stanwyck in *All I Desire*)—where highly emotional situations are underplayed to present an ironic discontinuity of feeling or a qualitative difference in intensity, usually visualized in terms of spatial distance and separation.

Such archetypal melodramatic situations activate very strongly an audience's participation, for there is a desire to make up for the emotional deficiency, to impart the different awareness, which in other genres is systematically frustrated to produce suspense: the primitive desire to warn the heroine of the perils looming visibly over her in the shape of the villain's shadow. But in the more sophisticated melodramas this pathos is most acutely produced through a 'liberal' mise-en-scène which balances different points of view, so that the spectator is in a position of seeing and evaluating contrasting attitudes within a given thematic framework—a framework which is the result of the total configuration and therefore inaccessible to the protagonists themselves. The spectator, say in Otto Preminger's *Daisy Kenyon* or a Nicholas Ray movie, is made aware of the slightest qualitative imbalance in a relationship and also sensitised to the tragic implications which a radical misunderstanding or a misconception of motives might have, even when this is not played out in terms of a tragic ending.

If pathos is the result of a skilfully displaced emotional emphasis, it is frequently used in melodramas to explore psychological and sexual repression, usually in conjunction with the theme of inferiority; inadequacy of response in the American cinema often has an explicitly sexual code: male impotence and female frigidity—a subject which allows for thematisation in various directions, not only to indicate the kinds of psychological anxiety and social pressures which generally make people sexually unresponsive, but as metaphors of unfreedom or a quasi-metaphysical 'overreaching' (as in Ray's *Bigger Than Life*). In Sirk, where the theme has an exemplary status, it is treated as a problem of 'decadence'—where intention, awareness, yearning, outstrip performance—sexual, social, moral. From the Willi Birgel character in *Zu Neuen Ufern* onwards, Sirk's most impressive characters are never up to the demands which their lives make on them, though some are sufficiently sensitive, alive and intelligent to feel and know about this inadequacy of gesture and response. It gives their pathos a tragic ring, because they take on suffering and moral anguish knowingly, as the just price for having glimpsed a better world and having failed to live it. A tragic self-awareness is called upon to compensate for lost spontaneity and energy, and in films like *All I Desire* or *There's Always Tomorrow*, where, as so often, the fundamental irony is in the titles themselves, this theme, which has haunted the European imagination at least since Nietzsche, is absorbed into an American small-town atmosphere, often revolving around the questions of dignity and responsibility, how to yield when confronted with true talent and true vitality—in short, those qualities that dignity is called upon to make up for.

In the Hollywood melodrama characters made for operettas play out the tragedies of humankind, which is how they experience the contradictions of American civilization. Small wonder they are constantly baffled and amazed, as Lana Turner is in *Imitation of Life,* about what is going on around them and within them. The discrepancy between seeming and being, of intention and result, registers as a perplexing frustration, and an ever-increasing gap opens between the emotions and the reality they seek to reach. What strikes one as the true pathos is the very mediocrity of the human beings involved, putting such high demands upon themselves, trying to live up to an exalted vision of man, but instead living out the impossible contradictions that have turned the American dream into its proverbial nightmare. It makes the best American melodramas of the fifties not only critical social documents but genuine tragedies, despite, or rather because of, the 'happy ending': they record some of the agonies that have accompanied the demise of the 'affirmative culture'. Spawned by liberal idealism, they advocate with open, conscious irony that the remedy is to apply more of the same. But even without the national disasters that were to overtake America in the 1960s, this irony, too, almost seems to belong to a different age.

Notes

1. A. Filon, *The English Stage,* London, 1897. Filon also offers an interesting definition of melodrama: 'When dealing with Irving, I asked the question, so often discussed, whether we go to the theatre to see a representation of life, or to forget life and seek relief from it. Melodrama solves this question and shows that both theories are right, by giving satisfaction to both desires, in that it offers the extreme of realism in scenery and language together with the most uncommon sentiments and events.'

2. See J. Duvignaud, *Sociologie du théâtre,* Paris, 1965, IV, 3, "Théâtre sans révolution, révolution sans théâtre".

3. About the ideological function of 19th-century Victorian melodrama, see M. W. Disher: 'Even in gaffs and saloons, melodrama so strongly insisted on the sure reward to be bestowed in this life upon the law-abiding that sociologists now see in this a Machiavellian plot to keep democracy servile to Church and State. . . . There is no parting the two strains, moral and political, in the imagination of the nineteenth-century masses. They are hopelessly entangled. Democracy shaped its own entertainments at a time when the vogue of Virtue Triumphant was at its height and they took their pattern from it. . . . Here are Virtue Triumphant's attendant errors: confusion between sacred and profane, between worldly and spiritual advancement, between self-interest and self-sacrifice' (*Blood and Thunder,* London, 1949, pp. 13–14). However, it ought to be remembered that there are melodramatic traditions outside the puritan-democratic world view: Catholic countries, such as Spain, Mexico (*cf.* Buñuel's Mexican films) have a very strong line in melodramas, based on the themes of atonement and redemption. Japanese melodramas have been 'highbrow' since the Monogatari stories of the 16th century and in Mizoguchi's films (*O Haru, Shinheike Monogatari*) they reach a transcendence and stylistic sublimation rivalled only by the very best Hollywood melodramas.

4. Hanns Eisler, *Composing for Film,* London, 1951.

5. Lilian Ross, *Picture,* London, 1958.

6. The impact of *Madame Bovary* via Willa Cather on the American cinema and the popular imagination would deserve a closer look.

7. *Brighton Film Review,* nos. 14, 15, 21.

8. *Ibid.,* nos. 19, 20.

9. I have not seen *A Woman's Secret* (1949) or *Born to Be Bad* (1950), either of which might include Ray in this category, and the Ida Lupino character in *On Dangerous Ground*

(1952)—blind, living with a homicidal brother—is distinctly reminiscent of this masochistic strain in Hollywood feminism.

   10. As a principle of mise-en-scène the dramatic use of staircases recalls the famous
Jessnertreppe of German theatre. The thematic conjunction of family and height/depth
symbolism is nicely described by Max Tessier: 'le héros ou l'héroine sont ballotés dans un
véritable scenic-railway social, où les classes sont rigoureusement compartimentées. Leur
ambition est de quitter à jamais un milieu moralement dépravé, physiquement éprouvant,
pour accéder au Nirvana de la grande bourgeoisie. . . . Pas de famille, pas de mélo! Pour
qu'il y ait mélo, il faut avant tout qu'il y ait faute, péché, transgression sociale. Or, quel est
le milieu idéal pour que se développe cette gangrène, sinon cette cellule familiale, liée à
une conception hiérarchique de la société?' (*Cinéma 71*, no. 161, p. 46).

Bibliography: Melodrama

This bibliography is by no means attempting to be comprehensive. It is offered by way of
an outline of how the subject might be approached.

THEATRE

M. W. Disher, *Blood and Thunder*, London, 1949.
A. Filon, *The English Stage*, London, 1897.
J. Duvignaud, *Sociologie du théâtre*, Paris, 1965.

NOVEL

W. C. Phillips, *Dickens, Reade and Collins*, New York, 1919.
L. A. Fiedler, *Love and Death in the American Novel*, London, 1967.

MUSIC

Hanns Eisler, *Composing for Film*, London, 1951.
T. W. Adorno, *Musiksoziologie*, Hamburg, 1968.
D. Cooke, *The Language of Music*, London, 1959.

CINEMA

H. Sachs, "Film Psychology," *Close-Up* 3, no. 5 (November 1928).
R. Durgnat, "Ways of Melodrama," *Sight and Sound*, August–September 1951.
E. Morin, *Le Cinéma ou l' homme imaginaire*, Paris, 1958.
J. Mitry, *Esthétique du cinéma*, Paris, 1962.
Cinématographie française, 7 December 1963.
B. Nichols, "Revolution and Melodrama," *Cinema* (USA) 6, no. 1 (1970).
J. L. Comolli, Sirk interview, *Cahiers du Cinéma* no. 189, April 1967.
Cinéma 71, special number on melodrama (no. 161).
Jean-Loup Bourget, *Positif*, no. 131 (October 1971).
Fernsehen und Film, special number on Sirk and melodrama, February 1971.
P. Willeman, "Distantiation and Douglas Sirk," *Screen*, Summer 1971.

MINNELLI AND MELODRAMA

GEOFFREY NOWELL-SMITH

Nowell-Smith establishes three central factors for an understanding of film melodrama: an internal history of the melodrama as formal system, a "social history" of the present class system and its contradictions, and something that might be considered a subset of the second: psychic determinations arising from the distinctive form of family life characterizing the bourgeoisie as its members are represented in melodrama.

His most provocative point overlaps with Laura Mulvey's claim in her article, "Douglas Sirk and Melodrama" (Australian Journal of Screen Theory, *no. 3 [1977]: 26 –30), that since melodramatic heroes, unlike tragic heroes, often lack an awareness of their fate or flaw, the style of the film may work to provide such a consciousness —for the viewer if not the hero. Nowell-Smith proposes a similar mechanism and an even more psychoanalytically inspired perspective: Taking the text as analogous to the patient, he claims that the forceful, relentless repression of desire returns to the body of the text as a symptom and that this return is manifest in the style or mise-en-scène of the film. What cannot be said or understood by characters is spoken by irruptions of intense or abnormal color, music, camera angle, composition, and so on.*

Nowell-Smith's suggestions help to give us a purchase on texts that at first may seem only to exaggerate family conflicts. By linking style to the return of the repressed and repression to the requirements of the class hierarchy and patriarchal system manifested in the nuclear family, he demonstrates a complex interdependence among his three central pivots for melodrama.

•

What this paper claims is that the genre or form that has come to be known as melodrama arises from the conjunction of a formal history proper (development of tragedy, realism, etc.), a set of social determinations, which have to do with the rise of the bourgeoisie, and a set of psychic determinations, which take shape around the family. The psychic and social determinations are connected because the family whose conflicts the melodrama enacts is also the bourgeois family, but a complexity is added to the problem by the fact that the melodrama is also a particular form of artistic representation. As artistic representation it is also (in marxist terms) ideology and (in Freudian terms) 'secondary revision', but it cannot be simply reduced to either. As artistic representation it does not 'reflect' or 'describe' social and psychic determinations. Rather, it *signifies* them. This act of signifying has two aspects: on the one hand it produces a narrated or represented content, the life of people in society; and on the other hand it narrates and represents to and from a particular standpoint or series of standpoints, 'subject positions'. Now it might be thought that the former aspect, concerning the content, is a question for social (historical-materialist) analysis, and the latter, concerning the form, a matter for psychology or psychoanalysis. What I shall claim is that this is not the case and that the positions of the narrating are also social positions, while what is narrated is also psychical. The 'subject positions' implied by the melodrama are those of bourgeois art in a bourgeois epoch, while the 'represented object' is that of the oedipal drama.

MELODRAMA AND TRAGEDY

Melodrama originally meant, literally, drama + melos (music) and this eighteenth-century sense survives in the Italian 'melodrama '—grand opera. In its early form, melodrama was akin to pastoral, and differentiated from tragedy in that the story usually had a happy end. Not much of the original meaning has survived into later—Victorian and modern—usages of the term, but the differentiation from tragedy has become, if anything, more marked. The principal differences are two, both of them the result of developments in art forms generally that began in the eighteenth century and were consolidated later. The first of these concerns modes of address and the second representation of the hero(ine). At the time it should be noted that in many other aspects the melodrama is the inheritor of many tragic concerns, albeit transposed to a new situation.

MELODRAMA AS BOURGEOIS FORM

One feature of tragic and epic forms up to (roughly) the eighteenth century is that they characteristically deal with kings and princes, while being written by, and for the most part addressed to, members of a less exalted social stratum. (The authors, even Homer, are, broadly speaking, 'intellectuals', while the audience is conceived of, however inaccurately, as 'the people'.) With the advent of the novel (cf. Scarron's *Le Roman bourgeois*) and the 'bourgeois tragedy' of the eighteenth century, the situation changes. Author, audience and subject matter are put on a place of equality. As Raymond Williams has noted, in a paper to a recent SEFT weekend school, the appeal is directly to 'our equals, your equals'. Mystified though it may be, the address is from one bourgeois to another bourgeois, and the subject matter is the life of the bourgeoisie. This movement of equalisation generally goes under the name of (or is conflated with) realism, but it also characterises forms which in other respects are not conspicuous for their realism, such as the melodrama.

Insofar as melodrama, like realism, supposes a world of equals, a democracy within the bourgeois stratum (alias bourgeois democracy), it also supposes a world without the exercise of social power. The address is to an audience which does not think of itself as possessed of power (but neither as radically dispossessed, disinherited, oppressed) and the world of the subject matter is likewise one in which only middling power relations are present. The characters are neither the rulers or the ruled, but occupy a middle ground, exercising local power or suffering local powerlessness, within the family or the small town. The locus of power is the family and individual private property, the two being connected through inheritance. In this world of circumscribed horizons (which corresponds very closely to Marx's definition of 'petty bourgeois ideology') patriarchal right is of central importance. The son has to become like his father in order to take over his property and his place within the community (or, in variant structures, a woman is widowed and therefore inherits, but the question posed is which man she can pass the property on to by remarriage; or, again, the father is evil and the son must grow up different from him in order to be able to redistribute the property at the moment of inheritance, etc., etc.). Notably, the question of law or legitimacy, so central to tragedy, is turned inward from 'Has this man a right to rule (over us)?' to 'Has this man a right to rule a family (like ours)?' This inward-turning motivates a more directly psychological reading of situations, particularly in the Hollywood melodrama of the '50s.

ACTION AND PASSION

Aristotle defined history as 'what Alcibiades did and suffered'. Doing and suffering, action and passion, are co-present in classical tragedy, and indeed in most art forms up to the romantic period. There is then a split, producing a demarcation of forms between those in which there is an active hero, inured or immune to suffering, and those in which there is a hero, or more often a heroine, whose role is to suffer. Broadly speaking in the American movie, the active hero becomes protagonist of the Western, the passive or impotent hero or heroine becomes protagonist of what has come to be known as melodrama. The contrast active/passive is, inevitably, traversed by another contrast, that between masculine and feminine. Essentially the world of the Western is one of activity/masculinity, in which women cannot figure except as receptacles (or occasionally as surrogate males). The melodrama is more complex. It often features women as protagonists, and where the central feature is a man there is regularly an impairment of his 'masculinity'—at least in contrast to the mythic potency of the hero of the Western. It cannot operate in the simple terms of a fantasy affirmation of the masculine and disavowal of the feminine, but the way it recasts the equation to allow more space for its women characters and for the representation of passion undergone throws up problems of its own. Insofar as activity remains equated with masculinity and passivity with femininity, the destiny of the characters, whether male or female, is unrealisable; he or she can only live out the impairment ('castration') imposed by the law. In their struggle for the achievement of sexual and social demands, men may sometimes win through, women never. But this fact about the plot structure is not just an element of realism, it reflects an imbalance already present in the conceptual and symbolic structure. 'Masculinity', although rarely attainable, is at least known as an ideal. 'Femininity,' within the terms of the argument, is not only unknown but unknowable. Since sexuality and social efficacy are recognisable only in a 'masculine' form, the contradictions facing the women characters are posed in more acutely problematic form from the outset. For both men and women, however, suffering and impotence, besides being the data of middle-class life, are seen as forms of a failure to be male—a failure from which patriarchy allows no respite.

THE GENERATION GAME

To describe as patriarchy the law which decrees suffering and impairment (if only as motors for dramatic action) and decrees them unequally for men and for women is also to raise the problem of generations. The castration which is at issue in the melodrama (and according to some writers in all narrative forms) is not an ahistorical, atemporal structure. On the contrary it is permanently renewed within each generation. The perpetuation of symbolic sexual division only takes place insofar as it is the father who perpetuates it. It is not just the place of the man relative to the woman, but that of the parent (male) relative to the children, which is crucial here. Melodrama enacts, often with uncanny literalness, the 'family romance' described by Freud—that is to say, the imaginary scenario played out by children in relation to their paternity, the asking and answering of the question, whose child am I (or would I like to be)? In addition to the problems of adults, particularly women, in relation to their sexuality, the Hollywood melodrama is also fundamentally concerned with the child's problems of growing into a sexual identity within the family, under the aegis of a symbolic law which the father incarnates. What is at stake (also for social-ideological reasons) is the survival of the family unit and the possibility for individuals of acquiring an identity which is also a place within the system, a place in which they can both be 'themselves' and 'at home', in which they can simultaneously enter, without contradiction, the symbolic order and bourgeois society. It is a condition of the drama that the attainment of such a place is not easy and does not happen without sacrifice, but it is very rare for it to be seen as radically impossible. The problems posed are always to some extent resolved. Only in Ophuls's *Letter from an Unknown Woman*, where Lisa dies after the death of her (fatherless) child, are all the problems laid out in all their poignancy, and none of them resolved.

HYSTERIA AND EXCESS

The tendency of melodrama to culminate in a happy end is not unopposed. The happy end is often impossible, and, what is more, the audience knows it is impossible. Furthermore, a 'happy end' which takes the form of an acceptance of castration is achieved only at the cost of repression. The laying out of the problems 'realistically' always allows for the generating of an excess which cannot be accommodated. The more the plots press towards a resolution, the harder it is to accommodate the excess. What is characteristic of the melodrama, both in its original sense and the modern one, is the way the excess is siphoned off. The undischarged emotion which cannot be accommodated within the action, subordinated as it is to the demands of family/lineage/inheritance, is traditionally expressed in the music and, in the case of film, in certain elements of the *mise-en-scène*. That is to say, music and *mise-en-scène* do not just heighten the emotionality of an element of the action; to some extent they substitute for it. The mechanism here is strikingly similar to that of the psychopathology of hysteria. In hysteria (and specifically in what Freud has designated as "conversion hysteria") the energy attached to an idea that has been repressed returns converted into a bodily symptom. The "return of the repressed" takes place, not in conscious discourse, but displaced on to the body of the patient. In the melodrama, where there is always material which cannot be expressed in discourse or in the actions of the characters furthering the designs of the plot, a conversion can take place into the body of the text. This is particularly the case with Minnelli. It is not just that the characters are often prone to hysteria, but that the film itself somatises its own unaccommodated excess, which thus appears displaced or in the wrong place. This is the case both in the musicals (*The Pirate, Meet Me in St. Louis,* etc.), which tend to be much more melodramatic than others from the same studio and where the music and dancing are the principal vehicles for the siphoning of the excess but where they may still be explosions of a material that is repressed rather than expressed; and in the dramas proper, where the extreme situations represented turn up material which itself cannot be represented within the convention of the plot and *mise-en-scène*. It should be stressed that the basic conventions of the melodrama are those of realism: i.e., what is represented consists of supposedly real events, seen either 'objectively' or as the summation of various discrete individual points of view. Often the 'hysterical' moment of the text can be identified as the point at which the realist representative convention breaks down. Thus in the scene in *The Cobweb* where the lake is being dragged for Stevie's body, there is no certainty either as to what is being represented (is the woman Stuart is talking to Meg or is it Karen?), or as to whose point of view, if anybody's, is being represented. The breakdown of the stable convention of representation allows such questions to be temporarily suspended in favour of what is, at one level, simple narrative confusion, but on another level can be seen as an enactment of a fantasy that involves all the characters whom the plot has drawn together. At the level of this collective fantasy, Stevie is Stuart's and Meg's 'child' and therefore the child Stuart could have had by Meg, did he not already have children by Karen (from whom he is estranged). The possibility of Stevie being dead brings this submerged fantasy to the surface, but not directly into the articulation of the plot. Realist representation cannot accommodate the fantasy, just as bourgeois society cannot accommodate its realisation.

PROVISIONAL CONCLUSION

Melodrama can thus be seen as a contradictory nexus, in which certain determinations (social, psychical, artistic) are brought together but in which the problem of the articulation of these determinations is not successfully resolved. The importance of melodrama (at least in the versions of it that are due to Ophuls, Minnelli, Sirk) lies precisely in its ideological failure. Because it cannot accommodate its problem, either in a real present or in an ideal future, but lays them open in their shameless contradictoriness, it opens a space which most Hollywood forms have studiously closed off.

AN INTRODUCTION TO THE AMERICAN HORROR FILM

ROBIN WOOD

Robin Wood combines a traditional preoccupation of genre study — the determination of recurrent themes or motifs — with a much less traditional choice of subject and thesis — the horror film as royal road to the repressed dimensions of contemporary society. Wood also combines Marx with Freud, by attending to film's relationship with ideology and by emphasizing the "return of the repressed" in horror films via the monster, which represents forms of sexuality that are inimical to the status quo. In this exemplary venture, Wood bypasses Lacanian interpretations of Freud in order to return to Herbert Marcuse and later disciples of the Frankfurt School approach to psychoanalysis and culture.

From Gad Horowitz, a follower of Marcuse, Wood borrows the central tension between repression and surplus repression. Surplus repression involves the repression of desires that could be expressed but that are treated as threatening to the existing order. It is these forms of surplus repression — bisexuality, homosexuality, female desire, and so forth — that the monster represents.

One of Wood's most interesting elaborations of this thesis involves the delineation of reactionary and progressive sides to the horror film genre, as his comparison of The Omen *and* The Texas Chainsaw Massacre *demonstrates. A similar dichotomy may well exist in film noir between the right-wing films, such as* Gilda *and* Thieves Highway, *that continue to offer hope and films, such as* D.O.A. *and* Kiss Me Deadly, *that deny any possible escape. So schematic a division of the genre may be oversimplified, but it provides a useful guideline for evaluating the politics of a film at the level of its deployment of genre conventions, and it does not require a self-reflexive or modernist "interrogation" of those conventions. Peter Biskind's recent book,* Seeing Is Believing *(New York: Pantheon, 1983), generalizes a similar, four-part taxonomy to postwar Hollywood films.*

Wood's argument is exceptionally clear. There is none of the density and obscurity that one sometimes finds in the writings of Lacanian and semiotically inclined critics. And yet this very clarity may be problematic in the sense that it is partly the result of a reductive operation that overlooks other aspects of the films in order to stress their figuration of surplus repression through the monster. For example, Wood takes the dismissive "it's only entertainment" attitude of audience and critics alike as proof that the horror film has charmed our psychic censor to let down its guard so that repressed material can be represented, as it is in jokes and dreams. However, many, including Freud, would add that the form of the joke or dream, which allows the material to slip past the censor, also transforms its effect. Hostility is expressed in a joke safely, in a socially acceptable manner that does not convey the threat that its balder expression would. Something similar seems to be at work in the horror film, but it may escape Wood's linear linkage between representation and repression. Wood sees contradictions embedded at a thematic level in horror films that Nowell-Smith sees embedded at a stylistic level in melodrama. Like Nowell-Smith, Wood views this process as clear-cut evidence of ideology at work, but the political effect of this representation of contradiction is not necessarily obvious. At the very least, the question of effect, whether measured in either empirical or theoretical and psychoanalytic terms, needs considerably more examination.

•

I. REPRESSION, THE OTHER, THE MONSTER

The most significant development—in film criticism, and in progressive ideas generally—of the last few decades has clearly been the increasing confluence of Marx and Freud, or more precisely of the traditions of thought arising from them: the recognition that social revolution and sexual revolution are inseparably linked and necessary to each other. From Marx we derive our awareness of the dominant ideology—the ideology of bourgeois capitalism—as an insidious all-pervasive force capable of concealment behind the most protean disguises, and the necessity of exposing its operation whenever and wherever possible. It is psychoanalytic theory that has provided (without Freud's awareness of the full revolutionary potential of what he was unleashing) the most effective means of examining the ways in which that ideology is transmitted and perpetuated, centrally through the institutionalization of the patriarchal nuclear family. The battle for liberation, the battle against oppression (whether economic, legal or ideological), gains enormous extra significance through the addition of that term "patriarchal," since patriarchy long *precedes* and far exceeds what we call capitalism. It is here, through the medium of psychoanalytic theory, that Feminism and Gay Liberation join forces with Marxism in their progress towards a common aim, the overthrow of patriarchal capitalist ideology and the structures and institutions that sustain it and are sustained by it.

Psychoanalytic theory, like Marxism, now provides various models, inflecting basic premises in significantly different ways. It is not certain that the Lacanian model promoted by (among others) *Screen* magazine is the most satisfactory (see Andrew Britton's article, "The Ideology of *Screen*," in *Movie* 26). On the evidence so far it seems certainly not the most potentially *effective*, leading either to paralysis or to a new academicism perhaps more sterile than the old, and driving its students into monastic cells rather than the streets. I want to indicate briefly a possible alternative model, developed out of Freud by Marcuse and given definitive formulation in a recent book by Gad Horowitz. *Repression* (University of Toronto Press): a model that enables us to connect theory closely with the ways we actually think and feel and conduct our lives—those daily practicalities from which the theorizing of *Screen* seems often so remote. The book's sub-title is *Basic and Surplus Repression in Psychoanalytic Theory: Freud, Reich, Marcuse.* It is the crucial distinction between basic and surplus repression that is so useful in relation to direct political militancy and so suggestive in relation to the reading of our cultural artifacts (among them our horror films) and, through them, our culture itself. Horowitz has devoted a dense, often difficult and closely argued book to the subject; in the space at my disposal I can offer only a bald and simplified account.

Basic repression is universal, necessary and inescapable. It is what makes possible our development from an uncoordinated animal capable of little beyond screaming and convulsions into a human being; it is bound up with the ability to accept the postponement of gratification, with the development of our thought and memory processes, of our capacity for self-control, of our recognition of and consideration for other people. Surplus repression, on the other hand, is specific to a particular culture and is the process whereby people are conditioned from earliest infancy to take on predetermined roles within that culture. In terms of our own culture, then: *basic* repression makes us distinctively human, capable of directing our own lives and co-existing with others; *surplus* repression makes us (if it works) into monogamous heterosexual bourgeois patriarchal capitalists ('bourgeois' even if we are born into the proletariat, for we are talking here of ideological norms rather than material status). *If* it works; if it doesn't, the result is either a neurotic or a revolutionary (or both), and if revolutionaries account for a very small proportion of the population, neurotics account for a very large one. Hardly surprising. All known existing societies are to some degree surplus-repressive, but the degree varies enormously, from the trivial to the overwhelming. Freud saw long ago that our own civilization had reached a point where the burden of repression was becoming all but insupportable, an insight Horowitz (following Marcuse) brilliantly relates to Marx's theory of alienated labour: the most immediately obvious characteristics of life in our culture are frustration, dissatisfaction, anxiety, greed, possessiveness, jealousy, neuroticism: no more than what psychoanalytic theory shows to be the logical product of patriarchal capitalism. What needs to be stressed is that the kind of challenges now being made to the system—and the kind of perceptions and recognitions that structure those challenges and give them impetus—become possible (become in the literal sense *thinkable*) only in the circumstances of the system's imminent disintegration. While the system retained sufficient conviction, credibility and show of coherence to suppress them, it did so. The struggle for liberation is not utopian, but a practical necessity.

Given that our culture offers an extreme example of surplus repressiveness, one can ask what, exactly, in the interests of alienated labour and the patriarchal family is repressed. One needs here both to distinguish between the concepts of *re*pression and *op*pression, and to suggest the continuity between them. In psychoanalytic terms, what is *re*pressed is not accessible to the conscious mind (except through analysis or, if one can penetrate their disguises, in dreams). We may also not be conscious of ways in which we are *op*pressed, but it is much easier to become so: we are oppressed by something "out there". One might perhaps define repression as fully internalized oppression (while reminding ourselves that all the groundwork of repression is laid in infancy), thereby suggesting both the difference and the connection. A specific example may make this clearer: our social structure demands the *re*pression of the bisexuality that psychoanalysis shows to be the natural heritage of every human individual, and the *op*pression of homosexuals: obviously, the two phenomena are not identical, but equally obviously they are closely connected. What escapes *re*pression has to be dealt with by *op*pression.

What, then, is repressed in our culture? First, sexual energy itself, together with its possible successful sublimation into non-sexual creativity—sexuality being the source of creative energy in general. The "ideal" inhabitant of our culture will be the individual whose sexuality is sufficiently fulfilled by the monogamous heterosexual union necessary for the reproduction of future ideal inhabitants, and whose sublimated sexuality (creativity) is sufficiently fulfilled in the totally non-creative and non-fulfilling labour (whether in factory or office) to which our society dooms the overwhelming majority of its members. The "ideal", in other words, is as close as possible to an automaton in whom both sexual and intellectual energy have been reduced to a minimum. Otherwise, the "ideal" is a contradiction in terms and a logical impossibility, hence the *necessary* frustration, anxiety and neuroticism of our culture.

Secondly, bisexuality—which should be understood both literally (in terms of possible sexual orientation and practice) and in a more general sense. Bisexuality represents the most obvious and direct affront to the principle of monogamy and its supportive romantic myth of "the one right person"; the homosexual impulse in both men and women represents the most obvious threat to the 'norm' of sexuality as reproductive and restricted by the "ideal" of family. But more generally we confront here the whole edifice of clear-cut sexual differentiation that bourgeois capitalist ideology erects on the flimsy and dubious foundations of biological difference: the social norms of masculinity and femininity, the social definitions of manliness and womanliness, the whole vast apparatus of oppressive male/female myths, the systematic repression from infancy ("blue for a boy") of the man's "femininity" and the woman's "masculinity", in the interests of forming human beings for specific predetermined social roles.

Thirdly, the particularly severe repression of female sexuality/creativity; the attribution to the female of passivity, her preparation for her subordinate and dependent role in our culture. Clearly, a crucial aspect of the repression of bisexuality is the denial to women of drives culturally associated with masculinity: activeness, aggression, self-assertion, organizational power, creativity itself.

Fourthly—and fundamentally—the repression of the sexuality of children, taking different forms from infancy, through "latency" and puberty, and into adolescence—the process moving, indeed, from *re*pression to *op*pression, from the denial of the infant's nature as sexual being to the veto on the expression of sexuality before marriage.

None of these forms of repression is necessary for the existence of civilization in some form (i.e., none is "basic")—for the development of our human-ness. Indeed, they impose limitations and restrictions on that development, stunting human potential. All are the outcome of the requirements of the particular, surplus-repressive, civilization in which we live.

Closely linked to the concept of repression—indeed, truly inseparable from it—is another concept necessary to an understanding of ideology on which psychoanalysis throws much light, the concept of "the Other": that which bourgeois ideology cannot recognize or accept but must deal with (as Barthes suggests in *Mythologies*) in one of two ways: either by rejecting and if possible annihilating it, or by rendering it safe and assimilating it, converting it as far as possible into a replica of itself. The concept of Otherness can be theorized in many ways and on many levels. Its psychoanalytic significance resides in the fact that it functions not simply as something external to the culture or to the self, but also as what is repressed (but never destroyed) in the self and projected outwards in order to be hated and disowned. A particularly vivid example—and one that throws light on a great many classical Westerns—is the relationship of the Puritan settlers to the Indians in the early days of America. The Puritans rejected any perception that the Indians had a culture, a civilization, of their own; they perceived them not merely as savage but, literally, as devils or the spawn of the Devil; and since the Devil and sexuality are inextricably linked in the Puritan consciousness, they perceived them as sexually promiscuous, creatures of unbridled libido. The connection between this view of the Indian and Puritan repression is obvious: a classic and extreme case of the projection onto the Other of what is repressed within the Self, in order that it can be discredited, disowned, and if possible annihilated. It is repression, in other words, that makes impossible the healthy alternative: the full recognition and acceptance of the Other's autonomy and right to exist.

Some versions, then, of the figure of the Other as it operates within our culture, of its relation to repression and oppression, and of how it is characteristically dealt with:

1. Quite simply, other people. It is logical and probable that under capitalism all human relations will be characterized by power, dominance, possessiveness, manipulation: the extension into relationships of the property principle. Given the subordinate and dependent position of women, this is especially true of the culture's central relationship, the male/female, and explains why marriage as we have it is characteristically a kind of mutual imperialism/colonization, an exchange of different forms of possession and dependence, both economic and emotional. In theory, relations between people of the same sex stand more chance of evading this contamination, but in practice most gay and lesbian relationships tend to rely on heterosexual models. The "otherness", the autonomy, of the partner, her/his right to freedom and independence of being, is perceived as a threat to the possession/dependence principle and denied.

2. Woman. In a male-dominated culture, where power, money, law, social institutions are controlled by past, present and future patriarchs, woman as the Other assumes particular significance. The dominant images of women in our culture are entirely male-created and male-controlled. Woman's autonomy and independence are denied; onto women men project their own innate, repressed femininity in order to disown it as inferior (to be called "unmanly"—i.e., like a woman—is the supreme insult).

3. The proletariat—in so far as it still has any autonomous existence, escaping its colonization by bourgeois ideology. It remains, at least, a conveniently

available object for projection: the bourgeois obsession with cleanliness, which psychoanalysis shows to be closely associated, as outward symptom, with sexual repression, and bourgeois sexual repression itself, find their inverse reflections in the myths of working-class squalor and sexuality.

4. Other cultures. If they are sufficiently remote, no problem: they can be simultaneously deprived of their true character and exoticized (e.g., Polynesian cultures as embodied by Dorothy Lamour). If they are inconveniently close, we already have the example of the American Indian: the procedure is very precisely represented in Ford's *Drums Along the Mohawk,* with its double vision of the Indians as "sons of Belial" fit only for extermination, or the Christianized, domesticated, servile and (hopefully) comic Blueback.

5. Ethnic groups within the culture. Again, an easily available projection-object (myths of black sexuality, "animality", etc.). Acceptable in either of two ways: either they keep to their ghettoes and don't trouble us with their "otherness", or they behave as we do and become replicas of the good bourgeois, their otherness reduced to the one unfortunate difference of colour. We are more likely to invite a Pakistani to dinner if he dresses in a business suit.

6. Alternative ideologies or political systems. The exemplary case is of course Marxism, the strategy that of parody. Still almost totally repressed within our preuniversity education system (despite the key importance of Marx—whatever way you look at it—in the development of twentieth-century thought), Marxism exists generally in our culture only in the form of bourgeois myth that renders it indistinguishable from Stalinism (rather like confusing the teachings of Christ with the Spanish Inquisition).

7. Deviations from ideological sexual norms—notably bisexuality and homosexuality. One of the clearest instances of the operation of the repression/projection mechanism: homophobia (the irrational hatred and fear of homosexuals) is only explicable as the outcome of the unsuccessful repression of bisexual tendencies: what is hated in others is what is rejected (but nonetheless continues to exist) within the self.

8. Children. When we have worked our way through all the other liberation movements, we may discover that children are the most oppressed section of the population (unfortunately, we cannot expect to liberate our children until we have successfully liberated ourselves). Most clearly of all, the "otherness" of children (see Freudian theories of infantile sexuality) is that which is repressed within ourselves, its expression therefore hated in others: what the previous generation repressed in us, and what we, in turn, repress in our children, seeking to mould them into replicas of ourselves, perpetuators of a discredited tradition.

All this may seem to have taken us rather far from our immediate subject. In fact, I have been laying the foundations, stone by stone, for a theory of the American horror film which (without being exhaustive) should provide us with a means of approaching the films seriously and responsibly. One could, I think, approach any of the genres from the same starting-point; it is the horror film that responds in the most clear-cut and direct way, because central to it is the actual dramatization of the dual concept the repressed/the Other, in the figure of the Monster. One might say that the true subject of the horror genre is the struggle for recognition of all that our civilisation *re*presses or *op*presses: its re-emergence dramatized, as in our nightmares, as an object of horror, a matter for terror, the "happy ending" (when it exists) typically signifying the restoration of repression. I think my analysis of what is repressed, combined with my account of the Other as it functions within our culture, will be found to offer a comprehensive survey of horror film monsters from German Expressionism on. It is possible to produce "monstrous" embodiments of virtually every item in the list. Let me preface this by saying that the general sexual content of the horror film has long been recognized, and the list of monsters representing a generalized sexual threat would be interminable; also, the generalized concept of "otherness" offered by the first item on my list cannot be represented by specific films.

Female sexuality. Earlier examples are the panther-woman of *Island of Lost Souls* and the heroine of *Cat People* (the association of women with cats runs right through and beyond the Hollywood cinema, cutting across periods and genres from *Bringing up Baby* to *Alien*); but the definitive Feminist horror film is clearly De Palma's *Sisters* (coscripted by the director and Louisa Rose), which is among the most complete and rigorous analyses of the oppression of women under patriarchal culture in the whole popular cinema.

The proletariat. I would claim here Whale's *Frankenstein,* partly on the strength of its pervasive class references, more on the strength of Karloff's costume: Frankenstein *could* have dressed his creature in top hat, white tie and tails, but in fact chose labourer's clothes. Less disputable, in recent years we have *The Texas Chainsaw Massacre,* with its monstrous family of retired, but still practising, slaughterhouse workers; the underprivileged devil-worshippers of *Race with the Devil;* and the revolutionary army of *Assault on Precinct 13.*

Other cultures. In the Thirties the monster was almost invariably foreign; the rebellious animal-humans of *Island of Lost Souls* (though created by the white man's science) on one level clearly signify a "savage", unsuccessfully colonized culture. Recently, one horror film, *The Manitou,* identified the monster with the American Indian. (*Prophecy* plays tantalizingly with this possibility—also linking it to urban blacks   before opting for the altogether safer and less interesting explanation of industrial pollution.)

Ethnic groups. The *Possession of Joel Delaney* links diabolic possession with Puerto Ricans; blacks (and a leader clad as an Indian) are prominent, again, in *Assault on Precinct 13's* monstrous army.

Alternative ideologies. The Fifties science-fiction cycle of invasion movies is generally regarded as being concerned with the Communist threat.

Homosexuality and bisexuality. Both Murnau's *Nosferatu* and Whale's *Frankenstein* can be claimed as implicitly (on certain levels) identifying their monsters with repressed homosexuality. Recent, less arguable, instances are Dr. Frank 'n' Furter of *The Rocky Horror Picture Show* (he, not his creation, is clearly the film's real monster) and, more impressively, the bisexual god of Larry Cohen's *Demon.*

Children. Since *Rosemary's Baby* children have figured prominently in horror films as the monster or its medium: *The Exorcist, The Omen,* etc. Cohen's two *It's Alive* films again offer perhaps the most interesting and impressive example. There is also the Michael of *Halloween*'s remarkable opening.

This offers us no more than a beginning, from which one might proceed to interpret specific horror films in detail as well as further exploring the genre's social significance, the insights it offers into our culture. I shall add here simply that these notions of repression and the Other afford us not merely a means of access but a rudimentary categorization of horror films in social/political terms, distinguishing the progressive from the reactionary; the criterion being the way in which the monster is presented and defined.

II.   RETURN OF THE REPRESSED

I want first to offer a series of general propositions about the American horror film, then attempt to define the particular nature of its evolution in the Sixties and Seventies.

1. Popularity and Disreputability

The horror film has consistently been one of the most popular and, at the same time, the most disreputable of Hollywood genres. The popularity itself has a peculiar characteristic that sets the horror film apart from other genres: it is restricted to aficionados and complemented by total rejection, people tending to go to horror films either obsessively or not at all. They are dismissed with contempt by the majority of reviewer critics, or simply ignored. (The situation has changed somewhat since *Psycho,* which conferred on the horror film something of the dignity that *Stagecoach* conferred on the Western, but the disdain still largely continues. I have read no serious or illuminating accounts of, for example, *Raw Meat, It's Alive,* or *The Hills Have Eyes.*) The popularity, however, also continues. Most horror films make money; the ones that don't are those with overt intellectual pretensions, obviously "difficult" works like *God Told Me To (Demon)* and *Exorcist II.* Another psychologically interesting aspect of this popularity is that many people who go regularly to horror films profess to ridicule them and go in order to laugh—which is not true, generally speaking, of the Western or the gangster movie.

2. Dreams and Nightmares

The analogy frequently invoked between films and dreams is usually concerned with the experience of the audience. The spectator sits in darkness, and the sort of involvement the entertainment film invites necessitates a certain switching-off of consciousness, a losing of oneself in a fantasy experience. But the analogy is also useful from the point of view of the filmmakers. Dreams—the embodiment of repressed desires, tensions, fears that our conscious mind rejects—become possible when the "censor" that guards our subconscious relaxes in sleep, though even then the desires can only emerge in disguise, as fantasies that are "innocent" or apparently meaningless.

One of the functions of the concept of "entertainment"—by definition, that which we don't take seriously, or think about much ("It's only entertainment")—is to act as a kind of partial sleep of consciousness. For the filmmakers as well as for the audience, full awareness stops at the level of plot, action, and character, in which the most dangerous and subversive implications can disguise themselves and escape detection. This is why seemingly innocuous genre movies can be far more radical and fundamentally undermining than works of conscious social criticism, which must always concern themselves with the possibility of reforming aspects of a social system whose basic rightness must not be challenged. The old tendency to dismiss the Hollywood cinema as escapist always defined escape merely negatively as escape *from,* but escape logically must also be escape *to.* Dreams are also escapes, from the unresolved tensions of our lives into fantasies. Yet the fantasies are not meaningless; they can represent attempts to resolve those tensions in more radical ways than our consciousness can countenance.

Popular films, then, respond to interpretation as at once the personal dreams of their makers and the collective dreams of their audiences—the fusion made possible by the shared structures of a common ideology. It becomes easy, if this is granted, to offer a simple definition of horror films: they are our collective nightmares. The conditions under which a dream becomes a nightmare are (a) that the repressed wish is, from the point of view of consciousness, so terrible that it must be repudiated as loathsome, and (b) that it is so strong and powerful as to constitute a serious threat. The disreputability noted above—the general agreement that horror films are not to be taken seriously—works clearly *for* the genre viewed from this position. The censor (in both the common *and* the Freudian sense) is lulled into sleep and relaxes vigilance.

3. The Surrealists

It is worth noting here that one group of intellectuals *did* take American horror movies very seriously indeed: the writers, painters, and filmmakers of the Surrealist movement. Luis Buñuel numbers *The Beast with Five Fingers* among his favorite films and paid homage to it in *The Exterminating Angel;* and Georges Franju, an heir of the Surrealists, numbers *The Fly* among *his.* The association is highly significant, given the commitment of the Surrealists to Freud, the unconscious, dreams, and the overthrow of repression.

4. Basic Formula

At this stage it is necessary to offer a simple and obvious basic formula for the horror film: normality is threatened by the Monster. I use "normality" here in a strictly non-evaluative sense, to mean simply "conformity to the dominant social norms"; one must firmly resist the common tendency to treat the word as if it were more or less synonymous with "health".

The very simplicity of this formula has a number of advantages:

a. It covers the entire range of horror films, being applicable whether the Monster is a vampire, a giant gorilla, an extraterrestrial invader, an amorphous gooey mass, or a child possessed by the Devil, and this makes it possible to connect the most seemingly heterogeneous movies.

   b. It suggests the possibility of extension to other genres: substitute for "Monster" the term "Indians," for example, and one has a formula for a large number of classical Westerns.

   c. Although so simple, the formula provides three variables: normality, the Monster, and, crucially, the relationship between the two. The definition of normality in horror films is in general boringly constant: the heterosexual monogamous couple, the family, and the social institutions (police, church, armed forces) that support and defend them. The Monster is, of course, much more protean, changing from period to period as society's basic fears clothe themselves in fashionable or immediately accessible garments—rather as dreams use material from recent memory to express conflicts or desires that may go back to early childhood.

   It is the third variable, the relationship between normality and the Monster, that constitutes the essential subject of the horror film. It, too, changes and develops, the development taking the form of a long process of clarification or revelation. The relationship has one privileged form: the figure of the doppelgänger, alter ego, or double, a figure that has recurred constantly in Western culture, especially during the past hundred years. The *locus classicus* is Stevenson's *Dr. Jekyll and Mr. Hyde,* where normality and Monster are two aspects of the same person. The figure recurs throughout two major sources of the American horror film, German Expressionist cinema (the two Marias of *Metropolis,* the presentation of protagonist and vampire as mirror reflections in *Nosferatu,* the very title of F. W. Murnau's lost Jekyll-and-Hyde film *Der Januskopf*), and the tales of Poe. Variants can be traced in such oppositions as Ahab/the white whale in *Moby Dick* and Ethan/Scar in *The Searchers.* The Westerns of Anthony Mann are rich in doubles, often contained within families or family patterns; *Man of the West,* a film that relates very suggestively to the horror genre, represents the fullest elaboration.

   I shall limit myself for the moment to one example from the horror film, choosing it partly because it is so central, partly because the motif is there less obvious, partially disguised, partly because it points forward to Larry Cohen and *It's Alive*: the relationship of Monster to creator in the *Frankenstein* films. Their identity is made explicit in *Son of Frankenstein,* the most intelligent of the Universal series, near the start of which the title figure (Basil Rathbone) complains bitterly that everyone believes "Frankenstein" to be the name of the monster. (We discover subsequently that the town has also come to be called Frankenstein, the symbiosis of Monster and creator spreading over the entire environment.) But we should be alerted to the relationship's true significance from the moment in the James Whale original where Frankenstein's decision to create his monster is juxtaposed very precisely with his decision to become engaged. The doppelgänger motif reveals the Monster as normality's shadow.

5. Ambivalence

The principle of ambivalence is most eloquently elaborated in A. P. Rossiter's *Angel with Horns,* among the most brilliant of all books on Shakespeare. Rossiter first expounds it with reference to Richard III. Richard, the "angel with horns," both horrifies us with his evil and delights us with his intellect, his art, his audacity; while our moral sense is appalled by his outrages, another part of us gleefully identifies with him. The application of this to the horror film is clear. Few horror films have totally unsympathetic Monsters (*The Thing* is a significant exception); in many (notably the *Frankenstein* films) the Monster is clearly the emotional centre, and much more human than the cardboard representatives of normality. The Frankenstein monster suffers, weeps, responds to music, longs to relate to people: Henry and Elizabeth merely declaim histrionically. Even in *Son of Frankenstein*—the film in which the restructured monster is explicitly designated evil and superhuman—the monster's emotional commitment to Ygor and grief over his death carries far greater weight than any of the other relationships in the film.

But the principle goes far beyond the Monster's being sympathetic. Ambivalence extends to our attitude to normality. Central to the effect and fascination of horror films is their fulfillment of our nightmare wish to smash the norms that oppress us and which our moral conditioning teaches us to revere. The overwhelming commercial success of *The Omen* cannot possibly be explained in terms of a simple, unequivocal *horror* at the devil's progress.

6. Freudian Theses

Finally, one can simply state the two elementary (and closely interconnected) Freudian theses that structure this article: that in a society built on monogamy and family there will be an enormous surplus of sexual energy that will have to be repressed; and that what is repressed must always strive to return.

Before considering how the horror film has developed in the past decade, I want to test the validity of the above ideas by applying them to a classical horror film. I have chosen Robert Florey's *Murders in the Rue Morgue* (1932)—because it is a highly distinguished example, and generally neglected; because its images suggest Surrealism as much as Expressionism; and because it occupies a particularly interesting place in the genre's evolution, linking two of the most famous, though most disparate, horror films ever made. On the one hand it looks back very clearly to *The Cabinet of Dr. Caligari:* the Expressionist sets and lighting, with Karl Freund as cinematographer; the fairground that provides the starting point for the action; the figure of the diabolical doctor, who shows off his exhibit and later sends it to kidnap the heroine; the flight over the rooftops. On the other hand it looks forward, equally clearly, to *King Kong*: instead of *Caligari's* sleepwalker, a gorilla, which falls in love with the heroine, abducts her at night and is shot down from a roof. It is as important to notice the basic motifs that recur obstinately throughout the evolution of the horror film in Western culture as it is to be aware of the detailed particularities of individual films. *Murders in the Rue Morgue* responds well to the application of my formula.

a. *Normality*. The film is quite obsessive about its heterosexual couples. At the opening, we have two couples responding to the various spectacles of the fairground; there is a scene in the middle where numerous carefree couples disport themselves picturesquely amid nature. Crucial to the film, however, is Pierre's love-speech to Camille on her balcony, with its exaggerated emphasis on purity: she is both a "flower" and a "star"; she is told not to be curious about what goes on in the houses of the city around them ("Better not to know"); she is also prevented from obtaining knowledge of the nature of Pierre's activities in the morgue (a "horrid old place"). Even the usual gay stereotype, Pierre's plump and effeminate friend, fits very well into the pattern. He is provided with a girl friend, to recuperate him into the heterosexual coupling of normality. His relationship with Pierre (they share an apartment, he wears an apron, cooks the dinner, and fusses) is a parody of bourgeois marriage, the incongruity underlining the relationship's repressive sexlessness. And he underlines the attempts at separating "pure" normality from the pervasive contamination of outside forces by complaining that Pierre "brings the morgue into their home."

   b. *The Monster. Murders in the Rue Morgue* has a divided Monster, a phenomenon not uncommon in the horror film. (In *The Cabinet of Dr. Caligari* the Monster is both Caligari and Cesar; in *Island of Lost Souls* both Dr. Moreau and his creatures.) Here the division is tripartite: Dr. Mirakle (Bela Lugosi), his servant-assistant, and Erik, "the beast with a human soul." The servant's role is small but important because of his appearance: half-human, half-animal, he bridges the gap between Mirakle and Erik. Scientist and ape are linked, however, in another way: Mirakle himself lusts after Camille, and Erik (the animal extension of himself) represents the instrument for the satisfaction of that lust. Together, they combine the two great, apparently contradictory, dreads of American culture as expressed in its cinema: intellectuality and eroticism.

   c. *Relationship.* The film's superficial project is to insist that purity-normality can be separated from contaminating eroticism-degradation; its deeper project is to demonstrate the impossibility of such a separation. In the opening sequence, the couples view a series of fairground acts as spectacles (the separation of stage from audience seeming to guarantee safety): an erotic dance by "Arabian" girls, a Wild Red Indian show, and finally Erik the ape. The association of the three is suggestive of the link between the horror film and the Western—the link of horror, Indians, and released libido. In each case the separation of show and audience is shown to be precarious: Pierre's sidekick asks his girl if she "could learn to do that dance" for him; two spectators adopt the name "apache" to apply to the savages of Paris; the audience enters the third booth between the legs of an enormous painted ape, where its phallus would be. Dr. Mirakle's introduction uses evolutionary theory to deny separation: Erik is "the darkness at the dawn of Man." His subsequent experiments are carried out to prove that Erik's blood can be "mixed with the blood of man"—and as the experiments all involve women, the sexual connotations are plain.

   Though not obvious, the "double" motif subtly structures the film. It comes nearest to explicitness in the effeminate friend's remark that Pierre is becoming fanatical, "like that Dr. Mirakle." But Pierre and Mirakle are paralleled repeatedly, both in the construction of the scenario and through the *mise-en-scène.* At the end of the balcony love scene Florey cuts from the lovers' kiss to Mirakle and Erik watching from their carriage. Later, the juxtaposition is reversed, the camera panning from Mirakle-Erik lurking in the shadows to Pierre-Camille embracing on the balcony; it is as if the Monster were waiting to be released by the kiss. Mirakle sends Camille a bonnet; she assumes it is from Pierre. After Pierre leaves her at night, there is a knock at her door. She assumes it is Pierre come back and opens; it is Mirakle. Bearing in mind that Mirakle and Erik are not really distinct from one another, one must see Pierre and this composite Monster paralleled throughout as rival mates for Camille, like Jonathan and Nosferatu, or like David Ladd and the underworld man of *Raw Meat*. (The motif's recurrence across different periods and different continents testifies to its importance.) At the climax, Pierre and Erik confront each other like mirror images on the rooftop, and Erik is shot down by Pierre: the hero's drive is to destroy the doppelgänger who embodies his repressed self.

Murders in the Rue Morgue is fascinating for its unresolved self-contradiction. In the fairground, Mirakle is denounced as a heretic, in the name of the Biblical/Christian tradition of God's creation of man; the whole notion of purity/normality clearly associates with this—explicitly, in the very prominent, carefully lit crucifix above Camille's bed. Yet Mirakle's Darwinian theories are also obviously meant to be correct. Erik and humanity are *not* separable; the ape exists in all of us; the "morgue" cannot be excluded from the "home."

The horror film since the Sixties has been dominated by five recurrent motifs. The list of examples offered in each case begins with what I take to be the decisive source-film of each trend—not necessarily the first, but the film that, because of its distinction or popularity, can be thought of as responsible for the ensuing cycle. I have included a few British films that seem to me American-derived *(Raw Meat,* arguably the finest British horror film, was directed by an American, Gary Sherman); they lie outside the main British tradition represented by Hammer Productions, a tradition very intelligently treated in David Pirie's book *A Heritage of Horror.* The lists are not, of course, meant to be exhaustive.

a. The Monster as human psychotic or schizophrenic: *Psycho, Homicidal, Repulsion, Sisters, Schizo.*

b. The revenge of Nature: *The Birds, Frogs, Night of the Lepus, Day of the Animals, Squirm.*

c. Satanism, diabolic possession, the Antichrist: *Rosemary's Baby, The Exorcist, The Omen, The Possession of Joel Delaney, The Car, God Told Me To (Demon),* and *Race With the Devil,* which, along with *High Plains Drifter,* interestingly connects this motif with the Western.

d. The Terrible Child (often closely connected to the above). To the first three films in (c) add: *Night of the Living Dead, Hands of the Ripper, It's Alive, Cathy's Curse;* also, although here the "children" are older, *Carrie* and *The Fury.*

e. Cannibalism: *Night of the Living Dead, Raw Meat, Frightmare, The Texas Chainsaw Massacre, The Hills Have Eyes.*

These apparently heterogeneous motifs are drawn deeper together by a single unifying master-figure: the Family. The connection is most tenuous and intermittent in what has proved, on the whole, the least interesting and productive of these concurrent cycles, the "revenge of Nature" films; but even there, in the more distinguished examples (outstandingly, of course, *The Birds,* but also in *Squirm*), the attacks are linked to, or seem triggered off by, familial or sexual tensions. Elsewhere, the connection of the Family to Horror has become overwhelmingly consistent: the psychotic/schizophrenic, the Antichrist and the child-monster are all shown as products of the family, whether the family itself is regarded as guilty (the "psychotic" films) or innocent (*The Omen*).

The "cannibalism" motif functions in two ways. Occasionally members of a family devour each other (*Night of the Living Dead,* and *Psycho's* Mrs. Bates is a metaphorical cannibal who swallows up her son). More frequently, cannibalism is the family's means of sustaining or nourishing itself (*The Texas Chainsaw Massacre, The Hills Have Eyes*). Pete Walker's revoltingly gruesome and ugly British horror film *Frightmare* deserves a note here, its central figure being a sweet and gentle old mother who has the one unfortunate flaw that she can't survive without eating human flesh, a craving guiltily indulged by her devoted husband.

If we see the evolution of the horror film in terms of an inexorable "return of the repressed," we will not be surprised by this final emergence of the genre's real significance—together with a sense that it is currently the most important of all American genres and perhaps the most progressive, even in its overt nihilism—in a period of extreme cultural crisis and disintegration, which alone offers the possibility of radical change and rebuilding. To do justice to the lengthy process of that emergence would involve a dual investigation too complex for the framework of this article: into the evolution of the horror film, and into the changing treatment of the family in the Hollywood cinema. I shall content myself here with a few further propositions.

1. The family (or marital) comedy in which the Thirties and Forties are so rich, turns sour (*Father of the Bride, The Long Long Trailer*) in the Fifties and peters out; the family horror film starts (not, of course, without precedents) with *Psycho* in 1960, and gains impetus with *Rosemary's Baby* and *Night of the Living Dead* toward the end of the decade.

2. As the horror film enters into its apocalyptic phase, so does the Western. *The Wild Bunch* appeared in 1969, the year after *Rosemary's Baby.* And *High Plains Drifter* (1973) fused their basic elements in a Western in which the Hero from the Wilderness turns out to be the Devil (or his emissary) and burns the town (American civilisation) to the ground after revealing it as fundamentally corrupt and renaming it Hell.

3. The family comedies that seemed so innocent and celebratory in the Thirties and Forties appear much less so in retrospect from the Seventies. In my book *Personal Views* I pointed to the remarkable anticipation in *Meet Me in St. Louis* of the Terrible Child of the Seventies horror film, especially in the two scenes (Halloween, and the destruction of the snow people) in which Margaret O'Brien symbolically kills parent figures. What is symbolic in 1944 becomes literal in *Night of the Living Dead,* where a little girl kills and devours her parents—just as the implications of another anticipatory family film of the early Forties, *Shadow of a Doubt,* becomes literally enacted in *It's Alive* (the monster as product of the family).

4. The process whereby horror becomes associated with its true milieu, the family, is reflected in its steady *geographical* progress toward America.

a. In the Thirties, horror is always foreign. The films are set in Paris (*Murders in the Rue Morgue*), Middle Europe (*Frankenstein, Dracula*) or on uncharted islands (*Island of Lost Souls, King Kong*); it is always external to Americans, who may be attacked by it physically but remain (superficially, that is) uncontaminated by it morally. The designation of horror as foreign stands even when the "normal" characters are Europeans. In *Murders in the Rue Morgue,* for example, the young couples, though nominally French, are to all intents and purposes nice clean-living Americans (with American accents); the foreignness of the horror characters is strongly underlined, both by Lugosi's accent and by the fact that nobody knows where he comes from. The foreignness of horror in the Thirties can be interpreted in two ways: simply, as a means of disavowal (horror exists, but is un-American), and, more interestingly and unconsciously, as a means of locating horror as a "country of the mind," as a psychological state: the films set on uncharted (and usually nameless) islands lend themselves particularly to interpretation of this kind.

b. The Val Lewton films of the Forties are in some ways outside the mainstream development of the horror film. They seem to have had little direct influence on its evolution (certain occasional haunted-house movies like *The Uninvited* and *The Haunting* may owe something to them), though they strikingly anticipate, by at least two decades, some of the features of the modern horror film. *Cat People* is centred on the repression of female sexuality, in a period where the Monster is almost invariably male and phallic. (Other rare exceptions are the panther-woman of *Island of Lost Souls* and, presumably, *Dracula's Daughter,* which I have not seen.) *The Seventh Victim* has strong undertones of sibling envy and sexual jealousy (the structure and editing of the last scene suggesting that Jacqueline's suicide is willed by her "nice" husband and sister rather than by the "evil" devil-worshippers), as well as containing striking anticipations of *Psycho* and *Rosemary's Baby;* it is also set firmly in America, with no attempt to disown evil as foreign.

Above all, *I Walked With A Zombie* explicitly locates horror at the heart of the family, identifying it with sexual repressiveness in the cause of preserving family unity. *The Seventh Victim* apart, horror is still associated with foreignness; Irena in *Cat People* is from Serbia, *Zombie* is set in the West Indies, *The Leopard Man* in Mexico, etc. Yet the best of the series are concerned with the undermining of such distinctions—with the idea that no one escapes contamination. Accordingly, the concept of the Monster becomes diffused through the film (closely linked to the celebrated Lewton emphasis on atmosphere, rather than overt shock), no longer identified with a single figure.

Zombie, one of the finest of all American horror films, carries this furthest. It is built on an elaborate set of apparently clear-cut structural oppositions— Canada-West Indies, white-black, light-darkness, life-death, science-black magic, Christianity-Voodoo, conscious-unconscious, etc.—and it proceeds systematically to blur all of them. Jessica is both living and dead; Mrs. Rand mixes medicine, Christianity, and voodoo; the figurehead is both St. Sebastian and a black slave; the black-white opposition is poetically undercut in a complex patterning of dresses and voodoo patches; the motivation of *all* the characters is called into question; the messenger-zombie Carrefour can't be kept out of the white domain.

c. The Fifties science fiction cycles project horror onto either extraterrestrial invaders or mutations from the insect world, but they are usually set in America; even when they are not (*The Thing*), the human characters are American. The films, apparently simple, prove on inspection often very difficult to "read." The basic narrative patterns of the horror film repeat themselves obstinately and continue to carry their traditional meanings, but they are encrusted with layers of more transient, topical material. *Them!* for example, seems to offer three layers of meaning. Explicitly, it sets out to cope with the fear of nuclear energy and atomic experiment: the giant ants are mutants produced by the radioactive aftermath of a bomb explosion; they are eventually destroyed under the guidance of a humane and benevolent science embodied in the comfortingly paternal figure of Edmund Gwenn. The fear of Communist infiltration also seems present, in the emphasis on the ants as a subversive subterranean army and on their elaborate communications system. Yet the film continues to respond convincingly to the application of my basic formula and its Freudian implications. The ants rise up from underground (the unconscious); they kill by holding their victims and injecting into them huge (excessive) quantities of formic acid (the release of repressed phallic energy); and both the opening and final climax of the film are centered on the destruction (respectively actual and potential) of family groups.

Since *Psycho*, the Hollywood cinema has implicitly recognized Horror as both American and familial. I want to conclude this section by briefly examining two key works of recent years that offer particularly illuminating and suggestive contrasts and comparisons: *The Omen* and *The Texas Chainsaw Massacre*.

One can partly define the nature of each by means of a chart of oppositions:

The Omen	*Massacre*
big budget	low budget
glossy production values	raw, unpolished
stars	unknown actors
bourgeois entertainment	nonbourgeois "exploitation"
Good Taste	Bad Taste
"good" family	"bad" family
the Monster imported from Europe	the Monster indigenously American
child destroys parents	parent-figures destroy "children"
traditional values reaffirmed	traditional values negated

I don't wish to make any claims for *The Omen* as a work of art: the most one could say is that it achieves a sufficient level of impersonal professional efficiency to ensure that the "kicks" inherent in its scenario are not dulled. (I would add here that my description above of *Massacre* as "raw, unpolished" refers to the overall effect of the film, as it seems to be generally experienced. Its *mise-en-scène* is, without question, everywhere more intelligent, more inventive, more cinematically educated and sophisticated than that of *The Omen*. Hooper's cinematic intelligence, indeed, becomes more apparent on every viewing, as one gets over the initial traumatizing impact and learns to respect the pervasive felicities of camera placement and movement.)

In obvious ways *The Omen* is old-fashioned, traditional, reactionary: the "goodness" of the family unit isn't questioned, "horror" is disowned by having the devil-child a product of the Old World unwittingly *adopted* into the American family, the devil-child and his independent-female guardian (loosely interpretable in "mythic" terms as representing child liberation and women's liberation) are regarded as purely evil (oh, for a cinematic Blake to reverse all the terms).

Yet the film remains of great interest. It is about the end of the world, but the "world" the film envisages ending is very particularly defined within it: the bourgeois capitalist patriarchal Establishment. Here "normality" is not merely threatened by the monster but totally annihilated: the state, the church, the family. The principle of ambivalence must once again be invoked: with a film so shrewdly calculated for box-office response, it is legitimate to ask what general satisfaction it offers its audience.

Superficially, the satisfaction of finding traditional values reaffirmed (even if "our" world is ending, it was still the good, right, true one); more deeply, and far more powerfully, under cover of this, the satisfaction of the ruthless logic with which the premise is carried through—the supreme satisfaction (masquerading as the final horror) being the revelation, as the camera cranes down in the last shot, that the Devil has been adopted by the President and First Lady of the United States. The translation of the film into Blakean terms is not in fact that difficult: the devil-child is its implicit hero, whose systematic destruction of the bourgeois Establishment the audience follows with a secret relish. *The Omen* would make no sense in a society that was not prepared to enjoy and surreptitiously condone the working out of its own destruction.

As Andrew Britton pointed out to me, *The Omen* and *The Texas Chainsaw Massacre* (together with numerous other recent horror films) have one premise disturbingly in common: the annihilation is inevitable, humanity is now completely powerless, there is nothing anyone can do to arrest the process. (Ideology, that is, can encompass despair, but not the imagining of constructive radical alternatives.) *The Omen* invokes ancient prophecy and shows it inexorably fulfilling itself despite all efforts at intervention; we infer near the opening of *Massacre* that the Age of Aquarius whose advent was so recently celebrated in *Hair* has already passed, giving way to the Age of Saturn and universal malevolence. Uncontrol is emphasized throughout the film: not only have the five young victims no control over their destiny, their slaughterers (variously psychotic and degenerate) keep losing control of themselves and each other.

This is partly (in conjunction with the film's relentless and unremitting intensity) what gives *Massacre* to such a degree (beyond any other film in my experience) the authentic quality of nightmare. I have had since childhood a recurring nightmare whose pattern seems to be shared by a very large number of people within our culture: I am running away from some vaguely terrible oppressors who are going to do dreadful things to me; I run to a house or car, etc., for help; I discover its occupants to be precisely the people I am fleeing. This pattern is repeated twice in *Massacre,* where Sally "escapes" from Leatherface first to his own home, then to the service station run by his father.

The application of my formula to *Massacre* produces interesting results: the pattern is still there, as is the significant relationship between the terms, but the definitions of "normality" and "monster" have become partly reversed. Here "normality" is clearly represented by the quasi-liberated, permissive young (though still forming two couples and a brother/sister family unit, hence reproducing the patterns of the past); the monster is the family, one of the great composite monsters of the American cinema, incorporating four characters and three generations, and imagined with an intensity and audacity that far transcend the connotations of the term "exploitation movie." It has a number of important aspects:

1. The image of the "Terrible House" stems from a long tradition in American (and Western capitalist) culture. (For a fuller treatment of this, see Andrew Britton's magisterial account of *Mandingo* in *Movie* 22.) Traditionally, it represents an extension or "objectification" of the personalities of the inhabitants. *Massacre* offers two complementary "terrible houses": the once imposing, now totally decayed house of Franklyn's and Sally's parents (where we keep *expecting* something appalling to happen), and the more modest, outwardly spruce, inwardly macabre villa of the monstrous family wherein every item of decor is an expression of the characters' degeneracy. The borderline between home and slaughterhouse (between work and leisure) has disappeared—the slaughterhouse has invaded the home, humanity has begun literally to "prey upon itself, like monsters of the deep." Finally, what the "terrible house" (whether in Poe's *The Fall of the House of Usher,* in *Psycho,* in *Mandingo,* or here) signifies is the dead weight of the past crushing the life of the younger generation, the future—an idea beautifully realized in the shot that starts on the ominous grey, decayed Franklyn house and tilts down to show Kirk and Pam, dwarfed in long shot, playing and laughing as they run to the swimming-hole, and to their doom.

2. The contrast between the two houses underlines the distinction the film makes between the affluent young and the psychotic family, representatives of an exploited and degraded proletariat. Sally's father used to send his cattle to the slaughterhouse of which the family are products.

3. The all-male family (the grandmother exists only as a decomposing corpse) also derives from a long American tradition, with notable antecedents in Ford's Westerns (the Clantons of *My Darling Clementine,* the Cleggses of *Wagonmaster*) and in *Man of the West.* The absence of Woman (conceived of as a civilizing, humanizing influence) deprives the family of its social sense and social meaning while leaving its strength of primitive loyalties largely untouched. In *Massacre,* Woman becomes the ultimate object of the characters' animus (and, I think,

the film's, since the sadistic torments visited on Sally go far beyond what is necessary to the narrative).

4. The release of sexuality in the horror film is always presented as perverted, monstrous, and excessive (whether it takes the form of vampires, giant ants, or Mrs. Bates), both the perversion and the excess being the logical outcome of repression. Nowhere is this carried further than in *Massacre*. Here sexuality is totally perverted from its functions, into sadism, violence, and cannibalism. It is striking that there is no suggestion anywhere that Sally is the object of an overtly sexual threat: she is to be tormented, killed, dismembered, eaten, but not raped. Ultimately, the most terrifying thing about the film is its total negativity, the repressed energies—represented most unforgettably by Leatherface and his continuously whirring phallic chainsaw—are presented as irredeemably debased and distorted. It is no accident that the four most intense horror films of the Seventies at "exploitation" level (*Night of the Living Dead, Raw Meat,* and *The Hills Have Eyes* are the other three) are all centered on cannibalism, and on the specific notion of present and future (the younger generation) being devoured by the past. Cannibalism represents the ultimate in possessiveness, hence the logical end of human relations under capitalism. The implication is that "liberation" and "permissiveness," as defined within our culture, are at once inadequate and too late—too feeble, too unaware, too undirected to withstand the legacy of long repression.

5. This connects closely with the recurrence of the "double" motif in *Massacre*. The young people are, on the whole, uncharacterized and undifferentiated (the film's energies are mainly with its monsters—as usual in the horror film, the characteristic here surviving the reversal of definitions), but in their midst is Franklyn, who is as grotesque, and almost as psychotic, as his nemesis Leatherface. (The film's refusal to sentimentalize the fact that he is crippled may remind one of the blind beggars of Buñuel.) Franklyn associates himself with the slaughterers by imitating the actions of Leatherface's brother the hitchhiker: wondering whether he, too, could slice open his own hand, and toying with the idea of actually doing so. (Kirk remarks, "You're as crazy as he is".) Insofar as the other young people are characterized, it is in terms of a pervasive petty malice. Just before Kirk enters the house to meet his death, he teases Pam by dropping into her hand a human tooth he has found on the doorstep; later, Jerry torments Franklyn to the verge of hysteria by playing on his fears that the hitchhiker will pursue and kill him. Franklyn resents being neglected by the others. Sally resents being burdened with him on her vacation. The monstrous cruelties of the slaughterhouse family have their more pallid reflection within "normality." (The reflection pattern here is more fully worked out in *The Hills Have Eyes,* with its stranded "normal" family besieged by its dark mirror-image, the terrible shadow-family from the hills, who want to kill the men, rape the women, and eat the baby.)

6. Despite the family's monstrousness, a degree of ambivalence is still present in the response they evoke. Partly, this is rooted in our sense of them as a *family*. They are held together—and torn apart—by bonds and tensions with which we

are all familiar—with which, indeed, we are likely to have grown up. We cannot cleanly dissociate ourselves from them. Then there is the sense that *they* are victims, too—of the slaughterhouse environment, of capitalism—*our* victims, in fact. Finally, they manifest a degraded but impressive creativity. The news reporter at the start describes the tableau of decomposing corpses in the graveyard (presumably the work of the hitchhiker, and perhaps a homage to his grandparents: a female corpse is posed in the lap of a male corpse in a hideous parody of domesticity) as "a grisly work of art." The phrase, apt for the film itself, also describes the art works among which the family live, some of which achieve a kind of hideous aesthetic beauty: the light-bulb held up by a human hand, the sofa constructed out of human and animal bones, surmounted by ornamental skulls, the hanging lamp over the dining-table that appears to be a shrunken human head. The film's monsters do not lack that characteristically human quality, an aesthetic sense, however perverted its form; also, they waste nothing, a lesson we are all taught as children.

7. Central to the film—and centred on its monstrous family—is the sense of grotesque comedy, which in no way diminishes (rather intensifies) its nightmare horror: Leatherface chasing Sally with the chainsaw, unable to stop and turn, skidding, wheeling, like an animated character in a cartoon; the father's response to Leatherface's devastations, which by that time include four murders and the prolonged terrorization of the heroine ("Look what your brother did to that door"); Leatherface dressed up in jacket and tie and fresh black wig for formal dinner with Grandpa; the macabre farce of Grandpa's repeated failures to kill Sally with the hammer. The film's sense of fundamental horror is closely allied to a sense of the fundamentally absurd. The family, after all, only carries to its logical conclusion the basic (though unstated) tenet of capitalism, that people have the right to live off other people. In twentieth-century art, the sense of the absurd is always closely linked to total despair (Beckett, Ionesco). The fusion of nightmare and absurdity is carried even further in *Death Trap*, a film that confirms that the creative impulse in Hooper's work is centred in his monsters (here, the grotesque and pathetic Neville Brand) and is essentially nihilistic.

The Texas Chainsaw Massacre, unlike *The Omen*, achieves the force of authentic art, profoundly disturbing, intensely personal, yet at the same time far more than personal, as the general response it has evoked demonstrates. As a "collective nightmare" it brings to a focus a spirit of negativity, an undifferentiated lust for destruction, that seems to lie not far below the surface of the modern collective consciousness. Watching it recently with a large, half-stoned youth audience, who cheered and applauded every one of Leatherface's outrages against their representatives on the screen, was a terrifying experience. It must not be seen as an isolated phenomenon: it expresses, with unique force and intensity, at least one important aspect of what the horror film has come to signify, the sense of a civilization condemning itself, through its popular culture, to ultimate disintegration, and ambivalently (with the simultaneous horror/wish-fulfillment of nightmare) celebrating the fact. We must not, of course, see that as the last word.

III. THE REACTIONARY WING

I suggested earlier that the theory of repression offers us a means towards a political categorization of horror movies. Such a categorization, however, can never be rigid or clear-cut. While I have stressed the genre's progressive or radical elements, its potential for the subversion of bourgeois patriarchal norms, it is obvious enough that this potential is never free from ambiguity. The genre carries within itself the capability of reactionary inflection, and perhaps no horror film is entirely immune from its operations. It need not surprise us that there is a powerful reactionary tradition to be acknowledged—so powerful it may at times appear the dominant one. Its characteristics are, in extreme cases, very strongly marked.

Before noting them, however, it is important to make one major distinction, between the reactionary horror film and the "apocalyptic" horror film. The latter expresses, obviously, despair and negativity, yet its very negation can be claimed as progressive: the "apocalypse", even when presented in metaphysical terms (the end of the world), is generally reinterpretable in social/political ones (the end of the highly specific world of patriarchal capitalism). The majority of the most distinguished American horror films (especially in the Seventies) are concerned with this particular apocalypse; they are progressive in so far as their negativity is not recuperable into the dominant ideology, but constitutes (on the contrary) the recognition of that ideology's disintegration, its untenability, as all it has repressed explodes and blows it apart. *The Texas Chainsaw Massacre, Sisters, Demon* are all apocalyptic in this sense; so are Romero's two *Living Dead* movies. (Having said that, it must be added that important distinctions remain to be made between these works).

Some of the characteristics, then, that have contributed to the genre's reactionary wing:

1. The designation of the monster as *simply* evil. In so far as horror films are typical manifestations of our culture, the *dominant* designation of the monster must necessarily be "evil": what is repressed (in the individual, in the culture) must always return as a threat, perceived by the consciousness as ugly, terrible, obscene. Horror films, it might be said, are progressive precisely to the degree that they refuse to be satisfied with this simple designation—to the degree that, whether explicitly or implicitly, consciously or unconsciously, they modify, question, challenge, seek to invert it. All monsters are by definition destructive, but their destructiveness is capable of being variously explained, excused and justified. To identify what is repressed with "evil incarnate" (a metaphysical, rather than a social, definition) is automatically to suggest that there is nothing to be done but strive to *keep* it repressed. Films in which the "monster" is identified as the Devil clearly occupy a privileged place in this group; though even the Devil can be presented with varying degrees of (deliberate of inadvertent) sympathy and fascination—*The Omen* should not simply be bracketed with *The Sentinel* for consignment to merited oblivion.

2. The presence of Christianity (in so far as it is given weight or presented as a positive force) is in general a portent of reaction. (This is a comment less on Christianity itself than on what it signifies within the Hollywood cinema and the dominant ideology.) *The Exorcist* is an instructive instance—its validity is in direct proportion to its failure convincingly to impose its theology.

3. The presentation of the monster as totally non-human. The "progressiveness" of the horror film depends partly on the monster's capacity to arouse sympathy; one can feel little for a mass of viscous black slime. The political (McCarthyite) level of Fifties science fiction films—the myth of Communism as total dehumanization—accounts for the prevalence of this kind of monster in that period.

4. The confusion (in terms of what the film wishes to regard as "monstrous") of *repressed* sexuality with sexuality itself. The distinction is not always clear-cut; perhaps it never can be, in a culture whose attitudes to sexuality remain largely negative and where a fear of sex is implanted from infancy. One can, however, isolate a few extreme examples where the sense of horror is motivated by sexual disgust.

A very common generic pattern plays on the ambiguity of the monster as the "return of the repressed" and the monster as punishment for sexual promiscuity (or, in the more extreme puritanical cases, for *any* sexual expression whatever: two teenagers kiss; enter, immediately, the Blob). Both the *Jaws* films (their sources in both Fifties McCarthyite science fiction and all those beach party/ monster movies that disappeared with the B feature) are obvious recent examples, Spielberg's film being somewhat more complex, less blatant, than Szwarc's, though the difference is chiefly one of ideological sophistication.

I want to examine briefly here some examples of the "reactionary" horror film in the Seventies, of widely differing distinction but considerable interest in clarifying these tendencies.

David Cronenberg's *Shivers* (formerly *The Parasite Murders*) is, indeed, of very special interest here, as it is a film single-mindedly about sexual liberation, a prospect it views with unmitigated horror. The entire film is premised on and motivated by sexual disgust. The release of sexuality is linked inseparably with the spreading of venereal disease, the scientist responsible for the experiments having seen fit (for reasons never made clear) to include a VD component in his aphrodisiac parasite. The parasites themselves are modelled very obviously on phalluses, but with strong excremental overtones (their colour) and continual associations with blood; the point is underlined when one enters the Barbara Steele character through her vagina. If the film presents sexuality in general as the object of loathing, it has a very special animus reserved for female sexuality (a theme repeated, if scarcely developed, in Cronenberg's subsequent *Rabid*). The parasites are spread initially by a young girl (the original subject of the scientist's experiments), the film's Pandora whose released eroticism precipitates general cataclysm; throughout, sexually aroused preying women are presented with a particular intensity of horror and disgust. *Shivers* systematically chronicles the breaking of every sexual-social taboo—promiscuity, lesbianism, homosexuality, age difference, finally incest—but each step is presented as merely one more addition to the accumulation of horrors. At the same time, the film shows absolutely no feeling for traditional relationships (or for human beings, for that matter): with its unremitting ugliness and crudity, it is very rare in its achievement of *total* negation.

The Brood, again, is thematically central to the concept of the horror film proposed here (its subject being the transmission of neurosis through the family structure) and the precise antithesis of the genre's progressive potential. It carries over all the major structural components of its two predecessors (as an *auteur,* Cronenberg is nothing if not consistent): the figure of the Scientist (here psychotherapist) who, attempting to promote social progress, precipitates disaster; the expression of unqualified horror at the idea of releasing what has been repressed; the projection of horror and evil onto women and their sexuality, the ultimate dread being of women usurping the active, aggressive role that patriarchal ideology assigns to the male. The film is remarkable for its literal enactment, at its climax, of the Freudian perception that, under patriarchy, the child becomes the woman's penis-substitute—Samantha Eggar's latest offspring representing, unmistakeably, a monstrous phallus. The film is laboriously explicit about its meaning: the terrible children are the physical embodiments of the woman's rage. But that rage is never seen as the logical product of woman's situation within patriarchal culture; it is blamed entirely on the woman's mother (the father being culpable only in his weakness and ineffectuality). The film is useful for offering an extremely instructive comparison with *Sisters* on the one hand and *It's Alive* on the other.

In turning from Cronenberg's films to *Halloween* I do not want to suggest that I am bracketing them together. John Carpenter's films reveal in many ways an engaging artistic personality: they communicate, at the very least, a delight in skill and craftsmanship, a pleasure in play with the medium, that is one of the essential expressions of true creativity. Yet the film-buff innocence that accounts for much of the charm of *Dark Star* can go on to combine (in *Assault on Precinct 13*) *Rio Bravo* and *Night of the Living Dead* without any apparent awareness of the ideological consequences of converting Hawks's fascists (or Romero's ghouls, for that matter) into an army of revolutionaries. The film buff is very much to the fore again in *Halloween,* covering the film's confusions, its lack of real *thinking,* with a formal/stylistic inventiveness that is initially irresistible. If nothing in the film is new, everything testifies to Carpenter's powers of assimilation (as opposed to mere imitation): as a resourceful amalgam of *Psycho, The Texas Chainsaw Massacre, The Exorcist* and *Black Christmas, Halloween* is cunning in the extreme.

The confusions, however, are present at its very foundation, in the conception of the monster. The opening is quite stunning both in its virtuosity and its resonances. The long killer's-point-of-view tracking-shot with which the film begins establishes the basis for the first murder as sexual repression: the girl is killed because she arouses in the voyeur-murderer feelings he has simultaneously to deny and enact in the form of violent assault. The second shot reveals the murderer as the victim's bewildered six-year-old brother. Crammed into those first two shots (in which *Psycho* unites with the Halloween sequence of *Meet Me in St. Louis*) are the implications for the definitive family horror film: the child-monster, product of the nuclear family and the small-town environment; the sexual repression of children; the incest taboo that denies sexual feeling precisely where the proximities of family life most encourage it. Not only are those implications not realized in the succeeding film, their trace is obscured and all but obliterated. The film identifies the killer with "the Bogeyman", as the embodiment of an eternal and unchanging evil which, by definition, can't be understood; and with the Devil ("those eyes . . . the Devil's eyes"), by none other than his own psychoanalyst (Donald Pleasence)—surely the most extreme instance of Hollywood's perversion of psychoanalysis into an instrument of repression.

The film proceeds to lay itself wide open to the reading Jonathan Rosenbaum offered in *Take One:* the killer's victims are all sexually promiscuous, the one survivor a virgin; the monster becomes (in the tradition of all those beach-party/monster movies of the late Fifties–early Sixties) simply the instrument of Puritan vengeance and repression rather than the embodiment of what Puritanism repressed.

Halloween is more interesting than that—if only because more confused. The basic premise of the action is that Laurie is the killer's real quarry throughout (the other girls merely distractions *en route*), because she is for him the reincarnation of the sister he murdered as a child (he first sees her in relation to a little boy who resembles him as he was then, and becomes fixated on her from that moment). This compulsion to reenact the childhood crime keeps Michael tied at least to the *possibility* of psychoanalytical explanation, thereby suggesting that Donald Pleasence may be wrong. If we accept that, then one tantalizing unresolved detail becomes crucial: the question of how Michael learned to drive a car. There are only two possible explanations: either he *is* the Devil, possessed of supernatural powers; or he has *not* spent the last nine years (as Pleasence would have us believe) sitting staring blackly at a wall meditating further horrors. (It is to Carpenter's credit that the issue is raised in the dialogue, not glossed over as an unfortunate plot necessity we aren't supposed to notice; but he appears to use it merely as another tease, a bit of meaningless mystification.) The possibility this opens up is that of reading the whole film against the Pleasence character: Michael's "evil" is what his analyst has been projecting onto him for the past nine years. Unfortunately, this remains merely a possibility in the material that Carpenter chose not to take up: it does not constitute a legitimate (let alone a coherent) reading of the actual film. Carpenter's interviews suggest that he strongly resists examining the connotative level of his own work; it remains to be seen how long this very talented filmmaker can preserve this false innocence.

At first glance, *Alien* seems little more than *Halloween* in outer space: more expensive, less personal, but made with similar professional skill and flair for manipulating its audiences. Yet it has several distinctive features that give it a limited interest in its own right: it clearly wants to be taken, on a fairly simple level, as a "progressive" movie, notably in its depiction of women. What it offers on this level amounts in fact to no more than a "pop" feminism that reduces the whole involved question of sexual difference and thousands of years of patriarchal oppression to the bright suggestion that a woman can do anything a man can do (almost). This masks (not very effectively) its fundamentally reactionary nature.

Besides its resemblance to *Halloween* in general narrative pattern and suspense strategies (Where is the monster hiding?—who will be killed next?—when?—how? etc.), *Alien* has more precise parallels with *The Thing*. There is the enclosed space, cut off from outside help; the definition of the monster as both non- and super-human; the fact that it feeds on human beings; its apparent indestructibility. Most clearly of all, the relationship of Ash, the robot science officer, to the alien is very close to that of Professor Carrington to the Thing; in both films, science regards the alien as a superior form of life to which human life must therefore be subordinate; in both films, science is initially responsible for bringing the monster into the community and thereby endangering the latter's existence.

What strikingly distinguishes *Alien* from both *Halloween* and *The Thing* (and virtually every other horror movie) is the apparently total absence of sexuality. Although there are two women among the space-ship's crew of seven, there is no "love interest", not even any sexual banter—in fact, with the characters restricted exclusively to the use of surnames, no recognition anywhere of sexual difference (unless we see Parker's ironic resentment of Ripley's domineeringness as motivated partly by the fact that she is a woman; but he reacts like that to all displays of authority in the film, and his actual phrase for her is "son-of-a-bitch"). Only at the end of the film, after all the men have been killed, is female sexuality allowed to become a presence (as Ripley undresses, not knowing that the alien is still alive and in the compartment). The film constructs a new "normality" in which sexual differentiation ceases to have effective existence—on condition that sexuality be obliterated altogether.

The term "son-of-a-bitch" is applied (by Ripley herself) to one other character in the film: the alien. The cinematic confrontation of its two "sons of bitches" is the film's logical culmination. Its resolution of ideological contradictions is clear in the presentation of Ripley herself: she is a "safe threat", set against the real threat of the alien. On the one hand, she is the film's myth of the "emancipated woman": "masculine", aggressive, self-assertive, she takes over the ship after the deaths of Kane and Dallas, rebelling against and dethroning both "Mother" (the computer) and father (Ash, the robot). On the other hand, the film is careful to supply her with "feminine", quasi-maternal characteristics (her care for Jones, the cat) and gives her, *vis-à-vis* the alien, the most reactionary position of the entire crew (it is she who is opposed to letting it on board, even to save Kane's life). She is, of course, in the film's terms, quite right; but that merely confirms the ideologically reactionary nature of the film in its attitude to the Other.

If male and female are superficially and trendily united in Ripley, they are completely fused in the alien (whose most striking characteristic is its ability to transform itself). The sexuality so rigorously repressed in the film returns grotesquely and terrifyingly in its monster (the more extreme the repression, the more excessive the monster). At first associated with femaleness (it begins as an egg in a vast womb), it attaches itself to the most "feminine" of the crew's males (John Hurt, most famous for his portrayal of Quentin Crisp) and enters him through the mouth as a preliminary to being "born" out of his stomach. The alien's phallic identity is strongly marked (the long reptilian neck); but so is its large, expandable mouth, armed with tiers of sharp metallic teeth. As a composite image of archetypal sexual dreads it could scarcely be bettered: the monstrous phallus combined with *vagina dentata*. Throughout the film, the alien and the cat are repeatedly paralleled or juxtaposed, an association that may remind us of the panther/domestic cat opposition in *Cat People* (the cats even have the same surname, the John Paul Jones of Tourneur's movie reduced here to a mere "Jones" or "Jonesey"). The film creates its image of the emancipated woman only to subject her to massive terrorization (the use of flashing lights throughout *Alien'*s climactic scenes strikingly recalls the finale of *Looking for Mr. Goodbar*) and enlist her in the battle for patriarchal repression. Having destroyed the alien, Ripley can become completely "feminine" —soft and passive, her domesticated pussy safely asleep.

It is not surprising, though disturbing and sad, that at present it is the reactionary horror film that dominates the genre. This is entirely in keeping with the overall movement of Hollywood in the past five years. Vietnam, Nixon and Watergate produced a crisis in ideological confidence which the Carter administration has temporarily resolved; *Rocky, Star Wars, Heaven Can Wait* (all overwhelming popular successes) are but the echoes of a national sigh of relief. *Sisters, Demon, Night of the Living Dead, The Texas Chainsaw Massacre* in their various ways reflect ideological disintegration and lay bare the possibility of social revolution; *Halloween* and *Alien,* while deliberately evoking maximum terror and panic, variously seal it over again.

This article owes a considerable debt to the work of Tony Williams. Tony has been writing an M. A. thesis on the horror film under my supervision, and in the last two years we have exchanged so many ideas that it would no longer be possible to sort out whose was which.

ENTERTAINMENT AND UTOPIA

RICHARD DYER

Attempts to define genres seem less satisfactory than analyses that examine the meanings conveyed by a particular genre, such as the musical. The success of this approach, as several of the articles assembled here demonstrate, is quite extraordinary: In clarity, cogency, and explanatory power, it compares favorably with other critical approaches. What it lacks in theoretical bite it makes up for in accessibility and use value.

Richard Dyer's article is a case in point. Dyer provides an extremely valuable perspective that enables us to link what is often considered pure entertainment, the Hollywood musical, with the very real contradictions of everyday life from which musicals help us to escape. He suggests that such films offer a utopian sensibility through style, gesture, song, and dance proposed as solutions to real needs and lacks like scarcity or the lack of community. Furthermore, these solutions are available within the terms of the socioeconomic order that creates the perception of these needs and lacks. In this way, musicals, like myth, attempt to resolve contradictions. Since the contradictions are real, they do not always succeed. Dyer's discussion of three particular films indicates some of the ways in which dissonance marks their surface and underlines the impossibility of the task, even as the basic momentum of the narrative carries us toward resolution and a happy ending.

Dyer's article is noteworthy also for its extended attempt to place the Hollywood musical by considering the general concept of entertainment in some detail. His distinction between a treatise on utopia and a work that conveys a utopian sensibility the way music conveys an emotive sensibility makes particularly good sense. Movies do not have to become didactic documentaries before they can join philosophical, theoretical, or sociological issues. That they do so more in the manner of myth than of science does not, as Dyer demonstrates, remove them from the realm of philosophic or utopian discourse: It does, however, require us to use different critical procedures if we are to analyze movies effectively.

•

This article is about musicals as entertainment. I don't necessarily want to disagree with those who would claim that musicals are also 'something else' (e.g., 'Art') or argue that entertainment itself is only a product of 'something more important' (e.g., political/economic manipulation, psychological forces), but I want to put the emphasis here on entertainment as entertainment. Musicals were predominantly conceived of, by producers and audiences alike, as 'pure entertainment'—the *idea* of entertainment was a prime determinant on them. Yet because entertainment is a commonsense, 'obvious' idea, what is really meant and implied by this never gets discussed.

Musicals are one of a whole string of forms—music hall, variety, TV spectaculars, pantomime, cabaret, etc.—that are usually summed up by the term 'show biz.' The idea of entertainment I want to examine here is most centrally embodied by these forms, although I believe that it can also be seen at work, *mutatis mutandis,* in other forms and I suggest below, informally, how this might be so. However, it is probably true to say that 'show biz' is the most thoroughly entertainment-oriented of all types of performance, and that notions of myth, art, instruction, dream and ritual may be equally important, even at the conscious level with regard to, say, Westerns, the news, soap opera, or rock music.

It is important, I think, to stress the cultural and historical specificity of entertainment. The kinds of performance produced by professional entertainment are different in audience, performers and above all intention from the kinds of performance produced in tribal, feudal or socialist societies. It is not possible here to provide the detailed historical and anthropological argument to back this up, but I hope the differences will suggest themselves when I say that entertainment is a type of performance produced for profit, performed before a generalised audience (the 'public') by a trained, paid group who do nothing else but produce performances which have the sole (conscious) aim of providing pleasure.

Because entertainment is produced by professional entertainers, it is also largely defined by them. That is to say, although entertainment is part of the coinage of everyday thought, nonetheless how it is defined, what it is assumed to be, is basically decided by those people responsible (paid) for providing it in concrete form. Professional entertainment is the dominant agency for defining what entertainment is. This does not mean, however, that it *simply* reproduces and expresses patriarchal capitalism. There is the usual struggle between capital (the backers) and labour (the performers) over the control of the product, and professional entertainment is unusual in that: (1) it is in the business of producing forms, not things, and (2) the work force (the performers themselves) is in a better position to determine the form of its product than are, say, secretaries or car workers. The fact that professional entertainment has been by and large conservative in this century should not blind us to the implicit struggle within it, and looking beyond class to divisions of sex and race, we should note the important role of structurally subordinate groups in society—women, blacks, gays—in the development and definition of entertainment. In other words, show business's relationship to the demands of patriarchal capitalism is a complex one. Just as it does not simply 'give the people what they want' (since it actually defines those wants), so, as a relatively autonomous mode of cultural production, it does not simply reproduce unproblematically patriarchal capitalist ideology. Indeed, it is precisely on seeming to achieve both these often opposed functions simultaneously that its survival largely depends.

Two of the taken-for-granted descriptions of entertainment, as 'escape' and as 'wish-fulfilment,' point to its central thrust, namely, utopianism. Entertainment offers the image of 'something better' to escape into, or something we want deeply that our day-to-day lives don't provide. Alternatives, hopes, wishes— these are the stuff of utopia, the sense that things could be better, that something other than what is can be imagined and maybe realised.

Entertainment does not, however, present models of utopian worlds, as in the classic utopias of Sir Thomas More, William Morris, *et al.* Rather the utopianism is contained in the feelings it embodies. It presents, head-on as it were, what utopia would feel like rather than how it would be organised. It thus works at the level of sensibility, by which I mean an effective code that is characteristic of, and largely specific to, a given mode of cultural production.

This code uses both representational and, importantly, non-representational signs. There is a tendency to concentrate on the former, and clearly it would be wrong to overlook them—stars are nicer than we are, characters more straightforward than people we know, situations more soluble than those we encounter.

All this we recognise through representational signs. But we also recognise qualities in non-representational signs—colour, texture, movement, rhythm, melody, camerawork—although we are much less used to talking about them. The nature of non-representational signs is not however so different from that of representational. Both are, in C. S. Peirce's terminology, largely iconic; but whereas the relationship between signifier and signified in a representational icon is one of resemblance between their appearance, their look, the relationship in the case of the non-representational icon is one of resemblance at the level of basic structuration.

This concept has been developed (among other places) in the work of Suzanne K. Langer, particularly in relation to music. We feel music (arguably more than any other performance medium), yet it has the least obvious reference to 'reality'—the intensity of our response to music can only be accounted for by the way music, abstract, formal though it is, still embodies feeling. Langer puts it thus in *Feeling and Form*:

The tonal structures we call 'music' bear a close logical similarity to the forms of human feeling—forms of growth and of attenuation, flowing and slowing, conflict and resolution, speed, arrest, terrific excitement, calm or subtle activation or dreamy lapses—not joy and sorrow perhaps, but the poignancy of both—the greatness and brevity and eternal passing of everything vitally felt. Such is the pattern, or logical form, of sentience; and the pattern of music is that same form worked out in pure measures, sound and silence. Music is a tonal analogue of emotive life.

Such formal analogy, or congruence of logical structures, is the prime requisite for the relation between a symbol and whatever it is to mean. The symbol and the object symbolized must have some common logical form.

Langer realises that recognition of a common logical form between a performance sign and what it signifies is not always easy or natural: 'The congruence of two given perceptible forms is not always evident upon simple inspection. The common *logical* form they both exhibit may become apparent only when you know the principle whereby to relate them.' This implies that responding to a performance is not spontaneous—you have to learn what emotion is embodied before you can respond to it. A problem with this as Langer develops it is the implication that the emotion itself is not coded, is simply 'human feeling'. I would be inclined, however, to see almost as much coding in the emotions as in the signs for them. Thus, just as writers such as E. H. Gombrich and Umberto Eco stress that different modes of representation (in history and culture) correspond to different modes of perception, so it is important to grasp that modes of experiential art and entertainment correspond to different culturally and historically determined sensibilities.

This becomes clear when one examines how entertainment forms come to have the emotional signification they do: that is, by acquiring their signification in relation to the complex of meanings in the social-cultural situation in which they are produced. Take the extremely complex history of tap dance—in black culture, tap dance has had an improvisatory, self-expressive function similar to that in jazz; in minstrelsy, it took on an aspect of jolly mindlessness, inane good hu-

	Energy: Capacity to act vigorously; human power, activity, potential.	Abundance: Conquest of scarcity; having enough to spare without sense of poverty of others; enjoyment of sensuous material reality.
Show Biz Forms	Dance—tap, Latin American, American Theatre Ballet; also 'oomph', 'pow', 'bezazz'—qualities of performance.	Spectacle; Ziegfeld, Busby Berkeley, MGM.
Sources of Show Biz Forms	Tap—black and white folk culture; American Theatre Ballet—modern dance plus folk dance plus classical ballet.	Court displays; high art influences on Ziegfeld, Cedric Gibbons (MGM) —and haute couture.
Gold Diggers of 1933	'Pettin' in the Park' (tap, roller skates; quick tempo at which events are strung together).	'Pettin' . . . ' (leisure park) 'We're in the Money' (showgirls dressed in coins) 'Shadow Waltz' (lavish sets; tactile, non-functional, wasteful clothing; violins as icon of high culture— expense).
Funny Face	'Think Pink' 'Clap Yo' Hands' (tap) 'Let's Kiss and Make Up' (tap and Astaire's longevity) Cellar dance.	'Think Pink' (use of materials and fabrics) 'Bonjour Paris' 'On How to Be Lovely' (creation of fashion image).
On the Town	'New York, New York' 'On the Town' 'Prehistoric Man' 'Come Up to My Place'.	'New York, New York' (cf. 'Bonjour Paris') 'Miss Turnstiles' (woman as commodity-fantasy)
Westerns	Chases, fights, bar-room brawls; pounding music (sixties onward).	Land—boundlessness and/or fertility.
TV News	Speed of series of sharp, short items; the 'latest' news; hand-held camera.	Technology of news-gathering—satellites, etc.; doings of rich; spectacles of pageantry and destruction.

Intensity	Transparency	Community
Intensity: Experiencing of emotion directly, fully, unambiguously, 'authentically,' without holding back.	Transparency: A quality of relationships—between represented characters (e.g., true love), between performer and audience ('sincerity').	Community: Togetherness, sense of belonging, network of phatic relationships (i.e., those in which communication is for its own sake rather than for its message).
'Incandescent' star performers (Garland, Bassey, Streisand); torch singing.	'Sincere' stars (Crosby, Gracie Fields); love and romance.	The singalong chorus numbers.
Star phenomenon in wider society; the blues.	Star phenomenon in wider society; 18th-century sentimental novel.	Pub entertainment *and* parlour balladry; choral traditions in folk and church.
'Forgotten Man' 'I've Got to Sing a Torch Song' (blues inflections)	'Shadow Waltz' (Keeler and Powell as couple in eye-to-eye contact).	Showgirls (wise-cracking interaction, mutual support—e.g., sharing clothes).
'How Long Has This Been Going On?'	'Funny Face' 'He Loves and She Loves' ''S Wonderful'	(?) Cellar dance.
'A Day in New York' ballet; climactic chase.	'You're Awful' (insult turned into declaration of love) 'Come up to My Place' (direct invitation)	'You Can Count on Me'
Confrontation on street; suspense.	Cowboy as 'man'— straight, straightforward, morally unambiguous, puts actions where his words are.	Townships; cowboy camaraderie.
Emphasis on violence, dramatic incident; selection of visuals with eye to climactic moments.	(?) 'Man of the people' manner of some newscasters, celebrities and politicians; (?) Simplification of events to allow easy comprehension.	The world rendered as global village; assumptions of consensus.

mour, in accord with minstrelsy's image of the Negro; in vaudeville, elements of mechanical skill, tap dance as a feat, were stressed as part of vaudeville's celebration of the machine and the brilliant performer. Clearly there are connections between these different significations, and there are residues of all of them in tap as used in films, television and contemporary theatre shows. This has little to do however with the intrinsic meanings of hard, short, percussive, syncopated sounds arranged in patterns and produced by the movement of feet, and everything to do with the significance such sounds acquire from their place within the network of signs in a given culture at a given point of time. Nevertheless, the signification is essentially apprehended through the coded non-representational form (although the representational elements usually present in a performance sign—a dancer is always 'a person dancing' —may help to anchor the necessarily more fluid signification of the non-representational elements; for example, a black man, a white man in blackface, a troupe, or a white woman tap-dancing may suggest different ways of reading the taps, because each relates to a slightly different moment in the evolution of the non-representational form, tap dance).

I have laboured this point at greater length than may seem warranted partly with polemic intent. Firstly, it seems to me that the reading of non-representational signs in the cinema is particularly undeveloped. On the one hand, the *mise-en-scène* approach (at least as classically developed in *Movie*) tends to treat the non-representational as a function of the representational, simply a way of bringing out, emphasising, aspects of plot, character, situation, without signification in their own right. On the the other hand, semiotics has been concerned with the codification of the representational. Secondly, I feel that film analysis remains notoriously non-historical, except in rather lumbering, simplistic ways. My adaptation of Langer seeks to emphasise not the connection between signs and historical events, personages or forces, but rather the history of signs themselves as they are produced in culture and history. Nowhere here has it been possible to reproduce the detail of any sign's history (and I admit to speculation in some instances), but most of the assertions are based on more thorough research, and even where they are not, they should be.

The categories of entertainment's utopian sensibility are sketched in the accompanying table together with examples of them. The three films used will be discussed below; the examples from Westerns and television news are just to suggest how the categories may have wider application; the sources referred to are the cultural, historical situation of the code's production.

The categories are, I hope, clear enough, but a little more needs to be said about 'intensity'. It is hard to find a word that quite gets what I mean. What I have in mind is the capacity of entertainment to present either complex or unpleasant feelings (e.g., involvement in personal or political events, jealousy, loss of love, defeat) in a way that makes them seem uncomplicated, direct and vivid, not 'qualified' or 'ambiguous' as day-to-day life makes them, and without those intimations of self-deception and pretence. (Both intensity and transparency can be related to wider themes in the culture, as 'authenticity' and 'sincerity' respectively; see Lionel Trilling's *Sincerity and Authenticity*.)

The obvious problem raised by this breakdown of the utopian sensibility is where these categories come from. One answer, at a very broad level, might be that they are a continuation of the utopian tradition in Western thought. George Kateb, in his survey of utopian thought, *Utopia and Its Enemies,* describes what he takes to be the dominant motifs in this tradition, and they do broadly overlap with those outlined above. Thus:

> ... when a man [sic] thinks of perfection ... he thinks of a world permanently without strife, poverty, constraint, stultifying labour, irrational authority, sensual deprivation ... peace, abundance, leisure, equality, consonance of men and their environment.

We may agree that notions in this broad conceptual area are common throughout Western thought, giving it, and its history, its characteristic dynamic, its sense of moving beyond what is to what ought to be or what we want to be. However, the very broadness, and looseness, of this common ground does not get us very far— we need to examine the specificity of entertainment's utopia.

One way of doing so is to see the categories of the sensibility as temporary answers to the inadequacies of the society which is being escaped from through entertainment. This is proposed by Hans Magnus Enzensberger in his article, 'Constituents of a Theory of the Media' (in *Sociology of Mass Communication,* edited by Dennis McQuail). Enzensberger takes issue with the traditional left-wing use of concepts of 'manipulation' and 'false needs' in relation to the mass media:

> The electronic media do not owe their irresistible power to any sleight-of-hand but to the elemental power of deep social needs which come though even in the present depraved form of these media. . . .
> Consumption as spectacle contains the promise that want will disappear. The deceptive, brutal and obscene features of this festival derive from the fact that there can be no question of a real fulfilment of its promise. But so long as scarcity holds sway, use-value remains a decisive category which can only be abolished by trickery. Yet trickery on such a scale is only conceivable if it is based on mass need. This need—it is a utopian one—is there. It is the desire for a new ecology, for a breaking-down of environmental barriers, for an aesthetic which is not limited to the sphere of the 'artistic'. These desires are not—or are not primarily—internalized rules of the games as played by the capitalist system. They have physiological roots and can no longer be suppressed. Consumption as spectacle is— in parody form—the anticipation of a utopian situation.

This does, I think, express well the complexity of the situation. However Enzensberger's appeal to 'elemental' and 'physiological' demands, although we do not need to be too frightened by them, is lacking in both historical and anthropological perspectives. I would rather suggest, a little over-schematically, that the categories of the utopian sensibility are related to specific inadequacies in society as follows:

Social Tension/Inadequacy/Absence	Utopian Solution
Scarcity (actual poverty in the society; poverty observable in the surrounding societies, e.g., Third World); unequal distribution of wealth	Abundance (elimination of poverty for self and others; equal distribution of wealth)
Exhaustion (work as a grind, alienated labour, pressures of urban life)	Energy (work and play synonymous), city dominated *(On the Town)* or pastoral return *(The Sound of Music)*
Dreariness (monotony, predictability, instrumentality of the daily round)	Intensity (excitement, drama, affectivity of living)
Manipulation (advertising, bourgeois democracy, sex roles)	Transparency (open, spontaneous, honest communications and relationships)
Fragmentation (job mobility, rehousing and development, high-rise flats, legislation against collective action)	Community (all together in one place, communal interests, collective activity)

The advantage of this analysis is that it does offer some explanation of why entertainment *works*. It is not just left-overs from history, it is not *just* what show business, or 'they', force on the rest of us, it is not simply the expression of eternal needs—it responds to real needs *created by society*. The weakness of the analysis (and this holds true for Enzensberger too) is in the give-away absences from the left-hand column—no mention of class, race or patriarchy. That is, while entertainment is responding to needs that are real, at the same time it is also defining and delimiting what constitutes the legitimate needs of people in this society.

I am not trying to recoup here the false needs argument—we are talking about real needs created by real inadequacies, but they are not the only needs and inadequacies of the society. Yet entertainment, by so orienting itself to them, effectively denies the legitimacy of other needs and inadequacies, and especially of class, patriarchal and sexual struggles. (Though once again we have to admit the complexity and contradictions of the situation—that, for instance, entertainment is not the only agency which defines legitimate needs, and that the actual role of women, gay men and blacks in the creation of show business leaves its mark in such central oppositional icons as, respectively, the strong woman type, e.g., Ethel Merman, Judy Garland, Elsie Tanner, camp humour and sensuous taste in dress and decor, and almost all aspects of dance and music. Class, it will be noted, is still nowhere.)

Class, race and sexual caste are denied validity as problems by the dominant (bourgeois, white, male) ideology of society. We should not expect show business to be markedly different. However, there is one further turn of the screw, and that is that, with the exception perhaps of community (the most directly working class in source), the ideals of entertainment imply wants that capitalism itself promises to meet. Thus abundance becomes consumerism, energy and intensity personal free-dom and individualism, and transparency freedom of speech. In other (Marcuse's) words, it is a partially 'one-dimensional' situation. The categories of the sensibility point to gaps or inadequacies in capitalism, but only those gaps or inadequacies that capitalism proposes itself to deal with. At our worse sense of it, entertainment pro-vides alternatives *to* capitalism which will be provided *by* capitalism.

However, this one-dimensionality is seldom so hermetic, because of the deeply contradictory nature of entertainment forms. In variety, the essential con-tradiction is between comedy and music turns; in musicals, it is between the narrative and the numbers. Both these contradictions can be rendered as one between the heavily representational and verisimilitudinous (pointing to the way the world is, drawing on the audience's concrete experience of the world) and the heavily non-representational and 'unreal' (pointing to how things could be bet-ter). In musicals, contradiction is also to be found at two other levels—within numbers, between the representational and the non-representational, and within the non-representational, and within the non-representational, owing to the dif-fering sources of production inscribed in the signs.

To be effective, the utopian sensibility has to take off from the real experiences of the audience. Yet to do this, to draw attention to the gap between what is and what could be, is, ideologically speaking, playing with fire. What musicals have to do, then (not through any conspiratorial intent, but because it is always easier to take the line of least resistance, i.e., to fit in with prevailing norms), is to work through these contradictions at all levels in such a way as to 'manage' them, to make them seem to disappear. They don't always succeed.

I have chosen three musicals which seem to me to illustrate the three broad tendencies of musicals—those that keep narrative and number clearly separated (most typically, the backstage musical); those that retain the division between narrative as problems and numbers as escape, but try to 'integrate' the numbers by a whole set of papering-over-the-cracks devices (e.g., the well-known 'cue for a song'); and musicals which try to dissolve the distinction between narrative and numbers, thus implying that the world of the narrative is also (already) utopian.

The clear separation of numbers and narrative in *Golddiggers of 1933* is broadly in line with a 'realist' aesthetic: the numbers occur in the film in the same way as they occur in life, that is, on stages and in cabarets. This 'realism' is of course reinforced by the social-realist orientation of the narrative, settings and characterisation, with their emphasis on the Depression, poverty, the quest for capital, 'gold-digging' (and prostitution). However, the numbers are not wholly contained by this realist aesthetic—the way in which they are opened out, in scale and in cinematic treatment (overhead shots, etc.), represents a quite marked shift from the real to the non-real, and from the largely representational to the largely nonrepresentational (sometimes to the point of almost complete abstraction). The thrust of the narrative is towards seeing the show as a 'solution' to the per-sonal, Depression-induced problems of the characters; yet the non-realist presentation of the numbers makes it very hard to take this solution seriously. It is 'just' escape, 'merely' utopian.

If the numbers embody (capitalist) palliatives to the problems of the narrative—chiefly, abundance (spectacle) in place of poverty, and (non-efficacious) energy (chorines in self-enclosed patterns) in place of dispiritedness—then the actual mode of presentation undercuts this by denying it the validity of 'realism'.

However, if one then looks at the contradiction between the representational and non-representational within the numbers, this becomes less clear-cut. Here much of the representational level reprises the lessons of the narrative—above all, that women's only capital is their bodies as objects. The abundant scale of the numbers is an abundance of piles of women; the sensuous materialism is the texture of femaleness; the energy of the dancing (when it occurs) is the energy of the choreographic imagination, to which the dancers are subservient. Thus, while the non-representational certainly suggests an alternative to the narrative, the representational merely reinforces the narrative (women as sexual coinage, women— and men—as expressions of the male producer).

Finally, if one then looks at the non-representational alone, contradictions once again become apparent—e.g., spectacle as materialism and metaphysics (that is, on the one hand, the sets, costumes, etc. are tactile, sensuous, physically exhilarating, but on the other hand, are associated with fairy-land, magic, the by-definition immaterial), dance as human creative energy and sub-human mindlessness.

In *Funny Face*, the central contradiction is between art and entertainment, and this is further worked through in the antagonism between the central couple, Audrey Hepburn (art) and Fred Astaire (entertainment). The numbers are escapes from the problems, and discomforts, of the contradiction—either by asserting the unanswerably more pleasurable qualities of entertainment (e.g., 'Clap Yo' Hands' following the dirge-like Juliette Greco–type song in the 'empathicalist', i.e., existentialist, *soirée*), or in the transparency of love in the Hepburn–Astaire numbers.

But it is not always that neat. In the empathicalist cellar club, Hepburn escapes Astaire in a number with some of the other beats in the club. This reverses the escape direction of the rest of the film (i.e., it is an escape from entertainment/ Astaire into art). Yet within the number, the contradiction repeats itself. Before Hepburn joins the group, they are dancing in a style deriving from Modern Dance, angular, oppositional shapes redolent in musical convention of neurosis and pretentiousness (*cf.* Danny Kaye's number, 'Choreography', in *White Christmas*). As the number proceeds, however, more show biz elements are introduced—use of syncopated clapping, forming in a vaudeville line-up, and American Theatre Ballet shapes. Here an 'art' form is taken over and infused with the values of entertainment. This is a contradiction between the representational (the dreary night club) and the non-representational (the oomph of music and movement) but also, within the non-representational, between different dance forms.

The contradiction between art and entertainment is thus repeated at each level.

In the love numbers, too, contradictions appear, partly by the continuation in them of troubling representational elements. In *Funny Face*, photographs of Hepburn as seen by Astaire, the fashion photographer, are projected on the wall as background to his wooing her and her giving in. Again, their final dance of reconciliation to ''S Wonderful' takes place on the grounds of a chateau, beneath the trees, with doves fluttering around them. Earlier, this setting was used as the finish for their fashion photography sequence. In other words, in both cases, she is reconciled to him only by capitulating to his definition of her. In itself, there is nothing contradictory in this—it is what Ginger Rogers always had to do. But here the mode of reconciliation is transparency and yet we can see the strings of the number being pulled. Thus the representational elements, which bespeak manipulation of romance, contradict the non-representational, which bespeaks its transparency.

The two tendencies just discussed are far more common than the third, which has to suggest that utopia is implicit in the world of the narrative as well as in the world of the numbers.

The commonest procedure for doing this is removal of the whole film in time and space—to turn-of-the-century America (*Meet Me in St. Louis, Hello Dolly!*), Europe (*The Merry Widow, Gigi, Song of Norway*), cockney London (*My Fair Lady, Oliver!, Scrooge*), black communities (*Hallelujah!, Cabin in the Sky, Porgy and Bess*), etc.—to places, that is, where it can be believed (by white urban Americans) that song and dance are 'in the air', built into the peasant/black culture and blood, or part of a more free-and-easy stage in American development. In these films, the introduction of any real narrative concerns is usually considerably delayed and comes chiefly as a temporary threat to utopia—thus reversing the other two patterns, where the narrative predominates and numbers function as temporary escapes from it. Not much happens, plot-wise, in *Meet Me in St. Louis* until we have had 'Meet Me in St. Louis', 'The Boy Next Door', 'The Trolley Song' and 'Skip to My Lou'—only then does father come along with his proposal to dismantle this utopia by his job mobility.

Most of the contradictions developed in these films are over-ridingly bought off by the nostalgia or primitivism which provides them with the point of departure. Far from pointing forwards, they point back, to a golden age—a reversal of utopianism that is only marginally offset by the narrative motive of recovery of utopia. What makes *On the Town* interesting is that its utopia is a well-known modern city. The film starts as an escape—from the confines of Navy life into the freedom of New York, and also from the weariness of work, embodied in the docker's refrain, 'I feel like I'm not out of bed yet', into the energy of leisure, as the sailors leap into the city for their day off. This energy runs through the whole film, *including the narrative*. In most musicals, the narrative represents things as they are, to be escaped from. But most of the narrative of *On the Town* is about the transformation of New York into utopia. The sailors release the *social* frustrations of the women—a tired taxi driver just coming off shift, a hard-up dancer reduced to belly-dancing to pay for ballet lessons, a woman with a sexual appetite that is deemed improper—not so much through love and sex as through energy. This sense of the sailors as a transforming energy is heightened by the sense of pressure on the narrative movement suggested by the device of a time-check flashed on the screen intermittently.

This gives a historical dimension to a musical, that is, it shows people making utopia rather than just showing them from time to time finding themselves in it. But the people are men—it is still men making history, not men and women together. (And the Lucy Schmeeler role is unforgivably male chauvinist.) In this context, the 'Prehistoric Man' number is particularly interesting. It centres on Ann Miller, and she leads the others in the take-over of the museum. For a moment, then, a woman 'makes history'. But the whole number is riddled with contradictions, which revolve round the very problem of having an image of a women acting historically. If we take the number and her part in it to pieces, we can see that it plays on an opposition between self-willed and mindless modes of being; and this play is between representational (R) and non-representational (NR) at all aesthetic levels.

Self-willed	*Mindless*
Miller as star (R)	Miller's image ("magnificent animal") (R)
Miller character—decision-maker in narrative (R)	Number set in anthropology museum—associations with primitivism (R)
Tap as self-expressive form (NR)	Tap as mindless repetitions (NR)
Improvisatory routine (R/NR)	

The idea of a historical utopianism in narrativity derives from the work of Ernest Bloch. According to Frederic Jameson in *Marxism and Form,* Bloch 'has essentially two different languages or terminological systems at his disposition to describe the formal nature of Utopian fulfilment: the movement of the world in time towards the future's ultimate moment, and the more spatial notion of that adequation of object to subject which must characterise that moment's content. . . . [these] correspond to dramatic and lyrical modes of the presentation of not-yet-being.'

Musicals (and variety) represent an extraordinary mix of these two modes— the historicity of narrative and the lyricism of numbers. They have not often taken advantage of it, but the point is that they could, and that this possibility is always latent in them. They are a form we still need to look at if films are, in Brecht's words on the theatre, to 'organise the enjoyment of changing reality'.

An earlier version of this article was used at a SEFT weekend school and at the BFI Summer School, where it greatly benefitted from comments and criticism offered.

BEYOND *VÉRITÉ:* EMILE DE ANTONIO AND THE NEW DOCUMENTARY OF THE SEVENTIES

THOMAS WAUGH

If it is fruitful to consider the documentary as a film genre with its own set of conventions (black-and-white photography, location sound, voice-over commentary) and typical forms (images that illustrate the assertions of a narrator, the interview, observation, the crisis structure of much cinéma vérité*), then it will also be fruitful to consider how this genre and its subgenres change over time. Tom Waugh's article is a brilliant feat of historical placement and critical assessment regarding the documentary film of the midseventies. Using Emile de Antonio's innovative work as his fulcrum, Waugh distinguishes the various documentary tendencies, which range from the raw, confrontational strategies of Newsreel to the tepid, placebo effects of network documentaries. He accurately pinpoints the crucial importance of sound—from the stentorian voice-over of some American documentary, to its alternatives in the personal or ironic commentary of French and Canadian direct cinema, to the complete rejection of commentary in American* cinéma vérité*. He also identifies the crucial parameters of one documentary and television staple, the interview, including the status of the interviewee as expert, authority, witness, or participant and as someone distinguished and readily recognized or typical and personally unknown. Finally, he contrasts the collagelike strategy of de Antonio's films and its effects on viewers with the more improvisational approach of* cinéma vérité *and the didactic approach of narrated documentaries to identify one central innovation of de Antonio's work: the invitation to viewers to take an active part in determining the meaning of interview statements, in comparing and assessing disparate claims by different individuals, and in noting and evaluating the effect of various juxtapositions of image and sound. De Antonio attempts to construct a cinema of intelligence, and Waugh's characterizations of it provide some of the essential background for my own examination of recent developments in "The Voice of Documentary," which follows.*

    Waugh's 1975 article touches on so many important points that it is hard to find fault with his comprehensiveness, though his criticism of cinéma vérité *may be somewhat heavy-handed. (For a more sympathetic perspective, see Colin Young's essay "Observation Cinema", listed in Further Readings.) The proliferation of films that echo de Antonio's basic strategies (*With Babies and Banners, The Wobblies, Atomic Cafe, Rosie the Riveter*) testifies to the accuracy of Waugh's assessment. Perhaps the form of documentary analysis that has developed most noticeably since his article first appeared is a concern with formal strategies —*

use of narrative structure, effects of the indexical quality of the photographic image, analysis of the rhetorical devices specific to visual communication — and their ideological effect. (See, for example, Annette Kuhn's "The Camera I—Observations on Documentary," in Screen *19, no. 2 [Summer 1978]: 71–83, or Dai Vaughn's article, "The Space between Shots," in Part 6.)*

•

The appearance of a whole series of impressive new documentaries over the last few years—*Painters Painting, I. F. Stone's Weekly, Attica, Antonia,* and *Hearts and Minds* are the best known—is a reminder that, with mid-decade suddenly upon us, the American documentary is not only showing remarkable signs of vitality but is also moving purposefully forward through the seventies in its own unique direction. And it is a direction which, for all its diversity, is markedly distinct from the cinéma vérité impulse which dominated the sixties. Despite the continuing voices of Wiseman, the Maysles and others still using the idiom of a decade ago, there is no doubt that the seventies have already added a new chapter to the history of the American documentary. *Gimme Shelter,* now five years old, and even *American Family,* almost three, already seem curiously dated in the shadow of this imposing new chapter.

A general overview of the new films is already long past due; even radical journals, let alone *The New York Times,* have shown a tendency toward a helter-skelter, ad hoc reception of each new film as it appears, rather than a more historical estimation of the new documents as parts of a totality. The Museum of Modern Art's recent retrospective of the films of Emile de Antonio, most recently the director of *Painters Painting* (1972) and the soon-to-be-released film on the Weather Underground, is an occasion to answer this need. De Antonio, long a dissenter from the cinéma vérité mainstream of the sixties—his first film, *Point of Order,* dates from 1963—is confirmed in his seven-film retrospective as the pioneer and the foremost practitioner of the new documentary sensibility which has at long last reached the fore. The increasing publicity which surrounds de Antonio's work, his elevation by *Rolling Stone* to the status of radical saint, reinforces the need for a comprehensive evaluation of this filmmaker's career in the cultural, political, and theoretical context which formed it.

The original impetus for the cinéma vérité, as is well known, had been a technological revolution, an upheaval as radical in its own way as the introduction of the talkies had been thirty years earlier. Upon the first introduction of the hand-held cameras and portable recorders in the late fifties, there was a sudden burst on both sides of the Atlantic of nonfiction films celebrating the new accessibility of "truth"—truth in the surface textures of audiovisual reality, in the immediacy of present time, and in the nuance of spontaneous behavior. Close on the heels of their French and Canadian contemporaries, Richard Leacock and others, grouped around Drew Associates, rushed into the streets with their "caméra-stylos" and discovered, as if for the first time, the vitality of "unmediated" existence. They talked of honesty, intimacy, and above all objectivity, as if these old brickbats of aesthetics had been invented along with the Nagra.

This claim to a new privileged grasp of reality, which supplanted the old "subjective" documentary modes of discourse, now appears in retrospect to have been somewhat naive. Leacock and the others were of course right to hate the old newsreel voice-overs which had hammered away at American audiences for generations, each inflection delivering its prepackaged interpretation of the "facts." (Later de Antonio was to derive a brilliant ironic effect from newsreel clips of Nixon's red-baiting days in *Milhouse,* his analysis of the Nixon phenomenon.) Yet the American voice-over with its abuses had not been the only alternative for the classical documentarist. The French had developed a distinguished tradition of the narrated documentary, in which sober and unobtrusive Gallic voice-overs were personal and suggestive rather than pontifical. Alain Resnais, and later Chris Marker, were the most celebrated arbiters of this genre of documentary. Accordingly, the French cinéma vérité movement (or the cinéma-direct as the Gallic manifestation of it is properly called) led by Jean Rouch used the spoken word as an essential material and structural principle. In fact, the cinéma-direct's most radical achievement was as a cinema of sounds. In contrast, the American filmmakers reacted to their heritage of the authoritarian voice-over with an affirmation of the supposed objectivity of the unmediated image, creating a predominantly visual documentary form. Their aesthetic of the image, spontaneous, random, and true, was in effect a gospel of subjectivity, and too often, as it turned out, of inarticulacy as well. The movement's most serious liability was not this subjectivity per se, but its persistent pretense of impartiality.

Most of the films of the era bore highly charged emotional statements beneath their posture of objectivity—uncritical adulation in *Stravinsky,* euphoria in *Woodstock,* condescension in *Happy Mothers' Day,* contempt in *Sixteen in Webster Groves,* contempt in *Titicut Follies. . . .* In fact, contempt was probably the predominant tone of the entire cinéma vérité movement (probably since contempt is the stance which comes most easily to Eastern liberalism when it interacts with middle America). And contempt is the most visible residue of the cinéma vérité in a film such as *Hearts and Minds* in its weakest moments.

If the artifacts of the cinéma vérité now seem in retrospect to have captured so much of the spirit of their age, it is their embrace of inarticulateness, spontaneity, and entrenched emotionalism—not their aspiration to objectivity—which above all seemed linked to the decade of campus disturbances, ghetto riots, assassinations, and a counterculture based on uncritical iconoclasm. Cinéma vérité bore the imprint of all the ambiguous romanticism of the Greening of America, its adventurism as well as its fervor.

The challenge to base the new consciousness in concrete change—and the Vietnam war—gave the counterculture its fatal test and provided the cinéma vérité with a challenge which proved equally fatal. It was a challenge as insurmountable as the Depression had been for twenties avant-gardism two generations earlier. Cinéma vérité per se had nothing to contribute to the real job that faced the counterculture; it merely reflected and reinforced a mood which in itself was not enough. As the war escalated and escalated, the cinéma vérité people were preoccupied with rock concerts and easy targets like police-chief conventions and boot-camps, some moving gracelessly into the commercial arena. To be sure, they often provided undeniably profound and touching works of art, but films which failed to meet the increasing need for explicit socio-political analysis to support the momentum of the alternative politics. This failure of Leacock, Wiseman, et al. was a particularly bitter one, because of their widespread reputation as social critics, and because of the broad-based, potentially activist, liberal audience they addressed. Documentary has a special mystique in the English-speaking world, an aura of social responsibility not shared by the fiction film, which is perhaps its legacy from Grierson. The filmmakers were far more involved in the mystique than in the social issues they dealt with.

Nevertheless, Leacock and his contemporaries had developed an expressive and flexible language which was available for radical social criticism even if they themselves declined to use it in that direction. And three distinct currents of dissident filmmaking did emerge in the Vietnam era, all more or less adapting this language to their own particular goals. The current with the most immediate and diffuse (and no doubt the least radical) impact was based on a series of controversial television documentaries which appeared sporadically during those years, both on PBS and the commercial networks. Here, as might be expected, analytic rigor and conscience were the necessary sacrifice to the medium's huge audience potential. Nevertheless, a number of creditable documentary examinations of domestic social problems appeared from time to time. These effectively continued the intermittent but impressive tradition of conscientious broadcasting initiated by Edward Murrow in his early fifties anti-McCarthy broadcasts. Morton Silverstein's 1967 expose of conditions for southern black migrants on Long Island farms, *What Harvest for the Reaper?*, was widely praised as a sequel to Murrow's classic denunciation of the same social evil in his 1960 *Harvest of Shame*. *What Harvest for the Reaper?* relied almost exclusively on cinéma vérité techniques, although it was structured by voice-over narration (like most television documentaries). A later film by Silverstein, *Banks and the Poor* (1970), also shown on PBS, is perhaps the most praiseworthy of this category of film during the Nixon era. It is a searing and moving indictment of the victimization of the urban poor by neighborhood banks and lending institutions. Its highlights include a hidden-camera scene in a ghetto loan office in which an unsuspecting loan shark does his pitch for a prospective client, and, most memorably, an interview with a tearful black woman whose house has just been repossessed through a liability of only a few dollars. The canned rebuttals and denials by bank officials, including David Rockefeller, offer sharp contrast with the authenticity of the vérité language as Silverstein uses it: a compelling Brechtian collage effect, the clash of document and actuality, is achieved which is, as we shall see, one of Emile de Antonio's trademarks. A 1968 CBS documentary, *Hunger in America,* by Martin Carr and Peter Davis, was less successful, clumsy with its interviewing, and more interested in snags in welfare distribution than in the roots of the problem under scrutiny.

Only a few critical assessments of the ongoing war made it to television, understandably. Only rarely did the networks' coverage of the war yield any insight as powerful as Silverstein's domestic analysis had been. The first breakthrough here was a controversial PBS broadcast of a long segment of Felix Greene's *Inside North Vietnam* (1968), a film CBS had originally planned to show before losing its nerve. This capsule tour of enemy territory also had a limited art house distribution despite federal harassment. More important was Peter Davis's critical look at the Department of Defense in 1971, only obliquely aimed at the war, *The Selling of the Pentagon*. This denunciation of the Pentagon's promotional activities was a masterful blend of the language of cinéma vérité (watching children play on display bombers, for example) and the traditional TV documentary structures (a voice-over commentary by Roger Mudd, official statements from the Pentagon denying all, etc.). Of course these few successes do not substantially alter the overwhelmingly dismal record of the network news departments during those years. But what else is new?

A second current of dissident documentary during these years was based on efforts by a number of Movement filmmakers, both individual and collective, to compensate for this media void. Few of these had any delusions about their potential for reaching a constituency anywhere as broad as a television audience, or even, for that matter, much broader than the already converted radical community. Impeccable in their directness and uncompromising in their anger, such filmmakers initiated a whole tradition of alternative radical documentary that is still going strong. This tradition's base was the network of radical communities scattered across the urban and campus centers of the country, its continuity often broken and its internal liaison often exceedingly fragile. This tradition tended to emphasize depth of impact rather than breadth, and for a while screening discussions were the pattern, until coordination problems proved too much.

In the early days, this movement's chief impetus came from the New York and San Francisco chapters of Newsreel, an organization whose pre-credits machine-gun logo is still the most recognizable symbol of this whole tradition. Newsreel's strategy of polarization and confrontation differed sharply from both the networks' stance of socially conscious journalism and de Antonio's emphasis on analysis. Such spokespeople as New York's Robert Kramer (before he turned to fiction) rejected analysis as a goal entirely, championing instead the notion of film as a weapon. The commitment towards analysis was an "illusion," as was the possibility of real dissent or of real understanding of the issues.[1] The early Newsreel film-weapons were often criticized by radicals for an "ultra-left disdain for quality (the larger the grain, the better the politics)."[2] In other words, the potential weaknesses of the cinéma vérité language used indiscriminately infected many of the films, and not only in terms of production values: thematic confusion, egotism, and ideological contradictions were rampant. Nevertheless, a number of competent, articulate films did come to be produced on both coasts and enjoyed a surprisingly large distribution on what was in the late sixties a burgeoning radical circuit. Such titles as *Garbage, Chicago, Boston Draft Resistance Group,* and *Meat Co-operative* stood out above the early glut of films during the first Nixon years. As the output of films slackened somewhat, they seemingly improved, and it is from this middle period that the movement's best films emerged: *People's War* (1969), another Vietnam-behind-the-lines film (an important documentary subgenre until quite recently, with its own special problems arising from varying degrees of Vietnamese official "co-authorship"); *Black Panther* and *The Woman's Film,* two of the San Francisco products, dealing with the radical black problematic and the organization of working-class women respectively, both relying heavily on cinéma vérité and interview techniques and representing the peak of Newsreel achievement both in terms of artistic impact and distribution range; *Richmond Oil Strike,* a 1970 chronicle of a California strike by white workers which has a special place in the Newsreel oeuvre for its stunning revelation of incipient revolutionary consciousness among white union members and their wives. With these latter two films, the Newsreel crews for once started to listen, and tapped what has become the alternative cinema's richest resource, the voices and consciousness of its working-class constituency. Such recent films as Julia Reichert's and Jim Klein's *Methadone: An American Way of Dealing* brilliantly demonstrate the flexibility and power of this resource.

Other Movement filmmakers, unaffiliated with Newsreel, were also notable. From Chicago, for example, came Howard Alk's and Mike Gray's *The Murder of Fred Hampton* and the former's *American Revolution Two,* both widely distributed and powerful documents heavily dependent on cinéma vérité language. The former in particular had a large audience and was highly praised despite its susceptibility to the rhetorical excesses of vérité. Much of its impact was due no doubt to the drama of the event it described (a frequent tendency of Newsreel films as well), in this case Hampton's assassination, which occurred halfway through the shooting of a proposed film on the Chicago Panthers. The result is a film on his death, half eulogistic, half journalistic; its most interesting feature is its de Antonio—style interplay of Chicago police Newspeak and its own vérité investigation of the evidence. Its ultimate effect, however, is undercut by the artists' overly sentimental approach to the subject (long indulgent closeups of bereaved Panther women), a frequent liability of white filmmakers when dealing with minority agitation or "other people's struggles," as one Movement veteran puts it.[3] In recent years this liability has been increasingly overcome by radical documentarists by either concentrating on struggles closer to home or by creating films about minority struggles which have genuine roots in the consciousness of their subjects.

Despite the continuing prolificacy of this alternative tradition, as evidenced by such strong recent films as *Winter Soldiers, Finally Got the News,* the methadone film, and the work of the Pacific Street Collective (*Frameup: The Imprisonment of Martin Sostre*), this current has always been plagued by serious distribution problems, both theoretical and actual. Most radical filmmakers of this orientation have always relied on existing Movement structures to exhibit and distribute their work, and the overall result has been neither efficient, systematic, nor continuous. Inevitably the old problematic of preaching to the converted has reasserted itself—the films by and large never reached a public beyond the circuit of the radical subculture, despite such attempts as Newsreel's experiments with street projections in ghetto neighborhoods, etc.; and the weakening of that circuit in the seventies was disastrous, though far from fatal, for alternative filmmaking. Nevertheless, the role of this current in stimulating and strengthening the Movement that has persisted over the years has been immeasurable and a worthy achievement in itself.

The third current of dissident documentary, what I have already referred to as the new documentary of the seventies, richly heterogeneous but epitomized by Emile de Antonio, avoids the pitfalls both of network compromise and the isolation of the radical circuit. Admittedly, its audience is not composed of workers, rightly a priority for radical filmmakers, or the minority communities that Newsreel tried to reach. Its constituency includes the radical subculture, but extends far beyond it to a wider base which often assures it a commercial viability (insofar as documentaries can ever be commercial) and a certain degree of independence as well. Speaking directly to the urban, liberal or intellectual middle class, it is able to retain much of its integrity as hard-nosed social inquiry. It is based on both the recognition of where the power really lies, and on the premise of the importance of the struggle on the theoretical front as well as on the barricades, in the realm of the liberal consciousness as well as in ghetto neighborhoods, and of the macrocosmic perspective as well as the microcosmic. Filmmakers with this inspiration, occasionally casual or vague about their target audience and usually middle-class intellectuals themselves, find a constituency of their peers and address themselves to the task of challenging the ideological foundation of that group. Most often such films rely on financing by wealthy liberals and on theatrical distribution in the urban and campus centers; some occasionally make it to the airwaves as well. Such filmmakers are hesitant to offer solutions—their contribution is often based on their ability to pose the correct questions, to penetrate and unsettle the liberal equilibrium. Contradictions are many—but ultimately radical discourse is extended to a broader base, and significantly enriched.

Emile de Antonio has set the pattern for the new documentary, and embodies its inspiration and its contradictions more than any other. As one encounters him presiding over his New York office-studio, one is struck by the incongruity of a battle taken up against the whole U.S. establishment by this congenial man with enormous energy, roving conversation, and a robust sense of outrage. A laureate of the Enemies List? As he looks out over Union Square he points to both the pinkness of the late afternoon sky and the spot where the huge Communist marches gathered during the thirties. He wryly recalls his participation in those marches, a leader of a contingent from Harvard (the beginning of decades of FBI surveillance of his career, as he discovered recently, thanks to the Freedom of Information Act). As he braces himself for his forthcoming lawsuit against the FBI and the CIA (invasion of privacy), an outcome of the much-publicized grand jury challenge to the new Weather Underground film, one senses the exhausting emotional investment of the man in his art and in his struggle to continue asking his own unique kind of questions. Yet for all his dedication to social change, and his continuously professed allegiance to Marxism, there seems a curious isolation on his part from the mainstream of both the Left and contemporary radical film culture. There is the suggestion that his now famous fascination with the Weather People stems partly from an affinity with them—an embattled obstinacy, a romantic bravado, a fierce self-dependence. As he lists the stages in his career—his years at prep school and Harvard, his service in the war, his shortlived teaching stint (English and philosophy at William and Mary), his aimless drift through the fifties engaging in short-term business operations and hovering on the periphery of the New York avant-garde (he points out Andy Warhol's headquarters across the street and recalls his support for Warhol at the beginning of the artist's career), his sudden, almost accidental emergence as a filmmaker—he constantly alludes to the irony that he should have made his first film when already "middle-aged," as he puts it, and that his political development should have most recently taken the course of support for a famous group of underground revolutionaries while already advancing through his fifties. The overall impression is one of deadly seriousness and moral fervor, and in this, his role in the perpetuation of past traditions of documentary conscience, his place in the continuum of causes, ideals, and outcries that is his legacy as a documentarist, is a clear one.

The new documentary of the seventies, then, finds its roots in this man's response to the political climate of the sixties. Like the filmmakers of the dissident television tradition and of the radical underground, de Antonio assimilated where necessary the strategies and aesthetics of the vérité mainstream which dominated the decade, but adapted them to the serious and modest form suitable to his moral, didactic purposes. This form, refusing the resources of both declamatory rhetoric and self-indulgent aestheticism, expanded the documentary's potential as a medium of genuine political interrogation. The pseudo-objective cinéma vérité of the sixties was ultimately bypassed by this cinema of open commitment, research, and analysis. The new American documentary recognized the camera's unavoidable subjectivity and harnessed it in the service of a conscious political orientation from the start. This seriousness, this modesty, and this commitment enabled this current to withstand the traps of commercial co-optation and political desublimation which *Woodstock* and its progeny so vividly epitomized.

Emile de Antonio, then, was hardly an eager young camera wizard like the cinéma vérité people when he made his first film, *Point of Order,* in 1963. It is significant that this first gesture of resistance to the formal and ideological orthodoxy of vérité was made by a middle-aged, ex-academic culture hobo who had never touched a camera; for the new documentary was not set off by a technological revolution as the cinéma vérité had been. Its roots were more in a modulation of sensibility. This shift from cinéma vérité to the new committed documentary echoed a similar transition forty years earlier, in which the first euphoric documentaries of the twenties were replaced by those strikingly subdued products of the thirties and forties. Despite the intervening introduction of sound technology, which of course had some thematic ramifications, it was not primarily technical refinement which distinguished the typical documentaries of the twenties—the avant-garde manifestos of Ivens, Ruttman, Cavalcanti, and Vertov, not to mention the Flahertian travelogues—from the restrained, earnest films of the next two decades—the sober products of the American New Deal and war effort, of the Grierson bodies in Britain and Canada, and of the Soviet First Five-Year Plan and after. Both transitions (1930 and 1970 being only schematic approximations of their dates) were characterized by a reassessment of the previous era's technical revolution, by a movement from "formlessness" to "form," from poesis to thesis, from the celebration of surfaces to the probing of meanings, from the ecstatic experimentation with new resources to their consolidation in the services of specific analysis, questions, and statements. Both the thirties and the seventies represent a period of technological stasis in the field of the documentary, a pause for the arsenal of the non-fiction filmmaker to be tested, expanded, and applied to new aesthetic and political problems, not remodeled.

Point of Order, de Antonio's first film, appeared in 1963, the same year as the release of Leacock's *Happy Mothers' Day*, well before the zenith of the cinéma vérité movement, and yet it deserves to be seen as an early reaction to that movement. In fact, side by side, *Point of Order* and *Happy Mothers' Day* offer a strikingly clear paradigm of the twofold direction open to documentarists in the decade or so to follow. Leacock's film, an often snide exploration of a South Dakota town's materialistic response to the local birth of quintuplets, represents the path almost unanimously taken during the sixties. De Antonio's film, rejected by the New York Film Festival because it was not a film, is an examination of the phenomenon of McCarthyism through a compilation of original video footage of the Army–McCarthy hearings of ten years earlier. It sketches the contours of a less crowded route.

The contrast between these two directions is fundamental: the Leacock film, pure poesis, a cinema of great intimacy yet of almost baroque stylization, at once a celebration of the present and an implied elegy for a mythological past; the de Antonio work, pure analysis, a cinema that is both public and visually austere, the documents of the past explored for their lessons for the present. *Happy Mothers' Day* expresses its eloquent despair in the lyrical-populist Flahertian tradition: it sees the ultimate betrayal of the American ideal in ordinary townspeople, but rejoices in the equanimity and grace of the babies' mother. De Antonio localizes the object of his despair at the very seat of power, in the Eisensteinian manner: he presents McCarthy, his cronies, and the ineffectual politicians he confronts (not to mention the clever lawyers on both sides) as the personifications of a corrupt and oppressive system, just as his Soviet predecessor saw the Tsarist officers, the ineffectual Kerensky, and the fat kulaks and priests as embodiments of reaction.

The divergence between these two directions is essentially one which is already well explored in this century's art forms: collage vs. improvisation. De Antonio's basic technique is "the use of a collage of people, voices, images, ideas to develop a story line or a didactic line, uninterrupted by external narration."[4] He compresses and analyzes an event, assembling and juxtaposing fragments of it. *Point of Order* represents this technique in its purest, most rudimentary form, since the act of assemblage and editing is the artist's only original contribution to the raw material. In contrast, Leacock extends and elaborates an event by intuitively circling about it, accumulating a wealth of random detail into a decoratively mythologized whole. The opposition suggested by these two approaches implies among other things the irreconcilability of mythological thought and analytic thought, of the Costa-Gavras and the Godards, of neo-mythologization and demythologization. For the radical filmmaker the implications are important. It is, of course, not surprising that it should have been the neo-mythologists who dominated the mainstream political cinema in the early and mid-sixties. It is a tragedy archetypally American that the Newspeak newsreel voice-over should have been replaced by a mythologization all the more insidious, the fetishization of the image by a sensibility of alienated, individualist Romanticism.

Television has naturally had a crucial influence on the work of both Leacock and de Antonio; and the opposition between the 1963 works of the two men demonstrates the distinctly different mode of this influence on each. Leacock was, as we have seen, one of the first to develop an integrated aesthetics from the new hardware of the late fifties, but the importance of television both in providing the economic stimulus for its development and the forum for the public assimilation of the new idiom it entailed cannot be over-emphasized. *Happy Mothers' Day* was in fact originally commissioned by ABC (and then drastically re-edited for the version that was finally broadcast); and the film is notable for its reliance on a filmic syntax made accessible by television, its assumption of its audience's televisual literacy. Although the Leacock version of the film is undeniably more piquant than the re-edited ABC one, it is nevertheless disturbingly guilty of the increasing tendency of television to "massage" its audience under the innocent guise of objectivity.

In contrast, though *Point of Order* is composed entirely of period television footage of the Army–McCarthy hearings, compressed in a ratio of 100 to one, the result is an incisive critique of the video medium itself, a documentary parallel of Elia Kazan's *A Face in The Crowd,* the 1957 Hollywood denunciation of the power of the tube. *Point of Order*'s impact as autocritique is stronger because of its documentary authenticity. The alienating effect of seeing video on the cinema screen, and the further effect of the ten-year lapse between shooting and compilation, give the film all the more analytic power. The object of analysis becomes not only the web of personality and issue involved in the historic Alice-in-Wonderland debate, but the medium itself and its power to lend dignity and legitimacy to scoundrels and demagogues and authority and inertia to the status quo. As de Antonio has often said, the two video cameras are the heroes of the film: visual rhetoric wields more weight than logic, and videogenic physiognomy and witty rejoinder have more force than conviction. Of course the televised Senate hearings were not the first manifestation of the video politics to come: with *Milhouse,* and the later separate release of the Nixon 1952 Checkers Speech segment of it, de Antonio was to trace its birth back even further. If the cinema has long had a clearly articulated tradition of autocritique, of metacinema, ranging from *Man with a Movie Camera* to *Le Gai Savoir, Point of Order* signified the coming of age of television with the now richly demonstrated possibility of the mode of metavideo.

At the same time, *Point of Order* was also an early revelation of the crucial potential of video as a tool of primary historical investigation. Period video footage now becomes an audiovisual historical record with the unassailable authority formerly held only by vintage newsreels (with the same inherent dangers, of course, given video's even greater need for editing—de Antonio himself once commented that he could have made McCarthy come out looking good). This authority is partly due to the naive, functional, purely denotative orientation of the original recording. Video's low density would seem also to minimize film's emphasis of random nuances, while it captures all of the rich fabric of audiovisual inflection and detail which written history omits. Ironically, the transfer of video from the television screen to the movie screen somehow serves to absolve it of whatever lack of credibility infects it in its original, functional context. It attains purity as a document.

In this light de Antonio appears the descendant of the first generation of Soviet cine-historians, Esther Shub and others, who had a comparable sense of the primary role of the film document as a raw material of historical research. Dziga Vertov's use of the cine-document was also highly skilled and all too rarely exercised, only in *Stride, Soviet!* and *Three Songs of Lenin* among his mature works. Vertov's use of newsreel footage in these films has a somewhat different orientation than Shub's or de Antonio's, more towards the modes of rhetoric and mythography than historiography proper. Nevertheless the basic maieutic rhythm arising from the conjunction of document and actuality in these films certainly anticipates de Antonio's essential strategy more than Shub's basically archival interest.

In any case, de Antonio's use of video documents, with their own freshness and impact, is his own unique contribution. Since video is a major component of the present cultural and ideological fabric of American society, it becomes, with *Point of Order,* an indispensable resource for radical documentarists of both socio-political and historiographical intent.

Thus, while the cinéma vérité movement and *Happy Mothers' Day* celebrated the present, *Point of Order* legitimized the past as an equally rich field of documentary exploration for Americans. History ceased to mean for the filmmaker either a visual illustration of conventional historiography, such as CBS's *Twentieth Century* and a host of other voice-overed, popularized historical films had been, or a pretext for heroic mythologization, as in the Spanish Civil War subgenre represented by *To Die in Madrid* (a worthy exercise in itself, as a prod to civilization's fading conscience, but hardly a tool of new historical investigation). Instead, the documentary became a genuine instrument of historiography, a medium for diachronic social analysis with its own validity and authority, relying on visual documents in the same way that the traditional writing of history relied on written documents. (Of course, an irony is to be savored in the use of a medium based technically on the ephemerality of the instant as an instrument for grasping the meaning of the past.) The discovery of this potential of film and video is no doubt parallel to the changing conception of the task of history, the new emphasis, for example, on the use of oral history and, oddly enough, of statistical analysis as well. As might be expected, Americans followed other groups as diverse as the Parisian Left Bank and the National Film Board in their discovery of the cinema as a medium of historical analysis, though it is to their credit that they discovered video as an indispensable resource in this pursuit and have used it most successfully since. And it is no doubt video's integral auditory component, incidentally, that makes it such a valuable resource—the new documentary's revolt against the tyranny of the image was implicit in de Antonio's turn to video as the material of his first film.

As it stands, *Point of Order* is still de Antonio's only film to have been televised nationally in the U.S., although there is now talk of broadcasting one or two of the others and virtually all of them have appeared on TV in most other Western countries. When it appeared, *Point of Order* was the most controversial and critically acclaimed documentary in years (it also provoked the most hate mail) and remains today one of the most commercially successful and widely distributed of his films. Financed, as was to be the pattern, with "liberal money," and produced by New Yorker Films' Daniel Talbot, it reached a theatrical audience unheard-of for postwar documentaries (thanks in no small way to a $100,000 distribution campaign financed by Walter Reade, another unheard-of feature of the film). It is no mean feat for a documentarist to reach such a constituency, to introduce the possibility of radical discourse to the deeply prejudiced and powerful, middle-class liberal audience, with its entrenched fear of Stalinist propaganda, as de Antonio can be said to have done with that first film. It is a goal on which de Antonio staked his subsequent career, and one which Newsreel has never even begun to entertain.

The simple factor which most ensures de Antonio's accessibility to the "unconverted" middle-brow or intellectual audience is his respect for the integrity of the document. He retains his audience's trust by refusing to superimpose an external explanation or commentary upon his evidence. The documents speak for themselves. His didacticism, in *Point of Order* as well as in his other films, is democratic in a real sense. The viewer must actively meet the challenge posed by a document rather than submit to an exegesis dictated in the authoritarian manner of Louis de Rochemont, Roman Karmen, or Walter Cronkite. As de Antonio himself explained:

I'm usually attacked for not jumping on McCarthy hard enough, or not explaining certain events with a voice-over narration. I've always thought that it's wrong to explain things to audiences. The material is there, and interpretations can be made. I mean, I could have stopped the film and inserted outside explanations, but I'm really not terribly interested in that. I disagree with that approach from every point of view aesthetically and even politically. I think it's a mistake to show everything. And I think this is what is most wrong with so-called didactic films, that they become so utterly didactic that they forget that a film is also a film.[5]

Nevertheless, in a later interview about his Vietnam film, he expands a notion of "democratic didacticism" which is crucial to his work, for all its anachronistic Griersonian ring:

I have been a teacher. My work is didactic. . . . I only want to think that this film on Vietnam is more complicated, has more levels of meaning than there are in a slogan or in a purely didactic message. I don't believe that such a message has any more sense than to shout in the street "Down with war!" If you do so, that doesn't mean anything. The goal of a truly didactic work is to go beyond that and to suggest the "why." I like to describe my own feelings as democratic with a small *d,* which means that if you don't want to teach things to people but to reveal things to them, you will permit them then to arrive at the same conclusion as yourself. That's a democratic didacticism, without having to say "firstly, secondly, thirdly." And that's why I insist on the word "reveal." A young American sees the film, and he doesn't hear de Antonio addressing him, but he can himself come to a conclusion about the war . . ."[6]

Grierson is thus not the only ghost conjured up by this fervent ideal—the echoes of Eisenstein as well, in particular his famous invocation of Marx in *Film Sense,* are too striking to pass over and too obvious to elaborate:

The spectator is compelled to proceed along that selfsame path that the author traveled in creating the image. The spectator not only sees the represented elements of the finished work, but also experiences the dynamic process of the emergence and assembly of the image just as it was experienced by the author. And this is, obviously, the highest possible degree of approximation to transmitting visually the author's perceptions and intention in all their fullness, to transmitting them with "that strength of physical palpability" with which they arose before the author in his creative work and his creative vision.

Relevant to this part of the discussion is Marx's definition of the course of genuine investigation: "Not only the results, but the road to it also is a part of truth. The investigation of truth must itself be true, true investigation is unfolded truth, the disjuncted members of which unite in the result." The strength of the method resides also in the circumstance that the spectator is drawn into a creative act in which his individuality is not subordinated to the author's individuality, but is opened up throughout the process of fusion with the author's intention . . ."[7]

Of course the question can arise whether de Antonio's appeal to a broad-based liberal audience is consistent with the Marxist principles he professes. It is a question not easily resolved. Is his divergence from the reformist ideology of the sixties more a theoretical one than an actual one, his analytic methodology merely a style based on a theoretically constructed model of an ideal spectator who doesn't actually exist? Does de Antonio's recent interest in the Weather People mean that his earlier faith in "democratic didacticism" has been revised? He claims not, yet the contradictions persist. They present themselves sharply indeed in de Antonio's next film after *Point of Order, That's Where the Action Is,* a fifty-minute BBC television assignment dealing with the 1965 New York mayoral race between John Lindsay, Abraham Beame, and William Buckley. The artist's first experience with a camera crew and his first encounter with an ongoing event, the result is his most journalistic film. It is also most remote from the acerbic tone of the "radical scavenging" for which he was to become famous, and the least inclined to escape from the confines of the bourgeois problematic within which it is posed. Compared to the other films, it has, predictably, the impersonal air of an assignment about it, but it is executed with skill and verve nonetheless.

The film interpolates a British perspective of an American election (a BBC voice-over introducing parties, candidates, and issues was probably unavoidable) with a running discussion of the urban problems which were the issues of the campaign. The vivid melange of vérité footage of campaign activity and interviews with both voters and candidates, lay and professional commentators, is flawlessly assembled. The most impressive aspect of the film is its continuation of the theme of media critique begun with *Point of Order.* De Antonio wittily undercuts the electoral system by including television spots by both major candidates, complete with unabashedly empty rhetoric and tasteless campaign songs (by

Ethel Merman in the Lindsay spot). There is also prolonged scrutiny of the candidates' platform demagoguery and a caustic critique of the Lindsay style by also-ran conservative Buckley. On the whole, *That's Where the Action Is* (it's the BBC's title, not his own) is a modest and promising second film; however, it fails to heighten the satirical bemusement in its view of electoral politics to any serious level of interrogation, and furthermore seems content with the classical sixties-liberal problematic of urban decay in its treatment of big-city problems (relying heavily on Daniel Moynihan for its commentary in this area). And ultimately the film's analysis of video politics is itself weakened by its own susceptibility to the charismatic attraction of candidate Lindsay. The photogenic, aristocratic liberal emerges relatively unscathed from the film, seeming to get the better share of the camera's attention (at one point he offers it a gigantic close-up hot dog). And in the long run he succeeds in charming the film's audience, despite the director's attempts to undercut his appeal, as much as he charmed most American liberals that year (as well as the majority of the voters).

However, if the film is unquestionably a minor work, it constitutes an important step in the artist's career. If *Point of Order* served as a manifesto of general aesthetic principle (democratic didacticism) and strategy (collage), expressed in their most basic form, *That's Where the Action Is* and de Antonio's subsequent film, *Rush to Judgment* (1966), point clearly to the complex form of cinema, the "document-dossier," which the four following "mature" works were to imitate and refine: *In the Year of the Pig* (1969), a discussion of American involvement in Vietnam; *America Is Hard to See* (1970), an analysis of the Eugene McCarthy presidential campaign of 1968; *Milhouse* (1971), a satirical portrait of Richard Nixon; and *Painters Painting* (1973), a historical survey of contemporary American (New York) painting.

In *Rush to Judgment,* de Antonio confirms the interview, that basic artifact of television culture (and the basic ingredient of the television film which he had just completed), as an integral element of his characteristic form of collage. The interview had been totally suppressed by Leacock and his colleagues but had always been a standard component of the European and Canadian cinéma-direct (not to mention the films of Godard). Despite the interview experiments in such early sound documentaries as Esther Shub's *Komsomol: Leaders of Electrification* (1932), Vertov's *Three Songs of Lenin* (1933) and Grierson's *Housing Problems* (1936), and occasional reliance on it in the theatrical newsreel medium, it was only with the coming of television that this technique had been perfected as a staple of audiovisual language. By the time de Antonio took it up, it had already been totally absorbed by his video-generation audience. Low-key and non-emphatic, the interview is essential to the functional orientation of his work. His art is an art of revelation, not astonishment, and "content," not style. His emphasis on "content" is the basis for his nostalgic admiration for the pre-television documentaries of the thirties (particularly those of Paul Strand) and his scorn for his cinéma vérité contemporaries:

Why did I make *Point of Order?* I wanted to make documentaries: the only documentaries I like had been made before World War II. Television and the Cold War had taken the content out of documentary . . .[8]

The audiovisual history of our time is the television out-take. Each hour, cameras, as impersonal as astronauts, grind away film and tape which the content-free networks will never transmit. Our television is content-free not because it is regulated but because it is commodity—not news or art or entertainment but a product . . .[9]

Dependence on the technical is also an aspect of no content. Cinéma vérité? Whose vérité? No one can fault the development of fast, light, mobile equipment. What is wrong is the space the best known practitioners of cinéma vérité occupy today: publicity films for rock groups.[10]

De Antonio relies on the interview, not only as a means of personal revelation (as with the cinéma-direct), but also, more importantly, as a medium of "content," in defiance of television's relegation of the interview to its most pedestrian, digestible, reliably content-free ingredient. The use of this traditionally innocuous device for historical analysis, personal reminiscence, or professional (or lay) opinion made such content fresh and accessible for an audience unaccustomed to finding such weighty matter therein. It becomes emphatic by virtue of its flatness. The long, static interview shots in *Rush to Judgment* and the later films force their content upon the spectator because of their visual austerity. De Antonio's film language is more sedate, more prosaic, as it were, and much cheaper—ultimately much more relevant to the double ideals of democracy and didacticism than the flamboyant, poetic language of the cinéma vérité. And this visual language is by no accident an affirmation of the vital role of speech, of dialogue, of logic in radical discourse.

The interview is also integral to de Antonio's historical perspective. The fundamental rhythm of his mature films is a systole-diastole between the document, a fragment from a past event, and the interview, a living segment of a present reflecting upon and analyzing that fragment. It is the basic Brechtian (and Sophoclean) structure of action in alternation with analysis. *Rush to Judgment,* de Antonio was proud to claim, was the first American film that "went into really big interviewing" and his retrospective defensiveness about its "boringness" is not at all warranted. Just as *That's Where the Action Is* had juxtaposed documents (visual and auditory) from an event, with commentary from observers of and participants in that event, *Rush to Judgment* assembled film and video material from the Dallas assassination and the investigation that followed it, with interviews with spectators of the events. The ultimate effect is a denunciation of the Warren Commission's (deliberate?) shortsightedness. De Antonio's collaboration with Mark Lane on the project, the author of the investigative book by the same title, is perhaps responsible for the only major flaw in this otherwise compelling film: there is an overall tendency to sensationalize rather than analyze the evidence that the film gradually accumulates in the defense of the scapegoat Oswald, and in addition, a rather explicit, almost homiletic tone due to the awkward appearances of Lane himself, who tends to belabor the points that have already been driven home by the documentary evidence and testimonies of witnesses.

Rush to Judgment's most interesting feature is its continuation of the previous film's excursion into the populist arena which is more normally considered the domain of Leacock, et al. Seen in the context of de Antonio's oeuvre, these two films and the later treatment of Eugene McCarthy's presidential campaign, *Amer-*

ica Is Hard to See, reveal a grass roots sensibility that is ultimately secondary within his vision of American society; these three films contain what might be called a digression from the more central preoccupation of the artist's career, that is, the American tragedy as seen in the roles of its chief protagonists, not its chorus (or its victims).

Rush to Judgment, filmed only on the brink of the age of fashionable dissent and far from the Eastern enclaves of radical chic, was also de Antonio's most dangerous film to produce until the Weather Underground film. For one thing, his customary rich liberal investors were nervous about such a touchy subject and the film had to be financed by British sympathizers, such as Tony Richardson and John Osborne. Realized with an amateur crew, terrorized while in production by local and federal police, and hampered by official hostility, the film provoked de Antonio's first real taste of the harassment that was to dog him for the rest of his career. Distribution was also a problem—theater owners were threatened with vandalism and the release date coincided with the outbreak of the Six Days War, which provided serious competition on the small screen. As a result, it was de Antonio's least widely distributed film. Recently, however, there has been renewed interest in it and there is even talk of it being broadcast on PBS.

Remarkable then for its very existence, *Rush to Judgment* is all the more impressive as an exploration of a popular response to bewildering political events:

What I wanted to show, at great length, was that one guy could take on the FBI—or two of us really, Mark Lane and I—and the Warren Report, and prove that they had lied, by filming people at great length describing events that had happened in Texas in November of 1963. I felt that the Warren Commission's investigations, or really lack of them, was outrageous, so I went down and filmed these witnesses. I like the idea of their slow Texas speech while telling a story—just ordinary working people, not Marxists or anything, just guys who worked for the railroad or whatever—and I didn't give a damn if people were bored by it or not. I liked it.[11]

De Antonio thus hits upon a basic principle of the French and Canadian cinéma-direct: not only can non-participant, non-expert subjects offer profound, illuminating discussions of the social forces which affect their lives, but their testimonies alone, by virtue of their very existence, can themselves in the specific socio-political context of their lives constitute the basis of a moving and provocative aesthetic/political experience. This insight was later the basis for Newsreel's most solid achievements, as we have already seen, in such films as *The Woman's Film* and *Richmond Oil Strike.* It is certainly telling to compare the dignity of the witnesses in *Rush to Judgment,* pictured in their unassuming living rooms (doilies in place) or in the open spaces of the assassination sight with the shallow, condescending portraits of ordinary Americans one encounters in the films of Leacock, Wiseman, or Barron. Unhappily, de Antonio seldom returns to build on this talent he shows in *Rush to Judgment* or to confirm the populist sensibility which is too often lacking in the consciousness of the New Left.

De Antonio's art is always highly evocative visually; he can extract as much visual power from a static close-up interview as exists in a Godard monologue or in a Pasolini close-up of a wrinkled extra. Nevertheless, the ultimate impact of his art is fundamentally aural. If the American vérité filmmakers banished the sound-track to a minor role (despite their delight in noise), the reverse is true of de Antonio. His films are essentially sound films or, more specifically, films of verbal language and dialogue. As with television journalism, the dominant logic of the de Antonio film is verbal and the image often functions simply as a contrapuntal accompaniment to the primary current of the film, its voices—voices arising out of the documents from the past, and voices from the present echoing, interpret-ing, mocking, judging, analyzing, exorcising them. The voices of the interview-ees regularly leave the image of the present and accompany the documents as they unfold, so that the past-present, document-actuality opposition becomes not only sequential but simultaneous. With *That's Where the Action Is* and *Rush to Judgment,* the voice-over, banished by the cinéma vérité as a vestige of a tyranni-cal past, is reclaimed and liberated. No longer the voice-over of *Twentieth Cen-tury* and *The March of Time,* it is the voice of a witness participating in a discourse extracting the meaning hidden by the image, bringing the reflection and the per-haps greater wisdom of the present to bear on the inscrutability of time past as it unrolls once again.

The word becomes the basic structural and organizational principle of the film:

> Words are very important in my film *(The Year of the Pig)* and in all of my work, and that's how I do the editing: I start with the transcription of the soundtrack and put all of these pages up on the walls of the big editing rooms where I work and begin to assemble the papers before the film: that's how the structure begins; then I take the film, and I go endlessly from the text to the film and from the film to the text, and I change them around, switching the sheets of paper with each other. I have a good visual memory. When you have so much filmed material, you think of a shot you want and the list of shots is no use because no list of shots can describe everything with precision (you know, the list of shots says: buffaloes, peasants, airplanes, medium shot of buffaloes and peasants). Even if it's well drawn up, it's not as exact as your own memory.[12]

It is no accident that this methodology is extremely similar to that followed by many of the cinéma-direct filmmakers. A related structural principle is implied by the ratios of document to actuality, both aural and visual, in this particular film: on the soundtrack, the interviews overwhelm the documentary sound in a ratio of eight to one, but the image track presents four times as much vintage document as it does de Antonio's own shots. Visual memory is restructured vocally, and only then is it useful to the present. Proust's voice extracted redemption from the unorganized mass of visual fragments in his memory; and the voice is no less the instrument for de Antonio's characters (and the other personae of the new docu-mentary, I. F. Stone, Antonia Brico, Tom Wicker, Dan Ellsberg, etc.) to confront the visual fragments from the past, and to shore these fragments against ruin. When the enemy has learned to hide its face behind a screen, only the faculty of speech exercised in naming it, denouncing it, can begin the confrontation with it.

In the Year of the Pig, de Antonio's Vietnam epic, separated by an interval of three years from the Dallas film, is the artist's only film to have reaped the dubi-ous honor of an Oscar nomination; fortunately it did not win (according to de Antonio because of a closed-shop town's hostility to a non-union film). And the monolith's infinite capacity to absorb even its most ardent opposition was temporarily forestalled (although this oversight can now be said to have been amply rectified by the Academy's later gestures toward Joseph Strick's *Interviews with My Lai Veterans* and now *Hearts and Minds,* in the true Hollywood tradition of hindsight, surrogate recognition). *In the Year of the Pig* was also one of de Antonio's three biggest commercial successes (along with *Point of Order* and *Painters Painting,* but none of his films has ever lost money), focusing as it did on the decade's most divisive national issue. Financed readily by various Peace Movement millionaires and such prominent liberals as Paul Newman, Leonard Bernstein, and Steve Allen, the film was one of the first documentaries about the Indochina struggle, and it still remains the best.

Yet, despite its place at the center of the anti-war movement in the late sixties, the film's mood seems in marked contrast to the predominant spirit of the movement as it now appears in retrospect. Instead of the passionate moralistic tone of the marches, de Antonio's rhetoric is cool, scholarly, and articulate. Its aim was to convince, not to inflame, to do the homework that the marchers had no time for. In contrast to the two famous French anti-war films of the period, *In the Year of the Pig* is notable for its shrewd, deliberate, cerebral tone: a far cry from *The Seventeenth Parallel,* Joris Ivens's epic tribute to the heroism of the North Vietnamese peasant defense, or the emotional, subjective *Far from Vietnam,* the collective statement of the Leftish fringes of the New Wave. In a cultural climate already charged with the divisive rhetoric of the war and distrustful of radical polemic, de Antonio's strategy was probably the right one. American liberals were ready for this cold chronological collage of documents arranged with the artist's customary matter-of-factness and unmediated by any external narration. The documents outlined with precision and clarity almost forty years of the history of the Vietnamese struggle; a counterpoint of long authoritative interviews with experts as diverse as a French scholar of Buddhist thought and American congressional leaders provided analysis and background at each stage of the chronology. The faces of the interlocuters repeatedly surface from the past, become familiar guides, and then vanish again as their voices continue on, disembodied, over the stream of visual artifacts. Motifs and refrains, both visual and aural, appear and disappear: early in the film a specially commissioned concerto of helicopter noises drones out of the silence in a deafening crescendo (when the projectionist resists the urge to turn down the volume, as occasionally happens), thereby introducing a major aural motif of the film and the war.

Much of the film's documentary footage came, predictably, from sympathetic sources—the NLF and North Vietnam. However, considerable amounts also originated with ABC, the BBC, and the French Army; and the film often achieves a dramatic emphasis because of this, with the editor's reversing the original intention of a clip through judicious cutting or juxtaposition. Again it is a question of the removal of newsreel and video material from its original context and exploiting the profound distanciation which results. Particularly the American television footage of the war now displays its startling contradictions when shown on a cinema screen, suddenly having lost the lulling effect that its continuous low-definition, saturation in American living rooms is said to have had. Media critique is thus once more de Antonio's stance:

There is nothing as bad that's happened concerning the war as the network's coverage of it, because it seems as if they're covering the war whereas in fact they're not. The networks have made the American people comfortable with the war—because it appears between commercials. There's never the question asked, "Why are we doing this? What is this war about?" It's never suggested by anything that occurs on television that we should even be interested in that type of question. Television is a way of avoiding coming to terms with the fact that we're in this war.[13]

In contrast to the previous film's populist flavor, a vivid record of ordinary people caught up in a political turmoil, *In the Year of the Pig* has little sense of public perspective of the war. The interviewer's encounters with the French scholar and Ho Chi Minh are no doubt highlights of the film; but, however indispensable the artist's attention to the experts and the protagonists to his analytical goals and his exposure of the folly and evil of the American leadership, there is a sense that this irrepressible Jeremiah might have profited from the cinéma vérité model of interest in ordinary people. The concluding credits of his film about American painting, *Painters Painting,* unroll over footage of expressionless crowds wandering around the Museum of Modern Art, and at this point one is suddenly struck by how much this film, as well as others of his oeuvre, would have been enriched by the reflection of the consciousness of such crowds. In *Year of the Pig,* de Antonio's short encounters with a deserter and with GI's on active duty are high points of the film, but this exploration of the human, everyday dimension of the war is tantalizingly brief. In *Painters Painting,* as in the art world in general, the absence of lay perspective is total.

With *Hearts and Minds,* Peter Davis makes some progress towards correcting this deficit, aiming for a populist perspective of the war which is not present in de Antonio. Davis's involvement with individual Americans who obediently waged the war is often sensitive and profound and almost compensates for occasional lapses into clumsiness and offense (the Saigon bordello cinéma vérité sequence) or facile crowd scenes which rival Leacock and Wiseman in their arrogance and undercut the sensitivity displayed elsewhere in the film. If de Antonio saw the war as a debacle of international imperialism and domestic intrigue, Davis sees it as a national tragedy, not primarily for the Vietnamese people (though he doesn't understate their suffering), but for the American people. Employing a characteristic de Antonio collage, though in a less rigorous, nonchronological manner, Davis confronts participants and witnesses both in the present and the past, from the Oklahoma ex-flier, who weeps as he remembers his bombing raids, to the infamous Colonel Patton, who, in a video tape from the late sixties, praises his men for being "good killers" (de Antonio used the same tape, but not in Davis's living color). A sense of national failure of spirit emerges from this application of the collage approach, despite the ideological confusion of the overall effect, the blurring of class lines in Davis's conception of the American people, and a tendency towards a muddled sentimentality. Like de Antonio, Davis also presents chief protagonists in the conflict—Ellsberg, Rostow, Westmoreland, etc., but what finally remains with the spectator is the impression of a community divided, defensive, penitent, and fearful. Davis's early television documentary, *The Selling of the Pentagon* (1971), is on the whole a much better film, ironically because network requirements apparently demanded more coherence (the topic was also much more compact and assailable—the public relations activities of the Defense Department). However, the topic was less amenable to the kind of populist sensibility which Davis later reveals in the best moments of *Hearts and Minds*. Morton Silverstein's TV films, as we have seen, represent the potential of television journalism to reflect the lives and viewpoints of ordinary people at its best.

Cinda Firestone's *Attica* is another recent documentary which builds upon de Antonio's formula in *Year of the Pig* (she is a former editor of his) and in addition shares in the populist sensibility which is the most important achievement of the radical underground current of films. She relies much more than her mentor on long interviews with her subjects, the participants and witnesses in the prison revolt. And unlike Davis, she does not lose sight of the political basis of the tragedy and resists the easy resources of sentimentality.

De Antonio's fifth film was *America Is Hard to See* (1970), a title taken from Robert Frost. It dealt with a single event from the recent past rather than an ongoing historical process of several decades like the Vietnam war. By restricting his focus to the McCarthy campaign for the presidency in 1968, de Antonio created a more concentrated, more specific kind of political analysis than the unwieldy subject of the war permitted. In addition, the McCarthy film was closer to its subject chronologically than any of the others, a time lapse of only two years separating document/event from recollection/analysis. This is a very short historical perspective indeed, but a dramatic one nevertheless: the abrupt changes in even the sartorial aspect of the campaigners as they emerge from the 1968 documents into the 1970 interviews, the pronounced oscillation between the 1968 campaign euphoria and the 1970 sober realism tinged with nostalgia, the hagiographical atmosphere with which only two years' hindsight surrounds the documentary appearances of Robert Kennedy and the references to Martin Luther King—all contribute to a sense of the uncontrollable acceleration of the historical process, two years having seen such a radical transformation of cast and ambience in the American political arena. The film is at times a critique of the naive enthusiasm of the McCarthy supporters, from the gloomy perspective of Nixonian 1970, and otherwise a meditation on the very real possibility of a reformist alternative politics within the system. *America Is Hard to See* is at once a (relatively) bright film and a highly ambiguous one. The victories in New Hampshire and Oregon are miracles captured on video, Johnson's resignation speech a tentative defeat of the enemy, and the charm and affable rationality of the chief protagonist of the film himself a refreshing glimpse of an apparently real, attractive alternative. Yet the awareness is always present that the film is, after all, a post-mortem, and the campaign so euphorically pursued and relived was indeed a failure.

Again, a low-key chronological approach follows the event from its beginning, slowly and conscientiously to its end. As a historian de Antonio is fastidious: he is careful to balance whatever mythologization is inevitable in his subject matter—

the heroics, the flag-waving, the paranoia, the despair—with a down-to-earth examination of the mechanics of electoral politics on the smallest level. He seeks out documents which show the moments of groundwork and individual effort which cumulatively make up the historical process. The potential of alternative politics is discovered in the images and voices of ordinary people with specific goals and in those of top strategists planning and then evaluating the maneuvers.

De Antonio's focus on specific topical issues—a Senate hearing, a war, a political campaign, etc.—does not mean that his interest is restricted to these events, as we have seen. The challenge of addressing abstract theoretical problems through immediate, topical subjects is a traditional one for the radical filmmaker: he or she must always satisfy the demands for the concrete and topical, by box-office and audience, and perhaps even by the photographic-representative nature of the medium, despite whatever interest he/she may have in more abstract or theoretical issues. It is to de Antonio's credit that he habitually succeeds in extending the microcosm to the macrocosm, yet never makes this extension in a way that is un-"democratic" or facile. The step from the specific to the general is never transparent and often difficult, yet it is always there implicitly, engaging his spectators to complete the connections themselves. It is perhaps this aspect of de Antonio's films that is most responsible for their extraordinary durability, a feature that is by no means a common one in the radical cinema.

The Army–McCarthy hearing, as we have seen, for example, becomes a pretext for an analysis of what de Antonio saw as a symptomatic emphasis on "technique" in American life.[14] In the same way, *Rush to Judgment* becomes an attempt "not to prove the innocence of Oswald, but to show how the American machine works,"[15] and *Year of the Pig* is an analysis of the media's role in legitimizing the politics of imperialism and monopoly capitalism. Similarly, *America Is Hard to See* contains a consciousness, beneath its surface optimism, of the grim inevitability that the system must ultimately defuse even this hope, using even dissent to entrench itself in its own inertia. From this viewpoint, de Antonio's entire oeuvre becomes a continuing Marcusean essay on the modern state and its manner of making its tyranny palatable. Yet the films continue, one by one, with no end in sight, and their presence contradicts de Antonio's apparent recognition of this fatality. The Weather film is certain to add an important new perspective to this continuing essay.

America Is Hard to See treated a personality as the symbol of the system's potential to renew itself from within; *Milhouse,* another, different kind of portrait, appeared a year later, and treated another personality, Nixon at the height of his power, as emblematic of the corruption of the System and its tenacious opposition to that self-renewal. "The film attacks the System, the credibility of the System, by focusing on the obvious and perfect symbol for that System."[16] De Antonio's blackest, most sardonic, and most despairing film, *Milhouse* is also his funniest, as he himself terms it, "the first real attempt at a real documentary comedy."[17] But immediately the Marcusean problematic again imposes itself: is the ability of the radical subculture to laugh at the enemy merely the reverse side of that enemy's power to absorb its dissent with just as much glee?

Though the filmmaker was to claim that *Milhouse* is not a personal attack, whatever else it may be, it *is* indeed an attack, *par excellence,* merciless and brilliant, worthy of Swift and Pope, delivered *ad hominem* and below the belt. De Antonio certainly deserved the honor of inclusion on Nixon's celebrated enemies list as much as anyone. *Milhouse* (its full title is *Milhouse, a White Comedy*) is predictably conducted as a chronological record of Nixon's career, in fact as a parody of the famous crisis-to-crisis chronology which Nixon himself set forth in his pre-presidential memoirs. The system which Nixon had manipulated continuously to his own advantage for over a quarter century is closely scrutinized. As with the previous films, the basic strategy is to remove documents from their original context and re-examine them in a context of (here, satiric) juxtaposition with actuality. The most memorable example is the infamous Checkers speech, where the nervous young candidate gravely tries out the ropes of the medium to which he would habitually resort when under attack over the next twenty years. Once removed from its intended context it becomes a monument of hilarity. An additional twist in *Milhouse* is the humor derived from the art of the out-take. This means of confronting the public man with the private man is developed here to perfection, often without cutting. The changes the Nixonian face undergoes as it confronts the video cameras constitute a sublime image of the duplicity fostered by the system of media politics. And Nixon's unwitting contributions to de Antonio's art of collage are more expressive of the man than any other moments in the film.

Although *ad hominem* mockery hardly seems a legitimate tool of "democratic didacticism," there is a stratum to the film of utmost gravity, developed by serious commentators in the traditional de Antonio style. The homework is done no less efficiently for the fun: the facts and the documents are presented with equal authoritativeness. De Antonio's scrutiny of the political personality from the earliest red-baiting and smear-campaign days to the smoothest White House piety is as methodical and thorough as it is irreverent.

It is ironic that *Milhouse,* that arch-example of an anti-exemplary biography, should provide the model for an important subgenre of the new documentary, the exemplary biography, the documentary homage. Jerry Bruck's *I. F. Stone's Weekly* and Jill Godmilow's *Antonia* are two of the best known of the new biographical films, all built more or less faithfully on the model provided by *Milhouse,* that is, the collage of vintage document and commentary, and the extensive use of interviews and monologues to penetrate the personality under examination. (The National Film Board of Canada's film biographies of Dr. Norman Bethune and John Grierson are two other admirable prototypes for this subgenre.) Such films, given the advantage of the posture of tribute rather than attack, have often been able to enlist the co-operation of their subjects, thereby making the invaluable addition of his or her own voice to the commentary, and varying amounts of cinéma vérité footage to the collage as well. The latter brings to the portrait the cinéma vérité's undeniable talent for capturing behavioral authenticity. In contrast to the accumulative effect of the new film portrait, those of the sixties relying solely on vérité language seem superficial indeed—Stravinsky, Fonda, Dylan, Cash, etc. De Antonio has demonstrated that the addition of historical background, contemporary and external commentary, and the direct on-camera confrontation with the subject are essential to the genre. Instead of the suggestive cinéma vérité cameo, limited by the counterculture's and the System's shared synchronic conception of the personality, we have in this way a more penetrating diachronic exploration of individuals, one elaborating their growth in relation to the social forces around them. Cinéma vérité reinforced individualist, behaviorist ideology; the de Antonio collage makes possible a new collective, materialist view of the human reality.

If *Milhouse* is de Antonio's most exaggerated rejection of the network and vérité ideal of "objectivity," *Painters Painting* (1973) hovers disturbingly close to that dubious standard which the filmmaker's previous career had so convincingly repudiated. Outside of the film, de Antonio made no secret of the definite reservations about contemporary painting which we might have expected from him:

If you consider American art since the war, it's a cold art for a cold war. It's an art "non-engagé." The best American painters have no point of view on the world. They have become part of the world of business. The rich families collect their works. McLuhan admires technology, as John Cage does in music, who has passed from music to technology. This is political, because you are upholding in this way American values; when you are neutral you defend the existing order: and that's the danger of McLuhan.[18]

And criticism of post-war American (official) art might well be the duty of an artist who has spent a decade of his life in films denouncing the triumph of technique over content—in politics, in communications, in film (including the film aesthetics of that group of New American independent filmmakers, most akin to the post-war movements in painting, whom de Antonio once termed "Jonas Mekas and his troupe of trend-sniffing mercenary cavalry"),[19] and in every phase of American life. However the viewer is hard-pressed to read such an attitude into *Painters Painting*. In fact, it is a film that even CBS might be proud to broadcast, it is so wary of evaluating the phenomenon under study. As a film, then, by an avowed Marxist about an artistic avant-garde, *Painters Painting* encapsules all of the contradictions in the murky relationships of the Left to such avant-gardes.

Predictably, de Antonio readily admits to such contradictions in the film:

. . . it's presented me with several problems personally, which anyone who has seen my work would guess, since I regard myself as a Marxist social critic of the existing social system in this country and yet the painters and the way in which they work are essentially manifestations of a very conservative aspect of America. The painting itself is not conservative (though it is apolitical) but it's part of a machine which runs this country. And so, if I have to make a choice between American painting and the attempt to turn men's [sic] minds and the search for a collective soul, then I'm more interested in what Mao is doing than in the art of my friends. And yet I'm making the film: perhaps it's something I have to do to get it out of my system.[20]

The film's virtually sole critical perception comes from the half-satirical encounter with Robert Scull, the self-styled Maecenas of the New York art world, and his since-jettisoned wife. The interview brings out only a momentary flash of the *Milhouse* de Antonio, as the realization half-emerges that virtually all contemporary painting depends on the whims of these dubiously motivated, superficially endowed, nouveaux riches, and on the personal tastes of the establishment art critics whose pontifical pronouncements on surfaces and textures are also part of the collage.

Still, as an uncritical chronicle of post-war painting (with an evaluation of its elitist audience, marketplace orientation, and incestuous, conspiratorial inspiration hardly implied), *Painters Painting* represents an additional refinement of the essay-collage form which de Antonio had been developing for a decade. Now the past-present, document-analysis oscillation is sharpened by the 35mm definition and brilliant acrylic color of the footage from the present. The documents recording the masters in the act, Pollack pouring, and de Kooning and the others doing whatever we are told they were doing, presented in reverent fifties black and white, form an evocative counterpoint with the color images of their completed work and of their successors working and talking a generation later. The tendency of the present generation of painters and sculptors to talk and conceptualize at least as much (and as well) as they create makes the interviews all the more penetrating. The only exception to the respectful bourgeois-Romantic perspective of Art adopted by the film as a whole arises from the interview with Andy Warhol. This artist is easily as fascinating on the screen as the haunting menagerie which he himself has led across it over the last ten years; and in the film, he is unique among the artists interviewed for his refusal to play the self-important, oracular role which attracts the others.

Painters Painting also continues the tendency of the historical films of the seventies to incorporate some elements of cinéma vérité into the structure of the collage. De Antonio balances the interviews, ranging from manifesto-like monologues to *Chelsea Girls* chitchat, with revealing though somewhat stiff footage of the personalities outside of the interview format. The flexibility of such an eclecticism is richly demonstrated.

However rewarding this film might be for some observers of Rockefeller Art who would not be disturbed by such a non-committal attitude, it is to be hoped that with this film (partly financed by the sale of paintings de Antonio himself had collected during the fifties from his artist friends), the artist has indeed "got it out of his system."

A far more rewarding film on avant-garde culture is Jean-Marie Straub's excellent short work on Schoenberg, also a film based on the structural principle of collage. In it Straub no doubt shares de Antonio's reverential attitude to his subject, but balances it not only with a clear elaboration of the historical context for Schoenberg's work, but also, importantly, with a statement by Brecht reflecting on the very problem the earlier biographical material had dealt with (anti-Semitism). The insight provoked by this disruption of the biographical moment with a (literally) Brechtian intervention is an achievement that de Antonio might profitably have imitated in *Painters Painting,* to redeem what otherwise is a disturbingly ambiguous homage to an avant-garde movement which could use more analysis than accolades.

Now that *Hearts and Minds* has finally succeeded in reaching its public, and public anticipation of the Weather Underground film is high, there seems no reason to doubt that the new documentary is in reasonably good health, with every possibility of expanding its audience even more. Despite the enormous debt that Davis clearly owes de Antonio, there are important differences between them. Davis belongs more to the tradition of liberal, humanitarian journalism than to that of incisive, political analysis, and thus bears less resemblance to de Antonio than to Marcel Ophuls, with whom he has already been compared in the popular press several times. Though both Davis and Ophuls use modified versions of the basic de Antonio "document-dossier" format, they share explicit moralistic, bourgeois-humanist perspectives of history which de Antonio has always been careful to avoid. For de Antonio, history is neither therapeutic or cathartic, nor, worse still, a paradigm of the moral relativity of human acts—it is instructive. Weeping over Vietnam with Davis and *mea culpa*ing over the Occupation with Ophuls only serve to becloud the social forces in play. De Antonio's review of *Hearts and Minds* in a 1974 *University Review* condemns the Davis film for "political emptiness," "an inability to understand either the United States or Vietnam," a "(sneering), japing, middle-class liberal superiority," and "patronizing attitudes"—in short it is "heartless" and "mindless."[21] De Antonio's objections are by and large valid; nevertheless Davis's film deserved the wide audience it reached even if it only serves to prevent Americans from forgetting Indochina as quickly as they seem to be doing. And it is to be praised for speaking to its audiences with moral and emotional force. It can't be denied that Davis's broad appeal is a tactical virtue which other more rigorous and uncompromising Vietnam films lack, for example *Year of the Tiger* by Deirdre English, Dave Davis, and Steve Talbot (a casualty of the official-tour-behind-the-lines syndrome), or the Jane Fonda and Haskell Wexler work, *Introduction to the Enemy* (a far superior film because it is more personal, but one apparently still restricted to the committed circuit). Of course the definitive film of the Vietnam war—and the Cold War—has still to be made. And de Antonio has provided the surest models with which to begin.

In the meantime, as the Weather film nears completion, the filmmaker has two projects in the conception phase. Both ideas are for fiction films, a shift in gears of no small consequence for a documentarist of his standing. Which project will materialize first, if either, is anybody's guess: a fictional treatment of Philip Agee's *Inside the Company: CIA Diary,* or a story of a famous radical filmmaker seen through the eyes of government agencies who keep him under surveillance(!). What is certain is that de Antonio, in leaving behind him (temporarily, it is to be hoped) the documentary mode of discourse, will not abandon the rich creative energy, the obstinate commitment to rationality and to change, and the clear-sighted historical consciousness which have made him one of the major American filmmakers of our time. It is perhaps this last dimension of his art, its investment in the importance of historical analysis, which has constituted his most significant contribution to American radical culture, and which will no doubt continue to do so with his new turn toward the mode of fiction.

Notes

1. Robert Kramer, quoted in "Newsreel: A Montage of Programmatic Comments by Newsreel Filmmakers," *Film Quarterly,* no. 22 (Winter 1968), p. 45.

2. Peter Biskind, quoted in "Radical American Film? A Questionnaire," *Cineaste,* 5, no. 4, p. 15.

3. *Ibid.*

4. Bernard Weiner, "Radical Scavenging: An Interview with Emile de Antonio," *Film Quarterly,* no. 25 (Fall 1971), p. 3.

5. *Ibid.,* p. 9.

6. Michel Ciment and Bernard Cohn, "Entretien avec Emile de Antonio," *Positif,* no. 113 (February 1970), p. 28. My translation.

7. Sergei M. Eisenstein, *Film Sense.* New York: Harcourt, Brace, 1942, p. 28.

8. Weiner, p. 8.

9. *Ibid.,* p. 10.

10. *Ibid.,* p. 10.

11. *Ibid.,* p. 8.

12. Ciment and Cohn, p. 30.

13. Weiner, p. 7.

14. *Ibid.,* p. 8.

15. *Ibid.,* p. 7.

16. *Ibid.,* p. 6.

17. *Ibid.,* p. 15.

18. Ciment and Cohn, p. 36.

19. Weiner, p. 10.

20. *Ibid.,* p. 14.

21. Emile de Antonio, "Visions of Vietnam," *University Review,* no. 41 (December 1974), p. 21.

THE VOICE OF DOCUMENTARY

BILL NICHOLS

This article tries to base a largely structural analysis of different documentary film styles not on a theoretical agenda but on the experiential effect that they have on a viewer. The resulting argument does not ignore theoretical concepts, but it seeks to recast them in terms that critics and filmmakers seem to share. As a result, this text can be seen as another attempt at one prevalent form of critical activity: the integration of two or more perspectives, for which Freud and Marx are the figures most often invoked. Here, the integration is between communication theory, Marxism, and semiotics.

In this text, I identify four different styles of documentary filmmaking, ranging from the didactic, voice-of-God style to cinéma vérité *but also including two recent forms: the string-of-interviews film, often used as a means of historical recall, and the self-reflexive film. This last type appears to address many of the problems discussed in Parts 4 and 5 of this volume, although its form results as much from debates within the arena of social science (anthropology in particular) as it does from debates within film theory or semiotics. Using the central concept of logical typing, I discuss the effect that each form's claim of access to reality has on a viewer. Other ways of accounting for effects—theories of subjectivity, the unconscious, or imaginary and symbolic communication—are not necessarily incompatible with the approach adopted here, but they are deeply rooted in the psychoanalytic perspective. My stress on the pragmatics of communication dwells more on the structure of a message than on the construction of a viewer. It is the openly complex, self-referential strategy of the self-reflexive form of documentary that seems the most promising, not because it possesses any inherent superiority but because it resolves a number of problems evident in the way in which the other forms make their claims about reality and their relation to it.*

Together with the articles by MacDougall and Williams and Rich, this article helps to broaden our understanding of documentary not as a special use of the film medium that affords a "privileged" view of reality but as a genre. The concerns expressed here avoid the terminology of semiotics (discours/histoire, énonciation/énoncé, imaginary/symbolic, apparatus), *but they join similar issues: how to understand images* of *the world as speech* about *the world and how to place that speech within formal, experiential, and historical contexts.*

•

It is worth insisting that the strategies and styles deployed in documentary, like those of narrative film, change; they have a history. And they have changed for much the same reasons: the dominant modes of expository discourse change; the arena of ideological contestation shifts. The comfortably accepted realism of one generation seems like artifice to the next. New strategies must constantly be fabricated to re-present "things as they are" and still others to contest this very representation.

In the history of documentary we can identify at least four major styles, each with distinctive formal and ideological qualities.[1] In this article I propose to examine the limitations and strengths of these strategies, with particular attention to one that is both the newest and in some ways the oldest of them all.[2]

The direct-address style of the Griersonian tradition (or, in its most excessive form, the March of Time's "voice of God") was the first thoroughly worked-out mode of documentary. As befitted a school whose purposes were overwhelmingly didactic, it employed a supposedly authoritative yet often presumptuous off-screen narration. In many cases this narration effectively dominated the visuals, though it could be, in films like *Night Mail* or *Listen to Britain,* poetic and evocative. After World War II, the Griersonian mode fell into disfavor (for reasons I will come back to later) and it has little contemporary currency—except for television news, game and talk shows, virtually all ads, and most documentary specials.

Its successor, *cinéma vérité,* promised an increase in the "reality effect" with its directness, immediacy, and impression of capturing untampered events in the everyday lives of particular people. Films like *Chronique d'un été, Le Joli Mai, Lonely Boy, Back-Breaking Leaf, Primary,* and *The Chair* built on the new technical possibilities offered by portable cameras and sound recorders which could produce synchronous dialogue under location conditions. In pure *cinéma vérité* films, the style seeks to become "transparent" in the same mode as the classical Hollywood style—capturing people in action, and letting the viewer come to conclusions about them unaided by any implicit or explicit commentary.

Sometimes mesmerizing, frequently perplexing, such films seldom offered the sense of history, context, or perspective that viewers seek. And so in the past decade we have seen a third style which incorporates direct address (characters or narrator speaking directly to the viewer), usually in the form of the interview. In a host of political and feminist films, witness-participants step before the camera to tell their story. Sometimes profoundly revealing, sometimes fragmented and incomplete, such films have provided the central model for contemporary documentary. But as a strategy and a form, the interview-oriented film has problems of its own.

More recently, a fourth phase seems to have begun, with films moving toward more complex forms where epistemological and aesthetic assumptions become more visible. These new self-reflexive documentaries mix observational passages with interviews, the voice-over of the film-maker with intertitles, making patently clear what has been implicit all along: documentaries always were forms of re-presentation, never clear windows onto "reality"; the film-maker was always a participant-witness and an active fabricator of meaning, a producer of cinematic discourse rather than a neutral or all-knowing reporter of the way things truly are.

Ironically, film theory has been of little help in this recent evolution, despite the enormous contribution of recent theory to questions of the production of meaning in narrative forms. In documentary the most advanced, modernist work draws its inspiration less from post-structuralist models of discourse than from the working procedures of documentation and validation practiced by ethnographic film-makers. And as far as the influence of film history goes, the figure of Dziga Vertov now looms much larger than those of either Flaherty or Grierson.

I do not intend to argue that self-reflexive documentary represents a pinnacle or solution in any ultimate sense. It is, however, in the process of evolving alternatives that seem, in our present historical context, less obviously problematic than the strategies of commentary, *vérité,* or the interview. These new forms may, like their predecessors, come to seem more "natural" or even "realistic" for a time. But the success of every form breeds its own overthrow: it limits, omits, disavows, represses (as well as represents). In time, new necessities bring new formal inventions.

As suggested above, in the evolution of documentary the contestation among forms has centered on the question of "voice." By "voice" I mean something narrower than style: that which conveys to us a sense of a text's social point of view, of how it is speaking to us and how it is organizing the materials it is presenting to us. In this sense "voice" is not restricted to any one code or feature, such as dialogue or spoken commentary. Voice is perhaps akin to that intangible, moiré-like pattern formed by the unique interaction of all a film's codes, and it applies to all modes of documentary.

Far too many contemporary film-makers appear to have lost their voice. Politically, they forfeit their own voice for that of others (usually characters recruited to the film and interviewed). Formally, they disavow the complexities of voice, and discourse, for the apparent simplicities of faithful observation or respectful representation, the treacherous simplicities of an unquestioned empiricism (the world and its truths exist; they need only be dusted off and reported). Many documentarists would appear to believe what fiction film-makers only feign to believe, or openly question: that film-making creates an objective representation of the way things really are. Such documentaries use the magical template of verisimilitude without the story teller's open resort to artifice. Very few seem prepared to admit through the very tissue and texture of their work that all film-making is a form of discourse fabricating its effects, impressions, and point of view.

Yet it especially behooves the documentary film-maker to acknowledge what she/he is actually doing. Not in order to be accepted as modernist for the sake of being modernist, but to fashion documentaries that may more closely correspond to a contemporary understanding of our position within the world so that effective political/formal strategies for describing and challenging that position can emerge. Strategies and techniques for doing so already exist. In documentary they seem to derive most directly from *A Man with a Movie Camera* and *Chronique d'un été* and are vividly exemplified in David and Judith MacDougall's Turkana trilogy *(Lorang's Way, Wedding Camels, A Wife Among Wives)*. But before discussing this tendency further, we should first examine the strengths and limitations of *cinéma vérité* and the interview-based film. They are well-represented by two recent and highly successful films: *Soldier Girls* and *Rosie the Riveter.*

Soldier Girls presents a contemporary situation: basic army training as experienced by women volunteers. Purely indirect or observational, *Soldier Girls* provides no spoken commentary, no interviews or titles, and, like Fred Wiseman's films, it arouses considerable controversy about its point of view. One viewer at Filmex interjected, "How on earth did they get the Army to let them make such an incredibly anti-Army film?" What struck that viewer as powerful criticism, though, may strike another as an honest portrayal of the tough-minded discipline necessary to learn to defend oneself, to survive in harsh environments, to kill. As in Wiseman's films, organizational strategies establish a preferred reading—in this case, one that favors the personal over the political, that seeks out and celebrates the irruptions of individual feeling and conscience in the face of institutional constraint, that re-writes historical process as the expression of an indomitable human essence whatever the circumstance. But these strategies, complex and subtle like those of realist fiction, tend to ascribe to the historical material itself meanings that in fact are an effect of the film's style or voice, just as fiction's strategies invite us to believe that "life" is like the imaginary world inhabited by its characters.

A pre-credit sequence of training exercises which follows three woman volunteers ends with a freeze-frame and iris-in to isolate the face of each woman. Similar to classic Hollywood-style vignettes used to identify key actors, this sequence inaugurates a set of strategies that links *Soldier Girls* with a large part of American *cinéma vérité (Primary, Salesman, An American Family,* the *Middletown* series). It is characterized by a romantic individualism and a dramatic, fiction-like structure, but employing "found" stories rather than the wholly invented ones of Hollywood. Scenes in which Private Hall oversees punishment for Private Alvarez and in which the women recruits are awakened and prepare their beds for Drill Sergeant Abing's inspection prompt an impression of looking in on a world unmarked by our, or the camera's, act of gazing. And those rare moments in which the camera or person behind it is acknowledged certify more forcefully that other moments of "pure observation" capture the social presentation of self we too would have witnessed had we actually been there to see for ourselves. When *Soldier Girls'* narrative-like tale culminates in a shattering moment of character revelation, it seems to be a happy coincidence of dramatic structure and historical events unfolding. In as extraordinary an epiphany as any in all of *vérité,* tough-minded Drill Sergeant Abing breaks down and confesses to Private Hall how much of his own humanity and soul has been destroyed by his experience in Vietnam. By such means, the film transcends the social and political categories which it shows but refuses to name. Instead of the personal becoming political, the political becomes personal.

We never hear the voice of the film-maker or a narrator trying to persuade us of this romantic humanism. Instead, the film's structure relies heavily on classical narrative procedures, among them: (1) a chronology of apparent causality which reveals how each of the three women recruits resolves the conflict between a sense of her own individuality and army discipline; (2) shots organized into dramatically revelatory scenes that only acknowledge the camera as participant-observer near the film's end, when one of the recruits embraces the film-makers as she leaves the training base, discharged for her "failure" to fit in; and (3) excellent performances from characters who "play themselves" without any inhibiting self-consciousness. (The phenomenon of filming individuals who play themselves in a manner strongly reminiscent of the performances of professional actors in fiction could be the subject of an extended study in its own right.) These procedures allow purely observational documentaries to asymptotically narrow the gap between a fabricated realism and the apparent capture of reality itself which so fascinated André Bazin.

This gap may also be looked at as a gap between evidence and argument.[3] One of the peculiar fascinations of film is precisely that it so easily conflates the two. Documentary displays a tension arising from the attempt to make statements about life which are quite general, while necessarily using sounds and images that bear the inescapable trace of their particular historical origins. These sounds and images come to function as signs; they bear meaning, though the meaning in not really inherent in them but rather conferred upon them by their function within the text as a whole. We may think we hear history or reality speaking to us through a film, but what we actually hear is the voice of the text, even when that voice tries to efface itself.

This is not only a matter of semiotics but of historical process. Those who confer meaning (individuals, social classes, the media and other institutions) exist within history itself rather than at the periphery, looking in like gods. Hence, paradoxically, self-referentiality is an inevitable communicational category. A class cannot be a member of itself, the law of logical typing tells us, and yet in human communication this law is necessarily violated. Those who confer meaning are themselves members of the class of conferred meanings (history). For a film to fail to acknowledge this and pretend to omniscience—whether by voice-of-God commentary or by claims of "objective knowledge"—is to deny its own complicity with a production of knowledge that rests on no firmer bedrock than the very act of production. (What then becomes vital are the assumptions, values, and purposes motivating this production, the underpinnings which some modernist strategies attempt to make more clear.)[4]

Observational documentary appears to leave the driving to us. No one tells us about the sights we pass or what they mean. Even those obvious marks of documentary textuality—muddy sound, blurred or racked focus, the grainy, poorly lit figures of social actors caught on the run—function paradoxically. Their presence testifies to an apparently more basic absence: such films sacrifice conventional, polished artistic expression in order to bring back, as best they can, the actual texture of history in the making. If the camera gyrates wildly or ceases functioning, this is not an expression of personal style. It is a signifier of personal danger, as in *Harlan County,* or even death, as in the street scene from *The Battle of Chile* when the camera man records the moment of his own death.

This shift from artistic expressiveness to historical revelation contributes mightily to the phenomenological effect of the observational film. *Soldier Girls, They Call Us Misfits,* its sequel, *A Respectable Life,* and Fred Wiseman's most recent film, *Models,* propose revelations about the real not as a result of direct argument, but on the basis of inferences we draw from historical evidence itself. For example, Stefan Jarl's remarkable film, *They Call Us Misfits,* contains a purely observational scene of its two 17-year-old misfits—who have left home for a life of booze, drugs, and a good time in Stockholm—getting up in the morning. Kenta washes his long hair, dries it, and then meticulously combs every hair into place. Stoffe doesn't bother with his hair at all. Instead, he boils water and then makes tea by pouring it over a tea bag that is still inside its paper wrapper! We rejoin the boys in *A Respectable Life,* shot ten years later, and learn that Stoffe has nearly died on three occasions from heroin overdoses whereas Kenta has sworn off hard drugs and begun a career of sorts as a singer. At this point we may retroactively grant a denser tissue of meaning to those little morning rituals recorded a decade earlier. If so, we take them as evidence of historical determinations rather then artistic vision—even though they are only available to us as a result of textual strategies. More generally, the aural and visual evidence of what ten years of hard living do to the alert, mischievous appearance of two boys—the ruddy skin, the dark, extinguished eyes, the slurred and garbled speech, especially of Stoffe— bear meaning precisely because the films invite retroactive comparison. The films produce the structure in which "facts" themselves take on meaning pre-

cisely because they belong to a coherent series of differences. Yet, though powerful, this construction of differences remains insufficient. A simplistic line of
historical progression prevails, centered as it is in *Soldier Girls* on the trope of
romantic individualism. (Instead of the Great Man theory we have the Unfortunate Victim theory of history—inadequate, but compellingly presented.)

And where observational cinema shifts from an individual to an institutional
focus, and from a metonymic narrative model to a metaphoric one, as in the
highly innovative work of Fred Wiseman, there may still be only a weak sense of
constructed meaning, of a textual voice addressing us. A vigorous, active, and
retroactive reading is necessary before we can hear the voice of the textual system
as a level distinct from the sounds and images of the evidence it adduces, while
questions of adequacy remain. Wiseman's sense of context and of meaning as a
function of the text itself remains weak, too easily engulfed by the fascination that
allows us to mistake film for reality, the impression of the real for the experience
of it. The risk of reading *Soldier Girls* or Wiseman's *Models* like a Rorschach test
may require stronger counter-measures than the subtleties their complex editing
and *mise-en-scène* provide.

Prompted, it would seem, by these limitations to *cinéma vérité* or observational cinema, many film-makers during the past decade have reinstituted direct
address. For the most part this has meant social actors addressing us in interviews
rather than a return to the voice-of-authority evidenced by a narrator. *Rosie the
Riveter,* for example, tells us about the blatant hypocrisy with which women were
recruited to the factories and assembly lines during World War II. A series of five
women witnesses tell us how they were denied the respect granted men, told to
put up with hazardous conditions "like a man," paid less, and pitted against one
another racially. *Rosie* makes short shrift of the noble icon of the woman worker
as seen in forties newsreels. Those films celebrated her heroic contribution to the
great effort to preserve the free world from fascist dictatorship. *Rosie* destroys
this myth of deeply appreciated, fully rewarded contribution without in any way
undercutting the genuine fortitude, courage, and political awareness of women
who experienced continual frustration in their struggles for dignified working
conditions and a permanent place in the American labor force.

Using interviews, but no commentator, together with a weave of compilation
footage as images of illustration, director Connie Field tells a story many of us
may think we've heard, only to realize we've never heard the whole of it before.

The organization of the film depends heavily on its set of extensive interviews
with former "Rosies." Their selection follows the direct-cinema tradition of filming ordinary people. But *Rosie the Riveter* broadens that tradition, as *Union
Maids, The Wobblies,* and *With Babies and Banners* have also done, to retrieve the
memory of an "invisible" (suppressed more than forgotten) history of labor
struggle. The five interviewees remember a past the film's inserted historical
images reconstruct but in counterpoint: their recollection of adversity and struggle contrasts with old newsreels of women "doing their part" cheerfully.

This strategy complicates the voice of the film in an interesting way. It adds a
contemporary, personal resonance to the historical compilation footage without

challenging the assumptions of that footage explicitly, as a voice-over commentary might do. We ourselves become engaged in determining how the women witnesses counterpoint these historical "documents" as well as how they articulate their own present and past consciousness in political, ethical, and feminist dimensions.

We are encouraged to believe that these voices carry less the authority of historical judgment than that of personal testimony—they are, after all, the words of apparently "ordinary women" remembering the past. As in many films that advance issues raised by the women's movement, there is an emphasis on individual but politically significant experience. *Rosie* demonstrates the power of the act of naming—the ability to find the words that render the personal political. This reliance on oral history to reconstruct the past places *Rosie the Riveter* within what is probably the predominant mode of documentary filmmaking today—films built around a string of interviews—where we also find *A Wive's Tale, With Babies and Banners, Controlling Interest, The Day After Trinity, The Trials of Alger Hiss, Rape, Word Is Out, Prison for Women, This Is Not a Love Story, Nuove Frontieras (Looking for Better Dreams),* and *The Wobblies.*

This reinstitution of direct address through the interview has successfully avoided some of the central problems of voice-over narration, namely authoritative omniscience or didactic reductionism. There is no longer the dubious claim that things are as the film presents them, organized by the commentary of an all-knowing subject. Such attempts to stand above history and explain it create a paradox. Any attempt by a speaker to vouch for his or her own validity reminds us of the Cretan paradox: "Epimenides was a Cretan who said, 'Cretans always lie.' Was Epimenides telling the truth?" The nagging sense of a self-referential claim that can't be proven reaches greatest intensity with the most forceful assertions, which may be why viewers are often most suspicious of what an apparently omniscient Voice of Authority asserts most fervently. The emergence of so many recent documentaries built around strings of interviews strikes me as a strategic response to the recognition that neither can events speak for themselves nor can a single voice speak with ultimate authority. Interviews diffuse authority. A gap remains between the voice of a social actor recruited to the film and the voice of the film.

Not compelled to vouch for their own validity, the voices of interviewees may well arouse less suspicion. Yet a larger, constraining voice may remain to provide, or withhold, validation. In *The Sad Song of Yellow Skin, The Wilmar 8, Harlan County, USA, This Is Not a Love Story,* or *Who Killed the Fourth Ward,* among others, the literal voice of the film-maker enters into dialogue but without the self-validating, authoritative tone of a previous tradition. (These are also voices without the self-reflexive quality found in Vertov's, Rouch's, or the MacDougalls' work.) Diary-like and uncertain in *Yellow Skin;* often directed toward the women strikers as though by a fellow participant and observer in *Wilmar 8* and *Harlan County;* sharing personal reactions to pornography with a companion in *Not a Love Story;* and adopting a mock ironic tone reminiscent of Peter Falk's Columbo in *Fourth Ward*—these voices of potentially imaginary assurance instead share doubts and emotional reactions with other characters and us. As a result they seem to refuse a privileged position in relation to other characters. Of course, these less assertive authorial voices remain complicit with the controlling voice of the textual system itself, but the effect upon a viewer is distinctly different.

Still, interviews pose problems. Their occurrence is remarkably wide-spread—from *The Hour of the Wolf* to *The MacNeil/Lehrer Report* and from *Housing Problems* (1935) to *Harlan County, USA*. The greatest problem, at least in recent documentary, has been to retain that sense of a gap between the voice of interviewees and the voice of the text as a whole. It is most obviously a problem when the interviewees display conceptual inadequacy on the issue but remain unchallenged by the film. *The Day After Trinity,* for example, traces Robert F. Oppenheimer's career but restricts itself to a Great Man theory of history. The string of interviews clearly identifies Oppenheimer's role in the race to build the nuclear bomb, and his equivocations, but it never places the bomb or Oppenheimer within that larger constellation of government policies and political calculations that determined its specific use or continuing threat—even though the interviews took place in the last few years. The text not only appears to lack a voice or perspective of its own, the perspective of its character-witnesses is patently inadequate.

In documentary, when the voice of the text disappears behind characters who speak to us, we confront a specific strategy of no less ideological importance than its equivalent in fiction films. When we no longer sense that a governing voice actively provides or withholds the imprimatur of veracity according to its own purposes and assumptions, its own canons of validation, we may also sense the return of the paradox and suspicion interviews should help us escape: the word of witnesses, uncritically accepted, must provide its own validation. Meanwhile, the film becomes a rubber stamp. To varying degree this diminution of a governing voice occurs through parts of *Word Is Out, The Wobblies, With Babies and Banners,* and *Prison for Women.* The sense of a hierarchy of voices becomes lost.[5] Ideally this hierarchy would uphold correct logical typing at one level (the voice of the text remains of a higher, controlling type than the voices of interviewees) without denying the inevitable collapse of logical types at another (the voice of the text is not above history but part of the very historical process upon which it confers meaning). But at present a less complex and less adequate sidetracking of paradox prevails. The film says, in effect, "Interviewees never lie." Interviewees say, "What I am telling you is the truth." We then ask, "Is the interviewee telling the truth?" but find no acknowledgement in the film of the possibility, let alone the necessity, of entertaining this question as one inescapable in all communication and signification.

As much as anyone, Emile de Antonio, who pioneered the use of interviews and compilation footage to organize complex historical arguments without a narrator, has also provided clear signposts for avoiding the inherent dangers of interviews. Unfortunately, most of the film-makers adopting his basic approach have failed to heed them.

De Antonio demonstrates a sophisticated understanding of the category of the personal. He does not invariably accept the word of witnesses, nor does he adopt rhetorical strategies (Great Man theories, for example) that limit historical understanding to the personal. Something exceeds this category, and in *Point of Order, In the Year of the Pig, Milhouse: A White Comedy,* and *Weather Underground,* among others, this excess is carried by a distinct textual voice that clearly judges the validity of what witnesses say. Just as the voice of John Huston in *The Battle of San Pietro* contests one line of argument with another (that of General Mark Clark, who claims the costs of battle were not excessive, with that of Huston, who suggests they were), so the textual voice of de Antonio contests and places the statements made by its embedded interviews, but without speaking to us directly. (In de Antonio and in his followers, there is no narrator, only the direct address of witnesses.)

This contestation is not simply the express support of some witnesses over others, for left against right. It is a systematic effect of placement that retains the gaps between levels of different logical type. De Antonio's overall expository strategy in *In the Year of the Pig,* for example, makes it clear that no one witness tells the whole truth. De Antonio's voice (unspoken but controlling) makes witnesses contend with one another to yield a point of view more distinctive to the film than to any of its witnesses (since it includes this very strategy of contention). (Similarly, the unspoken voice of *The Atomic Cafe*—evident in the extraordinarily skillful editing of government nuclear weapons propaganda films from the fifties—governs a preferred reading of the footage it compiles.) But particularly in de Antonio's work, different points of view appear. History is not a monolith, its density and outline given from the outset. On the contrary, *In the Year of the Pig,* for example, constructs perspective and historical understanding, and does so right before our eyes.

We see and hear, for example, US government spokesmen explaining their strategy and conception of the "Communist menace," whereas we do not see and hear Ho Chi Minh explain his strategy and vision. Instead, an interviewee, Paul Mus, introduces us to Ho Chi Minh descriptively while de Antonio's cutaways to Vietnamese countryside evoke an affiliation between Ho and his land and people that is absent from the words and images of American spokesmen. Ho remains an uncontained figure whose full meaning must be conferred, and inferred, from available materials as they are brought together by de Antonio. Such construction is a textual, and cinematic, act evident in the choice of supporting or ironic images to accompany interviews, in the actual juxtaposition of interviews, and even in the still images that form a pre-credit sequence inasmuch as they unmistakably refer to the American Civil War (an analogy sharply at odds with US government accounts of Communist invasion). By juxtaposing silhouettes of Civil War soldiers with GIs in Vietnam, the pre-credit sequence obliquely but clearly offers an interpretation for the events we are about to see. De Antonio does not subordinate his own voice to the way things are, to the sounds and images that are evidence of war. He acknowledges that the meaning of these images must be conferred upon them and goes about doing so in a readily understood though indirect manner.

De Antonio's hierarchy of levels and reservation of ultimate validation to the highest level (the textual system or film as a whole) differs radically from other approaches. John Lowenthal's *The Trials of Alger Hiss,* for example, is a totally subservient endorsement of Hiss's legalistic strategies. Similarly, *Hollywood on Trial* shows no independence from the perhaps politically expedient but disingenuous line adopted by the Hollywood 10 over thirty years ago—that HUAC's pattern of subpoenas to friendly and unfriendly witnesses primarily threatened the civil liberties of ordinary citizens (though it certainly did so) rather than posing a more specific threat to the CPUSA and American left (where it clearly did the greatest damage). By contrast, even in *Painters Painting* and *Weather Underground,* where de Antonio seems unusually close to validating uncritically what interviewees say, the subtle voice of his *mise en scène* preserves the gap, conveying a strong sense of the distance between the sensibilities or politics of those interviewed and those of the larger public to whom they speak.

De Antonio's films produce a world of dense complexity: they embody a sense of constraint and over-determination. Not everyone can be believed. Not everything is true. Characters do not emerge as the autonomous shapers of a personal destiny. De Antonio proposes ways and means by which to reconstruct the past dialectically, as Fred Wiseman reconstructs the present dialectically.[6] Rather than appearing to collapse itself into the consciousness of character witnesses, the film retains an independent consciousness, a voice of its own. The film's own consciousness (surrogate for ours) probes, remembers, substantiates, doubts. It questions and believes, including itself. It assumes the voice of personal consciousness at the same time as it examines the very category of the personal. Neither omniscient deity nor obedient mouthpiece, de Antonio's rhetorical voice seduces us by embodying those qualities of insight, skepticism, judgment, and independence we would like to appropriate for our own. Nonetheless, though he is closer to a modernist, self-reflexive strategy than any other documentary film-maker in America—with the possible exception of the more experimental feminist film-maker, Jo Ann Elam—de Antonio remains clearly apart from this tendency. He is more a Newtonian than an Einsteinian observer of events; he insists on the activity of fixing meaning, but it is meaning that does, finally, appear to reside "out there" rather than insisting on the activity of producing that "fix" from which meaning itself derives.

There are lessons here we would think de Antonio's successors would be quick to learn. But, most frequently, they have not. The interview remains a problem. Subjectivity, consciousness, argumentative form and voice remain unquestioned in documentary theory and practice. Often, film-makers simply choose to interview characters with whom they agree. A weaker sense of skepticism, a diminished self-awareness of the film-maker as producer of meaning or history prevails, yielding a flatter, less dialectical sense of history and a simpler, more idealized sense of character. Characters threaten to emerge as stars—flashpoints of inspiring, and imaginary, coherence contradictory to their ostensible status as ordinary people.[7]

These problems emerge in three of the best history films we have (and in the pioneering gay film, *Word Is Out*), undermining their great importance on other levels. *Union Maids, With Babies and Banners,* and *The Wobblies* flounder on the axis of personal respect and historical recall. The films simply suppose that things were as the participant-witnesses recall them, and lest we doubt, the film-makers respectfully find images of illustration to substantiate the claim. (The resonance set up in *Rosie the Riveter* between interviews and compilation footage establishes a perceptible sense of a textual voice that makes this film a more sophisticated, though not self-reflexive, version of the interview-based documentary.) What characters omit to say, so do these films, most noticeably regarding the role of the CPUSA in *Union Maids* and *With Babies and Banners*. *Banners*, for example, contains one instance when a witness mentions the helpful knowledge she gained from Communist Party members. Immediately, though, the film cuts to unrelated footage of a violent attack on workers by a goon squad. It is as if the textual voice, rather than provide independent assessment, must go so far as to find diversionary material to offset presumably harmful comments by witnesses themselves!

These films naively endorse limited, selective recall. The tactic flattens witnesses into a series of imaginary puppets conforming to a line. Their recall becomes distinguishable more by differences in force of personality than by differences in perspective. Backgrounds loaded with iconographic meanings transform witnesses further into stereotypes (shipyards, farms, union halls abound, or for the gays and lesbians in *Word Is Out*, bedrooms and the bucolic out-of-doors). We sense a great relief when characters step out of these closed, iconographic frames and into more open-ended ones, but such "release" usually occurs only at the end of the films, where it also signals the achievement of expository closure—another kind of frame. We return to the simple claim, "Things were as these witnesses describe them, why contest them?"—a claim which is a dissimulation and a disservice to both film theory and political praxis. On the contrary, as de Antonio and Wiseman demonstrate quite differently, things signify, but only if we make them comprehensible.[8]

Documentaries with a more sophisticated grasp of the historical realm establish a preferred reading by a textual system that asserts its own voice in contrast to the voices it recruits or observes. Such films confront us with an alternative to our own hypotheses about what kind of things populate the world, what relations they sustain, and what meanings they bear for us. The film operates as an autonomous whole, as we do. It is greater than its parts and orchestrates them: (1) the recruited voices, the recruited sounds and images; (2) the textual "voice" spoken by the style of the film as a whole (how its multiplicity of codes, including those pertaining to recruited voices, is orchestrated into a singular, controlling pattern); and (3) the surrounding historical context, including the viewing event itself, which the textual voice cannot successfully rise above or fully control. The film is thus a simulacrum or external trace of the production of meaning we undertake ourselves every day, every moment. We see not an image of imaginary unchanging coherence, magically represented on a screen, but the evidence of an historically rooted act of making things meaningful comparable to our own historically situated acts of comprehension.

With de Antonio's films, *The Atomic Cafe, Rape,* or *Rosie the Riveter* the active counterpointing of the text reminds us that its meaning is produced. This foregrounding of an active production of meaning by a textual system may also heighten our conscious sense of self as something also produced by codes that extend beyond ourselves. An exaggerated claim, perhaps, but still suggestive of the difference in effect of different documentary strategies and an indication of the importance of the self-reflexive strategy itself.

Self-reflexiveness can easily lead to an endless regression. It can prove highly appealing to an intelligentsia more interested in "good form" than in social change. Yet interest in self-reflexive forms is not purely an academic question. *Cinéma vérité* and its variants sought to address certain limitations in the voice-of-God tradition. The interview-oriented film sought to address limitations apparent in the bulk of *cinéma vérité,* and the self-reflexive documentary addresses the limitations of assuming that subjectivity and both the social and textual positioning of the self (as film-maker or viewer) are ultimately not problematic.

Modernist thought in general challenges this assumption. A few documentary film-makers, going as far back as Dziga Vertov and certainly including Jean Rouch and the hard-to-categorize Jean-Luc Godard, adopt the basic epistemological assumption in their work that knowledge and the position of the self in relation to the mediator of knowledge, a given text, are socially and formally constructed and should be shown to be so. Rather than inviting paralysis before a centerless labyrinth, however, such a perspective restores the dialectic between self and other: neither the "out there" nor the "in here" contains its own inherent meaning. The *process* of constructing meaning overshadows constructed meanings. And at a time when modernist experimentation is old-hat within the avant-garde and a fair amount of fiction film-making, it remains almost totally unheard of among documentary film-makers, especially in North America. It is not political documentarists who have been the leading innovators. Instead it is a handful of ethnographic film-makers like Timothy Asch (*The Ax Fight*), John Marshall (*Nai!*) and David and Judith MacDougall who, in their meditations on scientific method and visual communication, have done the most provocative experimentation.

Take the MacDougalls' *Wedding Camels* (part of the Turkana trilogy), for example. The film, set in northern Kenya, explores the preparations for a Turkana wedding in day-to-day detail. It mixes direct and indirect address to form a complex whole made up of two levels of historical reference—evidence and argument—and two levels of textual structure—observation and exposition.

Though *Wedding Camels* is frequently observational and very strongly rooted in the texture of everyday life, the film-makers' presence receives far more frequent acknowledgment than it does in *Soldier Girls,* or Wiseman's films, or most other observational work. Lorang, the bride's father and central figure in the dowry negotiations, says at one point, with clear acknowledgment of the film-makers' presence, "They [Europeans] never marry our daughters. They always hold back their animals." At other moments we hear David MacDougall ask questions of Lorang or others off-camera much as we do in *The Wilmar 8* or *In the Year of the Pig.* (This contrasts with *The Wobblies, Union Maids,* and *With Babies and Banners,* where the questions to which participant witnesses respond are not heard.) Sometimes these queries invite characters to reflect on events we observe in detail, like the dowry arrangements themselves. On these occasions they introduce a vivid level of self-reflexiveness into the characters' performance as well as into the film's structure, something that is impossible in interview-based films that give us no sense of a character's present but only use his or her words as testimony about the past.

Wedding Camels also makes frequent use of intertitles, which mark off one scene from another to develop a mosaic structure that necessarily admits to its own lack of completeness even as individual facets appear to exhaust a given encounter. This sense of both incompleteness and exhaustion, as well as the radical shift of perceptual space involved in going from apparently three-dimensional images to two-dimensional graphics that comment on or frame the image, generates a strong sense of a hierarchical and self-referential ordering.

For example, in one scene Naingoro, sister to the bride's mother, says, "Our daughters are not our own. They are born to be given out." The implicit lack of completeness to individual identity apart from social exchange then receives elaboration through an interview sequence with Akai, the bride. The film poses questions by means of intertitles and sandwiches Akai's responses, briefly, between them. One intertitle, for example, phrases its question more or less as follows, "We asked Akai whether a Turkana woman chooses her husband or if her parents choose for her." Such phrasing brings the film-maker's intervention strongly into the foreground.

The structure of this passage suggests some of the virtues of a hybrid style: the titles serve as another indicator of a textual voice apart from that of the characters represented. They also differ from most documentary titles, which, since the silent days of *Nanook,* have worked like a graphic "voice" of authority. In *Wedding Camels* the titles, in their mock-interactive structure, remain closely aligned with the particulars of person and place rather than appearing to issue from an omniscient consciousness. They show clear awareness of how a particular meaning is being produced by a particular act of intervention. This is not presented as a grand revelation but as a simple truth that is only remarkable for its rarity in documentary film. These particular titles also display both a wry sense of humor and a clear perception of the meaning an individual's marriage has for him or her as well as for others (a vital means of countering, among other things, the temptation of an ethnocentric reading or judgment). By "violating" the coherence of a social actor's diegetic space, intertitles also lessen the tendency for the interviewee to inflate to the proportions of a star-witness. By acting self-reflexively such strategies call the status of the interview itself into question and diminish its tacit claim to tell the whole truth. Other signifying choices, which function like Brechtian distancing devices, would include the separate "spaces" of image and intertitle for question/response; the highly structured and abbreviated question/ answer format; the close-up, portrait-like framing of a social actor that pries her away from a matrix of ongoing activities or a stereotypical background, and the clear acknowledgment that such fabrications exist to serve the purposes of the film rather than to capture an unaffected reality.

Though modest in tone, *Wedding Camels* demonstrates a structural sophistication well beyond that of almost any other documentary film work today. Whether its modernist strategies can be yoked to a more explicitly political perspective (without restricting itself to the small avant-garde audience that exists for the Godards and Chantal Akermans), is less a question than a challenge still haunting us, considering the limitations of most interview-based films.

Changes in documentary strategy bear a complex relation to history. Self-reflexive strategies seem to have a particularly complex historical relation to documentary form since they are far less peculiar to it than the voice-of-God, *cinéma vérité* or interview-based strategies. Although they have been available to documentary (as to narrative) since the teens, they have never been as popular in North America as in Europe or in other regions (save among an avant-garde). Why they have recently made an effective appearance within the documentary domain is a matter requiring further exploration. I suspect we are dealing with more than a reaction to the limitations of the currently dominant interview-based form. Large cultural preferences concerning the voicing of dramatic as well as documentary material seem to be changing. In any event, the most recent appearances of self-reflexive strategies correspond very clearly to deficiencies in attempts to translate highly ideological, written anthropological practices into a proscriptive agenda for a visual anthropology (neutrality, descriptiveness, objectivity, "just the facts," and so on). It is very heartening to see that the realm of the possible for documentary film has now expanded to include strategies of reflexivity that may eventually serve political as well as scientific ends.

Notes

1. Many of the distinctive characteristics of documentary are examined broadly in *Ideology and the Image* (Bloomington: Indiana University Press, 1981), pp. 170–284. Here I shall concentrate on more recent films and some of the particular problems they pose.

2. Films referred to in the article or instrumental in formulating the issues of self-reflexive documentary form include: *The Atomic Cafe* (USA, Kevin Rafferty, Jayne Loader, Pierce Rafferty, 1982), *Controlling Interest* (USA, SF Newsreel, 1978), *The Day After Trinity* (USA, Jon Else, 1980), *Harlan County, USA* (USA, Barbara Kopple, 1976), *Hollywood on Trial* (USA, David Halpern, Jr., 1976), *Models* (USA, Fred Wiseman, 1981), *Nuove Frontieras (Looking for Better Dreams)* (Switzerland, Remo Legnazzi, 1981), *On Company Business* (USA, Allan Francovich, 1981), *Prison for Women* (Canada, Janice Cole, Holly Dale, 1981), *Rape* (USA, Jo Ann Elam, 1977), *A Respectable Life* (Sweden, Stefan Jarl, 1980), *Rosie the Riveter* (USA, Connie Field, 1980), *The Sad Song of Yellow Skin* (Canada, NFB—Michael Rubbo, 1970), *Soldier Girls* (USA, Nick Broomfield, Joan Churchill, 1981), *They Call Us Misfits* (Sweden, Jan Lindquist, Stefan Jarl, c. 1969), *This Is Not a Love Story* (Canada, NFB—Bonnie Klein, 1981), *The Trials of Alger Hiss* (USA, John Lowenthal, 1980), *Union Maids* (USA, Jim Klein, Julia Reichert, Miles Mogulescu, 1976), *Who Killed the Fourth Ward?* (USA, James Blue, 1978), *The Wilmar 8* (USA, Lee Grant, 1980), *With Babies and Banners* (USA, Women's Labor History Film Project, 1978), *A Wive's Tale* (Canada, Sophie Bissonnette, Martin Duckworth, Joyce Rock, 1980), *The Wobblies* (USA, Stuart Bird, Deborah Shaffer, 1979), *Word Is Out* (USA, Mariposa Collective, 1977).

3. Perhaps the farthest extremes of evidence and argument occur with pornography and propaganda: what would pornography be without its evidence, what would propaganda be without its arguments?

4. Without models of documentary strategy that invite us to reflect on the construction of social reality, we have only a corrective act of negation ("this is not reality, it is neither omniscient nor objective") rather than an affirmative act of comprehension ("this is a text, these are its assumptions, this is the meaning it produces"). The lack of an invitation to assume a positive stance handicaps us in our efforts to understand the position we occupy; refusing a position proffered to us is far from affirming a position we actively construct. It is similar to the difference between refusing to "buy" the messages conveyed by advertising, at least entirely, while still lacking any alternative non-fetishistic presentation of commodities that can help us gain a different "purchase" on their relative use- and exchange-value. In many ways, this problem of moving from refusal to affirmation, from protest at the way things are to the construction of durable alternatives, is precisely the problem of the American left. Modernist strategies have something to contribute to the resolution of this problem.

5. After completing this article, I read Jeffrey Youdelman's "Narration, Invention and History" (*Cineaste*, 12:2, pp. 8–15) which makes a similar point with a somewhat different set of examples. His discussion of imaginative, lyrical uses of commentary in the thirties and forties is particularly instructive.

6. Details of de Antonio's approach are explored in Tom Waugh's "Emile de Antonio and the New Documentary of the Seventies," *Jump Cut* no. 10–11 (1976), pp. 33–39, reprinted here, and of Wiseman's in my *Ideology and the Image*, pp. 208–36.

7. An informative discussion of the contradiction between character witnesses with unusual abilities and the rhetorical attempt to make them signifiers of ordinary workers, particularly in *Union Maids,* occurs in Noel King's "Recent 'Political' Documentary — Notes on *Union Maids* and *Harlan County, USA*," *Screen* 22, no. 2 (1981): 7–18.

8. In this vein, Noel King comments: "So in the case of these documentaries (*Union Maids, With Babies and Banners, Harlan County, USA*) we might notice the way a discourse of morals or ethics suppresses one of politics and the way a discourse of a subject's individual responsibility suppresses any notion of a discourse on the social and linguistic formation of subjects" ("Recent 'Political' Documentary," p. 11). But we might also say, as the film makers seem to, "This is how the participants saw their struggle and it is well worth preserving" even though we may wish they did not do so slavishly. There is a difference between criticizing films because they fail to demonstrate the theoretical sophistication of certain analytic methodologies and criticizing them because their textual organization is inadequate to the phenomena they describe.

BEYOND OBSERVATIONAL CINEMA

DAVID MACDOUGALL

Following up on his article in the first volume of Movies and Methods, *David MacDougall here assesses the strengths and weaknesses of observational cinema's contribution to ethnographic film and concludes with a call for an alternative, participatory cinema. In the context in which representatives of one culture film representatives of another, MacDougall finds the "curiously lonely" approach of* cinéma vérité *dehumanizing. It denies the fact, let alone the complexity, of the filmmaking encounter itself, an event that in many ways recapitulates both the origins of anthropology in an imperialist era and the continuing process of acculturation. As MacDougall notes, "Beside such an extraordinary event, the search for isolation and invisibility seems a curiously irrelevant ambition."*

*His alternative approach involves an acknowledgement of the filmmaker's participation in the making of meaning. MacDougall argues that, in many instances, the underlying significance of events will not be apparent from everyday behavior and that the filmmaker's intervention and inquiries can help to "peel back the layers of culture and reveal its fundamental assumptions." This tactic, which David and Judith MacDougall exemplify supremely well in their Turkana trilogy (*Lorang's Way, Wedding Camels, *and* A Wife Among Wives*) is formulated principally by the filmmaker's intervention (for example, by requesting undirected discussion of a given topic), not by the act of viewing. As described here, participatory cinema may not acknowledge the act of participation in a way that the viewer can recognize, and it may thereby adopt the appearance of the* cinéma vérité *style that it seeks to replace. At the same time, the filmmaker's intervention can be acknowledged through textual conventions accessible to the viewer, such as interviews, audible questions, or comments directed to the filmmaker, camera, or viewer or interviews constructed in such a way as to call into question the convention of interviewing itself, as the MacDougalls do in* Wedding Camels. *At this point, the conception of participatory cinema begins to join modernist film aesthetics and structuralist methodologies, although it retains the "essential surface" of cinematic observation. It is precisely such a combination of the photographic record with the production of meaning that requires us to acknowledge the distinctive characteristics and qualities of a visual rather than a written anthropology.*

•

Truth is not a Holy Grail to be won: it is a shuttle which moves ceaselessly between the observer and the observed, between science and reality. —Edgar Morin

The past few years have seen a recommitment to the principle of observation in documentary filmmaking. The result has been fresh interest in the documentary film and a body of work which has separated itself clearly from the traditions of Grierson and Vertov.[1] Audiences have had restored to them the sense of wonder at witnessing the spontaneity of life that they felt in the early days of the cinema, seeing a train rush into the Gare de Ciotat. This sense has not grown out of the perfection of some new illusion, but out of a fundamental change in the relationship that filmmakers have sought to establish between their subjects and the viewer. The significance of that relationship for the practice of social science is now beginning to be felt as a major force in the ethnographic film. This would seem an appropriate moment to discuss the implications of the observational cinema as a mode of human inquiry.

In the past anthropologists were accustomed to taking their colleagues' descriptions of faith. It was rare to know more about a remote people than the person who had studied them, and one accepted his analysis largely because one accepted the scholarly tradition that had produced him. Few monographs offered precise methodological information or substantial texts as documentary evidence.

Ethnographic films were rarely more liberal in this regard. The prevailing style of filming and film editing tended to break a continuum of events into mere illustrative fragments. On top of this, ethnographic filmmaking was a haphazard affair. It was never employed systematically or enthusiastically by anthropologists as a whole. *Moana* (Flaherty, 1926) was the work of a geologist and explorer, *Grass* (Cooper and Schoedsack, 1925) of casual adventurers who later went on to make *King Kong* (1933). Until very recently most ethnographic films were the by-products of other endeavors: the chronicles of travelers, the political or idealistic visions of documentary filmmakers, and the occasional forays of anthropologists whose major commitment was to other methods. In most cases these films announced their own inadequacies. When they did not, neither were they wholly persuasive. One often wondered what had been concealed or created by the editing, the framing, or the narrator's commentary.

Even as good a film as *The Hunters* (Marshall, 1958) left important areas of doubt. Could one accept that this was how the !Kung conducted long hunts, given the fact that the film was compiled from a series of shorter ones? In Robert Gardner's *Dead Birds* (1963), how could one know that the thoughts attributed to the subjects were what they might really have been thinking?

Over the past few years ethnographic filmmakers have looked for solutions to such problems, and the new approaches to filming within our society have provided most of them. By focussing upon discrete events rather than upon mental constructs or impressions, and by seeking to render faithfully the natural sounds, structure, and duration of events, the filmmaker hopes to provide the viewer with sufficient evidence to judge for himself the film's larger analysis. Films like Marshall's *An Argument About a Marriage* (1969), Sandall's *Emu Ritual at Ruguri* (1969), and Asch's *The Feast* (1969) are all attempts of this kind. They are "observational" in their manner of filming, placing the viewer in the role of an observer, a witness of events. They are essentially revelatory rather than illustrative, for they explore substance before theory. They are, nevertheless, evidence of what the filmmaker finds significant.

To those of us who began making ethnographic films at the time that *cinéma vérité* and American direct cinema were revolutionizing documentary filmmaking, this approach to filming other cultures seemed all but inevitable. Its promise for social science appeared so obvious that it was difficult to understand the years of unrealized potential. Why, we often wondered, with time running out to document the world's vanishing cultures, had it not been anthropologists rather than journalists who had first fashioned such a use for the cinema and struggled for its perfection?

The observational direction in ethnographic filmmaking had, after all, begun vigorously enough. The very invention of the cinema was in part a response to the desire to observe the physical behavior of men and animals (Muybridge, 1887; Marey, 1893). Regnault and Baldwin Spencer quickly went beyond the popular interests of Lumière, making essentially observational film records of technology and ritual in traditional societies. Flaherty's work, for all its reflection of his own idealism, was rooted in the careful exploration of other people's lives. It heralded the achievements of such diverse filmmakers as Cooper and Schoedsack among the Bakhtiari of Iran, Stocker and Tindale in Australia, and Bateson and Mead in Bali. From then on, the ethnographic film fell heir to the fragmentation of image that had originated in the Soviet cinema and that began to dominate the documentary film with the coming of sound.

It could be said that the notion of the synchronous-sound ethnographic film was born at the moment Baldwin Spencer decided to take both an Edison cylinder recorder and a Warwick camera to Central Australia in 1901. It became a practical possibility in the late 1920's only to be neglected in documentary films until the 1950's. In 1935 Arthur Elton and Edgar Anstey demonstrated what could have been done more widely by taking sound cameras, bulky as they then were, into the slums of Stepney and documenting the lives of the inhabitants.[2] To say that they were ahead of their time is only to note with regret that they should not have been.

When highly portable synchronous-sound cameras were finally developed around 1960, few ethnographic filmmakers jumped at the chance to use them although long awaiting this event. Two exceptions were Jean Rouch in France and John Marshall in the United States. Indeed, Rouch's influence was to become a major force in European filmmaking. Marshall had already practised a makeshift kind of synchronous-sound filming in the 1950's among the !Kung and Gwi of the Kalahari. His observational approach foreshadowed the discoveries of the Drew Associates group and the Canadian Film Board in North America, although the originality of his early work only became evident with the release, long after *The Hunters,* of additional material from his Peabody-Harvard-Kalahari expeditions.

Filmmakers who followed an observational approach quickly divided along methodological lines. Unlike the followers of Rouch, those in the English-speaking world were hesitant to interact in any way with their subjects, except occasionally to interview them. Their adherence to this principle had an almost religious fervor and asceticism, as distinct from the speculative European approach as Calvinism is from Roman Catholicism.

It is this self-denying tendency of modern observational cinema that I should like to examine in particular. It is the tradition in which I was trained, and it has an obvious affinity to certain classical notions of scientific method. But this very orthodoxy could well make it a dangerously narrow model for ethnographic film-makers of the future.

Many of us who began applying an observational approach to ethnographic filmmaking found ourselves taking as our model not the documentary film as we had come to know it since Grierson, but the dramatic fiction film, in all its incarnations from Tokyo to Hollywood. This paradox resulted from the fact that of the two, the fiction film was the more observational in attitude. Documentaries of the previous thirty years had celebrated the sensibility of the filmmaker in confronting reality; they had rarely explored the flow of real events. Although this style had produced such masterpieces as Basil Wright's *Song of Ceylon* (1934) and Willard Van Dyke and Ralph Steiner's *The City* (1939), it was a style of synthesis, a style that used images to develop an argument or impression.

Each of the discrete images of such documentaries was the bearer of a predetermined meaning. They were often articulated like the images of a poem, juxtaposed against an asynchronous soundtrack of music or commentary. Indeed, poetry was sometimes integral to their conception, as in *The River* (Lorentz, 1937), *Night Mail* (Wright and Watt, 1936), and *Coalface* (Cavalcanti, 1936).

In contrast to this iconographic approach, the images of the fiction film were largely anecdotal. They were the pieces of evidence from which one deduced a story. The audience was told little. It was presented with a series of contiguous events. It learned by observing.

It seemed that such a relationship between viewer and subject should be possible with materials found in the real world. In our own society this had indeed become the approach of filmmakers like Leacock and the Maysles, who were fond of quoting Tolstoy's declaration that the cinema would make the invention of stories unnecessary. For the few of us interested in filming in other cultures, the films of the Italian neorealist period, with their emphasis upon the economic and social environment, seemed like mirror-images of the films we hoped could be made from real events in the ongoing lives of traditional peoples.

The natural voice of the fiction film is the third person: the camera observes the actions of the characters not as a participant but as an invisible presence, capable of assuming a variety of positions. To approximate such an approach in the nonfiction film, the filmmaker must find ways of making himself privy to human events without disturbing them. This is relatively easy when the event attracts more attention than the camera—what Morin (1962:4) calls "intensive sociality." It becomes difficult when a few people are interacting in an informal situation. Yet documentary filmmakers have been so successful in achieving this goal that scenes of the most intimate nature have been recorded without apparent embarrassment or pretense on the part of the subjects. The usual method is to spend so much time with one's subjects that they lose interest in the camera. Finally they must go on with their lives, and they do so in their accustomed ways. This may seem improbable to those who have not seen it happen, yet to filmmakers it is a familiar phenomenon.

In my own work I have often been struck by the readiness of people to accept being filmed, even in societies where one might expect a camera to be particularly threatening. This acceptance is of course aided by de-emphasizing the actual process of filming, both in one's manner and technique. While making *To Live with Herds* (1972) among the Jie of Uganda I used a special brace which allowed me to keep the camera in the filming position for twelve or more hours a day over a period of many weeks. I lived looking through the viewfinder. Because the camera ran noiselessly, my subjects soon gave up trying to decide when I was filming and when I was not. As far as they were concerned I was always filming, an assumption which no doubt contributed to their confidence that their lives were being seen fully and fairly. When I took out a still camera at the end of my stay everyone began posing—a clear sign that they had understood an essential quality of the cinema.

I would suggest that at times people can behave more naturally while being filmed than in the presence of an ordinary observer. A man with a camera has an obvious job to do, which is to film. His subjects understand this and leave him to it. He remains occupied, half-hidden behind his machine, satisfied to be left alone. As an unencumbered visitor, he would have to be entertained, whether as a guest or as a friend. In this, I think, lies both the strength and the weakness of the observational method.

The purpose behind this curiously lonely approach of observational cinema is arguably to film things that would have occurred if one had not been there. It is a desire for the invisibility of the imagination found in literature combined with the aseptic touch of the surgeon's glove—in some cases a legitimization, in the name of art or science, of the voyeur's peephole. It has even been reduced to a formula for anthropology:

Ethnographic film is film which endeavors to interpret the behavior of people of one culture to persons of another culture by using shots of people doing precisely what they would have been doing if the camera were not there (Goldschmidt, 1972).

Invisibility and omniscience. From this desire it is not a great leap to begin viewing the camera as a secret weapon in the pursuit of knowledge. The self-effacement of the filmmaker begins to efface the limitations of his own physicality. He and his camera are imperceptibly endowed with the power to witness the TOTALITY of an event. Indeed, they are expected to. Omniscience and omnipotence.

It is an approach that has produced some remarkable films. And for many filmmakers it has in practice a comforting lack of ambiguity. The filmmaker establishes a role for himself which demands no social response from his subjects, and he then disappears into the woodwork. Allan King's *Warrendale* (1966) and *A Married Couple* (1969) make the audience witnesses of scenes of private emotional anguish without reference to the presence of the film crew. In a film like *At the Winter Sea Ice Camp, Part II* (Balikci, 1968), from the Netsilik Eskimo series, the people seem altogether oblivious of Robert Young's camera. And in Frederick Wiseman's *Essene* (1972), a study of people striving painfully to live communally in a religious order, one has at times the curious sense of being the eye of God.

When films like these are functioning at their best, the people in them seem bearers of the immeasurable wealth and effort of human experience. Their lives have a weight that makes the film that caught but a fragment seem trivial, and we sit in a kind of awe of our own privileged observation of them. That emotion helps us accept the subjects' disregard of the filmmaker. For them to notice him would amount almost to a sacrilege—a shattering of the horizons of their lives, which by all rights should not include someone making a film about them. In the same way, some scholars are disturbed by descriptions of traditional societies in which the anthropologist is a feature of cultural contact.

Audiences are thus accomplices in the filmmaker's voluntary absence from his film—what Leacock calls "the pretense of our not being there" (Levin 1971: 204). From a scientific standpoint, the priorities of research also keep the filmmaker out, because to pay attention to him is to draw valuable time from the subject at hand. Finally, the literature and films we have grown up with have shaped our expectations: Aeneas is unaware of Virgil; the couple on the bed ignores the production crew of twenty standing round. Even in home movies people wince when someone looks at the camera.

Filmmakers begin as members of an audience and carry part of that inheritance with them. But the act of filming tends to interpose its own barriers between the observer and the observed. For one thing, it is difficult for a filmmaker to photograph himself as an element in the phenomenon he is examining—unless, like Jean Rouch and Edgar Morin in *Chronique d'un été* (1961), he becomes an "actor" before the camera. More often it is through his voice and the response of his subjects that we feel his presence.

Perhaps more important, the filmmaker exhausts most of his energy making his camera respond to what is before it. His concentration induces a certain passivity from which it is difficult for him to rouse himself. Active participation with his subjects suggests an altogether different psychic state. This may explain the rather frequent success of film as a contemplative art.

Among ethnographic filmmakers, another restraint is the special reverence that surrounds the study of isolated peoples. The fragility of these cultures and the rarity of filming them turns the filmmaker into an instrument of history—an obligation which, if accepted or even felt, must necessarily weigh down his efforts to pursue specific lines of inquiry.

This lofty view is often reinforced by an identification with his audience that may cause him to mimic, consciously or otherwise, their impotence. As members of an audience we readily accept the illusion of entering into the world of a film. But we do so in complete safety, because our own world is as close as the nearest light switch. We observe the people in the film without being seen, assured that they can make no claims upon us. The corollary of this, however, lies in our inability to reach through the screen and affect their lives. Thus our situation combines a sense of immediacy with an absolute separation. Only when we try to invade the world of the film do we discover the insubstantiality of its illusion of reality.

In his attempt to make us into witnesses, the observational filmmaker often thinks in terms of the image on the screen rather than his presence in the setting where events are occurring. He becomes no more than the eye of the audience, frozen into their passivity, unable to bridge the separation between himself and his subjects.

But it is finally scientific objectives that have placed the severest strictures on ethnographic film. Inevitably, the extraordinary precision of the camera-eye as a descriptive aid has influenced conceptions of the use to which film should be put, with the result that for years anthropologists have considered film pre-eminently as a tool for gathering data. And because film deals so overwhelmingly with the specific rather than the abstract, it is often considered incapable of serious intellectual articulation.

Certainly there are enough ethnographic films containing crude or dubious interpretations to explain, if not to justify, such a conclusion. Films risking more legitimate, if more difficult, kinds of analysis are often flawed in the attempt. Still others receive no credit because their contribution exists in a form that cannot be assessed in the terms of conventional anthropology. Each of these instances adds weight to the common impression that attempts to use film as an original medium of anthropology are simply pretexts for self-indulgence. What is more, each attempt that fails can be viewed as an opportunity lost to add to the fund of more routine ethnography.

With data-gathering as the objective, there is of course no real need for the making of films, but merely for the collection of footage upon which a variety of studies can later be based. Indeed, Sorenson (1967) suggests that footage might be collected with only this broad objective in view. Yet much bad anthropological writing is a similar gathering and cataloguing of information, deficient in thought or analysis. This is not far from the criticism that Evans-Pritchard levels at Malinowski:

> The theme is no more than a descriptive synthesis of events. It is not a theoretical integration . . . There is consequently no real standard of relevance, since everything has a time and space relationship in cultural reality to everything else, and from whatever point one starts one spreads oneself over the same ground (1962: 95).

The same criticism could be made of many existing ethnographic films. If it is a valid criticism, if ethnographic film is to become anything more than a form of anthropological note-taking, then attempts must continue to make it a medium of ideas. There will inevitably be more failures. But it seems probable that the great films of anthropology, as distinct from ethnography, are still to be made.

Curiously, it is the survival of the data within the context of thought, inescapable in the cinema, that is responsible for the impatience of many social scientists with film as a medium for anthropology. The glimpse gained of the original field situation may be so immediate and evocative that it proves tantalizing to those who would like to see more, and infuriating to those whose specific theoretical interests are not being served. Thus an ecologist may well dismiss as shallow a film in which the study of social relationships takes precedence over ecology.

Films prove to be poor encyclopedias because of their emphasis upon specific and delimited events viewed from finite perspectives. Yet surprisingly, it is often the supposed potency of film in this capacity that has led to its downfall. At first glance, film seems to offer an escape from the inadequacies of human perception and a factual check on the capriciousness of human interpretation. The precision of the photographic image leads to an uncritical faith in the camera's power to capture, not the images of events, but the events themselves—as Ruskin once said of some photographs of Venice, "as if a magician had reduced reality to be carried away into an enchanted land" (1886–1887:341). So persuasive is this belief in the magic of photography that it is assumed by scholars who in the rest of their research would challenge far more circumspect assumptions. When disillusionment comes, it is therefore profound.

The magical fallacy of the camera parallels the fallacy of omniscient observation. It may result from a tendency in viewing films to define what has been photographed by what one is seeing. The film image impresses us with its completeness, partly because of its precise rendering of detail, but even more because it represents a continuum of reality which extends beyond the edges of the frame and which therefore, paradoxically, seems not to be excluded. A few images create a world. We ignore the images that could have been, but weren't. In most cases we have no conception of what they might be.

It is possible that the sense of completeness created by a film also lies in the richness of ambiguity of the photographic image. Images begin to become signs of the objects they represent; yet unlike words or even pictographs, they share in the physical identity of the objects, having been produced as a kind of photochemical imprint of them. The image thus continually asserts the presence of the concrete world within the framework of a communicative system that imposes meaning.

The viewfinder of the camera, one could say, has the opposite function of the gunsight that a soldier levels at his enemy. The latter frames an image for annihilation; the former frames an image for preservation, thereby annihilating the surrounding multitude of images which could have been formed at that precise point in time and space. The image becomes a piece of evidence, like a potsherd. It also becomes, through the denial of all other possible images, a reflection of thought. In that double nature is the magic that can so easily dazzle us.

Observational cinema is based upon a process of selection. The filmmaker limits himself to that which occurs naturally and spontaneously in front of his camera. The richness of human behavior and the propensity of people to talk about their affairs, past and present, are what allow this method of inquiry to succeed.

It is, nevertheless, a method that is quite foreign to the usual practice of anthropology or, for that matter, most other disciplines. (Two exceptions are history and astronomy, which the barriers of time and distance require to function in the same way.) Most anthropological fieldwork involves, in addition to observation, an active search for information among informants. In the laboratory sciences, knowledge comes primarily from events that the scientist himself provokes. Thus the observational filmmaker finds himself cut off from many of the channels that normally characterize human inquiry. He is dependent for his understanding (or for the understanding of his audience) upon the unprovoked ways in which his subjects manifest the patterns of their lives during the moments he is filming them. He is denied access to anything they know but take for granted, anything latent in their culture which events do not bring to the surface.

The same methodological asceticism that causes him to exclude himself from the world of his subjects also excludes his subjects from the world of the film. Here the implications are ethical as well as practical. By asking nothing of his subjects beyond permission to film them, the filmmaker adopts an inherently secretive position. He has no need for further explanation, no need to communicate with his subjects on the basis of the thinking that organizes his work. There is, in fact, some reason for him not to do so for fear it may influence their behavior. In his insularity, he withholds the very openness that he asks from his subjects in order to film them.

In his refusal to give his subjects access to the film, the filmmaker refuses them access to himself, for this is clearly his most important activity when he is among them. In denying a part of his own humanity, he denies a part of theirs. If not in his personal demeanor, then in the significance of his working method, he inevitably reaffirms the colonial origins of anthropology. It was once the European who decided what was worth knowing about "primitive" peoples and what they in turn should be taught. The shadow of that attitude falls across the observational film, giving it a distinctively Western parochialism. The traditions of science and narrative art combine in this instance to dehumanize the study of man. It is a form in which the observer and the observed exist in separate worlds, and it produces films that are monologues.

What is finally disappointing in the ideal of filming "as if the camera were not there" is not that observation in itself is unimportant, but that as a governing approach it remains far less interesting than exploring the situation that actually exists. The camera is there, and it is held by a representative of one culture encountering another. Beside such an extraordinary event, the search for isolation and invisibility seems a curiously irrelevant ambition. No ethnographic film is merely a record of another society: it is always a record of the meeting between a filmmaker and that society. If ethnographic films are to break through the limitations inherent in their present idealism, they must propose to deal with that encounter. Until now they have rarely acknowledged that an encounter has taken place.

The main achievement of observational cinema is that it has once again taught the camera how to watch. Its failings lie precisely in the attitude of watching— the reticence and analytical inertia it induces in filmmakers, some of whom feel themselves agents of a universal truth, others of whom comment only slyly or by indirection from behind their material. In either case, the relationship between the observer, the observed, and the viewer has a kind of numbness.

Beyond observational cinema lies the possibility of a PARTICIPATORY CINEMA, bearing witness to the "event" of the film and making strengths of what most films are at pains to conceal. Here the filmmaker acknowledges his entry upon the world of his subjects and yet asks them to imprint directly upon the film their own culture. This should not imply a relaxation of the filmmaker's purposeful-ness, nor should it cause him to abandon the perspective that an outsider can bring to another culture. By revealing his role, the filmmaker enhances the value of his material as evidence. By entering actively into the world of his subjects, he can provoke a greater flow of information about them. By giving them access to the film, he makes possible the corrections, additions, and illuminations that only their response to the material can elicit. Through such an exchange a film can begin to reflect the ways in which its subjects perceive the world.

This is a process that goes back to Flaherty. Nanook participated in creating the film about himself, "constantly thinking up new hunting scenes for the film" (Flaherty 1950:15). During the filming of *Moana,* Flaherty projected his rushes each evening, building upon the suggestions that came from his subjects. Yet with the exception of Jean Rouch, few filmmakers today are able or willing to invite such insights.

To the degree that the elements of one culture are not describable in the terms of another, the ethnographic filmmaker must devise ways of bringing the viewer into the social experience of his subjects. This is partly an act of analysis, partly what Redfield called "the art of social science." But it can also be a process of collaboration—the filmmaker combining the skills and sensibilities of his sub-jects with his own. This requires that they and he, whatever their differences, be moved by at least some common sense of urgency.

Rouch and Morin's *Chronique d' un été,* about a disparate group of young Pari-sians, explores their lives within the context of their interest in the film itself. Despite the anonymity of the actual cameramen[3] (which is unfortunate), there is no pact made with the audience to ignore the role of the film's makers. On the contrary, it is the making of the film that binds them and their subjects together.

Chronique d' un été is an elaborate experiment which one would probably not expect to see transferred intact to a traditional society. Yet it is remarkable how few of the ideas of this extraordinary film managed to penetrate the thinking of ethnographic filmmakers in the decade after it was made. The approach proved too alien to an effort preoccupied with the needs of teaching or the urgency of preserving overall records of imperiled societies.

It is, of course, the value of such records that is open to question. They may be unable to answer future anthropological questions except in the most general manner. An exhaustive analysis of a social phenomenon usually requires that the data be collected with the full extent of that phenomenon in mind. It is clear from the body of Rouch's work that he views broad salvage anthropology, based upon no defined perspective, as more hazardous to the future understanding of extinct societies—and therefore to an understanding of man—than a study in which the investigator is passionately and intellectually engaged. If acutely perceived, he seems to say, the part may stand more accurately for the whole than the survey, which succeeds only in capturing the most superficial aspects of the whole. This is at odds with the view of Lévi-Strauss (1972) that anthropology is like astronomy, seeing human societies from after and only discerning their brightest constellations.

In Rouch's approach anthropology must therefore proceed by digging from within rather than observing from without, which all too easily gives an illusory sense of comprehension. Digging necessarily disturbs the successive strata through which one passes to reach one's goal. But there is a significant difference between this human archaeology and its material counterpart: culture is pervasive and expresses itself in all the acts of human beings, whether they are responding to customary or extraordinary stimuli. The values of a society lie as much in its dreams as in the reality it has built. Often it is only by introducing new stimuli that the investigator can peel back the layers of a culture and reveal its fundamental assumptions.

In the film that James Blue and I made among the Boran of Kenya (MacDougall and Blue, 1973), some of the information revealed resulted from just such a process. Without the participation of our subjects, certain aspects of their situation might well have remained unexpressed. Once, during a typical men's conversation over tea, we asked a man named Guyo Ali to raise the subject of the government's advocacy of birth control. The result was an explosion of disagreement from Iya Duba, the most conservative old man present. In his reply, he set forth his view of the logic of having many children in a pastoral society, followed by an impassioned defense of cattle and cattle herding, which he was unlikely to have delivered without some such strong provocation. It was in fact the clearest expression of Boran economic values that we encountered during our stay.

Involvement with one's subjects can become a kind of pose—the fleeting recognition of the film crew which gives a sense of candor but really reveals nothing. For a film to gain meaning from the breakdown of old narrative conventions, that recognition must develop into a genuine conversation.

Sometimes one hears only half of the conversation. The oldest examples go back to those ruminative testimonies of lonely people, of which *Paul Tomkowicz: Street-Railway Switch Man* (Kroitor, 1954) is perhaps the archetype and Jorge Preloran's *Imaginero* (1970) the most convincing document. Sometimes it becomes a performance—the compulsive talking of a subject stimulated by the camera, as in Shirley Clarke's *Portrait of Jason* (1967) or Tanya Ballantyne's *The Things I Cannot Change* (1967). The out-of-work father in the latter film cannot resist the offer to control the image of himself presented to the world. Yet he bears out Rouch's dictum: whatever he tries to be, he is only more himself.

Sometimes role-playing provides the necessary stimulus. In Rouch's *Jaguar* (1958–1967) his young protagonists respond to the invitation to act out an adventure for which they have long been eager. They use the pretext of the story to reveal a private image of themselves, just as Marcelline in *Chronique d'un été* uses the pretext of a film role to speak of her painful return from a concentration camp.

This is a kind of participation, but it remains one in which the film manipulates its subjects. A further step will be films in which participation occurs in the very conception and recognizes common goals. That possibility remains all but unexplored—a filmmaker putting himself at the disposal of his subjects and, with them, inventing the film.

The promise of a useful relationship between film and anthropology is still crippled by timidity on both sides. Its fulfillment will require an enlarging of the acceptable forms of both film and anthropology. Anthropology must admit forms of understanding which replace those of the written word. Film must create forms of expression reflecting anthropological thought. Films, rather than speculation, will finally demonstrate whether these possibilities are real. Ethnographic film-makers can begin by abandoning their preconceptions about what is good cinema. It is enough to conjecture that a film need not be an aesthetic or scientific per-formance: it can become the arena of an inquiry.

Notes

1. Many consider Vertov the father of observational cinema, and to the extent that he was committed to penetrating the existing world with the "kino eye" there can be no doubt of his influence. But Vertov's films reflected the prevailing Soviet preoccupation with syn-thesis, taking their temporal and spatial structures more from the perceptual psychology of the observer than from structures of the events being filmed. His was not a cinema of duration, in the sense that Bazin attributes it to Flaherty.

2. *Housing Problems,* made for the British Commercial Gas Association.

3. Roger Morillère, Raoul Coutard, Jean-Jacques Tarbès, and Michel Brault.

References

LITERATURE

EVANS-PRITCHARD, E. E.
1962   *Social anthropology and other essays.* Glencoe: Free Press.

FLAHERTY, ROBERT J.
1950   "Robert Flaherty talking," in *The cinema 1950.* Edited by R. Manvell. Har-mondsworth: Penguin.

GOLDSCHMIDT, WALTER
1972   Ethnographic film: definition and exegesis. *PIEF Newsletter of the American An-thropological Association* 3 (2): 1–3.

LEVIN, G. ROY
1971   *Documentary explorations.* New York: Doubleday.

MAREY, ÉTIENNE
1883   Emploi des photographies partielles pour étudier la locomotion de l'homme et des animaux. *Comptes rendus de l'Académie des Sciences* (Paris) 96: 1827–1831.

MORIN, EDGAR
1962   "Preface," in *The cinema and social science; a survey of ethnographic and socio-logical films,* by Luc de Heusch, 4–6. Reports and Papers in the Social Sciences 16. Paris: UNESCO.

MUYBRIDGE, EADWEARD
1887   *Animal locomotion: an electro-photographic investigation of consecutive phases of animal movements,* 16 volumes. Philadelphia: J. B. Lippincott Company.

RUSKIN, JOHN
1886–1887   *Praeterita: outlines of scenes and thoughts, perhaps worthy of memory, in my past life.* (New edition 1949, London: R. Hart Davis.)

SORENSON, E. RICHARD
1967   A research film program in the study of changing man. *Current Anthropology* 8: 443–469.

FILMS

ASCH, TIMOTHY

1968   *The Feast.* Center for Documentary Anthropology.

BALIKCI, ASEN

1968   *At the Winter Sea Ice Camp, Part II.* Educational Development Center.

BALLANTYNE, TANYA

1967   *The Things I Cannot Change.* National Film Board of Canada.

CAVALCANTI, ALBERTO

1936   *Coalface.* GPO (General Post Office) Film Unit.

CLARKE, SHIRLEY

1967   *Portrait of Jason.* Produced in association with Film Makers Distribution Center.

COOPER, MERIAN C., ERNEST B. SCHOEDSACK

1925   *Grass.* Famous-Players-Lasky.

1933   *King Kong.* RKO.

ELTON, ARTHUR, EDGAR ANSTEY

1935   *Housing Problems.* British Commercial Gas Association.

FLAHERTY, ROBERT J.

1922   *Nanook of the North.* Revillon Frères.

1926   *Moana, a Romance of the Golden Age.* Famous-Players-Lasky.

GARDNER, ROBERT

1963   *Dead Birds.* Film Study Center, Harvard University.

KING, ALLAN

1966   *Warrendale.* Allan King Associates.

1969   *A Married Couple.* Allan King Associates.

KROITOR, ROMAN

1953   *Paul Tomkowicz: Street-Railway Switch Man.* National Film Board of Canada.

LÉVI-STRAUSS, CLAUDE

1972   Interview with Edwin Newman, on *Speaking Freely.* ORTF-NET.

LORENTZ, PARE

1937   *The River.* Farm Security Administration.

MACDOUGALL, DAVID

1972   *To Live With Herds.* Film Images.

MACDOUGALL, DAVID, JAMES BLUE

1973   *Kenya Boran.* American Universities Field Staff.

MARSHALL, JOHN

1958   *The Hunters.* Film Study Center, Harvard University.

1969   *An Argument About a Marriage.* Center for Documentary Anthropology.

PRELORAN, JORGE

1970   *Imaginero.* Image Resources.

ROUCH, JEAN

1958–1967   *Jaguar.* Les Films de la Pléiade.

ROUCH, JEAN, EDGAR MORIN

1961   *Chronique d' un été.* Les Films de la Pléiade.

SANDALL, ROGER

1969   *Emu Ritual at Ruguri.* Australian Institute of Aboriginal Studies.

VAN DYKE, WILLARD, RALPH STEINER

1939   *The City.* American Documentary Films, Inc., for American Institute of Planners.

WISEMAN, FREDERICK

1972   *Essene.* Zipporah Films.

WRIGHT, BASIL

1934   *Song of Ceylon.* Ceylon Tea Propaganda Board.

WRIGHT, BASIL, HARRY WATT

1936   *Night Mail.* GPO (General Post Office) Film Unit.

THE AVANT-GARDE: HISTORY AND THEORIES

CONSTANCE PENLEY
AND JANET BERGSTROM

One of the most pervasive assumptions of film criticism informed by a semiotic, poststructural perspective is that challenges to the formal conventions of cinema will simultaneously be challenges to the habitual reception of cinema. The notion extends at least as far back as the Russian Formalists, and it has gradually prompted semiotic criticism to go beyond conventional narrative cinema to the avant-garde, where challenges to formal convention are part of the filmmaker's agenda. But the same notion also means looking at avant-garde cinema for the larger issues that may be at stake: identification, voyeurism, fetishism, the cinematic apparatus, women's image in film, political effect and effectiveness, and narrative itself. In this article, which reviews some recent and prominent writings on the avant-garde, Penley and Bergstrom identify a phenomenological and formalist impetus that leaves most of the larger issues aside. The characteristics that they find in the writings examined are similar to characteristics of the pioneering auteur critics, such individuals as V. F. Perkins, Andrew Sarris, and Robin Wood. These writings are clearly of value, but they adopt some assumptions that preclude engagement with the simultaneously aesthetic and ideological scrutiny of film that Penley and Bergstrom call for. By characterizing both the methodological assumptions of some prominent texts on the avant-garde and the institutional matrix from which these writings have emerged, the authors sharpen our historical perspective on one mode of critical inquiry.

   Characteristically, the emergence of critical detachment from a dominant critical paradigm occurs after an alternative mode of inquiry has gained some prominence. The alternative provides a perspective from which what was once an exhaustive, fully satisfying form of analysis becomes the restricted manifestation of a historically and methodologically limited vision. New assumptions generate new terminology and new ways of asking questions: the qualities of cinema assumed by the phenomenological and romantic critics whom Penley and Bergstrom assess become the effects of a cinematic apparatus that engenders "the illusion of perceptual mastery" and "the creation of a transcendental subject." However, by assuming that their readings are more exhaustive and more satisfying than the writings that they critique, Penley and Bergstrom may also repeat the rhetorical claim that they set out to overturn. P. Adams Sitney exchanged letters with Penley and Bergstrom in Screen *20, nos. 3–4: 151–59. The overall exchange helped to sharpen some issues, and it is recommended as supplementary reading. However, it introduces no significantly new insights, largely because Sitney dismisses semiotics as a "cultish fad." At the same time, he provides additional information. Whether that information supports his own contentions or those of Penley and Bergstrom is another question, on which the reader might keep an open mind.*

●

I

In the introduction to *A History of the American Avant-Garde Cinema*,[1] one of several scholarly treatments of avant-garde film published in the last three or four years, Marilyn Singer emphasises that avant-garde film requires both a new criticism and a new way of looking at film. Enough American critical work now exists on experimental film to enable us to ask if and to what degree it is essentially a new kind of criticism and a new way of looking at film.

Whether known as 'underground', 'independent', 'experimental' or 'avant-garde', this kind of film, produced outside the industry, usually by a single person, almost always on a very low budget, offers distinct challenges to film criticism, which for the most part has concentrated either on Hollywood commercial cinema or, at most, on 'art-house' films like those of Fellini, Antonioni and Bergman. The sixties marked a consolidation of American avant-garde film activity. The success of the film co-ops helped regularise distribution, the growth of film studies in the university ensured a large and serious audience. Anthology Film Archives, exclusively devoted to the avant-garde film, established itself in New York, and the work of the film-makers came to be powerful enough to demand consideration in the context of other American modernist art. Film-makers like Michael Snow, Hollis Frampton, Paul Sharits, Ernie Gehr, Joyce Wieland and Barry Gerson developed an international reputation and experimental film, itself influenced by minimalism and post-minimalism, began to influence the other arts.

All of the recent criticism is a response to this flourishing of American independent film, and, even though scholarly, sees itself as having an active function of supporting this film-making activity and of making the films more widely accessible, both physically and intellectually. Within the formal rigour of this critical work appears a necessary and important promotional tone. However, the desire to le-

gitimise the critical object is bound to insinuate itself into the methodology—
something which up to now has not been sufficiently considered by even the most
theoretically orientated of the new approaches to the avant-garde film. This is not at
all to say that active public support for this kind of cinema and theoretical work on it
should be kept separate. But the desire to 'prove', for example, that these films are
as sophisticated as other modernist art activity, that they have irrevocably changed
the face of *all* art, and that they are the most successful form for 20th-century
epistemological inquiry is going to inflect any presentation of these films' conceptual strategies and material realisations. As Christian Metz points out in his self-
ironic analysis of the metapsychology of the film analyst,[2] any critical discourse
attempting to valorise the object does not address the *properties* of cinematic language *per se;* these properties are offered instead to us as 'resources', 'riches',
'means of expression', this vocabulary revealing a very different project from that
of an analysis of how film functions.

We see this problem most clearly in *The Essential Cinema: Essays on the Films
in the Collection of Anthology Film Archives.*[3] Can a project involving definitively
establishing 'the monuments of cinematic art' (Introduction, p. v), a project
whose stated criteria, determined in advance, are that the films be 'sublime
achievements' and exhibit 'wholeness' and 'unity' (Introduction, *passim*), be
compatible with evolving a theory of film, or even a new kind of criticism? *The
Essential Cinema* permits any critical approach as long as each article substantiates the quality of its chosen monument: Seymour Stern's passionate anecdotal
piece on the making of Griffith's *Intolerance,* in which he offers the remarkable
argument that *'Intolerance, like The Birth of a Nation,* was produced and exhibited
in entire independence of the Hollywood film industry; although made in Hollywood, it was not of Hollywood' (p.37); Ken Kelman's thematic readings of
Buñuel, Vigo, and Bresson, his most controversial position being that Buñuel's
early films like *L' Age d' Or* and *Land Without Bread* were neither 'social criticism'
nor 'revolutionary' but that all of the seemingly 'socially conscious' scenes are
actually only 'counterpoint or background to the main theme and action of love'
(p. 122); P. Adams Sitney's rhetorical analysis of Bresson's *Pickpocket* in which
he catalogues the devices Bresson uses to present his metaphysic of predestina-
tion and acquisition of grace; and Annette Michelson's explicitly phenomenological approach, in which she argues that the important shift in Dziga Vertov's work
was from 'the articulation of a comprehensive and dialectical view of the world to
the exploration of the terrain of consciousness itself' (p. 100), that is, his evolution from an attempt at a historical materialist analysis to the concerns of phenomenology as epistemological enterprise: 'that philosophical phantasm of the
reflexive consciousness, the eye seeing, apprehending itself through its constitution of the world's visibility' (p. 98).

A History of the American Avant-Garde Cinema[4] is much more homogenous and
coherent in terms of its methodology even though its primary function, too, is to
present and explicate films which are almost all in the collection of Anthology Film
Archives, i.e., those films in the constellation of avant-garde masterpieces as
according to Anthology Film Archives. But is it a new criticism? One can see imme-

diately in these articles the much more important influence of the rigorous and thoroughgoing formalist art criticism of the sixties (e.g., *Artforum*) than that of literary criticism, which has up until now been the base of film criticism. Not only the careful descriptive mode, but the categories (when discussing the later 'structural' films) are those of the sixties criticism responding to minimalist and post-minimalist artwork: the function of repetition and other non-causal strategies, the devaluation of interpretation as a mode of viewing, the elimination of psychological interiority, the focus on the spectator's conscious relation to his or her own perceptual and logical activities, the shift of interest away from referential illusion, and an attention to the materials and processes specific to the medium.

But in order to characterise this 'new criticism', this 'new way of looking at film', it is necessary to recall the influence of the work of Annette Michelson on these critics, for the most part either her colleagues or former students. Michelson's approach to film, whether in analyses of Vertov, Eisenstein, Brakhage or Snow, has been explicitly phenomenological. She sees film as *the* 20th-century medium for epistemological inquiry. For her, as a phenomenological critic, the power of film is its striking capacity to serve as a grand metaphor of vision used to trace out the essence of all the activities of consciousness. As she says, 'Epistemological inquiry and cinematic experience converge, as it were, in reciprocal mimesis.'[5] To take a specific example of her phenomenological methodology at work in her analysis of Michael Snow's *Wavelength,* she says of the 45-minute 'zoom' of which the film is comprised: 'The film is a projection of a grand reduction; its "plot" is the tracing of spatio-temporal *données,* its "action" the movement of the camera as the movement of consciousness.'[6] In the work of Michelson, as well as that of P. Adams Sitney, the phenomenological approach is not meant to be an exterior analysis 'applied' to the film; for them, it is a description of both the intentional efforts of the film-makers and an analysis of the *nature* of film; in other words, their critical discourse justifies itself by the belief that their methodology mirrors filmic processes and that film is the perfect phenomenological scene: Merleau-Ponty called film the 'phenomenological art'.[7] In *Visionary Film* P. Adams Sitney finds an historical base for this in the work of Maya Deren: 'The potential for a phenomenology of cinema, which is implied in the notes on *Meditations on Violence,* later came to be realised by Stan Brakhage and Michael Snow, among others, whose achievements can, in part, be traced back to Maya Deren's vision' (p. 29). Sitney refers to the American avant-garde as 'mythologists of consciousness' (p. 332); on Sidney Peterson: 'It is specifically his use of radical techniques as metaphors for perception and consciousness . . . that elaborates Deren's central contribution . . . ' (p. 55); on Gregory Markopoulos: 'The ultimate aspiration of Markopoulos's form has been the mimesis of the human mind. In different degrees and in different ways this might be the aim of the American avant-garde film-maker in general' (p. 142); on Snow: 'In *Back and Forth* (1969) and *The Central Region* (1971) the film-maker elaborates on the metaphor of the moving camera as an imitation of consciousness' (p. 419).

Throughout *A History of the American Avant-Garde Cinema* we see the same emphasis. Writing of Maya Deren's *A Study on Choreography for the Camera* Lucy

Fisher says: 'Thus the fluid transitions of Beatty's dance movements seem to stand as analogues for the movements of consciousness' (p. 73); Stuart Liebman describes Brakhage's 'great project' as 'the representation of the movements of consciousness itself' (p. 97); Fred Camper insists that Jordan Belson's films are 'not images at all, but forms of consciousness' (p. 125); Ellen Feldman: 'The use of persistence of vision becomes the foundation for creating an analogy between the processes of viewing film and that of consciousness' (p. 149) and 'the film structure functions as both analogue and an instant of consciousness' (p. 149). In *The Essential Cinema*, Ken Kelman will add his voice to Michelson's and Sitney's in stating that Buñuel's *Land Without Bread* 'is a film concerned with consciousness' (p. 125) and that the process of Bruce Conner's *Report* is 'analogous to the process of thought' (p. 241). Phenomenology thus permeating all the new writing on avant-garde film, what sort of consequences does this have in terms of developing a methodology (methodologies) of film analysis? And further, how does this sort of criticism relate to current developments in theoretical work on film?

A History of the American Avant-Garde Cinema and *The Essential Cinema* for the most part consist of descriptions of films. Although the descriptions are often careful and rigorous in their demonstration of these films as 'analogues of consciousness' and/or subversions of filmic illusionism through consciousness, they seldom go beyond that.[8] But then, methodology is not a problem in a phenomenological approach: 'It is a matter of describing and not of explaining or analysing.' Phenomenology aims at a 'report (*compte rendu*) of space, time, of the "lived" world . . . It is also the attempt at a direct description of our experience as it is without respect to psychological genesis and causal explanation . . . '[9] This approach differs from much of the recent work in film theory, which concentrates on the construction of abstract systems in order to understand the mechanisms of the film, such as the notion of codes and their hierarchies in the filmic system (e.g., the important distinction between specific and nonspecific codes) and of 'textual system', not the reconstruction of *the* system of the film but a construction by the analyst of *a* system of the film according to the level and purpose of the analysis. That this degree of abstraction is able to remain close to the film can be seen in the work of, for example, Thierry Kuntzel,[10] in which semiological and psychoanalytic structures are worked in close relation to a minute description of the temporal engenderment of the film.

Much of the French and English theoretical work on film, a semiology informed by psychoanalytic theory, has concerned itself with phenomenology and cinema, but from a very different direction. Both Jean-Louis Baudry and Christian Metz have discussed the similarity between cinema and phenomenology. In 'The Imaginary Signifier' Metz says that 'it is true that the topographical apparatus of the cinema resembles the conceptual apparatus of phenomenology, with the result that the latter can cast light on the former' (p. 55).[11] What is also true is that the tautological structure of experimental films mirrors the phenomenological *gestalt:* the films are 'about' the spectator's spatio-temporal traversal of the film. Metz states that it is 'no accident that the main form of idealism in cinematic theory has been phenomenology.'[12] For both Baudry and Metz, it is not that cinema just happens miraculously to work like human perception (and like the psychical apparatus, e.g., projection, mirror structure, etc.); a certain wish-fulfilling placement of the spectator is implicit in the structure of the cinematic institution, the institution including the industry, the technological base and the spectator's 'desire to go to the cinema'. Cinema replays unconscious wishes the structures of which are shared by phenomenology: the illusion of perceptual mastery with the effect of the creation of a transcendental subject.

The American criticism discussed here takes the phenomenological *gestalt* of cinema, and of avant-garde film in particular, for granted, both theoretically and historically. It takes its critical cues from what it has determined to be the nature of film and especially of these films. Thus, everyone is in agreement. The filmmakers write their *Metaphors on Vision* (Brakhage), Snow will talk of his project of making a film (*Wavelength*) that would be 'a definitive statement of pure film space and time . . . all about seeing'.[13] Warhol will remind us to 'just look'. The films themselves will be seen as the exemplary phenomenological event by their very nature. Criticism's function will be to refine our seeing and affirm the modernist credo of knowledge through self-consciousness. The discourse about the object becomes (is the same thing as) the discourse of the object.

Another direct consequence of this phenomenological approach is its elimination of consideration of the spectator's unconscious relation to the film, the screen, the entire viewing situation, an aspect that has received much attention in French and English film theory. When the unconscious is discussed in this recent American work, it is either brought in as an example of one of the possible 'states of consciousness' presented by the film, or is incorrectly referred to as the 'subconscious', thus eliminating the radicalness of Freud's notion of the unconscious as alterity.

As a first step towards a theory of film there is a sense in which a phenomenological approach can be seen as essential. We are still getting to know this object 'film'. Any discipline must have a basis in careful description. The books under discussion often do an excellent job of written re-presentation of the films, often complex, requiring long hours of close work in projection rooms, at the editing table. Hopefully this 'phenomenology of cinema', even though limited to a descriptive mode, to an overly confining model of film as an 'analogue of consciousness' (thus eliminating consideration of the spectator's unconsciousness processes), can still serve an important first step, its mirroring exaltation of the film gradually giving way to a desire and an impetus to develop critical tools going beyond description into an analysis of the aesthetic, psychical and social functioning of cinema.

[Constance Penley]

II

Definitions of avant-garde or experimental cinema have always been controversial because they have always presupposed value judgments; even those offered in the most recent histories provoke the kinds of counter-examples which imply conflicting opinions about what counts as avant-garde cinema. Likewise, theories about what avant-garde film-making is, has been, or should be, which are often formulated in terms of film's alleged essential properties, also verge toward polemics, especially since the major theorists have been film-makers with incompatible views about the purposes and formal possibilities of cinematic innovation: Vertov, Eisenstein, Kuleshov, Dovzhenko, Epstein, Delluc, Léger, L'Herbier, Clair, Deren, Brakhage, Markopoulos, Peterson, Kubelka, Dreyer, Bresson, Godard, Frampton, Sharits, LeGrice, Gidal, Mulvey and Wollen, among others. Such a grouping of names challenges the oppositional distinctions which historians of the American avant-garde cinema commonly hold as definitive, namely: 16mm/35mm (amateur vs. professional film gauge and equipment); non-commercial/commercial; non-narrative/narrative; formalist/political; and sometimes also: abstract/representational; exclusion of language/use of language. Despite the long history of arguments (today as heated as ever) over what avant-garde might mean in connection with film, and in particular what socially generalisable meanings might be compatible with such arguments, American histories of avant-garde film have largely resolved such conflicts in terms of a formalist, anti-Hollywood stance, and an appreciation of the artist's personal vision in order to incorporate it into a history of stylistic innovation. The lack of discord which such histories present will seem more important later in this piece, when the institutional web binding these views together is made more explicit.

If one approaches the books under discussion for a definition of avant-garde, what answer is given?

When 'avant-garde' is used to describe an artistic movement, such as Cubism, it means that the movement is, for a time, *ahead of* critical acceptance. But when Cubism becomes absorbed into the mainstream of the tradition, it is no longer avant-garde. In connection with cinema, however, avant-garde does not mean 'in advance of' a developing film tradition; it is taken to mean, rather, *apart from* the commercial cinema. The avant-garde cinema is almost always seen—especially by its own historians—in terms of a development completely separate from that of the history of cinema. It is seen in terms of the 'art world' (painting, graphics, music, poetry, sometimes architecture) rather than the 'entertainment industry'. Thus John Hanhardt (associate curator of film at the Whitney Museum of American Art in New York) defines avant-garde film in his introductory essay to *A History of the American Avant-Garde Cinema* as 'the expression of an artist engaged in such vanguard aesthetic movements as surrealism, cubism, abstract expressionism or minimalism. This cinema subverts cinematic conventions by exploring the medium and its properties and materials, and in the process creates its own history separate from that of the classical narrative cinema' (p. 21).

Hanhardt's definition brings together the two major approaches to avant-garde cinema. It is discussed both through *comparison* with modernism, especially in the visual arts (as non-narrative), and in *opposition* to narrative cinema (as anti-narrative). In *The Cubist Cinema*,[14] Standish Lawder says that Cubism 'was a revolution in the manner of seeing. The real content of the Cubist painting was an analysis of vision. The object, that is, what was seen, became virtually unimportant' (p. 67).

Modernist art—and modernist criticism—emphasises the work of the signifier; but such work is discounted if it is organised around specific meanings. Thus Hanhardt warns his readers that, although the Surrealists loved *Potemkin,* and although Lawder can draw a formal comparison between Léger's *Ballet Mécanique* and the highly abstracted cream-separator sequence from Eisenstein's *The Old and the New,* 'it is important to remember, however, that for Eisenstein abstract imagery was used only in the service of the narrative, not as an end in itself' (p. 35).

Insofar as modernism is a modern formalism, it is by definition opposed to the possibility of a political avant-garde, which is necessarily concerned with meanings. Eisenstein is considered by formalist critics only in terms of formal innovation. His extensive theoretical work, all of which is explicitly concerned with how to present specific configurations of meaning to the spectator through particular kinds of formal choices, is selectively reduced by Hanhardt to being 'about editing (montage), composition, and a range of other basic issues' (p. 35). It is well known that Vertov's work has also been seen both as a model for avant-garde political film-making (Godard–Gorin's Dziga Vertov Group, for example) and as a treasury of formalist strategies.

On the other hand, the second part of Hanhardt's definition— 'this cinema subverts cinematic conventions by exploring the medium and its properties and materials'—refers to 'radical formalism', which represents an attempt to talk about a political avant-garde—or the avant-garde as political—while still restricting analysis to the play of the signifiers. Through the notion of deconstruction, this is now the most prevalent anti-narrative approach. It is argued that films which successfully work against (deconstruct) the dominant narrative conventions operate radical changes on conventional viewing habits and provoke a more distanced, critical spectator. The work of Noël Burch, in this connection, has been important and controversial.[15] However, basic problems with the conception of this notion have also encouraged its use as a gauge to measure formal innovation *per se* (a film is avant-garde insofar as it deconstructs), in which case inventories of deconstruction strategies are compiled with little attention as to how they progressively engender and govern textual movement or what the point of these strategies might be beyond creating an awareness of film-as-film. It is just this confusion about what 'radical' means in conjunction with formalism that permits definitions like Hanhardt's to conflate modernism and deconstruction.

Mixed in with the predominantly formalist orientation of contemporary avant-garde film criticism, and consistent with the anti-Hollywood stance, is the equation of avant-garde film with 'film-as-art' by nearly all its critics and historians. This equation has inverse consequences for commercial film, with rare exceptions. The Anthology Film Archives' manifesto, published as the introduction to *The Essential Cinema,* states that 'the art of the cinema surfaces primarily when it divests itself of commercial norms. The narrative commercial films included in our collection represent radical exceptions, cases where art has emerged despite the conditions of production and popular expectation' (p. x). (A list of the films in the collection is included in *The Essential Cinema.*) Although Anthology's selection committee describes its position as polemical, this attitude—which pits avant-garde film against commercial film as qualitative opposites—pervades almost all writing on avant-garde film depending on a constant analogy with the visual arts. The rhetoric of this criticism insists on an opposition between film as the expression of the artist's personal vision (or individual statement) versus a factory-produced market commodity (Hanhardt: 'factory = studio' [p. 20]) where film's visual and poetic qualities are sacrificed for a linear and verbalised plot.

Sarris's American *auteur* theory, of course, which was published in *Film Culture,* the house organ of American avant-garde cinema, attempted to re-evaluate (and elevate) Hollywood cinema precisely in terms of personal vision. For Steve Dwoskin, who argues for avant-garde film in similar terms in *Film Is,*[16] virtually everything except Hollywood cinema is avant-garde including the French New Wave, Italian Neo-realism, the British Free Cinema, and 'film as a political weapon'—Godard and Marker in France, Rocha and Brazilian *cinema novo,* Cuban film, American Newsreel, among others. Although in *Visionary Film,* P. Adams Sitney refuses the simplistic denial of the least Hollywood influence on American avant-garde film-makers and consistently draws attention to classical narrative conventions used and reworked, in particular by Anger, Markopoulos, Cornell, and Jacobs (such as the use of composition in depth, the off-screen look, the eye-line match, and more general editing and fictional strategies), it is only in David Curtis's *Experimental Cinema*[17] that the monolithic view of Hollywood gives way to a discussion of experiments within the industry itself. While brief, this is still the best general history available, and the only one to extend the frame of reference beyond the 'art world' to take into consideration social and economic reasons determining the availability of low-cost equipment, processing and distribution.

None of these habitual ways of describing avant-garde film pre-supposes a theory which could actually account for its specific characteristics, nor, certainly, which could distinguish film-as-art from film that isn't art, nor, presumably, which could clarify what is meant by personal vision. Anthology's proposal—'to define the art of the film in terms of selected works which indicate its essences and perimeters'(p. vi)—is put in terms of recognised works, not theoretical principles. So it will be more appropriate to consider what films these histories take as their subject. *Visionary Film* and *A History of the American Avant-Garde Cinema* are the first critical histories of American avant-garde film, and together with *The Essential Cinema* are based on the holdings of Anthology Film Archives. Although neither claims to be exhaustive or definitive, they discuss very nearly the same film-makers and cover the same years, placing the beginning in 1943 with Deren and Hammid's *Meshes of the Afternoon* and continuing through the early seventies with structural/minimal films—Snow, Gehr, Sharits, Frampton among others. This tacit critical and institutional consensus creates the impression that an official canon of important works and film-makers has already been decided. *A History of the American Avant-Garde Cinema* is closely identified with the Whitney Museum, which is one of the major New York avant-garde showcases, through John Hanhardt, who chose the films to be described in the history and wrote the introductory essay. Virtually all the essays, including Hanhardt's, were written by former students of the New York University (NYU) Cinema Studies Department. Sitney, who until fairly recently taught at NYU, is the director of publications and one of the founders and board members of Anthology Film Archives, and has long been associated with Jonas Mekas, another co-founder of Anthology, through their work together on *Film Culture* magazine.

Aside from the American avant-garde's pride in its unclassifiable diversity, this critical agreement is controversial because the histories are based on a single and avowedly idiosyncratic collection. Anthology states in its introductory manifesto that it intends to collect only masterpieces of film art. Elsewhere, film archives, as opposed to fine arts museums, attempt to collect (i.e., preserve) as many films as possible on the principle that present critical standards will, in time, give way to others. The fact that there is such consensus on the 'sublime achievements' (Anthology's phrase) of the American avant-garde according to the first scholarly books devoted to it suggests that a particular corpus and a particular interpretation of its development are quickly becoming standardised, thus threatening the critical recognition of those films which are not included. This kind of influence is not restricted to New York. To take just one European example, the new Centre Georges Pompidou in Paris (the Beaubourg) bought virtually Anthology's entire collection as its foundation collection of experimental film.

In addition to these general considerations, each of these books has certain debatable features. *A History of the American Avant-Garde Cinema* is limited by its conception as a museum catalogue designed to accompany a travelling exhibit of 'film art'. Each essay describes and comments on the films apparently chosen arbitrarily as representative of seven 'periods' of American avant-garde film history. The expressed aims of this collection—to develop a new criticism to deal with a new art object—are discussed above by Constance Penley. In comparison, *Visionary Film* covers far more films and is much more substantial in every way. It represents the first serious attempt to present a unified history of the American avant-garde film, and has provoked controversy for five main reasons: (a) Sitney's thesis that the most appropriate critical approach to 'visionary cinema' is to see it and Abstract Expressionism in terms of Romantic poetics; (b) the vagueness and indirect presentation of the key critical terms Sitney introduces, especially 'visionary' film and his genre categories (trance, mythopoeia, lyric, graphic, picaresque, structural, and participatory film); (c) the typology of genres: Sitney's history sees a progressive development of avant-garde genres out of one another (a 'historical morphology'); (d) the chapter on structural film, which loops the development of the American avant-garde back to Deren and the subjective film, suggesting that the structural film is motivated by the same Romantic quest for self-discovery; and (e) Sitney's suggestion throughout that 'the great unacknowledged aspiration of the American avant-garde film has been the cinematic reproduction of the human mind' (p. 408). *Visionary Film* is an important book because of the attention given to avant-garde film theory, which had received little critical attention before this. Even Deren's writings, though always acknowledged, have been viewed superficially, and Markopoulos's extremely interesting ideas about experimental narration are virtually unknown outside of the readers of *Film Culture*. From Sitney one gets a sense of the great diversity of options beyond what is usually flattened into an anti-Hollywood or film-as-art stance, which American avant-garde film-makers have considered, attempted, and very often written about. Hopefully *Visionary Film* will stimulate further and more systematic work on particular areas of film theory and history, and on textual studies of individual films.

Although Anthology's collection discussed and detailed in *The Essential Cinema* (edited of course by Sitney) makes narrative exceptions, predictably enough, for what has traditionally been seen as art cinema—the 'sublime achievements' of a Bresson, for example—it excludes such film-makers as Godard, Straub and Huillet, Duras, Rainer, Akerman, Rivette, Mulvey and Wollen, among many others, whose films constitute another direction, and an extremely vital one, of contemporary avant-garde film-making. Because they combine commercial and non-commercial aspects, narrative and non-narrative, and are constituted in different ways as political cinema, these films stand in contrast to prototypes of 'pure cinema', at any rate as they have usually been discussed. This exclusion is all the more interesting in that it parallels a blind spot in American avant-garde film criticism as well, which, though it seems like a methodological hodge-podge, is nonetheless unified through the priority given to formal description and the total absence of reference to film as a discursive practice. It is this combination of characteristics which permits one to call it formalist: a film's structure and formal properties are described step by step, outside any consideration of audience, social context, or the operations by which meaning is produced by and for the spectator. Sitney, for one, is interested in establishing a homology of structures between the American avant-garde film and 'the mind', but what those mental structures are is never made explicit.

A very important set of questions never arises in this criticism, central among which concerns filmic enunciation. According to Emile Benveniste, 'what characterises enunciation in general is the emphasis on the discursive relationship with a partner, whether it be real or imagined, individual or collective.'[18] What we think of as the classical, Hollywood-style fiction film tends to efface the marks of its construction (the organising half of the discursive relationship), as well as direct references to the spectator. Therefore the crucial question in determining the relationship of the spectator to the filmic discourse, how he or she is placed and thereby understands it, becomes: who 'speaks' beneath the deceptively neutral and objective voice of the 'third-person' narration. In other words, according to what logic(s) does the film make sense? In whose interest are the images and sounds recorded and ordered in a specific way, as one particular textual system? Who controls the look, and with it, the diegesis, and what kind of spectator does this presuppose? The same questions can be asked of *Wavelength, Marnie* or *Comment ça va*, a film in which they are discussed directly by the film's characters.

One way to characterise this group of film-makers is to say that they all investigate and analyse the question 'who speaks': the point of view from which the narrative is organised is specified, although the kind of address to the spectator differs vastly with each film. They also work explicitly with and against conventions governing different kinds of discourse in an attempt to reshape cinematic and, with varying degrees of directness, social conventions. One way to look at differences among them—as examples, think of Straub and Huillet's *Fortini-Cani,* Rivette's *Celine and Julie Go Boating,* Duras's *India Song,* Akerman's *News from Home,* Mulvey and Wollen's *Riddles of the Sphinx,* Rainer's *Film About a Woman Who,* Godard's *Comment ça va*—is to consider which discourses enter into a restricted play there, and how their interplay is controlled: discourses of historical writing, sexuality, theatre, cinema, those of the mass media—television, newspapers, radio, magazine advertising, discourses which turn on the family, colonialism, nationalism, among many others.

These concerns are also central to our work in *Camera Obscura,* particularly when the question of conflicting definitions and interests, the notion that every film is crossed by a heterogeneity of discourses, bears upon the representation of women. The films of Yvonne Rainer, Chantal Akerman and Marguerite Duras, although very different in some ways, are among those made by women who share a motivating interest in the status of the representation of woman—her desire, her self-image, the image others create of and for her. These films have been very helpful in suggesting possible approaches to the question 'who speaks' when what is at stake is the woman's voice/image, particularly in showing the difficulty in asking it: the status of 'woman' (daughter, mother, etc.) is unstable, which makes attempts to formulate what a 'woman's discourse' might be a tentative but, at the same time, an open question, one which is explored increasingly in women's films, as well as in feminist theory.

One of the ways this difficulty is brought out is by making the *I* of the enunciation problematic. In *News from Home,* the sound track establishes an *I—you* relationship through a mother's letters to her daughter, who has left her family in Belgium to make films in New York. This, and everything else we know about the mother or daughter, we know from the letters, except for the sound of the voice reading them, which we imagine to be the daughter's, and the images we see, which look almost like photographs in the fixity of their hold upon disconnected scenes, streets and subways in New York, with people randomly present or absent, none of them the *you* addressed in the letters. Another *I—you* relationship, between the subject of the enunciation (the point of view from which the narrative is organised) and the spectator, is caught among several representations: those the mother ceaselessly tries to piece together in the imaginary space of the letters (the family, present as 'news from home', the lack in the mother's life caused by her daughter's absence, the mother's attempts to visualise her daughter's life, to fit it into what she knows, and thus her constant demand for more news, more descriptions, a photograph) and the representations framing the letters—the sound of the woman's voice reading them, the city noises coming in, interfering with the words, the images.

One is tempted to identify the voice reading the letters with the daughter's, the visual point of view with hers, and, quickly, to conflate three different terms: the subject of the enunciation (the *I* who speaks, organises the narrative logic), the daughter, and Chantal Akerman, film-maker, who has said that *News from Home* is based on letters her mother sent her when she went to New York to make films. To do this, however, would be to take for granted the very terms the film establishes as difficult, and at best, fragile: both mother and daughter when they attempt to 'originate' representations, images, let's say, of their own desire. As in Rainer's *Film About a Woman Who* and much of Duras's work, autobiographical reference serves a complex function, one which draws on a woman's lived experience while at the same time complicating the question 'who speaks' by dispersing the origin of the enunciation across many positions; the film-maker, like the filmic system and its characters, is shaped by conflicting interests and desires. To understand the positions available to mother or daughter in *News from Home*, one has to take into account the symbolic structures which circumscribe them, just as to understand the options the various women referred to as 'she' see for themselves in *Film About a Woman Who*, as well as the overall logic of the film's manoeuvres, requires an analysis of the different discourses which ultimately determine them. Like research on the cinematic codes, this is a study which goes beyond the individual film. The work of *m/f* is very helpful in demonstrating this, and in *Camera Obscura* no. 2, Raymond Bellour's analysis of enunciation in *Marnie* shows some of the interests which shaped Hitchcock as 'enunciation' there, extending beyond him and the global text of his films to take in the psychical rules of the functioning of the classical cinematic institution, in particular the importance of the look (of the camera-director-male character/delegate) which controls the fiction through (at the expense of) the desired woman's body. Much of that issue of *Camera Obscura* is about the relationship of the look to the enunciating *I*.

It is important to ask these questions also of the many kinds of films which make up the New American Cinema, or of avant-garde film more generally. Surely the answers are not foregone conclusions, nor without interest or consequence. For one thing, many of the film-makers in this 'second avant-garde', to use Peter Wollen's phrase, have been very much influenced by experimental film. Within the American avant-garde itself, however, it is interesting to see how film-makers who were once considered paradigm formalists (Snow or Frampton, for example) are now beginning to be reconsidered in terms of fictional and representational strategies which deal more or less explicitly with questions of enunciation. This shift of attention to the entire process of signification, rather than limiting it to the play of the signifiers, will sooner or later necessitate changes in the official view of avant-garde film, and perhaps will also make a re-evaluation of the purposes of avant-garde film criticism seem important.

[Janet Bergstrom]

Notes

1. P. Adams Sitney, *Visionary Film: The American Avant-Garde,* Oxford University Press, 1974.

2. "The Imaginary Signifier," *Screen* 16 no. 2 (Summer 1975), p. 24.

3. P. Adams Sitney (ed.), *The Essential Cinema: Essays on the Films in the Collection of Anthology Film Archives,* New York University Press and Anthology Film Archives,

1975. (A 130-page bibliography on the films in Anthology's collection is included as an appendix.)

4. *A History of the American Avant-Garde Cinema*, The American Federation of Arts, 1976.

5. "Toward Snow," *Artforum*, June 1971, p. 30.

6. *Ibid.*, p. 32.

7. Maurice Merleau-Ponty, "The Film and the New Psychology," lecture to the Institut des Hautes Etudes Cinématographiques, March 13, 1945, trans. in *Sense and Non-sense*, Evanston, Ill.: Northwestern University Press, 1964, pp. 48–59.

8. P. Adams Sitney however makes a provocative link between phenomenology in cinema and American experimental film as a grand Romantic metaphor in his study of the 'visionary' film, a type of film which he see as predominant throughout the history of the American avant-garde (*Visionary Film*, p. 422). Although he merely notes it, this might be one of the more fruitful approaches to take to the question of the resemblances between cinema and the phenomenological scene.

9. Maurice Merleau-Ponty, *Phénoménologie de la perception*, Paris: Gallimard, 1945, p. ii.

10. Cf., e.g., "*Le défilement:* A View in Close-up," *Camera Obscura* no. 2, 1978.

11. Metz, *op. cit.* Cf. his description of the resemblance between the subject in phenomenology and cinema: 'The *"there is"* of phenomenology proper (philosophical phenomenology) as an ontic revelation to a perceiving-subject (= "perceptual *cogito*"), to a subject for which alone there can be anything, has close and precise affinities with the inauguration of the cinematic signifier in the ego as I have tried to define it, with the spectator falling back on himself as a pure instance of perception, the whole of the perceived being "over the way".'

12. *Ibid.*, p. 54.

13. Catalogue, 1967 International Film Festival of Knokke-le-Zoute.

14. *The Cubist Cinema*, New York University Press, 1975.

15. See especially *Afterimage* no. 5 and Stephen Heath's criticisms in *Screen* 17, no. 3 (Autumn 1976).

16. *Film Is*, London, 1975.

17. *Experimental Cinema*, London, 1971.

18. E. Benveniste, "L'appareil formel de l'énonciation," *Problèmes de linguistique générale*, Paris, 1974, p. 85.

Part 3
Feminist
Criticism

VISUAL PLEASURE AND NARRATIVE CINEMA

LAURA MULVEY

As working methodologies, psychoanalysis and semiotics can be used to different ends. Both have attracted the attention of feminists as ways of helping to understand how women are represented in the cinema. They have helped feminist critics to extend critiques stressing the limited, stereotypical roles assigned to most female characters to a broad examination of how the formal organization of a film is a function of ideology as well as of aesthetics. One particularly significant aspect of this examination has been inquiry into the ways in which formal organization —the textual system —promotes certain states of mind among viewers. This line of reasoning has received extended treatment in the writings of Laura Mulvey, as well as by Claire Johnston, Pam Cook, and many other writers whose works are in included Further Readings.

In this seminal article, which was written in 1975, Mulvey gives a sharply feminist twist to psychoanalytic theory. Taking Freud's account of sexuality and the unconscious as a basically accurate description of the place of women in a phallocentric order, Mulvey asks how the unconscious of patriarchal society has structured film form. Many would disagree with this premise as an unnecessary endorsement of Freud's essentialism and as an undervaluation of the social experience of mothering as a major determinant of both gender roles and the psychic internalizations that support them. See, for example, Nancy Chodorow's The Reproduction of Mothering *(Berkeley: University of California Press, 1978), which cites a wealth of psychoanalytic and sociological literature to support the contrary position. The most direct critique is Julia Lesage's "The Human Subject —You, IIe, or Me? Or, The Case of the Missing Penis" (originally published in* Jump Cut, *no. 4 [1974]: 26 27), which engendered an extended debate. Written prior to publication of Mulvey's article and directed expressly at points made in* Screen 15, *no. 2 (Summer 1974), an issue devoted to Brecht, Lesage's article reminds us that Freud's and Lacan's conception that the body of the woman is a threat to men because it signifies lack or castration is not the only reading of woman's body available, even in psychoanalytic literature. Her critique seemed to go unheard until recently. D. N. Rodowick's "The Difficulty of Difference" (*Wide Angle 5, *no. 1 [1982]: 4–15) broaches the topic of masochism, which Mulvey's essay suppresses, but it fails to make a radical break with Mulvey's assumptions. In Part 5, Gaylyn Studlar's article, "Masochism and the Perverse Pleasures of the Cinema," carries this critique further by arguing that visual pleasure derives primarily from masochistic sources. Thus, she overturns the basic premises of Mulvey's article and of others who have followed her lead. Studlar's article and the section of* Jump Cut, *no. 29 (1984) on women and representation (see in particular Jane Gaines's introduction) indicate that,* *after a period of remarkably strong influence, Mulvey's perspective is being displaced or contextualized by alternatives that are only now being heard.*

Mulvey's view of patriarchy and film form is seductively direct. Assuming that male visual pleasure is the controlling pleasure in cinema, she describes its two central forms: scopophilic pleasure that is linked to sexual attraction (voyeurism in extremis) and scopophilic pleasure that is linked to narcissistic identification (the introjection of ideal egos). Within the assumptions of the heterosexual orientation, which Mulvey does not contest, narcissistic identification works to strengthen the ego through same-sex identification (between boys and male stars, for example), while sexual attraction is of a different order, since it can weaken the ego in the interests of instinctual gratification. Mulvey then considers the consequences of the erotic attraction of male viewers for female characters, arguing that the attraction is ambivalent, since the feminine is seen not only as a lure but as a threat: the threat of sinking into the "half-light of the imaginary," the threat of castration conveyed by the "real absence of a penis" from the body of the woman. The reality of that absence has often been called into question by those who point out that absence is itself a conceptual and symbolic category. The existence of female genitalia must be denied in order to see the "lack" that Freud and our phallocentric culture proclaim. See the "Critique of Phallocentrism" in Anthony Wilden's System and Structure *2nd ed. (London: Tavistock, 1980, 278–301).*

For Mulvey, male ambivalence toward the image of woman propels the film text and the viewer toward nonmutually exclusive extremes: either to devalue, punish, or save woman, the guilty object, as Hitchcock's films do, or to make her a pedestal figure, a fetish, as von Sternberg and sometimes Hitchcock films do. These extremes leave no place for the female viewer. (In a later article, Mulvey describes how the female viewer must accept identification with a female heroine on the impossible terms of an aggressive, preoedipal sexuality or a passive, postoedipal one.) The possibilities for female sexual attraction (voyeuristic instead of narcissistic scopophilia) remain to be explored in comparable detail. See Mulvey's "Afterthoughts . . . Inspired by Duel in the Sun" *in* Framework, *nos. 15–17 (Summer 1981): 12–15.*

The alternative that Mulvey proposes is the refusal of visual pleasure as structured by a patriarchal order. Mulvey's own filmmaking work may be seen as an indication of the directions that such a refusal might take, while Claire Johnston's references in the next article to Chantal Akerman's work suggest another. (Mulvey's films include Penthesilea *[1974],* Riddles of the Sphinx *[1977], and* Crystal Gazing *[1982], all with Peter Wollen.) Of paramount importance to the development of a specifically feminist criticism is Mulvey's persuasive demonstration of the inadequacy of criticism that assigns formal or thematic meanings to works that can be described or explained objectively. She argues that scopophilic drives "pursue aims in indifference to perceptual reality, creating the imagised, eroticised concept of the world that forms the perception of the subject and makes a mockery of empirical objectivity." Such insight must be the starting-point for any affect-oriented feminist aesthetic.*

I. INTRODUCTION

A. A Political Use of Psychoanalysis

This paper intends to use psychoanalysis to discover where and how the fascination of film is reinforced by pre-existing patterns of fascination already at work within the individual subject and the social formations that have moulded him. It takes as starting point the way film reflects, reveals and even plays on the straight, socially established interpretation of sexual difference which controls images, erotic ways of looking and spectacle. It is helpful to understand what the cinema has been, how its magic has worked in the past, while attempting a theory and a practice which will challenge this cinema of the past. Psychoanalytic theory is thus appropriated here as a political weapon, demonstrating the way the unconscious of patriarchal society has structured film form.

The paradox of phallocentrism in all its manifestations is that it depends on the image of the castrated woman to give order and meaning to its world. An idea of woman stands as lynch pin to the system: it is her lack that produces the phallus as a symbolic presence, it is her desire to make good the lack that the phallus signifies. Recent writing in *Screen* about psychoanalysis and the cinema has not sufficiently brought out the importance of the representation of the female form in a symbolic order in which, in the last resort, it speaks castration and nothing else. To summarise briefly: the function of woman in forming the patriarchal unconscious is twofold, she first symbolises the castration threat by her real absence of a penis and second thereby raises her child into the symbolic. Once this has been achieved, her meaning in the process is at an end, it does not last into the world of law and language except as a memory, which oscillates between memory of maternal plenitude and memory of lack. Both are posited on nature (or on anatomy in Freud's famous phrase). Woman's desire is subjected to her image as bearer of the bleeding wound, she can exist only in relation to castration and cannot transcend it. She turns her child into the signifier of her own desire to possess a penis (the condition, she imagines, of entry into the symbolic). Either she must gracefully give way to the word, the Name of the Father and the Law, or else struggle to keep her child down with her in the half-light of the imaginary. Woman then stands in patriarchal culture as signifier for the male other, bound by a symbolic order in which man can live out his phantasies and obsessions through linguistic command by imposing them on the silent image of woman still tied to her place as bearer of meaning, not maker of meaning.

There is an obvious interest in this analysis for feminists, a beauty in its exact rendering of the frustration experienced under the phallocentric order. It gets us nearer to the roots of our oppression, it brings an articulation of the problem closer, it faces us with the ultimate challenge: how to fight the unconscious structured like a language (formed critically at the moment of arrival of language) while still caught within the language of the patriarchy. There is no way in which we can produce an alternative out of the blue, but we can begin to make a break by examining patriarchy with the tools it provides, of which psychoanalysis is not the only but an important one. We are still separated by a great gap from important issues for the female unconscious which are scarcely relevant to phallocentric theory: the sexing of the female infant and her relationship to the symbolic, the sexually mature woman as non-mother, maternity outside the signification of the phallus, the vagina. But, at this point, psychoanalytic theory as it now stands can at least advance our understanding of the status quo, of the patriarchal order in which we are caught.

B. Destruction of Pleasure as a Radical Weapon

As an advanced representation system, the cinema poses questions of the ways the unconscious (formed by the dominant order) structures ways of seeing and pleasure in looking. Cinema has changed over the last few decades. It is no longer the monolithic system based on large capital investment exemplified at its best by Hollywood in the 1930's, 1940's and 1950's. Technological advances (16mm, etc.) have changed the economic conditions of cinematic production, which can now be artisanal as well as capitalist. Thus it has been possible for an alternative cinema to develop. However self-conscious and ironic Hollywood managed to be, it always restricted itself to a formal mise-en-scène reflecting the dominant ideological concept of the cinema. The alternative cinema provides a space for a cinema to be born which is radical in both a political and an aesthetic sense and challenges the basic assumptions of the mainstream film. This is not to reject the latter moralistically, but to highlight the ways in which its formal preoccupations reflect the psychical obsessions of the society which produced it, and, further, to stress that the alternative cinema must start specifically by reacting against these obsessions and assumptions. A politically and aesthetically avant-garde cinema is now possible, but it can still only exist as a counterpoint.

The magic of the Hollywood style at its best (and of all the cinema which fell within its sphere of influence) arose, not exclusively, but in one important aspect, from its skilled and satisfying manipulation of visual pleasure. Unchallenged, mainstream film coded the erotic into the language of the dominant patriarchal order. In the highly developed Hollywood cinema it was only through these codes that the alienated subject, torn in his imaginary memory by a sense of loss, by the terror of potential lack in phantasy, came near to finding a glimpse of satisfaction: through its formal beauty and its play on his own formative obsessions. This article will discuss the interweaving of that erotic pleasure in film, its meaning, and in particular the central place of the image of woman. It is said that analysing pleasure, or beauty, destroys it. That is the intention of this article. The satisfaction and reinforcement of the ego that represent the high point of film history hitherto must be attacked. Not in favour of a reconstructed new pleasure, which cannot exist in the abstract, nor of intellectualised unpleasure, but to make way for a total negation of the ease and plenitude of the narrative fiction film. The alternative is the thrill that comes from leaving the past behind without rejecting it, transcending outworn or oppressive forms, or daring to break with normal pleasurable expectations in order to conceive a new language of desire.

II. PLEASURE IN LOOKING/FASCINATION WITH THE HUMAN FORM

A. The cinema offers a number of possible pleasures. One is scopophilia. There are circumstances in which looking itself is a source of pleasure, just as, in the reverse formation, there is pleasure in being looked at. Originally, in his *Three Essays on Sexuality*, Freud isolated scopophilia as one of the component instincts of sexuality which exist as drives quite independently of the erotogenic zones. At this point he associated scopophilia with taking other people as objects, subjecting them to a controlling and curious gaze. His particular examples centre around the voyeuristic activities of children, their desire to see and make sure of the private and the forbidden (curiosity about other people's genital and bodily functions, about the presence or absence of the penis and, retrospectively, about the primal scene). In this analysis scopophilia is essentially active. (Later, in *Instincts and Their Vicissitudes*, Freud developed his theory of scopophilia further, attaching it initially to pre-genital autoeroticism, after which the pleasure of the look is transferred to others by analogy. There is a close working here of the relationship between the active instinct and its further development in a narcissistic form.) Although the instinct is modified by other factors, in particular the constitution of the ego, it continues to exist as the erotic basis for pleasure in looking at another person as object. At the extreme, it can become fixated into a perversion, producing obsessive voyeurs and Peeping Toms whose only sexual satisfaction can come from watching, in an active controlling sense, an objectified other.

At first glance, the cinema would seem to be remote from the undercover world of the surreptitious observation of an unknowing and unwilling victim. What is seen on the screen is so manifestly shown. But the mass of mainstream film, and the conventions within which it has consciously evolved, portray a hermetically sealed world which unwinds magically, indifferent to the presence of the audience, producing for them a sense of separation and playing on their voyeuristic phantasy. Moreover, the extreme contrast between the darkness in the auditorium (which also isolates the spectators from one another) and the brilliance of the shifting patterns of light and shade on the screen helps to promote the illusion of voyeuristic separation. Although the film is really being shown, is there to be seen, conditions of screening and narrative conventions give the spectator an illusion of looking in on a private world. Among other things, the position of the spectators in the cinema is blatantly one of repression of their exhibitionism and projection of the repressed desire onto the performer.

B. The cinema satisfies a primordial wish for pleasurable looking, but it also goes further, developing scopophilia in its narcissistic aspect. The conventions of mainstream film focus attention on the human form. Scale, space, stories are all anthropomorphic. Here, curiosity and the wish to look intermingle with a fascination with likeness and recognition: the human face, the human body, the relationship between the human form and its surroundings, the visible presence of the person in the world. Jacques Lacan has described how the moment when a child recognises its own image in the mirror is crucial for the constitution of the ego. Several aspects of this analysis are relevant here. The mirror phase occurs at a time when the child's physical ambitions outstrip his motor capacity, with the result that his recognition of himself is joyous in that he imagines his mirror image to be more complete, more perfect than he experiences his own body. Recognition is thus overlaid with misrecognition: the image recognised is conceived as the reflected body of the self, but its misrecognition as superior projects this body outside itself as an ideal ego, the alienated subject, which, re-introjected as an ego ideal, gives rise to the future generation of identification with others. This mirror moment predates language for the child.

Important for this article is the fact that it is an image that constitutes the matrix of the imaginary, of recognition/misrecognition and identification, and hence of the first articulation of the I, of subjectivity. This is a moment when an older fascination with looking (at the mother's face, for an obvious example) collides with the initial inklings of self-awareness. Hence it is the birth of the long love affair/despair between image and self-image which has found such intensity of expression in film and such joyous recognition in the cinema audience. Quite apart from the extraneous similarities between screen and mirror (the framing of the human form in its surroundings, for instance), the cinema has structures of fascination strong enough to allow temporary loss of ego while simultaneously reinforcing the ego. The sense of forgetting the world as the ego has subsequently come to perceive it (I forgot who I am and where I was) is nostalgically reminiscent of that pre-subjective moment of image recognition. At the same time the cinema has distinguished itself in the production of ego ideals as expressed in particular in the star system, the stars centring both screen presence and screen story as they act out a complex process of likeness and difference (the glamorous impersonates the ordinary).

C. Sections II. A and B have set out two contradictory aspects of the pleasurable structures of looking in the conventional cinematic situation. The first, scopophilic, arises from pleasure in using another person as an object of sexual stimulation through sight. The second, developed through narcissism and the constitution of the ego, comes from identification with the image seen. Thus, in film terms, one implies a separation of the erotic identity of the subject from the object on the screen (active scopophilia), the other demands identification of the ego with the object on the screen through the spectator's fascination with and recognition of his like. The first is a function of the sexual instincts, the second of ego libido. This dichotomy was crucial for Freud. Although he saw the two as interacting and overlaying each other, the tension between instinctual drives and self-preservation continues to be a dramatic polarisation in terms of pleasure. Both are formative structures, mechanisms not meaning. In themselves they have no signification, they have to be attached to an idealisation. Both pursue aims in indifference to perceptual reality, creating the imagised, eroticised concept of the world that forms the perception of the subject and makes a mockery of empirical objectivity.

During its history, the cinema seems to have evolved a particular illusion of reality in which this contradiction between libido and ego has found a beautifully complementary phantasy world. In *reality* the phantasy world of the screen is subject to the law which produces it. Sexual instincts and identification processes have a meaning within the symbolic order which articulates desire. Desire, born with language, allows the possibility of transcending the instinctual and the imaginary, but its point of reference continually returns to the traumatic moment of its birth: the castration complex. Hence the look, pleasurable in form, can be threatening in content, and it is woman as representation/image that crystallises this paradox.

III. WOMAN AS IMAGE, MAN AS BEARER OF THE LOOK

A. In a world ordered by sexual imbalance, pleasure in looking has been split between active/male and passive/female. The determining male gaze projects its phantasy onto the female figure, which is styled accordingly. In their traditional exhibitionist role women are simultaneously looked at and displayed, with their appearance coded for strong visual and erotic impact so that they can be said to connote *to-be-looked-at-ness*. Woman displayed as sexual object is the leitmotif of erotic spectacle: from pin-ups to stripe-tease, from Ziegfeld to Busby Berkeley, she holds the look, plays to and signifies male desire. Mainstream film neatly combined spectacle and narrative. (Note, however, how in the musical song-and-dance numbers break the flow of the diegesis.) The presence of woman is an indispensable element of spectacle in normal narrative film, yet her visual presence tends to work against the development of a story line, to freeze the flow of action in moments of erotic contemplation. This alien presence then has to be integrated into cohesion with the narrative. As Budd Boetticher has put it:

What counts is what the heroine provokes, or rather what she represents. She is the one, or rather the love or fear she inspires in the hero, or else the concern he feels for her, who makes him act the way he does. In herself the woman has not the slightest importance.

(A recent tendency in narrative film has been to dispense with this problem altogether; hence the development of what Molly Haskell has called the 'buddy movie', in which the active homosexual eroticism of the central male figures can carry the story without distraction.) Traditionally, the woman displayed has functioned on two levels: as erotic object for the characters within the screen story, and as erotic object for the spectator within the auditorium, with a shifting tension between the looks on either side of the screen. For instance, the device of the show-girl allows the two looks to be unified technically without any apparent break in the diegesis. A woman performs within the narrative, the gaze of the spectator and that of the male characters in the film are neatly combined without breaking narrative verisimilitude. For a moment the sexual impact of the performing woman takes the film into a no-man's-land outside its own time and space. Thus Marilyn Monroe's first appearance in *The River of No Return* and Lauren Bacall's songs in *To Have and Have Not*. Similarly, conventional close-ups of legs (Dietrich, for instance) or a face (Garbo) integrate into the narrative a different mode of eroticism. One part of a fragmented body destroys the Renaissance space, the illusion of depth demanded by the narrative, it gives flatness, the quality of a cut-out or icon rather than verisimilitude to the screen.

B. An active/passive heterosexual division of labour has similarly controlled narrative structure. According to the principles of the ruling ideology and the psychical structures that back it up, the male figure cannot bear the burden of sexual objectification. Man is reluctant to gaze at his exhibitionist like. Hence the split between spectacle and narrative supports the man's role as the active one of forwarding the story, making things happen. The man controls the film phantasy and also emerges as the representative of power in a further sense: as the bearer of the look of the spectator, transferring it behind the screen to neutralise the extra-diegetic tendencies represented by woman as spectacle. This is made possible through the processes set in motion by structuring the film around a main controlling figure with whom the spectator can identify. As the spectator identifies with the main male[1] protagonist, he projects his look onto that of his like, his screen surrogate, so that the power of the male protagonist as he controls events coincides with the active power of the erotic look, both giving a satisfying sense of omnipotence. A male movie star's glamorous characteristics are thus not those of the erotic object of the gaze, but those of the more perfect, more complete, more powerful ideal ego conceived in the original moment of recognition in front of the mirror. The character in the story can make things happen and control events better than the subject/spectator, just as the image in the mirror was more in control of motor coordination. In contrast to woman as icon, the active male figure (the ego ideal of the identification process) demands a three-dimensional space corresponding to that of the mirror recognition, in which the alienated subject internalised his own representation of this imaginary existence. He is a figure in a landscape. Here the function of film is to reproduce as accurately as possible the so-called natural conditions of human perception. Camera technology (as exemplified by deep focus in particular) and camera movements (determined by the action of the protagonist), combined with invisible editing (demanded by realism), all tend to blur the limits of screen space. The male protagonist is free to command the stage, a stage of spatial illusion in which he articulates the look and creates the action.

C.1   Sections III. A and B have set out a tension between a mode of representation of woman in film and conventions surrounding the diegesis. Each is associated with a look: that of the spectator in direct scopophilic contact with the female form displayed for his enjoyment (connoting male phantasy) and that of the spectator fascinated with the image of his like set in an illusion of natural space, and through him gaining control and possession of the woman within the diegesis. (This tension and the shift from one pole to the other can structure a single text. Thus both in *Only Angels Have Wings* and in *To Have and Have Not,* the film opens with the woman as object of the combined gaze of spectator and all the male protagonists in the film. She is isolated, glamorous, on display, sexualised. But as the narrative progresses she falls in love with the main male protagonist and becomes his property, losing her outward glamorous characteristics, her generalised sexuality, her show-girl connotations; her eroticism is subjected to the male star alone. By means of identification with him, through participation in his power, the spectator can indirectly possess her too.)

But in psychoanalytic terms, the female figure poses a deeper problem. She also connotes something that the look continually circles around but disavows: her lack of a penis, implying a threat of castration and hence unpleasure. Ultimately, the meaning of woman is sexual difference, the absence of the penis as visually ascertainable, the material evidence on which is based the castration complex essential for the organisation of entrance to the symbolic order and the law of the father. Thus the woman as icon, displayed for the gaze and enjoyment of men, the active controllers of the look, always threatens to evoke the anxiety it originally signified. The male unconscious has two avenues of escape from this castration anxiety: preoccupation with the re-enactment of the original trauma (investigating the woman, demystifying her mystery), counterbalanced by the devaluation, punishment or saving of the guilty object (an avenue typified by the concerns of the *film noir*); or else complete disavowal of castration by the substitution of a fetish object or turning the represented figure itself into a fetish so that it becomes reassuring rather than dangerous (hence over-valuation, the cult of the female star). This second avenue, fetishistic scopophilia, builds up the physical beauty of the object, transforming it into something satisfying in itself. The first avenue, voyeurism, on the contrary, has associations with sadism: pleasure lies in ascertaining guilt (immediately associated with castration), asserting control and subjecting the guilty person through punishment or forgiveness. This sadistic side fits in well with narrative. Sadism demands a story, depends on making something happen, forcing a change in another person, a battle of will and strength, victory/ defeat, all occuring in a linear time with a beginning and an end. Fetishistic scopophilia, on the other hand, can exist outside linear time as the erotic instinct is focussed on the look alone. These contradictions and ambiguities can be illustrated more simply by using works by Hitchcock and Sternberg, both of whom take the look almost as the content or subject matter of many of their films. Hitchcock is the more complex, as he uses both mechanisms. Sternberg's work, on the other hand, provides many pure examples of fetishistic scopophilia.

C.2 It is well known that Sternberg once said he would welcome his films being projected upside down so that story and character involvement would not interfere with the spectator's undiluted appreciation of the screen image. This statement is revealing but ingenuous. Ingenuous in that his films do demand that the figure of the woman (Dietrich, in the cycle of films with her, as the ultimate example) should be identifiable. But revealing in that it emphasises the fact that for him the pictorial space enclosed by the frame is paramount rather than narrative or identification processes. While Hitchcock goes into the investigative side of voyeurism, Sternberg produces the ultimate fetish, taking it to the point where the powerful look of the male protagonist (characteristic of traditional narrative film) is broken in favour of the image in direct erotic rapport with the spectator. The beauty of the woman as object and the screen space coalesce; she is no longer the bearer of guilt but a perfect product, whose body, stylised and fragmented by close-ups, is the content of the film and the direct recipient of the spectator's look. Sternberg plays down the illusion of screen depth; his screen tends to be one-dimensional, as light and shade, lace, steam, foliage, net, streamers, etc, reduce the visual field. There is little or no mediation of the look through the eyes of the main male protagonist. On the contrary, shadowy presences like La Bessière in *Morocco* act as surrogates for the director, detached as they are from audience identification. Despite Sternberg's insistence that his stories are irrelevant, it is significant that they are concerned with situation, not suspense, and cyclical rather than linear time, while plot complications revolve around misunderstanding rather than conflict. The most important absence is that of the controlling male gaze within the screen scene. The high point of emotional drama in the most typical Dietrich films, her supreme moments of erotic meaning, take place in the absence of the man she loves in the fiction. There are other witnesses, other spectators watching her on the screen, their gaze is one with, not standing in for, that of the audience. At the end of *Morocco,* Tom Brown has already disappeared into the desert when Amy Jolly kicks off her gold sandals and walks after him. At the end of *Dishonoured,* Kranau is indifferent to the fate of Magda. In both cases, the erotic impact, sanctified by death, is displayed as a spectacle for the audience. The male hero misunderstands and, above all, does not see.

In Hitchcock, by contrast, the male hero does see precisely what the audience sees. However, in the films I shall discuss here, he takes fascination with an image through scopophilic eroticism as the subject of the film. Moreover, in these cases the hero portrays the contradictions and tensions experienced by the spectator. In *Vertigo* in particular, but also in *Marnie* and *Rear Window,* the look is central to the plot, oscillating between voyeurism and fetishistic fascination. As a twist, a further manipulation of the normal viewing process, which in some sense reveals it, Hitchcock uses the process of identification normally associated with ideological correctness and the recognition of established morality and shows up its perverted side. Hitchcock has never concealed his interest in voyeurism, cinematic and non-cinematic. His heroes are exemplary of the symbolic order and the law — a policeman (*Vertigo*), a dominant male possessing money and power (*Marnie*) — but their erotic drives lead them into compromised situations. The power to subject another person to the will sadistically or to the gaze voyeuristically is turned onto the woman as the object of both. Power is backed by a certainty of legal right and the established guilt of the woman (evoking castration, psychoanalytically speaking). True perversion is barely concealed under a shallow mask of ideological correctness—the man is on the right side of the law, the woman on the wrong. Hitchcock's skilful use of identification processes and liberal use of subjective camera from the point of view of the male protagonist draw the spectators deeply into his position, making them share his uneasy gaze. The audience is absorbed into a voyeuristic situation within the screen scene and diegesis which parodies his own in the cinema. In his analysis of *Rear Window,* Douchet takes the film as a metaphor for the cinema. Jeffries is the audience, the events in the apartment block opposite correspond to the screen. As he watches, an erotic dimension is added to his look, a central image to the drama. His girlfriend Lisa had been of little sexual interest to him, more or less a drag, so long as she remained on the spectator side. When she crosses the barrier between his room and the block opposite, their relationship is re-born erotically. He does not merely watch her through his lens, as a distant meaningful image, he also sees her as a guilty intruder exposed by a dangerous man threatening her with punishment, and thus finally saves her. Lisa's exhibitionism has already been established by her obsessive interest in dress and style, in being a passive image of visual perfection; Jeffries's voyeurism and activity have also been established through his work as a photo-journalist, a maker of stories and captor of images. However, his enforced inactivity, binding him to his seat as a spectator, puts him squarely in the phantasy position of the cinema audience.

In *Vertigo,* subjective camera predominates. Apart from one flash-back from Judy's point of view, the narrative is woven around what Scottie sees or fails to see. The audience follows the growth of his erotic obsession and subsequent despair precisely from his point of view. Scottie's voyeurism is blatant: he falls in love with a woman he follows and spies on without speaking to. Its sadistic side is equally blatant: he has chosen (and freely chosen, for he had been a successful lawyer) to be a policeman, with all the attendant possibilities of pursuit and investigation. As a result, he follows, watches and falls in love with a perfect image of female beauty and mystery. Once he actually confronts her, his erotic drive is to break her down and force her to tell by persistent cross-questioning. Then, in the second part of the film, he re-enacts his obsessive involvement with the image he loved to watch secretly. He reconstructs Judy as Madeleine, forces her to conform in every detail to the actual physical appearance of his fetish. Her exhibitionism, her masochism, make her an ideal passive counterpart to Scottie's active sadistic voyeurism. She knows her part is to perform, and only by playing it through and then replaying it can she keep Scottie's erotic interest. But in the repetition he does break her down and succeeds in exposing her guilt. His curiosity wins through and she is punished. In *Vertigo,* erotic involvement with the look is disorientating: the spectator's fascination is turned against him as the narrative carries him through and entwines him with the processes that he is himself exercising. The Hitchcock hero here is firmly placed within the symbolic order, in narrative terms. He has all the attributes of the partriachal superego. Hence the spectator, lulled into a false sense of security by the apparent legality of his surrogate, sees through his look and finds himself exposed as complicit, caught in the moral ambiguity of looking. Far from being simply an aside on the perversion of the police, *Vertigo* focuses on the implications of the active/looking, passive/looked-at split in terms of sexual difference and the power of the male symbolic encapsulated in the hero. Marnie, too, performs for Mark Rutland's gaze and masquerades as the perfect to-be-looked-at image. He, too, is on the side of the law until, drawn in by obsession with her guilt, her secret, he longs to see her in the act of committing a crime, make her confess and thus save her. So he, too, becomes complicit as he acts out the implications of his power. He controls money and words, he can have his cake and eat it.

IV. SUMMARY

The psychoanalytic background that has been discussed in this article is relevant to the pleasure and unpleasure offered by traditional narrative film. The scopophilic instinct (pleasure in looking at another person as an erotic object), and, in contradistinction, ego libido (forming identification processes) act as formations, mechanisms, which this cinema has played on. The image of woman as (passive) raw material for the (active) gaze of man takes the argument a step further into the structure of representation, adding a further layer demanded by the ideology of the patriarchal order as it is worked out in its favourite cinematic form—illusionistic narrative film. The argument returns again to the psychoanalytic background in that woman as representation signifies castration, inducing voyeuristic or fetishistic mechanisms to circumvent her threat. None of these interacting layers is intrinsic to film, but it is only in the film form that they can reach a perfect and beautiful contradiction, thanks to the possibility in the cinema of shifting the emphasis of the look. It is the place of the look that defines cinema, the possibility of varying it and exposing it. This is what makes cinema quite different in its voyeuristic potential from, say, strip-tease, theatre, shows, etc. Going far beyond highlighting a woman's to-be-looked-at-ness, cinema builds the way she is to be looked at into the spectacle itself. Playing on the tension between film as controlling the dimension of time (editing, narrative) and film as controlling the dimension of space (changes in distance, editing), cinematic codes create a gaze, a world, and an object, thereby producing an illusion cut to the measure of desire. It is these cinematic codes and their relationship to formative external structures that must be broken down before mainstream film and the pleasure it provides can be challenged.

To begin with (as an ending), the voyeuristic-scopophilic look that is a crucial part of traditional filmic pleasure can itself be broken down. There are three different looks associated with cinema: that of the camera as it records the pro-filmic event, that of the audience as it watches the final product, and that of the characters at each other within the screen illusion. The conventions of narrative film deny the first two and subordinate them to the third, the conscious aim being always to eliminate intrusive camera presence and prevent a distancing awareness in the audience. Without these two absences (the material existence of the recording process, the critical reading of the spectator), fictional drama cannot achieve reality, obviousness and truth. Nevertheless, as this article has argued, the structure of looking in narrative fiction film contains a contradiction in its own premises: the female image as a castration threat constantly endangers the unity of the diegesis and bursts through the world of illusion as an intrusive, static, one-dimensional fetish. Thus the two looks materially present in time and space are obsessively subordinated to the neurotic needs of the male ego. The camera becomes the mechanism for producing an illusion of Renaissance space, flowing movements compatible with the human eye, an ideology of representation that revolves around the perception of the subject; the camera's look is disavowed in order to create a convincing world in which the spectator's surrogate can perform with verisimilitude. Simultaneously, the look of the audience is denied an intrinsic force: as soon as fetishistic representation of the female image threatens to break the spell of illusion, and the erotic image on the screen appears directly (without mediation) to the spectator, the fact of fetishisation, concealing as it does castration fear, freezes the look, fixates the spectator and prevents him from achieving any distance from the image in front of him.

This complex interaction of looks is specific to film. The first blow against the monolithic accumulation of traditional film conventions (already undertaken by radical film-makers) is to free the look of the camera into its materiality in time and space and the look of the audience into dialectics, passionate detachment. There is no doubt that this destroys the satisfaction, pleasure and privilege of the 'invisible guest', and highlights how film has depended on voyeuristic active/passive mechanisms. Women, whose image has continually been stolen and used for this end, cannot view the decline of the traditional film form with anything much more than sentimental regret.

Note

1. There are films with a woman as main protagonist, of course. To analyse this phenomenon seriously here would take me too far afield. Pam Cook and Claire Johnston's study of *The Revolt of Mamie Stover* in Phil Hardy, ed., *Raoul Walsh*, Edinburgh, 1974, shows in a striking case how the strength of this female protagonist is more apparent than real.

relating to other things

*from — FortDa— precedbook
pleasure of not
seeing*

TOWARDS A FEMINIST FILM PRACTICE: SOME THESES

CLAIRE JOHNSTON

Claire Johnston's conception of feminist film practice involves a struggle for the means of signification. Our sense of ourselves as conscious, autonomous individuals depends on the effect of material practices that position us in relation to others. Going from Freud's theory of sexual position and identity through the elaborate recastings of this theory by Jacques Lacan, Johnston argues that existing practices identify the feminine as nonmale. Her movement over this difficult terrain of psychoanalytic semiotic theory provides a brief, helpful summary of the implications of psychoanalysis for feminism from a perspective close to Laura Mulvey's, and it is subject to similar criticisms. From this review, she draws the conclusion that feminist film practice must challenge the dominant film practice, whose means of signification are keyed to a patriarchal ideology that reconstitutes sexuality in hierarchical or oppositional terms: "It is this imaginary unit, the sutured coherence [that centers on the phallus as paradigm of male sexuality, marking the female as "object rather than the subject of desire"], the imaginary sense of identity set up by the classic film which must be challenged by a feminist film practice."

Johnston locates one instance of instructive challenge in Chantal Akerman's Jeanne Dielman, 23 Quai du Commerce—1080 Bruxelles. *(For further comment on Akerman's film, see Patricia Patterson and Manny Farber, "Kitchen Without Kitsch," in* Film Comment *13, no. 6 [1977]: 47–50, and Marsha Kinder, "Reflections on* Jeanne Dielman," *in* Film Quarterly *30, no. 4 [Summer 1977]: 2–8.) Responding to Julia Kristeva's call for a return to negation and refusal that provides pleasure (*jouissance*) through a rejection of patriarchal, ideological means of signification, Johnston calls for texts that unsettle the viewer and jar him or her loose from the overdetermined meanings of an oppressive sexual identity. Johnston warns that calls for textual, semiotic revolution risk being perceived as "anarchic" —outside specific historical conditions and existing political struggles. For her, Akerman's film both avoids anarchism through its ethnographic specificity and disturbs dominant cinematic signification by refusing to close off space into an envelope that "contains" our own subjectivity. (See Daniel Dayan's "The Tutor-Code of Classical Cinema" in the first volume of* Movies *and* Methods.*) The film allows for an eruption of* jouissance *that is "annulled in the act of murder, in the abolition of the phallus." Akerman seems to make possible a new vision of the feminine and of a symbolic order of exchange that is not governed by the Law of the Father and hence not by patriarchy.*

These points, which Johnston makes as theses, leave considerable room for debate on such issues as the extent to which avant-garde texts can alter something as fundamental as "subject position"; instead, avant-garde texts often seem to be refused by a well-developed and persistent subject, which is constituted by many more material practices than just the cinema. Also, the question of how feminism as a sexual identity (the nonmale) can undergo re-vision in terms that also acknowledge oppression by class, race, and nationality remains to be answered. Some may well doubt that the road to semiotic or poststructural interrogation is the best. It may seem overly intellectual, excessively idealized, or potentially elitist. However, it has the advantage of being the first rigorous theoretical critique of sexism and the cinema to emerge within academic scholarship, and as such it has enjoyed an institutional advantage, although that advantage may only be temporary. Even so, it may also propose a level and an intensity of debate that show how more content- or issue-oriented practices may unwittingly perpetuate formally the very ideology that they reject thematically. We will encounter that issue several times in this volume. It does not lend itself to very clear-cut resolution, except in polemic.

•

CLASSIC HOLLYWOOD CINEMA
AND THE IMAGINARY

The central question which psychoanalysis has raised for film theory in general and for feminist film theory in particular is what kind of reader the film text constructs, the positioning of the subject in relation to patriarchal ideology. In her essay 'Visual Pleasure and Narrative Cinema',[1] Laura Mulvey points to the fetishistic and sadistic aspects of the scopic drive which are at play in the classic film text and the problems this poses for development of a feminist cinema. But it is ultimately the question of the positioning of the subject in relation to patriarchy which determines the question of voyeuristic pleasure in relation to the female figure in the cinema. Voyeuristic pleasure itself cannot be eliminated from the cinema; indeed, it is vital for the cinema's survival and its development as a political weapon. Feminist cinema must include a challenge to the fetishistic and sadistic aspects of the scopic drive which Laura Mulvey demonstrates so convincingly, but it will also have to challenge in a very fundamental sense the entire notion of the specular text itself, which involves going beyond the question of the inscription of the look as discourse to the more general question of the way the specular text places the spectator in a certain way. This involves an examination of the cinema as a certain kind of enunciation *(énonciation)*, which, as Metz describes, suppresses 'all marks of the subject of the enunciation . . . in order that the viewer may have the impression of being that subject himself, but an empty, absent subject, a pure capacity for seeing'. Metz claims that the actual indentification with the characters on the screen in any film must be secondary to the prior identification with this 'instance of seeing' and that, in this situation, the viewer 'only retrieves himself as subject at the last moment, by a paradoxical identification with his own self'.

In this essay 'Histoire/Discours', Metz goes one step further than in 'The Imaginary Signifier'[2] in his analysis of the specular text by stressing the importance of the *histoire* (story) as a system, taking the distinction from Emile Benveniste in his examination of the constitution of subjectivity in language. It is the story which reconciles everything in the cinema precisely because it is always 'a story from nowhere, told by nobody, but received by someone (without which it would not exist)'. Metz then goes on to claim that for this reason it is therefore 'the receiver (or rather the receptacle) who tells it; while at the same time it is not told at all, since the receptacle is required merely as an empty space, within which the purity of the enunciation without the *énoncé* (statement) will resound all the better'. It is precisely this non-exhibitionistic aspect of the cinema, a fundamental denial of the look of the spectator, which, according to Metz, has channelled all classic cinema into the history mould, eradicating the notion of cinema as discourse. Metz goes on to qualify this by saying that this denial is in fact split. There is always a discourse which lies behind the history if we consider cinema as an institution, a concealed discourse, and it is this split in which film is both exhibitionist and at the same time secretive which characterises the dominant form voyeurism assumes in the cinema.

It is this idea of the spectator as an 'empty space', a 'receptacle' into which the enunciation resounds, the fundamental denial of the look of the spectator, which provides the basis for seeing the cinema as a process which locks the spectator into an imaginary unity, a particular sense of identity, analogous with but not reducible to the mirror phase described by Lacan. It is precisely this sense of unity, of identity, which provides an impression of 'truth', a reality effect in the spectator. As Metz observes, this creates a situation which leads to such notions as 'narrator as God or viewer as God; it is the "story" which exhibits itself, the story which reigns'. It is this conception of the specular text, this 'specularisation of reality', as Stephen Heath[3] has put it, which achieves a 'coherence of a subject outside contradiction', the sense of 'the individual as subject framed and narrated' which is rooted in the idea of identity: the imaginary. According to Lacan it is the imaginary which constitutes the subject through a speculary effect, a unifying reflection. This speculary, imaginary function also constitutes the limits without which syntagms and paradigms in language would be dissolved into an infinity of differences.

In *The Order of Things,* Michel Foucault analyses the painting 'Las Meninas' by Velasquez in terms of being in itself a representation of classical representation in that it depicts what is usually invisible: the spectator. The painting represents the 'reverse shot' of classical representation. In *Cahiers du Cinéma,* Jean-Pierre Oudart[4] takes this analysis one stage further in examining the specific role the cinema assigns to the imaginary. He sees the cinema as essentially the same kind of enunciation as that of classical representation, the spectator occupying the place left empty by the system of representation. What concerns Oudart is not the apparatus of the cinema itself, but the succession of 'views' produced through classic narrative forms and points of view set up in the film text: the oblique personal form of *histoire* with discourse concealed behind it. Oudart calls the articulation of narrative and image flow in which the film constantly poses an absence, a lack in relation to the subject, suture. Taking the paradigm of the classic cinema—the shot/reverse shot format—Oudart demonstrates how the possession of space by the spectator is illusory in the sense that he can only see what is represented in the axis of the glance of another spectator—the absent one of the reverse shot. Meaning is produced through a process of sealing the imaginary into the film through a system based on the dichotomy 'what I see' vs. the absent one in the shot/reverse shot format. This process involves a situation in which the glance of the absent one becomes, through the flow of the image, the glance of someone, thus liberating the imaginary and structuring the production of meaning in a certain way. The filmic field ('what I see') is the signifier, the absent one the signified. In the image flow the absent one continually destroys the balance of the filmic statement at the level of the signifier, creating a sense of loss; it is always incomplete at the level of the signified. In addition, the effect on the spectator must always be retroactive. When we finally know what the other field was, it is no longer on the screen. The meaning of any shot is thus given retrospectively. It represents a memory in the mind of the spectator. The suture in a representational process, therefore, remodels memory in the retroactive process of the signified linked to an anticipatory process of the signifier, in which it eternally attempts to stop up the eruption of hiatuses which the marks of enunciation as discourse constantly introduce into the imaginary unity of the story. In the sense that any mark referring to the subject of discourse *is not that subject,* the relation of subjectivity (i.e., that which poses the subject) is eternally fissured in the very process of enunciation. The subject is always elsewhere: only the marks of the subject can be located. The suturing process addresses itself precisely to this process of 'fading' by retroactively closing up the distance opened up between the subject and its mark, introducing 'stand-ins' to fill the gap opened up, establishing an imaginary unity. This imaginary unity is available as support for ideology and accountable for much of its force.

Lacan[5] discusses suture as the situation in which the subject becomes an effect of the signifier: this situation in which he/she is stood in for. It thus relates to the relationship of the individual as subject to the chain of his/her discourse, and is a process which constantly attempts to close or bind up the gap between the subject and the signifier. But in that as soon as the subject is posited, it is, in fact, elsewhere, this process is doomed to failure. To understand the implications of the process of suture for the whole question of ideology, and in particular its relationship to the imaginary and the symbolic, it is necessary to look at the *fort/da* game described by Freud. In the game the child constantly throws away and then retrieves a cotton reel: the child gives the Other, the outside, the possibility of holding signification in the acquisition of a symbol. In so doing the child superimposes the determination of the signifier over that of the signified. In this hypothesis of the mythical origin of language, two phonemes, A and O, come to represent for the child the presence and absence of the mother for the first time, and it is these categories of presence/absence which constitute the notion of difference upon which language is founded. With a co-extension of the two systems signifier/signified, therefore, according to Lacan, there are now four terms: presence and absence as signifier and presence and absence as signified. In this way, there is no necessary link between thing and sign, but only the relation of differences. In Lacanian theory, there is no identity but only difference: each element can only be seen in relation to all the other elements in the signifying chain. The crucial determinant is the signifier. He states:

It is in the chain of the signifier that meaning insists but that none of the elements 'consists' in the meaning of which it is at that moment capable.[6]

This implies the constant sliding of the signified under the signifier and a notion of retrospective meaning: meaning is only ensured in the last term of the phrase, with reference to the signifying chain at moments of captation. The signifier is, therefore, the mark of separation (inaugurated with the first cry of the child) by which identities and differences are established. The incidence of the signifier on the signified can only occur by evoking a third term as witness to its meaning—it only occurs at a place outside itself (the Other). It is therefore not possible to speak of a fully present (self-present) subject. He/she must be understood as essentially absent, and able to signify only because he/she produces him/herself in a position in relation to the signifier. Without the signifier there would be no subject. The suture constitutes an attempt to constantly fill up this gap between the subject and the signifier in a situation in which it is doomed forever to be the effect of the signifier, represented or stood in for.

Lacan[7] describes how in the mirror phase the child becomes fascinated with his/her image in the mirror as an identification. This identification in the mirror constitutes the first moment in which the child, still dominated by maternal dependency and autoeroticism, comes to form an image of him/herself separate from the fragmented mobility of the drives. In order to grasp this unity, therefore, the child must situate its identity in alienation. The mirror phase is the key moment for the imaginary order and the one in which the subject finds him/herself in relation to objects. It thus represents the threshold to positionality necessary for language and representation. Not only is the signifiable outside established as it is implicitly with the first cry and in the *fort/da* game, where, as we have seen, the subject becomes the effect of the signifier, but here that outside, the Other, is represented by an imaginary projection in the mirror. Thus for the first time this image of the subject becomes the means by which he/she can represent him/herself in a relatively fixed relation to external objects. In the mirror phase it is the unity characterising the ideal ego which is the basis for the child's necessary miscognition of itself as omnipotent in the face of his/her own lack of power and co-ordination by which all later identifications of the ego are inaugurated. This miscognition of primary narcissism prefigures that of the sutured coherence, the fiction of totality which marks the assumption of the I and with the gap which must forever be filled. Suture, then, is essentially bound up with the Imaginary, and functions over and against the Symbolic and the order of language.

Over and against the Imaginary there is the realm of desire, also set in motion by the play of presence/absence. Desire is essentially the difference between satisfaction sought and satisfaction obtained. The object of desire is thus the memory trace of a previous gratification which can never be attained, but will always be the lost object forever reincarnating itself in a series of objects. Desire is set in motion with the first cry and the posing of the first signifier, and with it a series of signifiers which are interchangeable, generating a perpetual metonymy which Leplanche and Leclaire describe as that which:

designates, covers or masks the gaping abyss of the subject . . . this metonymy like a scar, by its inexhaustible power of displacement, is made precisely to mark and mask the gap through which desire originates and into which it perpetually plunges on the bedrock of the death drive.[8]

It is the experience of loss which sets the metonymic process of desire in motion, the gap forever to be filled. In his analysis of suture as a process, Oudart tends to ignore the aspect of desire, because he is concerned to pinpoint the reality effect of classic representation. The question of desire is important because it adds another dimension to the notion of the suture in the analysis of the specular text, articulating image flow, the inauguration of narrative and its constant development as a series of enigmas (the hermeneutic code)—the perpetual narration of subject and desire in the classic Hollywood cinema. As Metz observes, the filmic system is essentially a displacement, 'a movement of negation, of destruction–construction', which is that of desire, and thus the death drive. The pleasure of the classic text, then, is intimately linked with the tracing of desire in image flow and narrative, the metonymic play of desire aiming at abolishing the gap forever opened up by the fact that desire must pass through the 'defiles' of the signifier.

PATRIARCHAL IDEOLOGY AND
THE REPRESSION OF THE FEMININE

The structuring of the subject through language leads to a radically different relationship to language for men and women under patriarchy deriving from women's negative entry into the Symbolic. This negativity can be located, as Juliet Mitchell has pointed out,[9] in the system of kinship itself. Juliet Mitchell's feminist reading of Freud draws heavily on the work of the anthropologist Lévi-Strauss and in particular his work on kinship systems,[10] in which he demonstrates how social communication operates essentially at three different levels: verbal communication, myth and the kinship system, which communicates through the exchange of women. In this sense, then, kinship studies and linguistics approach the same kinds of problems at different strategic levels pertaining essentially to the same field. Culture consists not simply of language to which we must all submit in order to achieve 'humanity', but also of rules stating how the games of communication should be played. Citing the system of kinship as the dominant means by which women are defined in patriarchal culture, Juliet Mitchell sees men as being defined predominantly by historical processes. Placed outside history, therefore, woman is to a large extent a message which is being communicated, a sign which is being exchanged in patriarchal culture. This points to a view of women as necessarily being guardians of negative and passive structural relations, without the social language of political practice, destined to form an identity in relation to negativity aimed at the demands of the system of reproduction.

The feminist re-reading of Freud, extended and modified by the work of Lacan, has focussed on how the acquisition of language and the child's entry into the Symbolic involves the organisation of sexuality around the fact of being and not being the phallus. This involves the examination of the movement from the world of difference outlined above, to that of sexual difference, brought about through the production of symbolic positions which force a meaning to the distinction male/female. With this movement goes the development of desire organised according to the demands of reproduction. The phallus is the privileged signifier in the child's entry into the Symbolic, the signifier *par excellence* of desire and of difference. The pre-oedipal subject is set in symbolic relations through the structuring of difference, but it is the identification necessitated by the whole question of having or not having the phallus which forces the transition from the Imaginary to the Symbolic, the Oedipus complex constituting a retrospective sanctioning of earlier differences and separations.

Juliet Mitchell characterises patriarchy and the Oedipus complex in the following terms:

The act of exchange holds society together (i.e., human society is different from animal organisation precisely because of the laws of exchange governing society in opposition to the natural family, laws of exchange resulting from the law—in all known societies—of the prohibition of incest, with its inevitable corollary, the Oedipus complex). The rules of kinship are the society.

The Law, then, has always rested with the father in patriarchal culture. In such a symbolic order, the child must renounce his/her pre-oedipal bisexuality and the mother as love object for the requirements of the Oedipus complex and assume his/her castration. Lacan states:

Freud revealed to us that it is thanks to the Name of the Father that man does not remain in the sexual service of the mother, and that aggression towards the father is at the principle of the Law and that the Law is at the service of desire, which it institutes through the prohibition of incest. It is therefore the assumption of castration which creates the lack through which desire is instituted. Desire is the desire for desire, the desire of the Other, and it is subject to the Law.[11]

The phallocentrism of patriarchal culture is founded on the paradigm of male sexuality—the penis. In the light of the fact of the privileged place of the phallus in patriarchal culture, therefore, entry into the Symbolic, for the girl in her lack of a penis, must necessarily be a negative entry. The Symbolic serves to break up the imaginary direction of the ego, allowing the child to take up finally a fixed position within language at the axis of the division between signifier/signified. This process is brought about by the intervention of the third term, which in patriarchal culture takes the form of the father who demands of the child that he/she acknowledge the fact of sexual difference and its implications. In this way, as Freud demonstrated, the Oedipus complex and the acceptance of symbolic castration of necessity forces a distinction between 'masculinity' and 'femininity', and with its dissolution and the child's acquisition of the superego (internalised source of morality and conscience) patriarchal culture reproduces itself. What marks patriarchy above all else is the prohibition of incestuous desire and a fundamental asymmetry between the sexes. The structural function of the phallus as *the* Signifier determines a positionality in relation to it, establishing sexual difference and ensuring the sexual reproduction of the species: the transference of the drives to the Symbolic Order for the purpose of reproduction.

Drawing from Freud, Juliet Mitchell makes a strong case for seeing femininity in patriarchal culture as essentially a secondary condition (in the light of the fact that the Oedipus complex faces the girl with a far more complex problem to solve) which can only be acquired partially and in a distorted form. In fact, Freud was the first to observe that women are inherently more bisexual than men. The human heritage of femininity, Juliet Mitchell suggests, can be seen as a secondary identity opened up by the Symbolic Order but not co-extensive with it. Perhaps the relationship of the feminine to the Symbolic can only be understood in its symptoms, as in the case of hysteria, which Freud saw as a disorder with 'feminine characteristics' in that it embodied both the representation of desire and its prohibition. In the asymmetry of patriarchal culture, then, woman is defined as other, as *that which is not male.*

Thus patriarchy formulates the mode of articulation between the Imaginary and the Symbolic in terms of castration, of absence, and this in turn determines what is the system of subjectivity in relation to sex in culture as a whole, and thus in language. Not only does our culture speak in the individual speech act, but we are spoken by it. The relations of subjectivity in language, as we have seen, are eternally fissured in the very process of enunciation. The subject is always elsewhere; only the marks of the subject can be located in language. The suturing process constantly retroactively attempts to close up this gap between the subject and its mark, transforming the codic aspect of the system of pronouns into the marks of the sexed subject in terms of woman as other: male/non-male. In the film text, then, the marks of the subject are overdetermined by patriarchal ideology giving a content to the dichotomy between personal and non-personal pronouns in terms of male/non-male. In its turn, non-male is conflated with the stereotype of 'femininity' in patriarchal culture: woman as locus of lack and castration fears or woman as image of lost maternal plenitude. In the economy of desire set up by systems of representation in patriarchy based on the incest taboo (prohibition of incest with the mother) woman as sign is destined to be forever the object rather than the subject of desire. Positioned and sexed by the mode of discourse as *histoire* of the classic Hollywood text, woman can only be exchanged as currency in the economy of desire in a perpetual play of metonymy. This point is made most clearly in Raoul Walsh's *The Revolt of Mamie Stover*[12] where the exchange of women is related explicitly to the circulation of money, a system which they do not have access to directly but only through a stereotyped sexuality. The refusal of such a positionality, as in the case of Cukor's *Sylvia Scarlett* and Tourneur's *Anne of the Indies*,[13] in the form of the masquerade renders the female figure an impossible sign, a trouble which must be eliminated from the text.

The repression of the feminine in the classic film text therefore consists of the reduction of sexual difference into the dichotomy male/non-male and in the system of exchange set up by the play of desire in the text. The process of suture is what articulates the workings of patriarchal ideology in the classic text, establishing through the constant filling up of gaps set up in the mode of representation an imaginary unity necessary as a support for patriarchal ideology. Althusser locates the problem of ideology as a system of representations: it is an imaginary relation. This formulation requires further clarification in the light of the psychoanalytic theory of ego construction. To the extent that ideology consists of the unity of a real relation and an imaginary relation, it utilises the imaginary unity of the mirror phase: such a unity makes it possible to act in society at all. But this is not to imply that the symbolic and patriarchal ideology is a separate realm. Ultimately Althusser's[14] definition of ideology derives from a notion of 'representation' rather than of 'signification'. But the products of signifying practices such as film do not represent anything outside themselves. They cannot serve as a simple means of expression because they are constituted through the very practices of signification themselves. As an operation, suture cannot simply be seen as a support for patriarchal ideology, which somehow pre-exists it. As we have seen, through a process of transformation of symbolic relations suture articulates a system of subjectivity in relation to sexual difference in the film text, which is then supported by an imaginary unity. As a process, a practice of signification, suture is an ideological operation with a particular function in relation to patriarchal ideology in that out of a system of differences it establishes a position in relation to the phallus. In so doing it places the spectator in relation to that position, and it is at this point that Althusser's imaginary aspect of ideology comes into play. It is this imaginary unity, the sutured coherence, the imaginary sense of identity set up by the classic film, which must be challenged by a feminist film practice to achieve a different constitution of the subject in relation to ideology.

FEMINIST FILM PRACTICE: 'JEANNE DIELMAN'

Undoubtedly the most important work to have been produced to date on the relationship between patriarchy and artistic practice is that of Julia Kristeva in *La Révolution du Langage Poétique*.[15] This book draws extensively on the work of Lacan and continues the interrogation of the metaphysical conception of the sign inaugurated by Jacques Derrida and others (the conception of sign as unity of signifier/signified in traditional linguistics) with the aim of restoring the materiality of the sign repressed by Western discourse since Plato. Julia Kristeva states: 'The subject never is, the subject is only the process of signification and only presents itself as the signifying practice'. Thus the acquisition of the sign is only a part of the process of signification. According to Julia Kristeva there is a division in Western discourse between the pheno-text—a unity, a symbolic system obeying the laws of communication—and the genotext, a semiotic process analogous to the primary process and the drives which language represses and which do not take the form of signification but can only emerge as an interruption in discourse. The semiotic is most clearly in evidence in psychotic discourse and in the poetic language of avant-gardist textual practice from the late nineteenth century onwards.

Julia Kristeva describes this structure as being set up by the 'thetic event', which creates the structure or system of exchange and communication on which signification is founded. In the Western episteme founded on the two monotheisms of Judaism and Christianity the 'thetic event' takes the form of castration, producing in its turn woman as

the other race, silent support of the symbolic function, permanent appeal to a forbidden incest, object of anguished masculine identification.

Thus in the form of patriarchy which founds Western discourse, woman is the 'unnameable', the 'unsaid'. In the economy of the speaking subject there is a certain type of relation between the unity of the symbolic and the semiotic process which is heterogeneous to it. The feminine, in so far as it can be expressed at all, exists in the face of the unifying instance of signifier/signified, which forms identity and the coherence of the sign. As such it is profoundly subversive. It is for this reason that Julia Kristeva has made a study of the position of women in China where there exists a totally different signifying practice involving a quite other relation between symbolic system and semiotic process. The semiotic as process, as free play of drives, gives rise in its infiltration into the structure of language, to the feminine in a repressed form. This involves the production of excess experienced as *jouissance,* opening up a radical heterogeneity in its process of *signifiance.* Poetic language is the primary example of such a process of *signifiance,* which puts the subject in crisis and with it the sign and social identity itself. It is an expenditure without exchange.

Julia Kristeva claims that for the first time in history conditions exist to relativise this unity in Western discourse, and here women and the feminine play a key role. In connection with this she places considerable emphasis on the idea of negativity and the process of *rejet* or 'throwing out', a movement of destruction linked to the death drive and experienced as *jouissance* as a fundamental expression of the semiotic modality and a condition of such a relativisation. In *The Pleasure of the Text*[16] Roland Barthes characterises the text of *jouissance* as one marked by a sense of loss; it is a text which

unsettles the reader's historical, cultural, psychological assumptions, the consistency of his tastes, values, memories, brings to a crisis his relation with language.

It is through this negativity and the expression of the destructive drives that structures previously repressed emerge, namely the feminine. At the same time there is always the risk of psychosis in such a project. It is pleasure on the side of the death drive which is the condition of putting the subject in process, but as Julia Kristeva rightly points out, a complete dissolution of unity and the symbolic system would mean the dissolution of sociality itself.

This putting of the subject in process in textual practice constitutes a revolutionary practice according to Julia Kristeva. As a contribution to the materialist theory of language her work is of fundamental importance, but for feminism this contribution is less clear. The central weakness of her position is that it fails to deal with the question of how such a textual practice can relate to political practice and to history. In pointing to the asymmetry of patriarchal culture and the precariousness of the Oedipus complex for women, she opens the way for an exploration of such questions, but ultimately sees the solution in terms of individual subjectivity, the relativisation of the Symbolic and in the notion of bisexuality. In the last analysis such a solution is anarchic in its implications.

Political practice must of necessity harness the semiotic, but in specific symbolic structures. As a political practice the Women's Movement poses the struggle at this point in history for a different Symbolic Order other than that consecrated by patriarchy in which the production of the new subject involves the setting up of an entirely different relation to the third term, one that is structurally analogous to but not the same as the third term of the Oedipus complex. This is manifest in the Movement's search for new forms of political organisation and practice. The task is not to relativise the Symbolic, as Julia Kristeva suggests, but to displace and undermine it through struggle in a project of transforming the Symbolic—a project posed in the last section of Laura Mulvey and Peter Wollen's film *Penthesilea*. This struggle will be necessarily linked to but distinct from the class struggle. As Serge Leclaire[17] points out, for women the phallus can never be a pure signifier; it is this different relationship which women have to absence which points to such a transformation.

Chantal Akerman's *Jeanne Dielman, 23 Quai du Commerce —1080 Bruxelles* is a film which poses this problem of absence in relation to woman in a fundamental sense. The film charts with an ethnographic precision three days in the life of a Belgian housewife/prostitute: the fixed identity encapsulated in the name and address of the title. Two systems are set up by the film: that of the framing—the ordering of physical space—and that of the diegesis—the ordering of temporal space. The framing consists of the cutting out of space in long, immobile takes, the human figure constantly coming in and going out of frame. There is no reverse shot, but the opening up of what suture attempts to fill. What dominates is the 'thetic', the symbolic cutting out of the field of vision, posing both absence and the fact of heterogeneity by the over-inscription of rigidity—the very representation of the repression of sexuality. The diegesis poses the narrative content of the film concerned with the filling up of temporal space, which again is articulated by the sense of lack, the filling of an absence: the dead husband, the absent son, the day itself, the world of objects, gestural language.

These two systems come together in a moment which is off-screen and elided in the diegesis: sexuality. A repressed sexuality erupting as *jouissance,* setting up a series of parapraxes, creating both the disorganisation of physical space and temporal gaps. This eruption of the semiotic, the drives, closed off from our view and unnarrated, in a moment of *jouissance,* constitutes an expenditure without exchange within the economy set up by the film text. As such it must be annulled in the act of murder, in the abolition of the phallus. The film ends with the re-establishment of the symbolic and of absence, the order of socio-familial constraints. The final frame is again one of plenitude, of absence and of paralysis.

Chantal Akerman's film is important for feminism because it resolutely refuses to present us with the security of the reverse shot of classic representation and instead foregrounds the 'thetic' aspect of the field of vision, the Symbolic Order, in all its harshness on the body of the woman as other, woman as non-male. In so doing it reveals the fragility of such a Symbolic Order by the over-inscription of absence and by the inscription of the drives as 'elsewhere'. The film's inscription of this asymmetry opens up the possibility of a different Symbolic Order, a different mode of articulation between the Imaginary and the Symbolic beyond the frame, the diegesis and our field of vision—but nevertheless present.

Notes

1. *Screen,* Autumn 1975.

2. *Screen,* Summer 1975.

3. "On Screen, In Frame: Film and Ideology," *Quarterly Review of Film Studies,* Autumn 1976.

4. *Cahiers du Cinéma,* no. 211 (April 1969); this article was utilised in English by Daniel Dayan in "The Tutor-Code of Classical Cinema" in *Film Quarterly,* vol. 27, no. 1, 1974, reprinted in *Movies and Methods,* vol. 1.

5. In *Ecrits,* Paris: Editions du Seuil, 1966. For a useful account of what is at stake in Lacan's notion of suture, a concept which appears throughout his writings, see Stephen Heath's chapter "On Suture" in *Questions of Cinema.*

6. In "The Insistence of the Letter in the Unconscious", in *Structuralism,* ed. Jacques Ehrmann, New York: Anchor Books, 1970.

7. "The Mirror Phase as Formative of the Function of the I", in *New Left Review,* no. 51 (1968).

8. "The Unconscious: A Psychoanalytic Study", in *Yale French Studies,* no. 48 (1972).

9. *Psychoanalysis and Feminism,* London: Allen Lane, 1974.

10. *The Elementary Structures of Kinship,* London: Eyre and Spottiswood, 1969.

11. *Ecrits.* "Du 'Trieb' de Freud et du Desir du Psychanalyste"—this text does not appear in the English version of *Ecrits.*

12. "The Place of Women in the Cinema of Raoul Walsh" by Pam Cook and Claire Johnston in *Raoul Walsh,* E.F.F., 1974.

13. "Femininity and the Masquerade: Anne of the Indies" by Claire Johnston in *Jacques Tourneur,* E.F.F., 1975.

14. "Ideology and the Ideological State Apparatuses" in *Lenin and Philosophy and Other Essays,* London: New Left Books, 1971. For a critique of Althusser's position see *Screen,* Autumn 1976.

15. Paris: Editions du Seuil, 1974.

16. New York: Hill and Wang, 1975.

17. *On Tue un Enfant,* Paris: Editions du Seuil, 1975.

JEANNE DIELMAN: DEATH IN INSTALLMENTS

JAYNE LOADER

Although there is considerable insistence that films establish a privileged reading through their style and structure, it is not entirely clear to what extent such a reading is governed more by the assumptions and priorities of a critical approach than by the film itself. Compare the last three paragraphs of Claire Johnston's article with Loader's extended discussion of Jeanne Dielman *here. Although Johnston and Loader share a feminist perspective, they arrive at opposed readings: Johnston sees in the act of murder "the abolition of the phallus," an "eruption of the semiotic," "of* jouissance" *that must subside back into "the order of socio-familial constraints."*

This annulment of pleasure underscores the fragility of a symbolic order that hinges on absence, and it holds out the possibility of another symbolic order beyond the constraints that hold the character, Jeanne Dielman, in place. Johnston's reading locates the film in an arena of contestation defined by signification and the production of meaning. In contrast, Loader locates the film in an arena of contestation defined by social practice and meaning. In other words, Loader's reading is more a style-sensitive thematic reading than it is a semiotic one. For Loader, Akerman's camera style reveals the oppressive condition of housewifery, whereas for Johnston it also establishes a "framing" to the diegetic events and their social relevance that produces significance by withholding the reverse shot. These innovative elements are ignored or dismissed by Loader, who concludes that the film, despite some of the best examination of the role of the traditional mother in feminist cinema, is dramatically conventional and politically retrograde. From Loader's viewpoint, the film's structure, style, and climactic act seem less to evoke a feminist alternative to the victim and victimizing role of housewife than to capitulate to conventions of patriarchal narrative, such as killing for freedom and "revenge and regeneration through violence," and to conventional narrative structure ("tension, climax, exhaustion").

Loader associates the act of murder with a rejection of disruptive "jouissance" by the character, whereas Johnston associates the murder not with the character but with the overall énonciation and with the opening up of an alternative order by the very rigidity of the framing. (Loader also makes inferences about Akerman's intentions in her conclusion, but her main argument against individual acts of violence can stand on its own merits. What is not clear is whether Akerman would not in fact agree with her.)

These two readings are quite different. Loader's demonstrates the continuing value of a socially oriented form of feminist critique that judges actions in a film against the efficacy of similar actions in society. This returns us to the question of the work of culture as a set of direct propositions about social conduct, a question that most psychoanalytic and poststructuralist work deflects toward forms of positioning for the viewer as viewer, not as social agent. Neither Johnston nor Loader needs to be "right" in her reading of Jeanne Dielman *for both to demonstrate the workings of two quite different feminist approaches.*

•

Chantal Akerman's *Jeanne Dielman, 23 Quai du Commerce —1080 Bruxelles,* recently subtitled in preparation for possible American release, is an ambiguous and difficult film but one that deserves serious consideration from both feminist and formalist critics. In presenting her portrait of a bourgeois Belgian housewife whose widowhood leads her to afternoon prostitution, Akerman elicits not only an intensely sensitive performance from Delphine Seyrig but startlingly contradictory responses from her audience as well. The vehemence and passion of these responses and the structure of the film itself lead one to question Akerman's politics and aesthetics that can only be answered in the context of the historiography and theory of women in the home: as workers who are essential in maintaining the capitalist system through production and reproduction, largely unrecognized and unpaid. The film raises further questions in terms of its contribution to the vital task of developing feminist art and feminist film language, providing a measure of how far we have come and of what remains undone.

My own answers to these questions are not encouraging ones: I find Akerman's film not only self-defeating in its depiction of the housewife's role and her so-called regeneration through violence at the film's end, but cavalier in its treatment of the complex role of women in the family. Akerman's solution to the fact of female oppression is unfortunately a common one, which is offered not only in several other contemporary films by women but in a significant number of women's novels as well: it is violence, directed at the first male who comes to hand. By his sex rather than his person, he is forced to stand for the oppressors of all the rest.

Jeanne Dielman examines three days in the life of its heroine, each day consuming approximately one hour of screen space. Much of the action of the film is shot in "real time"; if it takes Jeanne fifteen minutes to peel a batch of potatoes, then the fifteen minutes are presented on the screen without a cut. Yet the moments thus shown are of necessity carefully selected; three days must be compacted into three hours, rather than 72. Much of the film—and, for me, its strongest sections—is about housework; other moments capture Jeanne's interaction with her teenage son. Less time is taken up with her relations with the other people on the periphery of her life: the storekeepers who sell to her, a woman in her building whose baby she watches, the baby, neighbors on the street. She seems to have no friends. Only a small amount of time is devoted to the men who provide Jeanne's income: the clients she services as a prostitute each afternoon.

It is the housework that sticks in one's mind after the film is over and the housework that provides Jeanne's identity. The work is close to ritual, rigidly scheduled and repeated daily with slight variation and maximum efficiency; a process that appears impossible to sustain if one has not been at some point a housewife (or factory worker) oneself. As Barbara Ehrenreich and Deirdre English describe it:

Housework is maintenance and restoration: the daily restocking of the shelves and return of each cleaned and repaired object to its starting point in the family game of disorder. After a day's work, no matter how tiring, the housewife has produced no tangible object—except, perhaps, dinner; and that will disappear in less than half the time it took to prepare. She is not supposed to make anything, but to buy, and then to prepare or conserve what has been bought, dispelling dirt and depreciation as they creep up. And each housewife works alone.[1]

Since Jeanne Dielman's duties as housewife compose the bulk of the film's action, one can get a feel for the film's flow and pacing through scanning this list of them: Jeanne gets up, puts on her dressing gown, and chooses her son's clothes; she lights a fire in his room, picks up his shoes and takes them to the kitchen, where she shines them, lights the stove, grinds the coffee beans, and makes coffee; she wakes her son; he eats while she dresses; she says goodbye to him and gives him money taken from a blue and white china crock on the dining table; she washes the dishes, makes her son's bed and folds it into a couch, makes her own bed and lays a towel over her coverlet; she shops and runs errands, returns to her apartment, and begins to prepare dinner; she sits with her neighbor's child, eats her lunch, and returns the baby to its mother; the doorbell rings; she admits a man, takes his hat and coat, and leads him into the bedroom; she leads him to the front door, gives him his hat and coat, and takes money from him, which she puts in the blue china crock; she opens the window in her bedroom, puts the rumpled towel in the clothes hamper, bathes, cleans the tub, and dresses; she closes the bedroom window and takes dinner off the stove; her son comes home; they eat dinner immediately: soup, meat, and potatoes; she tells him not to read while eating; he puts his books away; she clears the table and helps him with his homework; she knits and glances through the newspaper, until it is time for them to take their evening walk around the block; they unfold his sofa bed; he reads while she undresses; she turns off the stove, kisses him, turns out the lights, and goes, at last, to sleep.

There exist subtle variations within this basic range of activities that give us clues to Jeanne's character and moods, but this structure—carefully designed and rigidly adhered to—forms the core of the film and accurately, poignantly captures the reality of housework and the housewife role for many women. Ann Oakley notes the frequency of such inflexible, self-imposed schedules in her study of contemporary English housewives, who use timetables and ritualized action in order to give their lives structure, to impart meaning to what seems to many a meaningless job:

Faced with housework as their job, they devise rules which give the work the kind of structure most employed workers automatically find in their job situation. Having defined the rules they then attempt to adhere to them, and to derive reward from carrying them out.[2]

The monotony, the crippling effect of such a process is powerfully illustrated in Akerman's film. We are initially bored with its slow pace, which admits no music, no camera movement, and no opticals as distraction, but we are ultimately carried into the rhythm of Jeanne's life: empathy is virtually unavoidable. The frustrations—the "mad housewife" syndrome so often presented in American film and fiction about women—are absent here for the most part; Jeanne is serene, methodical, almost madonna-like as she floats efficiently, effortlessly through the day. If she feels frustrations with her role or has fantasies of escape she represses them even, or especially, in the privacy of her own home.

The precision of Jeanne's motions is as clean and sharp as a good Swiss watch; we watch her dip veal in egg, meal, and flour without a wasted movement. She is presented as an automaton, geared for maximum efficiency and functioning perfectly, a victim of both the domestic science movement and the petit-bourgeois Belgian culture that produced her. The compulsiveness of Jeanne's housecleaning, the zeal with which she attacks crumbs and disorder, the serenity with which she accomplishes her tasks all point to a woman who has internalized the principle that "neglect of housecleaning is tantamount to child abuse."[3] And Akerman's controlled, formal style perfectly mirrors the inner feelings of her character, forcing us visually into her world.

The most striking formal technique in *Jeanne Dielman* is Akerman's use of the static camera. We see Jeanne's life as if it were a painting which we have all the time in the world to study; thus we are not manipulated by dollies in or out of space that force us to focus on some particular point of action, or by changing camera angles which hurtle us up or down emotionally. Akerman has said that she saw no reason to move the camera in her film, and for the most part I agree with her: her character's actions speak for themselves.[4] The static camera traps us as completely as Jeanne's static life traps her, and studying that world, we become a part of it. The contrast between the average viewer's boredom with Jeanne's life or voyeuristic obsession with its stasis in contrast to Jeanne's glacial calm is striking: we are forced to experience Jeanne's life and wonder how she stands living it.

Since Jeanne is the heart of the film, this is expressed visually by her placement in the still frame. She is centered precisely within it, and unless she moves
from one room to another, Akerman not only holds the camera steady but holds
the shot as well. There are no cuts except when absolutely necessary, and Jeanne
is almost always on screen. Akerman's cinema focuses our attention on her smallest gestures, gestures that reveal character but would be lost in a more flamboyant
film: a knife that almost slips when a potato is peeled, a light turned off unnec-
essarily, a facial expression of disquiet or of frustration, the curious act of making
coffee in a thermos in the morning for drinking at lunchtime. The effect of such
details, repeated and ritualized, is cumulative: slowly the portrait is pieced
together.

Akerman's mise-en-scène is subtle in structuring the way we view the separate elements of the film and gradually put them together. When Jeanne returns to
her apartment after a shopping trip, for example, Akerman presents the action with
one long shot in the apartment hallway; the elevator that will take Jeanne upstairs is
centered precisely in the middle of the frame, and mailboxes line the hall's left
side. Jeanne walks into the foyer and stops to check her mail, then walks away from
the camera toward the elevator, pushes the button, waits, and enters it. A simple
shot, but the use of a lens with very little depth of field which is focused sharply only
on the foreground mailboxes changes the nature of the shot. We see Jeanne walk out
of focus as she nears the elevator and stands waiting for it; as she nears her apartment, she becomes (visually) a different person. Suddenly the objects in the frame
outweigh her: we concentrate on the texture of the walls sharply in focus rather than
on the fuzzy female person. And the following shot sharpens the emotional impact
of the first. Jeanne is in the elevator, slowly being carried up past the lighted floors.
We don't see Jeanne but her mirror image, trapped in one half of the frame, with the
lights of the passing floors playing over her face. The slow trip becomes a poignant
metaphor; the woman trapped in a small, dark space while the world's lights flicker
by is an image whose real self is obscured. As Jeanne leaves the elevator, the angles
of the mirror's edges fragment her image further. And Akerman uses this particular
sequence of shots and the elevator itself only when Jeanne returns to her apartment,
never when she leaves it.

The apartment seems to have a life of its own, to have needs and demands which
manipulate Jeanne and structure her day much more substantially than do the
needs of either her living son or once-living husband; both of them are, she tells a
neighbor, "easy to please," blind to their surroundings or to what is on the table.[5]
It is the apartment that makes clear and tangible demands: it must be cleaned, its
dishes washed, its furniture polished, its rooms aired of unpleasant odors, its
voracious appetite for human attention, love, and labor appeased.[6] The cuts in the
film emphasize this fact; Akerman's camera often lingers lovingly in a room moments after Jeanne has left it or precedes her entrances by a few long feet of film
which show the quiet permanence of the apartment. Older than Jeanne, it will
survive her.

Much of the cutting in the film involves the physical presence of the house and
its maintenance. Because there is no camera movement, there is no invisible

editing and very few cuts on Jeanne's moving figure. Although Akerman occasionally moves from one room to another by cutting on the placement of Jeanne's figure within the frame, she is much more likely to cut on objects: a table in one shot is balanced by a bowl in the shot adjacent to it. By cutting on lights, sounds, and objects, Akerman emphasizes the overpowering presence of the apartment which, in its very ordinary state, has such an effect on the lives of its inhabitants.

A frequent kind of cut involves a movement from one room to the next; Jeanne turns out the light in the kitchen, and turns on the light in the living room. The cut is masked by the darkness between the two moments. Similar cuts are made with doors opening and closing, often in combination with turning on and off of lights. Such cuts make the film smoother than repeated jump cuts could have, providing natural fades without compromising Akerman's static frame or the illusions of naturalism and real time. The cuts also serve to emphasize Jeanne's compulsive nature and thrift: the lights are turned off to save electricity, the doors closed to save heat. The incessant turning on and off of lights, the rhythm of the opening and closing doors become additional rituals, visual and aural patterns that add another level of repetition to the film and emphasize its pace.

The lighting pattern in the elevator is one more example of these repeated physical motifs. A far more important one is the neon light that flashes into Jeanne's living room each evening. With its consistent, unchanging pattern (four regular flashes and a flicker) the neon light, which never goes out and is never washed out by the light sources in the room, becomes a visual metaphor for the lives of the film's characters and perhaps a foreshadowing of Jeanne's breakdown at the film's end: a "flicker" of life that is always contained by the more powerful pulsation and control of a larger pattern.

The three days of Jeanne's life are significantly different. If the first day is a usual day when everything goes smoothly, we see that the second day throws Jeanne slightly off balance. Because a client stays longer than usual, Jeanne burns the potatoes that were cooking on the stove. With her hair slightly mussed, she wanders from room to room with the pot of burned potatoes, wondering what to do with them. It is a powerful moment in the film, the first time we have ever seen her lose her composure or perform an action that is not completely efficient. Because Jeanne has no potatoes left in the house, she must go again to market. Dinner is late. And although she is quick to reassert the family routine by forcing her son to take their nightly walk around the block, although he would prefer to read, Sylvan destroys her day further by embarrassing questions and confessions about sex. Although Jeanne heads the questions off, the day is not what it should have been.

The third day is even more disrupted. Jeanne fails to button her robe completely and gets shoe polish on her cuff while polishing Sylvan's shoes. Both precision and efficiency are eroded. She moves in and out of rooms turning their lights on and off as she goes, with no idea of what to do once in them. She arrives too early at the post office and grocery and is unable to locate a button for Sylvan's coat at the several shops she visits. She washes her dishes over and over and kneads a meatloaf interminably. When her coffee tastes strange, she throws it out and makes a new pot but finds she cannot drink even that. At the restaurant where she usually goes after shopping, her usual waitress has already gotten off, and a stranger occupies her favorite seat. It is an older, business-like woman with short hair and no make-up who smokes and is engrossed in her work. Traditional, feminine Jeanne is literally displaced by a new kind of woman. At the shops Jeanne makes an attempt to talk to the sales people about her family; previously she had been pleasantly formal to them. She even tries for the first time to play with the baby she sits for, but it cries whenever she picks it up. She sits and stares into space. She is inactive. She responds sexually to her client and stabs him to death with her sewing scissors.

Given the role of the housewife as Akerman presents it, one could easily define Jeanne as a "victim of society" and her act of murder an act of liberation. But there is another aspect of the film that undercuts this interpretation: the psychologically and socially repressive role of the mother in the patriarchal family. While Jeanne's relationship with her apartment marks her as a social victim, her relationship with her son shows him to be victimized as well.

Jeanne is a victim who accepts her victim's role and forces her son to join her in it, and Akerman thus reveals the social role that many women have been compelled to assume: as conservative force in the family, transmitting patriarchal values to their children and assuring through their repression and subjugation the continuance of the dominant social order. The emergence of this role as a fullblown stereotype in male culture (Leo McCarey's *My Son John* is certainly a prime example; the woman in *The Harder They Come,* a more contemporary one) has led many women to deny its real social base and has kept feminists from giving it the serious treatment it deserves. The pitfalls Akerman risked in her attempt to do so are obvious: she presents Jeanne's role as repressor so graphically that her character becomes a difficult one to sympathize with. By zealously defending the family and internalizing its values, Jeanne seems to renounce all opposition and to accept the principle of male-dominated bourgeois society: "bad luck is your own fault."[7]

The idea of the mother as a monster within the home is not a new one in either film or literature, and in Dielman's interactions with her son, she exhibits the kind of character traits which Philip Wylie grouped together and labelled "Momism" in the 1940's. (A concept which peaked in popularity as women were forced back into their homes during the 50's, Momism allowed men to blame women for all the world's ills while never noticing that it was the active *repression* of women in post-war America that produced Mom in the first place.) Jeanne is rigidly compulsive and thrifty, completely invested in concepts of order and cleanliness, with no interests outside her home and no ideas. When her son asks her why she married his father, she explains that she did not want to marry him when he was rich; but that after he lost his money, she could not be talked *out* of the marriage. She finds mention of her husband's body distasteful and explains sex as something to submit to in order to produce children. The marriage to a weak, poor, and unattractive man indicates Jeanne's resolve to have a husband she could tower above as a beautiful and competent woman, and her relations with her son reveal her attempts to cast him in the same mold: as a weak man, without hope or thought of rebellion. As a stereotyped castrating mother, Jeanne Dielman is distinguishable from Mrs. Portnoy and Ma Jarred only by virtue of style.

Jeanne's conscious choice of her role in the victim/victimizer chain may seem at first glance to undercut Akerman's apparent intent in the film: to portray a woman who is a product of a specific class and social milieu, a woman shaped by society and by history. I believe, rather, that it reveals Akerman's sophisticated understanding of the role of women in the home, showing to what lengths some are forced to go in order to have autonomy in the only sphere allotted them; if such women seem monstrous, they become so only to defend themselves from almost overwhelming social forces. Just as Dorothy Arzner's Harriet Craig (in *Craig's Wife*) was willing to sacrifice everything, including her husband, in order to preserve the only place in the world where she had power and security, so Jeanne Dielman is similarly willing to make sacrifices to preserve her home. These include not only her physical prostitution but the renunciation of all genuine human relationships.

Jeanne's son Sylvan's character is not fully revealed, but he has clearly internalized many of the values of his mother and his culture. He corrects her lapses from proper motherhood immediately, reasserting the family routine when it threatens to break down. His only rebellion in the film is to suggest that the family walk be abandoned, but when Jeanne insists, he dutifully puts on his coat. His weakness is emphasized in his total lack of social life and in his failure to pass a school test by faking an illness.

The extent to which Sylvan has accepted Jeanne's values is illustrated by this remarkable interchange, uttered after he returns home on the second day to find dinner late:

Sylvan: Your hair's all tousled.
Jeanne: I let the potatoes boil too long.

That the two perfectly understand each other is one level of communication: to Sylvan, it is logical that a hitch in the day's schedule is enough to muss his mother's hair. That we know her hair is mussed because she hasn't had the time to comb it after an overlong sex act adds another level: the level in which Jeanne denies not only her sexual activities but the function she performs to support the family—as prostitute and as worker.

The sexually repressive nature of the family and its links with the authoritarian personality are perfectly realized in Jeanne's character, and it is in terms of sexuality that her role as agent of repression is most fully known. During the second evening, Sylvan attempts to talk to Jeanne about sex. In a remarkable monologue he describes his introduction to sex through a friend, who has told him, "The penis is a sword; the deeper you thrust it, the better it is." The pain and power associated with that image evokes his own secret fantasies about sex between his parents and a confusion of guilt over his father's death. Hating his father's sexual use of his mother made him wish for the father's death, but to Sylvan's cry for help and explanation and comfort, Jeanne coldly answers, "You shouldn't have worried." To end the discussion, she turns out the light.

The mother's refusal to deal with her own sexuality honestly and to recognize the sexual confusion of her children is one factor, Horkheimer argues, that contributes to the continuation of a repressive social order:

Under the pressure of such a family situation the individual does not learn to respect his mother in her concrete existence, that is, as this particular social and sexual being. Consequently, he is not only educated to repress his socially harmful impulses (a feat of immense cultural significance) but, because this education takes the problematic form of camouflaging reality, the individual also loses for good the disposition of part of his psychic energies. Reason and joy in its exercise are restricted; the suppressed inclination towards the mother reappears as a fanciful and sentimental susceptibility to all symbols of the dark, maternal and protective powers.[8]

When Jeanne hides the reality of not only her past sexual life with Sylvan's father but of her present sexual life with the clients who visit her regularly, monotonously, each weekday afternoon, not only sexuality but work is repressed. Jeanne denies that she works at all and is thus able to maintain the illusion that she is "only a housewife." Her self-definition does not include the concept of work, and by engaging in prostitution in her home, while the potatoes boil, Jeanne relegates it to the level of cleaning the bathtub or bleaching out a particularly nasty stain: sex becomes a necessary but bothersome choice.

Dielman's role as a prostitute becomes another facet of her role as both repressive agent and conservative social force. The prostitute complements the wife, and both are necessary in maintaining the status quo and preventing any real change from occurring. As a prostitute Dielman provides a socially acceptable outlet for drives which left unchecked might lead the individual to question the sexually repressive nature of society and to think of rebellion. If, as some feminists argue, the prostitute literalizes the sexual oppression of all women by calling it by its right name—an exchange of sex for money—and refuses to accept the nonnegotiable items (love, marriage, dinners) that most women bargain for, she may, in fact, avoid being a sexual victim herself. But by serving as a stabilizing force in bourgeois society, she perpetuates the sexual oppression of other women and leaves them and herself open to other forms of oppression.

The role of prostitute (a job many women have found capable of providing large amounts of money in a short time) allows Jeanne the luxury of maintaining that she is a housewife, with her dead husband's support replaced by that of the five johns she services. They replace the father as dispensers of cash while Jeanne serves as dispenser of culture.

As Jeanne misrepresents herself to Sylvan through lies and distortions, the camera similarly represses sexuality through its selection of the moments of time it chooses to show or to omit. Although Akerman shoots much of the film in real time, the sex between Jeanne and her first two clients is not shown at all. Possibly, Akerman is seeking to avoid any audience voyeurism. Because sex is in itself often interesting, omitting it altogether from the film is one way to make it seem unimportant, to prevent any sexual titillation from creeping into the film.

This seems a glib way of solving an important problem in cinema: how does one present sexuality, given the audience's conditioned responses to it as spectacle? Hard-core pornography teaches us that it is quite possible through repetition and the objectification of body parts to make the sex act seem as boring and mundane as washing dishes, as distasteful as cleaning the toilet. But by her failure to show Jeanne's physical prostitution, Akerman calls attention to it. She makes us not voyeurs but busybodies—we wonder what went on in the bedroom. By withholding knowledge of sex, she makes us preoccupied with it and forces us to identify not with Jeanne but with Sylvan, from whom knowledge is similarly withheld.

In the chain of rituals, of monotony, of the interchangeability of days and events which the film presents, the act of sex stands as an anomaly. Although sexual parts are interchangeable in filmed pornography, men and women are not; each person makes love differently. To preserve the illusion that Jeanne's clients (and all men) *are* identical, the filmmaker must not show their most personal, least interchangeable acts. In a film of such realism, this flaw or distortion is particularly noticeable and unfortunate.

On another level it destroys the credibility of the film. When we finally see Jeanne in bed with a client on the film's third day, we know something significant is about to happen. When we see her react sexually to the man, we are confused. Our lack of knowledge about her prior sexual behavior prevents us from understanding her: does she always respond, or is sexual response a further symptom of her disintegration? The film's point is muddied, Jeanne's act incomprehensible; does she kill the man because he made her respond despite herself or simply because she had a bad day?

While Akerman plays down the importance of the killing to the film as a whole, a look at the film's narrative structure reveals that the murder is demanded: the film has a conventional narrative structure despite its slow pacing and technical innovations.[9] It tells a story, sets up a conflict, and offers a solution to the conflict. It has a violent climax and period of reflective calm afterwards. The editing becomes faster as the climax approaches, and the revealing of new bits of information—the sexual act—piques our interest and lets us know that a solution to the conflict is near. Scissors left conveniently near the bed foreshadow the film's resolution.[10]

One can take the film's climax in at least two ways. My own reaction was to see Jeanne's act as a repressive one, a response to her sexual awakening. To accept this interpretation, one first has to believe that her breakdown is a positive thing; that a breakdown is preferable to a life of calm, controlled insanity and that sexual response could be the first step toward that breakdown and thus toward change. The film becomes a critical one—critical of Jeanne's role as repressed and conservative force while cognizant of the difficulties of change—while Jeanne's act is part of a desperate struggle to preserve the status quo in the face of forces that are threatening to change and overwhelm her. The film, then, illustrates the power of bourgeois, patriarchal culture and points out the degree to which most of us have internalized its mandates. Ending the film with a bloody Jeanne, sitting in a dark room with neon flashing over her face and the blue and white china crock prominently in the foreground, seemed to capture in a frame the hegemony of oppressive forces, the futility of isolated, individualized revolt.

Chantal Akerman intends that the film be read differently. She has said of the murder, "It was either him or her, and I'm glad it was him." The murder is seen as an act of liberation, one which, Akerman says, will "change her life."

Such a concept of problem-solving is neither particularly novel nor arguably feminist, which makes its use by women writers and filmmakers all the more distressing. It is understandable in such a work as Volker Schlöndorff and Margarethe Von Trotta's *Lost Honor of Katherina Blum,* where a young woman shoots the muck-raking reporter who has tormented her throughout the film. But the reporter is an old-fashioned villain, a symbol more of a certain kind of press than of male culture, and his death is as cathartic for the audience as the climactic shooting of any Western bad guy is likely to be. Nothing feminist about it.

Nor is there anything particularly feminist in the kind of solutions many of the heroines in contemporary women's fiction reach to their objectifications and oppression: Lois Gould's beautiful victim becomes a pseudo-man in *A Sea Change* and victimizes her female lover; Susan Reis Lukas's housewife/victim breaks out of her rut by having sex with two Puerto Rican boys who try to hustle her in *Stereopticon* and finishes the job by killing herself with a shiv; Judith Rossner's Theresa is murdered by a pick-up in *Looking for Mr. Goodbar* at precisely the moment when she decides to change her life and stop being a victim. And in Liliane Dreyfus's *Femmes au Soleil,* the heroine's conflict over whether to leave her comfortable, if stifling and superficial, bourgeois life for the love and adventure offered by a younger man is conveniently resolved when he is killed in a motorcycle accident. Death is the *deus ex machina;* as children end stories, badly written, with the words "and then she died," so many women authors and filmmakers resolve the conflicts set up in the bodies of their work.

The suicidal heroine of Dinah Brooke's *Death Games* resolves her love/hate relationship with her father by slipping into his bed after he's suffered a heart attack and performing fellatio on him until he dies. Brooke, like Akerman, portrays this act as a sign of social and sexual liberation for her heroine and, by analogy, for all women; a literal blow against patriarchal culture:

Children scream violently, struggling, hissing with rage, daughters become avenging demons. What is required is nourishment. Love. We will fight forever. We will never give up. We will spew up your aid, your allowances, your falseness; we will struggle for what we need. We cannot be denied. Our desires are as old and powerful as the earth. They are also your desires. If you deny them you will die. . . . We will all be destroyed by the hidden, silent, secret desire, never expressed. You have created such a huge world, such a stack of card houses, such false structures of governments, and bombs and money and boarding schools and ministries and hotels and banks and factories and development projects and armies to hide you, to protect you from your own desires. But do not be afraid. We will pursue you. We are your daughter, your soul. We will sneak up on you in the night and in the afternoon. We are your salvation. We will have you. We will find you out in spite of all your struggles and your power. Your power is nothing. It will scream, melt, explode in the heat of our desire, and of your own.[11]

Such alternatives are not attractive ones and offer little hope or encouragement to real women: absolute repression or a living out of all one's repressed desires for incest, sex, and death within the framework of a total war between men and women. Dusan Makavejev's *Sweet Movie* expresses these options perfectly through two different women: Miss World of 1984, who is objectified and mauled throughout the film until her famous chocolate bath makes her a living symbol of the union of sexual oppression and consumerism under capitalism; and the carefree "liberated woman," a revolutionary who acts on all her desires, including the castration of her only adult lover in a bed of sugar and the seduction and murder of little boys.

Many male filmmakers use the kill-for-freedom motif of *Jeanne Dielman,* not the least of them being Sam Peckinpah. Dustin Hoffman's rampage in *Straw Dogs* is as socially "justified" as Dielman's and proves him a man capable of action as hers proves her a conscious woman. Killing is used as proof of manhood in *The Marathon Man,* where the villains which Hoffman (again) vanquishes are hardly less odious than the somewhat gentle man Jeanne Dielman kills and are meant to stand for just as many cultural evils: anti-Semitism, fascism, blacklisting, and the immorality of the government. And the virtue of revenge and regeneration through violence is routinely offered as a solution to the moral dilemmas posed in scores of old and new films: *Walking Tall, Macon County Line, Buster and Billie, Death Wish.*

Is violence any more progressive politically when women perform it? Many women applauded when the heroine of Stephanie Rothman's *Velvet Vampire* murdered the man who tried to rape her after pretending to submit. But Rothman later shows us that her violence was not reserved for oppressive men alone but was generalized to include more sympathetic figures, women as well as men. Most male films about female rape victims become opportunities to depict the act of rape for the titillation of the male audience, no matter how those victims ultimately respond or revenge themselves: Margaux Hemingway's murder of her rapist in *Lipstick* was overshadowed by her lengthy rape, and Yvette Mimieux's murder of the rapist/jailer in *Jackson County Jail*—the Joanne Little case in white-face—solves nothing: not for Mimieux's character in the film and certainly not for the women who continue to be brutalized and raped inside jails and out of them.

When we study these films, we find that most of them support the social order, offering individual solutions to complex social problems: kill criminals rather than abolish the causes of crime, kill rapists rather than rearrange the sexual power structure that necessitates the act of rape. If there are films that criticize such solutions (as I would argue in the case of *Walking Tall*) then such criticism resides in the mise-en-scène, as in many *films noirs.* The plots are spoon-fed homilies to an audience that has been taught to expect what it gets: the message that violence is the acceptable way to handle all difficulties and a "natural" reaction to injustice.

The ending of Robert Altman's *Images* crystallizes the drawbacks of such responses to oppression. Although Susannah York kills her oppressive husband, who is probably contributing to her madness, she kills him only when she sees him as a mirror-image of herself. It is her own problems which haunt her and continue to haunt her after her husband's death: her husband is gone, but the greater problem, York's own, persists. Nor does Gerald Depardieu's self-castration in Ferrari's *Last Woman* solve the problems of machismo and egoism, as the pathetic final offering of his severed penis to his lover suggests, though it is certainly an act that "changed his life."

If we are to make real changes in our lives and in our cinema, we must offer not only new cinematic structures but serious solutions to the social problems that persist. If none are forthcoming, I feel it is better to be descriptive than prescriptive. Films which illustrate the extent of female oppression and the tenacity of patriarchy seem to me more feminist than those which offer cheap answers— answers that fall within the range of acceptable responses as defined by male-dominated bourgeois culture—to complex social, historical, and political problems. The sections of *Jeanne Dielman* which examine in minute detail the function and practice of housework and the role of the traditional mother within the repressive structure of the nuclear family are among the finest examples of feminist cinema yet produced, pioneering and carefully wrought in both form and content. I only wish Akerman had been content with this magnificent and unique achievement rather than succumbing to the demands of the traditional narrative film form that requires a bang-up ending and the culture that requires a neatly packaged and thoroughly acceptable message. In this case: killing is good for you.

Notes

1. Barbara Ehrenreich and Deirdre English, "The Manufacture of Housework," *Socialist Revolution* 5, no. 4 (October–December 1975): 6.

2. Ann Oakley, *Woman's Work* (New York: Vintage Books, 1974), p. 95.

3. Ehrenreich and English, p. 19.

4. The static camera becomes confusing at only one point in the film: the nightly walk around the block. Four shots show them on the block's four sides, but the streets could be anywhere. Without a tracking shot, we have no sense that the four streets interlock.

5. This proves to be delusion. When Jeanne starts to perform her role as a housewife *poorly,* her son is quick to notice, to button an open robe or tidy disarrayed hair. Her perfect performances are taken for granted, but she is never allowed to stray from the rigid bounds that circumscribe her role.

6. The house has something of the feel that Lotte Eisner described so well in German films and literature, mirrored by a linguistic structure that gives objects a life of their own: "they are spoken of with the same adjectives and verbs used to speak of human beings, they are endowed with the same qualities as people, they act and react in the same way . . . [the houses] seem to have an insidious life of their own when the autumn evening mists stagnate in the streets and veil their imperceptible grimace." See *The Haunted Screen* (Berkeley: University of California Press, 1969), p. 23.

7. Max Horkheimer, "Authority and the Family," in *Critical Theory* (New York: Herder and Herder, 1972), p. 121.

8. *Ibid.,* p. 121.

9. This and all references to Akerman's comments on *Jeanne Dielman* were discussed at a screening of the film at the Museum of Modern Art's *CineProbe* series, November 8, 1976.

10. If, as feminist film critic Barbara Halpern Martineau has convincingly argued in her lectures, most narrative films reflect a structure that is remarkably close to the conventional pattern of male sexual response (build-up of tension, climax, exhaustion), then Akerman's film falls well within this range rather than positing an alternative narrative structure that is female or feminist.

11. Dinah Brooke, *Death Games* (New York: Harcourt Brace Jovanovich, 1976), pp. 147–48.

IN THE NAME OF FEMINIST
FILM CRITICISM

B. RUBY RICH

Most of the articles included in the first volume of Movies and Methods *as examples of feminist criticism were written in the first few years of this approach. In this article, which was written in 1978, B. Ruby Rich looks back over those early years. She identifies an American, sociological approach and a British, theoretical approach to film. She finds that some films are still identified, very loosely, as feminist films. But that appellation identifies something of the social and political context to which they belong, not specific qualities of the films themselves. Therein lies the crisis: The lack of names to allow formal differentiation and acknowledgement of divergent political strategies renders the conceptualization of such differences impossible. Moreover, important qualities are not only unspoken, they are unspeakable. Language actively represses or disavows differences that threaten the prevailing categories of perception. Naming things previously unnamed has the power to establish the terms and categories of debate and action within the world. Rich's position here places her within the context of the Whorf-Sapir hypothesis, at least in its weak form, which intimately and dynamically associates the language that we speak with the reality that we speak of. To this context, she adds a conception of an ideological operation of active constraint, a repression, in language itself. Rich's urgency stems from a commitment to finding the words needed to name objects and experiences that feminist film criticism has left unnamed. Rich's suggestions have not been picked up, but that may be less because they lack value than because, like Lesage's early warning against a psychoanalytic model that posits woman as a threatening lack, they could not be heard within the context of the emerging Lacanian-feminist paradigm. One great strength of Rich's suggestions is the broad range of feminist filmmaking practices that she seeks to identify, a range much broader than the practices directed at signification or signifying practices themselves, which are usually identified with Chantal Akerman, Yvonne Rainer, and Marguerite Duras.*

A useful indication of how Rich's call has been taken up indirectly by those who desire to sustain a broad range of feminist culture appears in Sara Halprin's review of E. Ann Kaplan's book, Women and Film, *in* Jump Cut, *no. 29 (1984): 31–33.*

Like Johnston and Loader, Rich refers to Chantal Akerman's Jeanne Dielman, *among other films, as a focal point for feminist debate. With* Dielman *and* Mädchen in Uniform, *Rich finds that much of the critical reception subordinates feminist issues to other social or aesthetic priorities. Her discussion of* Jeanne Dielman *offers yet another perspective on a film that clearly has functioned as an important test case for feminist theory and practice.*

•

Whatever is unnamed, undepicted in images, whatever is omitted from biography, censored in collections of letters, whatever is mis-named as something else, made difficult-to-come-by, whatever is buried in the memory by the collapse of meaning under an inade-quate or lying language–this will become, not merely unspoken, but unspeakable. —Adrienne Rich[1]

The situation for women working in filmmaking and film criticism today is pre-carious. While our work is no longer invisible, and not yet unspeakable, it still goes dangerously unnamed. There is even uncertainty over what name might characterize that intersection of cinema and the women's movement within which we labor, variously called "films by women," "feminist film," "images of women in film" or "women's films." All are vague and problematic. I see the lack of proper name here as symptomatic of a crisis in the ability of feminist film criticism thus far to come to terms with the work at hand, to apply a truly feminist criticism to the body of work already produced by women filmmakers. This crisis points to a real difference between the name "feminist" and the other names that have traditionally been applied to film (i.e., "structuralist" for certain avant-garde films or "melodrama" for certain Hollywood films).[2] "Feminist" is a name which may have only a marginal relation to the film text, describing more persuasively the context of social and political activity from which the work sprang. Such a difference is due, on the one hand, to a feminist recognition of the links tying a film's aesthetics to its modes of production and reception; and, on the other hand, to the particular history of the cinematic field which "feminist" came to desig-nate—a field in which filmmaking-exhibition-criticism-distribution-audience have always been considered inextricably connected.

THE HISTORY

The great contribution of feminism, as a body of thought, to culture in our time has been that it has something fairly direct to say, a quality all too rare today. And its equally crucial contribution, as a process and style, has been wom-en's insistence on conducting the analysis, making the statements, in unsullied terms, in forms not already associated with the media's oppressiveness toward women. It is this freshness of discourse and distrust of traditional modes of articulation that placed feminist cinema in a singular position vis-à-vis both the dominant cinema and the avant-garde in the early 70's. By the "dominant," I mean Hollywood and all its corresponding manifestations in other cultures; but this could also be termed the Cinema of the Fathers. By the "avant-garde," I mean the experimental/personal cinema, which is positioned, by self-inclusion, within the art world; but this could also be termed the Cinema of the Sons. Being a business, the Cinema of the Fathers seeks to do only that which has been done before and proved successful. Being an art, the Cinema of the Sons seeks to do only that which has not been done before and so prove itself successful.

Into such a situation, at the start of the 70's, entered a feminist cinema. In place of the Fathers' bankruptcy of both form and content, there was a new and different energy; a cinema of immediacy and positive force now opposed the retreat into violence and the revival of a dead past which had become the dominant cinema's mainstays. In place of the Sons' increasing alienation and isolation, there was an entirely new sense of identification—with other women—and a corresponding commitment to communicate with this now-identifiable audience, a commitment which replaced, for feminist filmmakers, the elusive public ignored and frequently scorned by the male formalist filmmakers. Thus, from the start, its link to an evolving political movement gave feminist cinema a power and direction entirely unprecedented in independent filmmaking, bringing issues of theory/practice, aesthetics/meaning, process/representation into sharp focus.

Since the origin and development of feminist film work are largely unexamined, the following chronology sketches some of the major events of the 70's in North America and Great Britain. Three sorts of information are omitted as beyond the scope of this survey: (1) European festivals and publications, although some have been extremely significant; (2) beyond the first entry, the hundreds of films made by women during the decade; and (3) the publication in 1969–70 of key feminist writings such as *Sexual Politics, The Dialectic of Sex,* and *Sisterhood Is Powerful,* which must be remembered as the backdrop and theoretical impetus for these film activities.

1971:   Release of *Growing Up Female, Janie's Janie, Three Lives* and *The Woman's Film:* first generation of feminist documentaries.

1972:   First New York International Festival of Women's Films and the Women's Event at Edinburgh Film Festival. First issue of *Women & Film* magazine; special issues on women and film in *Take One, Film Library Quarterly* and *The Velvet Light Trap;* filmography of women directors in *Film Comment.*

1973:   Toronto Women and Film Festival, Washington Women's Film Festival, season of women's cinema at National Film Theatre in London and Buffalo women's film conference. Marjorie Rosen's *Popcorn Venus* (first book on women in film) and *Notes on Women's Cinema,* edited by Claire Johnston for British Film Institute (first anthology of feminist film theory).

1974:   Chicago Films by Women Festival. First issue of *Jump Cut* (quarterly on contemporary film emphasizing feminist perspective); two books on images of women in film: Molly Haskell's *From Reverence to Rape* and Joan Mellen's *Women and Their Sexuality in the New Film.*

1975:   Conference of Feminists in the Media, New York and Los Angeles. *Women & Film* ceases publication; *The Work of Dorothy Arzner* (BFI monograph edited by Johnston), and Sharon Smith's *Women Who Make Movies* (guide to women filmmakers).

1976:   Second New York International Festival of Women's Films (smaller, noncollective, less successful than first) and Womanscene, a section of women's films in Toronto's Festival of Festivals (smaller, noncollective, but comparable in choices to 1973).

1977:   First issue of *Camera Obscura* (journal of film theory founded largely by former *Women & Film* members, initially in opposition to it); Karyn Kay and Gerald Peary's *Women and the Cinema* (first anthology of criticism on women and film).

1978:   *Women in Film Noir* (BFI anthology edited by E. Ann Kaplan); special feminist issues of *Quarterly Review of Film Studies* and *New German Critique;* Brandon French's *On the Verge of Revolt: Women in American Films of the Fifties* (study on images of women).

1979:   Alternative Cinema Conference, bringing together over 100 feminists in the media for screenings, caucuses, and strategizing within the left; Feminism and Cinema Event at Edinburgh Film Festival, assessing the decade's filmmaking and theory and debating what might come next. Patricia Erens's *Sexual Stratagems: The World of Women in Film* (anthology on women and cinema).

It is immediately apparent from this chronology that the 1972–73 period marked a cultural watershed that has not since been equaled and that the unity, discovery, energy, and brave, we're-here-to-stay spirit of the early days underwent a definite shift in 1975, mid-decade. Since then, the field of vision has altered. There is increased specialization, both in the direction of genre studies (like *film noir*) and film theory (particularly semiotic and psychoanalytic); the start of sectarianism, with women partitioned off into enclaves defined by which conferences are attended or journals subscribed to; increased institutionalization, both of women's studies and cinema studies departments—twin creations of the 70's; a backlash emphasis on "human" liberation, which by making communication with men a priority can leave woman-to-woman feminism looking déclassé. Overall, there is a growing acceptance of feminist film as an area of study rather than as a sphere of action. And this may pull feminist film work away from its early political commitment, encompassing a wide social setting; away from issues of life that go beyond form; away from the combative (as an analysis of and weapon against patriarchal capitalism) into the merely representational.

The chronology also shows the initial cross-fertilization between the women's movement and cinema, which took place in the area of practice rather than in written criticism. The films came first. In fact, we find two different currents feeding into film work: one made up of women who were feminists and thereby led to film, the other made up of women already working in film and led therein to feminism. It was largely the first group of women who began making the films which were naturally named "feminist,"[3] and largely the second group of women, often in university film studies departments, who began holding the film festivals, just as naturally named "women and/in film." Spadework has continued in both directions, creating a new women's cinema and rediscovering the antecedents, with the two currents feeding our film criticism.

The past eight years have reduced some of the perils of which Adrienne Rich speaks. No longer are women "undepicted in images": even four years ago, Bonnie Dawson's *Women's Films in Print* could list over 800 available films by U.S. women alone, most depicting women. No longer are women omitted from all biography, nor are letters always censored. (In this respect, note the ongoing work of the four-woman collective engaged in "The Legend of Maya Deren Project" to document and demystify the life and work of a major, underacknowledged figure in American independent cinema.) No longer are women's films so hard to come by: the establishment of New Day Films (1972), the Serious Business Company (c. 1973–1983) and the Iris Films collective (1975) ensures the continuing distribution of films by or about women, although the chances of seeing any independently made features by women in a regular movie theatre are still predictably slim (with Jill Godmilow's *Antonia* and Claudia Weill's *Girl Friends* the only U.S. films to succeed so far). Returning to Rich's original warning, however, we reach the end of history's comforts and arrive at our present danger: "whatever is unnamed . . . buried in the memory by the collapse of meaning under an inadequate or lying language—this will become, not merely unspoken, but unspeakable." Herein lies the crisis facing feminist film criticism today; for after a decade of film practice and theory, we still lack our proper names. The impact of this lack on the films themselves is of immediate concern.

THE FILMS

One classic film rediscovered through women's film festivals indicates the sort of misnaming prevalent in film history. Leontine Sagan's *Maedchen in Uniform*, a 1931 German film, details the relationship between a student and her teacher in a repressive girls' boarding school.[4] The act of naming is itself a pivotal moment in the narrative. Toward the end of the film, the schoolgirls gather at a drunken party after the annual school play. Manuela has just starred as a passionate youth and, drunk with punch, still in boy's clothing, she stands to proclaim her happiness and love—naming her teacher Fraulein von Bernburg as the woman she loves. Before this episode, the lesbian substructure of the school and the clearly shared knowledge of that substructure have been emphasized; the school laundress even points to the prevalence of the Fraulein's initials embroidered on

the girls' regulation chemises as evidence of the adulation of her adolescent ad-
mirers. This eroticism was *not* in the closet. But only when Manuela stands and
names that passion is she punished, locked up in solitary—for her speech, not for
her actions.

Such is the power of a name and the valor of naming. It is ironic that the
inscription of the power of naming within the film has not forestalled its own
continuous misnaming within film history, which has championed its anti-fascism
while masking the lesbian origins of that resistance. The problem is even more
acute in dealing with contemporary films, where the lack of an adequate language
has contributed to the invisibility of key aspects of our film culture—an invisibility advantageous to the existing film tradition.

The women say, unhappy one, men have expelled you from the world of symbols and yet
they have given you names . . . their authority to accord names . . . goes back so far that the
origin of language itself may be considered an act of authority emanating from those who
dominate . . . they have attached a particular word to an object or a fact and thereby consider themselves to have appropriated it . . . The women say, the language you speak poi-
sons your glottis tongue palate lips. They say, the language you speak is made up of words
that are killing you . . . the language you speak is made up of signs that rightly speaking
designate what men have appropriated. Whatever they have not laid hands on . . . does not
appear in the language. This is apparent precisely in the intervals that your masters have
not been able to fill with their words . . . this can be found in the gaps, in all that which is
not a continuation of their discourse, in the zero. . . . (Monique Wittig)[5]

The act of misnaming functions not as an error, but as a strategy of the patriarchy. The lack of proper names facilitates derogatory name-calling; the failure to
assign meaningful names to contemporary feminist films eases the acquisition of
misnomers. Two key films of the 70's reveal this process and the disenfranchise-
ment we suffer as a result.

Chantal Akerman's *Jeanne Dielman* (1975) is a chronicle of three days in the
life of a Brussels housewife, a widow and mother who is also a prostitute. It is the
first film to scrutinize housework in a language appropriate to the activity itself,
showing a woman's activities in the home in real time to communicate the alienation of woman in the nuclear family under European post-war economic conditions. More than three hours in length and nearly devoid of dialogue, the film
charts Jeanne Dielman's breakdown via a minute observation of her performance
of household routines, at first methodical and unvarying, later increasingly disar-
ranged, until by film's end she permanently disrupts the patriarchal order by mur-
dering her third client. The film was scripted, directed, photographed and edited
by women with a consciously feminist sensibility.

The aesthetic repercussions of such a sensibility are evident throughout the
film. For example, the choice of camera angle is unusually low. In interviews,
Akerman explained that the camera was positioned at her own height; since she is
quite short, the entire perspective of the film is different from what we are used to
seeing, as shot by male cinematographers. The perspective of every frame thus
reveals a female ordering of that space, prompting a reconsideration of point-of-
view that I had felt before only in a few works shot by children (which expose the

power of tall adults in every shot) and in the films by the Japanese director Yasu-jiro Ozu (where the low angle has been much discussed by Western critics as an entry into the "oriental" detachment of someone seated on a tatami mat, observ-ing). Akerman's decision to employ only medium and long shots also stems from a feminist critique: the decision to free her character from the exploitation of a zoom lens and to grant her an integrity of private space usually denied in close-ups, thereby also freeing the audience from the insensitivity of a camera barreling in to magnify a woman's emotional crisis. Similarly, the activities of shopping, cooking and cleaning the house are presented without ellipses, making visible the extent of time previously omitted from cinematic depictions. Thus, the film is a profoundly feminist work in theme, style and representation; yet it has been criti-cally received in language devoted to sanctifying aesthetics stripped of political consequence.

Shortly after *Jeanne Dielman*'s premiere at the Cannes film festival, European critics extolled the film as "hyper-realist" in homage both to the realist film (and literary) tradition and to the super-realist movement in painting. Two problems arise with such a name: first, the tradition of cinematic realism has never included women in its alleged veracity; second, the comparison with super-realist painters obscures the contradiction between their illusionism and Akerman's anti-illusionism. Another name applied to *Jeanne Dielman* was "ethnographic," in keeping with the film's insistence on real-time presentation and non-elliptical editing. Again, the name negates a basic aspect by referring to a cinema of clini-cal observation, aimed at "objectivity" and noninvolvement, detached rather than engaged. The film's warm texture and Akerman's committed sympathies (the woman's gestures were borrowed from her own mother and aunt) make the name inappropriate.

The critical reception of the film in the *Soho Weekly News* by three different reviewers[6] points up the confusion engendered by linguistic inadequacy.[6] Jonas Mekas questioned, "Why did she have to ruin the film by making the woman a prostitute and introduce a murder at the end, why did she commercialize it?" Later, praising most of the film as a successor to *Greed,* he contended that the heroine's silence was more "revolutionary" than the murder, making a case for the film's artistic merit as separate from its social context and moving the work into the area of existentialism at the expense of its feminism. Amy Taubin consid-ered the film "theatrical" and, while commending the subjectivity of the camera-work and editing, she attacked the character of Jeanne: "Are we to generalize from Jeanne to the oppression of many women through their subjugation to activ-ity which offers them no range of creative choice? If so, Jeanne Dielman's pathol-ogy mitigates against our willingness to generalize." By holding a reformist position (i.e., she should vary her menu, change her wardrobe) in relation to a revolutionary character (i.e., a murderer), Taubin was forced into a reading of the film limited by notions of realism that she, as an avant-garde film critic, would have ordinarily tried to avoid: her review split the film along the lines of form/content, annexing the aesthetics as "the real importance" and rejecting the char-acter of Jeanne as a pathological woman. Again we find a notion of pure art set up in opposition to a feminism seemingly restricted to positive role models. Finally, Annette Michelson wrote a protest to Mekas which defended the film for "the sense of renewal it has brought both to a narrative mode and the inscription *within it* of feminist energies" (my italics). Yes, but at what cost? Here the effect of inadequate naming is precisely spelled out: the feminist energies are being spent to create work quickly absorbed into mainstream modes of art that renew themselves at our expense. Already, the renaissance of the "new narrative" is under way in film circles with nary a glance back at filmmakers like Akerman or Yvonne Rainer, who first incurred the wrath of the academy by reintroducing characters, emotions and narratives into their films.

The critical response to Rainer's recent films, especially *Film about a Woman Who,* adds instances of naming malpractice.[7] Much of the criticism has been in the area of formal textual analysis, concentrating on the "post-modernist" structures, "Brechtian" distancing or cinematic deconstruction of the works. Continuing the tactic of detoxifying films via a divide-and-conquer criticism, critic Brian Henderson analyzed the central section in *Film about a Woman Who* according to a semiological model, detailing the five channels of communication used to present textual information.[8] The analysis was exhaustive on the level of technique but completely ignored the actual meaning of the information (Rainer's "emotional accretions")—the words themselves and the visualization (a man and woman on a stark bed/table). At the opposite extreme, a *Feminist Art Journal* editorial condemned Rainer as a modernist, "the epitome of the alienated artist," and discounted her film work as regressive for feminists, evidently because of its formal strategies.[9]

Rainer's films deal with the relations between the sexes and the interaction of life and art within a framework combining autobiography and fiction. Whatever the intent of Rainer's filmmaking in political terms, the work stands as a clear product of a feminist cultural milieu. The films deal explicitly with woman as victim and the burden of patriarchal mythology; they offer a critique of emotion, reworking melodrama for women today, and even (*Kristina Talking Pictures*) provide an elegy to the lost innocence of defined male/female roles. The structure of the themes gives priority to the issues over easy identification with the "characters" and involves the audience in an active analysis of emotional process. Yet little of the criticism has managed to reconcile an appreciation for the formal elements with an understanding of the feminist effect. Carol Wikarska, in a short review for *Women & Film,* could only paraphrase Rainer's own descriptions in a stab at *Film about a Woman Who* seen in purely art-world terms.[10] More critically, the feminist-defined film journal *Camera Obscura* concentrated its first issue on Rainer but fell into a similar quandary. While an interview with Rainer was included, the editors felt obliged to critique the films in the existing semiological vocabulary, taking its feminist value for granted without confronting the points of contradiction within that methodology. The lack of vocabulary once again frustrates a complete consideration of the work.

Lest the similarity of these misnamings merely suggest critical blindness rather than a more deliberate tactic, an ironic reversal is posed by the response to

Anne Severson's *Near the Big Chakra*. Silent and in color, the film shows a series of 36 women's cunts photographed in unblinking close-up, some still and some moving, with no explanations or gratuitous presentation. Formally the film fits into the category of "structuralist" cinema: a straightforward listing of parts, no narrative, requisite attention to a predetermined and simplified structure, and fixed camera position (as defined by the namer—P. Adams Sitney). Yet Severson's image is so powerfully uncooptable that her film has never been called "structuralist" to my knowledge, nor—with retrospective revisionism—have her earlier films been so named. Evidently any subject matter that could make a man vomit (as happened at a London screening in 1973) is too much for the critical category, even though it was founded on the "irrelevance" of the visual images. Thus a name can be withheld by the critical establishment if its application alone won't make the film fit the category.

"Whatever they have not laid hands on . . . does not appear in the language you speak," wrote Monique Wittig. Here is the problem: not so much that certain names are used, but that other names are not—and therefore the qualities they describe are lost. Where patriarchal language holds sway, the silences, the characteristics that are unnamed, frequently hold the greatest potential strength. In Chantal Akerman's work, what is most valuable for us is her decoding of oppressive cinematic conventions and her invention of new codes of non-voyeuristic vision; yet these contributions go unnamed. In Yvonne Rainer's work, the issue is not one of this or that role model for feminists, not whether her women characters are too weak or too victimized or too individualistic. Rather, we can value precisely her refusal to pander (visually and emotionally), her frustration of audience expectation of spectacle (physical or psychic) and her complete reworking of traditional forms of melodrama and elegy to include modern feminist culture. Yet these elements, of greatest value to us, are not accorded critical priority.

The effect of not naming is censorship, whether caused by the imperialism of the patriarchal language or the underdevelopment of a feminist language. We need to begin analyzing our own films, but first it is necessary to learn to speak in our own name. The recent history of feminist film criticism indicates the urgency of that need.

"FEMINIST FILM CRITICISM: IN TWO VOICES"

There have been two types of feminist film criticism,[11] motivated by different geographical and ideological contexts, each speaking in a very different voice.

History of philosophy has an obvious, repressive function in philosophy; it is philosophy's very own Oedipus. "All the same, you won't dare speak your own name as long as you have not read this and that, and that on this, and this on that. . . . To say something in one's own name is very strange." (Gilles Deleuze)[12]

Speaking in one's own name versus speaking in the name of history is a familiar problem to anyone who has ever pursued a course of study, become involved in an established discipline, and then tried to speak out of personal experience or nonprofessional/nonacademic knowledge without suddenly feeling quite schizophrenic. Obviously it is a schizophrenia especially familiar to feminists. The distinction between one's own voice and the voice of history is a handy one by which to distinguish the two types of feminist film criticism. At least initially, these two types could be characterized as either American or British: the one, American, seen as sociological or subjective, often a speaking out in one's own voice; the other, British, seen as methodological or more objective, often speaking in the voice of history. (The work of the past few years has blurred the original nationalist base of the categories: for example, the Parisian perspective of the California-based *Camera Obscura.*)

The originally American, so-called sociological, approach is exemplified by early *Women & Film* articles and much of the catalogue writing from festivals of that same period. The emphasis on legitimizing women's own reactions and making women's contributions visible resulted in a tendency toward reviews, getting information out, a tendency to offer testimony as theory. Fruitful in this terrain, the weakness of the approach became the limits of its introspection, the boundaries established by the lack of a coherent methodology for moving out beyond the self. An example of this approach would be Barbara Halpern Martineau's very eccentric, subjective, and illuminating analyses of Nelly Kaplan and Agnes Varda films.[13] A dismaying example of the decadent strain of this approach was Joan Mellen's mid-70's book *Big Bad Wolves,* which offered personal interpretations of male characters and actors in a move to shift attention to the reformist arena of "human liberation."

The originally British, so-called theoretical, approach is exemplified by the British Film Institute monograph on women and film (see above), by articles in *Screen,* and by the initial issues of *Camera Obscura* (which, like the British writing, defers to the French authorities). Committed to using some of the most advanced tools of critical analysis, like semiology and psychoanalysis, this approach has tried to come to terms with *how* films mean—to move beyond regarding the image to analyzing the structure, codes, the general subtext of the works. Fruitful for its findings regarding signification, the weakness of the approach has been its suppression of the personal and a seeming belief in the neutrality of the analytic tools, so that the critic's feminist voice has often been muted by this methodocracy. Two of the most important products of this approach are pieces by Laura Mulvey and Claire Johnston.[14] Johnston has critiqued the image of woman in male cinema and finds her to be a signifier, not of woman, but of the absent phallus, a signifier of an absence rather than any presence. Similarly, Mulvey has analyzed the nature of the cinematic spectator and finds evidence—in cinematic voyeurism and in the nature of the camera look—of the exclusively male spectator as a production assumption.

Another way of characterizing these two approaches would be to identify the American (sociological, or in one's own voice) as fundamentally phenomenological, and the British (theoretical, or the voice of history) as fundamentally analytical. Johnston and Mulvey's texts taken together, for example, pose a monumental absence that is unduly pessimistic. The misplaced pessimism stems from their overvaluation of the production aspect of cinema, a misassumption that cinematic values are irrevocably embedded at the level of production and, once there, remain pernicious and inviolable. Woman is absent on the screen and she is absent in the audience, their analysis argues. And yet here a bit of phenomenology would be helpful, a moment of speaking in one's own voice and wondering at the source in such a landscape of absence. As a woman sitting in the dark, watching that film made by and for men with drag queens on the screen, what is my experience? Don't I in fact interact with that text and that context, with a conspicuous absence of passivity? For a woman's experiencing of culture under patriarchy is dialectical in a way that a man's can never be: our experience is like that of the exile, whom Brecht once singled out as the ultimate dialectician for that daily working out of cultural oppositions within a single body. It is crucial to emphasize here the possibility for texts to be transformed at the level of reception and not to fall into a trap of condescension toward our own developed powers as active producers of meaning.

The differences implicit in these two attitudes lead to quite different positions and strategies, as the following selection of quotations helps to point up.[15] When interviewed regarding the reason for choosing her specific critical tools (auteurist, structuralist, psychoanalytic), Claire Johnston replied: "As far as I'm concerned, it's a question of what is theoretically correct; these new theoretical developments cannot be ignored, just as feminists cannot ignore Marx or Freud, because they represent crucial scientific developments." In contrast to this vision of science as ideologically neutral would be the reiteration by such theoreticians as Adrienne Rich and Mary Daly that "you have to be constantly critiquing even the tools you use to explore and define what it is to be female." In the same interview as Johnston, Pam Cook elaborated their aim as: "Women are fixed in ideology in a particular way, which is definable in terms of the patriarchal system. I think we see our first need as primarily to define that place—the place that women are fixed in." In marked contrast to such a sphere of activity, the Womanifesto of the 1975 New York Conference of Feminists in the Media stated: "We do not accept the existing power structure and we are committed to changing it by the content and structure of our images and by the ways we relate to each other in our work and with our audience." In her own article, Laura Mulvey identified the advantage of psychoanalytic critiques as their ability to "advance our understanding of the status quo," a limited and modest claim; yet she herself went beyond such a goal in making (with Peter Wollen) *The Riddles of the Sphinx,* a film which in its refusal of patriarchal codes and feminist concerns represented in fact a Part Two of her original theory.

I have termed the British approach pessimistic, a quality which may be perceived by supporters as realistic or by detractors as colonized. I have termed the American approach optimistic, a quality which may be viewed by supporters as radical or by detractors as unrealistic, utopian. It is not surprising, however, that such a dualism of critical approach has evolved. In *Woman's Consciousness, Man's World,* Sheila Rowbotham points out:

There is a long inchoate period during which the struggle between the language of experience and the language of theory becomes a kind of agony.[16]

It is a problem common to an oppressed people at the point of formulating a new language with which to name that oppression, for the history of oppression has prevented the development of any unified language among its subjects. It is crucial for those of us working in the area of feminist film criticism to mend this rift, confront the agony, and begin developing a synthesis of maximally effective critical practice. Without names, our work remains anonymous, insecure, our continued visibility questionable.

ANTICLIMAX: THE NAMES

Without new names, we run the danger of losing title to films that we sorely need. By stretching the name "feminist" beyond all reasonable elasticity, we contribute to its ultimate impoverishment. At the same time, so many films have been partitioned off to established traditions, with the implication that these other names contradict or forestall any application of the name "feminist" to the works so annexed, that the domain of "feminist" cinema is fast becoming limited to that work concerned only with feminism as explicit subject matter. "Feminist," if it is to make a comeback from the loss of meaning caused by its all-encompassing overuse, requires new legions of names to preserve for us the inner strengths, the not-yet-visible qualities of these films still lacking in definition.

Because this need is so very urgent, I here offer an experimental glossary of names as an aid to initiating a new stage of feminist criticism. These names are not likely to be an immediate hit. First of all, it's all well and good to call for new names to appear in the night sky like so many constellations, but it's quite another thing to invent them and commit them to paper. Second, there's the inevitable contradiction of complaining about names and then committing more naming acts. Third, there's the danger that, however unwieldy, these new names might be taken as formulas to be applied willy-nilly to every hapless film that comes our way. The point, after all, is not to set up new power institutions (feminist banks, feminist popes, feminist names) but rather to open the mind to new descriptive possibilities. Not to require alternate glossaries of Talmudic herstory, but to suggest the revolutionary possibilities of non-patriarchal, non-capitalist imaginings.

Validative.

One of feminist filmmaking's greatest contributions is the body of films about women's lives, political struggles, organizing, etc. These films have been vaguely classified under the *cinéma vérité* banner, where they reside in decidedly mixed company. Since they function as a validation and legitimation of women's culture and individual lives, the name "validative" would be a better choice. It has the added advantage of aligning the work with products of oppressed peoples (with the filmmaker as insider), whereas the *cinéma vérité* label represents the oppressors, who make films as superior outsiders documenting alien, implicitly inferior cultures, often from a position of condescension. The feminist films of the early 70's were validative, and validative films continue to be an important component of feminist filmmaking. They may be ethnographic, documenting the evolution of women's lives and issues (as in *We're Alive,* a portrait and analysis of women in prison) or archaeological, uncovering women's hidden past (as in *Union Maids,* with its recovery of women's role in the labor movement, or Sylvia Morales's *Chicana,* the first film history of the Mexican-American woman's struggle). The form is well established, yet the constantly evolving issues require new films, such as *We Will Not Be Beaten,* a film on domestic violence culled from videotaped interviews with women. By employing the name "validative" in place of *cinéma vérité,* we can combat the patriarchal annexation of the woman filmmaker as one of the boys, i.e., as a professional who is not *of* the culture being filmed. It is a unifying name aimed at conserving strength.

Correspondence.

A different name is necessary for more avant-garde films, like those of Yvonne Rainer, Chantal Akerman, Helke Sander or Laura Mulvey/Peter Wollen. Looking to literary history, we find a concern with the role played by letters ("personal" discourse) as a sustaining mode for women's writing during times of literary repression. The publication of historical letters by famous and ordinary women has been a major component of the feminist publishing renaissance, just as the long-standing denigration of the genre as not "real" writing (i.e., not certified by either a publishing house or monetary exchange) has been an additional goad for the creation of feminist alternatives to the literary establishment. A cinema of "correspondence" is a fitting homage to this tradition of introspective missives sent out into the world. Equally relevant is the other definition of "correspondence" as "mutual response, the answering of things to each other," or, to take Swedenborg's literal Doctrine of Correspondence as an example, the tenet that "every natural object symbolizes or corresponds to some spiritual fact or principle which is, as it were, its archetype."[17] Films of correspondence, then, would be those investigating correspondences, i.e., between emotion and objectivity, narrative and deconstruction, art and ideology. Thus *Jeanne Dielman* is a film of correspondence in its exploration of the bonds between housework and madness, prostitution and heterosexuality, epic and dramatic temporality.

What distinguishes such films of correspondence from formally similar films by male avant-garde filmmakers is their inclusion of the author within the text. *Film about a Woman Who* corresponds to very clear experiences and emotional concerns in Rainer's life and *Jeanne Dielman* draws on the gestures of the women in Akerman's family, whereas Michael Snow's *Rameau's Nephew* uses the form to suppress the author's presence. (Of course, there is a tradition of "diary" movies by men as well as women, but, significantly, the presence of Jonas Mekas in most of his diary films—like that of Godard in *Numéro deux*—is of the filmmaker rather than the "man" outside that professional role.) Similarly, Helke Sander in *The All Around Reduced Personality* revises the ironic, distanced narration of modernist German cinema to include the filmmaker in a same first-person-plural with her characters, unlike her compatriot Alexander Kluge, who always remains external and superior to his characters. It is this resolute correspondence between form and content, to put it bluntly, that distinguishes the films of correspondence. Such films are essential to the development of new structures and forms for the creation and communication of feminist works and values; more experimental than validative, they are laying the groundwork of a feminist cinematic vocabulary.

Reconstructive.

Several recent films suggest another name, located midway between the two described above, and dealing directly with issues of form posed by the political and emotional concerns of the work. One such film is Sally Potter's *Thriller,* a feminist murder mystery related as a first-person inquiry by the victim: Mimi, the seamstress of Puccini's *La Bohème,* investigates the cause of her death and the manner of her life, uncovering in the process the contradictions hidden by the bourgeois male artist. Michelle Citron's *Daughter Rite* probes relations between women in the family, using dramatic sequences to critique *cinéma vérité* and optical printing to re-examine home movies, that U.S. index to domestic history. Both *Thriller* and *Daughter Rite* are reconstructive in their rebuilding of other forms, whether grand opera or soap opera, according to feminist specifications. At the same time both Potter and Citron reconstruct some basic cinematic styles (psychodrama, documentary) to create new feminist forms, in harmony with the desires of the audience as well as the theoretical concerns of the filmmakers. By reconstructing forms in a constructive manner, these films build bridges between the needs of women and the goals of art.

Medusan.

Humor should not be overlooked as a weapon of great power. Comedy requires further cultivation for its revolutionary potential as a deflator of the patriarchal order and an extraordinary leveler and reinventor of dramatic structure. An acknowledgment of the subversive power of humor, the name "Medusan" is taken from Helene Cixous's "The Laugh of the Medusa," in which she celebrates the potential of feminist texts "to blow up the law, to break up the 'truth' with laughter."[18] Cixous's contention that when women confront the figure of Medusa she will be laughing is a rejoinder to Freud's posing the "Medusa's head" as an incarnation of male castration fears. For Cixous, women are having the last laugh. And, to be sure, all the films in this camp deal with combinations of humor and sexuality. Vera Chytilova's *Daisies* was one of the first films by a woman to move in the direction of anarchic sexuality, though its disruptive humor was received largely as slapstick at the time. Nelly Kaplan's two films, *A Very Curious Girl* and *Nea,* also offer an explosive humor coupled with sexuality to discomfort patriarchal society (even though her fondness for "happy" endings that restore order has discomfited many feminist critics). Jan Oxenberg's *A Comedy in Six Unnatural Acts* is an excellent recent example of a Medusan film, attacking not just men or sexism but the heterosexually defined stereotypes of lesbianism; its success has been demonstrated by its raucous cult reception and, more pointedly, by its tendency to polarize a mixed audience along the lines not of class but of sexual preference. It is disruptive of homophobic complacency with a force never approached by analytical films of those defensive of lesbianism. Another highly Medusan film is Jacques Rivette's *Celine and Julie Go Boating* (which may be curious, as it is directed by a man, but production credits indicate a total collaboration with the four actresses and co-scenarists). Celine and Julie enter each other's lives by magic and books, joined in a unity of farce; once they are together, each proceeds to demolish the other's ties to men (an employer, a childhood lover) by using humor, laughing in the face of male fantasies and expectations and thus "spoiling" the relationships with a fungus of parody. The film has been criticized as silly, for Juliet Berto and Dominique Labourier do laugh constantly—at the other characters, themselves, the audience, acting itself—yet their laughter ultimately proves their finest arsenal, enabling them to rescue the plot's girlchild from a darkly imminent Henry Jamesian destruction simply through a laughing refusal to obey its allegedly binding rules. Again, *Celine and Julie* has consistently divided its audience according to whom it threatens: it has become a cult feminist movie even as the male critical establishment (except for Rivette fan Jonathan Rosenbaum) has denounced the film as silly, belabored, too obvious, etc.

Corrective Realism.

As mentioned earlier, the tradition of realism in the cinema has never done well by women. Indeed, extolling realism to women is rather like praising the criminal to the victim, so thoroughly have women been falsified under its banner. A feminist feature cinema, generally representational, is now developing with a regular cast of actresses, a story line, aimed at a wide audience and generally accepting of many cinematic conventions. The women making these films, however, are so thoroughly transforming the characterizations and the narrative workings of traditional realism that they have created a new feminist cinema of "corrective realism." Thus, in Margarethe von Trotta's *The Second Awakening of Christa Klages,* it is the women's actions that advance the narrative; bonding between women functions to save, not to paralyze or trap, the characters; running away brings Christa freedom, while holding his ground brings her male lover only death. The film has outrageously inventive character details, an attention to the minutiae of daily life, an endorsement of emotion and intuitive ties, and an infectious humor. Marta Meszaros's *Women* presents a profound reworking of socialist realism in its depiction of the friendship between two women in a Hungarian work hostel. The alternating close-ups and medium shots become a means of social critique, while the more traditional portrayal of the growing intimacy between the two women insistently places emotional concerns at the center of the film. Both films successfully adapt an existing cinematic tradition to feminist purposes, going far beyond a simple "positive role model" in their establishment of a feminist cinematic environment within which to envision their female protagonists and their activities.

These, then, are a few of the naming possibilities. However, it is not only the feminist films that demand new names, but also (for clarity) the films being made by men about women.

Projectile.

One name resurrected from the 50's by 70's criticism was Molly Haskell's recoining of the "woman's film," the matinee melodramas which, cleared of pejorative connotations, were refitted for relevance to women's cinematic concerns today. Wishful thinking. The name was Hollywood's and there it stays, demonstrated by the new "woman's films" that are pushing actual women's films off the screen, out into the dark. These are male fantasies of women—men's projections of themselves and their fears onto female characters. The name "projectile" identifies these films' true nature and gives an added awareness of the destructive impact of male illusions on the female audience. It is time the bluff was called on the touted authenticity of these works, which pose as objective while remaining entirely subjective in their conception and execution. The clearest justification for this name can be found in director Paul Mazursky's description of his *An Unmarried Woman:* "I don't know if this is a woman's movie or not. I don't know what that means anymore. . . . I wanted to get inside a woman's head. I've felt that all the pictures I've done, I've done with men. I put myself inside a man's head, using myself a lot. I wanted this time to think like a woman. That's one of the reasons there was so much rewriting. . . . There were many things the women I cast in the film . . . wouldn't say. They'd tell me why, and I'd say, 'Well, what would you say?' and I'd let them say that. I used a real therapist; I wanted a woman, and I had to change what she said based on what she is. In other words, the only thing I could have done was to get a woman to help me write it. I thought about that for a while, but in the end I think it worked out."[19] Films such as this one (and *The Turning Point, Pretty Baby, Luna,* and so on ad infinitum) are aimed fatally at us; they deserve to be named "projectile."

Certainly the names offered here do not cover all possibilities, nor can every film be fitted neatly into one category. But I hope their relative usefulness or failings will prompt a continuation of the process by others. The urgency of the naming task cannot be overstated.

WARNING SIGNS: A POSTSCRIPT

We are now in a period of normalization, a time that can offer feminists complacency as a mask for cooption. Scanning the horizon for signs of backlash and propaganda, we see the storm clouds within feminist film criticism are gathering most clearly over issues of form.

It has become a truism to call for new forms. Over and over, we have heard the sacred vows; you can't put new revolutionary subjects/messages into reactionary forms; new forms, a new anti-patriarchal film language for feminist cinema must be developed. While certainly true to an extent, form remains only one element of the work. And the valorization of form above and independent of other criteria has begun to create its own problems.

There is the misconception that form, unlike subject matter, is inviolate and can somehow encase the meaning in protective armor. But form is as cooptable as other elements. A recent analysis by critic Julianne Burton of the *cinema novo* movement in Brazil raised this exact point by demonstrating how the Brazilian state film apparatus took over the forms and styles of *cinema novo* and stripped them of their ideological significance as one means of disarming the movement.[20] If we fetishize the long take, the unmediated shot, etc., as feminist per se, then we will shortly be at loss over how to evaluate the facsimiles proliferating in the wake of such a definition. Furthermore, the reliance on form as the ultimate gauge of a film's worth sets up an inevitable hierarchy that places reconstructive films or films of correspondence at the top of a pyramid, leaving corrective realist or validative approaches among the baser elements. This itself is a complex problem. First, such a view reproduces the notion of history as "progress" and supposes that forms, like technology, grow cumulatively better and better; some believe in that sort of linear quality, but I don't. Second, recent criticism by Christine Gledhill (of film) and Myra Love (of literature) has questioned the naturalness of the Brechtian, postmodernist, deconstructive model as a feminist strategy, pointing out the real drawbacks of its endemic authoritarianism and ambiguity.[21] Third, our very reasons for supporting such work must at least be examined honestly. Carolyn Heilbrun's point should be well taken: "critics, and particularly academics, are understandably prone to admire and overvalue the carefully construed, almost puzzlelike novel [read: film], not only for its profundities, but because it provides them, in explication, with their livelihood."[22] Just as a generosity of criticism can provide the strongest support for feminist filmmakers, so acceptance of a variety of filmic strategies can provide the vigor needed by the feminist audience.

For we must look to the filmmaker and viewer for a way out of this aesthetic cul-de-sac. Aesthetics are not eternally embedded in a work like a penny in a cube of Lucite. They are dependent on and subject to the work's reception. The formal values of a film cannot be considered in isolation, cut off from the thematic correspondents within the text and from the social determinants without. Reception by viewers as well as by critics is key to any film's meaning. As my chronology indicates, feminist cinema arose out of a need not only on the part of the filmmakers and writers, but on the part of the women they knew to be their audience. Today we must constantly check feminist film work to gauge how alive this thread of connection still is, how communicable its feminist values are. We are in a time of transition now, when we still have the luxury of enjoying feminist work on its makers' own terms, without having to sift the sands paranoiacally for impostors. But this transitional period is running out: as the cultural lag catches up, the dominant and avant-garde cinema may begin to incorporate feminist success before we recognize what we've lost. The emphasis on form makes that incorporation easier. Burton ended her article with a call for the inscription of modes of production within the body of Third World film criticism. Therein lies a clue. Feminism has always emphasized process; now it's time that this process of production and reception be inscribed within the critical text. How was the film made? With what intention? With what kind of crew? With what relationship to the subject? How was it produced? Who is distributing it? Where is it being shown? For what audience is it constructed? How is it available? How is it being received? There is no need to establish a tyranny of the productive sphere over a film's definition, nor to authorize only immediately popular films, but it will prove helpful in the difficult times ahead of us to keep this bottom line of method and context in mind, to avoid painting ourselves into a corner.

Formal devices are progressive only if they are employed with a goal beyond aesthetics alone. Here, finally, is the end of the line. Feminist film criticism cannot solve problems still undefined in the sphere of feminist thought and activity at large. We all are continually borrowing from and adding to each other's ideas, energies, insights, across disciplines. We also need to develop lines of communication across the boundaries of race, class and sexuality. Last year in Cuba, I heard a presentation by Alfredo Guevara, founder and director of the Cuban Film Institute. He explained its efforts to educate the Cuban audience to the tricks of cinema, to demystify the technology, to give the viewers the means with which to defend themselves against cinematic hypnosis, to challenge the dominant ideology of world cinema, to create a new liberated generation of film viewers. I will never forget his next words: "We do not claim to have created this audience already, nor do we think it is a task only of cinema." The crisis of naming requires more than an etymologist to solve it.

Notes

Earlier versions of this article appeared in *Jump Cut,* no. 19 (1979) and *Heresies* no. 9 (1980).

Many of the ideas in the section on "The Names" originated in the context of a germinative discussion published as "Women and Film: A Discussion of Feminist Aesthetics," *New German Critique,* no. 13 (1978), pp. 83–107. I am grateful to the other participants in that discussion, including Michelle Citron, Julia Lesage, Judith Mayne, Anna Marie Taylor, and the three *New German Critique* editors, for their support. This piece has been strengthened by the opportunity to test my new ideas in a winter program at the Walker Art Center, Minneapolis, and at the 1979 Edinburgh Film Festival's Feminism and Cinema Event, where the last section on "Warning Signs" comprised a portion of my talk.

1. Adrienne Rich, "It is the Lesbian in Us," *Sinister Wisdom,* no. 3 (1977) and "The Transformation of Silence into Language and Action," *Sinister Wisdom,* no. 6 (1978). See also Mary Daly, *Beyond God the Father* (Boston: Beacon Press, 1973) for her pioneering analysis of naming as power.

2. "Melodrama" and "structuralist" cinema were the two names analyzed in papers presented by my co-panelists, William Horrigan and Bruce Jenkins, at the 1978 Purdue Conference on Film, where the ideas in this paper were first presented.

3. Women artists working in film continued, as before, to make avant-garde films, but those without feminist material lie outside my present concerns.

4. For a fuller discussion of the film, see my "*Maedchen in Uniform*: From Repressive Tolerance to Erotic Liberation," *Jump Cut,* nos. 24–25 (1981).

5. Monique Wittig, *Les Guérillères* (New York: Avon, 1973), pp. 112–14.

6. See *Soho Weekly News,* November 18 (p. 36), November 25 (p. 31), and December 9 (p. 35), all 1976.

7. See also my article, "The Films of Yvonne Rainer," *Chrysalis,* no. 2 (1977).

8. Presented at the International Symposium on Film Theory and Practical Criticism, Center for 20th-Century Studies, University of Wisconsin-Milwaukee, in 1975.

9. Cindy Nemser, "Editorial: Rainer and Rothschild, an Overview," *Feminist Art Journal* 4, no. 2 (1975): 4. The same issue contained Lucy Lippard's "Yvonne Rainer on Feminism and Her Film." Lippard, however, is the exception in her ability to handle both the formal value and feminist strengths of Rainer's work.

10. *Women & Film.* no. 7, p. 86; also *Camera Obscura,* no. 1 (1977).

11. Here I am considering only English-language feminist film criticism; there are other complex issues in French and German criticism, for example.

12. Gilles Deleuze, "I Have Nothing To Admit," *Semiotexte,* no. 6 (1977), p. 112.

13. See Barbara Halpern Martineau, "Nelly Kaplan" and "Subjecting Her Objectification, or Communism Is Not Enough" in *Notes On Women's Cinema,* ed. Claire Johnston (London: Society for Education in Film and Television, 1973).

14. See Claire Johnston, "Women's Cinema as Counter-Cinema" in *Notes on Women's Cinema* and Laura Mulvey, "Visual Pleasure and Narrative Cinema" in *Women and the Cinema,* ed. Karyn Kay and Gerald Peary (New York: Dutton, 1977), pp. 412–28, and reprinted in this volume.

15. Quotations are taken from: E. Ann Kaplan, "Interview with British Cine-Feminists" in *Women and the Cinema,* pp. 400–401; Barbara Charlesworth Gelpi and Albert Gelpi, *Adrienne Rich's Poetry* (New York: Norton, 1975), p. 115; Barbara Halpern Martineau, "Paris/Chicago" in *Women & Film,* no. 7, p. 11; Laura Mulvey, "Visual Pleasure and Narrative Cinema" (op. cit.), p. 414, as well as personal communications. See also E. Ann Kaplan, "Aspects of British Feminist Film Theory" in *Jump Cut,* nos. 12–13, for an in-depth examination of the British theories and their implications.

16. Sheila Rowbotham, *Woman's Consciousness, Man's World* (London: Penguin, 1973), p. 33. See also her statement (p. 32) that language always is "carefully guarded by the superior people because it is one of the means through which they conserve their supremacy."

17. *The Compact Edition of the Oxford English Dictionary.*

18. Helene Cixous, "The Laugh of the Medusa," *Signs* 1, no. 4 (1976): 888.

19. "Paul Mazursky Interviewed by Terry Curtis Fox," *Film Comment* 14, no. 2 (1978): 30–31.

20. These remarks by Burton are taken from memory of her talk at the 1979 Purdue Conference on Film. As stated, they are a simplification of complexities that she was at pains to elucidate without distortion.

21. Christine Gledhill, "Recent Developments in Feminist Criticism," *Quarterly Review of Film Studies* 3, no. 4 (1979); and Myra Love, "Christa Wolf and Feminism: Breaking the Patriarchal Connection," *New German Critique,* no. 17 (1979).

22. Carolyn G. Heilbrun, Introduction to May Sarton, *Mrs. Steven Hears the Mermaids Singing* (New York: Norton, 1974), p. xii.

THE RIGHT OF RE-VISION: MICHELLE CITRON'S *DAUGHTER RITE*

LINDA WILLIAMS
AND B. RUBY RICH

An early feminist article by Eileen McGarry, "Documentary, Realism, and Women's Cinema" (Women & Film 2, no. 7 [1975]), *sought to establish that documentary film operates under the constraints of formal coding and convention; if is not a form of privileged cinematic instance that somehow escapes cinematic and extracinematic constraints and mediations. She calls for a feminist exploration of the documentary that joins cinematic materialism—a concern with the material form of the cinema's signifying practices—with political materialism—a concern for the concrete social practices that underpin ideology. To a considerable degree, Michelle Citron's* Daughter Rite *appears to answer that call, especially as it has been explicated by Williams and Rich.*

Like MacDougall, who attempted in his article in Part 2 to specify an ethnographic documentary practice that steps beyond the limitations of observational cinema, Williams and Rich seek a feminist documentary practice that avoids the seductive appeal of cinéma vérité *style, which can be misrecognized as objective truth. While these authors may overstate the relation between* cinéma vérité *and truth in positing an identity about which many viewers would be skeptical, their description of the complex yet accessible structure of* Daughter Rite *is precise.*

Using Nancy Chodorow's The Reproduction of Mothering *as a theoretical guide to the familial issues examined in Citron's film, they analyze how it addresses a real social issue, the relations between daughters and mothers, through a formal strategy that emphasizes its own structure; how it loosens traditional identification with characters, be they fictional or "real"; and how it invites a reflective engagement of the viewer's emotions and intellect. The choice to put Chodorow in a place often reserved in film writing for an invocation of Jacques Lacan's theories is notable in itself, and it points to an emphatic stress on a social, rather than a strictly psychoanalytic, theory of family relations. However, the prime concern of the authors is with the structure of the film itself, namely, with how* Daughter Rite *uses familiar and accessible forms—cinéma vérité, soap opera, home movies, journals—both to critique and to renew the documentary form. In this effort, Citron's film, like the ethnographies of David and Judith MacDougall, which also adopt, subvert, and contextualize familiar documentary forms (see my article, "The Voice of Documentary," in Part 2), refuses to address only an audience of avant-garde or vanguard cultural workers and instead offers immediate bridges to other communities of women. The authors' emphasis on this strategy is of some importance, since it speaks to a potential division between those who advocate a rejection of dominant cinematic forms in order to found a radically distinct aesthetic and those who propose a critical reworking of dominant forms in order both to develop a distinct aesthetic and to address an audience constituted primarily on the basis of feminist or political issues, not of aesthetic or ideological ones.*

•

The vast majority of literary and visual images of motherhood comes to us filtered through a collective or individual male consciousness. . . . We need to know what, out of that welter of image-making and thought-spinning, is worth salvaging, if only to understand better an idea so crucial in history, a condition which has been wrested from the mothers themselves to buttress the power of the fathers. —Adrienne Rich[1]

Perhaps our current responsibility lies in humanizing our own activities so that they will communicate more effectively with all women. Hopefully we will aspire to more than women's art flooding the museum and gallery circuit (and screens). Perhaps a feminist art will only emerge when we become wholly responsible for our own work, for what becomes of it, who sees it, and who is nourished by it. For a feminist artist, whatever her style, the prime audience at this time is other women. —Lucy Lippard[2]

As Adrienne Rich indicates above, the image of motherhood has been one of the most censored and distorted of all the images produced by patriarchy. Only recently has this image been freed from the taboos and constraints of patriarchal culture to become a subject of psychological study and literary inspiration for feminists. Yet for a long time, within the form of the melodramatic "woman's film," the mother-daughter relationship has been a favorite theme, from *Stella Dallas* to *Mildred Pierce* to *The Turning Point*. The problem with such films, in spite of their focus on the complex of emotions contained in the mother-daughter bond, is that they are characterized by a hidden misogyny. Pretending to sanctify the institution of motherhood, they more often merely exalt its ideal while punishing and humiliating the individual women who participate in it.

At the heart of all these representations of the mother-daughter bond is a psychological truth that has been much discussed in recent writing[3] but which has perhaps been best described by Nancy Chodorow in her book, *The Reproduction of Mothering*.[4] Unlike a son who must ultimately repress or deny his original attachment and identification with the mother's body to take on a more abstract and less primally connected identification with the father, a daughter undergoes no such shift in gender identification; her primary identification with her mother remains with her always. This "Oedipal asymmetry" causes the daughter to continue to experience herself as unseparated, continuous with others. Continuous identification with a member of the same sex makes it more difficult for the daughter to separate off from her mother, to claim her own life. It is not surprising, then, that so much women's melodrama has centered upon the contradiction of an idealized mother love that, when actually represented as an ongoing relationship, turns into a stranglehold (cf. *Now Voyager, Imitation of Life*).

What often happens in these films is that the mother must learn to renounce her love for her daughter and to suffer nobly for some supposedly higher good— the daughter's increased social status achieved through marriage (*Stella Dallas*) or even the daughter's entrance into a career (*The Turning Point*). Thus narrative resolution usually occurs through the mother's sacrifice, a sacrifice that unhappily perpetrates a patriarchal definition of motherhood *as* sacrifice.

Given these problems, what are the alternatives for a radical feminist filmmaker who chooses to represent this most crucial relationship? In the past, the most popular format for feminists seeking to document the issues affecting women's lives has been the cinéma vérité documentary. But despite its efficacy as record, testimony, and organizing wedge, the documentary form has begun to be re-examined by feminist critics skeptical of its neutrality. The use of the documentary as a form of social evidence has fed the misconception that film can be equated with "truth." As with the fiction film, this "truth" is negotiated through an unspoken contract involving the spectator's absolute identification with the film's character as a real person and with the film's narrative as a spontaneous recording of a candid situation.

Daughter Rite,[5] Michelle Citron's recent film about mothers and daughters, avoids such misleading notions of truth by, first of all, subverting the audience's expectations of the documentary form. This subversion sets in motion an emotional chain-reaction that overcomes the limitations of identification and culminates in analysis. The filmmaker's central problem was how to make a film about relations of women within the family without producing either a first-person confessional film or a fictional portrait of a representative family. By reconstructing and juxtaposing four different forms (cinéma vérité, soap opera melodrama, home movies, journals), Citron problematizes identification itself—its false and easy notions of unity and truth. She thus opens to scrutiny a number of cherished cinematic assumptions to explore the mother-daughter bond in an entirely new way.

Instead of representing a single mother and daughter in a single representational mode, *Daughter Rite* represents a plurality of interwoven subjective approaches to two different mothers in a variety of modes. Significantly, neither mother is directly represented in any of the film's sections. The mothers appear to us only in the form of their daughters' often anger-filled memories of them. Thus Citron replaces more conventional and unitary *representation of* with multiple, overlapping and contradictory *relations to*. All of these relations to are characterized by very specific problems of identification with the mother that radically affect each daughter's sense of self.

The film opens with several sequences of re-edited home movie footage. The flickering 8mm films show a mother and two daughters at various stages of mother and girlhood, smiling and waving at the camera in typical poses of coy and narcissistic femininity—the kind frequently elicited by the home movie camera. In an early scene the mother and daughters ride a swan boat. The mother sits in the middle, a protective arm around each daughter, smoothing the hair of one, leading both in cheerful waves at the camera. Other scenes show: the mother and daughters in their Sunday best parading on the sidewalk of their suburban neighborhood; a large group of mothers watching as their daughters parade decorated baby carriages; the two little sisters in curlers washing dishes at home, presenting each clean dish for mother's approval.

These movies have been taken, as are most home movies, by a father-cameraman who is never seen. Nothing could be more true to life, more acceptable as unmediated reality, then a family's home movies. Yet by her techniques of rephotography, slowing down and repeating actions and gestures, Citron opens to question the neutrality of even this form of movie making to uncover a more problematic picture of family life than these superficially happy views of sunny family outings and domestic scenes would suggest. Just as feminist historians have called attention to the dilemma of searching out women within written history, which itself is patriarchal, so Citron calls attention to a similarly patriarchal vision of domestic life captured in home movies.

Where the father's camera portrays the mother as a happy mother goose, instinctively leading her flock to fulfill their natural destinies as daughters, wives and mothers, the daughter's re-photographing and re-editing of these haunting happy memories of the family album reveal a process of socialization that is neither very natural nor very happy. Optical step-frame printing repeats and slows the telling gestures with which the mother teaches her daughters their roles as proper young ladies. The natural flow of an image is interrupted to show, for example, the mother adjusting the same recalcitrant curl on her daughter's head. Repetition renders the gesture unnatural, constraining, obsessive. Repetition also reveals the ritualized imprinting of the mother's role: the same dish is repeatedly washed, dried and offered up for mother's approval by these tiny aspiring housewives; the same miniature baby carriages are wheeled again and again to mother's approving gaze.

In a striking scene that begins the film, one of the daughters repeatedly races an egg—balanced precariously on a spoon held in her mouth—to her mother at the far end of a field. As the film continues, we begin to understand that it is precisely the carrying of this egg—symbol of the daughter's role as the bearer of future generations and of the culture that nurtures them—that is at issue in this film.

Thus what the father films as the natural behavior of mother and daughters is re-filmed by the daughter-filmmaker as ritualized, learned behavior. Adrienne Rich has written that patriarchal culture depends upon the mother to act as a conservative influence, "imprinting future adults with patterned values even when the mother-child relationship might seem most individual and private."[6] By making us aware of the ritual nature of this imprinting, the home movie sections of *Daughter Rite* claim the daughter's right to wrest the image of the mother away from the "power of the fathers," to filter it back through her own consciousness. A first step in this re-filtering has thus been a necessary deconstruction of the father's image of both mother and daughter, a deconstruction that problematizes the daughter's own identification with the "truth" of these images.

Accompanying the home movie images from the past, in counterpoint to them, is the first-person voice of one of the daughters, now an adult filmmaker, speaking thoughtfully of the present: of the troubled, guilt-ridden, ongoing relationship with her mother. Speaking as if to a film diary, the daughter tells of her mother's divorce, of her move to Hawaii and of their occasional visits and phone calls. Thus past images of childhood combine with a present voice of adulthood that probes the confusing mixture of love, hate and guilt so typical of the adult relationship with our mothers.

The daughter's voice begins with the impetus for the film itself: her 28th birthday and the realization that she herself had been born when her own mother was 28. As we see the egg race in the home movies, the daughter confesses her uneasiness at not following in her mother's footsteps: she is neither married nor having a child. The fear that she will not be like her mother (and will not carry on that egg) is followed in succeeding sections of voice-over by its even more terrifying opposite: the matrophobic fear of, in fact, *becoming* the mother.[7] These two contradictory fears—of being either too much or not enough like our mothers—originate with the same root problem mentioned above: the difficulty young girls have sorting out and claiming their own independent identities.

Inevitably, the daughter's attempt to claim her own life by opposing the patriarchal limitations of the mother-daughter bond involves the expression of anger, even hatred, toward the mother. But this anger is not the indirect misogyny of the many so-called "woman's films." This is a more direct anger, with at least a potential for health-giving catharsis and change—a necessary exorcism of emotions that have poisoned the daughter's own view of herself. As she explains, "I hate my mother and, in hating her, hate myself."

Anger is equally manifest, though more oblique, in the sections which alternate with the home movie images and diary-style voice-over. Two women sit, ill at ease, in front of the camera. The scene is a familiar one in the 70's: the "common woman" consenting to share her experiences with a film crew to communicate with other women—in this case the story of her experience during childbirth with her own mother. The camera moves in closer, rather clumsily, for effect as the emotional register requires. When the film next returns to the two sisters, they are again facing the camera, speaking this time about their childhood: how they kept diaries, how their mother read those diaries, to what an extent their mother prohibited privacy to exert her own power over their lives.

We see no interlocutor, hear no questions, yet the women's self-consciousness and the camera's searching movements from one face to the other are convincing indicators of a spontaneous interview situation. It is only when the film returns for the third time to the domestic locus of the two sisters, who have moved from the formal environs of the dining room into the kitchen, that a shift in the style of representation moves the viewer to a shift in awareness. In the kitchen, the sisters for the first time ignore the camera entirely: there is no face-front address, nor any particular testimony. Instead, the sisters interact with each other, revealing through conversation and gesture a range of character and emotion (including humor) inaccessible in the more formal interview format. It is this very display of character that signals the artifice which has underlain the sisters' scenes from the start. No cinéma vérité documentary could ever capture this scene of intimacy, this sudden ease in front of the camera. The scenes have been acted all along: these women, not sisters at all, are in fact actresses engaged in a convincing replica of documentary behavior. And to complicate matters even further, these are not the same sisters who appear as children in the home movie sections.

Daughter Rite thus alternates the home movie and voice-over scenes with these adult sister scenes. But even within these latter scenes there is an alternation of modes—from quasi-vérité to staged fiction. In the second half of the film these staged scenes come more and more to resemble the stuff of soap opera. In one such scene, the two sisters sit on the floor rifling through Mom's record collection (all of these sister scenes take place in the mother's house although the mother herself is never there). They groan at her bad taste and surplus of Christmas music, then gradually edge into a discussion of finance. When the older sister displays astonishment at their mother's having asked her sister outright for money when she had coyly dropped hints about her pecuniary distress, no stagey organ music surges on the soundtrack, but the emotional notes are clearly those of soap opera: "I wish I had that kind of mother, but I don't."

Once the audience has been able to adjust successfully to the film's mixed modes, Citron is able to return to the earlier vérité style with stunning effect. The younger sister faces the camera and recounts a chilling tale of incestuous rape. The viewer is forced into a contradictory series of reactions: sympathy for the character, whether real-life or constructed; respect for the actress's performance, so true to life; anger at the filmmaker's exposure of this intimate moment, followed by a quick save as its artificiality is recalled; perhaps even anger at such trickery. In other words, the film's mixed-mode form of presentation profoundly criticizes the very forms in use without sacrificing the emotional connection binding the viewer to its workings. What seemed at the film's start to be a one-dimensional documentary truth has become, by its end, a more complex rendering of truths through these shifts to a more obviously manipulated, fictional style of representation.

Although the tone of the adult sisters scenes ranges from gossipy anecdote to intense emotion, these scenes are in strong contrast to the voice-over that accompanies the home movie sections. This daughter's voice has a more distanced, reflective, but also lyrical tone. Her recollections of her mother freely mix specific events from the recent past with more obscure accounts of dreams. Combined with the flickering images of the already dream-like slow-motion of the home movies, this disembodied, comparatively detached voice often achieves a more sympathetic understanding of the mother. Perhaps it is precisely due to its dream-like locus that such a sympathy can be expressed, for on the more realistic bedrock of the sister scenes, daily behavior still lags far behind any such fantasy resolution.

The film juxtaposes, for example, two similar instances in which the sisters and the voice of the filmmaker react to the revelation of the woman who lies behind the role of mother. In the last of the sister scenes, the two sisters rummage through their mother's bedroom, violating the same privacy they had earlier condemned her for violating when they were girls. While rummaging, they discover the mother's guilty secrets: her cache of dope (Valium and speed), her sexual and romantic fantasies (the books *Return to Peyton Place* and *Valley of the Dolls*— themselves the stuff of soap opera and melodrama). These secrets are undoubtedly similar to those that their mother, who used to read their diaries, once discovered about them. Like their mother, the sisters fail to sympathize with the genuine yearnings that lie behind these guilty pleasures; they can only disapprove of her misuse of drugs and bad taste in literature. For all their previous criticism of their mother's conventional acceptance of the role of mother, they are quite simply shocked to discover that this same mother could have such desires. "This is the woman who reads *Guideposts*?" one of them muses.

This final sister scene contrasts with the final episode of the film: the voice of the filmmaker (this, too, as we come to see, is a fictionalized voice) relates an incident in which her mother unexpectedly gave her the wedding pyjamas from her trousseau. Like the other mother's secret dope and cheap fiction, these pyjamas represent an aspect of her sexual being that has been tucked away in a drawer, long hidden from her daughters, the rest of the world, and perhaps even herself. But unlike the pills and cheap fiction, the pyjamas are a voluntary gift whose meaning and poignancy are understood by the filmmaker daughter, "It was as if she were handing me a little piece of her dreams."

Dreams are in fact used repeatedly by the voice of the filmmaker as one way of breaking out of the repetitive cycle in which the two sisters seem to be caught. In this cycle, the mother infantilizes the daughter until such time as the daughter can infantilize her in turn. The crippling effects of this infantilization are stressed in a scene in which one of the sisters tells how her mother's babying of her during her own birth-giving sapped her strength. Only when her mother left the room could she regain it.

The filmmaker, on the other hand, uses her dreams to imagine a more mysterious and powerful—though not always beneficent—mother. In the final episode of the film, her dream recounts the story of a mother who has, and can give, amazing strength, but whose strength is employed to strangely destructive ends. In this dream, the mother helps burn the filmmaker's sister who is dying of cancer of the jaw and has asked to be set on fire. The dream account tells how the mother takes control, burning and then burying the youngest daughter while the older sister, the filmmaker, stands in awe and appreciation of the herculean task. If this dream offers no solution to the actual relations of mother and daughter, it at least avoids the reductive infantilization of the sister scenes, offering an appreciation of the mother's power to give and take life.

Yet another of the filmmaker's dreams affords a more positive contrast to the sisters' view of the mother. The younger sister's cinéma vérité account of her rape by her stepfather is preceded by the filmmaker's dream of an attempt by both her mother and grandmother to get her to accept an injection from a giant needle, "for the good of mankind." In both the dream of the injection and the "reality" of the rape, the mother emerges as the final culprit, tacitly acknowledging her helplessness before the power of the father that rapes her daughter in one instance, wielding the phallic needle, symbol of that power, in the next. Here we see, most forcefully, the mother's role as "imprintor" of patriarchy. But the narrator's dream contains an obvious wish-fulfillment: the power of the daughter to refuse the needle and thus to refuse patriarchy (in her dream she cannot be injected so long as she does not consent to their right to give her the injection—unlike, of course, an actual rape!).

It is tempting—and we have already suggested some of the directions of this temptation—to compare the relative value of the different daughters' relationships to their mother to find a valorization of the more lyrical contemplative voice of the daughter filmmaker in the home movie sections of the film. But even here it is important to see that the film problematizes what could become an overly simplified solution. For this final image of the mother—an image which seems to offer a more positive and healing closure in which the daughter genuinely admires her mother—depicts the mother as killing off the daughter's sibling rival. Hardly an innocent choice of activity, this is a dream fantasy of troubling content that may raise as many problems as it solves.

But, as we have seen, this is the daughter's film. The girl who rode the swan boat in the home movies with a Brownie camera around her neck has grown up and taken over from Dad: now it is she who gets to peer through the lens, this time with X-ray eyes, to visualize the family. Toward the close of the film, in the home movie sections, there are many shots of Mom alone, looking vaguely heroic, extending her arm out over an expanse of water. This near noble portrait, along with the dream of reconciliation, perhaps comprise an acknowledgment of the *other* film, the one which could match with positives all the negatives of this film: the mother's film, of course, which no daughter could ever make, but which could speak the flip side of all we have heard as alternate readings of identical actions.

As it is, *Daughter Rite* reflects the generational imperialism whereby a decade of daughters has not infrequently sought to remake the mothers in our own renovated image. By summing up the emotional quandaries of the moment, Citron has at least opened the way to dialogue. In fact, after the last image fades and the screen goes blank, a voice speaks as though out of the collective memory. It is the voice of the mother, speaking as she might in her daughter's fantasy, in fact taken from a Deena Metzger story about a mother reading her daughter's writing: "'Why do you have to say all this,' she asks." For an answer, only the credits appear.

Daughter Rite is an important film for feminists due to the nature of the forms Citron has chosen to rework. The critique from within of the cinéma vérité format accomplishes a dual task. On the one hand, Citron is able to criticize its limitations, showing that cinema cannot deliver up the Truth, that character identification may lead only to individualized pathos, that the political is not merely the personal, nor the personal only the private, that the single-person portrait can only raise our level of knowledge in increments of one. Yet, at the same time, the film functions to redeem documentary, in that its form is accessible, related to the lives of women, a meaningful tradition and a still powerful taproot into the emotions as well as the intellects of viewers. By combining the mock documentary with the other introspective voice of narration which accompanies the home movies, Citron can validate the personal subjective documentary with qualification; rather than making it the only voice, she provides for a multiple approach to the truths of mothers and daughters. Furthermore, by replacing the usual individual with a synthetic character (whose experiences, in fact, were scripted out of materials derived from some forty interviews with mothers and daughters), Citron is able to break the traditional documentary dependence on the isolated life and extend the individual experience into the social sphere.

The title of the Lippard article quoted at the beginning of this article is a reference to the art likely to be most familiar to working-class women: the pink glass swan. In questioning what traditional art forms might offer a bridge of communication between feminist artists and the community of women outside of the art world, Lippard opens an area of inquiry to which Citron can also be seen as contributing. In her use of soap opera and home movies as two major modes of visualization, and of diary or journal as the narrative mode, Citron employs three "domestic" forms which will be familiar, and assimilable, to her audience. The home movies are explicitly re-viewed, while the soap opera form is implicitly critiqued by the play-off with cinéma vérité, which disrupts the credibility of both. Because of that disruption, making the viewer's identification with the characters a self-conscious one, the film also opens the route to an analysis of the normally authoritative narrative voice. We begin to subject the narrator-filmmaker to the same kind of distanced critique applied to her characters.

By establishing a harmony between its subject matter and formal strategies, *Daughter Rite* narrows the gap between the aesthetics of woman's culture and those of the avant-garde film. Because the forms themselves have developed out of a women's movement context, their use within the film is a political one. Since it is increasingly impossible for a filmmaker to jam both the purely political and the purely formal together into one work pleasing to anyone, or even internally consistent, Citron's solution of annexing popular forms, which she both revives and critiques, represents a significant innovation.[8]

The aesthetics of a film, particularly a feminist film, cannot be separated from its mode of production or its sphere of reception. The complex interplays of character identification, for example, are an effective strategy precisely because *Daughter Rite* was made with a woman's movement audience, schooled in the movement's documentary tradition, in mind. Similarly, the familial insights suggested by the film strike an immediate response in many viewers not only because of the synoptic scripting that drew on a range of individual pasts, but also because of the context within which *Daughter Rite* is received—a context characterized by an awareness of the issues of mother-daughter and sibling relations occurring within a rich feminist literature of fiction, poetry, philosophy, sociology and psychology. Even the film's attention to particular female characteristics—forms of conversation, gesture, even the love/hate relation to food preparation reflecting woman's contradictory nurturing/dieting impulses—reflect current issues under discussion within the women's movement.

Daughter Rite's formal invention similarly parallels issues under discussion by feminist film and television critics regarding the function of soap opera and its viability as a "woman's" form. Just as critics like Molly Haskell were able to find certain positive values in the "woman's film" (the respect for emotion, the displacing of action into talk and internal change), so now there is an ongoing re-examination of soap opera's emphasis on domestic life, its spinning out of conversation, and the relegation of events to off-screen space, providing an endless verbal replay that retards the forward movement of the narrative in order to explore the lateral repercussions of each action on everyone's life.[9]

Over the course of the past decade, there has been a dearth of work by filmmakers who are both committed to the woman's community as an audience and yet equally influenced by the developing theory of feminist critics. By daring to enter into this seeming limbo, Michelle Citron has succeeded in opening up a major new direction for feminist filmmaking. The emphasis on gesture, conversation, and other modes of communication between women moves *Daughter Rite*'s audience beyond the previously acknowledged boundaries of valorizing positive "images" or lamenting the eternal inscription of women within patriarchal language.

More important, because *Daughter Rite* is self-explanatory in its critiques and priorities, it represents a significant alternative to films that base their forms of subversion upon extra-filmic texts, thereby creating a protective shield beyond which inexplicability most women will not venture. Because the documentaries taken as the film's starting point are a mutual resource for both filmmaker and audience, and because soap operas have already entered the home (and women's consciousness) through television's inclusion in the daily rituals of domestic maintenance, Citron's work can potentially carry the pink glass swan back to the silver screen.

Notes

1. *Of Woman Born* (New York: Bantam, 1976) p. 45.

2. "The Pink Glass Swan: Upward and Downward Mobility in the Art World," *Heresies,* no. 1, p. 85.

3. See Nancy Friday, *My Mother/My Self: The Daughter's Search for Identity* (New York: Dell, 1978); Adrienne Rich, *Of Woman Born,* cited above; Dorothy Dinnerstein, *The Mermaid and The Minotaur* (New York: Harper and Row, 1976).

4. Berkeley: University of California Press, 1978.

5. Distributed by Iris Films, Box 5353, Berkeley, CA 94705.

6. Rich, p. 45.

7. Rich, p. 338. "Matrophobia can be seen as a womanly splitting of self, in the desire to become purged once and for all of our mother's bondage, to become individuated and free."

8. Citron is working in quite a different direction, for example, from that taken by Mulvey and Wollen in *Riddles of the Sphinx.* Like *Daughter Rite, Riddles* takes its subject

matter directly from the women's movement but it takes its formal strategies from theories of avant-garde film, placing itself within an ever widening gap between the avant-garde and the women's movement. Citron, however, begins with forms familiar to the woman's movement and builds from there.

9. See Tania Modleski, "The Search for Tomorrow in Today's Soap Operas: Notes on a Feminine Narrative Form," *Film Quarterly,* Fall 1979, pp. 12–20.

GENTLEMEN CONSUME BLONDES

MAUREEN TURIM

Maureen Turim's article pursues a question closely related to the question raised in the preceding article: In what way is the blatantly exploitative "sexual display" of Marilyn Monroe and Jane Russell in Gentlemen Prefer Blondes *offset or undercut by their own clearly communicated self-awareness of this display, by their "cynicism and cleverness"? Turim places this remake of Anita Loos's satiric novella of 1925 in the context of postwar American culture, where display of the female body took on particular connotations associated with commodity consumption. These connotations invite us to reflect on the linkage between the utopian sensibility conveyed by musicals and the premise that utopia can be realized on the terms of the capitalism that prompts the envisioning of an alternative realm in the first place, the premise that Richard Dyer discusses in his article in Part 2. In the framework of Turim's article, this linkage involves the channeling of sexual desire into heterosexual monogamy and a transformation of the body as signifier of personal style or individuality into a commodity. Not only is this commodity then put on display for the (male) viewer, its idealization as a commodity demonstrates the distinctive form of social organization that underpins capitalism, namely, the private ownership of the means of production and, in the patriarchal family, of reproduction.*

Turim's article demonstrates the applicability of some general theories of visual pleasure and the patriarchal ordering of narrative to a specific text. However, she warns in her addendum against overly generalized accounts of narrative or spectacle, since specific textual operations may not fit the broad theory and in fact may contradict it.

In this regard, Turim's position resembles that of several other authors in this volume—for example, Salt, Loader, Polan, Browne, and Andrew—who emphasize the primacy of specific analyses over general theories. To what extent

general theories, such as those advanced by Mulvey, Johnston, or Baudry,
account for the major effects of most films and to what extent they obscure
important differences among them remain central questions for contemporary
film theory and criticism. It seems very unlikely that these questions can be
answered in any general, all-encompassing manner. Instead, each particular
application and reassessment must be weighed in the balance. Turim's effort to
show the limit to which a "positive" image of women fully aware of their status
as objects of erotic desire and capable of exploiting it can be carried in a fifties
musical—a limit that falls short of feminist consciousness or group solidarity by
remaining "enlightened" self-interest—contributes significantly to an assessment
of visual pleasure and the image of women.

•

I. SATIRE/SEDUCTION—THE FILM
AS ENTERTAINMENT MACHINE

The line which separates celebration from satire in American culture is perniciously thin; no place is that lack of differentiation more evident than in Howard Hawks's *Gentlemen Prefer Blondes,* in which the excesses of the representation create a terrain of ambiguity fertile enough to support the perfect mass entertainment—a film whose ideological foundations are at once so evident and so hidden as to escape analysis.

Gentlemen, an elaborate Cinemascope Technicolor production of 1953, is in this light a totally different cultural artifact from the short volume Anita Loos wrote in 1925 which served as the source for the Broadway musical from which the film was derived. Loos's original work, first run as a serial in *Harper's Bazaar,* was more clearly a satire. The narrative takes the form of diary entries made by a flapper whose malapropisms, misspellings and child-like reasoning have the same force as Tom Sawyer's observations, ridiculing the surrounding society.

The transformation of diary into spectacle affects the possibility of a primarily satiric mode; in Hawks's film, the flapper and her best friend become two show-girls, objects continually on display for us, the viewing audience. Before examining the significance of this transformation, it is useful to trace the development of *Gentlemen* through the versions which lie between the magazine serial and the Fifties movie.

Edgar Selwyn persuaded Miss Loos to write a straight dramatic play based on her story, but after she signed the contract she discovered to her dismay that Florenz Ziegfeld, Jr. wanted to produce a musical version. . . . In collaboration with her husband, John Emerson, she wrote a comic play which starred brunette June Walker wearing a blonde wig to play Lorelei. . . . The show was successful both in New York and on the road, where at least three companies toured simultaneously.

Paramount Pictures bought the film rights. The studio officials, deciding to cast an unknown actress in the role of Lorelei, selected Ruth Taylor, a wide-eyed blonde. . . . Miss Loos said that John C. Wilson had repeatedly asked her to adapt her story as a stage musical comedy, but that she had been too busy writing movie scripts. . . . Miss Loos went to work on the book and co-authored the adaptation with Joseph Fields. . . . [They] kept the spirit of the original book and the atmosphere of the 20s but gave the story a somewhat different treatment. . . .

The plot was certainly farfetched, but the book was not the primary reason for the musical's phenomenal success. The dances, the music, the sumptuous sets, the costumes, the cast, and above all, Carol Channing as Lorelei made the production a fast-moving extravaganza with an emphasis on entertainment. Disregarding integrated score or songs that developed the action, *Gentlemen Prefer Blondes* followed the pattern of the old-fashioned musicals, which shunted plot aside to make way for elaborate musical production numbers.[1]

While the 1949 Broadway version contained many elements of the new brashness and sexual appeal infused into the original story by the addition of the musical performances, it remained deeply rooted in the Twenties, including an opening song about Prohibition and a closing number entitled "Keeping Cool with Coolidge." The Hawks film, then, was the first version to update the story, moving it to a Fifties setting, amplifying the sexual play/exchange against a backdrop of the increasing reification of consumerist values. The musical numbers are treated differently—there are fewer songs in the film and they are more integrated.

Marilyn Monroe and Jane Russell.

Gentlemen opens with a dance number which is both invitation and threat as the "two little girls from Little Rock" maneuver their bodies in a perfectly matched and coordinated assault which begins with them tossing their ermines at the audience/camera. The channels of signification are flooded; ermines tossed away, the fantastic power of being able to discard a commodity of so great an exchange value in order to expose a more precious commodity, the sexually cultivated self-aware female body. The number stresses the cooperative effort of the two, as lyrics are either delivered in unison, or, as when Lorelei delivers her verse on her retribution of the boy who once broke her heart and Dorothy, left off screen for the moment, comes back in to reunify the ranks for the chorus:

> I was young and determined
> To be wined and dined and ermined
> Every night opportunity would knock.

> For a kid from a small street,
> I did very well on Wall Street
> Although I never owned a share of stock.

> Men are the same way everywhere.

The lyrics enhance the provocation, opening a paradigm which informs the structure of the narrative—an opposition between the sexual display made of these women (their exploitation as objects within the film's narrative and for the film's appeal) and the women's expressed cynicism and cleverness (the satire in which the objects take on the role of critical subjects). This opposition between "come on" and "put down" provides the ambiguity which is essential to the ambiance of the sophisticated tease.

This opposition is also evidenced in a larger structural alternation between segments of musical performances and segments of other kinds of narrative development. The songs function as structural high points, intense, priviledged moments of the film's expressivity. Among the five songs, two can be distinguished as differing from the others; "Little Rock" and "Diamonds" stand apart since they are stage performances, therefore having double audiences (one represented in the film and the film's real audience) and both play on the codes of nightclub extravaganzas. These two performance numbers almost frame the narrative— "Little Rock" at the beginning and "Diamonds" close to the end. This framing function can be seen as extending to the songs in general since they are grouped towards the beginning and end of the film with a large narrative block uninterrupted by song comprising the film's center (from the cocktail party aboard ship to the hotel in Paris). Also, the songs are alternated with non-musical narrative sequences in the sections of the film in which they do occur:

OPENING SEGMENTS

STAGE	BACKSTAGE	BOAT	DECK	POOL	
"Little Rock"		"Bye, Bye, Baby"		"Anyone Here For Love?"	

CLOSING SEGMENTS

CAFE	BACKSTAGE	STAGE	BACKSTAGE	COURT	WEDDING
"When Love Goes Wrong"	CHEZ LOUIS	"Diamonds"		reprise "Diamonds"	reprise "Little Rock"

This alternation is important to the system of embedding, of narrative motivation operative in the film's use of songs. We are never given spectacle for its own sake—each instance of performance/seduction is grounded in a logical purpose, hardly "naturalistic," but not freestanding either. This embedding acts as a justifying force, tempering the eroticism—the film's audience is not watching an enticing performance directly exhibited for them, but rather the film's audience is witness to a nightclub performance directed at an audience within the film. So even though camera angles and distance increase and highlight the film audience's voyeurism and fetishism over what is attainable at the local establishment, this vision is made innocent. We need not consider ourselves voyeurs and fetishists, habitués of cheap strip shows—we prefer "sophisticated musical comedy."

A corollary function of the alternation of song and narrative segments is to structurally disperse and alternate moments of more intense titillation and provocation. The film as machine to entertain needs this pattern of dispersion; it is dependent on recurrent stimulation, not only on the sways, rhythms and beats, but also on the very fact of creating moments when the spectator is encouraged to partake of the forbidden vision, to watch with prurient pleasure. The success of the entertainment derives from this indulgence of an erotic vision, but not continually. Intermittence—privilege—must be associated with this vision if it is to retain its power within the spectator's imagination.

II. WOMAN OBJECT

Marilyn Monroe/Lorelei Lee—star persona and character—are flattened into a single myth. It is ironic that in a film about performances, acting is denied in favor of "matching." Even the Twenties locutions which remain ("Thank you ever so") become simply another of Marilyn's idiosyncracies, part of her essence as instantaneous artifact and pop art sex goddess, part of the arsenal along with quivering lips and dresses drawn tight across her hips.

A major force developed in the film is the contrast/complement relationship between Lorelei and Dorothy, between Monroe and Russell. For beneath an initial opposition, Blonde/Money versus Brunette/Love, is an overriding similarity which ideologically anchors certain traits and powers as inherently female. This shared quality is the skillful manipulation of men (in the attempt to regain an incriminating photo: "If we aren't able to empty his pockets between us, we aren't worthy of the name Woman."). The courtroom impersonation of Lorelei by Dorothy emphasizes this sameness beneath the superficial difference—the difference is marked ironically by the disguise, the affected manners, while the sameness is marked by the willingness and ability to so deceive.

Hawks himself has interpreted this united front as a joke, a "reversal" of the sexual structures of his other films' narratives:

> *Gentlemen Prefer Blondes* was only a joke. In the other films, you have two men who go out and try to find some pretty girls in order to have a good time. We thought of the opposite and took two girls who go out and find some men to have a good time: a perfectly modern story. It pleased me, it was funny. The two girls, Jane Russell and Marilyn Monroe, were so good together that each time I didn't know what scene to invent, I just had them walk back and forth and everyone adored it; they never tired of watching these two pretty girls walk. I built a staircase so that they could go up and down and as the girls were well-built . . .[2]

Somehow Hawks's words are more revealing than informative. They disclose that beneath the "joke" of depicting women in an active sexual role is their exploitation as objects being trotted back and forth, up and down the screen like ducks in a shooting gallery.

Dorothy/male object/love.

The characterization of Dorothy as connoisseur of the male body and yet fall-girl for old-fashioned romantic love blends the modern (sexual) woman with the Victorian. Her number, "Ain't There Anyone Here for Love?" has her satirizing the athletic cult as sexual sublimation while she actively displays a body in training for sexual activity. "Love" here clearly equals sex, as Dorothy flings herself at the oblivious musclemen saying, "I need a shoulder to lean on and a couple of arms to hold me," and calls out such teasers as, "Doubles, anyone?" Ideological transformation: Dorothy's "excessive" sexuality, her freely expressed lust, disappears behind "true love" for Malone. Desire is tamed before the film's end.

Lorelei/diamonds.

Lorelei's desire to marry for money, unlike Dorothy's sexual drive, undergoes no transformation. It is merely explained in practical terms as good business sense, the female parallel to any male commercial transaction. Like "Little Rock," "Diamonds" puts golddigging into a social context which makes it highly rational:

> A kiss may be grand
> But it won't pay the rental
> On your humble flat
> Or help you at the Automat.
>
> Men grow cold as girls grow old
> And we all lose our charms in the end.
> But square-cut or pear-shape
> These rocks don't lose their shape.

Over and over the lyrics say men are undependable and women have one commodity to exchange, and that for a limited time (youth). At one point Lorelei is choreographed as the center of a cluster of women, her song offered to them as advice: Get diamonds, a commodity of ever-rising exchange value; get diamonds, security. It is the clever logic of a deeply alienated woman. A dramatic lighting change punctuates the number, coming in the middle of the line, "Stiff-backed or stiff-kneed, you stand straight at Tiff'ny's." Later Lorelei explains to Gus's father, "A girl being pretty is like a man being rich. . . . If you had a daughter, you'd want her to marry a rich man." The Fifties capitalist must agree, for what is being embodied in Lorelei is the understanding of the exchange value of sex, although not uniquely, not even primarily as concerns the golddigger. Rather, Lorelei must be seen as just an exaggerated form of the role assigned all middle-class women in Fifties culture, while Dorothy complements this role by being transformed by romantic love. The amalgam of the two is the ideological prescription of the film.

In the reprise of "Little Rock" for the marriage ceremony at the film's end, the women boast, "At last we won the big crusade." About to attain the ultimate victory, marriage, the two women stand as equally successful. For love or money, with blondes or brunettes, marriage provides the closure for this film as it does for so many in which happiness/success of women is sustained as the hermeneutic question, the question which informs the narrative. Considering this closure, considering the film's function as machine to entertain through intermittent stimulation, considering the cloaking of this stimulation in a narrative framework of "good cultural object" which justifies and excuses the inclusion of the erotic, what is left to be said of the satire? Is the satire gutless, only a variant on bourgeois entertainment with no power to challenge? Is it just a frill, an embellishment, or perhaps even part of the cloaking of the exploitation? Is it not perhaps the satire which provides a pleasing and necessary ambiguity which disguises the seduction and diverts our attention from the ideological functioning of the film?

What must be remembered in arriving at the answer to these questions is the manner in which this film uses the female body. It is the hourglass figure, the lush, full body of Fifties fashion which sells the film. The female body is not only a sex object, but also an object of exchange; its value can be sold (prostitution) or it can be incorporated into another commodity which then can be sold (the film).

In the universe of consumerism, there is an object more beautiful, more precious, more striking than any other—heavier with connotations than even the automobile; it is the body. Its rediscovery after the era of puritanism under the sign of physical and sexual liberation; its omnipresence (and specifically the feminine body) in advertising, fashion, mass culture; the hygienic, dietetic, and therapeutic cults which surround it; the obsession with youth, elegance, virility/femininity, treatments, diets, and sacrificial practices attached to it; the Myth of Pleasure which envelops it—all are evidence that today the body has become a sacred object. It has literally been substituted for the soul in its moral and ideological function. . . .

The status of the body is culturally determined. In each culture the mode of organization of the relationship to the body reflects the mode of organization of the relationship to objects and the social relations. In a capitalist society the general laws of private property apply to the body, to the social practice and the mental representation of it.[3]

These comments by Baudrillard on the status of the body invite speculation on the specific treatment of the female body in *Gentlemen* in relationship to American culture of 1953. There is the same combination of gaudiness and elegance evidenced in the finned Cadillacs. There is a fullness which can be associated with fertility and prosperity. This film is the product of an age when a fortune can be made on the skillful marketing of air-brushed pin-ups, an age which no longer exists in its pure form (styles change), but which was influential in establishing the social relations and mental representations which have lingered on over more than twenty years to find a new form today.

III. THE REFERENCE AND THE
SYMBOLIC: IDEOLOGICAL FUNCTIONS

Is it by chance that "Piggy" Beekman, the object of Lorelei Lee's quest throughout the central portion of the film, is the owner of a South African diamond mine? Is it by chance that Lorelei Lee is a blonde? Is it by chance that the narrative centers on a voyage to France?

The referential code—the discrete references the text makes to social and historical phenomena—how do these references mobilize, reproduce and generate cultural mythologies, in Barthes's sense of this term? Capitalist values are at the base of *Gentlemen;* they are the assumption, the context. Racist, sexist and imperialist assumptions intriguingly surround the core depiction of consumerist values inherent in capitalism.

Piggy/South Africa/diamonds.

The text, even within its satire, treats this subject frivolously. The name "Piggy" is mildly satirical, but endearing. Piggy is ridiculous but not dangerous or evil. South Africa and diamond mines are part of a caricature, an idiosyncrasy, and are fundamentally depoliticized. When Piggy is first introduced to Lorelei, there is a shot of him, taken as her subjective vision, which has a diamond superimposed where his head should be. To Lorelei, Piggy has only one signification, wealth, which she intends to exploit, "to mine." If golddigging is justified within the film as the female form of capitalist enterprise, what underlies this "justification" is the assumption that capitalism and thus imperialism are unquestioned, natural. The satire does not touch this assumption.

Gentlemen prefer blondes.

Blondness as a criterion for sexual preference is racist. Consider a publicity still for silent screen star Colleen Moore: a photo of her in blackface, wearing an Afro wig, bore this caption—"What will I do if it's true that gentlemen prefer blondes?" Blondness is also easily appropriated for commercial reasons—consider the years of Clairol ads, followed by a more recent series lauding Hanes stockings as blonde models are placed in the fetishist glance of males with the slogan, "Gentlemen prefer Hanes." Blondness is a cultural fetish, the sexual ideal of a racist society.

France/the crossing on the Ile de France/
les chanteuses américaines.

Why does the theme of a voyage to France recur in the Fifties musicals—*An American in Paris* (1950), *April in Paris* and *On the Riviera* (1951), *The French Line* and *Gentlemen Prefer Blondes* (1953), *Silk Stockings* (1956), *Funny Face* (1957), *Gigi* (1958)? The luxury liner has its own mystique. It is a limited, intense time when anything goes, perfect for the portion of the narrative which necessitates complications, intrigues. The film can make use of this setting in innumerable imaginative ways: Lorelei surveying the passenger list or trapping herself in the porthole. France fits into the imaginary of musicals as a fantasy land of culture combined with risqué morality and sexual excitement, the blend which is the goal of the musical's structure.

Finally we come to the instance at which the reference and the symbolic become totally enmeshed. It is most helpful to this argument that Barthes, outside the context of this film, has already remarked on the relationship between women and diamonds which is so central to this film. He suggests that not only are diamonds considered a girl's best friend, but also that a girl is considered a diamond:

The classical props of the music-hall . . . Feathers, furs and gloves go on pervading the woman with their magical virtue even once removed, and give her something like the enveloping memory of a luxurious shell, for it is a self-evident law that the whole of striptease is given in the very nature of the initial garment: if the latter is improbable, as is the case with the woman in furs, the nakedness which follows remains itself unreal, smooth and enclosed like a beautiful slippery object, withdrawn by its very extravagance from human use: this is the underlying significance of the G-string covered with diamonds or sequins which is the end of the striptease. This ultimate triangle, by its pure and geometrical shape, by its hard and shiny material, bars the way to the sexual parts like a sword of purity, and definitively drives the woman back into a mineral world, the [precious] stone being here the irrefutable symbol of the absolute object, that which serves no purpose.[4]

Notes

1. Abe Laufe, *Broadway's Greatest Musicals* (New York: Funk & Wagnalls, 1969), pp. 133-34.

2. Jacques Becker, Jacques Rivette, François Truffaut, "Entretien avec Howard Hawks," *Cahiers du cinéma,* no. 56 (February 1956).

3. Jean Baudrillard, *La Société de consommation* (Paris: S.G.P.P., 1970), p. 196.

4. Roland Barthes, *Mythologies* (New York: Hill and Wang, 1972), p. 85.

Addendum

Looking back over this article, I realize I might now pose some of the questions it raises more forcefully. The question of adaptation and revision of the Loos book into a stage musical, into a film, with which the article begins could do more than raise the question of the difference in dominance between the satiric mode and the entertainment mode of celebration. It seems that these artifacts could be looked at from a perspective I have called elsewhere[1] "semiotic layering," that is, the accrual and transformations of meanings associated with an artifact as it passes through history, or as it is presented in different versions. In the case of *Gentlemen*, there is a curious shift of the Twenties heritage into the Fifties context which is then affected by our vantage point as analysts of the film in the late Seventies. The Twenties golddigger arose from the working class and the recesses of rural America alongside the other immigrant aspirants in America's rush for gold. It follows, then, that she should become a heroic figure of so many Thirties films as a reincarnation of a true-heart Susie, a working-class heroine who only *seems* to be lusting after money, but in fact seeks love, security, community, aspirations precariously mixed in the growth of sisterhood amongst the chorus, with a final marriage which appears to doom that vital, creative group activity. She is a golddigger in ironic appelation only; actually, she is the "good wife," as exemplified by Joan Blondell in *Footlight Parade* kicking her rival, the pretentious floozy, out the door. When the fifties *Gentlemen* returns to this golddigger myth, it is not just as renewal and updating into Fifties values, but it also holds on to the layers of meanings circulating in American popular culture for thirty years.

This explains the Pop Art, prefabricated texture of the Hawks film and of its "star," Marilyn Monroe (the quotations serve to remind us that she was still fighting for that status at the time of the film's production). Consider the availability of such curious manuals as the *Bonomo "Original" Hollywood "Success Course,"* published in 1945 (the quotes are in the "original" title).[2] Young Norma Jeans all over the country could study such texts, learning the correct answers to the questions proved in "Personality Tests" (pp. 81-82), such as "Do you laugh charmingly? Can you talk for half an hour without mentioning yourself? Have you looked at yourself in a triple mirror in the past two weeks?"

Obviously golddigging is to be taken very seriously in the Fifties as the entrance into the culture itself. I indicated this in the article by asserting that the amalgam of Lorelei and Dorothy was the ideological proscription of the film, telling us to temper an acceptance of the female position with both an understanding of the exchange value of sex and the channelling of the power of that sexuality into a romantic love; thus we again see the culture reifying contradictory values, that signal for the participants' suicidal deaths and bra advertisements.

It is interesting that, in the three years since the article first appeared, American culture has danced its way back to the high-heeled steps of the Fifties in which bustiers, cinched waists and tight skirts splash feminine charms in the face of the movement for feminist consciousness. Danskin brought out a leotard this year which resembles the "Playboy bunny" costumes used in the "Little Rock" opening number. Here we come to an analysis that overlaps with a topic which I am currently working on with Fina Bathrick, the role definition of fashion as transmitted through Hollywood films. These images have literally designed our lives for us, as we look in three-way mirrors before buying.

Another point that I find deserves some amplification is the analysis in the article of the psychoanalytic operation of the film as it manipulates the spectator through a network characterized by the body as source of spectacle by using such devices as doubling, repetition, alternation of denial and access, and the focusing on fragments as symbolic replacement which typifies fetishism. I want to make it clear that, in evoking these basic operations of fascination and pleasure, it is the specific ideological functions of their inscription in the film which is to be examined critically. The point is not to negatively critique all spectacle, as some film theorists have tended to do recently, but rather to show how the cultural references and ideological determinants of the commercial spectacle have in fact created a very restricted access to pleasure, to eroticism, to the viewing experience. This is what I tried to do in this article and continue to do elsewhere.[3]

To add, then, one point on this topic that is specific to *Gentlemen* which is not brought out in the article is the appeal of the two women performing movements in rhythmic coordination. How do we understand the fascination of what I called the "perfectly matched and coordinated assault" of this dancing team? Here I think we need to blend some very abstract psycho-perceptual concepts about the appeal of symmetry, rhyming and patterning within a visual field with an historical analysis of how lesbianism has served in male-oriented pornography to increase visual stimulation and to ultimately give twice as much power to the eye, which can penetrate even the liaisons which would appear to deny male entry.[4] Lesbians exist in pornography and advertising as a trope; they are not really women given to each other erotically rather than to men, but pseudo-lesbians given over to the gaze which truly possesses them. In *Gentlemen* the narrative assures us that, despite the bonds between Dorothy and Lorelei, their relationship is not self-sufficient; it seeks males for completion, so that when (heterosexual) love goes wrong, nothing goes right.

Notes

1. This was developed in a paper given at the Purdue Film Conference, 1979, called "Layers of Meaning: Enoch Arden and an Historically Wrought Semiotics."

2. Joe Bonomo, *Bonomo "Original" Hollywood "Success Course,"* (New York: Bonomo Culture Institute, 1945).

3. Here I refer to a paper I gave at the International Film Conference V: "Cinema and Language," Milwaukee, 1979, entitled, "Lifting the Veil: Women, Image and Desire."

4. *Ibid.*

THE PLACE OF WOMAN IN THE CINEMA OF RAOUL WALSH

PAM COOK AND
CLAIRE JOHNSTON

*This discussion of the image of women in the films of Raoul Walsh, and of Jane
Russell in particular, first appeared in 1974. It calls for a challenge to the
"delineation to the ideology of patriarchy—by which we mean the Law of the
Father—within the text of the film," a challenge that Laura Mulvey also makes.
Cook and Johnston's analysis is localized in the film itself; it does not extend to
the place of the viewer, but it draws on the same set of psychoanalytic semiotic
assumptions that Laura Mulvey does. Here, these assumptions are used to lay a
Lacanian conception of human communication over the narrative treatment of a
female heroine in order to resolve the apparent contradiction between the "strong
and independent" women in Walsh's films and the dominance of a patriarchal
capitalist order. Like Turim, these authors find the resolution of this contradiction
in the means by which a woman asserts her strength, namely "through the
exploitation of a fetishized image of woman to be exchanged within the circulation
of money." They trace the implications of this process of exploitation in
considerable detail, which, after an introduction to difficult Lacanian terminology,
becomes an exceptionally clear example of textual analysis. Referring to the
Cahiers du Cinéma editorial that identifies a group of Hollywood films riven by an
"internal criticism" (see "Cinema/Ideology/Criticism" in the first volume of
Movies and Methods), they place Walsh's films within this category of films that
cannot fully contain their own contradictions. Such films serve as reminders of
the radical disjunction between the discovery of internal but unacknowledged
criticism and the development of a feminist counter cinema. (The issues of
authorship, ideology, and feminism raised here are further explored in a review by
Colin MacCabe of the Edinburgh Film Festival book in which Cook and
Johnston's article first appeared and in a reply by Elizabeth Cowie in* Screen 16,
no. 1 [Spring 1975]: 128–34 and 134–39.)

•

PRESENTATION

The following analysis of the place of women in some of Raoul Walsh's
films relies on concepts borrowed from the psychoanalyst Jacques Lacan, whose
work constitutes a radical re-reading of Freud. The basis of that reading is the
insight that Freud thought his theory of the unconscious in terms of a conceptual
apparatus which he forged in the face of pre-Saussurian linguistics, anticipating
the discoveries of modern linguistics. Lacan therefore proceeds to a re-reading of

Freud's theory in the light of concepts produced by and for structural linguistics. This obviously involves the rejection of the vast bulk of post-Freudian psychoanalysis. Now that it has become clear that Freud conceived the unconscious as being structured like a language, any decipherment of the discourse of the unconscious must abandon all the unfortunately widespread misconceptions regarding the reading—i.e., selection—of "symptoms" and of the kind of sexual "symbolism" propagated by Jung.

J. Lacan distinguishes the *Symbolic* from the *Imaginary* and the *Real*. The Imaginary relationship with the other occurs in a dual situation which is primarily narcissistic. Aggressiveness and identification with the image of the other predominate at this stage. The *Symbolic* element is one that intervenes to break up an Imaginary relationship from which there is no way out. The child meets the "third element" upon birth; he enters a world ordered by a culture, law, and language, and is enveloped in that Symbolic order. Finally, Lacan distinguishes the *Other,* the locus from which the code emanates, from the Imaginary *other.* (M. Mannoni, *The Child, his 'Illness' and the Others,* London, 1970, p. 23n.)

The Other, as the locus of the Law (e.g., the law of the prohibition of incest), as the Word (i.e., the signifier as unit of the code) is the "Name-of-the-Father" around which the Symbolic order is constructed. The child, or indeed, any human being, as a subject of desire is constituted from the place of the Other: his "I" is a signifier in someone else's discourse and he has to find out how and where "I" fits into the social universe he discovers.

It has often been argued that there are a number of films directed by Raoul Walsh which appear to present women as strong and independent characters. The authors of the following essay take issue with this type of reading and attempt to demonstrate that women (e.g., Mamie Stover) in fact function as a signifier in a circuit of exchange where the values exchanged have been fixed by/in a patriarchal culture. Although Lévi-Strauss pointed out that real women, as producers of signs, could never be reduced to the status of mere tokens of exchange, i.e., to mere signs, the authors argue that, in films, the use of images of women and the way their "I" is constituted in Walshian texts play a subtle game of duplicity: in the tradition of classic cinema and 19th-century realism, the characters are presented as "autonomous individuals"; but the construction of the discourse contradicts this convention by reducing these "real" women to images and tokens functioning in a circuit of signs the values of which have been determined by and for men. In this way, the authors are attempting to help lay the foundations of a feminist film criticism as well as producing an analysis of a number of films directed by Walsh.

Between 1956 and 1957 Raoul Walsh made three films which centre around the social, cultural and sexual definition of women. At first sight, the role of woman within these films appears a "positive" one; they display a great independence of spirit, and contrast sharply with the apparent "weakness" of the male protagonists. The first film in this cycle depicts a woman occupying the central function in the narrative; the Jane Russell vehicle, *The Revolt of Mamie Stover,* tells the story of a bar-room hostess's attempts to buck the system and acquire wealth and social status within patriarchy. *The King and Four Queens,* made the same year, depicts five women who hide out in a burnt-out ghost town to guard hidden gold. *Band of Angels,* made the following year, tells the story of a Southern heiress who suddenly finds herself sold into slavery at the time of the American Civil War. Walsh prefigured the problematic of the independent woman before this period, most notably in a series of films he made in the 1940's, some of which starred the actress Ida Lupino, who later became one of the few women film-makers to work in Hollywood: *They Drive by Night, High Sierra* and *The Man I Love.* However, undoubtedly the most useful films for providing a reference point for this cycle are *Manpower* (1941) and *The Bowery* (1933); in these films, Walsh celebrates the ethic of the all-male group, and outlines the role which women are designated to play within it. Walsh depicts the male hero as being trapped and pinned down by some hidden event in his past. In order to become the Subject of Desire he must test the Law through transgression. To gain self-knowledge and to give meaning to memories of the past, he is impelled towards the primal scene and to the acceptance of a symbolic castration. For the male hero the female protagonist becomes an agent within the text of the film whereby his hidden secret can be brought to light, for it is in woman that his "lack" is located. She represents at one and the same time the distant memory of maternal plenitude and the fetishized object of his phantasy of castration — a phallic replacement and thus a threat. In *Manpower* Walsh depicts an all-male universe verging on infantilism—the camaraderie of the fire-fighters from the "Ministry of Power and Light". Sexual relationships and female sexuality are repressed within the film, and Marlene Dietrich is depicted as only having an existence within the discourse of men: she is "spoken", she does not speak. As an object of exchange between men, a sign oscillating between the images of prostitute and mother-figure, she represents the means by which men express their relationships with each other, the means through which they come to understand themselves and each other. *The Bowery* presents a similar all-male society, this time based totally on internal all-male rivalry; within this highly ritualised system the women ("the skirts") assume the function of symbols of this rivalry. Whatever the "positive" attributes assigned to them through characterization, woman as sign remains a function, a token of exchange in this patriarchal order. Paul Willemen in his article on *Pursued* describes the role of the female protagonist Theresa Wright/Thorley as the "specular image" of the male protagonist Robert Mitchum/Jeb: she is the place where he deposits his words in a desire to "know" himself through her.

In her book *Psychoanalysis and Feminism* Juliet Mitchell, citing Lévi-Strauss, characterises a system where women are objects for exchange as essentially a communications system.

The act of exchange holds a society together: the rules of kinship (like those of language to which they are near-allied) are the society. Whatever the nature of the society—patriarchal, matrilineal, patrilineal, etc.—it is always men who exchange women. Women thus become the equivalent of a sign which is being communicated.

In Walsh's oeuvre, woman is not only a sign in a system of exchange, but an empty sign. (The major exception in this respect is Mamie Stover, who seeks to transform her status as object for exchange precisely by compounding a highly articulated, fetishized image for herself.) The male protagonist's castration fears, his search for self-knowledge all converge on woman: it is in her that he is finally faced with the recognition of "lack". Woman is therefore the locus of emptiness: she is a sign which is defined negatively: something that is missing which must be located so that the narcissistic aim of the male protagonist can be achieved. The narrative structure of *Band of Angels* is particularly interesting in the light of this model. The first half of the story is concerned with events in Manty/Yvonne de Carlo's life which reduce her from the position of a lady to that of a slave to be auctioned in the slave market. Almost exactly half way through the story—at the "centre" of the film—Clark Gable appears and takes possession of her: from that moment the unfolding of his "dark secret" takes precedence. It becomes clear that Manty/Yvonne de Carlo's story was merely a device to bring into play the background (the slave trade, crumbling Southern capitalism) against which the "real" drama is to take place. Manty/Yvonne de Carlo is created in Clark Gable's image: half black and half white, she signifies the lost secret which must be found in order to resolve the relationship between Clark Gable and Sidney Poitier—the "naturalisation" of the slave trade.

One of the most interesting aspects of this *mise-en-scène* of exchange in which woman as sign is located is the way Walsh relates it directly and explicitly to the circulation of money within the text of the film. Marx states that under capitalism the exchange value of commodities is their inherent monetary property and that in turn money achieves a social existence quite apart from all commodities and their natural mode of existence. The circulation of money and its abstraction as a sign in a system of exchange serves as a mirror image for woman as sign in a system of exchange. However, in Walsh's universe, women do not have access to the circulation of money: Mamie Stover's attempt to gain access to it takes place at a time of national emergency, the bombing of Pearl Harbor, when all the men are away fighting—it is described as "theft". As a system, the circulation of money embodies phallic power and the right of possession; it is a system by which women are controlled. In *Band of Angels* Manty/Yvonne de Carlo is reduced to a chattel and exchanged for money on the slave market; she is exchanged for money because of her father's "dark secret" and because of his debt. In *The King and Four Queens* the women guard the gold but they cannot gain access to it directly. Its phallic power lies hidden in the grave of a dead husband, surrounded by sterility and devastation. Clark Gable gains access to it by asserting his right of possession by means of tossing a gold coin in the air and shooting a bullet through the middle of it, a trick which the absent males of the family all knew: the mark of the right of possession. The ticket system in *The Revolt of Mamie Stover* takes the analogy between money and women one stage further: men buy tickets at "The Bungalow" and at the same time they buy an image of woman. It is the symbolic expression of the right men have to control women within their imaginary system. This link between money and phallic power assumes its most striking image in Walsh's oeuvre when Jane Russell/Mamie, having accumulated considerable savings as a bar hostess in Pearl Harbor, declares her love for Richard Egan/Jimmy by asking him if she can place these savings in his safety deposit box at the bank: "there's nothing closer between friends than money". Recognising the significance of such a proposition, he refuses.

The Revolt of Mamie Stover is the only one of these films in which the female protagonist represents the central organising principle of the text. As the adventuress *par excellence* she is impelled to test and transgress the Law in the same way that all Walsh's heroes do: she would seem to function at first sight in a similar way to her male counterpart, the adventurer, within the narrative structure. But as the film reveals, her relationship to the Law is radically different. Her drive is not to test and transgress the Law as a means towards understanding a hidden secret within her past, but to transgress the forms of representation governing the classic cinema itself, which imprison her forever within an image. As the credits of the film appear on the screen, Jane Russell looks into the camera with defiance, before turning her back on America and walking off to a new life in Pearl Harbor. This look, itself a transgression of one of the classic rules of cinematography (i.e., "don't look into the camera") serves as a reference point for what is to follow. Asserting herself as the subject rather than the object of desire, this look into the camera represents a reaching out beyond the diegetic space of the film and the myths of representation which entrap her. The central contradiction of her situation is that she can only attempt to assert herself as subject through the exploitation of a fetishized image of woman to be exchanged within the circulation of money; her independence and her desire for social and economic status all hinge on this objectification. The forms of representation generated by the classic cinema—the myths of woman as pin-up, vamp, "Mississippi Cinderella"—are the only means by which she can achieve the objective of becoming the subject rather than the object of desire. The futility of this enterprise is highlighted at the end of the film when she returns once more to America in a similar sequence of shots; this time she no longer looks towards the camera, but remains trapped within the diegetic space which the film has allotted to her.

The film opens with a long-shot of a neon-lit city at night. Red letters appear on the screen telling us the time and place: SAN FRANCISCO 1941. *The Revolt of Mamie Stover* was made in 1956—the story is therefore set within the living memory/history of the spectator. This title is the first indication that the film will reactivate the memory of an anxiogenic situation: the traumatic moment of the attack on Pearl Harbor and the entry of the United States into the Second World War. Simultaneously, on the sound band, sleazy night-club music swells up (clipjoints, predatory prostitution, female sexuality exchanged for money at a time when the country, its male population and its financial resources are about to be put at risk). A police car (one of the many representations of the Law in the film) its siren wailing insistently over the music (a further indication of imminent danger) drives fast onto a dock-side where a ship is waiting. As it draws up alongside the ship, a female figure carrying a coat and a small suitcase gets out of the car and appears to turn back to look at the city from which she has obviously been expelled in a hurry. Jane Russell then looks straight into the camera (see above).

Up to this point the text has been multiply coded to signify danger/threat. The threat is closely associated with sexuality—besides the music, the red letters on the screen indicate red for danger and red for sex. Paul Willemen has pointed out that the "look" in *Pursued* is a threatening object: the *Cahiers du Cinéma* analysis of *Young Mr. Lincoln* also delineates Henry Fonda/Lincoln's "castrating stare" as having the same threatening significance. Besides this threatening "look," Jane Russell has other dangerous connotations: qualities of aggression, of preying on the male to attain her own ends. Her "look"—repeated many times during the film, directed towards men, and explicitly described at one point as "come hither"—doubly marks her as signifier of threat. In the absence of the male, the female might "take his place": at the moment of Jane Russell's "look" at the camera, the spectator is directly confronted with the image of that threat. The fact that this image has been expelled from a previous situation is also important: Jane Russell actually represents the repudiated idea: she *is* that idea. Thus the threat is simultaneously recognised and recuperated: the female cannot "take the place" of the male; she can only be "in his place"—his mirror image—the "you" which is the "I" in another place.

This moment of dual fascination between the spectator and Jane Russell is broken by the intervention of a third organising principle representing the narrative, as the titles in red letters "Jane Russell Richard Egan" appear over the female figure. The title has the effect of immediately distancing the spectator: it reminds him of the symbolic role of the narrative by locating Jane Russell as an imaginary figure. In psychoanalytic terms the concept "imaginary" is more complex than the word would immediately seem to imply. It is a concept central to the Lacanian formulation of the "mirror stage" in which the "other" is apprehended as the "other which is me", i.e., my mirror image. In the imaginary relationship the other is seen in terms of resemblance to oneself. As an imaginary figure in the text of the film Jane Russell's "masculine" attributes are emphasised: square jaw, broad shoulders, narrow hips, swinging, almost swashbuckling walk—"phallic" attributes which are echoed and re-echoed in the text; for example, in her aggressive language—she tells a wolf-whistling soldier to "go mend your rifle, soldier"; when Richard Egan/Jimmy fights Michael Pate/Atkins at the Country Club she shouts "give him one for me, Jimmy". The girls at "The Bungalow" hail her as "Abe Lincoln Stover". Jane Russell/Mamie is the imaginary *counterpart* of the absent spectator and the absent subject of the text: the mirror image they have mutually constructed and in whom both images converge and overlap.

Again, borrowing from Lacan, the function of the "Symbolic" is to intervene in the imaginary situation and to integrate the subject into the Symbolic Order (which is ultimately the Law, the Name of the Father). The narrative of *The Revolt of Mamie Stover,* in that it presents a particular model of the world historically, culturally and ideologically overdetermined, could be said to perform a symbolic function for the absent spectator. The anxiety-generating displacement Jane Russell/Mamie appears to threaten the narrative at certain points. For example, after having promised to marry Richard Egan/Jimmy, give up her job at "The Bungalow" and become "exclusively his", and having taken his ring in a symbolic exchange which is "almost like the real thing" and "makes it legal", Jane Russell/

Mamie leaves her man at the army camp and returns to "The Bungalow" to resign. However, she is persuaded by Agnes Moorhead/Bertha Parchman to continue working there, now that Michael Pate/Atkins has gone (been expelled), for a bigger share of the profits and more power. Richard Egan/Jimmy is absent, so he won't know. His absence is important: it recalls another sequence earlier in the narrative which shows in a quick succession of shots Richard Egan/Jimmy and the army away at war while Jane Russell/Mamie is at the same moment buying up all the available property on the island, becoming "Sto-Mame Company Incorporated" with Uncle Sam as her biggest tenant. Jane Russell/Mamie makes her biggest strides in the absence of men: she threatens to take over the power of exchange. By promising to marry and give it all up, she is reintegrated into an order where she no longer represents that threat. Richard Egan/Jimmy can be seen as the representative of the absent spectator and absent subject of the discourse in this structure: they are mutual constructors of the text—he is a writer who is constantly trying to write Jane Russell/Mamie's story for her. When Jane Russell/Mamie goes back to work at "The Bungalow" she in effect negates his image of her in favour of an image which suggests destruction and purging—"Flaming Mamie"—and becomes again a threatening displacement, reproduced and enlarged 7 foot high. When Richard Egan/Jimmy is confronted with this threatening image at the army camp, when a soldier shows him a photograph of her, a bomb drops and he is wounded. In the face of this renewed threat he returns to "The Bungalow" and in his final speech to Jane Russell/Mamie repudiates her as his imaginary counterpart; the narcissistic fascination with her is ended; he realises he can no longer control her image.

The symbolic level of the narrative in maintaining its order in the face of a threat is reasserted in the final sequence where the policeman at the dockside re-echoes Richard Egan/Jimmy's words of rejection: "Nothing's changed, Mamie. You aren't welcome here". Jane Russell/Mamie replies that she is going home to Leesburg, Mississippi (this is what Richard Egan/Jimmy was always telling her she must do). When the policeman remarks that she does not seem to have done too well, she replies: "If I told you I had made a fortune and given it all away, would you believe me?" When he says "No", she replies "I thought so". This exchange contains a final assertion that the protagonist cannot write her own story: she is a signifier, an object of exchange in a play of desire between the absent subject and object of the discourse. She remains "spoken": she does not speak. The final rhetorical question seals her defeat.

On the plane of the image, the symbolic order is maintained by an incessant production, within the text, of images for and of Jane Russell/Mamie from which she is unable to escape, and with which she complies through a *mise-en-scène* of exchange. In order to become the subject of desire, she is compelled to be the object of desire, and the images she "chooses" remain locked within the myths of representation governed by patriarchy. This *mise-en-scène* of exchange is initiated by her expulsion by the police at the dockside—the image of predatory whore is established. This image is elaborated during the next scene when the ship's steward tells Richard Egan/Jimmy about her reputation as sexual predator ("she ain't no lady"). Mamie interrupts the conversation, and realising that Richard Egan/Jimmy as a scriptwriter in Hollywood is interested in her, she suggests he should write and buy her story—the hard-luck story of a "Mississippi Cinderella". Growing emotional involvement with him leads her to reject the idea of being "written" in favour of "writing" her own story, and to seek out an image more consistent with the wealthy "hilltop" milieu of which Richard Egan/Jimmy is part, epitomised by Jimmy's girlfriend ("Miss Hilltop"). Jane Russell/Mamie asks Richard Egan/Jimmy to "dress her up and teach her how to behave"; he refuses. Their relationship from then on is characterised as one of transgression: they "dance without tickets" at the country club, away from the "four don'ts" of "The Bungalow". For her image as a performer and hostess at "The Bungalow" Jane Russell/Mamie has dyed her hair red and has assumed the name of "Flaming Mamie" ("Mamie's not beer or whisky, she's champagne only"). The image of "Flaming Mamie" is at one and the same time an assertion and a negation of female sexuality; sexually arousing ("Fellas who try to resist should hire a psychiatrist" intones the song) but at the same time the locus of sexual taboo ("Keep the eyes on the hands" she says in another number—they tell the story). It is at "The Bungalow" that the ticket system formalises this *mise-en-scène* of exchange; men literally buy an image for a predetermined period of time. (It is this concept of exchange of images which Jane Russell/Mamie finally discards when she throws the ticket away as she leaves the boat at the end of the film.) Reduced once again to the image of common prostitute when they go dancing at the country club and having decided to stay at "The Bungalow" in spite of Richard Egan/Jimmy, she finally assumes the iconography of the pin-up, with the "come hither" look; an image emptied of all personality or individuality; an image based on the effects of pure gesture. This image was prefigured in an extraordinary sequence at the beach when Jane Russell/Mamie jumps up from the sand where she has been sitting with Richard Egan/Jimmy in order to take a swim. As she does so, she turns back to look at him and her image becomes frozen into the vacant grin of a bathing suit advertisement. Talking about money, Jane Russell/Mamie describes herself at one point as a "have not"; this recurrent imbrication of images, the telling of story within a story which the film generates through a *mise-en-scène* of exchange, serves to repress the idea of female sexuality and to encase Jane Russell/Mamie within the symbolic order, the Law of the Father.

Walsh criticism to date has been dominated by the notion of "personality"; like the American adventurer *par excellence* he so often depicts, Walsh, as one of the oldest pioneers, has come to be regarded as of the essence of what is called "classic" Hollywood cinema—a cinema characterised traditionally by its linearity, its transparency: in short, the effect of "non-writing". Andrew Sarris has even gone so far as to say of him: "only the most virile director can effectively project a feminine vulnerability in his characters". This notion of authorship has been criticised by Stephen Heath in the following terms: "the function of the author (the effect of the idea of authorship) is a function of unity; the use of the notion of the author involves the organisation of the film . . . and in so doing, it avoids—this is indeed its function—the thinking of the articulation of the film text in relation to ideology". A view of Walsh as the originating consciousness of the Walsh oeuvre is, therefore, an ideological concept. To attribute such qualities as "virility" to Walsh is to foreclose the recognition of Walsh as subject within ideology. This feminist reading of the Walsh oeuvre rejects any approach which would attempt to delineate the role of women in terms of the influence of ideology or sociology, as such an approach is merely a strategy to supplement auteur analysis. We have attempted to provide a reading of the Walsh oeuvre which takes as its starting point Walsh as a subject within ideology and, ultimately, the laws of the human order. What concerns us specifically is the delineation of the ideology of patriarchy—by which we mean the Law of the Father—within the text of the film. As Lévi-Strauss has indicated: "The emergence of symbolic thought must have required that women, like works, should be things that were exchanged". The tasks for feminist criticism must therefore consist of a process of de-naturalisation: a questioning of the unity of the text; of seeing it as a contradictory interplay of different codes; of tracing its "structuring absences" and its relationship to the universal problem of symbolic castration. It is in this sense that a feminist strategy for the cinema must be understood. Only when such work has been done can a foundation for a feminist counter-cinema be established. Woman as signifier of woman under patriarchy is totally absent in most image-producing systems, but particularly in Hollywood where image-making and the fetishistic position of the spectator are highly developed. This is indeed why a study of "woman" within the Hollywood system is of great interest. A study of woman within Walsh's oeuvre, in particular, reveals "woman" as the locus of a dilemma for the patriarchal human order, as a locus of contradictions. *Cahiers du cinéma* in an editorial described such texts in the following terms: "an internal criticism is taking place which cracks the film apart at the seams. If one reads the film obliquely, looking for symptoms, if one looks beyond its apparent coherence one can see that it is riddled with cracks; it is splitting under an internal tension which is simply not there in an ideologically innocuous film. The ideology thus becomes subordinate to the text. It no longer has an independent existence; it is presented by the film". The function of "woman" in Walsh as the locus of "lack", as an empty sign to be filled, the absent centre of a phallocentric universe marks the first step towards the de-naturalisation of woman in the Hollywood cinema. In a frenzied imbrication of images (*The Revolt of Mamie Stover*) the Phallus is restored; but in this distanciation the first notes of the "swan-song of the immortal nature of patriarchal culture" (*cf.* Juliet Mitchell) can be heard.

Part 4
Structuralist Semiotics

SIGNIFICATION IN THE CINEMA

PAUL SANDRO

Paul Sandro's careful, detailed review of Christian Metz's first three volumes presents us with an extremely valuable introduction to the basic concerns of early film semiotics. Debts to phenomenology and linguistics are plain to see. Psychoanalysis, Marxism, or feminist criticism are well below the horizon. The principal tasks are taxonomic and descriptive. Metz's thorough efforts provide us with a useful set of critical categories, even if some basic classifications, such as the grand syntagmatique, *remain subject to debate. Many of the terms introduced and explained here have found their way into the everyday vocabulary of contemporary film theory. But, to some degree, this taxonomic effort has proved a cul-de-sac. Facts, terms, descriptive categories —these building blocks arise in connection with specific theories, not prior to them, and the theory of film as language or languagelike has had little explanatory power when it comes to questions of industry, ideology, aesthetics, history, or audience.*

Most contemporary theory, including Metz's more recent work, has taken a more purposeful, if not a political, direction. Classification has become subordinate to interrogation. An examination of the properties of the text as a thing apart, woven from more or less specific codes into a distinctive system, has yielded to an examination of the text as a production of meanings and positions for viewers, as many of the articles in Part 3 attest. Nonetheless, the strong association between linguistics and psychoanalysis continues, largely through the intermediary figure of Jacques Lacan, and, although priorities and principles may shift, many terms and assumptions persist. For these reasons, this highly compact introduction to Metz's early work makes an excellent starting point for our consideration of structuralist semiotic criticism.

•

Christian Metz. *Langage et cinéma*. Paris: Larousse, 1971. (*Language and Cinema*. Trans. Donna Jean Umiker-Sebeok. The Hague: Mouton, 1974.)

Essais sur la signification au cinéma. Vol. I. Paris: Klincksieck, 1968. (*Film Language: A Semiotics of the Cinema*. Trans. Michael Taylor. New York: Oxford University Press, 1974.) *Essais*. Vol. II. Paris: Klincksieck, 1972.

In his first and perhaps best-known article on signification in the cinema, Christian Metz described cinema as a means of expression without a code, a discourse which lacks the coherent body of governing constraints and clear articulations of *langue* but which signifies nevertheless as if by having already mobilized features of the more general category of *langage* (*Communications*, no. 4, 1964). As Metz indicates, the extrapolation of these Saussurian concepts from linguistics to the study of cinema is problematic. Even the notion of cinema as a kind of "*langage* without a code" is at best a loose image for what resists explanation in systematic terms, and the absence of a code raises a difficult theoretical question. If at its core cinema does not have a grammatical system comparable to *langue,* what organizes it as a *langage* whose process generates meaning?

While much of this article is directed against the excesses of those montage theorists who compared the splicing of shots to the creative manipulation of words and against the guidebook grammarians of "cinematic language," this negative gesture clears the way for some tentative affirmations about cinema as a signifying process. The assertion that even a close-up shot of a single object such as a revolver would more likely correspond to the speech utterance "Here is a revolver" than to the single word "revolver" affirms the presence of a visual discourse already at work in the shot (a continuous strip of film from one "take" which Metz calls the minimal unit of montage). As a minimal discursive unit, the shot is an *actualized* unit of signification, more like the speech utterance than the linguistic seme; it is one of an infinite number of constructions that may be generated. But unlike the speech utterance, its semes are not articulated by anything comparable to the discrete units of phonemic articulation. This actualized visual discourse, the "discours imagé," thus becomes the tentative basis for a permanent project, a semiology of the cinema, aimed at discovering *how* cinema signifies and attempting to be descriptive rather than normative. In the absence of a clearly defined "grammar" which could be seen to govern the logical relations among constitutive units, Metz initially seeks the principle of intelligibility for this cursive visual expression in larger rhetorical patterns (*Essais,* I, p. 119).

Metz's first volume of essays, published four years later and now translated as *Film Language,* includes the *Communications* article, essays on the impression of reality, on the phenomenology of the narrative in cinema, and on theoretical problems in modern cinema. But of crucial importance is one essay (*FL,* pp. 108–46) which ascribes a partial code to the temporal dimension of what Metz had previously described as a "*langage* without a code." It applies specifically to the "bande-images" (image-track), the succession of images which, together with the "bande sonore" (sound track), comprises the syntagmatic axis of filmic expression. The analytical model proposed in this key essay defines the categories of spatio-temporal logic linked to various kinds of sequential patterns that function as autonomous story segments in the image-track of the classical narrative film (roughly from the early thirties to 1955, with reservations as noted in *Essais,* II, pp. 202 and 204). The "large-scale syntagmatics of the image-track" is a paradigm of these sequential types (syntagmata), a code which defines the meaning of one syntagma in relation (or by opposition) to the others. For Metz, the foundation of such a code lies in the functional history of forms, the way a cultural logic attaches itself to a material, rather than in a pre-determined ontology: ever since its invention, cinema has been used to tell stories, to express spatio-temporal relationships; hence a code of syntagmatic devices which responds to this narrative function. The repeated intercutting of two series of filmed events, for example, may be considered as an article of code (the *alternating syntagma*) only because it has come to fill the need to show simultaneity between the events, as in the simplest chase scene or in scenes which depict enemy camps preparing for battle. Some of the syntagmata are not chronological (the *parallel syntagma* and *bracketed syntagma*), performing purely associative functions; one syntagma is chronological but not truly narrative (the *descriptive syntagma:* successive views of different elements in the setting to evoke a spatial state of being without directly advancing the story); others (the *scene,* the *episodic sequence,* and the *ordinary sequence*) are narrative and linear with varying degrees of continuity.

Yet as the only model of codification elaborated, the large-scale syntagmatics raised several important questions from the outset. Was this to be *the* code of cinematic language? If so, what would account for the meaning produced by other aspects of cinema not included in this schema, such as camera movements, optical effects, cutting rhythm, variations in lighting and color? And what about cinema's claim to the representation of reality? What system informs the animated icon which seems "always already" to signify by its "likeness" to "real" objects before they are filmed? Finally, how are the other expressive "materials" of cinema—words, music, sound effects—organized in relation to the "visual discourse"? Metz himself acknowledges these problems in his essays and in the accompanying notes—many of which were written several years after an essay was originally published in article form and thus mark an evolution in his thinking. But not until *Langage et cinéma* does he situate the large-scale syntagmatics in an extensive approach to the semiology of cinema. This approach departs significantly from the initial notion of cinema as a "*langage* without a code," describing the film as a discursive object informed by *many* codes, some—like the large-scale syntagmatics—being more or less specific to cinema as a signifying process, and others—such as "iconic codes of analogy"—being to a great degree "borrowed" from extra-cinematic resources. Moreover, this approach entails a complete re-evaluation of notions which underlie the idea of cinema as a "*langage* without a code," such as the relationship of a code to a given means of expression, the notion of specificity, and the notion of minimal units in a system of signification.

In *Language and Cinema* Metz does not assume the coherence of a body of codes which would constitute "cinematic language." He holds that term in abeyance for at least two reasons: first, the notion of *cinematic* language calls for a means to isolate what is specifically cinematic; second, any reference to language evokes a series of terminological distinctions which result from methodology appropriate for the analysis of strictly verbal expression and might prejudice one's approach to cinema, a means of expression with several semiotic dimensions.

MATERIAL OF EXPRESSION, CODE

Metz treats the question of specificity at several stages in his development, each time adding criteria which increase the difficulty of defining what "belongs" to cinema as a signifying process and what does not. Initially, he characterizes cinema as a composite of different kinds of expression "which may be distinguished from one another by their physical nature alone": cinema's "continuous moving photographs, its speech, its music, its sound effects."[1] In this respect, cinema differs from other means of expression which are not physical composites, such as classical music, where the "material" (*matière*) of the signifier "consists uniformly of 'musical sound,' the spoken language where it is limited to phonetic sound, writing where it is restricted to graphic lines, etc." (*LC,* p. 36). For this reason, even an initial definition of cinema in "technico-sensory terms" should focus on "a specific combination of several materials of expression" and not a single privileged material of expression (*LC,* p. 36). Metz uses Louis Hjelmslev's "*matière de l'expression*" throughout his study to designate what might be called the *raw* material of expression, "the (physical, sensorial) material nature of the signifier, or more exactly of the 'fabric' into which the signifiers are woven (for one reserves the term 'signifier' for the signifying form)" (*LC,* p. 208). Defining cinema's specificity in technico-sensory terms amounts to analyzing the combination of phenomenal traits common to all films; cinema would equal "the film" as a perceptual object. But the semiology of cinema is intent upon discovering *how* films signify, just as linguistics seeks to discover how verbal expression signifies. Approached in this way, cinema no longer designates the perceptual *object* film, but the body of relational systems which informs it. Cinema in this sense is an abstract, purely ideal whole formed by analysis which anticipates "a certain unity, which has yet to be determined. The film is an object in the real world, cinema is not" (*LC,* p. 24).

This definition of cinema complicates the question of specificity, for the diverse codes which inform various means of expression do not fall into place neatly, each one relating to only one kind of expression as defined by its "material." In fact, there is much overlapping, because the homogeneity of codes

is not a sensory one, but rather one of the order of logical coherence, of explanatory power, of classification, of generative capacity. If a code is a code it is because it provides a unified field of commutation, i.e., a (reconstructed) "domain" within which the transformations of the signifier correspond to variations of the signified, and within which a certain number of elements have meaning only in relation to each other. (*LC,* pp. 28–29)

Metz gives examples of some codes ("sémies hétérogènes") which call upon different materials of expression within a single field of commutation, and other codes in which the system of signifying oppositions may be "transposed in its entirety from one modality [material of expression] to another while its internal relational structure (*form* according to Hjelmslev) remains to a greater or lesser extent unchanged" (*LC,* p. 29). Yet at the same time, Metz cannot deny a certain correlation between material of expression and relational systems in some instances: "any rhythmic code—disregarding the figurative senses of the word 'rhythm'—requires in order to be manifested a material which presents the physical characteristic of temporality, and this is why rhythmic codes are only specific to *langages* [means of expression] whose material of expression satisfies this requirement."[2] Here it is crucial to note the difference "between a specificity defined *directly* according to material criteria and one that is defined in terms of codes, even if the specification of codes cannot be accomplished without a consideration of *certain traits* of the material of the signifier (and not of this material itself, taken as a whole and without analysis)" (*LC,* p. 43).

One example serves to clarify this distinction. The overall field of semiotic oppositions which characterizes the system of light and shade known as chiaroscuro passes essentially intact from painting to color photography. The "migration of the entire system" from painting to photography is possible because both means of expression share material characteristics that are pertinent to the manifestation of this system: both offer fixed, colored, visual images to the viewer. But what if "the same symbolism of chiaroscuro were adopted in a literary description and expressed with words? The vehicle, henceforth verbal, would have changed profoundly, but the internal ordering of signifying oppositions could, in the extreme, remain the same, or at least largely isomorphic, throughout this new migration" (*LC* Larousse, p. 162). At this point Metz distinguishes between two kinds of codical transposition, one in which the change from one means of expression to another does not involve the technico-sensory characteristics which are pertinent to the code in question and one in which it does:

Among the conditions necessary in order that a system of chiaroscuro exist and remain authentically such, there is none which specifies that it should be painted by hand or photographed; on the other hand, a chiaroscuro which would no longer be visual but expressed with the help of words would, strictly speaking, no longer be a chiaroscuro, but a description of chiaroscuro (the material transposition, this time, would have involved characteristics that are pertinent for any system of chiaroscuro). (*LC* Larousse, p. 163)

Only in the second case does Metz speak of true codical transposition; in the first, the code remains unchanged because the pertinent characteristics of the material of expression that it informs remain unchanged.

DEGREES AND MODES OF SPECIFICITY

If the specificity of cinema is to be defined in terms of codes, these distinctions are crucial: a code which informs a technico-sensory characteristic that is common to many kinds of expression (being able to do so in each case without codical transposition) would be less specific than a code which informs a characteristic that is manifested in only one or a few kinds of expression. One might thus speak of varying degrees of codical specificity. Metz lists several systems of intelligibility that the viewer of cinema must have mastered for "the comprehension and integration of the total message of the film" but which seem to have little or no cinematic specificity. Among these are two which relate to the perception and identification of filmed objects: "1. visual and auditory perception itself (systems for structuring space, 'figures' and 'backgrounds,' etc.) to the extent that it already constitutes a certain degree of intelligibility which is *acquired* and variable according to different cultures; 2. the recognition, identification, and enumeration of visual or auditory objects which appear on the screen, i.e., the capacity (which is cultural and acquired) to appropriately manipulate the material that the film presents" (*LC,* pp. 33–34). One is tempted to call these systems of intelligibility extra-cinematic or pre-cinematic because they are not linked directly to cinema as a signifying process. Yet, because they underlie the perception and identification of objects outside the film, they play a major part in the iconic aspect of signification within the film—that is, the representation of objects by visual analogy (partial likeness).[3] Cinema, conceived narrowly as a means for reproducing "reality," is in this respect a process for *transferring* codes: "to say that an image resembles its object is to say that, thanks to this resemblance, the decipherment of the image will be able to benefit from codes which intervened in the decipherment of the 'real object'" (*Essais* II, pp. 153–54). Perhaps more important is the idea that resemblance itself is codified, subject to quantitative and qualitative variables that in every culture enter into the determination of resemblance. Here Metz refers to the work of Abraham Moles on "degrees of iconicity" and to that of Pierre Francastel on the axes of resemblance in a single culture and on differences in the determination of resemblance among different cultures.

What Metz calls the "iconic codes of visual analogy" have a low degree of specificity to cinema because they inform many other types of visual texts whose materials are structured to "re-present" real objects by visual analogy (e.g., the figurative painting, the photograph, the photo-novel or photo-essay, the comic strip). At the same time, each of these means of expression is distinguished by more than its capacity to manifest a visual image whose configurations are informed by "iconic codes of visual analogy." Figurative painting is characterized by a single, immobile image obtained by hand; photography by a single, immobile image obtained mechanically; the comic strip by an immobile, multiple image obtained initially by hand; the photo-novel by an immobile, multiple image obtained mechanically; and cinema by a mobile and multiple image obtained mechanically and "combined with three sorts of sound elements (speech, music, sound effects) and written credits" (*LC,* p. 226). Metz has deliberately chosen these examples in order to "identify and enumerate (in the form of discrete units) the sensory characteristics to which a given code is intrinsically linked" (*LC,* p. 222). When the technical mode by which an image is produced has a bearing on the codes which may inform the image, he also includes technical criteria; hence, the hybrid term "technico-sensory characteristics" and his distinction between the mechanically recorded image and the image rendered by hand. The specificity of cinema defined in terms of codes is a notion of great internal complexity, which Metz describes for illustrative purposes according to a schema of overlapping circles (concentric circles and secants). Each circle stands for a technico-sensory characteristic which is common to a group of *langages* (means of expression) and which is informed by a class of codes requiring that characteristic in order to be manifested. The "iconic codes of visual analogy" constitute a first class for which only the characteristic "visual image" is required. (For more on these codes see *LC,* pp. 227–28; *Essais II,* pp. 151–62; and articles in *Communications* no. 15 [1970], especially "Sémiologie des messages visuels" by Umberto Eco whose work Metz frequently acknowledges.)

A second class of codes relates to the production of the iconic image in cinema by photography, what Metz calls a means of "mechanical duplication" (*LC,* p. 228). The film shares these codes with the photograph and the photo-novel but not with the drawing, the painting, the fresco, the comic strip, and the animated cartoon, whose images are composed initially by hand. In this second category are "photographic" codifications linked to phenomena such as angular incidence (shooting angles), shot scale (long shots, medium shots, close-ups), effects created by focal modifications, such as filters, lenses of different powers, and depth-of-focus effects regulated by the diaphragm opening (*LC*, p. 29).

These technical codes raise two problems. First, visual configurations linked to technical variations seem to constitute signifiers without "fixed signifieds," they serve to "denote" what is placed before the camera but seem to have no fixed meaning of their own. These configurations, as Metz explains later in relation to codes of movement, may become codified according to their use in a particular genre or period of films. Others take on a meaning only in the context of the film. Second, the characteristic of mechanical duplication involves the indexical aspect of signification which Metz stresses in an early essay on realism (*FL*, pp. 3–15) but does not develop with regard to codes in *LC*. A photograph implies the optical duplication performed by a camera, thus a straightforward causal link between the recorded image and its referent or model; the still photograph presents what Barthes has called an *avoir-été-là* (*Communications*, No. 4 [1964]; p. 47). By contrast, the characteristics of the hand-painted image do not imply the prior existence of a real object (model), only that of an artist (the brushstrokes and boundaries of applied pigment presenting a "trace" or index of his prior activity). At stake is the notion of pictorial realism, which, like that of resemblance, is subject in every culture to variables that enter into the determination of realism. In a general codification of pictorial realism, elements of the photographic codes to which Metz refers would necessarily come into play. Indeed, Metz's emphasis on camera *position* and optical modifications suggests that these codes involve many of the features which lead viewers in our culture to accept the photograph as an index of reality.

A third class of codes in Metz's schema of overlapping specificities relates to the image as it is placed in sequence with other images; the film is characterized in part by a *series* of images. The single painting or photograph does not share this characteristic of "successive plurality," but the fresco, the comic strip, the animated cartoon (all excluded from class two) and the photo-novel do. "This third circle is thus concentric with the first, that of general iconicity, and smaller than it (included in it). But in relation to the second, that of the mechanical image, it is in a position of intersection" (*LC*, p. 230). Psychologists and psychosociologists have studied the effects obtained by putting images into sequence. Of particular interest are: (1) the "logical relationships perceived by the spectator" among successive images (e.g., causality, opposition, simple juxtaposition); (2) "diverse means of expressing temporal relationships, such as simultancity, close consecution, remote consecution, between actions represented by the different images of the sequence"; (3) "more properly esthetic configurations: echoes of motifs or of graphic contours from one image to another (with the problem of 'transition'), violent contrasts between contiguous images, etc." (*LC*, pp. 230–31). Similar constructions, of course, play a crucial part in cinematic montage.

Metz has made it clear that his large-scale syntagmatics does not constitute an exclusive "ciné-langue" extrapolated from the effects of montage: "it constitutes only an attempt to elucidate *one* of the codes of the film, the one which organizes the most common spatio-temporal logic within the sequence; this logical *combinatoire* is only one of the systems which make up the 'grammar' of the cinema (and thus *a fortiori* which inform the total message of the film)" (*LC* Larousse, p. 143). (See *FL*, pp. 119–82 for a detailed presentation of the large-scale syntagmatics and a syntagmatic analysis of Jacques Rozier's *Adieu Philippine.*)

For the most part, the "image units" which make up the sequential patterns (syntagmata) of the large-scale syntagmatics are distinguished by the physical boundaries of the shot, each syntagma consisting of two or more single "takes." As Metz has noted, the large-scale syntagmatics pertains mainly to a tradition of montage which relies heavily on cutting:

The period that my large-scale syntagmatics covers is characterized by what Bazin used to call "classic cutting": analytical cutting which, in order to capture a complex segment of the action, preferred to fragment it in several successive shots rather than to turn it in continuity; one finds oneself, then, in one of the last seven types of my classification (autonomous segments formed by several shots). (*Essais II*, p. 204)

But in one notable example, the sequence-shot or "long take," the "image units" which make up an autonomous sequential pattern are distinguished *within* a single shot by a fourth characteristic of the film, *movement* (examples: "'linking through movement' from one image to the next, passage from a medium long shot to a close-up shot [or the reverse] as a procedure of montage which puts two different images in succession without recourse to 'cutting,' certain movements of the actors [called 'entries and exits from the field of vision'] which bring together several scenes in a single shot"; *LC* Larousse, p. 175). Because movement allows for a kind of "internal montage," it too is pertinent to the spatio-temporal logic of film narrative. This is why Metz has left open the possibility of a second codical formulation that would indicate which categories of narrative logic manifested in a series of individual shots could also be manifested within the sequence-shot.

The characteristic of movement, accompanied necessarily by that of sequentiality, thus comprises a fourth circle in Metz's schema of overlapping specificities. It is inside the third circle, which specifically defines sequentiality, and it excludes those means of expression with multiple but immobile images (e.g., comic strip, photo-novel, fresco). This fourth domain has a higher degree of cinematic specificity than group three because the film shares it with fewer other means of expression. At this stage in the analysis, the overlapping of domains defines a fifth area in the center which represents the logical product of circles two and four: means of expression having mobile and multiple images produced mechanically. Because the cartoon, the photograph, and the photo-novel, etc., are excluded, cinema shares this fifth area only with television (which, although distinguished by technical differences in transmission and psycho-sociological differences in reception, is seen by Metz as largely isomorphic; *LC*, p. 237).

Linked to this fifth area are configurations which result from camera movements (e.g., dolly shots, pan shots) or optical effects (e.g., zoom shots, dissolve, iris, fade) which may play an important part in "interior montage," as already noted. However, these configurations and others belonging to the cinematic process (e.g., slow motion, deliberate blur, wipe, stop-action shot) often have no signified in the sense of a stable and commonly accepted meaning. The dolly shot, for example, can "signify" in several ways. A forward dolly shot which moves in rapidly on a character's face can *announce* "an impending transition to subjectivity," as in David Lean's *Brief Encounter*, "and thus signal that the events which are henceforth going to appear on the screen are only mental evocations of the character whose face is in the process of filling the screen"; it can *describe* a scene, "introducing the spectator into a new setting which is presented to him little by little"; and it can *accompany* characters as they move when it is important to keep them at a fixed distance (*LC*, p. 133). Slow motion, another example, can create a dream atmosphere as in Vigo's *Zéro de conduite;* it can also dramatize moments of violence as in Peckinpah's *The Wild Bunch;* or it can "function in relation to time in the same way as the magnifying glass in relation to space," as in the German term *Zeitluppe,* temporal magnifying glass (*LC*, p. 133). The standard approach to the pansemic tendency of certain figures is to say that they "acquire a precise signified in each context, but that 'taken in themselves' they have no fixed value . . . one can at the most draw up a disparate list of their particularly frequent or particularly normalized uses" (*LC*, p. 133). "Something else, in addition" to these figures gives them meaning, but Metz notes that this "something else" can be of two kinds, each being supplemental in a different way.

The first kind, corresponding to common usage of the term context, is what Metz calls "syntagmatic context." It consists of elements which appear *along with* the given figure in the unfolding ("déroulement") of the film. But for these other elements to clarify the figure in question, they must themselves be made intelligible. (As "uninformed" configurations they have meaning only at the barest phenomenological level, thus *signifying* no more than the figure in question; *LC*, p. 134.) The notion of a clarifying context thus implies a textual operation; we are no longer dealing with elements of the "raw" filmic text but with those elements as they are analyzed, *informed* by diverse systems of intelligibility. The meaning given to a problematic figure will result only from a global operation, the production of meaning within the text by the interplay of codes as they inform the unique structure of selected and combined elements which underlies the coherence of every text. Metz's emphasis on textuality is important, for it situates the notion of code (an abstract system of differences) in relation to the actualized filmic discourse, "the activity of *integration* (or of disintegration)—the process of composition or 'writing'—by which the film, relying on . . . codes, modifies them, combines them, plays them one against the other, eventually arriving at its own individual system" (*LC*, p. 100). As we shall note, this distinction between code system and textual system not only corresponds in some ways to Chomsky's notion of a model of performance being generated from a model of competence, but it emphasizes as well the inescapable role of the interpreter in this operation. In the case of certain cinematic figures "without fixed signifieds," the filmic system alone may provide a necessary context.

But in other cases, a second kind of context may inform the figure. What Metz calls, for illustrative purposes, a "paradigmatic context" is not really a context at all, but a partial code consisting of "a relatively fixed number of 'meanings' [*acceptations*], even if this number is rather large, even if the different uses have at first glance nothing in common, and even if present studies are not in a position to furnish an exhaustive list of them" (*LC,* pp. 134–35). A given figure may have a more or less fixed signified in relation to certain genre of films (use within the western, the psycho-drama, the horror or science fiction story) or in relation to a period of films. Metz calls this kind of partial codification a sub-code because it concerns a smaller number of films than a code and because it is only a partial solution to a central "coding problem." In linguistics "each sub-code ('level of language,' or 'linguistic usage') augments and details in its own manner the production of the code, but these productions are already determined before any activity of this sort" (*LC,* p. 138). At the present stage of research in the semiology of cinema, these secondary codifications may appear as secondary only to a *potential* primary code which has yet to be elaborated:

the *place of the code* (the common core) seems to be made up of something which, in the absence of sufficiently definite structures, is not yet a code but rather the potential location (although already outlined) of diverse possible or future codifications, a *coding problem* and not yet a code, a question and not yet a response, a set of possibilities and not yet an organization of these possibilities. The "responses," the positive organizations, come into play only with the sub-codes. (*LC,* p. 138)

The sub-code as a paradigmatic "context" and the textual system as a syntagmatic context are, of course, interdependent; in fact, the sub-code as a response to a "coding problem" is forged logically by accumulated usage in textual systems, such that the figures involved acquire "a relatively fixed number of 'acceptations'" (*LC,* p. 134).

While presenting problems for the semiology of cinema, as Metz emphasizes, these codes and sub-codes of group five are linked to the combination of technico-sensory traits which are most specific to cinema, a combination which goes the furthest to distinguish cinematic expression from other means of visual expression. One must not forget, however, that cinema is also auditory. What Metz calls the "codes of sound composition" are common to radio (radioplays) as well as to cinema and television. These include (1) codes for the syntagmatic arrangement of auditive elements among themselves (e.g., musical codes, the language system [*langue*], sound effect codes); (2) codes which involve contrasts between foreground and background sounds, as elaborated, for example, in the work of Jean Epstein; (3) codes which concern the gradual transformation of noises into musical motifs; and (4) codes of counterpoint—interruption of music by words or vice versa (*LC,* pp. 232–33). Another group of codifications concerns the relationships between visual and auditory configurations. What Metz calls the codes of "audio-visual composition" are more specific to cinema because they are restricted to those means of expression capable of manifesting an audio-visual mix-ture. As examples, Metz mentions the reinforcement of the image-track by the sound track (or vice versa) and possible effects of contrast between them; rela-tionships between ordinary sound and *sound-off;* more complex use of *sound-off* called "asynchronism" by theorists of the period c. 1928–33; and relationships between the image-track and speech—what could be called the "registers of speech"; "the ordinary speech of 'dialogue,' monologue said to be 'internal' but which is not, 'sonorous first-person,' external commentary assigned to a speaker or an anonymous narrator" (*LC,* p. 233).

RELATIONS AMONG CODES

Metz's listing of codes does not purport to be exhaustive; nor is every code elaborated to the same degree as his large-scale syntagmatics. His purpose is rather to illustrate the complexity of the notion of specificity when defined in terms of codes. Not only is a given means of expression characterized by certain codes which, because they are linked to its more exclusive technico-sensory traits, are more specific to it, but also by a combination of codes, a specific *set* of codes which informs that means of expression. This second notion alone is insuf-ficient to define the scope of a "cinematic language system" because it merely "adds up" the codes "taxonomically" without regard for their interrelationships. That is why Metz needs the first notion of codical specificity to present a more dynamic picture of the combination of codes:

[Codes] are not regrouped, added to one another, or juxtaposed in just any manner; they are organized, articulated in terms of one another in accordance with a certain order, they contract unilateral hierarchies, similar in certain regards to those which, according to Ju-lien Greimas, are twisted about the semes of each lexeme or of each sememe. Thus a veritable *system of intercodical relations* is generated which is itself, in some sort, another code, and which—on the level of the codical, not of the material of expression—repre-sents what is most specific in each language system [*langage*]. (*LC,* p. 242)

Formulated in this manner, cinematic language would be a "super-system" of codes, an abstract body of systems conceptualized as a coherent whole before (or apart from) the production of meaning which results from its implication in filmic texts. (The actual production of meaning in films—the evidence of an activity of "construction-destruction," of selection and "relocation" [displacement], which transforms elements of the cinematic language system into the text's own logic [the textual system]—should not be confused with the cinematic language sys-tem, which represents only potential meanings. It has no discursive structure, only an abstract, paradigmatic one, and in this regard it is like Chomsky's model of competence.) Metz does not elaborate this super-system in any kind of defini-tive form; his schema of overlapping specificities merely begins this task by illus-trating "the relations of *unilateral implication* which come to successively 'embed' the less specific groups of codes in more specific groups of codes" (*LC,* p. 242). In fact, he is quite modest about this undertaking, emphasizing its incom-pleteness and maintaining a critical awareness of the methodology that makes it possible. Above all, Metz stresses what is perhaps the major problem with the notion of cinematic language when considered as a system of inter-codical relations: its apparent lack of internal coherence when compared to that of *langue*. Yet, curiously, these reservations taken altogether do not lead to an impasse, but help overcome one. They prompt him to question, in fact, the unitary status of *langue* itself, whose features, such as the single material of expression (phonic sound), the unmotivated sign, and the articulation of semes by phonemes, have been almost hypostatized as standards of comparison for the study of cinema. Whether cinema has been found to resemble verbal language (the idea of "ciné-langue") or not (Metz's initial notion of "*langage* without a code"), the methodology of linguistics, which permits the abstraction of a structural model of language in the first place, has remained deceptively transparent. Contrary to the wishes of Saussure, who envisioned the possibility of a general semiology, the role of methodology in defining the object of linguistics through an initial act of abstraction is often forgotten when one attempts to "extrapolate" notions from linguistics.

COHERENCE, METHOD OF ABSTRACTION

Saussure gave his notion of *langue* a kind of objective unity from the outset by basing it on the social function of verbal expression: *langue* is the system of governing constraints, abstracted from speech, which enables people to understand each other: "It is both a social product of the faculty of speech and a collection of necessary conventions that have been adopted by a social body to permit individuals to exercise that faculty" (*Course in General Linguistics,* trans. Wade Baskin [New York: McGraw-Hill, 1966], p. 9). The unified status of *langue* is assured from the beginning by the assumption that some system of intelligibility must account for the social reality of bilateral verbal exchange. Conditions are strikingly different in cinematic expression. Cinematic language is "used" only in one-way communication, first by specialists whose influence on it is strong, and then by viewers. Its status as a social object is affected by its esthetic function. As Metz has written, cinematic language is already an artistic language, and as such is more susceptible to influence by signifying structures that are common to a given period, genre, or film maker, structures whose occurrence in textual systems is persistent enough to become more or less stabilized in a "cinematic sub-code."

Grounding the system of *langue* in social reality justified a principle of selection capable of abstracting that system. Saussure isolated what he thought to be the common property of verbal expression, its constitutive principles, from individual utterances (*parole*) which include variations, distortions, and aspects (such as accent and intonation) considered to be non-pertinent to the system. The structural coherence of *langue* depends to a large extent on the discriminations of the analyst, who draws the line between what belongs to the system and what is considered to be variation or excess. This line has been repeatedly questioned in recent research. As Metz points out, work in generative grammar, in "secondary modeling systems" (the Soviet school), and in socio-, psycho-, ethno-, and neurolinguistics has begun to account for many aspects of *parole* that Saussure excluded from *langue*. By contrast with the apparent coherence of *langue* and the tendency of linguistic research even to systematize some of what was considered *parole,* cinema seems af first glance to be all *parole.* But Metz insists that "what one 'compares' most often, is, on the one hand, the *already largely analyzed* spoken language (for linguists have been working for a long time), and, on the other, the cinematic language system *before any analysis* (for the semiotics of the cinema does not yet exist)—such that this impression, which is so vivid, and so often invoked, of a large inequality in systematization, actually constitutes a situation which is rather delicate to interpret" (*LC,* p. 287).

MINIMAL UNITS

Still another feature of Saussure's initial act of abstraction compounds the situation. *Langue* as a system of signification is based on a single characteristic of verbal expression, articulated sound; the phoneme thus becomes the material constituent of the speech chain, the minimal distinctive unit of articulated language. The "arbitrary" linking of a signifier and a signified in the morpheme, composed by one or more phonemes, was to become the essential feature of Saussure's doctrine of the sign and provide one of the bases of structural semantics. The absence in cinema of anything comparable to the relatively fixed number of morphemes of *langue* led Metz initially to speak of cinema as a "*langage* without a code." The mistake, as he has noted subsequently, was in assuming that a given means of expression is defined by a *single* code whose minimal differential units are the basis for all expressed meaning. Because *langue* accounts only for the meaning of articulated "bits," and because of its "privileged" position in relation to the whole of speech, one may forget that other aspects of verbal expression (e.g., accent, intonation) produce meaning and that other codes may inform more complex combinations of these bits (e.g., units defined at the level of rhetoric or connotation). In order to free the semiology of cinema from the contaminating influence of linguistic categories, Metz felt obliged to emphasize the heterogeneity of verbal codes, a tactic which relativizes the status of *langue* with regard to the entire domain of verbal expression. This tactic is evident in the very fact that he titles his study *Langage et cinéma* rather than *Langage cinématographique.*

Studies in transformational grammar have shown that even *langue,* although it suggests a single code of digital units, functions more like a machine with several systemic components "(e.g., syntactic, transformational, and phonological components, lexical matrices, etc.), each articulated one after the other so that the output of one becomes the input of the next" (*LC,* p. 66). Metz points out that what is considered to be a minimal constitutive unit at one stage of the process may not even exist at an earlier one. For example, the English *do* in negative and interrogative phrases is considered in generative linguistics to be a pure *formant,* a simple grammatical tool lacking any particular signified, rather than a true *morpheme;* it is not present as a terminal unit of the "syntagmatic" (or "categorial") phase of syntactic generation, and is only introduced later in the transformational phase. One may thus speak of two kinds of minimal significative units, depending on their place in the linguistic process. Many of the minimal units at one level may coincide with minimal units at another (e.g., morphemes from the syntagmatic phase which remain identical throughout the transformation process), but this should not give the impression that there must be a "typical sign" or universal minimal unit for there to be systematic relations among codes.

Codes of verbal expression outside the strict definition of *langue* have minimal units of varying dimension: in French, "s'il vous plaît" is a minimal unit of the code of etiquette, but this unit is composed of several units of *langue*. The units of myth in Lévi-Strauss's *Structural Anthropology* and the units that Barthes isolates in codes of connotation are also of varying dimensions. The point is that the notion of minimal unit is only pertinent to the individual code which makes that unit significant, not to the entire means of expression (*langage* in the broadest sense) which can mobilize a multitude of codes.

In cinema (or elsewhere) no sovereign code exists which imposes its minimal units, which are always the same, on all parts of all films. These films, on the contrary, have a textual surface—which is temporal and spatial—a fabric in which multiple codes come to segment, each for itself, their minimal units which, throughout the entire length of the filmic discourse, are superimposed, overlap, and intersect without their boundaries necessarily coinciding. (*LC,* p. 194)

What characterizes a given means of expression in codical terms is thus "not *a code,* as those who search for 'the code of the cinema' would maintain, but a combination of several codes" (*LC,* p. 240). Metz's schema of overlapping specificities is an attempt to analyze this combination by abstracting methodologically the codes which pertain to the various technico-sensory characteristics of the film. To the extent that Metz sees this formalizing as a necessary step in the study of cinema, he is a structuralist, but clearly a wary one. For he knows at the same time that codes and systems of codes are products of the analyst, whose method for neutralizing the field of discourse, in order to abstract a differential system of potential meanings, carries its own epistemology. While acknowledging the need for methodology (and the need for it to remain visible), Metz wishes to bring to the study of signification in cinema a concern for the dynamism involved in the production of meaning, the discursive force of the film which is lost by abstracting a static structural model. Hence, his insistence on codical heterogeneity, on the link between codes and materials of expression, and on the dynamic interrelationships among the codes within a language system. Furthermore, the reader who is sensitive to a certain reductionism implicit in these analytical concepts will find that Metz never "reduces" films to codes. Codes are abstract, static, and general, while films are concrete, discursive, and particular.

THE TEXTUAL SYSTEM

Language and Cinema is primarily a study of codes as they apply in general to all films, but one may also study the individual film as a unique text informed by a multitude of codes. The two approaches are complementary but distinct through a shift in emphasis: the study of codes concerns the *potential* meaning of a given configuration, which may appear in any film, while the study of an individual film concerns the *discursive* or actualized meaning of that configuration in combination with others of the same film. What Metz calls the textual system (or singular system) represents an attempt to describe the dynamics of this combination, to specify the force of meaning implied in the unique ordering of codical elements which underlies the intelligibility of each film. And so, while Metz retains the notion of codes, he considers the film's unique combination of codical elements to be evidence of an active process of integration and displacement of codes, which should be of major interest in a structural study:

the system of the text is the process which *displaces* codes, deforming each of them by the presence of the others, contaminating some by means of others, meanwhile replacing one by another, and finally—as a temporarily "arrested" result of this general displacement— *placing* each code in a particular position in regard to the overall structure, a displacement which thus finishes by a positioning which is itself destined to be displaced by another text. (*LC,* p. 193)

Locating the force of meaning in the implied "work" of the textual system allows one to bypass consideration of the infinite variables of viewer affectivity.

It also offers a way to discuss cinema in terms of a creative activity without resorting to an essentialist notion of creative origin and speculating about intention. The text is evidence of a creative activity which *produces* meaning in the strict sense of *value-added:* "Whether the film is 'invention' or 'creation' is dependent solely upon the degree to which it is *operation,* i.e., to the extent to which it adds something to pre-existent codes, producing structural configurations which none of them alone could have anticipated" (*LC,* p. 104). Perhaps more than anything else in Metz's current work, his way of analyzing this *value-added* marks the critical shift he has made from his early writings. For the film's discursive force cannot be created *ex nihilo* as the abandoned notion of "*langage* without a code" would have it. Nor can it arise simply from the natural "expressivity of the world," an assumption in Metz's early writings which shows the influence of André Bazin. What Metz once described as the immanent meaning (*sens immanent*) of the world, which arises naturally and which the film takes up, is no longer taken for granted. Reality cannot give the film its expressive impetus quite so directly or naturally, for what we call reality presupposes "a set of codes without which this reality would not be accessible or intelligible, such that nothing could be said of it, not even that it is reality" (*LC,* p. 103). Thus the meaning that the signifying process generates "(the coefficient of modification and work which is appropriate to the text) does not intervene in relation to a simple, basic reality, not in some void which would strangely carry within itself the promise of a future and unfailing creativity, but in relation to codes" (*LC,* p. 104). Metz's debt to recent literary criticism is evident here, especially to Julia Kristeva's notion of the double-edged process of destruction/construction involved in the production of meaning of the text:

Just as the literary work, which can only exist thanks to some natural language, is nevertheless constructed against it rather than *in* it (since it is a working of the language, and since it is nourished by what this language lacks as much as by what it possesses)—so the overall system of a film consists essentially of a double and unique movement, a movement by which are "mobilized" diverse codes without which the film would have nothing on which to maintain its drive, a movement which relegates these very codes to a secondary position, and by which the filmic system is detached from them, by which it tells us that it is something more than these codes, that it is, strictly speaking, this difference itself, this re-impulsion. (*LC,* p. 104)

Yet, finally, this comparison between literary production and filmic production points up the difficult situation of cinema semiology. Because structural linguistics constitutes its object as the common property of verbal expression, the literary text may be readily viewed as evidence of a productive operation, carried on by specialists, both with and against "ordinary language" and with/against the systems of other texts. By contrast, cinema appears to have no "ordinary language" with/against which its texts can be constructed. It obviously does not have such a language if one defines language narrowly as a system which permits bilateral communication. Yet cinema is too clearly a signifying practice, with conventions of its own, to have no systematic underpinnings. The difficulty is in dealing with cinema's status as an esthetic practice. As such, cinema appears from the beginning to be a specialized language of visual and auditory devices, and the temptation is great to discount its conventions as mere technical knowhow, important only to film makers (since we "understand" the film *anyway*). But at the same time, the unfolding of the film, due largely to this technical knowhow, plays with/against perceptual conventions that are so common (yet complex) that one takes them for granted. Metz's schema of overlapping codical specificities begins to show how these codifications are potentially brought together in the cinematic process, and, in this way, he guards against too hasty a distinction between what is cinematic and what is extra-cinematic, what "belongs" to the film maker and what "belongs" to the viewer. The notion of "ordinary language" is built into this schema at the level of the least specific codes, those which shape the perception of reality and the identification of objects. These codes provide a basic level of intelligibility which the codes more specific to the cinematic process play upon. However, Metz's reflections on textuality go even further, suggesting that each film is also constructed with/against the most specific cinematic codes and with/against sub-codes that are forged by the textual systems of a given tradition or genre of films.

Notes

1. *Language and Cinema,* p. 36. All material cited from this work is taken from the Mouton translation unless indicated by brackets or by reference to the original Larousse edition. Those variations, and translations of passages from the second volume of *Essais,* are mine.

2. *LC* Larousse, p. 31. As in many other passages where Metz uses the French word *langage* in a deliberately general and ambiguous manner, the English term "means of expression" seems preferable to the translator's term "language system," for the emphasis is not on the system alone but on its link with the raw material that it "articulates" and informs. Earlier in the book, the translation "language system" merely forces a distinction which, for tactical reasons, Metz prefers to postpone until he can illustrate these links and

relate them to the notion of specificity. But in a critical passage, such as this one, where he begins to do so, the substitution of "language system" for *langage* undermines the dialectical value of the distinction by eliminating the general term which implies the links between material of expression and the codes which structure it.

3. It is important to note that the cinematic image is not exclusively *iconic,* but also shares *indexical* aspects of signification (based on a causal or existential relationship between referent and configuration) and *symbolic* aspects (based on an unmotivated relationship). See Metz's discussion of Peirce's three-part distinction in *Essais* II, pp. 151–62.

THE ANATOMY OF
A PROLETARIAN FILM:
WARNER'S *MARKED*
WOMAN

CHARLES ECKERT

Charles Eckert's article of 1974 remains one of the most lucid applications of structural Marxist and Freudian concepts to film criticism that we have. The fact that his own letter of self-criticism in the following issue of Film Quarterly *(see Addendum) is also one of the most vivid characterizations of what Eckert feared was an incompatible schism between idealist (structural) readings and materialist (Marxist-Freudian) ones makes this text an exceptionally valuable testing ground for methodological questions in general.*

Eckert's approach is quite different from that of Karyn Kay, who examined the same film in the first volume of Movies and Methods. *Kay's reading and interpretation were thematic; Eckert's is an attempt to posit a deep structure of oppositions traceable to real social contradictions (class conflict) but disguised by neutral operations analogous to those that Freud uses to explain dreamwork (the displacement of political and economic contradictions into ethical dilemmas and the condensation of the capitalist into the gangster). Eckert's contention that the attempt to resolve the real contradiction leads to "crystal-like growth" of the narrative, which continues until it succeeds in reworking the dilemma into a form that at least appears to be resolved, offers an instructive insight into why narratives take time, that is, why they need a lengthy middle when the beginning and end already bear the formal marks of closure. The middle presents difficulties and means of overcoming them by the time of the story's conclusion. (This point is pursued further in my* Ideology and the Image *[Bloomington: Indiana University*

Press, 1981], pp. 93–103, where the relation between narrative and paradox is discussed.) Eckert also suggests that the film has some Brechtian aspects by identifying intensely affective scenes that point to real social contradictions which stand apart from emotionally flat scenes that advance the narrative plot. This reading departs significantly from the terms of the essay by Louis Althusser that Eckert cites as his source, since Eckert relates the characters' melodramatic expressivity to real social conditions and their emotionless resignation to melodramatic fiction. This reverses the situation that Althusser describes, where reality is drab and monotonous and the melodramatic moments are charged with emotion. Whether the final effect is analogous to the one that Althusser proposes for Bertolazzi's play is thus open to question.

But the hardest question is the one Eckert asks in his letter: Can we treat films as myths? Do their structures, codes, sign systems, and analogies to mental operations replace the idealism of thinking about social conditions with the materialism of thought within the conditions of social existence? Are films myths, or are they products, ahistorical or historical? Can we marry an idealist structuralism with a material referent, or must we forge a materialist, historical theory of knowledge from the stuff of history itself, and what is that stuff if not forms of signification? Finally, what is the relation between mental operations (language, semiotics, psychodynamics) and material conditions (production, exchange, class, sex), and what forms of theory effectively unite them? Eckert's article and letter may not resolve all these questions, but they make exceptionally clear both the analytic procedures and the methodological problems inherent in a structuralism based on the analysis of contemporary culture as myth.

•

Marked Woman was produced by Warner Brothers–First National in 1937, based on an original script by Robert Rossen and Abem Finkel, and directed by Lloyd Bacon. It is, to give it its fullest definition, a topical, proletariat-oriented gangster film. As such, it must be understood within a complex tradition of films, and against a backdrop of Depression issues. The analysis I shall attempt respects the context of the film and centers upon three crucial problems.

The first concerns a striking contrast between the cool, rigidly controlled emotions typical of the scenes that develop the melodramatic plot and a different order of emotions spanning a spectrum from despair to rage, that appear in a series of interspersed scenes (and in the crucial final scene). The affective center of the film seems displaced into another dimension than the melodramatic, a dimension that the latter scenes define.[1] The second problem concerns the way in which the moral and social dilemmas are developed. And the third concerns the significance of the prime-mover of the plot, the gangster-racketeer: since he is a heavily stereotyped figure bringing with him not simply the swagger and jargon of dozens of previous incarnations but a specific aura of significances and values, understanding him requires what we might call a "theory of the gangster," the development of which will take us beyond *Marked Woman*.

However disconnected these analytical concerns may seem, they are, I believe, aspects of a single unified intellectual operation that affects almost every detail of the film. It may be helpful to define this operation and to sketch in the conclusions I will be moving towards before entering upon an extended analysis. My major contention is that the ultimate sources of *Marked Woman* and its tradition are in class conflict; but the level at which the film-makers perceive this conflict, and the level at which it is lived by the fictional characters and perceived by the audience, is existential rather than political or economic. It is in the lived experience of the Depression, in the resentment directed at those who "caused" the Depression, and in the sense of disparity between being poor and being rich, that this popular notion of class conflict originates.

The expression of the conflict in the films, however, is almost never overt. It is instead converted into conflicts of a surrogate nature—some ethical, some regional, some concerned with life-style, some symbolized by tonal or aesthetic overlays created by the makers of the films. The analysis of this elaborate secondary structure requires close attention to the processes of condensation and displacement by which latent content is converted into manifest content. I would like to avoid jargon for its own sake, but Freud's terms and their strict definitions are essential for an understanding of the processes involved (I shall give definitions at the appropriate point in the analysis). I hope to show that the effect of these operations is to attenuate conflicts at the level of real conditions and to amplify and resolve them at the surrogate levels of the melodrama. This solution is not always successful, however; it can lead to dialectical play between the real and disguised conflicts, the effect of which is to make the usually opaque operations transparent. I believe that this is what happens in *Marked Woman* and that it is the chief source of the atypical feel of the film and of the forceful and unsettling character of a number of its scenes.

But all of this can only be clarified after we have recalled the film and its topical basis. *Marked Woman* capitalized upon a sensational trial reported almost daily in the *New York Times* between May 14 and June 22, 1936. Because the details of this trial strongly influenced Rossen and Finkle, and because the trial provides a body of real analogues to the fiction of the film, I shall review it first. I will then give a summary of the film designed to make the disjuncture between the melodramatic and the strongly affective scenes apparent, while giving enough detail to familiarize the reader with the whole film and to provide material for the subsequent analysis.

THE TRIAL

Charles "Lucky Luciano" Lucania won his place in the pantheon of Depression Mafiosi by cornering a market more durable than liquor—the brothels of New York. His method was that of the simple "take-over," with promises of protection from the law and fair treatment for all concerned. The reasons why the State of New York decided to get Luciano were as politically and socially complex as those that drove Capone out of Chicago—and fortunately need not concern us here. The state's instrument was a task force set up under as ambitious a prosecutor-cum-politician as the country contained, Thomas E. Dewey.

Dewey began by raiding the brothels and arresting almost one hundred women as material witnesses. In its early stages the trial was high-spirited, with an absurdly Runyonesque cast: "Jo-Jo" Weintraub, Crazy Moe, "Little Davie" Betillo, Cokey Flo. But as the trial centered more and more upon the women, whose testimony would make or break the prosecution's case, the proceedings became a bleak window upon a world of exploitation, drab servitude and occasional terror.

Nancy Presser said that one of Luciano's men drove her into prostitution by threatening to "cut me up so that my own mother wouldn't know me."[2] And Thelma Jordan said "I knew what happened to girls who had talked about the combination. The soles of their feet and their stomachs were burned with cigar butts for talking too much. . . . I heard Ralph [Liguori] say that their tongues were cut when girls talked."[3] Liguori also threatened that if any of the women testified against the combination "their pictures would be sent to their home town papers with stories of what they were doing for a living."[4]

Another of the women, Helen Kelley, testified to the economics of prostitution. She had quit an underpaid job to become a prostitute and in her first week made $314. After a friendly booker persuaded her to quit and go straight she took a job as a waitress averaging twelve dollars per week. After a year of this she went back to the booker "to solve an economic problem."[5]

The conditions of the prostitutes' lives influenced Rossen and Finkle, as we shall see, but the real issue of the trial was the conviction of Luciano. To this end Dewey faced two obstacles—convincing the women that they would be protected from retaliation, and convincing the jury, and the public at large, that prostitutes were "worthy of belief" in a court of law. When he found that his star witness's life had been threatened, he spent hours persuading her to testify, and then fatuously described to the court the sense of "responsibility" that the experience had aroused in him. And when he had finally gotten his conviction, he assured the court that it was in no sense a personal victory; credit rather belonged to "the men who prepared the case through months of grueling, hard work. . . ."[6]

And where were the "confessed prostitutes" who had been barely "worthy of belief" at this moment of sharing the spoils? They left the House of Detention and "were sent to Special Prosecutor Thomas E. Dewey's offices in the Woolworth Building, where they received, as fees, sums ranging between $150 and $175"— barely a half week's earnings for a working prostitute. "Many said that they planned to return to their home town," or so the *Times* sentimentalized.[7]

From the trial Luciano went on to organize the prison at Dannemora, then the New York dock workers, then the international drug trade. Dewey became governor of the state of New York and candidate for the presidency in 1944 and 1948. The women, who had served both men equally well, disappeared, as they do in the film, into the fog.

THE FILM

Now let us summarize the film that Warner's made to capitalize upon this trial, with particular attention to the affective split referred to earlier. In the first sequence Johnny Vanning (Eduardo Cianelli) enters the Club Intime, a dinner-club that he had just taken over and intends to convert into a "classy" nightclub and gambling room. He informs the women who work there, among them Mary Dwight (Bette Davis), that he has all the clubs in town and the women who work in them "sewed up." He intends to "organize" the place and to give the women protection from the law. In the course of the sequence he fires one of the women who looks too old to be a hostess, is asked by Mary to let her stay on, relents, shows an interest in the outspoken Mary, and is repulsed by her. Emotionally, all of the dialogue is muted: Vanning is a study in icy cynicism; the women are apprehensive and morose. The tonalities established in this initial sequence are those that dominate the melodrama throughout.

The next scene shows us five of the women in an apartment they rent together: homey curtains, department-store art, an air of proletarian domesticity. They enter depressed, discussing whether they should continue to work for Vanning. One of them suggests that working in a factory or as a waitress would be preferable. Mary suddenly interrupts with the first strongly felt language in the film: "We've all tried this twelve-and-a-half-a-week stuff. It's no good. Living in furnished rooms. Walking to work. Going hungry a couple of days a week so you can have some clothes to put on your back. I've had enough of that for the rest of my life. So have you." And as for Vanning and his hoods, "I know all the angles. And I think I'm smart enough to keep one step ahead of them until I get enough to pack it all in and live on easy street the rest of my life. I know how to beat this racket." This insight into the real conditions of the women's lives is so strongly assertive that it momentarily diverts our attention from the melodrama. The dilemma is as real, and as compelling, as it was for the Helen Kelley of the trial.

In the third sequence, we are back at the Club. The women introduce themselves to the "chumps" who have come to be bilked of their money, then two of them sing songs compounded equally of cynicism and sentiment. Mary picks a man named Crawford who pays for his gambling losses with a bad check, leaves with Mary and is tailed to his hotel by Vanning's men. Mary returns to her room and is surprised by the visit of her innocent kid sister, Betty, in town for a football game. As the girls help Mary in her explanation that she is a fashion-model, the police enter with the news that Crawford has been killed and that Mary is implicated. All of the women are taken in, including Betty.

Enter David Graham (Humphrey Bogart), a jejune, dedicated prosecuting attorney who tells his chief that he thinks he can get Vanning with the aid of the women implicated in the murder. He takes Mary to his office and threatens to indict her if she does not testify against Vanning. Then, in the middle of the scene, Graham becomes pontifical and infuriates Mary:

Graham: Now, Mary, we're trying to help you.
Mary: I'm doing all right.
Graham: For how long? Until Vanning gets as much as he can out of you and then throws
          you in the ash can? Now, we're trying to put a stop to that—help people like
          you. But there's nothing we can do unless you're willing to help yourself. Now,
          why don't you give us a break?

Mary: (passionately): What kind of break have you ever given us? Outside of kicking us around every chance you get. There's only one kind of a break we want from you, and that's to leave us alone. (Voice rising) And let us make a living in our own way! Or is that asking too much? (Long pause) Anything else you want to know?

The outburst is over quickly, and the scene ends with Mary sullenly uncooperative. But we have been given another insight into the conditions and psychology of the women that diverts our attention back to the realities of the Luciano trial—and the Depression itself.

In a series of rapid scenes Vanning's lawyer Gordon (John Litel) develops a plan to ruin Graham: Mary will be told to "cooperate" but a bought witness will destroy Graham's case. When Mary is called in to see Graham again, she pretends to be terrified of Vanning, but otherwise willing to cooperate. The characterization of Graham in this scene seems intentionally self-righteous. He tells Mary, "You're not the only one in the world who was born with two strikes against them. I probably got kicked around just as much as you did. I didn't like it any better than you do. The only difference between us is that—well, I did something about it, you won't."

Pretending to be challenged by Graham, Mary agrees to testify. The emotions of the courtroom scene are largely played out in the faces of Mary and Betty. Mary allows herself to be accused of "entertaining" men after hours and grimly accepts the shame; Betty cannot look at her sister. The exchange between Graham and Mary at the end of the scene is cold: "Thanks for the ride." "So long chump, I'll be seeing you."

Back in the apartment the contained emotions of the courtroom explode. Betty is convinced that her friends will have read their story in the newspapers and that she cannot go back to school. In a scene of mercurial emotions she and Mary bicker, then collapse weeping in each other's arms: again it is the women's exploitation and despair that is forced on our attention.

In the next scene we discover Betty sitting alone in the apartment, obviously unhappy. Emmy Lou enters and invites her to a party at Vanning's where, under the spell of liquor and gaiety, Betty accepts the advances of an experienced lecher. When she returns to the apartment with a one-hundred-dollar bill, Mary knows where she has been and is furious. Betty says that she is no different from Mary, that she has the right to lead the same sort of life. Then she goes back to the party.

On a balcony, against a background of drunken high life, she is again cornered by her would-be seducer. As she struggles to escape him, Vanning comes out and strikes her for "putting on an act." Betty falls, hits her head and is killed. Emmy Lou, the only sympathetic witness, is warned to keep her mouth shut. Mary learns of Betty's disappearance from the party and confronts Vanning, with a threat to "get" him if anything has happened to Betty. She then goes to Graham—now reluctant to trust her—and says she will provide evidence against Vanning. While they talk Graham receives a report that Betty's body has been fished from the river.

Graham comes to the women's apartment and pleads with them to help him and Mary prosecute Vanning. But the women feel that the law isn't for them; besides, another gangster will take Vanning's place. Shortly after Graham leaves, defeated, Vanning enters. In the film's most powerful scene Mary accuses Vanning of Betty's death and swears she will tell the DA. Vanning calmly orders the other women into the next room, nods significantly to his strong-arm man, Charlie, and follows the women out.

It would seem that the melodrama can no longer be played out in terms of glacial confrontation. And yet it is. The camera stays in the room with Vanning and Mary's friends. First, in a long shot, we see a picture jump on the wall from the violence of the beating in the next room. As the beating continues, then is followed by a silence cut by an anguished scream, we move from one woman's face to another—each an ambiguous study in fear, rage and acceptance. Quite forcefully we are reminded that the women have no strength of their own, no recourse for help, and no choice but to accept this denigration by the men who exploit them. But it is their condition, not the cruelty of Vanning, that the visual treatment underlines.

Graham then sets out on a search for the only witness he can hope to shake, Emmy Lou. Vanning learns of Graham's search and sends his men to get her first. In a melodramatic chase scene, Emmy Lou escapes from her pursuers. In the following sequence we are in a hospital room with Mary and her three remaining friends. Mary is wrapped in bandages, her face swollen and her eyes bruised. Her friends assure her that she will be all right and that her scars can be disguised. Her reply is one of the most telling lines in the film: "I got things wrong with me that all the doctors in the world can't fix."

As Mary tells her friends that she can't pretend the beating didn't happen, Emmy Lou enters. Both she and Mary weep as they recall Betty, and Emmy Lou agrees to talk to the DA. One of the women argues against provoking Vanning: "You want to keep on living, don't you?" Mary, her voice partly muffled by her bandages, says, "If this is what you call living, I don't want any part of it. Always being afraid. . . . There must be some other way for me to live. If there isn't, I— well, I'd just as soon put a bullet in my head right now and end it." A powerful *Angst* penetrates this scene, for which the physical metaphors are Mary's battered face and listless voice. At this point Graham enters the room and is told that all of the women are ready to testify.

We are next in Vanning's jail cell. Gordon tells him he must make a deal, but Vanning says that he doesn't make deals. Then he launches into a speech that indicates to us that madness and the blindness of the gods have descended upon him—that he is now marked for destruction.

Vanning:	You think I care for money? All I care about is to make people do what I tell them.
Gordon:	You're crazy, Johnny.
Vanning:	Yes, maybe I am. Maybe I ain't. I just know one thing. I ain't gonna let no five crummy dames put the skids under me now. Get word to those dames. If they talk, sure as my name's Johnny Vanning, I'll get 'em.

In a brief scene, the women, who have been imprisoned for their own protection, look out the window and see one of Vanning's hoods staked out in the street. Then we are in the courtroom again. One by one the women take the stand and deliver damning evidence against Vanning and his men. Mary is the last, and as she recounts the details of her beating, she turns the right side of her face toward the camera. We see why she had screamed so desperately in the earlier scene: Charlie has cut an X in her cheek—Vanning's mark for those who double-cross him.

The verdict is assured, but Graham's summation and appeal to the jury remain to be heard. The speech obviously transcends its function in the trial and is directed at the audience as a kind of thinking through of all of the issues presented in the film.

You should consider not only Vanning the murderer, but also Vanning the Vice Czar, who at this very moment is exacting his staggering tribute from a supine and cowardly city. . . . Out of all the teeming millions of this great city only five girls had the courage to take their very lives in their hands and accuse Johnny Vanning. In spite of all the threats of reprisal . . . they were ready to appear before you to testify. And let me be the first to admit the truth of the accusations that were brought against these girls in a desperate effort to discredit them. Frankly they're . . . they're everything the defense has said they are. Their characters are questionable, their profession unsavory and distasteful. Oh, it's not been difficult to crucify them. But it has been difficult to crucify the truth. And that truth is that these girls in the face of sheer, stark terrorism did appear in court, expose themselves to the public gaze, told the truth about themselves, told the world what they really are. Well, then, surely you must believe that they were telling the truth when they testified that Johnny Vanning was responsible for the death of Betty Strauber.

In two short scenes the jury returns a verdict of guilty and the judge pronounces a sentence of 30 to 50 years, with the warning that if anything happens to the women the full sentence will be served. As reporters rush toward Graham, the five women rise slowly from their seats. "Well, that's that," Mary says. "Come on kids. Let's go." Then they walk unnoticed from the courtroom. As the women descend the steps, Graham appears at the door. He calls Mary back.

Graham:	You're the one who should be getting the congratulations, not me.
Mary:	Um um. I don't want them.
Graham:	But where will you go?
Mary:	Places.
Graham:	But what will you do?
Mary:	Oh, I'll get along, I always have.
Graham:	Mary, I'd like to help you.
Mary:	(curious . . . and interested): Why?
Graham:	Why . . . because I . . . because I think you've got a break comin' to you.
Mary:	(still curious): And?
Graham:	And I'd like to see that you get it.
Mary:	(suddenly dejected): What's the use of stalling? We both live in different worlds, and that's the way we've got to leave it.
Graham:	I don't want to leave it that way. I once said to you that if you ever started helping yourself I'd be the first one to go to bat for you, and that still goes. No matter what you do or where you go, we'll meet again.
Mary:	Goodbye, Graham. I'll be seeing you.

Mary descends the steps to join her friends as a melancholy blues theme swells on the sound track. As they walk into the engulfing fog, the camera picks them out in a series of close-ups. The women stare straight ahead, their faces erased of all emotion, almost of life—walking deliberately toward the fog as if they accepted it as their natural element. Behind them, in the bright doorway, there are voices: "How about a couple of pictures of our next DA?" "What do-you mean, DA? If he isn't our next governor, he ought to have his head examined."

STRUCTURE

Marked Woman is vintage Warner's *cinéma brut*—aesthetically spare, almost devoid of metaphoric effects achieved with the camera or lighting. Any veneer of meaning upon that projected by the faces and words of the actors most likely originates in our empathy for the women's conditions and the sense that these are mirrored in the barren *mise-en-scène*. Because of this aesthetic minimalism, the structural split that I have outlined in the previous summary is all the more forcefully experienced. One set of scenes develops a standard melodrama concerned with the outrages and the eventual destruction of a stereotyped villain. Another set, composed of Mary's outbursts to her friends and to Graham, her quarrels with Betty, the study of the women's faces while Mary is being beaten, Mary's thoughts of suicide, and the striking conclusion (all of them strongly affective), comprises a separate order of experience. And yet there seems to be some necessitous link between the two orders, as if one gave rise to the other or was a precondition of its existing: how else could they maintain so dialectical a relationship throughout the film?

Perhaps we can begin to understand the reasons for the split by looking closely at the scenes concerned with the real conditions of the women's lives. Each of these scenes is characterized by forceful emotion and some attempt to conceptualize the dilemmas that the women face. These attempts, as I shall show in detail later, are frustratingly confused: there is no clear analysis of their situation or the causes of their misery, but rather a muddled pointing at this, that, or maybe that— an obfuscation that paralyzes the mind. At this level the exploited have no exploiter—or, at best, a faceless one called "life" or "the way things are." The true exploiters—the capitalist system, sexism, pernicious ideologies—are vaguely immanent in some of Mary's outbursts, but recede like ghosts as quickly as they are glimpsed. The degree of emotion in these scenes seems directly related to their dead-endedness. There are no answers to the women's questions; the intense confrontation with reality leads only to a stifling semantic cul-de-sac from which they—and we—must escape. And the escape is exhilaratingly easy: we merely leap into the alternative reality of the melodrama.

This leap is typical of what are usually called "proletarian" or "socially conscious" films of the thirties and very early forties. One can specify the exact moment at which they occur in such films as *Public Enemy, Crime School, Dead End, Angels with Dirty Faces, Invisible Stripes, The Big Shot, They Drive by Night* and others. The leap is by its nature dialectical (from one order of experience to an opposite order); and we therefore encounter a series of inversions. To return to our immediate example, *Marked Woman,* we find, first of all, an inversion of emotions: from scenes of weeping, depression, and apathy we move to melodramatic scenes in which the characters project the sort of controlled affect epitomized in the terms "tough," "smart," and "smooth." Spontaneity has no place in this world; if the face breaks at all, it is into a smirk or a leer; and the expression is as calculated as a grammarian's comma. There is also an inversion of activities: from circular, frustrated behavior we move to highly motivated actions, saturated with purpose. One is out to serve one's interests, to rid society of corruption, to "get" somebody.

Obviously, all activities and emotions at this level are surrogate. And any return to the depiction of real conditions may bring this fact home to the audience and destroy the illusion, and the function, of the melodrama. In *Public Enemy, Crime School,* and similar films the depiction of real conditions is limited to the first third or half of the film. These depictions often function as explanations, and partial exonerations, for criminality. Once the melodrama asserts itself strongly, however, there is no break while it runs its course.

But it is precisely this clear function of the melodrama that is lacking in *Marked Woman.* Not only do the real conditions assert themselves in scenes throughout the film, they dominate the crucial final scene. The dialectic comes close to being a contradiction as we realize that the expected denouement of the melodrama has been frustrated. There is also, as a close viewing of the film would demonstrate, occasional penetration of the attitudes typical of the real conditions into the melodrama—alienation, apathy, and confusion. As I will show in the next section, the whole ethos of the melodrama is affected—the women are not altering their conditions, and the destruction of Vanning does not accomplish anything.

Certainly the massive dose of reality infused into the film by its topical sources could be responsible for these effects. But there are other and more proximate causes. Through analysis of passages in which the ethos is developed we can perhaps come closer to them.

ETHOS

Since every ethos presents itself as a unified body of polarized conceptions we need for our analysis a methodology attuned to polarity. The form of structural analysis developed by Lévi-Strauss, although idealist and limited in vision, can help us here. Two of Lévi-Strauss's insights are specially provocative: that a dilemma (or contradiction) stands at the heart of every living myth, and that this dilemma is expressed through layered pairs of opposites which are transformations of a primary pair. The impulse to construct the myth arises from the desire to resolve the dilemma; but the impossibility of resolving it leads to a crystal-like growth of the myth through which the dilemma is repeated, or conceived in new terms, or inverted—in short, subjected to intellectual operations that might resolve it or attenuate its force. We can best locate the important ethical dilemmas in *Marked Woman* by close inspection of individual scenes.

In preparation for what follows, an extensive structural analysis of *Marked Woman* was made, the recounting of which would demand more interest and patience than I can presume in a general audience. The method, however, is illustrated here. My selection of only a few passages for analysis is motivated by an additional consideration: the fact that *Marked Woman,* like most works of popular art, relies upon a few dilemmas and a limited number of transformations of them. It is initially difficult to grasp the relationships between transformations and to find one's way to the crucial dilemmas. Only concrete examples will illustrate what I mean. Let us begin with a very simple but typical transformational set found in a song sung by one of the women in an early nightclub scene (the two songs in the film, by Harry Warren and Al Dubin, seem expressly written to reflect the women's attitudes, or chosen because of their content).

> City people pity people
> Who don't know a lot
> About the night life,
> But they are wrong.
> Though they may be witty people,
> They don't know that folks
> Who lead the right life
> Still get along.
>
> To a plain old fashioned couple
> Let me dedicate my song.
>
> They're not sophisticated people,
> And though they're only common folk,
> You don't know how I envy people
> Like Mr. and Mrs. Doe.
>
> They don't know much about swing music,
> They wouldn't care for risqué jokes,
> But every morning birds sing music
> For Mr. and Mrs. Doe.

The lyric continues, developing variations on the basic oppositions found in these stanzas, so that we wind up with the following essential pairs (in the following analysis a colon means "is opposed to" and brackets indicate an implied term):

> witty people : people who lead the right life
> [modern people] : old fashioned people
> sophisticated people : common people
> swing music, risqué jokes : the music of birds
> wreath of holly : garden
> [nightclub life] : home life

All of these are rather obviously transformations of a simple, more basic pair, city life: small town life (with agrarian overtones). This opposition is amplified in the film through the use of many codes of dress, speech and taste. Working-class apartment decor clashes with penthouse decor, Mary's plain dresses with her silver lamé hostess gown, Emmy Lou's curled blond hair with Betty's plain brunette, Graham's law-school English with Mary's terse vernacular. The city: small town opposition, which has a long history in the Hollywood film, turns up frequently, and somewhat unexpectedly, in many gangster films. For instance, it utterly polarizes such films as *The Roaring Twenties, King of the Underworld, High Sierra,* and *It All Came True;* and it has crucial functions in *Little Caesar, The Big Shot, Public Enemy* and others. We can return to this opposition later; for the moment I merely want to define the primary opposition that the song transforms into many pairs. As we look over these oppositions we note that all of them are simple transformations, with one striking exception—the opposition "witty people": "people that lead the right life." We can reduce this to the crucial terms "witty" and "right." The opposition is at first sight illogical. "Witty" demands as its antonym a term that implies witlessness: the common adjective "dumb" (dumb cop, dumb blonde) is perhaps the proper one. "Right," of course, demands "wrong." As we read the opposition, then, we take "witty" as a metonym for "wrong" and "right" as a metonym for "dumb." Because the opposition demands interpretation, it is the most foregrounded and active in the song; and because of its doubled metonymic character it comes across as a pair of dilemmas: why, we ask, is wittiness wrong? Why is dumbness right? These simple dilemmas are, by context of the song, related to the primary opposition of city life and small town life. Before analyzing this relation let us note the appearance of these dilemmas in other parts of the film.

Mary Dwight's first outburst directed at Vanning contains these lines directed both at Vanning and at her conditions: "I know all the angles. And I think I'm smart enough to keep one step ahead of them until I get enough to pack it all in and live on easy street the rest of my life. . . . I know how to beat this racket." Mary's concerns, seen in the larger context of American puritanism, are self-centered and hedonistic, and therefore "wrong." If we miss the point here, we cannot miss it in Graham's remarks to Mary just before they receive news of Betty's death (a kind of moral punishment for Mary): "You know what's right and you know what's wrong. You know better but you just won't do anything about it. You choose to think that you can get through the world by outsmarting it. Well, I've learned that those kind of people generally end up by outsmarting themselves." And, finally, there is an almost syllogistic example in the argument between Mary and Betty:

Betty: If I can't live one way I can live another. Why not? I'm young and pretty and . . .
Mary: And dumb!
Betty: But you're smart! You can teach me the rest.

There are other examples which show the dilemma bound up in the use or disuse of one's wits. But how is it related to the regional opposition represented by city: small town? More specifically, is either opposition seminal for the other and therefore the "crucial" dilemma we are seeking? We should first recall some key references: Mary and Betty came from a small town; Betty feared returning because of a scandal; and the women in the Luciano trial were threatened with exposure in their home-town newspapers. Mary's wrong use of her wits should probably be seen, then, as a city-oriented trait, something she has learned through contact with men like Vanning. But there is something recessive about the city: small town opposition, and it seems more in keeping with the emphasis in the film to see the right: wrong opposition as seminal. If we did, we would arrive at a familiar characterization of the film: we would see it as a kind of exemplum or moral fable. And yet such a definition would have to ignore the scenes that seem most striking—those in which the women are depicted as disconsolate, angry or apathetic. These are not morally toned attitudes as are those of hedonistic ambition and egotism. If there were a primary pair to which all the oppositions we have so far mentioned were related, as well as the opposition between real conditions and melodrama, one would feel that the analysis was more true to the whole film and that it respected the complex interaction between ideas and emotions that the film maintains.

For a fresh start, let us look at a quite different set of oppositions, one found in a song sung immediately before the one already analyzed:

> Ain't it funny that paper money
> Don't seem like genuine jack?
> And every check has the knack
> Of jumpin' and bumpin' and bouncin' back?
> I like nothin' but silver dollars
> And I've collected a few.
> When silver starts in ringin',
> It rings so true.
>
> My silver dollar man,
> He ain't a tie-and-collar man.
> A rough and ready man,
> But he's a mighty steady man.
> And though he can't supply
> A lot of luxuries that I demand,
> He never leaves me till he leaves
> A bit of silver in my hand. . . .

Obviously the major function of the song is to valorize the poor: the poor man is the true man; she would love him even if he had no money (his poverty and his class valorize him). But there is more at work in the song. The principal oppositions are:

> rough and ready man : tie-and-collar man
> silver dollars : paper money
> [sufficiency] : luxury

Class consciousness (and class prejudice) figures strongly in this complex, however tritely conceived. And we are suddenly made aware of the absence of class oppositions of this sort in the song previously cited, and in the film as a whole. Prostitutes, the song reminds us, follow their trade, like the Helen Kelley of the trial, "to solve an economic problem." Only Mary's early allusions to making "twelve and a half a week" and going hungry two days out of seven strikes at the heart of her dilemma—and the force of this passage is vitiated by the immediate characterization of Mary as greedy for "easy street" luxuries to be won by the (wrong) use of her wits. Or at least it apparently is, since our attention is shifted to the ethical (and implicit regional) dilemmas defined earlier. This movement from incipient class or economic protest to ethical dilemma can be found elsewhere, and in crucial scenes: in Mary's encounters with Graham in his office, in Graham's visit to the apartment, in the hospital scene, and in the obtuse summary for the prosecution. But all of this only compounds our problem: what do we have here—merely obfuscation as the result of censorship, or another form of transformation?

Deduction has probably taken us as far as it can, so let us proceed inductively. If we posited that the roots of *Marked Woman* are in class opposition and that its ethos is the product of "displacement" as Freud defines this term (the substitution of an acceptable object of love, hate, etc., for a forbidden one), we would be able to see the relation between class opposition and ethical dilemma as both the product of censorship and as transformational. The irresolvability of crucial dilemmas in myths leads to their transformation into other dilemmas. The intent is to resolve the dilemma at another level, or to somehow attenuate its force. If class opposition is regarded as seminal, its displacement into ethical, regional and other oppositions can be seen as both the result of conscious censorship and a myth-like transposition of the conflict into new terms. The latter is an unconscious or less conscious procedure whereby the *force* of the opposition is diminished while its form and some of its substance are retained.

The effect in the film is for the ethical and regional dilemmas to function as displaced, and partly defused, class oppositions. They can still *feel* like class oppositions and be treated as such by the writers and director; the city with its penthouses and limousines can function as reified capitalism; wittiness can be allied to the manipulations of financiers; all of this can be given high resolution by the use of visual coding—skyscrapers, tuxedos, one-hundred-dollar bills; but every thrust of class or economic protest is sufficiently blunted to avoid breaking the skin.

But all of the relations I have examined need a more exact formulation, one that must include a major figure that I have so far only mentioned—the gangster. As the autarch of the universe the women inhabit, his class affiliations, his goals and his psychology need close examination.

THE GANGSTER

Unquestionably *Marked Woman*, like many films of its genre, transmits a sense of compassion for the poor and the exploited. But at the level of real conditions we cannot tell why the poor are poor nor who their exploiters are. Instead of real opposition and conflict we encounter substitute formations—principally dialectical movements between such feeling states as anger and apathy or despair and sentimentalism. Sentimentalism seems to function as the most retrograde of the many possible states. As a tendency toward passive compassion, toward meditative solipsism, it contains nothing insurrectionary, no components of hostility or criticism. It cannot be a coincidence that so many proletarian films head unerringly toward sentiment in their final reels. When, in *The Roaring Twenties,* Eddie (James Cagney) lies dying on the steps of a church while "Melancholy Baby" is heard on the sound track and his motherly friend Panama weeps over him, a lumpen *pietà* mitigates whatever social criticism the film has made.

Opposition is only fully manifested when we make the leap into melodrama. This leap is subjectively fulfilling and clarifying: the exploited now have an exploiter in the gangster—a figure subjected to an almost cosmic overdetermination. If displacement is the principal Freudian mechanism at work in the ethos, it is largely condensation that produces the gangster. Condensation, to give it its simplest definition, is a process whereby a number of discrete traits or ideas are fused in a single symbol. Each component is usually an abbreviated reference to something larger than itself, a sort of metonym that must be interpreted properly if we are to understand its discrete significance as well as its relation to other components in the symbol. By 1937 the figure of the gangster had acquired a remarkable symbolic richness. Every personal mannerism and every artifact of his world resonated with meaning. And he had also become a *vade mecum* for anyone in search of a scapegoat. The judge, in his presentence speech to Johnny Vanning, pronounces him "a low and brutal character, an unprincipled and aggressive egotist." Vanning is guilty of "every vicious and reprehensible crime."

Such attempts to blame the gangster for all important civic ills were, of course, abetted by the tabloid exposés of criminals like Luciano. But it would be shortsighted, and ultimately confusing, to look to real criminals for the prototypes of Johnny Vanning. We must start with the gangsters found in the films themselves and note their most common traits. Although the discussion will initially take us afield, it should lead us to a more exact understanding of Vanning, his relation to the women he exploits, and his function in the structure I have outlined. In a film made up of many specificities, he is the most generalized, and traditional, object.

We must distinguish, first of all, between two almost antithetical images of the gangster. The first obtained between 1927 and 1931 and was projected by such actors as John Gilbert, Conrad Nagel, Walter Huston, William Boyd, Lowell Sherman, Richard Dix and Monte Blue. The type is basically Anglo-Saxon, aristocratic, polished in speech and bearing, and dressed in the formal clothing of the wealthy (often white tie and tails or morning suits). The same actors could, and did, readily play the roles of aristocrats and pillars of the community. Walter Huston, for instance, appeared as a bank president in *American Madness* (1932) and as the President of the United States in *Gabriel Over the White House* (1933).

The class image of this species of gangster was frequently commented on by reviewers. Speaking of John Gilbert in *Four Walls* (1928) the *New York Times* reviewer said, "Mr. Horowitz is so careful regarding the cut of his clothes, the selection of his necktie, the spotlessness of his linen and the combing of his hair that one could never imagine him as a killer living on Manhattan's east side, but rather a broker with an apartment on Park Avenue."[8] And of Monte Blue in *Skin Deep* (1929), "The gangster chief is always to be seen attired in excellent taste. . . . Curiously enough, the master mind's henchmen are usually the lowest underworld types, presenting a ludicrous contrast."[9] Curious indeed, but not inexplicable. So much did the gangster resemble a blue-blood financier that he needed crude, proletarian sidekicks to make his criminality manifest.

The physical image, demeanor and speech were most important, but, in addition, the early gangster was often an explicit capitalist in his methods. Huston, in *The Ruling Class* (1931), headed what he called a "board of directors" who received checks according to what they had accomplished. And this whole group of gangsters frequently dealt in "gilt-edged securities," diversified their interests, and invested in businesses. Their principal occupation, of course, was bootlegging, an activity that required organization, the careful division of "territories," and legal and political manipulation.

Class conflict and implicit criticism of the world of business and finance are unmistakable in these films, lying so near the surface that they frequently shoulder their way free. It is interesting that films of this era dealing directly with capitalists and "millionaires," of which there were a great many, took the uncontroversial form of love romances, fantasies (inheriting a fortune) or comedies. The mask of the gangster film, fragile as it was, seems to have provided the right degree of displacement needed at this time for class criticism.

While this first generation of gangsters still dominated the screen, the second had made its appearance in the person of George Bancroft, the star of *Underworld* (1927), *Tenderloin* (1928), *Thunderbolt* (1929), and *The Mighty* (1929). Bancroft's lower-class origins were egregiously conveyed by his simpleton grin, his oversize hands and nose, his rough vitality and illiteracy. He is the most important progenitor of the type elaborated by Cagney, Robinson, Gable, Raft (in his early films), Carillo, Muni, McLaglen, and Eduardo Cianelli (Vanning). The shift in type must be the result of many forces. Before the stock-market crash the aristocratic gangster may have absorbed some of the resentment normally directed at the wealthy; but public attitudes were suddenly less mild; they were, indeed, sour and embittered. Instinct and a sense of the audience's mood must have played their parts, along with the rise of proletarian sympathies, the clamor against glorifying the criminal, "Latinizing" as a method of rendering the criminal comic (Raft, Carillo) or of making him an acceptable scapegoat (Cianelli), and other factors.

The end result, however, was to invert the class image in terms of physical appearance and life-style and to bring the forces of displacement and condensation into full, compensatory action. In general, the gangster retains his taste for formal dress, silk scarves and spats, but he usually looks *arriviste* or anthropoidal when wearing them. His capitalist affinities are more covertly projected by his language, his philosophy and his methods.

The advent of sound, of course, makes displacement into language possible and somewhat lessens the need for forceful visual coding. The gangster's speech, however, is not simply a substitute code—it is a partial disguise. The accent and vocabulary tell us that he is lower-class, and yet a lexicon of business terms surrounds him like an afflatus: "I got a *job* for you," "I *own* city hall," "This is a *business*," "Let's give him the *business*," "The *business* end of a gun." When, in *The Roaring Twenties,* a young lawyer tells Cagney, "This isn't my kind of law. I started out to be a corporation lawyer," Cagney, who has invested his bootlegging profits in a fleet of 2,000 cabs, says, "This is a corporation. We're making money." In the opening scene of *Marked Woman* Vanning strolls about the Club Intime giving orders in his broken Italianate English that demonstrate his organizational astuteness even as they reveal his illiteracy. But there is no need to elaborate this all too familiar element. What is important is its function as one trait in the condensed figure of the gangster.

Equally active are the conceptions that the gangster is egotistic, ruthlessly acquisitive, and ambitious to control or torment other people. The formation is, of course, the classic Freudian anal-sadistic. These two traits, when they appear in adults, are usually fused. It is important, therefore, to note that they are frequently presented as separate poles of the gangster's character, between which a contradiction may arise. A clear statement of the contradiction is Vanning's "You think I care for money? All I care about is to make people do what I tell them." The formulation is at least as old as *Little Caesar:* "Yeh, money's all right, but it ain't everything. Naaa, *be* somebody. Look hard at a buncha guys and know that they'll do anything ya tell 'em. Have your own way or nothin'. *Be* somebody!"

The anal-sadistic formation is, of course, appropriate to the real capitalist character, but the emphasis upon sadism to the exclusion of acquisitiveness has an obscuring effect upon the gangster's identity, since it tells us that the formal clothes, limousines and penthouses are not his goals in life. Capitalists, in popular mythology, may be predominantly interested in controlling people, too, but they are always interested in wealth, and their sadism is not self-destructive or insane. Their cruelty reflects their alienation and loneliness—they are men who can possess Xanadu but not Rosebud. This pernicious conception, designed to placate the dispossessed, is also latent in those scenes in which the gangster finds himself alone; but it is not central. The sadism of the gangster functions more as a device than a trait: when it asserts itself we know that he is marked for destruction and that the melodrama will shortly complete its course.

Robert Warshow's well-known analysis of the tragic arc of the gangster's life is germane here.[10] The definition is, however, almost exclusively formal and generic; although it accounts well for the gangster's function in the melodrama, it misses an important function of the melodrama itself. The class criticism displaced upon the gangster's methods, tastes and acquisitiveness is obscured by his transformation into a sadistic villain who deserves his death solely for his cruelty. His exploitative methods, unlike those of the wealthy, are ultimately crude and palpable, and he can be brought to the bar of justice or shot like a mad dog without guilt.

Clearly, many more forces impinge upon the portrait of a gangster like Vanning than upon his aristocratic predecessors. The total effect is to almost obscure his significance behind a semantic welter, making him both exploiter and one of the exploited, indeterminate in class, after money but contemptuous of it, deserving of his death but somehow pitiable. His most important function, however, is to be the exploiter, to cause civic corruption, and to create the existential hell that Mary Dwight and her friends awaken to every morning. Vanning's penthouse is the reified suffering of his enslaved "girls," and his white silk scarf is the badge of his class. But lest we smell out his precise identity, we are faced with his illiteracy, his disinterest in money, and his madness. The Charles Foster Kanes of Hollywood have their flaws, but they die in beds reeking of mystified capital, reverentially pitied by those they have exploited, awesome to the end. Only obfuscated capitalists like Vanning are sent to prison—or die, like Little Caesar, in the litter behind a billboard.

CONCLUSION

Throughout the analysis I have attempted to stick to the task of applied criticism. I have deliberately slighted discussions of methodology because the prospect of validating the several methods I employ and then pushing all of that abstract lumber ahead of me through so lengthy an analysis was, frankly, overwhelming (it would also make a monograph of what was intended to be an article). I trusted, I hope correctly, that the many methodological articles now appearing in film magazines would provide a rear-projection against which my analysis would seem to move. My essential ingredients are Marxist, Freudian, and structuralist; but I would argue that the mixture is not heretically eclectic: structures and their permutations are central to each form of analysis, making them complementary and intrinsically suited to the task of illuminating a work rooted in class conflict. The idealist tendency of structuralism does not, I believe, invalidate it for a specific role in an ongoing materialist criticism: the description of transformational operations. The *substance, causes,* and *significance* of these operations must, of course, be sought for in the material realms of history and psychology— and I have, at least, begun this search.

But I have not yet sorted out the relations between the levels of opposition that were defined in the discussion of the ethos. The analysis of the figure of the gangster serves, I believe, to support the contention that *Marked Woman* is rooted in class conflict. It would be absurd to argue that this insight exhausts the film; but it does satisfy the requirement for an *optimal* criticism: one that illuminates the aesthetics, form and content of a work, as well as its relation to its era and to its creators. Class opposition, as we have seen, is displaced into a number of surrogate conflicts, most of which obtain at the level of the melodrama where the exploited face an unequivocal exploiter. Ethical dilemmas appear first. The intensity with which they are expressed seems proportionate to the intensity of the real-life dilemmas they displace; and their muddled logic reflects, in part, a struggle between desires to articulate and to repress class conflicts. As we move up the chain of displacement to the regional oppositions, class conflict is more covertly represented; as a result, there is less need for obfuscations and the oppositions are clearly and richly developed through the use of many codes. There are, in addition, tonal overlays (toughness, sentimentality), which cover the film like a skin, masking the real and substitute conflicts alike, and enticing the audience into solipsism and false emotion.

Marked Woman was produced toward the end of a rather bone-weary tradition. It is often mindlessly trite and perfunctory. But its makers had read their way through a depressing court record of real exploitation and suffering, and they approached the task of making the film somewhat as adversaries. If, limited by ability, temperament, and studio realities, they could only produce another melodrama, they could at least deny it a full life. By centering their attention upon the women, they mitigated some of the worst effects of the melodramatic form—and most certainly lessened their personal sense of venality.

As the women descend from the courthouse steps we know that they face a world without Vanning, but one in which they will still be exploited. If their exploitation is not analyzed, it is at least acknowledged and located in the real world. And yet—and yet—the melancholy blues theme rises on the sound track. Sentimentalism beckons: after all they are only women and their lot is suffering. Suddenly everything that has been gained seems perilously compromised. But against the music the camera pits the faces of the women. Bette Davis and the other actresses, who must have understood it all better than the men they worked for, cut through the swelling mystification with tough, implacable expressions. Let the Warner's music weep; the women are as alienated as the street, and they will not be sentimentalized.

Notes

1. Readers familiar with Althusser's "The 'Piccolo Teatro': Bertolazzi and Brecht" reprinted in *For Marx,* trans. Ben Brewster (New York: Random House, 1969) will recognize both my indebtedness to this essay and the many ways in which I deviate from it. I have also benefited from Karyn Kay's study of *Marked Woman,* "Sisters of the Night," *The Velvet Light Trap,* Fall 1972, pp. 20–25.

2. *The New York Times,* May 26, 1936, p. 2. I follow the *Times* account throughout because of its immediacy. There are more elaborate reports in Hickman Powell, *Ninety Times Guilty* (New York: Harcourt, Brace and Co., 1939), and in issues of *Liberty* magazine published soon after the trial. Warner's acquired the rights to the *Liberty* material (which was based on interviews with only two informants, "Cokey Flo" Brown and Mildred Harris) and used it as the ostensible basis for the film.

3. *Ibid.,* p. 2.

4. *Ibid.,* p. 2.

5. *Ibid.,* May 21, p. 4.

6. *Ibid.,* June 8, p. 8.

7. *Ibid.,* June 13, p. 6.

8. *The New York Times Film Reviews,* I (New York Times and Arno Press: New York, 1970), p. 465.

9. *Ibid.,* p. 558.

10. "The Gangster as Hero" in *The Immediate Experience* (New York: Doubleday and Co., 1962), pp. 127–33.

Addendum: Shall We Deport Lévi-Strauss?

In a recent article, "The English Cine-Structuralists" (*Film Comment,* May–June 1973), I reviewed the work of a group of English critics whom I designated "auteur-structuralists," faulting some of them for what I considered an improper and unproductive application of the structural method of Lévi-Strauss to the study of directors. I also described Lévi-Strauss's method and discussed its application to other areas of film study (really my principal interest). My article was intended to be an informative survey of what had been done and a suggestive prolegomenon to what might be attempted. The article has now received attacks (considerate, but damaging) from Geoffrey Nowell-Smith and Brian Henderson, both of whom point up what can only be called the assiduous naiveté of portions of my article.[1] Perhaps I shouldn't bother to respond, but I fear that if I don't, my article will continue to stand in opposition to their criticisms; and I would like to rise in my pew and acknowledge this Rosemary's Baby—after all, acceptance brought Mia Farrow some measure of peace.

My article was written at a moment when I was only half-emerged from a fetishistic attachment to Lévi-Strauss's method. My infatuation had no grounds in theory; it was merely idolatry, deriving from a long-standing interest in myth and ritual and my sense that Lévi-Strauss had provided the logico-mathematical tools by which they were henceforth and forever to be comprehended. Films were like myths, I reasoned, since they were communal in origin (Hollywood, or a given studio, could constitute a community—why not?); and directors might function as creators of myths (I adduced Renoir and others on the subject of the artist as myth-maker). But soon after the article was sent off I encountered Marvin Harris's destructive exposé of Lévi-Strauss's idealist premises in his *The Rise of Anthropological Theory.* Harris, a Marxist anthropologist, meets Lévi-Strauss on his own grounds and demonstrates that his almost exclusive concern with mental structures arose from his early grounding of kinship structure in the theory of reciprocal gift-giving. Lévi-Strauss reasoned that men exchange gifts (the most important being women) because of a universal psychological need arising from "certain fundamental structures of the human mind." But, Harris asks, Candide-like, "if reciprocity is so fundamental to the human psyche, why do we have the ancient and contemporary condition of the opulent and powerful haves (possessing, among their valuables, more than their share of women) and the miserable have-nots?" In general, Harris argues, "Lévi-Strauss's picture of the human psychological landscape is . . . noteworthy for its disregard for the biopsychological, emotional, and affective drives and instincts. Hunger, sex, fear, love, are present, but they seem to be peripheral. More important for the French structuralist program is the basic propensity of the human mind to build logical categories by means of binary contrasts. For Lévi-Strauss such oppositions or dualities lie at the bottom of large portions if not the totality of sociocultural phenomena."[2] Harris's entire discussion, which surveys the history of idealism in French anthropology, should disabuse anyone of Lévi-Straussian hero-worship.

I still felt, however, that my article had value as a survey of a group of English auteur critics united by their use of structural method. But my unambitious history-of-ideas approach (Nowell-Smith begat Wollen begat Lovell) turns out to be inadequate because it is, as Nowell-Smith patiently demonstrates, "empiricist idealist"; because I was ignorant as to *why* this group of critics was attracted to structural method; and because my provincial Indiana situation led me to presume that English critics contacted each other's ideas (as I do) by reading criticism. But, Nowell-Smith informs us (in a passage as full of surprises as a piñata), the critics concerned were not attracted to structuralism because they wanted to import Lévi-Strauss into film study, but rather because they were seeking in the notion of structuralism "a materialist (or if you prefer objective) basis for the concept of authorship" redefined "as to take account both of the specifics of film production, which seem at first sight to deny the concept of the author/artist entirely, and of the equally specific authorial presence in the movie text." Equally surprising is Nowell-Smith's statement that some of the critics actually knew and talked to each other, apparently meeting at a sort of bar and grill called "London W.1." This is enough to send historians of ideas begging in the streets. And it has, of course, the deeper implications that a history of ideas is a helpless and false endeavor in the face of so diffuse a critical development. I only hope that my blind assumption that Lévi-Strauss was the "source" of their structuralist interests (which I based on Wollen's allusion) will stand corrected: it has already influenced Brian Henderson and exposed him to the same criticism I received. So, once and for all, there is no formal history of auteur-structuralism; and Nowell-Smith, Wollen, *et al.* were not attempting to employ Lévi-Strauss's method or to meet his standards.

This leaves standing the question of whether they should have been more demanding if they intended their structural analysis to be productive as well as corrective. I would still contend that the *Mythologiques* sets a standard for intelligence, subtlety, and conformity to its critical object (within its limited apprehension of its object) that bears comparison with the best of Barthes and Metz. It is because Lovell rather dabbles in structural analysis, for instance, that he is so exposed to Murray's disparagement of structuralist results.

But I may seem to be dragging Lévi-Strauss back through the transom after dismissing him through the door. Actually I am only attempting to bridge my way to the larger question of whether Lévi-Strauss's method has any future in film criticism. Brian Henderson masses a body of critics against structuralism itself in a long passage that cannot be easily summarized. I now substantially agree with what he says, having been educated by Harris and Julia Kristeva in particular,[3] but I would like to add my penny's worth on the kind of structuralism in which I am notoriously expert—Lévi-Strauss's.

The most fundamental question that one should ask, perhaps, is "Are films Lévi-Straussian myths?" I think that Harris has indirectly answered this. The idea that any social group, even a tightly knit production team, could constitute a single entity bent upon "thinking" through a social dilemma, or projecting its universal mental structures into a film, or however one wants to put it, is a patent denial of the way men truly think, relate, and create. The gain to the critic of this idealist gambit is very real: it severs films from their existential roots, obviates the need for an abundance of facts, and makes the refining of concepts both easy and seemingly important.

A less simple issue is the status of Lévi-Straussian "dilemmas" of the sort that I isolated and discussed in my recent article on *Marked Woman* (*Film Quarterly*, Winter 1973–74). In the conclusion I stated that "The idealist tendency of structuralism does not, I believe, invalidate it for a specific role in an ongoing materialist criticism: the description of transformational operations." I was forced into this pragmatism by an awareness of a methodological split that had developed in the process of writing the article. Beginning with an idealist structural analysis of *Marked Woman* I found that the transformations I was dealing with could only be *comprehended* through the Freudian operation of displacement, and *accounted for* by a recourse to the Marxist notion of class conflict and its censorship in ideology. Since both Freud and Marx are structuralist in the broadest sense of the term (they deal in polarities and their structured relationships), I reasoned that I was merely being eclectic in wedding them to Lévi-Strauss. Specifically, I argued that such shifts as that from class conflict to ethical dilemma could be described as both transformational *and* the results of repression or censorship. I thought of these operations as occurring in the minds of the writers and director (and, for what they add in interpretation, the actors) with the censoring influences of the studio and class ideology ranked behind them. But clearly these operations cannot be idealist and materialist at the same time: minds cannot operate simultaneously divorced from their own history and psychology and engaged in them. Lévi-Strauss's description of the mental act whereby one attempts to resolve a dilemma by "transforming" it into another dilemma connotes a pure mental activity—the activity of what Husserl calls a "transcendental ego" exalted above, severed from, the contingencies of psychology, biology, and society (except in so far as one is *thinking* about a *social* dilemma).[4] The transformations I described, if the term is to retain its Lévi-Straussian connotations, are no such things. They *are* displacements produced by censoring influences. They occur because of complex personal and socially responsive acts of inhibition, assertion, obfuscation, and so forth. This amounts to more than a confession of methodological incest, however. It also, as Brian Henderson makes clear, argues a different theory for what a film text is, since it views it as a product rather than a "found object" analogous to a Lévi-Straussian myth.

All of this does not lead me to repudiate the insights of *Marked Woman:* one of them, that ethical dilemmas displace class conflicts, is, I discover, an independent corroboration of the *Cahiers* contention in its analysis of *Young Mr. Lincoln* that morality represses politics. But if one is to do more than penetrate the deeply symptomatic surface of *Marked Woman,* one must know more—all that there is to know—about the film's several creators, their working conditions and social situations.

Henderson ends by citing the *Cahiers* analysis as probably the best thing going in terms of an exemplary combination of film theory and analytic method. Adopting it, or a close variant of it, means that we will not only have to forego the welfare-state comforts of idealist analysis, but also perhaps the more recently purchased luxuries of structures, codes, sign-systems, Nowell-Smith's authorial "structure in dominance," and the rest, and chart a retrograde course back into the dense, existential humus in which films, like all cultural events, reside. It's a little like coming out of a theater and discovering that the messy, contingent world is still there.

But whether or not one adopts *Cahiers'* specific proto-type—which is, of course, a custom job for *Young Mr. Lincoln* and will have to be modified for every use—film study is becoming increasingly demanding, just in terms of the organization of one's work, since everything needs to be pursued at once, presented at once, theoretically validated as it is presented, and subjected to scrutiny in terms of one's motivations for establishing categories and arriving at solutions (which, in turn, in the interest of truth, must be converted into problems of a new order). But maybe this is where film study is, since we are increasingly intolerant of self-serving narrowings of the field of inquiry ("I want to write about Delbert Mann") and expedient defenses for methods of study which "get results." In a sense this is less a choice between critical monism and holism than it is a growing conviction that monism won't work—a demand for a "totalizing" criticism, to use Frederic Jameson's term,[5] which has arisen with the disintegration of the whole formalist-idealist endeavor. At any rate, as my experience—and that of Graham Petrie at the hands of John Hess in the last issue of *Film Quarterly*—demonstrates, there is a stiff, cold wind blowing against partial, outmoded, or theoretically unsound forms of film criticism—and it just might blow many of them away.

Notes

1. Nowell-Smith, "I Was a Star-Struck Structuralist," *Screen* 14, no. 3 (Autumn 1973): 92–99; Henderson, "Critique of Cine-Structuralism I and II," *Film Quarterly* 17, no. 1 (Autumn 1973): 25–34; 17, no. 2 (Winter 1973–1974): 37–46.

2. Harris, *Rise* (New York, 1968), pp. 492–93.

3. Kristeva, "The System and the Speaking Subject," *Times Literary Supplement* (October 12, 1973), pp. 1249–50.

4. I am indebted here to Kristeva, *ibid.*

5. One should read the entirety of the final chapter of Jameson's *Marxism and Form* (Princeton, 1971), pp. 306–416.

THE SEARCHERS: AN AMERICAN DILEMMA

BRIAN HENDERSON

A quest to rescue someone who does not want to be rescued—that paradoxical mission links The Searchers *to a number of important recent films, as Brian Henderson indicates in this article. What accounts for the power of the original film and others indebted to it? Henderson's answer emphasizes the relations set up among the entire cast of characters and pays considerable attention to the seemingly secondary figure of Martin Pawley (Jeffrey Hunter), Ethan Edwards's (John Wayne's) fellow searcher. By analyzing the structural workings of the narrative, Henderson concludes that Martin figures as the Indian who has successfully entered the melting pot of an all-white society, in contrast to the "savage" Scar and the abducted Debbie, who becomes integrated into Indian culture. But, he argues, the implicit tensions take hold only when we see them as a displacement of the more topical, and pressing, tensions of racial conflict between blacks and whites in fifties America.*

Henderson seeks to adapt some of the critical strategies of Lévi-Strauss as mediated by Cahiers du Cinéma's *reading of* Young Mr. Lincoln *and Charles Eckert's reading of* Marked Woman. *As such, his article helps to demonstrate the methodological fruitfulness of structural analysis that regards individual films as similar to myth. Much of the more psychoanalytically oriented criticism treats the film text like a patient, reading symptoms of individual neurosis that may have social overtones. The approach pursued here places the text in the arena of collective discourse and ideology. If a question remains, it has to do with Henderson's assumption that the power of the film lies beyond the reach of author-oriented critics because it is tied to a level of deep structure involving black-white racial conflict. (See Peter Lehman's article on* The Searchers, *"Looking at Luke's Missing Reverse Shot,"* Wide Angle *4, no. 4 [1981]: 65-70, for an indication of how an auteur critic can come to surprisingly similar conclusions, and Peter Biskind's book,* Seeing Is Believing *[New York: Pantheon, 1983], for thematic readings of westerns and other genres that translate their tensions into contemporary issues of racism, juvenile delinquency, and anti-Communism.)*

Another question involves the uses to which Henderson puts Freud's processes of dreamwork. Henderson uses Freud's displacement concept to show how one form of racial conflict masks another. This departs somewhat from Eckert's use of displacement to show how class, economic conflict is shifted to individual, moral conflict. Displacement moves us to another order of problem, from economic to moral, instead of to another version of the same problem. The difference in usage suggests a kinship between Henderson's approach and allegorical readings that is much weaker in Eckert's case. It may also be that the power of The Searchers *lies more in the intricacy of the pattern of relationships among characters than it does in any particular interpretation of that pattern. Art, like dreams, can be said to be about relations, not about things, about the complex texture of certain patterns of interaction, not about our labels for those patterns. From this perspective, Henderson may place too much emphasis on uncovering the "real" nature of the ostensible conflict. He may downplay the intricacy with which a form of hierarchical, inside-outside conflict involving a valued object in need of rescue works itself out. Certainly, much more could be said about family in this film and its function as Ideal Law (following the* Cahiers *reading of* Young Mr. Lincoln*) or about the discovery that the object of heroic rescue efforts does not want to be saved, in which* The Searchers *differs significantly from such descendants as* Close Encounters of the Third Kind *and* Star Wars. *Even so, Henderson offers a lucid analysis of a complex film. So clear and comprehensible an argument can only help to define this particular method of structural inquiry and its alternatives.*

●

Dedicated to the memory of
James Blue, 1930–1980

In a 1979 article, Stuart Byron surveys the influence of John Ford's film *The Searchers* (1956) on several young directors and screenwriters.[1] "In one way or another," he concludes, "the film relates to Paul Schrader, John Milius, Martin Scorsese, Steven Spielberg, George Lucas, and Michael Cimino; to *Hardcore, Taxi Driver, Close Encounters of the Third Kind, Dillinger, Mean Streets, Big Wednesday, The Deer Hunter, The Wind and the Lion, Ulzana's Raid,* and *Star Wars* . . . When one film obsesses so much talent, it won't do just to call it a cult movie. *The Searchers* is the Super-Cult movie of the New Hollywood."

The film-makers Byron discusses do not hesitate to confirm his argument. Milius: "The best American movie—and its protagonist, Ethan Edwards, is the one classic character in films. I've named my own son Ethan after him. I've seen it 60 times." Schrader: "I make sure I see *The Searchers* at least once a year. God knows that there are movies that are better acted or better written, but *The Searchers* plays the fullest artistic hand." "Scorsese and I agree that *The Searchers* is the best American film, a fact that must have influenced *Taxi Driver.*" Scorsese: "The dialogue is like poetry! And the changes of expressions are so subtle, so magnificent! I see it once or twice a year." Spielberg: "*The Searchers* has so many superlatives going for it. It's John Wayne's best performance . . . It's a study in dramatic framing and composition. It contains the single most harrowing moment in any film I've ever seen. It is high on my twenty-favorite-film list." Spielberg says he has seen the film a dozen times, including twice on location with *Close Encounters of the Third Kind.*

Byron argues that four recent films in particular have a basic story structure identical to and inspired by *The Searchers: Taxi Driver, Close Encounters of the Third Kind, The Deer Hunter,* and *Hard Core.* In each, "an obsessed man searches for someone—a woman, a child, a best friend—who has fallen into the clutches of an alien people. But when found, the sought one doesn't want to be rescued."

There has been a good deal of writing on *The Searchers,* as film criticism goes. In "Critics on *The Searchers,*" Edward Buscombe summarizes the work of several Ford critics—John Baxter, J. A. Place, Andrew Sarris, Michael Wilmington, and Joseph McBride.

Despite their sense that the film is concerned with questions of history the critics do not in practice pay much attention to this. What is ultimately of concern is the artistry with which the film organizes the audience's responses to the characters . . . The actual way in which the critics deal with questions of character in the film . . . lead[s] us all the time towards articulating what it is the characters are like, what motivates them, how they understand each other and how they are to be understood by us . . . All these critics, then, to some extent treat the film as though it were a psychological novel.[2]

What Buscombe does not say, perhaps because it is obvious, is that critics of *The Searchers* have been notably focussed on one character in particular, Ethan Edwards. Indeed, preoccupation with Ethan and his motives has been a constant of commentary on the film since it first appeared. Lindsay Anderson, who did not like the film, was as centered on the character of Ethan as those later critics who esteem it supremely.

The Searchers begins with a promise . . . yet somehow, curiously, the effect is cold. . . . Lack of intensity in all [its] echoes reminds us that it is not enough just to set Ford down among the mesas . . . he has to have a story—or at least a theme. And the story of *The Searchers . . .* does not turn out to be a good one for him. In the first place there is too much of it. The pictures Ford has himself produced in the last ten years . . . have relied less and less on narrative and more and more on mood.

The Searchers is a long and complicated story, spread over eight or nine years. Moreover its hero, Ethan Edwards, is an unmistakable neurotic, devoured by an irrational hatred of Indians and half breeds, shadowed by some mysterious crime. His search for his little niece . . . abducted by Comanches seems . . . inspired less by love or honour than by an obsessive desire to do her to death as a contaminated creature. Now what is Ford, of all directors, to do with a hero like this?[3]

Even one of the trade magazines spoke of a "problem of motivation" in a review that appeared before the film's release.

The box office appeal of John Wayne combined with the imprint of John Ford makes *The Searchers* a contender for the big money stakes. It's a Western in the grand manner—handsomely mounted and in the tradition of *Shane.* . . . Yet *The Searchers* is somewhat disappointing. . . . Overlong and repetitive at 119 minutes there are subtleties in the basically simple story that are not adequately explained. . . . Wayne, the uncle of the kidnapped girl, is a complex character. His motivations, from the time he appears out of the southwest plains at his brother's ranch to his similar exit after he accomplishes his mission, are unclear. . . . Wayne is a bitter, taciturn individual throughout and the reasons for his attitude are left to the imagination of the viewer. (*Variety,* March 14, 1956)[4]

There is not one point in these passages but several: a centering on Ethan; a centering on Ethan's motives; and finding a problem with Ethan's motives, usually followed by an attempt to solve it. We have not space to sort these out so we treat the "preoccupation with Ethan" as a single thing.

T. S. Eliot has warned against critical fascination with a fascinating character. "Few critics have even admitted that *Hamlet* the play is the primary problem, and Hamlet the character only secondary."[5] Our analysis seeks to focus on *The Searchers* the film, not *The Searchers* the saga of Ethan Edwards. This attempt opposes the weight of prior commentary: it has never been doubted that *The Searchers* concerns the uneasy relations between the restless hero, half-civilized, half-savage, and the community he benefits.

Vladimir Propp counsels that the motivations of characters have nothing to do with the structure of narrative.

Motivations belong to the most inconstant and unstable elements of the tale. . . . Completely identical or similar acts are motivated in the most varied ways . . . [which] has no influence on the structure of the course of action. i.e., on the search as such. . . . One may observe in general that the feelings and intentions of the dramatic personas do not have an effect on the course of action in any instances at all."[6]

Propp's formulae on motivation hold good for the entire "structural analysis of the narrative" tradition—Lévi-Strauss, Greimas, Todorov, Barthes. Despite his motivational complications, Ethan does function rather conventionally as the hero of *The Searchers* in structural terms. His ambiguous motives do not prevent, they do not even qualify his performance of the hero's functions in the film. *

But *The Searchers* itself foregrounds the problem of Ethan and his motivations through the song that begins and ends the film. The first part of the song is played over the titles, its last words overlapping the figure of Ethan as he slowly approaches his brother's house: "What makes a man to wander? What makes a man to roam? What makes a man to leave bed and board and turn his back on home? Ride away, ride away, ride away." The second part of the song is played at the end of the film over images of the settlers entering the house and Ethan turning away. "A man will search in heart and soul, go searching way out there. His peace of mind he knows he'll find, but where, O Lord, O where? Ride away, ride away, ride away." The first part of the song poses a question that we expect the film to answer. The second part of the song also poses a question, but this time we know that the film will answer neither one. The second question is rhetorical, suggesting that Ethan will not find peace of mind and that his response to this is to ride

---

*There is a Proppian problem in the film's doubled hero: it is Martin who kills Scar, recovers Debbie, and marries Laurie, although arguably he does the first two as Ethan's helper. We deal with this in a separate essay.

away. (The second part of the song has another function: it tells us that Ethan *is* riding away, not just going back to feed his horse before going into the house.)

The song that frames *The Searchers* seems to parallel the poem that opens *Young Mr. Lincoln,* itself a series of questions. In the *Cahiers* reading, the main function of the poem is to pretend that its questions haven't been answered yet, whereas the film itself presumes the spectator's knowledge of Lincoln. Through this "feigned indecisiveness" the film effects a naturalization of the Lincoln myth. The function of the song in *The Searchers* is opposite to this. In *Lincoln* the audience knows the answers to the questions before the film begins; in *The Searchers* the audience does not know the answers to the questions even after the film is over.

To displace Ethan from the center of *The Searchers* thus seems to oppose the film itself; but the foregrounding of Ethan and his problems may be read as a ruse of the text (though not of its makers) to deflect attention from more important and hidden matters. This analysis of *The Searchers* seeks to explore different patterns of signification and to use different methods of criticism than prior criticism of the film has done. Of course it is a "reading" of the film, but it does not have the closed or completed quality that the notion of reading suggests; it will be enough if this analysis succeeds in displacing discussion of the film. Its point of departure is the extraordinary power of *The Searchers* as film-myth on a number of filmmakers, critics, and other viewers, a power that might also be defined by the number of intelligent viewers that the film intensely repels. The moral-psychological critics whom Buscombe discusses, who are also thoroughly "author-centered," tend to assume the film's power in a way that precludes raising it as a problem. Insofar as they consider it they attribute the film's impact on audiences to the artistry of its director. But if myth is viewed as a collective phenomenon then the power of a myth can only be explained by reference to the community that responds to it.

This analysis has several methodological inspirations. The first is Lévi-Straussian myth analysis with its Freudian emphasis on the unconscious dimension, and its Marxist emphasis on the materialist interpretation, of collective phenomena. From Lévi-Strauss we take the notion that myths (and other public narratives) have an unconscious component, formed by public conflicts rather than private ones. These are contradictions either in social life or in knowledge; they explain why listeners are stirred by myths and why myths are told again and again. When these conflicts fade in social life, the power of the myth is lessened until it "dies." The myth operates by transposing the terms of the actual conflict into other sets of terms, usually in the form of binary oppositions.* It is the resolution of the transposed oppositions, substituted for the real conflict, that gives the myth a palliative effect. That this effect is a kind of deception accounts for the pejorative sense of the word "mythical," even in Lévi-Strauss. He refuses to budge in calling

---

*Lévi-Strauss's binarism, his postulate that all myths (and kinship and totemistic structures) are built out of sets of binary oppositions, which he seems to ground in the structure of the brain itself, has been much attacked. The consensus now seems to be that binarism fits some situations well but as a universal principle of the formation of culture it is untenable.

myth "inauthentic" because it operates to deflect humans from identifying and resolving their actual problems. Finally, the operation of a myth—both its construction from actual conflicts and its impact on audiences—always has to do with the time in which the myth is told, not with the time that it tells of. Thus *The Searchers* has to do with 1956, not with the 1868–1873 period in which it is set.

We also draw upon the *Cahiers du cinéma* analysis of *Young Mr. Lincoln*,[7] which uses Lévi-Strauss, among other sources, but proceeds quite differently. Lévi-Strauss overlooks the text's specific modes of unfolding and elaboration in order to study its structure. *Cahiers* does its Lévi-Straussian and other analyses off-stage, then devotes its analysis to reading them back into the unfolding text. Our analysis also benefits from Charles Eckert's reading of *Marked Woman*,[8] notably its casual but effective combination of Lévi-Straussian method and ideological analysis and its analysis of the gangster as an overdetermined figure of displacement in many films.

The Searchers is explicitly concerned with a number of anthropological issues. On its surface it treats questions of kinship, race, marriage, and the relations between tribes. These questions also have to do with the identity, status, and responsibilities of individuals: who is responsible for the retrieval and burial of the dead, for the search and recovery of captives, for vengeance? Who can marry whom? Which marriages are binding? Which are not?

The wealth of anthropological material in *The Searchers* is itself a problem: how to proceed? Let us begin with two parallel sets of relationships that appear to structure the film. With ethnographic accuracy, the film designates Martin Pawley as one-eighth Cherokee by descent. As a child Martin was rescued (by Ethan) from an Indian raid that killed his parents; Martha and Aaron Edwards adopted him and raised him as a member of their family. Martin's parents were white settlers like the Edwards but, as our analysis will show, he functions as an Indian in the symbolics of the film, more precisely as an Indian who has become an adopted white. Martin marries Laurie Jorgenson, who is white.

Debbie Edwards is captured by Scar and his band when she is ten. She is raised as a Comanche until she reaches puberty, then becomes Scar's wife. The parallelism is evident. White woman is adopted and raised by red society, marries a red man; (part) red man is adopted and raised by white society, marries a white woman. This textual parallel poses an exchange between red and white tribes, at best a de facto exchange since there is no alliance between them. Indeed, both inter-tribal transfers take place in violence or as a result of violence; and each tribe subjects the outsider to a total reconditioning, designed to obliterate the effects of previous filiation, as part of its adoption process. * This is an "exchange" between warring tribes, between which there can be no lawful exchange and no lawful marriage.

*But note that Debbie remembers her white childhood and language "from always," whereas Martin is a total amnesiac about his childhood, which, though among whites, stands in metaphorically for his Indian ancestry. Similarly, it is Ethan later who "speaks good Comanch"; Martin speaks it hardly at all despite five years' travelling among the tribes.

Still, the film's parallel adoptions and marriages constitute a de facto exchange, an implied contract with reciprocal obligations to fulfill; but the film poses this symmetry only to collapse it. Indian law and adoption, intermarriage on Indian terms are not recognized by the white settlers or by the film that takes their part; only white law and adoption and intermarriage on white terms are recognized. The film's surface progress is toward "recovery of Debbie" but this implies, and the film hardly disguises it, a progress toward the destruction of Indian law and Indian society. This is accomplished in the final Ranger/Cavalry charge that destroys the Indian military force and, metonymically, Indian society itself. There can be only one law, one definition of persons and relationships. *The Searchers* presents the violent triumph of that law, annihilating everything that opposes it or that it defines as "other."

This "collapse" of the film's apparent structuring opposition is itself one of the film's principal ideological and semantic operations. It is certainly overdetermined, that is, required by a number of different systems at work in the film. Let us consider briefly the figure of Debbie. Her choice to stay with the Comanches and with Scar is overridden by Ethan and Martin. Only their methods differ: Ethan wants to shoot her, Martin wants to abduct her. But the text itself rides roughshod over Debbie by making her change her mind suddenly when Martin appears to take her away, a conspicuously unmotivated act in a film that elsewhere supplies too many motives.

The figure of Debbie functions as an object in several other senses also. In Propp and Greimas, she is the object of value transferred from the good kingdom to the evil kingdom and back, over whom hero and villain fight to the death. In Lévi-Straussian anthropology, she is a wife exchanged for whom no other wife can be returned—the offered Indian wife Look is repudiated; therefore she must be recovered. Debbie is equated with her sexuality, by Ethan and Laurie at least, so that, "contaminated" by Scar, she can only be disposed of. All this is overdetermined by the system of sexual identity and the system of subject formation of which it is a foundation. This system has a negative dimension—how men and women may not be portrayed—as well as a positive one. It is inconceivable that a man be cast in the Debbie role or a woman in the Martin role. In classical cinema, aside from some "women's pictures," named and produced as a distinct genre, a special case, a man cannot be the object of value except briefly, e.g., Dean Martin's capture in *Rio Bravo,* from which, however, he delivers himself. And a woman cannot except briefly be a seeker, a searcher, cannot be put in the place of performances, of proving herself through action, as Martin is. Nor can she serve apprenticeships, which make her the subject of a becoming. She is defined and valued always in herself not for herself, that is, as object. This means, among other things, that she cannot change her social or racial allegiance by her own choice—they are not hers to change.

Thus the system of sexual identity requires that the parallelism of adoptions/marriages collapse and that it collapse on the feminine side. What about the opposition between red and white laws? The shift from a conflict between two laws to a conflict within one law is also fundamental to the film's ideological and semantic operations. First of all, it obscures the fact that the white settlers and their government, for personal and public gain, destroyed many Indian civilizations and damaged others, subjecting the survivors to white law. The film recasts the struggle between red and white laws as a conflict within one law, an Ideal Law supposed to reign over all humans. Then it casts the Indians as criminals under this law and casts the white settlers, Rangers, and Cavalry as the law's agents, who punish the Indians for their transgressions. The film is precisely structured along this axis, beginning with horrible crimes by the Comanches, which follow no acts by whites but initiate the cycle of violence gratuitously, and proceeding through intermediate stages to their punishment by whites at the end.

This structure is ideological in the traditional sense: a distortion of history in the interests of a particular class; but it is also a psychoanalytic structure. The *Cahiers* reading of *Lincoln* elucidates this.

It is in the constantly renewed relationship of this group [the white settlers] with another (the Indians), in the dualism of Ford's universe that the inscription of the structural imperative of Law which dictates the deferment of desire and imposes exchange and alliance is realized, in violence, guided by the mediating action of the hero (often a bastard) who is placed at its intersection.[9]

Scar's crimes—rape, murder, dismemberment, burning—eminently violate the law that dictates postponement of pleasure. His acts stand in for the terrifying libido that must be repressed and, if unrepressed, must be punished drastically. His crimes "stand in" for libido because, of course, libido cannot be represented. The film doubles this nonrepresentability by not showing Scar's actions or even their consequences—we see not one dead body of the murdered family. These actions and their consequences are evoked only by Ethan's grimaces and outbursts and even he most often operates to suppress representation—"Don't let him go in there, Mose," "I buried Lucy back there with my own hands; I thought it best to keep it from you," "What do you want me to do, draw you a picture?" "As long as you live don't ever ask me that." This requires the viewer to project unconscious fantasies into the film, which greatly increases the viewer's involvement in it. Put oversimply, the viewer identifies unconsciously with Scar's acts and also with the need for punishing them. This process, which gives pleasure by exercising libido and ego reassurance by suppressing it, imaginatively reconstitutes the structure of the self, thereby promoting what has been called "the maintenance of the subject."

In both *Lincoln* and *The Searchers* there is an early crime and a subsequent movement, the bulk of each film, toward cancelling it. "It is from this ideal Law that originated the cancellation of the criminal act in the fiction [and] the position of the Mother as the figure of forbidden violence (pleasure)."[10] As *Cahiers* argues, Lincoln is both the figure of ideal law (taking it over from his mother and Mrs. Clay) and the agent of its inscription. This forbids his resort to physical force and thereby denies the film "the usual bisection of [Ford's] fiction and the sometimes truly epic inscription of Law thereby articulated."[11] In the case of *Lincoln,* this "produce[s] the Law as a pure prohibition of violence, whose result is a permanent indictment of the castrating effects of its discourse."[12] But the inscription of law in *The Searchers* is epic indeed—the consequence of colorful adventures by action heroes, leading to a death struggle between hero and villain and an exuberant charge on the enemy's village. The party of repression confronts the party of libido in open battle. These epic lures obscure the grim business of inscribing the law that dictates postponement of pleasure—which stands forth nakedly in *Lincoln*. (But isn't Lincoln's courtroom battle with J. Palmer Cass a kind of verbal epic?) Scar is scalped, i.e., castrated, for which his name as well as his crime has predestined him.

It is the character of the mother that incarnates the idealized figure of Ideal Law in Ford's fiction. . . . often, as in *Young Mr. Lincoln,* the widowed mother, guardian of the deceased father's law. It is for her that the men (the regiment) sacrifice the cause of their desire, and under her presidency that the Fordian celebration takes place; this in fact consists in a simulacrum of sexual relations from which all effective desire is banned.[13]

The mother who incarnates Ideal Law in *The Searchers* is evidently Martha. She is murdered in the initial crime, but it is she whom Ethan and Martin serve, for her that they pursue Debbie, recover her, and punish Scar and his followers. That she is the figure of forbidden pleasure is also clear: first for Ethan, who loves her without hope of fulfillment; second for her husband Aaron, who toils for her and, by staying on the frontier, gives up his life—"She just wouldn't let a man quit"; and, after her death, for Ethan and Martin, who devote their energies to her cause for five years, like Lincoln taking over the mother's function by looking after her children. But from this point there is a division in Ideal Law. When Debbie refuses to leave Scar, Ethan seeks to impose the law of postponing pleasure by shooting her. Laurie invokes the authority of Martha for this policy, "You know what Ethan will do if be has a chance? He'll put a bullet in her brain and tell you Martha would want it." But Martin is also acting for Martha when he does all that he can to protect Debbie, from Ethan as well as from Scar. This confusion at the heart of ideal law is one of the most disturbing aspects of *The Searchers;* it reverberates in every corner of the film.

The undoing of Debbie's adoption and marriage and of the Indian law that sanctions them turns us back to Martin's adoption and marriage and to the white law that sanctions them and prescribes their terms. Martin's adoption and marriage are the "relation left over" when the originally posed symmetry collapses, hence they are of particular interest. Martin's adoption is treated on the surface of the film as a long-accomplished fact, but beneath the surface the nature, meaning, and consequences of his adoption are far from settled. Even on its surface, the film uses the character of Ethan to question what has long been settled, notably the matter of Martin's "Indian blood" and his kinship status as an adopted Edwards (white). (It is only one duplicity of a frequently duplicitous film that Ethan is punished for his disturbing the social order by exclusion from the community, though this in some way is duplicitous also.) As in *Young Mr. Lincoln,* the unconscious material lies partly on the surface of the film but arranged so as to be partly unreadable. This makes analysis considerably more difficult than simply identifying unconscious structures. The surface of *The Searchers* is broken again and again by the edges of contradictions that lie at deeper levels. This implies, which is true, that the surface of the film is contradictory, even incoherent, in a different way. It is Ford's skill as a film-maker that covers over and disguises these breaks again and again, indeed that makes a flowing filmic text out of them.

We first see Martin riding a horse bareback and sliding off in front of the Edwardses' open side door; he is late for dinner. The wilderness outside the door, Max Steiner's exuberant theme, Martin's high spirits, his effortless transition from exterior to interior—these signify an ideal boyhood spent in oneness with nature. The film will soon shatter this idyll ruthlessly by taking away all of Martin's adopted family, except his hostile uncle, making him an orphan again. But it shatters the idyll even sooner by initiating another signification set: Martin's skin is quite dark and he wears a loose, colored shirt buttoned at the neck, giving him the appearance of an Indian. It is Indians who ride bareback and, in American mythology, it is only Indians who are completely at one with the environment. Martin steps tentatively into the room. The surface question: he is late for dinner, will he be scolded? covers another question: he is an Indian, will he be welcome at the table? Much of the textual problematic revolving around Martin is posed in this scene, though in disguised form. As it happens, Martin does have cause to worry on this particular evening, for his Uncle Ethan has returned. Martin is introduced and takes his seat sheepishly. Ethan looks at him suspiciously and says, "A fellow could mistake you for a 'breed.'" Martin says that he is one-eighth Cherokee; the rest English and Welsh. Martha recalls that it was Ethan who found Martin after Indians killed his parents; to which Ethan replies, "It just happened to be me. No need to make any more of it." Ethan just glares at Martin following this remark; Martha deflects his anger by saying, "More coffee, Ethan?" Then the dinner scene simply ends, in the way that Ford sometimes ends a scene, with no dramatic rounding out, no ellipsis marks. There is a cut to Martin sitting on the steps of the porch with the family dog, half turned toward the door, as though Ethan's hostility has expelled him from the family group. After a scene with the adults inside, Aaron joins Martha in the bedroom and closes the door while Ethan sits on the porch with the dog, as Martin did earlier.

In the morning, they ride after Jorgenson's cattle. When Martin calls Ethan "Uncle," Ethan says that he is not his uncle, and not to call him grandpa or Methuselah either, since he can whip him to a frazzle. What should Martin call him? Name is Ethan. The game of names between Ethan and Martin is another textual duplicity. "I am not your uncle" means that Martin is not kin to the Edwards children, to whom Ethan is uncle, but the rest of Ethan's discourse turns this into a point of personal bravado and frontier democracy.

The events following Scar's raid on the Edwardses reveal Ethan's deep knowledge of Comanche ways, of horses, of the wilderness. He rests his horse before riding to the rescue, so he rides by Martin, who has ridden his horse to death.* This

---

*We might pause at this figure of a cowboy lugging a saddle across the plains as two riders hurry by. Is this the same Martin who yesterday rode bareback and dressed and looked like an Indian boy? A day later he is grown up and looks like a white cowboy, a prime instance of the text's duplicity, gaining

and other incidents show that, despite Ethan's hostility, Martin has a great deal to learn from him. Others show that Ethan is a good guide and teacher during Martin's five-year apprenticeship. He lets Martin see and know only what he can handle — he does not let him see Martha's body or, later, Lucy's, does not mention that he found Lucy dead, etc. Ethan also holds Martin back, hoisting him by the collar like a schoolboy, to prevent his following Brad into the Comanche camp.

Ethan's hostility to Martin begins at the Edwards dinner table but is restrained there. On the trail it bursts forth in a string of insults and epithets. "Come on, blankethead" (twice). "What does a quarter-blood [sic] Cherokee know about the Comanche trick of sleepin' with his best pony by his side?" When Martin says he thinks they're being followed (he's right), Ethan says, "That's just the Injun in you."

A large figure of textual features has to do with Martin's kinship. Many of his wrangles with Ethan have to do with whether or not he is Debbie's "brother" or otherwise her kin so as to justify his searching for her year after year. As noted these discussions may also be read as treating Martin's status as an adopted white. The kinship question is treated by the text at several different levels and often these levels are mixed or fused.

When the Comanches attack the pursuit party, Martin almost faints after his first shot. Mose Harper takes his rifle, Martin revives and starts firing with his hand gun. This is "the young man's initiation in battle" — Anthony Perkins did this bit in *Friendly Persuasion* the same year. Below the surface, the issue is Martin's firing on his blood kinsmen. The film is quite attentive to where Martin's loyalties lie at this moment of decision. A parallel issue is raised when Martin inadvertently acquires a Comanche wife. He cannot send her back because Ethan says it will bring her tribe down on them; but Martin's misery at her being there, his kicking her away when she lies down beside him, makes clear where his loyalties lie. Ethan's calling her Mrs. Pawley and baiting Martin about her link up with his other jibes about Martin as an Indian.

The kinship issue is discussed explicitly when Ethan and Martin return to the Jorgenson ranch after about a year of searching. Ethan wants Martin to stay behind, apparently because he plans to shoot Debbie now that she is a woman and defiled by Comanches. The next morning Ethan rides off alone; with reluctant help from Laurie, Martin follows in order to stop Ethan from harming Debbie. In the bunkhouse the night before, Ethan and Martin have this discussion:

E: Jorgenson's been running my cattle with his own.
M: Your cattle? You mean Debbie's cattle.
E: He's agreed to take you on and split the increase in my herd while I'm gone. I'm pushing on tomorrow.
M: Well, I sure ain't gonna stay here. I started out looking for Debbie, I intend to keep on.

---

all the associations of boyhood, Indian, and nature boy in one scene and of young manhood and white cowboy in the next. Moreover, the character has grown up in a day; we have now seen him, or we think we have, as a boy in the warmth of home and then a grown man on his own on the trail the next afternoon.

E: Why?

M: Why? Well, because she's my—

E: She's your nothin'. She's no kin to you at all.

M: Well, I always thought she was—the way her folks took me in, they raised me—

E: That don't make you no kin.

M: All right, maybe it don't, but I intend to keep on lookin' anyway.

E: How? You got any horses or money to buy them? You ain't even got money for cartridges. Jorgenson's offering you a good living here. Martin, there's something I want you to know—

M: Ya. I know what you want me to know—that I got no kin. I got no money, no horses. All I got here is a bunch of dead man's clothes to wear. Well, you told me that already, so shut your mouth.

Later when they inspect recovered captives at the headquarters of a cavalry regiment, the officer asks them, "Who is this girl to you?" Martin says, "She's my—" Ethan cuts him off, "—niece." When they arrive at Scar's camp still later and are invited into his tent, Ethan tells Martin to wait outside. Martin pushes past him, saying, "Not likely." Ethan's remark may mean: I'll handle this business best without you, or You're too young for this; but it also includes: This is a family matter and you're not part of the family.

When Martin confronts Debbie, he appeals to their shared childhood to break through to her; but he is also seeking validation from her as the sole survivor of the family of his own claims to kinship by adoption.

M: Debbie—

D: Un mea.

M: Debbie, don't you remember? I'm Martin. I'm Martin, your brother. Remember? Debbie, remember back. Do you remember how I used to let you ride my horse and tell you stories? Don't you remember me, Debbie?

D: I remember—from always. At first, I prayed to you. Come and get me, take me home. You didn't come.

M: But I've come now, Debbie.

D: These are my people. Un mea, Go. Go, Martin, please.

E: Stand aside, Martin.

M: No you don't, Ethan. Ethan, no you don't.

E: Stand aside.

What is going on in this scene is both obvious and subtle, overt and hidden. The adopted white and the adopted red confront each other and declare their kinship to each other. Martin seeks her return to white society, but he does not regard her marriage to Scar as any sort of disgrace. As one who is himself adopted, he cannot fault her loyalty to her new tribe; but as an adopted white, indeed as her brother, he must try to bring her back by any means. It is interesting also that just following this scene affirming the kinship of Martin and Debbie, Ethan formally disowns his kinship to Debbie.

M: (reading) 'I, Ethan Edwards, being of sound mind* and without any blood kin, do hereby—

*Surely this is one of the film's little jokes.

E: Bequeath, it means leave.

M: bequeath all my property of any kind to Martin Pawley.' What do you mean you don't have any blood kin? Debbie's your blood kin.

E: Not no more she ain't.

M: Well, you can keep your will. (throws it back) I don't want any of your property. And don't think I've forgotten what you were fixin' to do to her. What kind of a man are you anyway?

E: She's been livin' with a buck! She's nothin but a—

M: Shut your dirty mouth. I hope you die.

E: That'll be the day.

Martin persists in asserting and acting on his kinship bond to Debbie despite all obstacles. One of these obstacles is Laurie, the woman he will marry. She reluctantly helps him to continue the search when Ethan abandons him after their first return home. On their second return home, they interrupt her wedding to Charlie McCorry and then prepare to join the Rangers and the Cavalry in an attack upon Scar.

L: Marty, you're not going, not this time.

M: Are you crazy?

L: It's too late. She's a woman grown now.

M: I've got to fetch her home.

L: Fetch what home? The leavings of a Comanche buck, sold time and again to the highest bidder? With savages . . .

M: Laurie, shut your mouth.

L: You know what Ethan will do if he has a chance—he'll put a bullet in her brain and tell you Martha would want it.

M: Only if I'm dead.

In front of Scar's camp, Clayton gives the order to go in at sun-up. Martin says, "Just a minute, Reverend, we go chargin' in they'll kill her and you know it." Ethan: "That's what I'm counting on." Martin: "I know you are." Clayton: "Son, there's more at stake here than your sister." Ethan agrees and tells Martin that a scalp on Scar's lance belonged to his mother. Martin is given pause, then says, "But that doesn't change anything. That changes nothing!" He proposes to sneak into the village to save Debbie before the attack and does so, disguising himself as an Indian—with blanket and no shirt, but with white man's gun and holster under his blanket. Ethan opposes this but Clayton agrees. Martin finds Debbie and wakes her, saying, "Debbie, it's your brother, Marty. I'm going to get you out of here." She is disoriented a moment then says, "Yes, Marty. Oh yes, Marty." He kills Scar, who has been alerted by Debbie's scream, and the Ranger attack begins. Ethan enters the village, scalps Scar, then rides after Debbie, separating her from Martin. Martin tries to pull Ethan from his horse but cannot. As Ethan rides after Debbie, Martin chases on foot, his hand on his gun, saying "No, Ethan, no!" Ethan does not shoot Debbie but picks her up and takes her home.

The Laurie-Martin relation deserves a note. Whether or not Martin is a kin to the Edwards family has no bearing on his marrying Laurie: but the unconscious content of the kinship point, that he is a red man adopted by white society, does bear upon it. Even on the surface of the text, if Martin is a "breed," a blankethead, if Ethan is discomfited by sitting at the family table with him, then a fortiori he should be opposed to Martin's marrying a white woman. Yet neither Ethan nor anyone else in the film even hints at this. In the bunkhouse scene Ethan notices Laurie's attraction to Martin with amusement as she kisses Martin goodnight. Also, in urging Martin to stay on at the Jorgenson ranch, he apparently accepts the inevitable match between Laurie and Martin. When they return the second time and Laurie appears in a wedding dress he says to Martin with a smile, "It looks like you two have a lot to talk about." He looks on the fight between Martin and Charlie McCorry with good-natured neutrality.

Martin is the evident favorite of Laurie from the beginning and, it seems, of her mother also. Her father seems not to care, with perhaps a preference for Charlie, for whatever reason. The film is well under way before we see Laurie at all. She is seen in long shot at the funeral, barely coming into medium shot in a frame with several other things happening also. She says a silent good-bye to Martin, who seems awkward until he turns from her and mounts his horse.

When Martin returns for one day a year later, Laurie calls his name irritably and kisses him, to both of which he responds as though barely awake. Laurie's mother asks if he knows her name. He says "Sure I do, her name's Laurie, but I darned near forgot just how pretty she was." The next morning, after more kissing, he suggests that they go steady; she replies that they've been going steady "since they was three" and it's about time he found out about it. Her claim to an early closeness could not be proved by Martin's behavior. Upon the second return, Martin offers to go away so that Laurie can marry Charlie; she replies that, if he does, she'll die. (Never was the break-up of a wedding done so inertly.) Laurie tries hard to prevent Martin from going to the final attack on Scar but he goes anyway. Despite her threats not to wait for him, Laurie does wait each time and joins him in the final tableau as they walk into the house.

In the sexual relationship with Laurie, Martin is almost totally passive. The idea of the relationship seems to be hers as does each step that furthers it or reinforces it. Of course this reversal of traditional roles is one of the running gags of the film. It is carried even to a bathtub scene in which the male is the object of voyeurism and horseplay and comically asserts his outraged modesty. Martin at no time displays physical desire for Laurie or a desire to marry her nor does he at any time hurry to get back to her. Martin is the love object whom Laurie chooses and seeks out. She conspicuously desires him, a desire that is presented as physical, indeed as violent, with hard kisses, pushes that knock down furniture, and a constantly agitated voice, alternating between a quaver and a screech.

The running argument between Ethan and Martin concerns in part the issue of kinship by blood *versus* kinship by adoption. In context this is strictly a family matter—Martin is not a blood kin of the Edwards family and therefore, to Ethan, he has no reason to continue to search for Debbie. But altered slightly—kinship reckoned by blood *only* versus kinship reckoned by adoption also—it is also an anthropological issue, having to do with the relations between races and societies.

In tracing "the Martin complex" through the film we have also traced the line of a textual duplicity. Martin functions now as part Indian, now as pure white, while in the unconscious symbolics of the film he functions as pure Indian. This "duplicity" is merely the effect of unconscious structures breaking the surface of the film at several points. It is now time to address those structures and to relate them to the dilemma of this film's power on audiences. If Martin functions as an Indian, is *The Searchers* readable as a myth about the adoption and integration of Indians in white society? Does this account for its power?

Of course, adoption is an ideological notion, a "savage" thinking of social problems and relations on the model of the family and family relations, precisely the sort of logic one finds in myths. In fact, there are historical grounds for considering the integration of Indians into American society under the rubric of "adoption," at least in that in American history the detribalization of Indians was a conscious policy.

Meanwhile, Congress proceeded to attempt Indian detribalization. In March of 1871, the treaty system of dealing with the Indians was ended by congressional enactment. The intent of the legislation was clear; Grant and Congress wanted the Indian civilized and Christianized. Since the tribal system was in the way, it would be circumvented. The Indian was supposed to finally become a full participant in American society, but he was to do it as individual, not as a member of a tribe.[14]

But this does not make integration of Indians into American society, including intermarriage, an issue that requires unconscious treatment or that stirs audiences profoundly. It may have been an issue in 1868, but it was hardly one in 1956. Indeed, there were very few anti-miscegenation statutes regarding Indians at any time.

Of the various laws which penalized illicit miscegenation, none applied to Indians, and only North Carolina's (and Virginia's for a very brief period) prohibited intermarriage. On the contrary, several colonists were willing to allow, even advocate, intermarriage with the Indians—an unheard of proposition concerning Negroes. . . . It is suggestive, too, that Virginia's statutory definition of mulattoes extended the taint of Negro ancestry through three generations and of Indian ancestry through only one.[15]

Winthrop Jordan demonstrates Thomas Jefferson's praise of the Indian and his denigration of blacks and argues that his views, while extreme, are emblematic of American views generally.[16] Jefferson believed that in altered circumstances Indians would become white men, a transformation he thought the Negro could never accomplish. He hoped for the cultural and physical amalgamation of Indians and white Americans. "In truth the ultimate point of rest and happiness for them is to let our settlements and theirs meet and blend together, to intermix, and become one people." Such amalgamation and identification were precisely what Jefferson most abhorred with the Negro.

Will Rogers, who made three films with Ford in the thirties, and who had more Indian blood than the Martin character in *The Searchers,* expressed the positive view Americans have had of the Indian, at least in modern times.

My ancestors didn't come over on the Mayflower, but they met the boat. . . . My father was one-eighth Cherokee Indian, and my mother was a quarter-blood Cherokee. I never got far enough in arithmetic to figure out just how much "Injun" that makes me, but there's nothing of which I am more proud than my Cherokee blood.[17]

The emotional impact of *The Searchers* can hardly come from the issue of the kinship status and marriageability of an Indian in white society in 1956. This issue cannot be the locus of that unconscious conflict in knowledge or social life that activates every effective myth and fixes the attention of its listeners, according to Lévi-Strauss. It becomes explicable only if we substitute black for red and read a film about red-white relations in 1868–1873 as a film about black-white relations in 1956.

What does the opposition "kinship by blood *versus* kinship by adoption" have to do with the situation of blacks in the United States in 1956? Of course, blacks were detribalized with utmost violence by the acts that took them into slavery. As servants of plantations their own social organization was forcibly structured in relation to white society; but the questions we have considered under the rubric of "adoption" perhaps arose only with the first freed slaves and runaways. As late as 1857, the Supreme Court ruled in the Dred Scott case that Negro slaves and their descendants were not citizens of the United States or of the individual states and that prohibiting slavery deprived persons of their property without due process of law under the Fifth Amendment. In 1863 the Emancipation Proclamation freed slaves in areas in rebellion against the United States. Constitutional amendments in 1865, 1868, and 1870 conferred citizenship on blacks ("all persons born or naturalized in the United States"), guaranteed their rights against the individual states, and guaranteed them the right to vote ("regardless of race, color, or previous condition of servitude").

On May 17, 1954, the Supreme Court announced *Brown* v. *Board of Education of Topeka*, its most important decision of modern times, some say the most important of its history. *Brown* held that in public education the doctrine of separate but equal was inherently unequal and therefore violated the black students' right to "equal protection of the laws" under the Fourteenth Amendment. Because it foresaw difficulties in desegregating schools kept apart for decades and (though it did not say so) anticipated resistance to its decision, the Court postponed its implementation decree for one year, while it considered briefs and oral arguments on the point.

May 1954–May 1955 saw heated debate of *Brown*, including many defiant statements against it. "I shall use every legal means at my command to continue segregated schools in Virginia." "[The South] will not abide by or obey this legislative decision by a political court." The Court's decision reduced the Constitution to "a scrap of paper"; any effort to integrate the South will lead to "great strife and turmoil." The Florida brief on enforcement cited a poll showing that three-fourths of the white leaders of the state disagreed with the *Brown* decision, that 30 percent disagreed "violently" and that 13 percent of peace officers said they would enforce state attendance laws at racially mixed schools.[18] The later "Southern Manifesto" by senators and congressmen from eleven states dismissed the Court's use of "naked judicial power" to legislate and pledged its signers to use all lawful means to reverse the decision and to prevent the use of force in its implementation.*

Resistance to school desegregation was far more fierce and lasted far longer than resistance to the ending of other segregation practices during this period.

Desegregation progressed at a relatively rapid rate in a relatively peaceable manner in most areas—from the restaurants of Washington to the buses of Montgomery to the ball-parks of the Texas League. One area alone was excepted: the schools. Streetcars and eating places and amusement parks were, after all, settings for transients who shared proximity for a limited period of time; schools were something else. There the contact would last for six or eight hours daily; it was from interaction with one another as much as attention devoted to lesson books or lectures that school children derived the essence of their education. And so it was the schoolhouse that became the arena for the South's fiercest resistance to the desegregation order of the Supreme Court.[19]

Fear of intermarriage between black and white was one ground of opposition to *Brown,* explicit and implicit. Several states mention it in their briefs and cross-examinations.[20] Miscegenation was not cited more often as a likely consequence of *Brown* because in 1955 twenty-nine states had statutes forbidding blacks and whites to marry. (These were struck down as unconstitutional only in 1967.)

It was in the midst of the *Brown* upheaval that the writing of the screenplay for *The Searchers* and other preparations for filming took place. The novel by Alan LeMay was published in 1954, Merian C. Cooper bought it that year for filming by John Ford with John Wayne, under a production company just formed by C. V. Whitney. According to *Motion Picture Herald,* the shooting of *The Searchers* took place between June 25 and August 27, 1955. (It was released on May 26, 1956.) I have not been able to determine exactly when Frank Nugent wrote the screenplay, but it was almost surely between early or mid-1954 and the first half of 1955, the period that coincides with the initial Brown uproar.

We cannot do here a detailed analysis of Nugent's adaptation of LeMay's novel, but several of the features of the film with which we have been most concerned were added by Nugent. In the novel Martin is 100 percent white; hence there is no conflict between Martin and Ethan about race;† but Ethan does try twice to shoot Debbie and Martin attempts to stop him. Martin does not enter Scar's village alone; he charges with the Rangers in the final battle and finds Debbie gone. Ethan is killed in the battle while running down an Indian girl he thinks is Debbie; she is not Debbie; she pulls a gun from a horse and shoots him. Debbie, who has not been Scar's (or anyone's) wife or mistress, but is described as a dusky Indian maiden, has escaped to the desert. Martin trails her there and starts to make love to her on the last page. Laurie has married Charlie McCorry much earlier.

---

*By 1970 much of the south was in substantial compliance with *Brown.* In 1971 the Court somewhat redefined the *Brown* standard around the notion of racial balance, and the focus of enforcement, and resistance, shifted to the North.

† In addition to the meanings we have traced, this change is simply good screen writing: it introduces a dramatic conflict between the two principals that heightens and transforms the significance of their external adventures.

There were two great issues involved in *Brown:* the substantive question of desegregating public schools and changing the relations between black and white races and the constitutional question of securing obedience to federal law. To certain Americans perhaps not enthusiastic about desegregation, *Brown* and the open declarations of defiance to it precipitated the most serious constitutional crisis since the Civil War and Reconstruction. In discussions at the time it was said again and again that decisions of the Supreme Court were "the law of the land" or "part of the law of the land." But whether one started from the desire for justice between the races or started from the need for compliance to law, one came logically to the same problem: how to achieve desegregation and what its consequences, near and far, were likely to be. If one began with law as an abstract principle one was perhaps more likely to approach the problem backwards and in an unconscious way. This is pervasively so in a realm of "savage thought" like the construction of fictions. It is an even more complicated process in a case like *The Searchers* where a structure pre-existing the *Brown* situation is adapted under its (unconscious) pressure. This is what Lévi-Strauss calls the *bricolage* principle: myth makes its structures out of the diverse materials at hand.

We have described the opposition between kinship by blood and kinship by adoption as a kind of mythic fulcrum—it carries both the family dispute of the story and (covertly) the social dispute of great concern to its audience. But how are we to understand the film's elaboration and treatment of the social issue, that is, of *Brown* and its consequences? At first glance, the film's treatment seems quite clear once the conversion from story issue to social issue is made.

As noted, the running argument of Ethan and Martin treats the issue explicitly. Martin asserts kinship by adoption by acting in all respects as though Debbie were literally his blood kin. He insists on participating in every stage of the search for her and, finally, on risking his life to save her. His devotion to her transcends other obligations and filiations; he defends her against Indians (Scar) and whites (Ethan and the attacking Cavalry) and leaves Laurie (twice) to secure Debbie's safety.

Ethan asserts Martin's lack of kinship to Debbie (and to himself) both as a general point of principle (the interview with the Cavalry officer) and as a means of dissuading him from continuing the search (the bunkhouse talk at the end of the first search). Ethan's insistence on literal blood lines in determining kinship, its privileges and obligations, is historically the position of the segregationist and white supremacist. Ethan returns to his brother's ranch from the Civil War in which he fought on the Southern side; he still wears his Confederate coat and carries his sabre. He refuses to recognize the surrender of the South and to take any oath subsequent to his oath to defend the Confederacy. These features mark Ethan as a white Southerner, displaced out West.* This identification occurs partly on the surface of the film but is rendered unreadable in various ways. For one

*In fact, the Central Texas region of *The Searchers* was settled mainly by Southerners before and after the Civil War. Aaron speaks of a neighbor's having gone back to chopping cotton. See Richard Maxwell Brown, *Strain of Violence* (New York: Oxford, 1975), Chapter 8, "The Violent Region of Central Texas," pp. 236–99.

thing, Ethan lacks a Southern accent, which would give the game away every time he spoke of race or looked at Martin askance. Also, John Wayne was associated by audiences with Westerners, not Southerners; the references to the Civil War are taken as character points or preface. There is no mention of the issues of the Civil War or, at any time, of blacks. Also, except for the dinner-table scene and the ride out after the lost cattle at the beginning, Ethan's anti-Indian attitudes are motivated by the plot—"He is bitter about Martha"; hence there is no reason to see them as the film's displacement of anti-black attitudes.

There is another signification set clustered around Ethan: that of outlawism. His not accepting the surrender of his side in a war that is long over makes him at least a figurative outlaw. He boasts that he still has his sabre, "didn't turn it into no ploughshare either." (That sabre, through the mediation of a green lieutenant, is later thrust up the ass of the Reverend Captain Clayton, symbol of religious and civil authority in the film.) Ethan was missing for three years between the end of the Civil War and 1868, when the film opens; there are hints that he was an outlaw during this time. "You fit a lot of descriptions," says Clayton. He shows up on the Texas frontier with a bagful of fresh \$20 pieces, about the origin of which he is vague. Ethan does shoot Futterman and his two men in the back, making no attempt to take them alive; and he takes back his gold pieces, given in trade for information. This episode gets Ethan and Martin in actual trouble with the law; Clayton takes Ethan's gun and orders him to Austin to answer questions. The Cavalry enters with news of Scar, Ethan's gun is returned, and the film drops the matter. Throughout the film, Ethan violates the religious and social law of his people by desecrating dead Indians, by scalping his enemies, by attempting to murder his kin for marrying a Comanche, etc.

Racism was always immoral and undemocratic but *Brown* made some of its most fundamental institutions illegal. Thus *The Searchers* specifically conjoins the figure of the white Southerner with the figure of the outlaw. (In the novel Ethan came right home after the Civil War and had no bagful of money or other indicia of the outlaw and he is no more anti-Indian than Martin or any of the other main characters.) After *Brown*, opposing the possibility of kinship by adoption, affirming kinship by blood only, places one outside the law. Thus Ethan's exclusion from the community at the end of the film is overdetermined by its unconscious structure.

Martin in effect wins the argument with Ethan by saving Debbie and by returning home to marry Laurie and settle in the community. Ethan returns home only to move on again. He is self-excluded from the community but, as Propp shows, this is functionally similar to forcible exclusion, just as self-dispatch and dispatch by another are equivalent functions. Note that the figure of the white Southerner often functions as a scapegoat on the race question. Our racial prejudice and our guilt for it are placed on his shoulders, then he is criticized, excluded, or lampooned, mythically purging us of them. Thus, in *The Searchers,* Ethan is excluded for our sins; that is why we find it so moving.

The film's ending thus enacts Martin's position; the adopted one marries and enters the community as an adult male. He enjoys the full rights of kinship. But it is not so simple as this, for a number of reasons. First, Martin and Ethan debate several issues, not just this one, and the film treats the issue of kinship and race in many ways besides their arguments. Secondly, what we have called "Martin's victory" is implicit in *Brown:* if the film merely affirmed the non-white's entry into white society and opposed those who oppose that entry, it might not have as great power on audiences as it has. At least it would not bear on the issue of greatest concern once *Brown* is a *fait accompli:* what will the consequences of desegregation be?

The film concerns not only the fact of adoption, the right to adoption under the new law of the land, but the nature and scope of adoption, its rights and obligations. Are the adopted ones equal in rights and obligations to those who have always belonged to the society? Martin wins the argument with Ethan, but what is the price of that victory?

The film does not deal with the adoption itself, the finding of Martin by Ethan, the growing up years, etc.—those matters in the forefront of discussion and awareness in the debate over *Brown.* Rather, it looks to the other end of the adoption spectrum, that which is implied in adoption but not immediately palpable to the senses or to the imagination: what will happen when the adopted one grows up and enters white society as an adult? Thus in *The Searchers* Martin's adoption is a *fait accompli,* a long-settled and accepted fact. The film focuses not on the adoption process, but on the status, rights, duties, and responsibilities of the adopted one when grown.

Although it is a myth about non-whites by and for whites, *The Searchers* may also be read as a manual for non-whites adopted by white society, telling them what they may expect and what is expected of them. In our analysis of the Martin complex in the film, we saw that Martin exhibits unwavering loyalty to the white community. He kills Indian men, spurns Indian wives, even defends his sister against other whites. He devotes five years to finding her, then risks his life to kill the villain and save her. Martin's passivity in regard to Laurie is also exemplary. The non-white can show no aggressiveness toward a white love-object; if Martin is the example, he can hardly show or feel desire at all. Martin postpones pleasure in the Freudian sense. Laurie offers herself and the pleasures of peaceful life at home again and again, but he refuses until his mission is done. This may be read diachronically (à la Propp) that Martin cannot marry Laurie and enter society as an adult until he has proven himself as fully white, indeed as whiter than white, by the incredible number of performances that he accomplishes. Or it may be read synchronically à la Lévi-Strauss and Lacan: Martin immediately enjoys full white citizenship and kinship (and even wins Laurie) but this creates a *debt,* according to this film an enormous debt, that he must discharge in exchange for this gift. The debt for the non-white is evidently far greater than for whites. On the opposite end of the spectrum from Martin, the good Indian (nigger), there is Scar, the bad Indian (nigger). Scar precisely cannot postpone pleasure—he rapes, murders, dismembers, burns; he is punished in the most brutal way: death, scalping, destruction of his society. The annihilating punishment that Scar receives is also a warning to adopted non-whites of what awaits their transgressions. Correlated with Scar's crimes is the fact that he remains with his tribe, with his people, whereas Martin renounces any tribal tie, loyalty, or memory; this is the pre-condition of adoption.

Our reading is non-reductive—the Indian-white ideological theme remains. There is in fact a kind of double displacement operating in the film at almost every moment, whereby literal events of the text may be read in the Indian-white register and then in the black-white register. But if our concern is the power of a myth, then it is the black-white discourse that must interest us. Power selects a myth; the myth does not create it. Black-white relations were such in 1956, and arguably now as well, that the issues *The Searchers* treats could not be treated directly. This hiddenness is the mark of conflicts of great power and the continuing power of *The Searchers* confirms audience contact with conflicts of great importance to itself but not understood by it. As the Rev. Jesse Jackson said recently, "Racism is the curse of the American soul." As long as this remains true, *The Searchers* is likely to retain its power.

Notes

An earlier version of this paper was delivered to the American Seminar on Film, supported by the National Endowment for the Arts, at Cambridge, Massachusetts, in November 1975. I am grateful to Swank Pictures, Inc., for making available a print of *The Searchers*.

1. Stuart Byron, "*The Searchers:* Cult Movie of the New Hollywood," *New York Magazine,* March 5, 1979, pp. 45–48.

2. Edward Buscombe, "Critics on *The Searchers,*" *Screen Education,* Winter 1975–1976, p. 50.

3. Quoted in Douglas Pye, "*The Searchers* and Teaching the Industry," in *ibid.,* p. 45.

4. Quoted in *ibid.,* p. 43.

5. T. S. Eliot, *Selected Essays* (New York: Harcourt, 1950), p. 12.

6. Vladimir Propp, *The Morphology of the Folktale* (Austin: University of Texas Press, 1963), pp. 75–78.

7. "John Ford's *Young Mr. Lincoln,* a collective text by the Editors of *Cahiers du cinéma.*" trans. Helene Lackner and Diana Matias, *Screen,* Autumn 1972.

8. Charles W. Eckert, "The Anatomy of a Proletarian Film: Warner's *Marked Woman,*" *Film Quarterly,* Winter 1973–1974, p. 10, reprinted here.

9. *Cahiers, op. cit.,* p. 40.

10. *Ibid.,* p. 42.

11. *Ibid.,* p. 42.

12. *Ibid.,* pp. 42–43.

13. *Ibid.,* p. 40.

14. Dwight W. Hoover, *The Red and the Black* (Chicago: Rand McNally, 1976), p. 146.

15. Winthrop D. Jordan, *White Over Black: American Attitudes Toward the Negro, 1550–1812* (Baltimore: Penguin, 1969), p. 163.

16. *Ibid.,* pp. 429–81.

17. *The Will Rogers Scrapbook,* ed. Bryan B. Sterling (New York: Grosset & Dunlap, 1976), p. 11.

18. Richard Kluger, *Simple Justice* (New York: Knopf, 1976), pp. 700–747.

19. *Ibid.,* p. 751.

20. *Ibid.,* pp. 6, 28, 672, 751, among others.

MILDRED PIERCE
RECONSIDERED

JOYCE NELSON

Joyce Nelson's terse, compelling analysis of Mildred Pierce *makes particularly vivid the relationship between purely formal devices, such as shot/reverse-shot and flashback, and social hierarchy, particularly as that relationship affects women. Nelson shows that the false suture achieved in the first few shots of the film deflects us from asking Who killed this man? to asking Why did Mildred Pierce kill this man? and that this process of blaming the woman will be resolved by a patriarchal police detective. Nelson makes instructive use of a number of abstract theoretical propositions about the nature of cinema, narrative, and communication in showing how Mildred's discourse is framed and controlled by the film.*

Nelson also makes some insightful observations about the three main male characters in the film's flashbacks and suggests that the most guilty party may well be Wally Fay. However, displacement of guilt to Mildred and ultimately to Veda makes Mildred Pierce's bid for economic independence appear a far greater crime than Wally Fay's comparable, and more underhanded, maneuvering. Nelson links this displacement to historical conditions at the end of World War II. It could also be linked to the forms of subliminal or camouflaging displacement that Charles Eckert discusses in his article on Marked Woman, *which recasts real economic conditions as moral dilemmas. Mildred's agonizing choice of whether to take the blame for her daughter's crime may be precisely such a displacement. (Parenthetically, Abraham Polonsky's* Force of Evil *may be a prime example of how moral dilemma and economic, class conflict can be yoked together: It is one of the few examples of such yoking in Hollywood film.)*

Nelson's analysis partakes of a number of methodological currents, particularly of the feminist current. At the same time, it is a pointed contribution to structuralist semiotic analysis, because of the precision with which it links its thematic concerns to effects of textual production. Nelson reminds us that a methodological separation can be made between the formal characteristics of a language system and pragmatics —the social uses and effects of language —but that such a separation is itself arbitrary. In actual practice, the codes and qualities of the cinema are as much a social matter as a formal one.

•

The opening shots of Warner Brother's *Mildred Pierce* (1945) suggest the dark ambience of film noir style: a long-shot of a rainy night street and a deserted car parked next to a California beach house, a dissolve to a slightly closer reframing—a composition in diagonals punctuated by the sound of two gun shots. Just moments into the film (shot three on the image track) there is a cut from this exterior to a medium-shot of murder victim Zachary Scott (as Monte Beragon) inside the beach house. Standing with his arms slightly outstretched, he looks almost directly at the camera. As the take continues uninterrupted, two bullets strike the full-length mirror behind him, then two more hit him in the chest; he folds his arms, leans forward and stumbles into a medium close-up, pausing momentarily before falling to the floor on his side. During the shot, the camera has panned with him to the left to show him in long-shot on the floor, as a gun is tossed next to him and he rolls onto his back. Shot four is a medium close-up on his face as he gasps the one word, 'Mildred,' and then closes his eyes. Shot four continues with a pan across his body to the right, a tilt up to the couch beside him, a pan across it to a long-shot of the shattered mirror as we hear a door close.

Considering the film in its entirety, we find that the opening seconds of both shots three and four are repeated within a flashback near the film's end. A crucial difference in the closing flashback, however, is that the shot of victim Scott looking almost directly at the camera (repetition of shot three) is here followed by a cut to a medium-shot of Ann Blyth (as Mildred Pierce's daughter Veda) holding the gun—the shot/reverse-shot which Daniel Dayan argues is the 'tutor-code' of narrative cinema's 'suturing' its point-of-view images.[1] By leaving shot three 'unsutured' until the closing flashback, the film obviously works in terms of the enigma code, raising questions which it will answer for the viewer. While any number of films may be said to rely on similar techniques—the withholding of reverse-shot to cause enigma—*Mildred Pierce* particularly interests me because it seems to frame and structure the viewer's response in the same way that its police detective character frames and controls Mildred's discourse.

One of the primary ways that the film structures our response is by providing a 'false suture' for shot three. This substitution for the reverse-shot is the work of other codes, and is purposely tentative and somewhat ambiguous. Following a long-shot of the corpse in the room, shot six returns to the rainy night street of the first two shots, with the car now being driven away from the house by an unidentifiable person. Shot seven begins with a dissolve to a high-angle, deep-focus crane shot of the Santa Monica pier at night. The camera moves to the right and cranes down as a woman enters frame-right and walks in long-shot with her back to the camera along the wet pier. Shot eight begins as a medium-shot, from hips to shoes, of the woman walking along the pier, viewed from the side in a tracking shot. The camera stops moving to let her pass it, then tilts up and pans slightly to the right to show her now in long-shot from behind. Shot nine is a medium-shot of the woman, the camera tracking in front of her as she walks. It is the first time we see her face (Joan Crawford as Mildred), which is alternately lighted and obscured as she moves in and out of the shadows. Her hands are in the pockets of her fur coat and she is crying as she looks out towards the water flowing beneath her.

The 'false suture' seems the result of a careful combination of both 'filmic' and 'cinematic' codes, to use Metz's distinction between conventions recruited to film from the wider cultural context (codes of behavior, dress, lighting, etc.) and conventions unique to cinema (montage, camera distance and angle, etc.). Both the beach house and the pier settings are stylistically similar—first seen in long-shot at night, with the camera distance and shadows obscuring the identification of the person in these exteriors. The cultural significance placed upon the last word of a dying person (also the first and only word spoken thus far in the film) makes the utterance 'Mildred' continue to resonate throughout this sequence. The only other medium-shot of a person's face aside from the victim's thus far in the film is shot nine, taken from the same camera angle. The human pain registered in shot three is here answered by culturally appropriate response—female tears. When, a few moments later, this woman is confronted by a suspicious policeman who prevents her suicide, and is then named 'Mildred' by Wally Fay (Jack Carson) as she leaves the pier, the answer to shot three as somebody's point of view has been provisionally given.

In terms of structuring viewer response, the 'false suture' depends primarily upon the use of the dissolve between shots six and seven: the car moving away from the beach house dissolves to the Santa Monica pier. This dissolve, which seems to be a mere temporal ellipsis jumping insignificant moments in the plot (the drive from beach house to pier), turns out to be the means for connecting two quite separate times, spaces, and character reactions which are not as directly related as the dissolve implies. Within the narrative, this dissolve would seem to be what Barthes calls a cardinal function, a 'risk-laden moment':

Indeed, there is a strong presumption that the mainspring of the narrative activity is to be traced to that very confusion between consecutiveness and consequence, what-comes-*after* being read in a narrative as what-is-*caused-by*. Narrative would then be a systematic application of the logical fallacy denounced by scholasticism under the formula *post hoc, ergo propter hoc*, which may well be the motto of Destiny whose 'language,' after all, finds its expression in narrative; and this 'telescoping' of logic and temporality is mainly achieved by the framework of cardinal functions. These functions may at first glance appear quite trivial. What makes them crucial is not their spectacular quality but rather the risk involved: the cardinal functions are the risk-laden moments of narrative.[2]

This dissolve, a crucial aspect in the sequentiality of the narrative discourse, a form in time, is irreversible. By its means, the proairetic code (the coordination of the actions represented) is based on contiguity—two sequences next to each other in viewing time. The metonymical substitution of Mildred for Veda, which we don't realize until the end of the film, and the false suture itself both work towards changing the nature of the narrative's central enigma: now the question the film will answer is no longer 'Who killed Monte Beragon?' but 'Why did Mildred kill Monte Beragon?', the latter question rising to the foreground and held there, as we shall see, by the chief detective. If we still are unsure about the answer to the first question, it is because the film utilizes this seeming insecurity about our own response to keep the murder central in its unfolding. I would argue that, as responsive viewers, we are placed in the same position as Mildred is by the chief detective; rushing towards its preconceived end, the structure of the film insisting upon its central enigma, *Mildred Pierce* forces us to deny certain emotions as irrelevant to the narrative context, to discard alternative readings based on different emphases in the plot, in short, to disregard our own experience of the film.

As others have noted,[3] the film has a convoluted use of time. The opening murder, Mildred at the pier, her drink with Wally in his nightclub, her attempt to frame him for the Beragon murder, her return home where she is apprehended by the police—all lead to the interrogation of Mildred by the chief detective in his office, an interrogation through which two lengthy segments from Mildred's past are articulated. Each segment from the past leads into the 'present' context, the detective's office. Following upon the second segment, Mildred's daughter Veda is brought into the office and revealed (verbally) as the murderer. This instigates the third segment from the past, a flashback which returns to the opening moments of the film: the Beragon murder, with the missing details (and the withheld reverse-shot) included. Then, moving into the present again, Veda is taken away by the police and Mildred leaves the office to be rejoined by first husband Bert, who is waiting outside.

All of the scenes within the present (which includes the third flashback) seem much more suggestive of film noir style than are the two lengthy segments from Mildred's past, her discourse. Thus, the film's present is characterized by greater contrasts in areas of light and dark, certain unsettling variations in camera distance and angle, claustrophobic sets and framing devices, lines and angles which splinter the composition of the frame, events taking place at night, a mood of suspicion and distrust. In comparison, the two segments from Mildred's past are more evenly illuminated, use little variation in camera angle, are more harmoniously composed with traditionally balanced three-shots and two-shots, mainly concern events taking place in the light of day, and attempt to clarify rather than cloud relationships.

However, the pace within the film's present seems much more urgent and involving, especially because it is exclusively concerned with a specific moment and act, the Beragon murder. Not only does the temporal structure insist upon the murder as the primary concern, giving it privileged status through repetition, but the two lengthy segments comprising Mildred's discourse (in which other matters are explored) culminate in a return to the present, with the chief detective invalidating her narration. He demands that she 'now tell us the truth'—that is, stay with the 'facts' of the Beragon murder only. The invalidation of Mildred's discourse is supported by the false suture through which we have been led to perceive her as possible Murderer. Thus, her discourse is framed at several levels: structurally, visually, verbally, and contextually. The present frames the past, noir style frames Thirties softer look, detective's works frame hers, and his office provides the present context.

Context and framing embody stylistic and structural tensions which can be usefully explored through the concepts of logical typing, analog and digital communication, as discussed by Nichols in "Style, Grammar, and the Movies":[4]

Analog communication involves continuous quantities with no significant gaps. There is no 'not' nor any question of 'either/or': everything is 'more or less' (for example, all nonconventionalized gestures, inflections, rhythms, and the context of communication itself). Digital communication involves discrete elements and discontinuities or gaps. It allows for saying 'not' and 'either/or' rather than 'both/and' (as in all denotative, linguistic communication). In nature, the digital is the instrument of the analog (it is of a lower logical type and higher order of organization). In our culture the instrumental relationship is reversed. The two forms are not in opposition and the general function of the digital is to draw boundaries within the analog—as with the on/off switch of a thermostat operating within a temperature continuum, or phonemes arbitrarily carved from a sound continuum.[5]

Since the two modes are not in opposition, we are concerned with *how* boundaries are drawn within the analog, *who* draws them, who controls and uses the digital. In our culture greater validity is given to the digital mode (facts over feelings, verbal proficiency over the inarticulate, language over gesture) and can lead to the suppression of the analog. This devaluation of the analog has had vast repercussions in our society and relates directly to the experience of oppression suffered by women and minorities. If we consider the interrelationship of the two modes in *Mildred Pierce,* we find the film a provocative example of the digital mode exploiting and suppressing the analogical.

The temporal continuum, the continuity between past and present, is stylistically and structurally broken up into discrete units: the present, with its emphasis upon the Beragon murder; the past, Mildred's discourse. It is the function of the chief detective to keep the binary opposition of Victim/Murderer in the foreground, reminding us of the missing latter term (and the withheld reverse-shot) each time he interrupts Mildred's discourse. In his concern for the facts relevant only to the Beragon murder, as if it were a pure moment which could be isolated from all the rest, he dismisses everything else. Though he is the agent who instigates Mildred's discourse and the termination point of each segment (present as on/off switch), he notes only the 'on' or 'off' nature of Mildred's relationships. His concern with one discrete moment out of the whole continuum is obvious when he tells Mildred she was the "key" to solving the murder: "The key turned, the door opened, and in walked the murderer"—enter Veda. Tricking Veda into revealing her guilt by saying 'Your mother told us everything,' he is then able to turn the narrative back to its primary moment—the repetition through flash-back of the murder in detail.

Speech is always both digital and analogical, and the chief detective cunningly exploits the analogical to the service of his digital concerns: his fatherly and seemingly sympathetic tone when addressing Mildred, the offer of a cigarette, are analogical means for his getting the facts as well as for denying the context, the police office.

Mildred's discourse stresses the gradual changes within her life over a long period of time, the gradients within the various relationships, the importance of context for action and behavior, the triadic nature of interrelationships rather than binary oppositions. For Mildred, the Beragon murder is not a discrete moment which can be ripped apart from the larger continuum and considered in isolation, nor is it the only crime. Her discourse unfolds a series of complex familial and business relationships within which a series of crimes occurs, all having to do with the present Beragon murder. These other crimes have no corpse, no climactic moment, no isolatable guilty party; rather they are wrapped up in the paradoxical injunctions recurring within the family and business relationships. Having more to do with feelings than facts, these devastating injunctions are perhaps as difficult for Mildred to pinpoint as they are for the viewer. They are nonetheless 'real' and complicate the Beragon murder.

However, such complexity is seemingly beyond the interests of the chief detective and the judicial system he serves, since both demand isolatable units which can be processed and punished. Just as the detective dismisses everything but the facts, the structure of the film prevents Mildred's discourse from dirtying a clean one, and keeps the murder in a pure state. In these terms, it is the function of the final flashback to further purify it by inserting the true reverse-shot, completing the true suture—tidying up. My vocabulary here isn't gratuitous since a kind of master antinomy in the film is the supposed opposition: greasiness/cleanliness. It could be argued that the amount of screen time given to Mildred's past should make it the central concern of the narrative. But it is precisely here that we can see the power of plot over story. The formal reordering of chronology, here coupled with voice-over flashback, reduces what could be the central diegesis to a digression:

Metadiegetic amplifications correspond to stories within stories, where narration is one degree removed (hence the name): 'a second-hand narration is constituted wherever a narrative agent . . . conducts the story inside the primary narration.' This secondary status is obviously a purely formal property and has nothing to do with value judgments.[6]

Clearly, in *Mildred Pierce* the secondary status given her discourse through the various framing devices has everything to do with value judgments. Just as the police chief has Mildred trapped in a classic double-bind (either she sacrifices herself by confessing, or she sacrifices the one she loves, her daughter), the film asks us to deny our own feelings that Mildred's discourse is the primary one. We, too, are given paradoxical injunctions. First we are led to think, because of the withheld reverse-shot, that the film will be a whodunit. Then, through the false suture, we are encouraged to suspect Mildred and switch our focus to why. As we begin to understand Mildred's problematic past and perhaps to admire her career efforts, the detective breaks in to insist that what we just experienced and felt is irrelevant ('now tell us the truth'), that, despite all the detail and involvement in Mildred's discourse, what should really concern us is the murder. And finally we are shown, through the flashback of the murder in detail, that we were wrong to suspect Mildred in the first place.

These techniques for shifting the ground beneath us at strategic moments are related to what could be seen as the film's central paradoxical injunction. Through the strikingly similar appearance of Joan Crawford and Ann Blyth, which is enhanced by almost identical dress and coiffure, and through the use of recurring two-shots in which their profiles are framed, the film strongly invites us to see Mildred and Veda as mirror images of each other. In fact, I would argue that what began as a metonymical substitution of Mildred for Veda in the false suture—essentially syntagmatic and based on contiguity—becomes, through the course of the film, a metaphorical substitution—essentially paradigmatic and based on similarity. If visually the film poses them as mirror images, structurally and thematically it interchanges them in relationship to Monte Beragon as his lover and murderer. On these important levels the film thus asks us to deny our intuition that the two characters are actually of different logical types. Throughout the film Veda's methods for getting ahead in the world are ruthless, devious, and cut-throat;

she is much more like Wally Fay and Monte Beragon. Mildred, on the other hand, is generous and honest, and in terms of business and familial interactions is unlike any of the other characters, especially Veda.

By confusing logical types, the film attempts to obscure the very real differences between the two women, and perhaps ultimately asks us to read the character of Mildred as a castrating bitch, within the same paradigm as the murderer. The confusion of different logical types will thus have important repercussions for the ways we perceive Mildred as a career woman.

If the film asks us to find similarities between Mildred and Veda, it is perhaps in order to de-emphasize the comparisons among the three men—Bert, Monte, and Wally Fay. Through the course of the two past segments, neither Bert nor Monte (Mildred's husbands) works for a living. 'With me, loafing is a science,' says Monte, while Bert has been pushed out of a job and seems in no rush to find another—'Might be nice if you left me alone once for just five minutes; when the time comes, I'll get a job.' Both have other women besides Mildred in their lives: Monte's 'sisters' and then Veda, Bert's Mrs. Beiderhoff. Each is connected with selling real estate: Bert's former job and Monte's means of support, selling off his own property bit by bit. Both like to gamble and leave Mildred facing a stack of unpaid bills. Since neither has an income, each eventually lives off the money Mildred earns while openly resenting her economic success.

The differences between the two husbands are class differences. Thus, Monte's leisure is characterized by French *bons mots,* playing polo, gambling, drinking and seduction, while Bert plays gin rummy with Mrs. Beiderhoff. As Mildred's business grows in success, Bert's potency decreases while Monte's does not. During the same evening of Mildred's first romantic involvement with Monte, Bert's favorite daughter, Kay, contracts pneumonia and dies. Monte's whisper during their love scene, 'You take my breath away,' becomes grotesquely elaborated in the scene following: daughter Kay gasping for breath in an oxygen tent. Eventually Bert is almost totally out of the picture, no longer involved with Mrs. Beiderhoff, and serving only as the agent of mediation between Mildred and Veda. Without an income, Bert plays a servile, asexual role, while Monte, also unemployed, retains his sexual attractiveness and actual status.

Wally Fay, the third man important in Mildred's life, is a fast-talking businessman, a real estate agent (Bert's more ambitious partner) with ruthless methods who will do just about anything to 'make a buck.' Unlike Bert and Monte, Wally always seems to be working, dislikes gambling and bad business risks, and is never visually connected with a home of his own; his locales are the office and nightclub. As I recall, at no time are these three men together in a scene. Rather, the triadic quality of the two past segments is the result of any two of the three male characters together with Mildred in a three-shot. In comparison to Bert and Monte (lower-class and aristocracy), Wally seems representative of an upwardly mobile middle-class, but of a specifically cut-throat kind. Not only is he the agent by which Bert becomes unemployed in the first place (forced out of the business by Wally), but he is the agent through whom Monte sells off his diminishing estate. Wally Fay is therefore crucially instrumental to the economic impotence of both Bert and Monte, and finally of Mildred.

Recalling the importance of boundaries and who draws them, I think part of what Mildred's discourse reveals to us is that Wally Fay is the guilty party, in terms of crimes of the marketplace. But the order in which information is given us in the film makes us read his character in a more sympathetic light than he deserves. For example, in one of the opening scenes in the film Mildred has brought Wally to the beach house, where the corpse still lies in the next room. Setting him up as the fall guy (though knowing all along that 'You can talk your way out of anything, can't you, Wally?'), Mildred moves into the bedroom while Wally talks to her from the bar: 'You know, I'm glad you didn't get sore at me the way I took you over the hurdles, Mildred. I didn't mean to cut up your business the way I did. I just got started and couldn't stop . . . I can't help myself. I see an angle and right away I start cutting myself a piece of throat. It's an instinct.' In a way, we treat his words as noise at this point, since the film asks us to concentrate on Mildred as the probable murderer, the corpse in the next room, the fact that she is framing him.

The Beragon murder must cast its shadow over Mildred's discourse in order to put things right. The only character who uses compassion in both business and personal relations, who can move out from under economic and social oppression without cutting throats, must be silenced and sent home. If Veda's crime was murder, Mildred's was independence—especially in economic terms. Obviously, running a restaurant chain is not all that far removed from running an efficient home kitchen, except for the important difference of earning an income. It is only when Mildred begins to earn money from her work that it 'smells of grease' to the other characters. If we place *Mildred Pierce* in history, we find that its release date (October 20, 1945) coincides with the transition to a post-war economy and the return of the troops. The relative economic freedom given to women as part of the war effort had to be revoked, the boundaries redrawn, especially in terms of who was to fill managerial positions and other high-paying, decision-making jobs. This puts the ideological work in the film within a better light. Our own feelings about Mildred as a competent, compassionate businesswoman worthy of her position have been framed by the digital binary oppositions insisted upon by the film: Victim/Murderer, real murderer/innocent suspect (true suture/false suture), important crime/unimportant crimes, facts/noise, present/past (primary discourse/secondary discourse). On these terms we are asked to read the final image in *Mildred Pierce* as a positive resolution. Mildred walks away from the camera in long-shot with Bert (now employed) towards a massive archway. The light of dawn bathes the image, while in the foreground two scrubwomen scour the steps of the Hall of Justice. Everything and everyone have been put back into their proper places: the murder solved, the murderer found, the couple re-enshrined in their correct roles, and women back on their knees, keeping the facade clean.

Notes

1. Daniel Dayan, "The Tutor-Code of Classical Cinema," *Film Quarterly,* Fall 1974, pp. 22–31. See also William Rothman, "Against 'The System of the Suture,'" *Film Quarterly,* Fall 1975, pp. 45–50, reprinted in *Movies and Methods*, vol. I.

2. Roland Barthes, "An Introduction to the Structural Analysis of Narrative," *New Literary History,* Winter 1975, p. 248.

3. See especially Parker Tyler, "Doubting the Evidence of the Senses," in *Magic and Myth of the Movies* (New York: Henry Holt & Company, 1947), pp. 211–29, and John Davis, "The Tragedy of Mildred Pierce," *Velvet Light Trap,* no. 6, pp. 27–30.

4. Bill Nichols, "Style, Grammar, and the Movies," *Film Quarterly,* Spring 1975, pp. 33–49, reprinted in *Movies and Methods,* vol. I.

5. Nichols, p. 33.

6. Tzvetan Todorov, "Some Approaches to Russian Formalism," *Twentieth Century Studies,* December 1972, p. 14. Todorov here examines concepts of diegetic amplification as developed by Genette.

THE SPECTATOR-IN-THE-TEXT: THE RHETORIC OF *STAGECOACH*

NICK BROWNE

Like Edward Branigan in his article, "The Point-of-View Shot," in Part 6, Nick Browne draws attention to a possible rhetoric of cinematic narrative. Browne's account is less taxonomic than Branigan's, and Browne's examination of how we read a fictional film and align ourselves for or against characters is far more complex than Branigan's straightforward reading of the point-of-view shot and its formal variations. The particular problem that Browne confronts is one of how the shot works at a rhetorical level, when our figurative point of view —our emotional identification —differs from our literal point of view —the physical position from which we see.

Browne chooses a sequence from John Ford's Stagecoach *to develop his point. (It may be that a considerable number of other scenes could be cited from other films where events unfold from the physical perspective of someone in authority but where we relate emotionally to someone who lacks authority or control.) In this sequence, we see events unfold from Lucy's position. She is an upright member of society. But we identify emotionally with Dallas, a prostitute. How can this be?*

Browne's argument stresses the complex dynamics of reading as an operation that all viewers perform (as opposed to interpretation, which critics perform). His insistence on reading leads him to reject the notion that we feel the narration to be in the events because the sequence has been edited to follow our natural course of attention. He also rejects the arguments expressed by Baudry in his article in Part 5 that position and point of view are even more deeply embedded in the cinematic apparatus: French theory, Browne argues, is wrong to enforce an analogy based on the position of the eye in photographic perspective, because what is optical and literal in that case corresponds only to the literal place of the viewer in the theater, not to his or her figurative place in the film. Thus, Browne strives to account for this figurative place and to show how it can differ not only from our position in a theater but from the point-of-view shots that create a bond of emotional identification between viewer and character.

A major component of Browne's account is his attention to temporal duration, to the sequencing of shots and what it means for the act of reading. In this way, he contributes to an area of film theory —theories of the sequence —that is still noticeably underdeveloped and to the study of expressive or analog codes. The pacing and tension that accompany Lucy's and Dallas's direction of gazes, the delay of the consequences that Lucy's initial response to Dallas suggests, the gradual involvement of the other characters with the question of social as well as physical position —these all enter into an act of reading that accounts for our own place far more specifically than Baudry's theory of a fundamental ideological effect seems capable of doing. Gradually and retrospectively, both in this sequence and throughout the film, we recognize that Dallas is the wronged one and that Lucy is the intolerant one. Browne may become somewhat overly technical and philosophical about how the narrative agency positions us relative to this fairly clear-cut case of sympathetic whore and moralistic married woman (some of the anomaly of our position surely originates with genre conventions and with fairly straightforward signals of character type conveyed by acting), but Browne's detail should not obscure the basic point, which is that the structuring effects of the point-of-view figure are less determining than theorists concerned with something like a general field theory contend. Browne maintains that the viewer engages in an active, retrospective reading that differentiates between several different kinds of place and position in a sophisticated way. He also demonstrates how John Ford employs strategies of judgment and metacommentary within a highly traditional narrative. Browne concludes that we are neither compelled by editing to share the point of view of the camera or a character, except physically, nor entirely free to supply judgments of our own. The last point becomes even more important when we consider that the so-called objective style of some cinéma vérité *documentary presumably leaves the viewer free to supply value judgments based on previous experience. Browne suggests that "freedom," both in documentary, I suspect, and in fiction, is subject to complex processes of reading. Thus, by adding an element of rhetorical analysis, Browne carries structural criticism forward into a domain where questions of the reader's activity become germane.*

●

The sequence from John Ford's *Stagecoach* shown in the accompanying stills raises the problem of accounting for the organization of images in an instance of the "classical" fiction film and of proposing the critical terms appropriate for that account. The formal features of these images—the framing of shots and their sequencing, the repetition of set-ups, the position of characters, the direction of their glances—can be taken together as a complex structure and understood as a characteristic answer to the rhetorical problem of telling a story, of showing an action to a spectator. Because the significant relations have to do with seeing—both in the ways the characters "see" each other and the way those relations are shown to the spectator—and because their complexity and coherence can be considered as a matter of "point of view," I call the object of this study the "specular text."

Explanations of the imagery of the classical narrative film are offered by technical manuals and various theories of editing. Here, though, I wish to examine the connection between the act of narration and the imagery, specifically in the matter of the framing and the angle of view determined by set-ups, by characterizing the narrating agency or authority which can be taken to rationalize the presentation of shots. An explanation of this kind necessarily involves clarifying in some detail the notion of the "position of the spectator." Thus we must characterize the spectator's implied position with respect to the action, the way it is structured, and the specific features of the process of "reading" (though not in the sense of "interpretation"). Doing so entails a description (within the terms of the narrative) of the relation of literal and fictional space that comprehends what seems, ambiguously, like the double origin of filmic images.

An inquiry into the forms of authority for the imagery and the corresponding strategies which implicate the viewer in the action has few precedents, yet it raises general but basic questions about filmic narration that begin to clarify existing accounts of the relation of narrative to image. The sequence from *Stagecoach* is interesting as a structure precisely because, in spite of its simplicity (it has no narrative or formal eccentricity), it challenges the traditional premises of critical efforts to account for the operation and effects of "classical" film style.

The traditional rationale for the presentation of imagery is often stated by the camera's relation to the spectator. For instance, a basically dramatic account has it that the shots should show essentially what a spectator would see it the action were played on a stage, and if at each moment he had the best view of the action (thus changing angles only supply "accents"). Editing would follow the spectator's natural course of attention as it is implied by the action of the *mise-en-scène*. In such a mode the question of agency—that is, who is "staging" and making these events appear in this way—is referred not to the author or narrator but to the action itself, fully embodied in the characters. Everything that happens must be exhibited clearly for the eye of the spectator. In this theory, all the structures of the presentation are directed to a place external to the scene of the action—to the final authority, the ideal spectator. Oudart's recent account (*Film Quarterly*, Fall 1974) proposes that imagery is paradigmatically referred to the authority of the glance of the "absent one," the off-screen character within the story who in the counter shot is depicted within the frame; the spectator "identifies" with the visual field of the "owner" of the glance. The "system of the suture" is an explanation that establishes the origin of the imagery by reference to the agency of character but, surprisingly, it does not consider (indeed it seems to deny) the final agency, the authority of the narrator. The traces of the action of the narrator may seem to be effaced by this system, but such an effect can only be the result of a certain more general rhetoric. Thus I am proposing an account in which the structure of the imagery, whatever its apparent forms of presentation, refers jointly to the action of an implied narrator (who defines his position with respect to the tale by his judgements) and to the imaginative action occasioned by his placing and being placed by the spectator. Neither the traditional nor the more recent theories seem fully adequate to this problematic.

Thus the problem that arises from *Stagecoach* is to explain the functioning of the narrator and the nature and effects of spectator placement: specifically describing and accounting for in detail a filmic rhetoric in which the agency of the narrator in his relation to the spectator is enacted jointly by the characters and the particular sequence of shots that show them. To describe this rhetoric in a rigorous and illuminating way means clarifying in filmic terms the notions of "narrative authority," "point of view," and "reading" and showing that these concepts are of use precisely because they arise naturally from the effort to account for the concrete structures of the text.

The moment in the story that the sequence depicts is the taking of a meal at the Dry Fork station on the stage's way to Lordsburg. Earlier in the film, the prostitute Dallas (the woman in the dark hat) has been run out of town by the Ladies' Law and Order League and has been put aboard the stagecoach. There she joined, among others, a cavalry officer's wife named Lucy (in the white hat) and Hatfield, her chivalrous but distant escort. Just before the present scene, the Ringo Kid (John Wayne), who has broken out of jail to avenge his brother's murder, had been ordered aboard by the sheriff when discovered by the side of the road. The sequence begins immediately after a vote among the members of the group to decide whether to go on to Lordsburg and ends shortly before the end of the scene when the group exits the station. For purposes of convenience I have called shots 4, 8, and 10, which are from the same set-up, series A and shots 3, 7, 9 and 11 series B.

One of the rationales that might be proposed to account for the set-ups, the spatial fields they show, the sequence of shots, is their relation to the "psychology" of the characters. How, if at all, are the set-ups linked to the visual attention, as with the glance or, say, the interests of a character in the story? In the shot/reverse shot pattern, which is sometimes, wrongly I think, taken as an exclusive paradigm of the "classical" style, the presence of the shot on the screen is "explained" or read as the depiction of the glance of the off-screen character, who, a moment later, is shown in the reverse shot. But because only a few shots of this sequence (or of most films) follow this pattern we shall be pressed to a different formulation. The general question is how the two set-ups of the two major series of shots—series A from the head of the table and series B from the left side—are to be explained.

Series A is related to the visual attention of the woman at the head of the table, Lucy. The connection between the shots and her view, especially in the modulation of the force and meaning of that view, must however be established. These shots from A are readable as the depiction of Lucy's glance only retrospectively, after series B has shown her at the head of the table and after the animation conveyed in the dolly forward has implied its significance. The point remains, however, that the shots of series A are finally clearly authorized by a certain disposition of attention of one of the characters.

In contrast to series A, the series B shots from the left of the table are like the opening and closing shots (1, 12) in not being associated with or justified spatially as the depiction of anyone's glance. Can the placement of these shots be justified either as the "best angle" for the spectator or as the depiction of some other more complex conception of "psychology" of character than an act of attention in a glance? Persons to whom these shots might be attributed as views would be Dallas or the outlaw Ringo, for they satisfy one condition: they are out of the A series frame. As series A shows, in this style the association of a shot with a glance is effected by a coincidence of geographical places, eye and camera. But here, quite plainly, neither Dallas nor Ringo is in a position to view from this angle. And in each shot, Lucy is in the frame.

To attribute the shots of series B—to justify their placement spatially—to some conception of character psychology requires some other justification than the mere representation of somebody's glance. What kind of psychological account could explain the alternation of these precise framings? What kind of mental disposition, ensemble of attitude, judgement, and intention is this framing significant of? Whose disposition? On what basis would such an attribution be effected? If establishing the interpretation of the framing depended on or was referred to a character's "state of mind," which in fact changes significantly over the course of the sequence for each of the major characters (Dallas, Ringo, and Lucy), how would it be possible to accommodate those changing feelings to the fixity of set-up? The fact of the fixity of set-up denies that the explanation for camera placement can as a principle be referred to a psychology of character(s) based on the kind of emotional changes—surprise, repudiation, naivete, humiliation—that eventuate in the sequence.

As another hypothesis we could say that the particular compositional features of series B are a presentation not of the "mind" of any single character but of a state of affairs within the group, a relationship among the parties. What is the state of affairs within this society that the framing depicts? These are two significant features of the composition from set-up B: the relation of Lucy in the immediate foreground to the group behind her, a group whose responsiveness to events repeats the direction of her own attention, and her relation, spatially, to Dallas and Ringo, who, excluded by the left edge of the frame, are outside. The permanent and underlying fact about the *mise-en-scène* which justifies the fixity of camera placement is its status as a social drama of alliance and antagonism between two social roles—Lucy, an insider, a married woman and defender of custom, and Dallas, outsider and prostitute who violates the code of the table. The camera set-ups and the spatial fields they reveal, the compositional exclusion of the outlaw couple and their isolation in a separate space, with the implied assertion of Lucy's custodial relation to the body of legitimate society, respond to and depict in for-

1

4a

Dallas: Thank you.

2

4b

Ringo: Set down here, ma'am.

3a

4c

3b

5

6a

8a

6b

8b

7a

9

Hatfield: May I find you another place,
Mrs. Mallory? It's cooler by the window.

7b

10

11a

12a

Lucy: Thank you.

11b

12b

11c

mal terms the social "positions" of the characters. In the kind of dramatic presentation they effect, the features of the framing are not justified as the depiction of personal psychology considered as changes of feeling; instead, by their emphasis on social positions, or types, they declare a psychology of intractable situations.

The framing of series B from the left of the table does not represent literally or figuratively any single person's view; rather, it might be said, it depicts, by what it excludes and includes, the interplay of social positions within a group. This asymmetry of social position of Lucy over Dallas extends as well to formal and compositional features of the sequence. Though set-up B represents both positions, Dallas's negatively, it makes Lucy's position privileged in the formal mechanism of narrative exposition. The fundamental narrative feature of the sequence is a modification and inflection of the logic of shot/counter shot. Here it is an alternation of series A and B around not two characters but either Lucy's eye or body. That is, in series A Lucy is present as an eye, as the formal beholder of the scene. Alternately, in B, Lucy is shown bodily dominating the foreground, and as the eye to which the views of series A are referred. Formally the narration proceeds by alternatingly shifting Lucy's presence from the level of the depicted action, as body (B), to the level of representation, as the invisible eye (A), making Lucy's presence the central point of spatial orientation and legibility. In shots 5 and 6, the close-up of the exchange of looks between the two women, the formal asymmetry is the difference of their frontality, and the shot of Lucy is from a place that Dallas could not literally occupy. Lucy's frontality (5) marks a dispossession, a displacement, that corresponds to Dallas's social "absence" in the entire sequence—to her exclusion from the frame in B, to her isolation as the object of Lucy's scornful glance in A. By contrast to Lucy's presence everywhere, as body and eye, Dallas's eye is never taken as the source of authority for a shot. Her eye is averted. She is always, in both A and B, the object of another's gaze—a condition that corresponds to the inferiority of her social position and to her formal invisibility—she cannot authorize a view.

The shots of set-up B, which might be called "objective," or perhaps "nobody's" shots, in fact refer to or are a representation of Lucy's social dominance and formal privilege. B shows a field of vision that closely matches Lucy's *conception* of her own place in that social world: its framing corresponds to her alliance with the group and to her intention to exclude the outsiders, to deny their claim to recognition. It is in other words not exactly a description of Lucy's subjectivity but an objectification of her social self-conception. Though Lucy is visible in the frame, series B might be said, metaphorically, to embody her point of view.

This explanation seems cogent as far as it goes. But there are some further issues that arise from the passage, in the way it is experienced, that suggest that the foregoing analysis of the justification of these formal features is incomplete as an account of the grounds for the effects the passage produces and theoretically limited in terms of explaining the strategies of framing and other premises of the narration.

Simply put, the experience of the passage is a feeling of empathy for Dallas's exclusion and humiliation, and a repudiation of Lucy's prejudice as unjust, two feelings brought together by a sense of inevitability of the conflict. There is in other words a curious opposition between the empathetic response of a spectator toward Dallas and the underlying premises of the mechanism of the narrative which are so closely related, formally, to Lucy's presence, point of view, and interests. It is this sense of incongruity between feeling and formal structure that occasions the following effort to consider the sequence in terms of the ways it produces its effects, that is, rhetorically.

One question about a formal matter, which draws attention to the limitations of a structural account based on a conception of the social order, is why the outsiders are seen from a position that is associated with Lucy's place at the table, her gaze. This fact, and the action of the audience within the film, casts doubt on two theories of agency. Our attention as spectators, in the shots of series B, does not follow the visual attention of any depicted characters. These shots might perhaps be read as statements of the "interests" of characters, the nature of their social positions, but that is already a kind of commentary or interpretation that needs explanation. The actions of the men at the bar, the audience within the film, disprove the traditional rationale for editing stated by reference to an ideal spectator: as "placed" spectators we anticipate, not follow, the movements of their attention (2, 3); the object of their attention is sometimes out of the frame (3b) we see and what they see is shown only from a view significantly different from any simply "accented" or "best view," indeed from a place they could not occupy; and sometimes (7b, 8) they have turned away, uninterested, but the screen doesn't go black. In general, an adequate account of the formal choices of the passage must be quite different from an account of the event as if it were staged for the natural attention of a spectator, depicted or real. To ask why the spectator sees in the way he does refers to a set of premises distinguishable from an account based on the attention of either a character or an ideal spectator. It refers to the concrete logic of the placement of the implied spectator and to the theory of presentation that accounts for the shaping of his response. Such an account makes the "position" of the spectator, the way in which he is implicated in the scene, the manner and location of his presence, his point of view, problematical.

It is this notion of the "position of the spectator" that I wish to clarify in so far as that notion illuminates the rhetorical strategies, particularly choice of set-up (implying scale and framing) that depicts the action. In contemporary French film theory, particularly in the work of Comolli and Baudry, the notion of the "place" of the spectator is derived from the central position of the eye in perspective and photographic representation. By literally substituting the epistemological subject, the spectator, for the eye in an argument about filmic representation, the filmic spectator is said to be "theological" and "centered" with respect to filmic images. Thus the theory of the filmic spectator is treated as if subject to the Derridian critique of center, presence, etc. French theory is wrong to enforce this analogy based on the position of the eye in photographic perspective, because what is optical and literal in that case corresponds only to the literal place of the spectator in the projection hall, and not at all to his figurative place in the film, nor to his place as subject to the rhetoric of the film, or reader or producer of the sense of the discourse. Outside of a French ideological project which fails to discriminate literal and figurative space, the notion of "place" of the spectator, and of "center," is an altogether problematic notion whose significance and function in critical discussion have yet to be explicated.

The sequence from *Stagecoach* provides the terms in which the notion of the position of the spectator might be clarified, provided we distinguish, without yet expecting full clarification, the different senses of "position." A spectator is (a) seated physically in the space of the projection hall and (b) placed by the camera in a certain fictional position with respect to the depicted action; moreover (c), insofar as we see from what we might take to be the eye of a character, we are invited to occupy the place allied to the place he holds, in, for example, the social system; and finally (d), in another figurative sense of place, it is the only way that our response can be accounted for, that we can identify with a character's position in a certain situation.

In terms of the passage at hand, the question is then: how can I describe my "position" as spectator in identifying with the humiliated position of one of the depicted characters, Dallas, when my views of her belong to those of another, fictional character, Lucy, who is in the act of rejecting her? What is the spectator's "position" in identifying with Dallas in the role of the passive character? Dallas in averting her eyes from Lucy's in shot 6 accepts a view of herself in this encounter as "prostitute" and is shamed. However, in identifying with Dallas in the role of outcast, presumably the basis for the evocation of our sympathy and pity, our response as spectator is not one of shame, or anything even analogous. We do not suffer or repeat the humiliation. I understand Dallas's feeling but I am not so identified with her that I re-enact it. One of the reasons for this restraint is that, though I identify with Dallas's abject position of being seen as an unworthy object by someone whose judgement she accepts, I identify with her as the object of another's action. Indeed, in a remarkable strategy, I am asked to see Dallas through Lucy's eyes. That as spectator I am sharing Lucy's view and, just as importantly, her manner of viewing is insisted on most emphatically by the dolly forward (4) and by disclosures effected by shot/counter shot, thus placing us in a lively and implicated way in a position fully associated with Lucy's place at the head of the table.

Insofar as I identify with Dallas, it is not by repeating her shame, but by imagining myself in her position (situation). The early scenes of the film have carefully prepared us to believe that this exclusion is an unjust act. When the climactic moment arrives, our identification with Dallas as an object of view is simultaneously established as the ground for repudiating the one whose view we share and are implicated in. Though I share Lucy's literal geographical position of viewing at this moment in the film, I am not committed to her figurative point of view. I can in other words repudiate Lucy's view of or judgement of Dallas without negating it as a view, in a way that Dallas herself, captive of the other's image, cannot. Because our feelings as spectators are not "analogous" to the interests and feelings of the characters, we are not bound to accept their views either of themselves or of others. Our "position" as spectator then is very different from the previous senses of "position": it is defined neither in terms of orientation within the constructed geography of the fiction, nor of social position of the viewing character. On the contrary, our point of view on the sequence is tied more closely to our attitude of approval or disapproval and is very different from any literal viewing angle or character's point of view.

Identification asks us as spectators to be two places at once, where the camera is and "with" the depicted person—thus its double structure of viewer/viewed. As a powerful emotional process it thus throws into question any account of the position of the spectator as centered at a single point or at the center of any simply optical system. Identification, this passage shows, necessarily has a double structure in the way it implicates the spectator in both the position of the one seeing and the one seen. This sequence however does establish a certain kind of "center" in the person of Lucy. Each of the shots is referred alternatingly to the scene before her eye or the scene of her body, but it is a "center" that functions as a principle of spatial legibility, and is associated with a literal point within the constructed space of the fiction. This center stands, though, as I have suggested, in a very complicated relation to our "position" as spectator. That is, the experience of the passage shows that our identification, in the Freudian sense of an emotional investment, is not with the center, either Lucy or the camera. Rather, if, cautiously, we can describe our figurative relation to a film in geographical terms of "in," "there," "here," "distance" (and this sequence, as part of its strategy as a fiction, explicitly asks us to by presenting action to us from the literal view of a character), then as spectators we might be said to formally occupy someone else's place, to be "in" the film, all the while being "outside" it in our seats. We can identify with a character and share her "point of view" even if the logic of the framing and selection of shots of the sequence denies that she has a view or a place within the society that the *mise-en-scène* depicts. There are significant differences between structures of shots, views, and identification: indeed, this sequence has shown, as a principle, that we do not "identify" with the camera but with the characters, and hence do not feel dispossessed by a change in shots. For a spectator, as distinct perhaps from a character, point of view is not definitively or summarily stated by any single shot or even set of shots from a given spatial location.

The way in which we as spectators are implicated in the action is as much a matter of our position with respect to the unfolding of those events in time as of their representation from a point in space. The effect of the mode of sequencing, the regular opposition of insiders and outsiders, is modulated in ways that shape the attitudes of the spectator/reader toward the action. This durational aspect emphasizes the process of inhabiting a text with its rhythms of involvement and disengagement in the action, and suggests that the spectator's position, his being in time, might appropriately be designated the "reader-in-the-text." His doubly structured position of identification with the features and force of the act of viewing and with the object in the field of vision are the visual terms of the dialectic of spectator placement. The rhetorical effort of shots 2–6 is directed to establishing the connection between shots and a "view," to endowing the position at the head of the table with a particular sense of a personalized glance. Shot 2, like 4, cannot at the moment it appears on the screen be associated with Lucy's glance. The shot/counter shot sequencing discloses Lucy's location, and the turn of the head (3b) establishes a spatial relation between A and B; the animation, or gesture, implied by the dolly forward, combined with the emotional intensity implied by the choice of scale (5, 6), is read in terms of a personalized agency and clarified by what is shown in the visible field, Lucy's stern face (5). It is a rhetoric that unites the unfolding shots and gives meaning to this depicted glance—affront. It creates with the discrete shots (2, 3, 4) the impression of a coherent act of viewing, a mental unity whose meaning must make itself felt by the viewer at the moment of confrontation (5, 6) to effect the sense of repudiation of Lucy's view and the abjectness of Dallas. It takes time—a sequence of shots, in other words—to convey and specify the meaning of an act of viewing.

Reading, as this instance shows, is, in part, a process of retrospection, situating what could not be "placed" at the moment of its origin and bringing it forward to an interpretation of the meaning of the present moment. As such it has a complex relation to the action and to the spatial location of viewing. But the process of reading also depends on forgetting. After the climactic moment (5, 6) signaling Dallas's averting her eyes, a different temporal strategy is in effect. Lucy has looked away in 7b and in subsequent shots from the head of the table, our attention is directed not so much to the act of showing and what it means— unawareness (2), recognition (4), rejection (6)—but rather in 8 and 10 is directed at the action within the frame. The spectator's forgetting of what the dramatic impact depended on just a few moments before (here the personalized force that accompanied the act of showing the shot as a glance) is an effect of placement that depends on an experience of duration which occludes a previous significance and replaces it with another, a process we might call fading.

The modulation of the effects of fading are what, to take another example, is at issue in the interpretation of the shots of both series A and B. I have argued above that the set-up and field of B correspond to Lucy's understanding of her place in the social system—to her point of view in the metaphorical sense. This interpretation corresponds to the general impression of the first six shots, taken together, as representing Lucy's manner of seeing. Shot 7 initiates a new line of dramatic action that poses the question of what Lucy will do now, and also begins a process not exactly of re-reading, but a search for a new reading of the meaning of the set-ups. At this moment (7b), Lucy has turned her attention away from Dallas and is now turned toward Hatfield; and Ringo, previously occupied with his table etiquette (2, 4), is looking (8b, 10) intently out of frame right. The initial sense of the set-up B is partially replaced by, but coexists with, another: that the depicted action in the frame is now being viewed by someone looking from outside the frame, namely Ringo, who is waiting expectantly for something to happen. The view from the left of the table is readable, not exactly as Lucy's self-conception as before, and not as a depiction of Ringo's glance, but as a representation of his interest in the scene, his point of view (again, in the metaphorical sense). Similarly, shots 8 and 10, showing Dallas and Ringo, no longer seem to characterize Lucy as the one doing the seeing, as in 4 and 6; they have become impersonal. The rigidity and opposition of set-ups A and B correspond to the rigidity of social position, but our reading of the changing secondary significances of the framing is an effect of fading that is responsive to acts of attention and seeing depicted within the frame.

Our anticipation, our waiting to see what will happen, is provoked and represented on the level of the action by the turning around of the audience-in-the-film (Billy and Doc Boone in 3b and 9). Our own feeling, because of our visual place to the left of the table, is closer to Ringo's than to theirs. Certainly the distention and delay of the climactic moment by a virtual repetition (9, 11a) of those shots of a hesitating Lucy (unnecessary for simple exposition) produce a sense of our temporal identification with Ringo (8b, 10), necessary for the success of the moment as drama—its uncertainty and resolution. The drama depends for the lesson it demonstrates not on Lucy's self-regard before a general public, as previously, but on being watched by the parties to be affected. It is Ringo's increasingly involved presence as an authority for a view, even though he mistakenly thinks he is being ostracized, that makes the absent place left by Lucy's departure so evidently intended as a lesson in manners, so accusingly empty. By these strategies and effects of duration—retrospection, fading, delay, and anticipation—the reading of emphasis on the act of showing or what is shown, the significance of angle and framing, can be modulated. Together these means define features of a rhetoric which, though different from the placement effected by visual structures, also locates and implicates the reader/ spectator in the text.

The spectator's place, the locus around which the spatial/temporal structures of presentation are organized, is a construction of the text which is ultimately the product of the narrator's disposition toward the tale. Such structures, which in shaping and presenting the action prompt a manner and indeed a path of reading, convey and are closely allied to the guiding moral commentary of the film. In this sequence the author has effaced himself, as in other instances of indirect discourse, for the sake of the characters and the action. Certainly he is nowhere visible in the same manner as the characters. Rather he is visible only through the materialization of the scene and in certain masked traces of his action. The indirect presence to his audience that the narrator enacts, the particular form of self-effacement, could be described as the masked displacement of this narrative authority as the producer of imagery from himself to the agency of his characters. That is, the film makes it appear as though it were the depicted characters to whom the authority for the presentation of shots can be referred—most evidently in the case of a depiction of a glance, but also, in more complex fashion, in the reading of shots as depictions of a "state of mind." The explanation of the presence of the imagery is referred by the film not to the originating authority, who stands invisible behind the action, but to his masks within the depicted space.

In accord with the narrator's efforts to direct attention away from his own activity, to mask and displace it, the narrator of *Stagecoach* has a visible persona, Lucy, perform a significant formal function in the narration: to constitute and to make legible and continuous the depicted space by referring shots on the screen alternately to the authority of her eye or the place of her body. The literal place of the spectator in the projection hall, where in a sense all the shots are directed, is a "center" that has a figurative correspondence on the level of the discourse in the "place" that Lucy occupies in the depicted space. But because Lucy performs her integrative function not exactly by her being at a place, the head of the table, but by enacting a kind of central consciousness that corresponds to a social and formal role, a role which for narrative purposes can be exploited by shifting the views representing the manner of her presence, the notion of "center" might be thought of not as a geographical place, but as a structure or function. As such, this locus makes it possible for the reader himself to occupy that role and himself to make the depicted space coherent and readable. For the spectator, the "center" is not just a point either in the projection hall or in the depicted geography, but is the result of the impression produced by the functioning of the narrative and of his being able to fictionally occupy the absent place.

Locating this function, "inscribing" the spectator's place on the level of the depicted action, has the effect of making the story seem to tell itself by reference not to an outside author but to a continuously visible, internal narrative authority. This governing strategy, of seeming to internalize the source of the exposition in characters, and thus of directing the spectator's attention to the depicted action, is supported by other features of the style: shot/counter shot, matching of glances, continuity.

Consequently, the place of the spectator in his relation to the narrator is established by, though not limited to, identifications with characters and the views they have of each other. More specifically his "place" is defined through the variable force of identification with the one viewing and the one viewed—as illustrated in the encounter between Lucy and Dallas. Though the spectator may be placed in the "center" by the formal function Lucy performs, he is not committed to her view of things. On the contrary, in the context of the film, that view is instantly regarded as insupportable. Our response to Dallas supports the sense that the spectator's figurative position is not stated by a description of where the camera is in the geography of the scene. On the contrary, though the spectator's position is closely tied to the fortunes and views of characters, our analysis suggests that identification, in the original sense of an emotional bond, need not be with the character whose view he shares, even less with the disembodied camera. Evidently, a spectator is several places at once—with the fictional viewer, with the viewed, and at the same time in a position to evaluate and respond to the claims of each. This fact suggests that, like the dreamer, the filmic spectator is a plural subject: in his reading he is and is not himself.

In a film, imagining ourselves in a character's place by identification, in respect to the actual situation, is a different process, indeed a different order of fiction than taking a shot as originating from a certain point within the fictional geography. The relation though between the literal space of the projection hall and the depicted space of the film image is continuously problematic for a definition of the "thatness" of the screen and for an account of the place of the spectator. If a discourse carries a certain impression of reality it is an effect not exactly of the image, but rather of the way the image is placed by the narrative or argument. My relation to an image on the screen is literal because it can be taken as being directed to a physical point, my seat (changing that seat doesn't alter my viewing angle on the action), as though I were the fixed origin of the view. On the other hand, the image can also be taken as originating from a point in a different kind of space, recognizably different in terms of habitability from that of the projection hall: it is from a fictional and changeable place implied by an origin contained in the image. The filmic image thus implies the ambiguity of a double origin—from both my literal place as spectator and from the place where the camera is within the imaginative space.

One structural result of the ambiguous relation of literal and depicted space and of the seemingly contradictory efforts of the text to both place and displace the spectator is the prohibition against the "meeting," though no such act is literally possible, of actor's and spectator's glances, a prohibition that is an integral feature of the sequence as a "specular text." In its effect on the spectator, the prohibition defines the different spaces he simultaneously inhabits before the screen. By denying his presence in one sense, the prohibition establishes a boundary at the screen that underscores the fact that the spectator can have no actual physical exchange with the depicted world, that he can do nothing relevant to change the course of the action. It places him irretrievably outside the action.

At the same time, the prohibition is the initial premise of a narrative system for the representation of fictional space and the means of introducing the spectator imaginatively into it. The prohibition effects this construction and engagement by creating an obliquity between our angle of viewing and that of the characters which works to make differences of angle and scale readable as representations of different points of view. As such it plays a central part in our process of identification or non-identification with the camera and depicted characters. It provides the author an ensemble of narrative forms—an imaginary currency consisting of temporary exchange, substitution, and identification—that enables us, fictionally, to take the place of another, to inhabit the text as a reader.

Establishing agency either by the authority of character or of spectator corresponds in its alternative rhetorical forms to the articulation of the ambiguity of the double origin of the image. In a particular text it is the narration that establishes and arbitrates the spectator's placement between these two spaces. *Stagecoach* makes definite efforts to imply that not only is the spectator not there, not present in his seat, but that the film-object originates from an authority within the fictional space. The narration seems to insist that the film is a free-standing entity, which a spectator, irrelevant finally to its construction, could only look on from the outside. On the other hand, in the ways that I have described, the film is directed in all its structures of presentation toward the narrator's construction of a commentary on the story and toward placing the spectator at a certain "angle" to it. The film has tried not just to direct the attention, but to place the eye of the spectator inside the fictional space, to make his presence integral and constitutive of the structure of views. The explanation the film seems to give of the action of narrative authority is a denial of the existence of a narrator different from character and an affirmation of the dominating role of fictional space. It is a spatial mode not determined by the ontology of the image as such but is in the last instance an effect of the narration.

Masking and displacement of narrative authority are thus integral to establishing the sense of the spectator "in" the text, and the prohibition to establishing the film as an independent fiction, different from dream in being the product of another, that can nevertheless be inhabited. Fascination by identification with character is a way the integrity of fictional space is validated and, because the spectator occupies a fictional role, is a way too that the film can efface the spectator's consciousness of his position. As a production of the spectator's reading, the sense of reality that the film enacts, the "impression of the real," protects the account the text seems to give of the absent narrator.

The cumulative effect of the narrator's strategy of placement of the spectator from moment to moment is his introduction into what might be called the moral order of the text. That is, the presentational structures which shape the action both convey a point of view and define the course of the reading, and are fundamental to the exposition of moral ideas—specifically a discussion about the relation of insiders to outsiders. The effect of the distinction between pure and impure is the point of the sequence, though as a theme it is just part of the total exposition. The sequence thus assists in the construction of attitudes toward law and custom and to those who live outside their strictures. It introduces the question of the exercise of social and customary (as distinguished from legal) authority. To the extent we identify with Ringo and Dallas—and the film continuously invites us to by providing multiple grounds: the couple's bravery, competence, and sincerity—the conventional order and the morality it enforces are put in doubt. Without offering a full interpretation of the theme of *Stagecoach,* which would I think be connected with the unorthodox nature of their love and the issue of Ringo's revenge and final exemption from the law by the sheriff, I can still characterize the spectator's position at this particular moment in the film.

It amounts to this: that, though we see the action from Lucy's eyes and are invited by a set of structures and strategies to experience the force and character of that view, we are put in the position finally of having to reject it as a view that is right or that we could be committed to. The sequence engages us on this point through effecting an identification with a situation in which the outsider is wronged and thus that challenges Lucy's position as the agent of an intolerant authority. We are asked, by the manner in which we must read, by the posture we must adopt, to repudiate Lucy's view, to see behind the moral convention that supports intolerance, to break out of a role that may be confining us. As such, the importance of the sequence in the entire film is the way it allies us emotionally with the interests and fortunes of the outsiders as against social custom, an identification and theme that, modulated in subsequent events, continue to the end of the film. The passage, lifted out of its context but drawing on dispositions established in previous sequences, is an illustration of the process of constructing a spectator's attitudes in the film as a whole through the control of point of view. Whether or not the Western genre can in general be characterized by a certain mode of identification, as for example in the disposition or wish to see the right done, and whether *Stagecoach* has a particularly significant place in the history of the genre by virtue of its treatment of outsiders, is an open question. In any case the reader's position is constituted by a set of views, identifications, and judgements that establish his place in the moral order of the text.

Like the absent narrator who discloses himself and makes his judgements from a position inseparable from the sequence of depicted events that constitute the narrative, the spectator, in following the story, in being subject of and to the spatial and temporal placement and effects of exposition, is in the process of realizing an identity we have called his position. Following the trajectory of identifications that establishes the structure of values of a text, "reading" as a temporal process could be said to continuously reconstruct the place of the narrator and his implied commentary on the scene. In this light, reading, as distinct from interpretation, might be characterized as a guided and prompted performance that (to the extent a text allows it, and I believe *Stagecoach* does) recreates the point of view enacted in a scene. As a correlative of narration, reading could be said to be the process of reenactment by fictionally occupying the place of the narrator.

Certain formal features of the imagery—framing, sequencing, the prohibition, the "invisibility" of the narrator—I have suggested, can be explained as the ensemble of ways authority implicitly positions the spectator/reader. As a method, this analysis of *Stagecoach* points to a largely unexplored body of critical problems associated with describing and accounting for narrative and rhetorical signifying structures. The "specular text" and the allied critical concepts of "authority," "reading," "point of view," and "position of the spectator," however provisional, might be taken then as a methodological initiative for a semiotic study of filmic texts.

Selected Bibliography

Baudry, Jean-Louis. "Ideological Effects of the Basic Cinematographic Apparatus," *Film Quarterly,* winter 1974–1975, reprinted here.

Cavell, Stanley. *The World Viewed,* New York: Viking Press, 1971.

Comolli, Jean-Louis. "Technique et Idéologie: Caméra, Perspective, Profondeur de Champ," *Cahiers du Cinéma,* May–June 1971, reprinted here in part.

Dayan, Daniel. "The Tutor-Code of Classical Cinema," *Film Quarterly,* Fall 1974, reprinted in *Movies and Methods,* vol. I.

Guzzetti, Alfred. "Narrative and the Film Image," *New Literary History,* Winter 1975.

Lubbock, Percy. *The Craft of Fiction.* New York: Viking Press, 1957.

S/Z AND *THE RULES*
OF THE GAME

JULIA LESAGE

Roland Barthes's S/Z *has proved an exceptionally influential book. It flirts with a schematic, reductive approach to a text while constantly insisting that the critic cannot fix meaning within a permanent mold. It introduces a procedure linking intensive microanalysis—a virtually word-by-word dissection of Balzac's novella "Sarrasine" —with expansive theorization, in which five global codes come together to produce the effect of realism and narrative pleasure. As Lesage stresses, Barthes's concept of code is so diffuse that it could almost be dispensed with entirely, but it plays an important theoretical role: It prevents the blockage of analysis by the long-cherished notion of artist as creator. Instead of tracing style back to its creator, Barthes traces textual effects back to the codes governing them and hence to a broad cultural, ideological milieu that goes far beyond the particular author or artist.*

Julia Lesage builds on Barthes's critical insights as she leads us through her own extension and application of Barthes's method to Jean Renoir's The Rules of the Game. *Her analysis may bear some of the traces of the "aesthetic history and analysis of the expressive uses of cinematic technique" that Barthes's approach supersedes, and it may assign meanings to stylistic features of the text in a more linear or mechanical manner than Barthes does, which raises some questions about the extent to which Barthes's method is a function more of sensibility than of procedure. But Lesage also offers a particularly vivid example of how literary criticism can be carefully and sensibly applied to film criticism.*

The emphasis that Lesage places on the internal operations of the text assumes that their importance lies in the effect that they have on viewers or readers; but, in contrast to those whose approaches are heavily indebted to a psychoanalytic approach, Lesage does not view the question of effect as particularly problematic. Of greater importance is the supple, finely meshed manner in which Barthes and Lesage combine broad cultural and narrative codes with detailed textual criticism. As a model of such a process, Lesage's article compares favorably with the more technical and hermetic readings of Citizen Kane *found in the set of seven articles that appeared in* Film Reader, *no. 1 (1975). It also offers the singular advantage of trying not to "read out" sociological themes from cultural works but to "read in" how cultural references form an essential part of the formal and ideological effect of a text. Of further interest is* Quarterly Review of Film Studies *7, no. 3 (1982), an issue devoted to analyses of* The Rules of the Game.

●

MY ENCOUNTER WITH *S/Z*

It is not often that a film teacher comes upon any book that will entirely change her/his approach to teaching film. Before I read *S/Z* by Roland Barthes, my own method in teaching basic film or film and literature courses on the college level was the same method which I had learned—a combination of aesthetic history and analysis of the expressive uses of cinematic technique. However, my own interests as a Marxist and feminist critic led me to seek more precise ways to define and teach about the interface of society and art. The first wave of women's film festivals led me to consider in greater detail the role of women in the arts, but I soon faced the limitations of the concept of "the image of . . ." as an approach to teaching film courses, the content of which could be about any oppressed group.

Barthes's *S/Z* was a book I wanted to buy as soon as I had leafed through it in the French edition before it had been translated. It has a fine summary outline in the back and it has a lot of "gimmicks" and sections which engage the reader wherever she/he starts—in the beginning, middle, or end. I knew it would be useful for me even before I read it because Barthes seemed most interested in the interaction between artistic and social convention. Furthermore, he was clearly motivated to write the text for a radical reason: to give readers an understanding of those conventions which form the bulk of the presentation of bourgeois ideology in art. By raising unconscious mechanisms to a conscious level, the radical scholar teaches with a specific end in mind, that of giving people greater options for control over their own lives. Knowledge is power.

In my own work on Godard, I had come to accept as a given Godard's axiom that all films are fiction—documentaries, too. All those films which have a narrative framework subordinate their elements to a certain end. I was aware of the pitfalls of the so-called objectivity of cinéma vérité, for all the viewer finally has of the original "pre-filmic" situation is a highly structured film. Barthes's treatment of literature in *S/Z* differs from most works of literary analysis in that he deemphasizes a purely internal analysis of a narrative art work and emphasizes the ways that elements from the writer's milieu have entered and are used on the microlevel of the text. In film, it would be as if he had done a lot of shot and single-frame analysis of the visual track. Because of his detailed look at precisely those types of things in literature that film critics look for in film study, I have tried to apply his approach to teaching and analyzing film, and it has proven useful in both classroom teaching and in feminist and Marxist film scholarship.

S/Z AND ITS FIVE CODES

We can see that *S/Z* reveals a teacher's mind, for in this book Barthes gives us not only a way to apply semiotic, structuralist, psychoanalytic, linguistic, and poetic concepts to the analysis of a single literary work but also a concrete example of such an analysis. He traces out the conventions and cultural codes in a single work of short fiction, Balzac's *Sarrasine*. At the same time, he explains the theoretical basis of such an analysis so as to enable others to do the same critical work themselves. Throughout his career, much of Barthes's scholarly work has functioned implicitly as a polemic against and explicitly as a corrective to current critical practice. In this case, with *S/Z*, he rejects the deadly finality of an *explication de texte* or an Aristotelian or New Critical analysis of *Sarrasine*. Barthes uncovers no definitive "meaning" for the work, but rather he opens it up to multiple readings. Indeed he implies that the work of the critic/teacher is to teach not only how a tightly plotted work gives the illusion of completeness, but also the many ways in which that illusion of completeness is but one determinant, albeit a primary one, of the text.

Barthes's work as a whole is useful for those who want to understand how works of art mediate social assumptions and cultural patterns from the artist's and audience's milieu. Since cultural objects and patterns, such as dress, food and drink, artifacts, traffic, architecture, etc., are the extra-cinematic material which forms the very stuff of narrative film, as do conventionally determined forms of verbal and gestural expression and human social interaction, film students can follow with interest Barthes's theory, summarized in *Elements of Semiology* and drawn upon in *S/Z,* about how such artifacts and conventions of communication and interaction are organized into whole coded systems which follow laws first traced out in the field of linguistics.[1] *S/Z* itself suggests whole new ways to think of a film as an art object and an index of culture at the same time. To open up cinema to both a semiotic and rhetorical analysis in the way Barthes opens up literature in *S/Z* would lead to an increased understanding—in political, historical, anthropological, and cultural terms—of how the film narrative, image, and sound track both incorporate and also shape cultural conventions.

Barthes labels codes and conventions as they function in a work of art because, as he emphasizes in keeping with his larger purpose as a teacher of literature, naming these codes and conventions is a critical act by which we literally make sense out of a work and by which we gain control over previously unconscious ideological mechanisms in art, our psyches, and our milieu.[2] He emphasizes that rereading a work allows us to "multiply its signifiers," that is, to find new perspectives on it, new understandings about how the work itself is constituted. He wants readers to learn to name and define not only gross narrative and ideological structures but also to work "back along the threads of meaning" (p. 12).

To read is to find meanings, and to find meanings is to name them; but these named meanings are swept toward other names; names call to each other, reassemble, and their grouping calls for further naming. (p. 11)

In *S/Z* and other works, Barthes presents a number of concepts which seem to have a direct applicability to film study. In *Writing Degree Zero* he first introduced his fruitful distinctions between "classic" and "modern" literature, i.e., between open and closed narrative works, distinctions which he maintains in *S/Z,* where he chooses to analyze a closed narrative, a specifically "classic" text.[3] This analysis in *S/Z* can be extended to feature films since most commercial film narratives depend on a conventional story form: indeed, in the twentieth century with the sweep of Modernism in other arts, it is film itself that has given a new life to the tightly plotted, closed narrative form established in the nineteenth century.

In discussing the application of *S/Z* to film study, I shall concentrate on one film which has a complex narrative but which ties up all its narrative threads at the end—Barthes's criterion for a "classic" text. I chose Jean Renoir's *The Rules of the Game* as an exemplary text because it is readily accessible and reasonably well known. Also, it seems to me, this film is one of the closest cinematic parallels we have to Balzac's work, since Renoir's themes about bourgeois society come straight from the tradition of the realist bourgeois novel and bourgeois drama. However, just as Barthes analyzed one work in order to point out pervasive trends in the bourgeois narrative tradition which are still existent, largely unconscious, and "ideological," most other films with a closed narrative form could have been used as well.

Barthes uses the term *code* in a deliberately looser way than film semioticians, such as Christian Metz or Raymond Bellour, who draw heavily on linguistic-oriented models of analysis.[4] Barthes's use of the word *code* is closely related to concepts of social and artistic convention and the rituals of everyday life. In this he is close to Umberto Eco, who presents a general theory of codes in *A Theory of Semiotics* (Eco seems heavily influenced by Barthes).[5] According to Eco, conventions are limited and generally predictable within any given culture, for culture structures its members' lives and even their very perceptual capacities through various sets of pre-established (yet historically changing) intellectual and behavioral models. It is only because of these that people define what they perceive, assign meaning to that, and respond significantly. Certain intellectual structures, such as language, are codes based on rigid rules. Others, such as visual or iconic codes, rhetorical ones, and—to a lesser degree—psychological ones, are looser and vary to a greater degree across history and across cultures.

In daily life and in art, conventions establish what is probable, plausible or obvious. They provide whole clusters of seemingly natural details, and the fact that these details and the conventions behind them are *unremarkable* means that ordinarily we do not notice or discuss them, that they are lost until named. What Barthes wants most to analyze in *S/Z* are the social and artistic codifications shaping that phenomenon we call "realism." What this notion of realism usually tells us is that there is some denotation, some external reality, some conclusion to which the literary or cinematic text necessarily points. An example of this is Bazin's notion of cinema as "a window on the world." What Barthes teaches in *S/Z* is that the illusion of realism in a narrative is founded on the integrated functioning of five levels of codes, all of which work together to suggest what seems to be the Meaning (often signaled by the denouement) and all of which suggest other previously established cultural meanings beyond themselves.

Barthes distinguishes five main areas of cultural coding, or as he calls the codes, five "voices." He wants to trace the play of these codes within a single narrative work. He says that each of the codes forms a braid or lacework, one strand being picked up, worked into the major pattern, and then left for a while, only to be returned to later; the interstices of the strands "are positions held and then left behind in the course of a gradual invasion of meaning" (p. 160). By themselves, the codes are merely expressive, but as they are intertwined artistically they are both manipulated and act upon each other to form that kind of meaning which results from a narrative work of art.

The five levels of coding that Barthes traces out in *Sarrasine* and which I shall discuss in detail in their applicability to film function as follows: (1) The enigmatic code structures the plot proper by implanting certain key questions or enigmas and then delaying the answers or giving false leads—thus giving us a story. (2) Action codes establish what actions are conventionally prescribed in certain situations and how much of each action is, must, or must not be shown. They let us know which actions are important or appropriate to present in a narrative. (3) Referential codes enter the text through explicit references to the established knowledge of the time, such as science, medicine, history, literature, or the visual arts; on a more vulgar level, the artist may also refer to popular assumptions and common sense—"what everyone knows." (4) The semic codes let us label persons and places in the narrative in an adjectival way. They "characterize" the character as a person with certain attributes and certain motives; these adjectival attributes (such as "undecided," "resolute," etc.) are the *semes*. (5) The symbolic code could also be called the psychoanalytic structuring of the text. Barthes draws primarily on Freud and Lévi-Strauss to describe the symbolic "economy" of a narrative and defines the major symbolic rhetorical device in literature as antithesis.

All five of these codes are bound by the heavy weight of convention and tradition—centuries of what Barthes calls the "what's already been written and done." The semic, symbolic and referential codes function more flexibly in the narrative than the enigmatic and action ones, the enigmatic being the most rigid and the symbolic, the most fluid of all. The codes determine specific moments in the text and suggestively reflect back to anterior moments or forward to ulterior moments in the narrative proper. They also relate to other texts and to the author's general ideological, historical and cultural milieu. All five levels are connotative and suggestive. Barthes described the relation between the way codes function sequentially in the text and the way they bear meaning that is "extra-textual" in the following way:

Analytically, connotation is determined by two spaces: a sequential space, a series of orders, a space subject to the successivity of sentences, in which meaning proliferates by layering; and an agglomerative space, certain areas of the text correlating other meanings outside the material text and, with them, forming a "nebula" of signifieds. (p. 8)

CONNOTATIONS IN FILM

Students of literature, sociology, art, and history study film as a way to study culture. One can trace out many large cultural myths and models in the film, such as assumptions about romantic love or the *parvenu*. Conventional ways of photographing women or of presenting the relations between social classes in film reveal as much about the cultural assumptions behind film as they contribute to the narrative. Yet if we are to understand how feature films mediate cultural structures, we must also understand how these cultural structures enter film. Older film studies, such as those of the auteur critics, could recognize, let us say, the feathers motif in the von Sternberg films as a symbolic or metaphoric representation of femininity. More technically oriented studies, such as those of the mise-en-scène critics, discuss the connotative functions and cultural basis of halo lighting, deep focus, or Cinemascope. In a Barthesian analysis, analysis of theme or of expressive cinematographic techniques unique to a given director or film would be of only partial interest. Small gestures, architecture, fashion, furniture, time of day, assumptions about urban life, cars and traffic, food and drink customs, courtship customs, etc., bring important subcodes to and are the visual "stuff" of narrative film. Such subcodes function in the characterization and plot but also obviously derive their meaning from associations drawn from the society at large. Barthes's approach is superior to that of the auteur critics in that he does not reduce the text to, or only concentrate on, those signifiers which express the predilections of a "creator." Rather he allows us to examine the ordinary ways that social coding enters into and is used by a work of art.

In an analysis of a single photographic image (in an essay which owes much in its methodology to Eco and Barthes) Stuart Hall notes how ideology—here equal to the sum of a society's connotations—functions to provide a favored reading of a newsphotograph, an image socially reputed to be "factual" and "objective."

Connotations add qualities and attributes to a denoted subject. Connotations refer subjects to social relations, social structure: to our routinized knowledge of social formation. Codes also refer objects to a structure of beliefs and valuations about the world.[6]

In social life, these domains of meanings are both distinct enough to mobilize a whole set of associative meaning—yet overlapping enough so that an object may refer to more than one "associative field". . . . These criss-crossing sedimentations of meaning link the areas of social life. Together they constitute the "map of meanings" in a culture.[7]

In literature the denotative principle, the "one which seems to establish and to close the reading" (p. 9), is enacted by the enigmatic code, which Barthes also calls the "voice of truth." The enigmatic code establishes the sequence and the order by which we "find out things" in the narrative and limits and controls what we shall attend to. I shall discuss this code at greater length later but here would also indicate that the same principle of a "nebula" of connotations being limited by the sequential ordering of a little "drama" or even just a single sentence also determines the way we interpret or attend to the visual connotations in an advertisement, in photojournalism, in television, and in silent and sound film. For example, in an essay, "The Rhetoric of the Image," Barthes earlier analyzed the composition of a single photograph in which he found a synchronous play of connotative elements but also a preferred meaning suggested by the caption.[8] Similarly in any narrative film—silent or sound, fiction or documentary—the "story" of the film provides the anchor for the other connotative codes. The narrative limits the polyvalent image to a certain range of emotional and social interpretation.

In an implicit general attack on the abusive structuring of leisure in advanced capitalist societies, Barthes insists that we must create, not consume, aesthetic meaning. Both because of the commercial nature of film viewing and because of the chronologically determined, closed nature of narrative film structure with its beginning, middle, and end, most people want to see a feature film only once. Perhaps they sit through the beginning "to catch what they missed" if they came in late. In economic terms, they pay for a ticket and consume a show. In the structure of what they see, narrative tension determines the pacing of all the codes. People who see films only once anticipate primarily the end of the story. In Barthes's terms they always repeat the same kind of chronological experience with the mind set that "this happens *before* or *after* that." Yet they and we stubbornly cling to the ideological belief that this first viewing is a "primary, naive, phenomenal reading which we will only, afterwards, have to 'explicate,' intellectualize" (p. 16). In a consumer society, the ideological function of such a belief is to valorize the craving for novelty, make everyone an authority on the "movies," and as a result make film studies as a discipline inherently suspect. Although some films seem more amenable to "instant" first reading, disposable like Kleenex and appealing completely to surface gratifications like pinball, and some films seem richer for multiple viewings, a Barthesian analysis opens up both kinds of texts to multiple readings, tracing out the ways in which the films use cultural significations and establish their own interconnected levels of meaning. It is *within* the context of such a reading that Barthes discusses the "richness" of a text like Balzac's *Sarrasine,* a richness which Barthes finds mainly on the level of symbolic interactions and reversals—which one could trace out only on rereading or reviewing a work.

It takes a reeducation to make people want to see films twice or more. We tend to reread poems several times but experience novels and films only once. Barthes attributes that to the dominance of the narrative level, or plot. Knowing this, most film teachers instinctively discuss the role of convention and connotation in the acting, cinematic technique, decor, use of genre structures, etc., as they try to push students to attend to more than the plot. By tracing out how the various levels of coding interact in a single film seen several or many times, we can reread the film in a new way each time we see it. Analytically, re-viewing a film "multiplies it in its variety and plurality" (p. 16) as we learn to attend to other levels of signification beyond the linear experience imposed by the plot. The critical act teaches us to create our own aesthetic experience and saves us from a dulling consumption of art.

Although he borrows from Aristotle's *Poetics* and from sociology in his own technique of analysis, Barthes is far from an Aristotelian who subordinates the parts to the whole, nor is he a sociologist who tabulates and analyzes cultural codes by means of literature. In *S/Z* he takes the novella *Sarrasine* and breaks it up into arbitrary convenient short sections which he calls *lexies.* After each section he notes the introduction of, passing, or working out of narrative enigmas, antitheses, cultural references, adjectivally describable connotations, and symbolic exchanges. Narrative enigmas are paced, never immediately answered; otherwise there would be no story. The other connotative and symbolic levels enter in as structured "noise" or counter-communication against the enigmas, and this "noise" makes up the whole texture of the work. In the implantation of the codes, in the pacing and gaps of their "play," Barthes sees the uniqueness of any given narrative and an indication of the quality of the work of art.

To undertake a project like *S/Z* with a film would mean to have a class study perhaps just one film a semester. The film should be videotaped or shown on an editor-viewer, but in front of a large class one could just stop the projector. A good published film script would provide another important aid. To analyze any feature film short section by short section, one should minimally note down the following: the semic codes, which frequently can be worked out on the synchronous microlevel of still photography or a single frame; the action codes, seen chronologically on the level of the shot and in the editing of action sequences; the narrative codes, which, as Christian Metz has shown at some length, are worked out mainly on the level of the sequence; and the symbolic codes, which fluidly move between the composition of the frame, the filming of the shot, the editing within a sequence, and the combination of sequences to form the film as a whole. Indeed, to accomplish the equivalent of *S/Z* about a single film, one might best make an analytical videotape, or rather a series of tapes. These would alternate shots of the film (several taken together as a "lexie") with one's own analysis, which could then make use of clips from other films, photographs, diagrams, taped sounds and noises, and any other appropriate audiovisual support.

To describe in detail the five levels of coding and how they function in film, I have drawn all my examples from a single film, *The Rules of the Game*, yet obviously, without the film at hand for demonstration and in an essay of this length, I cannot give a total reading of the work. I have chosen my references here merely to show how each code can be traced in the work. Optimally, on videotape one could break the film up into small parts and note in each part where the various codes enter and how they are worked out across the length of the film. This is Barthes's method in *S/Z*, which is as multivalent and open to different emphases in interpretation as the critical attitude he wants audiences to achieve.

NARRATIVE STRUCTURE AND THE CODE OF ENIGMAS

When Barthes discusses the narrative construction of a novel, he does not talk about narrative as a formal *structure* at all. A plot depends on a code of multiple enigmas, which code is experienced by the ordinary film viewer as tension or suspense. Upon re-viewing a film we can see more clearly how the enigmatic code functions: the film centers in on the subject-to-be of an enigma; it poses, formulates, and develops the enigma; and it retards and finally provides an answer. The author must delay answering the principal enigmas about the protagonists to keep the story going. The way he/she delays narrative resolution (by partial and incomplete answers, double entendres, ambiguities, or lies) often defines the tone of the work.

The narrative points to but does not tell the whole truth about a character, especially a protagonist. Human figures distinguish themselves and become characters as the author develops their traits so as to develop and resolve enigmas. Because of the demands of the enigmas, the author both suppresses some character traits and develops others. One of the goals of a Barthesian analysis is to map how certain traits of characters are revealed at certain points; we arrive at a topology of the plot, in which the space of the enigma corresponds to the space of the characterization, which is the semic space.

In the narrative, key structural elements (a gesture, a word, a locale) are first received as unimportant details. The gratuitousness of their introduction makes them seem natural. A narrative only progressively invests its key elements with their full meaning, but it uses what comes first—something we may not have understood fully when we first saw it—as evidence for what comes later. This is the narrative's defense against illogic. Circumstances are shown as compatible, and the characters' choices are seemingly made for a number of different, interconnecting reasons. Barthes calls these tactics "pseudo-logical liaisons." In fact, meaning must be delayed or suspended and circumstances must be manipulated in order to tell a story at all.

The enigmatic code is a sequential one and reduces the plurality and reversibility of meanings within a given text. It is this characteristic sequentiality and closure of meaning in "classic" narrative against which modernist artists have reacted in both literature and film. As the enigmatic code functions in a traditional narrative like *Sarrasine,* it provides "the voice of truth" since it sweeps the reader along temporally in a rush of pseudo-logical connections towards a promised final truth. In film, the syntactical form of the narrative is similarly shaped by this code, which imposes itself on the other codes in the editing, in the shot, or in the composition of the frame. The enigmatic code imposes a certain irreversible order on the presentation of information and limits the multiple expressive possibilities of the medium at any given time. The more a film maintains interest or suspense, the more we read the elements within it in terms of the enigmatic code. By the time we reach the narrative climax, many tentative meanings that had suggested themselves earlier in the work are ultimately suppressed.

The enigmas of *The Rules of the Game* deal mainly with sexual relations and how they will be handled within a given society. The first enigma is planted when André Jurieu, a trans-Atlantic pilot, is greeted by a crowd on his triumphal return to Le Bourget airport. He bitterly complains in a nationally broadcast radio interview that a certain woman, whom we find out in the next sequence is Christine de la Chesnaye, was not there to greet him. The enigma of André Jurieu's behavior and Christine de la Chesnaye's response occupies perhaps only the first third of the film, when Christine finally receives André at her husband's estate. Then, surrounded by the de la Chesnayes' whole circle of friends and house guests, she explains to all with pride that her *friendship* with André contributed to his success. This episode is—as Barthes calls any episode—both exemplum and signifier. The enigma of André Jurieu's love for Christine and what is to be done about it provides reasonable and sufficient cause for the final episode in which André is killed.

The other major enigma introduced early in the film is Robert de la Chesnaye's continued affair with the aristocrat Geneviève de Marrast in the face of his wife Christine's sincerity and love for him. Although this enigma seems quickly resolved (Robert phones Geneviève to arrange to tell her the affair is over), Christine sees him by accident in the woods kissing Geneviève goodbye. Here is a classic case of misunderstanding sustaining a major enigma, one necessary for moving the narrative to the climax. There must be a sexual rift between Robert and Christine although we must not doubt either one's sincerity. Furthermore, this mistake is introduced as something natural and accidental in the plot; it contributes to that confluence of circumstances which masks the artifice of the enigmatic code.

A costume party dominates the second half of the film. Numerous enigmas, involving the shifting sexual relations between more than half a dozen characters, are set and partially answered; lies and misunderstanding abound. It is at this point that the visual mise-en-scène of the film is crucial, for the audience's delight lies in the rapidity and simultaneity with which the multiple enigmatic situations flash before their eyes. For example, all these events happen almost simultaneously: Christine, thinking Robert loves Geneviève, has drunkenly gone off with a guest, Saint-Aubin, to the dining room. André, who loves Christine, attacks Saint-Aubin. The gamekeeper Schumacher knows his wife Lisette, Christine's maid, and Marceau, the poacher turned servant, are carrying on—in this scene he pursues Marceau with a pistol, firing, and being chased by Lisette and the other servants. Robert continues as master of ceremonies at the party, presiding at a stage show in front of guests. Geneviève and Jackie, a younger woman who is infatuated with André, faint and are carried off.

It is because Barthes does not try to present an Aristotelian analysis of plot but rather is concerned with analyzing the implantation, interaction, and resolution of multiple enigmas that his methodology is especially apt here. At this point in *The Rules of the Game,* the intrigue comes from the interweaving of all the love triangles. We ask, "What will Christine-Lisette-Geneviève-Jackie do?" and "What will André-Robert-Octave-Schumacher-Marceau do?" Certain enigmas predominate and move the plot further toward its conclusion. In particular, Christine's motives are ambiguously treated. At the masquerade party, all the action, which seemingly saturated the narrative with meaning, masked a major subquestion posed by the enigma, "What will Christine do?" That is, now we must ask, "What are Christine's motives and whom does she love?" Indeed this enigma is answered ambiguously right up to the end of the film, for in the last third of the movie, Christine tells first André and then Octave, a tacky, good-humored family friend, that she loves each one. Both must believe in her love for the film to arrive at its narrative climax, in which André is sent by Octave, in an act of generosity on Octave's part, to run off with Christine. Finally, the concluding moments of the film are dominated by our questioning of Octave's relation to all the love triangles. He is the one most intimate with Christine as a friend, the real threat to her marriage, yet he has also flirted with Lisette, making the gamekeeper jealous and setting up the preconditions for the denouement. Like Christine's, Octave's own motives ambiguously fluctuate and it is hard to answer, "What will he do?"

A final series of coincidences is piled one on top of another, yet all are necessary for the "coincidence" and narrative climax of André's death. Christine wears Lisette's (Schumacher's wife's) cape. Schumacher no longer chases Marceau, since both had been fired after the party; when he and Marceau see Christine in Lisette's cape with Octave, they assume Lisette and Octave will now have an affair. When Octave sends his good friend André off to the rendezvous with Christine, he gives André his coat. Thus Schumacher shoots André, thinking it is Octave cuckolding him. All of these circumstances are "naturalized" by the fact that all the characters have participated in the exhausting chase scene during the party (as has the audience) and their nerves are frayed; they act hastily, without thinking, and each presumably also acts desperately from passion and/or love. Each of these coinciding circumstances was prepared for long in advance, "determined" in multiple ways. It is only the rate at which coincidence is presented which accelerates at the climax of the film.

This discussion of the implantation of major enigmas in *The Rules of the Game* lacks Barthes's subtlety, for in *S/Z* he does not just point out the enigmas but shows *how* they are centered, phrased, retarded, and developed. For example, by having André chide Christine in a public speech over national radio for being at Le Bourget, Renoir establishes the enigma of what will happen to André's love with a good deal of wit, which is reinforced by images of the apparatus of microphones, wires and transmitters, and by the voice patterns of an excited woman interviewer and later of a standard interviewee, the flight engineer. The wit is developed further by the cut from the airport to Christine's bedroom; we see an extreme close up of the tubes of a radio apparatus, from which the same interview blares. Only when the camera moves up to frame Christine and Lisette in long shot do we realize that that was the back of an ordinary radio receiver and that we are in another place. Similarly when Christine enters her husband Robert's room, we hear the same radio program before we see Robert. When we realize that he is standing by his radio and listening to that program, we can imagine what he is thinking about his wife. All of this suggested and stated information is necessary for the development of the enigma, but the pacing of the visual and verbal details is especially witty in its use of an editing/sound technique which introduces sequences via the mechanism of the very radio program which gave rise to the original enigma. It is thus really only with the film at hand that one can best make the kind of demonstration that Barthes makes in *S/Z*.

SEMIC CODES

As mentioned earlier, a photograph is particularly rich in connoted or semic information.[9] In it we can usually find signified nationality, social class, erotic desirability, social situation, and threatening or non-threatening situation. These semic connotations are structured in an informal, "ideological" way. As Stuart Hall noted, in any given society, there is a lexicon of expressive features, which imposes on the polysemy or multiplicity of meaning inherent in any given situation not an invariable but a preferred meaning.

Barthes and Umberto Eco agree that we can label traits because of cultural stereotypes or "paradigms" of available images and sounds. Because of repetition through their constant usage in a culture, semic codes work through architectural, linguistic, fashion, culinary, etc. codes and subcodes. In a film semic connotation is borne not only by the visual image but also by stylistic subtleties in verbal language which connote class, emotion, irony, ignorance, etc. There are also whole other emotional subcodes related to noise and music, such as thriller sounds or romantic violins.[10]

Semes are adjectivally describable units of connotation. They are the labels we mentally attribute to character and locale. Because narrative film must utilize character to develop its enigmas and because there is a unique emphasis historically placed on the individual subject, semic connotation in cinema devolves mainly around the characters. We "read" the mise-en-scène to tell us something about them. Less frequently a sequence illustrates a theme not directly related to the actions of a character; such a sequence depends mainly on the connotated relation between images. Examples of this would be the sequence of neon lights in American cinema signifying "Broadway" or "going out on the town," or in *The Rules of the Game,* the death of the animals during the hunt.

More important, in film, both the content and the composition of the shots work to connote the social situation, motives, and emotions of the principal characters. In a single photograph, one can decide things about a person from body position, facial expression, gesture and especially from milieu. In the shot of a film, the character is also seen in movement; from speech and interaction with other characters we can make many more judgments about that person's social situation. There is a whole system at work of mutual and reciprocal expressions and recognition. Finally, as was noted earlier, narrative dominates and limits meaning so that we most frequently read a shot in terms of the story, which is what Barthes meant when he said that consumers (vs. creators) of texts end up receiving the same message.

We also read the semic codes historically because the way we label a character or situation is not only dependent on the sequential development of the text but also derives from our experience in the culture at large. Semic codes, similar to the action codes and codes of established cultural wisdom in the narrative, can be understood only in relation to previous mention in other texts. The units that we can label derive from "something that has been *already* seen, done, experienced; the code is the wake of that *already*" (p. 20). As Stuart Hall said in reference to newsphotographs, the sources of semic connotation are in the whole framework of social codes which are used in any discourse to convey second-order meanings. Connotations thus "have the whole social order embedded or hidden within them: social practices and beliefs, the rank-order of power and interest, a structure of legitimations."[11]

Since ideological and cultural codes change with history, we can read the semes in any film or novel as a dated literature of signifiers. The artist's milieu always differs from ours, and we've often seen a film where the audience noticed as unusual or even silly semic connotations taken as natural within the artist's milieu. For example, the semes of beauty or erotic desirability, especially as connoted by fashion, vary from culture to culture. In *The Rules of the Game,* because of the way they are dressed and filmed and because of their role in the plot, we know that Lisette and Christine are desirable women, more so than Geneviève. However, the film does not signal so directly the male characters' desirability, and one wonders what the visual/verbal codes of erotic desirability in relation to the men were in Renoir's milieu or even now in France? How do we judge the sexual desirability of Robert, André, Octave, Marceau, or Saint-Aubin?

In any given shot we can see how a certain physical space is detached as seme-filled. In fiction and film a person is a collection of semes, the sum of which identifies character. First of all, the filmmaker lets us know which character or object is important by keeping or putting that character in focus. Secondly, that character is seen more in the foreground and center frame. Lighting also expresses semes. Especially noticeable in *The Rules of the Game* is the halo of curls and fine wispy hairs around Christine's and Lisette's heads, which are made to shine by means of a strong spotlight just for that purpose—a light which then connotes "femininity." Close-ups connote a special interest in the individual subject, in that person's thoughts and emotions; such a psychological interest characterizes traditional narrative fiction as well as feature film.

In a film, as in the theater, directors carefully control costuming so as to present a certain kind of person appropriate for a certain role. Both film and theater depend on fashion stereotypes or the semic code of dress. Christine is dressed in white silk, white fur, or an innocent Tyrolean folk costume. She usually has a soft white lace collar. Geneviève is dressed in black, a mannish hunting costume, an ornate oriental robe, or a harem costume. Lisette, like Christine, wears white ruffles around her neck. The respective semes which costuming connotes for these women are naturalness, sweetness and femininity for Christine and Lisette, and sophistication and brittleness for Geneviève.

In the same way, Christine's room, with its dressing table and white decor, connotes the seme "femininity." Geneviève, on the other hand, lives in an apartment filled with bronze statues and hothouse flowers, and she entertains three men there with no women present. Her milieu connotes "worldliness," perhaps "ennui."

Barthes tabulates the semes in each *lexie* as they enter *Sarrasine*. A brief tabulation of some of the semes in *The Rules of the Game* would yield the following results: The *setting* frequently connotes worldliness, naturalness, mechanicity—especially in relation to Robert and his mechanical toys—artificiality, class, servitude, or richness. Some of these connotations Barthes also traced in *Sarrasine* and indicate a kind of subject matter and psychology dear to the bourgeoisie, i.e., the cost of being on top. The *dress code* connotes masculinity, femininity, eroticism, beauty, rigidity, informality, class, age, or sophistication. This code, combined with the gesture, voice, age, and movement codes, indicates how integral the capturing of, i.e., possessing, a beautiful young woman is as a function of bourgeois art. A beautiful woman seems classless; she has this asset to trade for social gain—but the very concept of beauty in art and the semes which connote erotic desirability have been constructed by those in power who can buy beauty, men. The semes of beauty that men capture in art are their own fantasies. The *gesture code* in *The Rules of the Game* connotes roughness, sincerity, petulance, understanding, cynicism, obedience, power, gentility—sometimes excess gentility, awkwardness, world-weariness, dislike, hospitality or sadness, as well as erotic intent. Again, gestures are clearly codified according to class and sex. The *movement code* connotes age, adeptness or awkwardness, determination. Verbal characteristics, such as *tone of voice* and *type of vocabulary,* often connote emotions, such as despair and humor, but they also convey important information about eroticism, power, and class.

In the scene immediately following the playlet at the masquerade party at La Colinère, Christine saw Geneviève embrace Robert and then run off with Saint-Aubin. After looking for Christine, Robert went into the dining room to change back into his evening jacket. Geneviève followed him and pressed him to go off with her. Octave, in a bear costume, had previously tried unsuccessfully to find someone to help him take it off. Here Geneviève's and Octave's costumes both connote their personalities—burly, awkward, unpolished, and maladroit Octave and jaded, sophisticated, and brittle Geneviève (note the metallic jewels). Robert is meticulous, paying careful attention to his clothes, and his face has that expression of world-weariness characteristic of him throughout the film. He stands with his back to Geneviève. She is pressuring him. Octave is trying to pull her away.

This entire scene between Geneviève and Robert, where Robert refuses to commit himself to her, takes place in the center of a large open space in a large cold-looking room, the stag in the background being reminiscent of the slaughter at the hunt. Stuffed birds on the table add to the impression of artificiality and these birds will later be seen knocked on the floor when disorder and chaos invade the party. In addition, these birds refer us back to the hunt and forward to the death of André since both the animals and André are killed as an extension of property rights. The art work that Robert possesses at La Colinère, a representative sample seen in this picture, consists of statues and paintings of the hunt, stuffed animal trophies, and mechanical toys. In this scene, where he tells Geneviève that he cannot leave with her, she realizes that his property and his obligations to his guests mean more to him than she does—the relation between propriety and property being one of the major themes in the film.

Barthes calls semic connotation that "noise" which both names and dissimulates the truth, and the richness of which often defines the artistic quality of the text. The density of semes, like the density of enigmas (connotation running parallel to enigma structure), varies within the text. It is the role of the critic to name the semes within the narrative and thus to define the personages. At times, a clustering of semes leads one to name larger *thematics* which define whole sequences within the work. In *The Rules of the Game* these semes expanded into thematics would be sincerity, naturalness, artifice and class; they are what Barthes calls meta-names.

THE CODES OF CULTURAL REFERENCE

Résumés of common knowledge, the cultural codes provide the syllogisms of the narrative ... with their major premise, based always on public opinion ("probable," as the old logic said).

Barthes makes this observation as he discusses why the hapless lover dies in *Sarrasine*. Like André Jurieu in *The Rules of the Game,* Sarrasine is killed because he is ignorant of or perhaps willfully ignores the complexity of social mores. What triumphs for the other characters in both novella and film is the reality principle, which for them turns out to be composed of social reality and institutional codes. The cultural codes which "form the premises of the major syllogisms of the narrative" in *The Rules of the Game* relate to the title of the film. Renoir presents explicitly the rules governing marriage and adultery in high society, the rules of the hunt, the rules governing relations between masters and servants, and the rules governing peer relationships (courtesy, friendship, honor, jealousy, gossip) among masters and among servants. Renoir's major theme here is about the suffocating nature of received ideas; the "rules of the game" have an all-pervasive, determining influence over whatever might be natural so that the natural becomes lost. Thus the film as a whole, in its entire narrative structure, criticizes through art the received cultural codes shaping both society and its own art.

Most people read a film as they read a novel, not attending to the social and cultural conventions, the artifice, behind the actions and words presented. Thus, even though *The Rules of the Game* raises the theme of social convention vs. nature, it still presents the flow of its own discourse as natural, as "life."

Although entirely derived from books, these codes, by a swivel characteristic of bourgeois ideology, which turns culture into nature, appear to establish reality, "Life." "Life," then, in the classic text, becomes a nauseating mixture of common opinions, a smothering layer of received ideas. (p. 206)

Within the flow of the narrative the codes of cultural reference invert their bookish origin and are implanted in the words and actions of the characters as something natural or proverbial. For example, in this film the characters comment on how lovers should and do behave (the social lore of love and lust) as if these were ideas everyone shared; the audience is not led to challenge such assumptions. Explicitly described in the film is the way nature must submit to society, and the most smoothly coordinated *social* event is the hunt, which leads us directly to criticize aristocratic abuse of Nature per se. Yet in the way things "happen," just as in any narrative film, the social events themselves flow along "naturally." We accept what happens among the characters as probable, likely, or natural, as "life."

In studying a film we should examine those cultural codes which the text explains (the rules of the game), which it assumes we know (masculinity/feminity, the psychology of persons of certain types, ages, nationalities, professions, etc.) or which the authors or characters just mention in passing ("We've all come here to hunt, not to write our memoirs!"[12]). Renoir carefully details the daily rituals and the codes of behavior between the de la Chesnayes, among the servants, and between the two groups. We expect a different pattern of behavior from Robert toward Christine than from Schumacher toward Lisette. The de la Chesnayes' marriage relies on codes of elegance, entertaining, courtesy, and hospitality. The servants' marriage is partially controlled by their work situation, Lisette preferring to be with her mistress Christine in Paris than with her husband at La Colinère (Lisette being a conventional name for the maid-*confidante* in French comedy). When Schumacher gives Lisette a present of a warm cloak (code of practicality), she dismisses his gift as not pretty. When he chases her would-be lover Marceau with a gun (code of jealousy for lower-class males), she pacifies him by saying she'll do anything he wants (psychology of the clever, dominated wife), even go back to his small town in Germany. This reflects the code of rural vs. urban mores, as Schumacher wants to get Lisette where she will not be able to flirt with other men, and also the code of ethnic psychology: rural Prussian vs. urban French.

In general, in narrative film, the audience calls upon its knowledge of a vulgar code of the psychology of human types. In *The Rules of the Game* the house guests at La Colinère quickly distinguish themselves as types. The General belongs to the *ancien régime*. The ingenue Jackie is a university student, which is supposed to account for her lack of sexual sophistication! Octave and an older woman factory owner are the jolly fat people, and the woman's conversation draws on codes of popular science and medicine, diets, and card games. A young homosexual male character enacts a highly coded role in the tradition that homosexuality in fiction is supposed to represent upper-middle-class decadence. Geneviève, presented in her own apartment earlier as the Paris sophisticate, is here forced into the stereotypical role of the cast-off lover. André Jurieu as well, even though the house guests receive him as a modern hero, enacts the role of a desperate lover.

Geneviève's whole character is sketched very quickly in an early sequence, which relies on our coded knowledge of the worldly woman. Whereas Christine wears white silk or ruffles, Geneviève is first seen wearing a black dress with a geometric lace design across her chest; she is smoking a cigarette held in a cigarette holder. She also entertains a group of men, serves mixed drinks (code of modernity), and cites a cynical line from Chamfort on the definition of love (code of "looseness"). When Robert comes to her apartment (geographical code—we see Trocadéro from the window), she wears an ornate Chinese kimono and receives him in a room containing Oriental Buddhas, potted plants, and cut flowers (codes of excess, exoticism, chinoiserie, artifice, art, flowers). When Geneviève presents her guests mixed drinks, that is part of the code of modern hospitality. The codes of modern life must be contrasted with the codes of tradition if we are to grasp the full savor of the General's cliche (as a member of the *ancien régime*), which he repeats twice in reference to Robert: "That La Chesnaye doesn't lack for class, and that's becoming rare."

Actually the whole modern world enters the film only schematically. In the first scene we have rapidly presented a variety of codes intended to indicate "Modern Life." These are the codes of radio transmitters; those of Paris geography—Le Bourget; of crowd psychology; of cheers—"Bravo"; of newsworthy events; of the techniques, vocabulary and psychology of news reportage—both on the part of the interviewer and the interviewees; of contemporary history—the Lindbergh flight; and of the techniques of police control. Just as the airplanes flying over Paris in World War I provide that jarring image of modernity in Proust's *Remembrance of Things Past* to remind us that, in fact, aristocratic mores are a thing of the past, so too this first airport sequence, packed with assumptions about modern life, establishes the parameters of the game in *The Rules of the Game*, the film then ending with the General's words about the loss of aristocratic standards.

What Renoir refuses to do, and this is one of the virtues of the film, is to say that the modern (André) is better than the aristocrat (Robert) even though the film indicts aristocratic decadence. The contrast between aristocratic and modern, particularly as expressed by the General's cliche and by André's inability to understand Christine's position, functions to show that neither the aristocrats nor the "moderns" can understand each other except in terms of trite, language and conceptual baggage. Indeed, the film presents this contrast between aristocrat and modern particularly ambiguously since Robert de la Chesnaye is a *nouveau riche* aristocrat, a Jew, and thus an outsider himself—which fact is harped on by some of the servants, who are more purist in such matters than their masters. To further complicate our attitude toward Robert, at the end he understands more than the other characters, yet he will smoothly cover over André's murder as an accident.

In general, we read the semic codes, the level of adjectival amplification, on the level of the single frame or across small gestures. As soon as we see a setting or a personage in film or in a photograph, we "label" it; that is, we rapidly interpret the semes insofar as they relate to characterization, mood, and the development of the plot. The codes of cultural reference work themselves out on a grosser scale, especially the dialogue. Often the two codes mesh. We can observe the art, architecture, gardens and statuary in La Colinère and derive the adjectival semes "French aristocrat" or "dignity." But we can also examine in more detail how Renoir introduces and uses established cultural codes related to art and to the manor house or country estate.

Studying film with videotape would allow one to go back and notice the implantation of cultural codes which would otherwise pass quickly by as "natural." We can readily distinguish those codes which are repeated often enough to become stereotypes (André's excess of despair as a frustrated lover), but we often miss smaller ones that are not reinforced by an essential relation to the developing enigmas. Once we understand how much a film utilizes information and assumptions formulated anterior to the film, it becomes irrevocably clear that what cinema captures is social truth and institutionalized knowledge, not unmediated reality.

THE ACTION CODES

Action codes tell us what is considered "normal" action in a culture and also how to present that action in a representation: certain details and the chronological ordering of these details seem necessary or appropriate in literary fiction and film. Action codes not only establish what actions are conventionally prescribed in certain situations (e.g., a kiss in a romantic scene) but also how much of each action must be or is shown. At the end of *S/Z* Barthes presents a list sequentially tabulating all the actions that were clearly definable in *Sarrasine,* and this list lets us see how conventional the range of actions in fiction is.

We know that very few complex actions—for example, surgery or cooking a meal—last as long on the screen as in real life. An exception is a filmed conversation when it is necessary for the audience to hear the whole thing. Even here, film technique rests on certain cultural assumptions. The conventional use of a series of close-ups to film a conversation assumes that the audience's knowledge of the "rules" of how a conversation flows from one person to another will provide the continuity between shots of two individuals, each seen separately.

Two other common types of action sequences in narrative film are what Christian Metz calls "ordinary" and "episodic" sequences; in the former, bits of unnecessary action are eliminated; in the latter, representative stages in the development of an event or relationship are shown.[13] Obviously the decision about which actions to show in the various shots of a sequence depends on previous portrayals of action in film as well as audience expectations about what is "representative" or "unnecessary."

All film theorists from Eisenstein and Pudovkin to contemporary writers on film semiotics have seen a close relationship between editing codes and the representation of human actions. Such a relationship is most obvious in invisible editing or action cutting, but more recently scholars, such as Laura Mulvey, Daniel Dayan, and Raymond Bellour, have demonstrated how the whole foundation of realist film editing—field and reverse cutting—is based on cultural assumptions about point of view, which is based in film on the human glance.[14]

In *The Rules of the Game* many actions are presented schematically, particularly the moments of courtship. In only one larger action, the hunt, do we see many of the component parts detailed; here, too, each of the many participants — both aristocrats and servants—is depicted doing only a few representative, clearly defined things. Of all the codes, the action codes are the hardest to analyze in detail on first viewing because they seem so ordinary and, taken together, create such an illusion of continuity that they "form the main armature" (p. 255) of the "classic" text. Yet the presentation of cinematic action is never more than artifice. Whoever sees a film

amasses certain data under some generic titles for action (*stroll, murder, rendezvous*), and this title embodies the sequence of actions; the sequence of actions exists when and because it can be given a name, it unfolds as this process of naming takes place, as a title is sought or confirmed. (p. 19)

The action codes, both in terms of the human actions presented within a shot and editing on the basis of action, often seem "natural." Because the narrative is "saturated" with mechanisms to create meaning, the audience fills in the causal chains, assuming continuity when really the filmic presentation is discontinuous. The seeming continuity in classical prose fiction and narrative feature films comes from the fact that the actions serve multiple functions: they have a purpose in the narrative and they have a connotative and symbolic value. Furthermore, these actions gain in sense and continuity as the traditional narrative makes them serve a double function: we see each action both as determined and as determining something else. In other words, actions, like the characters' choices, are over-determined.[15]

SYMBOLIC CODES

A fifth level of narrative coding which Barthes discusses, in addition to enigmatic, semic, referential (to establish knowledge), and action codes, is that of psychoanalytic or symbolic coding. Symbolic codes, or the *play* of symbols, as Barthes prefers to say, work themselves out in art in terms of motifs common to the culture as a whole. Thus psychoanalytic criticism of art or auteur analysis of film often seeks themes, motifs, or archetypes. These symbolic structures are extremely fluid and do not reflect social rituals and expectations as obviously or as directly as the referential, semic, and action codes do.

Barthes uses Freud's language, but his analysis of the symbolic "economy" of the text comes directly from Lévi-Strauss. The latter, in his *Structural Anthropology,* asserted that we should study language, kinship, and economics in linguistic terms and interpret society as a whole in terms of a theory of communication. To cite Lévi-Strauss:

> This endeavor is possible on three levels, since the rules of kinship and marriage serve to insure the circulation of women between groups, just as economic rules serve to insure the circulation of goods and services, and linguistic rules the circulation of messages. These three forms of communication are also forms of exchange which are obviously inter-related (because marriage relations are associated with economic prestations, and language comes into play at all levels). It is therefore legitimate to seek homologies between them and define the formal characteristics of each type considered independently and of the transformations which make the transition possible from one to another.[16]

According to Barthes one can enter the symbolic field of the text on any of three levels: language, kinship or sex, and commercial economy. Language operates on the basis of an economy that is "usually protected by the separation of opposites" (p. 215), i.e., paradigms. The major rhetorical device which carries the symbolic motifs of the text is the antithesis, each term of which is exclusive and fully meaningful in its own right. Middle-ground figures transgress the antithesis, "pass through the wall of opposites" (p. 215), and abolish difference. Barthes also analyzes the symbolic field of the narrative by discussing the economy of genres and the economy of bodies, which Lévi-Strauss would call kinship codes; as Barthes says, their "parts cannot be interchanged" (p. 215).[17]

Barthes considers two ways that capitalist economic relations are symbolized in or rather form the "symbolic economy" of *Sarrasine,* and his observations can also be applied to *The Rules of the Game.* The characters deal with each other personally by means of informal "contracts," and the narrative as a whole treats as *nouveau riche* capitalist (vs. aristocratic, land-based) wealth. In both language and commerce, paradigmatic barriers let us understand the bases of equivalencies and exchange, which are the foundation of all meaning (under capitalism such exchange depends on private property). In the classical narrative, representation depends on an order of just equivalencies, by means of which we can regularly distinguish contraries, sexes, and possessions. Yet it is only when an excessive element enters which interrupts the normal circulation of the antitheses, sexes, property relations, or contracts that the narrative begins. It is the transgressor that impels the narrative toward its climax or catastrophe. Symbolic and narrative requirements in a work of fiction finally merge, for narrative resolution not only means the final and irreversible "predicating" of the subject and the end of the story (for there is no more to say) but also the end of the symbolic search, what Barthes calls a symbolic closure or return to order.

In *The Rules of the Game* one can note a whole series of related symbolic antitheses which generally reinforce each other and which have a long tradition in the history of Western literature and art. Such antitheses include the following pairs: civilization/nature; sincerity/lies; ingenuousness/sophistication; simplicity/complexity; naive eros/eros socialized; organic life/artifacts; life/death; fecundity/emptiness; outdoors/indoors; lower/upper; servants/masters; the male camp/the female camp; richness/poverty; power/dependence; property/wildlife; childishness/maturity; the greenhouse/the manor house.

In addition, the characters are paired with doubles among the masters and the servants. The inflexible idealist Jurieu has his parallel on the servants' level in the inflexible Prussian gamekeeper Schumacher, who enacts his ritual bond with Jurieu by executing Jurieu. The poacher Marceau and Robert de la Chesnaye are specifically paired: Marceau shows Robert the art of poaching; Robert promotes Marceau to Marceau's long-dreamed-of role as a household servant; Marceau has dreams of elegance—in a uniform—and in the film Robert is the male who is most meticulously dressed. Both involved with mistresses and jealous rivals in one sequence, the two men share their views on women.

The servant Lisette is inseparable from Christine for she identifies with Christine completely. As the critic Philippe Esnault says, Lisette devours Christine with her eyes.[18] It is because Lisette loans Christine her cape when Christine goes off to the greenhouse with Octave that Schumacher thinks he is shooting his wife's lover. Also, Saint-Aubin is a double for Geneviève. After Christine discovers her husband's affair, she does not turn to André, as we might expect, but rather throws herself at one of the house guests, Saint-Aubin. He is otherwise an insignificant figure and one might wonder at his role as Christine's potential lover until his symbolic function as Geneviève's double is perceived: both are the accepted adulterous partners from the aristocrats' peer group—that is, for adultery within the "rules of the game." If she had had an affair with Saint-Aubin, Christine would not have left the group nor her social/marital obligations—as she had planned to do with either Octave or André. In the same way Robert had conducted an affair with Geneviève yet had felt fully responsible to both his marriage and his social ties. Thus the structure of doubles can be diagrammed as follows:

Upper-Class			Saint-Aubin/	
Masters	André	Christine	Geneviève	Robert
Servants	Schumacher	Lisette		Marceau
	Purists Fools	Untamed female eros & love	The erotic partners in adultery who will play by the rules	Male lovers who are socially adept

Not in this diagram is Octave, who at various points in the narrative acts as the *transgressor*.[19] In terms of class he is neither master nor servant, but a bohemian hanger-on in both the artistic and aristocratic worlds. (In Renoir's original outline for the film, Octave's economic dependence on the de la Chesnayes was made more explicit.) That Octave (the middle-class intellectual!) might be in a position to love either a servant, Lisette, or an aristocrat, Christine, also leads to André's death, for Schumacher thinks he is killing Octave meeting Lisette.

At first glance, because of André's speech over the national airwaves denouncing the absent Christine, it might seem that André is the interloper, transgressing the marriage bonds between Christine and Robert. Yet this conflict is settled rapidly; Christine's sincerity leads Robert to break off his affair with Geneviève. Indeed the whole opening incident could have led to closer relations between Christine and Robert. But the film would have ended there! The transgressor who moves the narrative is Octave, who demands that Christine and Robert invite André to La Colinère. Once at La Colinère, André is depressed at this friendly but formal reception by Christine and would leave except that he is encouraged by Octave to stay. Finally, Octave, who all along has been identified with Christine's father and who has offered her avuncular, asexual friendship and protection, succumbs to her declaration of love and her desire to flee her husband's milieu. Octave symbolically transgresses incest taboos. Lisette senses this and expresses her strong disapproval when Octave is about to elope with Christine, saying, "But imagine *those* two living together—I think that young people should live with the young and the old folks with the old." Reverting again to his role of offering Christine asexual love, Octave sends André off in his place and in his coat, causing not only André's death but also his own curse, his permanent exclusion from Christine and Robert's milieu.

Visually, Robert represents the ego, meticulously dressed for the right social occasion and showing on his face an extremely sensitive response to every social situation. Lisette and Christine—dressed in ruffles, filmed with halo lighting, shown smiling and in moments of sheer exuberance and joy—are pure feminine eros, a potential fecundating principle and the prizes sought after by men. In fact, they are dependent on both men and the social structure dominated by men. A principle that Lévi-Strauss states as an unquestioned given is that "in human society, it is the men who exchange the women and not vice versa."[20] *The Rules of the Game* partly deals with the two women's efforts to exert their emotional independence and to escape the limitations placed on that independence.

Geneviève in her dress and comportment represents eros socialized. She knows her place. Marceau and Schumacher competing for Lisette are the erotic id and the supergo in opposition. Octave and André are the two types of anal figures (as Norman O. Brown described the anality of the bourgeoisie in *Life Against Death*[21]). Octave, fat, unkempt, shaggy, is not only the avuncular protector of Christine but also a childlike figure, thus fit to be the friend of the petulant, idealistic, compulsive, and adolescent Jurieu.

Symbols are more diffuse than semes, which as we have seen are commonly accepted cultural indicators of qualities or adjectival "labels." As Barthes says in

Elements of Semiology, a symbol is an inadequate representation; e.g., a cross does not adequately express all of Christianity. A seme, on the other hand, conveys a fuller sense of its signified. Octave's *clumsiness* is conveyed rather fully by the way he moves, the de la Chesnayes' *richness* by the objects in their apartment, the architecture of their homes. On the other hand, Octave's pleas for someone to help him out of his bear's costume symbolize his sexuality and say something about his coming emergence from an avuncular role to that of Christine's potential lover. Geneviève, the sexually free woman, can finally be prevailed upon to help him out of the costume but she does so begrudgingly and in the process throws him to the floor.

To a large degree the semes can be read synchronically, on the level of the single image or on the level of the shot. The symbols, however, especially in the working out of the antitheses, mediations, and transgressions, proceed diachronically. Substitutions, such as those of figures serving as doubles, are worked out on the syntagmatic level, and are frequently metonymic substitutions in which the whole is represented by a related part. The dying rabbit in the hunt scene stands for helplessness, animal life, and fertility; the sacrificial death of André Jurieu, Christine's softness and love.

Barthes also finds implanted in the text other symbols, such as a child-woman figure or queen-servant relationships. Obviously in *The Rules of the Game* the hunt and the masquerade are symbol-laden episodes that need almost no dialogue. Barthes insists that both the semes and the symbols are multivalent and reversible, so that the seme "richness" or the antithesis "nature/civilization" can be borne by any of the figures in the narrative in a multiplicity of ways. These reversals can be seen, for example, if we consider Christine's use of lipstick as "artifice" and Robert's rejecting Geneviève as his effort to act "sincerely" in his marriage—although Christine is otherwise often associated with naturalness and ingenuousness and Robert with sophistication.

FILM AND LITERATURE

Language is symbolic representation; cinema is primarily iconic. That is, the relation of word to object in writing or speaking is purely arbitrary, while cinema is built on photography, which gives a two-dimensional representation analogously similar to its object. In literature, the description of the human body depends on the fragmentation of a whole into its parts for the sake of metaphoric or connotative description in *words;* this necessary fragmentation influences the way the enigmatic, action, symbolic, and semic codes are worked out in literature; literary authors paraphrase other texts previously established in the same verbal (spoken and written) mode. A photograph offers us its iconic codes and its connotations all at once. In feature films, once the subject has been established by the enigmas, the setting or specific objects in that setting can fully connote a character even though that character is not on screen. Metonymy or the representation of the whole by one of its related parts is the major rhetorical device which carries symbolic and semic coding in feature films.

Christian Metz has demonstrated that the minimal syntagmatic unit in film is the shot; the discussion in this article of synchronous connotation on the level of the single frame is not intended to establish the frame as a complete signifying unit. Obviously much of Barthes's discussion of the relation between linguistic syntax and the literary narrative cannot be applied directly to film. Yet, because audiences receive the syntactic flow of shots and the editing in a film as "natural," one could also work out the ideological role of the shot in the way that Barthes describes the ideological role of the sentence.

The shot often masks our awareness of how a film uses cultural codes. It rigidifies denotation, and "it yields meaning with the security of an 'innocent' nature: that of . . . syntax" (p. 264). Furthermore, since Metz demonstrates that all of narrative film's syntagmatic structures are dependent on intentionality or on the development of a "plot," one could well add a Barthesian analysis of film to Metz's analysis of film's major syntagmatic structures.[22] Just as a caption gives a preferred reading to a still photograph, so in feature films, as in classic literary narratives, the enigma "anchors" the connotations, actions, and symbols and structures the cinematic sequence form itself.

Since Barthes is mostly concerned with language in its relation to narrative discourse and with the play of meaning across a number of semiotic codes, of which verbal language is only one, his major methodological premises can well be applied to the study of film, which is still primarily a narrative art form. In addition his criteria for quality in traditional narrative art can help us evaluate popular culture, for Barthes does not build on some canon of great works but rather evaluates a closed narrative by its successful orchestration, integration, and manipulation of cultural and symbolic codes:

. . . a "good" narrative fulfills both the plurality and the circularity of the codes: ceaselessly correcting the causality of the anecdote by the metonymy of the symbols and, inversely, the simultaneity of the meanings by the operations which lead on and use up expectation to its end. (p. 77)

Notes

1. Roland Barthes, *S/Z,* trans. Richard Howard (New York: Farrar, Straus, and Giroux, 1974). Further citations from this edition are indicated by page numbers in the text. *Writing Degree Zero and Elements of Semiology,* trans. Annette Lavers and Colin Smith (Boston: Beacon, 1970).

2. The radical film/literary critic often seeks to raise unconscious ideological mechanisms to the level of consciousness so that we may "gain control" over them. Certainly those critics who combine a Marxist and a psychoanalytic approach, such as Christian Metz in his current work, have that intent. Such radical critical practice serves the function of both consciousness raising and theoretical investigation, but the notion of "gaining control" and ideological *change* must be dialectically related to a more general economic, social, and political movement for change in the society at large. "Where do correct ideas come from? . . ."

3. *Writing Degree Zero and Elements of Semiology.*

4. Christian Metz, *Language and Cinema,* trans. Donna Jean Umiker-Sebeok (The Hague: Mouton, 1974). Raymond Bellour is concerned with "segmentals" and "supra-

segmentals" in film, which are linguistic concepts. He presented a paper on the supra-segmentals in *Gigi* at the Milwaukee Film Conference in November 1975. See also his "The Obvious and the Code," *Screen* 15, no. 4 (1974–1975).

5. Umberto Eco, *A Theory of Semiotics,* trans. David Osmond-Smith (Bloomington: Indiana University Press, 1976).

6. Stuart Hall, "The Determinations of Newsphotographs," *Working Papers in Cultural Studies,* no. 3 (1972), p. 65 .

7. *Ibid.*

8. Roland Barthes, "Rhetoric of the Image," *Working Papers in Cultural Studies,* no. 1 (1971).

9. In semantics, a seme is a unit of the signified. The seme is that quality which is signified by the connotation, e.g., richness. Both Barthes and Eco conclude that in a semiotic sense the sum of all the connotations in a given society, the sum of all the "semes," defines the society's ideological presuppositions.

10. Umberto Eco, "Towards a Semiotic Inquiry into the Television Message," *Working Papers in Cultural Studies,* no. 3 (1972), p. 114.

11. Hall, p. 66.

12. *La Règle du jeu: L'Avant Scène du cinéma,* no. 52 (1965). Translation mine. All further citations of dialogue are cited and translated from here.

13. Christian Metz, *Film Language: A Semiotics of Cinema* (The Hague: Mouton, 1971).

14. Laura Mulvey, "Visual Pleasure and Narrative Cinema," *Screen* 16, no. 3 (1975), reprinted here. Daniel Dayan, "The Tutor Code of Classical Cinema," *Film Quarterly* 28, no. 1 (1974). Raymond Bellour, *"The Birds,"* trans. from *Cahiers du cinéma,* no. 216 (1969), available from the BFI Educational Advisory Service, 81 Dean Street, London W1.

15. Overdetermined is a Freudian concept, brought into current critical thought by Louis Althusser and frequently used by Barthes in *S/Z*. To paraphrase Althusser, one can apply his concept to the choices, motives, and actions of the characters within a traditional closed narrative: the characters' choices, motives, and actions are inseparable from the total structure of the narrative in which they are found, inseparable from their formal conditions of existence and from the instances they govern. The characters' actions and choices are radically affected by these instances, determining and also determined in the one and the same movement, and determined by the various levels and instances of the narrative they animate. The narrative work as a whole is also overdetermined, reflecting and responding to the contradictions of the society in which it was engendered. See Althusser's *For Marx,* trans. Ben Brewster (New York: Vintage, 1970), p. 201. For a detailed analysis of the function and mechanisms of overdetermination in a single film, see Charles Eckert, "The Anatomy of a Proletarian Film: Warner's *Marked Woman,"* *Film Quarterly* 17, no. 2 (1973–1974), reprinted here.

16. Claude Lévi-Strauss, *Structural Anthropology* (New York: Anchor, 1967), p. 82.

17. Following Lévi-Strauss and Jacques Lacan, Barthes sees sexual differentiation and the exchange value of women as a structural determinant of the creation of both linguistic meaning and commercial or interpersonal "contracts" or relations. Such an analysis of the interrelation between psychic-linguistic-economic structures is deterministic in its premises, and feminists, such as Juliet Mitchell, who accept these premises do not demonstrate how these structures change across history or under socialism or if they can be fundamentally altered at all. In this particular instance, I would only note in passing that proof of the inadequacy of Barthes's treatment of sexual symbolism is that he cannot deal with homosexuality and androgeny but must treat the story of a man's unwitting falling in love with a

castrato only in terms of the antithesis between and "transgression" of an essential maleness and an essential femaleness.

18. Philippe Esnault, "Le Jeu de la vérité," *L'Avant Scène du cinéma,* no. 52 (1965), p. 11.

19. Lévi-Strauss, p. 221.

20. *Ibid.,* p. 45.

21. Norman O. Brown, *Life Against Death: The Psychoanalytic Meaning of History* (Middletown, Conn.: Wesleyan University Press, 1959).

22. Metz, *Film Language: A Semiotics of Cinema.*

GODARD AND COUNTER CINEMA: *VENT D'EST*

PETER WOLLEN

Written in 1972, Peter Wollen's article on Vent d'Est (Wind from the East) *attempts to crystallize several important transitions: Jean-Luc Godard's own movement toward a more radically Other counter cinema; the growing recognition of an openly political avant-garde for which Godard served as a crucial reference point; the parallel appreciation of the relevance of Bertolt Brecht's theories for the cinema; and, under the influence of film semiotics, an increasing emphasis on the formal qualities and properties of narrative cinema as such. Wollen's seven succinct dichotomies capture the fusion of political and formal concerns that seemed at the time to be the guiding star for both a scientific yet engaged semiotics and a radical film practice. Neither has subsequently followed quite the incandescent trajectory that Wollen seems to envision, but this hardly detracts from the precision with which he characterizes a set of very important differences between the traditional realist text and the modernist one. It is also clear that a great deal of contemporary counter cinema—*Jeanne Dielman, Sally Potter's* Thriller, *the films of Laura Mulvey and Peter Wollen—has consistently employed many of the "seven cardinal virtues" Wollen describes here.*

There may be more than a coy reference to theology in Wollen's opposition of Hollywood's sins with counter cinema's virtues. In the introduction to this volume, I mentioned the confluence between moral or puritanical values and the political left. Wollen's article certainly belongs to the stream of contemporary critical theory that distrusts pleasure. Such work stresses both the need for the viewer to work—to gain knowledge actively rather than to absorb pleasure passively— and the formal mechanisms by which meaning is produced, not created. Whether assumptions underlying this approach require further examination, lest critiques

*couched in political, semiotic, or formal terms resort to an underlying but
undefended puritanism for rhetorical force, needs closer consideration than most
authors have given it. Whether such a morality is part of Godard's own stance
is another aspect of the question that invites further reflection.*

•

More and more radically Godard has developed a counter-cinema whose values
are counterposed to those of orthodox cinema. I want simply to write some notes
about the main features of this counter-cinema. My approach is to take seven of
the values of the old cinema, Hollywood–Mosfilm, as Godard would put it, and
contrast these with their (revolutionary, materialist) counterparts and contraries.
In a sense, the seven deadly sins of the cinema against the seven cardinal virtues.
They can be set out schematically in a table as follows:

Narrative transitivity	Narrative intransitivity
Identification	Estrangement
Transparency	Foregrounding
Single diegesis	Multiple diegesis
Closure	Aperture
Pleasure	Unpleasure
Fiction	Reality

Obviously, these somewhat cryptic headings need further commentary. First,
however, I should say that my overall argument is that Godard was right to break
with Hollywood cinema and to set up his counter-cinema and, for this alone, he is
the most important director working today. Nevertheless, I think there are various confusions in his strategy, which blunt its edges and even, at times, tend to
nullify it—mainly, these concern his confusion over the series of terms: fiction/
mystification/ideology/lies/deception/illusion/representation. At the end of
these notes, I shall touch on some of my disagreements. First, some remarks on
the main topics.

   1. Narrative transitivity v. narrative intransitivity. (One thing following another v. gaps and interruptions, episodic construction, undigested digression.)

   By narrative transitivity, I mean a sequence of events in which each unit (each
function that changes the course of the narrative) follows the one preceding it
according to a chain of causation. In the Hollywood cinema, this chain is usually
psychological and is made up, roughly speaking, of a series of coherent motivations. The beginning of the film starts with establishment, which sets up the basic
dramatic situation—usually an equilibrium, which is then disturbed. A kind of
chain reaction then follows, until at the end a new equilibrium is restored.

   Godard began to break with this tradition very early. He did this, at first, in two
ways, both drawn from literature. He borrowed the idea of separate chapters,
which enabled him to introduce interruptions into the narrative, and he borrowed
from the picaresque novel. The picaresque is a pseudo-autobiographical form
which for tight plot construction substitutes a random and unconnected series of
incidents, supposed to represent the variety and ups-and-downs of real life. (The

hero is typically marginal to society, a rogue-errant, often an orphan, in any case without family ties, thrown hither and thither by the twists and turns of fortune.)

By the time he arrives at *Vent d'Est,* Godard has practically destroyed all narrative transitivity. Digressions which, in earlier films, represented interruptions to the narrative have hypertrophied until they dominate the film entirely. The basic story, as much of it as remains, does not have any recognizable sequence, but is more like a series of intermittent flashes. Sometimes it seems to be following a definite order in time, but sometimes not. The constructive principle of the film is rhetorical, rather than narrative, in the sense that it sets out the disposition of an argument, point by point, in a sequence of 1–7, which is then repeated, with a subsidiary sequence of Theories A and B. There are also various figures of amplification and digression within this structure.

There are a number of reasons why Godard has broken with narrative transitivity. Perhaps the most important is that he can disrupt the emotional spell of the narrative and thus force the spectator, by interrupting the narrative flow, to re-concentrate and re-focus his attention. (Of course, his attention may get lost altogether.) Godard's cinema, broadly speaking, is within the modern tradition established by Brecht and Artaud, in their different ways, suspicious of the power of the arts—and the cinema, above all—to 'capture' its audience without apparently making it think, or changing it.

2. Identification v. estrangement. (Empathy, emotional involvement with a character v. direct address, multiple and divided characters, commentary.)

Identification is a well-known mechanism though, of course, in the cinema there are various special features which mark cinematic identification off as a distinct phenomenon. In the first place, there is the possibility of double identification with the star and/or with the character. Second, the identification can only take place in a situation of suspended belief. Third, there are spatial and temporal limits either to the identification or, at any rate, to the presence of the imago. (In some respects, cinematic identification is similar to transference in analysis, though this analogy should not be taken too far.)

Again, the breakdown of identification begins early in Godard's films and then develops unevenly after that, until it reaches a new level with *Le Gai Savoir.* Early devices include non-matching of voice to character, introduction of 'real people' into the fiction, characters addressing the audience directly. All these devices are also used in *Vent d'Est,* which takes especially far the device of allowing voices to float off from characters into a discourse of their own on the soundtrack, using the same voice for different characters, different voices for the same character. It also introduces the 'real-life' company into the film itself and, in a rather complicated figure, introduces Gian Maria Volonte, not simply as an actor (Godard shows the actors being made-up) but also as intervening in the process of 'image-building' As well as this, there is a long and extremely effective direct address sequence in which the audience is described—somewhat pejoratively—from the screen and invited into the world of representation.

It is hardly necessary, after the work of Brecht, to comment on the purpose of estrangement-effects of this kind. Clearly, too, they are closely related to the break-up of narrative transitivity. It is impossible to maintain 'motivational' coherence, when characters themselves are incoherent, fissured, interrupted, multiple and self-critical. Similarly, the ruse of direct address breaks not only the fantasy identification but also the narrative surface. It raises directly the question, 'What is this film for?', superimposed on the orthodox narrative questions, 'Why did that happen?' and 'What is going to happen next?' Any form of cinema which aims to establish a dynamic relationship between film maker and spectator naturally has to consider the problem of what is technically the register of discourse, the content of the enunciation, as well as its designation, the content of the enunciate.

3. *Transparency v. foregrounding.* ('Language wants to be over-looked'— Siertsema v. making the mechanics of the film/text visible and explicit.)

Traditional cinema is in the direct line of descent from the Renaissance discovery of perspective and reformulation of the art of painting, expressed most clearly by Alberti, as providing a window on the world. The camera, of course, is simply the technological means towards achieving a perfect perspective construction. After the Renaissance the painting ceased to be a text which could be 'read', as the iconographic imagery and ideographic space of pre-Renaissance painting were gradually rejected and replaced by the concept of pure representation. The 'language' of painting became simply the instrument by which representation of the world was achieved. A similar tendency can be seen at work with attitudes to verbal language. From the seventeenth century onwards, language was increasingly seen as an instrument which should efface itself in the performance of its task—the conveyance of meaning. Meaning, in its turn, was regarded as representation of the world.

In his early films Godard introduced the cinema as a topic in his narrative— the 'Lumière' sequence in *Les Carabiniers,* the film within a film in *Le Mépris.* But it was not until his contribution to *Loin du Vietnam* that the decisive step was taken, when he simply showed the camera on screen. In the post-1968 films the process of production is systematically highlighted. In *Vent d'Est* this shows itself not simply in taking the camera behind the scenes, as it were, but also in altering the actual film itself: thus the whole worker's control sequence is shown with the film marked and scratched, the first time that this has happened in Godard's work. In previous films, he had not gone further than using special film stock (*Les Carabiniers*) or printing sequences in negative (*Les Carabiniers, Alphaville*).

At first sight, it looks as if the decision to scratch the surface of the film brings Godard into line with other avant-garde film makers, in the American 'underground' especially. However this is not really the case. In the case of the American film makers, marking the film is best seen alongside developments in painting that have dominated, particularly in the USA, in recent years. Broadly speaking, this involves a reduction of film to its 'optical' substrate. Noise is amplified until, instead of being marginal to the film, it becomes its principal content. It may then be structured according to some calculus or algorithm or submitted to random coding. Just as, in painting, the canvas is foregrounded, so, in cinema, the film is foregrounded.

Godard, however, is not interested in this kind of 'de-signification' of the image by foregrounding 'noise' and then introducing a new constructive principle appropriate to this. What he seems to be doing is looking for a way of expressing negation. It is well known that negation is the founding principle of verbal language, which marks it off both from animal signal-systems and from other kinds of human discourse, such as images. However, once the decision is made to consider a film as a process of writing in images, rather than a representation of the world, then it becomes possible to conceive of scratching the film as an erasure, a virtual negation. Evidently the use of marks as erasures, crossing-out an image, is quite different from using them as deliberate noise or to foreground the optical substrate. It pre-supposes a different concept of 'film-writing' and 'film-reading'.

Some years ago, Astruc, in a famous article, wrote about *le caméra-stylo*. His concept of writing—*écriture*—was closer to the idea of style. Godard, like Eisenstein before him, is more concerned with 'image-building' as a kind of picto-graphy, in which images are liberated from their role as elements of representation and given a semantic function within a genuine iconic code, something like the baroque code of emblems. The sequences in which the image of Stalin is discussed are not simply—or even principally—about Stalin's politics, as much as they are about the problem of finding an image to signify 'repression'. In fact, the whole project of writing in images must involve a high degree of foregrounding, because the construction of an adequate code can only take place if it is glossed and commented upon in the process of construction. Otherwise, it would remain a purely private language.

4. *Single diegesis v. multiple diegesis.* (A unitary homogeneous world v. heterogeneous worlds. Rupture between different codes and different channels.)

In Hollywood films, everything shown belongs to the same world, and complex articulations within that world—such as flash-backs—are carefully signalled and located. The dominant aesthetic is a kind of liberalized classicism. The rigid constraints of the dramatic unities have been relaxed, but mainly because they were over-strict and limiting, whereas the basic principle remains unshaken. The world represented on the cinema must be coherent and integrated, though it need not observe compulsory, statutory constraints. Time and space must follow a consistent order. Traditionally, only one form of multiple diegesis is allowed— the play within a play—whereby the second, discontinuous diegetic space is embedded or bracketed within the first. (It should be added that there are some exemplary cases of transgression of single diegesis within literature, such as Hoffmann's *Life of Tomcat Murr,* which consists of Tomcat Murr's life—the primary diegesis—interleaved at random with pages from another text—the life of Kreisler—supposedly bound into the book by mistake by the bookbinder. The pages from the secondary diegesis begin and end in the middle of sentences and are in the wrong order, with some missing. A novel like Sterne's *Tristram Shandy,* however, simply embeds a number of different diegeses on the play-within-a-play model. Of course, by recursion this principle can be taken to breaking-point, as Borges has often pointed out.)

Godard uses film-within-a-film devices in a number of his early works. At the same time the primary diegesis begins to develop acute fissures and stresses. In

Le Mépris, for example, there is not only a film-within-a-film, but many of the principal characters speak different languages and can only communicate with each other through an interpreter (an effect entirely lost in some dubbed versions, which have to give the interpreter meaningless remarks to speak). The first radical break with single diegesis, however, comes with *Weekend,* when characters from different epochs and from fiction are interpolated into the main narrative: Saint-Just, Balsamo, Emily Brontë. Instead of a single narrative world, there is an interlocking and interweaving of a plurality of worlds.

At the same time that Godard breaks down the structure of the single diegesis, he also attacks the structure of the single, unitary code that expressed it. Not only do different characters speak different languages, but different parts of the film do too. Most strikingly, there is a rupture between soundtrack and images: indeed, the elaboration of this rupture dominates both *Le Gai Savoir* and *Pravda.* The text becomes a composite structure, like that of a medieval macaronic poem, using different codes and semantic systems. Moreover, these are not simply different, but also often contradictory. *Vent d'Est,* for instance, presents alternative ways of making a film (the Glauber Rocha sequence) only to reject them. It is one of the assumptions of contemporary linguistics that a language has a single, unitary semantic component, just as it has a single syntax. In fact, this is surely not the case. The semantic component of a language is composite and contradictory, permitting understanding on one level, misunderstanding on another. Godard systematically explores the areas of misunderstanding.

5. *Closure v. aperture.* (A self-contained object, harmonized within its own bounds, v. open-endedness, overspill, intertextuality—allusion, quotation and parody.)

It has often been pointed out that in recent years, the cinema has become 'self-conscious', in contrast to the 'innocent' days of Hollywood. In itself, however, 'self-consciousness' is quite compatible with closure. There is a use of quotation and allusion that simply operates to provide a kind of 'surplus' of meaning, as the scholastics used to say, a bonus for those who catch the allusion. The notorious 'Tell me lies' sequence in *Le Petit Soldat,* borrowed from *Johnny Guitar,* is of this kind: it does not make much difference whether you recognise it or not and, even if you do, it has no effect on the meaning of the sequence. Or else quotation can be simply a sign of eclecticism, primarily a stylistic rather than semantic feature. Or, as with Makavejev's use of quotation, the objective may be to impose a new meaning on material by inserting it into a new context: a form of irony.

Godard, however, uses quotation in a much more radical manner. Indeed, his fondness for quotation has always been one of the distinguishing characteristics of his films. At the beginning of his career, Godard used to give instructions to the cameraman almost entirely in terms of shots from previous films and, at a more explicit level, there are endless direct quotes, both from films and from painting and literature. Whole films contain obvious elements of pastiche and parody: *Une Femme est une Femme* is obviously derivative from the Hollywood musical, *Les Carabiniers* from Rossellini, *Le Mépris* is 'Hawks and Hitchcock shot in the manner of Antonioni' . . . it would be possible to go on endlessly.

However, as Godard's work developed, these quotations and allusions, instead of being a mark of eclecticism, began to take on an autonomy of their own, as structural and significant features within the films. It becomes more and more impossible to understand whole sequences and even whole films without a degree of familiarity with the quotations and allusions which structure them. What seemed at first to be a kind of jackdaw mentality, a personality trait of Godard himself, begins to harden into a genuine polyphony, in which Godard's own voice is drowned out and obliterated behind that of the authors quoted. The film can no longer be seen as a discourse with a single subject, the film maker/auteur. Just as there is multiplicity of narrative worlds, so too there is a multiplicity of speaking voices.

Again, this takes us back to the period before the rise of the novel, the representational painting, to the epoch of the battle of the books, the logomachia. Perhaps the author who comes most to mind is Rabelais, with his endless counterposition of quotations, his parodies, his citation of authorities. The text/film can only be understood as an arena, a meeting-place in which different discourses encounter each other and struggle for supremacy. Moreover these discourses take on an independent life of their own. Instead of each being corked up in its bottle with its author's name on it as a label, the discourses escape, and like genies, are let out to intermingle and quarrel.

In this sense, Godard is like Ezra Pound or James Joyce who, in the same way, no longer insist on speaking to us in their own words, but can be seen more as ventriloquist's dummies, through whom are speaking—or rather being written— palimpsests, multiple *Niederschriften* (Freud's word) in which meaning can no longer be said to express the intention of the author or to be a representation of the world, but must like the discourse of the unconscious be understood by a different kind of decipherment. In orthodox logic and linguistics, context is only important as an arbiter between alternative meanings (amphibologies, as they are called in logic). In Godard's films, the opposite process is at work: the juxtaposition and re-contextualization of discourses leads not to a separating-out of meanings but to a confrontation.

6. *Pleasure v. unpleasure.* (Entertainment, aiming to satisfy the spectator v. provocation, aiming to dissatisfy and hence change the spectator.)

The attack on 'entertainment' cinema is part of a broader attack on the whole of 'consumer society'. Cinema is conceived of as a drug that lulls and mollifies the militancy of the masses, by bribing them with pleasurable dreams, thus distracting them from the stern tasks which are their true destiny. It is hardly necessary to insist on the asceticism and Puritanism—repressiveness—of this conception that unflinchingly seeks to put the reality-principle in command over the pleasure-principle. It is true that the short-term (cinematic) dream is sometimes denounced in the name of a long-term (millenarian) dream, and short-term (false, illusory, deceptive) satisfactions contrasted with long-term (real, genuine, authentic) satisfactions, but this is exactly the kind of argument which is used to explain the accumulation of capital in a capitalist society by the saving principle and postponement of consumption.

Brecht was careful never to turn his back on entertainment and, indeed, he even quotes Horace in favour of pleasure as the purpose of the arts, combined, of course, with instruction. This is not to say that a revolutionary cinema should distract its spectators from realities, but that unless a revolution is desired (which means nothing less than coinciding with and embodying collective fantasies) it will never take place. The reality-principle only works together with the pleasure-principle when survival itself is at stake, and though this may evidently be the case in a revolutionary situation, it is not so in the advanced capitalist countries today. In a situation in which survival is—at least relatively—nonproblematic, the pleasure-principle and the reality-principle are antagonistic and, since the reality-principle is fundamentally adaptive, it is from the pleasure-principle that change must stem. This means that desire, and its representation in fantasy, far from being necessary enemies of revolutionary politics—and its cinematic auxiliary—are necessary conditions.

The problem, of course, concerns the nature of the fantasies on the one hand, and the way in which they are presented in the text/film on the other hand, the way in which fantasy scenarios are related to ideologies and beliefs and to scientific analysis. A revolutionary cinema has to operate at different levels—fantasy, ideology, science—and the articulation of these levels, which involve different modes of discourse and different positions of the subject, is a complicated matter.

In *Vent d'Est* the 'struggle against the bourgeois notion of representation' certainly does not rule out the presence of fantasy: fantasy of shooting the union delegate, fantasies of killing shoppers in a supermarket. Indeed, as long as there are images at all, it is impossible to eliminate fantasy. But the fantasies are almost entirely sado-masochistic in content, and this same fantasy content also seems to govern the relationship between film maker and spectator, rather on the lines of the relationship between the flute-player in the film and his audience. A great many of the devices Godard uses are designed to produce a collective working relationship between film maker and audience, in which the spectator can collaborate in the production/consumption of meaning. But Godard's view of collective work is conceived of in very imprecise terms. 'Criticism' consists of insults and interrogation. The fantasy content of the film is not articulated correctly with the ideology or political theory. This, in turn, seems to spring from a suspicion of the need for fantasy at all, except perhaps in the sado-masochistic form of provocation.

7. *Fiction v. reality.* (Actors wearing make-up, acting a story v. real life, the breakdown of representation, truth.)

Godard's dissatisfaction with fiction cinema begins very early. Already in *Vivre sa vie* non-fiction is introduced—the chapter on the economics and sociology of prostitution. There is almost no costume drama in Godard's career, until—ironically enough—*Vent d'Est*. Even within the framework of fiction, he has stuck to contemporary life. His science-fiction films (*Alphaville, Anticipation*) have all been set in a kind of future-in-the-present, without any paraphernalia of special effects or sets.

As with all the features I have described, the retreat from (and eventually attack on) fiction has proceeded unevenly through Godard's career, coming forward strongly in, for instance, *Deux ou trois choses,* then receding again. Especially since May 1968, the attack on fiction has been given a political rationale (fiction=mystification=bourgeois ideology) but, at the beginning, it is much more closely connected with Godard's fascination (Cartesian, rather than Marxist) with the misleading and dissembling nature of appearances, the impossibility of reading an essence from a phenomenal surface, of seeing a soul through and within a body or telling a lie from a truth. At times Godard seems almost to adopt a kind of radical Romanticism, which sees silence (lovers' silence, killers' silence) as the only true communication, when reality and representation, essence and appearance, irreducibly coincide: the moment of truth.

Obviously, too, Godard's attitude to fiction is linked with his attitude to acting. This comes out most clearly in *Une Femme Mariée,* when the actor is interrogated about his true self, his relationship to his roles. Godard is obsessed with the problem of true speech, lying speech and theatrical speech. (In a sense, these three kinds of speech, seen first in purely personal terms, are eventually politicized and given a class content. The bourgeoisie lies, the revisionists lie, though they should speak the truth, the revolutionaries speak the truth, or, rather, stammer an approach to the truth.) Godard has long shown a horror of acting, based originally on a 'logocentric' antipathy to anybody who speaks someone else's words, ironic in the circumstances. Eventually, Godard seems to have reformulated his attitude so that actors are distrusted for speaking other people's words as if they were their own. This accompanies his growing recognition that nobody ever speaks in their own words, hence the impossibility of genuine dialogue and the reduction of dialogue to reciprocal—or often unilateral—interviewing. In *Vent d'Est* there is almost no dialogue at all (only a number of variants of monologue) and this must relate to the caricature of collective work Godard puts forward.

Interviewing is, of course, the purest form of linguistic demand, and the demand Godard makes is for the truth. Yet it never seems to be forthcoming, not surprisingly, since it cannot be produced on demand. It is as if Godard has a lingering hope that if people could find their own words, they might produce it miraculously in our presence, but if not, then it has to be looked for in books, which are the residues of real words. This kind of problematic has been tormenting Godard throughout his cinematic career. In *A Bout de souffle,* for instance, there is the central contrast between Michel Poiccard/Laszlo Kovacs—an honest impostor—and Patricia, whose mania for honesty reveals her in the end as a deceiver.

The early films tend to explore this kind of problem as one between different levels, but in the post-1968 films, there seems to have been a kind of flattening out, so that fiction = acting = lying = deception = representation = illusion = mystification = ideology. In fact, as anybody reflecting on Godard's earlier films must surely know, these are all very different categories. Ideology, for instance, does not depend primarily on lies. It depends on the acceptance of common values and interests. Similarly mystification is different from deception: a priest does not deceive his congregation about the miracle of the mass in the same way that a conjurer deceives his audience, by hiding something from them. Again, the cinema is a form of representation, but this is not the same as illusion or 'trompe l'oeil'. It is only possible to obliterate these distinctions by defining each of them simply in terms of their departure from truth.

The cinema cannot show the truth, or reveal it, because the truth is not out there in the real world, waiting to be photographed. What the cinema can do is produce meanings, and meanings can only be plotted, not in relation to some abstract yardstick or criterion of truth, but in relation to other meanings. This is why Godard's objective of producing a counter-cinema is the right objective. But he is mistaken if the thinks that such a counter-cinema can have an absolute existence. It can only exist in relation to the rest of the cinema. Its function is to struggle against the fantasies, ideologies and aesthetic devices of one cinema with its own antagonistic fantasies, ideologies and aesthetic devices. In some respects this may bring it closer—or seem to bring it closer—to the cinema it opposes than *Vent d'Est* would suggest. *Vent d'Est* is a pioneering film, an avant-garde film, an extremely important film. It is the starting-point for work on a revolutionary cinema. But it is not that revolutionary cinema itself.

JAWS, IDEOLOGY, AND FILM THEORY

STEPHEN HEATH

Somewhat uncharacteristically, Stephen Heath dwells in this article on popular, commercial cinema rather than on theory per se or avant-garde practices—the emphasis of much poststructuralist writing. But in another respect the article is seminal, reaffirming its author's continuing concern for the popular film and making a very clear call to focus film theory on the study of narrative, genre, popular cinema and its reliance on the pleasurable reworkings of ideology as a source of profit and perpetuation. Heath argues that the complex relationships among pleasure, meaning, commodity or industry, signifying practice, and text pose the central challenges, not formalism or content analysis.

Like Henderson and Eckert, Heath locates a particular film (Jaws) in relation to a particular event or issue (Watergate). He makes the connection through the way in which the town's mayor tries to hush up a politically harmful revelation (the shark attacks may jeopardize tourism, which will harm the town's economy and deflate his own status). But Heath goes on to insist on a more complex reading of the film. In a very useful retrospective glance at Metz's early work, Heath develops a sharp distinction between study of the object cinema and the study of the operation cinema. The latter concerns the process of engaging, or even of constructing, the viewer and of making meaning pleasurable. An elaboration of some of these operations leads Heath to introduce some psychoanalytic concerns —displacement and subjectivity, for example —in a fairly offhand manner. More important, he demonstrates why a purely structuralist semiotics devoted to the object cinema had become perceived as inadequate (though still valuable) by 1976. In this light, his brief and engaging study of one film helps to mark the transition from a structuralist linguistic semiotics to a more fully psychoanalytic semiotics.

For a valuable alternative reading of Jaws *and of* The Godfather, *one can turn to Fredric Jameson's article, "Reification and Utopia in Mass Culture,"* Social Text, *no. 1 (Winter 1979): 130–48, where he makes several provocative points about the relation of mass culture to high culture and modernism and about the presence of both reifying and utopian elements in mass culture.*

•

Every review of the film *Jaws* begins with some reference to its status as *the* film, not so much super-production as super-product, the box-office record-breaker expected to gross more than a quarter of a billion dollars. But the product also *means* (part of its meaning, of course, is to be 'the most profitable movie in history'), and means as *entertainment,* a moving and pleasurable experience marketed and bought. Analysis must hold to this pleasure-meaning-commodity complex, what film turns and sells *on,* and recent developments in film theory— centered in Britain, with powerful influence in the United States, round the work of the journal *Screen* and feeding from there into film teaching—have been concerned to pose precisely the problems which arise from such an emphasis. Epitome of 'cinema', *Jaws* can perhaps provide a focus for discussion that will allow something of these problems to be understood.

At one level, the ideology of *Jaws* is clear enough, the province of a traditional 'content analysis'. *Jaws* is a Watergate film: Mayor Larry Vaughan of Amity, Long Island, serves his electors ('Amity needs summer dollars') by hushing up a shark attack ('I was acting in the town's best interest'); the white male middle-class—not a single black and, very quickly, not a single woman in the film—in the person of Police Chief Martin Brody will recognize its complicity (a literal slap in the face from the mother of a boy who dies when the beaches stay open) and pull the town through with a ordinary-guy brand of heroism born of fear-and-decency; order is fragile but possible, mistakes are made (Vaughan is simply weak, caught out serving his town, and Brody with him; the evil is something else, call it a shark) but you—Brody—can redeem them (kill the shark), and better than any screwball romantic myth (Quint, a vague memory of *Moby Dick,* of which *Jaws* is the middle-class remake) or any expert (Hooper, the whiz-kid with all the equipment finally defeated by the shark). Other elements draw out from this core with a symptomatic rightness: as, for example, the story Quint tells of the sinking of the *Indianapolis* in shark-infested waters after transporting the Hiroshima bomb ('1100 men went into the water, 360 men came out, anyway we delivered the bomb'), a story that functions to motivate Quint's character as determined shark-killer but that does so excessively, placing—in the play between Quint, Hooper and Brody as they wait out at sea in the summer of America's final year in Vietnam—destruction and conscience and manliness and menace and just-doing-the-job (the scene ends with the three men joining in a song—'Show me the way to go home'—interrupted by the shark outside trying to rip into their world).

This clear ideology, the narrative image of the film, is seen in the number of such elements held in a loose coherence round the central core, working in the space of the film. It is the working-space that is important; to remain at the level of a content analysis in these terms is to fail to engage with the ideological *operation* of the film, its production, as also, the two running together as a set of relations, with the pleasure derived from this film about a shark and its pursuers—in short, is to fail to engage with the fact of film.

The fact of film has been the concern of film theory in its attempts to define film as a specific object of study, and it is in this context that one can grasp the initial role of structuralism and the early 'structuralist' semiology. Semiological description brought consideration of the ways in which meanings are articulated in film; in particular, attention was given to the codes of the image (the construction of iconic signs, problems of denotation and connotation) and to the codes of the arrangement of film in sequences (the definition of syntagmatic units, the structures of film narrative). This last was a part of the work of the French theoretician Christian Metz, whose *Language and Cinema,* published in 1971, is a rigorous investigation of the whole idea of cinema as language, a mapping out of the difficulties involved in the linguistic analogy in order to give precision to the use of the term 'language' in respect of film.

Language and Cinema rests firmly (and finely) within the limits of 'structuralist' semiological description, a focus exactly on the object cinema as opposed to the operation cinema. Its effect, nevertheless, taken in conjunction with surrounding theoretical developments—the encounter of Marxism and psychoanalysis on the terrain of semiotics—to which Metz's own later work has responded, was to allow the 'language-and-cinema' problem to be henceforth understood as that of the study of film as *specific signifying practice. Signifying* indicates the recognition of film as system or series of systems of meaning, film as articulation. *Practice* stresses the process of this articulation, which it thus refuses to hold under the assumption of notions such as 'representation' and 'expression'; it takes film as a work of production of meanings and in so doing brings into the analysis the question of the positioning of the subject within that work, its relations to the subject, what kind of 'reader' and 'author' it constructs. *Specific* is the necessity for analysis to understand film in the particularity of the work it engages, the differences it sustains with other signifying practices, which does not, however, entail pulling film towards some aesthetic idea of a pure cinematicity (on a line with the idea of 'literarity' derived in literary criticism from Russian Formalism and often become a way of avoiding crucial issues of production and ideology in its appeal, precisely, to a technicist 'structuralist poetics'): specificity here is semiotic, and a semiotic analysis of film—of film as signifying practice—is the analysis of a heterogeneity, the range of codes and systems at work in film over and across its five matters of expression (moving photographic image, recorded phonetic sound, recorded noise, recorded musical sound, and writing; the latter as, for example, in the prominent 'Amity welcomes you' hoarding in *Jaws*). Specificity, that is, is at once those codes particular to cinema (codes of articulation of dialogue and image, codes of scale of shot, certain codes of narrative organisation, etc.) *and* the heterogeneity in its particular effects, its particular inscriptions of subject and meaning and ideology. Thus directed, the study of film is of neither 'contents' nor 'forms' but, breaking the deadlock of that opposition now become a locus classicus of obscurantism, of operations, of the process of film and the relations of subjectivity in that process.

Such a direction can further be seen as grasping in a fundamental intersection three component areas: the conditions of film production and distribution, the individual film, and the general apparatus of cinema. As was said earlier, the film industry manufactures film products, but these products mean and sell on meaning and pleasure; between *industry* and *text,* we also need a category like *machine,* cinema itself understood in its stock of constraints and definitions, its possibilities and points of determination, with respect to which film can be distinguished as specific signifying practice and a particular film seized dialectically in *its* operation. Each of the three areas can bring with it its own set of tasks and study procedures, but attention to their intersection is *constantly* important.

In the light of these propositions, let us come back to *Jaws,* to this particular film. Space will not permit detailed analysis of the movement of its filmic system; one or two fragmentary indications must serve to suggest the terms of that movement and lead on to some consideration of machine and industry, indications that will be developed from the opening shots of the film.

The first shot has the camera underwater veering rapidly forward through the seabed forest to the accompaniment of ominous rhythmic music. Cut to a group of young people at a nighttime beach party; the cut is heavily marked by changes in colour, from the coldish underwater tones to the rich orange-yellow reflections of a fire; in music, a youth is playing a harmonica, and in rhythm, the camera now tracks smoothly right along the group—faces kissing, smoking, drinking—until it stops on a young man looking off-frame. Eyeline cut to the girl who is revealed as the object of his gaze, followed by a cut to a high-angle shot down onto the party establishing its overall space. Then comes a run down to the sea, the girl shedding her clothes as the boy stumbles drunkenly after; as she swims out, the boy collapses; an underwater shot, now moving up to the surface between the girl's legs, precedes the shark's attack; the next morning the boy wakes, sits up into frame as we look out with him on the empty ocean.

For the narrative, this sequence is precisely and simply the beginning, the initial premise: the arrival of the shark. At the same time, however, it sets off a number of other series which knot together as figures over the film. Thus, for example, the presence of the shark is given in the very first shot with its violent underwater movement tied to no human point of view, and the underwater shot is then used in the first part of the film to signify the imminence of attack: we are placed as the shark as it rises to the girl and, later, to the little boy on the float. Once systematized, it can be used to cheat: it occurs to confirm the second day-time beach attack, but this is only two boys with an imitation fin. More impor-tant, the shot binds up with an immediate marking out in the sequence of a danger of sexuality and the displacement of the latter onto the shark: the girl leads the boy on; as she strips, he follows with 'I'm coming, I'm definitely coming'; when she is attacked, he lies on the beach moaning again 'I'm coming, I'm coming' (the novel has the report of the attack held up while the duty patrolman finishes reading a story about a woman who castrates an assailant with a knife secreted in her hair). One inexorable movement of the film is then to get rid of women; in an exact rhyming inversion of the girl's provocative run down to the sea where the shark is ready, Brody's wife runs—with a similar following shot, now from left to right—away from the sea, out of Quint's shark-hung lair ('Here's to swimming with bow-legged women!'), out of the film, as the men set off to deal with the evil, the boat seen in long shot through a trophy pair of shark's jaws. The stress on dismemberment—after the girl, all the victims are male, and the focus is on losing legs—finds its resonance in this context, as too does the scene where Quint and Hooper compare shark wounds (and drink to their legs!), as again does the apparently gratuitous image of the old man in the bathing cap with hanging breasts who comes to taunt Brody with his fear of the water. This excess over the narrative in the opening sequence disturbs the coherence of the end. In the former we look out with the boy over the menacing sea (a shot elsewhere repeated from Brody's point of view); in the latter we look with Brody and Hooper from the sea back to the land, the menace destroyed, Brody's fear overcome ('I used to hate the water, I can't imagine why'); a closing—rhymingly inverted—high-angle shot establishes the beach again, empty and clean. But what cannot be re-solved is the whole shark displacement; the elements of the first sequence are left hanging, and no woman comes back—here too *Jaws* is a white male film.

Such indications begin to show something of the multiple series working over the narrative in a film text, series that combine across the different matters of expression and codes in rhymes, repetitions, turns. In fact, film is potentially a veritable flux of affects, a plurality of intensities, and narrative functions to con-tain that affectivity, which is thus 're-released' as 'excess', 'disturbance', 'figure'—symptomatic demonstrations of the *work* of containment.

This engages the intersection with cinema the machine. Narrative is not essen-tial to cinema, but historically the latter is developed and exploited as a narrative form: *against* dispersion, *for* representation, where representation is less immedi-ately a matter of 'what is represented' than of positioning; narrative in cinema is first and foremost the organization of a point of view through the image-flow, the laying out of an intelligibility, the conversion of seen into scene as the direction of the viewing-subject.

The grounding of vision in the subject as the perspective of intelligibility is crucial. Cinema is implicated in a founding ideology of vision as truth (Lumière aims 'to reproduce life itself') but film, in its flux, can also produce discontinuities, disruptions, 'shocks'. Hence, from the start, there is a need to reconstruct that truth of vision, to establish ways for holding a film's relations as the coherence of the subject-eye—continuity techniques, matches, 30-degree and 180-degree rules, codes of framing, and so on. Indeed, the drama of vision becomes a constant reflexive fascination *in* films. Hitchcock's *Rear Window* is a supreme example, but *Jaws* is also relevant with its play on the unseen and unforeseeable, the hidden shark and the moments of violent irruption—the corpse in the boat-hull, the shark rearing from the water close behind Brody as he shovels chum. *Jaws,* moreover, has the whole film summarized in the images flickeringly reflected in Brody's glasses as he skims through the pages of the books about sharks, occasionally fixing a corresponding image—the whole film except, precisely, for Brody, the vision to come, the film's 'resolution'. Film is the constant process of a phasing-in of vision, the pleasure of that process—movement and fixity and movement again, from fragment (actually thematized in *Jaws* as dismemberment) to totality (the jubilation of the final image). Genres are different balances of the process, shifting regulations of the subject, particular closures of desire.

Genres are also necessities of the industry, the optimal exploitation of the production apparatus requiring the containment of creative work within established frameworks. This double determination brings us back once more to the complex of intersection: films are industrial products, and they mean, and they sell not simply on the particular meaning but equally on the pleasure of cinema, this yielding the return that allows the perpetuation of the industry (which is why part of the meaning of *Jaws* is to be the most profitable movie); a film is not reducible to its 'ideology' but is also the working over of that ideology in cinema, with the industry dependent on the pleasure of the operation. The problems for film theory today are those of an understanding of the fact of film in these terms.

Jaws has placed the focus here on the dominant American cinema. It then remains to stress that such an understanding is a point of development in certain areas of avant-garde film, posing the material conditions of film in the interests of alternative practices, other cinema. Film theory has continually to learn from those practices, which must indeed provide its very edge; as it has too, dialectically, to turn back into them, a moment of their advance in the transformation of the relations of subject and meaning in film. The study of Hollywood film (*Jaws* included), its strategies, its frictions, its pleasure, can have an importance in this context—if only that study be directed, critically and specifically, to Hollywood film itself as signifying practice.

Part 5
Psychoanalytic Semiotics

PSYCHOANALYSIS AND CINEMA: THE IMAGINARY DISCOURSE

CHARLES F. ALTMAN

Charles Altman's review of an issue of Communications *devoted to psychoanalysis and cinema plays a role for Part 5 similar to the role played by Paul Sandro's review of Christian Metz's early writing in Part 4. Altman notes the shifts in critical thinking that inform the psychoanalytical approach. Although many proponents of this approach claim it gradually evolved from structuralist linguistic approaches, Altman makes clear how this new perspective establishes quite different priorities, models, and insights. The absence of a distinct body of work seeking to legitimate or to place the psychoanalytic study of film historically is symptomatic for Altman of how French critical writing has tended to appropriate the rhetorical power of a whole series of disciplines that rose to prominence after World War II: existentialism, phenomenology, structural linguistics, "and now Freudian/Lacanian psychoanalysis." In France, more than in English-speaking countries, a dominant paradigm becomes taken for granted, and its connection with previous modes of thought is assumed. Hence, the jump from a structural linguistic semiotics to a psychoanalytic one may seem to be more arbitrary and radical to an outside observer than it does to a direct participant, for whom the prevailing pattern of thought gradually shifts. Unfortunately, few participants appear motivated to explain these shifts to outsiders as anything but a "natural" continuity. For that reason, Altman's review is extremely valuable.*

In the review, Altman identifies two major changes in emphasis between the psychoanalytic approach and a more classical, presemiotic one. (Altman's discussion here can be augmented by Heath's discussion of the difference between the object cinema and the operation cinema in the preceding article — a difference between linguistic and psychoanalytic semiotics.) These changes center on the metaphors or analogies used to describe the film experience, namely, the shift from seeing the screen as a window (Bazin) or frame (Mitry) to seeing it as a mirror (drawing heavily on French psychoanalyst Jacques Lacan's description of an infantile "mirror-stage," which Altman summarizes concisely). His discussion of how this shift poses an entirely new set of questions is exceptionally instructive. It suggests something both of the complex relationship between specific facts and the metaphors that derive from them and of how shifts in metaphor allow new theoretical questions to be asked and new film practices, especially modernist, reflexive practices, to be described or explained more adequately than they have been.

These points are pursued in Altman's discussion of the analogy between film and dream as a second change of focus, which moves away from a conception of film as a reflection of reality toward a conception of film as mental operation. Under this new tendency, film is a "thinking about" social conditions, rather than a manifestation of thought within the constraints of existing social conditions — just the characterization Charles Eckert hoped to avoid. The psychoanalytic approaches return to structural linguistics via the film-as-dream analogy, since they regard dreams within the rigorous framework of Freud's theory of dreamwork and of subsequent attempts to understand the operations of the unconscious as linguistic in nature.

Finally, Altman reminds us of the problems of reasoning by analogy. He points to three major drawbacks, including the strong possibility that such analogies trap the psychoanalytic commentator in an imaginary discourse. All in all, Altman's review is a compact but illuminating description of recent psychoanalytic approaches to film.

●

Christian Metz, Thierry Kuntzel, and Raymond Bellour, eds. *Communications* 23. Paris: Centre d'Etudes Transdisciplinaires, 1975.

What are we going to do about Frenchspeak? Should we learn this new jargon-laden language, which is slowly infiltrating the American scene through departments of French and comparative literature, through highly selective summer institutes, and through a few hermetic journals? Or can we afford to ignore, indeed to repress, this admittedly (some would say purposefully) difficult material? The problem is a serious one, for Frenchspeak threatens to split American film criticism as it has already fragmented the fields of French, English, and comparative literature. Frenchspeakers and traditional critics tend to avoid each other, recognizing that their presuppositions, their vocabulary, their very languages are different. The American Frenchspeak ghetto has complicated things by maintaining an elitist, separationist policy: initiation rites no longer are limited to a reading of Freud, Marx, and Saussure; now one must know Lacan, Althusser, and Derrida as well. Faced with such demands, traditional critics have naturally run to more familiar ground: rhetorical criticism, genre study, film history. The holier-than-thou attitude often adopted by both sides has served only to deepen the schism.

Can anything be done about this situation? Does the highly theoretical literature of Frenchspeak contain insights which might be of use to American film historians and critics? In short, do Frenchspeak and our native tongue have *anything* in common? Often it seems that they do not. The French approach elevates theory to the rank of a separate discipline, while American criticism, eminently practical in nature, often ignores it entirely. If anything is to be recuperated (a four-letter word in Frenchspeak) from the French theoretical project for the benefit of American practical criticism, I believe it must be located in the realm of methodology, of strategies for viewing the filmic text. Frenchspeak is primarily devoted to understanding *textuality,* while American practice concentrates on understanding *texts;* the problem of methodology represents the intersection of these two approaches. If we are to avoid a radical rift in American film scholarship it is essential that American critics have access at least to the methodological level implicit in French theory. To this end, I have concentrated in the following pages on providing the apparatus necessary for an understanding of recent developments in French film theory. Furthermore, I have chosen to stress the continuity between French innovations and American tradition rather than their differences.

In its composition, *Communications* 23 is an odd beast. The four articles written by the issue's organizers (Christian Metz, Thierry Kuntzel, Raymond Bellour) take up fully 250 of the issue's 350 pages, while the other ten articles, written largely by newcomers to the film scene and old hands from related fields, divide up the remainder. By any normal standards this is not a single issue, but four full-fledged books (Metz has 60,000 words, Kuntzel has 30,000 plus illustrations, Bellour has 60,000 plus illustrations, short articles have a total of 70,000 words), each reflecting a different interpretation of the issue's title: *Psychoanalysis and Cinema*. In spite of their differences, however, these articles share an attitude which provides the issue with its overall tonality: almost all the contributors accept and invoke Freudian psychology with the fervor of converts.

It is nevertheless important to distinguish between two major strains of Freudianism present in *Communications* 23—the one clearly on the way out, the other coming in. Since the early days of structuralism a specific Freudian analogue has often been used in conjunction with the analysis of classical narrative. According to this model, plots follow an Oedipal configuration: both the protagonist's desire and the text itself are generated by a search for the Father. Like Oedipus, the protagonist is thus a detective. Popularized in the writings of Roland Barthes, this approach tends to project emphasis onto plot patterns and thus onto the text as signified. The Oedipal strategy dominated French criticism of the sixties and early seventies and remains an underlying factor throughout *Communications* 23—it is even specifically recognized in the preface ("Horizon of the text: the Oedipus as generator of narrative forms"). The approach which now prevails, however, emphasizes the specificity of the filmic sign; it is more attuned to the complex interrelationships between text and spectator, and thus to the text as signifier. The new psychoanalytical model is provided by Lacan's notion of the *stade du miroir* or "mirror stage" (the relevant material is contained in Jacques Lacan, *Ecrits,* Paris: Le Seuil, 1966; especially "Le stade du miroir comme formateur de la fonction du Je").

According to Lacan, the infant develops between the ages of six to eighteen months from a state where his own mirror image appears to him as another child, to the point where he recognizes the image as himself. It is at this stage that the infant first fully realizes a notion of selfhood. Up to this moment he has related to himself only as a series of separate parts (*corps morcelé*); now, at a time when his powers of vision far outstrip his capacity for coordinated motor action, the child gains a sense of his own unity with the help of a mirror. The eyes are thus the very source of man's sense of Self. This *primary identification* at the same time presents a significant problem: the mirror image which the child identifies with himself is in fact not the child itself, but only an image. The life of the Self thus begins under the sign of a *misapprehension*. Lacan further suggests that this primary identification of the child with his image also involves identification of the child with the mother. Though this period is called the "mirror stage," the notion of mirror should not be taken literally; Lacan bases his findings on a variety of mirror-like situations where children fail to distinguish Self from Other (as in the phenomenon of transitivism, where a child attributes his own behavior to another child or even to a doll).

The mirror stage corresponds to the *Imaginary order*. It is followed by the Oedipal stage, during which the child accedes to the *Symbolic order,* the order of language and of the Father. In Lacan's scenario, the father is assumed absent during the mirror stage, which is dominated by the mother. Once the child achieves primary identification, however, the father intervenes, separating the child from the mother. This separation constitutes the child's first encounter with the Law-of-the-father (*Loi du père*), with which he will later identify. It is at this point that the child gains a symbolizing ability closely related to the acquisition of language. In order to represent the mother when she is absent (or any other absent object), the child must resort to meaningful linguistic oppositions (such as the *Fort! Da!* invoked by Freud). Eventually, the child succeeds in naming the cause of the mother's absence, and in so doing names the father. This *secondary identification* with the *Name-of-the-Father* (not the real father but a symbolic figure of the Father-as-Law) permits the child to rise above his dual relationship with the mother and to enter into the triadic relationship basic to the family. In this way the child finally becomes a subject entirely distinct from his parents, prepared to enter into the world of language and of culture and capable of articulating the difference between Imaginary and Real.

From this rapid overview of the heart of Lacanian doctrine I have omitted many important steps. In particular I have passed over Lacan's treatment of the child's relationship to the phallus and the accompanying theory of signification. Surprisingly enough, however, little more than this is needed to follow the seemingly labyrinthine ways of *Communications* 23. The following table reduces an already inadequate summary to a shadow of Lacan's complex system, but it may provide a convenient method of summing up:

Mirror Stage	*Oedipal Stage*
primary identification	secondary identification
importance of the mother	importance of the father
dual relationship	triadic relationship
image	language
Imaginary order	Symbolic order

It is against this background that most of the analyses presented in *Communications* 23 must be seen. The concerns of the issue may conveniently be divided into two major areas: metaphors for the screen and film as dream.

SCREEN/MIRROR

What is the screen and how do we understand it? In an effort to answer this question film theoreticians have often resorted to metaphors which explain indirectly the nature and function of the screen. For Bazin, "the screen is not a frame like that of a picture but a mask which allows only a part of the action to be seen" ("Theater and Cinema—Part Two," in *What Is Cinema?*, Hugh Gray, translator, Berkeley: University of California Press, 1967, p. 105). Later in the same essay, Bazin goes on to specify that the screen's masking action is like that of a window; we don't see the space which extends on all sides of the screen but we never doubt the existence of that space. We feel that if we could move to the left or the right a bit, we would be able to catch a glimpse of the objects and people masked by the screen's border. In other words, on-screen space always suggests off-screen space, thus producing a centrifugal configuration. This theory of the screen-as-window underlies Bazin's entire realist theory.

For Jean Mitry, the window metaphor is insufficient because it describes only one half of the screen dialectic. If the screen has a tendency to become a mask it also operates as a frame, organizing internal space and concentrating interest on specific spots within the frame. This centripetal function can exist alongside (or rather against) a centrifugal one because the screen's border has a double existence: it is at the same time the point where the frame stops and the point where it starts. Furthermore, when the screen is seen as a window, the image takes on a depth which suggests a relationship to perspective painting; seen as a frame, however, the screen appears flat and graphic, like the paintings of the cubists who privilege the picture plane over the object plane.

The entire history of film criticism and theory, often seen as a dialectic between formalist and realist positions, might just as well be seen as a dialectic between these two metaphors for the screen:

Window	*Frame*
centrifugal	centripetal
perspective	graphic
object plane	picture plane

Indeed, this model is so persuasive that it has tended to blind film theoreticians to what it does *not* explain. In particular, the window/frame approach takes the existence of the image for granted, bracketing the apparatus for producing the image (projector, dark room, bright light source, flat reflective surface) as well as the apparatus for consuming that image (the spectator, his eyes, mind, and body). To put it another way, the image is treated as pure signified, while the signifier and the actual process of signification are neglected. Even when the frame metaphor is invoked, and the flatness of the picture plane is stressed (as in Eisenstein's analyses of the dynamism of diagonal lines within the frame), emphasis is placed on the organization of objects or the movement of people rather than on the cinematic process whereby those objects and people are evoked. Though the window and frame metaphors appear diametrically opposed, they actually share an assumption of the screen's fundamental independence from the processes of production and consumption. The ability of the spectator to recognize objects and people is taken for granted and never analyzed.

It is in this context, I believe, that we must see the current French attempt to create a new metaphor for the screen, one which would take into account the process of signification itself. First suggested by Jean-Louis Baudry in "Cinéma: effets idéologiques produits par l'appareil de base" (*Cinéthique* 7–8, 1970, pp. 1–8; translated in *Film Quarterly* 28, Winter 1974–1975, pp. 39–47), this new metaphor is the *mirror* (the projected text thus being designated as *specular*). Cinema reconstitutes the conditions of Lacan's "mirror stage"—reduced motor activity and predominance of visual sensations—and thus sets up an Imaginary relationship between the film spectator and the world which he sees mirrored on the screen. At first glance this comparison seems somewhat gratuitous. If any screen should be compared to a mirror it is that of the television, which figuratively mirrors the bourgeois home interior where it is located (with the set on) whenever it is not literally reflecting the objects or people in front of it (with the set off). How can the movie screen be a mirror when it is incapable of reflecting the viewer's face? The key to this problem lies in the meaning of the word "mirror" as it is used by Lacan; the notion of "mirror stage" applies to far more than the specific situation of the child being held up in front of a mirror (though the availability of a mirror surely speeds up the process of primary identification). Any "transitive" situation, in which the individual confuses the Imaginary with the Real, constitutes a "mirror" experience. Thus Christian Metz is able to show how cinema, in comparison with the theater, has an Imaginary signifier. On the stage a chair is a chair—before, during, and after the performance. In cinema the chair which was actually present during the filming delegates its image to replace it when the film is projected. There is no chair on the screen, only its reflection—its mirror image, as it were. In this extended sense, the mirror metaphor seems quite applicable, particularly if it can help us recapture those aspects of the film experience which remain unavailable to the window/frame dialectic.

The key to recent French fascination with the mirror metaphor lies in the fact that the mirror image (and mirror stage) relationship constitutes by itself a dialectic: between subject and mirror image there exist at the same time an identity (they have exactly the same outline, characteristics, coloring, and so forth) and a difference (the subject is flesh and blood, the image only an image). In the words of Catherine B. Clément, the screen has a double function: "*to show* (the primal scene, seductions, the fantastic) and *to block* the view at the same time" ("Les charlatans et les hystériques," p. 220). The screen, in other words, is like a veil. The process of comprehending the screen image is thus not a simple, direct one, as phenomenology would have it, but a complex dialectic. Metz sums this up: "To understand the fiction film, I must at one and the same time identify with the character (= Imaginary procedure) so that he may benefit by analogical projection from all the patterns of understanding which I possess, and not identify with him (= return to the Real) so that the fiction may be perceived as such (= as

Symbolic): this is the *reality illusion* [le *semble-réel*]. Similarly, to understand the film (any film), I must perceive the photographed object as absent, its photograph as present, and the presence of this absence as significant" ("Le signifiant imaginaire," p. 41). This play of absence and presence is of course radically different from that implied by the window metaphor: there the absence/presence dialectic suggested by the notion of masking was entirely located within the signified, whereas the mirror dialectic handles the process of signification from the point of view of the signifier and its status as Imaginary. The mirror approach recaptures the extent to which the film viewer, like the child in the mirror stage, can make sense and unity only by at first accepting a lie, which then calls for correction. Fiction films mean nothing if we refuse to take them—at least provisionally—as reality. On the other hand, they cannot achieve their true status as fiction if we hold permanently to that illusion. Only a structured alternation which holds these two approaches in tension permits us to perceive a film as fiction. In this sense, the spectator who must begin his viewing by an Imaginary relationship (taking absence for presence) concludes it with a Symbolic one (structuring the absence/presence relationship through the notion of fiction).

It is instructive to note how, in a practical way, the mirror metaphor permits questions and raises problems unavailable to the window/frame dialectic. Until the late sixties, the window/frame dialectic might have handled the major issues in film theory and practice quite well. The two major oppositions on which idealist film theory was based could easily be accommodated to the window/frame opposition. In terms of epistemology:

frame: formalism:: window: realism

and in terms of technique:

frame: montage:: window: plan-séquence + deep focus

Today these strategies no longer seem so fundamentally opposed. Though they represent two different approaches to breaking up, to portraying reality, neither realism nor formalism questions the basic assumption that the spectator looks right through a transparent signifier in order to perceive a substantial signified. The change in position of Eisenstein is significant here: once seen as the hero of the frame/montage/formalism school, he is now opposed to Vertov as the goat, simply because his major commitment was to the signified rather than to a highlighting of the signifier.

The constitutive opposition (dialectic) of film theory in the past decade is thus no longer that of formalism to realism, but of classical narrative (defined as that narrative, however constituted, which hides, which represses the signifier) to modernist narrative (defined as that narrative which foregrounds the signifier, i.e., which takes the process of signification as its signified). To the extent that the classical-modernist opposition governs current film theory, the window/frame dialectic fails to structure that theory, for neither the window nor the frame points to the problem of signification, nor can either metaphor properly account for the reflexive text, which derives its identity from a portrayed disparity between reality and its representation. The mirror analogy, however, sets up a clear dialectic capable of handling both the classical/modernist opposition and the cinema-viewing situation on which it rests.

We can understand this capacity more clearly by schematizing the relationsᶜ ips implied by the above Metz quote:

$$\underrightarrow{\text{identification}} \text{IMAGINARY (absence taken as presence)}$$

$$\text{REAL (absence} \xleftarrow{\text{distantiation}}$$
$$\text{recognized as absence)}$$

That is, in order to understand the projected image (or any fiction, and thus doubly of any fiction film—Metz is not very clear on this distinction) we must begin with an entrance into the imaginary order, treating two entities as identical even though they are not (absence/presence, character/spectator). This is the mode proper to classical narrative, the stage at which it attempts to stall us, tempting us never to proceed to the next phase. The second logical step in the progression is a return to the Real. This can take place in many different ways: when we remember that "it's only a film" to lessen the effect of violence, when the film apparatus is foregrounded within the film itself, or simply when the lights come up and destroy the image on the screen. This return to the Real is the mode proper to modernist narrative, which would have us forget our primary filmic identification in favor of a radical distinction between Real and Imaginary. The Symbolic is constituted by neither one of these two tendencies, but by their simultaneous presence in a tension which we call *fiction*—which implies neither a wholesale confusion of Real with imaginary, nor the erection of a watertight barrier between them, but the structuring of the two tendencies in a dialectic. In this sense, the mirror metaphor proves its timeliness, its ability to organize the terminology which has become central to the enterprise of current film theory.

FILM/DREAM

The notion that films are somehow like dreams is by no means a new one. As early as 1916 Hugo Munsterberg had declared that "In the photoplay our imagination is projected on the screen" (*The Photoplay: A Psychological Study*, New York: Dover, 1970, p. 41). By 1949, Hugo Mauerhofer could speak of a "Cinema Situation" which shares with the dream situation a set of general attributes: the spectator's passive state, his comfort, his anonymity, his receptiveness, together inducing a withdrawal from reality. Mauerhofer even captures an important difference separating the two activities: "While in sleep we ourselves produce our dreams, in the cinema they are presented to us ready-made" ("Psychology of the Film Experience," *Penguin Film Review* 8, 1949, p. 106). In this analysis Mauerhofer agrees with his contemporary Parker Tyler, for whom "Hollywood is but the industrialization of the mechanical worker's daylight dream"

(*The Hollywood Hallucination,* New York: Creative Age Press, 1944, p. 237). In fact two generations of critics have labeled Hollywood a "dream factory" since Ilya Ehrenburg first coined the expression (*Die Traumfabrik: Chronik des Films,* Berlin: Malik-Verlag, 1931).

The problem with this impressionistic comparison is that it provides no more than a general appreciation of film's attraction and effect. Suzanne Langer's *Feeling and Form* (New York: Scribner, 1953) attempts to discover the specific characteristics which tie cinema to the dream experience. Langer claims that "Cinema is 'like' dream in the mode of its presentation; it creates a virtual present, an order of direct apparition. That is the mode of dream." Thus "the percipient of a moving picture sees with the camera . . . the camera is his eye . . . he takes the place of the dreamer" (pp. 412–13). These very interesting reflections, which foreshadow to a considerable extent the type of work done by the current French school (especially Baudry), were unfortunately never followed up by any systematic investigation of the relationships between film and dream.

One of the important projects of *Communications* 23 is to remedy that situation. From several different viewpoints the members of the Metz group have attempted to discover parallels between film viewing and dreaming, thus continuing a line of inquiry begun in France by Cohen-Séat and Wallon. For Baudry the most important analogy is provided by the state of regression common to film and dream ("Le dispositif: approches métapsychologiques de l'impression de réalité"). Given the theater's darkness, the spectator's relative passivity, his enforced immobility, as well as the hypnotic effect of the play of light and shadows, film necessarily induces "an artificial regressive state" (p. 69). In other words, secondary processes and the reality principle are shunted aside in favor of primary processes and the pleasure principle. "Cinema, like dreams, would thus correspond to a form of temporary regression" (pp. 70–71).

While generally agreeing with Baudry's thesis, Metz tends to attribute cinema's tendency to induce regression to another source ("Le film de fiction et son spectateur: Etude métapsychologique"). Instead of emphasizing the general film-viewing situation—darkness, reduced motor activity, anonymity—Metz leans on film's propensity for forming fictions ("fantasies" in Freud's terminology). Whatever dreamlike aspects film owes to the circumstances of its projection and viewing, it reinforces them by organizing the film's images into fictions. "The fiction film, while grinding *out* images and sounds which overload our zones of shadow and irresponsibility, grinds *up* our affectivity and inhibits our actions" (p. 112). Starting from the basic assumption that fiction films induce a dreamlike state in the viewer even more than other films, Metz reaches a rather startling conclusion. If a coherent fiction can induce a state of artificial regression like that found in dreaming subjects, then both film and dream must possess a method of disguising the rough edges which might otherwise wake the subject and his secondary processes. In dream, this method is well known under the name of "secondary elaboration," which combines the results of the other dream-work operations into a single and fairly coherent whole. According to Metz, "secondary elaboration (which in the production/perception of dreams is only one force among others, and not the main one at that) becomes in the production and in the perception of the film the dominant force, omnipresent, the force which weaves the mental fabric itself" (p. 123). Secondary elaboration keeps us within the dream/film world by rounding its contours, by making sure that it jars none of our expectations, by turning a deformed version of reality into a fiction so coherent that it no longer appears to be fiction.

Though Metz never suggests the parallel, his analysis of secondary elaboration has obvious consequences for our understanding of classical narrative. Nearly every word which has been said about classical narrative—seamless editing, motivated action and camera movement, absence of unexplained activity, and so forth—might have been said about the dream work's secondary elaboration. Here is a fertile notion which might permit us to tie the volumes of purely stylistic studies on classical narrative to a specific function within a large system. In this respect, Metz's article opens up new areas of investigation for traditional as well as Frenchspeak critics. In a similar way, in his article "Mise en scène: U.S.A." Marc Vernet demonstrates how psychoanalysis itself has contributed to the secondary elaboration of classical narrative. Vernet shows, apropos of films which are built around a psychoanalytic "cure," that "The most important contribution of psychoanalysis has been to furnish a new alibi for the structure of the American narrative film" (p. 233).

In his analysis of *The Most Dangerous Game* ("Le Travail du film, II"), Thierry Kuntzel provides a necessary complement to Metz's work. Where Metz stresses secondary elaboration, Kuntzel emphasizes the other aspects of the dream work: condensation, displacement, symbolization. A careful and extremely perceptive analysis of the opening sequence of *The Most Dangerous Game* permits Kuntzel to show that the Freudian notion of dream work can profitably be applied to film as an interpretational strategy, a methodology of reading. We no longer really need anyone to tell us that, for a variety of reasons, film is like dream. Instead, we need somebody to show us what difference that "fact" might make to our critical practice. This is the challenge that Kuntzel takes up. The problem would have been solved long ago except for an embarrassing difference between film and dream: according to Freud, dreams represent a deformation of material provided by the dreamer's "daily residue"; films, on the other hand, are not produced by the spectator, nor can they be said to relate directly to any given spectator's recent experiences. If the film represents the viewer's daylight dream, then the question remains: to what daily residue should this dream be related?

Kuntzel's solution to this problem has been to take introductory sequences (the murder of Elsie in *M*, the credits and the subsequent shipboard sequences in *King Kong* and *The Most Dangerous Game*, the airport shots which open *La Jetée*) as separable units which condense, displace, and symbolize the material of the remainder of the film. Instead of using the dream-work terms to describe the relationship between the dream's preconditions and the dream itself, he uses them to describe the relationship between the text's surface and deep structures (taking these as parallel to the dream's manifest and latent content). "There is no latent text *under* the manifest text constituted by the credit sequence, but *after* it

... another manifest text where are replayed in expanded form the elements which at first were expressed in laconic, abridged fashion—condensed, in Freud's terminology" (p. 148). The credit sequence is thus like the subject's dream, which at first is entirely unclear to him, because of its deformation of familiar events and relationships; the rest of the narrative untangles the dream material, explaining it by identifying the relationship latent within it. "The entire itinerary of *The Most Dangerous Game* serves to make the initial image [*figure*] *legible,* to progressively *reassure* the subject plunged *ex abrupto* into the uncertainty of the image" (p. 152). In other words, the spectator is *not* to be taken as homologous with the dreamer alone, as in previous film/dream analogies (including those of Metz and Baudry), but with two separate subjects: at first analogous to the dreamer (the introductory sequence representing his dream), the spectator subsequently becomes analogous to the analyst (the remainder of the film representing an explanation of the introductory "dream" material).

This strategy, which in Kuntzel's able hands can be so rewarding, nevertheless has its dangers. Consciousness serves as an absolute barrier separating the subject's daily life from his dream. Such absolute dividing lines exist in few films, however. Where does the "introductory sequence" end and its expanded form begin? Does Kuntzel's method apply only to those films which provide a clear line of demarcation between preliminary material and the body of the narrative? By choosing to analyze such films as *La Jetée, M,* and *The Most Dangerous Game* (which all provide an absolute barrier between two wholly separate parts), Kuntzel in fact suggests such a limitation. If this is the case, however, we will simply have reverted to the long accepted practice whereby one register in films possessing two clearly separate levels *(The Wizard of Oz, Woman in the Window, Belle de Jour)* is taken to have given rise, through the intermediary of a dreaming or hallucinating character, to the other register.

In the long run, Kuntzel's method fails to provide the link between the cinema-viewing situation and internal analysis of the film which his dream-work terminology seems to promise. Though it borrows its methodology from the dream work, Kuntzel's discourse eventually abandons all connections with the dream analogy. Perhaps it is for this reason that Kuntzel feels compelled to describe Freud's work as no more than an "intertext" for his own project (p. 183). But if Freud is only an intertext, and the terminology is separated from its specific dream context, then why should we grant any more status to Kuntzel's method than we would to any other? Once divorced from the dream situation to which Freud applies them, the dream-work terms revert to the level of any other stylistic labels, such as repetition, gradation, metaphor, or paradox. The Freudian terms may help us to understand textual interaction in selected films, but we should not be fooled into believing that the psychoanalytic source of the dream-work terminology lends it any particular status. In sum, Kuntzel's work departs both from the Metz/Baudry project of describing the cinema-viewing situation in terms of the dream apparatus and from the more general attempt to discover specific parallels between the Lacanian scenario and the film experience; instead Kuntzel provides a new type of interpretational strategy based on an appropriation rather than an application of the Freudian dream-work terminology.

CRITICISM/ANALOGY

As a mode of reasoning, analogy has always held a major place among the human sciences. Major, but largely unquestioned. To claim that one activity is homologous to another and to draw certain conclusions based on that analogy begs fundamental questions: Just how alike do the two activities have to be? What kind of conclusions does analogy authorize? Are there conclusions which are not proper? When Augustine compares David's victory over Goliath to Christ's defeat of the devil, he is implying that David and Christ share certain attributes, but he is definitely *not* suggesting that David shares Christ's divine nature. This kind of distinction is all the harder to establish when, as is often the case, analogy becomes a strategy for appropriating the rhetorical power of a modish discipline. Since the war France has passed through a number of these strategies; just as surely as medieval theology was valorized by the language of the Bible and the church fathers, so recent French critical discourse has been successively valorized by the languages of existential phenomenology, Saussurian linguistics, and now Freudian/Lacanian psychoanalysis. Literature is *like* language. The structure of the unconscious is *like* that of language. Without analogies of this sort the entire structuralist and poststructuralist critical enterprise would not exist. *Communications* 23 is no exception to this rule, for even its most basic claims are grounded on a constitutive analogy. The screen is *like* a mirror. Film is *like* dream. Yet when criticism depends on analogy it exposes itself to three fundamental problems, which are amply exemplified by *Communications* 23.

1. The Discourse of Analogy Is Incomplete

Let us for a moment take the analogical strategy of *Communications* 23 entirely on its own terms. The question still remains: is a visual metaphor like that of the mirror sufficient to capture the complexity of the film-viewing experience? We must conclude, I think, that it is not. Though one would hardly know it from reading *Communications* 23 (with the exception of a few lucid pages by Metz), films are not only light and shadow, they are sound as well. The French are not alone in forgetting this important fact, for sound certainly represents a universally neglected domain in film criticism and theory today. Ask any student about the mise-en-scène of a particular shot, the cutting pattern used in a given sequence, or the camera movement identified with a specific director, and chances are that a cogent and fairly detailed answer will soon be forthcoming. Ask the same student which theme was played with which scene, where the diegetic sounds were cut out, or whether asynchronous sound was used, and it's a good bet that these important aspects of the film will have been missed altogether. Indeed, all of our terminology suggests that films are visual affairs: *spectators* go to *see* a film at a special *viewing* in the *visual* arts building. Between terms like these and Lacan's preference for the visual metaphor, it is hardly surprising that psychoanalytic criticism should stress the video aspect of the film experience.

Even the Greeks, however, knew that the story of Narcissus is incomplete without that of Echo: the audio mirror completes the video mirror. In fact this familiar myth provides an elegant explanation of the relationship between image and sound tracks. Echo was once much more than she now is; she had the power to initiate speech. In fact she told such fascinating stories that Juno sat around by the hour listening to her, while Jove looked to his amours with no thought of his legal consort. Jealous as usual, Juno blamed her problems on Echo's loquaciousness and thus reduced the poor nymph to reproducing the sounds of those she meets. *Before the advent of sound film, the sound track (the radio) had the power to initiate speech. In fact it told such fascinating stories that the public stayed home by the hour listening to it. Jealous of the public's infidelity, Queen Cinema punished the poor sound track by removing its initiative and forcing it to reproduce the sounds mouthed by those on the image track.* When Echo met Narcissus, she was tantalized by his youthful beauty, but Narcissus, intent on his own reflection, had no time for Echo. She would have made overtures to him, but she could not speak without first having been spoken to. His world limited to two imaginary and thus unseizable lovers, Narcissus eventually died of grief.

Just as the unity of the subject in the mirror stage is achieved only at the price of mistaking an image for reality, so the unity of the sound film is purchased at the expense of a lie: a servile echo is taken as the actual voice of the character represented on the screen when in fact, with current technology, the sound recording which corresponds to any given image does not even appear on the film next to that image. Every unity is bought at the cost of a mistaken identity, and the sound/image unity is no exception. From its very beginnings the sound track is part of an *écart,* a splitting of the film phenomenon which turns cinema into something more akin to puppet theater or ventriloquism than to photography. More attention needs to be paid to the complexity engendered by film's two-track nature—and the unity-through-misapprehension model provided by the mirror stage appears tailor-made to encourage such attention—but little progress will be made if the Lacanian model is restricted to the visual image. Cinema depends on the reflection of sound as well as that of light. If cinema is to be compared to the visual mirror of Narcissus, then it must be likened to the audio mirror of Echo as well.

2. The Discourse of Analogy Is Programmatic

Freudian criticism has always had a tendency to be overly programmatic, the scenarios of childhood providing a program against which all adult texts are measured. To a surprising degree, Metz and Kuntzel are able to avoid this pitfall, by concentrating on what is particular to cinema (Metz) or by borrowing Freud's relational terms rather than his scenarios (Kuntzel). As a whole, however, the French intelligentsia have fallen prey to a programmatic impulse which often damages careful analysis. Raymond Bellour's analysis of *North by Northwest* ("le blocage symbolique") is a case in point. At times Bellour's reading takes the familiar course of Freudian symbol-chasing ("The miniaturization of the razor and the shaving brush suggests that the penis risks being reduced," p. 252) or willful overinterpretation (the play which Cary Grant never gets to see "must have been" *Oedipus Rex*). More serious, however, are those moments when Bellour's language reveals the programmatic, indeed allegorical style of his interpretation: Hitchcock "accomplishes the Oedipal itinerary of his hero by inscribing him logically in the problematics of the murder of the father. But why, one might ask, if Townsend is the father—assuming that we are justified in placing him in this position—have him be killed by Vandamm, when it is the symbolic destiny of Thornhill which is at stake?" (p. 244). *Assuming that we are justified in placing him in this position* [*le faire venir à cette place*]: in order to establish his critical discourse, Bellour must accommodate Hitchcock's film to the Freudian/Lacanian scenario, labeling each character according to a single preconceived program. Medieval allegorical interpretation operates in precisely the same fashion.

Bellour continues: "Three elements suggest that Townsend be entered in the father's slot [*inscrire Townsend à la place du père*]. The first, age, is a strong element: on the generational level, Townsend is obviously 'a father' for Thornhill. The second element, their shared last initial, is weak, in that nothing, for example in their first names, reinforces this phonic equivalency. The third is a neutral element, which gains its value only as a part of the overall structure: Townsend is not, is no longer married" (pp. 244–45). Now that we have Townsend cast in the role of father, we must provide a reason for doing so. If we were to apply Bellour's argument widely, however, every older man in every movie would have to be "entered in the father's slot" for every bachelor who shares his last initial (the "phonic" argument of course does not hold–*T* and *Th* produce the same sound in French but not in English). When Bellour announces, at the high point of his argument, that the mythical Kaplan "is none other than the Name-of-the-Father" (p. 263), I must admit that I bristle. For a structuralist psychoanalyst whose avowed purpose is to avoid interpretations based on content paradigms, Bellour is all too delighted to be able to adjust his plot *(North by Northwest)* to a Lacanian counterpart (the Oedipal stage). As Guattari suggests in his contribution to the issue ("Le Divan du pauvre"), structuralist psychoanalysis has nothing to say to us if it insists on returning to the programmatic model of the fifties.

3. The Discourse of Analogy Is Imaginary

How do we understand the cinematic text? In answer to this question the *Communications* team adopts a simple hypothesis: we can best understand cinema by comparing it to psychoanalysis. The cinematic signifier is like the Imaginary Other of the mirror stage, the cinematic apparatus recalls that of dreams, the cinema-viewing situation makes each of us a voyeur witnessing the primal scene. Such analogizing performs an essential function within the discourse of the *Communications* group: it focuses cinema's various aspects around a single constitutive metaphor (the cinema apparatus equals the psychic apparatus), thus providing the cinematic experience with a unity which it otherwise would lack. In other words, this strategy establishes the identity of cinema by finding cinema reflected in psychoanalysis.

In short, the very notion of analogy, so essential to Metz's concept of the "Imaginary signifier," itself sets up an Imaginary relationship not unlike that associated by Lacan with the mirror stage. When I say that one thing resembles another, and thus can be understood by reference to that other (e.g., the cinema-viewing situation and the mirror stage), I am claiming to establish the unity of one area by finding it reflected in another. As in the relationship between the child and his mirror image, however, I must deny the differences implicit in the reflection in order to create that unity. It is thus only by adopting an Imaginary discourse himself that Metz is able to demonstrate that cinema has an Imaginary signifier. As a method of reasoning, analogy presents the constant danger that critical language will remain a prisoner of Imaginary relationships.

IDEOLOGICAL EFFECTS OF THE BASIC CINEMATOGRAPHIC APPARATUS

JEAN-LOUIS BAUDRY

In this seminal article, Jean-Louis Baudry, like many others in this volume, uses an analogy to develop the implications of his argument. Baudry claims that the masking of social contradiction and difference in the cinema resembles the masking of our perception of still images by the illusion of movement. Baudry elaborates on the basic concept of apparent movement to construct an imposing theoretical argument. He draws from Louis Althusser the idea that relations to real conditions which do not help us to realize how those relations were constructed are ipso facto ideological. They lack the "knowledge effect" that a realization of their production would entail. This idea allows Baudry to posit that the cinema, based as it is on an illusion of movement that we mistake for actual movement, is based on a fundamentally ideological effect.

Baudry turns to Jacques Lacan to demonstrate that this ideological effect involves constituting the viewer as a transcendental subject or imaginary unity. The continuous unfurling of a universe before our eyes at the cinema confirms our own centrality: When our vision roams freely, liberated from the body, the world exists for it. Our sight is the world's point of origin and its source of coherence. Baudry summarizes Lacan's notion of the mirror-stage, likening it to our experience at the cinema, where we identify not only with characters but also with the camera as the surrogate for our desire for order, organization, and unity. We want a narrative that makes sense of disparate experiences, that confirms the self as the transcendent, all-knowing center of the world.

This turn toward Lacan and the psychoanalytic approach also turns us toward ideology, but ideology here remains at some remove from specific instances in the political, economic, or social arenas. It is an ideology of the subject and of subjectivity, which certainly underpins specific ideologies of class, gender, race, and nationality but which in isolation leads to an idealist conception of the subject or ego apart from specific historical conditions. Some, like Nick Browne, argue that such generalized effects fail to account for patterns of varied and conflictual ideological effect at particular levels of textual analysis. If Browne is right, Baudry's presentation shows that Altman's strictures about analogy are correct: The presentation constructs an imaginary coherence for the cinema by positing an attractive analogy in which the cinema masks difference in a way that resembles the masking of difference in the mirror-stage. Thus, Baudry's argument may be compelling and satisfying precisely because of its own effect, which is one of producing an imaginary unity for cinema. But, even if his analogy is overextended, Baudry may also be right: The potential of cinema for the production of knowledge may be severely constrained by the nature of the apparatus. That this apparatus renders the production of knowledge completely impossible, as Baudry seems to imply, remains very much in doubt. (The translation published here is a revised version of the one that appeared in Film Quarterly *28, no. 2 [Winter 1974–1975].*

•

At the end of *The Interpretation of Dreams,* when he seeks to integrate dream elaboration and its particular "economy" with the psyche as a whole, Freud assigns to the latter an optical model: "Let us simply imagine the instrument which serves in psychic productions as a sort of complicated microscope or camera." But Freud does not seem to hold strongly to this optical model, which, as Derrida has pointed out,[1] brings out the shortcomings of graphic representation in the area earlier covered by his work on dreams. Moreover, he will later abandon the optical model in favor of a writing instrument, the "mystic writing pad." Nonetheless this optical choice seems to prolong the tradition of Western science, whose birth coincides exactly with the development of the optical apparatus which will have as a consequence the decentering of the human universe, the end of geocentrism (Galileo).

But also, and paradoxically, the optical apparatus *camera obscura* will serve in the same period to elaborate in pictorial work a new mode of representation, *perspectiva artificialis.* This system, recentering or at least displacing the center (which settles itself in the eye), will assure the setting up of the "subject"[2] as the active center and origin of meaning. One could doubtless question the privileged position which optical instruments seem to occupy on the line of intersection of science and ideological productions. Does the technical nature of optical instruments, directly attached to scientific practice, serve to conceal not only their use in ideological products but also the ideological effects which they may themselves provoke? Their scientific base would assure them a sort of neutrality and help to prevent their being questioned.

But already a question: if we are to take account of the imperfections of these instruments, their limitations, by what criteria may these be defined? If, for example, one can speak of a restricted depth of field as a limitation, doesn't this term itself depend on a particular conception of reality for which such a limitation would not exist? Contemporary media are particularly in question here, to the extent that instrumentation plays a more and more important role in them and that their distribution is more and more extensive. It is strange (but is it so strange?) that emphasis has been placed almost exclusively on their influence, on the effects that they have as finished products, their content, the field of the signified if you like; the technical bases on which these effects depend and the specific characteristics of these bases have, however, been ignored. They have been protected by the inviolability that science is supposed to provide. We would like to establish for the cinema a few guidelines which will need to be completed, verified, improved.

We must first establish the place of the instrumental base in the set of operations which combine in the production of a film (we omit consideration of economic implications). Between "objective reality" and the camera, site of inscription, and between the inscription and projection are situated certain operations, a *work* which has as its result a finished product. To the extent that it is cut off from the raw material ("objective reality") this product does not allow us to see the transformation which has taken place.

Equally distant from "objective reality" and the finished product, the camera occupies an intermediate position in the work process which leads from raw material to finished product. Though mutually dependent from other points of view, *découpage* [shot breakdown before shooting] and *montage* [editing, done afterwards] must be distinguished because of the essential difference in the signifying raw material on which each operates: language (scenario) or image. Between the two complementary stages of production a mutation of signifying material takes place (neither translation nor transcription, obviously, for the image is not reducible to language) precisely in the place occupied by the camera. Finally, between the finished product (possessing exchange value, a commodity) and its consumption (use value) is introduced another operation effected by a set of instruments. Projector and screen restore the light lost in the shooting process and transform a succession of separate images into an unrolling which also restores, but according to another scansion, the movement seized from "objective reality."

Cinematographic specificity thus refers to a *work*, that is, to a process of transformation. The question becomes: is the work made evident, does consumption of the product bring about a "knowledge effect" [Althusser], or is the work concealed? If the latter, consumption of the product will obviously be accompanied by ideological surplus value. On the practical level, this poses the question of by what procedures the work can in fact be made "readable" in its inscription. These procedures must of necessity call cinematographic technique into play. But, on the other hand, going back to the first question, one may ask, do the instruments (the technical base) produce specific ideological effects, and are these effects themselves determined by the dominant ideology? In which case, concealment of the technical base will also bring about an inevitable ideological effect. Its inscription, its manifestation as such, on the other hand, would produce a knowledge effect, as actualization of the work process, as denunciation of ideology, and as critique of idealism.

THE EYE OF THE SUBJECT

Central in the process of production[3] of the film, the camera—an assembly of optical and mechanical instrumentation—carries out a certain mode of inscription characterized by marking, by the recording of differences of light intensity (and of wavelength for color) and of differences between the frames. Fabricated on the model of the *camera obscura,* it permits the construction of an image analogous to the perspective projections developed during the Italian Renaissance. Of course the use of lenses of different focal lengths can alter the perspective of an image. But this much, at least, is clear in the history of cinema: it is the perspective construction of the Renaissance which originally served as model. The use of different lenses, when not dictated by technical considerations aimed at restoring habitual perspective (such as shooting in limited or extended spaces which one wishes to expand or contract), does not destroy [traditional] perspective but rather makes it play the role of norm. Departure from the norm, by means of a wide-angle or telephoto lens, is clearly marked in comparison with so-called "normal" perspective. We will see in any case that the resulting ideological effect is still defined in relation to the ideology inherent in perspective. The dimensions of the image itself, the ratio between height and width, seem clearly taken from an average drawn from Western easel painting.

The conception of space which conditions the construction of perspective in the Renaissance differs from that of the Greeks. For the latter, space is discontinuous and heterogeneous (for Aristotle, but also for Democritus, for whom space is the location of an infinity of indivisible atoms), whereas with Nicholas of Cusa will be born a conception of space formed by the relation between elements which are equally near and distant from the "source of all life." In addition, the pictorial construction of the Greeks corresponded to the organization of their stage, based on a multiplicity of points of view, whereas the painting of the Renaissance will elaborate a centered space. ("Painting is nothing but the intersection of the visual pyramid following a given distance, a fixed center, and a certain lighting."—Alberti.) The center of this space coincides with the eye which Jean Pellerin Viator will so appropriately call the "subject." ("The principal point in perspective should be placed at eye level: this point is called fixed or subject."[4]) Monocular vision, which as Pleynet points out is what the camera has, calls forth a sort of play of "reflection." Based on the principle of a fixed point by reference to which the visualized objects are organized, it specifies in return the position of the "subject,"[5] the very spot it must necessarily occupy.

In focusing it, the optical construct appears to be truly the projection-reflection of a "virtual image" whose hallucinatory reality it creates. It lays out the space of an ideal vision and in this way asserts the necessity of a transcendence—metaphorically (by the unknown to which it appeals; here we must recall the structural place occupied by the vanishing point) and metonymically (by the displacement that it seems to carry out; a subject is both "in place of" and "a part for the whole"). Contrary to Chinese and Japanese painting, Western easel painting, presenting as it does a motionless and continuous whole, elaborates a total vision which corresponds to the idealist conception of the fullness and homogeneity of "being,"[6] and is, so to speak, representative of this conception. In this sense it contributes in a singularly emphatic way to the ideological function of art, which is to provide the tangible representation of metaphysics. The principle of transcendence which conditions and is conditioned by the perspective construction represented in painting and in the photographic image which copies from it seems to inspire all the idealist paeans to which the cinema has given rise:

This strange mechanism, parodying man's spirit, seems better to accomplish the latter's own tasks. This mimetic play, brother and rival of the intelligence, is, finally, a means of the discovery of Truth. (Cohen-Séat)

Far from leading us down the path of determinism, as one could legitimately believe, this art—the most positive of all, insensible to all that is not brute fact, pure appearance— presents us on the contrary the idea of a hierarchical universe, ordered in terms of an ultimate end. Behind what film gives us to see, it is not the existence of atoms that we are led to seek, but rather the existence of an 'other world' of phenomena, of a soul or of any other spiritual principle. It is in this revelation, above all, of a spiritual presence, that I propose we seek Poetry. (André Bazin)

PROJECTION: DIFFERENCE DENIED

Nevertheless, whatever the effects proper to optics generally, the movie camera differs from still photography by registering through its mechanical instrumentation a series of images. It might thus seem to counter the unifying and "substantializing" character of the single-perspective image, taking what would seem to be instants of time or slices from "reality" (but always a reality already worked upon, elaborated, selected). This might permit the supposition, especially since the camera moves, of a multiplicity of points of view which would neutralize the fixed position of the eye-subject and even nullify it. But here we must turn to the relation between the succession of images inscribed by the camera and their projection, bypassing momentarily the place occupied by editing, which plays a decisive role in the strategy of the ideology produced.

The projection operation (projector and screen) restores continuity of movement and the temporal dimension to the sequence of static images. The relation between the individual frames and the projection would resemble the relation between points and a curve in geometry. But it is precisely this relation and the restoration of continuity to discontinuous elements which poses a problem. The meaning effect produced does not depend only on the content of the images but also on the material procedures by which an illusion of continuity, dependent on persistence of vision, is restored from discontinuous elements. These separate frames have between them differences that are indispensable for the creation of an illusion of continuity, of continuous passage (movement, time). But only on one condition can these differences create this illusion: they must be effaced as differences.[7]

Thus on the technical level the question becomes one of the adoption of a very small difference between images, such that each image, in consequence of an organic factor [presumably persistence of vision], is rendered incapable of being seen as such. In this sense we could say that film—and perhaps this case is exemplary—lives on the denial of difference: differences are necessary for it to live, but it lives on their negation. This is indeed the paradox that emerges if we look directly at a strip of processed film: adjacent images are almost exactly repeated, their divergence being verifiable only by comparison of images at a sufficient distance from each other. We should remember, moreover, the disturbing effects which result during a projection from breakdowns in the recreation of movement, when the spectator is brought abruptly back to discontinuity—that is, to the body, to the technical apparatus which he had *forgotten*.

We might not be far from seeing what is in play on this material basis if we recall that the "language" of the unconscious, as it is found in dreams, slips of the tongue, or hysterical symptoms, manifests itself as continuity destroyed, broken, and as the unexpected surging forth of a marked difference. Couldn't we thus say that cinema reconstructs and forms the mechanical model (with the simplifications that this can entail) of a system of writing [*écriture*] constituted by a material base and a counter-system (ideology, idealism) which uses this system while also concealing it? On the one hand, the optical apparatus and the film permit the marking of difference (but the marking is already negated, we have seen, in the constitution of the perspective image with its mirror effect). On the other hand, the mechanical apparatus both selects the minimal difference and represses it in projection, so that meaning can be constituted; it is at once direction, continuity, movement. The projection mechanism allows the differential elements (the discontinuity inscribed by the camera) to be suppressed, bringing only the relation into play. The individual images as such disappear so that movement and continuity can appear. But movement and continuity are the visible expression (one might even say the projection) of their relations, derived from the tiny discontinuities between the images. Thus one may presume that what was already at work as the originating basis of the perspective image, namely the eye, the "subject," is put forth, liberated (in the sense that a chemical reaction liberates a substance) by the operation which transforms successive, discrete images (as isolated images they have, strictly speaking, no meaning, or at least no unity of meaning) into continuity, movement, meaning. With continuity restored, both meaning and consciousness are restored.[8]

THE TRANSCENDENTAL SUBJECT

Meaning and consciousness, to be sure: at this point we must return to the camera. Its mechanical nature not only permits the shooting of differential images as rapidly as desired but also destines it to change position, to move. Film history shows that, as a result of the combined inertia of painting, theater, and photography, it took a certain time to notice the inherent mobility of the cinematic mechanism. The ability to reconstitute movement is after all only a partial, elementary aspect of a more general capability. To seize movement is to become movement, to follow a trajectory is to become trajectory, to choose a direction is to have the possibility of choosing one, to determine a meaning is to give oneself a meaning. In this way the eye-subject, the invisible base of artificial perspective (which in fact only represents a larger effort to produce an ordering, regulated transcendence) becomes absorbed in, "elevated" to a vaster function, proportional to the movement which it can perform.

And if the eye which moves is no longer fettered by a body, by the laws of matter and time, if there are no more assignable limits to its displacement— conditions fulfilled by the possibilities of shooting and of film—the world will not only be constituted by this eye but for it.[9] The movability of the camera seems to fulfill the most favorable conditions for the manifestation of the "transcendental subject." There is a fantasmatization of objective reality (images, sounds, colors)—but of an objective reality which, limiting its powers of constraint, seems equally to augment the possibilities or the power of the subject.[10] As it is said of consciousness—and in point of fact we are concerned with nothing less—the image will always be image *of* something; it must result from a deliberate act of consciousness [*visée intentionelle*]. "The word intentionality signifies nothing other than this peculiarity that consciousness has of being consciousness *of* something, of carrying in its quality of *ego* its *cogitatum* within itself."[11] In such a definition could perhaps be found the status of the cinematographic image, or rather of its operation, the mode of working which it carries out. For it to be an image of something, it has to constitute this something as meaning. The image seems to reflect the world but solely in the naive inversion of a founding hierarchy: "The domain of natural existence thus has only an authority of the second order, and always presupposes the domain of the transcendental."[12]

The world is no longer only an "open and indeterminate horizon." Limited by the framing, lined up, put at the proper distance, the world offers up an object endowed with meaning, an intentional object, implied by and implying the action of the "subject" which sights it. At the same time that the world's transfer as image seems to accomplish this phenomenological reduction, this putting into parentheses of its real existence (a suspension necessary, we will see, to the formation of the impression of reality) provides a basis for the apodicity[13] of the ego. The multiplicity of aspects of the object in view refers to a synthesizing operation, to the unity of this constituting subject: Husserl speaks of "'aspects,' sometimes of 'proximity,' sometimes of 'distance,' in variable modes of 'here' and 'there,' opposed to an absolute 'here' (which is located—for me—in 'my own body' which appears to me at the same time), the consciousness of which, though it remains *unperceived,* always accompanies them. [We will see moreover what happens with the body in the *mise-en-scène* of projection.—J.-L. B.] Each 'aspect' which the mind grasps is revealed in turn as a unity synthesized from a multiplicity of corresponding modes of presentation. The nearby object may present itself as the same, but under one or another 'aspect.' There may be variation of visual perspective, but also of 'tactile,' 'acoustic' phenomena, or of other 'modes of presentation'[14] as we can observe in directing our attention in the proper direction."[15]

For Husserl, "the original operation [of intentional analysis] is to *unmask the potentialities implied* in present states of consciousness. And it is by this that will be carried out, from the noematic point of view, the eventual *explication, definition,* and *elucidation* of what is meant by consciousness, that is, its *objective meaning.*"[16] And again in the *Cartesian Meditations:* "A second type of polarization now presents itself to us, another type of synthesis which embraces the particular multiplicities of *cogitationes,* which embraces them all and in a special manner, namely as *cogitationes* of an identical self which, *active* or *passive,* lives in all the lived states of consciousness and which, through them, relates to all objects."[17]

Thus is articulated the relation between the continuity necessary to the constitution of meaning and the "subject" which constitutes this meaning: continuity is an attribute of the subject. It supposes the subject and it circumscribes its place. It appears in the cinema in the two complementary aspects of a "formal" continuity established through a system of negated differences and narrative continuity in the filmic space. The latter, in any case, could not have been conquered without exercising violence against the instrumental base, as can be discovered from most of the texts by film-makers and critics: the discontinuity that had been effaced at the level of the image could have reappeared on the narrative level, giving rise to effects of rupture disturbing to the spectator (to a *place* which ideology must both conquer and, in the degree that it already dominates it, must also satisfy: fill). "What is important in a film is the feeling of continuity which joins shots and sequences while maintaining unity and cohesion of movements. This continuity was one of the most difficult things to obtain."[18] Pudovkin defined montage as "the art of assembling pieces of film, shot separately, in such a way as to give the spectator the impression of continuous movement." The search for such narrative continuity, so difficult to obtain from the material base, can only be explained by an essential ideological stake projected in this point: it is a question of preserving at any cost the synthetic unity of the locus where meaning originates [the subject]—the constituting transcendental function to which narrative continuity points back as its natural secretion.[19]

THE SCREEN-MIRROR: SPECULARIZATION AND DOUBLE IDENTIFICATION

But another supplementary operation (made possible by a special technical arrangement) must be added in order that the mechanism thus described can play its role effectively as an ideological machine, so that not only the reworked "objective reality" but also the specific type of identification we have described can be represented.

No doubt the darkened room and the screen bordered with black like a letter of condolences already present privileged conditions of effectiveness—no exchange, no circulation, no communication with any outside. Projection and reflection take place in a closed space and those who remain there, whether they know it or not (but they do not), find themselves chained, captured, or captivated.

(What might one say of the function of the head in this captivation: it suffices to recall that for Bataille materialism makes itself headless—like a wound that bleeds and thus transfuses.) And the mirror, as a reflecting surface, is framed, limited, circumscribed. *An infinite mirror would no longer be a mirror.* The paradoxical nature of the cinematic mirror-screen is without doubt that it reflects *images* but not "*reality*"; the word reflect, being transitive, leaves this ambiguity unresolved. In any case this "reality" comes from behind the spectator's head and if he looked at it directly he would see nothing except the moving beams from an already veiled light source.

The arrangement of the different elements—projector, darkened hall, screen—in addition to reproducing in a striking way the *mise-en-scène* of Plato's cave (prototypical set for all transcendence and the topological model of idealism[20]) reconstructs the situation necessary to the release of the "mirror stage" discovered by Lacan. This psychological phase, which occurs between six and eighteen months of age, generates *via* the mirror image of a unified body the constitution or at least the first sketches of the "I" as an imaginary function. "It is to this unreachable image in the mirror that the specular image gives its garments."[21] But for this imaginary constitution of the self to be possible, there must be—Lacan strongly emphasizes this point—two complementary conditions: immature powers of mobility and a precocious maturation of visual organization (apparent in the first few days of life). If one considers that these two conditions are repeated during cinematographic projection—suspension of mobility and predominance of the visual function—perhaps one could suppose that this is more than a simple analogy. And possibly this very point explains the "impression of reality" so often invoked in connection with the cinema for which the various explanations proposed seem only to skirt the real problem. In order for this impression to be produced, it would be necessary that the conditions of a formative scene be reproduced. This scene would be repeated and reenacted in such a manner that the imaginary order (activated by a specularization which takes place, everything considered, in reality) fulfills its particular function of occultation or of filling the gap, the split, of the subject on the order of the signifier.[22]

On the other hand, it is to the extent that the child can sustain the look of another in the presence of a third party that he can find the assurance of an identification with the image of his own body. From the very fact that during the mirror stage is established a dual relationship, it constitutes, in conjunction with the formation of the self in the imaginary order, the nexus of secondary identification.[23] The origin of the self, as discovered by Lacan, in pertaining to the imaginary order effectively subverts the "optical machinery" of idealism which the projection room scrupulously reproduces.[24] But it is not as specifically "imaginary," nor as a reproduction of its first configuration, that the self finds a "place" in the cinema. This occurs, rather, as a sort of proof or verification of that function, a solidification through repetition.

The "reality" mimed by the cinema is thus first of all that of a "self." But, because the reflected image is not that of the body itself but that of a world already given as meaning, one can distinguish two levels of identification. The first, attached to the image itself, derives from the character portrayed as a center of secondary identifications, carrying an identity which constantly must be seized and reestablished. The second level permits the appearance of the first and places it "in action"—this is the transcendental subject whose place is taken by the camera which constitutes and rules the objects in this "world." Thus the spectator identifies less with what is represented, the spectacle itself, than with what stages the spectacle, makes it seen, obliging him to see what it sees; this is exactly the function taken over by the camera as a sort of relay.[25] Just as the mirror assembles the fragmented body in a sort of imaginary integration of the self, the transcendental self unites the discontinuous fragments of phenomena, of lived experience, into unifying meaning. Through it each fragment assumes meaning by being integrated into an "organic" unity. Between the imaginary gathering of the fragmented body into a unity and the transcendentality of the self, giver of unifying meaning, the current is indefinitely reversible.

The ideological mechanism at work in the cinema seems thus to be concentrated in the relationship between the camera and the subject. The question is whether the former will permit the latter to constitute and seize itself in a particular mode of specular reflection. Ultimately, the forms of narrative adopted, the "contents" of the image, are of little importance so long as an identification remains possible.[26] What emerges here (in outline) is the specific function fulfilled by the cinema as support and instrument of ideology. It constitutes the "subject" by the illusory delimitation of a central location—whether this be that of a god or of any other substitute. It is an apparatus destined to obtain a precise ideological effect, necessary to the dominant ideology: creating a fantasmatization of the subject, it collaborates with a marked efficacy in the maintenance of idealism.

Thus the cinema assumes the role played throughout Western history by various artistic formations. The ideology of representation (as a principal axis orienting the notion of aesthetic "creation") and specularization (which organizes the *mise-en-scène* required to constitute the transcendental function) form a singularly coherent system in the cinema. Everything happens as if, the subject himself being unable—and for a reason—to account for his own situation, it was necessary to substitute secondary organs, grafted on to replace his own defective ones, instruments or ideological formations capable of filling his function as subject. In fact, this substitution is only possible on the condition that the instrumentation itself be hidden or repressed. Thus disturbing cinematic elements—similar, precisely, to those elements indicating the return of the repressed—signify without fail the arrival of the instrument "in flesh and blood," as in Vertov's *Man with a Movie Camera*. Both specular tranquillity and the assurance of one's own identity collapse simultaneously with the revealing of the mechanism, that is, of the inscription of the film-work.

The cinema can thus appear as a sort of psychic apparatus of substitution, corresponding to the model defined by the dominant ideology. The system of repression (primarily economic) has as its goal the prevention of deviations and of the active exposure of this "model."[27] Analogously one could say that its "unconscious" is not recognized (we speak of the apparatus and not of the content of films, which have used the unconscious in ways we know all too well). To this unconscious would be attached the mode of production of film, the process of "work" in its multiple determinations, among which must be numbered those depending on instrumentation. This is why reflections on the basic apparatus ought to be possible to integrate into a general theory of the ideology of cinema.

Notes

1. Cf. on this subject Derrida's work "La Scène de l'écriture" in *L'Écriture et la différence* (Paris: Seuil).

2. [The term "subject" is used by Baudry and others not to mean the topic of discourse—though this is clearly involved—but rather the perceiving and ordering self, as in our term "subjective"—Tr.]

3. Obviously we are not speaking here of investment of capital in the process.

4. Cf. L. Brion Guerry, *Jean Pellerin Viator* (Paris: Belles Lettres, 1962).

5. We understand the term "subject" here in its function as vehicle and place of intersection of ideological implications, which we are attempting progressively to make clear, and not as the structural function which analytic discourse attempts to locate. It would rather take partially the place of the ego, of whose deviations little is known in the analytic field.

6. The perspective "frame" which will have such an influence on cinematographic shooting has as its role to intensify, to increase the effect of the spectacle, which no divergence may be allowed to split.

7. "We know that the spectator finds it impossible to notice that the images which succeed one another before his eyes were assembled end-to-end, because the projection of film on the screen offers an impression of continuity although the images which compose it are, in reality, distinct, and are differentiated moreover by variations in space and time.

"In a film, there can be hundreds, even thousands of cuts and intervals. But if it is shown for specialists who know the art, the spectacle will not be divulged as such. Only an error or lack of competence will permit them to seize, and this is a disagreeable sensation, the changes of time and place of action." Pudovkin, "Le Montage," in *Cinéma d' aujourd' hui et de demain* (Moscow, 1956).

8. It is thus first at the level of the apparatus that the cinema functions as a language: inscription of discontinuous elements whose effacement in the relationship instituted among them produces meaning.

9. "In the cinema I am simultaneously in this action and *outside* of it, in this space and out of this space. Having the power of ubiquity, I am everywhere and nowhere." Jean Mitry, *Esthétique et psychologie du cinéma* (Paris: P.U.F., 1965), p. 179.

10. The cinema manifests in a hallucinatory manner the belief in the omnipotence of thought, described by Freud, which plays so important a role in neurotic defense mechanisms.

11. Husserl, *Les Méditations cartésiennes* (Paris: Vrin, 1953), p. 28.

12. *Ibid.,* p. 18.

13. [Apodicity, in phenomenological terminology, indicates something of an ultimately irrefutable nature. See Husserl, *op. cit.* Here, Baudry is using the term critically— in a sense *ironically*—Tr.]

14. On this point it is true that the camera is revealed as incomplete. But this is only a

technical imperfection which, since the birth of cinema, has already in large measure been remedied.

15. *Ibid.,* p. 34, emphasis added.

16. *Ibid.,* p. 40.

17. *Ibid.,* p. 58.

18. Mitry, *op. cit.,* p. 157.

19. The lens, the "objective," is of course only a particular location of the "subjective." Marked by the idealist opposition interior/exterior, topologically situated at the point of meeting of the two, it corresponds, one could say, to the empirical organ of the subjective, to the opening, the fault in the organs of meaning, by which the exterior world may penetrate the interior and assume meaning. "It is the interior which commands," says Bresson. "I know this may seem paradoxical in an art which is all exterior." Also the use of different lenses is already conditioned by camera movement as implication and trajectory of meaning, by this transcendental function which we are attempting to define: it is the possibility of choosing a field as accentuation or modification of the *visée intentionelle.*

No doubt this transcendental function fits in the field of psychology without difficulty. This, moreover, is insisted upon by Husserl himself, who indicates that Brentano's discovery, intentionality, "permits one truly to distinguish the method of a descriptive science of consciousness, as much philosophical and transcendental as psychological."

20. The arrangement of the cave, except that in the cinema it is already doubled in a sort of enclosure in which the camera, the darkened chamber, is enclosed in another darkened chamber, the projection hall.

21. Lacan, *Écrits* (Paris: Seuil, 1966). See in particular "Le Stade du miroir comme formateur de la fonction du Je."

22. We see that what has been defined as impression of reality refers less to the "reality" than to the apparatus which, although being of an hallucinatory order, nonetheless founds this possibility. Reality will never appear except as relative to the images which reflect it, in some way inaugurated by a reflection anterior to itself.

23. We refer here to what Lacan says of identifications in liaison with the structure determined by an optical instrument (the mirror), as they are constituted, in the prevailing figuration of the ego, as lines of resistance to the advance of the analytic work.

24. "That the ego be 'in the right' must be avowed, from experience, to be a function of misunderstanding." Lacan, *op. cit.,* p. 637.

25. "That it sustains itself as 'subject' means that language permits it to consider itself as the stagehand or even the director of all the imaginary capturings of which it would otherwise only be the living marionette." *Ibid.,* p. 637.

26. It is on this point and in function of the elements which we are trying to put in place that a discussion of editing could be opened. We will at a later date attempt to make some remarks on this subject.

27. *Méditerranée,* by J.-D. Pollet and Philippe Sollers (1963), which dismantles with exemplary efficiency the "transcendental specularization" which we have attempted to delineate, gives a manifest proof of this point. The film was never able to overcome the economic blockade.

Translated by Alan Williams.

STORY / DISCOURSE: NOTES ON TWO KINDS OF VOYEURISM[1]

CHRISTIAN METZ

This short article has a significance for the psychoanalytic study of cinema that far exceeds its length. In it, Metz argues that voyeurism is a vital psychic mechanism associated with both cinema and video, and he distinguishes between histoire *—the story or narration, which is issued by an all-knowing but unseen intelligence —and* discours *—the act of telling, the material practice of making meaning, what Heath has called "specific signifying practices" and what others stress as combining the abstract rules of* langue *with the more concrete and variable instances of* parole, *speech. The opposition between* discours *and* histoire *allows Metz to highlight textual procedures that acknowledge their own means of production and the place of the author or speaker.* Histoire *is characteristically third-person, whereas* discours *is also first-person; ideally,* discours *acknowledges that the "I" of a story is only a representative of the subject or agent who produced the story.*

The difference proposed here by Metz within a fairly phenomenological and noncontentious framework takes on added importance when it is placed in an explicitly political framework. Metz himself refers to the classic founts of inspiration, Freud and Marx, but in a manner that makes the primacy of Freud and psychoanalysis for him clear. He asks if the cinematic institution is a matter of ideology. "The audience has the same ideology as the films that are provided for them; they fill the cinemas, and that is how the machine keeps turning. Of course. But it is also a question of desire, and hence of symbolic positioning." In the rest of the article, Metz explores the question of desire, position, and spectator.

Metz argues that histoire *is disguised* discours. Histoire *effaces its marks of* énonciation *and disguises itself as story. This invites a voyeuristic response, since it thus becomes an object presented by an agent who hides, rather than confronts our gaze. This also allows us not only to look but to engage or attend: To some degree, we become the authoring agency as we make sense of an unfolding story that no one seems to tell. In this manner, Metz reintroduces the idea of ideology that he dismissed as mere congruence (films and viewers share a common ideology; this sharing sustains the institution of cinema). Only now it is ideology as the construction of the very notion of viewer, something that holds us to a constricting, unjustifiably egocentric, voyeuristic, but pleasurable position. The notion that a text that hides its own means of production, its* énonciation, *its status as* discours *must be contested and replaced by an alternative cinematic practice lies behind much recent writing that champions Brechtian cinema, the avant-garde, or film theory itself as an interrogation or intervention that reveals what* histoire *tries to conceal. Whether this program, which informed a great deal of writing in* Screen *in the late seventies, provides an adequate model for a political cinema or an adequate critique of popular cinema remains open to debate. Increasingly, emphasis is being placed on questions of history and textual specificity that implicitly challenge the highly generalized cinematic qualities attributed to the customary viewing experience discussed here. But, far from detracting from Metz's contribution, the authors who propose these new emphases demonstrate how knowledge itself is a function of theories, models, and paradigms that are proposed, used, debated, and refused in an ongoing historical process and whose current state is in appreciable measure a consequence of specific past contributions. Readers may wish to read the response to Metz's article by Nowell-Smith, which follows it, first, since it provides an additional introduction.*

•

I'm at the cinema. The images of a Hollywood Film unfold in front of me. It doesn't even have to be Hollywood: the images of any film based on narration and representation—of any 'film', in fact, in the sense in which the word is most often used today—the kind of film which it is the film industry's business to produce. The film industry, and also, more generally, the *institution of cinema* in its present form. For these films do not only represent the millions that have to be invested, made to show a profit, recovered along with the profit, and then reinvested. Beyond this, they presuppose, if only to guarantee the financial feedback, that the audiences will come and buy their tickets and therefore that they will *want* to do so. The institution of cinema reaches far beyond the sector (or the aspect) which is usually thought of as directly commercial.

Is it, then, a question of 'ideology'? In other words, the audiences have the same ideology as the films that are provided for them; they fill the cinemas, and that is how the machine keeps turning. Of course. But it is also a question of desire, and hence of symbolic positioning. In Emile Benveniste's terms, the traditional film is presented as story, and not as discourse. And yet it is discourse, if we refer it back to the film-maker's intentions, the influence he wields over the general public, etc.; but the basic characteristic of this kind of discourse, and the very principle of its effectiveness as discourse, is precisely that it obliterates all traces of the enunciation, and masquerades as story. The tense of story is of course always the 'past definite';[2] similarly, the narrative plenitude and transparency of this kind of film is based on a refusal to admit that anything is lacking, or that anything has to be sought for; it shows us only the other side of the lack and the search, an image of satiety and fulfilment, which is always to some extent regressive: it is a formula for granting a wish which was never formulated in the first place.

We talk about political 'regimes', economic regimes; and in French we can also say that a car, depending on how its gear-box is constructed, can have three, or four, or five 'regimes'. Desire, too, has its regimes, its short-lived or long-lasting plateaux of economic stabilisation, its positions of equilibrium in relation to defence, its gain formations (fiction is one of these, since it presents the narrated without the narrator, rather like in dreams or phantasy): adjustments which are not easy to get right, which must first go through a long process of running-in (from 1895 on, the cinema tried out a lot of different ideas before finding what is now its standard formula; adjustments which social evolution produces, and will alter as time goes by, though (as with states of political equilibrium, again) not constantly, for there are not endless possibilities to choose between, and of those that are actually functioning, each is a self-contained machine which tends to perpetuate itself and is responsible for the mechanisms of its own reproduction (the memory of every film one has enjoyed acts as a model for the next one). This is true of the kind of films which fill our 'screens' today—external screens in the cinemas, and internal screens of the *fictional*, that is, of the imaginary which is provided for us by 'diegesis', an imaginary at once shielded and openly allowed.

How should I 'set' my own position as subject, in order to describe these films? I find myself writing these lines, which are also a tribute to one of the scholars who has been most aware of all the kinds of distancing from the statement which can be created by the enunciation as a separate instance, and all the repercussions with which the statement itself can be reinvested. So, for as long as it takes me to write this, I shall take up a particular listening-post in myself (not, of course, the only one), a post which will allow my 'object', the standard-issue film, to emerge as fully as possible. In the cultural psychodrama of 'positions' I shall adopt neither the role of the person who likes that kind of film nor the role of the person who does not like them. I shall let the words on these pages come from the person who likes to see these films in quotation marks, who likes to savour them as dated allusions (like a wine whose charm lies partly in our knowing its vintage), accepting the ambivalent coexistence of this anachronistic affection with the sadism of the connoisseur who wants to break open the toy and see into the guts of the machine.

Because the film I am thinking of is a very real phenomenon (socially, analytically), it cannot be reduced to a gimmick on the part of a few film-producers out to make money, and good at it. It also exists as our product, the product of the society which consumes it, as an *orientation of consciousness,* whose roots are unconscious, and without which we would be unable to understand the overall trajectory which founds the institution and accounts for its continuing existence. It is not enough for the studios to hand over a polished little mechanism labelled 'fiction film'; the play of elements still has to be realised, or more simply it has to occur: it has to *take place.* And this place is inside each one of us, in an economic arrangement which history has shaped at the same time as it was shaping the film industry.

I'm at the cinema. I am present at the screening of the film. *I am present.* Like the midwife attending a birth who, simply by her presence, assists the woman in labour, I am present for the film in a double capacity (though they are really one and the same) as witness and as assistant: I watch, and I help. By watching the film I help it to be born, I help it to live, since only in me will it live, and since it is made for that purpose: to be watched, in other words to be brought into being by nothing other than the look. The film is exhibitionist, as was the classical nineteenth-century novel with its plot and characters, which the cinema is now copying (semiologically), continuing (historically), and replacing (sociologically, since the written text has now moved in other directions).

The film is exhibitionist, and at the same time it is not. Or at least, there are several kinds of exhibitionism, and correspondingly several kinds of voyeurism, several possible ways of deploying the scopic drive, not all of which are equally reconciled to the fact of their own existence, but which attain in varying degrees to a relaxed, socially acceptable practice of the perversion. True exhibitionism contains an element of triumph, and is always bilateral, in the exchange of phantasies if not in its concrete actions: it belongs to discourse rather than story, and is based entirely on the play of reciprocal identifications, on the conscious acceptance of the to-and-fro movement between *I* and *you*. Through the *mise-en-scène* of its contrary impulsions, the perverted couple (which has its equivalents in the history of cultural productions) takes on the pressure of the voyeuristic desire—ultimately the same for both partners (as it was in its narcissistic origins, in the very young child)—in the never-ending alternation of its two sides: active/passive, subject/object, seeing/being seen. If there is an element of triumph in this kind of representation, it is because what it exhibits is not exactly the exhibited object but, via the object, the exhibition itself. The exhibited partner knows that he is being looked at, wants this to happen, and identifies with the voyeur whose object he is (but who also constitutes him as subject). This is a different economic regime, and a different tuning of desire: not that of the fiction film, but the one which classical theatre sometimes comes close to, when actor and spectator are in each other's presence, when the *playing* (of the actor, and the audience) is also a distribution of roles (of 'character parts') in a game, an active complicity which works both ways, a ceremony which is always partly civic, involving more than the private individual: a festival. The theatre still retains—even if only in the form of a caricature, of theatre as a social rendezvous when the play is one of those insipid offerings of the *théâtre de boulevard*—something of its Greek origins, of its initial atmosphere of citizenship, of public holidays, when a whole population put itself on display for its own enjoyment. (But even then there were the slaves, who did not go to the theatre, and who collectively made it possible for a certain kind of democracy to function, a democracy from which they were excluded.)

The film is not exhibitionist. I watch it, but it doesn't watch me watching it. Nevertheless, it knows that I am watching it. But it doesn't want to know. This fundamental disavowal is what has guided the whole of classical cinema into the paths of 'story', relentlessly erasing its discursive basis, and making it (at best) a beautiful closed object which must remain unaware of the pleasure it gives us (literally, over its dead body), an object whose contours remain intact and which cannot therefore be torn open into an inside and an outside, into a subject capable of saying 'Yes!'

The film knows that it is being watched, and yet does not know. Here we must be a little more precise. Because, in fact, the one who knows and the one who doesn't know are not completely indistinguishable (all disavowals, by their very nature, are also split into two). The one who knows is the cinema, the *institution* (and its presence in every film, in the shape of the discourse which is behind the fiction); the one who doesn't want to know is the film, the *text* (in its final version): the story. During the screening of the film, the audience is present, and aware of the actor, but the actor is absent, and unaware of the audience; and during the shooting, when the actor was present, it was the audience which was absent. In this way the cinema manages to be both exhibitionist and secretive. The exchange of seeing and being-seen will be fractured in its centre, and its two disjointed halves allocated to different moments in time: another split. I never see my partner, but only his photograph. This does not make me any less of a voyeur, but it involves a different regime, that of the primal scene and the keyhole. The rectangular screen permits all kinds of fetishisms, all the nearly-but-not-quite effects, since it can decide at exactly what height to place the barrier which cuts us off, which marks the end of the visible and the beginning of the downward tilt into darkness.

For this mode of voyeurism (which by now is a stable and finely tuned economic plateau) the mechanism of satisfaction relies on my awareness that the object I am watching is unaware of being watched. 'Seeing' is no longer a matter of sending something back, but of catching something unawares. That something which is designed to be caught unawares has been gradually put in place and organised in its function, and through a kind of institutional specialisation (as in those establishments which 'cater for special tastes') it has become story, the story of the film: what we go to see when we say 'I'm going to the cinema'.

The cinema was born much later than the theatre, in a period when social life was deeply marked by the notion of the *individual* (or its more elevated version, 'personality'), when there were no longer any slaves to enable 'free men' to form a relatively homogeneous group, sharing in the experience of a few major affects and so sparing themselves the problem of 'communication', which presupposes a torn and fragmented community. The cinema is made for the private individual (like the classical novel again, which unlike the theatre also partakes of 'story'), and in the spectator's voyeurism there is no need for him to be seen (it is dark in the cinema, the visible is entirely confined to the screen), no need for a knowing object, or rather an object that wants to know, an object-subject to share in the activity of the component drive. It is enough, and it is even essential—this is another, equally well-defined, path of gratification—that the actor should behave as though he were not seen (and therefore as though he did not see his voyeur), that he should go about his ordinary business and pursue his existence as foreseen by the fiction of the film, that he should carry on with his antics in a closed room, taking the utmost care not to notice that a glass rectangle has been set into one of the walls, and that he lives in a kind of aquarium, one which is simply a little less generous with its 'apertures' than real aquariums (this withholding of things being itself part of the scopic mechanism).

In any case, there are fish on the other side as well, their faces pressed to the glass, like the poor of Balbec watching the guests of the grand hotel having their meals.[3] The feast, once again, is not shared—it is a furtive feast and not a festive feast. Spectator-fish, taking in everything with their eyes, nothing with their bodies: the institution of the cinema requires a silent, motionless spectator, a *vacant* spectator, constantly in a sub-motor and hyper-perceptive state, a spectator at once alienated and happy, acrobatically hooked up to himself by the invisible thread of sight, a spectator who only catches up with himself at the last minute, by a paradoxical identification with his own self, a self filtered out into pure vision. We are not referring here to the spectator's identification with the characters of the film (which is secondary), but to his preliminary identification with the (invisible) seeing agency of the film itself as discourse, as the agency which *puts forward* the story and shows it to us. Insofar as it abolishes all traces of the subject of the enunciation, the traditional film succeeds in giving the spectator the impression that he is himself that subject, but in a state of emptiness and absence, of pure visual capacity ('content' is to be found only in what is seen): indeed, it is important that the spectacle 'caught unawares' should itself be unexpected, that it should bear (as every hallucinatory satisfaction does) the stamp of external reality. The regime of 'story' allows all this to be reconciled, since story, in Emile Benveniste's sense of the term, is always (by definition) a story from nowhere, that nobody tells, but which, nevertheless, somebody receives (otherwise it would not exist): so, in a sense, it is the 'receiver' (or rather, the receptacle) who tells it and, at the same time, it is not told at all, since the receptacle is required only to be a place of absence, in which the purity of the disembodied utterance will resonate more clearly. As far as all these traits are concerned it is quite true that the primary identification of the spectator revolves around the camera itself, as Jean-Louis Baudry has shown.

So, is this the mirror stage (as the same author goes on to claim)? Yes, to a large extent (this is, in fact, what we have been saying). And yet, not quite. For what the child sees in the mirror, what he sees as an other who turns into *I,* is after all the image of his own body; so it is still an identification (and not merely a secondary one) with something *seen.* But in traditional cinema, the spectator is identifying only with something *seeing:* his own image does not appear on the screen; the primary identification is no longer constructed around a subject-object, but around a pure, all-seeing and invisible subject, the vanishing point of the monocular perspective which cinema has taken over from painting. And conversely, the *seen* is all thrust back on to the pure object, the paradoxical object which derives its peculiar force from this act of confinement. So we have a situation in which everything has burst apart, and in which the double denial essential to the story's existence is preserved at all costs: that which is seen does not know that it is seen (if it did, this would necessarily mean that it was already, to some extent, a subject), and its lack of awareness allows the voyeur to be himself unaware that he is a voyeur. All that remains is the brute fact of seeing: the seeing of an outlaw, of an *Id* unrelated to any *Ego,* a seeing which has no features or position, as vicarious as the narrator-God or the spectator-God: it is the 'story' which exhibits itself, the story which reigns supreme.

Notes

1. *Histoire/Discours* in the French text. These terms are taken from Benveniste, and are usually translated as 'story/discourse'.

2. Metz uses the term *'accompli'*, which is strictly speaking not a tense but a verbal aspect stressing the completion of an action, and which has no exact equivalent in English.

3. This refers to an episode in Proust's *A la Recherche du temps perdu*.

A NOTE ON STORY / DISCOURSE

GEOFFREY NOWELL-SMITH

Geoffrey Nowell-Smith reminds us of one difference between contemporary and traditional psychoanalytic readings of art: Whereas in the past the emphasis was on the character of the artist, now it is on the psychodynamics of the relationship between text and audience. Nowell-Smith cites Metz's reference to a cinema of "good objects," which give pleasure to an audience that gets what it wants, since it shares a common ideology, as an unnecessary reduction of the complexity of cinema as commodity, but he defends Metz's more subtle treatment of cinema as experience. Even here, though, Nowell-Smith asks whether Metz has not relied too heavily on analogy in his discussion of the similarity of the cinematic experience to Lacan's mirror-phase. In the cinema, what we see is not direct reflections of ourselves but the idealized body images of others. Consequently, Metz stresses that our primary identification is not with characters who are Other—a secondary identification—but with the experience of seeing voyeuristically.

Christian Metz treats primary identification and the attendant experience of helping to author a story that no one seems to tell as the more fundamental form of identification. This has the consequence of downplaying history by associating ideology mainly with the constitution of a transhistorical, transcultural subject. Nowell-Smith wonders if primary identification as something "further back" in psychic experience has not been confused with primary identification as something more determining. For adults who have passed through the hypothetical mirror-phase, regressing toward it and its pattern of identification with the images of self and others will be counterbalanced, if not superseded, by the secondary identifications that are a function of particular characters and textual strategies. This is the area that Metz downplays with his notion of the cinema as a "good object" matching the ideology to which we already hold, but it is also the very vital and complex area traditionally examined by Marxist critics and cultural historians. Nowell-Smith generously allows that Metz's simplified notion of ideology in the political context need not detract from his more elaborate treatment of ideology in the psychoanalytic context. Metz does not demonstrate that these two conceptions of ideology are actually compatible. We seem to get two different views of ideology, depending on where we begin: with the social formation or with the discursive, semiotic formation, the audience or the spectator. Thus, we see not a genuine merger but rhetorical assertions that one has more explanatory power than the other. If dialectic is at work here, the moment of synthesis has yet to come.

•

Psychoanalytic study of art is as old as psychoanalysis—and in some form no doubt dates way beyond psychoanalysis proper, whether as science or as cure. But for the most part it has taken the form of a wild analysis, of pseudo-analysis, of characters and authors. Hamlet is neurotic, and so, we infer, was Shakespeare.[1] Psychoanalysis of the text, and of the intersubjective textual relation, is, however, relatively recent. Although some early analysts, including Freud himself, had certain ideas about how texts (or performances) might reproduce processes whose structure was first revealed in analysis, it is only in recent years, with the insertion of signification into the problematic of psychoanalysis, notably through the work of Jacques Lacan, that a reciprocal action has become possible and the psychoanalytic concept of the subject has become a necessary part of the study of signifying systems.

Structural linguistics—and the semiotics which followed from it—was for the most part resolutely objectivist. It studied signifying systems as objects *per se.* The system might denote relations between subjects or be used to transmit messages between persons presumed to be subjects. But the notion of the subject and its representation within language was not seriously called into question. The subject was outside the system—on the one hand as an irrelevance to objective study, but on the other hand also as foundation, negligible because taken for granted.

This state of affairs was challenged, initially, by the work of Lacan within the field of psychoanalysis proper. In his assault on the notion of a transcendent ego (the foundation of metaphysics as well as the implicit base of linguistic "science" and, need one add, the source of much neurotic unhappiness) Lacan showed that the subject is constructed in and through language, though in a relation of alterity to it. This discovery (itself based, at least in part, on the linguistic theories of Saussure and Jakobson) has profound implications for linguistics and for the study of all signifying forms. For one of the properties of language then becomes the relations that the subject can have to it and within it. As well as being a system of signs related among themselves, language incarnates meaning in the form of the series of positions it offers for the subject from which to grasp itself and its relations with the real.

In such a context the distinction which Saussure made, for formal reasons, between *langue* as system and *parole* as enactment has to be seen in a new light.

For on the side of *parole* it is not the words as such but the fact of speaking them—and of who is speaking them—that constitutes the decisive relation to language as system.

Within *parole* therefore (but with implications also for *langue*) another distinction suggests itself, which is that between *énonciation* and *énoncé*. Both these terms tend to be translated into English as "utterance", thereby obliterating the distinction, but basically *énonciation* (which I shall give henceforth as "enunciation") means the act whereby an utterance is produced, and *énoncé* (which I shall give as "statement") means what is thereby uttered in itself. This is not a distinction between form and content, nor yet one between context and text, but a distinction within the utterance itself between two forms, two contents and, indeed, two texts. Often there is no need to distinguish sharply between the two aspects. The enunciating instance can be either a matter of indifference (it doesn't much matter who says "The sun shines in August" or "The King died in 1909") or else it can appear to be fused with the statement itself (as in "I promised"). But it becomes clear on reflection that not only are the two instances distinct but they may even be in contradiction with each other. This is particularly the case when the relation between the addresser and the addressee is brought into the statement itself, as for example with the use of the personal pronouns "I" and "you". The majority of statements contain a grammatical subject and a predicate, and very often neither of these invokes either addresser or addressee directly—or if they do it is some other position than the one they occupy at the moment of enunciation. The subject of the enunciation thus regularly stands outside the enunciated statement, even if it is the same person—as in "I borrowed five pounds from your purse". But if we look at that last statement more closely we can see that, alongside the relation expressed in the statement (*énoncé*) itself, which registers money having been borrowed by one person from another, there is also a relation expressed in which I, the speaker, now enunciate and so engage my indebtedness to you who are being spoken to. An even more extreme case is provided by such phrases as "I lied to you", which implicates another subject than the one who recently lied, this being the subject who is now (hopefully) telling the truth.

The problem of the subject in language thus becomes one of enunciation, or rather of the relation, always potentially contradictory, between enunciation and statement, *énonciation* and *énoncé*. This leads on to a further distinction, systematised by the French linguist Emile Benveniste, between discourse and history. Discourse and history are both forms of enunciation, the difference between them lying in the fact that in the discursive form the source of the enunciation is present, whereas in the historical it is suppressed. History is always "there" and "then", and its protagonists are "he", "she" and "it". Discourse, however, always also contains, as its points of reference, a "here" and a "now" and an "I" and a "you".[2] Benveniste cites as examples of the historical form in language on the one hand the statements of historians proper and on the other hand passages from novels representing events.[3] What characterises statements of this type—besides certain grammatical features, such as the choice of tense—is the absence in the text of a point from which the enunciation stems. "Solon established the laws" or "The young man looked around the room" are statements which do not specify any subject of enunciation. The existence of the historian Glotz or the novelist Balzac is announced on the title page, but they conceal themselves at some point beyond, or outside, the text.

Discourse, by contrast, is always marked by the presence of a subject of the enunciation—whether this be the author/speaker as person or not. Discursive forms (or forms with a strong discursive element) include most oral communications and also oratory (even when written down), the essay, the letter and various forms of narrated fiction. A classic example of a novel visibly constructed around both a discursive and an historical order would be Laclos's *Les Liaisons dangereuses* in which (discounting for the moment the further problem of the relation of the author, Laclos, to the text) the events represented are always related through the discourse of the characters writing letters to each other.[4] But almost any fictional form contains discursive elements, either bracketed, as with direct speech reported in inverted commas, or integrated into the text as "free indirect" or as the standpoint of a narrator. Arguably the ambition of certain novelists, from Flaubert onwards, has been to collapse discourse into history and to naturalise events so that they seem to exist in a space defined from nowhere, but most often the effect has been the reverse. The modern novel, since Henry James, has been discursive *par excellence*.

But what of the cinema? Although the particular marks of discursive enunciation, the shifters—personal pronouns, tense, etc.—are present in the film through its use of written or spoken language, these are hardly sufficient to mark the film as a whole as discursive. Since speech in films is mostly bracketed—as the dialogue of particular characters—there arises the problem of a superior discursive or narrating instance, marked in some way in the structure of the film. The most prevailing assumption—and the one which Metz uses as his starting point—has been that the film is predominantly history and that, though there may be subjects of its statements (characters who are seen to speak and to perform actions) there is no way that the film as such (particularly the classic fiction film) identifies its own enunciation as proceeding from somewhere.

One way discourse can be integrated into the film—other than through the use of written language—is by "point of view".[5] Film narration generally proceeds by means of a series of shots, or by movements within the shot, which alter the angle from which a set of events is viewed. These changes of angle also constitute changes of point of view in so far as they successively incorporate vantage points external or internal to the action, and along, across or against the eyelines of the characters. But while an analysis of point of view may help us to individuate different discourses proceeding from the characters or from a point outside them, it does not yet solve the problem of the discourse of the film as such. Like phrases of dialogue, points of view are usually bracketed. When it is asked what is outside the brackets, or who or what does the bracketing, the answer usually remains the same. Particular discourses are all comprised within a meta-discourse, but this meta-discourse is not strictly speaking a discourse at all, but presents itself as history—a set of statements from which a subject of enunciation is absent.

It is here that psychoanalysis enters the picture. The psychoanalytic approach cannot rest content with the observation that the internal construction of a film is one which situates the events portrayed as lacking any enunciating subject. For psychoanalysis is crucially concerned with the intersubjectivity of the construction of meaning. In the absence of a subject of enunciation on the side of the film it is hard to see what position is possible for that other subject, that of the spectator him/herself. The spectating subject requires the relation to an other in order to situate itself, and somewhere the film must provide it with that other. (The objection that the spectating subject is comfortably situated in an armchair and knows perfectly well that it is so situated is here beside the point. Unless the film sustains a discourse towards that position—which is precisely what is at issue—then the relation screen/ armchair is indeed conductive to fetishism.)

Elsewhere[6] I have argued that a narrating instance can often be found in the form of the author. But the search for a "subject" of a film cannot be traced back in this way further than the discovery of a notional subject of its statements (énoncés). Particularly where a film is a studio product, a "real" subject with which the spectator might engage is simply not inscribed into the film. The engagement of the spectator, except at rare moments, is therefore always with one or another aspect of the fiction. The absence of a clearly marked superior instance— a "John Ford is telling me this" or a "Universal Studios" or whoever it may be— encourages the setting up of various forms of discursive relation which are not linguistically bound but are informed by other structures co-existent with cinematic-linguistic systems proper. Here we may distinguish those relations which, although not linguistically (or cine-linguistically) bound, are specific to the form of the fictional text, and those whose structure can be defined from outside the fictional network. In the former category we can include various positional identifications with the characters—"I am who the character is looking at", "I am she who he is looking at", "I am looking at them from where the camera is", etc. To the latter belong various relations which are normally defined in terms redolent of psythopathology—voyeurism, exhibitionism, etc.

Two things are important to note here. One is that these relations are going to be set up anyway. It is proper to any work of art to posit quite a complex set of relations through which it can be grasped (or not) by the reader/viewer.[7] The absence of a superior instance (or the concealment of this instance in the form of history) merely affects the scope and mobility of the others. Secondly it should be noted that all the relations so far mentioned are pre-eminently discursive, whatever other connotations some of them might also have. Exhibitionism, for example, is far from being just a nasty thing that dirty old men do to little girls. Quite apart from the fact that most exhibitionism in its "real" pathological manifestations takes place in a context of complicity (within couples, or in artistic performance) the point is that the terms of the structure are those in which a relation between subject and object, active and passive, is constructed around an axis of seeing. (The exhibitionist creates the other as subject by letting himself be seen, while at the same time alienating himself in that other, etc.) The film, therefore, can hold a discourse towards the spectator as that which exhibits itself to be seen, or for that matter, as that which enables the spectator to see (identification with the camera as voyeur) or as an alternation of the two. Not only is exhibitionism, as Metz notes, "of the order of discourse, not history" (which incidentally means that *what* is exhibited is to some extent irrelevant). It is also discursive articulation. History becomes discourse in so far as the exhibitionist/voyeurist relation (or, more simply, the relation of seeing and showing) presides over the construction of the film.

This state of affairs—including the aspect we may call a kind of necessary perversity of filmic construction—is not in fact all that different from what prevails in other art forms. In some ways the difference is only one of complexity. There are in the cinema so many more forms of potentially discursive relations to take account of. This has to do with the fact that the film is simultaneously spectacle, reproduction and narrative, and the organisation of (say) spectacle along the axis of narrative poses enormous problems of articulation. The voyeurist/exhibitionist relation often overlays somewhat uneasily on the construction of the film as narrative sequence. Hence the frequent difficulty in deciding which axis to privilege and whether the film as a whole has a single discursive structure at all (and by and large I would argue that usually it does not). But three points, I think, should be retained from Metz's attempts to "psychoanalyse" the filmic text (and the cinematic institution), even if the actual elaboration of them needs to be questioned.

One we have already mentioned: the tendency of films to disguise themselves as history and so to split the subject of enunciation into two halves—the "real" subject not inscribed in the film, and the fictive subjects within the textual relation with whose positionality the spectating subject engages. One important feature which we have not so far discussed is that it represents events as having been accomplished. The film is present (during viewing) to the spectator, but only as something which is already past and which has already fixed a resolution for the problems it evokes. In so far as the film is successfully contained within its historicity—both its pastness and its plenitude—it is inevitably regressive, placing the spectating subject not beyond but short of desire, in an imaginary fulfilment. (In this analysis the ideological functioning of films would be very dependent on their naturalization as history and also on the regression that accompanies it.) It is doubtful, however, to what extent the regression is actualised. This is not because people are not prone to regressing, in the cinema as at other times and places in their daily lives, but because the notion of a totally historical film is intrinsically self-defeating. Although the film may pose itself as history—thereby invoking a complex structure of disavowals, refusals of negativity, etc.—it cannot do so without laying itself open, in the course of construction of its own plenitude, to other possible appropriations by the spectator. If ultimately the spectator is led back by the filmic system to a regressive point, where the film confirms itself as identical to its own beginning (already an extreme case), the journey is one with many detours in any of which the spectator might get lost, and therefore, so to speak, refound.

A second point concerns the specific relation of filmic narrativity to the axis of viewing. In addition to the structures of voyeurism and exhibitionism already mentioned (and analysable, incidentally, in phenomenological and existentialist terms as well as in psychoanalytical), there arises the question of specularity and, in particular, of the mirror phase posited by Lacan as a necessary nodal point in the constitution of the subject.[8] Metz is right, I think, to emphasise, both in "Story/Discourse" and elsewhere, an essential difference between the mirror relation as such, in which the child captures its own image (or is captivated by it), and cinematic representation, in which the one thing you don't see is your own image reflected.[9] Here what is significant is the fact of the contradiction: the screen is like a mirror, and yet one in which you don't see yourself. Hence the poignance of the moment in *All That Heaven Allows* where Jane Wyman looks into the blank TV screen and sees her own face reflected back at her. But hence too the importance of mirror shots generally—the mirroring within the mirror by which identity (of characters and/or spectator) is variously doubled, split and recomposed. Because film is also narrative, however, the function of specularity can rarely be grasped, or impose itself, in a pure form. Not only do mirror shots perform a variety of functions,[10] but the specularity of the projected image itself will vary according to the range of identifications available to the spectator at any given time. These identifications, as Metz points out, are secondary and in a sense may be held not to inflect a primary identification of the spectator with him/ herself as pure see-er opposing the screen image as pure external seen. I am not so sure about this, First of all it goes along with a general overvaluation of perception as a datum, which is very un-Freudian, and secondly the very fact that something is posited as primary should make us instantly suspicious. To say something is primary is simply to locate it further back in the psychic apparatus. It does not, or should not, invite any conclusions about its efficacy. I would argue, therefore, that the so-called secondary identifications do tend to break down the pure specularity of the screen/spectator relation in itself and to displace it onto relations which are more properly intra-textual—i.e., relations to the spectator posited from within the image and in the movement from shot to shot.[11]

Thirdly, and last, we have the problem of the cinema as institution. As Metz remarks in "The Imaginary Signifier",[12] the cinematic institution is not just the cinema industry but also includes "the mental machinery—another industry— which spectators 'accustomed to the cinema' have internalised historically and which had adapted them to the consumption of films." This second apparatus stands in a complementary relation to the productive apparatus proper and is linked to it (and to a possible third apparatus, more narrowly psychical in scope) in so far as the demand which the productive apparatus supplies supposes a structure of wants which are socially and psychologically instituted. As Marx observes, whether the want satisfied by the commodity "corresponds to the belly or the fantasy" is of no consequence: in the case of the cinema it is clearly fantasy.[13] But Metz is guilty of a gross oversimplification on both economic and psychological levels when he equates the functioning of the institution with the production of films as "good objects" for the spectator (the term is Melanie Klein's) and with a supposed desire or want of the spectators to see the films that are actually produced. Such an equation leaves the terrain of psychoanalysis for that of the utilitarian psychology of Bentham and certainly departs from the terrain of Marxist economics (if indeed it was ever there) for the long exploded castles in the air of Say's law and the necessary harmony of supply and demand. When Metz further claims that the cinematic institution by definition produces more pleasure than unpleasure, the ideological mixture becomes even more suspect. What the cinema certainly does provide for the spectator is a use value, but whether this use value corresponds to pleasure in the Freudian sense is another question, which cannot be solved by recourse to tautology. It is yet another question again whether there is a correspondence between the exchange value realised by the producer and the use value obtained by the consumer. That there is some relation between what makes money for the producer and what gives pleasure to the audience is undeniable, but the relation is not an immediate one and by no means assumes equilibrium, let alone identity.

Fortunately, however, the functionalist and utilitarian equation is by no means necessary to Metz's hypothesis of the different apparatuses, and indeed runs counter to the main thrust of the argument. What is interesting to register here is the existence of different apparatuses, different economies (in the sense in which one can talk, for example, of a "libidinal economy") which are not homologous with each other but overlap and interfere with one another at various points. One such point of interference would be precisely the production of films as (ostensibly) history rather than discourse, which is in part guaranteed by the relative anonymity of the productive apparatus and by the production of films as marketable objects. Conversely the existence in filmic textual systems of multiple points of entry into relations which are discursive can be correlated both to the diverse inheritance of previous forms of art and entertainment assumed by the cinema and reprojected onto the world market, and to a psychoanalytic instance—the possible forms of subject position faced with the cinematic apparatus as such. The cinema is a place where a lot of cotters come to the comb. The task of film theory is to disentangle them, not just cut them all off.

Notes

1. Freud himself was not exempt from this. See J.-L. Baudry, "Freud et la 'création littéraire,'" in *Théorie d'Ensemble,* Paris: Editions du Seuil, 1968, pp. 148–74.

2. These are the terms known in linguistics (since Jakobson) as "shifters". Their characteristic is that they are not definable as places in a system of object relations, but only by reference to the subject of enunciation itself. As well as certain pronouns and adverbs, a number of verbal forms (in English mostly the compound tenses "I am eating", "I have eaten", "I shall eat") are discursive rather than historical, since they too acquire meaning in terms of the place of enunciation. See E. Benveniste, "Les relations de temps dans le verbe français," *Problèmes de linguistique générale,* Paris: Gallimard, 1966, pp. 237–50.

3. *Op. cit.,* pp. 240–41.

4. See T. Todorov, "Les Catégories de récit littéraire," *Communications* 8, pp. 125–51 (English translation in *Film Reader,* no. 2, Evanston, 1976). For Todorov the categories of history and discourse correspond (roughly) to those of *fabula* and *syuzhet* in the Russian Formalists.

5. See E. Branigan, "Formal Permutations of the Point-of-View Shot", *Screen* 16, no. 3 (Autumn 1975): 54–64, reprinted here.

6. "Six Authors in Pursuit of *The Searchers*", *Screen* 17, no. 1 (Spring 1976): 26–33.

7. As for example by Sartre in *Being and Nothingness*.

8. J. Lacan, "The Mirror-Phase as Formative of the Function of the I" (1949), *New Left Review*, no. 51 (September–October 1968), pp. 71–77.

9. C. Metz, "The Imaginary Signifier," *Screen* 16, no. 2 (Summer 1975): 48.

10. E.g., in Welles *(Kane, Lady from Shanghai)* a multiple splitting of the character, in Ophuls *(Letter from an Unknown Women)* an encounter with an ideal-ego in the form of an I-that-once-was, in Sirk *(Tarnished Angels)* imprisonment in images of the self, etc. Countless variations are possible. In Hawks *(Rio Bravo)*, needless to say, looking into the mirror merely means giving way to a fatal (feminine) narcissism.

11. See, for example, Nick Browne, "The Spectator-in-the-text: the Rhetoric of *Stagecoach*," *Film Quarterly* 29, no. 2 (Winter 1975–1976): 26–38, reprinted here. (An alternative version of the same article entitled "Rhétorique de texte speculaire" appeared in French in *Communications* 23, 1975.)

12. Metz, *op. cit.*, p. 19.

13. In *Capital,* Vol. I, Ch. 1. The formulation is both tentative and ironic, and Marx goes on to show (in Vols. II and III) that there is a big difference in the roles played by commodities, according to whether or not they are ware-goods (restoring and reproducing labour power).

ON THE NAKED THIGHS OF MISS DIETRICH

PETER BAXTER

This essay introduces us to one important current in recent psychoanalytic analysis. Avoiding the temptation to diagnose von Sternberg's mental disposition on the basis of his films, Peter Baxter also departs from the viewer-response criticism that is central to Metz's "Story/Discourse" and Baudry's "Ideological Effects." Instead, he dwells on the psychodynamics of the film text itself, which he treats not unlike a patient's dream. Baxter explains how the film becomes fascinating by its only partially successful efforts to mask the anxieties that every psychoanalyst knows abound in the universe of sexual desire.

Baxter's introduction is especially useful in detailing the relationship between desire and society. He argues that freedom cannot be allowed to threaten the relations of production in bourgeois society. His brief description of the relationships among family, desire, and class society is exceptionally lucid, although the class or Marxist component of the relationships may seem to have been somewhat neglected by the time we get to the end, which seems closer to an ahistorical constitution of the postoedipal child. The woman becomes a living reminder of the threat of castration for the male child, and the naked thighs of Miss Dietrich become an arresting/arrested image of object that male viewers dare not acknowledge, "nothing, a blank, a gap . . ."

A few questions arise. Some pertain to Baxter's attempt to adapt both Freud and Lacan to a feminist perspective. Is the patriarchal context for this perception of female genitalia as "nothing" sufficiently stressed, and is its pathology—in Freud or in patients—clearly described? (That question is also discussed in the introduction to Laura Mulvey's article in Part 3.) Other questions pertain to the hazards of textual psychoanalysis: When is a top hat a phallic symbol, and when is it just a top hat? How do latent psychic meanings correspond to other latent but historical meanings (regarding Weimar Germany, for instance)? Still, this analytic approach has considerable currency—for example, it figures in Robin Wood's discussion of horror films—and the discomfort that we feel with its claims that objects and actions which themselves are displacements of direct sexual meaning actually do have sexual meaning may as easily confirm the analysis as deny it: Our discomfort suggests that a psychic nerve has been touched. We laugh not because the explanation is ludicrous but to avoid acknowledging what our own mechanisms of repression help us to ignore. This is often the claim made by practitioners of this approach, and it certainly warrants consideration. Adopting Roman Jakobson's principle of metonomy and Freud's principle of fetishism as his two key concepts, Peter Baxter provides a remarkably clear model of a semiotic psychoanalysis of film texts and thereby helps us to pose these questions with particular urgency.

●

When Josef von Sternberg published his autobiography in 1965, *Newsweek's* review of it credited the director with having created the "Marlene Dietrich image," an image which had become "one of the great features of contemporary fantasy life." But we have not simply carried Marlene about with us in our heads: the image is and always has been material, circulating in that constant production of texts which we can call the social discourse. Given the nature of our society, given the absorption of textual production by commodity production, an examination of the function of the image in social discourse inevitably leads to an investigation of the way in which (as Henri Lefevre puts it in *The Sociology of Marx):* "Those who wield material (economic and political) power within the established social and juridical order also wield 'spiritual' power"[1]—power over intellectual and emotional life.

Spiritual power and material power are, of course, not separate forces. The latter subsumes the former, since it is the character of material production and consumption under given circumstances which determines the particular form of general human need. "Need," that is, is an abstraction; we can say that its historical, concrete and personal form is "desire," with peculiar and specific characteristics brought about in social practice. Despite its conventional divisions into production/

distribution/exhibition, the cinema constitutes one sector of this practice: here images circulate and needs assume from them the shape of particular desires. At the level of individual desire, which we are encouraged to believe is the most private, spontaneous aspect of our lives, we discover the formative traces of the relations of production obtaining in our society.

The "Marlene Dietrich image"—whether the image of Lola in *The Blue Angel* or the image as it has taken shape and been written up in a hundred different places—exemplifies society producing the impasse into which it casts its members on the level of the libido as much as on the level of economics: the desire for what cannot be avoided without a radical rupture with the world that has formed us.

We may well ask ourselves how the particular fascination of this image came into being, what its terms are, and why this image is so privileged and so familiar.

A certain still image of Dietrich has circulated in European and American discourse for a number of years. We know that this pose was not spontaneously assumed; according to John Baxter's source, "her casual pose on the stage with one leg upraised was arrived at only after much experiment, with more than a dozen possible attitudes tried and discarded."[2] What determined the choice of this pose, and what determined that it, more than anything else in the film, would be "remembered," that is, would reappear in one form or another in ensuing discourse?

Heinrich Mann told Emil Jannings that the success of *The Blue Angel* would depend not on his acting genius but "on the naked thighs of Miss Dietrich."[3] André Bazin has certainly seemed to admire "their almost mathematically perfect contours."[4] Yet other actresses in other films doubtlessly showed thighs neither less naked nor less perfect, and they, their legs and their films did not enter the mass consciousness and discourse in the same way.

From the first, there has been an enigma associated with this consciousness; as early as 1931, in one of the first Paris reviews of the film, Pierre Bost wrote of "une fille magnifique, aux jambes *inexplicablement* belles."[5]

Ado Kyrou claimed that Dietrich's considerable charm lay dormant and unspectacular until Sternberg breathed life into it ("il lui insuffla des poses provocantes"[6]). If we are not satisfied with such an answer, however, we must be prepared to pull down the whole edifice of Marlene's mystery and dismantle the fascination in which it holds us.

According to Jacques Lacan the Oedipus complex is the crucial gate by which the individual leaves the realm of nature and enters the realm of culture. But the Eden of infantile sexuality is not simply abandoned; the manner of leaving it decides the sexual identity of the future adult. And here is where I would locate the function of the "Marlene Dietrich image." I hope to demonstrate that this image is part of the discourse in which the family unconsciously receives the knowledge of the social relations that it is instrumental in producing. The image serves to maintain the individual in a state of attraction to a past which he can only repress. Such an image places limits on desire which cannot be detected, so desire becomes the expression in the individual of the social order.

Freedom cannot be allowed to threaten the relations of production characteristic of bourgeois society. The social discourse, a vast complex from which we draw and which we produce as the image of ourselves, must therefore say two things while seeming to say one. It must say freedom to create oneself in history, against the encroachments of time, and concurrently it must impose the limits of the individual which correspond with his usefulness in the forces of production. Like the dream, discourse at large must therefore consist of a manifest level of meaning and of a latent level where what must be known but must be repressed is worked out, where the unconscious is produced.

In *The Blue Angel* we can see how a textual unconscious of discontinuous and repetitive events resurrects those infantile moments during which the course of mature libidinal impulses is determined. Those moments determine patterns of family life and of desire which are handed on in the family's re-inscription of itself and the social structure on its children.

At the manifest level, *The Blue Angel* carries out a task which Western narrative has classically set for itself: to provide modern man with a model of the individual life he believes himself to lead. "I hope you all realize the consequences of your behavior," says Rath to his students. By means of a textual surface of consequences, of cause and effect in time, society in its discourse impresses responsibility upon its citizens. Between the linearity of the narrative and the circularity of the repressed text, the film is experienced like novelistic literature as (to borrow a nice phrase from Olivier Burgelin) "a sort of fantasy susceptible of being experienced at once as personal and as real." [7]

In the analysis of dreams, those which are the most difficult to interpret, those in which the dream thoughts are least accessible, are precisely those which have a particular surface clarity, those in which the work of what Freud called "secondary revision" has most fully proceeded. Among the systems which the dream work employs for adducing this clarity is the narrative. Freud specifically mentions, for example, the "narrative of the French Revolution" when he is talking about the form taken by one of the dreams he culled from literature on the subject; not simply the French Revolution but the *narrative* of the French Revolution was what supplied the dreamer with the principles for organizing his fantasy.

In an individual text, secondary revision is an aspect of the productive activity of a society forging its world, formulating conscious relationships within itself and between itself and nature. The great importance of Freud's discovery of the unconscious was to have made evident the struggle with which the social superstructure is erected and maintained in each individual.

Let us say, for the moment, that a work such as *The Blue Angel* can be considered as the result of a kind of narrative secondary revision. We may suppose that, as in the dream where the narrative is not to be ignored, there is a textual "other" to be taken into account, the importance of which may be gauged from the fact that the narrative exists precisely to sweep it from view, to repress it. What I would contend, however, is that it is exactly this repressed text that has been the key factor in attracting attention to this film, in fascinating the public; it is a text which cuts through the vagaries of changing fashion in a single historical era, which is perfectly understood by the spectator, but which is quickly and firmly relegated to the individual unconscious, and is present to the conscious mind in the form of and obsession with the "mystery" of the "Marlene Dietrich image."

In undertaking the analysis of this process which writes desire and repression in the moment of textual production, I shall work within the framework of Roman Jakobson's proposition that realist art proceeds metonymically, and relate this to Freud's view of fetishism. What is interesting for us is that in Freud's view metonymy decides for the fetishist the object which is going to be the focus of his desires, and which has the function of signifying his other true, although imaginary, object of desire, "the woman's (the mother's) penis that the little boy once believed in and . . . does not want to give up."[8]

The resolution of the Oedipal complex, according to Freud, is accomplished in two moments, one involving a real or imagined threat of castration, and the other involving the sight of the female genital organ, or in other words, fear for the loss of the genital organ and evidence that organ-less individuals exist. For a reason or reasons which Freud admits he is "frankly unable to explain,"[9] it sometimes occurs that the reaction to the threat and the sight is not successful in inducing the repression of the Oedipal desire; in certain instances the subject avoids having to completely give up his original belief in the female penis, and substitutes a fetish as its emblem: "it is as though the last impression before the uncanny and traumatic one is retained as a fetish . . . pieces of underclothing, which are so often chosen as a fetish, crystallize the moment of undressing, the last moment in which the woman could still be regarded as phallic."[10]

In *The Blue Angel*, a crucial incident occurs in the shot where Professor Rath— who has come to the cabaret to look for his miscreant students— stands looking up the spiral stairway from Lola's dressing room into her bedroom, as she at the top, only her ankles visible, removes her underpants and drops them over his shoulder.

This realization of a critical moment in libidinal development is, it seems to me, a privileged instant in the semantic constitution of the film, charging an object with phallic significance. It functions, I believe, as one of what Jacques Lacan has called *"points de capiton,"* "points like the buttons on a mattress or the intersections in quilting, where there is a 'pinning down' [*capitonnage*] of meaning, not to an object, but rather by 'reference back' to a symbolic function."[11] Here the symbolic reference is to one of the two critical events which resolve the Oedipus complex and order the individual's entry into society.

If we accept that this moment in *The Blue Angel* is a figuration of such a critical event, and that the underpants acquire such a phallic significance, then we can go on from there to demonstrate how the textual unconscious is written in the film in accordance with a system of exchanges and transformations.

In fact, these underpants figure as the currency in a circuit of exchange which takes them from Lola to Rath to Guste (the wife of the magician, Kiepert) to Goldstaub (a student), who is hidden behind the screen in the dressing room, and back to Rath before they are finally returned to Lola the next evening. But this circuitry embellishes the important central axis by which the underpants are transferred from Lola to Rath, and obscures the completion of the exchange which extends phallic value. Rath returns to the Blue Angel the following night to give back the pants and to find the hat which he realized he had left behind. In exchanging that for underpants, the former acquires the value of the latter: it becomes phallic, and as we shall see, thus becomes of the utmost importance to the functioning of the repressed text.

We can now see a new relevance in Heinrich Mann's wry comment on Miss Dietrich's naked thighs; for it is with Rath's glance upward between Lola's thighs, it is with the fixing of his glance by those drawers so casually draped over his shoulder, that a text determined by a systematic strategy of repression breaks surface in the narrative. On the one hand the narrative upholds the conventional, "official" relations of man and woman, while on the other hand infantile experience of a unique importance emerges which is tied around the Oedipus complex and more especially around its essential moment, castration. The glance as such figures that instant when the child either leaves the Oedipal situation by a certain path or is locked into it.

But in Freud's hypothesis, the glance only has the force in the context of the threat of castration. The climactic scene of *The Blue Angel* is nothing less than an image of the execution of this threat; it is surely this fact that is the dominant determinant of the scene's powerful effect.

Lola makes remarks which establish the connection between Kiepert and Rath, the professor of magic and the real professor. Moreover, they resemble each other in physique and dress. Their similarity is fraught with tension, tension of the kind— I will propose—that ensues when the child's identification with his father leads him to covet his father's prerogatives. For Kiepert is the man who has power over women. When Rath chooses a top hat to replace that slouch brim he had misplaced, he chooses a hat identical to Kiepert's. In this way he begins a process of encroachment on Kiepert's domain which ends in his own public humiliation at the Blue Angel, where the terrifying spectacle of castration is acted out.

Kiepert introduces Rath to the audience as "my best student." This reversal of position for the former professors is further signified by the difference in their costumes: Rath is a ridiculous version of Kiepert, his clown costume aping Kiepert's formal rig. His hat in this scene, a battered, crushed equivalent of Kiepert's topper, is the focus of attention. Kiepert removes it from Rath's head and demonstrates that it is "empty," as is his clown's head. Four times Kiepert runs the hat completely through with a dagger as it sits on the head of his pathetic stooge. He takes up a pistol and fires through it. He lifts the hat from Rath's head and a dove flies up and out of frame.

For the speaker of German the verb *vögeln* is a slang word meaning "to copulate." It is derived from *Vogel* meaning "bird." (There is an editorial comment to this effect in *The Interpretation of Dreams* with respect to Freud's analysis of one of his own dreams.)

In *The Blue Angel,* the dove nestled beneath Rath's hat—a piece of apparel which is, as we have seen, a phallic symbol—acquires by metonymy a meaning linguistically substantiated in the light of the German provenance of the film and its makers. As the dove flies out, Kiepert announces "Now has my Auguste a weight off his mind." In this sentence "weight" surely refers to something other than the dove. It refers to the weight of that pendant organ which is the site of the sensations troubling the mind of the child in the toils of the Oedipus complex.

The phallic significance attained with full force in the scene upon the stage of the Blue Angel is unequivocally one of the *points de capiton* by which we can come to know the repressed text; one which makes clear that castration is the matter which the narrative in its repressive function aims to distort. Only by "reading back" from such a point do we find that the main axis of the repressed text becomes intelligible and its system formulable. Around the sight of the female organ, and the threat of castration, the whole network of the fragmented and partially evident text spreads out. Such a context clarifies the nature of the relationship, linking together winged "creatures" on the stage (the seagulls, the cupids) with the postcards of Lola that fascinate Rath's students when they blow aside the feathers cunningly stapled over the thighs. And with this knowledge we come to a new understanding of the rage which overtakes the Professor when the finds his students so occupied. Siegfried Kracauer has likened these students to Nazis, calling them "born Hitler youths" for their treatment of Rath. Surely Wilhelm Reich, who wrote about sexual problems of German youth in *The Mass Psychology of Fascism,* would have had a better guide to a situation that is both the reverse of Kracauer's interpretation and more complex. Professor Rath is the agent of his student's oppression, the voice of society in the figure of the father. The struggle between the man and the boys in the first half of the film is vividly Oedipal. He forbids them their hearts' desire and threatens them with punishment. For a brief moment in the classroom, however, they rise up against him, they jubilantly resist, until another, stronger, father—the *Gymnasium* headmaster—intervenes and re-imposes an order that enforces submission and repression. Their rebellion quashed, the boys file out of the classroom and out of the film.

And Rath, who has himself given way to forbidden urges, who has regressed to an emotional state interdicted by the social order that has given him his status, who has let himself be patted and cooed over by Lola, enjoys only the transient elation of his wedding before suffering for himself—and thus cautioning each of us—the "consequences of his behavior." (It is interesting that, in the 1959 remake of the film, Professor Rath is eventually "saved" from Lola by the Headmaster himself, who leads the contrite and broken man out of the cabaret back into the streets of town and the paths of moral rectitude.)

But if Lola has continued to fascinate us over the years, it is because the film is not simply misogynist, and she is not simply a destructive female. Critics have returned again and again to details which are too closely linked to the fetishist side of the film to be ignored. From Jacques Spitz in 1930, who comments that Lola is so fated "to show her thighs that even in street clothes, her dress opens at every step,"[12] through Georges Sadoul's opinion of her "animal sexuality which [Sternberg] accentuated by spinning around her admirable thighs an artful play of garters and black lace,"[13] to Bosley Crowther's explicit description of "this insolent girl with the long legs, the bare thighs, the garters, the provocatively ornamented crotch,"[14] it is abundantly clear that the specific relationship of concealment and revelation rivets the attention. This suggests an effort, hardly understood even by these writers, to say what had been left unsaid so often: the reason that the fascinating power of *The Blue Angel* is so continuously compelling.

The commentary which englobes the film, reflecting and fixing its position in the discourse of society, includes in one place and another that famous still of Lola leaning back, grasping her knee, on the stage of the Blue Angel. This still is instructive in a course of distortion and censorship, and is significant for its relation to the fetish and to the insistent swell of the repressed text.

The photograph turns up, among other places, in Herman Weinberg's *Josef von Sternberg*.[15] Weinberg calls it the "most famous of all Sternberg's stills," which is undoubtedly true. I include Weinberg's use of it here in comparison with its appearance in John Baxter's book *The Cinema of Josef von Sternberg*.[16] In Baxter's illustration, the hand of some unknown censor has blacked out the area of the thighs where Lola's pants and garters are, blacked them out and attempted to make it look as if she is wearing a short skirt which casts a strong shadow over her legs and over the barrel on which she is sitting. These versions of the still occur together in *The Blue Angel* (New York: Simon and Schuster, 1968), the translation of the German version of the film; the censored print graces the cover that will be turned to public gaze, and the uncensored occurs among the illustrations (inside).

It should be obvious by now that this pose arrests the instant of fetishization, the instant before the child's glimpse of the female genital organ. Lola's leg tantalizes by almost revealing that anatomic feature. In other words, we are at the instant where it is still possible for the child to believe in the maternal phallus. But if the censor covers the indiscreetly revealed upper legs of Marlene Dietrich as Lola, he also imposes, in the blackness of his ink, his knowledge of what actually exists where the child desires the phallus: nothing, a blank, a gap, the kind of material lacuna which Freud himself came to understand as the formal signification of castration.

Yet censorship could not totally disguise in fact what it could not totally distort in art or in the dream. The concentration of phallic signifiers in this still, placed in a simultaneous relationship, drawn from the film where those relationships are worked out in a complex diachronic vector, defies complete distortion. The censor covers Lola's legs but leaves her in possession of the top hat. The gull still hangs from the wire, and those lascivious cherubs still flit about in the background; both of these function in the film as phallic signifiers, connected on the thread of meaning with the dove that flew out from under Rath's hat. Perhaps most awkward of all, however, for the censor's task is the direction of Guste's gaze, which ensures from inside the still what the eye outside the still will be drawn to.

Notes

1. Henri Lefevre, *The Sociology of Marx,* trans. Norbert Guterman (Harmondsworth: Penguin Books, 1972).

2. John Baxter, *The Cinema of Josef von Sternberg* (London: A. Zwemmer, 1971).

3. Herman Weinberg, *Josef von Sternberg* (New York: E. P. Dutton, 1967).

4. André Bazin, *What Is Cinema?* trans. Hugh Gray (Berkeley: University of California Press, 1971).

5. Pierre Bost, "Le Cinéma," *Les annales politiques et littéraires,* no. 96 (1 February), p. 130.

6. Ado Kyrou, *Amour, érotisme et cinéma,* ed. Eric Losfield (Paris: Le Terrain Vague, 1966).

7. Olivier Burgelin, in the special issue on Barthes of *L'Arc,* 1974.

8. Sigmund Freud, *Fetishism* (London: The Hogarth Press and The Institute of Pyschoanalysis, Vol. XXI, 1927 e).

9. *Ibid.*

10. *Ibid.*

11. Jacques Lacan, "Fonction et champ de la parole et du langage en psychanalyse" trans. Anthony Wilden in *The Language of the Self* (Baltimore: The Johns Hopkins Press, 1968).

12. Jacques Spitz, "L'Ange Bleu," *La Revue du cinéma,* October 1930, pp. 40–42.

13. Georges Sadoul, *Histoire du cinéma mondial des origines à nos jours* (Paris: Flammarion, 1949).

14. Bosley Crowther, *The Great Films: Fifty Golden Years of Motion Pictures* (New York: G. P. Putnam's Sons, 1967).

15. Weinberg, *op. cit.*

16. Baxter, *op. cit.*

THE VOICE IN THE CINEMA: THE ARTICULATION OF BODY AND SPACE

MARY ANN DOANE

Many critics have lamented the subordination of sound to image. The manifesto of Eisenstein, Pudovkin, and Alexandrov attacked just this point, calling for sound that was not merely redundant, whether it was synchronous or not. Certainly, film and television criticism tends to neglect sound, as Charles Altman has already observed. Mary Ann Doane takes a somewhat different approach. Rather than championing a neglected aspect of film, she attempts to describe how sound actually functions, together with image, to support a phantasm—an imaginary body that we attribute to or identify with characters or the film in its entirety. In the latter instance, the film offers itself as the possessor of unity, as an organic totality that sound and image both support. It is not that sound is necessary to achieve such unity—classical sculpture shows that it is not—but rather that the use of sound is limited to those manifestations that enhance the sense of unity and presence that gives the film "body." (The word appears between quotation marks because the physical body of an actor is quite different from the conceptual body of a film; Doane assumes that our response to both is essentially the same.)

Doane goes on to discuss the characteristics of the different manifestations of sound to which we are accustomed: lip synchronization; certification of a star's "presence" by the mechanical, minimally distorted reproduction of his or her voice, even when he or she is off screen; the spatial localization of speech so that voice and image appear to issue from the same geometric coordinates of the "diegesis" or fictional world; the special qualities and limitations of voice-over (as a disembodied voice of authority or knowledge) and voice-off (as testimony to the unseen presence of an actor's body); and interior monologue. These characteristics are discussed with admirable precision and parallel Edward Branigan's description of point-of-view figures in Part 6.

Doane concludes by stressing an important leitmotif in her argument: the psychoanalytic perspective that suggests particular, hypothetical meanings for image, body, and phantasm. She suggests that the pleasure of hearing, like the pleasure of seeing, is grounded in infantile experience that is formative of the subject. Although Doane includes an important caveat—"This is not simply to situate the experiences of infancy as the sole determinant in a system directly linking cause and effect but to acknowledge that the traces of archaic desires are never annihilated" —her primary argument stresses the determining function of infantile experience through a recasting of Lacan's mirror-phase into an acoustical reflection-phase. The voice of the father disrupts the presumed unity between child and mother, constituting that relationship as the "lost object of desire." The classic cinema, with its construction of a "fantasmatic body," seeks to reassure, to offer the pleasure of presence and plenitude that a more radical cinema might contest.

This description and this proposal leave the other determinants of acoustic pleasure unclear. The other determinants pertain to the noninfantile experiences of social reality and aesthetic order. Although Doane is concerned that the limited use of sound in classic cinema "conceals the work" of the text and thereby performs an ideological as well as a psychoanalytic function, the ideological overtones of her argument, which are both Marxist and feminist, stand in need of further elaboration. Her article's turn toward a psychoanalytic theory of acoustic pleasure is only one of several possible explanatory theories. Bringing several of these theories together would serve to advance us along a line of inquiry opened up by this pioneering examination of sound in the light of psychoanalytic theory.

SYNCHRONIZATION

The silent film is certainly understood, at least retrospectively and even (it is arguable) in its time, as incomplete, as lacking speech. The stylized gestures of the silent cinema, its heavy pantomime, have been defined as a form of compensation for that lack. Hugo Münsterberg wrote, in 1916, "To the actor of the moving pictures . . . the temptation offers itself to overcome the deficiency [the absence of "words and the modulation of the voice"] by a heightening of the gestures and of the facial play, with the result that the emotional expression becomes exaggerated."[1] The absent voice re-emerges in gestures and the contortions of the face—it is spread over the body of the actor. The uncanny effect of the silent film in the era of sound is in part linked to the separation, by means of intertitles, of an actor's speech from the image of his/her body.

Consideration of sound in the cinema (in its most historically and institutionally privileged form—that of dialogue or the use of the voice) engenders a network of metaphors whose nodal point appears to be the body. One may readily respond that this is only "natural"—who can conceive of a voice without a body?[2] However, the body reconstituted by the technology and practices of the cinema is a *fantasmatic* body, which offers a support as well as a point of identification for the subject addressed by the film. The purpose of this essay is simply to trace some of the ways in which this fantasmatic body acts as a pivot for certain cinematic practices of representation and authorizes and sustains a limited number of relationships between voice and image.

The attributes of this fantasmatic body are first and foremost unity (through the emphasis on a coherence of the senses) and presence-to-itself. The addition of sound to the cinema introduces the possibility of re-presenting a fuller (and organically unified) body, and of confirming the status of speech as an individual property right. The potential number and kinds of articulations between sound and image are reduced by the very name attached to the new heterogeneous medium—the "talkie." Histories of the cinema ascribe the stress on synchronization to a "public demand": "the public, fascinated by the novelty, wanting to be sure they were hearing what they saw, would have felt that a trick was being played on them if they were not shown the words coming from the lips of the actors."[3] In Lewis Jacobs's account, this fear on the part of the audience of being "cheated" is one of the factors which initially limits the deployment of sonorous material (as well as the mobility of the camera). From this perspective, the use of voice-off or voice-over must be a late acquisition, attempted only after a certain "breaking-in" period during which the novelty of the sound film was allowed to wear itself out. But, whatever the fascination of the new medium (or whatever meaning is attached to it by retrospective readings of its prehistory), there is no doubt that synchronization (in the form of "lip-sync") has played a major role in the dominant narrative cinema. Technology standardizes the relation through the development of the synchronizer, the Moviola, the flatbed editing table. The mixing apparatus allows a greater control over the establishment of relationships between dialogue, music, and sound effects, and, in practice, the level of the dialogue generally determines the levels of sound effects and music.[4] Despite a number of experiments with other types of sound/image relationships (those of Clair, Lang, Vigo, and, more recently, Godard, Straub, and Duras), synchronous dialogue remains the dominant form of sonorous representation in the cinema.

Yet, even when asynchronous or "wild" sound is utilized, the fantasmatic body's attribute of unity is not lost. It is simply displaced—the body *in* the film becomes the body *of* the film. Its senses work in tandem, for the combination of sound and image is described in terms of "totality" and the "organic."[5] Sound carries with it the potential risk of exposing the material heterogeneity of the medium; attempts to contain that risk surface in the language of the ideology of organic unity. In the discourse of technicians, sound is "married" to the image, and, as one sound engineer puts it in an article on postsynchronization, "one of the basic goals of the motion picture industry is to make the screen look alive in the eyes of the audience."[6]

Concomitant with the demand for a life-like representation is the desire for "presence," a concept which is not specific to the cinematic soundtrack but which acts as a standard to measure quality in the sound-recording industry as a whole. The term "presence" offers a certain legitimacy to the wish for pure reproduction and becomes a selling point in the construction of sound as a commodity. The television commercial asks whether we can "tell the difference" between the voice of Ella Fitzgerald and that of Memorex (and since our representative in the commercial—the ardent fan—cannot, the only conclusion to be drawn is that owning a Memorex tape is equivalent to having Ella in your living room). Technical advances in sound recording (such as the Dolby system) are aimed at diminishing the noise of the system, concealing the work of the apparatus, and thus reducing the distance perceived between the object and its representation. The maneuvers of the sound-recording industry offer evidence which supports Walter Benjamin's thesis linking mechanical reproduction as a phenomenon with contemporary society's destruction of the "aura" (which he defines as "the unique phenomenon of a distance, however close it may be"[7]). According to Benjamin,

[the] contemporary decay of the aura . . . rests on two circumstances, both of which are related to the increasing significance of the masses in contemporary life. Namely, the desire of contemporary masses to bring things 'closer' spatially and humanly, which is just as ardent as their bent toward overcoming the uniqueness of every reality by accepting its reproduction.[8]

Nevertheless, while the desire to bring things closer is certainly exploited in making sound marketable, the qualities of uniqueness and authenticity are not sacrificed—it is not any voice which the tape brings to the consumer but the voice of Ella Fitzgerald. The voice is not detachable from a body, which is quite specific—that of the star. In the cinema, cult value and the "aura" resurface in the star system. In 1930 a writer feels the need to assure audiences that postsynchronization as a technique does not necessarily entail substituting an alien voice for a "real" voice, that the industry does not condone a mismatching of voices and bodies.[9] Thus, the voice serves as a support for the spectator's recognition and his/her identification of, as well as with, the star.

Just as the voice must be anchored by a given body, the body must be anchored in a given space. The fantasmatic visual space which the film constructs is supplemented by techniques designed to spatialize the voice, to localize it, give it depth, and thus lend to the characters the consistency of the real. A concern for room tone, reverberation characteristics, and sound perspective manifests a desire to re-create, as one sound editor describes it, "the bouquet that surrounds the words, the presence on the voice, the way it fits in with the physical environment."[10] The dangers of post-synchronization and looping stem from the fact that the voice is disengaged from its "proper" space (the space conveyed by the visual image), and the credibility of that voice depends upon the technician's ability to return it to the site of its origin. Failure to do so risks exposure of the fact that looping is "narration masking as dialogue."[11] Dialogue is defined therefore, not simply in terms of the establishment of an I-you relationship, but as the necessary spatializing of that relationship. Techniques of sound recording tend to confirm the cinema's function as a *mise-en-scène* of bodies.

VOICE-OFF AND VOICE-OVER

The spatial dimension which monophonic sound is capable of simulating is that of depth—the apparent source of the sound may be moved forward or backward, but the lateral dimension is lacking due to the fact that there is no sideways spread of reverberation or of ambient noise.[12] Nevertheless, sound/image relationships established in the narrative film work to suggest that sound does, indeed, issue from that other dimension. In film theory, this work to provide the effect of a lateral dimension receives recognition in the term "voice-off." "Voice-off" refers to instances in which we hear the voice of a character who is not visible within the frame. Yet the film establishes, by means of previous shots or other contextual determinants, the character's "presence" in the space of the scene, in the diegesis. He/she is "just over there," "just beyond the frame-line," in a space which "exists" but which the camera does not choose to show. The traditional use of voice-off constitutes a denial of the frame as a limit and an affirmation of the unity and homogeneity of the depicted space.

Because it is defined in terms of what is visible within the rectangular space of the screen, the term "voice-off" has been subject to some dispute. Claude Bailblé, for instance, argues that a voice-off must always be a "voice-in" because the literal source of the sound in the theater is always the speaker placed behind the screen.[13] Yet, the space to which the term refers is not that of the theater but the fictional space of the diegesis. Nevertheless, the use of the term is based on the requirement that the two spaces coincide, "overlap" to a certain extent. For the screen limits what *can be seen* of the diegesis (there is always "more" of the diegesis than the camera can cover at any one time). The placement of the speaker behind the screen simply confirms the fact that the cinematic apparatus is designed to promote the impression of a homogeneous space—the senses of the fantasmatic body cannot be split. The screen is the space where the image is deployed while the theater as a whole is the space of the deployment of sound. Yet, the screen is given precedence over the acoustical space of the theater—the screen is posited as the site of the spectacle's unfolding and all sounds must emanate from it. (Bailblé asks, "What would be, in effect, a voice-off which came from the back of the theater? Poor little screen . . ."[14]—in other words, its effect would be precisely to diminish the epistemological power of the image, to reveal its limitations.)

The hierarchical placement of the visible above the audible, according to Christian Metz, is not specific to the cinema but a more general cultural production.[15] And the term voice-off merely acts as a reconfirmation of that hierarchy. For it only appears to describe a sound—what it really refers to is the visibility (or lack of visibility) of the source of the sound. Metz argues that sound is never "off." While a visual element specified as "off" actually lacks visibility, a "sound-off" is always audible.

Despite the fact that Metz's argument is valid and we tend to repeat on the level of theory the industry's subordination of sound to image, the term voice-off does name a particular relationship between sound and image—a relationship which has been extremely important historically in diverse film practices. While it is true that sound is almost always discussed with reference to the image, it does not necessarily follow that this automatically makes sound subordinate. From another perspective, it is doubtful that any image (in the sound film) is uninflected by sound. This is crucially so, given the fact that in the dominant narrative cinema, sound extends from beginning to end of the film—sound is never absent (silence is, at the least, room tone). In fact, the lack of any sound whatsoever is taboo in the editing of the soundtrack.

The point is not that we "need" terms with which to describe, honor, and acknowledge the autonomy of a particular sensory material, but that we must attempt to think the heterogeneity of the cinema. This might be done more fruitfully by means of the concept of space than through the unities of sound and image. In the cinematic situation, three types of space are put into play:

(1) The space of the diegesis. This space has no physical limits, it is not contained or measurable. It is a virtual space constructed by the film and is delineated as having both audible and visible traits (as well as implications that its objects can be touched, smelled, and tasted).

(2) The visible space of the screen as receptor of the image. It is measurable and "contains" the visible signifiers of the film. Strictly speaking, the screen is not audible although the placement of the speaker behind the screen constructs that illusion.

(3) The acoustical space of the theater or auditorium. It might be argued that this space is also visible, but the film cannot visually activate signifiers in this space unless a second projector is used. Again, despite the fact that the speaker is behind the screen and therefore sound appears to be emanating from a focused point, sound is not "framed" in the same way as the image. In a sense, it *envelops* the spectator.

All of these are spaces *for the spectator*, but the first is the only space which the characters of the fiction film can acknowledge (for the characters there are no voices-off). Different cinematic modes—documentary, narrative, avant-garde —establish different relationships among the three spaces. The classical narrative film, for instance, works to deny the existence of the last two spaces in order to buttress the credibility (legitimacy) of the first space. If a character looks at and speaks to the spectator, this constitutes an acknowledgment that the character is seen and heard in a radically different space and is therefore generally read as transgressive.

Nothing unites the three spaces but the signifying practice of the film itself together with the institutionalization of the theater as a type of meta-space which binds together the three spaces, as the *place* where a unified cinematic discourse unfolds. The cinematic institution's stake in this process of unification is apparent. Instances of voice-off in the classical film are particularly interesting examples of the way in which the three spaces undergo an elaborate imbrication. For the phenomenon of the voice-off cannot be understood outside of a consideration of the relationships established between the diegesis, the visible space of the screen, *and* the acoustical space of the theater. The place in which the signifier manifests itself is the acoustical space of the theater, but this is the space with which it is least concerned. The voice-off deepens the diegesis, gives it an extent which exceeds that of the image, and thus supports the claim that there is a space in the fictional world which the camera does not register. In its own way, it *accounts for* lost space. The voice-off is a sound which is first and foremost in the service of the film's construction of space and only indirectly in the service of the image. It validates both what the screen reveals of the diegesis and what it conceals.

Nevertheless, the use of the voice-off always entails a risk—that of exposing the material heterogeneity of the cinema. Synchronous sound masks the problem, and this at least partially explains its dominance. But the more interesting question, perhaps, is: how can the classical film allow the representation of a voice whose source is not simultaneously represented? As soon as the sound is detached from its source, no longer anchored by a represented body, its potential work as a signifier is revealed. There is always something uncanny about a voice which emanates from a source outside the frame. However, as Pascal Bonitzer points out, the narrative film exploits the marginal anxiety connected with the voice-off by incorporating its disturbing effects within the dramatic framework. Thus, the function of the voice-off (as well as that of the voice-over) becomes extremely important in *film noir*. Bonitzer takes as his example *Kiss Me Deadly*, a *film noir* in which the villain remains out of frame until the last sequences of the film. Maintaining him outside of the field of vision "gives to his sententious voice, swollen by mythological comparisons, a greater power of disturbing, the scope of an oracle—dark prophet of the end of the world. And, in spite of that, his voice is submitted to the destiny of the body . . . a shot, he falls—and with him in ridicule, his discourse with its prophetic accents."[16]

The voice-off is always "submitted to the destiny of the body" because it *belongs* to a character who is confined to the space of the diegesis, if not to the visible space of the screen. Its efficacity rests on the knowledge that the character can easily be made visible by a slight reframing which would re-unite the voice and its source. The body acts as an invisible support for the use of both the voice-over during a flashback and the interior monologue as well. Although the voice-over in a flashback effects a temporal dislocation of the voice with respect to the body, the voice is frequently returned to the body as a form of narrative closure. Furthermore, the voice-over very often simply initiates the story and is subsequently superseded by synchronous dialogue, allowing the diegesis to "speak for itself." In *Sunset Boulevard* the convention is taken to its limits: the voice-over narration is, indeed, linked to a body (that of the hero), but it is the body of a dead man.

In the interior monologue, on the other hand, the voice and the body are represented simultaneously, but the voice, far from being an extension of that body, manifests its inner lining. The voice displays what is inaccessible to the image, what exceeds the visible: the "inner life" of the character. The voice here is the privileged mark of interiority, turning the body "inside-out."

The voice-over commentary in the documentary, unlike the voice-off, the voice-over during a flashback, or the interior monologue, is, in effect, a *disembodied* voice. While the latter three voices work to affirm the homogeneity and dominance of diegetic space, the voice-over commentary is necessarily presented as outside of that space. It is its radical otherness with respect to the diegesis which endows this voice with a certain authority. As a form of direct address, it speaks without mediation to the audience, by-passing the "characters" and establishing a complicity between itself and the spectator—together they understand and thus *place* the image. It is precisely because the voice is not localizable, because it cannot be yoked to a body, that it is capable of interpreting the image, producing its truth. Disembodied, lacking any specification in space or time, the voice-over is, as Bonitzer points out, beyond criticism—it censors the questions "Who is speaking?" "Where?" "In what time?" and "For whom?"

This is not, one suspects, without ideological implications. The first of these implications is that the voice-off[17] represents a power, that of disposing of the image and of what it reflects, from a space absolutely *other* with respect to that inscribed in the image-track. *Absolutely other and absolutely indeterminant.* Because it rises from the field of the Other, the voice-off is assumed to know: this is the essence of its power. . . . The power of the voice is a stolen power, a usurpation.[18]

In the history of the documentary, this voice has been for the most part that of the male, and its power resides in the possession of knowledge and in the privileged, unquestioned activity of interpretation. This function of the voice-over has been appropriated by the television documentary and television news programs, in which sound carries the burden of "information" while the impoverished image simply fills the screen. Even when the major voice is explicitly linked with a body (that of the anchorman in television news), this body, in its turn, is situated in the non-space of the studio. In film, on the other hand, the voice-over is quite often dissociated from any specific figure. The guarantee of knowledge, in such a system, lies in its irreducibility to the spatio-temporal limitations of the body.

THE PLEASURE OF HEARING

The means by which sound is deployed in the cinema inplicate the spectator in a particular textual problematic—they establish certain conditions for understanding which obtain in the "intersubjective relation" between film and spectator. The voice-over commentary and, differently, the interior monologue and voice-over flashback speak more or less *directly to* the spectator, constituting him/her as an empty space to be "filled" with knowledge about events, character psychology, etc. More frequently, in the fiction film, the use of synchronous dialogue and the voice-off presuppose a spectator who *overhears* and, overhearing, is unheard and unseen himself. This activity with respect to the soundtrack is not unlike the voyeurism often exploited by the cinematic image. In any event, the use of the voice in the cinema appeals to the spectator's desire to hear, or what Lacan refers to as the invocatory drive.

In what does the pleasure of hearing consist? Beyond the added effect of "realism" which sound gives to the cinema, beyond its supplement of meaning anchored by intelligible dialogue, what is the specificity of the pleasure of hearing a voice with its elements escaping a strictly verbal codification—volume, rhythm, timbre, pitch? Psychoanalysis situates pleasure in the divergence between the present experience and the memory of satisfaction: "Between a (more or less inaccessible) memory and a very precise (and localizable) immediacy of perception is opened the gap where pleasure is produced."[19] Memories of the first experiences of the voice, of the hallucinatory satisfaction it offered, circumscribe the pleasure of hearing and ground its relation to the fantasmatic body. This is not simply to situate the experiences of infancy as the sole determinant in a system directly linking cause and effect but to acknowledge that the traces of archaic desires are never annihilated. According to Guy Rosolato, it is "the organization of the fantasm itself which implies a permanence, an insistence of the recall to the origin."[20]

Space, for the child, is defined initially in terms of the audible, not the visible: "It is only in a second phase that the organization of visual space insures the perception of the object as *external*" (p. 80). The first differences are traced along the axis of sound: the voice of the mother, the voice of the father. Furthermore, the voice has a greater command over space than the look—one can hear around corners, through walls. Thus, for the child the voice, even before language, is the instrument of demand. In the construction/hallucination of space and the body's relation to that space, the voice plays a major role. In comparison with sight, as Rosolato points out, the voice is reversible: sound is simultaneously emitted and heard by the subject himself. As opposed to the situation in seeing, it is as if "an 'acoustical' mirror were always in function. Thus, the images of entry and exit relative to the body are intimately articulated. They can therefore be confounded, inverted, favored one over the other" (p. 79). Because one can hear sounds behind oneself as well as those with sources *inside* the body (sounds of digestion, circulation, respiration, etc.), two sets of terms are placed in opposition: exterior/front/ sight and interior/back/hearing. And "hallucinations are determined by an imaginary structuration of the body according to these oppositions" (p. 80). The voice appears to lend itself to hallucination, in particular the hallucination of power over space effected by an extension or restructuration of the body. Thus, as Lacan points out, our mass media and our technology, as mechanical extensions of the body, result in "planeterizing" or "even stratospherizing" the voice.[21]

The voice also traces the forms of unity and separation *between* bodies. The mother's soothing voice, in a particular cultural context, is a major component of the "sonorous envelope" which surrounds the child and is the first model of auditory pleasure. An image of corporeal unity is derived from the realization that the production of sound by the voice and its audition coincide. The imaginary fusion of the child with the mother is supported by the recognition of common traits characterizing the different voices and, more particularly, of their potential for harmony. According to Rosolato, the voice in music makes appeal to the nostalgia for such an imaginary cohesion, for a "veritable incantation" of bodies.

The harmonic and polyphonic unfolding in music can be understood as a succession of tensions and releases, of unifications and divergences between parts which are gradually stacked, opposed in successive chords only to be resolved ultimately into their simplest unity. It is therefore the entire dramatization of separated bodies and their reunion which harmony supports. (p. 82)

Yet, the imaginary unity associated with the earliest experience of the voice is broken by the premonition of difference, division, effected by the intervention of the father whose voice, engaging the desire of the mother, acts as the agent of separation and constitutes the voice of the mother as the irretrievably lost object of desire. The voice in this instance, far from being the narcissistic measure of harmony, is the voice of interdiction. The voice thus understood is an interface of imaginary and symbolic, pulling at once toward the signifying organization of language and its reduction of the range of vocal sounds to those it binds and codifies, and toward original and imaginary attachments, "representable in the fantasm by the body, or by the corporeal mother, the child at her breast" (p. 86).

At the cinema, the sonorous envelope provided by the theatrical space together with techniques employed in the construction of the soundtrack work to sustain the narcissistic pleasure derived from the image of a certain unity, cohesion, and, hence, an identity grounded by the spectator's fantasmatic relation to his/her own body. The aural illusion of position constructed by the approximation of sound perspective and by techniques which spatialize the voice and endow it with "presence" guarantees the singularity and stability of a point of audition, thus holding at bay the potential trauma of dispersal, dismemberment, difference. The subordination of the voice to the screen as the site of the spectacle's unfolding makes vision and hearing work together in manufacturing the "hallucination" of a fully sensory world. Nevertheless, the recorded voice, which presupposes a certain depth, is in contradiction with the flatness of the two-dimensional image. Eisler and Adorno note that the spectator is always aware of this divergence, of the inevitable gap between the represented body and its voice. And for Eisler and Adorno this partially explains the function of film music: first used in the exhibition of silent films to conceal the noise of the projector (to hide from the spectator the "uncanny" fact that his/her pleasure is mediated by a machine), music in the "talkie" takes on the task of closing the gap between voice and body.[22]

If this imaginary harmony is to be maintained, however, the potential aggressivity of the voice (as the instrument of interdiction and the material support of the symptom—hearing voices—in paranoia) must be attenuated. The formal perfection of sound recording in the cinema consists in reducing not only the noise of the apparatus but any "grating" noise which is not "pleasing to the ear." On another level, the aggressivity of the filmic voice can be linked to the fact that sound is directed *at* the spectator—necessitating, in the fiction film, its deflection through dialogue (which the spectator is given only obliquely, to overhear) and, in the documentary, its mediation by the content of the image. In the documentary, however, the voice-over has come to represent an authority and an aggressivity which can no longer be sustained—thus, as Bonitzer points out, the proliferation of new documentaries which reject the absolute of the voice-over and, instead, claim to establish a democratic system, "letting the event speak for itself." Yet, what this type of film actually promotes is the illusion that reality speaks and is not spoken, that the film is not a constructed discourse. In effecting an "impression of knowledge," a knowledge which is given and not produced, the film conceals its own work and posits itself as a voice without a subject.[23] The voice is even more powerful in silence. The solution, then, is not to banish the voice but to construct *another* politics.

THE POLITICS OF THE VOICE

The cinema presents a spectacle composed of disparate elements—images, voices, sound effects, music, writing—which the *mise-en-scène,* in its broadest sense, organizes and aims at the body of the spectator, sensory receptacle of the various stimuli.   This is why Lyotard refers to classical *mise-en-scène* (in both the theater and the cinema) as a kind of somatography, or inscription on the body:

the mise-en-scène turns written signifiers into speech, song, and movements executed by bodies capable of moving, singing speaking; and this transcription is intended for other living bodies—the spectators—capable of being moved by these songs, movements, and words. It is this transcribing on and for bodies, considered as multi-sensory potentialities, which is the work characteristic of the mise-en-scène. Its elementary unity is polyesthetic like the human body: capacity to see, to hear, to touch, to move. . . . The idea of performance . . . even if it remains vague, seems linked to the idea of inscription on the body.[24]

Classical *mise-en-scène* has a stake in perpetuating the image of unity and identity sustained by this body and in staving off the fear of fragmentation. The different sensory elements work in collusion and this work denies the material heterogeneity of the "body" of the film. All of the signifying strategies for the deployment of the voice discussed earlier are linked with such homogenizing effects: synchronization binds the voice to a body in a unity whose immediacy can only be perceived as a given; the voice-off holds the spectacle to a space—extended but still coherent; and the voice-over commentary places the image by endowing it with a clear intelligibility. In all of this, what must be guarded is a certain "oneness."

This "oneness" is the mark of a mastery and a control and manifests itself most explicitly in the tendency to confine the voice-over commentary in a documentary to a single voice. For, according to Bonitzer, "when one divides that voice or, what amounts to the same thing, multiplies it, the system and its effects change. Off screen space ceases to be that place of reserve and interiority of the voice."[25] This entails not only or not merely increasing the number of voices but radically changing their relationship to the image, effecting a disjunction between sound and meaning, emphasizing what Barthes refers to as the "grain" of the voice[26] over and against its expressivity or power of representation. In the contemporary cinema, the names which immediately come to mind are those of Godard (who, even in an early film such as *Vivre Sa Vie* which relies heavily on synchronous sound, resists the homogenizing effects of the traditional use of voice-off by means of a resolute avoidance of the shot/reverse-shot structure--the camera quickly panning to keep the person talking *in frame*) and Straub (for whom the voice and sound in general become the marks of a non-progressive duration). The image of the body thus obtained is not one of imaginary cohesion but of dispersal, division, fragmentation. Lyotard speaks of the "post-modernist" text which escapes the closure of representation by creating its own addressee, "a disconcerted body, invited to stretch its sensory capacities beyond measure."[27] Such an approach, which takes off from a different image of the body, can be understood as an attempt to forge a politics based on an erotics. Bonitzer uses the two terms interchangeably, claiming that the scission of the voice can contribute to the definition of "another politics (or erotics) of the voice-off."[28] The problem is whether such an erotics, bound to the image of an extended or fragmented body and strongly linked with a particular signifying material, can found a political theory or practice.

There are three major difficulties with the notion of a political erotics of the voice. The first is that, relying as it does on the idea of expanding the range or re-defining the power of the senses, and opposing itself to meaning, a political erotics is easily recuperable as a form of romanticism or as a mysticism that effectively skirts problems of epistemology, lodging itself firmly in a mind/body dualism. Secondly, the overemphasis upon the isolated effectivity of a single signifying material--the voice--risks a crude materialism wherein the physical properties of the medium have the inherent and final power of determining its reading. As Paul Willemen points out, a concentration upon the specificities of the various "technico-sensorial unities" of the cinema often precludes a recognition that the materiality of the signifier is a "second order factor" (with respect to language understood broadly as symbolic system) and tends to reduce a complex heterogeneity to a mere combination of different materials.[29] Yet, a film is not a simple juxtaposition of sensory elements but a discourse, an enunciation. This is not to imply that the isolation and investigation of a single signifying material such as the voice is a fruitless endeavor but that the establishment of a direct connection between the voice and politics is fraught with difficulties.

Thirdly, the notion of a political erotics of the voice is particularly problematic from a feminist perspective. Over and against the theorization of the look as phallic, as the support of voyeurism and fetishism (a drive and a defense which, in Freud, are linked explicitly with the male),[30] the voice appears to lend itself readily as an alternative to the image, as a potentially viable means whereby the woman can "make herself heard." Luce Irigaray, for instance, claims that patriarchal culture has a heavier investment in seeing than in hearing.[31]   Bonitzer, in the context of defining a political erotics, speaks of "returning the voice to women" as a major component. Nevertheless, it must be remembered that, while psychoanalysis delineates a pre-oedipal scenario in which the voice of the mother dominates, the voice, in psychoanalysis, is also the instrument of interdiction, of the patriarchal order. And to mark the voice as an isolated haven within patriarchy, or as having an essential relation to the woman, is to invoke the spectre of feminine specificity, always recuperable as another form of "otherness." A political erotics which posits a new fantasmatic, which relies on images of an "extended" sensory body, is inevitably caught in the double bind which feminism always seems to confront: on the one hand, there is a danger in grounding a politics on a conceptualization of the body because the body has always been *the* site of women's oppression, posited as the final and undeniable guarantee of a difference and a lack; but, on the other hand, there is a potential gain as well--it is precisely because the body has been a major site of oppression that perhaps it must be the site of the battle to be waged. The supreme achievement of patriarchal ideology is that it has no outside.

In light of the three difficulties outlined above, however, it would seem unwise to base any politics of the voice *solely* on an erotics. The value of thinking the deployment of the voice in the cinema by means of its relation to the body (that of the character, that of the spectator) lies in an understanding of the cinema, from the perspective of a topology, as a series of spaces including that of the spectator--spaces which are often hierarchized or masked, one by the other, in the service of a representational illusion. Nevertheless, whatever the arrangement or interpenetration of the various spaces, they constitute a *place* where signification intrudes. The various techniques and strategies for deployment of the voice contribute heavily to the definition of the form that "place" takes.

Notes

1. Hugo Münsterberg, *The Film: A Psychological Study* (New York: Dover Publications, 1970), p. 49.

2. Two kinds of "voices without bodies" immediately suggest themselves—one theological, the other scientific (two poles which, it might be added, are not ideologically unrelated): (1) the voice of God incarnated in the Word; (2) the artificial voice of a computer. Neither seems to be capable of representation outside of a certain anthropomorphism, however. God is pictured, in fact, as having a quite specific body—that of a male patriarchal figure. *Star Wars* and *Battlestar Galactica* illustrate the tendencies toward anthropomorphism in the depiction of computers. In the latter, even a computer (named Cora) deprived of mobility and the simulacrum of a human form is given a voice which is designed to evoke the image of a sensual female body.

3. Lewis Jacobs, *The Rise of the American Film: A Critical History* (New York: Teachers College Press, 1968), p. 435.

4. For a more detailed discussion of this hierarchy of sounds and of other relevant techniques in the construction of the soundtrack see M. Doane, "Ideology and the Practices of Sound Editing and Mixing," paper delivered at the Milwaukee Conference on the Cinematic Apparatus, February 1978, in *Conference Proceedings* (Fall 1979).

5. *Ibid.*

6. W. A. Pozner, "Synchronization Techniques," *Journal of the Society of Motion Picture Engineers* 47, no. 3 (September 1946): 191.

7. Walter Benjamin, "The Work of Art in the Age of Mechanical Reproduction," in *Illuminations,* ed. Hannah Arendt, trans. Harry Zohn (New York: Schocken Books, 1969), p. 222.

8. *Ibid.,* p. 223.

9. George Lewin, "Dubbing and Its Relation to Sound Picture Production," *Journal of the Society of Motion Picture Engineers* 16, no. 1 (January 1931): 48.

10. Walter Murch, "The Art of the Sound Editor: An Interview with Walter Murch," interview by Larry Sturhahn, *Filmmaker's Newsletter* 8, no. 2 (December 1974): 23.

11. *Ibid.*

12. Stereo reduces this problem but does not solve it—the range of perspective effects is still limited. Much of the discussion which follows is based on the use of monophonic sound but also has implications for stereo. In both mono and stereo, for instance, the location of the speakers is designed to ensure that the audience hears sound "which is roughly coincident with the image." See Alec Nisbett, *The Technique of the Sound Studio* (New York: Focal Press Limited, 1972), pp. 530, 532.

13. C. Bailblé, "Programmation de l'écoute (2)," *Cahiers du cinéma,* no. 293 (October 1978), p. 9. My translation.

14. *Ibid.* My translation.

15. C. Metz, "Le perçu et le nommé," in *Essais sémiotiques* (Paris: Éditions Klincksieck, 1977), pp. 153–59.

16. Pascal Bonitzer, "Les silences de la voix," *Cahiers du Cinéma,* no. 256 (February–March 1975), p. 25. My translation.

17. Bonitzer uses the term "voice-off" in a general sense which includes both voice-off and voice-over, but here he is referring specifically to voice-over commentary.

18. Bonitzer, p. 26. My translation.

19. Serge Leclaire, *Démasquer le réel,* p. 64, quoted in C. Bailblé, "Programmation de l'écoute (3)," *Cahiers du Cinéma,* no. 297 (February 1979), p. 46. My translation.

20. Guy Rosolato, "La voix: entre corps et langage," *Revue française de psychanalyse,* no. 38 (January 1974), p. 83. My translation. My discussion of the pleasure of hearing relies heavily on the work of Rosolato. Further references to this article will appear in parentheses in the text.

21. Jacques Lacan, *The Four Fundamental Concepts of Psycho-analysis,* ed. Jacques-Alain Miller, trans. Alan Sheridan (London: The Hogarth Press and the Institute of Psychoanalysis, 1977), p. 274.

22. Hanns Eisler, *Composing for the Films* (New York: Oxford University Press, 1947), pp. 75–77.

23. Bonitzer, pp. 23–24.

24. Jean-François Lyotard, "The Unconscious as Mise-en-scène," in *Performance in Postmodern Culture,* ed. Michel Benamou and Charles Caramello (Madison: Coda Press, Inc., 1977), p.88.

25. Bonitzer, p. 31.

26. See Roland Barthes, "The Grain of the Voice," in *Image-Music-Text,* trans. Stephen Heath (New York: Hill and Wang, 1977), pp. 179–189.

27. Lyotard, p. 96.

28. Bonitzer, p. 31.

29. Paul Willemen, "Cinema Thoughts," paper delivered at Milwaukee Conference on Cinema and Language, March 1979, pp. 12 and 3.

30. See Laura Mulvey, "Visual Pleasure and Narrative Cinema," *Screen.* 16 (Autumn 1975), 6–18 and Stephen Heath, "Sexual Difference and Representation," *Screen,* 19 (Autumn 1978), 51–112.

31. For a fuller discussion of the relationship some feminists establish between the voice and the woman see Heath, "Sexual Difference," 83–84.

THE AVANT-GARDE AND ITS IMAGINARY

CONSTANCE PENLEY

Recent semiotic work is highly critical of dominant film practice, which, among other things, conceals its own work, presents discours *as* histoire, *and produces relations of voyeurism and fetishism within an imaginary domain structured to reassure the male viewer and underwrite the ideologies of patriarchy and capitalism — no small indictment. Thus, it comes as no surprise that a search for alternative models has ensued, in which what Colin MacCabe called "moments of*

*subversion" in classical narratives would expand into "strategies of subversion."
The works of Brecht, Godard, Oshima, and the avant-garde are often cited in this
context, and this is where Constance Penley's article makes a valuable
contribution.*

*Penley asks what insight into the political and formal possibilities of avant-
garde practice we can gain from recent theoretical developments. She summarizes
the work of Malcolm LeGrice and Peter Gidal, two important figures in the
English Co-op filmmaking movement, and then compares their political and
formal agendas with the theoretical arguments of Christian Metz, Thierry
Kuntzel, Raymond Bellour, Jean-Louis Baudry, and Jacques Lacan. In doing so,
she offers some dense but comprehensive summaries of considerable value
regarding important recent work by these writers. Even more pertinent is her
systematic critique of LeGrice and Gidal as insufficiently aware of the
fundamentally psychical nature of the cinematic apparatus; of course, she
assumes that the French psychoanalytic perspective is essentially correct—a
large assumption to be sure. Instead of stopping there, however, Penley proceeds
to suggest how a more appropriate "interrogation" of the cinematic apparatus
can be based on an emphasis on verbal commentary and a representational
impulse at the limits and margins of narrative, not on the idealism of abstract,
nonrepresentational materialist or reflexive practices championed by LeGrice and
Gidal. She associates the preferred road with Godard, Straub and Huillet, Mulvey
and Wollen, Akerman, Duras, Rainer, Mangolte, and Raynal, but she does not
examine the relationship between its principles and strategies and those of
psychoanalytic semiotics closely enough to demonstrate exactly how the pitfalls
that LeGrice and Gidal fail to escape can be avoided. However, Penley's
summaries and bibliography provide a useful starting point for such an analysis,
which might very well prove extremely instructive in the search for models of film
practice that innovate both politically and formally.*

•

Recent metapsychological approaches to film and cinema permit useful precisions
in thinking the relation of avant-garde strategies to a feminist filmmaking practice. Any juxtaposition of an avant-garde practice and an avowedly political practice is, and has been historically, problematic. We would like to look at some of
the presuppositions of a contemporary avant-garde from the point of view of
these recent metapsychological studies because we think they can illuminate
some of the difficulties often found in the juxtaposition of political and avant-
garde practice. We have a contemporary example of a provocative attempt to
bring these two practices together in the English Co-op filmmaking movement,
often described by its theoretician-filmmakers as a 'structural/materialist' cinema
aiming towards a 'politics of perception'. This movement sees its political efficacy in offering a cinematic experience completely outside of and against the
strategies and effects of dominant classical cinema, i. e., an identification with the
characters and diegesis capable of manipulating the spectator in ways which leave
the spectator unconscious of her or his own experiences in watching the film.

Christian Metz offers the hypothesis that the cinematic signifier is by its very nature linked to the imaginary and also argues that the cinematic institution describes a fetishistic structuration at every level—from the frame of the image to its socio-historical functioning. Taking the Freudian notion of 'dream-work' to an analysis of the progressive engenderment of the filmic text, Thierry Kuntzel has shown the operations of dream processes like condensation and displacement at work in the spectator's unconscious reading of the film—the 'other film' which takes place in the mind of the spectator. Jean-Louis Baudry proposes that the entire cinematographic apparatus is taken in a wish inherent to the human psyche whose roots can already be seen in the time of Plato, a wish for a return to that 'other scene', a movement which creates 'a fantasmatization of the subject' by simulating a subject-effect which is an artificial state of regression. The recent work of Raymond Bellour on cinema and hypnosis is an attempt to circumscribe filmic fascination/identification by analyzing the ways in which the film and the apparatus work together to organize stimuli of a hypnotic nature. Bellour also uses the concept of hypnosis as historical predecessor of both cinema and psychoanalysis to open a discussion of their collusion on a particularly 20th-century concern: the relation of subject to image, of the subject as a function *of* image.[1]

Given these recent theses on the psychical roots of the cinematic institution, the degree of 'imaginariness' of the cinematic signifier, and the levels of regression and identification involved in the spectator/screen relation, what is the place of this modernist practice which explicitly and militantly disavows any relation to 'illusionism', the imaginary, identification, and even to fiction? In what ways does it offer solutions to those problems, basic to any attempt to formulate a filmmaking practice which does not re-enact the illusions and manipulations of dominant film?

We will focus our discussion, for several reasons, around the theoretical writings which have come out of the English Co-op movement, mainly those of Malcolm LeGrice and Peter Gidal.[2] The first reason is that, as we have mentioned, this movement brings together more explicitly and more extremely than any other the problematic of a simultaneous political and formal avant-garde practice.[3] Many of these questions exist implicitly in the work and writings of other experimental filmmakers, even in the United States, where the two practices are almost unthinkable together, but for now we will take the most evident and articulated example. Also, as theoretical writings, the work of LeGrice and Gidal offers an already secondarized and rationalized version of their own activity, thus making it even more accessible to a discussion of the premises of this manner of thinking film.[4] LeGrice's writings, moreover, offer an account of his own and his contemporaries' filmmaking practice across a history of the abstract, formal avant-garde, thus opening up the possibility of a discussion of the historical placement of this avant-garde and the historical imaginary of this avant-garde, that is, their conception of their origins and influences, of their relation to the other arts and to the history of art.

The theoretical writings of Malcolm LeGrice and Peter Gidal are highly complementary, often citing each other's film-work for examples and validation of argument, yet differ in that LeGrice speaks from within a concerned historical reconstruction of the same movement for which Gidal polemically agitates with wide-ranging references to much recent French theoretical work including Derrida, Althusser and Kristeva. They are two of the most active filmmakers in the very movement which they are attempting to describe in terms of its historical, political, aesthetic and philosophical premises. In order not to collapse the particularities of the two arguments into one another, we will take them separately; hopefully the similarities will become evident, the differences will remain distinct.

ABSTRACT FILM AND BEYOND (Malcolm LeGrice)*

Malcolm LeGrice locates the roots of the filmic evolution he traces in the pre-cinematic painting of the Impressionist era, comparing the single brushmark style of the Impressionists to the grain of the photographic image and seeing the most significant philosophical parallels between painting and photography in their shared movement away from a religious view of the world to a

---

'Painting's mistake is the subject.
Cinema's mistake is the scenario.
Freed from this negative weight, the cinema
can become a gigantic microscope of things
never before seen and felt.'
—FERNAND LÉGER, L'Art du cinéma, 1923

---

scientific materialism: 'observation, experiment and technological determination' (9). In citing Cézanne for creating an awareness of the relativistic nature of perception, he establishes the beginning of an historical line of artists who 'make us aware of the flux of perception through process' (10). He traces also an evolution from one medium into another: 'Problems of modern art lead directly into film . . . Cubism, Expressionism, Dadaism, abstract art, Surrealism found not only their expression in films, but a new fulfillment on a new level' (Hans Richter, 20), and describes its simultaneous emergence across the different arts: Dadaist poetry, *Finnegans Wake*, Schönberg, Cubist and Futurist painting. Thus from the very beginning of the book, LeGrice establishes a cinematic essence prior even to the debut of film as a medium and describes the movement of its progressive refinement through the abstract experiments of the 20's up to the present minimalist-influenced 'structuralist' avant-garde. LeGrice stays very much within his own definition, often eliminating films, filmmakers and movements which do not fit into the framework of 'abstract' cinema; as he readily states, this is for him a political decision. He sees the first work on abstraction (Cubists, Impressionists) as 'opening up two significant possibilities: the first stems from considering painterly form as diagrammatic rather than pictorial representation, the second from

---

*The numbers in parentheses in this and subsequent sections refer to pages from the text discussed in that section.

direct perceptual response to the material and form of the work as an object itself'
(15). And the result of this: 'Art, instead of representing the world, could now be
a model for it, functioning as analogy rather than imitation' (16). Among the
many artistic experiments described in this reconstruction of the abstract movement is Viking Eggeling's attempt to arrive at a universal language of visual composition, a complete syntax of form-relationships. Eggeling called for a 'strict
discipline of the elements' (21) and said, 'Art is not the subjective explosion of
the individual, but becomes the organic language of mankind, which must be
basically free of misconceptions, clear-cut, so that it can become a vehicle for
communication (21). But accompanying this systematic, almost 'scientific' abstraction is a tendency which paradoxically haunts the entire history of the abstract avant-garde movement, a tendency towards a strong metaphysical component. LeGrice notes the profound influence of Kandinsky and his *Concerning the
Spiritual in Art* (1910) on the early formal filmmakers but has no answers for the
collusion of science and mysticism in the first formal avant-gardists to use the
most technologically advanced equipment ever available to filmmakers: John
Whitney used computers to generate meditative mandala imagery and Jordan
Belson used his sophisticated optical printing machinery to create cosmic images
of his inner religious experiences. For LeGrice it was crucial that the abstract
movement broke from the dominance of Kandinsky and moved towards an aesthetic of the 'finite and physical' (84). While charting the history of this 'intrinsic' movement towards abstraction, LeGrice offers simultaneously a normative
definition of what new form cinema should seek—one that is 'essentially "cinematic"—not dominated by literature or theater, nor for that matter by painting or
music' (32). Both in trying to note this movement inherent in the medium and in
arguing for cinematic specificity he must eliminate as not properly within the
definition some of those films which have even been considered *the* avant-garde
of cinema *(Un Chien Andalou, L'Age d'Or, La Coquille et le Clergyman, etc.)*.
They are eliminated (partially or wholly) from this evolution because of their use
of 'associative', 'symbolic' imagery and narrative—elements always susceptible
to being recuperated and becoming no different from dominant cinema's use of
these strategies for construction and manipulation of a passive spectator. It is only
the films or parts of the films which use 'procedure as the basis of content', that
is, films which 'draw attention to the material nature of the film itself and the
images on it as a photochemical reality' (35) that LeGrice will include in this
progressive movement. LeGrice speaks several times of the filmmakers' lack of
awareness of their own evolutionary direction, and also of their techniques as
being 'beyond the full grasp of the artists at that time' (48), 'a kind of path of the
early filmmakers which can only be known to us now' (48).

Providing some of the most crucial articulations of LeGrice's argument is
Dziga Vertov whose work he sees as an exemplary solution to the question of how
'radicalism in the formal aspect of cinema can be related to radical politics . . . the
link between politics and the mode of perception engendered in the film audience' (52). Since one of the aims of the book is to demonstrate the intrinsic
political thrust of formal cinema, the 'politics of perception' (135), he insistently

refers to Vertov's strategies, comparing them to those of the formal avant-garde. Vertov is cited for providing a revolutionary critique of dominant cinema and for rejecting narrative and fiction in his attempt to portray revolutionary daily life. For LeGrice, all of Vertov's work focused on the relation of perception and consciousness, i.e., the attempt to create a new revolutionary consciousness through extending the possibilities of perception. The entire thrust is toward creating the conscious spectator: 'the conscious alone can fight against magical suggestions of every kind' ('Consciousness or Sub-Consciousness', Dziga Vertov, 56). The

---

'Consciousness or Sub-Consciousness':

*'We rise against the collusion between the
"director-enchanter" and the public which is
submitted to the enchantment.
The conscious alone can fight against magical
suggestions of every kind.
The conscious alone can form a man of firm
convictions and opinions.
We need a conscious people, not an unconscious mass ready to yield to any suggestion.'*
            —DZIGA VERTOV, quoted by Malcolm
         LeGrice, 56

Kino-Eye can accomplish this because it is not a substitute for the human eye but 'a machine in its own terms capable of extending or creating a new perception' (58). Vertov's editing makes impossible the 'passive, cathartic, emotionally manipulated mode which is normal in the popular cinema culture.' And, 'this is further reinforced by the direct reference to the machinery' (60). *Man with a Movie Camera* is seen as a forerunner of recent films which explore self-referential structures: seeing the camera, the projector, the screen, the roll of film itself *in* the film can recall to the spectator the fact that s/he is watching a film and thus of his or her own perceptual processes. Vertov's materialism is seen taken up by the post-war European avant-garde—'strongly anti-romantic and clearly based in the psycho-physical as material phenomena' (87), and then, since 1966, 'the formal aspect of avant-garde film has exploded to become its mainstream' (105), culminating in 'an implicit search for a film which can function essentially on the psycho-physical rather than the psycho-interpretative level' (106). The aim of these films is to create an experience in which 'Action on the autonomic nervous system seeks to create a nervous response which is largely preconscious, the psychological reactions sought being a direct consequence of physical function' (106). In these films, which LeGrice refers to as 'perception training films', the single sort of information is that which concerns filmic processes, but the concern is not with an *intellection* of these processes, a mental act involving a semantic dimension, but a direct apprehension: 'the primacy of current experience over the illusory or retrospective.' As one of the most effective strategies in this attempt, LeGrice cites information theory—by reducing the information within the film to an extreme degree the spectator's awareness can be focused solely onto her or his perceptual response. Finally, LeGrice states the aim of all this deliberate and didactic reflexivity, this attention to the material processes of film and the changing perceptual responses of the spectator: 'to give the spectator an affirmation of his own reality'; and it is this attempt, seen as completely counteractive to the mode of popular cinema, that represents 'the most advanced and radical state of cinematic language and convention' (153).

'THEORY AND DEFINITION OF STRUCTURAL MATERIALIST FILM' (PETER GIDAL)

The polemicism of Peter Gidal at the same time narrows into more precise definitions and expands into a set of philosophical presuppositions the historical descriptions and conclusions of Malcolm LeGrice. The argument of Gidal resolves itself into a series of dichotomies which can be schematized as follows:

idealism/materialism[5]

ideology/knowledge

reproduction/production

narrative/non-narrative

illusionist time/real-time

signified/signifier

Each step of the argument pits one half of the dichotomy against the other as a polar opposite, both philosophically and politically. Just as for LeGrice, Gidal's argument turns around an analysis of the workings of classical film in order to posit certain avant-garde strategies as completely counter to the classical model. Here, too, the political efficacy of these films is in the construction of a self-conscious, perceptually aware spectator as the result of self-reflexive strategies. The first tactic of the structural/materialist film is the emptying from the cinematic signifier of all semantic, associative, symbolic, representational significance. Gidal argues that any sort of representation is always susceptible to becoming naturalized by the dominant ideology and used to manipulate the spectator. The only images not susceptible to this recuperation are images of actual filmic processes; Gidal emphasizes not *representations, reproductions* of these processes but the actual experience of the production process inscribed in the film. The viewing activity of the spectator is the deciphering, anticipation, correction,

---

*'All I want anyone to get out of my paintings,
and all I ever get out of them, is the fact that
you can see the whole idea without any confusion . . . what you see is what you see.'*
—FRANK STELLA, quoted by Peter Gidal, 19

clarification and analysis of this material process: 'Thus viewing such a film is at once viewing a film and viewing the "coming into presence" of the film, i.e., the system of consciousness that produces the work, that is produced by and in it' (2). The spectator is completely prevented from any sort of identification with these films because they are non-narrative: 'Narrative is authoritarian, manipulative and mystificatory' (4) because it represses the reality of material space and time and therefore illusionism is its only function. Instead of the illusionistic time of the narrative, Gidal offers the solution of 'real-time', in which the duration of the processes depicted and the time of watching the film are absolutely homogenous. The basic unit of film will then be duration: 'Point "a" to point "b" in duration as opposed to narrative.'[6]

Structural/materialist film is then at once object and procedure, a didactic aesthetic using reflexive strategies to ensure a conscious spectator: 'A filmic practice in which one watches oneself watching . . . Filmic reflexiveness is the presentation of consciousness to the self' (10).

THE IMAGINARY SIGNIFIER (CHRISTIAN METZ)

At the center of Christian Metz's discussion of the psychoanalytic constitution of the cinematic signifier[7] he warns that the film which would aim to be a film of intervention must take into consideration the higher degree of imaginariness of the cinematic signifier (in comparison to the theater, for example). Since the main thrust of LeGrice's and Gidal's arguments is that the structural/materialist film is constructed to eliminate the spectator's imaginary relation to the film and to prevent identification largely through a disavowal of narrative and fiction,

---

'Thus as a beginning it is absolutely essential to tear the symbolic from its own imaginary and return to it as a look. To tear it from it, but not completely, or at least not in the sense of ignoring it and fleeing from it (fearing it): the imaginary is also what has to be rediscovered precisely in order to avoid being swallowed up by it: a never ending task.'
—CHRISTIAN METZ, 'The Imaginary Signifier', 16

---

let us look at these specific claims in the light of the metapsychological points raised in the article of Christian Metz's which most directly addresses itself to these problems.

LeGrice and Gidal note that both the represented content and the sequential organization of film have an effect on the viewer; if one can successfully eliminate a certain kind of imagery ('symbolic', 'associative' images, images which are 'representations' or 'reproductions') and a certain kind of ordering of the images (editing which suppresses material space and time) then the spectator would be confronted with an image, a film which would call forth a direct and conscious response, a response focused on the subject's own act of perception. In 'The Imaginary Signifier' Metz emphasizes that what is 'characteristic of the cinema is not the imaginary that it may happen to represent, it is the imaginary that it is from the start' (48). Basic to the constitution of the cinematic signifier is that it is *absent*: unlike the theater, in which real persons share the time and space of the spectator, the cinema screen is always the 'other scene', it is a recording and what it records is not there at the moment of its projection. The most basic characteristic of the cinematic signifier is that it combines presence and absence—it is more 'there' than almost any other medium (because of its density of perceptual registers) and less 'there' at the same time (because it is always only a replica of what is no longer there). This combination of presence and absence also describes the characteristic functioning of the Imaginary:[8] according to Lacan the ego is constituted by an image—that is, something that is a reflection (which is there) of the body (which is not really there 'in' the mirror). Is presenting an image of a filmic process, even the process of the 'coming into presence' of the very film we are

---

> '*The image is the strict reflection of reality, its objectivity is contradictory to imaginary extravagance. But at the very same time, this reflection is a "double". The image is already imbibed with subjective powers which are going to displace it, deform it, project it into fantasy and dream. The imaginary enchants the image because the image is already a potential sorcerer. The imaginary proliferates on the image like its own natural cancer. It is going to crystallize and deploy human needs, but always in images. The image is the common place of the image and imagination.*'
> —EDGAR MORIN, Le Cinéma ou l'homme imaginaire, 1956

---

watching, a way of making that process, the image of that process, more 'there', less imaginary (because truly 'present'), more directly apprehendable by perception? If the cinematic signifier shares the characteristic structuration of the Imaginary, then to insist on the *presence*, the 'materiality' of the image, would that not be to simultaneously (unconsciousiy) insist on its *absence*, would it not risk moving the imaginary quotient up yet another notch? To show the film in its materiality—for example to film a strip of film, or to emphasize the screen as surface through projecting not images, but clear light onto the screen—is to show the film in its 'materiality' at the very moment that it is no longer film. The piece of film footage that we see is not the film, the film exists only when it is projected; the empty, white screen is also not the film, the film exists in a dialectic of image and screen—when we see a screen, even in all its 'materiality', we are just seeing a screen. And the same for the structural/materialist approach to demonstrating film *processes*–to show film in its stages of becoming a film, or disintegrating as film, is a little like the *fort-da* game as described by Lacan in which the child plays out obsessively, repetitively the concept of separation, of loss. (Another reading of this could be that of Melanie Klein in relation to the handling of the fetish-object: it is sometimes quasi-venerated, sometimes destroyed in a constant alternation of destruction and reparation.) Material 'possession' of the film is always at the price of losing the instance in which it is film as such. This is not to say that these strategies involving the demonstration of the material processes of film are not valuable; it is just to say that, no matter how 'scientific' these experiments may be, they have psychoanalytic roots in a play of possession and loss. These 'materialization' strategies comprise a non-acceptance of the imaginary inherent to the cinematic signifier itself. The imaginary can only be endlessly played out, its infinite metonymy can only be stopped into *fictions* of materiality, never materiality itself.

Thus the cinematic signifier is imaginary in terms of its very constitution as signifier. It is also imaginary, Metz argues, because the screen reactivates the mirror stage as described by Jacques Lacan (or at least the images have their power of fascination because the subject has already undergone the mirror stage). Any relation to image is imaginary, that is, since the ego itself is constituted by images (the first being the image of the subject in the mirror) and all the rest of the images being doubles of this double, then there is no way to detach images from this fundamental imaginary operation. (We will see later that this operation is also a relation of desire.)

In specifying the imaginariness of the cinematic signifier Metz shifts the grounds of all previous discussions of the processes of identification in film, maintaining that the primary identification (primary in terms of importance in relation to the subject-effect, that is) is not with the characters on the screen but with the subject's own activity of looking. The spectator is the constitutive instance of the film, of the cinematic signifier; the film would not exist without the sight (and hearing) of the spectator. 'In other words, the spectator *identifies with himself*, with himself as a pure act of perception: as condition of possibility of the perceived and hence as a kind of transcendental subject, anterior to every *there is*' (51). If the primary identification is with the subject's own act of perceiving, then the primary identification in film is with the camera and not with the characters or the depicted events. It also follows from Metz's determination of the act of seeing itself as the primary cinematic identification that the images themselves, that is, what the images depict (even what filmic processes they present) do not have that much to do with the fundamental form of cinematic identification, the identification which establishes the spectator as transcendental subject. Thus the avant-gardists' program of eliminating 'associative', 'symbolic', extra-referential significance from filmic images (we will take up later the question of whether this is even possible)—Peter Gidal's example of an image-moment of a leaf which is only a leaf and nothing more—would have relatively little effect in terms of subverting this most fundamental identification.

As for LeGrice and Gidal's argument that it is narrative which constructs and controls spectator identification, it is not completely sure that even the least 'montaged' avant-garde films escape some of the fundamental structures of narrative. In another text ('Métaphore/Métonymie ou la référent imaginaire'),[9] Metz has noted that even though avant-garde films don't use the usual metonymic discursive operation of classical film, they don't completely escape this regime because they have (among other things) a *point of view* in relation to a contiguous organization of images. (See also Stephen Heath's 'Narrative Space' on the primary narrative function of cinema relying on the look sutured into a metonymy of images.)[10]

LeGrice and Gidal also maintain that identification is eliminated in their films because, correlatively with eliminating narrative, fiction too is eliminated, 'fiction' here meaning images, series of images which refer the spectator to an illusory elsewhere, an imaginary space rather than the material reality of the spectator's own space and time. When Metz says that 'Every film is a fiction film' (47) he is not trying to say that every film, no matter how abstract, has the functional equivalent of a 'character' or that all films, at bottom, have a 'story'. Once again we are being referred back to the constitution of the cinematic signifier itself in which, as has been shown, it is always an imaginary referent since what it represents is not there, thus fictive. Is it even possible to avoid the construction of an 'elsewhere'? Isn't any art object, art process, exactly that, no matter how minimal, no matter how little the conceptualizations structured to happen in that space resemble a story? Even when the metonymic contiguity of the images is designed to construct a 'specifically cinematic' space as opposed to a three-dimensional scene of classical representation, this space is never 'there' in any material way, and as soon as it is 'elsewhere', there is no way of controlling the interactions of the film with the processes of memory and fantasy (always fictional) of the perceiving subject. The work of Thierry Kuntzel (especially 'Savoir, Pouvoir, Voir' and 'Le travail du film, 2')[11] marks out the structuring function of certain basic fantasies in the vision of the spectator, most importantly perversion (especially fetishism) and the primal scene. Fetishism and the primal scene are notable for their particular imbrication of vision and fiction since both the perversion and the primal fantasy function across the scopophilic drive. Both the fetishistic ritual and the primal scene serve the subject exactly as fictions, fictions which are fabricated in order for the subject to work through/defend itself against questions at the level of sexual significance. Although these two articles address themselves to the effect of these fantasies on the vision of the spectator of classical film, we will see later how these psychical structures which fictionalize the subject to himself may be inherent in the act of vision. Thus, several times over, at several levels, 'Every film is a fiction film' (47).

At the level of cinema as a social institution Metz speaks of the role of the cinema spectator as essentially voyeuristic: participating in a form of scopophilia not normally sanctioned by society, we sit in the theater in darkness and solitude looking towards the aperture of the screen as through a keyhole. This is one of the reasons why it is so startling when a character looks at us from the screen, catching us in our own voyeuristic activity. As Metz points out, the cinema as an institution functions to sanction this activity and film-viewing becomes authorized scopophilia, legalized voyeurism, desire within the limits of the law. The social situation of the spectator of, say, Malcolm LeGrice's *Little Dog for Roger* or Peter Gidal's *Room Film, 1973* would be different from that of the spectator in a commercial cinema. The films are presented as near-scientific investigations of perceptual processes. We come to them in a more active manner, knowing they will be difficult, challenging, and that we are coming to learn something, to be productive, not passive, spectators (Peter Gidal would say for knowledge and not for ideology). Here it is not just a matter of being temporarily authorized to exercise our scopophilic pleasure (legally yet still furtively, in the manner of classical cinema), we are asked by the films and the viewing situation to *investigate* and we are promised the sanction of science. As valuable as these strategies might be on one level, they also tend to suppress a knowledge of the imaginary of the image by asserting the objectivity of the images and the rationality of our relation to them.

'THE APPARATUS' (JEAN-LOUIS BAUDRY)

The previous discussion concerned recent work on the imaginary status of the cinematic signifier. Jean-Louis Baudry's work[12] considers the imaginary status of the entire apparatus, that is the cinema 'machine' which includes not only the instrumental base (camera, lens, projector, etc.) but also the subject, most importantly the subject of the unconscious, the subject as a desiring machine without which the cinematic institution could not (would have no reason to) function. Baudry's article gives the sketch for an historical reconsideration of the cinema not as a machine which came into existence *because of* the state of tech-

---

'. . . And here
the painting becomes
this enormous
thing which
moves
The wheel
Life
The machine
The human soul. . . .'
—BLAISE CENDRARS, 'Constructions',
1919, dedicated to Fernand Léger

---

nology at the end of the 19th century but as the most perfected material realization of an unconscious goal perhaps basic to the psychical functioning of the human mind—the wish to return, by simulation, to that 'other scene'. And, it is especially through artistic practice that the unconscious proposes to have itself represented. For Baudry all the other arts were 'dry runs' in this unconscious historical experiment to devise an apparatus which could simulate not 'reality' but a subject-effect or state. This state would be an artificial state of regression that

> 'We need Cinema in order to create the total
> art towards which all the others, since the be-
> ginning, have tended.'
> —RICCIOTTO CANUDO, 'La theorie des
> sept arts'

would return the subject to an earlier state of development, with its own forms of satisfaction, a state of relative narcissism in which desire could be 'satisfied' through confusing real perceptions (filmic images) with representations (the subject's own endogenous images) and then taking them for perceptions (something existing 'in reality'). In dream, there are no real perceptions coming from the exterior, only the subject's own representations hallucinated as perceptions. The impression of reality particular to this state, then, would be closest to that of the dream-effect and would thus have the same possibilities for figuration and refiguration of the form of desire inherent to it. This impression of reality that the spectator has in the cinema, and the consequent form of identification, has less to do with a successful rendering of the real than with the reproduction and repetition of a particular condition, a 'fantasmatization of the subject'.

Metz, then, displaces the primary cinematic identification from an identification with the signified contents appearing on the screen to the act of perception itself; Baudry displaces the question of identification from the degree of reality of the images on the screen to a more fundamental identification with the entire apparatus. (A basic difference between these positions is the more Lacanian emphasis of Metz on identification across the specular regime as opposed to Baudry's more Freudian emphasis on satisfaction through regression providing the base for the primary identification. However, as Baudry points out in his article, the form of archaic regression that he isolates 'does not exclude other processes of identification which derive from the specular regime of the ego, from its constitution as imaginary' (112).)

LeGrice's book offers some necessary historical precisions which could support Baudry's thesis in tracing the evolution of an urge to cinematic representation which pre-existed cinema and found its greatest perfection in cinema. Both authors would be able to say there was never any first invention of cinema (Baudry, 113). LeGrice documents both the ecstasy of visual artists at the time—the Futurists, Dadaists and Surrealists—in discovering a medium that offered possibilities beyond what they had been able to achieve in painting, and also charts this 'natural evolution' from the concerns of modern painting to film. (However it must be remembered that, although LeGrice documents this movement, he is also a part of it and has a tendency to force the idea of a natural evolution; his is a strategic reconstruction of art history according to the need to justify a certain kind of filmmaking practice as the 'natural' culmination of an evolution intrinsic and inevitable to the medium itself.) Therefore, both Baudry and LeGrice would trace an evolutionary movement from painting to film and within film itself: LeGrice's logic would be a formalist and idealist notion of inevitable aesthetic progress in the resolution of a series of formal problems posed by the medium itself (see Clement Greenberg); Baudry's logic would be that of the unconscious in its successive attempts to represent itself.

Our questions then on avant-garde strategies in relation to the functioning of the apparatus as outlined by Baudry:

(1) If the entire cinematic institution is taken in this grand historical wish-fulfilling fantasy, if the apparatus is always already a function of the archaic mode of identification which 'created' it and permits its functioning, then what is the particular aspect of this wish which is fulfilled by structural/materialist film?

(2) In what ways, to what degree do the experiments of the structural/materialist filmmakers subvert this archaic form of identification?

Further on in this paper we will present a thesis in answer to the first question of the particular psychical option filled by structural/materialist film, i.e., what sort of 'fantasmatization of the subject' it creates. We will argue that, rather than fulfilling a role of giving cinematic *pleasure* or *satisfaction* (the argument of most metapsychological studies of film, however they might differ in defining this), this sort of filmmaking represents an extreme form of cinema's possibilities for serving a *defensive* function for the spectator/subject. For the moment we would like to undertake a discussion of the second question, the degree to which the theoretical presuppositions of these filmmakers could provide strategies for subverting the overall functioning of the apparatus.

In *The Interpretation of Dreams* Freud offers an answer to the enigma of critical feelings in dreams, that is, when the thought 'this is only a dream' occurs in a dream.[13] This moment of critical judgment, this instant of 'reality' in the dream, Freud claims, is only a strategy to ensure that the anxiety arising in the dream is sufficiently suppressed for the dreamer to be able to continue sleeping and dreaming. Baudry has made the equation *apparatus* = dream-state. Therefore like the 'rational' and 'critical' thoughts which occur in dreams, anything that occurs within the apparatus, for example the images and sounds of the film, is susceptible to being 'desecondarized', 'derationalized' and even used to contribute to maintaining the state of dream. And the most perfect strategy to maintain this state: that moment of *the most extreme self-reflexivity*—that moment of insistence on the material and rational. The use of self-reflexive aesthetic strategies is almost the definition of avant-garde practice. LeGrice cites Vertov's exemplary practice of showing every stage of the production of a film, of demystifying the machinery and process, in order to reinforce the consciousness of the spectator (59). Throughout *Abstract Film and Beyond,* films are included or excluded to the degree to which they are properly materialist and self-reflexive, i.e., whether or not the images show the functioning of the camera, projector, editing equipment or use 'filmic material processes' as subject matter: celluloid scratches, splicing tape marks, processing stains, finger prints, image slip, etc. Both writers repeatedly emphasize that this sort of imagery must not be used for expressive ends but must allow solely 'an awareness of the implications of changing forms of visual/

kinetic information' (LeGrice, 115). If we take Metz's thesis that the primary identification is with the camera, then we must immediately question the 'objectivity' of the strategy of showing the spectator these 'protheses' of his own body, of his own vision: it is quite likely that this could *reinforce* the primary identification, which, as Metz argues, is the base of the construction of a transcendental subject. At a more sociological level, we can look back into cinema history (and its pre-history) and trace our fascination with machines to record and project images. Beaumont Newhall's *The History of Photography*[14] describes the frenzy surrounding the first public presentations of photographic equipment and the first demonstrations of 'how-it-works'. This high pitch of excitement was seen again at each innovation in film technology: the invention of sound, color, 3-D, cinemascope, etc. Films which demonstrate the possibilities of perception, in no matter how 'scientific' a framework, cannot help but play on this fascination. The following section will suggest, following Jean-Louis Baudry, some theses on the psychical roots of this exuberance.

Correlative with the axiom of self-reflexivity is the emphasis on these films as epistemological enterprise. 'Knowledge' and 'investigation' are the positive terms opposed to the negative ones 'ideology' and 'passivity'. However, the desire to know and to investigate is not entirely unproblematic: when an intellectual process is shown and examined it enters immediately into the sexual fantasy of infantile investigation. (From a more Lacanian perspective, one could say, as P. Aulagnier-Spairani does, 'Knowledge has the narrowest relation to desire and to the unveiling of that which is the cause of it.')[15] In their extreme form they slide from epistemology into epistemophilia (the concept denoting the perversion of the desire to know). This perversion comprises the attempted mastery of knowledge and the demonstration of the all-powerfulness of the subject. Attempted mastery of knowledge (or of desire) traps the subject in an imaginary relation, an endless circle of trying to *know,* and since the object of all knowing is a knowledge of desire, there is no end and no way out: especially if the subject's aim is *full knowledge.* It is only in accepting the limits, the loss of the possibility of total mastery, that some symbolizing advances through this imaginary web are possible.[16]

The strategies of this avant-garde cannot hope to offer means of subverting the apparatus if they ignore these levels of unconscious functioning, choosing instead to work on the codes of 'conscious' reception of the film. The 'expanded cinema' experiments of LeGrice, Annabel Nicolson, William Raban and others could appear to be a re-thinking of the problem of the place of the subject in (of) the apparatus. The entire space of the viewing situation is altered: multi-screen, multi-projection; often the artists place themselves between the space of the screen and the projector, interacting with both. But once again all of this effort is towards constructing a subject 'affirmed in his own reality', a situation in which 'one watches oneself watching': a construction of a conscious subject, unified and affirmed as the place of synthesis of all perceptions (a 'materialist' transcendental subject?). Given the level of address in these expanded cinema experiments it could be asked if they offer nothing but *a multiplication of effects,* all striving

towards a new recentering of the subject, this time not centered in a transcendental elsewhere but in the body of the subject himself.

In both Baudry's earlier essay 'Ideological Effects of the Basic Cinematographic Apparatus' and in 'The Apparatus', he argues the profound link of cinema and idealism. Both construct a subject whose function as perceiver and syn-
thesizer makes him the center of a universe (because he is the place through which
all signification must pass) which he then believes to have created himself and over
which he believes he has ultimate control. (Too, it is a philosophy of consciousness: if the subject is the origin of all vision and knowledge then there is nothing
hidden from the subject, no possibility for a part of him which functions unknown
and inaccessible to him—see Thierry Kuntzel's 'Savoir, Pouvoir, Voir' on the
relations of *seeing* and *knowing* in the idealist version of vision re-enacted by the
classical film.) In both essays, but especially in 'The Apparatus', idealism is presented as a psychoanalytic as well as philosophical phenomenon, idealism having
a great deal to do with the desire of the subject. As a response to the shortcomings
of reality, the subject wants to be able to change it according to his desire. The
cinematic apparatus structures for (with) the spectator a sensation of full vision
('Ideological Effects of the Basic Cinematographic Apparatus': Renaissance perspective inscribed in the instrumental base itself) and enables a confounding of
the order of satisfaction of desire with the order of reality ('The Apparatus':
simulation of dream-effect where representation can no longer be distinguished
from perception). Much of the historical material cited in *Abstract Film and Beyond* gives support to Baudry's thesis of the inherent idealism of the cinematographic apparatus. What is the most important for our interests is that the formal
film movement in its own self-description appears as *the most extreme expression
of this inherent idealism.* Jacques Lacan's essay 'Du regard comme objet petit a'[17]
(we will look more closely at this essay in the next section) stands as one of the
most important psychoanalytic critiques of the idealist (specifically phenomenological) notion of vision. Lacan describes the world as 'omnivoyeuristic': 'we are
looked-at beings in the spectacle of the world' (71). (Nous sommes des êtres
regardés, dans le spectacle du monde.') We can see only from one place, through
our own eyes: we can never see ourselves from the place where others see us and
our vision is thus always affected by the field of the other, the imagined look. The
fantasy that we find in the Platonic perspective inverts this relation: here we find
an absolute being to whom is transferred the quality of all-seeing. The ability to
reshape space and time in the 'cineplastics' of Elie Faure, the Kino-Eye of Dziga
Vertov which is more perfect than the human eye because it can go everywhere
and see everything, the cinema philosophy of the Futurists: 'This is how we de-
compose and recompose the universe according to our marvelous whims'; to document the avant-garde film movement, even the most 'abstract' strains of it, is to
cite the exuberance of artists who had at last found a perfect supplement to their
vision, a machine-eye capable of 'remaking the very figuration of life' (Ricciotto
Canudo).[18] Popular cinema only chained vision into outworn theatrical and novelistic forms but 'pure cinema', 'abstract cinema' was to be the liberation and joyful

education of vision in order to create the 'new man' of the 20th century. The rhetoric of the inheritors of this enterprise, the structural/materialist filmmakers, is quite different from this romantic idealism. LeGrice documents a movement away from the idealism of the early avant-gardists to the present 'cool' experiments and didactic exercises on human perception. But some striking similarities remain: the attempt to expand the capacities of vision and knowledge of a spectator 'affirmed in his own reality', a spectator completely conscious of his own activities in 'producing' the film. The subject constituted by the early avant-gardists and the structural/materialists is essentially the same even if one constructs its subject in the name of a romantic humanism and the other in the name of science and 'materialism'. Both play on an infantile wish to shape the real to the measure of the subject's own boundless desire.

Like almost all the other writers on experimental film (David Curtis, Standish Lawder, Gene Youngblood, etc.) LeGrice emphasizes the close dependence of the avant-garde aesthetic on technological development. More so than with popular cinema, all the advances in avant-garde 'film thought' have depended on the refinement and expansion of the technological possibilities: color processing, optical printers, quality of film stock, computers. The idealist tendency of the avant-garde could be in part determined by this close dependency on technology for

---

'Using war surplus anti-aircraft gun directors
. . . began the construction of an animation table,
which allowed sections to rotate according to pre-
programmed patterns, transforming very simple
forms into complex movements similar to oscillo-
scope or pendulum-pantograph figures.'
—JOHN WHITNEY, cited by Malcolm LeGrice, 80

---

many of its advances. In 'Ideological Effects of the Basic Cinematographic Apparatus' Baudry opens the questioning of 'the privileged position which optical instruments seem to occupy on the line of intersection of science and ideological products.' That is, the cinema, based as it is on optical equipment derived from science, tends to treat its own technology as neutral and free from ideological inscription. Baudry argues that the idealist spectator is partly a construction of the Renaissance perspective of the lens itself. It is true that the majority of the structural/materialist films work against the centering of the spectator by the Renaissance perspective inscribed in the physical construction of the lens. However, after making this (by now, automatic) critique of Renaissance representational space, the machine is often unquestioningly reabsorbed into the project to 'expand' vision. LeGrice rejects vitriolically the mystical tendency in filmmakers like Jordan Belson and Scott Bartlett who use highly sophisticated technology to create the blend of spiritualism and science particular to their work. He criticizes them for being regressive elements in the larger tendency towards non-psychological abstraction. It could be however that this mystical tendency is only the logical extreme of the 'materialist' avant-garde's own unconscious direction; it is for this reason that they reject them so violently.

The recent work of Raymond Bellour on cinema and hypnosis[19] includes an investigation of the place of the camera in the imaginary and symbolic of the late 19th and 20th centuries. He argues that machines (and particularly image-making machines) came to have the function of an ideal ego (*moi idéal*), that is, an extended and perfected model of our own capacities, which we then introject as an ego ideal (*idéal du moi*). In cinema, as in hypnosis, the introjection of the ego ideal takes over the function of reality testing, permitting external stimuli to be perceived as originating in the subject. Cinematic identification becomes a rhythm of projection, introjection, a constant dialectic of ideal ego/ego ideal. For Bellour, as well as for Metz, it is an unconscious identification with the camera which creates the primary subject-effect and filmic 'fascination' in general. No matter how 'aware' we are, then, of the functioning of the camera/projector in our perceptual functioning this aids us very little in thinking our unconscious relation to images, to the technological apparatus, and to the fundamental relation of the two. The structural/materialist movement seems to have taken up and synthesized both an idealism embedded in photographic and cinematographic technology itself and an idealism inherited from its art-historical tradition, this last seen in their continuation of the rhetoric of 'expanding consciousness through expanding vision' of the earlier abstract filmmakers and in their Greenbergian notion of progress-in-art as a series of solutions to formal problems logically intrinsic to the medium.

'THE LOOK AS SMALL OBJECT A' (JACQUES LACAN)

One of the most important theoretical bases for the recent metapsychological studies of film is the work of Jacques Lacan on the imaginary constitution of the subject ('The Mirror Phase as Formative of the Function of the I'),[20] and his more recent work on the specular regime ('Du regard comme objet petit a')[21]; in what ways are the structures of subjectivity worked at the level of the scopic drive? The four seminars grouped under the heading 'The look as small object a' offer a critique of the idealist notion of vision and project onto the act of vision itself the same dialectic of desire and lack at work in the unconscious.

For the structural/materialist filmmakers perception operates at a conscious or perhaps 'pre-conscious' level; Malcolm LeGrice states that the aim of these films is to create an experience in which 'Action on the autonomic nervous system seeks to create a nervous response which is largely preconscious, the psychological reactions sought being a direct consequence of physical function' (106).[22] Except for the complicated physiological exigencies, they think of perception as a fairly unproblematic act and their aim is its knowledge and mastery. For Lacan the scopic drive is very different from the other drives and the most problematic. First, Lacan makes a distinction between the *eye* and the *look*: the eye refers to the organ and its physical functioning, and the look is a matter of that which is 'always to some degree eluded' in vision (70). The look is exactly that which eludes us from philosophy's notion of the plenitude met by the contemplative subject, the unified and all-seeing subject; the look is the very inverse of consciousness. When Lacan says that 'in the domain

---

'The function of the blot and the look is, at one and the same time, that which commands the most secretly, and that which always escapes the grip of, that form of vision which finds its contentment in imagining itself as consciousness.'

—JACQUES LACAN, Le quatre
concepts fondamentaux de la
psychanalyse, 71

'. . . my body simultaneously sees and is seen. That which looks at all things can also look at itself and recognize, in what it sees, the "other side" of its power of looking. It sees itself seeing; it touches itself touching; it is visible and sensitive for itself . . . a self that is caught up in things, that has a front and a back, a past and a future. . . .'

—MAURICE MERLEAU-PONTY, The
Essential Writings of Merleau-Ponty

---

of vision small object a is the look' (97), he is attempting to describe the functioning of lack at the level of the scopic drive. 'Small object a' in the Lacanian algebra stands for, not the object of desire itself, but the experience of separation, separation from all the things that have been lost from the body (for example, the mother's breast which was once experienced as part of the infant's body).[23] The imaginary relation itself, through which the subject becomes a subject for himself, occurs only at the price of the subject envisaging his own body as *other* in the mirror; that is, the moment of the constitution of the ego is also a moment of separation.[24] Thus Lacan can say, in relation to the domain of vision integrated into the field of desire: 'In the dialectic of the eye and the look, there is no point of coincidence, only basic lure' (94). The look is not at all a look that can be seen, it is a look imagined by the subject in the field of the other: the look concerned here is very much the presence of the other as such. That is, the determinant look is not our own (the phenomenological notion of the intentionality of perception and the subject as master of the visual field) but the one from outside; this look pre-exists the subject in the same way that the symbolic and the 'real' pre-exist the subject's constitution through the imaginary. We think of ourselves as the subject of representation but within the always reciprocal (yet not symmetrical) structure of the look we are, virtually, the object of representation also. Lacan even speaks of the subject being '*photo-*

graphed' by the incarnated and returned light of its own look (98). There is, then, something in vision nowhere mastered by the subject: the look of the other pre-exists the subject's look; the subject's visual field is always organized in relation to the other's look that it is not (what Lacan calls the 'blot' [*la tache*]); the relation of the look to what one wants to see is always a relation of lure. Certainly the subject here is not an objective subject, nor the one of reflecting consciousness, but the subject of desire.

One could say that it is not correct to criticize the structural/materialist film-makers for not considering the unconscious level of vision, it is not, say, the area they are 'interested in.' However one of the most emphasized claims of these theoretician-filmmakers is that their films offer a relation to vision completely counter to that of dominant cinema; this is the very base of their argument that their films can be politically effective in a struggle against bourgeois ideology. Christian Metz has discussed the close links of phenomenology and cinema (that is why, he says, up to a point, a phenomenological description of cinema can be useful.)[25] Both phenomenology and cinema posit the subject as a pure instance of perception, a subject with full mastery of vision, a subject of consciousness. The premises of LeGrice and Gidal, based as they are on a denial of unconscious processes at the level of vision, image and the apparatus, extend, reinforce and finally erect into a set of theoretical presuppositions the idealist and phenomenological bases of dominant cinema.

The two dangers lying in wait for the subject-in-process of poetic language are psychosis and fetishism. (Julia Kristeva)[26]

In taking up again our question of what sort of fantasmatization of the subject the minimalist work constructs, let us first look at what fetishism in the work of art represents in this statement of Kristeva's. She sees it as 'the constant screening, concealment (*la dérobade*) of the symbolic, paternal, sacrificial function, producing an objectification of the pure signifier, more and more empty of meaning, insipid formalism.'[27] Here 'fetishism' is not being used in the commonly accepted sense of the sexual overvaluation of an object separated from the body, but in the sense of it as a psychical mechanism for transforming signification, the reworking of the fact of castration, that is, the attempt to fantasize a whole and unified body (a basic narcissistic wish).[28] Thus, the fetish is not related to a *thing,* but involves a *process,* a refusal of signification operated through a constant oscillation of meaning. The fetishistic disavowal rephallizes the mother in order to ensure the subject of the integrity of his own body: if the mother has the phallus, then she has always had it and the question of castration 'disappears'. These minimalist efforts, in their attempt to strip away all problematic significations and replace them with a hyper-rational and conscious knowledge, identify this enterprise as the cinema of the lack *par excellence:* it constructs emptiness and insufficiency only in order to fill it. Other writers have discussed the fetishistic structuration of classical film (Metz, Rose, Kuntzel) and others have gone so far as to equate the basic processes of aesthetic elaboration with fetishistic operations like disavowal, doubling, condensation, displacement, metaphorical and metonymical movements (Kristeva, Heath, Rosolato). Guy Rosolato says that the work of art fascinates by keeping in play oscillations of signification (simultaneously establishing and effacing meaning), generating for us a self-representation that would be a totality offered as inexhaustible.[29] But even if fetishism is basic to art-making, there are still degrees of it and the minimalist enterprise seems to offer a particularly pure and extreme example of the quest for an unproblematic center of significance, a unified and coherent subject, a position of pure mastery, a phallus which is not decomposable. And, it is through the look, that is, across the specular regime, that the subject assures himself of the integrity of the object and thus of his own body. The minimalist film-work, then, serves a defensive function for the spectator, assuring the subject control over his own body across an identification with the camera (as carrier of his look) which then reorganizes space, time and signification according to the needs of his own narcissism.[30]

A metapsychology of film must be able to account for the subject's relation to the film in terms of both the activity and the passivity of the sexual drives. The defenses against the drives are as important as the activity of the drives themselves and the notion of cinematic 'pleasure' will have to be complicated through an analysis of the possibilities of defense offered by cinema. Cinema, like perversion, offers an eroticization of the mechanisms of defense against the drives, the object of desire and the means of attaining it.

To say that minimalist film is the extreme example of the fetishism inherent in cinema is to recall at the same time the ambivalent position of fetishism in relation to the Law. (Christian Metz has said that the Law, at the level of cinematic signifier, is the codes.[31]) The fetishist attempts to substitute the rules of his own desire for the culturally predominant ones; the minimalist artist wants an easily manipulable abstract set of rules completely void of cultural signification. The totality of the denial of signification tends to affirm the potency of the paternal function, thus exhibiting a very strong identification with the Law. This is the risk with any aesthetic of transgression.

In terms of a political filmmaking practice, a practice whose emphasis is on transformation rather than transgression, is there any way to eliminate the imaginary relation between spectator and screen? Is there any way to systematically subvert this relation without ending up in the fetishistic impasse described above? Barthes (who, like Brecht, has always been suspicious of cinema) believes that the only solution is in 'complicating a relation with a situation'.[32] There is perhaps only one way to complicate this particular (imaginary) relation: language can offer us an oblique route through the image; it can 'unstick' us a little from the screen as Barthes would say. The films of Godard have systematically taken into account this work of language on image, as have those of Straub and Huillet and Laura Mulvey and Peter Wollen. Images have very little analytical power in themselves; their power of fascination and identification is too strong. This is why there must always be a commentary *on* the image simultaneously with the commentary *of* and *with* them.

Stephen Heath has argued that 'deconstruction is clearly the impasse of the formal device' and that a socio-historically more urgent practice would be a work not on 'codes' but on the operations of narrativization, which for him means 'the constructions and relations of meaning and subject in a specific signifying practice'. We have one example of a politically motivated avant-garde practice which addresses itself exactly to this area—the recent work of several women filmmakers focusing on feminist concerns is less a work on 'codes' and 'perceptual processes' than it is on narrative, fiction and the construction of another subject-relation to the screen. It is not the Modernist pressure towards finding the most 'advanced' solution to formal problems which motivates filmmakers like Chantal Akerman, Marguerite Duras, Yvonne Rainer, Babette Mangolte, Jackie Raynal and others to make films involving 'an action at the limits of narrative within the narrative film, at the limits of its fictions of unity' (Stephen Heath).[33] It is the pressure of a specific socio-historical situation which demands this response, a situation in which narrative and the subject placement it involves are dominant; that is, narrative which reunifies and rephallizes a spectator posed by the film as coherent and all-powerful. The strategies of these feminist filmmakers point to a manner of reworking subjectivity within an analysis of social/sexual relations which avoids the sorts of transgressions of the symbolic paternal function which risk ending in an identification with patriarchy. If filmic practice, like the fetishistic ritual, is an inscription of the look on the body of the mother, we must now begin to consider the possibilities and consequences of the mother returning the look.

Notes

1. See the bibliography following the article for the citations of these articles and other important contributions, especially those of Jacqueline Rose and Stephen Heath.

2. Deke Dusinberre's article 'St. George in the Forest' (*Afterimage,* no. 6, Summer 1976) offers a good overview of the different strains of the English avant-garde. According to this article, the writings of Gidal and LeGrice would not be representative of the whole English avant-garde and Dusinberre even states that 'the theoretical ambitions of those filmmakers who write about film (Gidal, LeGrice) lead to contributions which tend to complicate and/or obfuscate the immediate issues' (p. 17). However, many of their premises are taken up throughout the English Co-op movement. For example, see the new English review *Readings,* no. 1, February 1977, edited by Annabel Nicolson and Paul Burwell.

3. Throughout *Abstract Film and Beyond* 'abstract' and 'formal' are used somewhat interchangeably. In the first part of the book LeGrice uses the term 'abstract' 'very much as it has come to be generally applied to the visual arts, implying "non-representational."' But in Chapter III he gives it a more general meaning: 'Abstract implies the separation of qualities, aspects or generalizations from particular interests', that is, abstract art as analytic work which 'seeks to avoid representation in favor of nonreferential elements' (32). Thus a representational film (in the photographic sense) could contain some 'abstract' tendencies. LeGrice says that if it were not for the common use of abstract', 'concrete' would be better.

4. We realize that there is often a discrepancy between the theoretical writings of the filmmaker and the actual effects of the film-work. These filmmakers, however, consider their theoretical writings and their theoretical film-work to be homologous (but not identical) and the films are generated from their theoretical presuppositions. Our interest here is an analysis of the limits and the possibilities of those presuppositions for offering a theoretical matrix for a radical film practice.

5. Anne Cottringer's 'On Peter Gidal's "Theory and Definition of Structural/Materialist Film"' discusses Gidal's use of the concept 'materialism'. *Afterimage*, no. 6, Summer 1976, 86–95. See also Ben Brewster's review of *Structural Film Anthology, Screen* 17, no. 4 (Winter 1976–1977): 117–20.

6. 'Interview with Hollis Frampton', *Structural Film Anthology*, 71.

7. 'Le signifiant imaginaire', *Communications*, no. 23 (May 1975), pp. 3–55; translated by Ben Brewster as 'The Imaginary Signifier', *Screen*, Summer 1975, pp. 14–76.

8. Catherine Clément has given a very concise overview of the imaginary and symbolic in Lacan's system:

The imaginary, the symbolic and the real constitute the *structure of the subject* in Lacan's system. We will give two formulations of it, both representing what Lacan calls diagram L. The diagram in question divides the subject (S) up into four points which figure the instances which determine it: O, the Other; o' or I, the Ego; o, the other of the other, but under the irreducible form of the partial object of desire (object a). Thus the diagram in its simplified form ("D'une question prealable à tout traitement possible de la psychose" in *Écrits, 1966*):

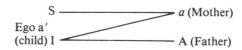

$$S \longrightarrow a \ (Mother)$$
Ego a'
(child) I $\longleftarrow$ A (Father)

This structure, which allows us to disintricate the axes of the real, the symbolic and the imaginary, must be placed in relation to the Oedipus complex, such as Freud extricated it, as a *triangle:* the father, the mother and the infant-subject between the two, for whom all the difficulty of being consists in situating himself between the two parental figuers. The whole history of the Oedipus complex occurs in this see-sawing between the figures of the mother and the father; the 'liquidation' of the Oedipus complex signifies, in a symbolic fashion, the entry into life, the end of infancy, the stabilization of identification. The structure of the subject as described by Lacan takes up these three terms, but transforms them in adding a fourth term: the subject himself, neither father, nor infant, nor mother, but the structure made up of these three terms. The Other is the place of Law, of cultural order. It is the place of the father which gives this law its particular figure; the partial object, called 'little a', is the place of impossible unsatisfying desire, of the giant body of the mother before the separation, of her body, then, forbidden by the Law; it is very much the place of the mother, total and partial at the same time, impossible to attain; finally, the o', the place of the infant, which depends on the other two places. There remains the subject. It is on the side of the real, whose entry into play appears as being excluded from the structure, or rather *foreclosed:* present and determinent, but unapparent and repressed, no longer there. The play of signifiers is the meeting of the two axes, imaginary and symbolic: the imaginary, between the place of the Ego and the place of the object of desire; the symbolic, between the Other and the absent subject of the combination. Thus is made precise the respective situations of the two instances; the symbolic is the order which establishes the subject in language, in *its* language, that of its father, of his father; the imaginary is that which reflects desire in the image that the subject has of himself. On the side of the imaginary is variety, diversity, the multiplicity of objects of desire in one's life; on the side of the symbolic is unicity, determination, the structuration of time. The imaginary, which comes to be hooked onto the panoply of the symbolic, lets itself be represented through the metaphor of *accessories*: objects of disguises, 'the set of imaginary figures', figures of theater; meanwhile the symbolic, in the panoply, represents the support where the variables of the subject attach themselves.' (*La Psychanalyse*, p. 50)

The imaginary is the order of perception, whereas the symbolic is the discursive order. Serge Leclaire explains the relation of the Imaginary to the Symbolic and the Real in this way:

The experience of the Real presupposes the simultaneous use of two correlative functions, the Imaginary function and the Symbolic function. That is Imaginary which, like shadows, has no existence of its own, and yet whose absence, in the light of life, cannot be conceived; that which, without power of distinction inundates singularity and thus escapes any truly rational grasp. That is Imaginary which is irremediably opposed or which is indistinctly confused, without any dialectical movement; the dream is Imaginary . . . just as long as it is not interpreted . . . no symbol can do without Imaginary support. (Anthony Wilden's translation from Serge Leclaire's 'A la recherche des principes d'une psychotherapie des psychoses', *L'Evolution psychiatrique* (1958), pp. 377–411)

Wilden adds:

The topographical regression of 'dream thoughts' to images in the dream might be described as a process of the Symbolic becoming Imaginary. (Anthony Wilden, *The Language of the Self: The function of Language in Psychoanalysis,* translations from Jacques Lacan with notes and commentary by Wilden (Dell, 1968), p. 92)

    9. In Christian Metz, *Le signifiant imaginaire: Psychanalyse et cinéma* (10/18, 1977), pp. 177–371.

    10. Stephen Heath, 'Narrative Space', *Screen,* Autumn 1976.

    11. Thierry Kuntzel, 'Savoir, Pouvoir, Voir', *Ça Cinéma,* no. 7–8 (May 1975), pp. 85–97; 'Le travail du film, 2', *Communications,* no. 23 (May 1975), pp. 136–89.

    12. Jean-Louis Baudry, 'Cinéma: effets idéologiques produits par l'appareil de base,' *Cinéthique,* no. 7–8 (1970, pp. 1–8. Published in an English translation by Alan Williams in *Film Quarterly* 27, no. 2 (Winter 1974–1975): pp. 39–47. Jean-Louis Baudry, 'Le dispositif: approches métapsychologiques de l'impression de réalité', *Communications,* no. 23 (1975): pp. 56–72. Published in an English translation by Bertrand Augst as 'The Apparatus' in *Camera Obscura,* no. 1 (December 1976).

    13. Sigmund Freud, *The Interpretation of Dreams* (New York: Avon Books, 1965), p. 526.

    14. Beaumont Newhall, *The History of Photography* (New York: Museum of Modern Art Press, 1965).

    15. Piera Aulagnier-Spairani, 'Le "désir de savoir" dans ses rapports à la transgression', *L'inconscient,* no. 1 (January 1967), pp. 109–25.

    16. There are also ideological reasons for this emphasis in LeGrice and Gidal. Gidal takes the Althusserian dichotomy between ideology and science even further than Althusser himself with the belief in the possibility of a pure (i.e. beyond ideology) scientific theory and pure practice of that theory. LeGrice's problematic notion of "knowledge" arises from an idealist notion of history as a progressive evolution (his book charts an inevitable 'tendency' with its achievements, regressions, successes in the direction of a greater abstraction and rationality) and a belief in technology (science) as a neutral and objective tool in helping to move from an outmoded form of consciousness to a more radical (more 'aware') form of consciousness.

    17. Jacques Lacan, *Le Séminaire: Les quatre concepts fondamentaux de la psychanalyse* (Seuil, 1973), pp. 65–109.

    18. Ricciotto Canudo, 'L'usine aux images', cited in *L'art du cinéma,* ed. Pierre Lherminier (Editions Seghers, 1960).

    19. This work was presented in his seminar at the Centre Universitaire Américain du Cinéma à Paris, Spring 1977.

    20. Jacques Lacan, 'Le stade du miroir comme formateur de la fonction du Je', *Écrits* (Paris: Seuil, 1966), pp. 93–100. Translated in English as 'The Mirror-Phase as Formative of the Function of the I', *New Left Review,* no. 51 (September–October 1968), pp. 71–77.

21. Jacques Lacan, 'Du regard comme objet petit a,' *Le Séminaire XI: Les quatres concepts fondamentaux de la psychanalyse* (Seuil, 1973), pp. 65–109.

22. There is a tendency toward a kind of pseudo-scientism in much recent avant-garde work, the artists making references to various areas of experimental research to legitimate their work. This tactic is a false solution to the minimalist problem of attempting to go beyond an author-oriented aesthetic by replacing subjectivity with the 'objectivity' of science. One of the problems with this tendency is that it is not at all sure that the present state of psychophysiological research could even permit distinguishing neatly between these different levels (conscious, preconscious, unconscious) or be able to determine if a certain 'psychological reaction' was a *direct* consequence of certain 'physical actions'.

23. Lacan's explication of 'object small a' with the example of the *fort-da* game:

'This spool is not the mother reduced to a little ball . . . –it is a little something of the subject which is detached from him while still being very much a part of him. This is the place to say, with Aristotle's imitation, that man thinks with his object. It is with his object that the infant leaps the boundaries of his domain transformed into holes, shafts and with which he commences his incantation. If it is true that the signifier is the first mark of the subject, how not to recognize here—from the single fact that this game is accompanied by one of the first oppositions to appear—that the object to which this opposition is applied in the act, the spool, is what we designate as the subject. To this object, we will give to it, ulteriorally, its name in the Lacanian algebra—little a.' (*Le Séminaire XI*, p. 60)

24. Of course, for Lacan, if the look is taken in the same dialectic as the unconscious, then vision too is organized in relation to the insufficiency which is the castration complex. In this article we will not go into the (for us) problematic status of castration as *the* lack which retrospectively gives symbolic significance to all the other experience of loss.

25. 'The Imaginary Signifier', section III. 4, 'On the idealist theory of the cinema', pp. 54–56.

26. Julia Kristeva, 'Le sujet en procès: le langage poétique', in *L'identité* (Editions Grasset & Fasquelle, 1977), p. 238.

27. *Ibid.*, p. 238.

28. The background for this discussion of fetishism in relation to film was first formulated in a paper by Sandy Flitterman and myself presented in Thierry Kuntzel's 'Travail du film' seminar at the Centre Universitaire Américain du Cinéma à Paris, November 1976.

29. Guy Rosolato, 'Difficultés à surmonter pour une esthétique psychanalytique', *Essais sur le Symbolique* (1965), pp. 121–28.

30. However precarious the subject's control of that experience might actually be, as Jackie Rose points out in 'The Imaginary—The Insufficient Signifier' (seminar paper, British Film Institute Education Advisory Service, November 1975). She cites Lacan for his discussion of the potential reversibility of this situation: the subject can always be seized by the object of his own look, he can become the *object* of representation.

31. 'The Imaginary Signifier', p. 15.

32. Roland Barthes, 'En sortant du cinéma', *Communications*, no. 23 (May 1975), p. 107.

33. Stephen Heath, 'Narrative Space', *Screen* 17, no. 3 (Autumn 1976), p. 109.

Bibliography

Auglagnier-Spariani, Piera. '"Le Désir de Savoir" dans ses rapports à la transgression', *L'inconscient*, no. 1 (January 1967), pp. 109–125.

Augst, Bertrand. '"The Apparatus": An Introduction', *Camera Obscura*, no. 1 (December 1976), pp. 97–101.

Barthes, Roland. 'En sortant du cinéma', *Communications,* no. 23, (May 1975), pp. 104–108.

Baudry, Jean-Louis. 'Cinéma: effets idéologiques produits par l'appareil de base', *Cinéthique,* no. 7–8, (1970), pp. 1–8. Published in an English translation by Alan Williams in *Film Quarterly* 27, no. 2 (Winter 1974–1975): pp. 39–47, reprinted here.

———. 'Le dispositif: approches métapsychologiques de l'impression de réalité', *Communications,* no. 23 (May 1975), pp. 56–72. Published in an English translation by Bertrand Augst and Jean Andrews in *Camera Obscura,* no. 1 (December 1976), pp. 104–126.

Bellour, Raymond. 'Le cinéma et l'hypnose', unpublished work presented at his seminar at the Centre Universitaire Américain du Cinéma, Paris, Spring 1977.

Brewster, Ben. Review of *Structural Film Anthology, Screen* 17, no. 4 (Winter 1976–1977), pp. 117–20.

Canudo, Ricciotto. 'L'usine aux images', *L'art du cinéma,* ed. Pierre Lherminier (Editions Seghers, 1960).

Clément, Catherine. 'L'imaginaire, le symbolique et le réel', Catherine Clément, François Gantheret, Bernard Mérigot, *La Psychanalyse* (Larousse, 1976).

Cottringer, Anne. 'On Peter Gidal's "Theory and Definition of Structural/Materialist Film"', *Afterimage,* no. 6 (Summer 1976), pp. 86–95.

Dusinberre, Deke. 'St. George in the Forest', *Afterimage,* no. 6 (Summer 1976).

Freud, Sigmund. *The Interpretation of Dreams* (Avon, 1965).

Gidal, Peter. *Structural Film Anthology* (British Film Institute, 1976).

Heath, Stephen. 'Lessons from Brecht', *Screen* 15, no. 2 (Summer 1974), pp. 103–129.

———. 'Film and System, Terms of Analysis, Part I', *Screen* 16, no. 1 (Spring 1975), pp. 7–78. 'Film and System, Terms of Analysis, Part II', *Screen* 16, no. 2 (Summer 1975), pp. 91–114.

———. 'Narrative Space', *Screen* 17, no. 3 (Autumn 1976), pp. 68–112.

Kristeva, Julia. 'Le sujet en procés: le langage poétique', in *L'identité* (Editions Grasset & Fasquelle, 1977), pp. 225–55.

Kuntzel, Thierry. 'Savoir, Pouvoir, Voir', *Ça Cinéma,* no. 7–8 (May 1975), pp. 85–97.

———. 'Le travail du film, 2', *Communications,* no. 23 (May 1975), pp. 136–89.

Lacan, Jacques. 'Le stade du miroir comme formateur de la fonction du Je', in *Écrits* (Seuil, 1966), pp. 93–100. Translated in English as 'The Mirror Phase as Formative of the Function of the "I"', *New Left Review,* no. 51 (September–October 1968).

———. 'Du regard comme objet petit a', *Le Séminaire XI: Les quatres concepts fondamentaux de la psychanalyse* (Seuil, 1973), pp. 65–109.

LeGrice, Malcolm. *Abstract Film and Beyond* (Studio Vista, England, 1977). Simultaneously published in the United States by M.I.T. Press.

MacCabe, Colin. 'Realism and the Cinema: Notes on Some Brechtian Theses', *Screen* 15, no. 2 (Summer 1974).

Metz, Christian. 'Le signifiant imaginaire', *Communications,* no. 23, (May 1975), pp. 3–55. Translated in English by Ben Brewster as 'The Imaginary Signifier' in *Screen* 16, no. 2 (Summer 1975), pp. 14–76.

———. 'Le film de fiction et son spectateur', *Communications,* no. 23 (May 1975), pp. 108–135. Translated in English by Alfred Guzzetti as 'The Fiction Film and Its Spectator' in *New Literary History,* Autumn 1976, pp. 75–105.

———. *'Le signifiant imaginaire: Psychanalyse et cinéma'* (10/18, 1977).

Newhall, Beaumont. *The History of Photography* (Museum of Modern Art, 1964).

Rose, Jacqueline. 'The Imaginary—The Insufficient Signifier', British Film Institute Educational Advisory Service seminar paper, November 1975.

———. 'Paranoia and Film System', *Screen* 17, no. 4 (Winter 1977): 85–105.

Rosolato, Guy. 'Difficultés à surmonter pour une esthétique psychanalytique', *Essais sur le symbolique* (Editions Gallimard, 1965), pp. 121–28.

———. 'Perversions sexuelles', *Encyclopédie Médico-Chirurgicale*, 37392 A[10]–37392 C[10] (Paris).

Wollen, Peter. 'The Two Avant-Gardes', *Studio International,* November–December 1975, pp. 77–85.

MASOCHISM AND THE PERVERSE PLEASURES OF THE CINEMA

GAYLYN STUDLAR

A number of writers have expressed reservations about the line of thought proposed in such articles as Claire Johnston's "Towards a Feminist Film Practice" and Laura Mulvey's "Visual Pleasure and Narrative Cinema." Relegation of the image of women in the cinema to absence or lack, to the nonmale, controlled by a scopophilic male gaze, leads some to take radical, even desperate, measures. For example, Peter Gidal vowed in 1978 never to present an image of a woman in his films, a "solution" that only reproduces the problem.

Those who are unsatisfied with this form of psychoanalytic reading, which tries to turn the methods and assumptions of phallocentric psychoanalysis to the advantage of feminist film theory, have contributed some helpful critiques, but they have not succeeded in proposing an effective counter theory within the domain of psychoanalysis itself. The time is ripe for such a theory, and Gaylyn Studlar's article is a pioneering introduction to some of the conceptual apparatus needed for the task.

Basically, Studlar draws on Gilles Deleuze's study of Sacher-Masoch's novels and through them of masochism to argue that there is a radical difference between sadism and masochism in origin and intent. The Freudian orthodoxy, adopted by most proponents of psychoanalytic film theory, posits these two perversions as reciprocal, the one finding its completion in the needs of the other. Studlar, like Deleuze, locates the origin of masochism in the preoedipal phase of infancy, where its goal is reunion with the mother. This contrasts with the oedipal origins of sadism, which desires to dominate or control the other. Sadism draws on the figuration of genital sexuality and the orgasm, masochism on pregenital sexuality and the pleasure of the symbiotic bond, a bond that is re-presented ambivalently (since it cannot be achieved with its true object, the mothering parent) in the form of recovery and loss, suspense, delay, fantasy, and punishment.

If masochism precedes sadism, and if it derives from the preoedipal, pregenital organization of sexuality, its implications for gender are very different from those of postoedipal, genitally organized sadism, for which women, the object of sadistic voyeurism, represent the threat of castration, not the power of the promise of plenitude and unity. Broadening the view of masochism beyond one of clinical "perversion," Studlar argues that masochism, like sadism, can ground an aesthetic. In this argument, we have the beginnings of a true counter theory of the spectator's relationship to visual pleasure and narrative cinema.

Like Nancy Chodorow in her pioneering book, The Reproduction of Mothering *(Berkeley: University of California Press, 1978), Studlar demonstrates the enormous importance of preoedipal sexuality for later gender development. (Chodorow places more emphasis on the social determinants involved and on the consequences of identifying the mothering function with women than Studlar does, but both return us to a formative range of experiences that recent poststructuralist psychoanalytic film theory has essentially ignored.) This return to the preoedipal period also allows her to link considerations of the cinema as a "dream-screen" (as described by Baudry and Eberwein) with a theory of visual pleasure based on masochistic structures. This is another valuable synthesis, since it meets a need that the stress on sadistic voyeurism and fetishistic scopophilia only partially satisfied. In opening up the possibilities for spectator positions that have not been determined by the consequences of the oedipal crisis and its patriarchal resolution, Studlar makes it possible to conceive of radical but less desperate alternatives to the pleasures of classical narrative cinema.*

This study offers an alternative model to the current discourse that emphasizes voyeurism aligned with sadism, the male controlling gaze as the only position of spectatorial pleasure, and a polarized notion of sexual difference with the female regarded as "lack." In 1978, Christine Gledhill wrote of the need to broaden the focus of feminist film theory, to question guiding theoretical assumptions, and to confront the complexity of "woman's place" within patriarchal culture.[1] In the context of feminist-psychoanalytic approaches to film, the hegemony of the Freudian-Lacanian-Metzian model has, unfortunately, reduced rather than enlarged the field of questions that feminist theory has asked about specific forms of enunciation in classic narrative cinema and the possibilities of subject positioning. While I do not assume to displace the dominant model, there is, I believe, an obvious call to question some of the assumptions that have shaped current trends.

My alternative model is derived from Gilles Deleuze's *Masochism: An Interpretation of Coldness and Cruelty.*[2] Deleuze employs a psychoanalytic-literary approach to the novels of Leopold von Sacher-Masoch, the namesake of masochism, to challenge basic Freudian tenets regarding the sado-masochistic duality and the etiology of masochism as a response to the father and castration fear. If the qualitative differences between sadism and masochism are disregarded and only the pain/pleasure content is considered, then the two perversions might well be considered to be complementary as Freud maintained, but Deleuze shows that only when masochism's formal patterns are recognized as reflections of a unique underlying psychoanalytic structure can the perversion be correctly defined as a distinct clinical entity or as an aesthetic:

Masochism is above all formal and dramatic: this means that its peculiar pleasure-pain complex is determined by a particular kind of formalism, and its experience of guilt by a specific story.[3]

Deleuze considers masochism to be a phenomenology of experience that reaches far beyond the limited definition of a perverse sexuality. Similarly, the masochistic aesthetic extends beyond the purely clinical realm into the arena of artistic form, language, and production of pleasure through a text.

Comparing Masoch's and Sade's novels, Deleuze concludes that Sade's intentions, formal techniques, and language are completely at odds with those of Masoch. These differences are but a reflection of differing psychoanalytic determinants. The Sadian discourse—denotative, scientific, unblinkingly direct in its obscene imperatives and descriptions—creates a fantastically cruel heterocosm based exclusively on the rule of reason. The governing sadistic fantasy expressed in Sade's work exalts the father "beyond all laws," says Deleuze, and negates the mother.[4] In contrast, Masoch's fictive world is mythical, persuasive, aesthetically oriented, and centered around the idealizing, mystical exaltation of love for the punishing woman. In her ideal form as representative of the powerful oral mother, the female in the masochistic scenario is not sadistic, but must inflict cruelty in love to fulfill her role in the mutually agreed upon masochistic scheme. Masoch writes in a typical passage from his most famous novel, "Venus in Furs":

To love and be loved, what joy! And yet how this splendour pales in comparison with the blissful torment of worshipping a woman who treats one as a plaything, of being the slave of a beautiful tyrant who mercilessly tramples one underfoot.[5]

As Deleuze notes, the paradox of the masochistic alliance as exemplified in Masoch's work is the subversion of the expected patriarchal positions of power/powerlessness, master/slave, with the ultimate paradox being the slave's (the male's) willingness to confer power to the female.[6]

An excerpt from Sade's *One Hundred and Twenty Days of Sodom* illustrates the blatant absurdity of equating sadism and masochism on a literary level, and, as Deleuze shows, on a psychoanalytic level as well:

This libertine requires a dozen women, six young, six old and if 'tis possible, six of them should be mothers and the other six daughters. He pumps out their cunts, asses, and mouths; when applying his lips to the cunt, he wants copious urine; when at the mouth, much saliva; when at the ass, abundant farts.[7]

Even when Sade chooses a woman as "heroine," she still acts out the criminally misogynistic impulse that is not satisfied with merely objectifying or demystifying women but must destroy them. In the masochistic text, the female is not one of a countless number of discarded objects but an idealized, powerful figure, both dangerous and comforting. Fetishization, fantasy, and idealizing disavowal replace the frenzied Sadian destruction of the female. While Sade's incessantly active libertines challenge the limits of human endurance and evil in endlessly repeated cycles of sex and violence, the masochistic world barely suggests sexual activity or violence. Deleuze remarks: "Of Masoch it can be said, as it cannot be of Sade, that no one has ever been so far with so little offence to decency."[8] In the masochistic aesthetic, dramatic suspense replaces Sadian accelerating repetition of action, intimacy between mutually chosen partners replaces the impersonality of masses of libertines and victims, idealized eroticism replaces the obscenity that threatens to burst the limits of conventional language in an attempt to match the unattainable, destructive Idea of Evil.[9] If Sade's writing is "structurally linked to crime and sex" as Roland Barthes has said,[10] then the work of Masoch reveals a formal and narrative pattern structurally linked to self-abasement and pre-Oedipal desire.

The formal structures of the masochistic aesthetic—fantasy, disavowal, fetishism, and suspense—overlap with the primary structures that enable classic narrative cinema to produce visual pleasure. These similarities raise fundamental questions about the relationship of cinematic pleasure to masochism, sexual differentiation, processes of identification, the representation of the female in film, and other issues in which a model derived from Deleuze's theory offers a radical alternative to those Freudian assumptions that have been adopted by most of psychoanalytic film theory.

The key question is: Why replace the line of thought represented by Christian Metz and Laura Mulvey, with its stress on the similarity between the structures of sadism and visual pleasure, with an emphasis on masochism's relationship to visual pleasure? What are the advantages?

By focusing on the pregenital period in the development of desire and sexual identity rather than on the phallic phase emphasized in Freud's studies, a consideration of the masochistic aesthetic and film shifts attention to a stage of psychosexual life that has been an overlooked determinant in the "sadistic" model of cinematic spectatorship. The "masochistic model" rejects a stance that has emphasized the phallic phase and the pleasure of control or mastery and therefore offers an alternative to strict Freudian models that have proven to be a dead end for feminist-psychoanalytic theory. In trying to come to terms with patriarchal society and the cinema as a construct of that society, current theoretical discourse has often inadvertently reduced the psychoanalytic complexity of spectatorship through a regressive phallocentrism that ignores a wider range of psychological influences on visual pleasure.

The approach presented here brings together two lines of theoretical work previously separated: (1) the analogy between the cinematic apparatus and the dream screen of the oral period of infancy pursued by Jean-Louis Baudry and Robert Eberwein,[11] and (2) the consideration of representation of the female, identification, and sexually differentiated spectatorship in the theories of Laura Mulvey, Claire Johnston, Mary Ann Doane, and others.[12] The "masochistic

ıld be viewed as an attempt to use the former approach to address the
f the latter.

ealt with the question of masochism in several essays; his views on the
perversion changed over the years, but he was consistent in his belief that Oedipal
conflict was the cause of the perversion. Guilt and fear of castration by the father
led the male child to assume a passive position in order to placate the father and
win his love. Being beaten by the father (or the female who provides the father's
disguise in the conscious fantasy) was "not only the punishment for the forbidden genital relation with the mother, but also a regressive substitute for it." The
punishment acquired "libidinal excitation," and "here," Freud declared, "we
have the essence of masochism."[13] Freud developed a theory of masochism as a
primary drive expressing the Death Instinct but was continually drawn into
reaffirming the complementary status of masochism and sadism. He stated that,
in the former, the heightened sadism of the superego was retained in the libido
 with the ego as "victim." In sadism, the Death Instinct was deflected outwards.[14]

Deleuze believes the superego/ego activities of sadism and masochism are
completely different, but, more important to a study of masochism and film, he
makes the mother the primary determinant in the structure of the masochistic
fantasy and in the etiology of the perversion.[15] Both love object and controlling
agent for the helpless child, the mother is viewed as an ambivalent figure during
the oral period. Whether due to the child's experience of real trauma, as Bernhard
Berliner asserts, or due to the narcissistic infant's own insatiability of demand,
the pleasure associated with the oral mother is joined in masochism with the need
for pain.[16] The masochistic fantasy cannot by its very nature fulfill its most primal
desire—"dual unity and the complete symbiosis between child and mother"—
except in the imagination.[17] As a consequence, death becomes the fantasy solution to masochistic desire.

The mother assumes her authority in masochism on the basis of her own importance to the child, not, as Freud maintained, because the father figure must be
"hidden" behind her in order to deflect the homosexual implications of the male
subject's fantasy. Roy Schafer identifies the child's fear of losing the mother as
the primary source of her authority.[18] Rooted in the fear of being abandoned by
the mother, masochism obsessively recreates the movement between concealment and revelation, disappearance and appearance, seduction and rejection. Posited as "lacking nothing," the mother is allied with the child in the disavowal of
the destruction of the superego. Deleuze maintains that the father's punishing
superego and genital sexuality are symbolically punished in the son, who must
expiate his likeness to the father. Pain symbolically expels the father and "fools"
the superego. It is not the son who is guilty, as in Freud's theory, but the father
who attempts to come between mother and child.[19] In Deleuze's view, fear of the
castrating father and Oedipal guilt cannot account for masochism's paradoxical
pain/pleasure structure. His denial of the importance of castration anxiety to the
perversion's formation constitutes a revision of Freudian theory that stands in
agreement with Michael de M'Uzan and Theodore Reik. M'Uzan deduces from
clinical observation that the masochist "fears nothing, not even castration."[20] In

his lengthy study *Masochism in Modern Man,* in which he details the social rather than sexual manifestations of masochism, Reik parallels M'Uzan's assessment: castration anxiety is not of major significance in the etiology of the perversion.[21]

It should be noted that Deleuze positions the male as the fantasizing subject of his construct. In this respect, his model might be regarded as sexist, although he notes that the female child can take the same position in relation to the oral mother.[22] Deleuze's model may also be approached from another perspective that makes it more applicable to a consideration of spectatorial response to film. The masochistic fantasy may be viewed as a situation in which the subject (male or female) assumes the position of the child who desires to be controlled *within* the dynamics of the fantasy. The sadistic fantasy (while not a simple reversal of instinct or aim) is one in which the subject takes the position of the controlling parent, who is not allied with the child (object) in a mutually agreed upon pact of pleasure/pain but who exercises (within the fantasy) a sadistic power over an unwilling victim.[23]

Masochism subverts traditional psychoanalytic notions regarding the origins of human desire and the mother's and father's roles in the child's psychic development. A theory of masochism that emphasizes pre-Oedipal conflicts and pleasures invites consideration of responses to film by spectators of both sexes that may conflict with conscious cultural assumptions about sexual difference, gender identity, and the separation of identification from object cathexis. A theory of masochistic desire also questions the complicity of most psychoanalytic film theory with phallocentrism as a formative instance in structuring identity and scopic pleasure. It also questions the pre-eminence of a pleasure based on a position of control rather than submission. In suggesting that the oral mother could be the primary figure of identification and power in clinical and aesthetic manifestations of masochism, Deleuze's theory of masochistic desire challenges the notion that male scopic pleasure must center around control—never identification with or submission to the female.

This article is derived from a book-length study of the films of Josef Von Sternberg that uses practical criticism to examine the masochistic aesthetic in film and the relationship between the formal elements of the aesthetic, the films' psychodynamics, and the specific forms of visual pleasure. With their submissive male masochist, the oral mother embodied in the ambivalent, alluring presence of Marlene Dietrich, and their ambiguous sexuality that has often been linked to "sado-masochism" and "degradation,"[24] the Von Sternberg/Dietrich collaborations offer themselves as a prime case study of the masochistic aesthetic in film.

Within the context of the post-modernist critique of realism, Von Sternberg's films have become the center of increasing interest. They are creations of sublime visual beauty and sensuality; dreamlike chiaroscuro and stifling decorative excess form the backdrop for melodrama pervaded by a diffuse sexuality. As many critics have remarked, the films are poetic but not symbolic, melodramatic and even tragic, but marked by a detached, ironic humor. In these narratives dominated by passion, even passion takes on a curiously distancing coldness. The films featuring Marlene Dietrich add the paradox of the dazzling yet androgynous female who is simultaneously moral and amoral, eminently proper yet irredeemably decadent.

As a result of their multiple layers of paradox, fascinating ambiguity of emotion, and almost transcendental visual beauty, Von Sternberg's films have again and again inspired attempts to explain their structure and meaning. They have just as frequently served as examples in theoretical treatises dealing with the representation of the female in narrative cinema or questions concerning the unconscious determinants of visual pleasure. Among the most important of these is Laura Mulvey's use of Von Sternberg's films to illustrate the concept of fetishistic scopophilia in her milestone article, "Visual Pleasure and Narrative Cinema." To her, Von Sternberg's *Morocco* typifies the kind of visual style and narrative structure which traps the female into a position of "to-be-looked-at-ness," of passive exhibitionism that oppresses women for the sake of the patriarchy's fetishistic aims. Mulvey regards such a female fetish as "reassuring rather than dangerous."[25] Although subscribing to Mulvey's thesis, Mary Ann Doane has referred to Dietrich's image as exemplifying the "excess of femininity . . . aligned with the *femme fatale* . . . and . . . necessarily regarded by men as evil incarnate."[26] Contrary to Doane, it is Dietrich's androgynous quality that is most often noted, and Carole Zucker has argued (with justification) that Dietrich's morality is "impossibly exalted" in the Von Sternberg films.[27] Adding to the controversy is Robin Wood's attempt to counter Mulvey's analysis of the role of the female in the films' narrative strategy and visual style. He argues that Von Sternberg is "fully aware" of the female's position as object for the male gaze and uses this as "an articulated theme" in *Blonde Venus* rather than an end product.[28] He has not, however, countered Mulvey's fundamental premise: that visual pleasure in classic narrative cinema is based on the workings of the castration complex.

Rather than develop a detailed textual analysis, this examination of the masochistic aesthetic and film explores the wider theoretical implications of masochism to cinematic pleasure. I will very briefly examine these implications in regard to five crucial issues: (1) the female defined as lack, (2) the male gaze defined by control, (3) the cause and function of disavowal and fetishism, (4) the dream screen, and (5) identification, particularly identification with the opposite sex.

THE FEMALE AS LACK

The female as cinematic image is often considered to be an ambivalent spectatorial pleasure for the male because she signifies the possibility of castration. She represents difference, nonphallus, lack. Undoubtably, the tension between attraction and fear is an ambivalence underlying much of cinema's representation of the female, but it is an oversimplication to collapse the entire signification of woman to phallic meaning.[29]

Within masochism, the mother is not defined as lack nor as "phallic" in respect to a simple transference of the male's symbol of power. She is powerful in her own right because she possesses what the male lacks—the breast and the womb.[30] Active nurturer, first source of love and object of desire, first environment and agent of control, the oral mother of masochism assumes all symbolic functions. Parallel to her idealization is a degrading disavowal of the father. "The father is nothing," says Deleuze, "he is deprived of all symbolic function."[31]

The infant's fantasy goal of re-fusion, of complete symbiosis with the mother is necessarily informed by ambivalence. The promise of blissful reincorporation into the mother's body and re-fusion of the child's narcissistic ego with the mother as ideal ego is also a threat. Only death can hold the final mystical solution to the expiation of the father and symbiotic reunion with the idealized maternal rule. The masochist imagines the final triumph of a parthenogenetic rebirth from the mother.[32]

Deleuze associates the good oral mother of masochism with the "ideal of coldness, solicitude, and death," the mythic extremes that crystallize her ambivalence.[33] The female reflects the fantasy of the desiring infant who regards the mother as both sacred and profane, loving and rejecting, frustratingly mobile yet the essence of rhythmic stability and stillness. In the masochist's suspension of the final "gratification" of death, the obsessive return to the moment of separation from the oral mother must be reenacted continuously as the masochistic *fort/da* game of desire that is the meeting point between fantasy and action.[34] Masochistic repetition sustains the paradoxical pain/pleasure structure of the perversion's psychodynamics and reflects the careful control of desire so necessary to sustaining the masochistic scenario even as it expresses the compulsive aspect of the fixation in infantile sexuality. Overriding the demands of the incest taboo, the castration complex, and progress into genital sexuality, masochism is a "subversive" desire that affirms the compelling power of the pre-Oedipal mother as a stronger attraction than the "normalizing" force of the father who threatens the alliance of mother and child.

The repetition of loss, of suffering, does not deter or confuse masochistic desire but inflames it, as graphically demonstrated in Von Sternberg's *The Devil Is a Woman.* His health broken, his career ruined by his involvement with "the most dangerous woman alive," Don Pasquale protests that he gains "no pleasure" in telling his friend Antonio about his road to ruin. It becomes obvious that he not only enjoys telling his story, but the retelling itself is the impetus for a new round robin in Don Pasquale's masochistic pursuit of Concha Perez. He allows himself to be shot in a duel to satisfy Concha's desire for another man (Antonio). Lying on his deathbed, he attains what he desires most, Concha and Death, one in the same, both still suspended, promised, but withheld. The eternal masochistic attitude of waiting and suspended suffering is maintained in all its tragedy and comic absurdity to the very end of this, the last Von Sternberg/Dietrich collaboration.

The ambivalence of separation/union from the mother, formalized in masochistic repetition and suspension, is an ambivalence shared by all human beings. Contrary to the Freudian view of familial dynamics, in which the mother has little psychological impact on her children's development, Deleuze, Schafer, Robert Stoller, Nancy Chodorow, and Janine Chasseguet-Smirgel regard the mother's influence and her *authority* as major factors in the child's development. The child's view of the powerful, loved, but threatening female during the pre-Oedipal stage is not obliterated by later stages of life—including the male's passage through the castration complex.[35] Hans Loewald suggests that, while the identification with the powerful pre-Oedipal mother is fundamental to the individual's organization of ego-reality, this same identification is the "source of the deepest dread."[36] Janine Chasseguet-Smirgel goes so far as to suggest that the contempt for women Freud believed was an inevitable male reaction to the perception of female "castration" is actually a pathological and defensive response to maternal power.[37]

In returning to the fantasies originating in the oral stage of development, the masochistic aesthetic opens the entirety of film to the existence of spectatorial pleasures divorced from issues of castration, sexual difference, and female lack. Current theory ignores the pleasure in submission that is phylogenetically older than the pleasure of mastery—for both sexes. In masochism, as in the infantile stage of helpless dependence that marks its genesis, pleasure does not involve mastery of the female but submission to her. This pleasure applies to the infant, the masochist, and the film spectator as well. Psychoanalytic film theory must reintegrate the powerful maternal image that is viewed as a complex, pleasurable "screen memory" by both male and female spectators, even in the patriarchal society.[38] As Janine Chasseguet-Smirgel asserts:

Now the woman as she is depicted in Freudian theory is exactly the opposite of the primal maternal imago as she is revealed in the clinical material of both sexes . . . the contradictions . . . throughout Freud's work on the problem of sexual phallic monism and its consequences, force us to take a closer notice of this opposition between the woman, as she is described by Freud, and the mother as she is known to the Unconscious. . . . If we underestimate the importance of our earliest relations and our cathexis of the maternal image, this means we allow paternal law to predominate and are in flight from our infantile dependence.[39]

Castration fear and the perception of sexual difference have no importance in forming the masochistic desire for complete symbiosis with the mother. The polarities of female lack/male phallus and the narrow view that the female in film can only function as the object of a sadistic male spectatorial possession must yield to other considerations.

The female in the masochistic aesthetic is more than the passive object of the male's desire for possession. She is also a figure of identification, the mother of plenitude whose gaze meets the infant's as it asserts her presence and her power. Von Sternberg's expression of the masochistic aesthetic in film offers a complex image of the female in which she is the object of the look but also the holder of a "controlling" gaze that turns the male into an object of "to-be-looked-at-ness." In *Morocco*, Private Tom Brown (Gary Cooper), a notorious "ladykiller," is reduced to the passive "feminine" position as object of Amy Jolly's appraising, steady gaze. Amy throws him a rose, which Brown then wears behind his ear. Operating within the limitations of the patriarchy, the Dietrich character in these films displays her ability to fascinate in confirmation of what Michel Foucault has called "power asserting itself in the pleasure of showing off, scandalizing, or resisting."[40] In response to the male gaze, Dietrich looks back or initiates the look. This simple fact contains the potential for questioning her objectification.

THE GAZE

While the pleasures of the cinematic apparatus as dream screen have been associated with oral phase pleasure by Jean-Louis Baudry and Robert Eberwein, the pleasures of viewing the female image in film have consistently been linked to the phallic phase, the castration complex, and the resulting physiological "needs" of the male spectator.

The structure of the look is one of the most important elements in defining visual pleasure. According to Laura Mulvey, narrative film is made for the pleasure of the male spectator alone, who "indirectly" possesses the female through the look, or rather the relay of looks created by the camera, the male star's gaze, and the spectator's own gaze. The woman is the bearer of the "burden of male desire," which is "born with language." She crystallizes the paradox of "the traumatic moment" of desire's birth—the castration complex, because she represents sexual difference. The male spectator escapes the castration anxiety the female image evokes either by a sadistic voyeurism (demystifying the female) or through fetishistic scopophilia. The latter, a "complete disavowal of castration," turns the female into a fetish, the signifier of the absent phallus.[41]

Mulvey's deterministic, polarized model leads to a crucial "blind spot" in her theory of visual pleasure, which has been noted by D. N. Rodowick. In "The Difficulty of Difference," Rodowick argues that Mulvey avoids the logical conclusion of her own theory that would necessitate pairing masochism, the passive submission to the object, with fetishistic scopophilia. Because of the "political nature of her argument," Rodowick concludes, Mulvey cannot admit that the masculine look contains passive elements and can signify *submission to* rather than *possession of* the female.[42]

In eliding a possible male spectatorial position informed by masochism, Mulvey is forced to limit the male gaze to one that only views the female as a signifier of castration and an object for possession. In reducing spectatorial pleasure to the workings of the castration complex, Mulvey also ignores the existence of pre-Oedipal desires and ambivalences that play a part in the genesis of scopophilia and fetishism as well as masochism. In Mulvey's construct of immutable polarities, the female "can exist only in relation to castration"; she is either the "bearer of guilt" or the "perfect product."[43]

Cinematic pleasure is much closer to masochistic scopic pleasure than to a sadistic, controlling pleasure privileged by Mulvey and also by Christian Metz. In Metz's *The Imaginary Signifier,* the voyeuristic separation of subject/screen object is used to align the spectator with sadism. "Voyeuristic desire, along with certain forms of sadism," says Metz, "is the only desire whose principle of distance symbolically and spatially evokes this fundamental rent." Metz believes that all voyeurism is sadistic to a degree and compares cinematic voyeurism to "unauthorized scopophilia" and its prototype, the child viewing the primal scene.[44]

Contrary to Metz, Jean Laplanche has shown how the spectatorial position in the primal gaze is aligned with masochism, not sadism. Laplanche considers masochism to be the "fundamental fantasy." He compares the infant's position to that of "Odysseus tied to the mast or Tantalus, on whom is imposed the spectacle of parental intercourse." Corresponding to the perturbation of pain is the "sympathetic excitation . . . the passive position of the child . . . [that] is not simply a passivity in relation to adult activity, but passivity in relation to adult fantasy intruding within him."[45] Parallel to Laplanche's description of the primal scene is Masoch's "A Childhood Memory and Reflection on the Novel." Ten-year-old Leopold von Sacher-Masoch, hiding in his aunt's bedroom closet, hears his aunt welcome her lover: "I did not understand what they were saying, still less what they were doing, but my heart began to pound, for I was acutely aware of my situation . . ." The husband interrupts the lovers' rendezvous. Madame Zenobia begins to beat him. She then discovers Leopold and whips him. "I must admit," Masoch writes, "while I writhed under my aunt's cruel blows, I experienced acute pleasure."[46] Not surprisingly, Von Sternberg's films also contain many scenes that evoke the situation of the child witnessing or overhearing parental intercourse. In Shanghai Express, Doc Harvey eavesdrops on the "negotiations" between Lily and the nefarious General Chang. Like the passive child who sees/overhears the primal scene and fantasizes both discovery and punishment, Doc is threatened with punishment for his curiosity and his desire: General Chang decides to blind him. In The Scarlet Empress, Alexei loves Catherine but is forced by her to prepare the royal bedchamber for the arrival of her lover, General Orloff. Alexei assumes the role of the child-spectator.

If Sade's novels are taken as the prototype of sadistic object relations, then it is obvious that the sadist is driven to consume or destroy the object in order to bring about the directly experienced pleasure of orgasm for himself. This negation cannot be exercised merely through the sadistic "look" — the active gaze. Orgasm is not the goal of the masochist, who is bound to the regime of pregenital sexuality. Masoch's heroes are forever swooning into a faint before the blissful moment of consummation. Closing the gap between the desiring masochistic subject and the object actually threatens the narcissistic gratification of the masochist who "gives nothing" and cannot endure the "anxiety [of giving] that must accompany orgasm."[47] Masochistic desire depends on separation to guarantee the structure of its ambivalent desire. To close the gap, to overcome separation from the mother, to fulfill desire, to achieve orgasm means death. The contracted, mutual alliance of the masochistic relationship guarantees distance/separation. Unlike sadism, which depends upon action and immediate gratification, masochism savors suspense and distance.

The spectator at the cinematic dream screen regresses to a similar state of orality as the masochist and also experiences a loss of ego-body boundary. Spectatorial pleasure is a limited one like the infantile, extragenital sexual pleasure that defines the masochist. Like the masochist, but unlike the sadist, to remain within the confines of normal spectatorship and not become, as Stephen Heath says, "a true voyeur,"[48] the spectator must avoid the orgasmic release that would effectively destroy the boundaries of disavowal and disrupt the magical thinking that defines his/her oral, infantile, and narcissistic use of the cinematic object. The spectator's narcissistic omnipotence is like the narcissistic, infantile omnipotence of the masochist, who ultimately cannot control the active partner. Immobile, surrounded in darkness, the spectator becomes the passive receiving object who is also subject. The spectator must comprehend the images, but the images cannot be controlled. On this level of pleasure, the spectator receives, but no object-related demands are made.

FETISHISM AND DISAVOWAL

The masochistic aesthetic appears to be a major site for developing a critique of theories of visual pleasure that hinge on the role of castration fear in the formation of male spectatorial pleasure. Masochism is not associated with castration fear, yet fetishism is an integral part of its dynamic. Disavowal and fetishism, the two common matrices of masochism and cinematic spectatorial pleasure, do not always reflect the psychic trauma of castration and sexual difference defined as feminine lack.

Recent psychoanalytic research into the pre-Oedipal period indicates that disavowal and fetishism are operative much, much earlier than the phallic stage and are not necessarily used as a defense against castration anxiety. Of particular importance to the study of visual pleasure and masochism is the view that fetishism and masochism evidence the prolonged need for primary identification with the "almighty pre-Oedipal mother."[49] If the mother/infant relationship is disturbed when the child's body boundaries are not well established, fetishism based on the disavowal of her loss may develop as a defensive maneuver to restore the mother's body, permit passive infant satisfaction, and protect primary identification.[50]

In summarizing various findings, Robert Dickes states that most pregenital research stands in direct opposition to Freud, i.e., that "the fetish represents more than the female phallus."[51] Dickes believes that the traditional view of the fetish as "a talisman in relieving phallic castration anxiety" is a "late stage of the development . . . ordinarily . . . never reached."[52] Most children, regardless of sex, use transitional objects to soothe the separation from the mother. If the child cannot accommodate itself to this separation, the transitional object may be retained and lead to fetishism. While Socarides believes fetishism "may have no etiological connection with phallic or genital sexuality," Wulff concludes that the fetish "represents a substitute for the mother's breast and the mother's body."[53]

Fetishism and disavowal are not exclusively male psychoanalytic manifestations, but males may be much more likely to develop such perversions because of problems in resolving gender identity (crossing over from primary to same-sex identification) unrelated to the existence of any sexually differentiated scopic drive.[54] Female perversion does exist; however, the extreme forms, in particular, are less "visible" than the male version because the female can "hide" impaired sexual function.[55] As a result, females may, as Charles Socarides believes, tend to exhibit "forms of fetishism not obviously associated with genital functioning," for example, ritualistic preparations for intercourse.[56] Although it is naive to assume that the identification of female scopophilia or fetishism would open a gap for the female spectator within dominant cinema, the pregenital origin of these manifestations calls into question the views that use them to exclude the female from the fundamental structures of cinematic pleasure or even from the possibility of libidinalized looking.

DREAM SCREEN

Masochistic fantasy is dominated by oral pleasure, the desire to return to the nondifferentiated body state of the mother/child, and the fear of abandonment (the state of nonbreast, nonplenitude). In a sense, these same wishes are duplicated by the film spectator who becomes a child again in response to the dream screen of cinema. This dream screen affords spectatorial pleasure in recreating the first fetish—the mother as nurturing environment. The spectator at the cinematic dream screen regresses to a state that Baudry says is analogous to the oral period.[57] Like the fetish objects that follow, the dream screen restores the sense of wholeness of the first symbiotic relationship as it restores the unity of the undifferentiated ego/ego ideal. It functions like a "good blanket" reuniting the spectator/child with the earliest object of desire that lessens the anxiety of the ego loosened from body boundaries.[58]

In restoring the first sleep environment of the dream screen, the cinematic apparatus re-establishes the fluid boundaries to self. In "The Unrememberable and the Unforgettable: The Passive Primal Repression," Alvan Frank discusses the psychic benefits of hallucinatory screen/breast experiences that create an absence of ego boundaries and permit the regression to earlier perceptual modes.[59] The cinema may also offer this type of psychic reparation in the re-creation of a screen phenomenon that gives access to the unremembered "memories" of earliest childhood experience.

The dream screen as the first hallucination of gratification is an essential notion to considering cinematic pleasure. Through imagination the child creates the mother and the breast. Just as the fantasized breast cannot offer real nourishment or interaction with the mother, the cinematic apparatus cannot provide intimacy or fusion with real objects. The spectator must disavow an absence: the dream screen offers only partial gratification of the symbiotic wish. The object/screen/images cannot be physically possessed or controlled by the spectator. The spectator's "misapprehension" of control over cinematic images is less a misapprehension than it is a disavowal of the loss of ego autonomy over image formation.

IDENTIFICATION

In restoring the pre-ego of primary narcissism, the cinema encourages a regression characterized by all the possibilities of identification and projection resembling the infantile mechanisms operative in perversions. The pleasures of perversion depend directly on a splitting kind of ego defense to solidify identity.[60] By satisfying the compulsion to repeat archaic stages of life, the artificial regression of the cinema enlarges and reintegrates the ego through different forms of ego-reality.[61] The cinematic spectator experiences infantile forms of object cathexis and identification normally repressed. Among the most important aspects of the release of repressed material are the pleasures of re-experiencing the primary identification with the mother and the pleasurable possibilities of gender mobility through identification. Loewald regards identification with the mother as essential to ego formation and the structuring of the personality:

. . . the primary narcissistic identity with the mother forever constitutes the deepest unconscious origin and structural layer of the ego and reality, and the motive force for the ego's "remarkable striving toward unification, synthesis."[62]

While the male's pre-Oedipal identification with the mother is repressed in adult life, for both male and female, same-sex identification does not totally exclude opposite-sex identification.[63] The wish to be both sexes—to *overcome* sexual difference—remains.

Although Freud recognized the bisexuality of every human being, he continually returned to an emphasis on the polarity between masculine and feminine—a polarity that has infiltrated feminist-psychoanalytic approaches to film. Recent research has revealed the vital importance of psychic androgyny (bisexuality) to understanding sexuality, identity, and the search for pleasure. In his study, "The Drive to Become Both Sexes," Lawrence Kubie details two prominent aspects of bisexuality: (1) the reverse of penis envy, and (2) the urge to become both sexes:

Overlooked is the importance of the reverse and complementary envy of the male for the woman's breast, for nursing as well as his envy for the woman's ability to conceive and to bring forth babies . . . from childhood and throughout life, on conscious, preconscious, and unconscious levels, in varying proportions and emphases, the human goal seems almost invariably to be *both* sexes, with the inescapable consequence that we are always attempting in every moment and every act both to affirm and deny our gender identities.[64]

Socarides, Zilboorg, and others have linked the male's fetishization of the female to this same urge to restore the wholeness of bisexuality—of having both male and female sexual characteristics. In Socarides's view, the male's identification with the pre-Oedipal mother expresses itself in "the wish for female genitalia, the wish for a child, and the wish to undo the separation from the mother."[65] Cathexis and identification are simultaneous in the dual aim of the bisexual urge.[66] The ability to simultaneously desire and also identify with the opposite sex has important implications for film spectatorship. When opposite-sex identification has been considered, it has most often been regarded as a problem for the female spectator rather than as a potential pleasure available to both sexes. The "masculinization" of the feminine spectator has been discussed by Mary Ann Doane and Laura Mulvey in terms of the female spectator's identification with the male position. In their view, this trans-sex identification is the result of the female's lack of a spectatorial position of her own, other than a masochistic-female/object identification.[67] Neglected are the possibilities of male identification with the female (even as an ideal ego) or his identification with a "feminized" masculine character.

Like the wish and counterwish for fusion with and separation from the mother, the wish to change gender identity, the "attempt to identify with and to become both parents," cannot be fulfilled in "reality."[68] Laplanche has stated that fantasy is one means of achieving the goal of reintegrating opposite-sex identification.[69] Otto Fenichel believed that scopophilic pleasure was dependent on taking the position, not of the observed same-sex participant in intercourse, but the opposite sex.[70] Through the mobility of multiple, fluid identifications, the cinema provides an enunciative apparatus that functions as a protective guise like fantasy or dream to permit the temporary satisfaction of what Kubie regards as "one of the deepest tendencies in human nature."[71]

Because pleasure in looking and, especially, looking at the dream screen of cinema and the female involves pregenital pleasures and ambivalences, the role and reaction of the sexually differentiated spectator must be approached in a completely different light. The pregenital pleasures of perversion are not limited to the enjoyment of the male spectator, nor available to the female only if she abandons masochistic identification with the "female object" and then identifies with a male spectatorial position defined only by control.

Prompted by the need to delineate the relationship of masochism and its formal structures to current psychoanalysis, a reconsideration of the role of pregenital states of psychic development holds great promise for opening new areas of exploration in the study of spectatorial pleasure. Many of the assumptions adopted by film theorists from Freudian metapsychology or Lacan seem inadequate in accounting for cinematic pleasure. To understand the structure of looking, visual pleasure must be connected to its earliest manifestations in infancy. As Edith Jacobson's work implies, as well as that of Stoller, Bak, Loewald, and others, the visual pleasure experienced in archaic stages is not automatically negated by later stages of the child's development.[72] The close resemblance of the cinematic apparatus to the structures of perversion and, specifically, to masochism warrants further investigation beyond the limitations imposed by current theoretical discourse if the nature of cinematic pleasure is to be understood in its full complexity and psychological significance.

Notes

1. Christine Gledhill, "Recent Developments in Feminist Criticism," *Quarterly Review of Film Studies* 3 (Fall 1978), pp. 457–93. In her 1984 revision of this article for *Re-Vision: Essays in Feminist Film Criticism* (Frederick, Md.: AFI-University Publications of America, 1984), Gledhill rearticulates her original critique.

2. Gilles Deleuze, *Masochism: An Interpretation of Coldness and Cruelty* (New York: George Braziller, 1971); Leopold von Sacher-Masoch, "Venus in Furs," trans. Jean McNeil, in Deleuze.

3. Deleuze, p. 95.

4. Deleuze, p. 52.

5. Sacher-Masoch, p. 129.

6. Deleuze, p. 80.

7. Donatien Alphonse François de Sade, *The 120 Days of Sodom and Other Writings*, trans. and ed. Austryn Wainhouse and Richard Seaver (New York: Grove Press, 1966), p. 577.

8. Deleuze, p. 31.

9. Deleuze, pp. 16–19. See also Roland Barthes, *Sade/Loyola/Fourier*, trans. Richard Miller (New York: Hill & Wang, 1976), pp. 31–37.

10. Barthes, p. 34.

11. Jean-Louis Baudry, "The Apparatus," *Camera Obscura* 1 (Fall 1976), pp. 105–26; Robert Eberwein, "Reflections on the Breast," *Wide Angle* 4, 3 (1981), pp. 48–53.

12. Laura Mulvey, "Visual Pleasure and Narrative Cinema," *Screen* 16 (Autumn 1975), pp. 6–18, reprinted here. Claire Johnston, *Notes on Women's Cinema* (London: Society for Education in Film and Television, 1973), pp. 2–4; Mary Ann Doane, "Misrecognition and Identity," *Cine-Tracts* 11 (Fall 1980), pp. 28–30; Doane, "Film and the Masquerade: Theorising the Female Spectator," *Screen* 23 (September–October 1982), pp. 74–87.

13. Sigmund Freud, "A Child Is Being Beaten" (1919), in *Sex and the Psychology of Love*, ed. Philip Rieff (New York: Macmillan, Collier Books, 1963), p. 117. See "The Economic Problem in Masochism", in *General Psychological Theory: Papers on Metapsychology*, ed. Philip Rieff (New York: Macmillan, Collier Books, 1963), pp. 190–93, for Freud's first essay to use the Death Instinct theory as an approach to the clinical and theoretical dilemmas. See also "Instincts and Their Vicissitudes" (1915) in *General Psychological Theory*, p. 25 and "Three Essays on the Theory of Sexuality," *Standard Edition of the Complete Psychological Works*, ed. James Strachey (London: Hogarth Press, 1953–66) Vol. 7, pp. 159–61.

14. Freud, "The Economic Problem in Masochism," pp. 190–91.

15. Deleuze, pp. 50–54. See also Bernhard Berliner, "On Some Psychodynamics of Masochism," *Psychoanalytic Quarterly* 16 (1947), pp. 459–71; Gustav Bychowski, "Some Aspects of Masochistic Involvement," *Journal of the American Psychoanalytic Association* 7 (April 1959), pp. 248–73; E. Bergler, *The Basic Neurosis* (New York: Grune and Stratton, 1949) for other views that locate masochism's genesis in the mother/child relationship. See Deleuze, pp. 111–12, on superego/ego.

16. Berliner, "Libido and Reality in Masochism," *Psychoanalytic Quarterly* 9 (1940), pp. 323–26, 333. Deleuze believes that the oral mother of masochism is the good mother who takes on the functions of the two "bad mothers of masochism," the uterine mother and the Oedipal mother. In the process, the functions are idealized and, as Deleuze explains, "This concentration of functions in the person of the good oral mother is one of the ways in which the father is cancelled out" (p. 55).

17. Bychowski, p. 260. The issue of why pain is necessary to masochism's dynamic of pleasure is still one of the most controversial in psychoanalysis. See Abram Kardiner, Aaron Karush, and Lionel Ovesey, "A Methodological Study of Freudian Theory III: Narcissism, Bisexuality, and the Dual Instinct Theory," *Journal of Nervous and Mental Disorders* 129 (1959), pp. 215–22. See also Deleuze, pp. 108–109.

18. Roy Schafer, "The Idea of Resistance," *International Journal of Psycho-Analysis* 54 (1973), p. 278.

19. Deleuze, p. 95. "Again, while the sense of guilt has great importance in masochism, it acts only as a cover, as the humorous outcome of a guilt that has already been subverted; for it is no longer the guilt of the child towards the father, but that of the father himself, and of his likeness in the child . . . When guilt is experienced 'masochistically,' it is already distorted, artificial and ostentatious" (p. 95). Deleuze's theory—that the father is the guilty one—is not as unusual as it might first appear. See Claude Lévi-Strauss, *The Raw and the Cooked*, trans. Johan and Doreen Weightman (New York: Harper & Row, 1969), p. 48.

20. Michael de M'Uzan, "A Case of Masochistic Perversion and an Outline of a Theory," *International Journal of Psycho-Analysis* 54 (1973), p. 462.

21. Theodore Reik, *Masochism in Modern Man,* trans. M. H. Beigel and G. M. Kruth (New York: Farrar, Straus, 1941), p. 428.

22. Deleuze, pp. 59–60.

23. See Victor Smirnoff, "The Masochistic Contract," *International Journal of Psycho-Analysis* 50 (1969), pp. 666–71, for an analysis of masochism heavily indebted to Deleuze's work, but which discounts the role of pain and emphasizes the role of the contractual alliance in the perversion. I must acknowledge my own debt to Marsha Kinder for suggesting this expansion of Deleuze's model.

24. Robin Wood, "Venus de Marlene," *Film Comment* 14 (March–April 1978), p. 60.

25. Mulvey, p. 14.

26. Doane, "Film and the Masquerade: Theorising the Female Spectator," p. 82. Doane refers to Dietrich's image as a stage performer. She takes Silvia Bovenschen's comments in "Is There a Feminine Aesthetic?" *New German Critique* 11 (Winter 1977), p. 130, and uses them to support her remarks on excess femininity. Bovenschen actually associates Dietrich with an "intellectual understatement" and refers to her becoming a "myth" despite "her subtle disdain for men." The complexity of Dietrich's image as discussed by Bovenschen does not support Doane's use of her statements to associate Dietrich with "an excess of femininity." David Davidson has placed Dietrich's Lola character in *The Blue Angel* within the tradition of the "amoral woman." He makes some interesting remarks on the "threatening" sexuality of these female characters in relation to Mulvey's theory.

27. Carole Zucker, "Some Observations on Sternberg and Dietrich," *Cinema Journal* 19 (Spring 1980), p. 21. Masochism's ambivalent stance toward the female ensures her alternation between coldness and warmth, sacrifice and torture, but, as Deleuze points out, the female in the masochistic scenario is not sadistic, She "incarnates instead the element of 'inflicting pain' in an exclusively masochistic situation" (p. 38). It is rarely the sexualized female who is judged guilty in Von Sternberg's films, but the representative of the superego and the father.

28. Wood, p. 61.

29. Claire Pajaczkowska discusses this point in "The Heterosexual Presumption: A Contribution to the Debate on Pornography," *Screen* 22 (1981), p. 86.

30. Deleuze, p. 56. Although the mothering agent might be considered to be a socially determined role rather than a strictly biological one, this alternative definition does not seem appropriate to this particular application of Deleuze and pregenital research. Interestingly, it has been suggested that in the pregenital stage, sexual difference is not an issue to the child except in terms of breast/nonbreast.

31. Deleuze, p. 56.

32. Deleuze, pp. 80–81; Bychowski, p. 260.

33. Deleuze, p. 49. The female in the masochistic scenario is a *femme fatale,* but a very specific kind. Her danger supersedes her portrayal as an "amoral," sexualized female who threatens social control. The "mystery" of the *femme fatale* of masochism is the mystery of the womb, rebirth, and the child's symbiotic bond with the mother. She represents the dialectical unity between liberation and death, the bonding of Eros with Thanatos that places the former in the service of the latter.

34. See Kaja Silverman, "Masochism and Subjectivity," *Framework* 12 (1980), p. 2. Silverman's discussion of the masochistic use of the *fort/da* game is most valuable; however, I cannot agree with her generalizations about cultural pleasure/instinctual unpleasure or with her reading of Freud (especially concerning transferrence of drive expression to a

contrary drive). She also approaches the idea that fetishism is related to identification (p. 6), a notion worth exploring in detail.

35. Schafer, p. 278. See also Robert Stoller, *Sexual Excitement* (New York: Simon and Schuster, 1979); Nancy Chodorow, *The Reproduction of Mothering: Psychoanalysis and the Sociology of Gender* (Berkeley: University of California Press, 1978); *Mothering: Essays in Feminist Theory*, ed. Joyce Trebilcot (Totowa, New Jersey: Rowman & Allanheld, 1984). While my brief consideration of Freud in this article necessitates a generalization about his stance on women, it should be noted that he did consider the influence of the mother, but, as demonstrated in his theories on masochism and various other symptomatologies, the father, penis envy, castration fear, and the emphasis on the phallic stage (and corresponding disinterest in pre-Oedipal or pregenital stages) effectively displace the mother from his work. See Viola Klein, *The Feminine Character: History of an Ideology* (New York: International Universities Press, 1949).

36.. Hans Loewald, *Papers on Psychoanalysis* (New Haven: Yale University Press, 1980), p. 165.

37. Janine Chasseguet-Smirgel, "Freud and Female Sexuality: The Consideration of Some Blind Spots in the Exploration of the Dark Continent," *International Journal of Psycho-Analysis* 57 (1976), p. 196.

38. Robert Dickes discusses the fetish as "screen memory" in "Fetishistic Behavior: A Contribution to Its Complex Development and Significance," *Journal of the American Psychoanalytic Association* 11 (1963), pp. 324–30. See also Anneliese Riess, "The Mother's Eye: For Better and for Worse," *The Psychoanalytic Study of the Child* 33 (1978), pp. 381–405.

39. Chasseguet-Smirgel, p. 281. Ethel Spector Person has suggested that infantile dependence may be the key to power relations in sexuality: "the limitations to sexual 'liberation,' meaning liberation from power contaminants, do not reside in the biological nature of sexuality, or in cultural or political arrangements, and certainly not in the sex difference, but may lie in the universal condition of infantile dependence" (p. 627). See "Sexuality as the Mainstay of Identity: Psychoanalytic Perspective," *Signs* 5 (Summer 1980).

40. Michel Foucault, *The History of Sexuality Vol. 1: An Introduction,* trans. Robert Hurley (New York: Pantheon Books, 1978), pp. 108–9.

41. Mulvey, pp. 13–14.

42. D. N. Rodowick, "The Difficulty of Difference," *Wide Angle* 5, 1 (1982), pp. 7–9.

43. Mulvey, pp. 11, 14.

44. Christian Metz, *The Imaginary Signifier,* trans. Celia Britton, Annwyl Williams, Ben Brewster, Alfred Guzzetti (Bloomington: Indiana University Press, 1982), pp. 59–63.

45. Jean Laplanche, *Life and Death in Psychoanalysis,* trans. Jeffrey Mehlman (Baltimore: Johns Hopkins University Press, 1976), p. 102.

46. Leopold von Sacher-Masoch, "A Childhood Memory and Reflection on the Novel," Appendix I in Deleuze, pp. 232–33.

47. Sylvan Keiser, "Body Ego During Orgasm," *Psychoanalytic Quarterly* 21 (April 1952), pp. 160, 193.

48. Stephen Heath, *Questions of Cinema* (Bloomington: Indiana University Press, 1981), p. 189.

49. P. J. Van der Leeuw, "The Preoedipal Phase of the Male," *The Psychoanalytic Study of the Child* 13 (1958), p. 369. See also Robert C. Bak, "Fetishism," *Journal of the American Psychoanalytic Association* 1 (1953), p. 291.

50. Van der Leeuw, pp. 352–74; Charles Socarides, "The Development of a Fetishistic Perversion: The Contribution of Preoedipal Phase Conflict," *Journal of the American Psychoanalytic Association* 8 (April 1960), pp. 307–9; Bak, p. 291. Bak maintains that the

normal male child thinks it is possible to identify with the mother and emulate her positive power (i.e., bear a child) while also repairing the separation from her (through fetishism) without endangering phallic integrity (p. 286). Joseph Solomon, "Transitional Phenomena and Obsessive-Compulsive States," in *Between Reality and Fantasy: Transitional Objects and Phenomena,* Simon A. Grolnick, Leonard Barkin, and Werner Muensterberger, eds. (New York: Jason Aronson, 1978), pp. 250–51, associates fetishism with the child's sense of body intactness derived from the mother.

51. Dickes, p. 320.

52. Dickes, p. 327.

53. M. Wulff, "Fetishism and Object Choice in Early Childhood," *Psychoanalytic Quarterly* 15 (1945), pp. 465–70. Socarides, p. 309. Brunswick, Lampl-de Groot, Jacobson, Kestenberg, Socarides, and a number of others link fetishistic perversion to the pre-Oedipal period. Most conclude that fetishism has little connection to the phallic period or genital sexuality in its formation, but this does not mean that a fetish cannot represent the phallus. Wulff qualifies the link between childhood fetishism and adult fetishism by noting the inconsistences in their relationship and the need for further research. Griselda Pollock has pointed out in "What's Wrong with Images of Women," *Screen Education* 24 (Autumn 1977), pp. 25–33, that Freud's theory of fetishism (as adopted by Mulvey in particular) cannot account for vaginal imagery in pornography.

54. Ralph Greenson, "Dis-Identifying from Mother: Its Special Importance for the Boy," *International Journal of Psycho-Analysis* 49 (1968), pp. 370–74; see also Nancy Chodorow, "Family Structure and Feminine Personality," in *Woman, Culture, and Society,* S. Rosaldo and L. Lamphere, eds. (Stanford, Calif.: Stanford University Press, 1978), p. 50; Chasseguet-Smirgel, pp. 281–84. In "Film and the Masquerade," Doane insists that the female is "constructed differently in relation to processes of looking" (p. 80).

55. Socarides, p. 304. See also Stoller, *Sexual Excitement,* pp. 7–13; Freud, "The Psychogenesis of a Case of Homosexuality in a Woman," in *Sexuality and the Psychology of Love,* pp. 133–59.

56. Socarides, p. 304.

57. Baudry, p. 125. "It may seem peculiar that desire which constituted the cine-effect is rooted in the oral structure of the subject. The conditions of projection do evoke the dialectics internal/external, swallowing/swallowed, eating/being eaten, which is characteristic of what is being structured during the oral phase . . . The relationship visual orifice/buccal orifice acts at the same time as analogy and differentiation, but also points to the relation of consecution between oral satisfaction, sleep, white screen of the dream on which dream images will be projected, beginning of the dream."

58. Judith S. Kestenberg and Joan Weinstock, "Transitional Objects and Body-Image Formation," in *Between Reality and Fantasy,* p. 82.

59. Alvan Frank, "The Unrememberable and the Unforgettable," *The Psychoanalytic Study of the Child* 24 (1969), p. 56. See also Ernst Kris, "On Preconscious Mental Processes," in *Organization and Pathology of Thought,* ed. David Rapaport (New York: Columbia University Press, 1951), p. 493.

60. W. Gillespie, "Notes on the Analysis of Sexual Perversion," *International Journal of Psychoanalysis* (1952), p. 397. See also Loewald, pp. 268–69, 401–2. See Chodorow, *Mothering,* on the splitting technique of ego defense, primary identification, and the oral stage, p. 60.

61. Loewald, pp. 16–17.

62. Loewald, p. 17.

63. Freud, "A Child Is Being Beaten," p. 129; Robert Stoller, "Facts and Fancies: An

Examination of Freud's Concept of Bisexuality," in *Women and Analysis,* ed. Jean Strouse (New York: Grossman, 1974), pp. 357–60.

64. Lawrence Kubie, "The Drive to Become Both Sexes," in *Symbols and Neurosis,* ed. Herbert J. Schlesinger (New York: International Universities Press, 1978), pp. 195, 202. See also Zilboorg and Kittay.

65. Socarides, p. 307; Gregory Zilboorg, "Masculine and Feminine; Some Biological and Cultural Aspects," *Psychiatry* 7 (1944), pp. 257–96; Eva Feder Kittay, "Womb Envy: An Explanatory Concept," in Trebicot, pp. 94–128.

66. Bruno Bettelheim, *Symbolic Wounds* (Glencoe, Ill.: The Free Press, 1954), p. 260.

67. Doane, "Film and the Masquerade," pp. 74–88; Laura Mulvey "Afterthoughts on 'Visual Pleasure and Narrative Cinema' Inspired by *Duel in the Sun,*" *Framework* 15/16/17 (Summer 1981), pp. 12–15.

68. Kubie, p. 211. See also Loewald, pp. 268–69.

69. Laplanche and J. B. Pontalis, *The Language of Psychoanalysis* (New York: W. W. Norton, 1973), pp. 243–46.

70. Otto Fenichel, "Scopophilic Instinct and Identification," in *Collected Papers of Otto Fenichel: First Series* (New York: W. W. Norton, 1953), p. 377.

71. Kubie, p. 211.

72. Edith Jacobson, *The Self and the Object World* (New York: International Universities Press, 1964).

Part 6
Countercurrents

THE NEGLECTED TRADITION
OF PHENOMENOLOGY
IN FILM THEORY

DUDLEY ANDREW

One of the things that get lost in the attention that semiotic approaches pay to the production of meaning, codes, positions, strategies, and effects is classic aesthetics. Much of what semiotic, structural, and psychoanalytic approaches have contributed are insights into texts as such, into discourse as a formal procedure that has psychic and ideological ramifications. In this, they are similar to communication or systems theory, although there has been surprisingly little cross-fertilization with these more North American approaches. All these methods, and classic Marxism, too, did not develop specifically from the attempt to come to grips with art, culture, or aesthetics. Applications abound, but in large measure they continue the founding impulse to unveil deep structures, codes, procedures, fissures, or gaps that tend to regard the text and its immediate experience as the husk within which the germ of discursive strategy and viewer response lie encrypted. These methods are not well equipped to generate a comprehensive aesthetics. They demonstrate a basic distrust of emotional response in the name of science, politics, knowledge as a rational enterprise, and this distrust suggests that the only aesthetic that can emerge will be centered on discipline, work, interrogation, and rationality. Few would call such an aesthetic complete.

Dudley Andrew's article reminds us of one alternative—phenomenology. He writes, "Indeed, phenomenologists have a longstanding distrust of pure reason, viewing rationality as a single mode of consciousness among others, a mode whose unquenchable thirst to swallow all experience must be restrained precisely because life itself tells us that experience is dearer and more trustworthy than schemes by which we seek to know and change it." The opposition would immediately seize on his turn of phrase, "life itself tells us," arguing that all experience, if meaningful, is mediated and structured by social classes, codes, systems, and so on. (See Metz's rejoinders in Film Language *[New York: Oxford University Press, 1974] to Pasolini's somewhat phenomenological semiotics for an extended example of precisely such a debate.) But that rebuttal is also an evasion. At best, it defers coming to grips with the moment of immediate experience; it refuses the probably no-win dare to find a means of linguistic expression capable of describing the unique qualities of experiential awareness. However, phenomenology is no stranger to contradiction, paradox, and mystery. Unlike more rational systems of thought, phenomenology embraces these qualities as perhaps ineffable but as also essential. It prizes the attempt to understand them. It seeks to found an aesthetic squarely upon them, on the ineffable tugs and pulls on our unconscious, the play on our emotions, the alterations of our consciousness that can perhaps be explained as effects of textual strategies but that also prompt us to*

*describe, if not to cherish, them. A tantalizing question remains: Is the phenomeno-
logical approach, whose history and methodology Andrew so aptly summarizes,
necessarily opposed to explanatory theories and political perspectives, or is there
perhaps some common ground that approaches like the sociology of everyday life
(represented by the work of such figures as Erving Goffman and Henri Lefebvre)
have already explored, often merging descriptive and explanatory categories
successfully?*

1

Countless American literary and film scholars who have been busy re-
tooling themselves for the kinds of structural project that floated to us from across
the Atlantic find themselves either bemused or frustrated to learn that the readings those tools have engendered are now repudiated by their very European
designers.

Even in its heyday, of course, the structural sand castle was eroded continually
from the outside. Such movements as the German Reader Response School or
Stanley Fish's audience theories specifically attacked structuralism's exclusive
orientation toward texts as did, in a more subtle way, the hermeneutics of Paul
Ricoeur.

But it is the interior erosion which has done the most damage, as former
promulgators of textual structuralism have turned to textuality or the "process"
of reading and writing. In coming to grips with the "event" of reading and the
activity of "rewriting," Roland Barthes's *S/Z* and *Pleasure of the Text* deny and
surpass the highly touted schematic models he generated in the mid-sixties, *Elements of Semiology* and "Introduction to the Structural Analysis of Narrative." In
the same tradition Edward Said's *Beginnings* has re-posed questions of origins and
of textual production which mainline structuralism had ruled out of bounds.

Barthes and Said still work within the domain of the textual but in them and in
others we can unmistakably measure a shift of interest from the text considered as
a formal structure to the dynamics of textuality taken to be a floating process of
structuration and deconstruction both writing and reading. Even old-guard semioticians like Umberto Eco have had to steer their "objective science of signs" into
the murky areas of the psyche where art, novelty and interpretation reign, weakening their structural model through overtaxation.

If we consider the development of intellectual movements to be dialectical in
nature, then all these signs of the collapse of rigid structuralism may suggest a
return to the problematic of phenomenology, for these two approaches to culture
have always been viewed as polar opposites.

This categorical opposition can be readily expressed by a double-column entry
list whose oversimplification has the advantage of mapping for us the terms and
the issues:

STRUCTURALISM/SEMIOTICS	PHENOMENOLOGY
Explanatory	Descriptive
Synchronic (System)	Diachronic (Origins)
Endistanced (Objective)	Immersed (Experimental)
Research Attitude	Research Attitude
(Rhetoric) Communications Model	(Art) Expression Model
Analytic (Revolutionary)	Synthetic (Revelatory)
Repositioning the Text	Repositioning the Self

While no sophisticated theorist working today would consider a literal return to the postwar phenomenological model, its terms and emphases indubitably throw structuralism into relief and provide an historical dimension to the struggle which, as I have already suggested, is currently deforming structuralism into something new and unrecognizable.

Literary and social theorists have recognized the importance of this historical progression. Structuralism was born out of the highly public Sartre–Lévi-Strauss debate, or out of Merleau-Ponty's move, late in his career, toward a theory of language; out of Jacques Lacan's shift in the 50's from a phenomenological stance toward a linguistically based structural psychoanalysis.

But in film this transition was hardly made and never recognized. There was no university film tradition to debate or develop the phenomenology inherent in the work of Bazin, Ayfre, Merleau-Ponty and others. Moreover, when, around 1963, film did begin to enter the university in a substantial way in both France and America, all three men had died, as had *La Revue internationale du filmologie,* the one journal devoted to theory along quasi-phenomenological grounds. Academically, then, our field was born in the era of Lévi-Strauss, an era offering few respectable alternatives to the semiotics and narrative structuralism which increasingly dominate our best journals. In film there was no one to challenge structuralism, and few to sense the dialectic out of which it had been spawned.

The fact that no phenomenological film theory ever self-consciously developed is a matter for regret only insofar as this lack of an opposing tradition locks us within a structuralist project and vocabulary. We can speak of codes and textual systems which are the results of signifying processes, yet we seem unable to discuss that mode of experience we call signification. More precisely, structuralism and academic film theory in general have been disinclined to deal with the "other-side" of signification, those realms of preformulation where sensory data congeal into "something that matters" and those realms of post-formulation where that "something" is experienced as mattering. Structuralism, even in its post-structural reach toward psychoanalysis and intertextuality, concerns itself only with that something and not with the process of its congealing nor with the event of its mattering.

To put it another way, the classification of general formal codes in the cinema, while necessary, must not retard the far more pressing tasks of describing the peculiar way meaning is experienced in cinema and the unique quality of the experience of major films. In neither of these cases will general codes take us very far. What is called for instead, and what I think we are beginning to receive from various camps, is a study of the zone of pre-formulation in which the psyche confronts a visual text intended for it, and the zone of post-formulation in which the psyche must come to terms with a surplus value unaccounted for by recourse to a science of signification.

2

The tradition behind this newer theoretical attitude lies in French phenomenology. Sartre, Merleau-Ponty, and Dufrenne have all attempted to describe perceptual, imaginative, and aesthetic experience, and all have shown interest in the cinema. From the positions they established between 1946 and 1955 a large number of film critics began to meditate on the cinema from what can only be called a phenomenological perspective.

A history of this scattered tradition is long overdue. As a first step I would like to sketch a typology of approaches which ought tentatively to be grouped together as phenomenological, in hopes that we can use the past to by-pass problems which bewilder current theory or to invite us to approach problems current theory ignores.

I. In 1945, Gilbert Cohen-Séat blew a loud bugle in the name of a new science, "filmologie." His *Essai sur les principles d'une philosophie de cinéma* became the rallying point of those anxious to organize a new and progressive science of cinema.

"Filmologie" from the first was marked with the phenomenological brand for it sought to describe cinema as a phenomenon among other phenomena, but one exerting a very special pressure on individuals and society. Cohen-Séat speaks of cinema as a social eruption controlled by an alien technology and creating a universal but impersonal dream. Through the breadth of its vision and the poetic quality of its "scientific" analysis, Cohen-Séat's book led a whole generation to review and reimagine the full cinematic complex in a fresh way and it immediately fathered several other investigations, the most well known of which is Edgar Morin's *Le Cinéma ou l'homme imaginaire*. In America, we should consider much of Cavell's *The World Viewed* in light of this effort to describe the experience, on both the personal and cultural level, of the very phenomenon of cinema in its totality. David Thomson's little-remembered *Movie Man* is likewise a descriptive foray into the experience of the movie complex. But neither of these works is so strong or sound as their French counterparts like Ayfre's *Cinéma et mystère,* Munier's *Contre l'image,* or Morin's brilliant book.

II. Since phenomenology has been dominated by the study of perception, we should expect to find film theory responding to Merleau-Ponty's landmark *Phenomenology of Perception*. Of course Merleau-Ponty himself wrote on the perceptual basis of cinema and, in the more significant *Eye and Mind,* on aesthetic perception in general.

The greatest cache of perception study in relation to film is the *Revue internationale de filmologie,* which from 1947 through 1960 published a steady stream of essays on cinema's relation to memory, cognition, time and space, psycho-physiology, daydreaming, illusion and so on. Ignored by American film students, the work of this journal nevertheless gave rise to several of Christian Metz's most important essays (especially those on the impression of reality, on daydreaming, and on perception of depth).

III. In both France and America perception studies in film have, for the most part, been carried out by scholars essentially outside cinema. Theorists interested more exclusively in film have usually attempted a study of the cinematic process itself. Here phenomenology requires that reflection recapture the experience in which a series of sounds and images, in confronting consciousness, constitutes a direction and a world, that is, a human signification. Jean Mitry's colossal *Esthétique et psychologie du cinéma* seeks to chronicle the movement of the cinematic experience from perception to the elaboration of a world and in certain films to an aesthetic plane from which we can review all our experience. Mitry's minute analyses of cinematic rhythm, subjective camera, reflexive montage, and so on constitute a vast phenomenological encyclopedia of traits of the cinema. Even Christian Metz, often considered a harsh opponent of phenomenology, embarked on his career with essays derived directly from Mitry, one on the impression of reality in cinema, another on the experience of narrative in film.

Metz here hovered about the two aspects of the film process most crucial for phenomenology: narrative and identification. Theses aspects have each received book-length study—the first in Albert Laffay's *Logique du cinéma* and the second in Jean-Pierre Meunier's *Les Structures de l'expérience filmique.*

Laffay's work has received quite a bit of attention, thanks again to Metz's enthusiasm for it. Meunier's 1968 treatise, however, is all but unknown. On the surface it appears to be a key to an overall phenomenological film theory, dedicated as it is to Merleau-Ponty's position and deriving explicitly from Sartre's writing on images and the imagination. Meunier hopes to describe, and account for, the peculiar fascination and momentum belonging to the various types of film, from home movies through narrative features. Identification is his key, unlocking the inner dynamics of genre upon genre by meditating on the viewer's shifting mode of consciousness in confrontation with various types and organizations of images.

IV. The first three types of phenomenological film study surveyed here have all aimed at the description of one or another sort of consciousness the spectator assumes in apprehending movies: a global response to the movie complex, a perceptual" stance in relation to the "animation and definition" of images, and a narrative stance implicating the spectator's consciousness through the processes of identification and individuation in relation to a sequence of images all directed toward some goal or experience.

All three of these descriptions essentially aim at what I have termed the zone of "pre-formulation." All attempt to describe as adequately as possible the experience of signification in cinema, comparing it to other forms of perception and imagination. There is also, however, a phenomenology which seeks to be adequate to that experience which lies on the hither side of signification, somewhere beyond the text. This venture can be divided into phenomenological film criticism on the one hand and a phenomenology of the act of interpretation (called hermeneutics) on the other.

What exists beyond the text and what kind of description can be adequate to it? Here we encounter the exciting and dangerous term "world." A film elaborates a world which it is the critic's job to flesh out or respond to. But what is this cinematic world?

After World War II a group of critics centered at the University of Geneva developed a technique of describing the world called up by the writing of any given author. In this so-called "Criticism of Consciousness" the boundaries between books dissolved as the transcendental author was seen to spew out fragments of a world which the critics learned to reconstitute.

Meditations on groups of films might also, then, be deemed phenomenological, making both auteur and genre studies the most prolix phenomenological endeavor in our field. Unquestionably André Bazin's writings are at the top of this category and provide its clearest model. In essays like "The Virtues and Limitations of Montage," "The Cinema of Exploration," and "Defense of Rossellini," he brilliantly circumscribes the unique worlds we experience respectively in fairy tale films, documentaries, and neorealism. His large studies of Welles, Chaplin, and the five directors subsumed under the title *Cinema of Cruelty* are the closest things we have to a phenomenological criticism in the manner of the Geneva School, for in all these he strives to erase the distinction between works and to join himself, as he was so able to do, to the creative energy of each auteur. Bazin's method essentially led him to elaborate the "world" of genre or auteur and then to pinpoint the source (be it economic, philosophic, political, etc.) capable of generating such a world.

Much of *Cahiers de cinéma* criticism developed as part of this project, especially the auteur and genre studies which have become so prevalent in America today. But few English-language critics have been able to mimic that speculative aura which struggles to go beyond the mere enumeration of repeated elements and to capture the quality of the experience we live through with an auteur or a genre. As always in the phenomenological criticism of any art, one finds casual impressionism standing beside decisive, law-discovering observation, the former masquerading as the latter.

V. To my mind the most important current phenomenological impulse in criticism stems from the hermeneutics of Paul Ricoeur. In effect Ricoeur wants to restrain the naive romanticism and exuberance of phenomenological criticism while retaining its goal of going beyond the text by means of fructifying experience of the text. The machinery by which texts have been produced or make sense must, he feels, be encountered head on. Ricoeur's debates with Lévi-Strauss and his monumental study of Freud[1] suggest that the first step of interpretation for him is a backward one which distrusts the text and seeks to explain its origins via semiotics, psychoanalysis, and a theory of ideology. This type of suspicion the

Geneva School was always afraid to entertain, preferring instead the romantic faith in the creative power of the individual author. Ricoeur knows that no author is completely in control of what his text says, that Freud, Marx, and de Saussure have taught us that texts are produced out of the interaction of massive systems far greater than personal consciousness. Nevertheless, this suspicious explanatory attitude, the attitude dominant among structuralists, must not suspend our experience of artworks. He finds that great works bear a "surplus of meaning" and of value which is qualified but not exhausted by analysis. And he calls for a "progressive and synthetic" hermeneutics to recover the gain in meaning which the artwork represents. Ultimately Ricoeur wants to clear enough space for us to be able to experience and reexperience artworks in a way which allows us to be adequate to them, to learn from them, to change our lives in relation to the meaning they suggest, rather than to protect ourselves from them through a structural analysis which can only discuss their possibility, not their actuality.

While Ricoeur's work has hardly been adapted to cinema studies, it should provide a model for those interested in contemplating the use of the phenomenological tradition in today's critical arena. For despite the fact that Ricoeur should be thought of as one who has passed through phenomenology and on to something else, his current work exemplifies the same concerns that motivate all the types of study surveyed here and put them in opposition to structuralism and semiotics. Since those concerns might better be thought of as an attitude toward research and toward the object of research, I would like to characterize that attitude in lieu of a conclusion.

3

Instead of elaborating an epistemology which is then applied in a second-level way to cinema, as do the structuralists, phenomenology has attempted to stay within the "hidden reason" of cinema itself and to make visible that "reason" on the run, so to speak. Opposed as they are in their basic approaches to research, these movements have quickly given off political overtones: structuralists are typed as cultural radicals while phenomenologists are accused of neutrality, if not rightism. The former, proceeding out of a higher logic, can envision a utopia of signs, of knowledge, and of communication, a cinema which will be clear, just, and demystified. The latter are anxious to change nothing but instead to comprehend a process which flows along perfectly well on its own. Indeed, phenomenologists have a longstanding distrust of pure reason, viewing rationality as a single mode of consciousness among others, a mode whose unquenchable thirst to swallow all experience must be restrained precisely because life itself tells us that experience is dearer and more trustworthy than schemes by which we seek to know and change it.

Perhaps now we can see why from Cohen-Séat to Meunier, phenomenologists have distrusted the "grammarians of cinema," be they Arnheim and Spottiswoode or Umberto Eco and Christian Metz. Instead of systematic grammars they write chapters on "Emotion in the Cinema" and on "Our Experience of Movement in the Cinema," because for them such experiences, both private and societal, must be the starting point and the ultimate goal of research. Grammars, lexicons, and structural studies in general can only remove us from the cinema and force us to focus on a second-level system (a logical system), which itself rests on a metaphysics or an epistemology masking a metaphysics.

Phenomenology wants to remain immune to the diseases, antibodies, and critical inoculations which have characterized the feverish world of structuralism for the past fifteen years. Second-level systems will always be vulnerable to, will in fact produce, the critiques which must destroy them. By according limitless value to experience and by granting all life processes an unquestioned respect, phenomenology seeks to put reason and language at the service of life or at least of human experience. If life and reality lie beyond human experience or our consciousness of it, as certain recent structuralists have avowed, then let's forget it anyway. And so from the most primitive descriptions of the peculiarities of perception in cinema, to our emotional involvement in the image, to the momentum of a narrative, to the constitution of a cinematic world, to the description of types of worlds (or genres) and to the life of our interpretation of them, phenomenology claims to be closer, not necessarily to truth, but to cinema and our experience of it. Since this is its object, it will happily let second-level philosophers and overly ambitious critics bicker and fight over "truth."

Note

1. See especially, Ricoeur's "Structure, Word, Event," *Philosophy Today* 12 (1968): 114–129, and of course his *Freud and Philosophy,* Yale University Press, 1969. I have tried to elaborate Ricoeur's potential for film criticism in an essay on *Sunrise* published in *Quarterly Review of Film Studies,* no. 3 (August 1977).

COLONIALISM, RACISM, AND REPRESENTATION: AN INTRODUCTION

ROBERT STAM AND LOUISE SPENCE

Discussion of Third World cinema represents an inevitable countercurrent
to the theory and practice of a predominately Western cinema. Many Western
filmmakers and critics are active supporters of efforts to develop progressive,
national cinemas in the Third World, and they are highly appreciative of the
differences of strategy and priorities that often develop. (For one vivid example

of these differences, see Julio Garcia Espinosa's "For an Imperfect Cinema" in Jump Cut, *no. 20 [1979]. Espinosa quotes Glauber Rocha's memorable distinction: "We are not interested in the problems of neurosis; we are interested in the problems of lucidity [where] lucid people are the ones who think and feel and exist in a world they can change, in spite of all the problems and difficulties.") Nevertheless, a great deal of theoretical momentum over the past ten years has gone into revising our historical understanding of Western cinema and refining our understanding of cinematic discourse, often from a Marxist or feminist perspective but sometimes from a purely formal one. Third World filmmakers have participated in this activity, and they have often produced films that extend or sharpen the terms of debate —São* Bernardo *(Leon Hirszman, Brazil, 1972– 1973),* Lucia *(Humberto Solas, Cuba, 1968), and* One Way or Another *(Sara Gomez, Cuba, 1977) are three noteworthy examples. But to a considerable degree the terms of analysis that continue to be applied to Third World films, and to women and members of minority groups in American and European films, are those of an older tradition that stresses the analysis of content and social stereotype.*

Robert Stam and Louise Spence acknowledge the value of that tradition as a starting point, but they go on to indicate its limitations and to propose an agenda that takes cognizance of recent examinations of cinematic discourse and textual specificity. For example, they point out how realism can function in various ways to color our reading of a text, in some instances confirming erroneous impressions derived from racist assumptions such as that Africa is a continent dominated by lions in the jungle, and in other, more Brechtian instances working to expose the causal network beneath surface appearances, such as the ways in which The Battle of Algiers *presents guerrilla insurrection as a response to colonial oppression.*

The authors' extended discussion of The Battle of Algiers *is a valuable example of how to read a Third World film. They show how cinematic conventions are subverted or reversed in the film, at the same time cautioning against any one-to-one correlations between structure and effect that would yield an abstract blueprint for "correct" filmmaking. They demonstrate, for example, how images of three Algerian women making up in front of mirrors escape the connotations of the mirror as a symbol of vanity in favor of the mirror as a revolutionary tool, although they may place too much stress on the role of lighting and too little on facial expression, offscreen looks, music, and narrative context.*

Basically, the shift from an emphasis on social image mediated by plot and character to an emphasis on reading as a function of narrative strategies, ranging from the uses of realism to questions of spectator positioning, is a welcome extension of new ways of looking into an area too long neglected. Like many of the articles in Part 5, this article pays special attention to the relationship between viewer and text, even opening up the question of "aberrant readings" occasioned by individual bias that goes "against the grain of the discourse." Thus, Stam and Spence provide both a welcome revision of some of the usual terms in which Third World films are received and discussed and a suggestive extension of the strategies of mise-en-scène and poststructural criticism to an area where they have been applied quite unevenly in the past. What still remains to be considered is how the distinctive, diverse qualities of Third World filmmaking might change or modify the assumptions and principles of the analytic methods developed inside dominant Western cultures. Just as poststructuralist methods may help us to locate the specific signifying practices of Third World film, Third World film may help us to locate the culturally specific, ideologically constrained limits of our own critical practices.

Racism and colonialism in the cinema have been the subject of many books and essays. The stereotyping of black Americans has been explored by Thomas Cripps in *Slow Fade to Black*,[1] by Daniel Leab in *From Sambo to Superspade*,[2] and by Donald Bogle in *Toms, Coons, Mulattoes, Mammies and Bucks*.[3] The pernicious distortion of African history and culture has been denounced by Richard Maynard in *Africa on Film: Myth and Reality*.[4] Ralph Friar and Natasha Friar's *The Only Good Indian*[5] chronicles the imagistic mistreatment dealt out to the Native American. Lester Friedman's *Hollywood's Image of the Jew*[6] documents the process by which most screen Jews have had to sacrifice all ethnic specificity in order to conform to a WASP-dominated assimilationist creed. Allen Woll's *The Latin Image in American Film*[7] focuses on the stereotypical 'bandidos' and 'greasers' common in Hollywood films about Latin America, while Pierre Boulanger's *Le Cinéma colonial*[8] exposes the caricatural vision of North Africa and the Near East displayed in such films as *Pépé le Moko* and *Lawrence of Arabia*. And Tom Engelhardt's essay 'Ambush at Kamakazi Pass'[9] places screen anti-Asiatic racism within the context of the war in Vietnam.

Our purpose here is not to review the research or criticise the conclusions of the aforementioned texts. Rather, we would like to sketch out the background of the questions raised in them, offer some preliminary definitions of key terms, and propose the outlines of a methodology in the form of a series of concerns addressable to specific texts and their representations. We would like both to build on and go beyond the methodologies implicit in existing studies. These studies of filmic colonialism and racism tend to focus on certain dimensions of film—social portrayal, plot, and character. While such studies have made an invaluable contribution by alerting us to the hostile distortion and affectionate condescension with which the colonised have been treated in the cinema, they have often been marred by a certain methodological naiveté. While posing legitimate questions concerning narrative plausibility and mimetic accuracy, negative stereotypes and positive images, the emphasis on realism has often betrayed an exaggerated faith in the possibilities of verisimilitude in art in general and the cinema in particular, avoiding the fact that films are inevitably constructs, fabrications, representations. The privileging of social portrayal, plot and character meanwhile, has led to the slighting of the specifically cinematic dimensions of the films; the analyses might easily have been of novels or plays rather than films. The insistence on 'positive images', finally, obscures the fact that 'nice' images might at times be as pernicious as overtly degrading ones, providing a bourgeois facade for paternalism, a more pervasive racism.

Although we are quite aware of the crucial importance of the *contextual,* that is, of those questions bearing on the cinematic industry, its processes of production, distribution and exhibition, those social institutions and production practices which construct colonialism and racism in the cinema, our emphasis here will be *textual* and *intertextual.*[10] An anti-colonialist analysis, in our view, must make the same kind of methodological leap effected by feminist criticism when journals like *Screen* and *Camera Obscura* critically transcended the usefully angry but methodologically flawed 'image' analysis of such critics as Molly Haskell and Marjorie Rosen in order to pose questions concerning the apparatus, the position of the spectator, and the specifically cinematic codes.[11] Our discussion draws from, and hopefully applies by extension to, the analysis of other oppressions, such as sexism, class subordination and anti-Semitism, to all situations, that is, in which difference is transformed into 'other'-ness and exploited or penalised by and for power.

SOME DEFINITIONS

We should begin, however, with some preliminary definitions. What do we mean by 'colonialism', 'the Third World' and 'racism'? By colonialism, we refer to the process by which the European powers (including the United States) reached a position of economic, military, political and cultural domination in much of Asia, Africa and Latin America. This process, which can be traced at least as far back as the 'voyages of discovery' and which had as its corollary the institution of the slave trade, reached its apogee between 1900 and the end of World War I (at which point Europe had colonised roughly 85 percent of the earth) and began to be reversed only with the disintegration of the European colonial empires after World War II.

The definition of the 'Third World' flows logically out of this prior definition of colonialism, for the 'Third World' refers to the historical victims of this process—to the colonised, neo-colonised or de-colonised nations of the world whose economic and political structures have been shaped and deformed within the colonial process. The colonial relation has to do with *structural* domination rather than with crude economic ('the poor'), racial ('the non-white'), cultural ('the backward') or geographical categories.[12]

Racism, finally, although not limited to the colonial situation (anti-Semitism being a case in point), has historically been both an ally and a product of the colonisation process. It is hardly accidental that the most obvious victims of racism are those whose identity was forged within the colonial process: blacks in the United States, Asians and West Indians in Great Britain, Arab workers in France, all of whom share an oppressive situation and the status of second-class citizens. We will define racism, borrowing from Albert Memmi, as 'the generalized and final assigning of values to real or imaginary differences, to the accuser's benefit and at his victim's expense, in order to justify the former's own privilege or aggression'.[13] Memmi's definition has the advantage of calling attention to the *uses* to which racism is put. Just as the logic of sexism leads to rape, so the logic of racism leads to violence and exploitation. Racism, for Memmi, is almost always a rationale for an already existing or contemplated oppression. Without ignoring the accumulated prejudices and cultural attitudes which prepared the way for racism, there is a sense in which it can be argued that racism comes 'in the wake' of concrete oppressions. Amerindians were called 'beasts' and 'cannibals' *because* white Europeans were slaughtering them and expropriating their land; blacks were slandered as 'lazy' *because* they were being exploited as slaves; Mexicans were caricatured as 'greasers' and 'bandidos' *because* the United States had seized half of their territory; and the colonised were ridiculed as lacking in culture and history *because* colonialism, in the name of profit, was destroying the basis of that culture and the memory of that history.

The same Renaissance humanism which gave birth to the code of perspective—subsequently incorporated, as Baudry points out, into the camera itself—also gave birth to the 'rights of man'. Europe constructed its self-image on the backs of its equally constructed Other—the 'savage', the 'cannibal'—much as phallocentrism sees its self-flattering image in the mirror of woman defined as lack. And just as the camera might therefore be said to inscribe certain features of bourgeois humanism, so the cinematic and televisual apparatuses, taken in their most inclusive sense, might be said to inscribe certain features of European colonialism. The magic carpet provided by these apparatuses flies us around the globe and makes us, by virtue of our subject position, its audiovisual masters. It produces us as subjects, transforming us into armchair conquistadores, affirming our sense of power while making the inhabitants of the Third World objects of spectacle for the First World's voyeuristic gaze.

Colonialist representation did not begin with the cinema: it is rooted in a vast colonial intertext, a widely disseminated set of discursive practices. Long before the first racist images appeared on the film screens of Europe and North America, the process of colonialist image-making, and resistance to that process, resonated through Western literature. Colonialist historians, speaking for the 'winners' of history, exalted the colonial enterprise, at bottom little more than a gigantic act of pillage whereby whole continents were bled of their human and material resources, as a philanthropic 'civilising mission' motivated by a desire to push back the frontiers of ignorance, disease and tyranny. Daniel Defoe glorified colonialism in *Robinson Crusoe* (1719), a novel whose 'hero becomes wealthy through the slave trade and through Brazilian sugar mills, and whose first thought, upon seeing human footprints after years of solitude, is to 'get (him) a servant'.[14]

Other European writers responded in more complex and ambiguous ways. The French philosopher Montaigne, writing at the end of the sixteenth century, suggested in 'Des Cannibales' that the Amerindian cannibalising of dead enemy warriors paled in horror when compared to the internecine warfare and torture practiced by European Christians in the name of a religion of love. Shakespeare has Caliban in *The Tempest,* whose name forms an anagram of 'cannibal', curse the European Prospero for having robbed him of his island: 'for I am all the subjects that you have/which first was mine own king'. (Aimé Césaire had to alter Shake-speare's character but slightly, in his 1969 version, to turn him into the anti-colo-nialist militant Caliban X.[15]) And Jonathan Swift, a century later in *Gulliver's Travels* (1726), portrays colonialism in satirical images that in some ways antici-pate Herzog's *Aguirre*:

A crew of pyrates are driven by a storm they know not whither; at length a Boy discovers Land from the Topmast; they go on shore to rob and plunder; they see an harmless people, are entertained with kindness, they give the country a new name, they take formal posses-sion of it for the king, they set up a rotten plank or a stone for a memorial, they murder two or three dozen of the natives, bring away a couple more by force for a sample, return home and get their Pardon. . . . And this execrable crew of butchers employed in so pious an expedition, is a modern colony sent to convert and civilise an idolatrous and barbarous people.[16]

The struggle over images continues, within literature, into the period of the begin-nings of the cinema. Conrad's *Heart of Darkness* (1902), published but a few years after the first Lumière screenings, describes colonialism in Africa as 'just robbery with violence, aggravated murder on a grand scale' and emphasises its racist under-pinnings. 'The conquest of the earth, which mostly means the taking it away from those who have a different complexion or slightly flatter noses than ourselves,' Con-rad has his narrator say, 'is not a pretty thing when you look into it too much.'[17] 'The settler,' Fanon writes, 'makes history; his life is an epoch, an Odyssey,' while against him 'torpic creatures, wasted by fevers, obsessed by ancestral customs, form an almost inorganic background for the innovating dynamism of colonial mercantilism.'[18] Since the beginnings of the cinema coincided with the height of European imperialism, it is hardly surprising that European cinema portrayed the colonised in an unflattering light. Indeed, many of the misconceptions concerning Third World peoples derive from the long parade of lazy Mexicans, shifty Arabs, savage Africans and exotic Asiatics that have disgraced our movie screens. Africa was portrayed as a land inhabited by cannibals in the Lubin comedy *Rastus in Zulu-land* (1910), Mexicans were reduced to 'greasers' in films like *Tony the Greaser* (1911) and *The Greaser's Revenge* (1914), and slavery was idealised, and the slaves degraded, in *The Birth of a Nation* (1915). Hundreds of Hollywood westerns turned history on its head by making the Native Americans appear to be intruders on what was originally their land, and provided a paradigmatic perspective through which to view the whole of the non-white world.

The colonialist inheritance helps account for what might be called the tenden-tiously flawed mimesis of many films dealing with the Third World. The innumer-able ethnographic, linguistic and even topographical blunders in Hollywood films are illuminating in this regard. Countless safari films present Africa as the land of 'lions in the jungle' when in fact only a tiny proportion of the African land mass could be called 'jungle' and when lions do not live in jungle but in grasslands. Hollywood films, in any case, show disproportionate interest in the animal, as opposed to the human life of Africa. And as regards human beings, the Western world has been oddly fascinated by Idi Amin, in many ways an atypical leader in the continent of Nyerere, Mugabe and Machel.

At times the 'flaw' in the mimesis derives not from the *presence* of distorting stereotypes but from the *absence* of representations of an oppressed group. *King of Jazz* (1930), for example, paid tribute to the origins of jazz by pouring (through superimposition) a series of musical ensembles, representing diverse European ethnic groups, into a gigantic melting pot, completely bypassing both Africa and Afro-Americans. Black Brazilians, similarly, formed a structuring absence within Brazilian cinema during the first few decades of this century, as film-makers exalted the already annihilated and mythically connoted 'Indian warrior' in preference to the more problematically present black, victim of a slavery abolished just ten years before the founding of Brazilian cinema. Many American films in the fifties gave the impression that there were no black people in America. The documentary-like *The Wrong Man* (Hitchcock, 1957), for example, shows the subways and even the prisons of New York City as totally devoid of blacks.

At other times the structuring absence has to do not with the people themselves but with a dimension of that people's history or institutions. A whole realm of Afro-American history, the slave revolts, is rarely depicted in film or is represented (as in the television series *Roots*) as a man, already dead, in a ditch. The revolutionary dimension of the black church, similarly, is ignored in favour of a portrayal which favours charismatic leaders and ecstatic songs and dances.[19] The exclusion of whites from a film, we might add paradoxically, can also be the result of white racism. The all-black Hollywood musicals of the twenties and thirties, like present-day South African films made by whites for black audiences, tend to exclude whites because their mere presence would destroy the elaborate fabric of fantasy constructed by such films.

The absence of the language of the colonised is also symptomatic of colonialist attitudes. The languages spoken by Third World peoples are often reduced to an incomprehensible jumble of background murmurs, while major 'native' characters are consistently obliged to meet the coloniser on the coloniser's linguistic turf (here westerns, with their Indian-pidgin English, again provide the paradigm). Anna, in *The King and I,* teaches the Siamese natives 'civilised' manners along with English. Even *Cuba* (directed by Richard Lester, 1980), a generally sympathetic portrait of the Cuban revolution, perpetuates a kind of linguistic colonialism by having the Cubans speak English in a variety of accents (many of which have nothing Hispanic about them beyond an occasional rolled *r*) not only to English-speaking characters, but also to one another. In other films, major nations are mistakenly attributed the wrong language. In *Latin Lovers* (directed by Mervyn Leroy, 1953), for example, Portuguese-speaking Brazilians, when they are not speaking English, are made to speak Spanish.[20]

In response to such distortions, the Third World has attempted to write its own history, take control of its own cinematic image, speak in its own voice. The colonialist wrote the colonised *out* of history, teaching Vietnamese and Senegalese children, for example, that their 'ancestors' were the Gauls. A central impulse animating many Third World films is precisely the effort to reclaim the past. Thus *Ganga Zumba* (directed by Carlos Diegues, 1963) memorialises the proud history of black rebellion in Brazil by focusing on the seventeenth-century fugitive slave republic called Palmares. *Emitai* (directed by Ousmane Sembene, 1972) deals with French colonialism and Senegalese resistance during the period of the Second World War. *Chronicle of the Years of Embers* (directed by Lakdar Hamina, 1975) recounts the Algerian revolution and *The Promised Land* (directed by Miguel Littin, 1973) renders homage to the short-lived 'socialist republic' of Marmaduke Grove as a way to examine both the contradictions and the revolutionary potential of the Chile of the Allende period.

Many oppressed groups have used 'progressive realism' to unmask and combat hegemonic images. Women and Third World film-makers have attempted to counterpose the objectifying discourse of patriarchy and colonialism with a vision of themselves and their reality as seen 'from within'. But this laudable intention is not always unproblematic. 'Reality' is not self-evidently given and 'truth' cannot be immediately captured by the camera. We must distinguish, furthermore, between realism as a goal—Brecht's 'laying bare the causal network'—and realism as a style or constellation of strategies aimed at producing an illusionistic 'reality effect'. Realism as a goal is quite compatible with a style which is reflexive and deconstructive, as is eloquently demonstrated by *El Otro Francisco* (directed by Sergio Giral, 1974), a Cuban film which deconstructs a romantic abolitionist novel by highlighting the historical realities (economic motivations on the part of the whites, armed resistance on the part of the blacks) elided by it, while at the same time underlining its own processes of construction as a filmic text.

POSITIVE IMAGES?

Much of the work on racism in the cinema, like early work on the representation of women, has stressed the issue of the 'positive image'. This reductionism, though not wrong, is inadequate and fraught with methodological dangers. The exact nature of 'positive', first of all, is somewhat relative: black incarnations of patience and gradualism, for example, have always been more pleasing to whites than to blacks. A cinema dominated by positive images, characterised by a bending-over-backwards-not-to-be-racist attitude, might ultimately betray a lack of confidence in the group portrayed, which usually itself has no illusions concerning its own perfection. ('Just because you're black don't make you right,' one black brother tells another in *Ashes and Embers,* directed by Haile Gerima.) A cinema in which all black actors resembled Sidney Poitier might be as serious a cause for alarm as one in which they all resembled Stepin Fetchit.

We should be equally suspicious of a naive integrationism which simply inserts new heroes and heroines, this time drawn from the ranks of the oppressed, into the old functional roles that were themselves oppressive, much as colonialism invited a few assimilated 'natives' to join the club of the 'elite'. A film like *Shaft* (1971) simply substitutes black heroes into the actantial slot normally filled by white ones, in order to flatter the fantasies of a certain (largely male) sector of the black audience. *Guess Who's Coming to Dinner* (directed by Stanley Kramer, 1967), as its title suggests, invites an elite black into the club of the truly human, but always on white terms. Other films, such as *In the Heat of the Night* (1967),

Pressure Point (1962), or the television series *Mod Squad,* place black characters in the role of law-enforcers. The ideological function of such images is not dissimilar to that pointed out in Barthes's famous analysis of the *Paris Match* cover which shows a black soldier in French uniform, eyes upraised, saluting what we presume to be the French flag. All citizens, regardless of their colour, can serve law and order, and the black soldier's zeal in serving the established law is the best answer to critics, black and white, of that society. The television series *Roots,* finally, exploited positive images in what was ultimately a cooptive version of Afro-American history. The series's subtitle, 'the saga of an American family', reflects an emphasis on the European-style nuclear family (retrospectively projected onto Kunta's life in Africa) in a film which casts blacks as just another immigrant group making its way toward freedom and prosperity in democratic America.

The complementary preoccupation to the search for positive images, the exposure of negative images or stereotypes, entails similar methodological problems. The positing and recognition of these stereotypes has been immensely useful, enabling us to detect structural patterns of prejudice in what had formerly seemed random phenomena. The exclusive preoccupation with images, however, whether positive or negative, can lead both to the privileging of characterological concerns (to the detriment of other important considerations) and also to a kind of essentialism, as the critic reduces a complex diversity of portrayals to a limited set of reified stereotypes. Behind every black child performer, from Farina to Gary Coleman, the critic discerns a 'pickaninny', behind every sexually attractive black actor a 'buck' and behind every attractive black actress a 'whore'. Such reductionist simplifications run the risk of reproducing the very racism they were initially designed to combat.

The analysis of stereotypes must also take cultural specificity into account. Many North American black stereotypes are not entirely congruent with those of Brazil, also a multi-ethnic New World society with a large black population. While there are analogies in the stereotypical images thrown up by the two cultures—the 'mammy' is certainly a close relation to the '*mae preta*' (black Mother), there are disparities as well. Brazilian historian Emilia Viotti da Costa argues, for instance, that the 'sambo' figure never existed, as reality or stereotype, in Brazilian colonial society.[21] The themes of the 'tragic mulatto' and 'passing for white', similarly, find little echo in the Brazilian context. Since the Brazilian racial spectrum is not binary (black *or* white) but nuances its shades across a wide variety of racial descriptive terms, and since Brazil, while in many ways oppressive to blacks, has never been a rigidly *segregated* society, no figure exactly corresponds to the North American 'tragic mulatto', schizophrenically torn between two radically separate social worlds.

An ethnocentric vision rooted in North American cultural patterns can lead, similarly, to the 'racialising', or the introjection of racial themes into, filmic situations which Brazilians themselves would not perceive as racially connoted. *Deus e Diabo na Terra do Sol* (*God and the Devil in the Land of the Sun,* directed by Glauber Rocha, 1964) was mistranslated into English as *Black God, White Devil,* suggesting a racial dichotomy not emphasised either in the original title or in the film itself. The humour of *Macunaíma* (1969), similarly, depends on an awareness of Brazilian cultural codes. Two sequences in which the title character turns from black to white, for example, occasionally misread as racist by North Americans, are in fact sardonic comments on Brazil's putative 'racial democracy'.

A comprehensive methodology must pay attention to the *mediations* which intervene between 'reality' and representation. Its emphasis should be on narrative structure, genre conventions, and cinematic style rather than on perfect correctness of representation or fidelity to an original 'real' model or prototype. We must beward of mistakes in which the criteria appropriate to one genre are applied to another. A search for positive images in *Macunaíma,* for example, would be fundamentally misguided, for that film belongs to a carnivalesque genre favouring what Mikhail Bakhtin calls 'grotesque realism'. Virtually all the film's characters are two-dimensional grotesques rather than rounded three-dimensional characters, and the grotesquerie is democratically distributed among all the races, while the most archly grotesque characters are the white industrialist cannibal and his ghoulish spouse. Satirical or parodic films, in the same way, may be less concerned with constructing positive images than with challenging the stereotypical expectations an audience may bring to a film. *Blazing Saddles* lampoons a whole range of ethnic prejudices, mocking audience expectations by having the whites sing 'Ole Man River' while the blacks sing 'I Get No Kick from Champagne'.

POLITICAL POSITIONING

One mediation specific to cinema is spectator positioning. The paradigmatic filmic encounters of whites and Indians in the western, as Tom Engelhardt points out, typically involve images of encirclement. The attitude toward the Indian is premised on exteriority. The besieged wagon train or fort is the focus of our attention and sympathy, and from this centre our familiars sally out against unknown attackers characterised by inexplicable customs and irrational hostility: 'In essence, the viewer is forced behind the barrel of a repeating rifle and it is from that position, through its gun sights, that he [sic] receives a picture history of western colonialism and imperialism.'[22] The possibility of sympathetic identifications with the Indians is simply ruled out by the point-of-view conventions. The spectator is unwittingly sutured into a colonialist perspective.

A film like *The Wild Geese* (directed by Andrew McLaglen, 1978) inherits the conventions of anti-Indian westerns and extends them to Africa. This glorification of the role of white mercenaries in Africa makes the mercenaries, played by popular heroic actors Richard Burton, Richard Harris and Roger Moore, the central focus of our sympathy. Even the gamblers and opportunists among them, recruited from the flotsam and jetsam of British society, are rendered as sympathetic, lively and humorous. Killing Africans *en masse,* the film implies, fosters camaraderie and somehow brings out their latent humanity. White Europe's right to determine Africa's political destiny, like the white American right to Indian land in the western, is simply assumed throughout the film.[23]

In *The Wild Geese,* the imagery of encirclement is used against black Africans, as the spectator, positioned behind the sight of mercenary machine guns, sees them fall in their hundreds. One of the crucial innovations of *Battle of Algiers* (directed by Gillo Pontecorvo, 1966) was to invert this imagery of encirclement and exploit the identificatory mechanisms of cinema on behalf of the colonised rather than the coloniser. Algerians, traditionally represented in cinema as shadowy figures, picturesquely backward at best and hostile and menacing at worst, are here treated with respect, dignified by close-ups, shown as speaking subjects rather than as manipulable objects. While never caricaturing the French, the film exposes the oppressive logic of colonialism and consistently fosters our complicity with the Algerians. It is through Algerian eyes, for example, that we witness a condemned Algerian's walk to his execution. It is from *within* the casbah that we see and hear the French troops and helicopters. This time it is the colonised who are encircled and menaced and with whom we identify.

One sequence, in which three Algerian women dress in European style in order to pass the French checkpoints and plant bombs in the European sector, is particularly effective in controverting traditional patterns of identification. Many critics, impressed with the film-makers' honesty in showing that the FLN committed terrorist acts against civilians, lauded this sequence for its 'objectivity'. (Objectivity, as Fanon pointed out, almost always works against the colonised.) But that *Battle of Algiers* shows such acts is ultimately less important than *how* it shows them; the signified of the diegesis (terrorist actions) is less important than the mode of address and the positioning of the spectator. The film makes us want the women to complete their task, not necessarily out of political sympathy but through the mechanisms of cinematic identification: scale (close shots individualise the three women); off-screen sound (we hear the sexist comments as if from the women's aural perspective); and especially point-of-view editing. By the time the women plant the bombs, our identification is so complete that we are not terribly disturbed by a series of close shots of the bombs' potential victims. Close-ups of one of the women alternate with close-ups of French people in a cafe, the eyeline matches suggesting that she is contemplating the suffering her bomb will cause. But while we might think her cruel for taking innocent life, we are placed within her perspective and admire her for having the courage to perform what has been presented as a dangerous and noble mission.

Other narrative and cinematic strategies are deployed in this sequence to solicit support for the three women. The narrative placement of the sequence itself presents their action as the fulfilment of the FLN promise, made in the previous sequence, to respond to the French terror bombing of the casbah. Everything here contributes to the impression that the bombing will be an expression of the rage of an entire people rather than the will of a fanatical minority. It is constructed, therefore, not as an individual emotional explosion but as a considered political task undertaken with reluctance by an organised group. The sequence consequently challenges the image of anti-colonialist guerrillas as terrorist fanatics lacking respect for human life. Unlike the Western mass media, which usually restrict their definition of 'terror' to anti-establishment violence—state repres-

sion and government-sanctioned aerial bombings are not included in the definition—*Battle of Algiers* presents anti-colonialist terror as a response to colonialist
violence. We are dealing here with what might be called the political dimension of
syntagmatic organisation; while the First World media usually present colonial
repression as a response to 'leftist subversion', *Battle of Algiers* inverts the sequencing. Indeed, examining the film as a whole, we might say that Pontecorvo
'highjacks' the techniques of mass-media reportage—hand-held cameras, frequent zooms, long lenses—to express a political point of view rarely encountered
in establishment-controlled media.

The *mise-en-scène*, too, creates a non-sexist and anti-colonialist variant on the
classic cinematic *topos:* women dressing in front of a mirror. The lighting highlights the powerful dignity of the women's faces as they remove their veils, cut
their hair and apply make-up so as to look European. The mirror here is not the
instrument of *vanitas,* but a revolutionary tool. The women regard themselves,
without coyness, as if they were putting on a new identity with which they do not
feel entirely comfortable. They perform their task in a disciplined manner and
without vindictive remarks about their future victims.

The film also highlights the larger social dimension of the drama in which the
women are involved. The colonial world, writes Fanon, is a world cut in two: 'In
the colonies it is the policeman and the soldier who are the official instituted go-
betweens, the spokesmen of the settler and his rule of oppression.'[24] The background imagery, readable thanks to the depth of field, shows that the French have
imposed their regime by what amounts to military occupation. The French are in
uniform, the Algerians in civilian dress. The casbah is the Algerian's home; for
the French it is an outpost on a frontier. The barbed wire and checkpoints remind
us of other occupations, thus eliciting our sympathy for a struggle against a foreign occupant. The proairetic 'code of actions', meanwhile, shows the soldiers
treating the Algerians with racist scorn and suspicion, while they greet the Europeans with a friendly 'bonjour'. They misperceive the three women as French and
flirtatious when in fact they are Algerian and revolutionary. Their sexism, furthermore, prevents them from seeing women, generally, as potential revolutionaries. In the negative dialectic of oppression, the slave (the colonised, the black,
the woman) knows the mind of the master better than the master knows the mind
of the slave.

Western attitudes toward non-Western peoples are also played on here. Has-
siba is first seen in traditional Arab costume, her face covered by a veil. So
dressed, she is a reminder of Arab women in other films who function as a sign of
the exotic. But as the sequence progresses, we become increasingly close to the
three women, though paradoxically, we become close to them only as they strip
themselves of their safsaris, their veils, and their hair. They transform themselves
into Europeans, people with whom the cinema more conventionally allows the
audience to identify. At the same time, we are made aware of the absurdity of a
system in which people warrant respect only if they look and act like Europeans.
The French colonialist myth of 'assimilation', the idea that select Algerians could
be first-class French citizens, is demystified. Algerians can assimilate, it is sug-

gested, but only at the price of shedding everything that is characteristically Algerian about them—their religion, their clothes, their language.[25]

If *Battle of Algiers* exploits conventional identification mechanisms on behalf of a group traditionally denied them, other films critique colonialism and colonialist point-of-view conventions in a more ironic mode.[26] *Petit à Petit* (directed by Jean Rouch, 1969) inverts the hierarchy often assumed within the discipline of anthropology, the academic offspring of colonialism, by having the African protagonist Damouré 'do anthropology' among the strange tribe known as the Parisians, interrogating them about their folkways. Europe, usually the bearer of the anthropological gaze, is here subjected to the questioning regard of the other. *How Tasty Was My Little Frenchman* (directed by Nelson Pereira dos Santos, 1971), meanwhile, updates Montaigne by persuading us to sympathise with Tupinamba cannibals.[27] The film plays ironically on the traditional identification with European heroes by placing the camera, initially, on American shores, so that the Amerindian discovers the European rather than the reverse. By the final shot, which shows the Frenchman's Tupinamba lover dining on him while manifesting no emotion beyond ordinary culinary pleasure, our 'natural' identification with the coloniser has been so completely subverted that we are quite indifferent to his fate.

The question of point of view is crucial then, but it is also more complex than might at first appear. The granting of point-of-view shots to the oppressed does not guarantee a non-colonialist perspective, any more than Hitchcock's granting of subjective shots to the female protagonist of *Marnie* inoculates that film from what is ultimately a patriarchal and infantilising discourse. The arch-racist *The Birth of a Nation* grants Gus, the sexually aggressive black man, a number of subjective shots as he admires little Flora. The racism in such a case may be said to be displaced from the code of editing onto the code of character construction, here inflected by the projection of white sexual paranoia onto the black male, in the case of Gus, and of patriarchal chivalry (tinged perhaps with authorial desire), in the case of Flora. The Brazilian film *João Negrinho* (directed by Oswaldo Censoni, 1954) is entirely structured around the perspective of its focal character, an elderly ex-slave. The film apparently presents all events from João's point of view so as to elicit total sympathy, yet what the film elicits sympathy *for* is in fact a paternalistic vision in which 'good' blacks are to leave their destiny in the hands of well-intentioned whites.

CODES AND COUNTER STRATEGIES

A more comprehensive analysis of character status as speaking subject as against spoken object would attend to cinematic and extra-cinematic codes, and to their interweaving within textual systems. In short, it must address the instances through which film speaks—composition, framing, scale, off- and on-screen sound, music—as well as questions of plot and character. Questions of image scale and duration, for example, are intricately related to the respect afforded a character and the potential for audience sympathy, understanding and identification. Which characters are afforded close-ups and which are relegated to the background? Does a character look and act, or merely appear, to be looked at and acted upon? With whom is the audience permitted intimacy? If there is off-screen commentary or dialogue, what is its relation to the image? *Black Girl* (directed by Ousmane Sembene, 1966) uses off-screen dialogue to foster intimacy with the title character, a Senegalese maid working in France. Shots of the maid working in the kitchen coincide with overheard slurs from her employers about her 'laziness'. Not only do the images point up the absurdity of the slurs—indeed, she is the *only* person working—but also the coincidence of the off-screen dialogue with close shots of her face makes us hear the comments as if through her ears.

An emphasis on identification, however, while appropriate to fiction films in the realist mode, fails to allow for films which might *also* show sensitivity to the point of view, in a more inconclusive sense, of the colonised or the oppressed, but in a rigorously distanced manner. A film like *Der Leone Have Sept Cabeças* (directed by Glauber Rocha, 1970), whose multi-lingual title already subverts the cultural positioning of the spectator by mingling the languages of five of Africa's colonisers, allows identification with none of its characters, because it is essentially a Brechtian 'tricontinental' fable which animates emblematic figures representing the diverse incarnations of coloniser and colonised in the Third World. 'Zumbi', named after the founder of the Brazilian fugitive slave republic Palmares, encapsulates the revolution in Africa and among the black diaspora; 'Samba' embodies the power of Afro-culture; and 'Xobu' figures in caricatural form the corruption of the black puppets of colonialism. To condemn such a film for not creating identification with the oppressed is to reduce the broad question of the articulation of narrative, cinematic and cultural codes to the single question of the presence or absence of a particular sub-code of editing.

The music track can also play a crucial role in the establishment of a political point of view and the cultural positioning of the spectator. Film music has an emotional dimension: it can regulate our sympathies, extract our tears or trigger our fears. The Ray Budd score in *The Wild Geese* consistently supports the mercenaries, waxing martial and heroic when they are on the attack, and maudlin when they emote. At one point, the Borodin air 'This Is My Beloved' musically eulogises one of the slain mercenaries. In many classical Hollywood films, African polyrhythms became aural signifiers of encircling savagery, a kind of synecdochic acoustic shorthand for the atmosphere of menace implicit in the phrase 'the natives are restless'. *Der Leone Have Sept Cabeças,* in contrast, treats African polyrhythms with respect, as music, while ironically associating the puppets of colonialism with 'La Marseillaise'. *Black and White in Color* employs music satirically by having the African colonised carry their colonial masters, while singing—in their own language—satirical songs about them ('My master is so fat, how can I carry him? . . . Yes, but mine is so ugly. . . .').

In many consciously anti-colonialist films, a kind of textual uneven development makes the film politically progressive in some of its codes but regressive in others. *Burn!* (directed by Gillo Pontecorvo, 1970), for example, a didactic assault on neo-colonialism, partially vitiates its message by imposing highly Europeanised choral music on its Third World setting.[28] *Compasso de Espera (Marking Time,* directed by Antunes Filho, 1973), a denunciation of Brazilian-style racism, subverts its pro-black position with a music track that mixes Erik Satie and Blood Sweat and Tears while ignoring the rich Afro-Brazilian musical heritage. On the other hand *Land in Anguish* (directed by Glauber Rocha, 1967) uses music to the opposite effect. Here, in a film dealing with Brazil's white political elite, Afro-Brazilian music serves as a constant reminder of the existence of the marginalised majority of blacks and mulattoes absent from the screen and not represented by that elite. Brazilian films in general, perhaps because of the ethnically 'polyphonic' nature of that society, are particularly rich in inter-codic contradiction, at times instituting a veritable battle of the codes on the music tracks. *The Given Word* (directed by Anselmo Duarte, 1962) sets in motion a cultural conflict between the Afro-Brazilian *berimbau* instrument and the bells of the Catholic Church, while *Tent of Miracles* (directed by Nelson Pereira dos Santos, 1976) counterpoints opera and samba to represent a larger conflict between Bahia's white elite and its subjugated *mestizos.*

ABERRANT READINGS

The filmic experience must inevitably be inflected by the cultural awareness of the audience itself, constituted outside the text and traversed by sets of social relations such as race, class and gender. We must allow, therefore, for the possibility of aberrant readings, readings which go against the grain of the discourse. Although fiction films are persuasive machines designed to produce specific impressions and emotions, they are not all-powerful; they may be read differently by different audiences. Hollywood's ill-informed portrayals of Latin-American life were sometimes laughed off the screen within Latin America itself. The Spanish version of *Dracula,* for example, made concurrently with the 1931 Bela Lugosi film, mingles Cuban, Argentine, Chilean, Mexican and peninsular Spanish in a linguistic hodge-podge that struck Latin-American audiences as quite ludicrous.

A particular audience's knowledge or experience can also generate a counterpressure to colonialist representations. Black Americans, presumably, never took Stepin Fetchit to be an accurate representation of their race as a whole. *One Potato Two Potato* (directed by Larry Peerce, 1964), a film about interracial marriage, provides a poignant narrative example, in which the experience of oppression inflects a character's reading of the film-within-the-film. The black husband, enraged by a series of racially motivated slights, attends a western in a drive-in movie theatre. Projecting his anger, he screams his support for the Indians, whom he sees as his analogues in suffering, and his hatred for the whites. His reading goes against the grain of the colonialist discourse.

The movement of an aberrant reading can also proceed in the opposite direction; an anti-racist film, when subjected to the ethnocentric prejudices of a particular critic or interpretative community, can be read in a racist fashion. A sequence in *Masculine, Feminine,* a quotation from LeRoi Jones's play *The Dutchman,* shows a blonde white woman in the metro accompanied by two black men. At the conclusion of the sequence, a shot of the woman's hand holding a revolver gives way, shortly thereafter, to the sound of gunfire and a title 'Nothing but a Woman/ and a Man/And a Sea of Blood.' Andrew Sarris, in his account of the sequence, ignores the visual and written evidence that it is the woman who wields the gun: ' . . .a Negro nationalist draws out a gun with phallic fury in the metro."[29] Here, cultural expectations inform the very perceptions of the viewer, who projects his own racial and sexual expectations onto the film.[30]

We must be aware, then, of the cultural and ideological assumptions spectators bring to the cinema. We must be conscious, too, of the institutionalised expectations, the mental machinery that serves as the subjective support to the film industry, and which leads us to consume films in a certain way. This apparatus has adapted most of us to the consumption of films which display high production values. But many Third World film-makers find such a model, if not repugnant, at least inappropriate—not only because of their critique of dominant cinema, but also because the Third World, with its scarcer capital and higher costs, simply cannot *afford* it. Significantly, such film-makers and critics argue for a model rooted in the actual circumstances of the Third World: a 'third cinema' (Solanas-Gettino), 'an aesthetic of hunger' (Rocha), and 'an imperfect cinema' (Espinosa). To expect to find First World production values in Third World films is to be both naive and ethnocentric. To prospect for Third World auteurs, similarly, is to apply a regressive analytical model which implicitly valorises dominant cinema and promises only to invite a few elite members of the Third World into an already established pantheon.

The objective of this study of filmic colonialism and racism, finally, is not to hurl charges of racism at individual film-makers or critics—in a systematically racist society few escape the effects of racism—but rather to learn how to decode and deconstruct racist images and sounds. Racism is not permanently inscribed in celluloid or in the human mind; it forms part of a constantly changing dialectical process within which, we must never forget, we are far from powerless.

Notes

We would like to express our appreciation to the members of the study group in racism, all graduate students in the Cinema Studies Program at New York University, for their suggestions and insights: Pat Keeton, Charles Musser, Richard Porton, Susan Ryan, Ella Shochat, and Ed Simmons.

1. Oxford, 1977.
2. Houghton Mifflin, 1976.
3. Bantam, 1974.
4. Hayden, 1974.
5. Drama, 1972.
6. Ungar, 1982.
7. UCLA Publications, 1980.
8. Seghers, 1974.
9. *Bulletin of Concerned Asian Scholars,* vol. 3 no. 1, Winter–Spring 1971.
10. For a discussion of the contextual dimension of racism in cinema, see "Racism in the Cinema: Proposal for a Methodological Model of Investigation", by Louise Spence

and Robert Stam, with the collaboration of Pat Keeton, Charles Musser, Richard Porton, Susan Ryan, Ella Shochat, and Ed Simmons, to be published in a forthcoming issue of *Critical Arts: A Journal for Media Studies.*

11. See, for example, Molly Haskell, *From Reverence to Rape* (New York: Holt, Rinehart and Winston, 1974) and Marjorie Rosen, *Popcorn Venus* (New York: Avon, 1974).

12. These notions of the Third World are imprecise because the Third World nations are not necessarily poor in resources (Mexico, Venezuela and Kuwait are rich in petroleum), nor culturally backward (as witnessed by the brilliance of contemporary Latin American literature), nor non-industrialised (Brazil is highly industrialised) nor non-white (Argentina is predominantly white).

13. Albert Memmi, *Dominated Man* (Boston: Beacon Press, 1968), p. 186.

14. Buñuel's film version of the novel mocks Defoe's protagonist by haunting him with surrealist dreams, turning him into a transvestite, and making it singularly difficult for him to make rational sense out of the tenets of Christianity to an inquisitive Friday. The film *Man Friday,* which we have not seen, reportedly tells the story from Friday's point of view. And in a recent Brazilian adaptation of the novel, black actor Grande Otelo subverts Defoe's classic by playing a Friday who refuses the coloniser's power to name, repeatedly telling the Englishman: 'Me Crusoe. *You* Friday!'

15. See Aimé Césaire, *Une Tempête* (Paris; Seuil, 1969).

16. Jonathan Swift, *Gulliver's Travels* (New York: Random House, 1958), p. 241.

17. Joseph Conrad, *Heart of Darkness* (New York: New American Library, 1950), p. 69.

18. Frantz Fanon, *The Wretched of the Earth* (New York: Grove Press, 1968), p. 51.

19. A recent example of this tendency is the ecstatic song led by James Brown in *The Blues Brothers* (directed by John Landis, 1980).

20. For a discussion of Hollywood's view of Brazil, see Sergio Augusto, "Hollywood Looks at Brazil: From Carmen Miranda to Moonraker", in Randal Johnson and Robert Stam, *Brazilian Cinema* (East Brunswick: Associated University Presses, 1982).

21. See Emilia Viotti da Costa, "Slave Images and Realities", in *Comparative Perspectives on Slavery in New World Plantation Societies* (New York: New York Academy of Sciences, 1977).

22. Engelhardt, *op. cit.*

23. In the racist hierarchies of *The Wild Geese,* white males stand at the apex, while women are treated as comically dispensable and blacks are relegated to the bottom. The film camouflages its racism, however, by two plot devices involving positive images: first, by including a token black (a positive image?) as a member of the mercenary force (genocide rendered palatable by 'integrating' its perpetrators) and second, by having the entire operation be undertaken on behalf of a black leader characterised as 'the best there is'. The African 'best', however, is embodied by a sick, helpless, dying 'good Negro' who must be literally carried on the backs of whites. In this white rescue fantasy, the black leader of the 70s speaks the Sidney Poitier dialogue of the 50s; he pleads for racial understanding. The blacks, he says, must forgive the white past, and whites must forgive the black present. Thus centuries of colonialism are cancelled out in the misleading symmetry of an aphorism.

24. Frantz Fanon. *op. cit.,* p. 38.

25. For a fuller discussion of this film, see Joan Mellen, *Filmguide to the Battle of Algiers* (Bloomington: Indiana University Press, 1973), and Robert Stam, *The Battle of Algiers: Three Women, Three Bombs,* Macmillan Films Study Extract, 1975.

26. Some Left critics dismissed *The Battle of Algiers* as a Hollywoodean Z-style exercise in political melodrama. Such critiques run the dangers of being (1) *ahistorical* (we must situate the film in the context of 1966); (2) politically *counter-productive* (the Left deprives itself of a powerful instrument of anti-colonialist persuasion); and (3) *ethnocentric* (offering an example of a kind of Left colonialism). While the Right asks all pro–Third World films to display high production values and be entertaining, a certain Left asks all pro–Third World films to be disconstructive, reflexive, and to display the precise variant of Marxism that the particular First World critic finds most sympathetic.

27. Montaigne's essay "Des Cannibales", was, ironically, based on interviews with Brazilian Indians then on display in Europe. The Indians, according to Montaigne, asked him three questions, only two of which he could remember: (1) Why were some people rich and others poor? (2) Why did Europeans worship kings who were no bigger than other people? Lévi-Strauss, more than three centuries later, claims to have been asked the same questions by Brazilian Indians.

28. The film also made the mistake of pitting one of the First World's most charismatic actors (Marlon Brando), as the coloniser, against a former peasant non-actor (Evaristo Marques), as the colonised, thus disastrously tipping the scales of interest, if not sympathy, in favour of the coloniser.

29. From Sarris's review in the *Village Voice,* September 29–October 6, 1966, included in *Masculine, Feminine* (New York: Grove Press, 1969), pp. 275–79.

30. In the case of Cuban films, ethnocentrism merges with anti-communism to distort the perception of First World critics. Many American critics, for example, identified very strongly with the alienated artist-intellectual protagonist of Alea's *Memories of Underdevelopment* (1968) and with his disabused view of the Cuban people. Seeing the film as an auteurist lament concerning the low level of cultural life in Cuba and the repressive nature of the Cuban regime, Andrew Sarris spoke for these critics (in his explanation of the award given the film by the National Society of Film Critics) when he claimed that what struck them most favourably was the film's 'personal and very courageous confrontation of the artist's doubts and ambivalences regarding the Cuban revolution'. Such critics completely missed the film's critique both of the protagonist and of pre-revolutionary Cuba.

RESPONSIBILITIES OF A GAY FILM CRITIC

ROBIN WOOD

In "To Have (Written) and Have Not (Directed)" in the first volume of Movies and Methods, *Robin Wood extracted elements of Hawksian vision from a film that had numerous contributors and constraints. The article was a model of auteur criticism. Since the mid seventies, Wood has shifted his critical emphasis and actively identified his writing with the politics of gay liberation. Along with other gay critics, such as Lee Atwell, Richard Dyer, Vito Russo, and Thomas Waugh, Wood has worked to establish a significant body of gay criticism both in academic and popular journals and in the gay press (for example,* The Body Politic, Christopher Street, *and* The Advocate*).*

At a slight lag, this criticism parallels the development of feminist film criticism. It constitutes an important countercurrent in its lively effort to merge personal and political concerns on the terrain of the social production of sexual identity and the cinematic representation of sexual politics. Gay criticism begins from a social perspective and proceeds to investigate the workings of culture in relation to that perspective, a procedure that often generates remarkably insightful results.

Here, Wood returns to his earlier auteur criticism, retaining the subject matter but radically changing the perspective. (In that respect, Wood's shift contrasts revealingly with Metz's, where the transformation from structural to psychoanalytic theory does not require a reassessment of earlier work.) This change in perspective compels Wood to address issues of ideology and sexual politics that have direct import for everyday life, and they become uppermost in his evaluations of Renoir, Bergman, and Hawks.

Wood now finds an ambiguity in Renoir and Hawks that he could not identify with precision before. In each case, it has to do with monogamy and sexual identity. Renoir focuses on the tension between human desire and existing social practices, while Hawks conveys the tension between these practices (namely, male camaraderie or domestic family life) and an indefinable chaos that lurks beyond the existing alternatives. Ingmar Bergman's explorations of human anguish pose a different problem by presenting anguish and neurosis as the human condition for which there is no alternative. His films foreclose the possibility of actively achieved change. In each case, Wood examines the director's oeuvre not in relation only to gay themes or the gay movement but in relation also to the interrelationship between aesthetics and ideology. By placing this question in a personal frame that minimizes theoretical abstractness, Wood shows us that thought and ideas can actively reshape our lives and that we do not have to repeat the misperceptions learned in a society that seeks to preserve its traditional forms. "Our emotions have to be educated," Wood writes, and it is to this valuable goal that Wood dedicates his recent writings.

First, my title. I intend equal emphasis on all three terms: *Gay Film Critic.* Critic: one concerned in problems of the interpretation and evaluation of art and artifacts. Film critic: one who makes the central area of that concern the cinema. Gay—not just the word and the fact it points to, but the word and fact asserted publicly: one who is conscious of belonging to one of society's oppressed minority groups, and who is ready to confront the implications of that for both his theory and his practice.

I can define what I mean here in relation to two types of gay critic who reject this equality of emphasis. First, the critic who for whatever reasons (many differ-

ent ones are conceivable, of widely varying respectability) resists the public revelation of his gayness, arguing (either as defensive self-justification or as a sincerely held principle) that it has nothing to do with his view of art—the view
conceived as "objective," and art conceived as something Out There that one can
be objective about. I cannot afford to be too contemptuous of this type, as I
belonged to it myself until quite recently, and in my case I was always half aware
that the defensive self-justification was of the flimsiest. A gay subtext is intermittently discernible running through my early work; a number of people, including
some who hadn't met me, have told me that they deduced that I was gay long
before I came out. But if these early writings are worth analyzing at all from the
gay viewpoint, it could only be as an analysis of self-oppression—an alternating
pattern of peeping out of the closet door and then quickly slamming it shut, and
pasting over the chinks with placards on which words like Marriage, Family,
Health, and Normality were loudly displayed—and with self-oppression becoming, as it always must, the oppression of others. (See, especially, the treatment of
homosexual relations in the account of *Les Biches* in the book on Chabrol I co-
authored with Michael Walker, for the most embarrassing moments of which I
must accept responsibility.)

The other type of gay critic places the emphasis strongly, sometimes exclusively, on "gay," and concerns himself strictly with works that have *direct* bearing
on gayness, approaching them from a political-propagandist viewpoint: do they
or do they not further the gay cause? He will find it necessary to review Fassbinder's *Fox*, but will probably ignore Godard's *Tout va bien*. My choice of examples
here is not arbitrary. The objection to such criticism is not merely that it is aesthetically restrictive but that it implies an inadequate, and insufficiently radical,
grasp of what the Gay Liberation Movement stands for at its best, of its more
general social significance. Godard's film, in which gayness is nowhere alluded
to, seems to me to have far greater positive importance for Gay Liberation than
Fassbinder's sour determinism, with its incidental reinforcing of gay stereotypes
for the bourgeois audience ("the truth about the homosexual milieu," as the English Establishment critics greeted it).

Positively, I am able to point to two British colleagues who amply fulfill, in
their very different ways, my conception of the gay film critic's responsibilities:
Richard Dyer and Andrew Britton. The latter's article on Eisenstein in the forthcoming *Framework* strikes me as exemplary in this respect.

The change in my critical position and practice which many people have
noted—some with favor, some with dismay—has been centrally determined by
my coming out, and by the changes in my personal life connected with that.
Critics are not, of course, supposed to talk personally. It is regarded as an embarrassment, as bad taste, and besides it is an affront to the famous ideal of "objectivity." The typical bourgeois Establishment reaction to any form of personal revelation might be typified by a remark by Philip Strick in his ignominious review of
my last book in *Sight and Sound*—a review that managed to trivialize every issue
in sight—where my coming out in print was described as "telling us about his
love life." Yet I believe there will always be a close connection between critical

theory, critical practice, and personal life; and it seems important that the critic should be aware of the personal bias that must inevitably affect his choice of theoretical position, and prepared to foreground it in his work.

I don't believe that any theory exists in a vacuum or as Truth. Every theory is the product of the needs of particular people within a particular culture at a particular stage of its development, and can only properly be understood within its context. Our gravitation, as human individuals within, and determined by, our culture, toward one or other of the available critical positions, will depend upon our personal needs, on the way we wish to lead our lives, on the sort of society we would like to build, on the particularities of our involvement in the social process. Such a view presupposes a constantly developing, dynamic relationship between criticism and art, between individual and work. There is in a sense no such thing as "the films of Ingmar Bergman," existing as an entity that criticism could finally and definitively describe and interpret and place in the museum. Rather, the films exist as experienced and perceived by the viewer, with the precise nature of the experiencing depending on the viewer's position in society and within ideology. Our sense of the *use* of art generally, and of the particular uses to which particular works allow themselves to be put, will vary from generation to generation, shifting in accordance with our sense of personal and social needs.

What I propose to do is, first, define what Gay Liberation means to me, the kind of significance I attach to the movement, the kinds of social intervention I see it capable of making; and then reconsider certain films and directors (not necessarily or centrally concerned with gayness) that already meant a great deal to me before my coming out, in an attempt to indicate the nature of the shift in my critical practice, the somewhat different kinds of interest and emphasis I would now bring to an interpretation and evaluation of them.

As most commonly expressed in the newspapers, periodicals, etc., of our Establishment (not to mention various Gay Society discussions I have attended), the aim of the Gay Liberation Movement would appear to be read as that of gaining acceptance and equal rights for homosexuals within existing society. My basic argument is that such an aim is totally inadequate. Acceptance of the homosexual by society has its obvious corollary and condition: acceptance of society by the homosexual. To see the incongruity of this, one has only to consider the dominant ideological norms of the society within which we live. As far as love and sexuality are concerned, those norms are marriage (in the form of legalized heterosexual monogamy) and the nuclear family (with the alternative, at once complementary and incompatible, of exclusive romantic love). Between them they offer homosexuals the terms on which they might be acceptable: the aping of heterosexual marriage and family (with poodles instead of children) or *l'amour fou,* preferably culminating in suicide or alcoholism.

Of crucial importance to Gay Liberation is its very close, logical connection with Women's Liberation. The present status of both has been made possible by the increasing public acceptance of birth control, with its implicit acknowledgment that the aim of sex is not necessarily procreation, and its consequent undermining of the tyrannical and repressive norm of monogamy and family. The common logical aim of both movements must be, it seems to me, to attack and undermine the dominant ideological norms on all levels. This offers the gay critic a brief that is enormously more open and comprehensive than the examination of the ways in which homosexuals have been presented on the screen (though that might of course become a perfectly legitimate focus of her or his attention, provided the wider implications were always kept in view). The attack, for instance, could—indeed, should—be directed at the economic structures of capitalism that support the norms, as they are embodied in the structure of the film industry itself as well as in its products. Being neither a practiced political nor a sociological thinker, I am going to restrict myself to questions of sexuality and love.

When dealing with ideology it is always necessary to ask not only what it *ex*presses but what it *re*presses. The opposed, largely contradictory, ideological positives our culture offers (monogamy and family, romantic love) have one obvious feature in common: the insistence on exclusivity and mutual possession, with "fidelity" thought of basically in sexual terms and sexuality mystified as "sacred." Beyond this, there is the furtive extra-marital affair, with its penalties of tension, secrecy, distrust, recrimination, etc. What is repressed is the possibility that people might relate freely to each other, on a non-pairing basis, without imposing restrictions on each other's liberty. The dominant ideology has a word for this: promiscuity, a term loaded with pejorative connotations. According o ideology's double standards, there is some difference between male promiscuity and female promiscuity. A heterosexual man who is promiscuous acquires a certain glamour and is a Casanova; a woman who is promiscuous is a bitch, a tart, a slut, a whore. By and large, however, ideology has no place for promiscuity (or, as I prefer to call it, relating freely to one another) as an asserted life-style or a possible norm.

My shift in terminology is also a shift in meaning. "Promiscuity" is always exclusively sexual, and the notion of it within ideology has the function of separating sexuality from love. "Relating freely to each other," on the other hand, involves potentially the whole person—*including* his or her sexuality, without which the relating wouldn't be free, but not *restricted* to it. (This is not to denigrate the pleasure of quite casual sexual relations, or to suggest that every relationship should be "complete," whatever that might mean.) Much the same distinction could be made if one substituted for "promiscuity" the term "permissiveness"—a term popularly understood almost entirely in sexual terms rather than in terms of free human relationships. The term has the added objectionability that it implies that someone or something ("society") is doing the permitting; and to acknowledge society's right to permit is to acknowledge its right to prohibit. In general, ideology's method of dealing with the unthinkable notion of free relationships is to trivialize or dirty it, so that it becomes difficult to imagine what it might actually entail or how it might work.

In *Life Against Death,* Norman O. Brown defines the central characteristic of capitalist man as dissatisfaction, with anxiety as its inevitable companion: the desire to own more, coupled with the fear of losing what one has. Anxiety, or insecurity, certainly seems fundamental to the possessiveness that characterizes most of our sexual relationships. Parenthetically, as a person whose personal insecurity reaches proportions one might describe as grotesque, I must stress that I don't wish to appear to speak from some superior "liberated" position wherein I have solved all life's problems within my own life. On the contrary, I speak as one struggling and floundering frantically among the mess and confusion of sexual relationships as they currently exist; I am prey to all the contaminations of the jealousy, possessiveness, and exclusivity that I attack. One must, however, recognize— otherwise there could never be any progress—that ideas must always outstrip emotions. Our emotions have to be educated, and emotional education is the most painful of all processes, because the education is resisted at every point by what we call our instincts but might more reasonably think of as our ideological structuring. Only with ideas can we confront ideology.

I shall move in a while to two strongly contrasted directors with whose work I' have, as a critic, been associated—Bergman and Howard Hawks—attempting to suggest ways in which their work might be re-read from the perspective I have outlined. I shall not spell out in detail the differences between my approach now and my books on these two directors, as this would be deducible for those who have read them and boring for those who haven't, but I hope for the former group a critical reflection back over my past work will be implicit. First, however, I want to talk briefly about a film that, long among my favorites, has grown in meaning and in richness for me over the past year: Jean Renoir's *The Rules of the Game*. I have come to re-read the film precisely in the context I have defined: our entrapment in ideological notions of love and sexuality, with their emphasis on pairing, choice, and exclusivity; and the continuously repressed but insistent vision of the potential loveliness of genuinely shared relationships, in which none of the participants feels excluded, in which love is recognized as a life-principle that transcends the exclusive romantic attachment. To anticipate, one can evoke here one of Renoir's favorite words, and the force it gets from the context of his work: generosity.

Two general or recurrent features of Renoir's work must be made present here. One is the notion (influenced perhaps by the childhood described in *Renoir, My Father*, and the background of French Impressionism) of life as continual flux. He quotes Antoine Lavoisier's "In nature nothing is lost, nothing is created, everything is transformed" as one of his favorite texts. The other is the recurring relationship-pattern in his films (at once an extension and a questioning of the "eternal triangle") of one to three—usually one woman to three men (*The Golden Coach, Elena et Les Hommes, Diary of a Chambermaid, French Can-Can*, and *Rules of the Game* itself, where there are in fact four men if one counts St. Aubin), though in *The River* there is one man to three women. The addition of a third option crucially affects the significance of the triangle, which in our culture has always been firmly associated with exclusivity and the necessity for choice (usually, the conflict is between marriage, family and romantic love, the opposed and complementary ideological poles). If three, why not four, five—or twenty?

The film was initially received (and is still, by some people) as virulent social satire, an attack on a decadent ruling class on the eve of its inevitable dissolution. Confronted with this view, Renoir's own response was one of amazement: "But I love those people. . . . I would love to have lived in that world." It is consistently analyzable, I think, in terms of a tension between the two impulses these responses suggest.

There's another way of looking at the film's rich ambiguity of effect: it can be read as a film about people who go too far, or as a film about people who can't quite go far enough. Many have commented on the difficulty of defining what, precisely, *are* the rules of the game. In fact, every character has his or her own rules, or a personal variation on an implied complex of rules. In only two characters do the rules appear clear-cut and rigid in their application: Schumacher (Gaston Modot) and Lisette (Paulette Dubost). One aspect of the film's astonishingly complex yet precise formal organization can be suggested by pointing to three things about them: (1) they are husband and wife; (2) the rules they enforce are the most strongly contrasted of any represented in the film, indeed diametrically opposed; and (3) it is the dual action of their application of their rules that produces the climactic catastrophe. The rules of Schumacher, the gamekeeper from Alsace (who is deliberately presented, in 1939, as an embryonic Fascist), are centered on strict and repressive notions of marital fidelity, the ownership of wife by husband, that give him the moral right to shoot both wife and lover in the event of discovered infidelity. The rules of Lisette, the Parisian ladies' maid, are centered on notions of free sexual play as long as it remains frivolous and unengaged. When it comes to seriousness, the priorities are narrowly social-ideological; Octave (Renoir) is too old for Christine (Nora Gregor), and couldn't afford to keep her in the luxury she's used to.

Between these two—with their equally defined and entrapping, if opposite, sets of rules—come the film's central characters, who all exist in states of varying uncertainty and confusion as to what the rules are. And Christine's uncertainty is significantly the most extreme. From her point of view, the ambiguity of the film can be put another way: the story of a woman trying desperately to understand what her role should be or the story of a woman who can't quite accept that all roles are traps and refuse them all—with the roles defined in terms of the relationships available with particular men. It is important to recognize that the society Renoir depicts is inhabited almost entirely by outsiders: the Marquis is Jewish, Christine is from Vienna, André Jurieu (Roland Toutain) is from the modern world of aeroplanes and public heroes, Octave is a perpetual outsider wherever he is. The character who seems chiefly to embody our idea of a stable aristocratic society is the General, an old man whose constant refrain is that everything is passing away.

It is a society in which all order is at a stage of potential or imminent collapse; and this can be seen either in terms of a closing down or an opening up (the film encourages both readings). "I don't want fences, and I don't want rabbits," the Marquis tells Schumacher, and the remark has very clear parallels with the paradoxes of the characters' sexual behavior throughout the film. I have no knowledge of the actual domestic commitments of rabbits—their familial organization may be as impeccably bourgeois as it appears in the books of one of my favorite authors, Beatrix Potter—but in popular imagery rabbits always have connotations of promiscuity; "breeding like rabbits" doesn't refer merely to the number of offspring but to presumed sexual habits. The emphasis throughout the hunt is on the mindless slaughter of rabbits, the detailed imagery evoking the strongest sympathetic response toward what is being destroyed.

The tension I have described can be illustrated succinctly with the beautiful little scene in which, after her discovery of her husband's adulterous relationship with Geneviève (Mila Parély), Christine confronts her rival in her room and enlists her in an ambiguously motivated complicity. On the one hand, Christine's reaction to the shock (she had previously believed completely in her husband's fidelity) is to play what she takes to be "the game" by rejecting all seriousness; she wants Geneviève to keep her husband occupied, not so that she can develop her relationship with André—whom she describes at this point as "too sincere"—but so that she can play around. On the other hand, the possibility of freely shared relationships is nowhere closer to the surface of the film than in this scene, which culminates in a moment of relaxed conviviality and exchange between two women (the demonstrations of how Tyrolean dances go) of a kind very rare in the cinema, where women are habitually seen from the male viewpoint as rivals for the man, their possible uniting repressed. The whole film can be read as structured on continuously shifting couplings (I don't intend the sexual meaning here) which cut completely across all the divisions of sex, class, social role; virtually all the characters have a "duet scene" at some point in the film. The obvious exception is André and Geneviève—the two Octave suggests near the beginning that it would be most convenient to pair off.

Renoir's method and the film's visual style are crucial to its meaning. His creative collaboration with actors—*all* the actors—is well known. The camera style emphasizes the structure-patterns of the scenario by never allowing us more than transitory identification with one character at the expense of others. The constant reframings, in which the camera excludes some to include others, the continual entrances into and exits from the frame, the division of our attention between foreground and background—the style might be aptly described as perpetual visual promiscuity, quite breaking down the traditional one-to-one relationship of spectator to protagonist to which the cinema has habituated us. The Renoiresque principle of emotional generosity is everywhere frustrated in its free functioning by the characters' insistence on sexual pairing, and everywhere expressed and celebrated through the "promiscuity" of the camera style and the direction of actors.

Ultimately, *The Rules of the Game* is circumscribed within the ideological assumptions about pairing (Renoir never overtly questions this on a sexual level), yet it is precisely such assumptions that provoke every disaster in the film. It hovers continuously on the verge of a new acceptance. Hence the final ambiguity of effect. The film is at once an elegy to a lost society and one of the most progressive ever made. The world it creates is of the past, yet it everywhere points toward a possible future.

If I were to rewrite my early books now, the one on Bergman (published in 1969) would certainly cause me the greatest problems, and be the one in need of the most drastic revision. When I wrote it, my sense of identification with its subject was extraordinarily intense. Beneath the apparently happy surface of a firmly traditional marriage-and-family situation, I was experiencing the sort of anguish and desperation that Bergman's films so compellingly communicate, and accepting it as unchangeable, as "the human condition." Now, it is precisely this tendency of the films to impose themselves as "the human condition" that most worries me. In a supremely revealing moment of the interview-book *Bergman on Bergman,* the filmmaker asserts his innocence of any ideology, a substance by which his films are apparently completely uncontaminated. He seems to be using the term in a sense somewhat different from that in which it is usually employed in current film criticism; he means by it a *conscious* structure of social-political ideas. Yet the innocence clearly extends beyond that. There is no awareness that an ideology might exist in one's work, and centrally structure and determine it, without one's being conscious of it. The lack of an explicit social-political dimension to Bergman's work has often been noted; ten years ago I quite failed to see the force of such an objection, my own work as a critic having precisely the same lack.

Another, related way of considering the limitations of Bergman's work is via Andrew Sarris's objection that the films are repeatedly flawed by eruptions of "undigested clinical material." The obstinate recurrence of certain narrative and relationship structures in Bergman's work (structures which, I have argued elsewhere, are basically psychological, the characters representing projections of the artist's inner tensions) is plainly neurotic, and testifies to that central principle of neurosis: resistance wherein the neurosis defends itself against cure. What the films repeatedly assert, with impressive intensity and conviction, is that life under the conditions in which it is lived is intolerable, therefore . . . At which point a shutter comes down. The "therefore" should continue: "therefore we must strive to change the conditions." The shutter asserts, "the conditions are something called 'the human predicament'; they can't be changed."

In Bergman's films, neurotic resistance goes hand in hand with the resistance to any concept of ideology. Since I wrote my book he has made what I consider two of his finest films, *The Passion of Anna* and *The Touch*—though neither seems to be in general very highly regarded, and my admiration for them is not without reservations. Both films contain important elements, both in style and narrative structure, that suggest a desire on Bergman's part to open out his work, to pass beyond the stalemate in which it constantly threatens to get trapped. An extended analysis of these films would take the form of examining the conflict between these innovative elements and the resistance to them. More briefly, one can assert that nowhere more than in *Passion* has the intolerability of possessive relationships—the lies, subterfuges, resentments, frustrations, jealousies, eruptions of "psychic and physical violence," the ultimate mutual destructiveness—been more ruthlessly or vividly analyzed. Yet the films continue, doggedly, to assert all this as a fact of life, as the human condition, rather than as ideologically determined. Even *Passion,* with its relatively open structure and its excitingly spontaneous, exploratory style, can never seriously envisage the possibility that things might be changed.

In any assessment of Bergman's work I would not wish to give much prominence to *Face to Face,* which seems to me one of his very worst films, actively offensive in its self-indulgence. If I focus on it here, it is because it is his first work to deal openly with gayness, and because its treatment of gays provides so precise an index of the limitations of Bergman's work.

Near the beginning of a film devoted to portraying the inner anguish of an individual, defined in terms of personal psychology, the notion of "world revolution" is reduced in passing to a game for 14-year-olds; no possible connection is suggested between the two. Of the three gay characters, two are presented as stereotypical. (The treatment of the actor, Michael Stromberg, is more detailed and sympathetic in the published script, which one might read as a sign that Bergman was actually repressing his own sense of other possibilities in the finished film; the sympatheticness, however, takes the form of suggesting that the character shares in the general anguish.) The third, the character portrayed by Erland Josephsson, is presented favorably by Bergman, the penalty for which is that his gayness is essentially monogamous—a minimal adaptation of the dominant sexual ideology—and that he suffers. Any possible alternative to the dominant ideological assumptions about relationships is firmly put down. We are left with the familiar Bergman pattern: the heroine, tormented in adulthood by her experiences as a child, moves toward forgiveness and reconciliation across the generations. In Bergman's world, as nothing can be changed, all that people can hope for is to learn to forgive each other for the pain they inflict.

I suspect that, were I to re-read my early books, the one on Hawks (1968) would embarrass me least. By and large, I continue to admire the same Hawks films I admired when I wrote it, for some of the same reasons, and my delight in them is undiminished. My way of seeing them, however, has changed and widened somewhat.

First, I want to consider the ambiguous relation of Hawks's work to the dominant ideology. In some ways the films are very firmly and obviously within the ideology: sexist (they celebrate masculinity and, however aggressive the women may be, male dominance is always reasserted at the end) and racist (white Americanness is a taken-for-granted token of superiority, and foreigners are either comic or subservient, and frequently both). These are more Hollywood than Hawks, though of course one can't clearly separate the two; they could be paralleled in the work of most mainstream American directors. Though they have to be noted, it seems legitimate to place the emphasis on the Hawksian particularities, the features that distinguish him.

The films might be said to belong loosely to an alternative American tradition (represented at its best by *Huckleberry Finn* and at its worst by Hemingway) which says no to established society, to the development of civilization conceived as the supreme good. What is striking is the almost total absence in the films of home, marriage, and family—and not only concretely but as concepts. The opposition between the adventure films and the comedies has been perceived in various ways, but both have in common the rejection of established order. The adventure films create an alternative order, cut off from mainstream civilization, centered on the male group; the comedies subvert order, throwing everything into chaos. The two sets of films are by and large very different in tone and rhythm. The adventure films are leisurely, measured, with an overall serenity that grows steadily up to *Rio Bravo* and *Hatari!* and then decreases abruptly in the films of Hawks's old age; the comedies are fast, frenetic, tense, with hysteria constantly threatened and sometimes taking over. In both sets the concept of chaos is important, but it is quite differently defined. In the adventure films it is *out there* (the Andes mountains, the Arctic wastes, etc.) and menacing; in the comedies it is *inside,* a positive force awaiting its chance to disrupt the established order, appalling yet also exhilarating and liberating.

The role of women in Hawks's films is always problematic. In many respects they remain male fantasy-figures; no one would wish to claim them for the Feminist cause, despite their aliveness and independence. With very few exceptions (*Red Line 7000,* for example), the women are always hostile to each other, unable to unite, conceived as instant, automatic rivals for the male, as in *Only Angels Have Wings* and *To Have and Have Not.* Their great interest—apart from the intensely vivid and dynamic, if male-orientated, performances Hawks usually gets from his actresses—lies in the total absence, in the adventure films at least, of any logical role for them. The point becomes very clear if one juxtaposes them with John Ford's women, who have a very well-defined, thoroughly traditional role: they are wives and mothers, mainstay of the home, at once the motivation behind the building of civilization and the guarantee of its continuance and transmission. In Hawks there is no positively conceived civilization, no home, no marriage. Woman becomes problematic by her very presence—which in Hawks is always a very insistent presence, far removed from the little lady left waving tearfully goodbye at the start to await the hero's return at the end. Hawks's solution (always uneasy, never satisfying, but central to the vitality of the films) is to break down as far as possible the division between male and female; always, in the adventure films, by making the woman aggressive and "masculine."

Many critics have noted a gay subtext running through Hawks's work, constantly suppressed, yet always insisting on some form of ambiguous, half-grudging expression. It goes right back to the silent period. *Fig Leaves* contains a remarkable scene in which a man "acts" a woman in a mock courtship with his friend; *A Girl in Every Port* (which actually ends with the woman ousted and the male relationship reaffirmed at her expense) was the first of two films Hawks has described as "a love story between men." He has of course never acknowledged gayness in his films and would repudiate any suggestion of it; nonetheless, one might see the term "love story" as a giveaway.

There are obvious examples of male relations so close as to become at least sexually ambiguous: Thomas Mitchell's feeling for Cary Grant in *Only Angels Have Wings,* or Kirk Douglas and Dewey Martin in the other "love story between men," *The Big Sky.* There is also, from the Forties on, a whole procession of young male actors, usually playing second fiddle or sidekick to the hero (but the relationship always characterized by an underlying tension or conflict—that conflict in which, according to *Bringing Up Baby's* psychiatrist, the love impulse expresses itself), who are fairly obvious gay icons in appearance and behavior, if not always in offscreen actuality: Montgomery Clift, Dewey Martin, Ricky Nelson, the young James Caan.

In view of this continually present, half-suppressed, sexual ambiguity in both male and female roles, the notion of chaos in Hawks—and the films' ambivalent attitudes to it—takes on a new interest. It is closely connected to one of the most striking, consistent, and peculiar features of his work: the fascination with role-reversal. This takes a great variety of forms. In *Gentlemen Prefer Blondes* and *The Ransom of Red Chief* (Hawks's episode in *O. Henry's Full House),* the reversal is between child and adult; in *Monkey Business* and *Hatari!* the sophisticated and the primitive change places, become reversible, the distinction blurred. Most striking here is Elsa Martinelli's initiation into the Warusha tribe, and the subsequent scene where her tribal paint is replaced with cold cream. *Hatari!* also reverses humans and animals; it opens with truck and jeep converging on a rhinoceros, and ends (almost) with baby elephants converging on a woman. Most bizarrely and puzzlingly, one has in *The Thing* the reversal of human and vegetable.

But most pervasive—and surely the crucial and explanatory instance—is the reversal, in film after film, of male and female. Existing within sexist ideology, the films never manage to assert equality: it is funny for men to dress as women, but generally attractive for women to dress as men (and they are in uniform, not drag). Yet the notion of potential reversibility is very strong. One small, intriguing point: the interchangeability of Angie Dickinson in *Rio Bravo* and James Caan in *El Dorado.* Both are conceived in terms of their relationship to John Wayne, a relationship based on both affection and antagonism; both are gamblers; both are seen doing the same bit of business with a pack of cards; both are identified partly by their idiosyncratic adornments (Dickinson by her feathers, Caan by a picturesque hat); both follow or stand by Wayne after they have been dismissed—in the long tradition of Hawks's heroines. And both have the same line of dialogue, addressed in both cases to Wayne: "I always make you mad, don't I?"

The logical end of the characterizing tendencies of Hawks's work is bisexuality: the ultimate overthrow of social order, and the essential meaning of the chaos the films both fear and celebrate. Ultimately it is always contained (Andrew Britton would say "repressed") within Hawks's classicism, which is also the classicism of pre-Sixties Hollywood. Yet it seems to me nevertheless the secret source of the oeuvre's richness, vitality, and fascination.

A BRECHTIAN CINEMA?
TOWARDS A POLITICS OF
SELF-REFLEXIVE FILM

DANA POLAN

A historian of recent film theory would be obliged to note the tendentious tone that accompanied the introduction of the structuralist, semiotic, and psychoanalytic approaches. These approaches, highly developed, with a dense vocabulary and broad range of critical concepts, have done much to fertilize film study and have certainly contributed to the flowering of Marxist, gay, and feminist studies. At the same time, they have met with strong resistance. This resistance, which sometimes takes the form of attack, has often been much stronger than the attacks on traditional, openly political approaches, which can be dismissed as vulgar or insufficiently rigorous. But they can also be less threatening, since they have never conveyed quite the same combination of mystery and disruptive presence as the new approaches seem to. (Rebels at the gate or critics in the court are easier to understand than those who belong to vaguely defined cults whose members do not speak the same language but appear to believe that their own is the best.) When methodologies are championed in writings that are as difficult and obscure as they are intelligent; when their adherents refuse to adopt the prevailing, humanist assumptions; when schools, masters, and disciples seem to speak with a single voice about a common body of writings and authorities and to exclude all other views, the sense of threat is bound to be heightened.

Dana Polan's article provides an extremely valuable perspective on these problems. His target is the tendency to overstate, or the inclination to construct an imaginary enemy, the better to destroy it. That is one important aspect of what he calls "terrorist semiotics," in which those few who own the means of semiotic interrogation appropriate knowledge as their intellectual capital. One important example involves the claim that we can identify "effects" —ideological effects, knowledge effects, reality effects, and so on—although there is no supporting evidence for such effects on actual viewers. The effects in question may indeed be difficult to measure, since they are often unconscious and since they seem to constitute the very subjectivity that formulates responses. Such subjectivity is unaware of its own constituted nature. We think that our thoughts and feelings are our own: cogito, ergo sum.

However, the most important example that Polan provides deals with self-reflexive and self-critical films. He takes issue with the ideas that coercion or bribery forces us into relationship with a text and that only reflexivity can rupture such a relationship. He reviews the writings of Bertolt Brecht to argue that recent theory has stripped away Brecht's political side and left us with a new, purely formalist Brecht. In short, Polan sees that reflexivity's claim to be a political, anti-ideological, knowledge-oriented operation is a formal device whose political value depends on the context. As he demonstrates, Daffy Duck cartoons, Mary Hartman Mary Hartman, and the avant-garde are all reflexive. Failing or playfully refusing to conceal the work of the text is far more common than many theorists claim.

Rebuttals are possible. For example, it could be argued that self-reflexiveness is not the same as revealing the work of production. It is not the same as using strategies of subversion to decenter the viewer's subjectivity. It is not the same as revealing the materiality of the medium or the imaginary dimension of the unity and coherence that we think is "naturally" there. Some might wonder whether Polan's efforts at substantive qualification need a sociological or institutional explanation. Don't most methods that become elevated to governing paradigms become charged with emotional tensions, since compliance with the paradigm is a vital ingredient in the reception and perceived value of most research? It is just that these tensions are easier to see in poststructuralist work than in work achieved with older, better-accepted methods that undercut fewer critical assumptions and that have a well-defined place in the universe of competing methods. Sorting out these objections is precisely what Polan calls for. If clarification proves Polan to be wrong in some measure, his article will still have served a worthy purpose by calling into question the criteria that make generalizations about art or communication admissible.

In a 1940's Bugs Bunny cartoon, Elmer Fudd, once again forced by destiny and by narrative to chase Bugs, fires several times at his fleeing nemesis. The bullets fail to have their desired effect. Of course, the lack of deadliness is a typical quality of Warners' cartoons bullets, but this time Bugs stops and comments to the audience: "Folks, those bullets are fake; we're saving the real ones for the boys overseas."

For me, this moment aptly demonstrates the attitudes an artwork can adopt towards the material world and the dynamics of history. First, a distance from worldly reality, a distance inherent in art and which makes it art. This is a distance of codes and of constructions—a distance which, if it allows the work to be a form of knowledge, does so only in a mediated or in a non-scientific fashion.[1] The cartoon is first of all a cartoon and not something else. Second, a distance in which the work turns in on itself and speaks about its own artistic conventions and pre-suppositions. This is an attitude of self-reflexivity, of the text making strange its own formal devices. For example, at the moment in question the cartoon explicitly signals its cartoon-ness. Finally, there is a third attitude which the cartoon brings to the foreground at this moment: a movement out of the self-enclosed world of the artwork toward a real world which the mediations of art usually leave behind. The cartoon reminds us of an activity—killing—which cartoons normally distort. These attitudes—the inherent one which makes art art and not something else, and the forced ones which appear as a conjunction of or a conflict between self-reflexivity and social awareness—form the primary concerns of this essay.

To me, the two most important signs, if we may call them that, in my title are the question mark and the word "towards." For a skepticism motivates this paper, a discontent which manifests itself as a set of tentative forays into an *over*charted region. To raise the question of the politics—intrinsic or otherwise—of self-reflexive film is to re-invoke issues of central importance in the history of film theory, if not art theory in general. How does film relate to a reality? To an audience? What is form? What is content? How are they political? If they are not political, how can they be made so? Here I don't pretend to be able to answer such awesome questions but merely to propose some movements towards their investigation, movements towards a politics of self-reflexive film.

In their recent manifestation, debates on these issues have generally come to revolve around a single object of inquiry: viewing. What does it mean to view a film? What happens ideologically when we view a world on a screen before us? At first glance, the activity of viewing may seem to be simple, both in its workings and in its ability to be understood. Yet the surface simplicity obscures a deeper intricacy. In *Reading Capital,* French philosopher Louis Althusser suggests that the great achievement of the modern age—an achievement which describes that age's break with the past—has been the "discovery and training in the meaning of the 'simplest' acts of existence: seeing, listening, speaking, reading . . ." Freud, he suggests, pinpointed the dimensions of speaking, Marx those of reading. Similarly, recent criticism of the visual arts—such as that criticism of painting by Pierre Francastel and John Berger or of film by recent writers in *Screen*—is attempting, I would suggest, to understand ways of seeing.

Indeed, recent film theory's "critique of illusionism" derives from the same theoretical impulse as the critique of empiricism put forward by Althusser and others. To these theorists, empiricism or illusionism depends upon a conception of the subject-object duality as easily bridged.[2] The world manifests truth and all one has to do is contemplate the world or its identical embodiment in human activity—texts—to gain insights into that meaning.

André Bazin epitomizes the film version of this optimistic theory of the possibilities of meaning. With such notions as the close-up as window to the soul, as the destructiveness of conscious artistic intervention, and film as the revelation of the spiritual life *(vie intérieure)* of the world, Bazin becomes the target for many, if not most, newer theories which see film as a production of meaning, as a site of work in the viewer's consciousness.

Narrative, and its ostensible canonization in Hollywood, also becomes a target. In *S/Z,* Roland Barthes clearly sees the hermeneutic and the proairetic codes (the codes of suspense and of the logic of actions, respectively) as the most determined and determining codes of fiction. Similarly, Noël Burch in an interview in *Women and Film* (No. 5–6) declares linearity—i.e., narrative—to be an inherent code of what he calls the "dominant cinema." Against narrative and against transparency, critics and artists suggest a whole range of deconstructive devices. Many of these strategies are based on a notion of work. Empiricism, it is claimed, invites passivity; all one has to do is contemplate and texts will deliver up their meaning. Subjects—be they viewing subjects, reading subjects, or historical subjects—will unite automatically with objects and with the knowledge of objects. To counter the encouragement of passivity many recent critics push for a difficult art, an art that forces its audience into an active interpretive response. The problem of passivity further provides the impetus for a rediscovery of Brecht who, for recent critics, has become the master of deconstruction, the champion of formal subversion. Burch, for example in *Theory of Film Practice,* adopts Brecht's theory but only after declaring it necessary to eliminate Brecht's concern for content. A new Brecht—Brecht the formalist—arises.

But there is also, and foremost, Brecht the realist. And it is this Brecht who will provide my perspective here. I believe that radical aesthetics—including film aesthetics—is falling prey to the rise of a new ahistorical formalism. This formalism is present first in attacks on particular types of cinema practice and cinema structure—the practices, as I have mentioned, of narrative and of representation.

But more recently, with the French and British rediscovery of Freud through Jacques Lacan, the attack on representation has become even more pronounced. Whereas formerly a certain type of film practice which was alone in effecting a particular audience response (namely, passivity) was singled out for attack, now the very practice of representation undergoes criticism as being ideologically reactionary. In this view, the very structure of film viewing—audiences sitting before a screen and watching from a particular viewpoint (or perspective)—contributes to the constitution of the subject as a viewing subject—that is, a subject safely elevated by self-confidence to a privileged, unchallenged position vis-à-vis the screen world. Thus in an article on television in a recent issue of *Screen* (Summer 1977), Gillian Skirrow and Stephen Heath go so far as to declare that "there is a generality of ideology before the 'institution' of any particular ideological position." Certainly, the recent critics often differ as to the sorts of films which contribute most to this non-challenge to the supposed passivity of viewing. But at its limit, this psychological model suggests that the very (f)act of seeing a film, regardless of the film story, turns spectators into non-acting subjects. In his essay on "Diderot, Brecht, Eisenstein," (*Screen,* Summer 1974), Roland Barthes banishes content from art and declares that "representation is not defined directly by imitation: even if one gets rid of notions of the 'real,' of the *'vraisemblable,'* of the copy, there will still be representation for so long as a subject casts his gaze towards a horizon on which he cuts out an apex." Barthes is thereby able to declare that Brecht and Eisenstein are pre-political artists since they don't break out of a presentational model. Jean-Pierre Oudart's examination of the influence of classical perspective on film and Jean-Louis Baudry's description of the ideological effects of the basic cinematographic apparatus also move in the same direction. This rejection of representation suggests not only a subversion from within but also from without. Critics and artists push for new artistic experiences which will call the traditional boundaries of the arts into question. But the overriding question remains: is this sort of aesthetic undermining the political?

In part, an answer depends on what we mean by political. To give a definition obviously open to disagreement, I would suggest that the political concerns itself with analyzing the contradictions of a particular historical situation. Obviously, the recent formalistic critics might contend that the formal innovations of works which challenge viewing experiences serve as such an investigation of historical contradictions. For example, in the 1972 postscript to *Signs and Meaning in the Cinema,* Peter Wollen declares that a new art would cause the spectator to "produce fissures and gaps in the space of his own consciousness (*fissures and gaps which exist in reality but which are repressed by an ideology, characteristic of bourgeois society,* which insists on the 'wholeness' and integrity of each individual consciousness)" (p. 162, my emphasis). Wollen partially covers his own tracks by declaring that such a repression is *characteristic* of and not intrinsic to bourgeois society, but that disclaimer is itself uncharacteristic of the radical formalist approach where a rigid either/or divides the progressive from the reactionary. The new aesthetic bases itself on a belief that texts repress, that they lead to a domination of their subjects by placing those subjects in a particular position, physically, formally, perhaps ideologically. A text, in this sense, is an ensemble of codes which rationalize a particular way of relating to the world and they make this rationalization attractive by not interfering with the fetishistic or voyeuristic perspective of the viewing subject. In his essay, "The Politics of Separation" (*Screen,* Winter 1975–1976), Colin MacCabe goes so far as to call this seduction "the bribe of identity," thereby situating textual persuasion in the realm of crime.

It seems to me though that his sort of position leaves a lot of points unanswered or at least ambiguous. Before we can examine the validity of certain subversive strategies as answers, we need to make sure that the problem has been correctly understood. We need to examine the notion of textual domination.

Such a notion, especially as a critique of representation, rests upon a great number of assumptions. I would like to concentrate on two of these: that texts confirm the world and blind us to contradictions, and that submission to a text means submission to its ideology. The belief in a bribe of identity sees the texts as a complicity of codes, a rhetoric which hides its own rhetorical nature. Thus critics like MacCabe see the text as a force of domination over spectators. However, we need to rigorously investigate such an argument. What does domination, in terms of a work of art, mean?

All texts dominate. Without a degree of code sharing between art makers and art receivers, the artwork becomes a noise. To alter MacCabe's economic metaphor (which he obviously does not mean as a metaphor), texts aren't bribes; they are contracts in which spectators or readers willingly agree to relate to codes in a certain way and, I would contend, with knowledge usually of the workings of many of these codes. The signs of the contract appear throughout the texts; they may become familiar to us but precisely because they are signs, we have to learn them to be able to read or to view. And yet submission to a contractual promise is only one side of the working of a text. Information theory emphasizes not only that information ceases without a common code but also that it ceases if a transgression of codes does not appear, a transgression actually inherent in the system and which expands it. Art, all art, bases itself not just on confirmation but also on contradiction. Literary critic Frank Kermode has alternatively described this interplay as one between credulity and skepticism (in *The Sense of an Ending*) or between recognition and deception ("Novels: Recognition and Deception," *Critical Inquiry*, no. 1). To a large extent, what we refer to as self-reflexivity represents one more strategy in the interplay of a technique intrinsic to *and actually defining the process of art*. One sort of pleasure comes from precisely this interplay of credulity and skepticism (which may explain why detective fiction—which in many ways ideally embodies many of the workings of the code of suspense—is so popular). Self-reflexive art appeals in part because it heightens this intrinsic interplay.

If we survey the development of the literary and dramatic arts, we continually come across examples of art which signal awareness of their own artifice. Literary critics often point to Laurence Sterne's 18th-century novel *Tristram Shandy* as a special highpoint of conscious artistic artifice; in a revealing comment, Russian Formalist critic Viktor Shklovsky called it "the most typical novel in world literature." Yet in the same literary period, Henry Fielding's *Tom Jones* goes as far as Sterne's book in uncovering the codes which a reading of literature depends upon. Fielding, for example, explicitly invokes the model of a contract by comparing the novel to a meal where there is a certain interplay between the fixed order of courses and the changing identities of the foods within that order. But the difference between *Tristram Shandy* and *Tom Jones* is one of degree, not a break. Similarly, both texts are no more than a *logical* culmination of a tendency and a characteristic of art. But the recent formal aesthetic has little awareness of degrees. Roland Barthes, for example, has declared that modernism was not really a possibility for art until 1850; he thereby ignores the fact that every artistic period is an interplay between tradition and artistic revolution. We need to examine different types and degrees of artifice and relate them both to the history of their production and of their reception.

Standard humanist literary and art criticism has long been able to accommodate transgressions of the rules. The usual schema is to see such transgressions as necessary to a progress that otherwise would stultify. Critics have long been able to situate modernism in a non-revolutionary aesthetic. One could cite many examples of this accommodation. Recently two books of literary criticism (Robert Alter's *Partial Magic* and Albert Guerard's *The Triumph of the Novel*) have celebrated what both authors call "the Great Other Tradition," thereby expanding the establishment, the canon, the Great Books of the Western World, beyond the limits proscribed by F. R. Leavis.[3] Both critics (and there are many others) turn aesthetic disturbances into positive, humanist values. To be more precise, they recognize literary, formal innovation for what it is: a non-threatening, typical component of art. Guerard, for example, refers to the novel's powers of "illuminating and imaginative distortion": literature can introduce an imbalance for the precise purpose of establishing a higher balance. Today's revolution is tomorrow's handservant of the established order. In its literal sense, the term avant-garde suggests nothing more than an advance force, a forward branch of the establishment.

The Russian Formalist Viktor Shklovsky argued for art as *ostranenie*: a making strange of the world. And indeed if art confirms, it also makes strange the normal order of things. Suspension of belief accompanies suspension of disbelief. But recent criticism often obscures this condition. Hollywood has been declared a paradigm of a fundamental lack of irony, of a celebration of art as transparency. The heritage of recent film critics from literary critical models with their high art/ popular art distinction is obvious. Recent radical literary criticism has committed historical and theoretical errors by adhering to a conception of the novel based on 19th century forms. In fact, the 19th-century novel is only one type of literature—and one that is itself not without its ironies and formal subversions. Similarly, there is no one type of Hollywood film; indeed, very few actual Hollywood productions would fit the abstract category of transparency which recent criticism has instituted as the Hollywood paradigm.

With the new formalistic critics a particular conception of Hollywood cinema is made to monolithically serve as the type of all classical films. A few exceptions crop up: the nonconformist auteurs like Nick Ray or Sam Fuller or Douglas Sirk. But Hollywood itself is defined as conformist, as the ultimate briber, the ultimate concealer of codes.

All art is distanced. This is as true of Hollywood as of Laurence Sterne or Aristophanes. We learn to read through this distance from material reality, but we also learn to want new distances. Hollywood not only presents unreality as reality; it also openly acknowledges its unreality. In his book *America in the Movies,* Michael Wood even suggests that unreality can become formulaic. Campiness is not only a subgenre of films but a tendency of most if not all Hollywood films, and Wood suggests that this distance represents one cause of Hollywood's appeal. As he exclaims, Hollywood is "the only place in the world where anyone says, 'Santa Maria, it had slipped my mind.'"

For example, the Hollywood cartoon—a staple of Hollywood production— embodies many of the formal techniques claimed to be deconstructive. And yet, if any *political* concern can be attributed to these cartoons, that is so only in the etymological sense of political: that which deals with the *polis,* with the universal relations of people to each other and to the world. To modify my initial comments, films demonstrate not three attitudes *but two.* Films differ significantly not so much in their degrees of formal complexity as in their political attitude, their sense of the changing and changeable nature of the world. I would suggest that what I initially described as a separate category of attitude—namely, conscious and deliberate self-reflexivity—may be nothing other than an expansion and making manifest of inherent qualities of art.

This difference of attitude—between textual artifice (forced or not) and social attitude—is the difference between art and political art. Let's take a closer look at a Hollywood cartoon for an example. *Duck Amuck* (1953) is a virtual culmination of the experimental possibilities of the Hollywood cartoon.[4] The subject of the cartoon is the nature of animation technique itself. In *Duck Amuck,* Daffy Duck undergoes victimization at the hand of his animator, ultimately revealed to be none other than Bugs Bunny. Bugs tortures Daffy by playing with such film coordinates as framing, background sound, and color. In an article on *Duck Amuck* in *Film Comment,* Richard Thompson rightly notes that the film manifests a high degree of emphasized formal complexity: "The film is extremely conscious of itself as an act of cinema, as is much of Jones' work. . . . *Duck Amuck* is a good example of Noël Burch's dialectic idea of film elements: foreground and background, space and action, character and environment, image and soundtrack are all in conflict with one another." Yet Burch's dialectic idea, as he himself notes, is far from political and so is *Duck Amuck.* If *Duck Amuck* is a metaphor for the confusions of life (as Thompson suggests), it is a disengaged metaphor at best for it fails to examine confusion through a politicized perspective. Indeed, the source of Daffy Duck's *angst* reveals itself to be none of the agents of social domination in the real world, but merely Bugs Bunny—another fictive character, whose power is tautological in origin. The film opens up a formal space and not a political one in viewer consciousness. *Duck Amuck* closes in on itself, fiction leads to and springs from fiction, the text becomes a loop which effaces social analysis. This is the project of all non-political art, realist or self-reflexive.

We may approach this issue from another direction if we examine those theories that deal with classical or traditional art's supposed function vis-à-vis the daily workings of the material world. The recent critics contend, as the earlier quote from Peter Wollen suggests, that bourgeois art works to instill a complacency in the viewer, a complacency both about the art object itself *and* about the world outside of art. *But there is nothing necessarily consoling or optimistic about conventional art. Similarly, life under capitalism is not necessarily one of complacency and isolation from an awareness of contradiction.* It depends on what kind of contradiction we're talking about. That our day-to-day expectations can be thwarted is a normal and accepted possibility of everyday life. The conventional work of art does not banish contradiction; rather, it works by divorcing contradiction from its social causes. Existence under capitalism is often little more than a continual succession of disappointments, of subversions, all of which fissure our self-unity and social unity as acting subjects. Art doesn't deny this malaise; it merely hides and denies its bases in historical forces. This is why contemporary culture can accommodate formally subversive art; as long as such an art does not connect its formal subversion to an analysis of social situations, such art becomes little more than a further example of the disturbances that go on as we live through a day. And a work of art which defeats formal expectations does not lead to protest against a culture that deals continually in the defeating of expectations. This, I would suggest, explains much of the appeal of *Mary Hartman, Mary Hartman.* It may also help to explain the morbid underside of fan fascination with Hollywood—an underside of scandal magazines and, ultimately, of the elevation of such trashy books as Kenneth Anger's *Hollywood Babylon* into coffee table respectability. We are used to having our realities deconstructed and so too it does not bother us to see the reality of the movie screen world deconstructed. In an article on *Mary Hartman, Mary Hartman* in *Socialist Revolution* (no. 30), Barbara Ehrenreich suggests that the TV series represents the triumph of contradiction: a show which attacks the consumer world is sponsored to sell the very sort of products its content disdains. And it succeeds. Ehrenreich presents this plenitude of contradictions as a stumbling block to socialist theories of popular culture. If it were merely a question of art inspiring blind optimism, criticism would be easy. Shows like *Mary Hartman, Mary Hartman* have made pessimism, discontent, and irony marketable. Such success suggests that we need to deal with this realm of contradiction which obscures political contradiction.

And here we return to Brecht. Brecht also sees a distance between art and political art. Art automatically embodies a distancing, a making strange. But there's nothing yet political about that. To be political, art for Brecht has to be made so. In his essay, "The Modern Theatre Is the Epic Theatre," Brecht uses the example of opera to present his conception of art as possessing intrinsic qualities of distance from reality to which the artist can add a sense of political engagement. As is well known, Brecht's theory of art reception emphasizes conscious knowledge over intuition. So does his theory of art creation. Like his teacher, Erwin Piscator, Brecht sees art as filling a *programmed* function. This implies conscious attention to form and to content.

This emphasis on conscious intention probably most separates Brecht from the Hungarian Marxist critic Georg Lukács. Lukács's approach to literary creation seems to fall quite often into an intuitionist theory of creation: "Lasting typologies based on a perspective of this sort [i.e., based on the "selection of the essential and the subtraction of the inessential"] owe their effectiveness not to the artist's understanding of day-to-day events but to his *unconscious* possession of a perspective independent of and reaching beyond his understanding of the contemporary scene" (*Realism in Our Time,* my emphasis). This belief on Lukács's part in unconscious awareness leads Brecht to call him a formalist, for it is precisely a belief like Lukács's that the 19th-century masters had the answers *and* that these answers are still relevant to the 20th century which signals a refusal to situate literary production within the actual workings of history.

In fact, Brecht's aesthetic suggests that we need to expand and clarify the notion of realism. Significantly, Brecht referred to his own artistic project as a realism. Realism is no more (and no less) than a type of attitude to the world and to art. Realism is not a natural quality; it is a social quality. Brecht's theory most significantly distinguishes between realism—which he saw as the overriding impulse of his art—and unrealism, the setting up of false or limited or reified attitudes toward the world and worldly possibilities. In "Against Gyorg Lukács," he defines realism as "discovering the causal complexes of society/unmasking the prevailing view of things as the view of those who rule it." Realism, thus, is a form of knowledge, a picturing of reality. To judge the efficacy of a particular realism, "one must compare the depiction of life in a work with the life that is being depicted." Like the Lacanian theories of the subject which recent critics draw upon, Brecht's theory depends on a notion of positioning, of the subject's place in the circuit of communication. But Brecht diverges from these critics in an essential way. For Brecht the attitudinal position of the viewing subject springs

from an attitudinal position in the work—the political artwork embodies a difference between the way things are and the way they can be. Brecht's formal experimentation depends on content in two ways. First, form must change to reflect
changing realities; otherwise, the formalism of a Lukács may result. Second,
Brecht's political theatre is a theatre of possibility—a theatre showing that life
doesn't only have to take on the forms it generally does. Political art compares an
image of human beings as "unalterable" to one of them as "alterable and able to
alter" (quoted from "The Modern Theatre Is the Epic Theatre"). As such, the
new theatre shows that formal arrangements of life can change. We can do things
we never thought possible. But the partial grounding in Brecht of groups like the
Living Theatre—groups which disconnect the potentials of activism from its
social(ist) responsibility—suggests that qualifications need to be placed on the
sorts of possibilities that a Brechtian political art would encourage. Not all possibilities are equally valid; Brecht chooses validity on the basis of socialist perspective. Hence, content once again makes its entrance. It is what the work says about
the real world that matters. The artist must pay close attention to the world of
possibility his/her work promises.

For Brecht, political art plays off a political re-definition of credulity and skepticism. To avoid the new world of possibility appearing as nothing but noise, the
artwork must also make use of the old world as a standard. Meaning, and its
realization in action, comes from the differences between the two world views.
Political art defamiliarizes the world. But it does so by playing off our connections to that world.

This reading of Brecht has two important implications for our discussion. First
of all, if the political text invites production from the spectator, this production is
a source of pleasure. Obviously, Brecht sees the theatre as a site of learning, but
that learning—that accession to knowledge—brings and is immersed in pleasure. The spectator finds joy in comparing a world view which he or she now
realizes is a strangling one to a world view of possibilities. Pleasure comes from
knowing the world can be remade. Pleasure, as Brecht says in Note 2 of "A Short
Organum for the Theatre" is "the noblest function that we have found for the
'theatre.'" Or as he says later in the Organum, the audience "must be entertained
with the wisdom that comes from the solution of problems, with the anger that is
a practical expression of sympathy with the underdog, with the respect due to
those who respect humanity . . . *in short, with whatever delights those who are
producing something*" (my emphasis).

Second, insofar as Brecht's political art includes the presence of the familiar
world *and* yet presents a more attractive world, Brechtian art is an art of identification. In examining Brecht's theories, critics have too often declared that the
theories allow no place for identification. In fact, Brecht's theory of art embodies
two identifications: one empathetic and unquestioning—the one connected to
the reified vision of the world—and a critical one—a new perspective of knowledge from which the old way is scrutinized. In his essay on "Alienation Effects in
Chinese Acting," Brecht is emphatic about the need for identification in political
theatre: "the audience identifies itself with the actor as being an observer, and
accordingly develops his attitude of observing or looking on."

Brecht's argument suggests that we need to pay a more open attention to *degrees* of identification and pleasure. At the very least, we can distinguish three possible forms of pleasure in a work of art. There is the pleasure of familiarity. This is the pleasure of uncritical, reified realism. Then there is pleasure which comes from art's dehumanization or from forced self-reflexivity. This is the pleasure of art as form, as aesthetic emotion, as Kant suggested. This is a pleasure which, as Barthes contends in *The Pleasure of the Text,* derives its force by shying away from history, by trying to be outside ideology (although such an attempt is itself ideological). Then there is the pleasure elaborated by Brecht, the pleasure of an art which finally realizes the dream of the Roman poet Horace in his *Ars Poetica* (which Brecht continually refers to): to please and instruct. To please through instruction. To instruct through pleasure. An art whose content is a combination of the world and a better version of the world.

We also need to examine instances of defamiliarization in popular art. In a valuable article on audience response in *Jump Cut,* no. 4, Chuck Kleinhans distinguishes between self-reflexive and self-critical films, the latter being films which directly examine both their form and their content. If, as I have claimed, all films embody a self-reflexivity, then we need to go on to examine differing uses and degrees of self-criticism. Of course, such self-criticism is not necessarily in itself political. We need to go back to Brecht's notion of conscious political criticism, but we also need to be more receptive to the *possibility* that such a critical mode may be operative in films of the so-called dominant cinema. This whole realm of investigation seems a promising one. But only if we can get beyond the dismissive attitude currently in fashion and move toward a knowledge important not only because it is knowledge but also because it matters.

Notes

I originally presented this paper at a panel on self-reflexive film at the annual conference of the Society for Cinema Studies in March 1977. I have modified it somewhat for publication.

1 Coming from Kant who saw practical reason and imagination as distinct regions of the human mind, 19th-century Romanticism tended to privilege the artwork as a special and superior activity of the creative portion of the intellect. In contrast, a politically aware criticism places an emphasis on seeing artworks as results of practical human activity rather than a transcendent creative talent above and beyond social responsibility. Thus, the use of terms like *code* and *text* to refer to aspects of an artwork has a deliberate and polemical intent behind it. Such usage stresses that artworks are constructions, that they are objects produced by people and for people in particular social situations.

Unlike Romanticism's theory of organicism, which treats the artwork as a unified (organic) whole, the notion of the text concentrates on the individual elements and how they go together. For example, *Cahiers du Cinéma's* famous analysis of *Young Mr. Lincoln* extracts two elements from the text—its attitudes toward sexuality and politics—to examine how the film's ostensible unity actually conceals a set of divergent and even contradictory impulses.

Codes are rules of communication whose application appears from text to text. Effective communication can only occur when senders and receivers share knowledge of the codes. The notion of the code is important in the examination of artistic media since it raises questions about the very extent to which we can consider an artistic text as an act of communication, and about the extent to which convention and rules govern the traditions and transgressions in art production and reception.

2. The subject–object distinction has been one of the central concerns of philosophy throughout its history. The distinction concerns human beings and the possible ways in which they can come to know about and perhaps understand the world around them. Marx, for example, suggests that people can best live in the world not as passive observers but as active participants. Those film critics who attack film illusionism and its notion of film as a window on the world generally direct their attack against two targets. First, they criticize the passivity which illusionist film seems to force spectators into. Second, they attack the impression which illusionist film seems to convey of a world which one can understand simply by viewing it.

3. In this study of English literature, *The Great Tradition,* moralist literary critic F. R. Leavis declared that the privilege of being part of *the* great tradition belonged exclusively to Jane Austen, George Eliot, Henry James, and Joseph Conrad. Thus he excluded writers ranging from Dickens whom he felt was too popular in appeal to James Joyce whose experiments he believed represented a "dead end." Many of the literary scholars who have criticized Leavis have done so simply to argue for the writers he leaves out rather than to question the very notion of a great tradition no matter who its members might be.

4. The screenplay for *Duck Amuck* has appeared in Richard Thompson's article on the film in *Film Comment* 11, no. 1 (January–February 1975): 42–43.

THE POINT-OF-VIEW SHOT

EDWARD BRANIGAN

Branigan's article could be characterized as descriptive or formal criticism, but it could also be profitably considered a contribution to a rhetoric of cinema. As such, it provides us with a rigorous taxonomy of the point-of-view figure, which all too often is spoken of as having a single form. There is little here of what a phenomenologist would call the experiential quality of being moved to share a point of view with characters, and there is little here that addresses desire or ideology—the cornerstones of psychoanalysis and Marxism. Rhetorical criticism is another countercurrent in contemporary film study. Branigan's own footnotes and references indicate his interest in aligning with the concerns of structural analysis, but his article can just as easily be viewed in the context of Brian Henderson's early writings, which Henderson, in Critique of Film Theory *(New York: Dutton, 1980), characterizes as contributions to a rhetoric of cinema.*

In the same book, Henderson himself asks whether semiotics has not rendered the rhetorical project untenable. However, the continuing usefulness of Henderson's early articles, of Noël Burch's Theory of Film Practice, *and of*

Branigan's article and other similar pieces indicates that semiotics has not become the all-encompassing methodology that some believed it would. Although countertendencies often lack the prestige or the fashionableness of the approaches that dominate a given historical period, they exert a broadening and leavening influence that has enormous value for the longer-range development of critical method. New zones of activity will eventually be designated prestigious or fashionable. The mixture of genuine value and temporary allure is inevitable when scholarship shares the consequences of commodity fetishization with other social products. And these new zones of scholarly activity may very well arise where countertendencies have prepared the way. Certainly, psychoanalysis was picked up off the dingy backstreets of literary criticism where it had subsisted for many decades. Decked out in new clothes, it was admitted proudly through the front door of academia, although not without a few loud coughs and aloof stares. Phenomenology, rhetorical criticism, auteur study, critical theory, systems theory, and other approaches are the backstreets of film scholarship today, yet they all provide lively, engaging approaches to cinema. Which will remain relatively obscure and which will gain in appeal remains open to speculation. Meanwhile, Branigan's article vividly demonstrates the values of a descriptive rhetoric. A few categories may be too tightly identified with narrative —point-of-view figures can also appear in documentary, sometimes to quite different effect —but his clarity of exposition and his suggestions of overlap with other approaches mark this contribution as exemplary.

1. THE ELEMENTS OF POV

An analysis of three films made in Hollywood in the 1930s showed that nearly 40 percent[1] of the cuts create what Noël Burch calls proximate spatial articulations; that is, the space revealed by shot A is adjacent to or near that of shot B—perhaps within the same room   but at no point does it overlap or coincide with the space of shot B.[2] A number of techniques have been developed to link these proximate spaces into spatial, and often temporal, continuity.[3] One such technique is the eyeline match; and a subset of the eyeline match is the point-of-view (POV) shot.

The POV shot is a shot in which the camera assumes the position of a subject in order to show us what the subject sees. More precisely, the POV shot is composed of six elements usually distributed in *two* shots as follows:

Shot A: Point/Glance
    1. *Point:*   establishment of a point in space.
    2. *Glance:*   establishment of an object, usually off-camera, by glance
                   from the point.
Between Shots A and B:
    3. *Transition:* temporal continuity or simultaneity.

Shot B: Point/Object
    4. *From Point:*   the camera locates at the point, or very close to the point, in space defined by element one above.
    5.*Object:*   the object of element two above is revealed.
Shots A and B:
    6. *Character:*   the space and time of elements one through five are justified by—referred to—the presence and normal awareness of a subject.

The sixth element is a narrative construction and underlies every shot in a POV structure. The six elements are specific instances, respectively, of the six general units of classical representation: origin, vision, time, frame, object, and mind.

At first glance, the specific elements of the POV shot appear trivial. However, let us examine them closer to see how a change in any *one* operates to subvert or de-stabilize the POV shot as a six-element structure.

Element one ('point') is the establishment of a point in space. Its importance may be illustrated by the cases in which no point is established or more than one point is established. An example of the former would be the case where a glance is established by dialogue ("Hey, look at this!") *but* no point is established because the screen is black or the camera too far away (on the top of a building, say) or the character is off-screen. An example of the establishment of too many points would be a shot of two heads turning in opposite directions (*Four Nights of a Dreamer,* Bresson, 1971) or, as in the opening of *Last Year at Marienbad* (Resnais, 1962), the establishment of five simultaneous glances in different directions. The latter film is particularly disorientating for the viewer because it *also* includes conventional eyeline matches and POV shots. In this way, the viewer is placed in a position of profound uncertainty with respect to the unfolding of space.

Element two ('glance') is the establishment of an off-camera object by glance. Whether or not a glance has occurred may be a matter of degree. Cues which may be present include the following: eye movement, head movement, body movement (e.g., walking to a door to answer a knock prior to a shot of the door swinging open in front of the camera), the beam of a flashlight carried by a character, a new—perhaps sudden—camera angle or camera distance, camera movement (e.g., a dolly-in), zoom, dialogue ("Hey, look at this!"), an intertitle, off-camera sound, music (a common device of horror films), the length of a shot (a character becomes fixated by an object), and perhaps even larger narrative structures (for instance, has everyone who has entered the room confronted the object? do we know that someone is hiding in a particular place, e.g., *Dial M for Murder,* Hitchcock, 1954?).

In *Psycho* (Hitchcock, 1960) we see Sam from the chest down as he says to Marion, lying on a bed, "You never did eat your lunch, did you?" We then see a lunch tray on a table. We cannot ascribe this view to Sam because we were unable to see whether he was looking at Marion or the lunch tray. The shot of the tray is an ambiguous, unclaimed voice in the film.

It is important to note that the concept of 'glance' implies the existence of a sentient observer in whose viewpoint we may participate. This does not mean, however, that the POV shot is limited to humans or even to living things. One low-budget horror film (*Cult of the Cobra*, Lyon, 1955), utilizing elliptical-shaped distortion in the image, offers the POV of a killer snake as it winds toward a sleeping victim. *Jaws* (Spielberg, 1975) opens with an underwater, traveling POV of a shark[4] and *Benji* (Camp, 1974) features repeated POV shots of a dog as well as other subjective structures including flashbacks by the dog. A distorted image is used to represent an alien's POV in *It Came From Outer Space* (Arnold, 1953). In *Vampyr* (Dreyer, 1932) there is an extended sequence from the optical POV of a dead man. Here, the glance is established by emphasizing the wide, staring eyes of the dead man; it is this *vision* which founds the representation and permits the metaphorical exchange of properties between the dead and the living. If the dead man's eyes were closed, the structure would become more complicated because the underlying POV (of a living person) fails—is deviant—when the person's eyes are closed (there is no glance).

Other metaphorical POVs occur in *Blood and Roses* (Vadim, 1960) where we share the viewpoint of an invisible spirit with the aid of a narrator and stirring window curtains. In *2001: A Space Odyssey* (Kubrick, 1968) the vision of a computer is represented by an extreme wide angle lens and in *Westworld* (Crichton, 1973) by a special optical printer effect which divides the film image into tiny squares. In *The Steel Helmet* (Fuller, 1950) we see the POV of a statue of Buddha.[5] Again, the representation of 'eyes' in statuary, portraits, etc. produces a 'look'— betrays a sentience—vital to the POV structure. Indeed would it even be possible to represent the view of, say, a rock? Such a camera angle would probably be reinterpreted in terms of some *other,* less remote sentience—such as an omniscient view, an author's eccentric framing, etc.

The omission of elements one and two ('point/glance') within a larger structure may create a tension of ambiguity. In Yasujiro Ozu's *Floating Weeds* (1959) and *Tokyo Story* (1953) there occur POV shots where a man looks at a flower in *Floating Weeds* and tombstones in *Tokyo Story*. However, later in the respective scenes, the POV structure is undermined, or evolves, when the point/object shot is repeated—the flower, the tombstones—without the point/glance shot—a man in each case. Thus the flower and the tombstones now seem almost to exist independently, in their own right. We then realize that our first view may not, in fact, have been a POV shot; that the men may not have been looking at the objects (only thinking of them, or if looking, not seeing, or whatever); that initially we were snared in the structure of the POV shot and the larger narrative structure (a reference to flowers in the dialogue; the sadness of death) in order to be set free at a later time. The narration at this later time has also evolved: it no longer has a specific origin (the men); rather, it has become larger, more general, more plural.

Element three ('transition') is any device which implies temporal continuity or simultaneity. There is no requirement of temporal continuity *within* shots A (point/glance) and B (point/object); all that is required is that the last fragment of shot A (elements one and two) be temporally joined to the first fragment of shot B (elements four and five); that is, it is elements, not shots, which must be continuous. Without temporal continuity, or at least simultaneity, the resultant structure will be deviant. For example, in a party scene, we cut to a close-up of a person (point/glance) then cut to what that person sees (point/object), but the second shot reveals an earlier time before the party has begun or a later time when the party is over—empty room, dirty glasses, etc. The structure is deviant. This is, in fact, the form of the traditional subjective flashback or flashforward: with additional marks signifying character memory this could be a flashback. As it stands, however, it is a deviant POV where a character seemingly glances into a corner of the room and sees a past or future space. A startling example of such a POV occurs in a Louis XVI style bedroom in the final scene of *2001: A Space Odyssey*.

In element four ('from point') the camera moves to that point, or nearly so, established by element one of the POV structure. This implies the spatial continuity of shots A and B. When the camera does not move to the point previously established, a deviant structure is generated, such as the cut to a new scene. In *Early Summer* (Ozu, 1951) we track down a hallway in front of two women who are creeping forward to catch a glimpse of the man one of them was supposed to marry in an arranged marriage. The tracking movement continues as we cut to the apparent viewpoint of the women. We soon realize, however, that we are in a different hallway, that the hallway is empty, that we are approaching an empty room. Here, Ozu utilizes an important secondary cue of spatial position—the so-called subjective traveling shot; that is, if a person is moving while looking at an object, then the point/object shot must also move. Ozu, however, uses the moving camera in this instance not in an effort to create 'smooth' film style, but a style that actually stresses the structures on which it is based.[6]

The subjective tracking shot is a common device and may be found in such diverse films as *Shoeshine* (DeSica, 1946), *Cleo from 5 to 7* (Varda, 1962), *Napoléon* (Gance, 1927), *Pinocchio* (the camera hops along as Jiminy Cricket, Disney, 1940), *Hair* (Foreman, 1979), and a great number of times in *Cat and Mouse* (Lelouch, 1975). Notice that it incorporates additional parameters—such as the angle and speed of the camera movement—which are part of the POV structure and thus may reinforce or undermine the structure as a whole. What, for instance, do we say of a subjective tracking shot which is moving 'too fast' for the character to keep up or where the character suddenly spurts out in front of the camera?[7]

More frequently, the secondary cues exist to reinforce spatial orientation. The cues may involve elements of the *mise-en-scène*. In *The General* (Keaton, 1926), for instance, we see Buster Keaton under a table lean toward a hole in the tablecloth, and then we see a long shot of the room framed by a ragged oval—which, of course, is the hole in the tablecloth and confirms that we are indeed located at a point previously seen. In *Vampyr* we watch as a coffin lid is lowered over the camera and various faces peer into the coffin through a small window. Other secondary cues relate to sound (the breathing of a character, say) or to the camera. Angle, for example, is often directly tied to the posture of a subject; a low angle for someone seated, a high angle for someone standing, and a very high angle for

King Kong (*King Kong,* Guillermin, 1976) and a killer grizzly (*Grizzly,* Girdler, 1976). Low camera height may be tied to the POV of a child. Often the lateral tilt of a camera, whether the image is completely inverted or tilted to a lesser degree, is strongly marked as subjective. In *Bambi* (Walt Disney, 1942) Bambi twists his head to look at some opossums hanging from their tails upside down on a branch. The next animated drawing is rotated 180 degrees so that we see the animals from Bambi's inverted viewpoint, hanging 'straight up' and so apparently defying gravity. Upside down views are also the result of unusual character position in *Pinocchio* (Walt Disney, 1940), Buster Keaton's *Seven Chances* (1925), Harold Lloyd's *A Sailor-Made Man* (Newmeyer, 1921), *Charley Varrick* (Siegel, 1973—upside down airplane) and *The Tin Drum* (Schlondorff, 1979—baby's POV from the birth canal) as well as from looking through a periscope in *The Three Muske-teers* (Lester, 1973) and a camera in *The Record of a Tenement Gentleman* (Ozu, 1947)[8]—though in the latter case it is not clear if anyone is looking through the camera! We also see a tumbling image as an airplane plunges out of control (*King Kong,* Cooper and Schoedsack, 1933), a car crashes (*On Dangerous Ground,* Ray, 1951), a character falls (*Days of Youth,* Ozu, 1929), leaps from a building (*The Bird with the Crystal Plumage,* Argento, 1970)[9] or hides in a spinning barrel (*Dark Passage,* Daves, 1947).

Dr. Jekyll and Mr. Hyde (Mamoulian, 1932), the comedy short *So You Want to Be a Detective* (Bare, 1948), and especially *Lady in the Lake* (Montgomery, 1946) are virtual catalogues of contextual cues. Almost the entire Montgomery film is shot from the private eye of a detective. At various times we see the detective's arms, feet, his shadow, his image in mirrors, the smoke from his cigarette, as well as extreme close-ups of a telephone receiver, lips approaching for a kiss, and a slap in the face which shakes the camera. Characters also speak directly into the camera. It has even been suggested that there should have been an intermittent blacking out of the screen to indicate occasional blinking of the hero's eyes.[10] The possible secondary cues seem endless.

The fifth element ('object') reveals the object suggested by element two of the POV structure. There is the possibility that the object, or part of the object, is actually seen in shot A. In that case element five functions to reveal the object either from a new angle or new distance or both. In *Psycho* we see Marion as well as a police car through the back window of her car; next we see the police car from Marion's point of view in the car mirror. These shots alternate through thirteen shots. A more common situation is an object picked up by a character followed by a closer view of what is seen.

Consider, however, the possibility for disruption of the POV structure should the camera, instead of revealing the object, turn in another direction (from the original point or from a new point). We would then see an object which we believe a character to be looking at, but which, in fact, he is not. In *An Autumn Afternoon* (Ozu, 1962) Hirayama enters his friend Kawai's home and calls out, "Hello. Hello." We see him at the end of a hallway looking toward camera. There is now a cut to an empty hallway and we hear a woman off-camera call, "Come in!" Since we cannot see either Hirayama or the woman, the exact location of the hallway remains a mystery. The absence of Hirayama suggests it might be a POV shot taken from the opposite end of the hallway we saw in the preceding shot. We expect the woman to appear in this hallway to greet Hirayama, but from what direction, and will she come toward the camera? She enters at left middle ground but goes to the far end of the hallway. The shot has not been a POV shot, but one taken in a new hallway at right angles to the entrance hall. We then realize that Hirayama has been blocked from our view by a partially closed partition at the end.

A more radical disruption of a POV structure occurs in *Equinox Flower* (Ozu, 1958). An apparent point/object shot of a hospital window is undermined when one of two women looking up at it says, "Mother's room is around there," which suggests that they may or may not be able to see the window from their vantage point. This ambiguity raises a second question: did we as viewers see the mother's hospital room or was it just around a corner? Note particularly that the two questions are independent of one another; one question may be answered in the affirmative, the other in the negative. The ambiguity achieved here is almost total and is never resolved. In both of the examples from *Equinox Flower* and *An Autumn Afternoon,* space has been separated from character and narrative but not to the extent that the films become non-narrative; rather, character and narrative are simply refused as the *preeminent* ways for the viewer to organize, unify, and understand the production of space.[11]

Finally, element six is the coherence inscribed within the structure ('character') which justifies the unity and meaning of all the elements. In chapter 4, we examined the out-of-focus POV shot (the perception structure) which represents the special perceptual circumstances of a subject—drunk, dizzy, drugged, etc. By analogy we may say that the non-distorted, or in-focus, POV shot represents *no* special perceptual circumstances; that is, normal awareness. A shot in *Spellbound* (Hitchcock, 1945) perfectly illustrates the close relation between the POV and perception shots as it alternates between the two structures: a letter goes in and out of focus according to the distance it is held from a character (whose eyesight is poor). A POV shot, therefore, requires the presence of a character but more than a 'body' is necessary—the character must be 'aware' and 'looking' in a normal way. What, for instance, is the status of a POV shot when the character is asleep, blindfolded, blind, or dead? Element six answers the question *how* the elements of the POV structure are to be unified and related to character (according to categories like memory, dream, perception, etc.).[12] Strictly speaking, it is not character (which is a rather complex notion), but a mere presence or awareness that is required.[13]

A stunning use of the presence and absence of character awareness in a POV structure occurs in *Notorious* (Hitchcock, 1946). Alicia (Ingrid Bergman) is a spy for the United States and has married Alexander Sebastian (Claude Rains) in order to penetrate an organization he heads. She wants to obtain a key to a locked door and on a pretext sends Sebastian to get the key from his mother who has been suspicious of her. A POV sequence begins with a pan to Alicia's glance (1) followed by a shot revealing her view down a hallway as Sebastian goes to his mother's room (2). We return to Alicia still watching (3) and again repeat the hallway shot from the set-up of 2 (4). There is then a repeat of Alicia watching from the set-up of 3 (5) and a repeat of the hallway shot from the same set-ups as 2 and 4 (6). Up to this moment there exists a six-shot POV structure containing three point/glance shots alternating with three point/object shots. We even hear a muffled conversation between Sebastian and his mother—from Alicia's *aural* POV in the hallway. Finally, in shot 6 we see Sebastian emerge from his mother's room and walk toward the camera. We expect him to stop and speak toward the camera, i.e., to Alicia. But no, he walks by the camera which pans with him (recall, incidentally, that the sequence began with a pan) to a door which he opens. There is now a cut to the interior of a room (7) where we see Sebastian enter in the background and, in the foreground, we are surprised to see none other than Alicia! Somehow, after her last glance down the hallway (5) and while we were ostensibly seeing her POV (6) for the third time, she slipped away from us, stealthily 'leaving' her viewpoint behind. Her purpose in not waiting for Sebastian was to feign unconcern about the key—to pretend she had other important things to do and that the key was of no importance. Sebastian is indeed misled. In the process, however, the viewer has also become a victim of her scheme for we were deceived into believing she was in the hallway when in fact she had secretly departed, concealing her intentions even from us. Thus the sequence builds a firm POV structure—providing the viewer secure expectations—only to subvert the structure at the end by precipitously withdrawing a fundamental element—the character whose view it is.[14] Our expectations have been overturned, but we gain, through the action of *space itself,* a deeper understanding of Alicia's character and intentions—the state of her awareness.

2. THE FRAMING OF POV

The elements of the POV structure require a transition device since the camera must physically shift between element one (point) and element four (from point). This shift is the physical correlate for a shift in narrative perception from, for instance, omniscient and voyeuristic to subjective and personal. The device may take the form of a simple cut to a new camera set-up, an optical printer effect (dissolves, fades, wipes, etc.), or camera movement, in which case we watch while the camera repositions. For example, the repositioning of the camera to assume a woman's POV in *Le Plaisir* (Ophuls, 1952) also reveals the woman's decision to kill herself by leaping from a window, and a camera movement in *Dial M for Murder* (Hitchcock, 1954) moves around and behind an unsuspecting victim to end as the murderer's POV. In certain situations where the camera begins close to the subject (point) a fast pan, rack focus, zoom, etc., may be sufficient to indicate a transition from element one (point) to element four (from point) even though the camera set-up has not, in actuality, changed. In fact, we may say that neither a change in camera set-up nor camera movement is necessary to a change in narration. What is important is not the camera as an absolute reference point but the relation among camera, character, object and a perceiver's hypothesis about this relation. A character, for example, may effect a POV structure by moving toward the camera and assuming its point in space.[15] Whatever transition device is used, of course, must imply temporal continuity or simultaneity (element three).

Since the initial angle of shot A (point/glance) may be any angle, we choose shot B (point/object) as a reference and take the line running from the subject's eyes to the object as a reference line. The POV structure is then classified according to the placement of shot B with respect to this line. Figure 1 represents alternative sites for the location of shot B. It displays a range of possibilities for the framing (element four) of the POV structure.

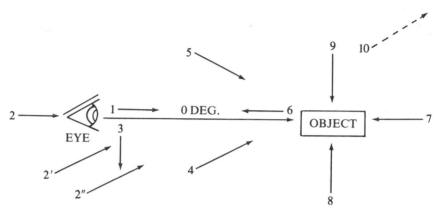

Figure 1 (overhead view): Alternate Sites for the Location of Shot B (Point/Object) Following Shot A (Point/Glance).

Set-up 1 is the classic POV shot—from the subject's eyes. Set-up 2 is a 're-verse angle'—from behind the subject, usually over one shoulder. In addition to being 'less subjective' than the POV shot, it is a more stable articulation since we view the direct spatial relation of subject and object. Set-up 2' is just to the side of the subject whom we do not see. The camera position is indicated by an indirect cue; for instance, in a conversation the person we see looks to one side of the camera at the subject whom we do not see. When the angular difference between camera and subject is small, set-up 2' is essentially the classic POV; as the difference increases—toward, say, 30 degrees—set-up 2' becomes less subjective and the address to the viewer less personal, more voyeuristic (set-up 2").

Set-up 3 is a deviant POV—discussed earlier in conjunction with examples from *An Autumn Afternoon* and *Equinox Flower*—where the camera reveals an object which we believe a subject to be looking at but which, in fact, he is not. It, as well as set-up 10, is a false eyeline match since we do not see the space implied by the directed glance. Set-up 4 is the typical eyeline match, especially when it marks the return to a familiar (previous) angle. It shows what a character sees and when, but not from where the character looks.

Set-up 5 is the mirror image of set-up 4. It is an important camera location because, for example, where the object is a person, by crossing the 180-degree line one can make it appear that two people are looking in opposite directions (as in *Sylvia Scarlett,* Cukor, 1935). Similarly, one can cross the line to make it appear that two people are not looking at each other when, in fact, they are.

Set-up 6 represents the POV of the object and usually occurs when the object is a person. Set-up 7 is a reverse angle of the object. It usually occurs when the object is a person. In *Seven Samurai* (Kurosawa, 1954) it follows a point/glance shot as an alternative to set-ups 1 or 2. In *Enter the Dragon* (Clouse, 1973) set-up 7 guarantees a preceding POV and shows the object of a return glance from a second person. The full sequence is as follows: a woman glances, then we cut to a man about to attack her who is looking at something. There is then a rack focus back to what he is looking at: a shard of glass which the woman is holding in front of the camera. This proves that the first part of the shot completed a POV of the woman and that the second part completes a return glance from the man.

Set-ups 8 and 9 are de-stabilizing shots since in their resemblance to set-up 1—the classic POV—they imply a false space for the subject. And finally, set-up 10—discussed earlier in conjunction with *Early Summer*—is also de-stabilizing since it represents a jump into a new space or new scene.

The move away from the strict subjectivity of set-up 1 is a move through a continuous spectrum as illustrated by set-ups 2' and 2". Is set-up 2" still 'mostly subjective' because of its relative proximity to set-up 2' or have we reached a break point where 2" must be related to set-ups 2 or 4? Differences in the framing of space—such as changes in angle from set-ups 1 through 4—allow the viewer to become aware of things the character is not. This additional knowledge, in turn, must be justified by the viewer through postulating a non-character source of narration.

3. A REPERTORY OF SIMPLE STRUCTURES

There are two major variants of the POV structure and a number of simple structures. The usual form of the POV is shot A (point/glance) followed by shot B (point/object). This 'prospective' POV is the form we have discussed up to now. A major alternative form of the POV is the 'retrospective' or discovered POV where the order of the shots is reversed: shot A *follows* shot B. For example, two men are conversing in an office about a woman suspected of murder. There is a pause in the conversation (or is it the end of the scene?). We then see a high-angle, extreme long shot of the woman sitting on a park bench (shot B). Then we cut to one of the men looking out of the window of the office (shot A). A reverse angle confirms he is looking at the woman from the office window. The conversation now resumes with one man aware that the woman is nearby. The difference between the prospective and retrospective POV is on the order of 'the man sees the woman' as opposed to 'the woman is seen by the man.'

The discovered POV is less common in Hollywood films than the prospective POV. Herbert Lightman, discussing a particular discovered POV, concedes that "certain elements of surprise and suspense were established. But," he continues,

for several seconds the audience was lost, so that a good deal of the dialogue went by unnoticed while the audience struggled to orient itself. Obviously, whatever originality was achieved by the use of the device was outweighed by the confusion that followed and by the loss of dramatic meaning within the sequence.[16]

Noël Burch, by contrast, celebrates discovered and quasi-POV shots and other structures precisely for their ability to *disorient* spectators, renew perception, and contest narrative primacy.[17]

We shall now examine a number of simple variants of the POV structure including structures which may be termed closed, delayed, open, continuing, cheated, multiple, embedded, or reciprocal structures.

The closed POV takes the form: A, B, A. The point/glance shot is repeated. For example, in *The General* we see two point/object shots where we look out from under a table and later where we watch the General being loaded by Union troops. Each time we return to the original point/glance shot after the point/object shot—Keaton under the table, Keaton and girl in the woods.

The closed POV has a high degree of narrative stability because the repetition of shot A (an overdetermination) serves to re-establish time, place, and what we've seen. The repetition also signals the end of a 'subjective' view. The audience is fully prepared for the camera to establish a new relation vis-à-vis the characters.

Further, time is momentarily suspended in the closed POV as in the traditional subjective flashback or during an intertitle; that is, we do not expect events to be happening to the characters while we are looking at an object or until we fully recognize the repetition (closure) of shot A. The closed POV would seem to be a common structure in traditional Hollywood cinema.

In *Vampyr,* however, the closed POV is undermined. We see David Gray outside an inn looking in a door toward camera; he glances up (shot A). We cut to a shot of the roof (shot B), then pan and tilt down to discover Gray walking along a wall *back* (?) toward the door and looking in the door again.[18] Thus it is not clear what has been happening while we have been looking at the roof. This illustrates a structural principle of the film whereby the camera is unable to 'keep up' with the events (i.e., it is not omniscient) and consequently there is a profound tension between on-screen and off-screen space.

The formal variants of the closed POV take the form: A′, B, A″ where A″ is a minor variant of A′, such as a new angle or new distance in which the subject is seen, at least momentarily, still frozen in his glance before the narrative action resumes. Either A′ or A″ or both may be reverse angles. Also common is the structure A, B, and then instead of cutting back to shot A or moving the camera back to A, we see the subject—after a decent interval—step in front of the camera, in effect creating a reverse angle to remind us of our special viewpoint. There also exist permutations similar to the above modelled on B, A, B. This discovered and closed POV structure is often used, for example, to emphasize an object or the sudden appearance of an object.

A second simple structure is the delayed or suspended POV. It is a special sort of temporally deviant POV where shots A and B are separated from one another for narrative reasons. It often occurs in detective, suspense, or horror films where a character clearly sees something (point/glance) yet the point/object shot is withheld from the audience for a number of shots (while another person is summoned to look at this extraordinary thing) or a number of scenes (when the character is killed by the object). It is also possible that the object is *not yet present* to be seen so that a character's glance becomes *premature*. In *King Kong* (Cooper and Schoedsack, 1933) there is a scene on shipboard, before reaching Skull Island, where the heroine (Fay Wray) rehearses a series of terrified reactions for the benefit of a movie camera. The cameraman shouts directions to her. Following a terrified glance, and in place of an object shot, the scene concludes with a bystander remarking, "What's he think she's really going to see?" The rehearsal is, of course, also *for us:* it suggests what we are destined to see later in the film—the monster—and what the heroine's (first!) reaction will be.[19]

The inverse of the delayed POV is the case where a point/object shot is given but the point/glance shot is withheld; that is, a discovered and delayed POV. Although early in *Jaws* (Spielberg, 1975) we see the gliding, underwater viewpoint of a shark, we do not see the shark itself until much later. In a cemetery scene of *The Omen* (Donner, 1976), a series of bizarrely framed shots (from behind trees, rocks, etc.) along with unusual music portend the eventual appearance of those who watch from hiding. Throughout *Wolfen* (Wadleigh, 1981) special camera movements signal the presence of unseen creatures. The first third of *Dark Passage* (Daves, 1947) contains several extended sequences from the delayed POV of Vincent Parry whose face is kept hidden from the audience until plastic surgery has provided him with a 'new' face (that of Humphrey Bogart).

Another example of a discovered and delayed POV occurs in *The Quiller Memorandum* (M. Anderson, 1966). We see a high-angle shot of the hero climbing into a car, then window curtains fall across the image. We now realize that someone was watching our hero, but who? Note the result if, after the window curtains fall across the image, we see the face of the person who is watching (the person steps in front of the camera). The shot began as an 'objective' view (the hero climbs into a car) but then became fully subjective by running through the elements of POV in reverse order and completing the structure by showing the person whose view we share. (An example may be found during a phone conversation in *The L-Shaped Room,* Forbes, 1963.) Furthermore, the shot could just as well continue and shift back into an objective view (for example, we hear the person walk away but continue to see the street). All of this could have occurred within a single, fixed camera set-up which illustrates the fact that the 'shot' is not a decisive term in the POV structure or, for that matter, in the system of narration. The elements of representation may be scattered in various ways in any number of shots, a single shot, or fragment of a shot. What is crucial is that there exist a representation of the elements—a point, glance, transition, etc.

Finally, it should be mentioned that just as the example from *King Kong* revealed that a glance may be premature so, too, may an object be premature; that is, we see something important which a character has overlooked or not yet discovered (one thinks of Hitchcock films). The premature glance is symptomatic of horror films while the premature object is symptomatic of suspense films.[20]

The delayed POV, of course, is not limited to horror and suspense films. The final eight shots of *An Autumn Afternoon* (Ozu, 1962) utilize a premature object in a delayed POV structure. After the wedding of his daughter, which he has arranged, Hirayama returns home a bit drunk. His head lolls forward as he sits at a table (shot 1). We then see an empty downstairs corridor leading to the daughter's now vacant room (2) followed by the stairs leading to her room (3). Next, we see three shots of the interior of her darkened room (4, 5, 6). Finally, we return to the downstairs corridor and, surprisingly, see Hirayama standing in profile staring off left (7). While we were upstairs, Hirayama must have revived, gotten up, and walked to the corridor where he now looks at the stairs we saw in shot 3. Note that shot 3 was not subjective since Hirayama had not yet arrived in the corridor; neither is shot 7 subjective since we do not see what Hirayama is looking at, though it must be something like what was seen in shot 3. Shots 3 and 7 placed together would be subjective (a discovered POV) except that they are separated by a series of spaces in the daughter's room. Thus the POV is delayed and curiously attenuated; character never quite connects up to, or masters, the space. Hirayama faces the absence of a daughter while the viewer is left with a slight, but unbridgeable, gap in space.

The delayed POV structure may be resolved in a number of ways. Other types of shots may be employed, such as reverse angles (earlier we discussed how these shots were related to the POV). Also larger narrative structures may interact and further delay the POV structure; for example, the POV may be resolved by a later shot but we may not be aware that it was resolved until still later when a narrator explains to us the significance of the shot.[21] Whether or not a flashback structure is employed, the missing shot—when it is recognized—will have retrospective significance because it completes an earlier POV structure; we now know, for example, that the killer is that person we have seen throughout the film.

Related to the delayed POV is the open POV. In this structure, although a point/glance is firmly established, we *never* see the object. Examples include the Indian torture victims of *Ulzana's Raid* (Aldrich, 1972); cloud formations which are earnestly discussed in *Ohayo* (Ozu, 1959); a troop of marching soldiers in *La Grande Illusion* (Renoir, 1937); and, after we see a series of roofs with TV antennas, we do not see the roof which has no TV antenna in *Fahrenheit 451* (Truffaut, 1966). The Renoir example shows that the open POV may be used to isolate certain non-visual aspects of the object which may be important in the narrative enterprise. Though we do not see the marching soldiers, we hear their fifes and the thud of their feet. These aspects of the event are emphasized in the dialogue.

Another simple variant of the POV structure is the continuing POV where one character looks at several objects or one object a number of times. The objects are typically rendered by cutting from object to object or by camera movement—the subjective traveling shot. If the point/object structure continues long enough, it may be necessary to insert a re-establishing shot (i.e., point/glance). The re-establishing shot functions to remind us of our special viewpoint—although, as *Lady in the Lake* demonstrates, one does not easily lose track of the viewpoint—as well as to change the narration momentarily and so introduce another level (hierarchy) of narrative codes.[22] In the classic Hollywood conversation of alternating medium close-ups, the re-establishing shot is often a reverse angle.

In *Psycho* simple two-shot POV structures are repeated in chains to create a continuing POV. There are sixteen POV sequences of six or more shots in the film, including at one point forty-two consecutive shots of Marion driving her car and what she sees from behind the wheel (although the sequence does not always maintain temporal continuity). The sustained viewpoint of the continuing POV[23] tends to implicate the viewer in the experience or fate of the character.

In a famous analysis of the Bodega Bay scene from *The Birds* (Hitchcock, 1963) Raymond Bellour demonstrates the importance of the glance.[24] If we segment the scene in a new way by linking the glance to other elements in order to form structures, we discover four simple POVs and five continuing POVs.[25] The final POV in the scene is particularly interesting. It shows Melanie (shot 81) looking at her blood (82) which she has wiped from her head after an attack by a seagull (78). This POV occurs after a series of shots which have already been marked as subjective—we share Melanie's view as her boat approaches a pier on which Mitch waits (shots 60–76). But now shots 80 and 83—which continue to show the pier and Mitch as the boat approaches and which *enclose* Melanie's final POV (81–82)—*cannot* be subjective because Melanie's glance toward the pier and Mitch (which was the basis of the previous POV series, 60–76) has been interrupted and diverted by the attack of the seagull (78). Thus we see both what Melanie *would have seen* if there had been no attack (80, 83), as well as seeing what she *does* see, namely, evidence of the attack (81, 82). In a fundamental way, the attack by the seagull drives the narrative forward by disrupting the expected view of the pier and Mitch. The passage from equilibrium to disequilibrium (homogeneity to heterogeneity)—so vital to narrative[26]—is here stated in terms of the tension between two POV structures—what should have been seen (based on 60–76) and what was instead seen (81–82)—leaving shots 80 and 83 (Mitch on the pier) intermediate between the two structures as a kind of excess vision, the emblem of a narrative violence which will be reinvested in the narrative to ensure its continuation. This excess vision also represents Melanie's unfulfilled desire for Mitch. Her desire—signified through her look (e.g., shot 76)—is postponed by the seagull attack (instead of Mitch she sees blood, shot 82). Her desire, in fact, will continue to be deferred until the 'end' of the narrative, which is exactly the re-grouping (realignment) of desire as stated through the space of character vision.

A similar example of excess vision may be found in *Dark Passage*. We see Irene Jansen (Lauren Bacall) from the POV of Vincent Parry (Humphrey Bogart) although he is not looking at her.[27] He is distracted by, and reading aloud, a newspaper which contains a letter written by Irene about Vincent. Thus we see what Vincent *would have seen* had he looked, and, in a more fundamental way, we see what he *will come* to see and to desire as the narrative progresses. The deviant POV here reveals two rather complicated times—a conditional perfect[28] and a future time (cf. the earlier discussion of a premature glance and premature object). This illustrates the fact that with respect to the viewer the film image cannot simply be considered as always in the present tense.[29] A wide range of temporal references is possible through the movement of narration.

The continuing POVs of *The Birds* illustrate another important trait of POV structures. A common variant allows the framing of the object (element four—'from point') to be somewhat closer to the object than the character's actual position—though the angle typically is still from that position. This compromise gives the *audience* a better view of the object.[30] The 'cheated' or 'forged' POV is acceptable, of course, depending on the degree to which the camera is cheated toward the object, and it becomes more acceptable if these shots are, as in *The Birds,* firmly embedded within an extensive, continuing POV which uses other, indisputably subjective shots from the correct distance. That is, if other cues are sufficiently strong—such as camera angle and movement, repeated character glances, narrative context, etc.—then a certain play is permitted in camera distance and in the composition of the point/object shot. Various secondary cues, described earlier, may also be ignored or cheated. In *King Kong* (Cooper and Schoedsack, 1933) a POV shot through the underbrush showing natives dancing is followed by a series of much closer shots of the natives and from a variety of angles before we return to the original glance from the bushes. Here, the play within the POV structure may be altogether too free. This does not, however, negate the subjective overtones of the sequence (the natives being watched) so much as argue for a very weak POV structure or, more likely, a reflective subjectivity (see chapters 4 and 6).

Another simple structure is the multiple or 'interlocking' POV.[31] It results when several characters see the same object, and takes the form, or some fragment of the form: A, (B), C, (B), D, E, (B) where B is the object and the other shots are of persons. Note that when a POV is offered for two people who appear together in a single shot, the structure is 'less subjective' than if offered as the view of only one person.

In *Spellbound* (Hitchcock, 1945) a multiple POV is compressed into an A, (B), C pattern. Characters A and C are in different rooms but the object shot, B (of an arriving car), is taken from an ambiguous angle so that it serves both characters. Another way to think of the sequence is as a deviant, closed POV where the same view is enclosed by two characters—the heroine (Ingrid Bergman) and a would-be suitor (John Emery). Together they watch the arrival of the man (Gregory Peck) who eventually is to win the love of the heroine. The complete (i.e., the underlying) form of this sequence would be A, (B), A, C, (B'), C where B' is a different angle than B corresponding to the different spatial location of C.

An embedded POV results when a POV structure of one character is nested or contained within a larger POV structure of another character. For example, in *Psycho* we see Marion inside her car glance (shot A) at a policeman outside the car who then glances (shot B) at her car license plate (shot C). Marion is still watching the policeman (repetition of shot A) as he looks up (repetition of shot B). One characteristic of this structure is that, while we have seen something from Marion's viewpoint, we have also seen something that she cannot see: the license plate. Note, too, that the first appearance of shot B functions both as the point/object shot of A and the point/glance shot for C. The elements of the POV structure need not be distributed in a fixed pattern of two elements per shot.

When the object of a glance is also a person, then it is possible to alternate POV structures—as in a conversation—centered about two or more points. This is the reciprocal POV. A character need not stare directly into the camera (for that involves another convention) but the eyes must be very near the line of the camera.

Strictly speaking the reciprocal POV takes the form: (A, B), (closer B, A), (closer A, B). This represents three POV structures, each fully defined, from A to B, B to A, A to B. An example occurs at the end of *La Femme infidèle* (Chabrol, 1968). Of special interest is the final shot of that film, which begins as a point/object shot of the wife from the husband's viewpoint. When the camera tracks back it may still be a point/object shot (the husband is walking away with the police while looking over his shoulder); but when the camera begins to zoom as well as track in a new direction, the nature of the shot changes. Indeed we watch while the shot slowly *changes* in narration. In the traditional Hollywood film the complete model of the reciprocal POV is often abridged so that the point/object shot functions also as the point/glance shot for the next series. Hence the above, complete model would be rendered in only four shots instead of six: (A, [B], [A], B). In *Psycho* such a series is created by alternating close-ups of Marion and a police officer through nineteen shots.

The use of a mirror or other reflective surface in the *mise-en-scène* in conjunction with a POV structure may result in rather complex permutations. The mirror image, for example, alters direction (by 180 degrees) as well as space—the image appears to be in front of the camera when, in fact, it is behind the camera. In addition, the mirror represents two objects: itself and its reflected image. Further, when the reflection is that of the subject (not to mention another mirror), a form of reciprocal POV is generated (a fully reflexive POV). Thus a mirror may, depending on the circumstances, undermine one or more of five elements of the POV structure—all except the transition element.

A sequence in *Vertigo* (Hitchcock, 1958) illustrates the complexity which may result when a mirror is utilized with a POV structure. 'Scottie' (James Stewart) is secretly following Madeleine (Kim Novak), who has disappeared into a room. He partially opens a door (point/glance) (shot 1) and we see her in a floral shop from his point in space (point/object) (shot 2). Madeleine casually moves about the shop and then begins walking toward the camera. Has she suddenly discovered Scottie spying on her? Will she discover him? Next there is a match on action (shot 3) as Madeleine turns away from the camera but the shot disorients us in the manner of a jump cut because we still see her from virtually the same frontal angle and her turning motion is in the 'wrong' direction. Gradually it becomes apparent that we are looking into a *mirror* which is mounted inside the room near the opening of the door through which we still see Scottie peering. Madeleine has not seen Scottie, but has walked closer to the door possibly in order to admire herself in the mirror. Although shot 3 completes a closed POV by returning to Scottie's initial glance, there is a sense in which the mirror image merely *continues* the glance of Scottie (cf. the scale of Madeleine in shot 3 with shot 2). Thus we now see in a single shot both Scottie and the object of his glance (although the image is reversed in the mirror); it is as if the elements of the POV structure were compacted into a single composition. Nonetheless, it cannot be a literal POV shot because the disorienting reversal of the image (in the mirror) demonstrates that the camera placement of shot 3 does not in fact coincide with Scottie's point in space. Thus shot 3 becomes a strange sort of eyeline match accomplished within a single composition, or better, an unusual form of the perception shot where the near repetition and disorienting reversal of the image become the mark of Scottie's heightened attention and growing obsession with Madeleine.

Even without Scottie's glance, however, the mirror image would be subjective if Madeleine has walked closer to admire herself because it would represent a space generated by the look of Madeleine. (The next chapter will explore this type of subjectivity.) By exhibiting herself in the mirror, Madeleine makes herself into an object for us and indeed cooperates in becoming the very kind of object required by Scottie's voyeuristic gaze. Unknown to Scottie and to the viewer, Madeleine is in fact aware that he is watching and, moreover, she is secretly luring him into a trap. In short, the mirror functions to hold one or both subjectivities, but in an uncertain way and at one remove from the characters. The effect is disquieting.

Notes

This selection is reprint of Chapter 5 of Edward Branigan's *Point of View in the Cinema: A Theory of Narration and Subjectivity in Classical Film* (New York and Berlin: Mouton Publishers, 1984). In the following notes, references to chapters and sections are to this book.

1. This figure results from a shot-by-shot tabulation of all transitions (cuts, dissolves, fades, wipes, etc.) of *Ever in My Heart* (Mayo, 1933) (37 percent), *Four Daughters* (Curtiz, 1938) (38.5 percent), and *His Girl Friday* (Hawks, 1939) (40.6 percent, which includes 6.6 percent cross-cutting via the telephone). A cut was not deemed a proximate articulation if the same character, though against different backgrounds, was common to both shots.

2. Noël Burch, *Theory of Film Practice,* trans. Helen Lane (New York: Praeger, 1973), ch. 1 "Spatial and Temporal Articulations," p. 9.

3. See, e.g., Karel Reisz and Gavin Millar, *The Technique of Film Editing* (New York: Hastings House, 2nd ed., 1968), sec. 3, "Principles of Editing," pp. 211–72.

4. Stephen Heath, "*Jaws,* Ideology and Film Theory," *The Times Higher Education Supplement* 231 (March 26, 1976), p. 11; reprinted in the following: *Framework* 2 (4) (Autumn 1976), p.27; *Film Reader* 2 (January 1977), p. 167; *Ciné-Tracts* 1 (1) (Spring 1977); and in this volume.

5. Phil Hardy, *Samuel Fuller* (New York: Praeger, 1970), pp. 100–101.

6. Donald Richie's description of the shot is inaccurate in a number of respects. Cf. also his judgment of the shot ("simple sloppiness") with the aesthetic of Noël Burch, *op. cit.,* pp. 6, 16 ("It is only through systematic and thorough exploration of the *structural* possibilities inherent in the cinematic parameters . . . that film will be liberated from the old narrative forms and develop new 'open' forms . . ."). Richie, *Ozu* (Berkeley and Los Angeles: University of California Press, 1974), p. 112.

7. Both of these possibilities are exploited in Oshima's *The Story of a Man Who Left His Will on Film;* see ch. 7, sec. 3 and 4.

8. Kristin Thompson and David Bordwell, "Space and Narrative in the Films of Ozu," *Screen* 17 (2) (Summer 1976), pp. 69–70.

9. In ch. 7, sec. 4 and 5, we will discuss an altogether different use of an inverted viewpoint as well as the POV of a character who leaps from a building in Oshima's *The Story of a Man Who Left His Will on Film.*

10. Lewis Herman, *A Practical Manual of Screen Playwriting* (New York: New American Library, 1952), p. 250. Jean Epstein in 1921 suggested the possibility of interrupting subjective images with flashes of black to represent the blinking of eyelids; see Jean Mitry, *Esthétique et psychologie du cinéma,* vol. 2 (Paris: Editions Universitaires, 1965), p. 62.

11. Edward Branigan, "The Space of *Equinox Flower,*" *Screen* 17 (2) (Summer 1976), esp. sec. 1.

12. See David Bordwell and Kristin Thompson's analysis of the subjective devices employed in the Albert Hall scene in *The Man Who Knew Too Much* (Hitchcock, 1934), *Film Art: An Introduction* (Reading, Mass.: Addison-Wesley, 1979), pp. 242–43; see also the general discussion of element six (mind) in ch. 3, sec. 4.

13. There is a subtle but important distinction here between a character, and the presence or awareness of a character. We may want to say that 'character' is a more complex effect of the text (cf. ch. 4, n. 17) and that much less is needed to found a POV shot; for instance, the presence of an animal can give rise to a POV shot. Further, the POV shot of an invisible spirit (*Blood and Roses,* Vadim, 1960) demonstrates that we need not see the character at all though we must at least understand, or accept (= reading hypothesis), that there is *some* presence or awareness *at work.* The example of the invisible spirit suggests something of the problem of "effaced" narrators (ch. 8, sec. 1) where objects are presented without explicitly revealing the method of the seeing of those objects. (Cf. a discovered, open POV where objects are shown but never the point/glance.) Presence or awareness in its most general form is the element of representation, mind. This element is responsible for the feeling that artworks ultimately present us with a "disengaged memory of a volition" (see ch. 3, sec. 5, discussion of "mind").

14. The reverse structure is also possible: An objective view may suddenly become subjective by a character moving in to take it over, with or without the immediate knowledge of the viewer. Less transgressive, but still jolting, is the case where the shot appears objective but is, actually, already the view of a character. Examples of both kinds from Fellini's *8½* are discussed in ch. 7; the latter in sec. 1 and the former in sec. 5. The problems encountered in analyzing a sequence when one shot appears subjective but is, actually, already objective are discussed in ch. 3, sec. 3.

15. An example from Fellini's *8½* is discussed in ch. 7, sec. 5.

16. Herbert Lightman, "The Subjective Camera," *American Cinematographer* 27 (2) (February 1946), p. 66, reprinted in Lewis Jacobs, ed., *The Movies as Medium* (New York: Farrar, Straus and Giroux, 1970), p. 63.

17. Burch, pp. 15, 78–80.

18. For an analysis of this sequence including stills see Mark Nash, "*Vampyr* and the Fantastic," *Screen* 17 (3) (Autumn 1976), pp. 41, 45–46.

19. Thierry Kuntzel, lecture on *King Kong* (University of Wisconsin, Madison, Spring 1976).

20. Cf. the distinction drawn by Hitchcock between surprise and suspense in François Truffaut, *Hitchcock* (New York: Simon and Schuster, 1967), pp. 50–52, 185. This book contains many suggestive comments by Hitchcock about character subjectivity.

21. The delayed POV illustrates the fact that in terms of the five narrative codes of Roland Barthes, the POV structure, in general, contains a built-in hermeneutic code.

Depending on the precise form, the POV structure may ask the following: What object is someone looking at? Who is looking at the object? What is the spatial or other relation of person and object? What will be the reaction of the person to the object? etc. For a definition of the hermeneutic see ch. 2.

22. The "failure" of *Lady in the Lake* (Montgomery, 1946) has been attributed to the fact that, in order to internalize a character's look, one has to know the character. Christian Metz, "Current Problems of Film Theory: C. Metz on J. Mitry's *L'esthétique et psychologie du Cinéma*, v. II," *Screen* 14 (1–2) (Spring 1973), p 47. One cannot know a character from a purely personal narrational stance (I, or I see) because psychology is an external construct which depends upon the perspective of an *a*personal narrational voice. Cf. Roland Barthes, "An Introduction to the Structural Analysis of Narrative," *New Literary History* 6 (2) (Winter 1975), p. 263, and in the same issue, J. M. Lotman, "Point of View in a Text," pp. 351–52. Similarly, one does not understand a film as the personal view of the film-maker (as a real-life person) because there is no context within which to locate the filmmaker. Even if the auteur appears in the film, we cannot recognize the "auteur" who placed him or her within the narration. There is always some filmic voice beyond which it is impossible to go and thus a film will always have an apersonal component. See ch. 3, sec. 2; and ch. 8, sec. 1.

23. There may be limits to the continuing POV. See the discussion of *Lady in the Lake* (Montgomery, 1946) by Metz, pp. 47–48.

24. Raymond Bellour, "*Les Oiseaux:* Analyse d'une séquence," *Cahiers du cinéma* 216 (October, 1969), pp. 24–38 (includes stills); a translation is available through the British Film Institute Educational Advisory Service (London).

25. Roughly, in terms of shots and utilizing Bellour's shot breakdown, the POV sequences are as follows: the fisherman's POV (shots 11–12), Mitch's POV (closed, 57–59), Melanie's POV (closed, 34–36; 81–82), and Melanie's continuing POV (15–24; closed, 25–31; closed, 37–43; 43–56; closed, 60–76). As one can readily see, Melanie's vision dominates the scene and only she has continuing POVs.

26. See, e.g., Stephen Heath, "Film and System: Terms of Analysis", Pt. I in *Screen* 16 (1) (Spring 1975), pp. 48–50; Tzvetan Todorov, "The Grammar of Narrative", *The Poetics of Prose* trans. Richard Howard (Ithaca, N.Y.: Cornell University Press, 1977), pp. 111, 118; "Narrative Transformations", *ibid.,* pp. 232–33; "The Principles of Narrative," *Diacritics* (Fall 1971), pp. 37–44.

27. Actually this shot would be better described as a "cheated" POV, or perhaps as a weak reflective subjectivity or even as a non-subjective shot, because our view of Irene in medium close-up is too close to be from Vincent's position in the room. Later in the scene we see Irene in medium long shot from Vincent's POV. Since the early part of *Dark Passage* is heavily subjective, a viewer will be expecting POV sequences and be more liberal in judging what counts as a POV sequence.

28. Cf. ch. 4, sec. 4, esp. the examples from *By the Law* and *Dark Passage*. See also appendix, n. 136 on counterfactuals.

29. See the discussion of the myth of the present tense image in appendix, text accompanying n. 125. The deviant POV here is better understood as a new level of narration. In addition to the problem of time noted in the text, there has been a failure of vision (glance) and an absence of character awareness (cf. the earlier analysis of the hallway scene in *Notorious*).

30. When a character is reading a paper, a cheated POV, with the camera closer to the paper, is often used to make it easier for us to read it. An example of the general strategy to

provide the audience with a better view can be seen in the seating arrangement around a table where the characters are bunched together and a large space is deliberately left open for the camera to shoot through. This adjustment of the *mise-en-scène* prevents a character from blocking our view and allows us to see all of the faces. The cheated POV is related to a dynamic perception shot (see ch. 4, sec. 3).

31. David Bordwell has suggested the term "interlocking" POV and analyzes its use in Dreyer's *La Passion de Jeanne d'Arc* (1927); *The Films of Carl-Theodor Dreyer* (Berkeley and Los Angeles: University of California Press, 1981), pp. 81–84.

STATISTICAL STYLE ANALYSIS OF MOTION PICTURES

BARRY SALT

Like those who have brought structuralism, psychoanalysis, formalism, or semiotics to film study, Barry Salt introduces us to a foreign methodology, statistics, that may contribute fruitfully to the analysis of film. Like structuralist semiotic methods, which ignore questions of aesthetics or a phenomenological level of affectivity in order to explore the production of meaning, the text as a set of discursive strategies, Salt's approach treats the text quite roughly, tearing it up into shot lengths, camera movements, and shot types (close-up, medium shot, and so on). This encourages us to reexamine some venerable assertions of film study regarding directorial style: Otto Preminger and John Stahl made films in which average shot lengths are comparable to those in Jean Renoir's, and Henry Hathaway made films where shots were shorter than in some of Eisenstein's.

A great deal of recent work in film history does not even refer to the categories that Barry Salt examines: directorial style, montage, deep focus, camera movement, shot type. In many instances, these categories are seen to belong to a history of origins —dating the "first" close-up, for example —or to an amateur criticism that is not well equipped to answer questions about technology or industrial practice. The individual film and individual filmmaker become secondary as attention shifts to industrial practice and microeconomic questions or to economics, technology, aesthetics, and ideology at the large-scale level of the coming of sound or the introduction of color. Salt counters this current, drawing our attention back to the films themselves, perhaps also reminding us how extraordinarily difficult it is to suspend a study of the characteristics of individual films and a study of general cultural tendencies within a single analytic framework.

Salt's approach may also point up a limitation of statistical analysis. Salt finds that statistical study does not support Sarris's claim that Howard Hawks's His Girl Friday *had more "fluidity of camera movement" and "faster" editing than Lewis Milestone's* The Front Page. *He finds more instances of camera movement in* The Front Page *and the same average shot length but a less typical or classical distribution of shot lengths. He concludes that "objectively, [The Front Page] has far greater fluidity of camera movement" and that the difference in effect is "due solely to the extra speed of delivery of the dialogue" and to more "business" by the actors. These assessments tend to conflate a statistical "fact" with an aesthetic impression. Frequency of camera movement does not necessarily translate into fluidity. For a long-take style, the exact contextual placement and thematic relevance of the long takes would be as important as the frequency of their occurrence. In these considerations of long takes and camera movements as elements of style, we may find that the differences between Renoir and Preminger or between Hathaway and Eisenstein that statistics erase are once again significant. That statistical analysis does not resolve all the problems or put them on an objective, scientific footing will come as no surprise. In contrast to some champions of semiotics, Salt does not claim that his method will. Nevertheless, statistical analysis adds another tool to our critical-historical repertoire and challenges us either to substantiate certain long-standing claims, or to abandon them. To do that is to do a great deal.*

It is nowadays fairly widely accepted that individual styles can be recognized for at least some film directors in the formal aspects of their films as well as in the content. However, just what constitutes these individualities of style has up to now been more a matter of loose assertion than demonstration, and indeed there have been some rather questionable suggestions on these points. This is hardly surprising since most of the ideas advanced have been suggested by people without any knowledge of how a film is actually put together, after seeing one or two projections of the films considered. Thus from time to time one reads statements such as "Fritz Lang, like Renoir, tends to film in long shot," references to a director's fondness for long takes, and so on. The feeling often seems to be that many directors have sharply different styles that are easily recognized. This is an attractive idea, but when one looks into the matter more carefully it becomes doubtful that the situation is that simple. To lend some objectivity to this area, and also in emulation of the statistical analyses of features of literary and musical style that have been in progress since the thirties,[1] the preliminary work reported here has been done.

The obvious approach in searching for individual characteristics in the formal side of a director's films is to consider those variables that are most directly under the director's control; also to a certain extent those that are easiest to quantify.

First, we might expect the duration of shots to vary from director to director, some preferring to shoot a script scene with fewer and longer takes than others. Hence the number of shots of different lengths in a sample of films was determined. Also, for the same films I determined the number of shots of different types in terms of closeness of the camera to the actors: i.e., whether the shots were close-ups, medium shots, etc. (The definition of these types of shots was as follows: Big Close-Up shows head only, Close-Up shows head and shoulders, Medium Close Shot includes body from waist up, Medium Shot includes hip to head of upright actors, Medium Long Shot shows body from below the knee upwards, Long Shot shows the full height of the body, and Very Long Shot shows the actor small in the frame.)

A further classification of shots in terms of camera movement was made. In this case it is to be noted that where small pans and tilts up to several degrees were made merely to keep the actors nicely framed, which is an automatic operation by the camera operator from the early thirties onward, the shots were classified as static, as were those where the camera was rigidly fixed relative to the actors, the background behind them moving, e.g., an actor filmed in a car. The angle of shots—whether low or high angle—and the extent of angling were not generally considered, though they could well have been.

These analyses could be extended in various directions—an obviously important quantity being the strength of cut or, more exactly, the nature of shot transition from each shot to the next, using some quantitative consideration of strength of shot transition.

Though it would not be simple, it would be possible to give a rough measure of the strength of a cut in terms of the angular change of camera position and change of closeness to the actors (or other objects) across the cut—due allowance being made for the fundamentally different cases of an action filmed with multiple cameras simultaneously, and for the action being reperformed for the second camera position after the cut. Further factors also have to be introduced for amount of movement in the frame in cuts on action, and for sound continuity across the cut.

METHODS OF ANALYSIS

To establish the existence of an individual formal style in the work of a director, it is necessary to compare not only a sufficient number of his films with each other, but also—which is always forgotten—to compare his films with films of similar genre made by other directors at the same time. This is essential to avoid describing as characteristic of a director's work features which are in fact shared with the work of other directors. An even more absolute norm for any period is really needed as well, to give a standard of comparison that reflects the technical and other constraints on the work of filmmakers at that time and place— namely the analysis of a large number of films both good and bad chosen completely at random.

In parentheses, it should be said that this comparative approach should be applied to the discussions of the singularities of content as well as of form in a director's work. It this were done it would eliminate a lot of the wild overinterpretation of films that continues to be produced.

The particular sample of films examined in this study for comparison with the group of early thirties Renoir films is some way from fulfilling these conditions; though chosen pretty much at random (in the sense that they were obtained by people other than the present writer for other purposes), they are all usually considered *good* films; there are no bad or mediocre films of the thirties among them. A few silent films are included to give some pointers for future research.

The statistics of interest to us can be derived from the post-production cutting continuity of a film if this is available. (Production companies almost always have had these made in recent decades.) Alternately, the statistics can be taken directly from a print of the film, as these were. In this case it is slightly easier and faster to work with 16mm copies, and the quickest method of extracting the shot lengths is with a synchronizer, and the other quantities with a variable speed moviola, though in general any film-viewing machine can be used.

For comparative purposes the number of shots for each range of shot lengths considered has been normalized to correspond to the number there would be if the movie was 90 minutes long. The actual number can be reclaimed by multiplying by the ratio of the actual length of the film to ninety minutes. The shot lengths can be left in film feet (to the nearest half foot) for either 16mm or 35mm as the case may be, as the laborious conversion to seconds gives nothing useful at this stage. However, the average shot length is given in seconds in the table below.

In justification of the estimation by sampling of the quantities in some cases, note that for instance in *Le Million* the first 1000 ft. give an average shot length (A.S.L.) of 5.19 ft., the next 1000 ft. an A.S.L. of 5.47 ft., and the remaining 896 ft. an A.S.L. of 5.26 ft. against an overall A.S.L. for the whole film of 5.31 ft. Here the fluctuation of the A.S.L. is only a few percent from the parts, each about 27 minutes long, to the whole, and this variation is of the same order in all the quantities we examine. So a 30- to 40-minute sample should give satisfactory results, though of course analysis of the whole film is preferable. This sort of result also suggests that differences in quantities have to be well above 10 percent to be significant for style considerations, and that those differences below are not; and it also shows that there is no point in pushing accuracy of measurement too far. The nearest second is quite enough for measurement of average shot length, for instance.

The distributions of types of shot are analyzed in terms of numbers of each type per 500 shots rather than for a standard 90 minutes, as the latter approach would depend on the average shot length as well, and not give directly, as we have here, the relative probability of the director choosing a particular type of shot. It might be useful to consider the relative total times spent in each type of shot during the course of the film, as also giving an indication of the director's preference for the use of that type of shot, but this possibility is declined for the moment on the assumption that the results would be much the same as those we do obtain.

SHOT LENGTH DISTRIBUTIONS AS FOR 90-MINUTE FILM

(NUMBER OF SHOTS IN RANGE OF LENGTH INDICATED)

35mm feet	0–1	2–8	9–15	16–22	23–29	30–36	37–43	44–50	51–57	58–64	65–71	72–78	79–85	86–92	93–99	100+
The Hired Man	18	720	150	24	12	6										
Erotikon	9	561	227	31	17											
Kameradschaft	0	116	147	63	42	42	11	11	11							
The Front Page	18	232	13	31	31	9	23	4	9	13	0	0	0	0	4	
The Big Sleep	8	240	101	49	23	21	8	3	8	8	8	0	8	3		

16mm feet	0–½	1–3½	4–6½	7–9½	10–12½	13–15½	16–18½	19–21½	22–24½	25–27½	28–30½	31–33½	34–36½	37–39½	40–42½	43–45½	46+
Hallelujah	0	276	141	35	44	30	17	5	3								1
Public Enemy	9	259	119	55	22	16	10	0	0	3	0	0	3	3			
Le Million	15	314	137	68	36	18	13	4	5	2	0	1	2	0	1		
La Chienne	2	78	61	42	21	27	15	8	6	7	5	4	2	3	1	3	5
Boudu	0	122	137	60	34	18	8	5	4	5	5	3	5	1	2	1	
Toni	2	79	53	39	17	17	12	3	15	3	11	4	3	0	0	3	4
Partie de Campagne	7	171	74	43	41	21	16	16	11	2	0	2	2				
Sylvia Scarlett	24	244	96	36	56	8	8	0	4	4	8	4	4				
His Girl Friday	16	158	50	37	30	18	11	7	9	7	0	5	9				4

RESULTS OF THE ANALYSIS

Looking at the frequency distributions of shot length, a considerable similarity of overall shape is apparent. This is a surprise; a greater diversity for different film-makers was expected. The profiles of the distributions approximate in nearly all cases to that of the Poisson distribution—the distribution of randomly arrived at events or quantities observed with such things as the distance between cars on a highway.[2] However, there are small deviations in two directions from the shapes of the Poisson distributions appropriate to the different average shot lengths: there are somewhat more short shots (of smaller length than average) in the case of *Le Million, Hallelujah, Sylvia Scarlett* and *The Public Enemy,* perhaps indicating a conscious desire to keep the shots short; and alternatively, in the case of the Renoir films and *Kameradschaft,* there are a larger number of very lengthy shots, no doubt indicating a conscious desire to keep the shots going as long as possible without departing from conventional procedures of shooting a film. The extremely anomalous case of *The Front Page* can only reflect definite and individual ideas that Milestone had at that time about how to break a script up into shots.

Altogether, as far as shot length distributions are concerned, the differentiation of Renoir's films from the rest is not great, and there is no real differentiation of the other films one from another (with the single exception noted above), other than would be equally well provided by the average shot length taken alone. However, when we move on to look at the distribution of types of shot by camera distance it is apparent that we have a more definite differentiation of directors—Renoir's films are more like each other with respect to this quantity, which we shall call *closeness of shot,* than they are like other directors' films, and the films by the various other directors considered also differ appreciably one from the other. The exception to this are two films by Howard Hawks, which are also more like each other than any other films are like them. Clair and Wellman concentrate about equally on the more distant shots (more than Renoir does), Pabst has virtually no close-ups in *Kameradschaft* and a heavy concentration on medium shots, *Sylvia Scarlett* has a strong concentration on closer shots, and so on.

As far as the silent films analyzed are concerned, the general shape of the shot length distribution is the same as for the sound films, indicating that the distribution has no connection with the lengths of particular lines of dialogue spoken in particular shots in sound films. However, the average shot length is shorter for the silent films, a not surprising result, though that it should be as short as 5.5 seconds in 1918 for *The Hired Man* is a little unexpected. But we are incredibly ignorant of the state of the American dramatic film around the end of the First World War, a time when the methods of Griffith were being developed and elaborated by others.

If we look at the types of shot used in these silent films, the large number of close-ups in the American film stands out against Stiller's films; it is possible that to use less close-ups has always been a general European tendency. (See also the other films studied.) Noting also the emergence of shots with camera movement,

Films (in Chronological Order)	Average Shot Length
INTOLERANCE (Griffith, 1916, 168 min.)	7 sec.
°THOMAS GRAAL'S BEST FILM (Stiller, 1917, 62 min.)	9.sec.
°THE HIRED MAN (Schertzinger, 1918, 65 min.)	5.5 sec.
°EROTIKON (Stiller, 1921, 100 min.)	6.5 sec.
NAPOLEON (Gance, 1925, 145 min. at 21 f.p.s.)	5 sec.
BATTLESHIP POTEMKIN (Eisenstein, 1925, 54 min. at 16 f.p.s.)	4 sec.
°HALLELUJAH (Vidor, 1929, 105 min.)	9 sec.
°THE PUBLIC ENEMY (Wellman, 1931, 85 min.)	9 sec.
KAMERADSCHAFT (Pabst, 1931, 85 min.)	13 sec.
LE MILLION (Clair, 1931, 80 min.)	13 sec.
A NOUS LA LIBERTE (Clair, 1931, 97 min.)	9.5 sec.
°LA CHIENNE (Renoir, 1931, 94 min.)	19 sec.
°BOUDU SAUVE DES EAUX (Renoir, 1932, 83 min.)	15 sec.
°TONI (Renoir, 1934, 90 min.)	19 sec.
THE OLD-FASHIONED WAY (Beaudine, 1934)	8.5 sec.
LE CRIME DE M. LANGE (Renoir, 1935, 80 min.)	21 sec.
LIVES OF A BENGAL LANCER (Hathaway, 1935)	5.5 sec.
°SYLVIA SCARLETT (Cukor, 1935, 95 min.)	10 sec.
°PARTIE DE CAMPAGNE (Renoir, 1936, 45 min.)	14 sec.
SAN FRANCISCO (Van Dyke, 1936)	9 sec.
HOTEL DU NORD (Carné, 1938)	17 sec.
IN OLD CHICAGO (King, 1938)	9 sec.
°HIS GIRL FRIDAY (Hawks, 1940, 92 min.)	13 sec.
THE GRAPES OF WRATH (Ford, 1940, 129 min.)	10 sec.
CITIZEN KANE (Welles, 1941, 119 min.)	12 sec.
DIVE BOMBER (Curtiz, 1941)	7 sec.
PASSAGE TO MARSEILLES (Curtiz, 1944)	6.5 sec.
WILSON (King, 1944)	12 sec.
LEAVE HER TO HEAVEN (Stahl, 1945)	8 sec.
HANGOVER SQUARE (Brahm, 1945)	10 sec.
THE SPANISH MAIN (Borzage, 1945, 99 min.)	9.5 sec.
NIGHT AND DAY (Curtiz, 1946)	9 sec.
°THE BIG SLEEP (Hawks, 1946, 114 min.)	12 sec.
THE YEARLING (Brown, 1946, 130 min.)	9.5 sec.
IVAN THE TERRIBLE (Eisenstein, 1946, 99 min. and 90 min.)	7.5 sec. (each part)
NIGHTMARE ALLEY (Goulding, 1947)	12 sec.
FOREVER AMBER (Preminger, 1947)	18 sec.
OH, YOU BEAUTIFUL DOLL (Stahl, 1949)	19 sec.
RASHOMON (Kurosawa, 1950, 88 min.)	13 sec.
DETECTIVE STORY (Wyler, 1951)	15 sec.
CAPTAIN HORATIO HORNBLOWER (Walsh, 1951)	8.5 sec.
PICKUP ON SOUTH STREET (Fuller, 1953)	11 sec.
YOUNG BESS (Sidney, 1953)	12 sec.
SEVEN SAMURAI (Kurosawa, 1954, 160 min.)	8 sec.
WRITTEN ON THE WIND (Sirk, 1957, 92 min.)	11 sec.
WILD STRAWBERRIES (Bergman, 1958, 90 min.)	9.5 sec.
FROM HELL TO TEXAS (Hathaway, 1958) (Scope)	6.5 sec.
LES QUATRE CENT COUPS (Truffaut, 1959, 93 min.) (Scope)	14 sec.
ONE, TWO, THREE (Wilder, 1960) (Scope)	14 sec.
UN HOMME ET UNE FEMME (Lelouch, 1966, 147 min.)	12 sec.
OEDIPUS REX (Pasolini, 1967, 110 min.)	7 sec.
IF (Anderson, 1968, 111 min.)	9.5 sec.
THEY SHOOT HORSES, DON'T THEY? (Pollack, 1969, 129 min.)	12.5 sec.

° Analyzed in this study.

it is apparent even from the bare figures that the characteristic American style is taking definite shape, a style that was not altogether of Griffith's creation, since he avoided using pans and tilts.

Camera movements do not seem, on the evidence available so far, to be so characteristic of a director's work as closeness of shot. There is still a certain amount of resemblance amongst Renoir's films in this respect; however, the large number of tracks in *La Chienne* must be noted, and the very small number (for Renoir) in *Boudu.* This is undoubtedly intentional, and probably relates to Renoir's statement with respect to the style of his films that he did different things in each of them—a statement that is superficially somewhat surprising.

His Girl Friday has been included in the analyses because chance presented the opportunity of a comparison with *The Front Page,* and the possibility of checking an assertion of Andrew Sarris about the two films. He wrote of *His Girl Friday,* "Hawksian fluidity of camera movement and invisibility of editing was actually faster than in Lewis Milestone's classical montage in *The Front Page.*"[3] Now *The*

NUMBER OF SHOTS PER 500 SHOTS WITH GIVEN CAMERA MOVEMENT

Film	Pan	Tilt	Pan with Tilt	Track	Track with Pan	Crane
THOMAS GRAAL'S BEST FILM	0	0	0	0	0	0
THE HIRED MAN	4	7	0	10	0	0
EROTIKON	0	0	0	0	0	0
HALLELUJAH	3	0	0	3	3	0
THE PUBLIC ENEMY	36	3	3	36	18	0
KAMERADSCHAFT	61	25	12	76	51	0
LE MILLION	16	4	2	2	0	2
LA CHIENNE	45	9	3	44	17	0
BOUDU	30	1	0	7	7	0
TONI	45	8	8	23	25	0
PARTIE DE CAMPAGNE	58	12	0	23	21	0
SYLVIA SCARLETT	22	4	0	15	11	0
HIS GIRL FRIDAY	82	0	0	20	9	0
THE BIG SLEEP	77	3	1	36	64	0
THE FRONT PAGE	0	0	6	39	65	0

(With the exception of BOUDU, LA CHIENNE and LE MILLION these quantities are estimated from 30-40 minute samples of the films.)

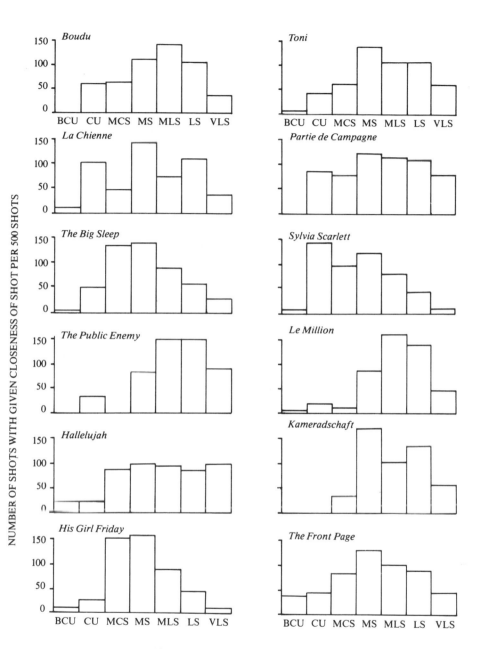

Front Page when analyzed has a far greater number of tracks of both kinds than the Hawks film; objectively it has far greater fluidity of camera movement. The average shot length of both movies is the same; however, the Milestone film achieves this by having a larger number of very short shots and a larger number of very long shots, and this latter is certainly not a classical feature by any reasonable definition of classical. *The Front Page* does have somewhat more close-ups, which might be considered more of a tendency in a classical direction, if we assume that classical means something like the style of *Sylvia Scarlett,* but this is hardly enough to override the previously mentioned aspects of *The Front Page.* In fact, from the data we have here, and from unbiased further inspection of *His Girl Friday,* noting particularly the way the sequence of violent action just after the escape of Earl Williams is shot and edited, one can see that there is only a moderate difference in the styles of the two films. The greater effect of speed in *His Girl Friday* is due solely to the extra speed of delivery of the dialogue (count the words per minute) and the addition of lots of business in the acting. Andrew Sarris is the most perceptive writer on the style of films, but the indulgence of his prejudices and his reliance on screenings only can lead him to make serious mistakes, despite his praiseworthy espousal of a comparative method. It is indeed even possible for an experienced film-maker who bases his judgments on one screening of a film to be mistaken about these matters.

There are further incidental benefits to be gained from this approach to film style analysis in the emergence of all sorts of detailed points about film construction while one is actually analyzing the film on the editing table. To give just one example, when comparing *Boudu, Le Million,* and *Hallelujah,* which are all pretty much static-camera films, one becomes aware that without sound *Le Million* is a rather boring film to watch, but the other two are not. The statistical results indicate partly why this is so: Renoir and Vidor in general get the camera in closer to the actors. But the points that become apparent only on the viewer are that in cross-cutting between parallel actions, Renoir cuts while the actors in each shot are still moving rather than between points of repose, and also that in *Le Million* there are a number of unnecessary cuts—shots that could have been continued from one of the chosen camera positions are cut short, and the camera position changed for no apparent reason at all, the change being too small to add any dynamic impulse to the film.

SEQUENTIAL PATTERNS

In all these films superficial inspection of the preliminary lists of shot lengths written down in order reveals no patterning in the way the different lengths follow one another, except for very rare appearances of pairs of shots of approximately equal length, and one or two occurrences of three successive shots of roughly the same length. That there is no overall patterning in the succession of shot lengths in the films considered is suggested, though of course it is not proven, by the conformity of the shot length distributions to the Poisson type of random distribution. Nevertheless, it would be of interest to apply Markov chain analysis not only to shot lengths, but also to some of the other shot characteristics, or parameters, particularly the previously suggested strength of shot transition. (Markov chain analysis means finding the influence on the characteristics of a shot of those of the preceding shot, and in the second-order analysis finding the influence of particular characteristics in the *two* previous shots on the next shot, and so on to higher orders.) There could be patterns in the higher orders of the succession of shot characteristics which are not visible to superficial inspection of the list of shots.

AVERAGE SHOT LENGTH

The average shot lengths that could be easily obtained for a number of films are tabulated here, and some reflections on these follow. Unfortunately, figures for some typical silent films of the twenties have not been obtained, but my subjective impression is that the average shot length in American and most European films stabilized at several seconds, but that exceptionally Gance, and following him Eisenstein, pushed on to using even shorter shots as illustrated by the figures here. This trend had virtually no effect on other film-makers, probably at least partly because sound intervened.

Also, when looking at these results, strong doubt begins to arise about the accuracy of André Bazin's ideas about pigeonholing directors of the late thirties and the forties into two classes, those using long takes and deep focus, and those not. In fact, the average shot length for *Citizen Kane* is about average for its period, and, on the other hand, the figure for Carné's *Hôtel du Nord* is similar to that for Renoir's films. Also, if anyone really cared to look, they would see that there is only a handful of deep-focus shots in any of Wyler's films, such as *Mrs. Miniver,* when Gregg Toland was not behind the camera.

A further note of caution is suggested by these figures about the too easily accepted claim that shot lengths increased with the introduction of CinemaScope and wide screen. (All American films were composed for wide screen after 1954.) This may or may not be true, but one certainly cannot be sure at this stage. Look at the figures for *Written on the Wind,* made by Douglas Sirk, who has been claimed to be a master of wide screen. Also note the near equality of average shot length for Henry Hathaway's *Lives of a Bengal Lancer* (1935) and *From Hell to Texas* (1958 and in Scope).

Although the values for average shot lengths collected here are not extensive enough to be entirely conclusive, they strongly support the impression that the average of the A.S.L. for Hollywood movies in the late thirties and early forties was 9–10 seconds, and there was an increase in this average of a few seconds through the latter part of the forties as more and more directors strove for longer takes. This tendency was commented on at the time,[4] and culminated of course in *Rope.* The introduction of Scope and wide screen came after this development and was not its cause.

CONCLUSION

However that may be, it is also important to note that average shot lengths for the work of different directors at any period cover a continuous range, and there is no sharp distinction between directors, although there is a tendency for a director to stick to approximately the same A.S.L. This continuous distribution of films along a dimension of form also emerges in the other dimensions of film form considered here, that is, in closeness of shot and in camera movement, as can be seen by looking at the bar chart presentation of the results for different films. It is speculated that the same is really true with respect to other aspects of style in the mainstream of cinema which are more difficult to quantify, such as style of acting and dialogue, of treatment of sound (i.e., amount of background music, etc.), of lighting and image composition.

The evidence presented here runs counter to the idea of "montage style" and "deep-focus style" and "wide-screen style" as pigeon-holes into which films can be neatly fitted, and it is further suggested that such terms are misleading if used as exact analytic tools.

At this stage it seems possible that a sufficient characterization of formal style for the films of a director might be obtained from their average shot length, plus the two distributions of numbers of shots according to types of shot (by camera closeness and movement). But shot length distribution should continue to be taken till it is clearer whether the non-Poisson distribution for *The Front Page* is a true anomaly or whether similar deviations occur in other films. This could well be the case for a number of films made after 1960, for instance. It might also be advisable to subdivide the classification Big Close-Up by the introduction of the category Choker Close-Up, which is already used in the film industry to describe a shot that shows part of the face only. And it might be worthwhile to collect numbers of high-angle and low-angle shots in a film; some style distinctions and developments might emerge through this quantity also. For instance, it seems that Howard Hawks used a greater number of high-angle and even low-angle shots in the thirties than he did later; his style changed.

Thorough extension of the investigation to the films of other directors than Renoir means taking, say, all the films of Howard Hawks made in the late thirties and comparing them in the ways indicated with one another and with a presumably random selection of about 20 (or more) films made in Hollywood during the same period in the same genres. And so on for such other directors as seem relevant in that period and other periods.

Several times the number of films so far analyzed need to be dealt with before definite conclusions about statistical style analysis can be arrived at. However, the results so far are based on more objective facts than have ever been used in the field of style comment before. The methods used can obviously be applied also to sections of a film when one is considering the interactions between, and relations of, form and content. And they can decide questions of attribution, such as who really directed *The Mortal Storm,* Borzage or Saville. A few hours with a film on a moviola is always more instructive than watching a second screening of it and then retiring to an armchair and letting one's imagination run riot.

Notes

1. H. B. Lincoln (ed.), *The Computer and Music,* Cornell, 1970; Dolezel and Bailey (eds.), *Statistics and Style,* Elsevier, 1969.

2. July 1983: As a result of further figures that I have collected for shot length distributions, which have been analysed with the advice and assistance of the statisticians Laurence Baxter and Valerie Isham and with the help of detailed calculations made by Wai Ling Chan, I have now concluded that the shot length distributions of the bulk of ordinary films are best described by the lognormal distribution and *not* the Poisson distribution. However it is possible that for films with long average shot lengths (roughly speaking, greater than 20 seconds) the best-fitting standard statistical distribution may be the gamma distribution. My earlier mistake indicates the dangers of generalizations based on inadequate data.

3. A. Sarris, *The Primal Screen,* Simon & Schuster, 1973, p.59.

4. *American Cinematographer,* December 1972.

THE SPACE BETWEEN SHOTS

DAI VAUGHN

Another important countercurrent involves the question of how problems of film theory can be articulated in the vocabulary not of an intellectual methodology but of film practice. Some theoretical statements are so theoretical in tone, syntax, and level of abstraction that they seem to imply that no one but theorists ever considers the problems thus addressed. This is no doubt correct, if we mean that no one else considers these problems in quite the same way, but it is far from correct if we mean that no one else considers them at all. (Some might argue that, in considering a similar problem differently, we are really considering a different problem.) Dai Vaughn, continuing some of David MacDougall's perspectives and preoccupations, shows how questions of ethics, which others may want to subsume under politics or ideology, become for practitioners questions centered on institutions, equipment, and technique. These day-to-day realities establish systems of constraint that limit possibilities and favor certain choices over others. But within these constraints —similar to those that narrative imposes to "contain" the treatment of visual space within the requirement of representing a fictional place —there is a multitude of choices. A filmmaker may have recourse to systems of belief in formulating his or her ethical positions, but they only become revealed through style, structure, or technique. For filmmakers who seek it, Vaughn argues, honesty becomes a technical problem.

Using examples drawn from his experience as an editor on a BBC television series, "The Space Between Words," conceived in the spirit of American cinéma vérité, *Vaughn demonstrates some of the concrete ethical choices that an editor confronts. Voicing the fear that editing is "a mutilation visited upon some defenseless simulacrum of life," Vaughn addresses some of the intricate questions that emerge once we accept film as a distinct form of discourse. He discusses why the goal of "objective" style is not only impossible but also an important part of the way in which institutions, such as the BBC, formulate their own guidelines for documentary work (despite the contradictory if not paradoxical injunctions that this may require). For contrast, Vaughn explains how the concept of "open-ended" style served as a valuable guide in the production of "Space Between Words" and demonstrates how criteria of relevance or significance involve concrete choices that tacitly manifest ethical positions.*

It could be an intriguing exercise to translate Vaughn's (or MacDougall's) argument into semiotic terms or to rephrase semiotic arguments in the vocabulary of practitioners. What is retained, and what is lost in translation? How do differences in assumptions and articulation produce perspectives that cannot be matched or made congruent? One reason for pursuing this point is to clarify the kind of questions raised by Constance Penley's comparison of certain avant-garde practices with a number of psychoanalytic semiotic theories: What forms of congruence are possible between theory and practice? When do individuals use the same words and mean different things? When do different words mean almost the same thing? Finally, what are the most direct and vital links between speaking in the language of film and speaking about film?

For those who bewail its absence, honesty is a moral problem. For those who try to achieve it, it is a technical one. At their first transmission, in mid-1972, Roger Graef's *Space Between Words* series aroused a good deal of fresh controversy about the relationship between *cinéma vérité* and truth. But most of the discussion was of a purely moralistic character in that the desiderata of 'objectivity' were dissected with scant regard for the realities of the film language in which it was, or was not, held to find expression. What has been lacking is an assessment of the problem by a technician on day-to-day terms with the demands of his medium. My own qualification for hazarding an opinion is that I was film editor on three of the *Space Between Words* programmes, and was in close touch with colleagues on all five; but there is little in what I shall say that is not the stuff of common discourse in the canteens of television companies.

The justification for concern with apparent trivia is that the answers we give to questions raised by new developments in documentary technique will help determine our views on censorship, access, democracy and control in broadcasting; and our views on these subjects have practical consequences. Policy decisions based upon a shaky understanding of the medium are likely to be bad ones.

Almost simultaneously with the first transmission of the *Space Between Words* series, the BBC were circulating to their staff a little green booklet called *Principles and Practice in Documentary Programmes*. This 'guide to conduct' received a hostile response from the press; but it did represent a rare attempt to link the ethics of television with its practical procedures. My purpose in referring to it here is not to revive a lapsed polemic but to illustrate the importance of the attempt with an example of practical recommendations based on what seems to be a faulty analysis:

A producer's ethics are principally concerned with: (1) what he may, or may not, simulate; (2) what he should, or should not, select for showing on the screen. The need for some element of simulation has been explained under II. METHOD but the precise extent to which this may be done is clearly a matter of great delicacy, and is frequently a cause of misunderstanding. For example, it is virtually impossible to convey an accurate impression of a board meeting or discussion by filming it as it happens. In real life nobody can predict the order in which various people will speak. The director, cameraman and sound man will find it impossible to follow a rapid and spontaneous interchange. Furthermore, the presence of the film crew will create in itself an artificial situation which can lead to self-consciousness and exhibitionism. Therefore the producer must to some extent prepare such a discussion. So long as the result on the screen gives a true picture of the real type of discussion (which the producer witnessed during his research), and so long as it is an accurate impression of the personalities involved, such preparation is not only ethically permissible, but necessary. (p. 20)

And II. METHOD offers the following:

He [the producer on research] sees what *really* happens when people go about their daily lives without the knowledge that a television audience is watching. He sees how a man *really* behaves when he is not putting on a show for the camera . . . (p. 8) Recent developments in cameras, microphones and film stocks have reduced technical preparations to a minimum, and made it increasingly possible to shoot things at the first attempt and with little pre-arrangement. But even the purest piece of '*ciné vérité*' can never be—and indeed should never be—totally free of the day-to-day business of directing. (p. 11)

The above will be seen to contain some surprising assumptions:

(1) A shot of someone speaking is more truthful than a shot of someone listening.

(2) Someone who is aware of the camera is aware of the television audience.

(3) People's considered adaptation to the camera is more real than their spontaneous response.

(4) What the director sees when the camera is absent is what would be happening if he himself were absent.

(5) The director can judge the reality of what happens this time by reference to what happened last time.

(6) The purpose is to portray a 'type' of incident, not to record a particular one.

(7) To ask for an 'accurate impression' does not beg all the important questions.

It is only fair to point out that the context from which these quotations come is not an encouragement to unbridled simulation but a warning to producers not to go too far—though anyone who stepped beyond these recommendations would surely be engaged in pure fiction. But the underlying assumptions which the quotations reveal form part of a consistent attitude towards the medium which can best be understood in an historical perspective.

In 1955, documentary films looked much as they had looked for the previous twenty years. They were shot in 35mm, budget permitting, with any synch sound recorded directly onto optical track or, latterly, transferred to optical from tape. People were rehearsed in their everyday activities so that they could perform them convincingly in front of the crowd of technicians with their forbidding mass of equipment, cables and lights. The finished film usually had a commentary and, frequently, music. I cannot recall what television documentaries were like at that time, but I know that few people in the short-film world saw television as a potential outlet for their talents.

Then, in the late 50s and early 60s, there came a succession of technical developments, each of which, being seized upon by film-makers tired of the old formulae, gave birth to an element of what was soon to become a new style. The first was the general introduction of magnetic sound stock, which can be cut into pieces and endlessly rearranged in a way that optical cannot, and which opened up the possibilities for disjunctive editing of sound and picture—for doing with ease what must have cost Jennings considerable effort. Denis Mitchell and John Read were able to pioneer the technique of 'voice over', in which people's recorded comments are laid—and usually hacked around a bit—to fit whatever visuals the film-maker chooses. Already the participants in a film are one step further from knowing what is being done to them.

The second development was a by-product of the first. Magnetic sound cannot be put together with a cement joiner (or rather it can, but the joins click). After about three years of trial and error, someone invented a satisfactory device for joining magnetic sound with ordinary clear sticky tape; and it was quickly realised that this could equally be used for joining picture. With it came a new freedom. The cement joiner made an overlapping join, so that every time we changed a cut we lost two frames, and every time we put something back we had to replace the loss with black spacing, and could no longer see how the cut worked. There was therefore an inhibition against making alterations. But with the tape joiner, which makes a butt join, we could try out any idea, however unpromising, knowing that if we did not like it we could try something else. With the invention of the tape joiner, documentary became an editor's medium.

The next two developments came simultaneously in 1963, with the appearance of a silent-running 16mm camera (the Eclair) and a professional-quality lightweight tape recorder (the Nagra). Almost overnight it became possible to shoot synch with portable equipment; and this, combined with the gradually improved resolution of film emulsion, swung the balance in favour of 16mm as a professional gauge. This in turn meant less expensive film stock, with the result that higher shooting ratios were considered acceptable. The script finally became obsolete. The new type of documentary, shot with small crews, which was relatively cheap and could be made in a hurry, was ideally suited to the needs of television, where the difference in definition between 16mm and 35mm was least important. Had the technical innovations happened in a different order, it is quite possible that what we know as the Mitchell style would not have been the one to develop from a challenge to a language, and ultimately to an orthodoxy, in the space of ten years: but they didn't, and it did.

Yet it was an orthodoxy ill-suited to the orthodox. It was a style in which nothing could be safely judged in advance—by the participants, by the executives or even by the film-makers; a style in which responsibility was indeterminately distributed (a thing which administrators never like) between a director who did not know what the cameraman was seeing, a cameraman who did not know what was going to happen next and an editor with more permutations to choose from than he could try out in a lifetime. Moreover, it was a style which drew upon a formal vocabulary—of vox pop,* voice over, montage, talking head, musical interlude, significant juxtapositions of any and all elements—so vast and flexible as to make the expression of attitude through the very form of the film not merely possible but inevitable. Yet there was no knowing whose attitude it was. It might have been the director's. It might have been the editor's. It might conceivably have been nobody's. Films have their own logic.

The public always distrusted the style, suspecting it of wilful distortion. The usual complaint was that things were taken out of context: to which the only reply is, 'How much context does a quotation require—a paragraph, a volume, a lifetime's experience?' Behind the inanities of tabloid opinion and the fulminations of 'Disgusted' lay very real ethical problems; but they were problems which presented themselves with each choice of camera angle, with each cut, with each decision to put something in or to leave something out. Such problems are not amenable to blanket legislation.

Recognising this, the BBC drew up its code of practice not as a table of requirements but as a set of guidelines to the individual conscience of the director. (Their failure to recognise other technicians as creative contributors derives not from aesthetic theory but from institutional predisposition.) However, in facing the moral ambiguities of a style in which the elements are more lifelike than ever before, yet the overall result bears less resemblance than ever to simple actuality—as if poetry had been achieved by collage from a company report—the BBC group seems to have clutched for reassurance at straws of the earlier tradition, evincing an apparent nostalgia for the well-made British documentary left behind with the waning of the Grierson impetus—all polish and no boots.

It further appears that, in attempting to draw general guidelines from specific examples, they have, in a most curious fashion, transferred the requirement for generality back upon the particular instance. Thus in their example of a board-room meeting they seem to be saying that what is required is an 'impression' of a 'type' of event rather than the record of an actual one. But the way of generality is treacherous. When, say, an Education Authority complain that one of their schools has been portrayed in an untypical or abnormal light, they understand by typical and normal not an intuitive statistical average of what usually goes on in

---

*Short piece of film representing what is supposed to be the spontaneous reaction or opinion of a man, woman or child in the street.

that school, but an adherence to the type or norm laid down for it, from which the confusion of daily troubles is seen as ephemeral deviation. In other words, authorities' idea of what is typical is what they like to imagine happens. And this is precisely what you get if you allow the board to rehearse their meeting. Perhaps the BBC's inclination towards this conception of the typical can be explained as one bureaucracy understanding the needs of others. (It was not for nothing that the Grierson style—the style of optical sound and cement joiner—recommended itself to the agencies of government and the managements of industry.) But perhaps it would be kinder to explain it as a gentlemanly hankering for a tradition in which, even if the film-makers had to be taken on trust, the participants had at least some sort of control over the image of reality they projected.

But while the BBC looks in one direction for its lost certitudes, documentary has been moving in another. This time the technical innovations have been less dramatic. While continued improvements in film emulsion have made it possible to shoot a high proportion of subjects with available light—or, at worst, with the replacement of ordinary light-bulbs by photofloods—cameraman and sound-recordists, freed by the crystal pulse from the necessity of being roped together like mountaineers, have developed incredible virtuosity in working in unison to follow, steadily and continuously, the most confused discussion or complicated action. Meanwhile editors, feeling their language has become stale with over-use, having seen the techniques of Godard and Ichikawa absorbed and exploited to the point of gimmickry, uneasy with the morality of subordinating real people's real experiences to a paramusical structure, and bored with being able to sit at home watching the box and snap their fingers to cue in the voice-over, have become fascinated by the experience of 'real time' which present-day rushes, in their continuity, frequently offer.

The result is the style, exemplified by the *Space Between Words* series, which has been labelled 'objective'. My own belief is that the subjective/objective duality is one of those which, like classic/romantic or intellectual/emotional, is useful only where it is too crude to be interesting: but since the word is with us, it may be worth our while to ask whether this series can legitimately be described as objective in some sense in which other documentaries cannot, and to discuss the bearing of this style upon the ethical problems of film-making.

Before the films were embarked upon, a number of assurances were given to those whose participation was required, in return for which the unit were granted freedom to shoot whatever, and wherever, they wished:

(1) The unit would never intentionally influence the course of events (for example, by revealing to one participant information gained from another).

(2) The unit would shoot only what was relevant to the specified theme of each film, and nothing, however interesting, that was not. (This could scarcely withstand legal scrutiny; but it was not meant to. The spirit was clear.)

(3) No one would be asked to do anything, or to repeat anything, for the benefit of the camera. (If we missed something, it stayed missed.)

(4) The finished films would have no commentary beyond a brief, explanatory introduction (i.e., people's actions would not be subjected to verbal interpretation).

(5) There would be no interviews. (This assurance was not given for all the films, but it was fundamental in winning the cooperation of the trade unionists— a group particularly sensitive to the way their statements are used on television.)

(6) If there were objections on grounds of 'security' to the use of anything which had been filmed, such as classified diplomatic information, it would not be included; and if necessary the record would be erased or exposed to light immediately. (Such destruction of material was never requested; and I recall only three remarks, out of a hundred and five hours of rushes, which I was asked to omit from the films.)

These assurances, in addition to merely gaining the necessary consent to film, enabled the work to proceed in an atmosphere of relative trust. As a further preparation, the crew made a point of being on location, with their equipment, for anything up to a fortnight before the start of shooting so that their presence, being familiar, would cause the minimum distraction.

Indeed, one remarkable feature of the *Space Between Words* series is their success in conveying the impression that the protagonists were wholly unaffected by the presence of the camera—or at least were indifferent to it. Indifference, it must be clearly said, is not the same as unawareness: in fact the impression of normality owes a good deal to those occasional moments in which someone glances uninterestedly towards the camera, acknowledging its presence, then continues with what he is doing. On the other hand, it is easier to be indifferent to something if it is relatively inconspicuous: and the fact that the series was shot almost entirely with available light, so that people did not find themselves plunged into an extraordinary environment of glaring and shifting lamps, was paramount in permitting them to behave naturally.

But again, it is disarmingly easy to equate 'naturally' with 'normally'—to allow ourselves to believe that because people seem relaxed in the presence of the camera they are behaving exactly as they would if it were not there. These distinctions, though crucial, are rarely made. It needs only one extra person to enter a room—let alone a whole film crew—for the pattern of behaviour to be completely altered. The extent of this alteration will vary from one situation to another; but in all situations it can only be estimated by guesswork. Of course, it can be argued that what happens in the presence of a camera is as much a reality as what happens in its absence, and that one's only responsibility to truth is to ensure that the viewer knows the people know they are being filmed. (In case anyone is inclined to claim that this can be taken as obvious, I should point out that some viewers have already asked whether the *Space Between Words* was not shot with concealed cameras, despite the evidence that the cameraman is clearly moving around among the desks of a classroom and filming from eye-level.) It was in recognition of this argument that the American wing of the *cinéma vérité* movement, represented by the Drew–Leacock team, went to great lengths to ensure the accidental presence of technicians and mike-booms in picture: but the fact that this technique rapidly degenerated into cliché is proof enough that it was alien to the nature of documentary. Even those occasional glances at the camera—a more discreet way of making the same point—are scarcely an integral element of film style. They may never happen to occur, or may all happen to be cut out in an editing process dictated by other requirements: and this will neither enhance nor diminish the truthfulness of what we are seeing.

If this sort of shooting can be called objective it is only in the trivial sense that it is less predetermined than ever by the intentions of an individual—the director. But the cameraman cannot be looking everywhere at once; and his choice of angle will reflect his moment-to-moment judgment of what is important. A sound recordist, faced with an unruly classroom, must choose between using a wide-angle mike to pick up the ambient noise or a narrow-angle mike to pick up what people are saying. Alternatively, he can choose to mix between several mikes, thus either sacrificing his mobility or increasing the number of technicians required to carry booms. At one noisy moment in the *School* film the teacher leaned forward to say to a boy, 'I can't hear you. I can't hear you.' The cameraman zoomed in, but the recordist was not able to adjust his position quickly enough. The result was that, although the teacher was in close-up, her words were almost drowned out; and the effect, in the finished film, was to throw emphasis upon her difficulties. Our professional honesty would have deterred us from simulating such an effect in the dubbing theatre. Yet was it truth or falsehood?

Most people, if pressed for their definition of the 'objective' view of an event, might define it as that view which would be obtained by an invisible observer with no preconceptions. But what qualities are we to attribute to our hypothetical observer? Can he watch from all directions? Can he perceive the overall pattern of the action together with the minute, telltale gestures, simultaneously and with equal attention? If he has no preconceptions, can he have any criteria of relevance or even of interest? And if he were to transfer all his observations to film, how long would it take us to look at it? Eternity would not exhaust it. The objective observer is a chimera.

Criteria of relevance are, of course, central to the editing process. I was recently obliged to look through some material which had been omitted from the very first assemblies of the *Space Between Words* films. It was an acutely boring experience: not because nothing was happening on the screen (there is never nothing happening); but because the camera was failing at these moments to reveal anything interesting about it. Despite his infatuation with the 'real-time' experience—and hence with the eventual extinction of his office—the editor finds himself, willy-nilly, making cuts; firstly to overcome camera run-outs and wobbles; then to eliminate longueurs and repetitions; next to clarify points of confusion created by the earlier cuts; and finally, with resignation, to allow the film to take on that form to which it seems to aspire. And if at times he begins to feel that editing is less a creative act than a mutilation visited upon some defenceless simulacrum of life, he is nevertheless forced by the logic of his craft to acknowledge the distinction between film and reality: that film is about something, whereas reality is not. (Andy Warhol's 24-hour look at the Empire State Building has the purely philosophic value of defining a limit. Like Duchamp's urinal, it needs not to be seen but merely to have been done.)

The way in which a 'slice of life' takes on the quality of being 'about' something can be illustrated by another example from *School*. The last two days of shooting afforded us two conversation sequences (neither, incidentally, used in the transmitted programme): in the one, the teacher on whom we had mainly concentrated said that a course of seminars conducted by the American educationist had greatly enlarged her understanding and increased her confidence; in the other, she said that the course seemed to have undermined her previous technique without putting anything better in its place. There was nothing particularly surprising about this. People's moods change, and they appear to contradict themselves. But for us the problem was how to end the film: and behind our jokes about using the happy ending for the American version lay an awareness that the note on which we chose to end would reverberate back through the programme and would express a view of the significance of the teacher's experience, whilst to juxtapose both possible endings would merely express confusion.

A further point emerges from this example: that, for all the differences of approach and method, the way cinematic elements function in these films is not dissimilar from the way they function in other films. In *Family* there is a sequence in which, after a gradual increase in emotional stress between the mother and the son, the father is shown withdrawn in concentration upon mending a child's toy. This shot is perfectly genuine, in the sense that it happened at the point which it occupies in the film. Yet it owes its remarkably moving effect not to its genuineness but to its poetic appropriateness. A shot of a father mending a toy could be taken in any family, at practically any time, with or without marital tension. And a Pudovkin could have perceived the possibilities of the shot and used it in just this way.

People have an eye for reality. In the films on which I worked there are one or two cutaways—as opposed to synchronous listening shots—which strike a false note for me, and which seem to do so for others. Yet the fact remains that a 'genuine' shot works not because it is genuine but because it *appears* genuine. The *Space Between Words* films can be analysed with much the same critical vocabulary as can other films. The differences quarantine themselves in the area where moral uncertainty resides—that of the film-makers' subjectivity. The problems are in one respect worse than those which the BBC's booklet evades, for the Mitchell style left no one in doubt that what he was seeing was poetry. It is we, not the audience, who must take the responsibility if dubious conclusions about the real world are based upon the false premises of our errors.

Cinéma vérité is not an elixir of truth. A film based upon no criteria of significance would be an amorphous mess; and criteria presuppose attitudes and judgments. How are these judgments made? In practice, on the *Space Between Words* series, they were made over the course of lengthy discussions between the technicians involved: the camera and sound crew, who could assess the relationship of what they had shot to the event as a whole; the director and researcher, who were frequently not present during the shooting (since they wished to keep intrusion and distraction to a minimum, and were in some cases fully employed in trying to discover what would happen next), but whose many conversations with those concerned gave them an overall understanding of the situation; and the editor, who could judge the potential of the rushes unprejudiced by prior knowledge of what they were supposed to reveal. In addition, the films were frequently checked for comprehensibility and apparent implication with projectionists, office staff and a random assortment of cutting-room personnel, each of whose criticisms revealed the vantage-point of his own philosophy.

But this was merely an extension, based upon conscious recognition, of that dispersal of responsibility brought about by the hand-held camera and the enlarged shooting ratio. (The convergence between methods of procedure evolved to suit new equipment and insights into human communication gained from the subject-matter of the films would almost merit a study in itself.) What we must ask is not only how, but on what basis, decisions were made: what were the guiding considerations; and did they differ from those governing the making of other documentaries?

Our overriding concern was that, just as the process of film-making should be as open-ended as was consistent with the need to produce finished programmes, the finished programmes should, so far as possible, reflect this open-endedness. We did not set out to prove anything, but simply to explore communication in several contexts with the aid of film. We did not assume from the start that communication between people was generally good or generally bad; and even the assumption that good communication was better than bad communication came under scrutiny. Though each of us, inevitably, had preconceptions (or moral values) which influenced his interpretation of events, we tried not to allow the structure of the films to be a mere expression of any one interpretation. For example, though some of us were struck by a parallelism between the manner adopted by management towards workers and that adopted by shop stewards towards members, we resisted using cinematic juxtaposition to make this a 'point'.

There can be few editors who have not been disturbed by the ability of their medium to suggest that a subject has been exhausted. The mere act of cutting a sequence into a coherent shape, the craftsman's compulsion to resolve irresolution and tidy up mess, contributes to a tradition whereby the viewer sails under sealed orders: and the very structure of the film conspires with the well-turned commentary to rob it of that penumbra of incomprehensibility which would preserve its link with reality and encourage the viewer to grant it further thought. Comprehensibility has a way of implying comprehensiveness: and anything that can be told comprehensively in an hour can only be a lie. In the *Space Between Words* series we tried to curb the encroachment of craftsmanship upon significance. We wished to leave people free to draw conclusions from the films as nearly as possible in the way one draws them from life, and hoped to avoid setting the familiar pattern of expectations within which the alert viewer watches for a clue to the stance of the *auteur*.

Some critics have seen in this an abrogation of responsibility. The *Socialist Worker* condemned the *Work* film for not condemning capitalism (apparently doubting capitalism's ability to condemn itself). But for anyone not committed to propaganda—which I would define as the conscious suppression of facts which might sustain a point of view other than one's own—our approach was a natural concomitant of that respect for 'real time' engendered by the style of shooting which present-day equipment permits. It has its dangers. On the other hand, we cannot boast of leaving our films open-ended and at the same time complain if people draw from them conclusions we dislike. (Some reviewers have not merely drawn nasty meanings from the films, but have attributed those meanings to us and have proceeded to attack us for them. This is tiresome.) On the other hand, in our anxiety to avoid using film language to communicate a closed message we risk forgetting that without this language a film communicates nothing at all. A further danger is that of being carried away by our own enthusiasm into believing that we have achieved some sort of transcendental impartiality. Throughout the series we were concerned to avert misconception of one sort and another. In *School,* for instance, we had to give adequate account of the disruptive potential of thirty recalcitrant children without implying that the teacher was simply unable to control the class. But to seek to avert misconception presupposes a judgment of what constitutes a true conception: and this judgment must be exercised by fallible and prejudiced human beings. The notion of objectivity does not help.

We crave the security of absolute distinctions, and tend to argue as if a difference in degree were no sort of difference at all. But if the *Space Between Words* series shares its syntax with *Rescued by Rover,* and if its distinctiveness appears at times to boil down to no more than the reinstatement of the unities of time, place and action, and if we seem to have difficulty in defining its characteristics by other than negative statements, perhaps some measure of its success can be found in the extent to which those who have seen it discuss the subject-matter rather than the films and the extent to which they find in the films implications beyond those of which we ourselves were conscious.

The question which remains to be asked is whether this series indicates a direction in which television might usefully develop. The style is expensive, requiring as it does a high shooting ratio (so that the unforeseeable moments of real revelation will be captured) and a superlatively skilled camera and sound team (who will be in the right place when they happen): and in a system where merit must bargain with money in the accountant's language the cost-barrier may frequently prove insurmountable. But this problem may soon be overcome by the development of high-quality portable videotape units; since videotape, unlike film, can be erased and used again.

A more serious difficulty is that of overall length. Overtly poetic films in the tradition of the last ten years can accommodate themselves with relative ease to slot-lengths fixed for the convenience of programme planners: their constituent elements can, if sometimes with resentment, be dismantled and reassembled in a different form. But a film in the style of *Space Between Words* requires a finite time to reveal the significance of its subject; and what we lose by shortening it is not just the significance of what is cut out, but the enhanced comprehension which this shed on what is left in: so that the film is not merely shortened but impoverished. Each film has its optimum length, defined by the point at which the increasing enrichment of cross-references is overtaken by the repetitiousness of diminishing returns.

However, if we set aside these practical considerations, we may allow ourselves the fantasy of a television service in which every aspect of our social lives would be reflected in a public mirror less distorting than any to which we have been accustomed, and in which the sheer volume of such programmes would do a good deal to cancel out the lingering effects of prejudice in any one film-maker. Indeed, it is not impossible that the portable video unit might eliminate entirely the ethical problems which currently beset the BBC. New problems would of course arise. The pessimistic side of this fantasy is the vision of a world in which people would be held to account for their unguarded utterances and the element of performance would therefore invade all our activities and relationships, with spontaneity retreating into the hermetic isolation of the inner life. But which would then be the artifice and which the reality? And is this or is it not an inevitable consequence of a more open society—whatever its technological detail—in which matters of public significance would be released from the confinement of private grudge? To put it at its simplest, would not many people rather act out their predicament before a ciné camera than state this case at a public meeting?

This brings me to my final point, which I deliberately sidestepped at an earlier stage. Among the people who were not consulted in the shaping of the films were the participants. This conforms with time-hallowed practice, which is usually defended on the grounds that the judgment of those who appear in a film would be vitiated by pride, vanity, modesty or embarrassment. Perhaps it would; and perhaps to argue our way beyond such impediments would take longer than current production schedules allow; and perhaps the attempt, through open discussion with the crew, to reach agreements between conflicting parties on what constituted a truthful account of a given event would bear more resemblance to a psychiatric encounter session than to a civilised chat between colleagues, and the film would end in ribbons. But perhaps that is a better use for some films than transmission, and perhaps our budgets should allow for it. There is something to be said for an art which is grounded, as therapy, in a real situation; and since television is a collaborative art, it may as well be collaborative therapy. The results might in fact be impressive.

I am aware that these democratic conclusions can be reached from other directions. If I have chosen to approach them through a consideration of film technique and equipment, it is because this is the context in which the ethical choices present themselves to those who actually work in the medium.

CLASS AND ALLEGORY IN CONTEMPORARY MASS CULTURE: *DOG DAY AFTERNOON* AS A POLITICAL FILM

FREDRIC JAMESON

Identifying a clearly Marxist form of contemporary film criticism is a more difficult task than one might think. Even as many move to appropriate the term for critical work that (it is claimed) demonstrates an integration of Freud with Marx, Saussure with Marx, or Lévi-Strauss with Marx, the specifically Marxist aspects of such criticism often defy identification. Debates between defenders of the approaches of the Birmingham Centre for the Study of Contemporary Culture, which examines culture broadly and locates it within a class context, and of the more psychoanalytic film-oriented approach of Screen *magazine or the debates between* Screen *and* Jump Cut *reflect a noticeable discomfort with loose, often vague allusions to* class, contradiction, dialectic, *and other key Marxian concepts in much contemporary criticism.*

Fredric Jameson's article takes a sophisticated, highly dialectical approach to a particular film and demonstrates the possibilities for a Marxist critical response that contrasts markedly with those of semiotic and psychoanalytic critics. Jameson's angle of incidence more closely resembles that of Hegelian Marxism than of psychoanalytic semiotics, although it is extremely well informed about this and other alternatives. One very clear advantage of his approach is that it effectively sidesteps the need for an interpretive elite that interrogates and decodes popular culture to expose the production of meaning, the work of ideology to achieve hegemony, the veiled operation of an "apparatus," the effect of "structuring absences," and the irruptions of contradiction through gaps, fissures, and caesuras that would otherwise go undetected. (This does not mean that Jameson's writing style is simple. It is not; it is, rather, Germanic or dialectical, although it is also clear and compelling within the admittedly difficult terms of that tradition.)

Instead of calling for a critical vanguard or interpretive elite, of which he would necessarily be a member, Jameson has another agenda. The central item in it is to identify and understand the historical conditions that make it possible for all to see the concrete representation of class conflict. What Jameson calls the figurability *of class contradiction arises when such contradiction can be grasped imaginatively as well as conceptually—something eminently possible in the visual medium of film, although from Jameson's perspective it has seldom been achieved in recent times, because class has generally been viewed as a static category, a separate stratum or unit that can be studied individually. Method acting, which figures classes as static but contending, provides a good example of this view. Method acting celebrates the antihero and reduces the politics of marginality to psychologized, personalized alienation. As a result, we do not see class conflict as such but only its individual consequences.*

In contrast, Jameson argues, Dog Day Afternoon *discovers in the triangulation between Al Pacino's bank robber, the local police chief, and the F.B.I. officer a powerful figuration of class contradiction. Most important, that the F.B.I. officer is the central agent of narrative movement shows how the relationality of classes can be represented. He is a tangible solution to the question of how to make the source and function of real power today materially evident, of how to imbue it with the reality of appearance. The question is complicated by the need to find a persona for a concept (in this case, the concept of power) when the essence of that concept in its modern form lies precisely in its impersonality.*

Jameson, then, does not unveil a subtext or system of hidden operations that constitutes the ideological secret of cinema by the very fact of its concealment. Rather, he tries to put his analytic finger on what is already evident—materially apparent—in the film; as such, it is something to which a viewer can be sensitive, even if he or she cannot name it. Here, he sidesteps the other great dilemma that faces an interpretive elite: the question of whether veiled, obscured, subtextual "effects" can be said to have an actual effect and, if they can, how, especially when it is claimed that these effects somehow "expose" ideology that the film seems to endorse. (The Cahiers du Cinéma *article on* Young Mr. Lincoln *in the first volume of* Movies and Methods *would be one example of a reading that discovers veiled, disruptive effects; others might be Claire Johnston's reading of* The Revolt of Mamie Stover, *in Part 3, and Colin MacCabe's of* American Graffiti, *in "Theory and Film: Principles of Realism and Pleasure,"* Screen 17, *no. 3 [Autumn 1976]: 7–27.)*

Jameson's concern for directing criticism toward problems of representation, toward what is there for all to see, that is, for the figurability of class consciousness and of the relationality of the two fundamentally opposed classes, challenges other forms of Marxist cultural criticism. Like Charles Eckert's article in Part 4, Jameson's argument echoes concepts in Althusser's article on Bertolazzi and Brecht, especially the idea that method acting, like melodrama, camouflages alienation with expressivity and thereby masks or displaces the real conditions of existence. Other aspects of Jameson's article may remind us of Nick Browne's interest in understanding a film rhetoric that can separate identification with character from camera placement and formal point of view. With Dog Day Afternoon, *this involves asking how our sympathies can remain with Sonny even when we see him and the events from the F.B.I. agent's perspective. The question of naming developed in the articles in Part 3 is also rejoined. All in all, these moments of return and this central preoccupation with how the visual signification of cinema can be brought into relationship with necessarily abstract structural concepts gives Jameson's article the force of an (open-ended) conclusion. He brings the desire and the debate that fuel much contemporary film criticism to a focus: how to give satisfactory formulation to the relationships among history, ideology, language, and culture.*

One of the most persistent leitmotivs in American liberalism's ideological arsenal, one of the most effective anti-Marxist arguments developed by the rhetoric of liberalism and anti-communism, is the notion of the disappearance of class. The argument is generally conveyed in the form of an empirical observation, but can take a number of different forms, the most important ones being either the appeal to the unique development of social life in the United States, or the notion of a qualitative break, a quantum leap, between the older industrial systems and what now gets to be called post-industrial society. In the first version of the argument, we are told that the existence of the frontier (and, when the real frontier disappeared, the persistence of that 'inner' frontier of a vast continental market unimaginable to Europeans) prevented the formation of the older, strictly European class antagonisms, while the absence from the United States of a classical aristocracy of the European type is said to account for the failure of a classical bourgeoisie to develop in this country—a bourgeoisie which would then, following the continental model, have generated a classical proletariat over against itself. This is what we may call the American mythic explanation, and seems to flourish primarily in those American studies programmes which have a vested interest in preserving the specificity of their object and in preserving the boundaries of their discipline.

The second version is a little less parochial and takes into account what used to be called the Americanisation, not only of the older European societies, but also, in our time, that of the Third World as well. It reflects the realities of the transition of monopoly capitalism into a more purely consumer state on what is for the first time a global scale; and it tries to take advantage of the emergence of this new stage of monopoly capitalism to suggest that classical Marxist economics is no longer applicable. According to this argument, a social homogenisation is taking place in which the older class differences are disappearing, and which can be described either as the embourgeoisement of the worker, or better still, the transformation of both bourgeois and worker into that new grey organisation person known as the consumer. Meanwhile, although most of the ideologues of a post-industrial stage would hesitate to claim that value as such is no longer being produced in consumer society, they are at least anxious to suggest that ours is becoming a 'service economy' in which production of the classical type occupies an ever dwindling percentage of the work force.

Now if it is so that the Marxian concept of social class is a category of nineteenth-century European conditions, and no longer relevant to our situation today, then it is clear that Marxism may be sent to the museum where it can be dissected by Marxologists (there are an increasing number of those at work all around us today) and can no longer interfere with the development of that streamlined and post-modern legitimation of American economic evolution in the seventies and beyond, which is clearly the most urgent business on the agenda now that the older rhetoric of a classical New Deal–type liberalism has succumbed to unplanned obsolescence. On the left, meanwhile, the failure of a theory of class seemed less important practically and politically during the anti-war situation of the 1960's, in which attacks on authoritarianism, racism, and sexism had their own internal justification and logic, and were lent urgency by the existence of the Vietnam war, and content by the collective practice of social groups, in particular students, blacks, browns and women. What is becoming clearer today is that the demands for equality and justice projected by such groups are not (unlike the politics of social class) intrinsically subversive. Rather, the slogans of populism and the ideals of racial justice and sexual equality were already themselves part and parcel of the Enlightenment itself, inherent not only in a socialist denunciation of capitalism, but even and also in the bourgeois revolution against the *ancien régime*. The values of the civil rights movement and the women's movement and the anti-authoritarian egalitarianism of the student's movement are thus pre-eminently co-optable because they are already—as ideals—inscribed in the very ideology of capitalism itself; and we must take into account the possibility that these ideals are part of the internal logic of the system, which has a fundamental interest in social equality to the degree to which it needs to transform as many of its subjects or its citizens into identical consumers interchangeable with everybody else. The Marxian position—which includes the ideals of the Enlightenment but seeks to ground them in a materialist theory of social evolution—argues on the contrary that the system is structurally unable to realise such ideals even where it has an economic interest in doing so.

This is the sense in which the categories of race and sex as well as the generational ones of the student movement are theoretically subordinate to the categories of social class, even where the former seem practically and politically a great deal more relevant. Yet it is not adequate to argue the importance of class on the basis of an underlying class reality beneath a relatively more classless appearance. There is, after all, a reality of the appearance just as much as a reality behind it; or, to put it more concretely, social class is not merely a structural fact but also very significantly a function of class consciousness, and the latter, indeed, ends up producing the former just as surely as it is produced by it. This is the point at which dialectical thinking—not merely the static and superficial notions of appearance and reality already mentioned, but the most involuted and historicising Hegelian variety—becomes unavoidable. In what follows, I will try to avoid it as much as possible, but an initial point has to be made, without which the intent of the rest will not be clear. It is simply this: that we cannot speak of an underlying 'essence' of things, of a fundamental class structure inherent in a system in which one group of people produces value for another group, unless we allow for the dialectical possibility that even this fundamental 'reality' may be 'realer' at some historical junctures than at others, and that the underlying object of our thoughts and representations —history and class structure—is itself as profoundly historical as our own capacity to grasp it. We may take as the motto for such a process the following still extremely Hegelian sentence of the early Marx: 'It is not enough that thought should seek to realise itself; reality must also strive towards thought.' In the present context, the 'thought' towards which reality strives is not only or even not yet class consciousness: it is rather the very preconditions for such class consciousness in social reality itself, that is to say, the requirement that, for people to become aware of the class, the classes be already in some sense perceptible as such. This fundamental requirement we will call, now borrowing a term from Freud rather than from Marx, the requirement of *figurability*,[1] the need for social reality and everyday life to have developed to the point at which its underlying class structure becomes *representable* in tangible form. The point can be made in a different way by underscoring the unexpectedly vital role that culture would be called on to play in such a process, culture not only as an instrument of self-consciousness but also even before that as a symptom and a sign of possible self-consciousness in the first place. The relationship between class consciousness and figurability, in other words, demands something more basic than abstract knowledge, and implies a mode of experience that is more visceral and existential than the abstract certainties of economics and Marxian social science: the latter merely continue to convince us of the informing presence, behind daily life, of the logic of capitalist production. To be sure, as Althusser tells us, the concept of sugar does not have to taste sweet; nonetheless, in order for genuine class consciousness to be possible, we have to begin to sense the abstract truth of class through the tangible medium of daily life in vivid and experiential ways, and to say that class structure is becoming representable means that we have now gone beyond mere abstract understanding and entered that whole area of personal fantasy, collective storytelling, narrative figurability, which is the domain of culture and no longer that of abstract sociology or economic analysis. To become figurable—that is to say, visible in the first place, accessible to our imaginations—the classes have to be able to become in some sense characters in their own right: this is the sense in which the term allegory in our title is to be taken as a working hypothesis.

We will have thereby also already begun to justify an approach to commercial film, as that medium where, if at all, some change in the class character of social reality ought to be detectable, since social reality and the stereotypes of our experience of everyday social reality are the raw material with which commercial film and television are inevitably forced to work. This is my answer, in advance, to critics who object *a priori* that the immense costs of commercial films, which inevitably place their production under the control of multinational corporations, make any genuinely political content in them unlikely, and on the contrary ensure commercial film's vocation as a vehicle for ideological manipulation. No doubt this is so, if we remain on the level of the intention of the individual film-maker, who is bound to be limited consciously or unconsciously by his or her objective situation. But it is to fail to reckon with the political content of daily life, with the political logic which is already inherent in the raw material with which the film-maker must work: such political logic will then not manifest itself as an overt political message, nor will it transform the film into an unambiguous political statement. But it will certainly make for the emergence of profound formal contradictions to which the public cannot but be sensitive, whether or not it yet possesses the conceptual instruments to understand what those contradictions mean.

Now it would seem that I've made things much too easy for myself by choosing to illustrate this process with a film, *Dog Day Afternoon,* that seems to have a great deal more overt political content than we would normally expect to find in a Hollywood production. In fact, we have only to think of the CIA-type espionage thriller, or the police show on television, to realise that overt political content of that kind is so omnipresent as to be inescapable in the entertainment industry. It is indeed as though the major legacy of the sixties was to furnish a whole new code, a whole new set of thematics—that of the political—with which, after that of sex, the entertainment industry could reinvest its tired paradigms, without any danger to itself or to the system; and we should take into account the possibility that it is the overtly political or contestatory parts of *Dog Day Afternoon* which will prove the least functional from a class point of view.

But before this becomes clear, we will want to start a little further back, with the anecdotal material in which the film takes its point of departure. The event itself is not so far removed in time that we cannot remember it for what it was; or more precisely, remember what the media found interesting about it, what made it worthwhile transforming into a feature story in its own right an otherwise banal bank robbery and siege with hostages, of the type with which countless newscasts and grade B movies have familiarised us in the past. Three novelties distinguished the robbery on which *Dog Day Afternoon* was to be based: first, the crowd sympathised with the bank robbery, booing at the police and evoking the then still very recent Attica prison massacre; second, the bank robber turned out to be a homosexual, or, more properly, to have gone through a homosexual marriage ceremony with a trans-sexual, and indeed later claimed to have committed the robbery in order to finance his partner's sex-change operation; finally, the television cameras and on-the-spot telephone interviews were so heavily involved in the day-long negotiations as to give a striking new twist to the concept of the 'media event': and to this feature, we should probably add the final subnovelty that the robbery took place on the climactic day of the Nixon–Agnew nominating convention (August 22, 1972).[2] A work of art that had been able to do justice to any one of these peculiarities by itself would have been assured of an unavoidable political resonance. The Sidney Lumet film, 'faithfully' incorporating all three, ended up having very little; and it is probably too easy, although not incorrect, to say that they cancel each other out by projecting a set of circumstances too unique to have any generalisable meaning, literature, as Aristotle tells us, being more philosophical than history in that it shows us what can happen, where the latter only shows us what did happen. Indeed, I believe a case can be made for the ideological function of overexposure in commercial culture: it seems to me just possible that the repeated stereotypical use of otherwise disturbing and alien phenomena in our present social conjuncture—political militancy, student revolt, resistance to and hatred of authority—has an effect of containment for the system as a whole. To name something is to domesticate it, to refer to it repeatedly is to persuade a fearful and beleaguered middle-class public that all of that is part of a known and catalogued world and thus somehow in order. Such a process would then be the equivalent, in the realm of everyday social life, of that co-operation by the media, that exhaustion of novel raw material, which is one of our principal techniques for defusing threatening and subversive ideas. If something like this is the case, then clearly *Dog Day Afternoon,* with its wealth of anti-social detail, may be thought to work overtime in the reprocessing of alarming social materials for the reassurance of suburban movie-goers.

Turning to those raw materials themselves, it is worth taking a passing glance at what the film did not become. Ours is, after all, a period and a public with an appetite for the documentary fact, for the anecdotal, the *vécu,* the *fait divers,* the true story in all its sociological freshness and unpredictability. Not to go as far back as the abortive yet symptomatic 'nonfiction novel'', nor even the undoubted primacy of non-fiction over fiction on the bestseller lists, we find particularly striking embodiment of this interest in a whole series of recent experiments on American television with the fictional documentary: narrative reports, played by actors, of sensational crimes like the Manson murders, or of otherwise curious *fait divers* like a flying saucer sighting by a bi-racial couple, President Truman's meeting with General MacArthur, or an ostracism at West Point. We would have understood a great deal if we could explain why *Dog Day Afternoon* fails to have anything in common with these fictional documentaries, which are far and away among the best things achieved by American television. I believe that the latter's success is at least in part to be attributed to the distance which such pseudo-documentaries maintain between the real-life fact and its representation. The more powerful of them preserve the existence of a secret in their historical content, and, at the same time that they purport to give us a version of the events, exacerbate our certainty that we will never know for sure what really did happen. This structural disjunction between form and content clearly projects a very different aesthetic strategy from those of classical Griersonian documentary, of Italian neo-realism, or of *Kino-pravda* or *ciné vérité,* to name only three of the older attempts to solve the problem of the relationship between movies and fact or event, attempts which now seem closed to us.

But it is equally clear that *Dog Day Afternoon* has none of the strengths of any of these strategies and does not even try for them: the juxtaposition, however, has the benefit of dramatising and reinforcing all of the recent French critiques of representation as an ideological category. What sharply differentiates the Lumet film from any of the television pseudo-documentaries just mentioned is precisely, if you will, its unity of form and content: we are made secure in the illusion that the camera is witnessing everything exactly as it happened and that what it sees is all there is. The camera is absolute presence and absolute truth: thus, the aesthetic of representation collapses the density of the historical event, and flattens it back out into fiction. The older values of realism, living on in commercial film, empty the anecdotal raw material of its interest and vitality; while, paradoxically, the patently degraded techniques of television narrative, irremediably condemned by their application to and juxtaposition with advertising, end up preserving the truth of the event by underscoring their own distance from it. Meanwhile, it is the very splendour of Al Pacino's virtuoso performance which marks it off from any possibility of *verismo* and irreparably condemns it to remain a Hollywood product: the star system is fundamentally, structurally, irreconcilable with neo-realism. This is indeed the basic paradox I want to argue and to deepen in the following remarks: that it is what is good about the film that is bad about it, and what is bad about it that is on the contrary rather good in many ways; that everything which makes it a first-rate piece of film-making, with bravura actors, must render it suspect from another point of view, while its historical originality is to be sought in places that must seem accidental with respect to its intrinsic qualities. Yet this is not a state of things that could have been remedied by careful planning: it is not a mismatch that could have been avoided had the producers divided up their material properly, and planned a neo-realist documentary on the one hand, and a glossy robbery film on the other. Rather, we have to do here with that unresolvable, profoundly symptomatic thing which is called a contradiction, and which we may expect, if properly managed and interrogated, to raise some basic issues about the direction of contemporary culture and contemporary social reality.

What is clear from the outset is that *Dog Day Afternoon* is an ambiguous product at the level of reception; more than that, that the film is so structured that it can be focused in two quite distinct ways, which seem to yield two quite distinct narrative experiences. I've promised to show that one of these narratives suggests an evolution, or at least a transformation, in the figurable class articulation of everyday life. But this is certainly not the most obvious or the most accessible reading of the film, which initially seems to inscribe itself in a very different and for us today surely much more regressive tradition. This is what we may loosely call, in the nontechnical sense, the existential paradigm. In its middle-brow media usage in current American culture, this term has come to designate things like *Catch-22* or some of Norman Mailer's novels. Existentialism here means neither Heidegger nor Sartre, but rather the anti-hero of the sad sack, Saul Bellow–type, and a kind of self-pitying vision of alienation (also meant in its media rather than its technical sense), frustration, and above all–yesterday's all-American concept–the 'inability to communicate'. Whether this particular narrative paradigm be the cause or the effect of the systematic psychologisation and privatisation of the ideology of the fifties and early sixties, it is clear that things change more slowly in the cultural and narrative realm than they do in the more purely ideological one, so that writers and film-makers tend to fall back on paradigms such as this who would otherwise have no trouble recognising a dated, no longer fashionable idea. Meanwhile, this 'unequal development' of the narrative paradigms through which we explain daily life to ourselves is then redoubled by another trend in contemporary consumerism, namely the return to the fifties, the nostalgia fad or what the French call *la mode rétro,* in other words the deliberate substitution of the pastiche and imitation of past styles for the impossible invention of adequate contemporary or post-contemporary ones (as in a novel like E. L. Doctorow's *Ragtime*). Thus, as if it were not enough that the political and collective urgencies of the sixties consigned the anti-hero and the anti-novel to the ash-can of history, we now find them being revived as a paradoxical sign of the good old days when all we had to worry about were psychological problems, momism, and whether television would ruin American culture. I would argue, for instance, not only that *One Flew Over the Cuckoo's Nest* is a typical fifties nostalgia film, which revives all of the stereotypical protests of that bygone individualistic era, but also that, virtually a Czech film in disguise, it reduplicates that particular time lag by another, more characteristically Central European form of 'unequal development'.

Method acting was the working out of the ideology of the anti-hero in that relatively more concrete realm of theatrical style, voice, gesture, which borders on the behavioural stances and gestural idiom, the interpersonal languages, of everyday life, where it is indeed the stylisation and effect of elements already present in the parts of the American community, and also the cause and model of newer kinds of behaviour that adapt it to the street and to the real world. Here for the first time perhaps we can understand concretely how what is best about *Dog Day Afternoon* is also what is least good about it: for Al Pacino's performance by its very brilliance thrusts the film further and further back into the antiquated paradigm of the anti-hero and the method actor. Indeed, the internal contradiction of his performance is even more striking than that: for the anti-hero, as suggested, was predicated on non-communication and inarticulacy, from Flaubert's Frédéric Moreau and Kafka's K all the way to Bellow, Bernard Malamud, Philip Roth, and the rest; and the agonies and exhalations of method acting were perfectly calculated to render this asphyxiation of the spirit that cannot complete its sentence. But in Pacino's second-generation reappropriation of this style something paradoxical happens, namely, that the inarticulate becomes the highest form of expressiveness, the wordless stammer proves voluble, and the agony over uncommunicatability suddenly turns out to be everywhere fluently comprehensible.

At this point, then, something different begins to happen, and Sonny's story ceases to express the pathos of the isolated individual or the existential loner in much the same way that the raw material from which it is drawn—that of marginality or deviancy—has ceased to be thought of as anti-social and has rather become a new social category in its own right. The gesture of revolt and the cry of rage begin to lose their frustration—the expression 'impotent rage' had been a stereotype of American storytelling from William Faulkner, indeed from Frank Norris and Theodore Dreiser, on—and to take on another meaning. Not because of any new political content to be sure: for Sonny's robbery, the politics of marginality, is not much more than part of the wild-cat strikes of contemporary everyday life; but rather simply because the gesture 'projects' and is understood. We mentioned the support of the crowd (both in real life and in the Lumet movie), but that is only the most conventional inscription of this tangible resonance of Sonny's gesture within the film. More significant, it seems to me, is the manifest sympathy of the suburban movie-going audience itself, which from within the tract housing of the *société de consommation* clearly senses the relevance to its own daily life of the re-enactment of this otherwise fairly predictable specimen of urban crime. Unlike the audience of the Bogart films, who had to stand by and watch the outcast mercilessly destroyed by the monolithic and omnipotent institution of Society, this one has witnessed the collapse of the system's legitimacy (and the sapping of the legitimations on which it was based): not only the Vietnam war, least of all Watergate, most significantly surely the experience of inflation itself, which is the privileged phenomenon through which a middle class suddenly comes to an unpleasant consciousness of its own historicity—these are some of the historical reasons for that gradual crumbling of those older Protestant ethic–type values (respect for law and order, for property, and institutions) which allows a middle-class audience to root for Sonny. In the longer run, however, the explanation must be sought in the very logic of the commodity system itself, whose programming ends up liquidating even those ideological values (respect for authority, patriotism, the ideal of the family, obedience to the law) on which the social and political order of the system rests. Thus the ideal consumer—compared to his Protestant ethic ancestors, with their repressive ethics of thrift and work and self-denial—turns out to be a far more doubtful quantity than they were when it comes to fighting foreign wars or honouring your debts or cheating on your income taxes. 'What kind of a crime', Brecht once said, 'is the robbing of a bank, compared to the founding of a bank?' And it is clear that for the citizens of some multinational stage of post-monopoly capitalism, the practical side of daily life is a test of ingenuity and game of wits between the consumer and the giant faceless corporation.

These, then, are the people who understand Sonny's gesture, and whose sympathies are strangely intersected and at least arrested by the whole quite different counter-cultural theme of homosexuality. Yet they have their counterpart within the film, not so much in the street crowd, which is only a chorus-like sign of this implicit public for Sonny's act, as rather in the hostages themselves, the women employees of the branch bank, whose changing attitudes towards Sonny thus become a significant part of what the film has to show us. I would argue that in that second reading of the film I want to suggest, the relationship of form and background reverses itself, and the Sonny character—the hero, as we have seen of a more conventional anti-hero plot—now becomes a simple pretext for the emergence and new visibility of something more fundamental in what might otherwise simply seem the background itself. This more fundamental thing is the sociological equivalent of that wholesale liquidation of older ideological values by consumer society on which we have already commented: but here it takes the more tangible form of the ghettoisation of the older urban neighbourhoods. The phenomenon is not an historically extremely recent one; nor is it unknown either to sociological journalism or to literature itself, where in one sense its representations may be said to go all the way back to Balzac's description of the corrosive and solvent effect of the money economy and the market system on the sleepy *Gemeinschaften* of the older provincial towns.

What is less well understood is the degree to which this process, which in the United States was significantly accelerated after the end of World War II and, contemporaneous with the introduction of television and the launching of the Cold War, was the result of deliberate political decisions that can be identified and dated. The post-war federal highway programme and the momentum given to the construction of individual family dwellings by veterans' housing bills are essential components in the new corporate strategy. According to Stanley Aronowitz in his book *False Promises:*

The 1949 Housing Act introduced the idea of federal assistance for private development of the centre cities, an approach to urban renewal vigorously pushed by the General Electric Company, large banks and insurance companies. The centre cities were not to be the site of housing redevelopment for working class people. . . . These political and economic decisions effectively determined the pattern of individual and residential development for the next generation. The white working class was fated for dispersal; the centre cities were to be reserved for the very poor and the relatively affluent. In the circumstances, durable goods purchases—cars, washing machines, one-family houses—began to absorb an increasing proportion of workers' incomes and had an enormous impact on work patterns.[3]

We may add that this vision of the future was first systematically tried out on Newark, New Jersey, which may thus fairly lay claim to something of the ominous and legendary quality which surrounds the names of the targets of World War II strategic bombing experiments.

Now my purpose in summarising these facts was not only informational, although I believe we need never apologise for anything which helps to put an only too frequently ahistorical experience of the present into something like historical perspective; rather, I want to underscore a fundamental distortion in the way in which we have traditionally tended to deplore such developments in contemporary American society as the destruction of the inner city and the rise of shopping centre culture. On the whole I think it would be fair to say that we have thought of these developments as inevitable results of a logic of consumer society which neither individuals nor politicians could do very much to reverse; even radicals have been content to stress the continuity between the present-day atomisation of the older communities and social groups and Marx's analysis of the destructive effects of classical capitalism, from the enclosure stage all the way to the emergence of the factory system. What is new today, what can be sensed in the excerpt from *False Promises* quoted above just as much as in *Dog Day Afternoon* itself, is the dawning realisation that someone was responsible for all that, that such momentous social transformations were not merely part of the developing logic of the system—although they are certainly that too—but also and above all the consequences of the decisions of powerful and strategically placed individuals and groups. Yet the re-emergence of these groups—the renewed possibility of once again catching sight of what Lukács would have called the subject of that history of which the rest of us are still only just the objects—this is not to be understood as the result of increased information on our part, nor as the consequence of a more polemic and sceptical history-writing on the part of so-called revisionist historians; rather, our very possibility of rewriting history in this way is itself to be understood as the function of a fundamental change in the historical situation itself, and of the power and class relations that underlie it.

Before we say what the change is, however, we want to remember how vividly *Dog Day Afternoon* explores the space which is the result of these historical changes, the ghettoised neighbourhood with its decaying small businesses gradually being replaced by parking lots or chain stores. It is no accident indeed that the principal circuit of communication of the film passes between the mom-and-pop store in which the police have set up their headquarters, and the branch bank—the real-life original was appropriately enough a branch of Chase Manhattan—in which Sonny is holding his hostages. Thus it is possible for the truth of recent urban history to be expressed within the framework of the bank scenes themselves: it is enough to note, first, that everyone in the branch is nothing but a salaried employee of an invisible multinational empire, and then, as the film goes on, that the work in this already peripheral and decentred, fundamentally colonised, space is done by those doubly second-class and underpayable beings who are women, and whose structurally marginal situation is thus not without analogy to Sonny's own, or at least reflects it in much the same way that a Third World proletariat might reflect minority violence and crime in the First. One of the more realistic things about recent American commercial culture, indeed, has been its willingness to recognise and to represent at least in passing the strange coexistence and superposition in the America of today of social worlds as rigidly divided from each other as in a caste system, a kind of post-Bowery and/or permanent Third World existence at the heart of the First World itself.

Yet this kind of perception does not in itself constitute that renewed class consciousness we evoked at the beginning of this article, but as such merely provides the material for a rhetoric of marginality, for a new and more virulent populism. The Marxian conception of class, indeed, must be distinguished from the academic bourgeois sociological one above all by its emphasis on relationality. For academic sociology, the social classes are understood in isolation from each other, on the order of sub-cultures or independent group 'life styles': the frequently used term 'stratum' effectively conveys this view of independent social units, which implies in turn that each can be studied separately, without reference to one another, by some researcher who goes out into the field. So we can have monographs on the ideology of the professional stratum, on the political apathy of the secretarial stratum, and so forth. For Marxism, however, these empirical observations do not yet penetrate to the structural reality of the class system, which it sees as being essentially dichotomous, at least in that latest and last social formation of prehistory which is capitalism: 'The whole of society', a famous sentence of the *Communist Manifesto* tells us, 'is increasingly split into two great hostile camps, into two great classes directly confronting one another: the bourgeoisie and the proletariat.' To which we must only add, (1) that this underlying starkly dichotomous class antagonism only becomes fully visible empirically in times of absolute crisis and polarisation, that is to say, in particular, at the moment of social revolution itself; and (2) that in a henceforth world-wide class system the oppositions in question are evidently a good deal more complicated and difficult to reconstruct than they were within the more representational, or figurable, framework of the older nation state.

This said, it is evident that a Marxian theory of classes involves the restructuring of the fragmentary and unrelated data of empirical bourgeois sociology in a holistic way: in terms, Lukács would say, of the social *totality,* or, as his antagonist

Althusser would have it, of a 'pre-given complex hierarchical structure of dominant and subordinate elements'. In either case, the random sub-groupings of academic sociology would find their place in determinate, although sometimes ambivalent, structural positions with respect to the dichotomous opposition of the two fundamental social classes themselves, about which innovative recent work— I'm thinking, for the bourgeoisie, of Sartre's Flaubert trilogy; for the proletariat, of the Aronowitz book already quoted from—has demonstrated the mechanisms by which each class defines itself in terms of the other and constitutes a virtual anti-class with respect to the other, and this, from overt ideological values all the way down to the most apparently non-political, 'merely' cultural features of everyday life.

The difference between the Marxian view of structurally dichotomous classes and the academic sociological picture of independent strata is however more than a merely intellectual one: once again, consciousness of social reality, or on the other hand the repression of the awareness of such reality, is itself ' determined by social being' in Marx's phrase and is therefore a function of the social and historical situation. Thus a remarkable sociological investigation has confirmed the view that these two approaches to the social classes—the academic and the Marxist—are themselves class conditioned and reflect the structural perspectives of the two fundamental class positions themselves. It is those on the higher rungs of the social ladder who tend to formulate their view of the social order, looking down at it, as separate strata; while those on the bottom looking up tend to map their social experience in terms of the stark opposition of 'them' and 'us'.[4]

But if this is so, then the representation of victimised classes in isolation— whether in the person of Sonny himself as a marginal, or the bank's clerical workers as an exploited group—is not enough to constitute a class system, let alone to precipitate the beginning of a consciousness of class in its viewing public. Nor are the repeated references to the absent bank management sufficient to transform the situation into a genuine class relationship, since this term does not find concrete representation—or *figuration,* to return to our earlier term—within the filmic narrative itself. Yet such representation is present in *Dog Day Afternoon,* and it is this unexpected appearance, in a part of the film where one would not normally look at it, that constitutes its greatest interest in the present context, our possibility of focusing it being as we have argued directly proportional to our ability to let go of the Sonny story and to relinquish those older narrative habits that programme us to follow the individual experiences of a hero or an anti-hero, rather than the explosion of the text and the operation of meaning in other, random narrative fragments.

If we can do this—and we have begun to do so when we are willing to reverse the robbery itself, and read Sonny's role as that of a mere pretext for the revelation of that colonised space which is the branch bank, with its peripheralised or marginalised work force—then what slowly comes to occupy the film's centre of gravity is the action outside the bank itself, and in particular the struggle for precedence between the local police and the FBI officials. Now there are various ways of explaining this shift of focus, none of them wrong: for one thing, we can observe that, once Sonny has been effectively barricaded inside the bank, he can no longer initiate events, the centre of gravity of the narrative as such then passing to the outside. More pertinently still, since the operative paradox of the film—underscored by Al Pacino's acting—is the fundamental likeability of Sonny, this external displacement of the acting can be understood as the narrative attempt to generate an authority figure who can deal directly with him without succumbing to his charm. But this is not just a matter of narrative machinery: properly interrogated, we can understand it as an ideological problem as well, as part of the internal needs of present-day legitimation, as a narrative answer to the fundamental question: how to imagine authority today, how to conceive imaginatively—that is in non-abstract, non-conceptual form—of a principle of authority that can express the essential impersonality and post-individualistic structure of the power structure of our society while still operating among real people, in the tangible necessities of daily life and individual situations of repression?

It is clear that the figure of the FBI agent represents a narrative solution to this ideological contradiction, and the nature of the solution is underscored by the characterological styles of the FBI agent and the local police chief, whose impotent rages and passionate incompetence are there, not so much to humanise him, as rather to set off the cool and technocratic expertise of his rival. In one sense of course this contrast is what has nowadays come to be called an intertextual one. This is not really the encounter of two characters, who represent two 'individuals', but rather the encounter of two narrative paradigms, indeed, of two narrative stereotypes: the clean-cut Efrem Zimbalist–type FBI agents, with their fifties haircuts, and the earthy urban cop whose television embodiments are so multiple as to be embarrassing—*The FBI Story* meets *Dragnet* or *Kojak*! Yet one of the most effective things in the film, and the most haunting impression left by *Dog Day Afternoon* in the area of performance, is surely not so much the febrile heroics of Al Pacino as rather their stylistic opposite, the starkly bland and emotionless, expressionless coolness of the FBI man himself. This gazing face, behind which decision-making is reduced to (or developed into) pure technique, yet whose judgments and assessments are utterly inaccessible to spectators either within or without the filmic frame, is one of the most alarming achievements of recent American movie-making, and may be said to embody something like the truth of a rather different but equally actual genre, the espionage thriller, where it has tended to remain obfuscated by the cumbersome theological apparatus of a dialectic of Good and Evil.

Meanwhile, the more existential and private-tragic visions of this kind of figure—I'm thinking of the lawman in *Bonnie and Clyde*—project a nemesis which is still motivated by personal vindictiveness, so that the process of tracking the victim down retains a kind of passion of a still recognisable human type. Arthur Penn's more recent *Missouri Breaks* then tried to make an advance on this personalised dramatisation of the implacability of social institutions by endowing its enforcer with a generalised paranoia; but it is not really much of an improvement and the vision remains locked in the pathos of a self-pitying and individualistic vision of history.

In *Dog Day Afternoon,* however, the organisation man is neither vindictive nor paranoid; he is in this sense quite beyond the good and evil of conventional melodrama, and inaccessible to any of the psychologising stereotypes that are indulged in most of the commercial representations of the power of institutions; his anonymous features mark a chilling and unexpected insertion of the real into the otherwise relatively predictable framework of the fiction film—and this, not, as we have pointed out earlier, by traditional documentary of montage techniques, but rather through a kind of dialectic of connotations on the level of the style of acting, a kind of silence or charged absence in a sign-system in which the other modes of performance have programmed us for a different kind of expressiveness.

Now the basic contrast, that between the police chief and the FBI agent, dramatises a social and historical change which was once an important theme of our literature but to which we have today become so accustomed as to have lost our sensitivity to it: in their very different ways, the novels of John O'Hara and the sociological investigations of C. Wright Mills documented a gradual but irreversible erosion of local and state-wide power structures and leadership or authority networks by national, and in our own time multinational, ones. Think of the social hierarchy of Gibbsville coming into disillusioning contact with the new wealth and the new political hierarchies of the New Deal era; think—even more relevantly for our present purposes—of the crisis of figurability implied by this shift of power from the face-to-face experiences of small-town daily life in the older communities to the abstraction of nation-wide power (a crisis already suggested by the literary representations of 'politics' as a specialised theme in itself).

The police lieutenant thus comes to incarnate the very helplessness and impotent agitation of the local power structure, and with this inflection of our reading, with this interpretive operation, the whole allegorical structure of *Dog Day Afternoon* suddenly emerges in the light of day. The FBI agent—now that we have succeeded in identifying what he supersedes—comes to occupy the place of that immense and decentralised power network which marks the present multinational stage of monopoly capitalism. The very absence in his features becomes a sign and an expression of the presence/absence of corporate power in our daily lives, all-shaping and omnipotent and yet rarely accessible in figurable terms, that is to say, in the representable form of individual actors or agents. The FBI man is thus the structural opposite of the secretarial staff of the branch bank: the latter present in all their existential individuality, but inessential and utterly marginalised, the former so depersonalised as to be little more than a marker—in the empirical world of everyday life, of *faits divers* and newspaper articles—of the place of ultimate power and control.

Yet with even this shadowy embodiment of the forces of those multinational corporate structures that are the subjects of present-day world history, the possibility of genuine figuration, and with it the possibility of a kind of beginning of an adequate class consciousness itself, is given. Now the class structure of the film becomes articulated in three tiers: the first, that newly atomised petty bourgeoisie of the cities whose 'proletarianisation' and marginalisation is expressed both by the women employees on the one hand, and by the lumpens on the other, Sonny and his accomplice, but also the crowd itself, an embodiment of the logic of marginality that runs all the way from the 'normal' deviancies of homosexuality and petty crime to the pathologies of Sal's paranoia and Ernie's trans-sexuality. On a second level, the impotent power structures of the local neighbourhoods, which represent something like the national bourgeoisies for the Third World, colonised and gutted of their older content, left with little more than the hollow shells and external trappings of authority and decision making. Finally, of course, that multinational capitalism into which the older ruling classes of our world have evolved, and whose primacy is inscribed in the spatial trajectory of the film itself as it moves from the ghettoised squalour of the bank interior to that eerie and impersonal science fiction landscape of the airport finale: a corporate space without inhabitants, utterly technologised and functional, a place beyond city and country alike—collective, yet without people, automated and computerised, yet without any of that older utopian or dystopian clamour, without any of those still distinctive qualities that characterised the then still 'modern' and streamlined futuristic vision of the corporate future in our own recent past. Here—as in the blank style of acting of the FBI agents—the film makes a powerful nonconceptual point by destroying its own intrinsic effects and cancelling an already powerful, yet conventional, filmic and performative language.

Two final observations about this work, the one about its ultimate aesthetic and political effects, the other about its historical conditions of possibility. Let us take the second problem first: we have here repeatedly stressed the dependence of a narrative figuration of class consciousness on the historical situation. We have stressed both the dichotomous nature of the class structures, and the dependence of class consciousness itself on the logic of the social and historical conjuncture. Marx's dictum, that consciousness is determined by social being, holds for class consciousness itself no less than for any other form. We must now therefore try to make good our claim, and say why, if some new and renewed possibility of class consciousness seems at least faintly detectable, this should be the case now and today rather than ten or twenty years ago. But the answer to this question can be given concisely and decisively; it is implicit in the very expression 'multinational corporation', which—as great a misnomer as it may be (since all of them are in reality expressions of American capitalism)—would not have been invented had not something new suddenly emerged which seemed to demand a new name for itself. It seems to be a fact that after the failure of the Vietnam war, the so-called multinational corporations—what used to be called the 'ruling classes' or later on the 'power elite' of monopoly capitalism—have once again emerged in public from the wings of history to advance their own interests. The failure of the war, Richard Barnet and Ronald Muller argue in their book *Global Reach*,

. . . has meant that the advancement of world capitalist revolution now depends more on the initiative of corporations and less on governments. The increasingly political pretensions of the global corporation are thus unavoidable but they inevitably mean more public exposure, and exposure carries with it the risk of increased hostility.[5]

But in our terms, the psychological language of the authors of *Global Reach* may be translated as 'class consciousness', and with this new visibility capitalism becomes objectified and dramatised as an actor and as a subject of history with an allegorical intensity and simplicity that had not been the case since the 1930's.

Now a final word about the political implications of the film itself and the complexities of the kind of allegorical structure we have imputed to it. Can *Dog Day Afternoon* be said to be a political film? Surely not, since the class system we have been talking about is merely implicit in it, and can just as easily be ignored or repressed by its viewers as brought to consciousness. What we have been describing is at best something pre-political, the gradual rearticulation of the raw material of a film of this kind in terms and relationships which are once again, after the anti-political and privatising 'existential' paradigms of the forties and fifties, recognisably those of class.

Yet we should also understand that the use of such material is much more complicated and problematical than the terminology of representation would suggest. Indeed, in the process by which class structure finds expression in the triangular relationship within the film between Sonny, the police chief and the FBI man, we have left out an essential step. For the whole qualitative and dialectical inequality of this relationship is mediated by the star system itself, and in that sense—far more adequately than in its overt thematics of the media exploitation of Sonny's hold-up—the film can be said to be about itself. Indeed we read each of the major actors in terms of his distance from the star system: Sonny's relationship to Maretti is that of superstar to character actor (Charles Durning), and our reading of this particular narrative is not a direct passage from one character or *actant* to another, but passes through the mediation of our identification and decoding of the actors' status as such. Even more interesting and complex than this is our decoding of the FBI agent, whose anonymity in the filmic narrative is expressed very precisely through his anonymity within the framework of the Hollywood star system. The face is blank and unreadable precisely because the actor is himself unidentifiable. In fact, of course, it is only within the coding of the Hollywood system that he is unfamiliar, for the actor in question (James Broderick), in another world, is a permanent feature of a durable and well-known television series, *Family*. But the point is precisely that in this respect television and its system of references is another world; not merely that the television actor becomes an unknown in a Hollywood production, but even more, that television comes itself to figure, with respect to Hollywood films, that new and impersonal multinational system which is coming to supersede the more individualistic one of an older national capitalism and an older commodity culture. Thus, the external, extrinsic sociological fact or system of realities finds itself inscribed within internal intrinsic experience of the film in what Sartre in a suggestive and too-little known concept in his *Psychology of Imagination* calls the analogon:[6] that structural nexus in our reading or viewing experience, in our operations of decoding or aesthetic reception, which can then do double duty and stand as the substitute and the representative within the aesthetic object of a phenomenon on the outside which cannot in the very nature of things be 'rendered' directly. This complex of intra- and extra-aesthetic relationships might then schematically be represented as in Figure 1. Here we find an ultimate formal confirmation of our initial hypothesis, that what is bad about the film is what is best about it, and that

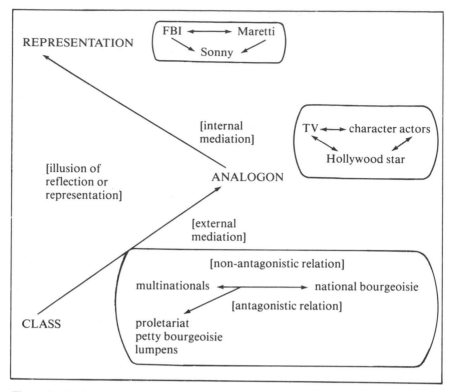

Figure 1. Analogon: the relationships of *Dog Day Afternoon*.

the work is a paradoxical realisation in which qualities and defects form an inextricable dialectical unity. For it is ultimately the star system itself—that commodity phenomenon most stubbornly irreconcilable with any documentary or *ciné vérité* of exploration of the real—which is thus responsible for even that limited authenticity which *Dog Day Afternoon* is able to achieve.

At this point I should formulate the basic presupposition of the present study. This is that there is a radical incompatibility between the possibilities of an older national language or culture (which is still the framework in which literature is being produced today) and the transnational, world-wide organisation of the economic infrastructure of contemporary capitalism. The result of this contradiction is a situation in which the truth of our social life as a whole—in Lukács's terms, as a totality—is increasingly irreconcilable with the possibilities of aesthetic expression or articulation available to us; a situation about which it can be asserted that if we can make a work of art from our experience, if we can give experience the form of a story that can be told, then it is no longer true, even as individual experience; and if we can grasp the truth about our world as a totality, then we may find some purely conceptual expression for us, but we will no longer be able to maintain an imaginative relationship to it. In current psychoanalytic terminology, we will thus be unable to insert ourselves, as individual subjects, into an ever more massive and impersonal or transpersonal reality outside ourselves. This is the perspective in which it becomes a matter of more than mere intellectual curiosity to interrogate the artistic production of our own time for signs of some new, so far only dimly conceivable, collective forms which may be expected to replace the older individualistic ones (those either of conventional realism or of a now conventionalised modernism); and it is also the perspective in which an indecisive aesthetic and cultural phenomenon like *Dog Day Afternoon* takes on the values of a revealing symptom.

Notes

This article first appeared in a special issue of *College English* 38, no. 8 (April 1977) on "Mass Culture, Political Consciousness, and English Studies." The version here contains a few minor amendments.

1. My rendering of Freud's term *Darstellbarkeit* in *The Interpretation of Dreams,* Chap. VI, especially section d.

2. For a useful survey of the newspaper coverage of the Wojtowicz robbery, see Eric Holm, "Dog Day Aftertaste," *Jump Cut,* no. 10–11 (June 1976), pp. 3–4.

3. New York: McGraw-Hill, 1973, p. 383.

4. Ralf Dahrendorf, *Class and Class Conflict in Industrial Society* (Stanford, Calif.: Stanford University Press, 1959), pp. 280–89.

5. See Richard J. Barnet and Ronald E. Muller, *Global Reach* (New York: Simon & Schuster, 1974), p. 68.

6. Jean-Paul Sartre, *The Psychology of Imagination* (New York: Washington Square Press, 1968), pp. 21–71; analogon here translated as 'the analogue'.

FURTHER READINGS

As an additional aid the following suggestions for further readings are offered. They are selective rather than exhaustive and drawn more heavily from published articles than from books.

HISTORICAL CRITICISM

Abel, Richard, *French Cinema: The First Wave, 1915–1929* (Princeton, N.J.: Princeton University Press, 1984).

Altman, Charles, "Towards a Historiography of American Film," *Cinema Journal* 16, no. 2 (1977): 1–25.

Baxter, Peter, "On the History and Ideology of Film Lighting," *Screen* 16, no. 3 (Autumn 1975): 83–106.

Bordwell, David, "Our Dream-Cinema: Western Historiography and the Japanese Film," *Film Reader,* no. 4 (1975): 45–62.

Burton, Julianne, "The Hour of the Embers: On the Current Situation of Latin American Cinema," *Film Quarterly* 30, no. 1 (Fall 1976): 33–44.

Buscombe, Edward, "Introduction: Metahistory of Film," *Film Reader,* no. 4 (1979): 11–15.

Campbell, Russell, "Radical Cinema in the 30s," *Jump Cut,* no. 14 (1977): 23–25.

Cannella, Mario, "Ideology and Aesthetic Hypotheses in the Criticism of Neo-Realism," *Screen* 14, no. 4 (Winter 1973–1974): 5–60.

Comolli, Jean-Louis, "Historical Fiction: A Body Too Much," *Screen* 19, no. 2 (Summer 1978): 41–53.

Eckert, Charles, "Shirley Temple and the House of Rockefeller," *Jump Cut,* no. 2 (1974): 1, 17–20.

———, "The Carol Lombard in Macy's Window," *Quarterly Review of Film Studies* 3, no. 1 (Winter 1978): 1–21.

Gomery, Douglas, "The Picture Palace: Economic Sense or Hollywood Nonsense," *Quarterly Review of Film Studies* 3, no. 1 (Winter 1978): 23–36.

———, "Hollywood, the National Recovery Administration, and the Question of Monopoly Power," *Journal of the University Film Association* 31, no. 2 (Spring 1979): 47–52.

————, *The Hollywood Studio System* (London: Macmillan, 1985).

Gomery, Douglas, and Robert Allen, *Film History: Theory and Practice* (New York: Random House, 1985).

Gomery, Douglas, and Janet Staiger, "The History of World Cinema: Models for Economic Analysis," *Film Reader,* no. 4 (1979): 35–44.

Harvey, Sylvia, *May '68 and Film Culture* (London: British Film Institute, 1978).

Kindem, Gorham A., "Hollywood's Conversion to Color: the Technological, Economic, and Aesthetic Factors," *Journal of the University Film Association* 31, no. 2 (Spring 1979): 29–36.

Musser, Charles, "The Eden Musée in 1898: The Exhibitor as Creator," *Film and History* 11, no. 4 (December 1981): 73–83.

Nichols, Bill, "Whatever Happened to Saturday Night?" *Queen's Quarterly* 86, no. 3 (Fall 1979): 383–408 (on changes in studio structure and alternatives to Hollywood).

Salt, Barry, "Film Style and Technology in the Forties," *Film Quarterly* 30, no. 1 (Fall 1976): 46–57.

————, "Film Style and Technology in the Thirties," *Film Quarterly* 31, no. 1 (Fall 1977): 19–32.

Staiger, Janet, "Dividing Labor for Production Control: Thomas Ince and the Rise of the Studio System," *Cinema Journal* 18, no. 2 (Spring 1979): 16–25.

Stam, Robert, and Randal Johnson, "Beyond Cinema Novo," *Jump Cut,* no. 21 (1979): 13–18.

Straw, Will, "The Myth of Total Cinema," *Cine-Tracts* 3, no. 1 (Winter 1980): 8–16.

Thomas, Sari, ed., *Film Culture* (Metuchen, N.J.: Scarecrow Press, 1982).

Thompson, Kristin, and David Bordwell, "Linearity, Materialism, and the Study of Early American Cinema," *Wide Angle* 5, no. 3 (1983): 4–15.

Thompson, Kristin, David Bordwell, and Janet Staiger, *The Classic Hollywood Cinema: Film Style and Modes of Production to 1960* (New York: Columbia University Press, 1985).

Tribe, Keith, "History and the Production of Memories," *Screen* 18, no. 4 (Winter 1977–1978): 41–53.

GENRE CRITICISM

Altman, Charles, "The American Film Musical," *Wide Angle* 2, no. 2 (1978): 10–12.

————, "Towards a Theory of Genre Film," in *Film: Historical-Theoretical Speculations* (Pleasantville, N.Y.: Redgrave Press, 1979).

————, *Genre: The Musical* (London: Routledge & Kegan Paul, 1981).

Bordwell, David, "The Art Cinema as a Mode of Film Practice," *Film Criticism* 4, no. 1 (Fall 1979): 56–64.

Carroll, Noël, "Nightmare and the Horror Film: The Symbolic Biology of Fantastic Beings," *Film Quarterly* 29, no. 3 (Spring 1981): 16–25.

Cunningham, Stuart, "The 'Force-Field' of Melodrama," *Quarterly Review of Film Studies* 6, no. 4 (Fall 1981): 347–64.

Fell, John, "Motive, Mischief, and Melodrama: The State of Film Narrative in 1907," *Film Quarterly* 33, no. 3 (Spring 1980): 30–37.

Feuer, Jane, "The Self-Reflexive Musical and the Myth of Entertainment," *Quarterly Review of Film Studies* 2, no. 3 (August 1977): 313–25.

———, "Hollywood Musicals: Mass Art as Folk Art," *Jump Cut*, no. 23 (1980): 23–25.

———, *The Hollywood Musical* (Bloomington: Indiana University Press, 1982).

Film Criticism 6, no. 1 (Fall 1982), issue on horror and fantasy.

Henderson, Brian, "Romantic Comedy Today: Semi-Tough or Impossible?" *Film Quarterly* 31, no. 4 (Summer 1978): 11–23.

Kawin, Bruce, "Me Tarzan, You Junk: Violence, Sexism, and Moral Education in the Paranoia Film," *Take One* 6, no. 4 (March 1978): 29–33.

Kleinhans, Chuck, "Contemporary Working Class Heroes," *Jump Cut*, no. 2 (1974): 11–14.

———, "Types of Audience Response: From Tear-Jerkers to Thought-Provokers," *Jump Cut*, no. 4 (1974): 21–23.

———, "Reading About the Avant-Garde," *Jump Cut*, no. 6 (1975): 21–25.

Kuhn, Annette, "The Camera I: Observations on Documentary," *Screen* 19, no. 2 (Summer 1978): 71–83.

———, "Women's Genres," *Screen* 25, no. 1 (1984): 18–29.

Lesage, Julia, "The Political Aesthetics of the Feminist Documentary Film," *Quarterly Review of Film Studies* 3, no. 4 (Fall 1978): 507–523.

Linton, James, "But It's Only a Movie," *Jump Cut*, no. 17 (1978): 16–19.

Locke, John, "Independent Film, Experimental Film, Avant-Garde Film: A Clarification," *Parachute*, no. 10 (1978): 16–17.

Mulvey, Laura, "Notes on Sirk and Melodrama," *Movie*, no. 25 (Winter 1977–1978): 53–57.

Nichols, Bill, "Revolution and Melodrama," *Cinema* (U.S.) 6, no. 1 (1970): 42–47.

Pollock, Griselda, Geoffrey Nowell-Smith, and Stephen Heath, "Dossier on Melodrama," *Screen* 18, no. 2 (1977): 105–119.

Rodowick, D. N., "Madness, Authority, and Ideology in the Domestic Melodrama of the 1950s," *The Velvet Light Trap*, no. 19 (1982): 40–45.

Schatz, Thomas, "The Structural Influence: New Directions in Film Genre Study," *Quarterly Review of Film Studies* 2, no. 3 (August 1977): 302–312.

———, *Hollywood Genres: Formulas, Filmmaking, and the Studio System* (New York: Random House, 1981).

Schrader, Paul, "Notes on Film Noir," *Film Comment* 8, no. 1 (Spring 1972): 8–13.

Sobchack, Vivian, *The Limits of Infinity: The American Science Fiction Film* (New York: A. S. Barnes, 1980).

Wide Angle 4, no. 2 (1980), entire issue on melodrama.

Wollen, Peter, "'Ontology' and 'Materialism' in Film," *Screen* 17, no. 1 (Spring 1976): 7–23 (on the avant-garde).

Wood, Robin, "The American Family Comedy: From *Meet Me in St. Louis* to *The Texas Chainsaw Massacre*," *Wide angle* 3, no. 2 (1979): 5–11.

Wright, Will, *Sixguns and Society: A Structural Study of the Western* (Berkeley: University of California Press, 1975).

Young, Colin, "Observational Cinema," in *Principles of Visual Anthropology,* ed. Paul Hockings (The Hague: Mouton Publishers, 1975), pp. 65–80.

FEMINIST CRITICISM

Artel, Linda, and Susan Wengraf, "Positive Images," *Jump Cut,* no. 18 (1978): 30–31.

Bergstrom, Janet, "Rereading the Work of Claire Johnston," *Camera Obscura,* nos. 3–4 (1979): 21–31.

———, "*Jeanne Dielman, 23 Quai du Commerce—1080 Bruxelles,*" *Camera Obscura,* no. 2 (1977): 115–121 (review and interview).

Burton, Julianne, "Seeing, Being, Being Seen: *Portrait of Teresa,* or Contradictions in Sexual Politics in Contemporary Cuba," *Social Text,* no. 4 (1981): 79–95.

Citron, Michelle, Julia Lesage, Judith Mayne, B. Ruby Rich, and Anna Maria Taylor, "Women and Film: A Discussion of Feminist Aesthetics," *New German Critique,* no. 13 (Winter 1978): 83–107.

Cook, Pam, "'Exploitation' Films and Feminism," *Screen* 17, no. 2 (Summer 1976): 122–27.

Cowie, Elizabeth, "Women, Representation, and the Image," *Screen Education,* no. 23 (Summer 1977): 15–23.

Doane, Mary Ann, "Woman's Stake: Filming the Female Body," *October,* no. 17 (Summer 1981): 23–36.

Erens, Patricia, *Sexual Stratagems: The World of Women in Film* (New York: Horizon Press, 1979).

Feuer, Jane, "Living with Our Pain and Love," *Jump Cut,* no. 23 (1980): 12–13 (on *Daughter Rite*).

Fischer, Lucy, "Image of Woman as Image: The Optical Politics of *Dames,*" *Film Quarterly* 30, no. 1 (Fall 1976): 2–11.

———, "The Lady Vanishes: Women, Magic, and the Movies," *Film Quarterly* 33, no. 1 (Fall 1979): 30–40.

Gaines, Jane, "Women and Representation," *Jump Cut,* no. 29 (1984): 25–27.

Gledhill, Christine, "Recent Developments in Feminist Criticism," *Quarterly Review of Film Studies* 3, no. 4 (1978): 457–93.

Grosz, Stephen, and Bruce McAuley, "*Self-Health* and *Healthcaring,*" *Camera Obscura,* no. 7 (1981): 129–35.

Heresies, no. 16 (1983), entire issue on film and video.

Johnston, Claire, "Re-Thinking Political Cinema," *Jump Cut,* nos. 12–13 (1976): 55–56.

———, "The Subject of Feminist Film Theory Practice," *Screen* 21, no. 2 (Summer 1980): 27–34.

Jump Cut, no. 24–25 (1981), special section on lesbians and film.

Kaplan, E. Ann, "Aspects of British Feminist Film Theory," *Jump Cut,* no. 9 (1975): 9–11.

————, "Investigating the Heroine: Sally Potter's *Thriller*," *Millennium Film Journal*, nos. 10–11 (1981–1982): 115–22.

————, "Theories of Melodrama: A Feminist Perspective," *Women and Performance* 1, no. 1 (1983).

————, *Women and Film: Both Sides of the Camera* (London and New York: Methuen, 1983).

————, ed., *Women in Film Noir* (London: British Film Institute, 1978).

Koch, Gertrude, "Why Women Go to the Movies," trans. Marc Silberman, *Jump Cut*, no. 27 (1983): 51–53.

Kuhn, Annette, *Women's Pictures: Feminism and Cinema* (London: Routledge & Kegan Paul, 1982).

Lauretis, Teresa de, *Alice Doesn't* (Bloomington: Indiana University Press, 1984).

Lyon, Elizabeth, "Discourse and Difference," *Camera Obscura* no. 3–4 (1979): 14–20 (a review of feminist film theory).

Martineau, Barbara, "*The Lacemaker* and *Free Breathing*," *Jump Cut*, no. 19 (1978): 12–14.

Mayne, Judith, "The Woman at the Keyhole: Women's Cinema and Feminist Criticism," *New German Critique*, no. 23 (1981): 27–43.

Mulvey, Laura, "Feminism, Film, and the Avant-Garde," *Framework*, no. 10 (1979): 3–10.

————, "Afterthoughts on 'Visual Pleasure and Narrative Cinema' Inspired by *Duel in the Sun*," *Framework*, nos. 15–17 (1981): 12–15.

Perlmutter, Ruth, "Feminine Absence: A Political Aesthetics in Chantal Akerman's *Jeanne Dielman, 23 Quai du Commerce—1080 Bruxelles*," *Quarterly Review of Film Studies* 4, no. 2 (Spring 1979): 125–33.

Rosenthal, Pam, "Notes on Female Bonding," *Jump Cut*, no. 19 (1978): 3–4.

Silverman, Kaja, "Male Subjectivity and Celestial Satire: *It's a Wonderful Life*," *Framework*, no. 14 (Spring 1981): 16–22.

Waldman, Diane, "There's More to a Positive Image Than Meets the Eye," *Jump Cut*, no. 18 (1978): 31–32.

STRUCTURALIST SEMIOTICS

Barthes, Roland, "The Third Meaning," *Artforum* 11, no. 5 (1973); also in *Image-Music-Text* (New York: Hill and Wang, 1977).

Bellour, Raymond, "The Obvious and the Code," *Screen* 15, no. 4 (Winter 1974–1975): 7–17.

————, "To Analyze, To Segment," *Quarterly Review of Film Studies* 1, no. 3 (1976): 331–45.

————, "Cine-Repetitions," *Screen* 20, no. 2 (Summer 1979): 65–72.

Bergstrom, Janet, "Alternation, Segmentation, Hypnosis: Interview with Raymond Bellour," *Camera Obscura*, nos. 3–4 (1979): 71–103.

Buscombe, Edward, "Ideas of Authorship," *Screen* 14, no. 3 (Autumn 1973): 75–85 and Stephen Heath, "Comment on 'The Idea of Authorship,'" 86–91 (two critiques of auteur theory).

Cook, David, "Some Structural Approaches to Cinema: A Survey of Recent Models," *Cinema Journal* 14, no. 3 (1975): 41–54.

Eckert, Charles, "The English Cine-Structuralists," *Film Comment* 9, no. 3 (1973): 46–51.

Eco, Umberto, "On the Contribution of Film to Semiotics," *Quarterly Review of Film Studies* 2, no. 1 (February 1977): 1–14.

Enclitic 5–6, No. 2/1 (1981–1982), entire issue on textual analysis of films.

Fell, John, "Vladimir Propp in Hollywood," *Film Quarterly* 30, no. 3 (Spring 1977): 19–28.

———, "Structuring Charts and Patterns in Film," *Quarterly Review of Film Studies* 3, no. 3 (1978): 311–88.

Harman, Gilbert, "Semiotics and the Cinema," *Quarterly Review of Film Studies* 2, no. 1 (February 1977): 15–24 (a critical view of the contribution of semiotics).

Heath, Stephen, "Film and System: Terms of Analysis," *Screen* 16, no. 1 (Spring 1975): 7–77; and *Screen* 16, no. 2 (Summer 1975): 91–113.

Jacobs, Lea, "*Now Voyager:* Some Problems of Enunciation and Sexual Difference," *Camera Obscura,* no. 7 (1981): 89–104.

Kinder, Marsha, and Beverle Houston, "Insiders and Outsiders in the Films of Nicholas Roeg," *Quarterly Review of Film Studies* 1, no. 3 (1976): 331–45.

Kuntzel, Thierry, "The Treatment of Ideology in the Textual Analysis of Film," *Screen* 14, no. 3 (Autumn 1973): 43–54.

———, "Le Défilement: A View in Close-Up," *Camera Obscura,* no. 2 (1977): 51–65.

———, "The Film Work 2," *Camera Obscura,* no. 5 (1980): 7–69.

———, "Sight, Insight, and Power: Allegory of the Cave," *Camera Obscura,* no. 6 (1980): 91–110.

MacCabe, Colin, "Realism and the Cinema: Notes on Some Brechtian Theses," *Screen* 15, no. 2 (Summer 1974): 7–27.

Metz, Christian, "Aural Objects," *Yale French Studies,* no. 60 (1980): 24–32.

Pasolini, Pier Paolo, "Pasolini on Semiotics," *Framework,* no. 3 (Spring 1976): 16–21 (three articles that elaborate on "The Cinema of Poetry," included in the first volume of *Movies and Methods*).

Rohdie, Sam, "Metz and Film Semiotics: Opening the Field," *Jump Cut,* no. 7 (1975): 22–24.

———, "Narrative Structures," *Film Reader,* no. 2 (1977): 11–14.

Ropars, Marie-Claire, "The Graphic in Filmic Writing," *Enclitic* 5–6, no. 2/1 (1981–1982) (on *Breathless*).

Suleiman, Susan, "Freedom and Necessity: Narrative Structure in *The Phantom of Liberty,*" *Quarterly Review of Film Studies* 3, no. 3 (Summer 1979): 277–95.

Walsh, Martin, "Political Formations in the Cinema of Jean-Marie Straub," *Jump Cut,* no. 4 (1974): 12–17.

Williams, Linda, "Hiroshima and Marienbad: Metaphor and Metonomy," *Screen* 17, no. 1 (Spring 1976): 34–39.

Wood, Robin, "Old Wine, New Bottles: Structuralism or Humanism?" *Film Comment* 12, no. 6 (1976): 22–25.

PSYCHOANALYTIC SEMIOTICS

Altman, Charles, "Moving Lips: Cinema as Ventriloquism," *Yale French Studies,* no. 60 (1980): 67–79.

Baudry, Jean-Louis, "The Apparatus," *Camera Obscura,* no. 1 (1976): 104–126.

Bellour, Raymond, "Psychosis, Neurosis, Perversion," *Camera Obscura,* nos. 3–4 (1979): 104–134.

Bergstrom, Janet, "Enunciation and Sexual Difference," *Camera Obscura,* nos. 3–4 (1979): 33–69.

Britton, Andrew, "Pursued: A Reply to Paul Willemen," *Framework,* no. 4 (1976): 4–14 (a reply to Willemen's "The Fugitive Subject").

———, "The Ideology of *Screen,*" *Movie,* no. 26 (1978–1979): 2–28.

Browne, Nick, "Griffith's Family Discourse: Griffith and Freud," *Quarterly Review of Film Studies* 6, no. 1 (Winter 1981): 67–80.

Doane, Mary Ann, "Misrecognition and Identity," *Cine-Tracts* 3, no. 3 (Fall 1980): 25–32.

Elsaesser, Thomas, "Primary Identification and the Historical Subject: Fassbinder and Germany," *Cine-Tracts* 3, no. 3 (Fall 1980): 43–52.

Flitterman, Sandy, "Woman, Desire, and the Look: Feminism and the Enunciative Apparatus in Cinema," *Cine-Tracts,* no. 5 (Fall 1978): 63–68.

Heath, Stephen, "On Screen, In Frame: Film and Ideology," *Quarterly Review of Film Studies* 1, no. 3 (August 1976): 251–65.

Lauretis, Teresa de, "Imaging, " *Cine-Tracts* 3, no. 3 (Fall 1980): 3–12.

Leaming, Barbara, "Towards a Psychoanalytic Reading of a Contemporary American Film," *Cine-Tracts* 1, no. 3 (1978): 15–29.

MacCabe, Colin, "Theory and Film: Principles of Realism and Pleasure," *Screen* 17, no. 3 (Autumn 1976): 7–27.

Metz, Christian, "The Imaginary Signifier," *Screen* 16, no. 2 (Summer 1975): 14–76; also in *The Imaginary Signifier* (Bloomington: Indiana University Press, 1982).

Rose, Jacqueline, "Paranoia and the Film System," *Screen* 17, no. 4 (1977): 85–104.

Silverman, Kaja, "Masochism and Subjectivity," *Framework,* no. 12 (1980): 2–9.

———, *The Subject of Semiotics* (New York: Oxford University Press, 1983).

Spellerberg, James, "Technology and Ideology in the Cinema," *Quarterly Review of Film Studies* 2, no. 3 (August 1977): 288–301.

Willemen, Paul, "The Fugitive Subject," in Phil Hardy, ed., *Raoul Walsh* (Colchester, England: Vineyard Press, 1974), pp. 62–91.

Williams, Alan, "Is Sound Recording Like a Language?" *Yale French Studies,* no. 60 (1980): 51–66.

Williams, Linda, "Film Body: An Implantation of Perversions," *Cine-Tracts* 3, no. 4 (Winter 1981): 19–35.

Debate on Psychoanalysis and Feminism
(arranged chronologically)

Brewster, Ben, and Colin MacCabe, "Editorial," *Screen* 15, no. 1 (Spring 1974): 4–10.

Lesage, Julia, "The Human Subject—You, He, or Me? Or, The Case of the Missing Penis," *Jump Cut,* no. 4 (1974): 26–27, reprinted in *Screen* 16, no. 2 (1975): 77–82.

Brewster, Ben, Stephen Heath, and Colin MacCabe, "Comment," *Screen* 16, no. 2 (1975): 83–90, reprinted in *Jump Cut,* no. 9 (1975): 27–28.

Kleinhans, Chuck, "Ventriloquist Psychoanalysis," *Jump Cut,* no. 9 (1975): 30–32.

Buscombe, Edward, Christine Gledhill, Allan Lovell, and Christopher Williams, "Psychoanalysis and Film," *Screen* 16, no. 4 (Winter 1975–1976): 119–30.

———, "Why We Have Resigned from the Board of *Screen,*" *Screen* 17, no. 2 (1976): 106–109.

Brewster, B., "Reply," *Screen* 17, no. 2 (1976): 110–16.

COUNTERCURRENTS

Andrew, Dudley, *Concepts in Film Theory* (New York: Oxford University Press, 1984) (an overview of concepts and issues at the center of recent work).

Aronowitz, Stanley, "Film—The Art Form of Late Capitalism," *Social Text,* no. 1 (Winter 1979): 110–29.

Benson, Thomas W., "*Joe*: An Essay in the Rhetorical Criticism of Film," *Journal of Popular Culture* (Winter 1974): 610–18.

Blowers, Geoffrey H., and Mildred M. McCoy, "The Phenomenological Analysis of Cinematic Episodes: A Cross-cultural Repertory Grid Analysis of a Narrative Film Segment," unpublished manuscript, Department of Psychology, University of Hong Kong, 1984.

Bordwell, David, "Eisenstein's Epistemological Shift," *Screen* 15, no. 4 (Winter 1974–1975): 32–46 (formal analysis).

Britton, Andrew, "Sexuality and Power, or the Two Others," *Framework,* no. 6 (1977): 7–11, 39; and no. 7 (1978): 4–11.

Browne, Nicholas, "Narrative Point of View: The Rhetoric of *Au Hasard, Balthazar,*" *Film Quarterly* 31, no. 1 (Fall 1977): 19–31.

Burch, Noël, and Jorge Dana, "Propositions," *Afterimage,* no. 5 (1975): 40–66.

Burton, Julianne, "Cultural Colonialism and the American Dream," *Jump Cut,* no. 6 (1975): 5–7.

Cahiers du Cinéma extracts, "Film and Popular Memory," *Edinburgh Magazine,* no. 2 (1977): 18–36.

Carroll, John, *Toward a Structural Psychology of Cinema* (New York: Mouton, 1980).

Cavell, Stanley, "Leopards in Connecticut," *Quarterly Review of Film Studies* 2, no. 2 (1977): 141–58.

Durgnat, Raymond, "Through a Looking Sign," *Quarterly Review of Film Studies* 8, no. 4 (Fall 1983): 3–18.

Dyer, Richard, "Homosexuality and Film Noir," *Jump Cut,* no. 16 (1977): 18–21.

————, *Gays and Film* (London: British Film Institute, 1979).

Garcia Espinosa, Julia, "For an Imperfect Cinema," *Jump Cut,* no. 20 (1979): 24–26 (from *Cine Cubano,* nos. 66–67).

Jameson, Fredric, "Reification and Utopia in Mass Culture," *Social Text,* no. 1 (Winter 1979): 130–48.

Jenkins, Bruce, "Structures of Perceptual Engagement in Film: Towards a Technology of Embodiment," *Film Reader,* no. 2 (1977): 141–46.

Jump Cut, no. 16 (1977), special section on gays and film.

Lehman, Peter, "Looking at Luke's Missing Reverse Shot: Psychoanalysis and Style in John Ford's *The Searchers,*" *Wide Angle* 4, no. 4 (1981): 65–70.

Nowell-Smith, Geoffrey, "On the Writing of the History of Cinema: Some Problems," *Edinburgh Magazine,* no. 2 (1977): 8–12.

Rothman, William, *Hitchcock: The Murderous Gaze* (Cambridge, Mass.: Harvard University Press, 1982).

Salt, Barry, *Film Style and Technology: History and Analysis* (London: Starwood, 1983).

Thompson, Kristin, *Eisenstein's Ivan the Terrible: A Neoformalist Analysis* (Princeton, N.J.: Princeton University Press, 1981).

Thompson, Kristin, and David Bordwell, "Space and Narrative in the Films of Ozu," *Screen* 17, no. 2 (Summer 1976): 41–73 (formal analysis).

INDEX

Subjects or names mentioned in or clearly apparent from the table of contents are not included here.